KW-223-744

ROGET'S THEMATIC DICTIONARY OF QUOTATIONS

BLOOMSBURY

First published 1988

Second edition published 1990
Third edition published 1997

Bloomsbury Publishing Limited, 38 Soho Square,
London W1V 5DF

A CIP catalogue record for this book is available from the British Library

ISBN 0 7475 3116 1

10 9 8 7 6 5 4 3 2 1

Compiled and typeset by
Market House Books Ltd., Aylesbury

Printed in England by Clays Ltd, St Ives plc

CONTENTS

Acknowledgments	vi
Introduction	vii
The Quotations	1
Appendix	441

ACKNOWLEDGMENTS

Editors

Fran Alexander
John Daintith
Anne Stibbs

Contributors

Peter Blair
Matthew Bland
Elizabeth Bonham
Deborah Chapman
Sue Cope
Eve Daintith
Hazel Egerton
Rosalind Fergusson
Joan Gallagher
Joanna Gosling
Jock Graham
Lawrence Holden
Alan Isaacs
Amanda Isaacs
Valerie Illingworth
Stephen Jones
Jonathan Law
Sandra McQueen
Elizabeth Martin
Jennifer Monk
David Pickering
Kathy Rooney
Mark Salad
Ruth Salomon
Jessica Scholes
Gwynneth Shaw
Mary Shields
Kate Smith
Tracey Smith
Edmund Wright

INTRODUCTION

This book is a companion volume to the *Bloomsbury Dictionary of Quotations* (first published in 1987), which is arranged alphabetically by author. The present volume contains quotations listed in that work but many other quotations have been added.

Here we have classified over 10,000 quotations under about 800 thematic headings. These are arranged alphabetically. Many of them are subjects that one might expect – 'big issues' such as *love*, *marriage*, *youth*, *age*, *death*, etc., but we have also included current topics such as *cars*, *computers*, *environment*, and *Middle East*. At the beginning of each entry there is a list of cross references to related themes. For example, those interested in *adultery* are also advised to read about *sex*, *unfaithfulness*, and *marriage*.

In general, the quotations under a theme are things said **about** the subject, but we have also used quotations that are **examples** of a theme. For instance, under the heading *epitaphs* will be found quotations that are epitaphs as well as things said about epitaphs. The entry on *last words* contains examples of last words, *Goldwynisms* gives a selection of Goldwyn's supposed sayings, *insults* provides the reader with a number of possibilities, and so on.

Within a thematic entry itself, the quotations are arranged alphabetically by author; for the first appearance of an author within an entry, the author's dates and a brief biographical note are given. This is followed by any explanatory note that may be required and the source, if it is known. Anonymous quotations come at the beginning of a thematic entry and biblical quotations will be found alphabetized under **Bible** within the entry. One of the interesting features of this method of organization is the juxtaposition of different viewpoints on the same subject.

The thematic arrangement is ideal for seeking an apt quotation on a particular theme. But it is also an interesting and amusing book through which to browse. For example, under the entry *politicians* a wide variety of quotations appear, from Shakespeare, through Curzon and Churchill, to references to John Major and Paddy Ashdown.

In addition, the Appendix contains a List of Themes, a List of Names of the authors of the quotations, and a Keyword Index.

The **List of Themes** is a useful quick guide to the themes used in the book.

The **List of Names** provides the reader with the opportunity of seeking *bon mots* from their favourite personalities, the themes under which each author is represented are listed, thus providing an entirely different way of making use of the thematic arrangement.

The **Keyword Index** is based on the *keyword* or *-words* in a quotation, directing the user to the theme under which a particular quotation is listed. So readers who remember only one or two words of a quotation can complete it correctly and find the source. As Dorothy Parker once said,

'I might repeat to myself a list of quotations beautiful from minds profound –
If I can remember any of the damn things.'

We hope that this book will help jog the memory as well as providing an informative and enjoyable selection.

The Editors

A

ABILITY

1 The superior man is distressed by his want of ability.

Confucius (K'ung Fu-tzu; 551–479 BC) Chinese philosopher. *Analects*

2 I don't even know how to use a parking meter, let alone a phone box.

Diana, Princess of Wales (1961–) Former wife of Prince Charles. Replying to allegations that she had been making nuisance telephone calls. *The Times*, 22 Aug 1994

3 One should oblige everyone to the extent of one's ability. One often needs someone smaller than oneself.

Jean de La Fontaine (1621–95) French poet. *Fables*, II, 'Le Lion et le Rat'

4 Intelligence is quickness to apprehend as distinct from ability, which is capacity to act wisely on the thing apprehended.

A. N. Whitehead (1861–1947) British philosopher. *Dialogues*, 135

ABORTION

1 If men could get pregnant, abortion would be a sacrament.

Florynce R. Kennedy (1916–) US lawyer, civil rights activist, and feminist. *Ms*, 'The Verbal Karate of Florynce R. Kennedy, Esq.' Gloria Steinem, Mar 1973

2 It serves me right for putting all my eggs in one bastard.

Dorothy Parker (1893–1967) US writer and wit. On going into hospital for an abortion. *You Might As Well Live* (J. Keats)

3 No woman has an abortion for *fun*.

Joan Smith (1953–) British writer and journalist. *Misogynies*

4 The greatest destroyer of peace is abortion because if a mother can kill her own child what is left for me to kill you and you to kill me? There is nothing between.

Mother Teresa (Agnes Gonxha Bojaxhui; 1910–) Yugoslavian missionary in Calcutta. *Nobel Peace Prize Lecture*

ABSENCE

See also separation

1 Long absent, soon forgotten.

Proverb

2 Out of sight, out of mind.

Proverb

3 When the cat's away, the mice will play.

Proverb

4 Absence makes the heart grow fonder,
Isle of Beauty, Fare thee well!

Thomas Haynes Bayly (1797–1839) British writer. *Isle of Beauty*

5 What's become of Waring
Since he gave us all the slip?

Robert Browning (1812–89) British poet. *Waring*

6 Absence is to love what wind is to fire; it extinguishes the small, it inflames the great.

Bussy-Rabutin (Roger de Rabutin, Comte de Bussy; 1618–93) French soldier and writer. *Histoire amoureuse des Gaules*

7 What's the good of a home, if you are never in it?

George Grossmith (1847–1912) British singer and comedian. *The Diary of a Nobody*, Ch. 1

8 Has anybody here seen Kelly?
Kelly from the Isle of Man?

C. W. Murphy (19th century) British songwriter. *Has Anybody Here Seen Kelly?*

9 We seek him here, we seek him there,
Those Frenchies seek him everywhere.
Is he in heaven? – Is he in hell?
That damned elusive Pimpernel?

Baroness Orczy (1865–1947) British novelist. *The Scarlet Pimpernel*, Ch. 12

10 Why art thou silent! Is thy love a plant
Of such weak fibre that the treacherous air
Of absence withers what was once so fair?

William Wordsworth (1770–1850) British poet. *Miscellaneous Sonnets*, III

ABSTINENCE

See also alcohol, self-denial, sex, smoking

1 He neither drank, smoked, nor rode a bicycle. Living frugally,saving his money, he died early, surrounded by greedy relatives. It was a great lesson to me.

John Barrymore (1882–1942) US actor. *The Stage*, Jan 1941 (J. P. McEvoy)

2 If someone asks for a soft drink at a party, we no longer think he is a wimp.

Edwina Currie (1946–) British politician. Speech, Dec 1988

3 Teetotallers lack the sympathy and generosity of men that drink.

W. H. Davies (1871–1940) British poet. *Shorter Lyrics of the 20th Century, Introduction*

4 It was a brilliant affair; water flowed like champagne.

William M. Evarts (1818–1901) US lawyer and statesman. Describing a dinner given by US President Rutherford B. Hayes (1877–81), an advocate of temperance. Attrib.

5 If you resolve to give up smoking, drinking

and loving, you don't actually live longer; it just seems longer.

Clement Freud (1924–) British Liberal politician and broadcaster. *The Observer*, 27 Dec 1964

6 Mr Mercaptan went on to preach a brilliant sermon on that melancholy sexual perversion known as continence.

Aldous Huxley (1894–1964) British novelist. *Antic Hay*, Ch. 18

7 My experience through life has convinced me that, while moderation and temperance in all things are commendable and beneficial, abstinence from spirituous liquors is the best safeguard of morals and health.

Robert E. Lee (1807–70) US general. Letter, 9 Dec 1869

8 The few bad poems which occasionally are created during abstinence are of no great interest.

Wilhelm Reich (1897–1957) Austrian-born US psychiatrist. *The Sexual Revolution*

9 The people who are regarded as moral luminaries are those who forego ordinary pleasures themselves and find compensation in interfering with the pleasures of others.

Bertrand Russell (1872–1970) British philosopher. *Sceptical Essays*

10 Lastly (and this is, perhaps, the golden rule), no woman should marry a teetotaller, or a man who does not smoke.

Robert Louis Stevenson (1850–94) Scottish writer. *Virginibus Puerisque*

11 She belongs to a Temperance Society and wears one of those badges in the shape of a bow of ribbon to show that she would never take a drink, not even brandy if she were dying. Of course by temperance they all mean the opposite – total abstinence.

Elizabeth Taylor (1912–75) British writer. *Angel*

12 Though in silence, with blighted affection, I pine,
Yet the lips that touch liquor must never touch mine!

G. W. Young (19th century) British writer. *The Lips That Touch Liquor*

ACADEMICS

See also education, intellectuals

1 A professor is one who talks in someone else's sleep.

W. H. Auden (1907–73) British poet. Attrib.

2 First come I; my name is Jowett.
There's no knowledge but I know it.
I am Master of this college:
What I don't know isn't knowledge.

H. C. Beeching (1859–1919) British academic. Referring to Benjamin Jowett, master of Balliol College, Oxford. *The Masque of Balliol*

3 It's no use trying to be *clever* – we are all clever here; just try to be *kind* – a little kind.

F. J. Foakes Jackson (1855–1941) British academic. Advice given to a new don at Jesus College, Cambridge. Noted in A. C. Benson's Commonplace Book

4 Like so many ageing college people, Pnin had long ceased to notice the existence of students on the campus.

Vladimir Nabokov (1899–1977) Russian-born US novelist. *Pnin*, Ch. 3

5 I am the Dean of Christ Church, Sir:
There's my wife; look well at her.
She's the Broad and I'm the High;
We are the University.

Cecil Arthur Spring-Rice (1859–1918) British diplomat. *The Masque of Balliol*

ACCIDENTS

See also chance, disaster, misfortune

1 The Act of God designation on all insurance policies; which means, roughly, that you cannot be insured for the accidents that are most likely to happen to you.

Alan Coren (1938–) British humorist and writer. *The Lady from Stalingrad Mansions*, 'A Short History of Insurance'

2 Accidents will occur in the best-regulated families.

Charles Dickens (1812–70) British novelist. *David Copperfield*, Ch. 28

3 My good man, I'm not a strawberry.

Edward VII (1841–1910) King of the United Kingdom. Rebuking a footman who had spilt cream on him. *The Last Country Houses* (C. Aslat)

4 Heard there was a party. Came.

Beatrice Lillie (Constance Sylvia Munston, Lady Peel; 1898–1989) Canadian-born British actress. On arriving breathlessly at a friend's house seeking help after a car crash. Attrib.

5 O Diamond! Diamond! thou little knowest the mischief done!

Isaac Newton (1642–1727) British scientist. Said to a dog that set fire to some papers, representing several years' work, by knocking over a candle. *Wensley-Dale...a Poem* (Thomas Maude)

6 There are no small accidents on this circuit.

Ayrton Senna (1960–94) Brazilian motor racing driver. Remark made before the 1994 San Marino Grand Prix, during which he was killed. *The Independent*, 22 Dec 1994

7 Knocked down a doctor? With an ambulance? How could she? It's a contradiction in terms.

N. F. Simpson (1919–) British dramatist. *One-Way Pendulum*, I

8 The chapter of accidents is the longest chapter in the book.

John Wilkes (1725–97) British politician. Attrib. in *The Doctor* (Southey), Vol. IV

ACCUSATION

See also responsibility

1 I do not know the method of drawing up an indictment against an whole people.

Edmund Burke (1729–97) British politician. *Speech on Conciliation with America* (House of Commons, 22 Mar 1775)

2 Never make a defence or apology before you be accused.

Charles I (1600–49) King of England. Letter to Lord Wentworth, 3 Sept 1636

3 *J'accuse.*
I accuse.

Émile Zola (1840–1902) French novelist. Title of an open letter to the French President, denouncing the French army's conduct in the Dreyfus affair. *L'Aurore*, 13 Jan 1898

ACHIEVEMENT

See also effort, success

1 Ye shall know them by their fruits. Do men gather grapes of thorns, or figs of thistles?
Even so every good tree bringeth forth good fruit; but a corrupt tree bringeth forth evil fruit.
A good tree cannot bring forth evil fruit, neither can a corrupt tree bring forth good fruit.
Every tree that bringeth not forth good fruit is hewn down, and cast into the fire.
Wherefore by their fruits ye shall know them.

Bible: Matthew 7:16–20

2 Be not afraid of growing slowly, be afraid only of standing still.

Chinese Proverb

3 Our greatest glory is not in never falling, but in rising every time we fall.

Confucius (K'ung Fu-tzu; 551–479 BC) Chinese philosopher. *Analects*

4 One never notices what has been done; one can only see what remains to be done.

Marie Curie (1867–1934) Polish chemist. Letter to her brother, 18 Mar 1894

5 We never do anything well till we cease to think about the manner of doing it.

William Hazlitt (1778–1830) British essayist. *On Prejudice*

6 I do not want to die...until I have faithfully made the most of my talent and cultivated the seed that was placed in me until the last small twig has grown.

Käthe Kollwitz (1867–1945) German sculptor and graphic artist. *Diaries and Letters*, 15 Feb 1915

7 For, as I suppose, no man in this world hath lived better than I have done, to achieve that I have done.

Thomas Malory (1400–71) English writer. *Morte d'Arthur*, Bk. XVII, Ch. 16

8 Log-cabin to White House.

W. M. Thayer (1820–98) US writer. The title of his biography of James Garfield, US president

9 To achieve great things we must live as though we were never going to die.

Marquis de Vauvenargues (1715–47) French soldier and writer. *Réflexions et maximes*

ACTING

See also action, actors, cinema, criticism, plays, theatre

1 Theatre director: a person engaged by the management to conceal the fact that the players cannot act.

James Agate (1877–1947) British theatre critic. Attrib.

2 It's not whether you really cry. It's whether the audience thinks you are crying.

Ingrid Bergman (1915–1982) Swedish film and stage actress. *Halliwell's Filmgoer's and Video Viewer's Companion*

3 Acting is the expression of a neurotic impulse. It's a bum's life. Quitting acting, that's the sign of maturity.

Marlon Brando (1924–) US film star. *Halliwell's Filmgoer's and Video Viewer's Companion*

4 For the theatre one needs long arms; it is better to have them too long than too short. An *artiste* with short arms can never, never make a fine gesture.

Sarah Bernhardt (Sarah Henriette Rosine Bernard; 1844–1923) French actress. *Memories of My Life*, Ch. 6

5 Pray to God and say the lines.

Bette Davis (Ruth Elizabeth Davis; 1908–89) US film star. Advice to the actress Celeste Holm. Attrib.

6 It is easier to get an actor to be a cowboy than to get a cowboy to be an actor.

John Ford (Sean O'Feeney; 1895–1973) US film director. Attrib.

7 It is. But not as hard as farce.

Edmund Gwenn (1875–1959) British actor. On his deathbed, in reply to the comment 'It must be very hard'. *Time*, 30 Jan 1984

8 Acting is therefore the lowest of the arts, if it is an art at all.

George Moore (1852–1933) Irish writer and art critic. *Mummer-Worship*

9 The art of acting consists in keeping people from coughing.

Ralph Richardson (1902–83) British actor. *The Observer*

10 In music, the punctuation is absolutely strict, the bars and the rests are absolutely defined. But our punctuation cannot be quite strict, because we have to relate it to the audience. In other words, we are continually changing the score.

Ralph Richardson *The Observer Magazine*, 'Tynan on Richardson', 18 Dec 1977

11 Imagination! imagination! I put it first years ago, when I was asked what qualities I thought

necessary for success upon the stage.
Ellen Terry (1847–1928) British actress. *The Story of My Life*, Ch. 2

12 Ladies, just a little more virginity, if you don't mind.
Herbert Beerbohm Tree (1853–1917) British actor and theatre manager. Directing a group of sophisticated actresses. *Smart Aleck* (H. Teichmann)

ACTION

See also acting

1 Barking dogs seldom bite.
Proverb

2 Doing is better than saying.
Proverb

3 Easier said than done.
Proverb

4 Footprints on the sands of time are not made by sitting down.
Proverb

5 Saying is one thing, and doing another.
Proverb

6 Let's meet, and either do, or die.
Francis Beaumont (1584–1616) English dramatist. *The Island Princess*, II:2

7 He who desires but acts not, breeds pestilence.
William Blake (1757–1827) British poet. *The Marriage of Heaven and Hell*, 'Proverbs of Hell'

8 Liberty's in every blow!
Let us do or die!
Robert Burns (1759–96) Scottish poet. *Scots, Wha Hae*

9 Deliberation is the work of many men. Action, of one alone.
Charles De Gaulle (1890–1970) French general and statesman. *War Memoirs*, Vol. 2

10 Suit the action to the word, the word to the action; with this special observance, that you o'erstep not the modesty of nature.
William Shakespeare (1564–1616) English dramatist. *Hamlet*, III:2

11 If to do were as easy as to know what were good to do, chapels had been churches, and poor men's cottages princes' palaces.
William Shakespeare *The Merchant of Venice*, I:2

12 So many worlds, so much to do,
So little done, such things to be.
Alfred, Lord Tennyson (1809–92) British poet. *In Memoriam A.H.H.*, LXXIII

13 It's dogged as does it. It ain't thinking about it.
Anthony Trollope (1815–82) British novelist. *Last Chronicle of Barset*, Ch. 61

14 We already know enough to begin to cope with all the major problems that are now threatening human life and much of the rest of life on earth. Our crisis is not a crisis of information; it is a crisis of decision of policy and action.
George Wald (1906–) US biochemist. *Philosophy and Social Action*

ACTORS

General quotes

See also acting, cinema, criticism, plays, theatre

1 An actor's a guy who, if you ain't talking about him, ain't listening.
Marlon Brando (1924–) US film star. *The Observer*, 'Sayings of the Year', Jan 1956

2 An actor is something less than a man, while an actress is something more than a woman.
Richard Burton (Richard Jenkins; 1925–84) British actor. *Halliwell's Filmgoer's and Video Viewer's Companion*

3 Never meddle with play-actors, for they're a favoured race.
Miguel de Cervantes (1547–1616) Spanish novelist. *Don Quixote*, Pt. II, Ch. 11

4 Remember you are a star. Never go across the alley even to dump garbage unless you are dressed to the teeth.
Cecil B. de Mille (1881–1959) US film producer and director. *Halliwell's Filmgoer's and Video Viewer's Companion*

5 Actors should be treated like cattle.
Alfred Hitchcock (1889–1980) British film director. Said in clarification of a remark attributed to him, 'Actors are like cattle'. *Quote, Unquote* (N. Rees)

6 At one time I thought he wanted to be an actor. He had certain qualifications, including no money and a total lack of responsibility.
Hedda Hopper (1890–1966) US writer. *From Under My Hat*

7 They didn't act like people and they didn't act like actors. It's hard to explain. They acted more like they knew they were celebrities and all. I mean they were good, but they were *too* good.
J. D. Salinger (1919–) US novelist. *The Catcher in the Rye*, Ch. 17

Specific quotes

8 Can't act. Can't sing. Can dance a little.
Anonymous Studio report after Fred Astaire's first screen test

9 John Wayne is dead.
The hell I am
Anonymous Inscription on a wall in Bermondsey Antique Market, together with a ghostly denial. *Evening Standard*, 1980

10 If she was a victim of any kind, she was a victim of her friends.
George Cukor (1899–1983) US film director. Referring to Marilyn Monroe. *On Cukor* (Gavin Lambert)

11 Garrick was pure gold beat out into thin leaf.

James Boswell (1740–95) Scottish lawyer and writer. Referring to David Garrick.

12 I remember Sarah Bernhardt's funeral perfectly. I have never had to wait so long to cross the street.

Eric Dunstan *Ego* 9, 14 Oct 1946

13 I'm just a lucky slob from Ohio who happened to be in the right place at the right time.

Clark Gable (1901–60) US film actor. Attrib.

14 Olivier's was, to my mind, the definitive Macbeth. Olivier had murder in his heart from the moment he came on the stage.

John Gielgud (1904–) British actor. *An Actor and His Time*

15 Chaplin is no business man – all he knows is that he can't take anything less.

Samuel Goldwyn (Samuel Goldfish; 1882–1974) Polish-born US film producer. Attrib.

16 You can't direct a Laughton picture. The best you can hope for is to referee.

Alfred Hitchcock (1889–1980) British film director.

17 She looked as though butter wouldn't melt in her mouth – or anywhere else.

Elsa Lanchester (1902–86) British-born US actress. Referring to Maureen O'Hara. Attrib.

18 Goodbye Norma Jean
Though I never knew you at all
You had the grace to hold yourself
While those around you crawled.
They crawled out of the woodwork
And they whispered into your brain
Set you on the treadmill
And made you change your name.

Bernie Taupin (1950–) British songwriter. Lyrics for a song by Elton John. *Candle in the Wind*; referring to Marilyn Monroe

19 I don't pretend to be an ordinary housewife.

Elizabeth Taylor (1932–) British-born US actress. Interview

20 As Romeo Irving reminded me of a pig who has been taught to play the fiddle. He did it cleverly, but would be better employed in squealing.

Ellen Terry (1847–1928) British actress. *Notes on Irving*

21 This whole thing is like a cross between a very severe virus and getting married.

Emma Thompson (1959–) British actress. Receiving an Oscar for Best Actress, 1993.

22 Ah, every day dear Herbert becomes *de plus en plus Oscarié*. It is a wonderful case of nature imitating art.

Oscar Wilde (1854–1900) Irish-born British dramatist. Referring to Beerbohm Tree's unconscious adoption of some of the mannerisms of a character he was playing in one of Wilde's plays. *Great Theatrical Disasters* (G. Brandreth)

ADAPTABILITY

See also change

1 Remember that to change your mind and follow him who sets you right is to be none the less free than you were before.

Marcus Aurelius (121–180 AD) Roman emperor. *Meditations*, Bk. VIII, Ch. 16

2 Mahomet made the people believe that he would call a hill to him…when the hill stood still, he was never a whit abashed, but said, 'If the hill will not come to Mahomet, Mahomet will go to the hill.'

Francis Bacon (1561–1626) English philosopher. Often misquoted as 'If the mountain will not come to Mohammed'. *Essays*, 'Of Boldness'

3 President Robbins was so well adjusted to his environment that sometimes you could not tell which was the environment and which was President Robbins.

Randall Jarrell (1914–65) US author. *Pictures from an Institution*, Pt. I, Ch. 4

4 As time requireth, a man of marvellous mirth and pastimes, and sometimes of as sad gravity, as who say: a man for all seasons.

Robert Whittington (16th century) English writer. Referring to Sir Thomas More; after Erasmus. *Vulgaria*, Pt. II, 'De constructione nominum'

ADDICTION

1 Cocaine isn't habit-forming. I should know – I've been using it for years.

Tallulah Bankhead (1903–68) US actress. *Pentimento* (Lillian Hellman), 'Theatre'

2 Every form of addiction is bad, no matter whether the narcotic be alcohol or morphine or idealism.

Carl Gustav Jung (1875–1961) Swiss psychoanalyst. *Memories, Dreams, Reflections*, Ch. 12

ADDRESSES

1 Addresses are given to us to conceal our whereabouts.

Saki (Hector Hugh Munro; 1870–1916) British writer. *Cross Currents*

2 Three addresses always inspire confidence, even in tradesmen.

Oscar Wilde (1854–1900) Irish-born British dramatist. *The Importance of Being Earnest*, III

ADMIRATION

See also compliments, love, praise, respect, wonder

1 Miss J. Hunter Dunn, Miss J. Hunter Dunn,

Furnish'd and burnish'd by Aldershot sun.

John Betjeman (1906–84) British poet. *A Subaltern's Love Song*

2 Here's looking at you, kid.

Humphrey Bogart (1899–1957) US film star. *Casablanca*

3 A fool always finds a greater fool to admire him.

Nicolas Boileau (1636–1711) French writer. *L'Art poétique*, I

4 There is a garden in her face,
Where roses and white lilies grow;
A heav'nly paradise is that place,
Wherein all pleasant fruits do flow.
There cherries grow, which none may buy
Till 'Cherry ripe' themselves do cry.

Thomas Campion (1567–1620) English poet. *Fourth Book of Airs*

5 I do think better of womankind than to suppose they care whether Mister John Keats five feet high likes them or not.

John Keats (1795–1821) British poet. Letter to Benjamin Bailey, 18 July 1818

6 'There is a report that Piso is dead; it is a great loss; he was an honest man, who deserved to live longer; he was intelligent and agreeable, resolute and courageous, to be depended upon, generous and faithful.' Add: 'provided he is really dead'.

Jean de La Bruyère (1645–96) French satirist. *Les Caractères*

7 On Richmond Hill there lives a lass,
More sweet than May day morn,
Whose charms all other maids surpass,
A rose without a thorn.

Leonard MacNally (1752–1820) Irish dramatist and poet. *The Lass of Richmond Hill*

8 Many a man has been a wonder to the world, whose wife and valet have seen nothing in him that was even remarkable. Few men have been admired by their servants.

Michel de Montaigne (1533–92) French essayist. *Essais*, III

9 Charlie is my darling, my darling, my darling,
Charlie is my darling, the young Chevalier.

Carolina Nairne (1766–1845) Scottish songwriter. Referring to Bonnie Prince Charlie. *Charlie is my Darling*

10 Not to admire, is all the art I know
To make men happy, and to keep them so.

Alexander Pope (1688–1744) British poet. *Imitations of Horace*, 'To Mr. Murray'

11 Where'er you walk, cool gales shall fan the glade,
Trees, where you sit, shall crowd into a shade:
Where'er you tread, the blushing flow'rs shall rise,
And all things flourish where you turn your eyes.

Alexander Pope *Pastorals*, 'Summer'

12 But search the land of living men,
Where wilt thou find their like agen?

Walter Scott (1771–1832) Scottish novelist. *Marmion*, I

13 The barge she sat in, like a burnish'd throne,
Burn'd on the water. The poop was beaten gold;
Purple the sails, and so perfumed that
The winds were love-sick with them; the oars were silver,
Which to the tune of flutes kept stroke and made
The water which they beat to follow faster,
As amorous of their strokes. For her own person,
It beggar'd all description.

William Shakespeare (1564–1616) English dramatist. *Antony and Cleopatra*, II:2

14 Age cannot wither her, nor custom stale
Her infinite variety. Other women cloy
The appetites they feed, but she makes hungry
Where most she satisfies.

William Shakespeare *Antony and Cleopatra*, II:2

15 'A was a man, take him for all in all,
I shall not look upon his like again.

William Shakespeare *Hamlet*, I:2

16 Who is Silvia? What is she,
That all our swains commend her?
Holy, fair, and wise is she.

William Shakespeare *The Two Gentlemen of Verona*, IV:2

17 He was a great patriot, a humanitarian, a loyal friend – provided, of course, that he really is dead.

Voltaire (François-Marie Arouet; 1694–1778) French writer. Giving a funeral oration. Attrib.

18 The sweetest thing that ever grew
Beside a human door!

William Wordsworth (1770–1850) British poet. *Lucy Gray*

ADULTERY

See also marriage, sex, unfaithfulness

1 What men call gallantry, and gods adultery,
Is much more common where the climate's sultry.

Lord Byron (1788–1824) British poet. *Don Juan*, I

2 I have looked on a lot of women with lust. I've committed adultery in my heart many times. God recognises I will do this and forgives me.

Jimmy Carter (1924–) US statesman and president. Remark

3 Sara could commit adultery at one end and weep for her sins at the other, and enjoy both operations at once.

Joyce Cary (1888–1957) British novelist. *The Horse's Mouth*, Ch. 8

4 Do you seriously expect me to be the first Prince of Wales in history not to have a mistress?

Charles, Prince of Wales (1948–) Eldest son of Elizabeth II. *The Daily Mail*, Dec 1994

5 There were three of us in this marriage, so it was a bit crowded.

Diana, Princess of Wales (1961–) Former wife of Prince Charles. On the relationship between her husband and Camilla Parker-Bowles.

6 I say I don't sleep with married men, but what I mean is that I don't sleep with happily married men.
Britt Ekland (1942–) Swedish film actress. Attrib.

7 You know, of course, that the Tasmanians, who never committed adultery, are now extinct.
W. Somerset Maugham (1874–1965) British novelist. *The Bread-Winner*

8 Madame, you must really be more careful. Suppose it had been someone else who found you like this.
Duc de Richelieu (1766–1822) French statesman. Discovering his wife with her lover. *The Book of Lists* (D. Wallechinsky)

9 With all my heart. Whose wife shall it be?
John Horne Tooke (1736–1812) British clergyman, politician, and etymologist. Replying to the suggestion that he take a wife. Attrib.

ADVERTISING

1 Any publicity is good publicity.
Proverb

2 It pays to advertise.
Anonymous Already current by c. 1912 when Cole Porter used it as the title of an early song.

3 Advertising is the most fun you can have with your clothes on.
Jerry Della Femina (1936–) Advertising executive. *From those wonderful folks who gave you Pearl Harbor*

4 Half the money I spend on advertising is wasted, and the trouble is I don't know which half.
Viscount Leverhulme (1851–1925) British industrialist. *Confessions of an Advertising Man* (D. Ogilvy)

5 Freedom of the press in Britain is freedom to print such of the proprietor's prejudices as the advertisers don't object to.
Hannen Swaffer (1879–1962) British journalist. Attrib.

Advertising Slogans

6 A diamond is forever.

7 A Mars a day helps you work rest and play.

8 Drinka pinta milka day.

9 Go to work on an egg.

10 Guinness is good for you.

11 Heineken refreshes the parts other beers cannot reach.

12 I'd like to teach the world to sing.
Coca Cola

13 I'll bet he drinks Carling Black Label.

14 It beats as it sweeps as it cleans.
Hoover

15 It's fingerlickin' good.
Kentucky Fried Chicken

16 It's the real thing.
Coca Cola

17 Sch... you know who.
Schweppes

18 The bank that likes to say yes.
Trustee Savings Bank

19 Vorsprung durch Technik.
Audi

ADVICE

1 A good scare is worth more than good advice.
Proverb

2 Don't teach your grandmother to suck eggs.
Proverb

3 He that has no children brings them up well.
Proverb

4 He that has no wife, beats her oft.
Proverb

5 Advice would be more acceptable if it didn't always conflict with our plans.
Anonymous

6 Advice is seldom welcome; and those who want it the most always like it the least.
Earl of Chesterfield (1694–1773) English statesman. Letter to his son, 29 Jan 1748

7 Your business is to put me out of business.
Dwight D. Eisenhower (1890–1969) US general and statesman. Addressing a graduating class at a university. *Procession* (J. Gunther)

8 I intended to give you some advice but now I remember how much is left over from last year unused.
George Harris (1844–1922) US congressman. Said when addressing students at the start of a new academic year. *Braude's Second Encyclopedia* (J. Braude)

9 It is a good thing to follow the first law of holes; if you are in one, stop digging.
Denis Healey (1917–) British Labour politician. Speech, May 1988

10 I advised her on what clothes she should wear, how to deal with the press and even helped her practise her public speaking.
James Hewitt (1958–) British army officer. Referring to Princess Diana, with whom he had a relationship. *The Independent*, 3 Oct 1994

11 On my twenty-first birthday my father said, 'Son, here's a million dollars. Don't lose it.'
Larry Niven (1938–) US science-fiction writer. When asked 'What is the best advice you have ever been given?'. Attrib.

12 One gives nothing so freely as advice.

Duc de la Rochefoucauld (1613–80) French writer. *Maximes*, 110

13 Don't tell your friends their social faults, they will cure the fault and never forgive you.

Logan Pearsall Smith (1865–1946) US writer. *Afterthoughts*

14 No one wants advice – only corroboration.

John Steinbeck (1902–68) US novelist.

15 It's queer how ready people always are with advice in any real or imaginary emergency, and no matter how many times experience has shown them to be wrong, they continue to set forth their opinions, as if they had received them from the Almighty!

Annie Sullivan (1866–1936) US teacher of the handicapped. Letter, 12 June 1887

16 I have lived some thirty years on this planet, and I have yet to hear the first syllable of valuable or even earnest advice from my seniors.

Henry David Thoreau (1817–62) US writer. *Walden*, 'Economy'

17 Are you in trouble? Do you need advice? Write to Miss Lonelyhearts and she will help.

Nathaniel West (Nathan Weinstein; 1903–40) US novelist. *Miss Lonelyhearts*

AFFECTATION

See also ostentation

1 We have become a grandmother.

Margaret Thatcher (1925–) British politician and prime minister. Remark, Mar 1989

2 Don't you sit there and sigh gal like you was Lady Nevershit.

Arnold Wesker (1932–) British dramatist. *Roots*, III

3 She keeps on being Queenly in her own room with the door shut.

Edith Wharton (1862–1937) US novelist. *The House of Mirth*, Bk. II, Ch. 1

AFTERLIFE

See also death, heaven

1 CLOV. Do you believe in the life to come?
HAMM. Mine was always that.

Samuel Beckett (1906–89) Irish novelist and dramatist. *Endgame*

2 That which is the foundation of all our hopes and of all our fears; all our hopes and fears which are of any consideration: I mean a Future Life.

Joseph Butler (1692–1752) British churchman. *The Analogy of Religion*, Introduction

3 We have no reliable guarantee that the afterlife will be any less exasperating than this one, have we?

Noël Coward (1899–1973) British dramatist. *Blithe Spirit*, I

4 We sometimes congratulate ourselves at the moment of waking from a troubled dream; it may be so the moment after death.

Nathaniel Hawthorne (1804–64) US novelist and writer. *American Notebooks*

5 Death is nothing at all. I have only slipped away into the next room. I am I and you are you. Whatever we were to each other, that we are still.... What is death but negligible accident? Why should I be out of mind because I am out of sight? I am waiting for you, for an interval, somewhere very near just around the corner. All is well.

Henry Scott Holland (1847–1918) British Anglican clergyman. Attrib.

6 Is there another life? Shall I awake and find all this a dream? There must be, we cannot be created for this sort of suffering.

John Keats (1795–1821) British poet. Letter, 1820

7 My doctrine is: Live that thou mayest desire to live again – that is thy duty – for in any case thou wilt live again!

Friedrich Wilhelm Nietzsche (1844–1900) German philosopher. *Eternal Recurrence*

8 After your death you will be what you were before your birth.

Arthur Schopenhauer (1788–1860) German philosopher. *Parerga and Paralipomena*

9 The dread of something after death –
The undiscover'd country, from whose bourn
No traveller returns.

William Shakespeare (1564–1616) English dramatist. *Hamlet*, III:1

10 I am going a long way
With these thou seest – if indeed I go
(For all my mind is clouded with a doubt) –
To the island-valley of Avilion;
Where falls not hail, or rain, or any snow,
Nor ever wind blows loudly; but it lies
Deep-meadow'd, happy, fair with orchard lawns
And bowery hollows crown'd with summer sea,
Where I will heal me of my grievous wound.

Alfred, Lord Tennyson (1809–92) British poet. *Idylls of the King*, 'The Passing of Arthur'

11 One world at a time.

Henry David Thoreau (1817–62) US writer. On being asked his opinion of the hereafter. Attrib.

AGE

See also longevity, old age, youth

1 Never too late to learn.

Proverb

2 There's many a good tune played on an old fiddle.

Proverb

3 All evil comes from the old. They grow fat on

ideas and young men die of them.

Jean Anouilh (1910–87) French dramatist. *Catch as Catch Can*

4 I am past thirty, and three parts iced over.

Matthew Arnold (1822–88) British poet and critic. Letter to A. H. Clough, 12 Feb 1853

5 I refuse to admit that I am more than fifty-two, even if that does make my sons illegitimate.

Nancy Astor (1879–1964) US-born British politician. Attrib.

6 I think your whole life shows in your face and you should be proud of that.

Lauren Bacall (1924–) US actress. Remark, Mar 1988

7 Age will not be defied.

Francis Bacon (1561–1626) English philosopher. *Essays*, 'Of Regiment of Health'

8 A man that is young in years may be old in hours, if he have lost no time.

Francis Bacon *Essays*, 'Of Youth and Age'

9 The only thing I regret about my past life is the length of it. If I had my past life over again I'd make all the same mistakes – only sooner.

Tallulah Bankhead (1903–68) US actress. *The Times*, 28 July 1981

10 What is an adult? A child blown up by age.

Simone de Beauvoir (1908–86) French writer. *La Femme rompue*

11 If thou hast gathered nothing in thy youth, how canst thou find any thing in thine age?

Bible: Ecclesiasticus 25:3

12 No man also having drunk old wine straightway desireth new: for he saith, The old is better.

Bible: Luke 5:39

13 Old age is ... a lot of crossed off names in an address book.

Ronald Blythe (1922–) British author. *The View in Winter*

14 Being now come to the years of discretion.

The Book of Common Prayer *Order of Confirmation*

15 Therefore I summon age
To grant youth's heritage.

Robert Browning (1812–89) British poet. *Rabbi ben Ezra*, XIII

16 Ah well, perhaps one has to be very old before one learns how to be amused rather than shocked.

Pearl Buck (1892–1973) US novelist. *China, Past and Present*, Ch. 6

17 A lady of a 'certain age', which means
Certainly aged.

Lord Byron (1788–1824) British poet. *Don Juan*, VI

18 A man is as old as he's feeling,
A woman as old as she looks.

Mortimer Collins (1827–76) British writer. *The Unknown Quantity*

19 Youth is a blunder; manhood a struggle; old age a regret.

Benjamin Disraeli (1804–81) British statesman. *Coningsby*, Bk. III, Ch. 1

20 I am resolved to grow fat and look young till forty, and then slip out of the world with the first wrinkle and the reputation of five-and-twenty.

John Dryden (1631–1700) British poet and dramatist. *The Maiden Queen*, III

21 Men are but children of a larger growth;
Our appetites as apt to change as theirs,
And full as craving too, and full as vain.

John Dryden *All for Love*, IV

22 The years between fifty and seventy are the hardest. You are always being asked to do things, and you are not yet decrepit enough to turn them down.

T. S. Eliot (1888–1965) US-born British poet and dramatist. *Time*, 23 Oct 1950

23 Here I am, an old man in a dry month,
Being read to by a boy, waiting for rain.

T. S. Eliot *Gerontion*

24 *Si jeunesse savait; si vieillesse pouvait.*
If only youth knew, if only age could.

Henri Estienne (1528–98) French scholar. *Les Prémices*

25 At sixteen I was stupid, confused, insecure and indecisive. At twenty-five I was wise, self-confident, prepossessing and assertive. At forty-five I am stupid, confused, insecure and indecisive. Who would have supposed that maturity is only a short break in adolescence?

Jules Feiffer (1929–) US writer, cartoonist, and humorist. *The Observer*, 3 Feb 1974

26 Though the Jazz Age continued, it became less and less an affair of youth. The sequel was like a children's party taken over by the elders.

F. Scott Fitzgerald (1896–1940) US novelist. *The Crack-Up*

27 At twenty years of age, the will reigns; at thirty, the wit; and at forty, the judgement.

Benjamin Franklin (1706–90) US scientist and statesman. *Poor Richard's Almanack*

28 A diplomat is a man who always remembers a woman's birthday but never remembers her age.

Robert Frost (1875–1963) US poet. Attrib.

29 When you're my age, you just never risk being ill – because then everyone says: Oh, he's done for.

John Gielgud (1904–) British actor. *Sunday Express* Magazine, 17 July 1988

30 She may very well pass for forty-three
In the dusk, with a light behind her!

W. S. Gilbert (1836–1911) British dramatist. *Trial by Jury*

31 'Old Cary Grant fine. How you?'

Cary Grant (Archibald Leach; 1904–86) British-born US film star. Replying to a telegram sent to his agent inquiring: 'How old Cary Grant?'. *The Filmgoer's Book of Quotes* (Leslie Halliwell)

32 You will recognize, my boy, the first sign of old age: it is when you go out into the streets of

London and realize for the first time how young the policemen look.

Seymour Hicks (1871–1949) British actor-manager. *They Were Singing* (C. Pulling)

33 What do the ravages of time not injure? Our parents' age (worse than our grandparents') has produced us, more worthless still, who will soon give rise to a yet more vicious generation.

Horace (Quintus Horatius Flaccus; 65–8 BC) Roman poet. *Odes*, III

34 Whenever a man's friends begin to compliment him about looking young, he may be sure that they think he is growing old.

Washington Irving (1783–1859) US writer. *Bracebridge Hall*, 'Bachelors'

35 It is sobering to consider that when Mozart was my age he had already been dead for a year.

Tom Lehrer (1928–) US university teacher and songwriter. *An Encyclopedia of Quotations about Music* (N. Shapiro)

36 I am just turning forty and taking my time about it.

Harold Lloyd (1893–1971) US silent-film comedian. Reply when, aged 77, he was asked his age. *The Times*, 23 Sept 1970

37 Growth is a greater mystery than death. All of us can understand failure, we all contain failure and death within us, but not even the successful man can begin to describe the impalpable elations and apprehensions of growth.

Norman Mailer (1923–) US writer. *Advertisements for Myself*

38 But at my back I always hear
Time's winged chariot hurrying near;
And yonder all before us lie
Deserts of vast eternity.

Andrew Marvell (1621–78) English poet. *To His Coy Mistress*

39 A man is only as old as the woman he feels.

Groucho Marx (Julius Marx; 1895–1977) US comedian. Attrib.

40 I am old enough to be – in fact am – your mother.

A. A. Milne (1882–1956) British writer. *Belinda*

41 How soon hath Time, the subtle thief of youth,
Stolen on his wing my three-and-twentieth year!

John Milton (1608–74) English poet. *Sonnet*: 'On Being Arrived at the Age of Twenty-three'

42 Do you think my mind is maturing late,
Or simply rotted early?

Ogden Nash (1902–71) US poet. *Lines on Facing Forty*

43 At 50, everyone has the face he deserves.

George Orwell (Eric Blair; 1903–50) British novelist. Last words in his manuscript notebook, 17 Apr 1949.

44 Each generation imagines itself to be more intelligent than the one that went before it, and wiser than the one that comes after it.

George Orwell Book Review

45 From forty to fifty a man is at heart either a stoic or a satyr.

Arthur Pinero (1855–1934) British dramatist. *The Second Mrs Tanqueray*, I

46 One of the pleasures of middle age is to *find out* that one WAS right, and that one was much righter than one knew at say 17 or 23.

Ezra Pound (1885–1972) US poet. *ABC of Reading*, Ch. 1

47 You know, by the time you reach my age, you've made plenty of mistakes if you've lived your life properly

Ronald Reagan (1911–) US politician and president. *The Observer*, 'Sayings of the Week', 8 Mar 1987

48 It is fun to be in the same decade with you.

Franklin D. Roosevelt (1882–1945) US Democratic president. After Churchill had congratulated him on his 60th birthday. *The Hinge of Fate* (Winston S. Churchill), Ch. 4

49 I have always felt that a woman has the right to treat the subject of her age with ambiguity until, perhaps, she passes into the realm of over ninety. Then it is better she be candid with herself and with the world.

Helena Rubinstein (1882–1965) Polish-born US cosmetics manufacturer. *My Life for Beauty*, Pt. I, Ch. 1

50 The young have aspirations that never come to pass, the old have reminiscences of what never happened.

Saki (Hector Hugh Munro; 1870–1916) British writer. *Reginald at the Carlton*

51 The young man who has not wept is a savage, and the old man who will not laugh is a fool.

George Santayana (1863–1952) US philosopher. *Dialogues in Limbo*, Ch. 3

52 When I was young, I was told: 'You'll see, when you're fifty. I am fifty and I haven't seen a thing.

Erik Satie (1866–1925) French composer. From a letter to his brother. *Erik Satie* (Pierre-Daniel Templier), Ch. 1

53 Thou hast nor youth nor age;
But, as it were, an after-dinner's sleep,
Dreaming on both.

William Shakespeare (1564–1616) English dramatist. *Measure for Measure*, III:1

54 Doth not the appetite alter? A man loves the meat in his youth that he cannot endure in his age.

William Shakespeare *Much Ado About Nothing*, II:3

55 Crabbed age and youth cannot live together:
Youth is full of pleasure, age is full of care;
Youth like summer morn, age like winter weather;
Youth like summer brave, age like winter bare.

William Shakespeare *The Passionate Pilgrim*, XII

56 All that the young can do for the old is to shock them and keep them up to date.

George Bernard Shaw (1856–1950) Irish dramatist and critic. *Fanny's First Play*

57 It's a funny thing about that bust. As time

goes on it seems to get younger and younger.

George Bernard Shaw Referring to a portrait bust sculpted for him by Rodin. *More Things I Wish I'd Said* (K. Edwards)

58 One's prime is elusive. You little girls, when you grow up, must be on the alert to recognize your prime at whatever time of your life it may occur. You must then live it to the full.

Muriel Spark (1918–) British novelist. *The Prime of Miss Jean Brodie*, Ch. 1

59 The mark of the immature man is that he wants to die nobly for a cause, while the mark of the mature man is that he wants to live humbly for one.

Wilhelm Stekel (1868–1940) Viennese psychiatrist. *The Catcher in the Rye* (J. D. Salinger), Ch. 24

60 Men come of age at sixty, women at fifteen.

James Stephens (1882–1950) Irish novelist. *The Observer*, 'Sayings of the Week', 1 Oct 1944

61 I was born old and get younger every day. At present I am sixty years young.

Herbert Beerbohm Tree (1853–1917) British actor and theatre manager. *Beerbohm Tree* (Hesketh Pearson)

62 Life begins at forty.

Sophie Tucker (Sophia Abuza; 1884–1966) Russian-born US singer. Attrib.

63 From birth to age eighteen, a girl needs good parents. From eighteen to thirty-five, she needs good looks. From thirty-five to fifty-five, she needs a good personality. From fifty-five on, she needs good cash.

Sophie Tucker Attrib.

64 There are no old men any more. *Playboy* and *Penthouse* have between them made an ideal of eternal adolescence, sunburnt and saunaed, with the grey dorianed out of it.

Peter Ustinov (1921–) British actor. *Dear Me*, Ch. 18

65 It is charming to totter into vogue.

Horace Walpole (1717–97) British writer. Letter to G. A. Selwyn, 1765

66 No woman should ever be quite accurate about her age. It looks so calculating.

Oscar Wilde (1854–1900) Irish-born British dramatist. *The Importance of Being Earnest*, III

67 One should never trust a woman who tells one her real age. A woman who would tell one that, would tell one anything.

Oscar Wilde *A Woman of No Importance*, I

68 The older one grows the more one likes indecency.

Virginia Woolf (1882–1941) British novelist. *Monday or Tuesday*

69 My heart leaps up when I behold
A rainbow in the sky:
So was it when my life began;
So is it now I am a man;
So be it when I shall grow old,
Or let me die!
The Child is Father of the Man;
And I could wish my days to be
Bound each to each by natural piety.

William Wordsworth (1770–1850) British poet. *My Heart Leaps Up*

70 One that is ever kind said yesterday:
'Your well-belovèd's hair has threads of grey,
And little shadows come about her eyes.'

W. B. Yeats (1865–1939) Irish poet. *The Folly of Being Comforted*

71 Where, where but here have Pride and Truth,
That long to give themselves for wage,
To shake their wicked sides at youth
Restraining reckless middle age?

W. B. Yeats *On hearing that the Students of our New University have joined the Agitation against Immoral Literature*

72 Though leaves are many, the root is one;
Through all the lying days of my youth
I swayed my leaves and flowers in the sun;
Now I may wither into the truth.

W. B. Yeats *The Coming of Wisdom with Time*

73 Wine comes in at the mouth
And love comes in at the eye;
That's all we shall know for truth
Before we grow old and die.

W. B. Yeats *A Drinking Song*

74 Be wise with speed,
A fool at forty is a fool indeed.

Edward Young (1683–1765) British poet. *Love of Fame*, II

AGGRAVATION

1 This is adding insult to injuries.

Edward Moore (1712–57) British dramatist. *The Foundling*, V

2 The point is that nobody likes having salt rubbed into their wounds, even if it is the salt of the earth.

Rebecca West (Cicely Isabel Fairfield; 1892–1983) British novelist and journalist. *The Salt of the Earth*, Ch. 2

AGREEMENT

1 My cousin Francis and I are in perfect accord – he wants Milan, and so do I.

Charles V (1500–58) Holy Roman Emperor. Referring to his dispute with Francis I of France over Italian territory. *The Story of Civilization* (W. Durant), Vol. 5

2 I am always of the opinion with the learned, if they speak first.

William Congreve (1670–1729) British Restoration dramatist. *Incognita*

3 'My idea of an agreeable person,' said Hugo Bohun, 'is a person who agrees with me.'

Benjamin Disraeli (1804–81) British statesman. *Lothair*, Ch. 35

4 We seldom attribute common sense except to

those who agree with us.

Duc de la Rochefoucauld (1613–80) French writer. *Maximes*, 347

5 Very like a whale.

William Shakespeare (1564–1616) English dramatist. *Hamlet*, III:2

6 Our agenda is now exhausted. The secretary general is exhausted. All of you are exhausted. I find it comforting that, beginning with our very first day, we find ourselves in such complete unanimity.

Paul Henri Spaak (1899–1972) Belgian statesman. Concluding the first General Assembly meeting of the United Nations.

7 Ah! don't say you agree with me. When people agree with me I always feel that I must be wrong.

Oscar Wilde (1854–1900) Irish-born British dramatist. *The Critic as Artist*, Pt. 2

8 If two men on the same job agree all the time, then one is useless. If they disagree all the time, then both are useless.

Darryl F. Zanuck (1902–79) US film producer. *The Observer*, 'Sayings of the Week', 23 Oct 1949

AGRICULTURE

See also countryside

1 We plough the fields, and scatter
The good seed on the land,
But it is fed and watered
By God's Almighty Hand.
He sends the snow in winter,
The warmth to swell the grain,
The breezes and the sunshine,
And soft refreshing rain.

Jane Montgomery Campbell (1817–78) British hymn writer. Hymn

2 Three acres and a cow.

Jesse Collings (1831–1920) British politician. Slogan used in his land-reform propaganda

3 You English bastard, you give my cows BSE then you want to know how I feel.

Georges Hourmann French cattle farmer. . *The Guardian Weekend*, 28 Dec 1996

4 Is my team ploughing,
That I was used to drive?

A. E. Housman (1859–1936) British scholar and poet. *A Shropshire Lad*, 'Bredon Hill'

5 'O Mary, go and call the cattle home,
And call the cattle home,
And call the cattle home,
Across the sands of Dee.'
The western wind was wild and dank with foam,
And all alone went she.

Charles Kingsley (1819–75) British writer. *The Sands of Dee*

6 This bread I break was once the oat,
This wine upon a foreign tree
Plunged in its fruit;
Man in the day or wind at night
Laid the crops low, broke the grape's joy.

Dylan Thomas (1914–53) Welsh poet. *This bread I break*

AIDS

1 Everywhere I go I see increasing evidence of people swirling about in a human cesspit of their own making.

James Anderton (1932–) British Chief Constable of Greater Manchester. Referring to AIDS

2 It could be said that the Aids pandemic is a classic own-goal scored by the human race against itself.

Princess Anne (1950–) The Princess Royal, only daughter of Elizabeth II. Remark, Jan 1988

3 We hope people will learn to love condoms. In the past people like Casanova had lots of fun with their condoms.

David Cox TV producer. Remark, Mar 1987

4 My message to the businessman of this country when they go abroad on business is that there is one thing above all they can take with them to stop them catching AIDS, and that is the wife.

Edwina Currie (1946–) British politician. *The Observer*, 15 Feb 1987

5 Every time you sleep with a boy you sleep with all his old girlfriends.

Government-sponsored AIDS advertisement, 1987

6 We're all going to go crazy, living this epidemic every minute, while the rest of the world goes on out there, all around us, as if nothing is happening, going on with their own lives and not knowing what it's like, what we're going through. We're living through war, but where they're living it's peacetime, and we're all in the same country.

Larry Kramer (1935–) US dramatist and novelist. *The Normal Heart*

ALCOHOL

See also abstinence, drinks, drunkenness, public houses

1 A cask of wine works more miracles than a church full of saints.

Proverb

2 Adam's ale is the best brew.

Proverb

3 A good drink makes the old young.

Proverb

4 He who drinks a little too much drinks much too much.

Proverb

5 Take a hair of the dog that bit you.

Proverb

6 There's many a slip 'twixt the cup and the lip.
Proverb

7 When the wine is in, the wit is out.
Proverb

8 If all be true that I do think,
There are five reasons we should drink;
Good wine – a friend – or being dry –
Or lest we should be by and by –
Or any other reason why.
Dean Aldrich (1647–1710) English poet. *Reasons for Drinking*

9 I feel no pain, dear mother, now
But oh, I am so dry!
O take me to a brewery
And leave me there to die.
Anonymous Shanty

10 So who's in a hurry?
Robert Benchley (1889–1945) US humorist. When asked whether he knew that drinking was a slow death. Attrib.

11 He is believed to have liked port, but to have said of claret that 'it would be port if it could'.
Richard Bentley (1662–1742) English academic. *Bentley* (R. C. Jebb)

12 Woe unto them that rise up early in the morning, that they may follow strong drink; that continue until night, till wine inflame them!
Bible: Isaiah 5:11

13 Drink no longer water, but use a little wine for thy stomach's sake and thine often infirmities.
Bible: I Timothy 5:23

14 When the ruler of the feast had tasted the water that was made wine, and knew not whence it was: (but the servants which drew the water knew;) the governor of the feast called the bridegroom,
And saith unto him, Every man at the beginning doth set forth good wine; and when men have well drunk, then that which is worse: but thou hast kept the good wine until now.
Bible: John 2:9–10

15 No man also having drunk old wine straightway desireth new: for he saith, The old is better.
Bible: Luke 5:39

16 Look not thou upon the wine when it is red, when it giveth his colour in the cup, when it moveth itself aright.
At the last it biteth like a serpent, and stingeth like an adder.
Bible: Proverbs 23:31–32

17 If we heard it said of Orientals that they habitually drank a liquor which went to their heads, deprived them of reason and made them vomit, we should say: 'How very barbarous!'
Jean de La Bruyère (1645–96) French satirist. *Les Caractères*

18 The heart which grief hath cankered
Hath one unfailing remedy – the Tankard.
C. S. Calverley (1831–84) British poet. *Beer*

19 Alcohol is like love: the first kiss is magic, the second is intimate, the third is routine. After that you just take the girl's clothes off.
Raymond Chandler (1888–1959) US novelist. *The Long Good-bye*

20 So was hir joly whistle wel y-wet.
Geoffrey Chaucer (c. 1342–1400) English poet. *The Canterbury Tales*, 'The Reve's Tale'

21 I must point out that my rule of life prescribed as an absolutely sacred rite smoking cigars and also the drinking of alcohol before, after, and if need be during all meals and in the intervals between them.
Winston Churchill (1874–1965) British statesman. Said during a lunch with the Arab leader Ibn Saud, when he heard that the king's religion forbade smoking and alcohol. *The Second World War*

22 Apart from cheese and tulips, the main product of the country is advocaat, a drink made from lawyers.
Alan Coren (1938–) British humorist and writer. Referring to Holland. *The Sanity Inspector*, 'All You Need to Know about Europe'

23 Then trust me, there's nothing like drinking
So pleasant on this side the grave;
It keeps the unhappy from thinking,
And makes e'en the valiant more brave.
Charles Dibdin (1745–1814) British actor and dramatist. *Nothing like Grog*

24 'Did you ever taste beer?' 'I had a sip of it once,' said the small servant. 'Here's a state of things!' cried Mr Swiveller.... 'She *never* tasted it – it can't be tasted in a sip!'
Charles Dickens (1812–70) British novelist. *The Old Curiosity Shop*, Ch. 57

25 First you take a drink, then the drink takes a drink, then the drink takes you.
F. Scott Fitzgerald (1896–1940) US novelist. *Ackroyd* (Jules Feiffer), '1964, May 7'

26 Best while you have it use your breath,
There is no drinking after death.
John Fletcher (1579–1625) English dramatist. With Jonson and others. *The Bloody Brother*, II:2

27 And he that will go to bed sober,
Falls with the leaf still in October.
John Fletcher *The Bloody Brother*, II:2

28 A taste for drink, combined with gout,
Had doubled him up for ever.
W. S. Gilbert (1836–1911) British dramatist. *The Gondoliers*, I

29 Let schoolmasters puzzle their brain,
With grammar, and nonsense, and learning,
Good liquor, I stoutly maintain,
Gives genius a better discerning.
Oliver Goldsmith (1728–74) Irish-born British writer. *She Stoops to Conquer*, I

30 He that goes to bed thirsty rises healthy.
George Herbert (1593–1633) English poet. *Jacula Prudentum*

31 Malt does more than Milton can
To justify God's ways to man.

A. E. Housman (1859–1936) British scholar and poet. *A Shropshire Lad*, 'The Welsh Marches'

32 Claret is the liquor for boys; port for men; but he who aspires to be a hero must drink brandy.

Samuel Johnson (1709–84) British lexicographer. *Life of Johnson* (J. Boswell), Vol. III

33 No, Sir; there were people who died of dropsies, which they contracted in trying to get drunk.

Samuel Johnson Scornfully criticizing the strength of the wine in Scotland before the Act of Union in response to Boswell's claim that there had been a lot of drunkenness. *Tour to the Hebrides* (J. Boswell)

34 Come, let me know what it is that makes a Scotchman happy!

Samuel Johnson Ordering for himself a glass of whisky. *Tour to the Hebrides* (J. Boswell)

35 My friends should drink a dozen of Claret on my Tomb.

John Keats (1795–1821) British poet. Letter to Benjamin Bailey, 14 Aug 1819

36 O, for a draught of vintage! that hath been
Cool'd a long age in the deep-delved earth.

John Keats *Ode to a Nightingale*

37 O for a beaker full of the warm South,
Full of the true, the blushful Hippocrene,
With beaded bubbles winking at the brim,
And purple-stained mouth.

John Keats *Ode to a Nightingale*

38 Even though a number of people have tried, no one has yet found a way to drink for a living.

Jean Kerr (1923–) US dramatist. *Poor Richard*

39 Frenchmen drink wine just like we used to drink water before Prohibition.

Ring Lardner Jnr (1885–1933) American humorist. *Wit's End* (R. E. Drennan)

40 It takes a good deal of physical courage to ride a horse. This, however, I have. I get it at about forty cents a flask, and take it as required.

Stephen Leacock (1869–1944) English-born Canadian economist and humorist. *Literary Lapses*, 'Reflections on Riding'

41 If die I must, let me die drinking in an inn.

Walter Map (c. 1140–c. 1209) Welsh clergyman and writer. *De Nugis Curialium*

42 The tranquilizer of greatest value since the early history of man, and which may never become outdated, is alcohol, when administered in moderation. It possesses the distinct advantage of being especially pleasant to the taste buds.

Nathan Masor (1913–) Attrib.

43 I've made it a rule never to drink by daylight and never to refuse a drink after dark.

H. L. Mencken (1880–1956) US journalist. *New York Post*, 18 Sept 1945

44 No man is genuinely happy, married, who has to drink worse gin than he used to drink when he was single.

H. L. Mencken *Prejudices*, 'Reflections on Monogamy'

45 Then to the spicy nut-brown ale.

John Milton (1608–74) English poet. *L'Allegro*

46 A torchlight procession marching down your throat.

John L. O'Sullivan (1813–95) US writer. Referring to whisky. *Collections and Recollections* (G. W. E. Russell), Ch. 19

47 *In vino veritas.*
Truth comes out in wine.

Pliny the Elder (Gaius Plinius Secundus; 23–79 AD) Roman scholar. *Natural History*, XIV

48 It is WRONG to do what everyone else does – namely, to hold the wine list just out of sight, look for the second cheapest claret on the list, and say, 'Number 22, please'.

Stephen Potter (1900–69) British writer. *One-Upmanship*, Ch. 14

49 A good general rule is to state that the bouquet is better than the taste, and vice versa.

Stephen Potter *One-Upmanship*, Ch. 14

50 It is the unbroken testimony of all history that alcoholic liquors have been used by the strongest, wisest, handsomest, and in every way best races of all times.

George Edward Bateman Saintsbury (1845–1933) British writer and critic. *Notes on a Cellar-Book*

51 People may say what they like about the decay of Christianity; the religious system that produced green Chartreuse can never really die.

Saki (Hector Hugh Munro; 1870–1916) British writer. *Reginald on Christmas Presents*

52 By insisting on having your bottle pointing to the north when the cork is being drawn, and calling the waiter Max, you may induce an impression on your guests which hours of laboured boasting might be powerless to achieve. For this purpose, however, the guests must be chosen as carefully as the wine.

Saki *The Chaplet*

53 It provokes the desire, but it takes away the performance. Therefore much drink may be said to be an equivocator with lechery.

William Shakespeare (1564–1616) English dramatist. *Macbeth*, II:3

54 I am only a beer teetotaller, not a champagne teetotaller.

George Bernard Shaw (1856–1950) Irish dramatist and critic. *Candida*

55 Alcohol is a very necessary article…It enables Parliament to do things at eleven at night that no sane person would do at eleven in the morning.

George Bernard Shaw *Major Barbara*, II

56 Gin was mother's milk to her.

George Bernard Shaw *Pygmalion*, III

57 Well, then, my stomach must just digest in its waistcoat.

Richard Brinsley Sheridan (1751–1816) British dramatist. On being warned that his drinking would destroy the coat of his stomach. *The Fine Art of Political Wit* (L. Harris)

58 Another little drink wouldn't do us any harm.

Edith Sitwell (1887–1964) British poet and writer. *Façade*, 'Scotch Rhapsody'

59 Selwyn Macgregor, the nicest boy who ever committed the sin of whisky.

Muriel Spark (1918–) British novelist. *The Go-Away Bird*, 'A Sad Tale's Best for Winter'

60 Fifteen men on the dead man's chest
Yo-ho-ho, and a bottle of rum!
Drink and the devil had done for the rest –
Yo-ho-ho, and a bottle of rum!

Robert Louis Stevenson (1850–94) Scottish writer. *Treasure Island*, Ch. 1

61 There are two things that will be believed of any man whatsoever, and one of them is that he has taken to drink.

Booth Tarkington (1869–1946) US novelist. *Penrod*, Ch. 10

62 It's a Naive Domestic Burgundy, Without Any Breeding. But I think you'll be Amused by its Presumption.

James Thurber (1894–1961) US humorist. *Men, Women and Dogs*

63 'Joe,' I said, 'was perhaps the first great nonstop literary drinker of the American nineteenth century. He made the indulgences of Coleridge and De Quincey seem like a bit of mischief in the kitchen with the cooking sherry.'

James Thurber *Alarms and Diversions*, 'The Moribundant Life...'

64 I prefer temperance hotels – although they sell worse kinds of liquor than any other kind of hotels.

Artemus Ward (Charles Farrar Browne; 1834–67) US humorous writer. *Artemus Ward's Lecture*

65 I hadn't the heart to touch my breakfast. I told Jeeves to drink it himself.

P. G. Wodehouse (1881–1975) British humorous novelist. *My Man Jeeves*

66 It was my Uncle George who discovered that alcohol was a food well in advance of modern medical thought.

P. G. Wodehouse *The Inimitable Jeeves*, Ch. 16

67 I must get out of these wet clothes and into a dry Martini.

Alexander Woollcott (1887–1943) US journalist. *Reader's Digest*

68 Father, dear father, come home with me now,
The clock in the steeple strikes one.

Henry Clay Work (1832–84) US songwriter. A temperance song. *Come Home, Father*

AMBITION

See also desire

1 He who rides a tiger is afraid to dismount.

Proverb

2 *Per ardua ad astra.*
Through hardships to the stars!

Anonymous Motto of the Royal Air Force.

3 Ah, but a man's reach should exceed his grasp,
Or what's a heaven for?

Robert Browning (1812–89) British poet. *Andrea del Sarto*

4 Man partly is and wholly hopes to be.

Robert Browning *A Death in the Desert*

5 You seem to have no real purpose in life and won't realize at the age of twenty-two that for a man life means work, and hard work if you mean to succeed.

Jennie Jerome Churchill (1854–1921) US-born British hostess and writer. Letter to Winston Churchill, 26 Feb 1897. *Jennie* (Ralph G. Martin), Vol. II

6 I have found some of the best reasons I ever had for remaining at the bottom simply by looking at the men at the top.

Frank More Colby (1865–1925) US editor. *Essays*, II

7 If thy heart fails thee, climb not at all.

Elizabeth I (1533–1603) Queen of England. Written on a window in reply to Walter RALEIGH's line. *Worthies of England* (Fuller), Vol. I

8 Hitch your wagon to a star.

Ralph Waldo Emerson (1803–82) US poet and essayist. *Society and Solitude*, 'Civilization'

9 I would like to throw an egg into an electric fan.

Oliver Herford (1863–1935) British-born US humorist. When asked if he really had no ambition beyond making people laugh. Attrib.

10 I am going to build the kind of nation that President Roosevelt hoped for, President Truman worked for and President Kennedy died for.

Lyndon B. Johnson (1908–73) US statesman. *The Sunday Times*, 27 Dec 1964

11 A slave has but one master; an ambitious man has as many masters as there are people who may be useful in bettering his position.

Jean de La Bruyère (1645–96) French satirist. *Les Caractères*

12 The shades of night were falling fast,
As through an Alpine village passed
A youth, who bore, 'mid snow and ice,
A banner with the strange device,
Excelsior!

Henry Wadsworth Longfellow (1807–82) US poet. Opening of a poem best known as a Victorian drawing-room ballad, and the butt of many music-hall jokes. Excelsior means 'higher' (Latin). *Excelsior*

13 If you would hit the mark, you must aim a little above it;

Every arrow that flies feels the attraction of earth.

Henry Wadsworth Longfellow *Elegiac Verse*

14 Fain would I climb, yet fear I to fall.

Walter Raleigh (1554–1618) English explorer. Written on a window pane. For the reply *see* ELIZABETH I. Attrib.

15 Ambition should be made of sterner stuff.

William Shakespeare (1564–1616) English dramatist. *Julius Caesar*, III:2

16 I have no spur
To prick the sides of my intent, but only
Vaulting ambition, which o'er-leaps itself,
And falls on th' other.

William Shakespeare *Macbeth*, I:7

17 And he that strives to touch the stars,
Oft stumbles at a straw.

Edmund Spenser (1552–99) English poet. *The Shepherd's Calendar*, 'July'

18 There is always room at the top.

Daniel Webster (1782–1852) US statesman. When advised not to become a lawyer because the profession was overcrowded. Attrib.

19 Well, good luck to you, kid! I'm going to write the Great Australian Novel.

Patrick White (1912–90) British-born Australian novelist. *The Vivisector*, 112

AMERICA

See also Americans

1 Our society distributes itself into Barbarians, Philistines, and Populace; and America is just ourselves, with the Barbarians quite left out, and the Populace nearly.

Matthew Arnold (1822–88) British poet and critic. *Culture and Anarchy*, Preface

2 God bless the USA, so large,
So friendly, and so rich.

W. H. Auden (1907–73) British poet. *On the Circuit*

3 Yankee Doodle came to town
Riding on a pony;
Stuck a feather in his cap
And called it Macaroni.

Edward Bangs (fl. 1775) US songwriter. *Yankee Doodle; or Father's Return to Camp*

4 O beautiful for spacious skies,
For amber waves of grain,
For purple mountain majesties
Above the fruited plain!
America! America!
God shed His grace on thee
And crown thy good with brotherhood
From sea to shining sea!

Katharine Lee Bates (1859–1929) US writer and poet. *America the Beautiful*

5 I called the New World into existence to redress the balance of the Old.

George Canning (1770–1827) British statesman. Speech, 12 Dec 1826

6 This is virgin territory for whorehouses.

Al Capone (1899–1947) Italian-born US gangster. Talking about suburban Chicago. *The Bootleggers* (Kenneth Allsop), Ch. 16

7 How beautiful it would be for someone who could not read.

G. K. Chesterton (1874–1936) British writer. Referring to the lights on Broadway. Attrib.

8 America is the only nation in history which miraculously has gone directly from barbarism to degeneration without the usual interval of civilization.

Georges Clemenceau (1841–1929) French statesman. Attrib.

9 Patriotism is easy to understand in America; it means looking out for yourself while looking out for your country.

Calvin Coolidge (1872–1933) US president. Attrib.

10 The business of America is business.

Calvin Coolidge Speech, Washington, 17 Jan 1925

11 Poor Mexico, so far from God and so near to the United States!

Porfirio Díaz (1830–1915) Mexican general and statesman. Attrib.

12 Whatever America hopes to bring to pass in this world must first come to pass in the heart of America.

Dwight D. Eisenhower (1890–1969) US general and statesman. Inaugural address, 1953

13 America is a country of young men.

Ralph Waldo Emerson (1803–82) US poet and essayist. *Society and Solitude*, 'Old Age'

14 Our country is the world – our countrymen are all mankind.

William Lloyd Garrison (1805–79) US abolitionist. *The Liberator*, 15 Dec 1837

15 New York...that unnatural city where every one is an exile, none more so than the American.

Charlotte Perkins Gilman (1860–1935) US writer. *The Living of Charlotte Perkins Gilman*

16 The United States is like a gigantic boiler. Once the fire is lighted under it there is no limit to the power it can generate.

Lord Grey (1862–1933) British statesman. *Their Finest Hour* (Winston S. Churchill), Ch. 32

17 The United States, I believe, are under the impression that they are twenty years in advance of this country; whilst, as a matter of actual verifiable fact, of course, they are just about six hours behind it.

Harold Hobson (1904–92) British theatre critic and writer. *The Devil in Woodford Wells*, Ch. 8

18 The American system of

rugged individualism.

Herbert Clark Hoover (1874–1964) US statesman. Speech, New York, 22 Oct 1928

19 It created in me a yearning for all that is wide and open and expansive. Something that will never allow me to fit in in my own country, with its narrow towns and narrow roads and narrow kindnesses and narrow reprimands.

Anthony Hopkins (1937–) Welsh actor. *The Independent*, 12 Feb 1994

20 The United States has to move very fast to even stand still.

John Fitzgerald Kennedy (1917–63) US statesman. *The Observer*, 'Sayings of the Week', 21 July 1963

21 'Tis the star-spangled banner; O long may it wave
O'er the land of the free, and the home of the brave!

Francis Scott Key (1779–1843) US lawyer. *The Star-Spangled Banner*

22 Give me your tired, your poor,
Your huddled masses yearning to breathe free,
The wretched refuse of your teeming shore,
Send these, the homeless, tempest-tossed to me,
I lift my lamp beside the golden door!

Emma Lazarus (1849–87) US poet and philanthropist. Used as an inscription on the Statue of Liberty. *The New Colossus*

23 In other countries, art and literature are left to a lot of shabby bums living in attics and feeding on booze and spaghetti, but in America the successful writer or picture-painter is indistinguishable from any other decent business man.

Sinclair Lewis (1885–1951) US novelist. *Babbitt*, Ch. 14

24 In an English ship, they say, it is poor grub, poor pay, and easy work; in an American ship, good grub, good pay, and hard work. And this is applicable to the working populations of both countries.

Jack London (1876–1916) US novelist. *The People of the Abyss*, Ch. 20

25 First the sweetheart of the nation, then the aunt, woman governs America because America is a land of boys who refuse to grow up.

Salvador de Madariaga y Rogo (1886–1978) Spanish diplomat and writer. *The Perpetual Pessimist* (Sagitarius and George)

26 If there is any country on earth where the course of true love may be expected to run smooth, it is America.

Harriet Martineau (1802–76) British writer. *Society in America*, Vol. III, 'Marriage'

27 The immense popularity of American movies abroad demonstrates that Europe is the unfinished negative of which America is the proof.

Mary McCarthy (1912–89) US novelist. *On the Contrary*

28 I believe the US is a truly monstrous force in the world, now off the leash for obvious reasons.

Harold Pinter (1930–) British dramatist. *The Independent*, 20 Sept 1993

29 The national dish of America is menus.

Robert Robinson (1927–) British writer and broadcaster. BBC TV programme, *Robinson's Travels*, Aug 1977

30 I pledge you, I pledge myself, to a new deal for the American people.

Franklin D. Roosevelt (1882–1945) US Democratic president. Speech accepting nomination for presidency, Chicago, 2 July 1932

31 America...where law and customs alike are based on the dreams of spinsters.

Bertrand Russell (1872–1970) British philosopher. *Marriage and Morals*

32 In the United States there is more space where nobody is than where anybody is. That is what makes America what it is.

Gertrude Stein (1874–1946) US writer. *The Geographical History of America*

33 I like to walk around Manhattan, catching glimpses of its wild life, the pigeons and cats and girls.

Rex Todhunter Stout (1886–1975) US writer. *Three Witnesses*, 'When a Man Murders'

34 I found there a country with thirty-two religions and only one sauce.

Talleyrand (Charles Maurice de Talleyrand-Périgord; 1754–1838) French politician. *Autant en apportent les mots* (Pedrazzini)

35 America is a large, friendly dog in a very small room. Every time it wags its tail it knocks over a chair.

Arnold Toynbee (1889–1975) British historian. Broadcast news summary, 14 July 1954

36 By the waters of Babylon we sit down and weep, when we think of thee, O America!

Horace Walpole (1717–97) British writer.
On the eve of the American Revolution. Letter to Mason, 12 June 1775

37 Up from the meadows rich with corn,
Clear in the cool September morn,
The clustered spires of Frederick stand
Green-walled by the hills of Maryland.

John Greenleaf Whittier (1807–92) US poet. *Barbara Frietchie*

38 There exists in the world today a gigantic reservoir of good will toward us, the American people.

Wendell Lewis Willkie (1892–1944) US lawyer and businessman. *One World*, Ch. 10

39 Sometimes people call me an idealist. Well, that is the way I know I am an American. America is the only idealistic nation in the world.

Woodrow Wilson (1856–1925) US statesman. Speech, Sioux Falls, 8 Sept 1919

40 America...is the prize amateur nation of the world. Germany is the prize professional nation.

Woodrow Wilson Speech, Aug 1917. *Mr Wilson's War* (John Dos Passos), Pt. III, Ch. 13

41 New York is a small place when it comes to the part of it that wakes up just as the rest is going to bed.

P. G. Wodehouse (1881–1975) British humorous novelist. *My Man Jeeves*, 'The Aunt and the Sluggard'

42 America is God's Crucible, the great Melting-Pot where all the races of Europe are melting and re-forming!

Israel Zangwill (1864–1926) British writer. *The Melting Pot*, I

AMERICANS

1 Good Americans, when they die, go to Paris.

Thomas Gold Appleton (1812–84) US writer. *Autocrat of the Breakfast Table* (O. W. Holmes), Ch. 6

2 A Boston man is the east wind made flesh.

Thomas Gold Appleton Attrib.

3 There is nothing the matter with Americans except their ideals. The real American is all right; it is the ideal American who is all wrong.

G. K. Chesterton (1874–1936) British writer. *New York Times*, 1 Feb 1931

4 Scratch an American and you get a Seventh Day Adventist every time.

Lord Hailsham (1907–) British Conservative politician. *The Observer*, 'Sayings of the Week', 1 June 1969

5 I am willing to love all mankind, *except an American.*

Samuel Johnson (1709–84) British lexicographer. *Life of Johnson* (J. Boswell), Vol. III

6 Does that mean that because Americans won't listen to sense, you intend to talk nonsense to them?

John Maynard Keynes (1883–1946) British economist. Said before a monetary conference, 1944 or 1945.

7 There won't be any revolution in America... The people are too clean. They spend all their time changing their shirts and washing themselves. You can't feel fierce and revolutionary in a bathroom.

Eric Linklater (1889–1974) Scottish novelist. *Juan in America*, Pt. V, Ch. 3

8 No one can kill Americans and brag about it. No one.

Ronald Reagan (1911–) US politician and president. *The Observer*, 'Sayings of the Week', 27 Apr 1986

9 An American is either a Jew, or an anti-Semite, unless he is both at the same time.

Jean-Paul Sartre (1905–80) French writer. *Altona*

10 That strange blend of the commercial traveller, the missionary, and the barbarian conqueror, which was the American abroad.

Olaf Stapledon (1886–1950) British philosopher and science-fiction writer. *Last and First Men*, Ch. 3

11 Americans have been conditioned to respect newness, whatever it costs them.

John Updike (1932–) US novelist. *A Month of Sundays*, Ch. 18

12 American writers want to be not good but great; and so are neither.

Gore Vidal (1925–) US novelist. *Two Sisters*

13 MRS ALLONBY. They say, Lady Hunstanton, that when good Americans die they go to Paris.
LADY HUNSTANTON. Indeed? And when bad Americans die, where do they go to?
LORD ILLINGWORTH. Oh, they go to America.

Oscar Wilde (1854–1900) Irish-born British dramatist. *See* Thomas Gold APPLETON. *A Woman of No Importance*, I

14 Like so many substantial Americans, he had married young and kept on marrying, springing from blonde to blonde like the chamois of the Alps leaping from crag to crag.

P. G. Wodehouse (1881–1975) British humorous novelist. *Wodehouse at Work to the End* (Richard Usborne), Ch. 2

ANALOGY

See also similarity

1 Though analogy is often misleading, it is the least misleading thing we have.

Samuel Butler (1835–1902) British writer. *Notebooks*

2 She, and comparisons are odious.

John Donne (1573–1631) English poet. *Elegies*, 8, 'The Comparison'

3 My mistress' eyes are nothing like the sun;
Coral is far more red than her lips' red.

William Shakespeare (1564–1616) English dramatist. *Sonnet 130*

4 And yet, by heaven, I think my love as rare
As any she belied with false compare.

William Shakespeare *Sonnet 130*

5 Jeeves coughed one soft, low, gentle cough like a sheep with a blade of grass stuck in its throat.

P. G. Wodehouse (1881–1975) British humorous novelist. *The Inimitable Jeeves*, Ch. 13

ANCESTRY

See also aristocracy, family

1 I am my own ancestor.

Duc d'Abrantes (1771–1813) French general. Said on being made a duke. Attrib.

2 I can trace my ancestry back to a protoplasmal primordial atomic globule. Consequently, my family pride is something in-conceivable. I can't help it. I was born sneering.

W. S. Gilbert (1836–1911) British dramatist. *The Mikado*, I

3 The difference between us is that my family begins with me, whereas yours ends with you.

Iphicrates (d. 353 BC) Athenian general. Reply to a descendant of Harmodius (an Athenian hero), who had derided Iphicrates for being the son of a cobbler. Attrib.

4 Being Southerners, it was a source of shame to some members of the family that we had no recorded ancestors on either side of the Battle of Hastings.

Harper Lee (1926–) US writer. *To Kill a Mockingbird*, Pt. I, Ch. 1

5 I don't know who my grandfather was; I am much more concerned to know what his grandson will be.

Abraham Lincoln (1809–65) US statesman. Taking part in a discussion on ancestry. Attrib.

ANGER

1 The man who gets angry at the right things and with the right people, and in the right way and at the right time and for the right length of time, is commended.

Aristotle (384–322 BC) Greek philosopher. *Nicomachean Ethics*, Bk. IV

2 When they heard these things, they were cut to the heart, and they gnashed on him with their teeth.

Bible: Acts 7:54

3 Never go to bed mad. Stay up and fight.

Phyllis Diller (1917–) US writer and comedienne. *Phyllis Diller's Housekeeping Hints*

4 Anger is one of the sinews of the soul.

Thomas Fuller (1608–61) English historian. *The Holy State and the Profane State*

5 Spleen can subsist on any kind of food.

William Hazlitt (1778–1830) British essayist. *On Wit and Humour*

6 Anger has overpowered him, and driven him to a revenge which was rather a stupid one, I must acknowledge, but anger makes us all stupid.

Johanna Spyri (1827–1901) Swiss writer. *Heidi*, Ch. 23

7 Anger supplies the arms.

Virgil (Publius Vergilius Maro; 70–19 BC) Roman poet. *Aeneid*, Bk. I

ANIMALISM

See also evolution, lust, mankind, sex

1 My brain: it's my second favourite organ.

Woody Allen (Allen Stewart Konigsberg; 1935–) US film actor. *Sleeper*

2 But oh, the farmyard world of sex!

Harley Granville-Barker (1877–1946) British actor and dramatist. *The Madras House*, IV

3 Be a good animal, true to your animal instincts.

D. H. Lawrence (1885–1930) British novelist. *The White Peacock*, Pt. II, Ch. 2

4 It's all this cold-hearted fucking that is death and idiocy.

D. H. Lawrence *Lady Chatterley's Lover*, Ch. 14

5 The soul started at the knee-cap and ended at the navel.

Wyndham Lewis (1882–1957) British novelist. *The Apes of God*, Pt. XII

6 – 'Do you come here often?'
'Only in the mating season.'

Spike Milligan (1918–) British comic actor and author. *The Goon Show*

7 The wren goes to't, and the small gilded fly
Does lecher in my sight.

William Shakespeare (1564–1616) English dramatist. *King Lear*, IV:6

ANIMALS

See also cats, dogs, horses, rabbits

1 There was a young lady of Riga,
Who went for a ride on a tiger;
They returned from the ride
With the lady inside,
And a smile on the face of the tiger.

Anonymous

2 The fox knows many things – the hedgehog one *big* one.

Archilochus (c. 680–c. 640 BC) Greek poet. Attrib.

3 And God said, Let the earth bring forth the living creature after his kind, cattle, and creeping thing, and beast of the earth after his kind: and it was so.

Bible: Genesis 1:24

4 Tiger! Tiger! burning bright
In the forests of the night,
What immortal hand or eye
Could frame thy fearful symmetry?

William Blake (1757–1827) British poet. *Songs of Experience*, 'The Tiger'

5 Rats!
They fought the dogs and killed the cats,
And bit the babies in the cradles.

Robert Browning (1812–89) British poet. *The Pied Piper of Hamelin*

6 And the muttering grew to a grumbling;
And the grumbling grew to a mighty rumbling;
And out of the houses the rats came tumbling.

Robert Browning *The Pied Piper of Hamelin*

7 Wee, sleekit, cow'rin', tim'rous beastie,
O what a panic's in thy breastie!

Robert Burns (1759–96) Scottish poet. *To a Mouse*

8 Whenever you observe an animal closely, you feel as if a human being sitting inside were making fun of you.

Elias Canetti (1905–94) Bulgarian-born novelist. *The Human Province*

9 The devil's walking parody
On all four-footed things.

G. K. Chesterton (1874–1936) British writer. *The Donkey*

10 Animals are such agreeable friends – they ask

no questions, they pass no criticisms.

George Eliot (Mary Ann Evans; 1819–80) British novelist. *Scenes of Clerical Life*, 'Mr Gilfil's Love Story', Ch. 7

11 Mary had a little lamb,
Its fleece was white as snow,
And everywhere that Mary went
The lamb was sure to go.

Sarah Josepha Hale (1788–1879) US writer. *Poems for Our Children*, 'Mary's Little Lamb'

12 'Twould ring the bells of Heaven
The wildest peal for years,
If Parson lost his senses
And people came to theirs,
And he and they together
Knelt down with angry prayers
For tamed and shabby tigers
And dancing dogs and bears,
And wretched, blind, pit ponies,
And little hunted hares.

Ralph Hodgson (1871–1962) British poet. *The Bells of Heaven*

13 The stars grew bright in the winter sky,
The wind came keen with a tang of frost,
The brook was troubled for new things lost,
The copse was happy for old things found,
The fox came home and he went to ground.

John Masefield (1878–1967) British poet. *Reynard the Fox*

14 I never nurs'd a dear gazelle,
To glad me with its soft black eye
But when it came to know me well,
And love me, it was sure to die!

Thomas Moore (1779–1852) Irish poet. *Lalla Rookh*

15 Dogs, like horses, are quadrupeds. That is to say, they have four rupeds, one at each corner, on which they walk.

Frank Muir (1920–) British writer and broadcaster. *You Can't Have Your Kayak and Heat It* (Frank Muir and Denis Norden), 'Ta-ra-ra-boom-de-ay!'

16 The cow is of the bovine ilk;
One end is moo, the other, milk.

Ogden Nash (1902–71) US poet. *The Cow*

17 Nothing can be more obvious than that all animals were created solely and exclusively for the use of man.

Thomas Love Peacock (1785–1866) British novelist. *Headlong Hall*, Ch. 2

18 *Exit, pursued by a bear.*

William Shakespeare (1564–1616) English dramatist. Stage direction. *The Winter's Tale*, III:3

19 There are two things for which animals are to be envied: they know nothing of future evils, or of what people say about them.

Voltaire (François-Marie Arouet; 1694–1778) French writer. Letter, 1739

20 Let dogs delight to bark and bite,
For God hath made them so;
Let bears and lions growl and fight,
For 'tis their nature too.

Isaac Watts (1674–1748) English theologian and hymn writer. *Divine Songs for Children*, 'Against Quarrelling'

21 Feather-footed through the plashy fen passes the questing vole.

Evelyn Waugh (1903–66) British novelist. *Scoop*, Bk. I, Ch. 1

22 I think I could turn and live with animals, they're so placid and self-contained,
I stand and look at them long and long.

Walt Whitman (1819–92) US poet. *Song of Myself*, 32

ANTICIPATION

See also expectation

1 A stitch in time saves nine.

Proverb

2 Don't cross the bridge till you get to it.

Proverb

3 The early bird catches the worm.

Proverb

4 Don't count your chickens before they are hatched.

Aesop (6th century BC) Reputed Greek writer of fables. *Fables*, 'The Milkmaid and her Pail'

5 To swallow gudgeons ere they're catched,
And count their chickens ere they're hatched.

Samuel Butler (1612–80) English satirist. *Hudibras*, Pt. II

6 He told me never to sell the bear's skin before one has killed the beast.

Jean de La Fontaine (1621–95) French poet. *Fables*, V, 'L'Ours et les deux Compagnons'

7 To travel hopefully is a better thing than to arrive, and the true success is to labour.

Robert Louis Stevenson (1850–94) Scottish writer. *Virginibus Puerisque*

APOLOGIES

See also regret

1 Very sorry can't come. Lie follows by post.

Charles Beresford (1846–1919) British naval officer. Reply, by telegram, to a dinner invitation at short notice from Edward, Prince of Wales. *The World of Fashion 1837–1922* (R. Nevill), Ch. 5

2 Miss Otis regrets she's unable to lunch today.

Cole Porter (1893–1964) US songwriter. *Hi Diddle Diddle*, Miss Otis Regrets

3 Love means never having to say you're sorry.

Erich Segal (1937–) US writer. *Love Story*

4 Mr. Speaker, I said the honorable member was a liar it is true and I am sorry for it. The honourable member may place the punctuation where he pleases.

Richard Brinsley Sheridan (1751–1816) British dramatist. On being asked to apologize for calling a fellow MP a liar. Attrib.

5 It is a good rule in life never to apologize. The

right sort of people do not want apologies, and the wrong sort take a mean advantage of them.

P. G. Wodehouse (1881–1975) British humorous novelist. *The Man Upstairs and Other Stories*

APPEARANCE

See also appearances, beauty, clothes, cosmetics, eyes

1 Fine feathers make fine birds.

Proverb

2 Handsome is as handsome does.

Proverb

3 A homely face and no figure have aided many women heavenward.

Minna Antrim (1861–?) US writer. *Naked Truth and Veiled Allusions*

4 Take a close-up of a woman past sixty! You might as well use a picture of a relief map of Ireland!

Nancy Astor (1879–1964) American-born British politician. When asked for a close-up photograph. Attrib.

5 But if a woman have long hair, it is a glory to her: for her hair is given her for a covering.

Bible: I Corinthians 11:15

6 Alas, after a certain age every man is responsible for his face.

Albert Camus (1913–60) French existentialist writer. *The Fall*

7 Ears like bombs and teeth like splinters:
A blitz of a boy is Timothy Winters.

Charles Causley (1917–) British poet and broadcaster. *Timothy Winters*

8 It was a blonde. A blonde to make a bishop kick a hole in a stained-glass window.

Raymond Chandler (1888–1959) US novelist. *Farewell, My Lovely*, Ch. 13

9 Sunburn is very becoming – but only when it is even – one must be careful not to look like a mixed grill.

Noël Coward (1899–1973) British dramatist. *The Lido Beach*

10 The ring so worn, as you behold,
So thin, so pale, is yet of gold.

George Crabbe (1754–1832) British poet. *His Mother's Wedding Ring*

11 The most delightful advantage of being bald – one can hear snowflakes.

R. G. Daniels (1916–93) British magistrate. *The Observer*, 'Sayings of the Week', 11 July 1976

12 He had but one eye, and the popular prejudice runs in favour of two.

Charles Dickens (1812–70) British novelist. Said by Mr Squeers. *Nicholas Nickleby*, Ch. 4

13 It was not a bosom to repose upon, but it was a capital bosom to hang jewels upon.

Charles Dickens Describing Mrs Merdle. *Little Dorrit*, Bk. I, Ch. 21

14 I am so changed that my oldest creditors would hardly know me.

Henry Stephen Fox (1791–1846) British diplomat. Remark after an illness. Letter from Byron to John Murray, 8 May 1817

15 There is a great difference between painting a face and not washing it.

Thomas Fuller (1608–61) English historian. *Church History*, Bk. VII

16 The flowers that bloom in the spring,
Tra la,
Have nothing to do with the case.
I've got to take under my wing,
Tra la,
A most unattractive old thing,
Tra la,
With a caricature of a face.

W. S. Gilbert (1836–1911) British dramatist. *The Mikado*, II

17 Where's the cheek that doth not fade,
Too much gaz'd at? Where's the maid
Whose lip mature is ever new?

John Keats (1795–1821) British poet. *Fancy*, I

18 It always seemed to me that men wore their beards, like they wear their neckties, for show. I shall always remember Lewis for saying his beard was part of him.

D. H. Lawrence (1885–1930) British novelist. *St Mawr*

19 There was an Old Man with a beard,
Who said, 'It is just as I feared! –
Two Owls and a Hen,
Four Larks and a Wren,
Have all built their nests in my beard!'

Edward Lear (1812–88) British artist and writer. *Book of Nonsense*

20 A smile that snapped back after using, like a stretched rubber band.

Sinclair Lewis (1885–1951) US novelist. Attrib.

21 The Lord prefers common-looking people. That is why he makes so many of them.

Abraham Lincoln (1809–65) US statesman. *Our President* (James Morgan), Ch. 6

22 He looks as if he had been weaned on a pickle.

Alice Roosevelt Longworth (1884–1980) US hostess. Referring to John Calvin Coolidge, US president 1923–29. *Crowded Hours*

23 Gentlemen always seem to remember blondes.

Anita Loos (1891–1981) US novelist. *Gentlemen Prefer Blondes*, Ch. 1

24 In high school and college my sister Mary was very popular with the boys, but I had braces on my teeth and got high marks.

Betty MacDonald (1908–58) US writer. *The Egg and I*, Ch. 2

25 There's a man outside with a big black moustache.

– Tell him I've got one.

Groucho Marx (Julius Marx; 1895–1977) US comedian. *Horse Feathers*

26 To Crystal, hair was the most important thing on earth. She would never get married because you couldn't wear curlers in bed.

Edna O'Brien (1936–) Irish novelist. *Winter's Tales*, 8, 'Come into the Drawing Room, Doris'

27 Men seldom make passes
At girls who wear glasses.

Dorothy Parker (1893–1967) US writer. Attrib.

28 All I say is, nobody has any business to go around looking like a horse and behaving as if it were all right. You don't catch horses going around looking like people, do you?

Dorothy Parker *Horsie*

29 Had Cleopatra's nose been shorter, the whole face of the world would have changed.

Blaise Pascal (1623–62) French philosopher and mathematician. *Pensées*, II

30 To church; and with my mourning, very handsome, and new periwig, make a great show.

Samuel Pepys (1633–1703) English diarist. *Diary*, 31 Mar 1667

31 My nose is huge! Vile snub-nose, flat-nosed ass, flat-head, let me inform you that I am proud of such an appendage, since a big nose is the proper sign of a friendly, good, courteous, witty, liberal, and brave man, such as I am.

Edmond Rostand (1868–1918) French poet and dramatist. *Cyrano de Bergerac*, I:1

32 In the spring...your lovely Chloë lightly turns to one mass of spots.

Ronald Searle (1920–) British cartoonist. *The Terror of St Trinian's*, Ch. 7

33 LORD NORTHCLIFFE. The trouble with you, Shaw, is that you look as if there were famine in the land.
G.B.S. The trouble with you, Northcliffe, is that you look as if you were the cause of it.

George Bernard Shaw (1856–1950) Irish dramatist and critic. Attrib.

34 Why not be oneself? That is the whole secret of a successful appearance. If one is a greyhound why try to look like a Pekinese?

Edith Sitwell (1887–1964) British poet and writer. *Why I Look As I Do*

35 A short neck denotes a good mind...You see, the messages go quicker to the brain because they've shorter to go.

Muriel Spark (1918–) British novelist. *The Ballad of Peckham Rye*, Ch. 7

36 But Shelley had a hyper-thyroid face.

John Collings Squire (1884–1958) British journalist. *Ballade of the Glandular Hypothesis*

37 ...his nicotine eggyellow weeping walrus Victorian moustache worn thick and long in memory of Doctor Crippen.

Dylan Thomas (1914–53) Welsh poet. *Under Milk Wood*

38 Very hard for a man with a wig to keep order.

Evelyn Waugh (1903–66) British novelist. *Decline and Fall*, Pt. I, Ch. 3

39 Enclosing every thin man, there's a fat man demanding elbow-room.

Evelyn Waugh *Officers and Gentlemen*, Interlude

40 But there are other things than dissipation that thicken the features. Tears, for example.

Rebecca West (Cicely Isabel Fairfield; 1892–1983) British novelist and journalist. *Black Lamb and Grey Falcon*, 'Serbia'

41 Grief has turned her fair.

Oscar Wilde (1854–1900) Irish-born British dramatist. Referring to the fact that a recently-bereaved lady friend had dyed her hair blonde. Attrib.

42 Big chap with a small moustache and the sort of eye that can open an oyster at sixty paces.

P. G. Wodehouse (1881–1975) British humorous novelist. *The Code of the Woosters*

43 The stationmaster's whiskers are of a Victorian bushiness and give the impression of having been grown under glass.

P. G. Wodehouse *Wodehouse at Work to the End* (Richard Usborne), Ch. 2

APPEARANCES

See also appearance, deception, hypocrisy

1 All that glitters is not gold.

Proverb

2 Appearances are deceptive.

Proverb

3 Never judge from appearances.

Proverb

4 Still waters run deep.

Proverb

5 Things are not always what they seem.

Proverb

6 Vice is often clothed in virtue's habit.

Proverb

7 You can't tell a book by its cover.

Proverb

8 The lamb that belonged to the sheep whose skin the wolf was wearing began to follow the wolf in the sheep's clothing.

Aesop (6th century BC) Reputed Greek writer of fables. *Fables*, 'The Wolf in Sheep's Clothing'

9 The French are wiser than they seem, and the Spaniards seem wiser than they are.

Francis Bacon (1561–1626) English philosopher. *Essays*, 'Of Seeming Wise'

10 No-wher so bisy a man as he ther nas,
And yet he semed bisier than he was.

Geoffrey Chaucer (c. 1342–1400) English poet. Referring to the man of law. *The Canterbury Tales*, Prologue

11 Keep up appearances; there lies the test
The world will give thee credit for the rest.

Charles Churchill (1731–64) British poet. *Night*

12 I may not hope from outward forms to win
The passion and the life, whose fountains are within.

Samuel Taylor Coleridge (1772–1834) British poet. *Dejection: An Ode*

13 Appearances are not held to be a clue to the truth. But we seem to have no other.

Ivy Compton-Burnett (1892–1969) British novelist. *Manservant and Maidservant*

14 No man could be so wise as Thurlow looked.

Charles James Fox (1749–1806) British Whig politician. *Lives of the Lord Chancellors* (Campbell), Vol. V

15 Ah, pray make no mistake,
We are not shy;
We're very wide awake,
The moon and I.

W. S. Gilbert (1836–1911) British dramatist. *The Mikado*, II

16 An' for all 'is dirty 'ide
'E was white, clear white, inside
When 'e went to tend the wounded under fire!

Rudyard Kipling (1865–1936) Indian-born British writer. *Gunga Din*

17 Strip the phoney tinsel off Hollywood and you'll find the real tinsel underneath.

Oscar Levant (1906–72) US pianist and actor. Attrib.

18 And you cannot tell by the way a party looks or how he lives in this town, if he has any scratch, because many a party who is around in automobiles, and wearing good clothes, and chucking quite a swell is nothing but a phonus bolonus and does not have any real scratch whatever.

Damon Runyon (1884–1946) US writer. *More than Somewhat*, 'The Snatching of Bookie Bob'

19 Things are entirely what they appear to be and *behind them*...there is nothing.

Jean-Paul Sartre (1905–80) French writer. *Nausea*

20 Care I for the limb, the thews, the stature, bulk, and big assemblance of a man! Give me the spirit.

William Shakespeare (1564–1616) English dramatist. *Henry IV, Part Two*, III:2

21 Through tatter'd clothes small vices do appear;
Robes and furr'd gowns hide all.

William Shakespeare *King Lear*, IV:6

22 Our purses shall be proud, our garments poor;
For 'tis the mind that makes the body rich;
And as the sun breaks through the darkest clouds,
So honour peereth in the meanest habit.

William Shakespeare *The Taming of the Shrew*, IV:3

23 It is only shallow people who do not judge by appearances.

Oscar Wilde (1854–1900) Irish-born British dramatist. *The Picture of Dorian Gray*, Ch. 2

ARCHITECTURE

See also houses, stately homes

1 Sir Christopher Wren
Said, 'I am going to dine with some men.
If anybody calls
Say I am designing St Paul's.'

Edmund Clerihew Bentley (1875–1956) British writer. *Biography for Beginners*

2 A very stately palace before him, the name of which was Beautiful.

John Bunyan (1628–88) English writer. *The Pilgrim's Progress*, Pt. I

3 You have to give this much to the Luftwaffe – when it knocked down our buildings it did not replace them with anything more offensive than rubble. We did that.

Charles, Prince of Wales (1948–) Eldest son of Elizabeth II. *See also* SITWELL. *The Observer*, 'Sayings of the Week', 6 Dec 1987

4 Like a carbuncle on the face of an old and valued friend.

Charles, Prince of Wales Referring to a proposed modern extension to the National Gallery. Speech, 1986

5 'Fan vaulting'...an architectural device which arouses enormous enthusiasm on account of the difficulties it has all too obviously involved but which from an aesthetic standpoint frequently belongs to the 'Last-supper-carved-on-a-peach-stone' class of masterpiece.

Osbert Lancaster (1908–86) British cartoonist. *Pillar to Post*, 'Perpendicular'

6 What has happened to architecture since the second world war that the only passers-by who can contemplate it without pain are those equipped with a white stick and a dog?

Bernard Levin (1928–) British journalist. *The Times*, 1983 can contemplate it a white stick and a dog

7 Sculpture to me is like poetry, and architecture like prose.

Maya Lin Architect and sculptor. *The Observer*, 'Sayings of the Week', 14 May 1994

8 I declare this thing open – whatever it is.

Prince Philip (1921–) The consort of Queen Elizabeth II. Opening a new annex at Vancouver City Hall. Attrib.

9 No person who is not a great sculptor or painter can be an architect. If he is not a sculptor or painter, he can only be a *builder*.

John Ruskin (1819–1900) British art critic and writer. *Lectures on Architecture and Painting*

10 When we build let us think that we build for ever.

John Ruskin *The Seven Lamps of Architecture*, Ch. 6, 'The Lamp of Memory'

11 Architecture in general is frozen music.

Friedrich Wilhelm Joseph von Schelling (1775–1854) German philosopher. *Philosophie der Kunst*

12 Many of my buildings are condemned now in advance.

Richard Seifert (1910–) British architect. He designed Centre Point, London and other office block schemes. *The Observer*, 'Sayings of the Week', 6 Aug 1972

13 How simple-minded of the Germans to imagine that we British could be cowed by the destruction of our ancient monuments! As though any havoc of the German bombs could possibly equal the things we have done ourselves!

Osbert Sitwell (1892–1969) British writer. *See also* CHARLES, PRINCE OF WALES. *The Collected Essays, Journalism and Letters of George Orwell*, Vol. III

14 It's beige! My color!

Elsie De Wolfe (1865–1950) US designer. On first sighting the Acropolis. *Elsie de Wolfe* (J. Smith)

15 In *Architecture* as in all other *Operative* Arts, the *end* must direct the *Operation*. The *end* is to build well. Well building hath three Conditions. *Commodity, Firmness,* and *Delight*.

Henry Wotton (1568–1639) English poet and diplomat. *Elements of Architecture*, Pt. I

ARGUMENTS

1 It takes two to make a quarrel.

Proverb

2 Least said soonest mended.

Proverb

3 For every why he had a wherefore.

Samuel Butler (1612–80) English satirist. *Hudibras*, Pt. I

4 There is only one way under high heaven to get the best of an argument – and that is to avoid it.

Dale Carnegie (1888–1955) US lecturer and writer. *Dale Carnegie's Scrapbook*

5 Many a long dispute among divines may be thus abridged: It is so. It is not so. It is so. It is not so.

Benjamin Franklin (1706–90) US scientist and statesman. *Poor Richard's Almanack*

6 In every age and clime we see,
Two of a trade can ne'er agree.

John Gay (1685–1732) English poet and dramatist. *Fables*

7 Scholars dispute, and the case is still before the courts.

Horace (Quintus Horatius Flaccus; 65–8 BC) Roman poet. *Ars Poetica c. 8* BC

8 'It's like the question of the authorship of the *Iliad*,' said Mr Cardan. 'The author of that poem is either Homer or, if not Homer, somebody else of the same name.'

Aldous Huxley (1894–1964) British novelist. *Those Barren Leaves*, Pt. V, Ch. 4

9 It takes in reality only one to make a quarrel. It is useless for the sheep to pass resolutions in favour of vegetarianism while the wolf remains of a different opinion.

Dean Inge (1860–1954) British churchman. *Outspoken Essays*

10 Sir, I have found you an argument; but I am not obliged to find you an understanding.

Samuel Johnson (1709–84) British lexicographer. *Life of Johnson* (J. Boswell), Vol. IV

11 Though a quarrel in the streets is a thing to be hated, the energies displayed in it are fine; the commonest man shows a grace in his quarrel.

John Keats (1795–1821) British poet. Letter

12 When men understand what each other mean, they see, for the most part, that controversy is either superfluous or hopeless.

Cardinal Newman (1801–90) British theologian. Sermon, Oxford, Epiphany 1839

13 Quarrels would not last so long if the fault were on only one side.

Duc de la Rochefoucauld (1613–80) French writer. *Maximes*, 496

14 The most savage controversies are those about matters as to which there is no good evidence either way.

Bertrand Russell (1872–1970) British philosopher. *Unpopular Essays*

15 I love argument, I love debate. I don't expect anyone just to sit there and agree with me, that's not their job.

Margaret Thatcher (1925–) British politician and prime minister. *The Times*, 1980

16 I did not know that we had ever quarrelled.

Henry David Thoreau (1817–62) US writer. On being urged to make his peace with God. Attrib.

17 I am, sir for the last time in my life, Your Humble Servant Horace Walpole.

Horace Walpole (1717–97) British writer. Ending a letter written to an uncle with whom he had recently quarrelled. *Horace Walpole* (R. Ketton-Cremes)

18 I am not arguing with you – I am telling you.

James Whistler (1834–1903) US painter. *The Gentle Art of Making Enemies*

19 No question is ever settled
Until it is settled right.

Ella Wheeler Wilcox (1850–1919) US poet. *Settle the Question Right*

ARISTOCRACY

See also ancestry, class, Houses of Parliament, nobility, stately homes, titles

1 One has often wondered whether upon the whole earth there is anything so unintelligent, so unapt to perceive how the world is really going, as an ordinary young Englishman of our upper class.

Matthew Arnold (1822–88) British poet and critic. *Culture and Anarchy*, Ch. 2

2 Like many of the upper class
He liked the sound of broken glass.

Hilaire Belloc (1870–1953) French-born British poet. *See also* Evelyn WAUGH. *New Cautionary Tales*, 'About John'

3 The nobility of England, my lord, would have snored through the Sermon on the Mount.

Robert Bolt (1924–95) British playwright. *A Man for All Seasons*

4 We, my lords, may thank heaven that we have something better than our brains to depend upon.

Earl of Chesterfield (1694–1773) English statesman. Speech, House of Lords. *The Story of Civilization* (W. Durant), Vol. 9

5 Democracy means government by the uneducated, while aristocracy means government by the badly educated.

G. K. Chesterton (1874–1936) British writer. *New York Times*, 1 Feb 1931

6 The Stately Homes of England
How beautiful they stand,
To prove the upper classes
Have still the upper hand.

Noël Coward (1899–1973) British dramatist. *Operette*, 'The Stately Homes of England'

7 If human beings could be propagated by cutting, like apple trees, aristocracy would be biologically sound.

J. B. S. Haldane (1892–1964) British geneticist. *The Inequality of Man*, title essay

8 There are no credentials They do not even need a medical certificate. They need not be sound either in body or mind. They only require a certificate of birth – just to prove that they are first of the litter. You would not choose a spaniel on these principles.

David Lloyd George (1863–1945) British Liberal statesman. Budget Speech, 1909

9 A fully equipped Duke costs as much to keep up as two Dreadnoughts, and Dukes are just as great a terror, and they last longer.

David Lloyd George Speech, Limehouse, 30 July 1909

10 An aristocracy in a republic is like a chicken whose head has been cut off: it may run about in a lively way, but in fact it is dead.

Nancy Mitford (1904–73) British writer. *Noblesse Oblige*

11 He is without strict doubt a Hoorah Henry, and he is generally figured as nothing but a lob as far as doing anything useful in this world is concerned.

Damon Runyon (1884–1946) US writer. *Short Takes*, 'Tight Shoes'

12 Kind hearts are more than coronets,
And simple faith than Norman blood.

Alfred, Lord Tennyson (1809–92) British poet. *Lady Clara Vere de Vere*, VI

13 If the French noblesse had been capable of playing cricket with their peasants, their chateaux would never have been burnt.

George Macaulay Trevelyan (1876–1962) British historian. *English Social History*, Ch. XIII

14 My Lord Bath, you and I are now two as insignificant men as any in England.

Robert Walpole (1676–1745) British statesman. Said to William Pulteney, Earl of Bath, when they were promoted to the peerage (1742). *Political & Literary Anecdotes* (W. King)

15 The sound of the English county families baying for broken glass.

Evelyn Waugh (1903–66) British novelist. *See also* Hilaire BELLOC. *Decline and Fall*, Prelude

16 Unlike the male codfish which, suddenly finding itself the parent of three million five hundred thousand little codfish, cheerfully resolves to love them all, the British aristocracy is apt to look with a somewhat jaundiced eye on its younger sons.

P. G. Wodehouse (1881–1975) British humorous novelist. *Wodehouse at Work to the End* (Richard Usborne), Ch. 5

ARMY

See also officers, soldiers, war, weapons

1 Oh! the grand old Duke of York
He had ten thousand men;
He marched them up to the top of the hill,
And he marched them down again.
And when they were up they were up,
And when they were down they were down,
And when they were only half way up,
They were neither up nor down.

Anonymous Traditional

2 Conduct…to the prejudice of good order and military discipline.

Anonymous Army Act, 40

3 The chief attraction of military service has consisted and will consist in this compulsory and irreproachable idleness.

Leo Tolstoy (1828–1910) Russian writer. *War and Peace*, Bk. VII, Ch. 1

4 An army is a nation within a nation; it is one of the vices of our age.

Alfred de Vigny (1797–1863) French writer. *Servitude et grandeur militaire*, 1

5 Ours is composed of the scum of the earth.

Duke of Wellington (1769–1852) British general and statesman. Of the British army. Remark, 4 Nov 1831

6 The army ages men sooner than the law and philosophy; it exposes them more freely to germs, which undermine and destroy, and it shelters them more completely from thought, which stimulates and preserves.

H. G. Wells (1866–1946) British writer. *Bealby*, Pt. VIII, Ch. 1

ARROGANCE

See also conceit, egotism, pride

1 The need to be right – the sign of a vulgar mind.

Albert Camus (1913–60) French existentialist writer. *Notebooks*, 1935–42

2 I am sure no man in England will take away my life to make you King.

Charles II (1630–85) King of England. To his brother James following revelation of Popish Plot fabricated by Titus Oates. Attrib.

3 He was like a cock who thought the sun had risen to hear him crow.

George Eliot (Mary Ann Evans; 1819–80) British novelist. *Adam Bede*

4 If this young man expresses himself in terms too deep for *me*,
Why, what a very singularly deep young man this deep young man must be!

W. S. Gilbert (1836–1911) British dramatist. *Patience*, I

5 There, but for the Grace of God, goes God.

Herman J. Mankiewicz (1897–1953) US journalist and screenwriter. Said of Orson Welles in the making of *Citizen Kane*. Also attributed to others. *The Citizen Kane Book*

6 The bullet that is to kill me has not yet been moulded.

Napoleon I (Napoleon Bonaparte; 1769–1821) French emperor. In reply to his brother Joseph, King of Spain, who had asked whether he had ever been hit by a cannonball. Attrib.

7 What His Royal Highness most particularly prides himself upon, is the excellent harvest.

Richard Brinsley Sheridan (1751–1816) British dramatist. Lampooning George IV's habit of taking credit for everything good in England. *The Fine Art of Political Wit* (L. Harris)

8 A LADY. This landscape reminds me of your work.
WHISTLER. Yes madam, Nature is creeping up.

James Whistler (1834–1903) US painter. *Whistler Stories* (D. Seitz)

9 Well, not bad, but there are decidedly too many of them, and they are not very well arranged. I would have done it differently.

James Whistler His reply when asked if he agreed that the stars were especially beautiful one night. Attrib.

10 The Admiral of the Atlantic salutes the Admiral of the Pacific.

Wilhelm II (1859–1941) King of Prussia and Emperor of Germany. Telegram sent to Czar Nicholas II during a naval exercise. *The Shadow of the Winter Palace* (E. Crankshaw)

11 All men think all men mortal, but themselves.

Edward Young (1683–1765) British poet. *Night Thoughts*

ART

See also artists, arts, painting, design

1 The works of art, by being publicly exhibited and offered for sale, are becoming articles of trade, following as such the unreasoning laws of markets and fashion; and public and even private patronage is swayed by their tyrannical influence.

Prince Albert (1819–61) The consort of Queen Victoria. Referring to the Great Exhibition. Speech, Royal Academy Dinner, 3 May 1851

2 The object of art is to give life a shape.

Jean Anouilh (1910–87) French dramatist. *The Rehearsal*

3 The lower one's vitality, the more sensitive one is to great art.

Max Beerbohm (1872–1956) British writer. *Seven Men*, 'Enoch Soames'

4 It would follow that 'significant form' was form behind which we catch a sense of ultimate reality.

Clive Bell (1881–1964) British art critic. *Art*, Pt. I, Ch. 3

5 Art is the only thing that can go on mattering once it has stopped hurting.

Elizabeth Bowen (1899–1973) Irish novelist. *The Heat of the Day*, Ch. 16

6 Art for art's sake.

Victor Cousin (1792–1867) French philosopher. Lecture, Sorbonne, 1818

7 Art is a jealous mistress.

Ralph Waldo Emerson (1803–82) US poet and essayist. *Conduct of Life*, 'Wealth'

8 Works of art, in my opinion, are the only objects in the material universe to possess internal order, and that is why, though I don't believe that only art matters, I do believe in Art for Art's sake.

E. M. Forster (1879–1970) British novelist. *Art for Art's Sake*

9 …I rarely draw what I see. I draw what I feel in my body.

Barbara Hepworth (1903–75) British sculptor. *World of Art Series* (A. M. Hammersmith)

10 In terms of conceptual art, the sheep had already made its statement.

Damien Hirst (1965–) British artist. Referring to the vandalizing of one of his works, which featured a preserved dead sheep. *The Observer*, 'Sayings of the Week', 21 Aug 1994

11 Art has to move you and design does not, unless it's a good design for a bus.

David Hockney (1937–) British painter, draughtsman and printmaker. Remark, Oct 1988

12 In free society art is not a weapon…Artists are not engineers of the soul.

John Fitzgerald Kennedy (1917–63) US statesman. Address at Dedication of the Robert Frost Library, 26 Oct 1963

13 But the Devil whoops, as he whooped of old: 'It's clever, but is it art?'

Rudyard Kipling (1865–1936) Indian-born British writer. *The Conundrum of the Workshops*

14 Art is not a special sauce applied to ordinary

cooking; it is the cooking itself if it is good.

W. R. Lethaby (1857–1931) British architect. *Form in Civilization*, 'Art and Workmanship'

15 I do not know whether he draws a line himself. But I assume that his is the direction...It makes Disney the most significant figure in graphic art since Leonardo.

David Low (1871–1963) New-Zealand-born newspaper cartoonist. *Walt Disney* (R. Schickel), Ch. 20

16 In England, pop art and fine art stand resolutely back to back.

Colin MacInnes (1914–76) British novelist. *England, Half English*, 'Pop Songs and Teenagers'

17 Art is not a mirror to reflect the world, but a hammer with which to shape it.

Vladimir Mayakovsky (1893–1930) Soviet poet. *The Guardian*, 11 Dec 1974

18 Nothing unites the English like war. Nothing divides them like Picasso.

Hugh Mills (1913–71) British screenwriter. *Prudence and the Pill*

19 To be aristocratic in Art one must avoid polite society.

George Moore (1852–1933) Irish writer and art critic. *Enemies of Promise* (Cyril Connolly), Ch. 15

20 All art deals with the absurd and aims at the simple. Good art speaks truth, indeed *is* truth, perhaps the only truth.

Iris Murdoch (1919–) Irish-born British novelist. *The Black Prince*, 'Bradley Pearson's Foreword'

21 All art constantly aspires towards the condition of music.

Walter Pater (1839–94) British critic. *The Renaissance*, 'The School of Giorgione'

22 When I was their age, I could draw like Raphael, but it took me a lifetime to learn to draw like them.

Pablo Picasso (1881–1973) Spanish painter. Visiting an exhibition of drawings by children. *Picasso: His Life and Work* (Ronald Penrose)

23 Burnings of people and (what was more valuable) works of art.

A. L. Rowse (1903–) British historian and critic. *Historical Essays* (H. R. Trevor-Roper)

24 Life without industry is guilt, and industry without art is brutality.

John Ruskin (1819–1900) British art critic and writer. *Lectures on Art*, 3, 'The Relation of Art to Morals', 23 Feb 1870

25 Fine art is that in which the hand, the head, and the heart of man go together.

John Ruskin *The Two Paths*, Lecture II

26 The trouble, Mr Goldwyn is that you are only interested in art and I am only interested in money.

George Bernard Shaw (1856–1950) Irish dramatist and critic. Turning down Goldwyn's offer to buy the screen rights of his plays. *The Movie Moguls* (Philip French), Ch. 4

27 Skill without imagination is craftsmanship and gives us many useful objects such as wickerwork picnic baskets. Imagination without skill gives us modern art.

Tom Stoppard (1937–) Czech-born British dramatist. *Artist Descending a Staircase*

28 Art is not a handicraft, it is the transmission of feeling the artist has experienced.

Leo Tolstoy (1828–1910) Russian writer. *What is Art?*, Ch. 19

29 What a delightful thing this perspective is!

Paolo Uccello (1397–1475) Italian painter. *Men of Art* (T. Craven)

30 ...any authentic work of art must start an argument between the artist and his audience.

Rebecca West (Cicely Isabel Fairfield; 1892–1983) British novelist and journalist. *The Court and the Castle*, Pt. I, Ch. 1

31 Art is the imposing of a pattern on experience, and our aesthetic enjoyment is recognition of the pattern.

A. N. Whitehead (1861–1947) British philosopher. *Dialogues*, 228

32 Art never expresses anything but itself.

Oscar Wilde (1854–1900) Irish-born British dramatist. *The Decay of Lying*

33 All Art is quite useless.

Oscar Wilde *The Picture of Dorian Gray*, Preface

34 Art is the most intense mode of individualism that the world has known.

Oscar Wilde *The Soul of Man Under Socialism*

ARTHURIAN LEGEND

1 What were they going to do with the Grail when they found it, Mr Rossetti?

Max Beerbohm (1872–1956) British writer. Caption to a cartoon

2 On either side the river lie
Long fields of barley and of rye,
That clothe the wold and meet the sky;
And thro' the field the road runs by
To many-tower'd Camelot.

Alfred, Lord Tennyson (1809–92) British poet. *The Lady of Shalott*, Pt. I

3 An arm
Rose up from out the bosom of the lake,
Clothed in white samite, mystic, wonderful.

Alfred, Lord Tennyson *Idylls of the King*, 'The Passing of Arthur'

ARTISTS

General quotes

See also art, painting

1 Poets and painters are outside the class system, or rather they constitute a special class of their own, like the circus people and the gipsies.

Gerald Brenan (Edward Fitzgerald Brenan; 1894–1987) British writer. *Thoughts in a Dry Season*, 'Writing'

2 Remember I'm an artist. And you know what that means in a court of law. Next worst to an actress.

Joyce Cary (1888–1957) British novelist. *The Horse's Mouth*, Ch. 14

3 Beware of the artist who's an intellectual also. The artist who doesn't fit.

F. Scott Fitzgerald (1896–1940) US novelist. *This Side of Paradise*, Bk. II, Ch. 5

4 I don't advise any one to take it up as a business proposition, unless they really have talent, and are crippled so as to deprive them of physical labor.

Grandma Moses (Anna Mary Robertson Moses; 1860–1961) US primitive painter. Referring to painting. *The New York Times*, 'How Do I Paint?', 11 May 1947

5 An amateur is an artist who supports himself with outside jobs which enable him to paint. A professional is someone whose wife works to enable him to paint.

Ben Shahn (1898–1969) US artist. Attrib.

6 What is an artist? For every thousand people there's nine hundred doing the work, ninety doing well, nine doing good, and one lucky bastard who's the artist.

Tom Stoppard (1937–) Czech-born British dramatist. *Travesties*, I

7 A painter should not paint what he sees, but what will be seen.

Paul Valéry (1871–1945) French poet and writer. *Mauvaises Pensées et Autres*

8 An artist is someone who produces things that people don't need to have but that he – for *some* reason – thinks it would be a good idea to give them.

Andy Warhol (Andrew Warhola; 1926–87) US pop artist. *From A to B and Back Again*, 'Atmosphere'

9 A living is made, Mr Kemper, by selling something that everybody needs at least once a year. Yes, sir! And a million is made by producing something that everybody needs every day. You artists produce something that nobody needs at any time.

Thornton Wilder (1897–1975) US novelist and dramatist. *The Matchmaker*, II

Specific quotes

10 It is comparatively easy to achieve a certain unity in a picture by allowing one colour to dominate, or by muting all the colours. Matisse did neither. He clashed his colours together like cymbals and the effect was like a lullaby.

John Berger (1926–) British author and art critic. *Toward Reality*

11 When Sir Joshua Reynolds died
All Nature was degraded;
The King dropped a tear in the Queen's ear,
And all his pictures faded.

William Blake (1757–1827) British poet. *On Art and Artists*

12 One of the reasons why medieval and renaissance architecture is so much better than our own is that the architects were artists. Bernini, one of the great artists of seventeenth-century Rome, was a sculptor.

Kenneth Clark (1903–83) British art historian. *Civilisation*

13 I do not paint a portrait to look like the subject, rather does the person grow to look like his portrait.

Salvador Dali (1904–89) Spanish painter. *Diary of a Genius*

14 The Epstein makes me feel physically sick. The wretched woman has two sets of breasts and a hip joint like a merry thought.

John Galsworthy (1867–1933) British novelist. Letter to Edward Garnett, 14 June 1925

15 His subjects are softened and sentimentalised too much. It is not simple unaffected nature that we see, but nature sitting for her picture.

William Hazlitt (1778–1830) British essayist. Referring to Thomas Gainsborough's pictures.

16 If people dug up the remains of this civilization a thousand years hence, and found Epstein's statues and that man Ellis, they would think we were just savages.

Doris Lessing (1919–) British novelist. *Martha Quest*, Pt. I, Ch. 1

17 I paint objects as I think them, not as I see them.

Pablo Picasso (1881–1973) Spanish painter. *Cubism* (John Golding)

18 I should desire that the last words which I should pronounce in this Academy, and from this place, might be the name of – Michael Angelo.

Joshua Reynolds (1723–92) British portrait painter. Discourse to Students of the Royal Academy, 10 Dec 1790

19 See what will happen to you if you don't stop biting your fingernails.

Will Rogers (1879–1935) US actor and humorist. Message written on a postcard of the Venus de Milo that he sent to his young niece

20 Nobody cares much at heart about Titian, only there is a strange undercurrent of everlasting murmur about his name, which means the deep consent of all great men that he is greater than they.

John Ruskin (1819–1900) British art critic and writer. *The Two Paths*, Lecture II

21 If Botticelli were alive today he'd be working for *Vogue*.

Peter Ustinov (1921–) British actor. *The Observer*, 'Sayings of the Week', 21 Oct 1962

22 No I ask it for the knowledge of a lifetime.

James Whistler (1834–1903) US painter. Replying to the taunt, during the Ruskin trial, that he was asking a fee of 200 guineas for two days' painting. *Lives of the Wits* (H. Pearson)

ARTS

1 Every man's work, whether it be literature or music or pictures or architecture or anything else, is always a portrait of himself.

Samuel Butler (1835–1902) British writer. *The Way of All Flesh*, Ch. 14

2 The artistic temperament is a disease that afflicts amateurs.

G. K. Chesterton (1874–1936) British writer. *Heretics*, Ch. 17

3 No poet, no artist of any sort, has his complete meaning alone. His significance, his appreciation is the appreciation of his relation to the dead poets and artists.

T. S. Eliot (1888–1965) US-born British poet and dramatist. *Tradition and the Individual Talent*

4 Yes, the work comes out more beautiful from a material that resists the process, verse, marble, onyx, or enamel.

Théophile Gautier (1811–72) French poet and critic. *L'Art*

5 The excellence of every art is its intensity, capable of making all disagreeables evaporate, from their being in close relationship with beauty and truth.

John Keats (1795–1821) British poet. Letter to G. and T. Keats, 21 Dec 1817

6 The whole of art is an appeal to a reality which is not without us but in our minds.

Desmond MacCarthy (1877–1952) British writer and theatre critic. *Theatre*, 'Modern Drama'

7 Music begins to atrophy when it departs too far from the dance...poetry begins to atrophy when it gets too far from music.

Ezra Pound (1885–1972) US poet. *ABC of Reading*, 'Warning'

8 The secret of the arts is to correct nature.

Voltaire (François-Marie Arouet; 1694–1778) French writer. *Épîtres*, 'À M. de Verrière'

ASSASSINATION

See also killing, murder

1 They really are bad shots.

Charles De Gaulle (1890–1970) French general and statesman. Remark after narrowly escaping death in an assassination attempt. *Ten First Ladies of the World* (Pauline Frederick)

2 Assassination has never changed the history of the world.

Benjamin Disraeli (1804–81) British statesman. Speech, House of Commons, 1 May 1865

3 My fellow citizens, the President is dead, but the Government lives and God Omnipotent reigns.

James A. Garfield (1831–81) US statesman. Speech following the assassination of Lincoln.

4 Will no one rid me of this turbulent priest?

Henry II (1133–89) King of England. Referring to Thomas Becket, Archbishop of Canterbury; four of Henry's household knights took these words literally, hurried to Canterbury, and killed Becket in the cathedral (Dec 1170). Attrib.

5 Assassination is the extreme form of censorship.

George Bernard Shaw (1856–1950) Irish dramatist and critic. *The Shewing-Up of Blanco Posnet*, 'The Limits of Toleration'

ASTRONOMY

See also moon, space, stars, sun, universe

1 There is one glory of the sun, and another glory of the moon, and another glory of the stars: for one star differeth from another star in glory.

Bible: I Corinthians 15:41–42

2 ...in my studies of astronomy and philosophy I hold this opinion about the universe, that the Sun remains fixed in the centre of the circle of heavenly bodies, without changing its place; and the Earth, turning upon itself, moves round the Sun.

Galileo Galilei (1564–1642) Italian scientist. Letter to Cristina di Lorena, 1615

3 *Eppur si muove.*
Yet it moves.

Galileo Galilei Referring to the Earth. Remark supposedly made after his recantation (1632) of belief in the Copernican system. Attrib.

4 Astronomy teaches the correct use of the sun and the planets.

Stephen Leacock (1869–1944) English-born Canadian economist and humorist. *Literary Lapses*, 'A Manual of Education'

ATHEISM

See also God, religion

1 An atheist is one point beyond the devil.

Proverb

2 God never wrought miracle to convince atheism, because his ordinary works convince it.

Francis Bacon (1561–1626) English philosopher. *Essays*, 'Of Atheism'

3 For none deny there is a God, but those for whom it maketh that there were no God.

Francis Bacon *Essays*, 'Of Atheism'

4 I am an atheist still, thank God.

Luis Buñuel (1900–83) Spanish film director. *Luis Buñuel: an Introduction* (Ado Kyrou)

5 An atheist is a man who has no invisible means of support.

Harry Emerson Fosdick (1878–1969) US baptist minister. Attrib.

6 Perhaps if I wanted to be understood or to

understand I would bamboozle myself into belief, but I am a reporter; God exists only for leader-writers.

Graham Greene (1904–91) British novelist. *The Quiet American*

7 If you don't find a God by five o'clock this afternoon you must leave the college.

Benjamin Jowett (1817–93) British theologian. Responding to a conceited young student's assertion that he could find no evidence for a God. Attrib.

8 He was an embittered atheist (the sort of atheist who does not so much disbelieve in God as personally dislike Him).

George Orwell (Eric Blair; 1903–50) British novelist. *Down and Out in Paris and London*, Ch. 30

9 It has been said that the highest praise of God consists in the denial of Him by the atheist, who finds creation so perfect that he can dispense with a creator.

Marcel Proust (1871–1922) French novelist. *À la recherche du temps perdu: Le Çôté de Guermantes*

AUDIENCES

1 Long experience has taught me that in England nobody goes to the theatre unless he or she has bronchitis.

James Agate (1877–1947) British theatre critic. *See also* Artur SCHNABEL. *Ego*, 6

2 Ladies and gentlemen, unless the play is stopped, the child cannot possibly go on.

John Philip Kemble (1757–1823) British tragic actor. Announcement to the audience when the play he was in was continually interrupted by a child crying. *A Book of Anecdotes* (D. George)

3 Those people on the stage are making such a noise I can't hear a word you're saying.

Henry Taylor Parker (1867–1934) US music critic. Rebuking some talkative members of an audience, near whom he was sitting. *The Humor of Music* (L. Humphrey)

4 A nice respectable, middle-class, middle-aged maiden lady, with time on her hands and the money to help her pass it...Let us call her Aunt Edna...Aunt Edna is universal, and to those who feel that all the problems of the modern theatre might be saved by her liquidation, let me add that...She is also immortal.

Terence Rattigan (1911–77) British dramatist. *Collected Plays*, Vol II, Preface

5 I know two kinds of audience only – one coughing and one not coughing.

Artur Schnabel (1882–1951) Austrian concert pianist. *See also* James AGATE. *My Life and Music*, Pt. II, Ch. 10

6 I quite agree with you, sir, but what can two do against so many?

George Bernard Shaw (1856–1950) Irish dramatist and critic. Responding to a solitary hiss heard amongst the applause at the first performance of *Arms and the Man* in 1894. *Oxford Book of Literary Anecdotes*

AUTHORITARIANISM

See also tyranny

1 *Roma locuta est; causa finita est.*
Rome has spoken; the case is concluded.

St Augustine of Hippo (354–430) Bishop of Hippo. *Sermons*, Bk. I

2 Then cometh the end, when he shall have delivered up the kingdom to God, even the Father; when he shall have put down all rule and all authority and power.
For he must reign, till he hath put all enemies under his feet.
The last enemy that shall be destroyed is death.

Bible: I Corinthians 15:24–26

3 Dictators ride to and fro upon tigers which they dare not dismount. And the tigers are getting hungry.

Winston Churchill (1874–1965) British statesman. *While England Slept*

4 I will have this done, so I order it done; let my will replace reasoned judgement.

Juvenal (Decimus Junius Juvenalis; 60–130 AD) Roman satirist. *Satires*, VI

5 Big Brother is watching you.

George Orwell (Eric Blair; 1903–50) British novelist. *Nineteen Eighty-Four*

6 I am painted as the greatest little dictator, which is ridiculous – you always take some consultations.

Margaret Thatcher (1925–) British politician and prime minister. *The Times*, 1983

7 I don't mind how much my ministers talk – as long as they do what I say.

Margaret Thatcher *The Times*, 1987

8 As for being a General, well, at the age of four with paper hats and wooden swords we're all Generals. Only some of us never grow out of it.

Peter Ustinov (1921–) British actor. *Romanoff and Juliet*, I

AUTUMN

See months, seasons

B

BABIES

See also birth, children, pregnancy

1 There is no more sombre enemy of good art than the pram in the hall.

Cyril Connolly (1903–74) British journalist. *Enemies of Promise*, Ch. 3

2 Every baby born into the world is a finer one than the last.

Charles Dickens (1812–70) British novelist. *Nicholas Nickleby*, Ch. 36

3 These wretched babies don't come until they are ready.

Elizabeth II (1926–) Queen of the United Kingdom. Remark, Aug 1988

4 Other people's babies –
That's my life!
Mother to dozens,
And nobody's wife.

A. P. Herbert (1890–1971) British writer and politician. *A Book of Ballads*, 'Other People's Babies'

5 A loud noise at one end and no sense of responsibility at the other.

Ronald Knox (1888–1957) British Roman Catholic priest. Attrib.

6 Sweetes' li'l' feller,
Everybody knows;
Dunno what to call 'im,
But he's mighty lak' a rose!

Frank L. Stanton (1857–1927) US journalist and poet. *Sweetes' Li'l' Feller*

BEAUTY

See also admiration, appearance, compliments

1 A good face is a letter of recommendation.

Proverb

2 Beauty is only skin-deep.

Proverb

3 Beauty is potent but money is omnipotent.

Proverb

4 Small is beautiful.

Proverb

5 My Love in her attire doth show her wit,
It doth so well become her:
For every season she hath dressings fit,
For winter, spring, and summer.
No beauty she doth miss,
When all her robes are on;
But beauty's self she is,
When all her robes are gone.

Anonymous Madrigal

6 You know, you can only perceive real beauty in a person as they get older.

Anouk Aimee (1932–) French actress. Remark, Aug 1988

7 There is no excellent beauty that hath not some strangeness in the proportion.

Francis Bacon (1561–1626) English philosopher. *Essays*, 'Of Beauty'

8 Beauty and the lust for learning have yet to be allied.

Max Beerbohm (1872–1956) British writer. *Zuleika Dobson*, Ch. 7

9 Exuberance is Beauty.

William Blake (1757–1827) British poet. *The Marriage of Heaven and Hell*, 'Proverbs of Hell'

10 For beauty being the best of all we know
Sums up the unsearchable and secret aims
Of nature.

Robert Bridges (1844–1930) British poet. *The Growth of Love*

11 Beauty sat with me all the summer day,
Awaiting the sure triumph of her eye;
Nor mark'd I till we parted, how, hard by,
Love in her train stood ready for his prey.

Robert Bridges *The Growth of Love*

12 It is better to be first with an ugly woman than the hundredth with a beauty.

Pearl Buck (1892–1973) US novelist. *The Good Earth*, Ch. 1

13 Beauty in distress is much the most affecting beauty.

Edmund Burke (1729–97) British politician. *On the Sublime and Beautiful*, Pt. III

14 She walks in beauty, like the night
Of cloudless climes and starry skies;
And all that's best of dark and bright
Meet in her aspect and her eyes.

Lord Byron (1788–1824) British poet. *She Walks in Beauty*

15 SONYA. I'm not beautiful.
HELEN. You have lovely hair.
SONYA. No, when a woman isn't beautiful, people always say, 'You have lovely eyes, you have lovely hair.'

Anton Chekhov (1860–1904) Russian dramatist. *Uncle Vanya*, III

16 There is nothing ugly; *I never saw an ugly thing in my life:* for let the form of an object be what it may, – light, shade, and perspective will always make it beautiful.

John Constable (1776–1837) British landscape painter. Letter to John Fisher, 23 Oct 1821

17 Love built on beauty, soon as beauty, dies.

John Donne (1573–1631) English poet. *Elegies*, 2, 'The Anagram'

18 One girl can be pretty – but a dozen are only a chorus.

F. Scott Fitzgerald (1896–1940) US novelist. *The Last Tycoon*

19 Against the beautiful and the clever and the successful, one can wage a pitiless war, but not against the unattractive.

Graham Greene (1904–91) British novelist. *The Heart of the Matter*

20 Glory be to God for dappled things –
For skies of couple-colour as a brindled cow;
For rose-moles all in stipple upon trout that swim.

Gerard Manley Hopkins (1844–99) British Jesuit and poet. *Pied Beauty*

21 Beauty in things exists in the mind which contemplates them.

David Hume (1711–76) Scottish philosopher. *Essays*, 'Of Tragedy'

22 Beauty is altogether in the eye of the beholder.

Margaret Wolfe Hungerford (c. 1855–97) Irish novelist. Also attributed to the US soldier and writer Lew Wallace (1827–1905). *Molly Bawn*

23 A thing of beauty is a joy for ever:
Its loveliness increases; it will never
Pass into nothingness; but still will keep
A bower quiet for us, and a sleep
Full of sweet dreams, and health, and quiet breathing.

John Keats (1795–1821) British poet. *Endymion*, I

24 'Beauty is truth, truth beauty,' – that is all
Ye know on earth, and all ye need to know.

John Keats *Ode on a Grecian Urn*

25 Was this the face that launch'd a thousand ships
And burnt the topless towers of Ilium?
Sweet Helen, make me immortal with a kiss.

Christopher Marlowe (1564–93) English dramatist. *Doctor Faustus*, V:1

26 Oh, thou art fairer than the evening air
Clad in the beauty of a thousand stars.

Christopher Marlowe *Doctor Faustus*, V:1

27 You're the most beautiful woman I've ever seen, which doesn't say much for you.

Groucho Marx (Julius Marx; 1895–1977) US comedian. *Animal Crackers*

28 Beauty stands
In the admiration only of weak minds
Led captive.

John Milton (1608–74) English poet. *Paradise Regained*, Bk. II

29 I hate that aesthetic game of the eye and the mind, played by these connoisseurs, these mandarins who 'appreciate' beauty. What *is* beauty, anyway? There's no such thing. I never 'appreciate', any more than I 'like'. I love or I hate.

Pablo Picasso (1881–1973) Spanish painter. *Life with Picasso* (Françoise Gilot and Carlton Lake), Ch. 2

30 And when I told them how beautiful you are
They didn't believe me! They didn't believe me!

M. E. Rourke (20th century) US songwriter and lyricist. *They Didn't Believe Me* (song)

31 There are no ugly women, only lazy ones.

Helena Rubinstein (1882–1965) Polish-born US cosmetics manufacturer. *My Life for Beauty*, Pt. II, Ch. 1

32 All she has to do is to walk around and about Georgie White's stage with only a few light bandages on, and everybody considers her very beautiful, especially from the neck down.

Damon Runyon (1884–1946) US writer. *Furthermore*, 'A Very Honourable Guy'

33 Remember that the most beautiful things in the world are the most useless, peacocks and lilies for instance.

John Ruskin (1819–1900) British art critic and writer. *The Stones of Venice*, Vol. I, Ch. 2

34 I always say beauty is only sin deep.

Saki (Hector Hugh Munro; 1870–1916) British writer. *Reginald's Choir Treat*

35 Beauty itself doth of itself persuade
The eyes of men without an orator.

William Shakespeare (1564–1616) English dramatist. *The Rape of Lucrece*, I

36 From fairest creatures we desire increase,
That thereby beauty's rose might never die.

William Shakespeare *Sonnet 1*

37 For she was beautiful – her beauty made
The bright world dim, and everything beside
Seemed like the fleeting image of a shade.

Percy Bysshe Shelley (1792–1822) British poet. *The Witch of Atlas*, XII

38 Half light, half shade,
She stood, a sight to make an old man young.

Alfred, Lord Tennyson (1809–92) British poet. *The Gardener's Daughter*

39 But Lancelot mused a little space;
He said, 'She has a lovely face;
God in his mercy lend her grace,
The Lady of Shalott.'

Alfred, Lord Tennyson *The Lady of Shalott*, Pt. IV

40 A woman of so shining loveliness
That men threshed corn at midnight by a tress,
A little stolen tress.

W. B. Yeats (1865–1939) Irish poet. *The Secret Rose*

41 All changed, changed utterly:
A terrible beauty is born.

W. B. Yeats *Easter 1916*

BED

See also idleness, rest, sleep

1 Early to bed and early to rise, makes a man healthy, wealthy and wise.

Proverb

2 Go to bed with the lamb, and rise with the lark.

Proverb

3 I'm Burlington Bertie:

I rise at ten-thirty.
W. F. Hargreaves (1846–1919) British songwriter. *Burlington Bertie*

4 I have, all my life long, been lying till noon; yet I tell all young men, and tell them with great sincerity, that nobody who does not rise early will ever do any good.
Samuel Johnson (1709–84) British lexicographer. *Tour to the Hebrides* (J. Boswell)

5 O! it's nice to get up in the mornin',
But it's nicer to stay in bed.
Harry Lauder (Hugh MacLennon; 1870–1950) Scottish music-hall artist. Song

6 It was such a lovely day I thought it was a pity to get up.
W. Somerset Maugham (1874–1965) British novelist. *Our Betters*, II

7 And so to bed.
Samuel Pepys (1633–1703) English diarist. *Diary*, 6 May 1660 and *passim*

8 Not to be abed after midnight is to be up betimes.
William Shakespeare (1564–1616) English dramatist. *Twelfth Night*, II:3

9 Early to rise and early to bed makes a male healthy and wealthy and dead.
James Thurber (1894–1961) US humorist. *Fables for Our Time*, 'The Shrike and the Chipmunks'

BEGINNING

See also prophecy

1 A journey of a thousand leagues begins with a single step.
Chinese Proverb

2 Fingers were made before forks, and hands before knives.
Proverb

3 From small beginnings come great things.
Proverb

4 Great oaks from little acorns grow.
Proverb

5 The first step is the hardest.
Proverb

6 No task is a long one but the task on which one dare not start. It becomes a nightmare.
Charles Baudelaire (1821–67) French poet. *My Heart Laid Bare*

7 She looked at him, as one who awakes:
The past was a sleep, and her life began.
Robert Browning (1812–89) British poet. *The Statue and the Bust*

8 The distance doesn't matter; it is only the first step that is difficult.
Marquise du Deffand (Marie de Vichy-Chamrond; 1697–1780) French noblewoman. Referring to the legend of St Denis, who is traditionally believed to have carried his severed head for six miles after his execution. Letter to d'Alembert, 7 July 1763

9 From today and from this place there begins a new epoch in the history of the world.
Goethe (1749–1832) German poet and dramatist. On witnessing the victory of the French at the battle of Valmy. *The Story of Civilization* (W. Durant), Vol. II

10 'Tis always morning somewhere in the world.
Richard Henry Horne (1803–84) English writer. *Orion*, Bk III, Ch. 2

11 There is an old saying 'well begun is half done' – 'tis a bad one. I would use instead – Not begun at all until half done.
John Keats (1795–1821) British poet. Letter, 1817

12 We stand today on the edge of a new frontier.
John Fitzgerald Kennedy (1917–63) US statesman. Said on his nomination as Presidential candidate. Speech, Democratic Party Convention, 15 July 1960

13 Are you sitting comfortably? Then I'll begin.
Julia S. Lang (1921–) British broadcaster. Introduction to the story in *Listen with Mother*.

BELIEF

See also faith, religion

1 Believe nothing of what you hear, and only half of what you see.
Proverb

2 Seeing is believing.
Proverb

3 Vain are the thousand creeds
That move men's hearts: unutterably vain;
Worthless as wither'd weeds.
Emily Brontë (1818–48) British novelist. *Last Lines*

4 If Jesus Christ were to come to-day, people would not even crucify him. They would ask him to dinner, and hear what he had to say, and make fun of it.
Thomas Carlyle (1795–1881) Scottish historian and essayist. *Carlyle at his Zenith* (D. A. Wilson)

5 *Action will furnish belief*, – but will that belief be the true one?
This is the point, you know.
Arthur Hugh Clough (1819–61) British poet. *Amours de voyage*, V

6 Believe it or not.
R. L. Ripley (1893–1949) US writer. Title of newspaper column

7 I believe because it is impossible.
Tertullian (c. 160–225 AD) Carthaginian father of the church. The usual misquotation of 'It is certain because it is impossible.'. *De Carne Christi*, V

8 If there were a verb meaning 'to believe falsely', it would not have any significant first person, present indicative.

Ludwig Wittgenstein (1889–1951) Austrian philosopher. *A Certain World* (W. H. Auden)

BEQUESTS

1 When you have told anyone you have left him a legacy the only decent thing to do is to die at once.

Samuel Butler (1835–1902) British writer. *Samuel Butler: A Memoir* (Festing Jones), Vol. 2

2 I'm sorry to hear that, sir, you don't happen to have the shilling about you now, do you?

Tom Sheridan (1775–1817) Son of the dramatist Richard Brinsley Sheridan. To his father, on learning that he was to be cut off in his will with a shilling. *The Fine Art of Political Wit* (L. Harris)

3 The man who leaves money to charity in his will is only giving away what no longer belongs to him.

Voltaire (François-Marie Arouet; 1694–1778) French writer. Letter, 1769

BETRAYAL

See also treason

1 And forthwith he came to Jesus, and said, Hail, master; and kissed him.
And Jesus said unto him, Friend, wherefore art thou come? Then came they, and laid hands on Jesus, and took him.

Bible: Matthew 26:49–50

2 Just for a handful of silver he left us,
Just for a riband to stick in his coat.

Robert Browning (1812–89) British poet. *The Lost Leader*

3 I hate the idea of causes, and if I had to choose between betraying my country and betraying my friend, I hope I should have the guts to betray my country.

E. M. Forster (1879–1970) British novelist. *Two Cheers for Democracy*, 'What I Believe'.

4 I'm waiting for the cock to crow.

William Morris Hughes (1864–1952) Australian statesman. Said in parliament, after being viciously critized by a member of his own party. *The Fine Art of Political Wit* (L. Harris)

5 He...felt towards those whom he had deserted that peculiar malignity which has, in all ages, been characteristic of apostates.

Lord Macaulay (1800–59) British historian. *History of England*, Vol. I, Ch. 1

6 I let down my friends, I let down my country. I let down our system of government.

Richard Milhous Nixon (1913–94) US president. *The Observer*, 'Sayings of the Week', 8 May 1977

7 *Et tu, Brute?*
You too, Brutus?

William Shakespeare (1564–1616) English dramatist. Said by Julius Caesar. *Julius Caesar*, III:1

BIBLE

See also religion

1 He will find one English book and one only, where, as in the *Iliad* itself, perfect plainness of speech is allied with perfect nobleness; and that book is the Bible.

Matthew Arnold (1822–88) British poet and critic. *On Translating Homer*

2 Candidates should not attempt more than six of these.

Hilaire Belloc (1870–1953) French-born British poet. Suggested addition to the Ten Commandments. Attrib.

3 There's a great text in Galatians,
Once you trip on it, entails
Twenty-nine distinct damnations,
One sure, if another fails.

Robert Browning (1812–89) British poet. *Soliloquy of the Spanish Cloister*

4 It's just called 'The Bible' now. We dropped the word 'Holy' to give it a more mass-market appeal.

Editor (Hodder & Stoughton) *The Daily Telegraph*, 30 Dec 1989

5 I have spent a lot of time searching through the Bible for loopholes.

W. C. Fields (1880–1946) US actor. Said during his last illness. Attrib.

6 We have used the Bible as if it was a constable's handbook – an opium-dose for keeping beasts of burden patient while they are being overloaded.

Charles Kingsley (1819–75) British writer. *Letters to the Chartists*, 2

7 The English Bible, a book which, if everything else in our language should perish, would alone suffice to show the whole extent of its beauty and power.

Lord Macaulay (1800–59) British historian. *Essays and Biographies*, 'John Dryden'. *Edinburgh Review*

8 The number one book of the ages was written by a committee, and it was called The Bible.

Louis B. Mayer (1885–1957) Russian-born US film producer. Comment to writers who had objected to changes in their work. *The Filmgoer's Book of Quotes* (Leslie Halliwell)

9 There's a Bible on that shelf there. But I keep it next to Voltaire – poison and antidote.

Bertrand Russell (1872–1970) British philosopher. *Kenneth Harris Talking To:* 'Bertrand Russell' (Kenneth Harris)

10 The Bible is literature, not dogma.

George Santayana (1863–1952) US philosopher. *Introduction to the Ethics of Spinoza*

11 LORD ILLINGWORTH. The Book of Life begins with a man and a woman in a garden.
MRS ALLONBY. It ends with Revelations.

Oscar Wilde (1854–1900) Irish-born British dramatist. *A Woman of No Importance*, I

BIOGRAPHY

1 The Art of Biography
Is different from Geography.
Geography is about Maps,
But Biography is about Chaps.

Edmund Clerihew Bentley (1875–1956) British writer. *Biography for Beginners*

2 A well-written Life is almost as rare as a well-spent one.

Thomas Carlyle (1795–1881) Scottish historian and essayist. *Critical and Miscellaneous Essays*, 'Richter'

3 History is the essence of innumerable biographies.

Thomas Carlyle *Critical and Miscellaneous Essays*, 'History'

4 Campbell has added another terror to death.

John Singleton Copley (1772–1863) US-born British lawyer. Referring to Lord Campbell's controversial *Lives of the Lord Chancellors* (1845–47), from which Lyndhurst was excluded because he was still alive

5 There is properly no history; only biography.

Ralph Waldo Emerson (1803–82) US poet and essayist. *Essays*, 'History'

6 Just how difficult it is to write biography can be reckoned by anybody who sits down and considers just how many people know the real truth about his or her love affairs.

Rebecca West (Cicely Isabel Fairfield; 1892–1983) British novelist and journalist. *Vogue* magazine

BIRDS

1 That's the wise thrush; he sings each song twice over,
Lest you should think he never could recapture
The first fine careless rapture!

Robert Browning (1812–89) British poet. *Home Thoughts from Abroad*

2 With my cross-bow
I shot the albatross.

Samuel Taylor Coleridge (1772–1834) British poet. *The Rime of the Ancient Mariner*, I

3 It was the Rainbow gave thee birth,
And left thee all her lovely hues.

W. H. Davies (1871–1940) British poet. *The Kingfisher*

4 On a tree by a river a little tom-tit
Sang 'Willow, titwillow, titwillow!'

W. S. Gilbert (1836–1911) British dramatist. *The Mikado*, II

5 Thou wast not born for death, immortal Bird!
No hungry generations tread thee down;
The voice I hear this passing night was heard
In ancient days by emperor and clown:
Perhaps the self-same song that found a path
Through the sad heart of Ruth, when sick for home,
She stood in tears amid the alien corn;
The same that oft-times hath
Charm'd magic casements, opening on the foam
Of perilous seas, in faery lands forlorn.

John Keats (1795–1821) British poet. *Ode to a Nightingale*

6 Ye living lamps, by whose dear light
The nightingale does sit so late,
And studying all the summer night,
Her matchless songs does meditate.

Andrew Marvell (1621–78) English poet. *The Mower to the Glow-worms*

7 A Nightingale Sang in Berkeley Square.

Eric Maschwitz (20th century) British songwriter. Song title

8 To hear the lark begin his flight,
And singing startle the dull night,
From his watch-tower in the skies,
Till the dappled dawn doth rise.

John Milton (1608–74) English poet. *L'Allegro*

9 Sweet bird, that shunn'st the noise of folly,
Most musical, most melancholy!

John Milton Referring to the nightingale. *Il Penseroso*

10 Hail to thee, blithe Spirit!
Bird thou never wert,
That from Heaven, or near it,
Pourest thy full heart
In profuse strains of unpremeditated art.

Percy Bysshe Shelley (1792–1822) British poet. *To a Skylark*

11 Ethereal minstrel! pilgrim of the sky!
Dost thou despise the earth where cares abound?

William Wordsworth (1770–1850) British poet. *To a Skylark*

12 O Nightingale, thou surely art
A creature of a 'fiery heart'.

William Wordsworth *O Nightingale*

13 The pious bird with the scarlet breast,
Our little English robin.

William Wordsworth *The Redbreast chasing the Butterfly*

14 Thrice welcome, darling of the spring!
Even yet thou art to me
No bird, but an invisible thing,
A voice, a mystery.

William Wordsworth *To the Cuckoo*

BIRTH

See also babies, life and death, pregnancy

1 A woman when she is in travail hath sorrow, because her hour is come: but as soon as she is delivered of the child, she remembereth no more the anguish, for joy that a man is born into the world.

Bible: John 16:21

2 For all men have one entrance into life, and the like going out.

Bible: Wisdom 7:6

3 My mother groan'd, my father wept,
Into the dangerous world I leapt;
Helpless, naked, piping loud,

Like a fiend hid in a cloud.
William Blake (1757–1827) British poet. *Songs of Experience*, 'Infant Sorrow'

4 For man's greatest crime is to have been born.
Pedro Calderón de la Barca (1600–81) Spanish dramatist. *La Vida es Sueño*, I

5 The history of man for the nine months preceding his birth would, probably, be far more interesting and contain events of greater moment than all the three-score and ten years that follow it.
Samuel Taylor Coleridge (1772–1834) British poet. *Miscellanies, Aesthetic and Literary*

6 If men had to have babies they would only ever have one each.
Diana, Princess of Wales (1961–) Wife of Prince Charles. *The Observer*, 'Sayings of the Week', 29 July 1984

7 Birth may be a matter of a moment. But it is a unique one.
Frédérick Leboyer (1918–) French obstetrician. *Birth Without Violence*

8 I'll simply say here that I was born Beatrice Gladys Lillie at an extremely tender age because my mother needed a fourth at meals.
Beatrice Lillie (Constance Sylvia Munston, Lady Peel; 1898–1989) Canadian-born British actress. *Every Other Inch a Lady*, Ch. 1

9 MACBETH. I bear a charmed life, which must not yield
To one of woman born.
MACDUFF. Despair thy charm;
And let the angel whom thou still hast serv'd
Tell thee Macduff was from his mother's womb
Untimely ripp'd.
William Shakespeare (1564–1616) English dramatist. *Macbeth*, V:8

10 The explanation is quite simple. I wished to be near my mother.
James Whistler (1834–1903) US painter. Explaining to a snobbish lady why he had been born in such an unfashionable place as Lowell, Massachusetts. Attrib.

BITTERNESS

1 The dupe of friendship, and the fool of love; have I not reason to hate and to despise myself? Indeed I do; and chiefly for not having hated and despised the world enough.
William Hazlitt (1778–1830) British essayist. *On the Pleasure of Hating*

2 It is very difficult to get up resentment towards persons whom one has never seen.
Cardinal Newman (1801–90) British theologian. *Apologia pro Vita Sua* (1864), 'Mr Kingsley's Method of Disputation'

3 He gave a deep sigh – I saw the iron enter into his soul!
Laurence Sterne (1713–68) Irish-born British writer. *A Sentimental Journey*, 'The Captive. Paris'

BLESSING

See also prayer

1 Matthew, Mark, Luke and John,
The bed be blest that I lie on.
Thomas Ady (17th century) English poet. *A Candle in the Dark*

2 I see the moon,
And the moon sees me;
God bless the moon,
And God bless me.
Anonymous *Gammer Gurton's Garland*

3 Thank you, sister. May you be the mother of a bishop!
Brendan Behan (1923–64) Irish playwright. Said to a nun nursing him on his deathbed. Attrib.

4 The Lord bless thee, and keep thee:
The Lord make his face shine upon thee, and be gracious unto thee:
The Lord lift up his countenance upon thee, and give thee peace.
Bible: Numbers 6:24–26

5 And the peace of God, which passeth all understanding, shall keep your hearts and minds through Christ Jesus.
Bible: Philippians 4:7

6 'God bless us every one!' said Tiny Tim, the last of all.
Charles Dickens (1812–70) British novelist. *A Christmas Carol*

BLINDNESS

See also disability

1 A nod is as good as a wink to a blind horse.
Proverb

2 How reconcile this world of fact with the bright world of my imagining? My darkness has been filled with the light of intelligence, and behold, the outer day-light world was stumbling and groping in social blindness.
Helen Keller (1880–1968) US writer and lecturer. *The Cry for Justice* (ed. Upton Sinclair)

3 Ask for this great deliverer now, and find him
Eyeless in Gaza at the mill with slaves.
John Milton (1608–74) English poet. *Samson Agonistes*

4 O dark, dark, dark, amid the blaze of noon,
Irrecoverably dark, total eclipse,
Without all hope of day!
John Milton *Samson Agonistes*

5 When I consider how my light is spent
Ere half my days in this dark world and wide,
And that one talent which is death to hide
Lodged with me useless.
John Milton *Sonnet*: 'On his Blindness'

6 He clapped the glass to his sightless eye,

And 'I'm damned if I see it', he said.

Henry John Newbolt (1862–1938) British poet. Referring to Lord Nelson at the Battle of Copenhagen. *Admirals All*

7 And so I betake myself to that course, which is almost as much as to see myself go into my grave – for which, and all the discomforts that will accompany my being blind, the good God prepare me!

Samuel Pepys (1633–1703) English diarist. The closing words of Pepys's *Diary*; he lived another 34 years and did not go blind. *Diary*, 31 May 1669

BOASTS

1 I have done almost every human activity inside a taxi which does not require main drainage.

Alan Brien (1925–) British critic. *Punch*, 5 July 1972

2 CAPTAIN. I'm never, never sick at sea!
ALL. What never?
CAPTAIN. No, never!
ALL. What, *never*?
CAPTAIN. Hardly ever!

W. S. Gilbert (1836–1911) British dramatist. *HMS Pinafore*, I

3 All my shows are great. Some of them are bad. But they are all great.

Lew Grade (Lewis Winogradsky; 1906–) British film and TV producer. Attrib.

4 If, drunk with sight of power, we loose
Wild tongues that have not Thee in awe,
Such boastings as the Gentiles use,
Or lesser breeds without the Law.

Rudyard Kipling (1865–1936) Indian-born British writer. *Recessional*

5 I can piss the old boy in the snow.

Max Liebermann (1847–1935) German painter. Remark to an artist who said he could not draw General Paul von Hindenburg's face. *Conversations with Stravinsky* (Igor Stravinsky and Robert Craft)

6 And when we open our dykes, the waters are ten feet deep.

Wilhelmina (1880–1962) Queen of the Netherlands. Replying to a boast by Wilhelm II that his guardsmen were all seven feet tall. Attrib.

BOATS

See also navy, sea

1 There's something wrong with our bloody ships today.

Earl Beatty (1871–1936) British admiral. Remark during Battle of Jutland, 30 May 1916. Attrib.

2 All rowed fast but none so fast as stroke.

Desmond Coke (1879–1931) British writer. Popular misquotation, derived from the passage: 'His blade struck the water a full second before any other…until…as the boats began to near the winning post, his own was dipping into the water *twice* as often as any other.'. *Sandford of Merton*

3 As idle as a painted ship
Upon a painted ocean.

Samuel Taylor Coleridge (1772–1834) British poet. *The Rime of the Ancient Mariner*, I

4 Jolly boating weather,
And a hay harvest breeze,
Blade on the feather,
Shade off the trees
Swing, swing together
With your body between your knees.

William Johnson Cory (1823–92) British schoolmaster and poet. *Eton Boating Song*

5 Fair stood the wind for France
When we our sails advance.

Michael Drayton (1563–1631) English poet. *Agincourt*

6 For you dream you are crossing the Channel, and tossing about in a steamer from Harwich
Which is something between a large bathing machine and a very small second-class carriage.

W. S. Gilbert (1836–1911) British dramatist. *Iolanthe*, II

7 There is nothing – absolutely nothing – half so much worth doing as simply messing about in boats.

Kenneth Grahame (1859–1932) Scottish writer. *The Wind in the Willows*, Ch. 1

8 The little ships, the unforgotten Homeric catalogue of *Mary Jane* and *Peggy IV*, of *Folkestone Belle*, *Boy Billy*, and *Ethel Maud*, of *Lady Haig* and *Skylark*…the little ships of England brought the Army home.

Philip Guedalla (1889–1944) British writer. Referring to the evacuation of Dunkirk. *Mr. Churchill*

9 No man will be a sailor who has contrivance enough to get himself into a jail; for being in a ship is being in a jail, with the chance of being drowned…A man in a jail has more room, better food, and commonly better company.

Samuel Johnson (1709–84) British lexicographer. *Life of Johnson* (J. Boswell), Vol. I

10 I'd like to get you
On a slow boat to China.

Frank Loesser (1910–69) US songwriter. *Slow Boat to China*

11 It was the schooner Hesperus,
That sailed the wintry sea;
And the skipper had taken his little daughter,
To bear him company.

Henry Wadsworth Longfellow (1807–82) US poet. *The Wreck of the Hesperus*

12 Quinquireme of Nineveh from distant Ophir
Rowing home to haven in sunny Palestine,
With a cargo of ivory,
And apes and peacocks,
Sandalwood, cedarwood, and sweet white wine.

John Masefield (1878–1967) British poet. *Cargoes*

13 Dirty British coaster with a salt-caked smoke stack,
Butting through the Channel in the mad March days,
With a cargo of Tyne coal,
Road-rail, pig-lead,

Firewood, iron-ware, and cheap tin trays.
John Masefield *Cargoes*

14 Now the sunset breezes shiver,
And she's fading down the river,
But in England's song for ever
She's the Fighting Téméraire.
Henry John Newbolt (1862–1938) British poet. *The Fighting Téméraire*

15 Only fools and passengers drink at sea.
Alan John Villiers (1903–) Australian naval commander. *The Observer*, 'Sayings of the Week', 28 Apr 1957

See courage, danger, frankness, impertinence

BOOKS

See also criticism, fiction, literature, novels, publishing, reading, writing

1 Books and friends should be few but good.
Proverb

2 Some books are undeservedly forgotten; none are undeservedly remembered.
W. H. Auden (1907–73) British poet. *The Dyer's Hand*, 'Reading'

3 Some books are to be tasted, others to be swallowed, and some few to be chewed and digested.
Francis Bacon (1561–1626) English philosopher. *Essays*, 'Of Studies'

4 Books must follow sciences, and not sciences books.
Francis Bacon *Proposition touching Amendment of Laws*

5 It is all very well to be able to write books, but can you waggle your ears?
J. M. Barrie (1860–1937) British novelist and dramatist. Speaking to H. G. Wells. *Barrie: The Story of A Genius* (J. A. Hamerton)

6 When I am dead, I hope it may be said:
'His sins were scarlet, but his books were read.'
Hilaire Belloc (1870–1953) French-born British poet. *Epigrams*, 'On His Books'

7 Child! do not throw this book about;
Refrain from the unholy pleasure
Of cutting all the pictures out!
Preserve it as your chiefest treasure.
Hilaire Belloc *The Bad Child's Book of Beasts*, 'Dedication'

8 And further, by these, my son, be admonished: of making many books there is no end; and much study is a weariness of the flesh.
Bible: Ecclesiastes 12:12

9 I keep my books at the British Museum and at Mudie's.
Samuel Butler (1835–1902) British writer. *The Humour of Homer*, 'Ramblings in Cheapside'

10 'Tis pleasant, sure, to see one's name in print;
A book's a book, although there's nothing in't.
Lord Byron (1788–1824) British poet. *English Bards and Scotch Reviewers*

11 A good book is the purest essence of a human soul.
Thomas Carlyle (1795–1881) Scottish historian and essayist. Speech made in support of the London Library. *Carlyle and the London Library* (F. Harrison)

12 'What is the use of a book,' thought Alice, 'without pictures or conversation?'
Lewis Carroll (Charles Lutwidge Dodgson; 1832–98) British writer. *Alice's Adventures in Wonderland*, Ch. 1

13 Go, litel book, go litel myn tragedie.
O moral Gower, this book I directe To thee.
Geoffrey Chaucer (c. 1342–1400) English poet. *Troilus and Criseyde*, 5

14 Due attention to the inside of books, and due contempt for the outside, is the proper relation between a man of sense and his books.
Earl of Chesterfield (1694–1773) English statesman. Letter to his son, 10 Jan 1749

15 Books cannot always please, however good;
Minds are not ever craving for their food.
George Crabbe (1754–1832) British poet. *The Borough*, 'Schools'

16 Books, we are told, propose to *instruct* or to *amuse*. Indeed!...The true antithesis to knowledge, in this case, is not *pleasure*, but *power*. All that is literature seeks to communicate power; all that is not literature, to communicate knowledge.
Thomas De Quincey (1785–1859) British writer. *Letters to a Young Man*

17 A book is not harmless merely because no one is consciously offended by it.
T. S. Eliot (1888–1965) US-born British poet and dramatist. *Religion and Literature*

18 Books are made not like children but like pyramids...and they're just as useless! and they stay in the desert!...Jackals piss at their foot and the bourgeois climb up on them.
Gustave Flaubert (1821–80) French novelist. Letter to Ernest Feydeau, 1857

19 Learning hath gained most by those books by which the printers have lost.
Thomas Fuller (1608–61) English historian. *The Holy State and the Profane State*

20 A book may be amusing with numerous errors, or it may be very dull without a single absurdity.
Oliver Goldsmith (1728–74) Irish-born British writer. *The Vicar of Wakefield*, Advertisement

21 Few books today are forgivable.
R. D. Laing (1927–89) British psychiatrist. *The Politics of Experience*, Introduction

22 Get stewed:
Books are a load of crap.
Philip Larkin (1922–85) British poet. *A Study of Reading Habits*

23 To every man who struggles with his own soul in mystery, a book that is a book flowers once, and seeds, and is gone.

D. H. Lawrence (1885–1930) British novelist. *Phoenix*, 'A Bibliography of D.H.L.'

24 Never judge a cover by its book.

Fran Lebowitz (1950–) US writer. *Metropolitan Life*

25 There can hardly be a stranger commodity in the world than books. Printed by people who don't understand them; sold by people who don't understand them; bound, criticized and read by people who don't understand them; and now even written by people who don't understand them.

Georg Christoph Lichtenberg (1742–99) German physicist and writer. *Aphorisms*

26 In recommending a book to a friend the less said the better. The moment you praise a book too highly you awaken resistance in your listener.

Henry Miller (1891–1980) US novelist. *The Books In My Life*

27 Who kills a man kills a reasonable creature, God's image; but he who destroys a good book, kills reason itself, kills the image of God, as it were in the eye.

John Milton (1608–74) English poet. *Areopagitica*

28 A good book is the precious life-blood of a master spirit, embalmed and treasured up on purpose to a life beyond life.

John Milton *Areopagitica*

29 The books one reads in childhood, and perhaps most of all the bad and good bad books, create in one's mind a sort of false map of the world, a series of fabulous countries into which one can retreat at odd moments throughout the rest of life, and which in some cases can even survive a visit to the real countries which they are supposed to represent.

George Orwell (Eric Blair; 1903–50) British novelist. *Riding Down from Bangor*

30 At last, an unprintable book that is readable.

Ezra Pound (1885–1972) US poet. Referring to *Tropic of Cancer* by Henry Miller.

31 An anthology is like all the plums and orange peel picked out of a cake.

Walter Raleigh (1861–1922) British scholar. Letter to Mrs Robert Bridges, 15 Jan 1915

32 I have known her pass the whole evening without mentioning a single book, or *in fact anything unpleasant* at all.

Henry Reed (1914–86) British poet and dramatist. *A Very Great Man Indeed*

33 When a new book is published, read an old one.

Samuel Rogers (1763–1855) British poet. Attrib.

34 We all know that books burn – yet we have the greater knowledge that books cannot be killed by fire. People die, but books never die. No man and no force can abolish memory...In this war, we know, books are weapons.

Franklin D. Roosevelt (1882–1945) US Democratic president. Message to American Booksellers Association, 23 Apr 1942

35 If a book is worth reading, it is worth buying.

John Ruskin (1819–1900) British art critic and writer. *Sesame and Lilies*, 'Of Kings' Treasuries'

36 All books are divisible into two classes, the books of the hour, and the books of all time.

John Ruskin *Sesame and Lilies*, 'Of Kings' Treasuries'

37 How long most people would look at the best book before they would give the price of a large turbot for it!

John Ruskin *Sesame and Lilies*, 'Of Kings' Treasuries'

38 A library is thought in cold storage.

Herbert Samuel (1870–1963) British Liberal statesman. *A Book of Quotations*

39 Children...have no use for psychology. They detest sociology. They still believe in God, the family, angels, devils, witches, goblins, logic, clarity, punctuation, and other such obsolete stuff... When a book is boring, they yawn openly. They don't expect their writer to redeem humanity, but leave to adults such childish illusions.

Isaac Bashevis Singer (1904–91) Polish-born US writer. Speech on receiving the Nobel Prize for Literature. *The Observer*, 17 Dec 1978

40 A best-seller is the gilded tomb of a mediocre talent.

Logan Pearsall Smith (1865–1946) US writer. *Afterthoughts*, 'Art and Letters'

41 No furniture so charming as books.

Sydney Smith (1771–1845) British clergyman and essayist. *Memoir* (Lady Holland)

42 Books are good enough in their own way, but they are a mighty bloodless substitute for life.

Robert Louis Stevenson (1850–94) Scottish writer. *Virginibus Puerisque*

43 My brother-in-law wrote an unusal murder story. The victim got killed by a man from another book.

Robert Sylvester (1907–75) US writer.

44 A good book is the best of friends, the same to-day and for ever.

Martin Farquhar Tupper (1810–89) British writer. *Proverbial Philosophy*, 'Of Reading'

45 Books, I don't know what you see in them...I can understand a person reading them, but I can't for the life of me see why people have to write them.

Peter Ustinov (1921–) British actor. *Photo-Finish*

46 There is no such thing as a moral or an immoral book. Books are well written, or badly written.

Oscar Wilde (1854–1900) Irish-born British dramatist. *The Picture of Dorian Gray*, Preface

BOOK, SONG, AND PLAY TITLES

1 Who's Afraid of Virginia Woolf?

Edward Albee (1928–) US dramatist. Play title

2 Lucky Jim.

Kingsley Amis (1922–95) British novelist. Title of novel

3 The Ugly Duckling.

Hans Christian Andersen (1805–75) Danish writer. Story title

4 Eating People Is Wrong.

Malcolm Bradbury (1932–) British academic, novelist, and critic. From a song 'The Reluctant Cannibal' by Michael Flanders and Donald Swann. Book title

5 Room at the Top.

John Braine (1922–86) British novelist. From Daniel Webster's remark 'There is always room at the top'. Book title

6 Tender Is the Night.

F. Scott Fitzgerald (1896–1940) US novelist. From the 'Ode to a Nightingale' (John Keats): 'Already with thee! tender is the night'. Book title

7 When the Kissing Had to Stop.

Constantine FitzGibbon From 'A Toccata at Galuppi's' (Robert Browning): 'What of soul was left, I wonder, when the kissing had to stop'. Book title

8 Diamonds Are Forever.

Ian Fleming (1908–64) British writer. From the advertising slogan 'A Diamond is Forever' for De Beers Consolidated Mines. Book title

9 'Tis Pity She's a whore.

John Ford (c. 1586–c. 1640) English dramatist. Play title

10 Goodbye to All That.

Robert Graves (1895–1985) British poet. Book title

11 A Woman Killed with Kindness.

Thomas Heywood (c. 1574–1641) English dramatist. Play title

12 The Light that Failed.

Rudyard Kipling (1865–1936) Indian-born British writer. Novel title

13 Shoot all the bluejays you want, if you can hit 'em, but remember it's a sin to kill a mockingbird.

Harper Lee (1926–) US writer. *To Kill a Mockingbird*, Pt. II, Ch. 10

14 Sergeant Pepper's Lonely Hearts Club Band.

John Lennon (1940–80) British rock singer. Song title (with Paul McCartney)

15 None But the Lonely Heart.

Richard Llewellyn (1907–83) British writer. Adapted from the English title of Tchaikovsky's song 'None But the Weary Heart' (original words by Goethe). Book title

16 Of Human Bondage.

W. Somerset Maugham (1874–1965) British novelist and doctor. From the title of one of the books in *Ethics* (Spinoza). Book title

17 The Moon and Sixpence.

W. Somerset Maugham From a review of his novel *Of Human Bondage*, 'Like so many young men, was so busy yearning for the moon that he never saw the sixpence at his feet'. (*Times Literary Supplement*). Book title

18 The Heart Is a Lonely Hunter.

Carson McCullers (1917–67) US novelist. From the poem 'The Lonely Hunter' (William Sharp): 'My heart is a lonely hunter that hunts on a lonely hill'. Book title

19 Gone With the Wind.

Margaret Mitchell (1909–49) US novelist. From the poem *Non Sum Qualis Eram* (Ernest Dowson): 'I have forgot much, Cynara! Gone with the wind...'. Book title

20 The Moon's a Balloon.

David Niven (1909–83) British actor. From e. e. cummings, '&': 'Who knows if the moon's a balloon, coming out of a keen city in the sky – filled with pretty people?'. Book title

21 A Dance to the Music of Time.

Anthony Powell (1905–) British novelist. From the name of a painting by Nicolas Poussin. Book title

22 A Bridge Too Far.

Cornelius Ryan Lieut. General Sir Frederick Browning said to Field Marshal Montgomery 'But, sir, we may be going a bridge too far'; referring to the airborne attack to capture eleven bridges over the Rhine, including the bridge at Arnhem, prior to the invasion of Germany (1944). Book title

23 Fanny by Gaslight.

Michael Sadleir (1888–1957) British author. Book title

24 Look Homeward, Angel!

Thomas Wolfe (1900–38) US novelist. From 'Lycidas' by John Milton. Book title

BOREDOM

See also bores

1 Nothing happens, nobody comes, nobody goes, it's awful!

Samuel Beckett (1906–89) Irish novelist and dramatist. *Waiting for Godot*, I

2 I wanted to be bored to death, as good a way to go as any.

Peter De Vries (1910–93) US novelist. *Comfort me with Apples*, Ch. 17

3 You ought not to be ashamed of being bored. What you ought to be ashamed of is being boring.

Lord Hailsham (1907–) British Conservative politician. *The Observer*, 'Sayings of the Week', 12 Oct 1975

4 Symmetry is tedious, and tedium is the very basis of mourning. Despair yawns.

Victor Hugo (1802–85) French writer. *Les Misérables*, Vol. II, Bk. IV, Ch. 1

5 The effect of boredom on a large scale in history is underestimated. It is a main cause of revolutions, and would soon bring to an end all the static Utopias and the farmyard civilization of the Fabians.

Dean Inge (1860–1954) British churchman. *The End of an Age*, Ch. 6

6 Is not life a hundred times too short

for us to bore ourselves?

Friedrich Wilhelm Nietzsche (1844–1900) German philosopher. *Jenseits von Gut und Böse*

7 When you're bored with yourself, marry and be bored with someone else.

David Pryce-Jones (1936–) British author and critic. *Owls and Satyrs*

BORES

See also boredom

1 *Bore,* n. A person who talks when you wish him to listen.

Ambrose Bierce (1842–?1914) US writer and journalist. *The Devil's Dictionary*

2 Society is now one polish'd horde,
Form'd of two mighty tribes, the *Bores* and *Bored.*

Lord Byron (1788–1824) British poet. *Don Juan*, XIII

3 Sir, you are like a pin, but without either its head or its point.

Douglas William Jerrold (1803–57) British dramatist. Speaking to a small thin man who was boring him. Attrib.

4 He is not only a bore but he bores for England.

Malcolm Muggeridge (1903–90) British writer. Referring to Sir Anthony Eden. In *Newstatesmanship* (E. Hyams), 'Boring for England'

5 A bore is a man who, when you ask him how he is, tells you.

Bert Leston Taylor (1866–1921) US journalist. Attrib.

6 Somebody's boring me, I think it's me.

Dylan Thomas (1914–53) Welsh poet. Remark made after he had been talking continuously for some time. *Four Absentees* (Rayner Heppenstall)

7 He is an old bore; even the grave yawns for him.

Herbert Beerbohm Tree (1853–1917) British actor and theatre manager. Referring to Israel Zangwill. *Beerbohm Tree* (Hesketh Pearson)

8 A healthy male adult bore consumes each year one and a half times his own weight in other people's patience.

John Updike (1932–) US novelist. *Assorted Prose*, 'Confessions of a Wild Bore'

9 Dear Frank, we believe you; you have dined in every house in London – *once.*

Oscar Wilde (1854–1900) Irish-born British dramatist. Interrupting Frank Harris's interminable account of the houses he had dined at. Attrib.

BORROWING

1 Borrowed garments never fit well.

Proverb

2 I don't trust a bank that would lend money to such a poor risk.

Robert Benchley (1889–1945) US humorist. To a bank that granted his request for a loan. Attrib.

3 Be not made a beggar by banqueting upon borrowing, when thou hast nothing in thy purse: for thou shalt lie in wait for thine own life, and be talked on.

Bible: Ecclesiasticus 18:33

4 One of the mysteries of human conduct is why adult men and women all over England are ready to sign documents which they do not read, at the behest of canvassers whom they do not know, binding them to pay for articles which they do not want, with money which they have not got.

Gerald Hurst (1877–1957) British writer and judge. *Closed Chapters*

5 The human species, according to the best theory I can form of it, is composed of two distinct races, the men who borrow, and the men who lend.

Charles Lamb (1775–1834) British essayist. *Essays of Elia*, 'The Two Races of Men'

6 Borrowers of books – those mutilators of collections, spoilers of the symmetry of shelves, and creators of odd volumes.

Charles Lamb *Essays of Elia*, 'The Two Races of Men'

7 Not everyone is a debtor who wishes to be; not everyone who wishes makes creditors.

François Rabelais (1483–1553) French satirist. *Pantagruel*, Bk. III, Ch. 3

8 Neither a borrower nor a lender be;
For loan oft loses both itself and friend,
And borrowing dulls the edge of husbandry.
This above all: to thine own self be true,
And it must follow, as the night the day,
Thou canst not then be false to any man.

William Shakespeare (1564–1616) English dramatist. *Hamlet*, I:3

9 Thank God, that's settled.

Richard Brinsley Sheridan (1751–1816) British dramatist. Handing one of his creditors an IOU. *Wit, Wisdom, and Foibles of the Great* (C. Shriner)

10 It is not my interest to pay the principal, nor my principle to pay the interest.

Richard Brinsley Sheridan To his tailor when he requested the payment of a debt, or of the interest on it at least. Attrib.

11 My dear fellow, be reasonable; the sum you ask me for is a very considerable one, whereas I only ask you for twenty-five pounds.

Richard Brinsley Sheridan On being refused a further loan of £25 from a friend to whom he already owed £500. *Literary and Scientific Anecdotes* (W. Keddie)

12 Let us all be happy, and live within our means, even if we have to borrer the money to do it with.

Artemus Ward (Charles Farrar Browne; 1834–67) US humorous writer. *Science and Natural History*

13 I don't owe a penny to a single soul – not

counting tradesmen, of course.

P. G. Wodehouse (1881–1975) British humorous novelist. *My Man Jeeves*, 'Jeeves and the Hard-Boiled Egg'

BOSNIA AND HERCEGOVINA

1 The region is undergoing ethnic cleansing.

Anonymous Referring to Bosnia-Hercegovina. Serbian radio, reported in *The Times*, 21 May 1992

2 If there is ever another war in Europe, it will come out of some damned silly thing in the Balkans.

Bismarck (1815–98) German statesman. Remark to Ballen, shortly before Bismarck's death

3 Defend us, or let us defend ourselves.

Alija Izetbegovic (1925–) Bosnian president (1990–). Pleading for an end to ethnic cleansing and the siege of Sarajevo. Speech to the UN, 8 Sept 1993

4 The Americans don't really understand what's going on in Bosnia. To them it's the unspellables killing the unpronouncables.

P. J. O'Rourke (1947–) US writer. *The Sun*, 1993

5 The most painful thing for me is seeing the fathers of human rights turning away from what is clearly genocide. By pulling the thread holding Bosnia together, they are pulling apart civilisation in Europe.

Haris Silajdzic (1945–) Bosnian prime minister (1993–96). *The Times*, 29 Dec 1993

BREVITY

See also sermons, speeches, verbosity

1 Good things, when short, are twice as good.

Baltasar Gracián (1601–58) Spanish writer. *The Art of Worldly Wisdom*

2 I strive to be brief, and I become obscure.

Horace (Quintus Horatius Flaccus; 65–8 BC) Roman poet. *Ars Poetica*

3 ?

Victor Hugo (1802–85) French writer. The entire contents of a telegram sent to his publishers asking how *Les Misérables* was selling; the reply was '!'. *The Literary Life* (R. Hendrickson)

4 But the shortest works are always the best.

Jean de La Fontaine (1621–95) French poet. *Fables*, X, 'Les Lapins'

5 Brevity is the soul of lingerie.

Dorothy Parker (1893–1967) US writer. *While Rome Burns* (Alexander Woollcott)

6 Trust the man who hesitates in his speech and is quick and steady in action, but beware of long arguments and long beards.

George Santayana (1863–1952) US philosopher. *Soliloquies in England*, 'The British Character'

7 Brevity is the soul of wit.

William Shakespeare (1564–1616) English dramatist. *Hamlet*, II:2

8 Men of few words are the best men.

William Shakespeare *Henry V*, III:2

9 Nurse unupblown.

Evelyn Waugh (1903–66) British novelist. Cable sent after he had failed, while a journalist serving in Ethiopia, to substantiate a rumour that an English nurse had been blown up in an Italian air raid. *Our Marvelous Native Tongue* (R. Claiborne)

BRIBERY

See also corruption

1 When their lordships asked Bacon
How many bribes he had taken
He had at least the grace
To get very red in the face.

Edmund Clerihew Bentley (1875–1956) British writer. *Baseless Biography*

2 To a shower of gold most things are penetrable.

Thomas Carlyle (1795–1881) Scottish historian and essayist. *History of the French Revolution*, Pt. I, Bk. III, Ch. 7

3 I have often noticed that a bribe...has that effect – it changes a relation. The man who offers a bribe gives away a little of his own importance; the bribe once accepted, he becomes the inferior, like a man who has paid for a woman.

Graham Greene (1904–91) British novelist. *The Comedians*, Pt. I, Ch. 4

4 Though authority be a stubborn bear, yet he is oft led by the nose with gold.

William Shakespeare (1564–1616) English dramatist. *The Winter's Tale*, IV:3

BRITAIN

See also British, British Empire, England, Ireland, patriotism, Scotland, Wales

1 Great Britain has lost an Empire and has not yet found a role.

Dean Acheson (1893–1971) US lawyer and statesman. Speech, Military Academy, West Point, 5 Dec 1962

2 A nation of shop-keepers are very seldom so disinterested.

Samuel Adams (1722–1803) US revolutionary leader. Referring to Britain, following the Declaration of Independence, 4 July 1776. Speech, Philadelphia, 1 Aug 1776

3 You must not miss Whitehall. At one end you will find a statue of one of our kings who was beheaded; at the other the monument to the man who did it. This is just an example of our attempts to be fair to everybody.

Edward Appleton (1892–1965) British physicist. Referring to Charles I and Cromwell. Speech, Stockholm, 1 Jan 1948

4 Land of Hope and Glory, Mother of the Free,

How shall we extol thee, who are born of thee?
Wider still and wider shall thy bounds be set;
God who made thee mighty, make thee mightier
yet.

A. C. Benson (1862–1925) British writer. *Land of Hope and Glory*

5 Britain has lived for too long on borrowed time, borrowed money and even borrowed ideas.

James Callaghan (1912–) British politician and prime minister. *The Observer*, 'Sayings of the Week', 3 Oct 1976

6 God save our Gracious King,
Long live our noble King,
God save the King.
Send him victorious,
Happy and glorious.

Henry Carey (c. 1690–1743) English poet and musician. *God Save the King*

7 When the British warrior queen,
Bleeding from the Roman rods,
Sought, with an indignant mien,
Counsel of her country's gods.

William Cowper (1731–1800) British poet. *Boadicea*

8 Britain is not a country that is easily rocked by revolution...In Britain our institutions evolve. We are a Fabian Society writ large.

William Hamilton (1917–) Scottish MP. *My Queen and I*, Ch. 9

9 We may be a small island, but we are not a small people.

Edward Heath (1916–) British politician and prime minister. *The Observer*, 'Sayings of the Week', 21 June 1970

10 Sir, it is not so much to be lamented that Old England is lost, as that the Scotch have found it.

Samuel Johnson (1709–84) British lexicographer. *Life of Johnson* (J. Boswell), Vol. III

11 This is a very fine country to be acutely ill or injured in, but take my advice and do not be old and frail or mentally ill here – at least not for a few years. This is definitely not a good country to be deaf or blind in either.

Keith Joseph (1918–94) British politician. *The Observer*, 'Sayings of the Week', 1 July 1973

12 Once, when a British Prime Minister sneezed, men half a world away would blow their noses. Now when a British Prime Minister sneezes nobody else will even say 'Bless You'.

Bernard Levin (1928–) British journalist. *The Times*, 1976

13 When Britain first, at heaven's command,
Arose from out the azure main,
This was the charter of the land,
And guardian angels sung this strain:
'Rule, Britannia, rule the waves;
Britons never will be slaves.'

James Thomson (1700–48) British poet. *Alfred: a Masque*, Act II

14 I should like to help Britain to become a Third Programme country.

Ellen Cicely Wilkinson (1891–1947) British feminist and politician. *The Observer*, 'Sayings of the Week', 2 Feb 1947

BRITISH

See also Britain, English, Irish, Scots, Welsh

1 A young Scotsman of your ability let loose upon the world with £300, what could he not do? It's almost appalling to think of; especially if he went among the English.

J. M. Barrie (1860–1937) British novelist and dramatist. *What Every Woman Knows*, I

2 There are no countries in the world less known by the British than these selfsame British Islands.

George Henry Borrow (1803–81) British writer. *Lavengro*, Preface

3 The British love permanence more than they love beauty.

Hugh Casson (1910–) British architect. *The Observer*, 'Sayings of the Week', 14 June 1964

4 It must be owned, that the Graces do not seem to be natives of Great Britain; and I doubt, the best of us here have more of rough than polished diamond.

Earl of Chesterfield (1694–1773) English statesman. Letter to his son, 18 Nov 1748

5 The maxim of the British people is 'Business as usual'.

Winston Churchill (1874–1965) British statesman. Speech, Guildhall, 9 Nov 1914

6 They are the only people who like to be told how bad things are – who like to be told the worst.

Winston Churchill Speech, 1921

7 Of all noxious animals, too, the most noxious is a tourist. And of all tourists the most vulgar, ill-bred, offensive and loathsome is the British tourist.

Francis Kilvert (1840–79) British diarist and clergyman. *Diary*, 5 Apr 1870

8 The spread of personal ownership is in harmony with the deepest instincts of the British people. Few changes have done more to create one nation.

Nigel Lawson (1932–) British Conservative politician. Speech, Jan 1988

9 It is beginning to be hinted that we are a nation of amateurs.

Lord Rosebery (1847–1929) British statesman. Rectorial Address, Glasgow, 16 Nov 1900

10 Other nations use 'force'; we Britons alone use 'Might'.

Evelyn Waugh (1903–66) British novelist. *Scoop*, Bk. II, Ch. 5

BRITISH EMPIRE

1 The loss of India would mark and consummate the downfall of the British Empire. That great organism would pass at a stroke out of life into history. From such a catastrophe there could be no recovery.

Winston Churchill (1874–1965) British statesman. Speech to Indian Empire Society, London, 12 Dec 1930

2 I have not become the King's First Minister in order to preside over the liquidation of the British Empire.

Winston Churchill Speech, Mansion House, 10 Nov 1942

3 It is only when you get to see and realize what India is – that she is the strength and the greatness of England – it is only then that you feel that every nerve a man may strain, every energy he may put forward, cannot be devoted to a nobler purpose than keeping tight the cords that hold India to ourselves.

Lord Curzon (1859–1925) British politician. Speech, Southport, 15 Mar 1893

4 How is the Empire?

George V (1865–1936) King of the United Kingdom. Last words. *The Times*, 21 Jan 1936

5 'Can't' will be the epitaph of the British Empire – unless we wake up in time.

Oswald Mosley (1896–1980) British politician. Speech, Manchester, 9 Dec 1937

6 His Majesty's dominions, on which the sun never sets.

Christopher North (John Wilson; 1785–1854) Scottish writer. *Noctes Ambrosianae*, 20 Apr 1829

7 The Empire is a Commonwealth of Nations.

Lord Rosebery (1847–1929) British statesman. Speech, Adelaide, 18 Jan 1884

8 We the English seem, as it were, to have conquered and peopled half the world in a fit of absence of mind.

John Robert Seeley (1834–95) British historian. *The Expansion of England*, I

BUREAUCRACY

1 A memorandum is written not to inform the reader but to protect the writer.

Dean Acheson (1893–1971) US lawyer and statesman. Attrib.

2 The best way to kill an idea is to take it to a meeting.

Anonymous

3 I'm surprised that a government organization could do it that quickly.

Jimmy Carter (1924–) US statesman and president. Visiting Egypt, when told that it took twenty years to build the Great Pyramid. *Presidential Anecdotes* (P. Boller)

4 A committee is a cul-de-sac down which ideas are lured and then quietly strangled.

Barnett Cocks (1907–) British political writer. *New Scientist*, 1973

5 Whatever was required to be done, the Circumlocution Office was beforehand with all the public departments in the art of perceiving – HOW NOT TO DO IT.

Charles Dickens (1812–70) British novelist. *Little Dorrit*, Bk. I, Ch. 10

6 A Royal Commission is a broody hen sitting on a china egg.

Michael Foot (1913–) British Labour politician and journalist. Speech, House of Commons, 1964

7 A difficulty for every solution.

Herbert Samuel (1870–1963) British Liberal statesman. Referring to the Civil Service. Attrib.

8 The working of great institutions is mainly the result of a vast mass of routine, petty malice, self interest, carelessness, and sheer mistake. Only a residual fraction is thought.

George Santayana (1863–1952) US philosopher. *The Crime of Galileo*

9 My life's been a meeting, Dad, one long meeting. Even on the few committees I don't yet belong to, the agenda winks at me when I pass.

Gwyn Thomas (1913–81) British writer. *The Keep*, I

10 The British civil service...is a beautifully designed and effective braking mechanism.

Shirley Williams (1930–) British politician. Speech, Royal Institute of Public Administration, 11 Feb 1980

BUSINESS

See also capitalism

1 In Dublin's fair city, where the girls are so pretty,
I first set my eyes on sweet Molly Malone,
As she wheeled her wheelbarrow, through streets broad and narrow,
Crying, Cockles and mussels! alive, alive, O!

She was a fishmonger, but sure 'twas no wonder,
For so were her father and mother before.

Anonymous *Cockles and Mussels*

2 Today's sales should be better than yesterday's – and worse than tomorrow's.

Anonymous

3 Who will change old lamps for new ones?... new lamps for old ones?

The Arabian Nights (c. 1500) A collection of tales from the East. *The History of Aladdin*

4 You ask me what it is I do. Well actually, you know,
I'm partly a liaison man and partly P.R.O.
Essentially I integrate the current export drive
And basically I'm viable from ten o'clock till five.

John Betjeman (1906–84) British poet. *Executive*

5 Here's the rule for bargains: 'Do other men, for they would do you.' That's the true business precept.

Charles Dickens (1812–70) British novelist. *Martin Chuzzlewit*, Ch. 11

6 Whenever you see a successful business,

someone once made a courageous decision.
Peter F. Drucker

7 The longest word in the English language is the one following the phrase: 'And now a word from our sponsor.'
Hal Eaton

8 A business that makes nothing but money is a poor kind of business.
Henry Ford (1863–1947) US car manufacturer. Interview

9 No nation was ever ruined by trade.
Benjamin Franklin (1706–90) US scientist and statesman. *Essays*, 'Thoughts on Commercial Subjects'

10 Remember that time is money.
Benjamin Franklin *Advice to a Young Tradesman*

11 The salary of the chief executive of the large corporation is not a market award for achievement. It is frequently in the nature of a warm personal gesture by the individual to himself.
John Kenneth Galbraith (1908–) US economist. *Annals of an Abiding Liberal*

12 Where wealth and freedom reign, contentment fails,
And honour sinks where commerce long prevails.
Oliver Goldsmith (1728–74) Irish-born British writer. *The Traveller*

13 Cherry ripe, ripe, ripe, I cry.
Full and fair ones; come and buy.
Robert Herrick (1591–1674) English poet. *Hesperides*, 'Cherry Ripe'

14 When you are skinning your customers, you should leave some skin on to grow so that you can skin them again.
Nikita Khrushchev (1894–1971) Soviet statesman. Said to British businessmen. *The Observer*, 'Sayings of the Week', 28 May 1961

15 He is the only man who is for ever apologizing for his occupation.
H. L. Mencken (1880–1956) US journalist. Referring to the businessman. *Prejudices*, 'Types of Men'

16 A friendship founded on business is better than a business founded on friendship.
John D. Rockefeller (1839–1937) US industrialist.

17 A dinner lubricates business.
William Scott (1745–1836) British jurist. *Life of Johnson* (J. Boswell), 1791

18 The customer is always right.
H. Gordon Selfridge (1857–1947) US-born businessman. Slogan adopted at his shops

19 A snapper-up of unconsidered trifles.
William Shakespeare (1564–1616) English dramatist. *The Winter's Tale*, IV:2

20 The big print giveth and the fine print taketh away.
J. Fulton Sheen (1895–1979) US Roman Catholic archbishop. Referring to his contract for a television appearance. Attrib.

21 People of the same trade seldom meet together but the conversation ends in a conspiracy against the public, or in some diversion to raise prices.
Adam Smith (1723–90) Scottish economist. *The Wealth of Nations*

22 You never expected justice from a company, did you? They have neither a soul to lose nor a body to kick.
Sydney Smith (1771–1845) British clergyman and essayist. *Memoir* (Lady Holland)

23 I have heard of a man who had a mind to sell his house, and therefore carried a piece of brick in his pocket, which he shewed as a pattern to encourage purchasers.
Jonathan Swift (1667–1745) Irish-born Anglican priest and writer. *The Drapier's Letters*, 2 (4 Aug 1724)

24 It's just like having a licence to print your own money.
Lord Thomson of Fleet (1894–1976) Canadian-born British newspaper proprietor. Speaking about commercial television. Attrib.

25 All business sagacity reduces itself in the last analysis to a judicious use of sabotage.
Thorstein Bunde Veblen (1857–1929) US social scientist. *The Nature of Peace*

26 If Max gets to Heaven he won't last long. He will be chucked out for trying to pull off a merger between Heaven and Hell...after having secured a controlling interest in key subsidiary companies in both places, of course.
H. G. Wells (1866–1946) British writer. Referring to Lord Beaverbrook. *Beaverbrook* (A. J. P. Taylor)

27 The trouble with the profit system has always been that it was highly unprofitable to most people.
Elwyn Brooks White (1899–1985) US journalist and humorist. Attrib.

28 For many years I thought what was good for our country was good for General Motors, and vice versa.
Charles Erwin Wilson (1890–1961) US engineer. Said in testimony to the Senate Armed Services Committee, Jan 1953. Attrib.

29 Business underlies everything in our national life, including our spiritual life. Witness the fact that in the Lord's Prayer the first petition is for daily bread. No one can worship God or love his neighbour on an empty stomach.
Woodrow Wilson (1856–1925) US statesman. Speech, New York, 1912

C

CAMBRIDGE

See also England, Oxford

1 Oxford is on the whole more attractive than Cambridge to the ordinary visitor; and the traveller is therefore recommended to visit Cambridge first, or to omit it altogether if he cannot visit both.

Karl Baedeker (1801–59) German publisher. *Baedeker's Great Britain*, 'From London to Oxford'

2 For Cambridge people rarely smile,
Being urban, squat, and packed with guile.

Rupert Brooke (1887–1915) British poet. *The Old Vicarage, Grantchester*

3 The King to Oxford sent a troop of horse,
For Tories own no argument but force:
With equal skill to Cambridge books he sent,
For Whigs admit no force but argument.

William Browne (1692–1774) English physician. A reply to TRAPP. *Literary Anecdotes* (Nichols), Vol. III

4 Spring and summer did happen in Cambridge almost every year.

Vladimir Nabokov (1899–1977) Russian-born US novelist. *The Real Life of Sebastian Knight*, Ch. 5

5 This is the city of perspiring dreams.

Frederic Raphael (1931–) British author. *The Glittering Prizes: An Early Life*, III

6 The King, observing with judicious eyes
The state of both his universities,
To Oxford sent a troop of horse, and why?
That learned body wanted loyalty;
To Cambridge books, as very well discerning
How much that loyal body wanted learning.

Joseph Trapp (1679–1747) English churchman and academic. Written after George I donated the Bishop of Ely's library to Cambridge; for a reply see BROWNE. *Literary Anecdotes* (Nichols), Vol. III

CANNIBALISM

1 Eating people is wrong.

Michael Flanders (1922–75) British comedian and songwriter. *The Reluctant Cannibal*

2 The better sort of Ishmaelites have been Christian for many centuries and will not publicly eat human flesh uncooked in Lent, without special and costly dispensation from their bishop.

Evelyn Waugh (1903–66) British novelist. *Scoop*, Bk. II, Ch. 1

CAPITALISM

See also business, commercialism

1 It is closing time in the gardens of the West.

Cyril Connolly (1903–74) British journalist. *The Condemned Playground*

2 Property has its duties as well as its rights.

Thomas Drummond (1797–1840) British engineer and statesman. Letter to the Earl of Donoughmore, 22 May 1838

3 If I had to give a definition of capitalism I would say: the process whereby American girls turn into American women.

Christopher Hampton (1946–) British writer and dramatist. *Savages*, Sc. 16

4 It is the unpleasant and unacceptable face of capitalism but one should not suggest that the whole of British industry consists of practices of this kind.

Edward Heath (1916–) British politician and prime minister. Referring to the Lonrho Affair. Speech, House of Commons, 15 May 1973

5 ...militarism...is one of the chief bulwarks of capitalism, and the day that militarism is undermined, capitalism will fail.

Helen Keller (1880–1968) US writer and lecturer. *The Story of My Life*

6 We cannot remove the evils of capitalism without taking its source of power: ownership.

Neil Kinnock (1942–) British politician. *Tribune*, 1975

7 Under capitalism we have a state in the proper sense of the word, that is, a special machine for the suppression of one class by another.

Lenin (Vladimir Ilich Ulyanov; 1870–1924) Russian revolutionary leader. *The State and Revolution*, Ch. 5

8 Not every problem someone has with his girlfriend is necessarily due to the capitalist mode of production.

Herbert Marcuse (1898–1979) German-born US philosopher. *The Listener*

9 Capitalist production begets, with the inexorability of a law of nature, its own negation.

Karl Marx (1818–83) German philosopher and revolutionary. *Das Kapital*, Ch. 15

10 Man is the only creature that consumes without producing.

George Orwell (Eric Blair; 1903–50) British novelist. *Animal Farm*, Ch. 1

11 I have gone to war too...I am going to fight capitalism even if it kills me. It is wrong that people like you should be comfortable and well fed while all around you people are starving.

Sylvia Pankhurst (1882–1960) British suffragette. *The Fighting Pankhursts* (David Mitchell)

12 Property is theft.

Pierre Joseph Proudhon (1809–65) French socialist. *Qu'est-ce que la Propriété?*, Ch. 1

13 Property is organised robbery.

George Bernard Shaw (1856–1950) Irish dramatist and critic. *Major Barbara*, Preface

14 Lenin was the first to discover that capitalism 'inevitably' caused war; and he discovered this only when the First World War was already being fought. Of course he was right. Since every great state was capitalist in 1914, capitalism obviously 'caused' the First World War; but just as obviously it had 'caused' the previous generation of Peace.

A. J. P. Taylor (1906–90) British historian. *The Origins of the Second World War*, Ch. 6

15 The public be damned. I am working for my stockholders.

William Henry Vanderbilt (1821–85) US railway chief. Refusing to speak to a reporter, who was seeking to find out his views on behalf of the public.

CARS

See also travel

1 I think that cars today are almost the exact equivalent of the great Gothic cathedrals...the supreme creation of an era, conceived with passion by unknown artists.

Roland Barthes (1915–80) French philosopher.

2 Eighty per cent of the people of Britain want more money spent on public transport – in order that other people will travel on the buses so that there is more room for them to drive their cars.

John Selwyn Gummer (1939–) British politician and Secretary of State for the Environment. *The Independent*, 14 Oct 1994

3 Motorists (as they used to be called) were utterly irresponsible in their dealings with each other and with the pedestrian public; for their benefit homicide was legalised. The basic principles of Equality were flouted, while the opposing principle of Envy was disastrously encouraged.

L. P. Hartley (1895–1972) British novelist. *Facial Justice*, Ch. 5

4 The car has become the carapace, the protective and aggressive shell, of urban and suburban man.

Marshall McLuhan (1911–81) Canadian sociologist. *Understanding Media*, Ch. 22

5 *Rush hour:* that hour when traffic is almost at a standstill.

J. B. Morton (1893–1979) British journalist. *Morton's Folly*

6 You have your own company, your own temperature control, your own music – and don't have to put up with dreadful human beings sitting alongside you.

Steven Norris (1945–) British politician and Under-Secretary of State, Department of Transport. Explaining why he prefers using his private car to public transport. *The Independent*, 9 Feb 1995

7 It is the overtakers who keep the undertakers busy.

William Ewart Pitts (b. 1900) British chief constable. *The Observer*, 'Sayings of the Week', 22 Dec 1963

CATHOLICISM

See also Christianity, Protestantism, religion

1 A priest is a man who is called Father by everyone except his own children who are obliged to call him Uncle.

Italian proverb

2 *Ad majorem Dei gloriam.*
To the greater glory of God.

Anonymous Motto of the Jesuits

3 I expect you know my friend Evelyn Waugh, who, like you, your Holiness, is a Roman Catholic.

Randolph Churchill (1911–68) British political journalist. Remark made during an audience with the Pope

4 I have a Catholic soul, but a Lutheran stomach.

Erasmus (1466–1536) Dutch humanist, scholar, and writer. Replying to criticism of his failure to fast during Lent. *Dictionnaire Encyclopédique*

5 The Papacy is not other than the Ghost of the deceased Roman Empire, sitting crowned upon the grave thereof.

Thomas Hobbes (1588–1679) English philosopher. *Leviathan*, Pt. IV, Ch. 37

6 There is no idolatry in the Mass. They believe God to be there, and they adore him.

Samuel Johnson (1709–84) British lexicographer. *Life of Johnson* (J. Boswell), Vol. II

7 We know these new English Catholics. They are the last words in Protest. They are Protestants protesting against Protestantism.

D. H. Lawrence (1885–1930) British novelist. *Phoenix*, 'Review of Eric Gill, *Art Nonsense*'

8 Since God has given us the papacy, let us enjoy it.

Leo X (Giovanni de' Medici; 1475–1521) Pope (1513–21). *Men of Art* (T. Craven)

9 I was fired from there, finally, for a lot of things, among them my insistence that the Immaculate Conception was spontaneous combustion.

Dorothy Parker (1893–1967) US writer. *Writers at Work, First Series* (Malcolm Cowley)

10 The Pope! How many divisions has *he* got?

Joseph Stalin (J. Dzhugashvili; 1879–1953) Soviet statesman. When urged by Pierre Laval to tolerate Catholicism in the USSR to appease the Pope, 13 May 1935. *The Second World War* (W. S. Churchill), Vol. I, Ch. 8

11 Becoming an Anglo-Catholic must surely be a sad business – rather like becoming an amateur conjurer.

John St Loe Strachey (1901–63) British politician. *The Coming Struggle for Power*, Pt. III, Ch. 11

12 'God knows how you Protestants can be expected to have any sense of direction,' she said. 'It's different with us. I haven't been to mass for years, I've got every mortal sin on my conscience, but I know when I'm doing wrong. I'm still a Catholic.

Angus Wilson (1913–91) British novelist. *The Wrong Set*, 'Significant Experience'

CATS

See also animals

1 Cruel, but composed and bland,
Dumb, inscrutable and grand,
So Tiberius might have sat,
Had Tiberius been a cat.

Matthew Arnold (1822–88) British poet and critic. *Poor Matthias*

2 Macavity, Macavity, there's no one like Macavity,
There never was a Cat of such deceitfulness and suavity.
He always has an alibi, and one or two to spare:
At whatever time the deed took place –
MACAVITY WASN'T THERE!

T. S. Eliot (1888–1965) US-born British poet and dramatist. *Macavity: The Mystery Cat*

3 I have noticed that what cats most appreciate in a human being is not the ability to produce food which they take for granted – but his or her entertainment value.

Geoffrey Household (1900–88) British writer. *Rogue Male*

4 When I observed he was a fine cat, saying, 'why yes, Sir, but I have had cats whom I liked better than this'; and then as if perceiving Hodge to be out of countenance, adding, 'but he is a very fine cat, a very fine cat indeed.'

Samuel Johnson (1709–84) British lexicographer. *Life of Johnson* (J. Boswell), Vol. IV

5 If a fish is the movement of water embodied, given shape, then cat is a diagram and pattern of subtle air.

Doris Lessing (1919–) British novelist. *Particularly Cats*, Ch. 2

6 When I play with my cat, who knows whether she is not amusing herself with me more than I with her?

Michel de Montaigne (1533–92) French essayist. *Essais*, II

7 If a dog jumps onto your lap it is because he is fond of you; but if a cat does the same thing it is because your lap is warmer.

A. N. Whitehead (1861–1947) British philosopher. *Dialogues*

CAUTION

See also prudence

1 Better be safe than sorry.

Proverb

2 Don't put all your eggs in one basket.

Proverb

3 He that fights and runs away, may live to fight another day.

Proverb

4 He who sups with the devil should have a long spoon.

Proverb

5 If you trust before you try, you may repent before you die.

Proverb

6 Keep your mouth shut and your eyes open.

Proverb

7 Keep your weather-eye open.

Proverb

8 Look before you leap.

Proverb

9 And all should cry, Beware! Beware!
His flashing eyes, his floating hair!
Weave a circle round him thrice,
And close your eyes with holy dread,
For he on honey-dew hath fed,
And drunk the milk of Paradise.

Samuel Taylor Coleridge (1772–1834) British poet. *Kubla Khan*

10 Chi Wen Tzu always thought three times before taking action. Twice would have been quite enough.

Confucius (K'ung Fu-tzu; 551–479 BC) Chinese philosopher. *Analects*

11 Take example by your father, my boy, and be very careful o' vidders all your life.

Charles Dickens (1812–70) British novelist. *Pickwick Papers*, Ch. 13

12 Don't go into Mr McGregor's garden: your Father had an accident there; he was put in a pie by Mrs McGregor.

Beatrix Potter (1866–1943) British children's writer. *The Tale of Peter Rabbit*

13 The only way to be absolutely safe is never to try anything for the first time.

Magnus Pyke (1908–92) British scientist, television personality, and writer. BBC radio programme

CENSORSHIP

See also pornography, prudery

1 Whenever books are burned men also in the end are burned.

Heinrich Heine (1797–1856) German poet and writer. *Almansor*

2 There is in our hands as citizens an instrument to mould the minds of the young and to create great and good and noble citizens for the future.

Edward Shortt (1862–1935) Home Secretary (1919–22);

President of the British Board of Film Censors (1929–35). Referring to the British Board of Film Censors.
Remark, 1929

3 Censorship is more depraving and corrupting than anything pornography can produce.

Tony Smythe (1938–) Chairman of the National Council for Civil Liberties, Great Britain. *The Observer*, 'Sayings of the Week', 18 Sept 1972

4 God forbid that any book should be banned. The practice is as indefensible as infanticide.

Rebecca West (Cicely Isabel Fairfield; 1892–1983) British novelist and journalist. *The Strange Necessity*, 'The Tosh Horse'

CERTAINTY

See also self-confidence

1 If a man will begin with certainties, he shall end in doubts, but if he will be content to begin with doubts, he shall end in certainties.

Francis Bacon (1561–1626) English philosopher. *The Advancement of Learning*, Bk. I, Ch. 5

2 Of that there is no manner of doubt –
No probable, possible shadow of doubt –
No possible doubt whatever.

W. S. Gilbert (1836–1911) British dramatist. *The Gondoliers*, I

CHANCE

See also accident, luck, opportunity

1 Throw out a sprat to catch a mackerel.

Proverb

2 I returned, and saw under the sun, that the race is not to the swift, nor the battle to the strong, neither yet bread to the wise, nor yet riches to men of understanding, nor yet favour to men of skill; but time and chance happeneth to them all.
For man also knoweth not his time: as the fishes that are taken in an evil net, and as the birds that are caught in the snare; so are the sons of men snared in an evil time, when it falleth suddenly upon them.

Bible: Ecclesiastes 9:11–12

3 I shot an arrow into the air,
It fell to earth, I knew not where.

Henry Wadsworth Longfellow (1807–82) US poet. *The Arrow and the Song*

4 Accidental and fortuitous concurrence of atoms.

Lord Palmerston (1784–1865) British statesman. Speech, House of Commons, 1857

5 When you take the bull by the horns... what happens is a toss up.

William Pett Ridge (1860–1930) British novelist. *Love at Paddington Green*, Ch. 4

CHANGE

See also conservatism, constancy, progress, transience

1 Can the Ethiopian change his skin, or the leopard his spots? then may ye also do good, that are accustomed to do evil.

Bible: Jeremiah 13:23

2 All reform except a moral one will prove unavailing.

Thomas Carlyle (1795–1881) Scottish historian and essayist. *Critical and Miscellaneous Essays*, 'Corn Law Rhymes'

3 The time's come: there's a terrific thundercloud advancing upon us, a mighty storm is coming to freshen us up....It's going to blow away all this idleness and indifference, and prejudice against work....I'm going to work, and in twenty-five or thirty years' time every man and woman will be working.

Anton Chekhov (1860–1904) Russian dramatist. *Three Sisters*, I

4 Variety's the very spice of life
That gives it all its flavour.

William Cowper (1731–1800) British poet. *The Task*

5 Most women set out to try to change a man, and when they have changed him they do not like him.

Marlene Dietrich (Maria Magdalene von Losch; 1901–92) German-born film star. Attrib.

6 Come mothers and fathers
Throughout the land
And don't criticize
What you can't understand.

Bob Dylan (Robert Allen Zimmerman; 1941–) US popular singer. *The Times They Are A-Changin'*

7 Man is so made that he can only find relaxation from one kind of labour by taking up another.

Anatole France (Jacques Anatole François Thibault; 1844–1924) French writer. *The Crime of Sylvestre Bonnard*

8 One must never lose time in vainly regretting the past nor in complaining about the changes which cause us discomfort, for change is the very essence of life.

Anatole France Attrib.

9 Everything flows and nothing stays.

Heraclitus (c. 535–c. 475 BC) Greek philosopher. *Cratylus* (Plato), 402a

10 You can't step into the same river twice.

Heraclitus *Cratylus* (Plato), 402a

11 Change is not made without inconvenience, even from worse to better.

Richard Hooker (c. 1554–1600) English theologian. *English Dictionary* (Johnson), Preface

12 There is a certain relief in change, even though it be from bad to worse; as I have found in travelling in a stage-coach, that it is often a comfort to shift one's position and be bruised in a new place.

Washington Irving (1783–1859) US writer. *Tales of a Traveller*, 'To the Reader'

13 An old Dutch farmer, who remarked to a companion once that it was not best to swap horses in mid-stream.

Abraham Lincoln (1809–65) US statesman. Speech, 9 June 1864

14 Well, I find that a change of nuisances is as good as a vacation.

David Lloyd George (1863–1945) British Liberal statesman. On being asked how he maintained his cheerfulness when beset by numerous political obstacles. Attrib.

15 The wind of change is blowing through the continent. Whether we like it or not, this growth of national consciousness is a political fact.

Harold Macmillan (1894–1986) British politician and prime minister. Speech, South African Parliament, 3 Feb 1960

16 At last he rose, and twitched his mantle blue:
To-morrow to fresh woods, and pastures new.

John Milton (1608–74) English poet. *Lycidas*

17 Poor old Daddy – just one of those sturdy old plants left over from the Edwardian Wilderness, that can't understand why the sun isn't shining any more.

John Osborne (1929–94) British dramatist. *Look Back in Anger*, II.2

18 Through all the changing scenes of life.

Nahum Tate (1652–1715) Irish-born English poet. *New Version of the Psalms*, 'Through all the Changing'

19 And slowly answer'd Arthur from the barge:
'The old order changeth, yielding place to new,
And God fulfils himself in many ways.'

Alfred, Lord Tennyson (1809–92) British poet. *Idylls of the King*, 'The Passing of Arthur'

CHARACTER

1 Monday's child is fair of face, Tuesday's child is full of grace; Wednesday's child is full of woe, Thursday's child has far to go; Friday's child is loving and giving, Saturday's child works hard for its living; and the child that's born on the Sabbath day, is fair and wise and good and gay.

Proverb

2 If you wish to know what a man is, place him in authority.

Yugoslav Proverb

3 Every man is as Heaven made him, and sometimes a great deal worse.

Miguel de Cervantes (1547–1616) Spanish novelist. *Don Quixote*, Pt. II, Ch. 4

4 He was as fresh as is the month of May.

Geoffrey Chaucer (c. 1342–1400) English poet. Referring to the squire. *The Canterbury Tales*, Prologue

5 Souninge in moral vertu was his speche,
And gladly wolde he lerne, and gladly teche.

Geoffrey Chaucer Referring to the clerk. *The Canterbury Tales*, Prologue

6 From a timid, shy girl I had become a woman of resolute character, who could not longer be frightened by the struggle with troubles.

Anna Dostoevsky (1846–1918) Russian diarist and writer. *Dostoevsky Portrayed by His Wife*

7 What e'r he did was done with so much ease,
In him alone, 'twas Natural to please.

John Dryden (1631–1700) British poet and dramatist. *Absalom and Achitophel*, I

8 A patronizing disposition always has its meaner side.

George Eliot (Mary Ann Evans; 1819–80) British novelist. *Adam Bede*

9 I am a man for whom the outside world exists.

Théophile Gautier (1811–72) French poet and critic. *Journal des Goncourt*, 1 May 1857

10 We ought to give up the metaphysical assumption that character is something for which people are responsible.

Jonathan Glover British philosopher. *The Independent*, 13 Feb 1995

11 Talent develops in quiet places, character in the full current of human life.

Goethe (1749–1832) German poet and dramatist. *Torquato Tasso*, I

12 Strong enough to answer back to desires, to despise distinctions, and a whole man in himself, polished and well-rounded.

Horace (Quintus Horatius Flaccus; 65–8 BC) Roman poet. *Satires*, II

13 A tart temper never mellows with age, and a sharp tongue is the only edged tool that grows keener with constant use.

Washington Irving (1783–1859) US writer. *The Sketch Book*, 'Rip Van Winkle'

14 What is character but the determination of incident? What is incident but the illustration of character?

Henry James (1843–1916) US novelist. *Partial Portraits*, 'The Art of Fiction'

15 He was a vicious man, but very kind to me. If you call a dog *Hervey*, I shall love him.

Samuel Johnson (1709–84) British lexicographer. *Life of Johnson* (J. Boswell), Vol. I

16 A very unclubable man.

Samuel Johnson Referring to Sir John Hawkins. *Life of Johnson* (J. Boswell), Vol. I

17 I recognize that I am made up of several persons and that the person that at the moment has the upper hand will inevitably give place to another. But which is the real one? All of them or none?

W. Somerset Maugham (1874–1965) British novelist. *A Writer's Notebook*

18 It is with narrow-souled people as with narrow-necked bottles: the less they have in them, the more noise they make in pouring it out.

Alexander Pope (1688–1744) British poet. *Thoughts on Various Subjects*

19 Children with Hyacinth's temperament don't know better as they grow older; they merely know more.

Saki (Hector Hugh Munro; 1870–1916) British writer. *Hyacinth*

20 There is no such thing as psychological. Let us say that one can improve the biography of the person.

Jean-Paul Sartre (1905–80) French writer. *The Divided Self* (R. D. Laing), Ch. 8

21 A certain person may have, as you say, a wonderful presence: I do not know. What I do know is that he has a perfectly delightful absence.

Idries Shah (1924–96) British author. *Reflections*, 'Presence and Absence'

22 His life was gentle; and the elements
So mix'd in him that Nature might stand up
And say to all the world 'This was a man!'

William Shakespeare (1564–1616) English dramatist. Referring to Brutus. *Julius Caesar*, V:5

23 A man of great common sense and good taste, – meaning thereby a man without originality or moral courage.

George Bernard Shaw (1856–1950) Irish dramatist and critic. Referring to Julius Caesar. *Caesar and Cleopatra*, Notes

24 I'm not hard – I'm frightfully soft. But I will not be hounded.

Margaret Thatcher (1925–) British politician and prime minister. *Daily Mail*, 1972

25 He is a man of brick. As if he was born as a baby literally of clay and decades of exposure have baked him to the colour and hardness of brick.

John Updike (1932–) US novelist. *Rabbit, Run*

26 There aren't many left like him nowadays, what with education and whisky the price it is.

Evelyn Waugh (1903–66) British novelist. *Decline and Fall*, Pt. I, Ch. 7

27 I've met a lot of hardboiled eggs in my time, but you're twenty minutes.

Billy Wilder (Samuel Wilder; 1906–) Austrian-born US film director. *Ace in the Hole*

CHARITY

See also generosity, help, parasites

1 Charity begins at home.

Proverb

2 The living need charity more than the dead.

George Arnold (1834–65) US poet and humorist. *The Jolly Old Pedagogue*

3 In charity there is no excess.

Francis Bacon (1561–1626) English philosopher. *Essays*, 'Of Goodness, and Goodness of Nature'

4 Feed the World
Let them know it's Christmas.

Band Aid Song written to raise money for the relief of famine in Ethiopia. *Do They Know It's Christmas?*

5 Don't bother to thank me. I know what a perfectly ghastly season it's been for you Spanish dancers.

Tallulah Bankhead (1903–68) US actress. Said on dropping fifty dollars into a tambourine held out by a Salvation Army collector. *With Malice Toward All* (D. Hermann)

6 Though I speak with the tongues of men and of angels, and have not charity, I am become as sounding brass, or a tinkling cymbal.
And though I have the gift of prophecy, and understand all mysteries, and all knowledge; and though I have all faith, so that I could remove mountains, and have not charity, I am nothing.
And though I bestow all my goods to feed the poor, and though I give my body to be burned, and have not charity, it profiteth me nothing.
Charity suffereth long, and is kind; charity envieth not; charity vaunteth not itself, is not puffed up,
Doth not behave itself unseemly, seeketh not her own, is not easily provoked, thinketh no evil;
Rejoiceth not in iniquity, but rejoiceth in the truth;
Beareth all things, believeth all things, hopeth all things, endureth all things.
Charity never faileth: but whether there be prophecies, they shall fail; whether there be tongues, they shall cease; whether there be knowledge, it shall vanish away.
For we know in part, and we prophesy in part.
But when that which is perfect is come, then that which is in part shall be done away.
When I was a child, I spake as a child, I understood as a child, I thought as a child: but when I became a man, I put away childish things.
For now we see through a glass, darkly; but then face to face: now I know in part; but then shall I know even as also I am known.
And now abideth faith, hope, charity, these three; but the greatest of these is charity.

Bible: I Corinthians 13:1–13

7 Now as touching things offered unto idols, we know that we all have knowledge. Knowledge puffeth up, but charity edifieth.

Bible: I Corinthians 8:1

8 But a certain Samaritan, as he journeyed, came where he was: and when he saw him, he had compassion on him,
And went to him, and bound up his wounds, pouring in oil and wine, and set him on his own beast, and brought him to an inn, and took care of him.
And on the morrow when he departed, he took out two pence, and gave them to the host, and said unto him, Take care of him; and whatsoever thou spendest more, when I come again, I will repay thee.

Bible: Luke 10:33–35

9 All our doings without charity are nothing worth.

The Book of Common Prayer *Collect, Quinquagesima Sunday*

10 Charity begins at home, is the voice of the world.

Thomas Browne (1605–82) English physician and writer. *Religio Medici*, Pt. II

11 I have always heard, Sancho, that doing good to base fellows is like throwing water into the sea.

Miguel de Cervantes (1547–1616) Spanish novelist. *Don Quixote*, Pt. I, Ch. 23

12 Charity is the power of defending that which we know to be indefensible. Hope is the power of being cheerful in circumstances which we know to be desperate.

G. K. Chesterton (1874–1936) British writer. *Heretics*, Ch. 12

13 No people do so much harm as those who go about doing good.

Mandell Creighton (1843–1901) British churchman. *Life*

14 I'm not interested in the bloody system! Why has he no food? Why is he starving to death?

Bob Geldof (1952–) Irish rock musician. *The Observer*, 'Sayings of the Week', 27 Oct 1985

15 She's the sort of woman who lives for others – you can always tell the others by their hunted expression.

C. S. Lewis (1898–1963) British academic and writer. *The Screwtape Letters*

16 In the field of world policy; I would dedicate this nation to the policy of the good neighbor.

Franklin D. Roosevelt (1882–1945) US Democratic president. First Inaugural Address, 4 Mar 1933

17 When they will not give a doit to relieve a lame beggar, they will lay out ten to see a dead Indian.

William Shakespeare (1564–1616) English dramatist. *The Tempest*, II:2

18 If you see anybody fallen by the wayside and lying in the ditch, it isn't much good climbing into the ditch and lying by his side.

H. R. L. Sheppard (1880–1937) British clergyman. *Dick Sheppard* (Carolyn Scott)

19 The white man knows how to make everything, but he does not know how to distribute it.

Sitting Bull (c. 1834–90) US Sioux Indian chief. Attrib.

20 You find people ready enough to do the Samaritan, without the oil and twopence.

Sydney Smith (1771–1845) British clergyman and essayist. *Memoir* (Lady Holland)

21 To keep a lamp burning we have to keep putting oil in it.

Mother Teresa (Agnes Gonxha Bojaxhui; 1910–) Yugoslavian missionary in Calcutta. *Time*, 'Saints Among Us', 29 Dec 1975

22 As for doing good, that is one of the professions which are full.

Henry David Thoreau (1817–62) US writer. *Walden*, 'Economy'

23 I have always depended on the kindness of strangers.

Tennessee Williams (1911–83) US dramatist. *A Streetcar Named Desire*, II:3

CHARM

1 It's a sort of bloom on a woman. If you have it, you don't need to have anything else; and if you don't have it, it doesn't much matter what else you have.

J. M. Barrie (1860–1937) British novelist and dramatist. *What Every Woman Knows*, I

2 All charming people have something to conceal, usually their total dependence on the appreciation of others.

Cyril Connolly (1903–74) British journalist. *Enemies of Promise*, Ch. 16

3 Oozing charm from every pore,
He oiled his way around the floor.

Alan Jay Lerner (1918–86) US songwriter. *My Fair Lady*, II:1

4 It is absurd to divide people into good and bad. People are either charming or tedious.

Oscar Wilde (1854–1900) Irish-born British dramatist. *Lady Windermere's Fan*, I

CHAUCER

1 Chaucer notwithstanding the praises bestowed on him, I think obscene and contemptible; he owes his celebrity merely to his antiquity.

Lord Byron (1788–1824) British poet. Attrib.

2 Chaucer, I confess, is a rough diamond; and must be polished e'er he shines.

John Dryden (1631–1700) British poet and dramatist. *Preface to the Fables*

3 I read Chaucer still with as much pleasure as any of our poets. He is a master of manners and of description and the first tale-teller in the true enlivened, natural way.

Alexander Pope (1688–1744) British poet. Attrib.

4 Mr. C. had talent, but he couldn't spel. No man has a right to be a lit'rary man onless he knows how to spel. It is a pity that Chawcer, who had geneyus, was so unedicated. He's the wus speller I know of.

Artemus Ward (Charles Farrar Browne; 1834–67) US humorous writer. *Chaucer's Poems*

CHILDREN

See also babies, family, innocence of childhood, youth

1 Spare the rod and spoil the child.

Proverb

2 There's only one pretty child in the world, and every mother has it.
Proverb

3 It was no wonder that people were so horrible when they started life as children.
Kingsley Amis (1922–95) British novelist. *One Fat Englishman*, Ch. 14

4 Only those in the last stage of disease could believe that children are true judges of character.
W. H. Auden (1907–73) British poet. *The Orators*, 'Journal of an Airman'

5 Children sweeten labours, but they make misfortunes more bitter.
Francis Bacon (1561–1626) English philosopher. *Essays*, 'Of Parents and Children'

6 Children have never been very good at listening to their elders, but they have never failed to imitate them.
James Baldwin (1924–87) US writer. *Esquire*, 1960

7 I am married to Beatrice Salkeld, a painter. We have no children, except me.
Brendan Behan (1923–64) Irish playwright. Attrib.

8 I wish I'd been a mixed infant.
Brendan Behan *The Hostage*, II

9 Alas! That such affected tricks
Should flourish in a child of six!
Hilaire Belloc (1870–1953) French-born British poet. *Cautionary Tales*, 'Godolphin Horne'

10 A trick that everyone abhors
In little girls is slamming doors.
Hilaire Belloc *Cautionary Tales*, 'Rebecca'

11 Desire not a multitude of unprofitable children, neither delight in ungodly sons.
Bible: Ecclesiasticus 16:1

12 But when Jesus saw it, he was much displeased, and said unto them. Suffer the little children to come unto me, and forbid them not: for of such is the kingdom of God.
Bible: Mark 10:14

13 Verily I say unto you, Except ye be converted, and become as little children, ye shall not enter into the kingdom of heaven.
Bible: Matthew 18:3

14 And whoso shall receive one such little child in my name receiveth me.
But whoso shall offend one of these little ones which believe in me, it were better for him that a millstone were hanged about his neck, and that he were drowned in the depth of the sea.
Bible: Matthew 18:5–6

15 He that spareth his rod hateth his son: but he that loveth him chasteneth him betimes.
Bible: Proverbs 13:24

16 You can do anything with children if you only play with them.
Bismarck (1815–98) German statesman. Attrib.

17 'Twas on a Holy Thursday, their innocent faces clean,
The children walking two and two, in red and blue and green.
William Blake (1757–1827) British poet. *Songs of Innocence*, 'Holy Thursday'

18 There is no finer investment for any community than putting milk into babies.
Winston Churchill (1874–1965) British statesman. Radio Broadcast, 21 Mar 1943

19 Boys do not grow up gradually. They move forward in spurts like the hands of clocks in railway stations.
Cyril Connolly (1903–74) British journalist. *Enemies of Promise*, Ch. 18

20 It is only rarely that one can see in a little boy the promise of a man, but one can almost always see in a little girl the threat of a woman.
Alexandre Dumas, fils (1824–95) French writer. Attrib.

21 Anybody who hates children and dogs can't be all bad.
W. C. Fields (1880–1946) US actor. Attrib.

22 To bear many children is considered not only a religious blessing but also an investment. The greater their number, some Indians reason, the more alms they can beg.
Indira Gandhi (1917–84) Indian stateswoman. *New York Review of Books*, 'Indira's Coup' (Oriana Fallaci)

23 Three little maids from school are we,
Pert as a school-girl well can be,
Filled to the brim with girlish glee.
W. S. Gilbert (1836–1911) British dramatist. *The Mikado*, I

24 Look at little Johnny there,
Little Johnny Head-in-Air.
Heinrich Hoffman (1809–74) German writer. *Struwwelpeter*, 'Johnny Head-in-Air'

25 Anything to me is sweeter
Than to see Shock-headed Peter.
Heinrich Hoffman *Struwwelpeter*, 'Shock-headed Peter'

26 The business of being a child interests a child not at all. Children very rarely play at being other children.
David Holloway (1924–) Literary editor. *The Daily Telegraph*, 15 December 1966

27 One of the most obvious facts about grown-ups to a child is that they have forgotten what it is like to be a child.
Randall Jarrell (1914–65) US author. *Third Book of Criticism*

28 The legitimate desire to have a child cannot be interpreted as the right to have a child at any cost.
John Paul II (Karol Wotjyla; 1920–) Polish pope. *The Times*, 1 Aug 1994

29 A child deserves the maximum respect; if you ever have something disgraceful in mind, don't ignore your son's tender years.

Juvenal (Decimus Junius Juvenalis; 60–130 AD) Roman satirist. *Satires*, XIV

30 The real menace in dealing with a five-year-old is that in no time at all you begin to sound like a five-year-old.

Jean Kerr (1923–) US dramatist. *Please Don't Eat the Daisies*

31 At every step the child should be allowed to meet the real experiences of life; the thorns should never be plucked from his roses.

Ellen Key (Karolina Sofia Key; 1849–1926) Swedish writer. *The Century of the Child*, Ch. 3

32 Boys are capital fellows in their own way, among their mates; but they are unwholesome companions for grown people.

Charles Lamb (1775–1834) British essayist. *Essays of Elia*, 'The Old and the New Schoolmaster'

33 A child's a plaything for an hour.

Mary Lamb (1764–1847) Sister of Charles Lamb. *Parental Recollections*

34 Kids haven't changed much, but parents seem increasingly unhappy with the child raising phase of their lives.

Penelope Leach British writer and child-care specialist. Remark, Oct 1988

35 Where are the children I might have had? You may suppose I might have wanted them.
Drowned to the accompaniment of the rattling of a thousand douche bags.

Malcolm Lowry (1909–57) British novelist. *Under the Volcano*, Ch. 10

36 Part of the reason for the ugliness of adults, in a child's eyes, is that the child is usually looking upwards, and few faces are at their best when seen from below.

George Orwell (Eric Blair; 1903–50) British novelist. *Essays*

37 The nice thing about having relatives' kids around is that they go home.

Cliff Richard (1940–) British pop singer. Remark, Nov 1988

38 Parents learn a lot from their children about coping with life.

Muriel Spark (1918–) British novelist. *The Comforters*, Ch. 6

39 There are only two things a child will share willingly – communicable diseases and his mother's age.

Dr Benjamin Spock (1903–) US pediatrician and psychiatrist. Attrib.

40 I have a big house – and I hide a lot.

Mary Ure (1933–75) British actress. Explaining how she coped with her large family of children. Attrib.

41 Never have children, only grandchildren.

Gore Vidal (1925–) US novelist. *Two Sisters*

42 The English are growing demented about children. When I was a boy the classroom had icicles inside every window at this time of year. We were savagely beaten three times a week...

Auberon Waugh (1939–) British novelist. *The Diaries of Auberon Waugh 1976–1985*, 'January 25, 1979'

43 A food is not necessarily essential just because your child hates it.

Katherine Whitehorn (1926–) British journalist. *How to Survive Children*

CHINA

1 Nothing and no one can destroy the Chinese people. They are relentless survivors. They are the oldest civilized people on earth. Their civilization passes through phases but its basic characteristics remain the same. They yield, they bend to the wind, but they never break.

Pearl Buck (1892–1973) US novelist. *China, Past and Present*, Ch. 1

2 Even if they're functioning out of ignorance, they are still participating and must be suppressed. In China, even one million people can be considered a small sum.

Deng Xiaoping (1904–) Chinese communist statesman. Referring to the pro-democracy demonstrators in Tiananmen Square. *The Times*, 5 June 1989

3 My grandmother's feet had been bound when she was two years old. Her mother...first wound a piece of white cloth about twenty feet long round her feet, bending all the toes except the big toe inward and under the sole. Then she placed a large stone on top to crush the arch.

Jung Chang (1952–) Chinese writer and lecturer. *Wild Swans*, Ch. 1

4 In spring 1989...I saw the buildup of demonstrations from Chengdu to Tiananmen Square. It struck me that fear had been forgotten to such an extent that few of the millions of demonstrators perceived danger. Most seemed to be taken by surprise when the army opened fire.

Jung Chang *Wild Swans*, Epilogue

5 Like spring, I treat my comrades warmly.
Like summer, I am full of ardor for my revolutionary work.
I eliminate my individualism as an autumn gale sweeps away fallen leaves
And to the class enemy, I am cruel and ruthless like harsh winter.

Lei Feng (1940–62) Chinese soldier. *The Four Seasons*

6 The Chinese do not draw any distinction between food and medicine.

Lin Yutang (1895–1976) *The Importance of Living*, Ch. 9, Sect. 7

7 If some Western politician claims he is in a position to use the normal Western methods to feed and clothe 1.2 billion Chinese, we would be happily prepared to elect him president of China.

Li Peng (1928–) Chinese prime minister. *The Independent*, 6 July 1994

8 Letting a hundred flowers blossom and a hundred schools of thought contend is the policy for promoting the progress of the arts and the sciences.

Mao Tse-Tung (1893–1976) Chinese communist leader. *Quotations from Chairman Mao Tse-Tung*, Ch. 32

9 Even the Hooligan was probably invented in China centuries before we thought of him.

Saki (Hector Hugh Munro; 1870–1916) British writer. *Reginald on House-Parties*

10 We have won the initial triumph in putting down the riot…a resolute struggle against the extremely small number of people who created the riot.

The Chinese Communist Party Central Committee and State Council Referring to the massacre in Tiananmen Square. *Letter to the People*, June 1989

CHIVALRY

See also courtesy

1 A gentleman is any man who wouldn't hit a woman with his hat on.

Fred Allen (1894–1956) US comedian. Attrib.

2 Even nowadays a man can't step up and kill a woman without feeling just a bit unchivalrous.

Robert Benchley (1889–1945) US humorist. *Chips off the Old Benchley*, 'Down in Front'

3 Somebody has said, that a king may make a nobleman, but he cannot make a gentleman.

Edmund Burke (1729–97) British politician. Letter to William Smith, 29 Jan 1795

4 He was a verray parfit gentil knight.

Geoffrey Chaucer (c. 1342–1400) English poet. Referring to the knight. *The Canterbury Tales*, Prologue

5 Madame, I would have given you another!

Alfred Jarry (1873–1907) French surrealist dramatist. On being reprimanded by a woman for firing his pistol in the vicinity of her child, who might have been killed. *Recollections of a Picture Dealer* (A. Vollard)

6 Some say that the age of chivalry is past, that the spirit of romance is dead. The age of chivalry is never past, so long as there is a wrong left unredressed on earth.

Charles Kingsley (1819–75) British writer. *Life* (Mrs C. Kingsley), Vol. II, Ch. 28

7 For he's one of Nature's Gentlemen, the best of every time.

W. J. Linton (1812–97) British writer. *Nature's Gentleman*

8 It is almost a definition of a gentleman to say that he is one who never inflicts pain.

Cardinal Newman (1801–90) British theologian. *The Idea of a University*, 'Knowledge and Religious Duty'

9 O, young Lochinvar is come out of the west,
Through all the wide Border his steed was the best.

Walter Scott (1771–1832) Scottish novelist. *Marmion*, V

10 So faithful in love, and so dauntless in war,
There never was knight like the young Lochinvar.

Walter Scott *Marmion*, V

11 A bow-shot from her bower-eaves,
He rode between the barley-sheaves,
The sun came dazzling thro' the leaves
And flamed upon the brazen graves
Of bold Sir Lancelot.

Alfred, Lord Tennyson (1809–92) British poet. *The Lady of Shalott*, Pt. III

CHOICE

1 Any colour, so long as it's black.

Henry Ford (1863–1947) US car manufacturer. Referring to the colour options offered for the Model-T Ford car. Attrib.

2 Two roads diverged in a wood, and I –
I took the one less traveled by,
And that has made all the difference.

Robert Frost (1875–1963) US poet. *The Road Not Taken*

3 More ways of killing a cat than choking her with cream.

Charles Kingsley (1819–75) British writer. *Westward Ho!*, Ch. 20

4 We have to believe in free will. We've got no choice.

Isaac Bashevis Singer (1904–91) Polish-born US writer. *The Times*, 21 June 1982

5 The American Standard translation *orders* men to triumph over sin, and you can call sin ignorance. The King James translation makes a promise in 'Thou shalt', meaning that men will surely triumph over sin. But the Hebrew word, the word *timshel* – 'Thou mayest' – that gives a choice. It might be the most important word in the world. That says the way is open.…For if 'Thou mayest' – it is also true that 'Thou mayest not'.

John Steinbeck (1902–68) US novelist Referring to Genesis, 4:7. *East of Eden*, Ch. 24

CHRISTIANITY

See also Catholicism, Protestantism, religion

1 There is a green hill far away,
Without a city wall,
Where the dear Lord was crucified,
Who died to save us all.

C. F. Alexander (1818–95) British hymn writer. *There is a Green Hill Far Away*

2 'Christianity, of course but why journalism?'

Arthur Balfour (1848–1930) British statesman. In reply to Frank Harris's remark, '…all the faults of the age come from Christianity and journalism'. *Autobiography* (Margot Asquith), Ch. 10

3 Onward, Christian soldiers,
Marching as to war,
With the Cross of Jesus
Going on before.

Sabine Baring-Gould (1834–1924) British author and hymn writer. *Onward Christian Soldiers*

4 Beware lest any man spoil you through

philosophy and vain deceit, after the tradition of men, after the rudiments of the world, and not after Christ.

Bible: Colossians 2:8

5 Where there is neither Greek nor Jew, circumcision nor uncircumcision, Barbarian, Scythian, bond nor free; but Christ is all, and in all.

Bible: Colossians 3:11

6 Take heed to yourselves, that your heart be not deceived, and ye turn aside, and serve other gods, and worship them.

Bible: Deuteronomy 11:16

7 There is neither Jew nor Greek, there is neither bond nor free, there is neither male nor female: for ye are all one in Christ Jesus.

Bible: Galatians 3:28

8 But the fruit of the Spirit is love, joy, peace, longsuffering, gentleness, goodness, faith, Meekness, temperance: against such there is no law.

Bible: Galatians 5:22–23

9 Therefore the Lord himself shall give you a sign; Behold, a virgin shall conceive, and bear a son, and shall call his name Immanuel.
Butter and honey shall he eat, that he may know to refuse the evil, and choose the good.

Bible: Isaiah 7:14–15

10 He shall feed his flock like a shepherd: he shall gather the lambs with his arm, and carry them in his bosom, and shall gently lead those that are with young.

Bible: Isaiah 40:11

11 He it is, who coming after me is preferred before me, whose shoe's latchet I am not worthy to unloose.

Bible: John 1:27

12 The next day John seeth Jesus coming unto him, and saith, Behold the Lamb of God, which taketh away the sin of the world.

Bible: John 1:29

13 For God so loved the world, that he gave his only begotten Son, that whosoever believeth in him should not perish, but have everlasting life.

Bible: John 3:16

14 Then spake Jesus again unto them, saying, I am the light of the world: he that followeth me shall not walk in darkness, but shall have the light of life.

Bible: John 8:12

15 I am the good shepherd: the good shepherd giveth his life for the sheep.

Bible: John 10:11

16 Jesus said unto her, I am the resurrection, and the life: he that believeth in me, though he were dead, yet shall he live.

Bible: John 11:25

17 Jesus saith unto him, I am the way, the truth, and the life: no man cometh unto the Father, but by me.

Bible: John 14:6

18 Come unto me, all ye that labour and are heavy laden, and I will give you rest.
Take my yoke upon you, and learn of me; for I am meek and lowly in heart: and ye shall find rest unto your souls.
For my yoke is easy, and my burden is light.

Bible: Matthew 11:28–30

19 Then said Jesus unto his disciples, If any man will come after me, let him deny himself, and take up his cross, and follow me.

Bible: Matthew 16:24

20 How very hard it is
To be a Christian!

Robert Browning (1812–89) British poet. *Easter-Day*, I

21 It was just one of those parties which got out of hand.

Lenny Bruce (1925–66) US comedian. Referring to the Crucifixion. *The Guardian*, 10 May 1979

22 He who begins by loving Christianity better than Truth will proceed by loving his own sect or church better than Christianity, and end by loving himself better than all.

Samuel Taylor Coleridge (1772–1834) British poet. *Aids to Reflection: Moral and Religious Aphorisms*

23 His Christianity was muscular.

Benjamin Disraeli (1804–81) British statesman. *Endymion*, Bk. 1, Ch. 14

24 Christianity has done a great deal for love by making a sin of it.

Anatole France (Jacques Anatole François Thibault; 1844–1924) French writer. *The Garden of Epicurus*

25 What about it? Do you want to crucify the boy?

Lew Grade (Lewis Winogradsky; 1906–) British film and TV producer. Referring to the revelation that an actor portraying Christ on television was living with a woman to whom he was not married. Attrib.

26 Christianity is part of the Common Law of England.

Matthew Hale (1609–76) English judge. *Historia Placitorum Coronae* (ed. Sollom Emlyn)

27 Tell me the old, old story
Of unseen things above,
Of Jesus and His glory
Of Jesus and His love.

Katherine Hankey (1834–1911) British hymn writer. *Tell Me the Old, Old Story*

28 A local cult called Christianity.

Thomas Hardy (1840–1928) British novelist. *The Dynasts*, I:6

29 The Christian religion not only was at first attended with miracles, but even at this day cannot be believed by any reasonable person without one. Mere reason is insufficient to convince us of its veracity: and whoever is moved by faith to assent to it, is conscious of a continued miracle in his own person, which subverts all the principles of his understanding, and gives him a determination to believe what is most contrary to custom and experience.

David Hume (1711–76) Scottish philosopher. *Essays*, 'Of Miracles' without one all the principles of his understanding

30 Christianity accepted as given a metaphysical system derived from several already existing and mutually incompatible systems.

Aldous Huxley (1894–1964) British novelist. *Grey Eminence*, Ch. 3

31 There must be several young women who would render the Christian life intensely difficult to him if only you could persuade him to marry one of them.

C. S. Lewis (1898–1963) British academic and writer. *The Screwtape Letters*

32 Ride on! ride on in majesty!
In lowly pomp ride on to die.

Henry Hart Milman (1791–1868) British poet and historian. *Ride On*

33 Fight the good fight with all thy might,
Christ is thy strength and Christ thy right,
Lay hold on life, and it shall be
Thy joy and crown eternally.

John Monsell (1811–75) British hymn writer. Hymn

34 No kingdom has ever had as many civil wars as the kingdom of Christ.

Baron de Montesquieu (1689–1755) French writer. *Lettres persanes*

35 I call Christianity the one great curse, the one enormous and innermost perversion, the one great instinct of revenge, for which no means are too venomous, too underhand, too underground and too petty – I call it the one immortal blemish of mankind.

Friedrich Wilhelm Nietzsche (1844–1900) German philosopher. *The Antichrist*

36 Christianity has made of death a terror which was unknown to the gay calmness of the Pagan.

Ouida (Marie Louise de la Ramée; 1839–1908) British novelist. *The Failure of Christianity*

37 All hail, the power of Jesus' name!
Let angels prostrate fall.

Edward Perronet (1726–92) British hymn writer. Hymn

38 Whether you think Jesus was God or not, you must admit that he was a first-rate political economist.

George Bernard Shaw (1856–1950) Irish dramatist and critic. *Androcles and the Lion*, Preface, 'Jesus as Economist'

39 Who dreamed that Christ has died in vain?
He walks again on the Seas of Blood,
He comes in the terrible Rain.

Edith Sitwell (1887–1964) British poet and writer. *The Shadow of Cain*

40 The Church's one foundation
Is Jesus Christ her Lord;
She is His new creation
By water and the Word.

Samuel. J. Stone (1839–1901) US hymn writer. Hymn

41 Well, you might try getting crucified and rising again on the third day.

Talleyrand (Charles Maurice de Talleyrand-Périgord; 1754–1838) French politician. Giving his opinion upon what action might impress the French peasantry. Attrib.

42 Christianity is the most materialistic of all great religions.

William Temple (1881–1944) British churchman. *Reading in St John's Gospel*, Vol. I, Introduction

43 And so the Word had breath, and wrought
With human hands the creed of creeds
In loveliness of perfect deeds,
More strong than all poetic thought.

Alfred, Lord Tennyson (1809–92) British poet. *In Memoriam A.H.H.*, XXXVI

44 The blood of the martyrs is the seed of the Church.

Tertullian (c. 160–225 AD) Carthaginian father of the church. Traditional misquotation: more accurately, 'Our numbers increase as often as you cut us down: the blood of Christians is the seed.'. *Apologeticus*, L

45 See how these Christians love one another.

Tertullian *Apologeticus*, XXXIX

46 Fraser…left his children unbaptized – his wife did it secretly in the washing basin.

Virginia Woolf (1882–1941) British novelist. *Jacob's Room*, Ch. 9

CHRISTMAS

See also Christianity

1 I have often thought, says Sir Roger, it happens very well that Christmas should fall out in the Middle of Winter.

Joseph Addison (1672–1719) British essayist. *The Spectator*, 269

2 Once in royal David's city
Stood a lowly cattle shed,
Where a Mother laid her Baby
In a manger for His bed:
Mary was that Mother mild,
Jesus Christ her little Child.

C. F. Alexander (1818–95) British hymn writer. *Once in Royal David's City*

3 As I sat on a sunny bank,
On Christmas Day in the morning,
I spied three ships come sailing by.

Anonymous *As I sat on a Sunny Bank*

4 God rest you merry, gentlemen,
Let nothing you dismay.

Anonymous *God Rest you Merry*

5 The holly and the ivy,
When they are both full grown,
Of all the trees that are in the wood,
The holly bears the crown.
The rising of the sun

And the running of the deer,
The playing of the merry organ,
Sweet singing in the choir.

Anonymous *The Holly and the Ivy*

6 For unto us a child is born, unto us a son is given: and the government shall be upon his shoulder: and his name shall be called Wonderful, Counsellor, The mighty God, The everlasting Father, The Prince of Peace.
Of the increase of his government and peace there shall be no end, upon the throne of David, and upon his kingdom, to order it, and to establish it with judgment and with justice from henceforth even for ever. The zeal of the Lord of hosts will perform this.

Bible: Isaiah 9:6–7

7 And she brought forth her firstborn son, and wrapped him in swaddling clothes, and laid him in a manger; because there was no room for them in the inn.

Bible: Luke 2:7

8 And there were in the same country shepherds abiding in the field, keeping watch over their flock by night.
And, lo, the angel of the Lord came upon them, and the glory of the Lord shone round about them: and they were sore afraid.
And the angel said unto them, Fear not: for, behold, I bring you good tidings of great joy, which shall be to all people.

Bible: Luke 2:8–10

9 Now when Jesus was born in Bethlehem of Judaea in the days of Herod the king, behold, there came wise men from the east to Jerusalem, Saying, Where is he that is born King of the Jews? for we have seen his star in the east, and are come to worship him.
When Herod the king had heard these things, he was troubled, and all Jerusalem with him.

Bible: Matthew 2:1–3

10 And when they were come into the house, they saw the young child with Mary his mother, and fell down, and worshipped him: and when they had opened their treasures, they presented unto him gifts; gold, and frankincense, and myrrh.
And being warned of God in a dream that they should not return to Herod, they departed into their own country another way.

Bible: Matthew 2:11–12

11 O little town of Bethlehem,
How still we see thee lie;
Above thy deep and dreamless sleep
The silent stars go by.

Phillips Brooks (1835–93) US Episcopal bishop. *O Little Town of Bethlehem*

12 Christians awake, salute the happy morn,
Whereon the Saviour of the world was born.

John Byrom (1692–1763) British poet and hymn writer. *Hymn for Christmas Day*

13 Fortified in their front parlours, at Yuletide men
are the more murderous. Drunk, they defy battle-
axes, bellow of whale-bone and dung.

Geoffrey Hill (1932–) British poet. Mercian Hymns, XXVI, 'Offa's Bestiary'

14 'Twas the night before Christmas, when all through the house
Not a creature was stirring, not even a mouse;
The stockings were hung by the chimney with care,
In hopes that St Nicholas soon would be there.

Clement Clarke Moore (1779–1863) US writer. In *Troy Sentinel*, 23 Dec 1823, 'A Visit from St. Nicholas'

15 Good King Wenceslas looked out,
On the Feast of Stephen;
When the snow lay round about,
Deep and crisp and even.

John Mason Neale (1818–66) British churchman. *Good King Wenceslas*

16 O come all ye faithful,
Joyful and triumphant,
O come ye, O come ye to Bethlehem.

Frederick Oakeley (1802–80) British churchman. Translated from the Latin hymn, *Adeste Fideles. O Come All Ye Faithful*

17 It came upon the midnight clear,
That glorious song of old,
From Angels bending near the earth
To touch their harps of gold;
'Peace on the earth; good will to man
From Heaven's all gracious King.'
The world in solemn stillness lay
To hear the angels sing.

E. H. Sears (1810–76) US clergyman. *That Glorious Song of Old*

18 While shepherds watch'd their flocks by night,
All seated on the ground,
The Angel of the Lord came down,
And Glory shone around.

Nahum Tate (1652–1715) Irish-born English poet. *Supplement to the New Version of the Psalms*, 'While Shepherds Watched'

19 At Christmas play and make good cheer,
For Christmas comes but once a year.

Thomas Tusser (1524–80) English farmer. *Five Hundred Points of Good Husbandry*, 'The Farmer's Daily Diet'

20 To perceive Christmas through its wrapping becomes more difficult with every year.

Elwyn Brooks White (1899–1985) US journalist and humorist. *The Second Tree from the Corner*

CHURCH

See also clergy, religion

1 And I say also unto thee, That thou art Peter, and upon this rock I will build my church; and the gates of hell shall not prevail against it.
And I will give unto thee the keys of the kingdom of heaven: and whatsoever thou shalt bind on

earth shall be bound in heaven: and whatsoever thou shalt loose on earth shall be loosed in heaven.

Bible: Matthew 16:18–19

2 For where two or three are gathered together in my name, there am I in the midst of them.

Bible: Matthew 18:20

3 The Vatican is an oppressive regime which, like a bat, fears the light.

Leonardo Boff (1938–) Brazilian theologian. Said on leaving the Roman Catholic Church. *The Observer*, 5 July 1992

4 I see it as an elderly lady, who mutters away to herself in a corner, ignored most of the time.

George Carey (1935–) British churchman; Archbishop of Canterbury. Referring to the Church of England. *Reader's Digest*, Mar 1991

5 And of all plagues with which mankind are curst,
Ecclesiastic tyranny's the worst.

Daniel Defoe (1660–1731) British journalist and writer. *The True-Born Englishman*, Pt. II

6 How is it that the Church produced no geometers in her autocratic reign of twelve hundred years?

John Draper (1811–1882) British-born US chemist. *The Conflict Between Science and Religion*

7 It is hard to tell where MCC ends and the Church of England begins.

J. B. Priestley (1894–1984) British novelist. *New Statesman*, 20 July 1962, 'Topside Schools'

8 The Church exists for the sake of those outside it.

William Temple (1881–1944) British churchman. Attrib.

CHURCHILL

See also politicians, World War II

1 It hasn't taken Winston long to get used to American ways. He hadn't been an American citizen for three minutes before attacking an ex-secretary of state!

Dean Acheson (1893–1971) US lawyer and statesman. At a ceremony in 1963 to make Churchill an honorary American citizen, Churchill obliquely attacked Acheson's reference to Britain losing an empire. *Randolph Churchill* (K. Halle)

2 Then comes Winston with his hundred-horse-power mind and what can I do?

Stanley Baldwin (1867–1947) British statesman. *Stanley Baldwin* (G. M. Young), Ch. 11

3 I thought he was a young man of promise; but it appears he was a young man of promises.

Arthur Balfour (1848–1930) British statesman. Said of Winston Churchill on his entry into politics, 1899. *Winston Churchill* (Randolph Churchill), Vol. I

4 He is a man suffering from petrified adolescence.

Aneurin Bevan (1897–1960) British Labour politician. *Aneurin Bevan* (Vincent Brome), Ch. 11

5 The nation had the lion's heart. I had the luck to give the roar.

Winston Churchill (1874–1965) British statesman. Said on his 80th birthday

6 The first time you meet Winston you see all his faults and the rest of your life you spend in discovering his virtues.

Lady Constance Lytton (1869–1923) British suffragette. *Edward Marsh* (Christopher Hassall), Ch. 7

7 Winston has devoted the best years of his life to preparing his impromptu speeches.

F. E. Smith (1872–1930) British lawyer and politician. Attrib.

8 Simply a radio personality who outlived his prime.

Evelyn Waugh (1903–66) British novelist. *Evelyn Waugh* (Christopher Sykes)

CINEMA

See also Goldwynisms

1 If my books had been any worse I should not have been invited to Hollywood, and if they had been any better I should not have come.

Raymond Chandler (1888–1959) US novelist. *The Life of Raymond Chandler* (F. MacShane)

2 There's a big trend in Hollywood of taking very good European films and turning them into very bad American films. I've been offered a few of those, but it's really a perverse activity. I'd rather go on the dole.

Roddy Doyle (1958–) Irish novelist and playwright. *The Independent*, 25 Apr 1994

3 I was born at the age of twelve on a Metro-Goldwyn-Mayer lot.

Judy Garland (Frances Gumm; 1922–69) US film star. *The Observer*, 'Sayings of the Week', 18 Feb 1951

4 I like a film to have a beginning, a middle and an end, but not necessarily in that order.

Jean-Luc Godard (1930–) French film director. Attrib.

5 Photography is truth. And cinema is truth twenty-four times a second.

Jean-Luc Godard *Le Petit Soldat*

6 Why should people go out and pay money to see bad films when they can stay at home and see bad television for nothing?

Samuel Goldwyn (Samuel Goldfish; 1882–1974) Polish-born US film producer. *The Observer*, 'Sayings of the Week', 9 Sept 1956

7 A wide screen just makes a bad film twice as bad.

Samuel Goldwyn Attrib.

8 The very meaninglessness of life forces man to create his own meaning. If it can be written or thought, it can be filmed.

Stanley Kubrick (1928–) US film director. *Halliwell's Filmgoer's and Video Viewer's Companion*

9 In Hollywood, if you don't have happiness you send out for it.

Rex Reed (1938–) US columnist and actor. *Colombo's Hollywood*, 'Hollywood the Bad' (J. R. Colombo)

10 They only got two things right, the camels and the sand.

Lowell Thomas (1892–1981) US author and broadcaster. Referring to the film *Lawrence of Arabia*. Obituary, *The Times*, 29 Aug 1981

11 Take that black box away. I can't act in front of it.

Herbert Beerbohm Tree (1853–1917) British actor and theatre manager. Objecting to the presence of the camera while performing in a silent film. *Hollywood: The Pioneers* (K. Brownlow)

12 Thanks to the movies, gunfire has always sounded unreal to me, even when being fired at.

Peter Ustinov (1921–) British actor. *Dear Me*, Ch. 7

13 Westerns are closer to art than anything else in the motion picture business.

John Wayne (Marion Michael Morrison; 1907–79) US film actor. *Halliwell's Filmgoer's and Video Viewer's Companion*

14 Me? Tarzan?

Johnny Weissmuller (1904–84) US swimmer and film actor. Reacting to an invitation to play Tarzan. Attrib.

15 When you get the personality, you don't need the nudity.

Mae West (1892–1980) US actress. *The Observer*, 'Sayings of the Week', 4 Aug 1968

CIVILIZATION

See also culture

1 Civilization is a method of living, an attitude of equal respect for all men.

Jane Addams (1860–1935) US social worker. Speech, Honolulu, 1933

2 I wish I could bring Stonehenge to Nyasaland to show there was a time when Britain had a savage culture.

Hastings Banda (1906–) Malawi statesman. *The Observer*, 'Sayings of the Week', 10 Mar 1963

3 The three great elements of modern civilization, Gunpowder, Printing, and the Protestant Religion.

Thomas Carlyle (1795–1881) Scottish historian and essayist. *Critical and Miscellaneous Essays*, 'The State of German Literature'

4 The modern world...has no notion except that of simplifying something by destroying nearly everything.

G. K. Chesterton (1874–1936) British writer. *All I Survey*

5 In essence the Renaissance was simply the green end of one of civilization's hardest winters.

John Fowles (1926–) British novelist. *The French Lieutenant's Woman*, Ch. 10

6 I think it would be a good idea.

Mahatma Gandhi (Mohandas Karamchand Gandhi; 1869–1948) Indian national leader. On being asked for his view on Western civilization. Attrib.

7 There is precious little in civilization to appeal to a Yeti.

Edmund Hillary (1919–) New Zealand mountaineer. *The Observer*, 'Sayings of the Week', 3 June 1960

8 As civilization advances, poetry almost necessarily declines.

Lord Macaulay (1800–59) British historian. *Literary Essays Contributed to the 'Edinburgh Review'*, 'Milton'

9 The degree of a nation's civilization is marked by its disregard for the necessities of existence.

W. Somerset Maugham (1874–1965) British novelist. *Our Betters*, I

CLARITY

See also communication, confusion

1 Oh! rather give me commentators plain,
Who with no deep researches vex the brain;
Who from the dark and doubtful love to run,
And hold their glimmering tapers to the sun.

George Crabbe (1754–1832) British poet. *The Parish Register*, 'Baptisms'

2 It's odd how people waiting for you stand out far less clearly than people you are waiting for.

Jean Giraudoux (1882–1944) French dramatist. *Tiger at the Gates*, I

3 When man's whole frame is obvious to a flea.

Alexander Pope (1688–1744) British poet. *The Dunciad*, IV

CLASS

See also aristocracy, equality, public, snobbery

1 There's one law for the rich, and another for the poor.

Proverb

2 You can measure the social caste of a person by the distance between the husband's and wife's apartments.

Alfonso XIII (1886–1941) Spanish monarch. Attrib.

3 I often, therefore, when I want to distinguish clearly the aristocratic class from the Philistines proper, or middle class, name the former, in my own mind *the Barbarians*.

Matthew Arnold (1822–88) British poet and critic. *Culture and Anarchy*, Ch. 3

4 When Adam delved and Eve span,
Who was then the gentleman?

John Ball (d. 1381) English priest. Text of sermon

5 Yet it is better to drop thy friends, O my daughter, than to drop thy 'H's'.

C. S. Calverley (1831–84) British poet. *Proverbial Philosophy*, 'Of Friendship'

6 One of those refined people who go out to sew for the rich because they cannot bear contact with the poor.

Colette (1873–1954) French novelist. *The Other One*

7 Servants should not be ill. We have quite enough illnesses of our own without them adding to the symptoms.

Lady Diana Cooper (1892–1986) British actress and writer. *Diana Cooper* (Philip Ziegler)

8 He bade me observe it, and I should always find, that the calamities of life were shared among the upper and lower part of mankind; but that the middle station had the fewest disasters.

Daniel Defoe (1660–1731) British journalist and writer. *Robinson Crusoe*, Pt. I

9 O let us love our occupations,
Bless the squire and his relations,
Live upon our daily rations,
And always know our proper stations.

Charles Dickens (1812–70) British novelist. *The Chimes*, '2nd Quarter'

10 He differed from the healthy type that was essentially middle-class – he never seemed to perspire.

F. Scott Fitzgerald (1896–1940) US novelist. *This Side of Paradise*, Bk. I, Ch. 2

11 All shall equal be.
The Earl, the Marquis, and the Dook,
The Groom, the Butler, and the Cook,
The Aristocrat who banks with Coutts,
The Aristocrat who cleans the boots.

W. S. Gilbert (1836–1911) British dramatist. *The Gondoliers*, I

12 He combines the manners of a Marquis with the morals of a Methodist.

W. S. Gilbert *Ruddigore*, I

13 Bow, bow, ye lower middle classes!
Bow, bow, ye tradesmen, bow, ye masses!

W. S. Gilbert *Iolanthe*, I

14 All the world over, I will back the masses against the classes.

William Ewart Gladstone (1809–98) British statesman. Speech, Liverpool, 28 June 1886

15 Dialect words – those terrible marks of the beast to the truly genteel.

Thomas Hardy (1840–1928) British novelist. *The Mayor of Casterbridge*, Ch. 20

16 '*Bourgeois*,' I observed, 'is an epithet which the riff-raff apply to what is respectable, and the aristocracy to what is decent'.

Anthony Hope (Sir Anthony Hope Hawkins; 1863–1933) British novelist. *The Dolly Dialogues*

17 You may be the most liberal Liberal Englishman, and yet you cannot fail to see the categorical difference between the responsible and the irresponsible classes.

D. H. Lawrence (1885–1930) British novelist. *Kangaroo*, Ch. 1

18 A Social-Democrat must never forget that the proletariat will inevitably have to wage a class struggle for Socialism even against the most democratic and republican bourgeoisie and petty bourgeoisie.

Lenin (Vladimir Ilich Ulyanov; 1870–1924) Russian revolutionary leader. *The State and Revolution*, Ch. 10

19 An Englishman's way of speaking absolutely classifies him
The moment he talks he makes some other Englishman despise him.

Alan Jay Lerner (1918–86) US songwriter. *My Fair Lady*, I:1

20 I'm not interested in classes...Far be it from me to foster inferiority complexes among the workers by trying to make them think they belong to some special class. That has happened in Europe but it hasn't happened here yet.

John Llewellyn Lewis (1880–1969) US labour leader. *The Coming of the New Deal* (A. M. Schlesinger, Jnr), Pt. 7, Ch. 25

21 Said Marx: 'Don't be snobbish, we seek to abolish
The 3rd Class, not the 1st.'

Christopher Logue (1926–) British poet and dramatist. *Christopher Logue's ABC*, 'M'

22 The history of all hitherto existing society is the history of class struggles.

Karl Marx (1818–83) German philosopher and revolutionary. *The Communist Manifesto*, 1

23 The one class you do *not* belong to and are not proud of at all is the lower-middle class. No one ever describes himself as belonging to the lower-middle class.

George Mikes (1912–87) Hungarian-born British writer. *How to be Inimitable*

24 Only on the third class tourist class passengers' deck was it a sultry overcast morning, but then if you do things on the cheap you must expect these things.

Spike Milligan (1918–) British comic actor and author. *A Dustbin of Milligan*

25 We have nothing to lose but our aitches.

George Orwell (Eric Blair; 1903–50) British novelist. Referring to the middle classes. *The Road to Wigan Pier*, Ch. 13

26 I don't think one 'comes down' from Jimmy's university. According to him, it's not even red brick, but white tile.

John Osborne (1929–94) British dramatist. *Look Back in Anger*, II:1

27 You can be in the Horse Guards and still be common, dear.

Terence Rattigan (1911–77) British dramatist. *Separate Tables*: 'Table Number Seven'

28 U and Non-U, An Essay in Sociological Linguistics.

Alan Strode Campbell Ross (1907–78) British professor of linguistics. Essay title, *Noblesse Oblige*, 1956

29 There are two classes in good society in England. The equestrian classes and the neurotic classes.

George Bernard Shaw (1856–1950) Irish dramatist and critic. *Heartbreak House*

30 I am a gentleman. I live by robbing the poor.

George Bernard Shaw *Man and Superman*

31 I have to live for others and not for myself; that's middle class morality.

George Bernard Shaw *Pygmalion*

32 It is impossible for one class to appreciate the wrongs of another.

Elizabeth Cady Stanton (1815–1902) US suffragette. *History of Woman Suffrage* (with Susan B. Anthony and Mathilda Gage), Vol. I

33 The charm of Britain has always been the ease with which one can move into the middle class.

Margaret Thatcher (1925–) British politician and prime minister. *The Observer*, 'Sayings of the Week', 27 Oct 1974

34 The ship follows Soviet custom: it is riddled with class distinctions so subtle, it takes a trained Marxist to appreciate them.

Paul Theroux (1941–) US-born writer. *The Great Railway Bazaar*, Ch. 30

35 For generations the British bourgeoisie have spoken of themselves as gentlemen, and by that they have meant, among other things, a self-respecting scorn of irregular perquisites. It is the quality that distinguishes the gentleman from both the artist and the aristocrat.

Evelyn Waugh (1903–66) British novelist. *Decline and Fall*, Pt. I, Ch. 6

36 No writer before the middle of the 19th century wrote about the working classes other than as grotesque or as pastoral decoration. Then when they were given the vote certain writers started to suck up to them.

Evelyn Waugh Interview. *Paris Review*, 1963

37 Bricklayers kick their wives to death, and dukes betray theirs; but it is among the small clerks and shopkeepers nowadays that it comes most often to the cutting of throats.

H. G. Wells (1866–1946) British writer. *Short Stories*, 'The Purple Pileus'

38 Margaret Thatcher's great strength seems to be the better people know her, the better they like her. But, of course, she has one great disadvantage – she is a daughter of the people and looks trim, as the daughters of the people desire to be. Shirley Williams has such an advantage over her because she's a member of the upper-middle class and can achieve that kitchen-sink-revolutionary look that one cannot get unless one has been to a really good school.

Rebecca West (Cicely Isabel Fairfield; 1892–1983) British novelist and journalist. Said in an interview with Jilly Cooper. *The Sunday Times*, 25 July 1976

39 Really, if the lower orders don't set us a good example, what on earth is the use of them?

Oscar Wilde (1854–1900) Irish-born British dramatist. *The Importance of Being Earnest*, I

40 The constitution does not provide for first and second class citizens.

Wendell Lewis Willkie (1892–1944) US lawyer and businessman. *An American Programme*, Ch. 2

CLASSICS

1 They were a tense and peculiar family, the Oedipuses, weren't they?

Max Beerbohm (1872–1956) British writer. *Max: A Biography* (D. Cecil)

2 So they told me how Mr Gladstone read Homer for fun, which I thought served him right.

Winston Churchill (1874–1965) British statesman. *My Early Life*, Ch. 2

3 Nor can I do better, in conclusion, than impress upon you the study of Greek literature which not only elevates above the vulgar herd, but leads not infrequently to positions of considerable emolument.

Thomas Gaisford (1799–1855) British classicist. Christmas Day Sermon at Oxford. *Reminiscences of Oxford* (Revd W. Tuckwell)

4 To the Greeks the Muse gave native wit, to the Greeks the gift of graceful eloquence.

Horace (Quintus Horatius Flaccus; 65–8 BC) Roman poet. *Ars Poetica*

5 Thou hadst small Latin, and less Greek.

Ben Jonson (1573–1637) English dramatist. *To the Memory of William Shakespeare*

6 The classics are only primitive literature. They belong in the same class as primitive machinery and primitive music and primitive medicine.

Stephen Leacock (1869–1944) English-born Canadian economist and humorist. *Homer and Humbug*

7 Every man with a belly full of the classics is an enemy of the human race.

Henry Miller (1891–1980) US novelist. *Tropic of Cancer*, 'Dijon'

8 Nobody can say a word against Greek: it stamps a man at once as an educated gentleman.

George Bernard Shaw (1856–1950) Irish dramatist and critic. *Major Barbara*, I

9 We were taught as the chief subjects of instruction Latin and Greek. We were taught very badly because the men who taught us did not habitually use either of these languages.

H. G. Wells (1866–1946) British writer. *The New Machiavelli*, Bk. I., Ch. 3

CLASSIFICATION

See also generalizations

1 One of the unpardonable sins, in the eyes of most people, is for a man to go about unlabelled. The world regards such a person as the police do an unmuzzled dog, not under proper control.

T. H. Huxley (1825–95) British biologist. *Evolution and Ethics*

2 The young Cambridge group, the group that stood for 'freedom' and flannel trousers and flannel shirts open at the neck, and a well-bred sort of emotional anarchy, and a whispering, murmuring sort of voice, and an ultra-sensitive sort of manner.

D. H. Lawrence (1885–1930) British novelist. *Lady Chatterley's Lover*, Ch. 1

3 Decades have a delusive edge to them. They are not, of course, really periods at all, except as any other ten years would be. But we, looking at them, are caught by the different name each bears, and give them different attributes, and tie labels on them, as if they were flowers in a border.

Rose Macaulay (1889–1958) British writer. *Told by an Idiot*, Pt. II, Ch. 1

CLEANNESS

1 Bath twice a day to be really clean, once a day to be passably clean, once a week to avoid being a public menace.

Anthony Burgess (John Burgess Wilson; 1917–93) British novelist. *Mr Enderby*, Pt. I, Ch. 2

2 MR PRITCHARD. I must dust the blinds and then I must raise them.
MRS OGMORE-PRITCHARD. And before you let the sun in, mind it wipes its shoes.

Dylan Thomas (1914–53) Welsh poet. *Under Milk Wood*

3 Have you ever taken anything out of the clothes basket because it had become, relatively, the cleaner thing?

Katherine Whitehorn (1926–) British journalist. *The Observer*, 'On Shirts', 1964

CLERGY

See also Church, religion

1 I always like to associate with a lot of priests because it makes me understand anti-clerical things so well.

Hilaire Belloc (1870–1953) French-born British poet. Letter to E. S. P. Haynes, 9 Nov 1909

2 This is a true saying, If a man desire the office of a bishop, he desireth a good work.
A bishop then must be blameless, the husband of one wife, vigilant, sober, of good behaviour, given to hospitality, apt to teach;
Not given to wine, no striker, not greedy of filthy lucre; but patient, not a brawler, not covetous.

Bible: I Timothy 3:1–3

3 As for the British churchman, he goes to church as he goes to the bathroom, with the minimum of fuss and no explanation if he can help it.

Ronald Blythe (1922–) British author. *The Age of Illusion*

4 The idea that only a male can represent Christ at the altar is a most serious heresy.

George Carey (1935–) British churchman; Archbishop of Canterbury. *Reader's Digest*, Apr 1991

5 Make him a bishop, and you will silence him at once.

Earl of Chesterfield (1694–1773) English statesman. When asked what steps might be taken to control the evangelical preacher George Whitefield. Attrib.

6 It is no accident that the symbol of a bishop is a crook, and the sign of an archbishop is a double-cross.

Dom Gregory Dix (1901–52) British monk. Letter to *The Times*, 3 Dec 1977 (Francis Bown)

7 For clergy are men as well as other folks.

Henry Fielding (1707–54) British novelist. *Joseph Andrews*, Bk II, Ch. 6

8 That whisky priest, I wish we had never had him in the house.

Graham Greene (1904–91) British novelist. *The Power and the Glory*, Pt. I

9 In old time we had treen chalices and golden priests, but now we have treen priests and golden chalices.

John Jewel (1522–71) English bishop. *Certain Sermons Preached Before the Queen's Majesty*

10 A man who is good enough to go to heaven, is good enough to be a clergyman.

Samuel Johnson (1709–84) British lexicographer. *Life of Johnson* (J. Boswell), Vol. II

11 I would burn the bloody bitches.

Anthony Kennedy British churchman; vicar of Lutton with Gedney. Referring to women priests. *The Times*

12 Damn it all, another Bishop dead, – I verily believe they die to vex me.

Lord Melbourne (1779–1848) British statesman. Attrib.

13 How can a bishop marry? How can he flirt? The most he can say is, 'I will see you in the vestry after service.'

Sydney Smith (1771–1845) British clergyman and essayist. *Memoir* (Lady Holland)

14 I never saw, heard, nor read, that the clergy were beloved in any nation where Christianity was the religion of the country. Nothing can render them popular, but some degree of persecution.

Jonathan Swift (1667–1745) Irish-born Anglican priest and writer. *Thoughts on Religion*

15 There is a certain class of clergyman whose mendicity is only equalled by their mendacity.

Frederick Temple (1821–1902) British churchman. Remark at a meeting of the Ecclesiastical Commissioners. *Years of Endeavour* (Sir George Leveson Gower)

16 But the churchmen fain would kill their church,
As the churches have kill'd their Christ.

Alfred, Lord Tennyson (1809–92) British poet. *Maud*, V

17 If I were a cassowary

On the plains of Timbuctoo,
I would eat a missionary,
Cassock, band, and hymn-book too.

Samuel Wilberforce (1805–73) British churchman. Also attrib. to W. M. Thackeray. Attrib.

CLOCKS

1 My poor fellow, why not carry a watch?

Herbert Beerbohm Tree (1853–1917) British actor and theatre manager. Remark made to a man carrying a grandfather clock. *Beerbohm Tree* (Hesketh Pearson)

2 My grandfather's clock was too large for the shelf.
So it stood ninety years on the floor.

Henry Clay Work (1832–84) US songwriter. *Grandfather's Clock*

3 But it stopped short – never to go again –
When the old man died.

Henry Clay Work *Grandfather's Clock*

CLOTHES

See also appearance, beauty, fashion, nakedness

1 It is not only fine feathers that make fine birds.

Aesop (6th century BC) Reputed Greek writer of fables. *Fables*, 'The Jay and the Peacock'

2 She just wore
Enough for modesty – no more.

Robert Williams Buchanan (1841–1901) British poet and writer. *White Rose and Red*, I

3 I go to a better tailor than any of you and pay more for my clothes. The only difference is that you probably don't sleep in yours.

Clarence Seward Darrow (1857–1938) US lawyer. Reply when teased by reporters about his appearance. *2500 Anecdotes* (E. Fuller)

4 'Good heavens!' said he, 'if it be our clothes alone which fit us for society, how highly we should esteem those who make them.'

Marie Ebner von Eschenbach (1830–1916) Austrian writer. *The Two Countesses*

5 The sense of being well-dressed gives a feeling of inward tranquillity which religion is powerless to bestow.

C. F. Forbes (1817–1911) British writer. *Social Aims* (Emerson)

6 Those who make their dress a principal part of themselves, will, in general, become of no more value than their dress.

William Hazlitt (1778–1830) British essayist. *On the Clerical Character*

7 A sweet disorder in the dress
Kindles in clothes a wantonness.

Robert Herrick (1591–1674) English poet. *Hesperides*, 'Delight in Disorder'

8 Whenas in silks my Julia goes
Then, then (methinks) how sweetly flows
That liquefaction of her clothes.

Robert Herrick *Hesperides*, 'Upon Julia's Clothes'

9 Fine clothes are good only as they supply the want of other means of procuring respect.

Samuel Johnson (1709–84) British lexicographer. *Life of Johnson* (J. Boswell), Vol. II

10 The uniform 'e wore
Was nothin' much before,
An' rather less than 'arf o' that be'ind.

Rudyard Kipling (1865–1936) Indian-born British writer. *Gunga Din*

11 How do you look when I'm sober?

Ring Lardner Jnr (1885–1933) American humorist. Speaking to a flamboyantly dressed stranger who walked into the club where he was drinking. *Ring* (J. Yardley)

12 Brevity is the soul of lingerie.

Dorothy Parker (1893–1967) US writer. *While Rome Burns* (Alexander Woollcott)

13 Where did you get that hat?
Where did you get that tile?

James Rolmaz (19th century) British songwriter. *Where Did You Get That Hat?*

14 Not a gentleman; dresses too well.

Bertrand Russell (1872–1970) British philosopher. Referring to Anthony Eden. *Six Men* (A. Cooke)

15 His socks compelled one's attention without losing one's respect.

Saki (Hector Hugh Munro; 1870–1916) British writer. *Ministers of Grace*

16 Costly thy habit as thy purse can buy,
But not express'd in fancy; rich, not gaudy;
For the apparel oft proclaims the man.

William Shakespeare (1564–1616) English dramatist. *Hamlet*, I:3

17 The only man who really needs a tail coat is a man with a hole in his trousers.

John Taylor (20th century) The editor of the *Tailor and Cutter*. *The Observer*, 'Shouts and Murmurs'

18 You can say what you like about long dresses, but they cover a multitude of shins.

Mae West (1892–1980) US actress. *Peel Me a Grape* (J. Weintraub)

19 Hats divide generally into three classes: offensive hats, defensive hats, and shrapnel.

Katherine Whitehorn (1926–) British journalist. *Shouts and Murmurs*, 'Hats'

20 Then the little man wears a shocking bad hat.

Duke of York and Albany (1763–1827) The second son of George III. Referring to Horace Walpole. Attrib.

COLD WAR

1 We all know the Iron Curtain has been demolished, but in its place an economic and social curtain might come down.

József Antall (1932–93) Hungarian statesman *The Independent*, 29 Oct 1992

2 Let us not be deceived – we are today in the midst of a cold war.

Bernard Baruch (1870–1965) US financier and presidential adviser. Speech, South Carolina Legislature, 16 Apr 1947

3 An iron curtain has descended across the Continent.

Winston Churchill (1874–1965) British statesman. The phrase 'iron curtain' was originally coined by Joseph Goebbels. Address, Westminster College, Fulton, USA, 5 Mar 1946

4 We must not let the iron curtain be replaced with a veil of indifference.

Bill Clinton (William Jefferson C.; 1946–) US politician and president. Speech to NATO, 10 Jan 1994

5 Now we are in a period which I can characterize as a period of cold peace.

Trygve Lie (1896–1968) Norwegian lawyer. *The Observer*, 'Sayings of the Week', 21 Aug 1949

6 Europe has not yet freed itself from the heritage of the Cold War and is in danger of plunging into a Cold Peace.

Boris Yeltsin (1931–) Russian statesman. *The Independent*, 6 Dec 1994

COMFORT

See also endurance, sympathy

1 The crash of the whole solar and stellar systems could only kill you once.

Thomas Carlyle (1795–1881) Scottish historian and essayist. Letter to John Carlyle, 1831

2 For this relief much thanks. 'Tis bitter cold,
And I am sick at heart.

William Shakespeare (1564–1616) English dramatist. *Hamlet*, I:1

3 I beg cold comfort.

William Shakespeare *King John*, V:7

4 Like a bridge over troubled water,
I will ease your mind.

Paul Simon (1942–) US singer. *Bridge Over Troubled Water*

COMMERCIALISM

See also business, economics, money

1 My fear will be that in 15 years time Jerusalem, Bethlehem, once centres of strong Christian presence, might become a kind of Walt Disney Theme Park.

George Carey (1935–) British churchman; Archbishop of Canterbury. *The Observer*, 12 Jan 1992

2 My greatest fear for a vision of the theatre in the year 2000 would be a sort of elongated panto season, followed by two or three shows featuring stars of sitcoms in the classics of their choice.

Richard Eyre (1943–) British artistic director of the Royal National Theatre. *The Observer*, 'Sayings of the Week', 26 Feb 1994

3 Our democratic capitalist society has converted Eros into an employee of Mammon.

Octavio Paz (1914–) Mexican poet, critic, and diplomat. *The Observer*, 'Sayings of the Week', 19 June 1994

4 The large print giveth, but the small print taketh away.

Tom Waits (1949–) US rock musician. *Small Change*

COMMITMENT

1 In for a penny, in for a pound.

Proverb

2 Never do things by halves.

Proverb

3 One cannot be a part-time nihilist.

Albert Camus (1913–60) French existentialist writer. *The Rebel*

4 Catholics and Communists have committed great crimes, but at least they have not stood aside, like an established society, and been indifferent. I would rather have blood on my hands than water like Pilate.

Graham Greene (1904–91) British novelist. *The Comedians*, Pt. III, Ch. 4

5 I love being at the centre of things.

Margaret Thatcher (1925–) British politician and prime minister. *Reader's Digest*, 1984

6 Miss Madeleine Philips was making it very manifest to Captain Douglas that she herself was a career; that a lover with any other career in view need not – as the advertisements say – apply.

H. G. Wells (1866–1946) British writer. *Bealby*, Pt. V, Ch. 5

COMMUNICATION

See also clarity, conversation, language, letter-writing, speech

1 Only connect!

E. M. Forster (1879–1970) British novelist. *Howards End*, Epigraph

2 Unless one is a genius, it is best to aim at being intelligible.

Anthony Hope (Sir Anthony Hope Hawkins; 1863–1933) British novelist. *The Dolly Dialogues*

3 The medium is the message. This is merely to say that the personal and social consequences of any medium…result from the new scale that is introduced into our affairs by each extension of ourselves or by any new technology.

Marshall McLuhan (1911–81) Canadian sociologist. *Understanding Media*, Ch. 1

4 What have we to say to India?

John Ruskin (1819–1900) British art critic and writer. Referring to the completion of the British-Indian cable. Attrib.

COMMUNISM

See also Marxism, Russia, socialism

1 Its relationship to democratic institutions is that of the death watch beetle – it is not a Party, it is a conspiracy.

Aneurin Bevan (1897–1960) British Labour politician. Referring to the Communist Party. *Tribune*

2 Socialism with a human face.

Alexander Dubček (1921–92) Czechoslovak statesman. A resolution by the party group in the Ministry of Foreign Affairs, in 1968, referred to Czechoslovak foreign policy acquiring 'its own defined face'. Attrib.

3 Every year humanity takes a step towards Communism. Maybe not you, but at all events your grandson will surely be a Communist.

Nikita Khrushchev (1894–1971) Soviet statesman. Said to Sir William Hayter, June 1956

4 Communism is Soviet power plus the electrification of the whole country.

Lenin (Vladimir Ilich Ulyanov; 1870–1924) Russian revolutionary leader. Political slogan of 1920, promoting the programme of electrification.

5 There's no such thing in Communist countries as a load of old cod's wallop, the cod's wallop is always fresh made.

Robert Morley (1908–92) British actor. *Punch*, 20 Feb 1974

6 Communism is like prohibition, it's a good idea but it won't work.

Will Rogers (1879–1935) US actor and humorist. *Autobiography*, Nov 1927

7 For us in Russia communism is a dead dog, while, for many people in the West, it is still a living lion.

Alexander Solzhenitsyn (1918–) Soviet novelist. *The Listener*, 15 Feb 1979

8 Every communist has a fascist frown, every fascist a communist smile.

Muriel Spark (1918–) British novelist. *The Girls of Slender Means*, Ch. 4

9 The party is the rallying-point for the best elements of the working class.

Joseph Stalin (J. Dzhugashvili; 1879–1953) Soviet statesman. Attrib.

10 Communism continued to haunt Europe as a spectre – a name men gave to their own fears and blunders. But the crusade against Com munism was even more imaginary than the spectre of Communism.

A. J. P. Taylor (1906–90) British historian. *The Origins of the Second World War*, Ch. 2

11 Lenin's method leads to this: the party organization at first substitutes itself for the party as a whole. Then the central committee substitutes itself for the party organization, and finally a single dictator substitutes himself for the central committee.

Leon Trotsky (Lev Davidovich Bronstein; 1879–1940) Russian revolutionary. *The Communist Parties of Western Europe* (N. McInnes), Ch. 3

COMPLAINTS

1 We have first raised a dust and then complain we cannot see.

Bishop Berkeley (1685–1753) Irish churchman and philosopher. *Principles of Human Knowledge*, Introduction

2 The world is disgracefully managed, one hardly knows to whom to complain.

Ronald Firbank (1886–1926) British novelist. *Vainglory*

3 If you are foolish enough to be contented, don't show it, but grumble with the rest.

Jerome K. Jerome (1859–1927) British humorist. *Idle Thoughts of an Idle Fellow*

4 Nay, Madam, when you are declaiming, declaim; and when you are calculating, calculate.

Samuel Johnson (1709–84) British lexicographer. Commenting on Mrs Thrales's discourse on the price of children's clothes. *Life of Johnson* (J. Boswell), Vol. III

5 I want to register a complaint. Do you know who sneaked into my room at three o'clock this morning?
– Who?
Nobody, and that's my complaint.

Groucho Marx (Julius Marx; 1895–1977) US comedian. *Monkey Business*

COMPLIMENTS

See also admiration, beauty, flattery, love, praise

1 She isn't a bad bit of goods, the Queen! I wish all the fleas in my bed were as good.

Miguel de Cervantes (1547–1616) Spanish novelist. *Don Quixote*, Pt. I, Ch. 30

2 She is Venus when she smiles;
But she's Juno when she walks,
And Minerva when she talks.

Ben Jonson (1573–1637) English dramatist. *The Underwood*, 'Celebration of Charis, V. His Discourse with Cupid'

3 Your eyes shine like the pants of my blue serge suit.

Groucho Marx (Julius Marx; 1895–1977) US comedian. *The Cocoanuts*

4 Shall I compare thee to a summer's day?
Thou art more lovely and more temperate.
Rough winds do shake the darling buds of May,
And summer's lease hath all too short a date.

William Shakespeare (1564–1616) English dramatist. *Sonnet 18*

5 Won't you come into the garden? I would like my roses to see you.

Richard Brinsley Sheridan (1751–1816) British dramatist. Said to a young lady. Attrib. in *The Perfect Hostess*

6 She would rather light candles than curse the darkness, and her glow has warmed the world.

Adlai Stevenson (1900–65) US statesman. Referring to Eleanor Roosevelt. Address, United Nations General Assembly, 9 Nov 1962

7 What, when drunk, one sees in other women, one sees in Garbo sober.

Kenneth Tynan (1927–80) British theatre critic. *The Sunday Times*, 25 Aug 1963

8 Of this blest man, let his just praise be given, Heaven was in him, before he was in heaven.

Izaak Walton (1593–1683) English writer. Referring to Dr Richard Sibbes. Written in a copy of *Returning Backslider* by Richard Sibbes

9 Roses are flowering in Picardy,
But there's never a rose like you.

Frederic Edward Weatherly (1848–1929) British lawyer and songwriter. *Roses of Picardy*

COMPOSERS

See musicians

COMPROMISE

1 It takes two to tango.

Proverb

2 We know what happens to people who stay in the middle of the road. They get run over.

Aneurin Bevan (1897–1960) British Labour politician. *The Observer*, 9 Dec 1953

3 For the flesh lusteth against the Spirit, and the Spirit against the flesh: and these are contrary the one to the other: so that ye cannot do the things that ye would.

Bible: Galatians 5:17

4 All government, indeed every human benefit and enjoyment, every virtue, and every prudent act, is founded on compromise and barter.

Edmund Burke (1729–97) British politician. *Speech on Conciliation with America* (House of Commons, 22 Mar 1775)

5 Compromise used to mean that half a loaf was better than no bread. Among modern statesmen it really seems to mean that half a loaf is better than a whole loaf.

G. K. Chesterton (1874–1936) British writer. *What's Wrong with the World*

COMPUTERS

See also technology

1 I'm afraid of a world where somebody exceedingly clever could wipe all the information off everybody's computers.

A(ntonia) S(usan) Byatt (1936–) British writer. *The Guardian*, 31 May 1995

2 In these days of computer viruses, asking if you may put your disk into someone's computer is the technological equivalent of unsafe sex.

Ruth Dudley Edwards *The Independent*, 9 Jan 1995

3 I've heard that myth quite seriously expressed in my church – that the beast in the Book of Revelation will be a monster computer.

Bill Ellis British specialist in modern folklore. *The Independent*, 13 Dec 1994

4 It's like a light bulb. When it's broken, unplug it, throw it away and plug in another.

Marcian Hoff (1937–) US computer engineer. Explaining how he would repair a computer chip

5 The most participatory form of mass speech yet developed...a never-ending worldwide conversation.

The three US Federal Court judges in Pennsylvania who ruled that the Communications Decency Act, proposed in 1996 with the aim of regulating the Internet, represented an unconstitutional infringement of free speech. Referring to the Internet. *The Guardian*, 5 Dec 1996

6 You have riches and freedom here but I feel no sense of faith or direction. You have so many computers, why don't you use them in the search for love?

Lech Walesa (1943–) Polish trade unionist. Speech, Dec 1988

CONCEIT

See also arrogance, boasts, egotism, pride

1 I'm the greatest!

Muhammad Ali (Cassius Clay; 1942–) US boxer. Remark, often said after his fights

2 A man...must have a very good opinion of himself when he asks people to leave their own fireside, and encounter such a day as this, for the sake of coming to see him. He must think himself a most agreeable fellow.

Jane Austen (1775–1817) British novelist. *Emma*, Ch. 13

3 It was prettily devised of Aesop, 'The fly sat upon the axletree of the chariot-wheel and said, what a dust do I raise.'

Francis Bacon (1561–1626) English philosopher. *Essays*, 'Of Vain-Glory'

4 To give an accurate and exhaustive account of that period would need a far less brilliant pen than mine.

Max Beerbohm (1872–1956) British writer. *1880*

5 If ever he went to school without any boots it was because he was too big for them.

Ivor Bulmer-Thomas (1905–93) British writer and politician. Referring to Harold Wilson. Remark, Conservative Party Conference, 1949

6 Vanity plays lurid tricks with our memory.

Joseph Conrad (Teodor Josef Konrad Korzeniowski; 1857–1924) Polish-born British novelist. *Lord Jim*

7 I know he is, and he adores his maker.

Benjamin Disraeli (1804–81) British statesman. Replying to a remark made in defence of John Bright that he was a self-made man; often also attrib. to Bright referring to Disraeli. *The Fine Art of Political Wit* (L. Harris)

8 We are so vain that we even care for the

opinion of those we don't care for.

Marie Ebner von Eschenbach (1830–1916) Austrian writer. *Aphorism*

9 I am the Captain of the *Pinafore*;
And a right good captain too!

W. S. Gilbert (1836–1911) British dramatist. *HMS Pinafore*, I

10 I have a left shoulder-blade that is a miracle of loveliness. People come miles to see it. My right elbow has a fascination that few can resist.

W. S. Gilbert *The Mikado*, II

11 All my shows are great. Some of them are bad. But they are all great.

Lew Grade (Lewis Winogradsky; 1906–) British film and TV producer. *The Observer*, 'Sayings of the Week', 14 Sept 1975

12 Conceit is the finest armour a man can wear.

Jerome K. Jerome (1859–1927) British humorist. *Idle Thoughts of an Idle Fellow*

13 He fell in love with himself at first sight and it is a passion to which he has always remained faithful. Self-love seems so often unrequited.

Anthony Powell (1905–) British novelist. *A Dance to the Music of Time: The Acceptance World*, Ch. 1

14 Self-love is the greatest of all flatterers.

Duc de la Rochefoucauld (1613–80) French writer. *Maximes*, 2

15 Besides Shakespeare and me, who do you think there is?

Gertrude Stein (1874–1946) US writer. Speaking to a friend she considered knew little about literature. *Charmed Circle* (J. Mellow)

16 The Jews have produced only three originative geniuses: Christ, Spinoza, and myself.

Gertrude Stein *Charmed Circle* (J. Mellow)

17 Vanity dies hard; in some obstinate cases it outlives the man.

Robert Louis Stevenson (1850–94) Scottish writer. *Prince Otto*

18 I think, historically, the term 'Thatcherism' will be seen as a compliment.

Margaret Thatcher (1925–) British politician and prime minister. Remark, Oct 1985

19 I think I have become a bit of an institution – you know, the sort of thing people expect to see around the place.

Margaret Thatcher Remark, July 1987

20 He would like to destroy his old diaries and to appear before his children and the public only in his patriarchal robes. His vanity is immense!

Sophie Tolstoy (1844–1919) Russian writer. *A Diary of Tolstoy's Wife, 1860–1891*

21 Isn't it? I know in my case I would grow intolerably conceited.

James Whistler (1834–1903) US painter. Replying to the pointed observaton that it was as well that we do not see ourselves as others see us. *The Man Whistler* (H. Pearson)

22 A LADY. I only know of two painters in the world: yourself and Velasquez.
WHISTLER. Why drag in Velasquez?

James Whistler *Whistler Stories* (D. Seitz)

23 No, no, Oscar, you forget. When you and I are together we never talk about anything except me.

James Whistler Cable replying to Oscar Wilde's message: 'When you and I are together we never talk about anything except ourselves'. *The Gentle Art of Making Enemies*

24 I cannot tell you that, madam. Heaven has granted me no offspring.

James Whistler Replying to a lady who had inquired whether he thought genius hereditary. *Whistler Stories* (D. Seitz)

25 Nothing, except my genius.

Oscar Wilde (1854–1900) Irish-born British dramatist. Replying to a US customs official on being asked if he had anything to declare. Attrib.

26 To love oneself is the beginning of a lifelong romance.

Oscar Wilde *An Ideal Husband*, III

27 Who am I to tamper with a masterpiece?

Oscar Wilde Refusing to make alterations to one of his own plays. Attrib.

CONFLICT

See also opposites

1 Attack is the best form of defence.

Proverb

2 Fight fire with fire.

Proverb

3 He who lives by the sword dies by the sword.

Proverb

4 Without Contraries is no progression. Attraction and Repulsion, Reason and Energy, Love and Hate, are necessary to Human existence.

William Blake (1757–1827) British poet. *The Marriage of Heaven and Hell*, 'The Argument'

5 No, when the fight begins within himself,
A man's worth something.

Robert Browning (1812–89) British poet. *Bishop Blougram's Apology*

6 Two souls dwell, alas! in my breast.

Goethe (1749–1832) German poet and dramatist. *Faust*, Pt. I

7 Two loves I have, of comfort and despair,
Which like two spirits do suggest me still;
The better angel is a man right fair,
The worser spirit a woman colour'd ill.

William Shakespeare (1564–1616) English dramatist. *Sonnet 144*

CONFORMITY

See also orthodoxy

1 Who spits against the wind, it falls in his face.
Proverb

2 When in Rome, live as the Romans do: when elsewhere, live as they live elsewhere.
St Ambrose (c. 339–397) Bishop of Milan. Advice to St Augustine

3 Take the tone of the company you are in.
Earl of Chesterfield (1694–1773) English statesman. Letter to his son, 9 Oct 1747

4 Whoso would be a man must be a nonconformist.
Ralph Waldo Emerson (1803–82) US poet and essayist. *Essays*, 'Self-Reliance'

5 Uniformity isn't bad, as some people still think, because if the quality is good, it satisfies. People are never happy who want change.
L. P. Hartley (1895–1972) British novelist. *Facial Justice*, Ch. 13

6 Why do you have to be a nonconformist like everybody else?
James Thurber (1894–1961) US humorist. Attrib. Actually a cartoon caption by Stan Hunt in the *New Yorker*

CONFUSION

1 Well, my deliberate opinion is – it's a jolly strange world.
Arnold Bennett (1867–1931) British novelist. *The Title*, I

2 I can't say I was ever lost, but I was bewildered once for three days.
Daniel Boone (1734–1820) US pioneeer. Reply when asked if he had ever been lost. Attrib.

3 'Curiouser and curiouser!' cried Alice.
Lewis Carroll (Charles Lutwidge Dodgson; 1832–98) British writer. *Alice's Adventures in Wonderland*, Ch. 2

4 I believe that I have created a lot of cognitive dissonance in the minds of people who are comfortable with stereotypes.
Hillary Clinton (1947–) US lawyer and First Lady. *The Observer*, 'Sayings of the Week', 15 May 1994

5 This world is very odd we see,
We do not comprehend it;
But in one fact we all agree,
God won't, and we can't mend it.
Arthur Hugh Clough (1819–61) British poet. *Dipsychus*, Bk. II

6 Bewitched, Bothered and Bewildered.
Lorenz Hart (1895–1943) US songwriter. From the musical *Babes in Arms*. Song title

7 I had nothing to offer anybody except my own confusion.
Jack Kerouac (1922–69) US novelist. *On the Road*, Pt. II

8 I don't want you to think I'm not incoherent.
Harold W. Ross (1892–1951) US journalist. *The Years with Ross* (James Thurber)

9 For mine own part, it was Greek to me.
William Shakespeare (1564–1616) English dramatist. *Julius Caesar*, I:2

10 That blessed mood,
In which the burthen of the mystery,
In which the heavy and the weary weight
Of all this unintelligible world,
Is lightened.
William Wordsworth (1770–1850) British poet. *Lines composed a few miles above Tintern Abbey*

CONSCIENCE

See also integrity

1 Conscience, I say, not thine own, but of the other: for why is my liberty judged of another man's conscience?
Bible: I Corinthians 10:29

2 Conscience is the internal perception of the rejection of a particular wish operating within us.
Sigmund Freud (1856–1939) Austrian psychoanalyst. *Totem and Taboo*

3 Conscience is a coward, and those faults it has not strength enough to prevent it seldom has justice enough to accuse.
Oliver Goldsmith (1728–74) Irish-born British writer. *The Vicar of Wakefield*, Ch. 13

4 Conscience is the inner voice that warns us somebody may be looking.
H. L. Mencken (1880–1956) US journalist. *A Mencken Chrestomathy*

5 Thus conscience does make cowards of us all;
And thus the native hue of resolution
Is sicklied o'er with the pale cast of thought.
William Shakespeare (1564–1616) English dramatist. *Hamlet*, III:1

CONSERVATION

See also ecology, environment

1 I gave my beauty and my youth to men. I am going to give my wisdom and experience to animals.
Brigitte Bardot (1934–) French film actress. Referring to her animal-rights campaign. *The Guardian*, 1987

2 Contrary to popular mythology, it is not my Department's mission in life to tarmac over the whole of England.
Paul Channon (1935–) British politician. Speech, Sept 1988

3 Population growth is the primary source of environmental damage.
Jacques Cousteau (1910–) French naval officer and underwater explorer. Remark, Jan 1989

4 Trees are poems that the earth writes upon the sky. We fell them down and turn them into paper that we may record our emptiness.

Kahlil Gibran (1833–1931) Lebanese mystic and poet. *Sand and Foam*

5 Green politics is not about being far left or far right, but far-sighted.

David Icke (1952–) Green Party spokesman. Speech, Green Party conference, Sept 1989

6 The biggest waste of water in the country by far is when you spend half a pint and flush two gallons.

Prince Philip (1921–) The consort of Queen Elizabeth II. Speech, 1965

7 Simply having a convention which says you must not make species extinct does not make a blind bit of difference.

Prince Philip Referring to the UN treaty on world conservation, Mar 1989. *The Sunday Correspondent*, 31 Dec, 1989

8 Our English countryside is one of the most heavily man-made habitats in Europe. To make it into a green museum would be to belie its whole history.

Nicholas Ridley (1929–93) British politician. Speech, Nov 1988

CONSERVATISM

See also change

1 All conservatism is based upon the idea that if you leave things alone you leave them as they are. But you do not. If you leave a thing alone you leave it to a torrent of change.

G. K. Chesterton (1874–1936) British writer. *Orthodoxy*, Ch. 7

2 I love everything that's old: old friends, old times, old manners, old books, old wine.

Oliver Goldsmith (1728–74) Irish-born British writer. *She Stoops to Conquer*, I

3 You can't teach the old maestro a new tune.

Jack Kerouac (1922–69) US novelist. *On the Road*, Pt. I

4 I do not know which makes a man more conservative – to know nothing but the present, or nothing but the past.

John Maynard Keynes (1883–1946) British economist. *The End of Laisser-Faire*, I

5 What is conservatism? Is it not adherence to the old and tried, against the new and untried?

Abraham Lincoln (1809–65) US statesman. Speech, 27 Feb 1860

6 You can't teach an old dogma new tricks.

Dorothy Parker (1893–1967) US writer. *Wit's End* (R. E. Drennan)

7 The radical invents the views. When he has worn them out, the conservative adopts them.

Mark Twain (Samuel Langhorne Clemens; 1835–1910) US writer. *Notebooks*

CONSTANCY

See also change, conservatism

1 A foolish consistency is the hobgoblin of little minds, adored by little statesmen and philosophers and divines. With consistency a great soul has simply nothing to do.

Ralph Waldo Emerson (1803–82) US poet and essayist. *Essays*, 'Self-reliance'

2 Consistency is contrary to nature, contrary to life. The only completely consistent people are the dead.

Aldous Huxley (1894–1964) British novelist. *Do What you Will*

3 *Plus ça change, plus c'est la même chose.*
The more things change, the more they stay the same.

Alphonse Karr (1808–90) French writer. *Les Guêpes*, Jan 1849

4 For men may come and men may go
But I go on for ever.

Alfred, Lord Tennyson (1809–92) British poet. *The Brook*

5 Still glides the Stream, and shall for ever glide;
The Form remains, the Function never dies.

William Wordsworth (1770–1850) British poet. *The River Duddon*, 'After-Thought'

CONTEMPT

See also ridicule

1 She was nothing more than a mere good-tempered, civil and obliging young woman; as such we could scarcely dislike her – she was only an Object of Contempt.

Jane Austen (1775–1817) British novelist. *Love and Friendship*

2 'You threaten us, fellow? Do your worst,
Blow your pipe there till you burst!'

Robert Browning (1812–89) British poet. *The Pied Piper of Hamelin*

3 He looked at me as if I was a side dish he hadn't ordered.

Ring Lardner Jnr (1885–1933) American humorist. Referring to W. H. Taft, US president (1909–13). *The Home Book of Humorous Quotations* (A. K. Adams)

CONTENTMENT

See also happiness, satisfaction

1 Live with the gods. And he does so who constantly shows them that his soul is satisfied with what is assigned to him.

Marcus Aurelius (121–180 AD) Roman emperor. *Meditations*, Bk. V, Ch. 27

2 Sweet Stay-at-Home, sweet Well-content.

W. H. Davies (1871–1940) British poet. *Sweet Stay-at-Home*

3 Here with a Loaf of Bread beneath the Bough,
A Flask of Wine, a Book of Verse – and Thou
Beside me singing in the Wilderness –
And Wilderness is Paradise enow.

Edward Fitzgerald (1809–83) British poet. A Book of Verse is not mentioned in the original Persian, where a common pair of words meaning wine and meat on a skewer occur; it has been suggested that Fitzgerald mistranslated deliberately. *The Rubáiyát of Omar Khayyám*

4 Notwithstanding the poverty of my outside experience, I have always had a significance for myself, and every chance to stumble along my straight and narrow little path, and to worship at the feet of my Deity, and what more can a human soul ask for?

Alice James (1848–92) US diarist. *The Diary of Alice James* (ed. Leon Edel)

5 If I had not been born Perón, I would have liked to be Perón.

Juan Perón (1895–1974) Argentine statesman. *The Observer*, 'Sayings of the Week', 21 Feb 1960

6 Nought's had, all's spent,
Where our desire is got without content.
'Tis safer to be that which we destroy,
Than by destruction dwell in doubtful joy.

William Shakespeare (1564–1616) English dramatist. *Macbeth*, III:2

7 O, this life
Is nobler than attending for a check,
Richer than doing nothing for a bribe,
Prouder than rustling in unpaid-for silk.

William Shakespeare *Cymbeline*, III:3

CONTRACEPTION

See also sex

1 Vasectomy means not ever having to say you're sorry.

Larry Adler (1914–) US harmonica player and entertainer. Attrib.

2 I want to tell you a terrific story about oral contraception. I asked this girl to sleep with me and she said 'no'.

Woody Allen (Allen Stewart Konigsberg; 1935–) US film actor. *Woody Allen: Clown Prince of American Humor* (Adler and Feinman), Ch. 2

3 He no play-a da game. He no make-a da rules!

Earl Butz (1909–) US politician. Referring to the Pope's strictures against contraception. Remark, 1974

4 The command 'Be fruitful and multiply was promulgated according to our authorities, when the population of the world consisted of two people.

Dean Inge (1860–1954) British churchman. *More Lay Thoughts of a Dean*

5 It is now quite lawful for a Catholic woman to avoid pregnancy by a resort to mathematics, though she is still forbidden to resort to physics and chemistry.

H. L. Mencken (1880–1956) US journalist. *Notebooks*, 'Minority Report'

6 Contraceptives should be used on every conceivable occasion.

Spike Milligan (1918–) British comic actor and author. *The Last Goon Show of All*

7 Skullion had little use for contraceptives at the best of times. Unnatural, he called them, and placed them in the lower social category of things along with elastic-sided boots and made-up bow ties. Not the sort of attire for a gentleman.

Tom Sharpe (1928–) British novelist. *Porterhouse Blue*, Ch. 9

8 Protestant women may take the Pill. Roman Catholic women must keep taking the *Tablet*.

Irene Thomas (1920–) British writer. *The Tablet* is a British Roman Catholic newspaper. Attrib.

CONVERSATION

See also speech

1 Although there exist many thousand subjects for elegant conversation, there are persons who cannot meet a cripple without talking about feet.

Chinese proverb.

2 I have but ninepence in ready money, but I can draw for a thousand pounds.

Joseph Addison (1672–1719) British essayist. Comparing his ability to make conversation and to write. *Life of Johnson* (Boswell)

3 JOHNSON. Well, we had a good talk.
BOSWELL. Yes, Sir; you tossed and gored several persons.

James Boswell (1740–95) Scottish lawyer and writer. *Life of Johnson*, Vol. II

4 Questioning is not the mode of conversation among gentlemen.

Samuel Johnson (1709–84) British lexicographer. *Life of Johnson* (J. Boswell), Vol. II

5 That is the happiest conversation where there is no competition, no vanity but a calm quiet interchange of sentiments.

Samuel Johnson *Life of Johnson* (J. Boswell), Vol. II

6 Beware of the conversationalist who adds 'in other words'. He is merely starting afresh.

Robert Morley (1908–92) British actor. *The Observer*, 'Sayings of the Week', 6 Dec 1964

7 Ideal conversation must be an exchange of thought, and not, as many of those who worry most about their shortcomings believe, an eloquent exhibition of wit or oratory.

Emily Post (1873–1960) US writer. *Etiquette*, Ch. 6

8 Conversation has a kind of charm about it, an insinuating and insidious something that elicits secrets from us just like love or liquor.

Seneca (c. 4 BC–65 AD) Roman author. *Epistles*

9 Teas,
Where small talk dies in agonies.

Percy Bysshe Shelley (1792–1822) British poet. *Peter Bell the Third*

10 There is no such thing as conversation. It is an illusion. There are intersecting monologues, that is all.

Rebecca West (Cicely Isabel Fairfield; 1892–1983) British novelist and journalist. *There Is No Conversation*, Ch. 1

11 A good listener is not someone who has nothing to say. A good listener is a good talker with a sore throat.

Katherine Whitehorn (1926–) British journalist. Attrib.

CORRUPTION

See also bribery, decline

1 Among a people generally corrupt, liberty cannot long exist.

Edmund Burke (1729–97) British politician. Letter to the Sheriffs of Bristol, 1777

2 Corruption, the most infallible symptom of constitutional liberty.

Edward Gibbon (1737–94) British historian. *Decline and Fall of the Roman Empire*, Ch. 21

3 The hungry sheep look up, and are not fed,
But, swoln with wind and the rank mist they draw,
Rot inwardly, and foul contagion spread.

John Milton (1608–74) English poet. *Lycidas*

4 As killing as the canker to the rose.

John Milton *Lycidas*

5 All things can corrupt perverted minds.

Ovid (Publius Ovidius Naso; 43 BC–17 AD) Roman poet. *Tristia*, Bk. II

6 Any institution which does not suppose the people good, and the magistrate corruptible is evil.

Robespierre (1758–94) French lawyer and revolutionary. *Déclaration des Droits de l'homme*, 24 Apr 1793

7 Something is rotten in the state of Denmark.

William Shakespeare (1564–1616) English dramatist. *Hamlet*, I:4

8 For sweetest things turn sourest by their deeds:
Lilies that fester smell far worse than weeds.

William Shakespeare *Sonnet 94*

9 A reformer is a guy who rides through a sewer in a glass-bottomed boat.

James J. Walker (1881–1946) US politician. Speech, New York, 1928

10 All those men have their price.

Robert Walpole (1676–1745) British statesman. *Memoirs of Sir Robert Walpole* (W. Coxe)

COSMETICS

See also appearance

1 Most women are not so young as they are painted.

Max Beerbohm (1872–1956) British writer. *A Defence of Cosmetics*

2 Wherever one wants to be kissed.

Coco Chanel (1883–1971) French dress designer. When asked where one should wear perfume. *Coco Chanel, Her Life, Her Secrets* (Marcel Haedrich)

3 In the factory we make cosmetics. In the store we sell hope.

Charles Revson (1906–75) US business tycoon. *Fire and Ice* (A. Tobias)

COUNTRYSIDE

See also agriculture, ecology, flowers, Nature, trees

1 I nauseate walking; 'tis a country diversion,
I loathe the country and everything that relates to it.

William Congreve (1670–1729) British Restoration dramatist. *The Way of the World*, IV:4

2 God made the country, and man made the town.

William Cowper (1731–1800) British poet. *The Task*

3 Ever charming, ever new,
When will the landscape tire the view?

John Dyer (1700–58) British poet. *Grongar Hill*

4 There is nothing good to be had in the country, or, if there is, they will not let you have it.

William Hazlitt (1778–1830) British essayist. *Observations on Wordsworth's* 'Excursion'

5 When I am in the country I wish to vegetate like the country.

William Hazlitt *On Going a Journey*

6 Here of a Sunday morning
My love and I would lie,
And see the coloured counties,
And hear the larks so high
About us in the sky.

A. E. Housman (1859–1936) British scholar and poet. *A Shropshire Lad*, 'Bredon Hill'

7 It must be generations since anyone but highbrows lived in this cottage...I imagine most of the agricultural labourers round here commute from London.

Anthony Powell (1905–) British novelist. *A Dance to the Music of Time: The Kindly Ones*, Ch. 2

8 O, Brignal banks are wild and fair,
  And Gretna woods are green,
And you may gather garlands there
  Would grace a summer queen.

Walter Scott (1771–1832) Scottish novelist. *Rokeby*, III

9 Under the greenwood tree
Who loves to lie with me,

And turn his merry note
Unto the sweet bird's throat,
Come hither, come hither, come hither.
Here shall he see
No enemy
But winter and rough weather.

William Shakespeare (1564–1616) English dramatist. *As You Like It*, II:5

10 Anybody can be good in the country.

Oscar Wilde (1854–1900) Irish-born British dramatist. *The Picture of Dorian Gray*, Ch. 19

COURAGE

See also endurance, heroism, patriotism

1 The sons of the prophet were brave men and bold,
And quite unaccustomed to fear,
But the bravest by far in the ranks of the Shah
Was Abdul the Bulbul Amir.

Anonymous *Abdul the Bulbul Amir*

2 Because of my title, I was the first to enter here. I shall be the last to go out.

Duchesse d'Alençon (d. 1897) Bavarian-born duchess. Refusing help during a fire, 4 May 1897, at a charity bazaar in Paris. She died along with 120 others. Attrib.

3 No coward soul is mine,
No trembler in the world's storm-troubled sphere:
I see Heaven's glories shine,
And faith shines equal, arming me from fear.

Emily Brontë (1818–48) British novelist. *Last Lines*

4 Perhaps your fear in passing judgement is greater than mine in receiving it.

Giordano Bruno (1548–1600) Italian philosopher. Said to the cardinals who excommunicated him, 8 Feb 1600. Attrib.

5 And though hard be the task,
'Keep a stiff upper lip.'

Phoebe Cary (1824–71) US poet. *Keep a Stiff Upper Lip*

6 Down these mean streets a man must go who is not himself mean; who is neither tarnished nor afraid.

Raymond Chandler (1888–1959) US novelist. *The Simple Art of Murder*

7 The Red Badge of Courage.

Stephen Crane (1871–1900) US writer. *Title of novel*

8 Boldness, and again boldness, and always boldness!

Georges Jacques Danton (1759–94) French political activist. Speech, French Legislative Committee, 2 Sept 1792

9 Oliver Twist has asked for more.

Charles Dickens (1812–70) British novelist. *Oliver Twist*, Ch. 2

10 I'll bell the cat.

Archibald Douglas (1449–1514) Scottish nobleman. Of his proposed capture of Robert Cochrane (executed 1482); the phrase 'bell the cat' was earlier used by Eustache Deschamps in his *Ballade: Le Chat et les souris*

11 None but the Brave deserves the Fair.

John Dryden (1631–1700) British poet and dramatist. *Alexander's Feast*

12 Courage is the price that Life exacts for granting peace.

Amelia Earhart (1898–1937) US flyer. *Courage*

13 Come cheer up, my lads! 'tis to glory we steer,
To add something more to this wonderful year;
To honour we call you, not press you like slaves,
For who are so free as the sons of the waves?
Heart of oak are our ships,
Heart of oak are our men:
We always are ready;
Steady, boys, steady;
We'll fight and we'll conquer again and again.

David Garrick (1717–79) British actor and manager. *Heart of Oak*

14 The boy stood on the burning deck
Whence all but he had fled;
The flame that lit the battle's wreck
Shone round him o'er the dead.

Felicia Dorothea Hemans (1793–1835) British poet. *Casabianca*

15 It is better to be the widow of a hero than the wife of a coward.

Dolores Ibarruri (1895–1989) Spanish politician. Speech, Valencia, 1936

16 If the creator had a purpose in equipping us with a neck, he surely meant us to stick it out.

Arthur Koestler (1905–83) Hungarian-born British writer. *Encounter*, May 1970

17 Then out spake brave Horatius,
The Captain of the Gate:
'To every man upon this earth
Death cometh soon or late.
And how can man die better
Than facing fearful odds,
For the ashes of his fathers,
And the temples of his Gods?'

Lord Macaulay (1800–59) British historian. *Lays of Ancient Rome*, 'Horatius', 27

18 The stubborn spear-men still made good
Their dark impenetrable wood,
Each stepping where his comrade stood,
  The instant that he fell.

Walter Scott (1771–1832) Scottish novelist. *Marmion*, VI

19 Once more unto the breach, dear friends, once more;
Or close the wall up with our English dead.

William Shakespeare (1564–1616) English dramatist. *Henry V*, III:1

20 He was a bold man that first eat an oyster.

Jonathan Swift (1667–1745) Irish-born Anglican priest and writer. *Polite Conversation*, Dialogue 2

21 Half a league, half a league,
Half a league onward,
All in the valley of Death
Rode the six hundred.

Alfred, Lord Tennyson (1809–92) British poet. *The Charge of the Light Brigade*

22 Into the jaws of Death,
Into the mouth of Hell.

Alfred, Lord Tennyson *The Charge of the Light Brigade*

23 Fortune favours the brave.

Terence (Publius Terentius Afer; c. 190–159 BC) Roman poet. *Phormio*

24 The three-o'-clock in the morning courage, which Bonaparte thought was the rarest.

Henry David Thoreau (1817–62) US writer. *Walden*, 'Sounds'

COURTESY

See also chivalry, etiquette, manners, respect

1 Civility costs nothing.

Proverb

2 If a man be gracious and courteous to strangers, it shews he is a citizen of the world.

Francis Bacon (1561–1626) English philosopher. *Essays*, 'Of Goodness and Goodness of Nature'

3 The English are polite by telling lies. The Americans are polite by telling the truth.

Malcolm Bradbury (1932–) British academic and novelist. *Stepping Westward*, Bk. II, Ch. 5

4 Courtesy is not dead – it has merely taken refuge in Great Britain.

Georges Duhamel (1884–1966) French writer. *The Observer*, 'Sayings of Our Times', 31 May 1953

COWARDICE

See also self-preservation

1 Probably a fear we have of facing up to the real issues. Could you say we were guilty of Noël Cowardice?

Peter De Vries (1910–93) US novelist. *Comfort me with Apples*, Ch. 8

2 None but a coward dares to boast that he has never known fear.

Marshal Foch (1851–1929) French soldier. Attrib.

3 He led his regiment from behind
He found it less exciting.

W. S. Gilbert (1836–1911) British dramatist. *The Gondoliers*, I

4 When the foeman bares his steel,
Tarantara! tarantara!
We uncomfortable feel.

W. S. Gilbert *The Pirates of Penzance*, II

5 To a surprising extent the war-lords in shining armour, the apostles of the martial virtues, tend not to die fighting when the time comes. History is full of ignominious getaways by the great and famous.

George Orwell (Eric Blair; 1903–50) British novelist. *Who Are the War Criminals?*

6 The summer soldier and the sunshine patriot will, in this crisis, shrink from the service of their country.

Thomas Paine (1737–1809) British writer. *Pennsylvania Journal*, 'The American Crisis'

7 Some craven scruple
Of thinking too precisely on th' event.

William Shakespeare (1564–1616) English dramatist. *Hamlet*, IV:4

8 I dare not fight; but I will wink and hold out mine iron.

William Shakespeare *Henry V*, II:1

9 Cowards die many times before their deaths:
The valiant never taste of death but once.

William Shakespeare *Julius Caesar*, II:2

CREATION

1 The Hand that made us is divine.

Joseph Addison (1672–1719) British essayist. *The Spectator*, 465

2 In the beginning God created the heaven and the earth.
And the earth was without form, and void; and darkness was upon the face of the deep. And the Spirit of God moved upon the face of the waters.
And God said, Let there be light: and there was light.
And God saw the light, that it was good: and God divided the light from the darkness.
And God called the light Day, and the darkness he called Night. And the evening and the morning were the first day.

Bible: Genesis 1:1–5

3 And God called the dry land Earth; and the gathering together of the waters called he Seas: and God saw that it was good.
And God said, Let the earth bring forth grass, the herb yielding seed, and the fruit tree yielding fruit after his kind, whose seed is in itself, upon the earth: and it was so.

Bible: Genesis 1:10–11

4 And God made two great lights: the greater light to rule the day, and the lesser light to rule the night: he made the stars also.

Bible: Genesis 1:16

5 And God said, Let the earth bring forth the living creature after his kind, cattle, and creeping thing, and beast of the earth after his kind: and it was so.

Bible: Genesis 1:24

6 And God said, Let us make man in our image, after our likeness: and let them have dominion over the fish of the sea, and over the fowl of the air, and over the cattle, and over all the earth, and over every creeping thing that creepeth upon the earth.
So God created man in his own image, in the image of God created he him; male and female created he them.

And God blessed them, and God said unto them, Be fruitful, and multiply, and replenish the earth, and subdue it: and have dominion over the fish of the sea, and over the fowl of the air, and over every living thing that moveth upon the earth.
Bible: Genesis 1:26–28

7 When the stars threw down their spears,
And watered heaven with their tears,
Did he smile his work to see?
Did he who made the Lamb make thee?
William Blake (1757–1827) British poet. *Songs of Experience*, 'The Tiger'

8 Little Lamb, who made thee?
Dost thou know who made thee?
William Blake *Songs of Innocence*, 'The Lamb'

9 Whan that the month in which the world bigan,
That highte March, whan God first maked man.
Geoffrey Chaucer (c. 1342–1400) English poet. *The Canterbury Tales*, 'The Nun's Priest's Tale'

10 'Who *is* the Potter, pray, and who the Pot?'
Edward Fitzgerald (1809–83) British poet. *The Rubáiyát of Omar Khayyám*

11 I cannot forgive Descartes; in all his philosophy he did his best to dispense with God. But he could not avoid making Him set the world in motion with a flip of His thumb; after that he had no more use for God.
Blaise Pascal (1623–62) French philosopher and mathematician. *Pensées*, II

12 For suddenly it was clear to me that virtue in the creator is not the same as virtue in the creature. For the creator, if he should love his creature, would be loving only a part of himself; but the creature, praising the creator, praises an infinity beyond himself.
Olaf Stapledon (1886–1950) British philosopher and science-fiction writer. *Star Maker*, Ch. 13

13 'Do you know who made you?' 'Nobody, as I knows on,' said the child, with a short laugh… 'I 'spect I grow'd.'
Harriet Beecher Stowe (1811–96) US novelist. *Uncle Tom's Cabin*, Ch. 20

14 Which beginning of time according to our Chronologie, fell upon the entrance of the night preceding the twenty third day of *Octob.*, in the year of the Julian Calendar, 710.
James Ussher (1581–1656) Irish churchman. Referring to the Creation, as described in Genesis, which, he had calculated, took place on 22 Oct 4004 BC. *The Annals of the World*

15 God made everything out of nothing. But the nothingness shows through.
Paul Valéry (1871–1945) French poet and writer. *Mauvaises Pensées et autres*

16 The art of creation
is older than the art of killing.
Andrei Voznesensky (1933–) Soviet poet. *Poem with a Footnote*

CRICKET

See also sport and games

1 It's not in support of cricket but as an earnest protest against golf.
Max Beerbohm (1872–1956) British writer. Said when giving a shilling towards W. G. Grace's testimonial. *Carr's Dictionary of Extraordinary English Cricketers*

2 I do love cricket – it's so very English.
Sarah Bernhardt (Sarah Henriette Rosine Bernard; 1844–1923) French actress. On seeing a game of football. *Nijinsky* (R. Buckle)

3 They came to see me bat not to see you bowl.
W. G. Grace (1848–1915) British doctor and cricketer. Refusing to leave the crease after being bowled first ball in front of a large crowd. Attrib.

4 It's more than a game. It's an institution.
Thomas Hughes (1822–96) British novelist. Referring to cricket. *Tom Brown's Schooldays*, Pt. II, Ch. 7

5 There's a breathless hush in the Close tonight –
Ten to make and the match to win –
A bumping pitch and a blinding light,
An hour to play and the last man in.
Henry John Newbolt (1862–1938) British poet. *Vitaï Lampada*

6 I tend to believe that cricket is the greatest thing that God ever created on earth…certainly greater than sex, although sex isn't too bad either.
Harold Pinter (1930–) British dramatist. *The Observer*, 5 Oct 1980

7 I have always looked upon cricket as organised loafing.
William Temple (1881–1944) British churchman. Address to parents when headmaster of Repton School.

8 If the French noblesse had been capable of playing cricket with their peasants, their chateaux would never have been burnt.
George Macaulay Trevelyan (1876–1962) British historian. *English Social History*, Ch. XIII

9 It requires one to assume such indecent postures.
Oscar Wilde (1854–1900) Irish-born British dramatist. Explaining why he did not play cricket. Attrib.

CRIME

See also murder, theft

1 And surely your blood of your lives will I require; at the hand of every beast will I require it, and at the hand of man; at the hand of every man's brother will I require the life of man. Whoso sheddeth man's blood, by man shall his blood be shed: for in the image of God made he man.
Bible: Genesis 9:5–6

2 How many crimes committed merely because their authors could not endure being wrong!

Albert Camus (1913–60) French existentialist writer. *The Fall*

3 He is the Napoleon of crime.

Arthur Conan Doyle (1856–1930) British writer. Referring to Professor Moriarty. *The Final Problem*

4 How we ever actually managed to do any burgling, I don't know. We were all off our tits on drugs.

Noel Gallagher (1967–) British pop musician in the group Oasis. *The Guardian Weekend*, 4 Jan 1997

5 If poverty is the mother of crime, stupidity is its father.

Jean de La Bruyère (1645–96) French satirist. *Les Caractères*

6 Crime, like virtue, has its degrees.

Jean Racine (1639–99) French dramatist. *Phèdre*, IV:2

7 We're barking mad about crime in this country. We have an obsession with believing the worst, conning ourselves that there was a golden age – typically 40 years before the one we're living in.

Nick Ross (1947–) British broadcaster. *Radio Times*, 26 June–2 July 1993

8 There is a statistical terrorism inflicted on society by crime figures.

Lady Runciman of Doxford (1936–) *The Times*, 20 Jan 1995

9 I came to the conclusion many years ago that almost all crime is due to the repressed desire for aesthetic expression.

Evelyn Waugh (1903–66) British novelist. *Decline and Fall*, Pt. III, Ch. 1

CRITICISM

See also actors, compliments, insults, poets, writers

1 I am bound by my own definition of criticism: a disinterested endeavour to learn and propagate the best that is known and thought in the world.

Matthew Arnold (1822–88) British poet and critic. *Essays in Criticism*, First Series, 'Functions of Criticism at the Present Time'

2 There is less in this than meets the eye.

Tallulah Bankhead (1903–68) US actress. Referring to a revival of a play by Maeterlinck. *Shouts and Murmurs* (A. Woollcott), 'Capsule Criticism'

3 Too much counterpoint; what is worse, Protestant counterpoint.

Thomas Beecham (1879–1961) British conductor. Said of J. S. Bach. *The Guardian*, 8 Mar 1971

4 Of all fatiguing, futile, empty trades, the worst, I suppose, is writing about writing.

Hilaire Belloc (1870–1953) French-born British poet. *The Silence of the Sea*

5 Criticism of a long-running play; the text is: 'Jesus Christ the same yesterday, and today, and for ever'.

Robert Benchley (1889–1945) US humorist. Attrib.

6 And why beholdest thou the mote that is in thy brother's eye, but considerest not the beam that is in thine own eye?

Bible: Matthew 7:3

7 He who discommendeth others obliquely commendeth himself.

Thomas Browne (1605–82) English physician and writer. *Christian Morals*, Pt. I

8 A great deal of contemporary criticism reads to me like a man saying: 'Of course I do not like green cheese: I am very fond of brown sherry.'

G. K. Chesterton (1874–1936) British writer. *All I Survey*

9 To see him act, is like reading Shakespeare by flashes of lightning.

Samuel Taylor Coleridge (1772–1834) British poet. Referring to Kean. *Table Talk*

10 I never realized before that Albert married beneath him.

Noël Coward (1899–1973) British dramatist. After seeing a certain actress in the role of Queen Victoria. *Tynan on Theatre* (K. Tynan)

11 This paper will no doubt be found interesting by those who take an interest in it.

John Dalton (1766–1844) British scientist. Said on many occasions when chairing scientific meetings. Attrib.

12 If you hear that someone is speaking ill of you, instead of trying to defend yourself you should say: 'He obviously does not know me very well, since there are so many other faults he could have mentioned'.

Epictetus (c. 60–110 AD) Stoic philosopher. *Enchiridion*

13 He played the King as though under momentary apprehension that someone else was about to play the ace.

Eugene Field (1850–95) US poet and journalist. Referring to Creston Clarke's performance in the role of King Lear. Attrib.

14 It is not good enough to spend time and ink in describing the penultimate sensations and physical movements of people getting into a state of rut, we all know them too well.

John Galsworthy (1867–1933) British novelist. Referring to D. H. Lawrence's *Sons and Lovers*. Letter to Edward Garnett, 13 Apr 1914

15 Funny without being vulgar.

W. S. Gilbert (1836–1911) British dramatist. Referring to Sir Henry Irving's *Hamlet*. Attrib.

16 My dear chap! Good isn't the word!

W. S. Gilbert Speaking to an actor after he had given a poor performance. Attrib.

17 We were as nearly bored as enthusiasm would permit.

Edmund Gosse (1849–1928) British writer and critic. Referring to a play by Swinburne. *Biography of Edward Marsh* (C. Hassall)

18 There are two things which I am confident I

can do very well: one is an introduction to any literary work, stating what it is to contain, and how it should be executed in the most perfect manner; the other is a conclusion, shewing from various causes why the execution has not been equal to what the author promised to himself and to the public.

Samuel Johnson (1709–84) British lexicographer. *Life of Johnson* (J. Boswell), Vol. I

19 It is burning a farthing candle at Dover, to shew light at Calais.

Samuel Johnson Referring to the impact of Sheridan's works upon the English language. *Life of Johnson* (J. Boswell), Vol. I

20 You *may* abuse a tragedy, though you cannot write one. You may scold a carpenter who has made you a bad table, though you cannot make a table. It is not your trade to make tables.

Samuel Johnson Referring to the qualifications needed to indulge in literary criticism. *Life of Johnson* (J. Boswell), Vol. I

21 This man I thought had been a Lord among wits; but, I find, he is only a wit among Lords.

Samuel Johnson Referring to Lord Chesterfield. *Life of Johnson* (J. Boswell), Vol. I

22 They teach the morals of a whore, and the manners of a dancing master.

Samuel Johnson Referring to Lord Chesterfield's *Letters*. *Life of Johnson* (J. Boswell), Vol. I

23 Yes, Sir, many men, many women, and many children.

Samuel Johnson When asked by Dr Blair whether any man of their own time could have written the poems of Ossian. *Life of Johnson* (J. Boswell), Vol. I

24 Difficult do you call it, Sir? I wish it were impossible.

Samuel Johnson On hearing a famous violinist. *Johnsonian Miscellanies* (ed. G. B. Hill), Vol. II

25 They are forced plants, raised in a hot-bed; and they are poor plants; they are but cucumbers after all.

Samuel Johnson Referring to Gray's *Odes*. *Life of Johnson* (J. Boswell), Vol. IV

26 The pleasure of criticizing robs us of the pleasure of being moved by some very fine things.

Jean de La Bruyère (1645–96) French satirist. *Les Caractères*

27 They are great parables, the novels, but false art. They are only parables. All the people are *fallen angels* – even the dirtiest scrubs. This I cannot stomach. People are not fallen angels, they are merely people.

D. H. Lawrence (1885–1930) British novelist. Referring to the novels of Dostoyevsky. Letter to J. Middleton Murray and Katherine Mansfield, 17 Feb 1916

28 His verse exhibits…something that is rather like Keats's vulgarity with a Public School accent.

F. R. Leavis (1895–1978) British literary critic. Referring to Rupert Brooke. *New Bearings in English Poetry*, Ch. 2

29 I cried all the way to the bank.

Liberace (Wladzin Valentino Liberace; 1919–87) US pianist and showman. Said when asked whether he minded being criticized. *Liberace: An Autobiography*, Ch. 2

30 People who like this sort of thing will find this is the sort of thing they like.

Abraham Lincoln (1809–65) US statesman. A comment on a book. Attrib.

31 His writing bears the same relation to poetry which a Turkey carpet bears to a picture. There are colours in the Turkey carpet out of which a picture might be made. There are words in Mr Montgomery's writing which, when disposed in certain orders and combinations, have made, and will make again, good poetry. But, as they now stand, they seem to be put together on principle in such a manner as to give no image of anything 'in the heavens above, or in the earth beneath, or in the waters under the earth'.

Lord Macaulay (1800–59) British historian. *Literary Essays Contributed to the 'Edinburgh Review'*, 'Mr. Robert Montgomery's Poems'

32 It was a book to kill time for those who like it better dead.

Rose Macaulay (1889–1958) British writer. Attrib.

33 I was so long writing my review that I never got around to reading the book.

Groucho Marx (Julius Marx; 1895–1977) US comedian. Attrib.

34 People ask you for criticism, but they only want praise.

W. Somerset Maugham (1874–1965) British novelist. *Of Human Bondage*, Ch. 50

35 Yea, marry, now it is somewhat, for now it is rhyme; before, it was neither rhyme nor reason.

Thomas More (1478–1535) English lawyer and scholar. On reading an unremarkable book recently rendered into verse by a friend of his. *Apophthegms* (Bacon), 287

36 Prolonged, indiscriminate reviewing of books involves constantly *inventing* reactions towards books about which one has no spontaneous feelings whatever.

George Orwell (Eric Blair; 1903–50) British novelist. *Confessions of a Book Reviewer*

37 She ran the whole gamut of the emotions from A to B.

Dorothy Parker (1893–1967) US writer. Referring to a performance by Katharine Hepburn on Broadway. Attrib.

38 This is not a novel to be tossed aside lightly. It should be thrown with great force.

Dorothy Parker Book review. *Wit's End* (R. E. Dremman)

39 'Tis hard to say, if greater want of skill
Appear in writing or in judging ill.

Alexander Pope (1688–1744) British poet. *An Essay on Criticism*

40 Damn with faint praise, assent with civil leer,
And, without sneering, teach the rest to sneer.

Alexander Pope *Epistle to Dr. Arbuthnot*

41 I never read anything concerning my work. I

feel that criticism is a letter to the public which the author, since it is not directed to him, does not have to open and read.

Rainer Maria Rilke (1875–1926) Austrian poet. *Letters*

42 Very good, but it has its *longueurs*.

Antoine de Rivarol (1753–1801) French writer and wit. Giving his opinion of a couplet by a mediocre poet. *Das Buch des Lachens* (W. Scholz)

43 The Stealthy School of Criticism.

Dante Gabriel Rossetti (1828–82) British painter and poet. Letter to the *Athenaeum*, 1871

44 Wagner has lovely moments but awful quarters of an hour.

Gioacchino Rossini (1792–1868) Italian operatic composer. Remark made to Emile Naumann, April 1867. *Italienische Tondichter* (Naumann)

45 I have seen, and heard, much of Cockney impudence before now; but never expected to hear a coxcomb ask two hundred guineas for flinging a pot of paint in the public's face.

John Ruskin (1819–1900) British art critic and writer. On Whistler's painting 'Nocturne in Black and Gold'. Letter, 18 June 1877

46 For I am nothing if not critical.

William Shakespeare (1564–1616) English dramatist. *Othello*, II:1

47 It does not follow...that the right to criticize Shakespeare involves the power of writing better plays. And in fact...I do not profess to write better plays.

George Bernard Shaw (1856–1950) Irish dramatist and critic. *Three Plays for Puritans*, Preface

48 It is disappointing to report that George Bernard Shaw appearing as George Bernard Shaw is sadly miscast in the part. Satirists should be heard and not seen.

Robert E. Sherwood (1896–1955) US writer and dramatist. Reviewing a Shaw play

49 It had only one fault. It was kind of lousy.

James Thurber (1894–1961) US humorist. Remark made about a play. Attrib.

50 A strange, horrible business, but I suppose good enough for Shakespeare's day.

Victoria (1819–1901) Queen of the United Kingdom. Giving her opinion of *King Lear*. *Living Biographies of Famous Rulers* (H. Thomas)

51 I do not think this poem will reach its destination.

Voltaire (François-Marie Arouet; 1694–1778) French writer. Reviewing Rousseau's poem 'Ode to Posterity'. Attrib.

52 As far as criticism is concerned, we don't resent that unless it is absolutely biased, as it is in most cases.

John Vorster (Balthazar Johannes Vorster; 1915–83) South African politician. *The Observer*, 'Sayings of the Week', 9 Nov 1969

53 My dear fellow a unique evening! I wouldn't have left a turn unstoned.

Arthur Wimperis (1874–1953) British screenwriter. Replying when asked his opinion of a vaudeville show. *Fifty Years of Vaudeville* (E. Short)

54 I saw it at a disadvantage – the curtain was up.

Walter Winchell (1879–1972) US journalist. Referring to a show starring Earl Carroll. *Come to Judgment* (A. Whiteman)

55 Trivial personalities decomposing in the eternity of print.

Virginia Woolf (1882–1941) British novelist. *The Common Reader*, 'Jane Eyre'

56 *Middlemarch*, the magnificent book which with all its imperfections is one of the few English novels for grown up people.

Virginia Woolf *The Common Reader*, 'George Eliot'

57 He is all blood, dirt and sucked sugar stick.

W. B. Yeats (1865–1939) Irish poet. Referring to Wilfred Owen. *Letters on Poetry to Dorothy Wellesley*, Letter, 21 Dec 1936

CRITICS

1 I will try to account for the degree of my aesthetic emotion. That, I conceive, is the function of the critic.

Clive Bell (1881–1964) British art critic. *Art*, Pt. II, Ch. 3

2 A man must serve his time to every trade
Save censure – critics all are ready made.

Lord Byron (1788–1824) British poet. *English Bards and Scotch Reviewers*

3 Reviewers are usually people who would have been poets, historians, biographers,...if they could; they have tried their talents at one or at the other, and have failed; therefore they turn critics.

Samuel Taylor Coleridge (1772–1834) British poet. *Lectures on Shakespeare and Milton*, I

4 I make my pictures for people, not for critics.

Cecil B. de Mille (1881–1959) US film producer and director. *Halliwell's Filmgoer's and Video Viewer's Companion*

5 A good critic is one who narrates the adventures of his mind among masterpieces.

Anatole France (Jacques Anatole François Thibault; 1844–1924) French writer. *The Literary Life*, Preface

6 I sometimes think
His critical judgement is so exquisite
It leaves us nothing to admire except his opinion.

Christopher Fry (1907–) British dramatist. *The Dark is Light Enough*, II

7 Asking a working writer what he thinks about critics is like asking a lamp-post how it feels about dogs.

Christopher Hampton (1946–) British writer and dramatist. *The Sunday Times Magazine*, 16 Oct 1977

8 What is a modern poet's fate?
To write his thoughts upon a slate;
The critic spits on what is done,
Gives it a wipe – and all is gone.

Thomas Hood (1799–1845) British poet. *Alfred Lord Tennyson, A Memoir* (Hallam Tennyson), Vol. II, Ch. 3

9 Critics are more malicious about poetry than about other books – maybe because so many manqué poets write reviews.

Elizabeth Jennings (1926–) British poet. Remark, Dec 1987

10 There is a certain race of men that either imagine it their duty, or make it their amusement, to hinder the reception of every work of learning or genius, who stand as sentinels in the avenues of fame, and value themselves upon giving Ignorance and Envy the first notice of a prey.

Samuel Johnson (1709–84) British lexicographer. *The Rambler*

11 A fly, Sir, may sting a stately horse and make him wince; but one is but an insect, and the other is a horse still.

Samuel Johnson *Life of Johnson* (J. Boswell), Vol. I

12 Dear Roger Fry whom I love as a man but detest as a movement.

Edward Howard Marsh (1872–1953) British civil servant and writer. Roger Fry (1866–1934) was an artist and art critic, who championed the postimpressionists. *Edward Marsh* (Christopher Hassall), Ch. 11

13 Insects sting, not from malice, but because they want to live. It is the same with critics – they desire our blood, not our pain.

Friedrich Wilhelm Nietzsche (1844–1900) German philosopher. *Miscellaneous Maxims and Reflections*

14 Nor in the critic let the man be lost.

Alexander Pope (1688–1744) British poet. *An Essay on Criticism*

15 They will review a book by a writer much older than themselves as if it were an over-ambitious essay by a second-year student…It is the little dons I complain about, like so many corgis trotting up, hoping to nip your ankles.

J. B. Priestley (1894–1984) British novelist. *Outcries and Asides*

16 The greater part of critics are parasites, who, if nothing had been written, would find nothing to write.

J. B. Priestley *Outcries and Asides*

17 I doubt that art needed Ruskin any more than a moving train needs one of its passengers to shove it.

Tom Stoppard (1937–) Czech-born British dramatist. *Times Literary Supplement*, 3 June 1977

18 I had another dream the other day about music critics. They were small and rodent-like with padlocked ears, as if they had stepped out of a painting by Goya.

Igor Stravinsky (1882–1971) Russian-born US composer. *The Evening Standard*, 29 Oct 1969

19 A whipper-snapper of criticism who quoted dead languages to hide his ignorance of life.

Herbert Beerbohm Tree (1853–1917) British actor and theatre manager. Referring to A. B. Walkley. *Beerbohm Tree* (Hesketh Pearson)

20 A critic is a man who knows the way but can't drive the car.

Kenneth Tynan (1927–80) British theatre critic. *New York Times Magazine*, 9 Jan 1966

21 A good drama critic is one who perceives what is happening in the theatre of his time. A great drama critic also perceives what is not happening.

Kenneth Tynan *Tynan Right and Left*, Foreword

CRUELTY

See also hurt, nastiness, violence

1 The wish to hurt, the momentary intoxication with pain, is the loophole through which the pervert climbs into the minds of ordinary men.

Jacob Bronowski (1908–74) British scientist and writer. *The Face of Violence*, Ch. 5

2 Man's inhumanity to man
Makes countless thousands mourn!

Robert Burns (1759–96) Scottish poet. *Man was Made to Mourn*

3 Fear is the parent of cruelty.

J. A. Froude (1818–94) British historian. *Short Studies on Great Subjects*, 'Party Politics'

4 A cruel story runs on wheels, and every hand oils the wheels as they run.

Ouida (Marie Louise de la Ramée; 1839–1908) British novelist. *Wisdom, Wit and Pathos*, 'Moths'

5 Whipping and abuse are like laudanum: You have to double the dose as the sensibilities decline.

Harriet Beecher Stowe (1811–96) US novelist. *Uncle Tom's Cabin*, Ch. 20

CULTURE

See also civilization, philistinism

1 Culture, the acquainting ourselves with the best that has been known and said in the world, and thus with the history of the human spirit.

Matthew Arnold (1822–88) British poet and critic. *Literature and Dogma*, Preface

2 Culture is the passion for sweetness and light, and (what is more) the passion for making them prevail.

Matthew Arnold *Literature and Dogma*, Preface

3 Culture is an instrument wielded by professors to manufacture professors, who when their turn comes will manufacture professors.

Simone Weil (1909–43) French philosopher. *The Need for Roots*

4 Mrs Ballinger is one of the ladies who pursue Culture in bands, as though it were dangerous to meet it alone.

Edith Wharton (1862–1937) US novelist. *Xingu*, Ch. 1

CURIOSITY

See also interfering, wonder

1 Ask no questions and hear no lies.

Proverb

2 Curiosity killed the cat.

Proverb

3 Be not curious in unnecessary matters: for more things are shewed unto thee than men understand.

Bible: Ecclesiasticus 3:23

4 'If everybody minded their own business,' the Duchess said in a hoarse growl, 'the world would go round a deal faster than it does.'

Lewis Carroll (Charles Lutwidge Dodgson; 1832–98) British writer. *Alice's Adventures in Wonderland*, Ch. 6

5 There is no such thing on earth as an uninteresting subject; the only thing that can exist is an uninterested person.

G. K. Chesterton (1874–1936) British writer. *Heretics*, Ch. 1

6 The world is but a school of inquiry.

Michel de Montaigne (1533–92) French essayist. *Essais*, III

7 I ofen looked up at the sky an' assed meself the question – what is the stars, what is the stars?

Sean O'Casey (1884–1964) Irish dramatist. *Juno and the Paycock*, I

8 Curiosity will conquer fear even more than bravery will.

James Stephens (1882–1950) Irish novelist. *The Crock of Gold*

9 Disinterested intellectual curiosity is the life blood of real civilisation.

George Macaulay Trevelyan (1876–1962) British historian. *English Social History*, Preface

CURSES

1 A plague o' both your houses!
They have made worms' meat of me.

William Shakespeare (1564–1616) English dramatist. *Romeo and Juliet*, III:1

2 Curses are like young chickens, they always come home to roost.

Robert Southey (1774–1843) British poet. *The Curse of Kehama*, Motto

3 'The curse is come upon me,' cried
The Lady of Shalott.

Alfred, Lord Tennyson (1809–92) British poet. *The Lady of Shalott*, Pt. III

4 She has heard a whisper say,
A curse is on her if she stay
To look down to Camelot.

Alfred, Lord Tennyson *The Lady of Shalott*, Pt. II

CUSTOM

See also habit

1 *O tempora! O mores!*
What times! What customs!

Cicero (106–43 BC) Roman orator and statesman. *In Catilinam*, I

2 Custom, then, is the great guide of human life.

David Hume (1711–76) Scottish philosopher. *An Enquiry Concerning Human Understanding*

3 But to my mind, though I am native here
And to the manner born, it is a custom
More honour'd in the breach than the
observance.

William Shakespeare (1564–1616) English dramatist. *Hamlet*, I:4

4 Custom calls me to't.
What custom wills, in all things should we do't,
The dust on antique time would lie unswept,
And mountainous error be too highly heap'd
For truth to o'erpeer.

William Shakespeare *Coriolanus*, II:3

CYNICISM

1 One is not superior merely because one sees the world in an odious light.

Vicomte de Chateaubriand (1768–1848) French diplomat and writer. Attrib.

2 Cynicism is an unpleasant way of saying the truth.

Lillian Hellman (1905–84) US dramatist. *The Little Foxes*, I

3 A cynic is a man who, when he smells flowers, looks around for a coffin.

H. L. Mencken (1880–1956) US journalist. Attrib.

4 Cynicism is humour in ill-health.

H. G. Wells (1866–1946) British writer. *Short Stories*, 'The Last Trump'

5 A man who knows the price of everything and the value of nothing.

Oscar Wilde (1854–1900) Irish-born British dramatist. A cynic. *Lady Windermere's Fan*, III

D

DAMNATION

See also devil, hell

1 Blot out his name, then, record one lost soul more,
One task more declined, one more footpath untrod,
One more devils'-triumph and sorrow for angels,
One wrong more to man, one more insult to God!

Robert Browning (1812–89) British poet. *The Lost Leader*

2 You will be damned if you do – And you will be damned if you don't.

Lorenzo Dow (1777–1834) British churchman. Speaking of Calvinism. *Reflections on the Love of God*

3 Now hast thou but one bare hour to live,
And then thou must be damn'd perpetually!
Stand still, you ever-moving spheres of heaven,
That time may cease, and midnight never come.

Christopher Marlowe (1564–93) English dramatist. *Doctor Faustus*, V:2

4 Ugly hell, gape not! come not, Lucifer!
I'll burn my books!

Christopher Marlowe *Doctor Faustus*, V:2

DANCING

1 On with the dance! let joy be unconfined;
No sleep till morn, when Youth and Pleasure meet
To chase the glowing Hours with flying feet.

Lord Byron (1788–1824) British poet. *Childe Harold's Pilgrimage*, III

2 Will you, won't you, will you, won't you, will you join the dance?

Lewis Carroll (Charles Lutwidge Dodgson; 1832–98) British writer. *Alice's Adventures in Wonderland*, Ch. 10

3 Dance, dance, dance little lady.

Noël Coward (1899–1973) British dramatist. Title of song

4 I have discovered the dance. I have discovered the art which has been lost for two thousand years.

Isadora Duncan (1878–1927) US dancer. *My Life*

5 Any time you're Lambeth way,
Any evening, any day,
You'll find us all doin' the Lambeth walk.

Douglas Furber (1885–1961) British songwriter. *Doin' the Lambeth Walk*

6 My men, like satyrs grazing on the lawns,
Shall with their goat-feet dance an antic hay.

Christopher Marlowe (1564–93) English dramatist. *Edward the Second*, I:1

7 Come, and trip it as you go
On the light fantastic toe.

John Milton (1608–74) English poet. *L'Allegro*

8 ...although one may fail to find happiness in theatrical life, one never wishes to give it up after having once tasted its fruits. To enter the School of the Imperial Ballet is to enter a convent whence frivolity is banned, and where merciless discipline reigns.

Anna Pavlova (1881–1931) Russian ballet dancer. *Pavlova: A Biography* (ed. A. H. Franks), 'Pages of My Life'

DANGER

1 Any port in a storm.

Proverb

2 If you play with fire you get burnt.

Proverb

3 Defend us from all perils and dangers of this night.

The Book of Common Prayer *Morning Prayer, Prayer of St Chrysostom*

4 Dangers by being despised grow great.

Edmund Burke (1729–97) British politician. Speech, House of Commons, 11 May 1792

5 Of course I realized there was a measure of danger. Obviously I faced the possibility of not returning when first I considered going. Once faced and settled there really wasn't any good reason to refer to it.

Amelia Earhart (1898–1937) US flyer. Referring to her flight in the 'Friendship'. *20 Hours: 40 Minutes – Our Flight in the Friendship*, Ch. 5

6 Believe me! The secret of reaping the greatest fruitfulness and the greatest enjoyment from life is to *live dangerously!*

Friedrich Wilhelm Nietzsche (1844–1900) German philosopher. *Die Fröhliche Wissenschaft*, Bk. IV

7 There's a snake hidden in the grass.

Virgil (Publius Vergilius Maro; 70–19 BC) Roman poet. *Eclogue*, Bk. III

DAY

1 Now the day is over,
Night is drawing nigh,
Shadows of the evening
Steal across the sky.

Sabine Baring-Gould (1834–1924) British author and hymn writer. *The Evening Hymn*

2 The day begins to droop, –
Its course is done:
But nothing tells the place
Of the setting sun.

Robert Bridges (1844–1930) British poet. *Winter Nightfall*

3 Where the quiet-coloured end of evening smiles,

Miles and miles.

Robert Browning (1812–89) British poet. *Love among the Ruins*, I

4 The day Thou gavest, Lord, is ended,
The darkness falls at Thy behest.

John Ellerton (1826–93) British churchman. *A Liturgy for Missionary Meetings*

5 Awake! for Morning in the Bowl of Night
Has flung the Stone that puts the Stars to Flight:
And Lo! the Hunter of the East has caught
The Sultan's Turret in a Noose of Light.

Edward Fitzgerald (1809–83) British poet. *The Rubáiyát of Omar Khayyám*

6 The Curfew tolls the knell of parting day,
The lowing herd winds slowly o'er the lea,
The plowman homeward plods his weary way,
And leaves the world to darkness and to me.

Thomas Gray (1716–71) British poet. *Elegy Written in a Country Churchyard*

7 Oh, what a beautiful morning!
Oh, what a beautiful day!

Oscar Hammerstein (1895–1960) US lyricist. From the musical *Oklahoma. Oh, What a Beautiful Morning*

8 Sweet day, so cool, so calm, so bright,
The bridal of the earth and sky.

George Herbert (1593–1633) English poet. *Virtue*

9 The candles burn their sockets,
The blinds let through the day,
The young man feels his pockets
And wonders what's to pay.

A. E. Housman (1859–1936) British scholar and poet. *Last Poems*, 'Eight O'Clock'

10 Under the opening eye-lids of the morn.

John Milton (1608–74) English poet. *Lycidas*

11 Now came still Evening on, and Twilight grey
Had in her sober livery all things clad.

John Milton *Paradise Lost*, Bk. IV

12 Midnight brought on the dusky hour
Friendliest to sleep and silence.

John Milton *Paradise Lost*, Bk. V

13 Three o'clock is always too late or too early for anything you want to do.

Jean-Paul Sartre (1905–80) French writer. *Nausea*

DEATH

See also afterlife, assassination, drowning, epitaphs, equality in death, execution, funerals, killing, last words, life and death, love and death, memorials, mortality, mourning, murder, obituaries, posterity, suicide

1 A man can die but once.

Proverb

2 A piece of churchyard fits everybody.

Proverb

3 As soon as man is born he begins to die.

Proverb

4 Dead men tell no tales.

Proverb

5 Death defies the doctor.

Proverb

6 Death is the great leveller.

Proverb

7 Fear of death is worse than death itself.

Proverb

8 Never speak ill of the dead.

Proverb

9 Nothing is certain but death and taxes.

Proverb

10 The good die young.

Proverb

11 The old man has his death before his eyes; the young man behind his back.

Proverb

12 There will be sleeping enough in the grave.

Proverb

13 It's not that I'm afraid to die. I just don't want to be there when it happens.

Woody Allen (Allen Stewart Konigsberg; 1935–) US film actor. *Without Feathers*, 'Death (A Play)'

14 God grants an easy death only to the just.

Svetlana Alliluyeva (1926–) Russian writer; daughter of Joseph Stalin. *Twenty Letters to a Friend*

15 As Amr lay on his death-bed a friend said to him: 'You have often remarked that you would like to find an intelligent man at the point of death, and to ask him what his feelings were. Now I ask *you* that question. Amr replied, 'I feel as if heaven lay close upon the earth and I between the two, breathing through the eye of a needle.'

Amr Ibn Al-As (d. 664) Arab conqueror of Egypt. *The Harvest of a Quiet Eye* (Alan L. Mackay)

16 O Death, where is thy sting-a-ling-a-ling,
O Grave, thy victoree?
The bells of hell go ting-a-ling-a-ling
For you but not for me.

Anonymous Song of World War I

17 Swing low sweet chariot,
Comin' for to carry me home,
I looked over Jordan an' what did I see?
A band of Angels coming after me,
Comin' for to carry me home.

Anonymous *Swing Low, Sweet Chariot*

18 He's gone to join the majority.

Petronius Arbiter (1st century AD) Roman satirist. Referring to a dead man. *Satyricon: Cena Trimalchionis*, 42

19 Now he is dead! Far hence he lies
In the lorn Syrian town;
And on his grave, with shining eyes,

The Syrian stars look down.

Matthew Arnold (1822–88) British poet and critic. *Obermann Once More*

20 I have often thought upon death, and I find it the least of all evils.

Francis Bacon (1561–1626) English philosopher. *An Essay on Death*

21 I do not believe that any man fears to be dead, but only the stroke of death.

Francis Bacon *An Essay on Death*

22 Men fear death, as children fear to go in the dark; and as that natural fear in children is increased with tales, so is the other.

Francis Bacon *Essays*, 'Of Death'

23 It is natural to die as to be born; and to a little infant, perhaps, the one is as painful as the other.

Francis Bacon *Essays*, 'Of Death'

24 To die will be an awfully big adventure.

J. M. Barrie (1860–1937) British novelist and dramatist. *Peter Pan*, III

25 Graveyards have a morbid reputation. Many people associate them with death.

Bishop of Bath and Wells (1935–) British churchman. Remark, Apr 1988

26 What I like about Clive
Is that he is no longer alive.
There is a great deal to be said
For being dead.

Edmund Clerihew Bentley (1875–1956) British writer. *Biography for Beginners*

27 The physician cutteth off a long disease; and he that is today a king tomorrow shall die.

Bible: Ecclesiasticus 10:10

28 Behold, I shew you a mystery; We shall not all sleep, but we shall all be changed,
In a moment, in the twinkling of an eye, at the last trump: for the trumpet shall sound, and the dead shall be raised incorruptible, and we shall be changed.
For this corruptible must put on incorruption, and this mortal must put on immortality.
So when this corruptible shall have put on incorruption, and this mortal shall have put on immortality, then shall be brought to pass the saying that is written, Death is swallowed up in victory.
O death, where is thy sting? O grave, where is thy victory?

Bible: I Corinthians 15:51–55

29 For all flesh is as grass, and all the glory of man as the flower of grass. The grass withereth, and the flower thereof falleth away.

Bible: I Peter 1:23–24

30 Lord, now lettest thou thy servant depart in peace, according to thy word:
For mine eyes have seen thy salvation,
Which thou hast prepared before the face of all people;
A light to lighten the Gentiles, and the glory of thy people Israel.

Bible: Luke 2:29–32

31 And I looked, and behold a pale horse: and his name that sat on him was Death, and Hell followed with him. And power was given unto them over the fourth part of the earth, to kill with sword, and with hunger, and with death, and with the beasts of the earth.

Bible: Revelations 6:8

32 Its visits,
Like those of angels, short, and far between.

Robert Blair (1699–1746) Scottish poet. *The Grave*

33 In the hour of death, and in the day of judgement.

The Book of Common Prayer *Morning Prayer, Prayer of St Chrysostom*

34 Any amusing deaths lately?

Maurice Bowra (1898–1971) British scholar. Attrib.

35 For I say, this is death, and the sole death,
When a man's loss comes to him from his gain,
Darkness from light, from knowledge ignorance,
And lack of love from love made manifest.

Robert Browning (1812–89) British poet. *A Death in the Desert*

36 It is important what a man still plans at the end. It shows the measure of injustice in his death.

Elias Canetti (1905–94) Bulgarian-born novelist. *The Human Province*

37 Days and moments quickly flying,
Blend the living with the dead;
Soon will you and I be lying
Each within our narrow bed.

Edward Caswall (1814–78) British hymn writer. Hymn

38 He had been, he said, a most unconscionable time dying; but he hoped that they would excuse it.

Charles II (1630–85) King of England. *History of England* (Macaulay), Vol. I, Ch. 4

39 Alack he's gone the way of all flesh.

William Congreve (1670–1729) British Restoration dramatist. *Squire Bickerstaff Detected*, attrib.

40 We perish'd, each alone:
But I beneath a rougher sea,
And whelm'd in deeper gulphs than he.

William Cowper (1731–1800) British poet. *The Castaway*

41 He'd make a lovely corpse.

Charles Dickens (1812–70) British novelist. *Martin Chuzzlewit*, Ch. 25

42 Because I could not stop for Death,
He kindly stopped for me;
The carriage held but just ourselves
And Immortality.

Emily Dickinson (1830–86) US poet. *The Chariot*

43 Our journey had advanced;
Our feet were almost come
To that odd fork in Being's road,

Eternity by term.

Emily Dickinson *Our Journey had Advanced*

44 Death be not proud, though some have called thee
Mighty and dreadful, for, thou art not so.

John Donne (1573–1631) English poet. *Holy Sonnets*, 10

45 Any man's death diminishes me, because I am involved in Mankind; And therefore never send to know for whom the bell tolls; it tolls for thee.

John Donne *Devotions*, 17

46 Sin brought death, and death will disappear with the disappearance of sin.

Mary Baker Eddy (1821–1910) US religious leader. *Science and Health, with Key to the Scriptures*

47 So death, the most terrifying of ills, is nothing to us, since so long as we exist, death is not with us; but when death comes, then we do not exist. It does not then concern either the living or the dead, since for the former it is not, and the latter are no more.

Epicurus (341–270 BC) Greek philosopher. *Letter to Menoeceus*

48 Death is my neighbour now.

Edith Evans (1888–1976) British actress. Said a week before her death. BBC radio interview, 14 Oct 1976

49 It hath been often said, that it is not death, but dying, which is terrible.

Henry Fielding (1707–54) British novelist. *Amelia*, Bk. III, Ch. 4

50 Strange, is it not? that of the myriads who
Before us pass'd the door of Darkness through,
Not one returns to tell us of the Road,
Which to discover we must travel too.

Edward Fitzgerald (1809–83) British poet. *The Rubáiyát of Omar Khayyám*

51 He hath shook hands with time.

John Ford (c. 1586–c. 1640) English dramatist. *The Broken Heart*, V:2

52 Death destroys a man, the idea of Death saves him.

E. M. Forster (1879–1970) British novelist. *Howards End*, Ch. 27

53 Dere's no more work for poor old Ned,
He's gone whar de good niggers go.

Stephen Foster (1826–64) US composer of popular songs. *Uncle Ned*

54 If Mr Selwyn calls again, shew him up: if I am alive I shall be delighted to see him; and if I am dead he would like to see me.

Henry Fox (1705–74) British politician. Said during his last illness. George Selwyn was known for his morbid fascination for dead bodies. *George Selwyn and his Contemporaries* (J. H. Jesse), Vol. III

55 Something lingering, with boiling oil in it, I fancy.

W. S. Gilbert (1836–1911) British dramatist. *The Mikado*, II

56 I am told he makes a very handsome corpse, and becomes his coffin prodigiously.

Oliver Goldsmith (1728–74) Irish-born British writer. *The Good-Natured Man*, I

57 Can storied urn or animated bust
Back to its mansion call the fleeting breath?
Can honour's voice provoke the silent dust,
Or flatt'ry soothe the dull cold ear of death?

Thomas Gray (1716–71) British poet. *Elegy Written in a Country Churchyard*

58 Here rests his head upon the lap of Earth
A youth to fortune and to fame unknown.
Fair Science frown'd not on his humble birth,
And Melancholy mark'd him for her own.

Thomas Gray *Elegy Written in a Country Churchyard*

59 Grieve not that I die young. Is it not well
To pass away ere life hath lost its brightness?

Lady Flora Hastings (1806–39) British poet. *Swan Song*

60 Death is still working like a mole,
And digs my grave at each remove.

George Herbert (1593–1633) English poet. *Grace*

61 Anno domini – that's the most fatal complaint of all in the end.

James Hilton (1900–54) British novelist. *Good-bye, Mr Chips*, Ch. 1

62 Death...It's the only thing we haven't succeeded in completely vulgarizing.

Aldous Huxley (1894–1964) British novelist. *Eyeless in Gaza*, Ch. 31

63 Our civilization is founded on the shambles, and every individual existence goes out in a lonely spasm of helpless agony.

William James (1842–1910) US psychologist and philosopher. *Varieties of Religious Experience*

64 Who doesn't regret Lazarus was not
Questioned about after-lives? Of course
He only reached death's threashold. I fear what
Dark exercises may with cunning powers
Do when I am brought
To my conclusion.

Elizabeth Jennings (1926–) British poet and writer. *The Fear of Death*

65 I die because I do not die.

St John of the Cross (Juan de Yepes y Alvarez; 1542–91) Spanish churchman and poet. *Coplas del alma que pena por ver a dios*

66 It matters not how a man dies, but how he lives. The act of dying is not of importance, it lasts so short a time.

Samuel Johnson (1709–84) British lexicographer. *Life of Johnson* (J. Boswell), Vol. II

67 I am able to follow my own death step by step. Now I move softly towards the end.

Pope John XXIII (Angelo Roncalli; 1881–1963) Italian churchman. Remark made two days before he died. *The Guardian*, 3 June 1963

68 Above ground I shall be food for kites; below I shall be food for mole-crickets and ants. Why rob one to feed the other?

Juang-zu (4th century BC) Chinese Taoist philosopher.

When asked on his deathbed what his wishes were regarding the disposal of his body. *Famous Last Words* (B. Conrad)

69 All right, my lord creator, Don Miguel, you too will die and return to the nothing whence you came. God will cease to dream you!

Miguel de Unamuno y Jugo (1864–1936) Spanish writer. *Mist*

70 Darkling I listen; and, for many a time
I have been half in love with easeful Death,
Call'd him soft names in many a mused rhyme,
To take into the air my quiet breath;
Now more than ever seems it rich to die,
To cease upon the midnight with no pain,
While thou art pouring forth thy soul abroad
In such an ecstasy!

John Keats (1795–1821) British poet. *Ode to a Nightingale*

71 I shall soon be laid in the quiet grave – thank God for the quiet grave – O! I can feel the cold earth upon me – the daisies growing over me – O for this quiet – it will be my first.

John Keats In a letter to John Taylor by Joseph Severn, 6 Mar 1821

72 Teach me to live, that I may dread
The grave as little as my bed.

Thomas Ken (1637–1711) English bishop. *An Evening Hymn*

73 In the long run we are all dead.

John Maynard Keynes (1883–1946) British economist. *Collected Writings*, 'A Tract on Monetary Reform'

74 That is the road we all have to take – over the Bridge of Sighs into eternity.

Søren Kierkegaard (1813–55) Danish philosopher. *Kierkegaard Anthology* (Auden)

75 O pity the dead that are dead, but cannot make
the journey, still they moan and beat
against the silvery adamant walls of life's exclusive city.

D. H. Lawrence (1885–1930) British novelist. *The Houseless Dead*

76 The dead don't die. They look on and help.

D. H. Lawrence Letter

77 I detest life-insurance agents. They always argue that I shall some day die, which is not so.

Stephen Leacock (1869–1944) English-born Canadian economist and humorist. *Literary Lapses*

78 It's better to die than become a victim of the whole dying industry – religion, morticians, politicians.

Timothy Leary (1920–96) US hippy leader. *The Guardian*, 2 Dec 1995

79 There is a Reaper whose name is Death,
And, with his sickle keen,
He reaps the bearded grain at a breath,
And the flowers that grow between.

Henry Wadsworth Longfellow (1807–82) US poet. *The Reaper and the Flowers*

80 It is the only disease you don't look forward to being cured of.

Herman J. Mankiewicz (1897–1953) US journalist and screenwriter. Referring to death. *Citizen Kane*

81 Cut is the branch that might have grown full straight,
And burned is Apollo's laurel-bough,
That sometime grew within this learned man.

Christopher Marlowe (1564–93) English dramatist. *Doctor Faustus*, Epilogue

82 The grave's a fine and private place,
But none, I think, do there embrace.

Andrew Marvell (1621–78) English poet. *To His Coy Mistress*

83 Either he's dead or my watch has stopped.

Groucho Marx (Julius Marx; 1895–1977) US comedian. *A Day at the Races*

84 My husband is dead.
– I'll bet he's just using that as an excuse.
I was with him to the end.
– No wonder he passed away.
I held him in my arms and kissed him.
– So it was murder!

Groucho Marx *Duck Soup*

85 Dying is a very dull, dreary affair. And my advice to you is to have nothing whatever to do with it.

W. Somerset Maugham (1874–1965) British novelist. *Escape from the Shadows* (Robin Maugham)

86 Alas! Lord and Lady Dalhousie are dead, and buried at last,
Which causes many people to feel a little downcast.

William McGonagall (1830–1902) Scottish poet. *The Death of Lord and Lady Dalhousie*

87 Whom the gods love dies young.

Menander (c. 341–c. 290 BC) Greek dramatist. *Dis Exapaton*

88 One dies only once, and it's for such a long time!

Molière (Jean Baptiste Poquelin; 1622–73) French dramatist. *Le Dépit amoureux*, V:3

89 Oh well, no matter what happens, there's always death.

Napoleon I (Napoleon Bonaparte; 1769–1821) French emperor. Attrib.

90 And in the happy no-time of his sleeping
Death took him by the heart.

Wilfred Owen (1893–1918) British poet. *Asleep*

91 It costs me never a stab nor squirm
To tread by chance upon a worm.
'Aha, my little dear,' I say,
'Your clan will pay me back one day.'

Dorothy Parker (1893–1967) US writer. *Sunset Gun*, 'Thought for a Sunshiny Morning'

92 She closed her eyes; and in sweet slumber lying
her spirit tiptoed from its lodging-place.
It's folly to shrink in fear, if this is dying;

for death looked lovely in her lovely face.

Petrarch (Francesco Petrarca; 1304–74) Italian poet. *Triumphs*

93 The surgeon is quiet, he does not speak.
He has seen too much death, his hands are full of it.

Sylvia Plath (1932–63) US poet and writer. *Winter Trees*, 'The Courage of Shutting-Up'

94 I mount! I fly!
O grave! where is thy victory?
O death! where is thy sting?

Alexander Pope (1688–1744) British poet. *The Dying Christian to his Soul*

95 Here am I, dying of a hundred good symptoms.

Alexander Pope *Anecdotes by and about Alexander Pope* (Joseph Spence)

96 How often are we to die before we go quite off this stage? In every friend we lose a part of ourselves, and the best part.

Alexander Pope Letter to Jonathan Swift, 5 Dec 1732

97 The hero is strangely akin to those who die young.

Rainer Maria Rilke (1875–1926) Austrian poet. *Duineser Elegien*, VI

98 I shall have more to say when I am dead.

Edwin Arlington Robinson (1869–1935) US poet. *John Brown*

99 When I am dead, my dearest,
Sing no sad songs for me;
Plant thou no roses at my head,
Nor shady cypress tree:
Be the green grass above me
With showers and dewdrops wet;
And if thou wilt, remember,
And if thou wilt, forget.

Christina Rossetti (1830–74) British poet. *When I am Dead*

100 He who pretends to look on death without fear lies. All men are afraid of dying, this is the great law of sentient beings, without which the entire human species would soon be destroyed.

Jean Jacques Rousseau (1712–78) French philosopher. *Julie, or the New Eloise*

101 To that dark inn, the grave!

Walter Scott (1771–1832) Scottish novelist. *The Lord of the Isles*, VI

102 His morning walk was beneath the elms in the churchyard; 'for death,' he said, 'had been his next-door neighbour for so many years, that he had no apology for dropping the acquaintance.'

Walter Scott *The Legend of Montrose*, Introduction

103 I have a rendezvous with Death
At some disputed barricade.

Alan Seeger (1888–1916) US poet. *I Have a Rendezvous with Death*

104 The rest is silence.

William Shakespeare (1564–1616) English dramatist. *Hamlet*, V:2

105 Why, he that cuts off twenty years of life
Cuts off so many years of fearing death.

William Shakespeare *Julius Caesar*, III:1

106 O mighty Caesar! dost thou lie so low?
Are all thy conquests, glories, triumphs, spoils,
Shrunk to this little measure?

William Shakespeare *Julius Caesar*, III:1

107 Ay, but to die, and go we know not where;
To lie in cold obstruction, and to rot;
This sensible warm motion to become
A kneaded clod; and the delighted spirit
To bathe in fiery floods or to reside
In thrilling region of thick-ribbed ice.

William Shakespeare *Measure for Measure*, III:1

108 Full fathom five thy father lies;
Of his bones are coral made;
Those are pearls that were his eyes;
Nothing of him that doth fade
But doth suffer a sea-change
Into something rich and strange.

William Shakespeare *The Tempest*, I:2

109 He that dies pays all debts.

William Shakespeare *The Tempest*, III:2

110 Nothing in his life
Became him like the leaving it: he died
As one that had been studied in his death
To throw away the dearest thing he ow'd
As 'twere a careless trifle.

William Shakespeare *Macbeth*, I:4

111 But thoughts, the slaves of life, and life, time's fool,
And time, that takes survey of all the world,
Must have a stop.

William Shakespeare *Henry IV, Part One*, V:4

112 His nose was as sharp as a pen, and
'a babbl'd of green fields.

William Shakespeare Referring to Falstaff on his deathbed. *Henry V*, II:3

113 I care not; a man can die but once; we owe God a death.

William Shakespeare *Henry IV, Part Two*, III:2

114 Death is the veil which those who live call life:
They sleep, and it is lifted.

Percy Bysshe Shelley (1792–1822) British poet. *Prometheus Unbound*, III

115 It is a modest creed, and yet
Pleasant if one considers it,
To own that death itself must be,
Like all the rest, a mockery.

Percy Bysshe Shelley *The Sensitive Plant*, III

116 I cannot forgive my friends for dying: I do not find these vanishing acts of theirs at all amusing.

Logan Pearsall Smith (1865–1946) US writer. *Trivia*

117 I do really think that death will be marvellous...If there wasn't death, I think you couldn't go on.

Stevie Smith (Florence Margaret Smith; 1902–71) British poet. *The Observer*, 9 Nov 1969

118 The whole of his life had prepared Podduyev for living, not for dying.

Alexander Solzhenitsyn (1918–) Soviet novelist. *Cancer Ward*, Pt. I, Ch. 8

119 Sleep after toil, port after stormy seas,
Ease after war, death after life does greatly please.

Edmund Spenser (1552–99) English poet. *The Faerie Queene*, I:9

120 Under the wide and starry sky
Dig the grave and let me lie.
Glad did I live and gladly die,
– And I laid me down with a will.
This is the verse you grave for me:
'Here he lies where he longed to be;
Home is the sailor, home from sea,
And the hunter home from the hill.'

Robert Louis Stevenson (1850–94) Scottish writer. *Underwoods*, Bk. I, 'Requiem'

121 Even so, in death the same unknown will appear as ever known to me. And because I love this life, I know I shall love death as well. The child cries out when from the right breast the mother takes it away, in the very next moment to find in the left one its consolation.

Rabindranath Tagore (1861–1941) Indian poet and philosopher. *Gitanjali*

122 Row upon row with strict impunity
The headstones yield their names to the element.

Allen Tate (1899–1979) US poet. *Ode to the Confederate Dead*

123 A day less or more
At sea or ashore,
We die – does it matter when?

Alfred, Lord Tennyson (1809–92) British poet. *The Revenge*, XI

124 I, born of flesh and ghost, was neither
A ghost nor man, but mortal ghost.
And I was struck down by death's feather.

Dylan Thomas (1914–53) Welsh poet. *Before I knocked*

125 After the first death, there is no other.

Dylan Thomas *A Refusal to Mourn the Death, by Fire, of a Child in London*

126 Do not go gentle into that good night,
Old age should burn and rave at close of day;
Rage, rage, against the dying of the light.

Dylan Thomas *Do not go gentle into that good night*

127 There is not any book
Or face of dearest look
That I would not turn from now
To go into the unknown
I must enter, and leave, alone,
I know not how.

Edward Thomas (1878–1917) British poet. *Lights Out*

128 Go and try to disprove death. Death will disprove you, and that's all!

Ivan Turgenev (1818–83) Russian novelist. *Fathers and Sons*, Ch. 27

129 While I thought that I was learning how to live, I have been learning how to die.

Leonardo da Vinci (1452–1519) Italian artist. *Notebooks*

130 There's no repentance in the grave.

Isaac Watts (1674–1748) English theologian and hymn writer. *Divine Songs for Children*, 'Solemn Thoughts of God and Death'

131 For he who lives more lives than one
More deaths than one must die.

Oscar Wilde (1854–1900) Irish-born British dramatist. *The Ballad of Reading Gaol*, III:37

132 Dead! and…never called me mother.

Mrs Henry Wood (1814–87) British novelist. *East Lynne* (dramatized version; the words do not occur in the novel)

133 Three years she grew in sun and shower,
Then Nature said, 'A lovelier flower
On earth was never sown;
This child I to myself will take;
She shall be mine, and I will make
A Lady of my own.

William Wordsworth (1770–1850) British poet. *Three Years she Grew*

134 We are laid asleep
In body, and become a living soul:
While with an eye made quiet by the power
Of harmony, and the deep power of joy,
We see into the life of things.

William Wordsworth *Lines composed a few miles above Tintern Abbey*

DEBAUCHERY

See also animalism, lust, pleasure, sex

1 A fool bolts pleasure, then complains of moral indigestion.

Minna Antrim (b. 1861) US writer. *Naked Truth and Veiled Allusions*

2 A great many people have come up to me and asked how I manage to get so much work done and still keep looking so dissipated.

Robert Benchley (1889–1945) US humorist. *Chips off the Old Benchley*, 'How to Get Things Done'

3 *Debauchee*, n. One who has so earnestly pursued pleasure that he has had the misfortune to overtake it.

Ambrose Bierce (1842–?1914) US writer and journalist. *The Devil's Dictionary*

4 So, we'll go no more a roving
So late into the night,
Though the heart be still as loving,
And the moon be still as bright.

Lord Byron (1788–1824) British poet. *So, we'll go no more a roving*

5 I've over-educated myself in all the things I

shouldn't have known at all.

Noël Coward (1899–1973) British dramatist. *Wild Oats*

6 No one ever suddenly became depraved.

Juvenal (Decimus Junius Juvenalis; 60–130 AD) Roman satirist. *Satires*, II

7 We're poor little lambs who've lost our way,
Baa! Baa! Baa!
We're little black sheep who've gone astray,
Baa-aa-aa!
Gentleman-rankers out on the spree,
Damned from here to Eternity,
God ha' mercy on such as we,
Baa! Yah! Bah!

Rudyard Kipling (1865–1936) Indian-born British writer. *Gentleman-Rankers*

8 Home is heaven and orgies are vile
But you need an orgy, once in a while.

Ogden Nash (1902–71) US poet. *Home, 99.44100% Sweet Home*

9 Once: a philosopher; twice: a pervert!

Voltaire (François-Marie Arouet; 1694–1778) French writer. Turning down an invitation to an orgy, having attended one the previous night for the first time. Attrib.

DECEPTION

See also appearances, hypocrisy, insincerity, lying

1 To deceive oneself is very easy.

Proverb

2 Beware of false prophets, which come to you in sheep's clothing, but inwardly they are ravening wolves.

Bible: Matthew 7:15

3 Almost every man wastes part of his life in attempts to display qualities which he does not possess, and to gain applause which he cannot keep.

Samuel Johnson (1709–84) British lexicographer. *The Rambler*

4 You can fool some of the people all the time and all the people some of the time; but you can't fool all the people all the time.

Abraham Lincoln (1809–65) US statesman. Attrib.

5 False face must hide what the false heart doth know.

William Shakespeare (1564–1616) English dramatist. *Macbeth*, I:7

6 You can fool too many of the people too much of the time.

James Thurber (1894–1961) US humorist. *Fables for Our Time*, 'The Owl Who Was God'

7 I have invented an invaluable permanent invalid called Bunbury, in order that I may be able to go down into the country whenever I choose.

Oscar Wilde (1854–1900) Irish-born British dramatist. *The Importance of Being Earnest*, I

DECISION

See also determination

1 Tender-handed stroke a nettle,
And it stings you for your pains;
Grasp it like a man of mettle,
And it soft as silk remains.

Aaron Hill (1685–1750) British poet and dramatist. *Verses Written on Window*

2 Like all weak men he laid an exaggerated stress on not changing one's mind.

W. Somerset Maugham (1874–1965) British novelist. *Of Human Bondage*, Ch. 37

3 If someone tells you he is going to make 'a realistic decision', you immediately understand that he has resolved to do something bad.

Mary McCarthy (1912–89) US novelist. *On the Contrary*

DECLINE

1 And though the Van Dycks have to go
And we pawn the Bechstein grand,
We'll stand by the Stately Homes of England.

Noël Coward (1899–1973) British dramatist. *Operette*, The Stately Homes of England

2 That's Why the Lady Is a Tramp.

Lorenz Hart (1895–1943) US songwriter. From the musical *Babes in Arms*. Song title

3 It is the logic of our times,
No subject for immortal verse –
That we who lived by honest dreams
Defend the bad against the worse.

C. Day Lewis (1904–72) British poet. *Where are the War Poets?*

4 From morn
To noon he fell, from noon to dewy eve,
A summer's day, and with the setting sun
Dropped from the zenith, like a falling star.

John Milton (1608–74) English poet. *Paradise Lost*, Bk. I

5 Macmillan seemed, in his very person, to embody the national decay he supposed himself to be confuting. He exuded a flavour of moth-balls.

Malcolm Muggeridge (1903–90) British writer. *Tread Softly For You Tread on My Jokes*, 'England, whose England'

6 It is only a step from the sublime to the ridiculous.

Napoleon I (Napoleon Bonaparte; 1769–1821) French emperor. Remark following the retreat from Moscow, 1812. Attrib.

7 We have on our hands a sick man – a very sick man.

Nicholas I (1796–1855) Tsar of Russia. Referring to Turkey, the 'sick man of Europe'; said to Sir G. H. Seymour, British envoy to St Petersburg, Jan 1853. Attrib.

8 Now there are fields where Troy once was.

Ovid (Publius Ovidius Naso; 43 BC–17 AD) Roman poet. *Heroides*, Bk. I

9 There may have been disillusionments in the

lives of the medieval saints, but they would scarcely have been better pleased if they could have foreseen that their names would be associated nowadays chiefly with racehorses and the cheaper clarets.

Saki (Hector Hugh Munro; 1870–1916) British writer. *Reginald at the Carlton*

10 I shall be like that tree; I shall die from the top.

Jonathan Swift (1667–1745) Irish-born Anglican priest and writer. Predicting his own mental decline on seeing a tree with a withered crown. *Lives of the Wits* (H. Pearson)

11 I dreamed there would be Spring no more,
That Nature's ancient power was lost.

Alfred, Lord Tennyson (1809–92) British poet. *In Memoriam A.H.H.*, LXIX

12 The difference between our decadence and the Russians' is that while theirs is brutal, ours is apathetic.

James Thurber (1894–1961) US humorist. *The Observer*, 'Sayings of the Week', 5 Feb 1961

13 I started at the top and worked my way down.

Orson Welles (1915–85) US film actor. *The Filmgoer's Book of Quotes* (Leslie Halliwell)

14 Plain living and high thinking are no more.

William Wordsworth (1770–1850) British poet. *Sonnets*, 'O friend! I know not'

15 Milton! thou shouldst be living at this hour:
England hath need of thee; she is a fen
Of stagnant waters: altar, sword, and pen,
Fireside, the heroic wealth of hall and bower,
Have forfeited their ancient English dower
Of inward happiness.

William Wordsworth *Sonnets*, 'Milton! thou shouldst'

DEFEAT

See also loss

1 'Tis better to have fought and lost,
Than never to have fought at all.

Arthur Hugh Clough (1819–61) British poet. *Peschiera*

2 Of all I had, only honour and life have been spared.

Francis I (1494–1547) King of France. Referring to his defeat at the Battle of Pavia, 24 Feb 1525; usually misquoted as 'All is lost save honour.'. Letter to Louise of Savoy (his mother), 1525

3 A man can be destroyed but not defeated.

Ernest Hemingway (1899–1961) US novelist. *The Old Man and the Sea*

4 Woe to the vanquished.

Livy (Titus Livius; 59 BC–17 AD) Roman historian. *History*, V:48

5 When I am dead and opened, you shall find 'Calais' lying in my heart.

Mary I (1516–58) Queen of England. *Chronicles* (Holinshed), III

6 Every man meets his Waterloo at last.

Wendell Phillips (1811–84) US reformer. Speech, Brooklyn, 1 Nov 1859

7 Well, I have one consolation, No candidate was ever elected ex-president by such a large majority!

William Howard Taft (1857–1930) US statesman. Referring to his disastrous defeat in the 1912 presidential election. Attrib.

8 It is the beginning of the end.

Talleyrand (Charles Maurice de Talleyrand-Périgord; 1754–1838) French politician. Referring to Napoleon's defeat at Borodino, 1813. Attrib.

9 Another year! – another deadly blow!
Another mighty empire overthrown!
And we are left, or shall be left, alone.

William Wordsworth (1770–1850) British poet. Napoleon defeated Prussia at the Battles of Jena and Anerstädt, 14 Oct 1806. *Sonnets*, 'Another year!'

DELUSION

1 But yet the light that led astray
Was light from Heaven.

Robert Burns (1759–96) Scottish poet. *The Vision*

2 Take care, your worship, those things over there are not giants but windmills.

Miguel de Cervantes (1547–1616) Spanish novelist. *Don Quixote*, Pt. I, Ch. 8

3 Didn't I tell you, Don Quixote, sir, to turn back, for they were not armies you were going to attack, but flocks of sheep?

Miguel de Cervantes *Don Quixote*, Pt. I, Ch. 18

4 Take the life-lie away from the average man and straight away you take away his happiness.

Henrik Ibsen (1828–1906) Norwegian dramatist. *The Wild Duck*, V

5 Many people have delusions of grandeur but you're deluded by triviality.

Eugène Ionesco (1912–94) French dramatist. *Exit the King*

DEMOCRACY

See also class, government, majority, public, republic

1 Democracy means government by discussion but it is only effective if you can stop people talking.

Clement Attlee (1883–1967) British statesman and Labour prime minister. *Anatomy of Britain* (Anthony Sampson)

2 One man shall have one vote.

John Cartwright (1740–1824) British writer. *People's Barrier Against Undue Influence*

3 Democracy means government by the uneducated, while aristocracy means government by the badly educated.

G. K. Chesterton (1874–1936) British writer. *New York Times*, 1 Feb 1931

4 Populism is on the increase – a populism that

rejects anything different, anyone with a different-coloured skin, or a different race or religion. This is the real danger and unspoken risk that threatens to pollute democracy.

Jacques Delors (1925–) French politician and European statesman. *The Independent*, 19 May 1994

5 Some comrades apparently find it hard to understand that democracy is just a slogan.

Mikhail Gorbachov (1931–) Soviet statesman. *The Observer*, 'Sayings of the Week', 1 Feb 1987

6 Democracy can't work. Mathematicians, peasants, and animals, that's all there is – so democracy, a theory based on the assumption that mathematicians and peasants are equal, can never work. Wisdom is not additive; its maximum is that of the wisest man in a given group.

Robert Heinlein (1907–88) US science-fiction writer. *Glory Road*, Ch. 20

7 Democracy is only an experiment in government, and it has the obvious disadvantage of merely counting votes instead of weighing them.

Dean Inge (1860–1954) British churchman. *Possible Recovery?*

8 The vote is the most powerful instrument ever devised by man for breaking down injustice and destroying the terrible walls which imprison men because they are different from other men.

Lyndon B. Johnson (1908–73) US statesman. Address on signing Voting Rights Bill, Washington, DC, 6 Aug 1965

9 No man is good enough to govern another man without that other's consent.

Abraham Lincoln (1809–65) US statesman. Speech, 1854

10 The ballot is stronger than the bullet.

Abraham Lincoln Speech, 19 May 1856

11 This country, with its institutions, belongs to the people who inhabit it. Whenever they shall grow weary of the existing government, they can exercise their constitutional right of amending it, or their revolutionary right to dismember or overthrow it.

Abraham Lincoln First Inaugural Address, 4 Mar 1861

12 ...that government of the people, by the people, and for the people, shall not perish from the earth.

Abraham Lincoln Speech, 19 Nov 1863, dedicating the national cemetery on the site of the Battle of Gettesburg

13 To have good government, you often need less, not more, democracy.

Kishore Mahbubani (1948–) Singaporean diplomatist. *The Observer*, 'Sayings of the Week', 17 Apr 1994

14 Man's capacity for evil makes democracy necessary and man's capacity for good makes democracy possible.

Reinhold Niebuhr (1892–1971) US churchman. Quoted by Anthony Wedgwood Benn in *The Times*, 18 Jul 1977

15 Democracy passes into despotism.

Plato (429–347 BC) Greek philosopher. *Republic*, Bk. 8

16 I think if the people of this country can be reached with the truth, their judgment will be in favor of the many, as against the privileged few.

Eleanor Roosevelt (1884–1962) US writer and lecturer. *Ladies' Home Journal*

17 We must be the great arsenal of democracy.

Franklin D. Roosevelt (1882–1945) US Democratic president. Broadcast address to Forum on Current Problems, 29 Dec 1940

18 We must be thoroughly democratic and patronise everybody without distinction of class.

George Bernard Shaw (1856–1950) Irish dramatist and critic. *John Bull's Other Island*

19 It's not the voting that's democracy; it's the counting.

Tom Stoppard (1937–) Czech-born British dramatist. *Jumpers*

20 Development requires democracy, the genuine empowerment of the people.

Aung San Suu Kyi (1945–) Burmese politician and human rights activist. *The Times*, 22 Nov 1994

21 A committee should consist of three men, two of whom are absent.

Herbert Beerbohm Tree (1853–1917) British actor and theater manager. *Beerbohm Tree* (H. Pearson)

22 I shall not vote because I do not aspire to advise my sovereign on the choice of her servants.

Evelyn Waugh (1903–66) British novelist. *A Little Order*

23 Democracy means simply the bludgeoning of the people by the people for the people.

Oscar Wilde (1854–1900) Irish-born British dramatist. *The Soul of Man under Socialism*

24 The world must be made safe for democracy.

Woodrow Wilson (1856–1925) US statesman. Address to Congress, asking for a declaration of war 2 Apr 1917

DENIAL

1 I am the spirit that always denies.

Goethe (1749–1832) German poet and dramatist. *Faust*, Pt. I

2 No, I am no one's contemporary – ever.
That would have been above my station...
How I loathe that other with my name.
He certainly never was me.

Osip Mandelstam (1891–1938) Russian poet. *Poems*, No. 141

3 I am not a crook.

Richard Milhous Nixon (1913–94) US president. Attrib., 17 Nov 1973

4 He would, wouldn't he?

Mandy Rice-Davies (1944–) British call girl. Of Lord Astor, when told that he had repudiated her evidence at the trial of Stephen Ward, 29 June 1963

DEPARTURE

See also dismissal, parting

1 Come, dear children, let us away;

Down and away below.

Matthew Arnold (1822–88) British poet and critic. *The Forsaken Merman*

2 She left lonely for ever
The kings of the sea.

Matthew Arnold *The Forsaken Merman*

3 Once I leave, I leave. I am not going to speak to the man on the bridge, and I am not going to spit on the deck.

Stanley Baldwin (1867–1947) British statesman. Statement to the Cabinet, 28 May 1937

4 Adieu, adieu! my native shore
Fades o'er the waters blue.

Lord Byron (1788–1824) British poet. *Childe Harold's Pilgrimage*, I

5 My native Land – Good Night!

Lord Byron *Childe Harold's Pilgrimage*, I

6 Let us go then, you and I,
When the evening is spread out against the sky
Like a patient etherized upon a table.

T. S. Eliot (1888–1965) US-born British poet and dramatist. *The Love Song of J. Alfred Prufrock*

7 And they are gone: aye, ages long ago
These lovers fled away into the storm.

John Keats (1795–1821) British poet. *The Eve of Saint Agnes*, XLII

8 She's leaving home after living alone for so many years.

John Lennon (1940–80) British rock musician. *She's Leaving Home* (with Paul McCartney)

DESIGN

See also art

1 Demand bare walls in your bedroom, your living room and your dining room. Built-in furniture takes the place of much of the furniture which is expensive to buy…Demand concealed or diffused lighting. Demand a vacuum cleaner. Buy only practical furniture and never buy 'decorative' pieces. If you want to see bad taste, go into the houses of the rich. Put only a few pictures on your walls and none but good ones.

Le Corbusier (Charles-Édouard Jeanneret; 1887–1965) French architect.

2 A machine for living in.

Le Corbusier Referring to a house. *Towards a New Architecture*

3 It is not this or that tangible steel or brass machine which we want to get rid of, but the great intangible machine of commercial tyranny which oppresses the lives of us all.

William Morris (1834–96) British designer, artist, and poet.

4 Nothing should be made by man's labour which is not worth making or which must be made by labour degrading to the makers.

William Morris

5 Art will make our streets as beautiful as the woods, as elevating as the mountain-side: it will be a pleasure and a rest, and not a weight upon the spirits to come from the open country into a town. Every man's house will be fair and decent, soothing to his mind and helpful to his work.

William Morris

6 Today industrial design has put murder on a mass-production basis.

Victor Papanek *Design for the Real World*

7 It will be a great day when cutlery and furniture designs (to name but two) swing like the Supremes.

Michael Wolff

8 The tall modern office building is the machine pure and simple…the engine, the motor and the battleship the works of the century.

Frank Lloyd Wright (1869–1959) US architect.

DESIRE

See also hunger, lust, thirst

1 Give me my golf clubs, fresh air and a beautiful partner, and you can keep my golf clubs and the fresh air.

Jack Benny (Benjamin Kubelsky; 1894–1974) US actor. Attrib.

2 Those who restrain Desire, do so because theirs is weak enough to be restrained.

William Blake (1757–1827) British poet. *The Marriage of Heaven and Hell*, 'Those who restrain Desire…'

3 Sooner murder an infant in its cradle than nurse unacted desires.

William Blake *The Marriage of Heaven and Hell*, 'Proverbs of Hell'

4 Man's Desires are limited by his Perceptions; none can desire what he has not perceived.

William Blake *There is no Natural Religion*

5 A sight to dream of, not to tell!

Samuel Taylor Coleridge (1772–1834) British poet. *Christabel*, I

6 O, she is the antidote to desire.

William Congreve (1670–1729) British Restoration dramatist. *The Way of the World*, IV:14

7 Someday I'll wish upon a star.

E. Y. Harburg (1896–1981) US songwriter. From the musical *The Wizard of Oz. Over the Rainbow*

8 Somewhere over the rainbow,
Way up high:
There's a land that I heard of
Once in a lullaby.

E. Y. Harburg From the musical *The Wizard of Oz. Over the Rainbow*

9 Ship me somewheres east of Suez, where the best is like the worst,
Where there aren't no Ten Commandments, an' a man can raise a thirst:

For the temple-bells are callin', an' it's there that I would be –
By the old Moulmein Pagoda, looking lazy at the sea.

Rudyard Kipling (1865–1936) Indian-born British writer. *The Road to Mandalay*

10 All I want is a room somewhere,
Far away from the cold night air;
With one enormous chair...
Oh, wouldn't it be loverly?

Alan Jay Lerner (1918–86) US songwriter. *My Fair Lady*, I:1

11 There is wishful thinking in Hell as well as on earth.

C. S. Lewis (1898–1963) British academic and writer. *The Screwtape Letters*, Preface

12 There is nothing like desire for preventing the thing one says from bearing any resemblance to what one has in mind.

Marcel Proust (1871–1922) French novelist. *À la recherche du temps perdu: Le Côté de Guermantes*

13 Appetite comes with eating.

François Rabelais (1483–1553) French satirist. *Gargantua*, Bk. I, Ch. 5

14 That she belov'd knows nought that knows not this:
Men prize the thing ungain'd more than it is.

William Shakespeare (1564–1616) English dramatist. *Troilus and Cressida*, I:2

15 There are two tragedies in life. One is to lose your heart's desire. The other is to gain it.

George Bernard Shaw (1856–1950) Irish dramatist and critic. *Man and Superman*, IV

16 Desire is the very essence of man.

Benedict Spinoza (Baruch de Spinoza; 1632–77) Dutch philosopher. *Ethics*

17 As soon as you stop wanting something you get it. I've found that to be absolutely axiomatic.

Andy Warhol (Andrew Warhola; 1926–87) US pop artist. Attrib.

18 And pluck till time and times are done
The silver apples of the moon
The golden apples of the sun.

W. B. Yeats (1865–1939) Irish poet. *The Song of Wandering Aengus*

DESPAIR

See also sorrow

1 And about the ninth hour Jesus cried with a loud voice, saying, Eli, Eli, lama sabachthani? that is to say, My God, my God, why hast thou forsaken me?

Bible: Matthew 27:46

2 The name of the slough was Despond.

John Bunyan (1628–88) English writer. *The Pilgrim's Progress*, Pt. I

3 A castle called Doubting Castle, the owner whereof was Giant Despair.

John Bunyan *The Pilgrim's Progress*, Pt. I

4 Not, I'll not, carrion comfort, Despair, not feast on thee;
Not untwist – slack they may be – these last strands of man
In me or, most weary, cry *I can no more.* I can;
Can something, hope, wish day come, not choose not to be.

Gerard Manley Hopkins (1844–99) British Jesuit and poet. *Carrion Comfort*

5 Don't despair, not even over the fact that you don't despair.

Franz Kafka (1883–1924) Czech novelist. *Diary*

6 The mass of men lead lives of quiet desperation.

Henry David Thoreau (1817–62) US writer. *Walden*, 'Economy'

DESTINY

See also purpose

1 What must be, must be.

Proverb

2 Whatever may happen to you was prepared for you from all eternity; and the implication of causes was from eternity spinning the thread of your being.

Marcus Aurelius (121–180 AD) Roman emperor. *Meditations*, Bk. X, Ch. 5

3 Everything that happens happens as it should, and if you observe carefully, you will find this to be so.

Marcus Aurelius *Meditations*, Bk. IV, Ch. 10

4 I felt as if I were walking with destiny, and that all my past life had been but a preparation for this hour and this trial.

Winston Churchill (1874–1965) British statesman. *The Gathering Storm*, Ch. 38

5 Which brings me to my conclusion upon Free Will and Predestination, namely – let the reader mark it – that they are identical.

Winston Churchill *My Early Life*, Ch. 3

6 Whatever Nature has in store for mankind, unpleasant as it may be, men must accept, for ignorance is never better than knowledge.

Enrico Fermi *Atoms in the Family* (Laura Fermi)

7 'Tis all a Chequer-board of Nights and Days
Where Destiny with Men for Pieces plays:
Hither and thither moves, and mates, and slays,
And one by one back in the Closet lays.

Edward Fitzgerald (1809–83) British poet. *The Rubáiyát of Omar Khayyám*, XLIX

8 The Moving Finger writes; and, having writ,
Moves on: nor all thy Piety nor Wit
Shall lure it back to cancel half a Line,
Nor all thy Tears wash out a Word of it.

Edward Fitzgerald *The Rubáiyát of Omar Khayyám*, LI

9 And that inverted Bowl we call The Sky,
Whereunder crawling coop't we live and die,
Lift not thy hands to *It* for help – for It
Rolls impotently on as Thou or I.

Edward Fitzgerald *The Rubáiyát of Omar Khayyám*, LII

10 Drink! for you know not whence you came, nor why:
Drink! for you know not why you go, nor where.

Edward Fitzgerald *The Rubáiyát of Omar Khayyám*, LXXIV

11 Tempt not the stars, young man, thou canst not play
With the severity of fate.

John Ford (c. 1586–c. 1640) English dramatist. *The Broken Heart*, I:3

12 I go the way that Providence dictates with the assurance of a sleepwalker.

Adolf Hitler (1889–1945) German dictator. Referring to his successful re-occupation of the Rhineland, despite advice against the attempt. Speech, Munich, 15 Mar 1936

13 Do not try to find out – we're forbidden to know – what end the gods have in store for me, or for you.

Horace (Quintus Horatius Flaccus; 65–8 BC) Roman poet. *Odes*, I

14 Who can foretell for what high cause
This darling of the Gods was born?

Andrew Marvell (1621–78) English poet. *The Picture of Little T.C. in a Prospect of Flowers*

15 And yet the order of the acts is planned,
The way's end destinate and unconcealed.
Alone. Now is the time of Pharisees.
To live is not like walking through a field.

Boris Pasternak (1890–1960) Russian Jewish poet and novelist. *Hamlet* (trans. Henry Kamen)

16 We may become the makers of our fate when we have ceased to pose as its prophets.

Karl Popper (1902–94) Austrian-born British philosopher. *The Observer*, 28 Dec 1975

17 Man never found the deities so kindly
As to assure him that he'd live tomorrow.

François Rabelais (1483–1553) French satirist. *Pantagruel*, Bk. III, Ch. 2

18 Fate sits on these dark battlements, and frowns;
And as the portals open to receive me,
Her voice, in sullen echoes, through the courts,
Tells of a nameless deed.

Ann Radcliffe (1764–1823) British novelist. *The Mysteries of Udolpho*

19 There's a divinity that shapes our ends,
Rough-hew them how we will.

William Shakespeare (1564–1616) English dramatist. *Hamlet*, V:2

20 As flies to wanton boys are we to th' gods –
They kill us for their sport.

William Shakespeare *King Lear*, IV:1

21 The ancient saying is no heresy:
Hanging and wiving goes by destiny.

William Shakespeare *The Merchant of Venice*, II:9

22 One God, one law, one element,
And one far-off divine event,
To which the whole creation moves.

Alfred, Lord Tennyson (1809–92) British poet. *In Memoriam A.H.H.*, CXXXI

23 I embrace the purpose of God and the doom assigned.

Alfred, Lord Tennyson *Maud*, III

24 We are merely the stars' tennis-balls, struck and bandied
Which way please them.

John Webster (1580–1625) English dramatist. *The Duchess of Malfi*, V:4

25 Every bullet has its billet.

William III (1650–1702) King of England. *Journal* (John Wesley), 6 June 1765

DETERMINATION

See also decision, endurance, inflexibility, persistence, stubbornness

1 He who hesitates is lost.

Proverb

2 Where there's a will there's a way.

Proverb

3 Don't listen to anyone who tells you that you can't do this or that. That's nonsense. Make up your mind, you'll never use crutches or a stick, then have a go at everything. Go to school, join in all the games you can. Go anywhere you want to. But never, never let them persuade you that things are too difficult or impossible.

Douglas Bader (1910–82) British fighter pilot. Speaking to a fourteen-year-old boy who had had a leg amputated after a road accident. *Flying Colours* (Laddie Lucas)

4 There is no such thing as a great talent without great will-power.

Honoré de Balzac (1799–1850) French novelist. *La Muse du département*

5 Let us determine to die here, and we will conquer.
There is Jackson standing like a stone wall. Rally behind the Virginians.

Barnard Elliot Bee (1824–61) US soldier. Said at the First Battle of Bull Run, 1861; hence Gen Thomas Jackson's nickname, 'Stonewall Jackson'. *Reminiscences of Metropolis* (Poore), II

6 We will not go to Canossa.

Bismarck (1815–98) German statesman. A declaration of his anti-Roman Catholic policy; the Emperor Henry IV had submitted to Pope Gregory VII at Canossa, N. Italy, in 1077. Speech, Reichstag, 14 May 1872

7 The spirit burning but unbent,
May writhe, rebel – the weak alone repent!

Lord Byron (1788–1824) British poet. *The Corsair*, II

8 I purpose to fight it out on this line, if it takes all summer.

Ulysses Simpson Grant (1822–85) US general. Dispatch to Washington, 11 May 1864

9 I will be conquered; I will not capitulate.

Samuel Johnson (1709–84) British lexicographer. Referring to his illness. *Life of Johnson* (J. Boswell), Vol. IV

10 I have not yet begun to fight.

John Paul Jones (1747–92) Scottish-born US naval commander. Retort when informed his ship was sinking. *Life and Letters of J. P. Jones* (De Koven), Vol. I

11 I shall return.

Douglas Macarthur (1880–1964) US general. Message (11 Mar 1942) on leaving for Australia from Corregidor Island (Philippines), which he had been defending against the Japanese

12 What though the field be lost?
All is not lost – the unconquerable will,
And study of revenge, immortal hate,
And courage never to submit or yield:
And what is else not to be overcome?

John Milton (1608–74) English poet. *Paradise Lost*, Bk. I

13 Look for me by moonlight;
Watch for me by moonlight;
I'll come to thee by moonlight, though hell
should bar the way!

Alfred Noyes (1880–1958) British poet. *The Highwayman*

14 *Ils ne passeront pas.*
They shall not pass.

Marshal Pétain (1856–1951) French marshal. Attrib; probably derived from General R.-G. Nivelle's Order of the Day, *'Vous ne les laisserez pas passer'* (June 1916). It is also attributed to the Spanish politician Dolores Ibarruri.

15 We are not now that strength which in old days
Moved earth and heaven; that which we are, we are;
One equal temper of heroic hearts,
Made weak by time and fate, but strong in will
To strive, to seek, to find, and not to yield.

Alfred, Lord Tennyson (1809–92) British poet. *Ulysses*

DEVIL

See also damnation, hell

1 The devil is not so black as he is painted.

Proverb

2 And he said unto them, I beheld Satan as lightning fall from heaven.

Bible: Luke 10:18

3 And he asked him, What is thy name? And he answered, saying. My name is Legion: for we are many.

Bible: Mark 5:9

4 And there was war in heaven: Michael and his angels fought against the dragon; and the dragon fought and his angels,
And prevailed not; neither was their place found any more in heaven.
And the great dragon was cast out, that old serpent, called the Devil, and Satan, which deceiveth the whole world: he was cast out into the earth, and his angels were cast out with him.

Bible: Revelations 12:7–9

5 And that no man might buy or sell, save he that had the mark, or the name of the beast, or the number of his name.
Here is wisdom. Let him that hath understanding count the number of the beast: for it is the number of a man; and his number is Six hundred threescore and six.

Bible: Revelations 13:17–18

6 O Thou! Whatever title suit thee –
Auld Hornie, Satan, Nick, or Clootie.

Robert Burns (1759–96) Scottish poet. *Address to the Devil*

7 Wherever God erects a house of prayer,
The Devil always builds a chapel there;
And 'twill be found, upon examination,
The latter has the largest congregation.

Daniel Defoe (1660–1731) British journalist and writer. *The True-Born Englishman*, Pt. I

8 It is so stupid of modern civilization to have given up believing in the devil when he is the only explanation of it.

Ronald Knox (1888–1957) British Roman Catholic priest. *Let Dons Delight*

9 It is no good casting out devils. They belong to us, we must accept them and be at peace with them.

D. H. Lawrence (1885–1930) British novelist. *Phoenix*, 'The Reality of Peace'

10 High on a throne of royal state, which far
Outshone the wealth of Ormus and of Ind,
Or where the gorgeous East with richest hand
Showers on her kings barbaric pearl and gold,
Satan exalted sat, by merit raised
To that bad eminence.

John Milton (1608–74) English poet. *Paradise Lost*, Bk. II

11 Sometimes
The Devil is a gentleman.

Percy Bysshe Shelley (1792–1822) British poet. *Peter Bell the Third*

DIARIES

1 Let diaries, therefore, be brought in use.

Francis Bacon (1561–1626) English philosopher. *Essays*, 'Of Travel'

2 Only good girls keep diaries. Bad girls don't have the time.

Tallulah Bankhead (1903–68) US actress. Attrib.

3 With the publication of his Private Papers in 1952, he committed suicide 25 years after his death.

Lord Beaverbrook (1879–1964) British newspaper owner and politician. Referring to Earl Haig. *Men and Power*

4 I do not keep a diary. Never have. To write a diary every day is like returning to one's own vomit.

Enoch Powell (1912–) British politician. *Sunday Times*, 6 Nov 1977

5 What is a diary as a rule? A document useful to the person who keeps it, dull to the contemporary who reads it, invaluable to the student, centuries afterwards, who treasures it!

Ellen Terry (1847–1928) British actress. *The Story of My Life*, Ch. 14

6 I never travel without my diary. One should always have something sensational to read in the train.

Oscar Wilde (1854–1900) Irish-born British dramatist. *The Importance of Being Earnest*, II

DICKENS

See also criticism, writers

1 We were put to Dickens as children but it never quite took. That unremitting humanity soon had me cheesed off.

Alan Bennett (1934–) British playwright. *The Old Country*, II

2 It does not matter that Dickens' world is not life-like; it is alive.

Lord Cecil (1902–86) British writer and critic. *Early Victorian Novelists*

3 Of Dickens's style it is impossible to speak in praise. It is jerky, ungrammatical, and created by himself in defiance of rules...No young novelist should ever dare to imitate the style of Dickens.

Anthony Trollope (1815–82) British novelist. *Autobiography*

4 One would have to have a heart of stone to read the death of Little Nell without laughing.

Oscar Wilde (1854–1900) Irish-born British dramatist. Lecturing upon Dickens. *Lives of the Wits* (H. Pearson)

DIFFERENCE

See also individuality, opposites, similarity, taste

1 Every man after his fashion.

Proverb

2 Every one to his taste.

Proverb

3 One man's meat is another man's poison.

Proverb

4 There is more than one way to skin a cat.

Proverb

5 There is no accounting for tastes.

Proverb

6 There's nowt so queer as folk.

Proverb

7 All colours will agree in the dark.

Francis Bacon (1561–1626) English philosopher. *Essays*, 'Of Unity in Religion'

8 If we cannot now end our differences, at least we can help make the world safe for diversity.

John Fitzgerald Kennedy (1917–63) US statesman. Speech, American University (Washington, DC), 10 June 1963

DIPLOMACY

See also tact

1 It is better for aged diplomats to be bored than for young men to die.

Warren Austin (1877–1962) US politician and diplomat. When asked if he got tired during long debates at the UN. Attrib.

2 There are three groups that no British Prime Minister should provoke: the Vatican, the Treasury and the miners.

Stanley Baldwin (1867–1947) British statesman. A similar remark is often attributed to Harold Macmillan. Attrib.

3 An honest broker.

Bismarck (1815–98) German statesman. His professed role in the diplomacy of 1878, including the Congress of Berlin. Speech, Reichstag, 19 Feb 1878

4 The healthy bones of a single Pomeranian grenadier.

Bismarck A price too high for Germany to pay regarding the Eastern Question. Speech, Reichstag, 5 Dec 1876

5 To jaw-jaw is better than to war-war.

Winston Churchill (1874–1965) British statesman. Speech, Washington, 26 June 1954

6 An appeaser is one who feeds a crocodile – hoping that it will eat him last.

Winston Churchill Attrib.

7 When you have to kill a man it costs nothing to be polite.

Winston Churchill Justifying the fact that the declaration of war against Japan was made in the usual diplomatic language. *The Grand Alliance*

8 America has all that Russia has not. Russia has things America has not. Why will America not reach out a hand to Russia, as I have given my hand?

Isadora Duncan (1878–1927) US dancer. Speaking in support of Russia following the 1917 Revolution. Speech, Symphony Hall, Boston, 1922

9 REPORTER: If Mr Stalin dies, what will be the effect on international affairs?
EDEN: That is a good question for you to ask, not a wise question for me to answer.

Anthony Eden (1897–1977) British statesman. Interview on board the *Queen Elizabeth*, 4 Mar 1953

10 Treaties are like roses and young girls – they last while they last.

Charles De Gaulle (1890–1970) French general and statesman. Attrib.

11 I met the great little man, the man who can be silent in several languages.

James Guthrie Harbord (1866–1947) US general.

Referring to Colonel House. *Mr Wilson's War* (John Dos Passos), Ch. 3

12 Official dignity tends to increase in inverse ratio to the importance of the country in which the office is held.

Aldous Huxley (1894–1964) British novelist. *Beyond the Mexique Bay*

13 The great nations have always acted like gangsters, and the small nations like prostitutes.

Stanley Kubrick (1928–) US film director. *The Guardian*, 5 June 1963

14 All diplomacy is a continuation of war by other means.

Chou En Lai (1898–1976) Chinese statesman.

15 *La cordiale entente qui existe entre mon gouvernement et le sien.*
The friendly understanding that exists between my government and hers.

Louis Philippe (1773–1850) King of France. Referring to an informal understanding reached between Britain and France in 1843. The more familiar phrase, 'entente cordiale', was first used in 1844. Speech, 27 Dec 1843

16 The reluctant obedience of distant provinces generally costs more than it is worth.

Lord Macaulay (1800–59) British historian. *Historical Essays Contributed to the 'Edinburgh Review'*, 'Lord Mahon's War of the Succession'

17 Let them especially put their demands in such a way that Great Britain could say that she supported both sides.

Ramsey MacDonald (1866–1937) British statesman and prime minister. Referring to France and Germany. *The Origins of the Second Word War* (A. J. P. Taylor), Ch. 3

18 Austria will astound the world with the magnitude of her ingratitude.

Prince Schwarzenberg (1800–52) Austrian statesman. On being asked whether Austria was under any obligation to Russia for help received previously. *The Fall of the House of Habsburg* (E. Crankshaw)

19 A diplomat these days is nothing but a headwaiter who's allowed to sit down occasionally.

Peter Ustinov (1921–) British actor. *Romanoff and Juliet*, I

20 No nation is fit to sit in judgement upon any other nation.

Woodrow Wilson (1856–1925) US statesman. Address, Apr 1915

21 An ambassador is an honest man sent to lie abroad for the good of his country.

Henry Wotton (1568–1639) English poet and diplomat. *Life* (Izaak Walton)

DISABILITY

See also blindness

1 If there are any of you at the back who do not hear me, please don't raise your hands because I am also nearsighted.

W. H. Auden (1907–73) British poet. Starting a lecture in a large hall. In *Book of the Month Club News*, Dec 1946

2 I'm a coloured, one-eyed Jew.

Sammy Davis Jnr (1925–90) US singer. When asked what his handicap was during a game of golf. Attrib.

DISAPPOINTMENT

See also disillusion, expectation

1 Unhappiness is best defined as the difference between our talents and our expectations.

Edward de Bono (1933–) British physician and writer. *The Observer*, 'Sayings of the Week', 12 June 1977

2 The best laid schemes o' mice an' men
Gang aft a-gley,
An' lea'e us nought but grief an' pain
For promis'd joy.

Robert Burns (1759–96) Scottish poet. *To a Mouse*

3 Mountains will heave in childbirth, and a silly little mouse will be born.

Horace (Quintus Horatius Flaccus; 65–8 BC) Roman poet. *Ars Poetica*

4 A mountain in labour shouted so loud that everyone, summoned by the noise, ran up expecting that she would be delivered of a city bigger than Paris; she brought forth a mouse.

Jean de La Fontaine (1621–95) French poet. *Fables*, V, 'La Montagne qui accouche'

5 Levin wanted friendship and got friendliness; he wanted steak and they offered spam.

Bernard Malamud (1914–86) US novelist. *A New Life*, VI

6 Look in my face; my name is Might-have-been.
I am also called No-more, Too-late, Farewell.

Dante Gabriel Rossetti (1828–82) British painter and poet. *The House of Life*, 'A Superscription'

7 Oh, I wish that God had not given me what I prayed for! It was not so good as I thought.

Johanna Spyri (1827–1901) Swiss writer. *Heidi*, Ch. 11

8 He said that he was too old to cry, but it hurt too much to laugh.

Adlai Stevenson (1900–65) US statesman. Said after losing an election, quoting a story told by Abraham Lincoln. Speech, 5 Nov 1952

DISASTER

See also accidents

1 Bad news travels fast.

Proverb

2 Let us hope...that a kind of Providence will put a speedy end to the acts of God under which we have been labouring.

Peter De Vries (1910–93) US novelist. *The Mackerel Plaza*, Ch. 3

3 An Act of God was defined as *something which no reasonable man could have expected.*

A. P. Herbert (1890–1971) British writer and politician. *Uncommon Law*

4 Beautiful Railway Bridge of the Silv'ry Tay!
Alas, I am very sorry to say
That ninety lives have been taken away
On the last Sabbath day of 1879,
Which will be remember'd for a very long time.

William McGonagall (1830–1902) Scottish poet. *The Tay Bridge Disaster*

DISCONTENT

See also envy

1 And sigh that one thing only has been lent
To youth and age in common – discontent.

Matthew Arnold (1822–88) British poet and critic. *Youth's Agitations*

2 The idiot who praises, with enthusiastic tone,
All centuries but this, and every country but his own.

W. S. Gilbert (1836–1911) British dramatist. *The Mikado*, I

3 So have I loitered my life away, reading books, looking at pictures, going to plays, hearing, thinking, writing on what pleased me best. I have wanted only one thing to make me happy, but wanting that have wanted everything.

William Hazlitt (1778–1830) British essayist. *English Literature*, Ch. XVII, 'My First Acquaintance with Poets'

4 How is it, Maecenas, that no one lives contented with his lot, whether he has planned it for himself or fate has flung him into it, but yet he praises those who follow different paths?

Horace (Quintus Horatius Flaccus; 65–8 BC) Roman poet. *Satires*, I

5 Ever let the fancy roam,
Pleasure never is at home.

John Keats (1795–1821) British poet. *Fancy*, I

6 I am sick o' wastin' leather on these gritty pavin'-stones,
An' the blasted English drizzle wakes the fever in my bones;
Tho' I walks with fifty 'ousemaids outer Chelsea to the Strand,
An' they talks a lot o' lovin', but wot do they understand?
Beefy face an' grubby 'and –
Law! Wot do they understand?
I've a neater, sweeter maiden in a cleaner, greener land!

Rudyard Kipling (1865–1936) Indian-born British writer. *The Road to Mandalay*

7 He disdains all things above his reach, and preferreth all countries before his own.

Thomas Overbury (1581–1613) English poet. *Miscellaneous Works*, 'An Affectate Traveller'

8 When in disgrace with fortune and men's eyes
I all alone beweep my outcast state,
And trouble deaf heaven with my bootless cries,
And look upon myself, and curse my fate,
Wishing me like to one more rich in hope
Featur'd like him, like him with friends possess'd,
Desiring this man's art, and that man's scope,
With what I most enjoy contented least.

William Shakespeare (1564–1616) English dramatist. *Sonnet 29*

9 While not exactly disgruntled, he was far from feeling gruntled.

P. G. Wodehouse (1881–1975) British humorous novelist. *The Code of the Woosters*

10 I'd rather be
A Pagan suckled in a creed outworn;
So might I, standing on this pleasant lea,
Have glimses that would make me less forlorn;
Have sight of Proteus rising from the sea;
Or hear Old Triton blow his wreathed horn.

William Wordsworth (1770–1850) British poet. *Sonnets*, 'The world is too much with us'

DISCOVERY

See also exploration, science, space

1 *Eureka!*
I have found it!

Archimedes (c. 287–212 BC) Greek mathematician. An exclamation of joy supposedly uttered as, stepping into a bath and noticing the water overflowing, he saw the answer to a problem and began the train of thought that led to his principle of buoyancy. Attrib.

2 Look, stranger, at this island now
The leaping light for your delight discovers.

W. H. Auden (1907–73) British poet. *Look, Stranger*

3 They are ill discoverers that think there is no land, when they can see nothing but sea.

Francis Bacon (1561–1626) English philosopher. *The Advancement of Learning*, Bk. II, Ch. 7

4 God could cause us considerable embarrassment by revealing all the secrets of nature to us: we should not know what to do for sheer apathy and boredom.

Goethe (1749–1832) German poet and dramatist. *Memoirs* (Riemer)

5 Then felt I like some watcher of the skies
When a new planet swims into his ken;
Or like stout Cortez when with eagle eyes
He star'd at the Pacific – and all his men
Look'd at each other with a wild surmise –
Silent, upon a peak in Darien.

John Keats (1795–1821) British poet. *On first looking into Chapman's Homer*

6 I do not know what I may appear to the world, but to myself I seem to have been only like a boy playing on the sea-shore, and diverting myself in now and then finding a smoother pebble or a prettier shell than ordinary, whilst the great ocean of truth lay all undiscovered before me.

Isaac Newton (1642–1727) British scientist. *Isaac Newton* (L. T. More)

7 The people – could you patent the sun?

Jonas E. Salk (1914–95) US virologist. On being asked who owned the patent on his polio vaccine. *Famous Men of Science* (S. Bolton)

8 Discovery consists of seeing what everybody has seen and thinking what nobody has thought.
Albert Szent-Györgyi (1893–1986) Hungarian-born US biochemist. *The Scientist Speculates* (I. J. Good)

DISEASE

1 A disease known is half cured.
Proverb

2 'Pray, Mr. Abernethy, what is a cure for gout' was the question of an indolent and luxurious citizen.
'Live upon sixpence a day – and earn it,' was the cogent reply.
John Abernethy (1764–1831) English surgeon. *Medical Portrait Gallery*, Vo. II (Thomas J. Pettigrew)

3 We are led to think of diseases as isolated disturbances in a healthy body, not as the phases of certain periods of bodily development.
Sir Clifford Allbutt (1836–1925) *Bulletin of the New York Academy of Medicine*, 4:1000, 1928 (F. H. Garrison)

4 Screw up the vise as tightly as possible – you have rheumatism; give it another turn, and that is gout.
Anonymous

5 Once I am sure a patient has terminal cancer I tell them straight, I say, 'Its time to go visit with the grand-children.' They seem to appreciate it.
Anonymous Said by a doctor from New Mexico. *The Encyclopedia of Alternative Medicine and Self-Help* (ed. Malcolm Hulke)

6 Before this strange disease of modern life,
With its sick hurry, its divided aims.
Matthew Arnold *The Scholar Gipsy*

7 Only those in the last stage of disease could believe that children are true judges of character.
W. H. Auden (1907–73) British poet. *The Orators*, 'Journal of an Airman'

8 Cure the disease and kill the patient.
Francis Bacon (1561–1626) English philosopher. *Essays*, 'Of Friendship'

9 The remedy is worse than the disease.
Francis Bacon *Essays*, 'Of Seditions and troubles'

10 GOUT, n. A physician's name for the rheumatism of a rich patient.
Ambrose Bierce (1842–c. 1914) US writer and journalist. *The Devil's Dictionary*

11 Diseases crucify the soul of man, attenuate our bodies, dry them, wither them, shrivel them up like old apples make them so many anatomies.
Robert Burton (1577–1640) English scholar and churchman. *The Anatomy of Melancholy*, 1

12 Evil comes at leisure like the disease; good comes in a hurry like the doctor.
G. K. Chesterton (1874–1936) British writer. *The Man who was Orthodox*

13 Life is an incurable disease.
Abraham Cowley (1618–67) English poet. *To Dr Scarborough*

14 There is a dread disease which so prepares its victim, as it were, for death…a disease in which death and life are so strangely blended, that death takes a glow and hue of life, and life the gaunt and grisly form of death – a disease which medicine never cured, wealth warded off, or poverty could boast exemption from – which sometimes moves in giant strides, and sometimes at a tardy sluggish pace, but, slow or quick, is ever sure and certain.
Charles Dickens (1812–70) British novelist. *Nicholas Nickleby*, Ch. 49

15 Epidemics have often been more influential than statesman and soldiers in shaping the course of political history, and diseases may also colour the moods of civilizations.
René and Jean Dubos (1901–82; 1918–) *The White Plague*, Ch. 5

16 Disease is an experience of mortal mind. It is fear made manifest on the body.
Mary Baker Eddy (1821–1910) US religious reader and scientist. *Science and Health*, Ch. 14

17 To think that a bottle of wine or a truffled pâté, or even a glass of beer, instead of being absorbed and eliminated by the system in the usual manner, should mine its way through the thighs, knees, calves, ankles, and instep, to explode at last in a fiery volcano in one's great toe, seems a mirth-provoking phenomenon to all but him who is immediately concerned.
George Herman Ellwanger (fl. 1897) *Meditations on Gout*, 'The Malady'

18 Time had robbed her of her personal charms, and that scourge of the human race, the gout, was racking her bones and sinews.
Hannah Farnham Lee (1780–1865) Referring to Catherine de Medici. *The Huguenots in France and America*

19 Many a diabetic has stayed alive by stealing the bread denied him by his doctor.
Martin H. Fischer (1879–1962) *Fischerisms* (Howard Fabing and Ray Marr)

20 Cancer's a Funny Thing:
I wish I had the voice of Homer
To sing of rectal carcinoma,
Which kills a lot more chaps, in fact,
Than were bumped off when Troy
was sacked…
J. B. S. Haldane (1892–1964) British geneticist. Written while mortally ill with cancer. *JBS* (Ronald Clark)

21 If gentlemen love the pleasant titillation of the gout, it is all one to the Town Pump.
Nathaniel Hawthorne (1804–64) US writer. *The Town Pump*

22 Some people are so sensitive they feel snubbed if an epidemic overlooks them.
Frank (Kin) Hubbard (1868–1930) US humorist and journalist. *Abe Martin's Broadcast*

23 Gout is to the arteries what rheumatism

is to the heart.

Henri Huchard (1844–1910) *Lancet*, 1:164, 1967 (D. Evan Bedford)

24 We're all going to go crazy, living this epidemic every minute, while the rest of the world goes on out there, all around us, as if nothing is happening, going on with their own lives and not knowing what it's like, what we're going through. We're living through war, but where they're living it's peacetime, and we're all in the same country.

Larry Kramer (1935–) US dramatist and novelist. *The Normal Heart*

25 It is the only disease you don't look forward to being cured of.

Herman J. Mankiewicz (1897–1953) US journalist and screenwriter. Referring to death. *Citizen Kane*

26 While there are several chronic diseases more destructive to life than cancer, none is more feared.

Charles H. Mayo (1865–1939) US physician. *Annals of Surgery*, 83:357, 1926

27 Fever the eternal reproach to the physicians.

John Milton (1608–74) English poet. *Paradise Lost*, Bk. XI

28 I have Bright's disease and he has mine.

S. J. Perelman Attrib.

29 The Muse but serv'd to ease some friend, not Wife,
To help me through this long disease, my life.

Alexander Pope (1688–1744) British poet. *Epistle to Dr. Arbuthnot*

30 Cur'd yesterday of my disease,
I died last night of my physician.

Matthew Prior (1664–1721) British poet. *The Remedy Worse than the Disease*

31 Diseases are the tax on pleasures.

John Ray (1627–1705) English naturalist. *English Proverbs*

32 The diseases which destroy a man are no less natural than the instincts which preserve him.

George Santayana (1863–1952) Spanish-born US philosopher, poet, and critic. *Dialogues in Limbo*, 3

33 Preachers say, Do as I say, not as I do. But if the physician had the same disease upon him that I have, and he should bid me do one thing, and himself do quite another, could I believe him?

John Selden (1584–1654) English historian. *Table Talk*

34 Disease is not of the body but of the place.

Seneca (c. 4 BC–65 AD) Roman writer. *Epistulae ad Lucilium*

35 Not even remedies can master incurable diseases.

Seneca *Epistulae ad Lucilium*

36 The development of industry has created many new sources of danger. Occupational diseases are socially different from other diseases, but not biologically.

Henry E. Sigerist (1891–1957) *Journal of the History of Medicine and Allied Sciences*, 13:214, 1958

37 The man of the present day would far rather believe that disease is connected only with immediate causes for the fundamental tendency in the modern view of life is always to seek what is more convenient.

Rudolf Steiner (1861–1925) Austrian philosopher, founder of anthroposophy. *The Manifestations of Karma*, Lecture III

38 The old saw is that 'if you drink wine you have the gout and if you do not drink wine the gout will have you.'

Thomas Sydenham (1624–89) *Works*, 'A Treatise on Gout and Dropsy'

39 Decay and disease are often beautiful, like the pearly tear of the shellfish and the hectic glow of consumption.

Henry David Thoreau (1817–62) US writer. *Journal*, 11 June 1852

40 The art of medicine consists of amusing the patient while Nature cures the disease.

Voltaire (1694–1788) French writer. Attrib.

41 I would like to remind those responsible for the treatment of tuberculosis that Keats wrote his best poems while dying of this disease. In my opinion he would never have done so under the influence of modern chemotherapy.

Arthur M. Walker (1896–1955) *Walkerisms* (Julius L. Wilson)

DISILLUSION

See also disappointment, innocence of childhood

1 The price one pays for pursuing any profession or calling is an intimate knowledge of its ugly side.

James Baldwin (1924–87) US writer. *Nobody Knows My Name*

2 If you live long enough, you'll see that every victory turns into a defeat.

Simone de Beauvoir (1908–86) French writer. *Tous les hommes sont mortels*

3 The coach has turned into a pumpkin and the mice have all run away.

Ladybird Johnson (1912–) Wife of Lyndon B. Johnson. Said after Lyndon Johnson gave up the presidency. *The Vantage Point* (Lyndon B. Johnson)

4 I have protracted my work till most of those whom I wished to please have sunk into the grave; and success and miscarriage are empty sounds.

Samuel Johnson (1709–84) British lexicographer. *Dictionary of the English Language*

5 One stops being a child when one realizes that telling one's trouble does not make it better.

Cesare Pavese (1908–50) Italian novelist and poet. *The Business of Living: Diaries 1935–50*

DISMISSAL

See also departure

1 You have sat too long here for any good you have been doing. Depart, I say, and let us have done with you. In the name of God, *go!*

Leopold Amery (1873–1955) British statesman. Said to Neville Chamberlain using Cromwell's words. Speech, House of Commons, May 1940

2 You have delighted us long enough.

Jane Austen (1775–1817) British novelist. *Pride and Prejudice*, Ch. 18

3 It is not fit that you should sit here any longer!...you shall now give place to better men.

Oliver Cromwell (1599–1658) English soldier and statesman. Speech to the Rump Parliament, 22 Jan 1655

4 Take away that fool's bauble, the mace.

Oliver Cromwell Speech dismissing Parliament, 20 Apr 1653

5 Go, and never darken my towels again!

Groucho Marx (Julius Marx; 1895–1977) US comedian. *Duck Soup*

6 There comes a time in every man's life when he must make way for an older man.

Reginald Maudling (1917–77) British politician. Remark made on being replaced in the shadow cabinet by John Davies, his elder by four years. *The Guardian*, 20 Nov 1976

7 We Don't Want To Lose You But We Think You Ought To Go.

Paul Alfred Rubens (1875–1917) British dramatist and songwriter. Title of song

8 Stand not upon the order of your going,
But go at once.

William Shakespeare (1564–1616) English dramatist. *Macbeth*, III:4

9 Dropping the pilot.

John Tenniel (1820–1914) British illustrator and cartoonist. Caption of a cartoon. The cartoon refers to Bismarck's resignation portraying him as a ship's pilot walking down the gangway of the ship while Wilhelm II watches from the deck. *Punch*, 29 Mar 1890

DOCTORS

See also disease, drugs, health and healthy living, illness, medicine, remedies

1 I am dying with the help of too many physicians.

Alexander the Great (356–323 BC) King of Macedon. Attrib.

2 And he said unto them, Ye will surely say unto me this proverb, Physician, heal thyself: whatsoever we have heard done in Capernaum, do also here in thy country.

Bible: Luke 4:23

3 The doctor found, when she was dead,
Her last disorder mortal.

Oliver Goldsmith (1728–74) Irish-born British writer. *Elegy on Mrs. Mary Blaize*

4 I suppose one has a greater sense of intellectual degradation after an interview with a doctor than from any human experience.

Alice James (1848–92) US diarist. *The Diary of Alice James* (ed. Leon Edel), 27 Sept 1890

5 It is incident to physicians, I am afraid, beyond all other men, to mistake subsequence for consequence.

Samuel Johnson (1709–84) British lexicographer. *Life of Johnson* (J. Boswell), Vol. I

6 My doctor has advised me to cut back on predictions.

Conor Cruise O'Brien (1917–) Irish writer and editor. *The Times*, 11 Nov 1994

7 Who shall decide when doctors disagree?

Alexander Pope (1688–1744) British poet. *Moral Essays*, III

8 Cur'd yesterday of my disease,
I died last night of my physician.

Matthew Prior (1664–1721) British poet. *The Remedy Worse than the Disease*

9 First they get *on*, then they get *honour*, then they get *honest*.

Humphrey Rolleston (1862–1944) British physician. Referring to physicians. *Confessions of an Advertising Man* (David Ogilvy)

10 Physicians are like kings, – they brook no contradiction.

John Webster (1580–1625) English dramatist. *The Duchess of Malfi*, V:2

DOGS

See also animals

1 A huge dog, tied by a chain, was painted on the wall and over it was written in capital letters 'Beware of the dog.'

Petronius Arbiter (1st century AD) Roman satirist. Latin, *Cave canem. Satyricon: Cena Trimalchionis*, 29

2 The woman who is really kind to dogs is always one who has failed to inspire sympathy in men.

Max Beerbohm (1872–1956) British writer. *Zuleika Dobson*

3 It's the one species I wouldn't mind seeing vanish from the face of the earth. I wish they were like the White Rhino – six of them left in the Serengeti National Park, and all males.

Alan Bennett (1934–) British playwright. Referring to dogs. *Getting On*, I

4 The great pleasure of a dog is that you may make a fool of yourself with him and not only will he not scold you, he will make a fool of himself too.

Samuel Butler (1835–1902) British writer. *Notebooks*

5 'Tis sweet to hear the watch-dog's honest bark
Bay deep-mouthed welcome as we draw near home;
'Tis sweet to know there is an eye will mark
Our coming, and look brighter when we come.

Lord Byron (1788–1824) British poet. *Don Juan*, I

6 Anybody who hates children and dogs can't be all bad.

W. C. Fields (1880–1946) US actor. Attrib.

7 The dog, to gain some private ends,
Went mad and bit the man.

Oliver Goldsmith (1728–74) Irish-born British writer. *Elegy on the Death of a Mad Dog*

8 The man recovered of the bite,
The dog it was that died.

Oliver Goldsmith *Elegy on the Death of a Mad Dog*

9 Stop running those dogs on your page. I wouldn't have them peeing on my cheapest rug.

William Randolph Hearst (1863–1951) US newspaper owner. Referring to the publication of Thurber's drawings by one of his editors. *The Years with Ross* (James Thurber)

10 A door is what a dog is perpetually on the wrong side of.

Ogden Nash (1902–71) US poet. *A Dog's Best Friend Is His Illiteracy*

11 I am His Highness' dog at Kew;
Pray tell me sir, whose dog are you?

Alexander Pope (1688–1744) British poet. On the collar of a dog given to Frederick, Prince of Wales

12 That indefatigable and unsavoury engine of pollution, the dog.

John Sparrow (1906–92) British lawyer and academic. Letter to *The Times*, 30 Sep 1975

13 I loathe people who keep dogs. They are cowards who haven't got the guts to bite people themselves.

August Strindberg (1849–1912) Swedish dramatist. *A Madman's Diary*

14 Daddy wouldn't buy me a bow-wow, bow-wow.
I've got a little cat
And I'm very fond of that.

Joseph Tabrar (20th century) US songwriter. *Daddy Wouldn't Buy Me A Bow-wow* (song)

DOOMSDAY

1 That at what time ye hear the sound of the cornet, flute, harp, sackbut, psaltery, dulcimer, and all kinds of musick, ye fall down and worship the golden image that Nebuchadnezzar the king hath set up:
And whoso falleth not down and worshippeth shall the same hour be cast into the midst of a burning fiery furnace.

Bible: Daniel 3:5–6

2 Immediately after the tribulation of those days shall the sun be darkened, and the moon shall not give her light, and the stars shall fall from heaven, and the powers of the heavens shall be shaken:
And then shall appear the sign of the Son of man in heaven: and then shall all the tribes of the earth mourn, and they shall see the Son of man coming in the clouds of heaven with power and great glory.
And he shall send his angels with a great sound of a trumpet, and they shall gather together his elect from the four winds, from one end of heaven to the other.

Bible: Matthew 24:29–31

3 'Tis the Last Judgment's fire must cure this place,
Calcine its clods and set my prisoners free.

Robert Browning (1812–89) British poet. *Childe Roland to the Dark Tower Came*, XI

4 Don't wait for the Last Judgement. It takes place every day.

Albert Camus (1913–60) French existentialist writer. *The Fall*

5 When all the world dissolves,
And every creature shall be purified,
All place shall be hell that is not heaven.

Christopher Marlowe (1564–93) English dramatist. *Doctor Faustus*, II:1

DOUBT

See also indecision, scepticism, uncertainty

1 If a man will begin with certainties, he shall end in doubts, but if he will be content to begin with doubts, he shall end in certainties.

Francis Bacon (1561–1626) English philosopher. *The Advancement of Learning*, Bk. I, Ch. 5

2 And immediately Jesus stretched forth his hand, and caught him, and said unto him, O thou of little faith, wherefore didst thou doubt?

Bible: Matthew 14:31

3 He who shall teach the child to doubt
The rotting grave shall ne'er get out.

William Blake (1757–1827) British poet. *Auguries of Innocence*

4 All we have gained then by our unbelief
Is a life of doubt diversified by faith,
For one of faith diversified by doubt:
We called the chess-board white, – we call it black.

Robert Browning (1812–89) British poet. *Bishop Blougram's Apology*

5 His doubts are better than most people's certainties.

Lord Hardwicke (1690–1764) English judge. Referring to Dirleton's *Doubts. Life of Johnson* (J. Boswell)

6 Negative Capability, that is, when a man is capable of being in uncertainties, mysteries, doubts, without any irritable reaching after fact and reason.

John Keats (1795–1821) British poet. Letter to G. and T. Keats, 21 Dec 1817

7 The trouble with the world is that the stupid are cocksure and the intelligent full of doubt.

Bertrand Russell (1872–1970) British philosopher. *Autobiography*

8 Those obstinate questionings

Of sense and outward things,
Fallings from us, vanishings;
Blank misgivings of a Creature
Moving about in worlds not realised,
High instincts before which our mortal nature
Did tremble like a guilty thing surprised.

William Wordsworth (1770–1850) British poet. *Ode. Intimations of Immortality*, IX

DREAMS

1 Dreams and predictions ought to serve but for winter talk by the fireside.

Francis Bacon (1561–1626) English philosopher. *Essays*, 'Of Prophecies'

2 It was a dream of perfect bliss,
Too beautiful to last.

Thomas Haynes Bayly (1797–1839) British writer. *It was a Dream*

3 So I awoke, and behold it was a dream.

John Bunyan (1628–88) English writer. *The Pilgrim's Progress*, Pt. I

4 I do not know whether I was then a man dreaming I was a butterfly, or whether I am now a butterfly dreaming I am a man.

Chuang Tse (*or* Zhuangzi; c. 369–286 BC) Chinese philosopher. *Chuang Tse* (H. A. Giles), Ch. 2

5 The people's prayer, the glad diviner's theme,
The young men's vision, and the old men's dream!

John Dryden (1631–1700) British poet and dramatist. *Absalom and Achitophel*, I

6 Last night I dreamt I went to Manderley again.

Daphne Du Maurier (1907–89) British novelist. *Rebecca*, Ch. 1

7 Underneath the arches
We dream our dreams away.

Bud Flanagan (Robert Winthrop; 1896–1968) British comedian. *Underneath the Arches*

8 God pity a one-dream man.

Robert Goddard (1882–1945) US physicist. *Broca's Brain* (Carl Sagan; 1980)

9 Castles in the air – they're so easy to take refuge in. So easy to build, too.

Henrik Ibsen (1828–1906) Norwegian dramatist. *The Master Builder*, III

10 Alas, all the castles I have, are built with air, thou know'st.

Ben Jonson (1573–1637) English dramatist. *Eastward Ho*, II:2

11 All men dream: but not equally. Those who dream by night in the dusty recesses of their minds wake in the day to find that it was vanity: but the dreamers of the day are dangerous men, for they may act their dream with open eyes, to make it possible.

T. E. Lawrence (1888–1935) British soldier and writer. *Seven Pillars of Wisdom*, Ch. 1

12 Abou Ben Adhem (may his tribe increase!)
Awoke one night from a deep dream of peace,
And saw, within the moonlight in his room,
Making it rich, and like a lily in bloom,
An angel writing in a book of gold…

Leigh Hunt (1784–1859) British poet. *Abou Ben Adhem and the Angel*

13 Many's the long night I've dreamed of cheese – toasted, mostly.

Robert Louis Stevenson (1850–94) Scottish writer. *Treasure Island*, Ch. 15

14 Dreams are true while they last, and do we not live in dreams?

Alfred, Lord Tennyson (1809–92) British poet. *The Higher Pantheism*

15 I have spread my dreams under your feet.
Tread softly because you tread on my dreams.

W. B. Yeats (1865–1939) Irish poet. *He wishes For The Cloths of Heaven*

DRINKS

See also alcohol, drunkenness, water

1 The infusion of a China plant sweetened with the pith of an Indian cane.

Joseph Addison (1672–1719) British essayist. *The Spectator*, 69

2 I the Trinity illustrate,
Drinking watered orange-pulp –
In three sips the Arian frustrate;
While he drains his at one gulp.

Robert Browning (1812–89) British poet. *Soliloquy of the Spanish Cloister*

3 I am willing to taste any drink once.

James Cabell (1879–1958) US novelist and journalist. *Jurgen*, Ch. 1

4 While the bubbling and loud-hissing urn
Throws up a steamy column, and the cups,
That cheer but not inebriate, wait on each,
So let us welcome peaceful evening in.

William Cowper (1731–1800) British poet. *The Task*

5 Tea for Two, and Two for Tea.

Otto Harback (1873–1963) US dramatist. From the musical *No! No! Nanette.* Song title

6 Coffee which makes the politician wise,
And see through all things with his half-shut eyes.

Alexander Pope (1688–1744) British poet. *The Rape of the Lock*, III

7 Here thou great Anna! whom three realms obey,
Dost sometimes counsel take – and sometimes Tea.

Alexander Pope *The Rape of the Lock*, III

8 Our trouble is that we drink too much tea. I see in this the slow revenge of the Orient, which has diverted the Yellow River down our throats.

J. B. Priestley (1894–1984) British novelist. *The Observer*, 'Sayings of the Week', 15 May 1949

9 I think it must be so, for I have been drinking it for sixty-five years and I am not dead yet.

Voltaire (François-Marie Arouet; 1694–1778) French writer. On learning that coffee was considered a slow poison. Attrib.

DROWNING

1 The western tide crept up along the sand,
And o'er and o'er the sand,
And round and round the sand,
As far as eye could see.
The rolling mist came down and hid the land:
And never home came she.

Charles Kingsley (1819–75) British writer. *The Sands of Dee*

2 O Lord, methought what pain it was to drown,
What dreadful noise of waters in my ears,
What sights of ugly death within my eyes!

William Shakespeare (1564–1616) English dramatist. *Richard III*, I:4

3 Nobody heard him, the dead man,
But still he lay moaning:
I was much further out than you thought
And not waving but drowning.

Stevie Smith (Florence Margaret Smith; 1902–71) British poet. *Not Waving But Drowning*

DRUGS

1 A drug is that substance which, when injected into a rat, will produce a scientific report.

Anonymous

2 Hark! The herald angels sing
Beecham's pills are just the thing.
Peace on earth and mercy mild;
Two for man and one for child.

Anonymous Apparently the result of a Beecham's advertisement in a hymnbook.

3 I'm proving that if you're on drugs then you're in trouble because those drugs aren't working. I'm clean and I'm beating you.

Linford Christie (1960–) British athlete. *The Independent*, 10 June 1994

4 Thou hast the keys of Paradise, oh,
just, subtle, and mighty opium!

Thomas De Quincey (1785–1859) British essayist and critic. *Confessions of an English Opium-Eater*, Pt. II

5 Alarmed successively by every fashionable medical terror of the day, she dosed her children with every specific which was publicly advertised or privately recommended. No creatures of their age had taken such quantities of Ching's lozenges, Godbold's elixir, or Dixon's anti-bilious pills. The consequence was, that the dangers, which had at first been imaginary, became real: these little victims of domestic medicine never had a day's health: they looked, and were, more dead than alive.

Maria Edgeworth (1767–1849) British novelist. *Patronage*

6 A man who cannot work without his hypodermic needle is a poor doctor. The amount of narcotic you use is inversely proportional to your skill.

Martin H. Fischer (1879–1962) *Fischerisms* (Howard Fabing and Ray Marr)

7 Half the modern drugs could well be thrown out the window except that the birds might eat them.

Martin H. Fischer *Fischerisms* (Howard Fabing and Ray Marr)

8 A hundred doses of happiness are not enough: send to the drug-store for another bottle – and, when that is finished, for another...There can be no doubt that, if tranquillizers could be bought as easily and cheaply as aspirin they would be consumed, not by the billions, as they are at present, but by the scores and hundreds of billions. And a good, cheap stimulant would be almost as popular.

Aldous Huxley (1894–1963) British writer. *Brave New World Revisited*, Ch. 8

9 What is dangerous about the tranquillizer is that whatever peace of mind they bring is a packaged peace of mind. Where you buy a pill and buy peace with it, you get conditioned to cheap solutions instead of deep ones.

Max Lerner (1902–92) Russian-born US teacher, editor, and journalist. *The Unfinished Country*, 'The Assault on the Mind'

10 I will lift up mine eyes unto the pills. Almost everyone takes them, from the humble aspirin to the multi-coloured, king-sized three deckers, which put you to sleep, wake you up, stimulate and soothe you all in one. It is an age of pills.

Malcolm Muggeridge (1903–90) British writer and editor. *The New Statesman*, 3 Aug 1962

11 Two great European narcotics, alcohol and Christianity.

Friedrich Wilhelm Nietzsche (1844–1900) German philosopher. *The Twilight of the Idols*, 'Things the Germans Lack'

12 Imperative drugging – the ordering of medicine in any and every malady – is no longer regarded as the chief function of the doctor.

William Osler *Aequanimitas, with Other Addresses*, 'Medicine in the Nineteenth Century'

13 The treatment with poison medicines comes from the West.

Huang Ti (The Yellow Emperor, 2697 BC–2597 BC) *Nei Ching Su Wen*, Bk. 4

14 I owe my reputation to the fact that I use digitalis in doses the text books say are dangerous and in cases that the text books say are unsuitable.

Karel Frederik Wenckebach (1864–1940) *Lancet*, 2:633, 1937

15 Cocaine is God's way of saying you're

making too much money.

Robin Williams (1952–) US actor. *Screen International*, 15 Dec 1990

DRUNKENNESS

See also alcohol

1 There are more old drunkards than old doctors.

Proverb

2 His mouth has been used as a latrine by some small animal of the night.

Kingsley Amis (1922–95) British novelist. Describing a hangover. *Lucky Jim*

3 Come landlord, fill the flowing bowl,
Until it doth run over…
For tonight we'll merry, merry be,
Tomorrow we'll be sober.

Anonymous *Come, Landlord, Fill the Flowing Bowl*

4 What shall we do with the drunken sailor
Early in the morning?
Hoo-ray and up she rises
Early in the morning.

Anonymous *What shall we do with the Drunken Sailor?*

5 Ha, ha, ha, you and me,
Little brown jug, don't I love thee!

Anonymous *The Little Brown Jug*

6 One reason I don't drink is that I want to know when I am having a good time.

Nancy Astor (1879–1964) American-born British politician. Attrib.

7 For when the wine is in, the wit is out.

Thomas Becon (1512–67) English Protestant churchman. *Catechism*, 375

8 Others mocking said, These men are full of new wine.

Bible: Acts 2:13

9 Wine is a mocker, strong drink is raging: and whosoever is deceived thereby is not wise.

Bible: Proverbs 20:1

10 Man, being reasonable, must get drunk;
The best of life is but intoxication.

Lord Byron (1788–1824) British poet. *Don Juan*, II

11 It's my opinion, sir, that this meeting is drunk.

Charles Dickens (1812–70) British novelist. *Pickwick Papers*, Ch. 33

12 I am as sober as a Judge.

Henry Fielding (1707–54) British novelist. *Don Quixote in England*, III:14

13 If merely 'feeling good' could decide, drunkenness would be the supremely valid human experience.

William James (1842–1910) US psychologist and philosopher. *Varieties of Religious Experience*

14 A branch of the sin of drunkenness, which is the root of all sins.

James I (1566–1625) King of England. *A Counterblast to Tobacco*

15 A man who exposes himself when he is intoxicated, has not the art of getting drunk.

Samuel Johnson (1709–84) British lexicographer. *Life of Johnson* (J. Boswell), Vol. III

16 Better sleep with a sober cannibal than a drunken Christian.

Herman Melville (1819–91) US novelist. *Moby Dick*, Ch. 3

17 I am as drunk as a lord, but then, I am one, so what does it matter?

Bertrand Russell (1872–1970) British philosopher. *Bertrand Russell, Philosopher of the Century* (Ralph Schoenman)

18 No, thank you, I was born intoxicated.

George William Russell (1867–1935) Irish poet and dramatist. Refusing a drink that was offered him. *10,000 Jokes, Toasts, and Stories* (L. Copeland)

19 But I'm not so think as you drunk I am.

John Collings Squire (1884–1958) British journalist. *Ballade of Soporific Absorption*

20 Come, Robert, you shall drink twice while I drink once, for I cannot permit the son in his sober senses to witness the intoxication of his father.

Horace Walpole (1717–97) British writer. Explaining why he filled his son's glass twice for every glass he drank himself. Attrib.

DUTY

See also obligation

1 From a very early age, I had imbibed the opinion, that it was every man's duty to do all that lay in his power to leave his country as good as he had found it.

William Cobbett (1763–1835) British journalist and writer. *Political Register*, 22 Dec 1832

2 Do your duty and leave the rest to the Gods.

Pierre Corneille (1606–84) French dramatist. *Horace*, II:8

3 England expects every man will do his duty.

Lord Nelson (1758–1805) British admiral. Signal hoisted prior to the Battle of Trafalgar, 1805.

4 When a stupid man is doing something he is ashamed of, he always declares that it is his duty.

George Bernard Shaw (1856–1950) Irish dramatist and critic. *Caesar and Cleopatra*, III

5 Sunset and evening star,
And one clear call for me!
And may there be no moaning of the bar
When I put out to sea.

Alfred, Lord Tennyson (1809–92) British poet. *Crossing the Bar*

E

ECOLOGY

See also conservation, environment

1 Over increasingly large areas of the United States, spring now comes unheralded by the return of the birds, and the early mornings are strangely silent where once they were filled with the beauty of bird song.

Rachel Carson (1907–64) US biologist. *The Silent Spring*

2 As cruel a weapon as the cave man's club, the chemical barrage has been hurled against the fabric of life.

Rachel Carson *The Silent Spring*

3 Man has been endowed with reason, with the power to create, so that he can add to what he's been given. But up to now he hasn't been a creator, only a destroyer. Forests keep disappearing, rivers dry up, wild life's become extinct, the climate's ruined and the land grows poorer and uglier every day.

Anton Chekhov (1860–1904) Russian dramatist. *Uncle Vanya*, I

4 It will be said of this generation that it found England a land of beauty and left it a land of beauty spots.

Cyril Joad (1891–1953) British writer and broadcaster. *The Observer*, 'Sayings of Our Times', 31 May 1953

5 We are living beyond our means. As a people we have developed a life-style that is draining the earth of its priceless and irreplaceable resources without regard for the future of our children and people all around the world.

Margaret Mead (1901–78) US anthropologist. *Redbook*, 'The Energy Crisis – Why Our World Will Never Again Be the Same.'

6 The Irish Sea is naturally radioactive, the Sellafield discharges are less radioactive than the sea they are discharged into.

Cecil Parkinson (1931–) British politician. Speech, Nov 1987

7 We are wealthy and wasteful but this can't go on. If we don't eat dog biscuits, we could end up eating our dog instead.

Magnus Pyke (1908–92) British scientist, television personality, and writer. *The Observer*, 'Sayings of the Week', 12 Jan 1975

8 Had we gone the way of France and got 60 per cent of our electricity from nuclear power, we should not have environmental problems.

Margaret Thatcher (1925–) British politician and prime minister. Speech, Oct 1988

9 To the average British farmer, organic farming is about as relevant as caviar and a flight on Concorde.

Oliver Walston (1941–) Speech, Jan 1989

ECONOMICS

1 Don't spoil the ship for a ha'porth of tar.

Proverb

2 A budget is a method of worrying before you spend instead of afterwards.

Anonymous

3 John Stuart Mill
By a mighty effort of will
Overcame his natural bonhomie
And wrote 'Principles of Political Economy'.

Edmund Clerihew Bentley (1875–1956) British writer. *Biography for Beginners*

4 Respectable Professors of the Dismal Science.

Thomas Carlyle (1795–1881) Scottish historian and essayist. Referring to economists. *Latter-Day Pamphlets*, 1

5 Provided that the City of London remains as at present, the Clearing-house of the World.

Joseph Chamberlain (1836–1914) British politician. Speech, Guildhall, London, 19 Jan 1904

6 I am not prepared to accept the economics of a housewife.

Jacques Chirac (1932–) French politician. Referring to Margaret Thatcher. Remark, July 1987

7 Annual income twenty pounds, annual expenditure nineteen nineteen six, result happiness. Annual income twenty pounds, annual expenditure twenty pounds ought and six, result misery.

Charles Dickens (1812–70) British novelist. *David Copperfield*, Ch. 12

8 If freedom were not so economically efficient it certainly wouldn't stand a chance.

Milton Friedman (1912–) US economist. Remark, Mar 1987

9 When every blessed thing you hold
Is made of silver, or of gold,
You long for simple pewter.
When you have nothing else to wear
But cloth of gold and satins rare,
For cloth of gold you cease to care –
Up goes the price of shoddy.

W. S. Gilbert (1836–1911) British dramatist. *The Gondoliers*, I

10 Having a little inflation is like being a little pregnant.

Leon Henderson (1895–1986) US economist. Attrib.

11 I will not be a party to debasing the currency.

John Maynard Keynes (1883–1946) British economist. On refusing to pay more than a small tip on having his shoes polished, whilst on a visit to Africa. *John Maynard Keynes* (C. Hession)

12 Economics is a subject that does not greatly respect one's wishes.

Nikita Khrushchev (1894–1971) Soviet statesman. Attrib.

13 It is clear that Britain is coming out of recession and confidence is returning...the green shoots of economic spring are appearing once again.

Norman Lamont (1942–) British politician. Speech, 9 Oct 1991

14 Inflation in the Sixties was a nuisance to be endured, like varicose veins or French foreign policy.

Bernard Levin (1928–) British journalist. *The Pendulum Years*, 'Epilogue'

15 One nanny said, 'Feed a cold'; she was a neo-Keynesian. Another nanny said, 'Starve a cold'; she was a monetarist.

Harold Macmillan (1894–1986) British politician and prime minister. Maiden speech, House of Lords, 1984

16 Population, when unchecked, increases in a geometrical ratio. Subsistence only increases in an arithmetical ratio.

Thomas Robert Malthus (1766–1834) British clergyman and economist. *Essays on the Principle of Population*

17 A nation is not in danger of financial disaster merely because it owes itself money.

Andrew William Mellon (1855–1937) US financier. Attrib.

18 In the days when the nation depended on agriculture for its wealth it made the Lord Chancellor sit on a woolsack to remind him where the wealth came from. I would like to suggest we remove that now and make him sit on a crate of machine tools.

Prince Philip (1921–) The consort of Queen Elizabeth II. Speech, Aug 1986

19 Recession is when a neighbour loses his job; depression is when you lose yours.

Ronald Reagan (1911–) US politician and president. *The Observer*, 'Sayings of the Week', 26 Oct 1980

20 If all economists were laid end to end, they would not reach a conclusion.

George Bernard Shaw (1856–1950) Irish dramatist and critic. Attrib.

21 Give me a one-handed economist! All my economists say, 'on the one hand...on the other'.

Harry S. Truman (1884–1972) US statesman. *Presidential Anecdotes* (P. Boller)

22 From now, the pound is worth 14 per cent or so less in terms of other currencies. It does not mean, of course, that the pound here in Britain, in your pocket or purse or in your bank, has been devalued.

Harold Wilson (1916–95) British politician and prime minister. Speech after devaluation of the pound, 20 Nov 1967

23 One man's wage rise is another man's price increase.

Harold Wilson *The Observer*, 'Sayings of the Week', 11 Jan 1970

EDITORS

See also books, journalism, newspapers, publishing

1 Where were you fellows when the paper was blank?

Fred Allen (1894–1956) US comedian. Said to writers who heavily edited one of his scripts. Attrib.

2 He made righteousness readable.

James Bone (1872–1962) British journalist. Referring to C. P. Scott, former editor of *The Manchester Guardian*. Attrib.

3 An editor is one who separates the wheat from the chaff and prints the chaff.

Adlai Stevenson (1900–65) US statesman. *The Stevenson Wit*

EDUCATION

See also academics, classics, examinations, indoctrination, learning, punishment

1 Soon learnt, soon forgotten.

Proverb

2 What we must look for here is, first, religious and moral principles; secondly, gentlemanly conduct; thirdly, intellectual ability.

Thomas Arnold (1795–1842) British educator. Address to the Scholars at Rugby

3 My object will be, if possible to form Christian men, for Christian boys I can scarcely hope to make.

Thomas Arnold Letter on appointment as Headmaster of Rugby, 1828

4 Universities incline wits to sophistry and affectation.

Francis Bacon (1561–1626) English philosopher. *Valerius Terminus of the Interpretation of Nature*, Ch. 26

5 Studies serve for delight, for ornament, and for ability.

Francis Bacon *Essays*, 'Of Studies'

6 It is Oxford that has made me insufferable.

Max Beerbohm (1872–1956) British writer. *More*, 'Going back to School'

7 The dread of beatings,
Dread of Being Late
And greatest dread of all, the dread of games.

John Betjeman (1906–84) British poet. *Summoned by Bells*

8 The true University of these days is a collection of books.

Thomas Carlyle (1795–1881) Scottish historian and essayist. *Heroes and Hero-Worship*, 'The Hero as Man of Letters'

9 'Reeling and Writhing, of course, to begin with,' the Mock Turtle replied; 'and then the different branches of Arithmetic – Ambition, Distraction, Uglification, and Derision.'

Lewis Carroll (Charles Lutwidge Dodgson; 1832–98) British writer. *Alice's Adventures in Wonderland*, Ch. 9

10 His English education at one of the great public schools had preserved his intellect perfectly and permanently at the stage of boyhood.

G. K. Chesterton (1874–1936) British writer. *The Man Who Knew Too Much*

11 Education is simply the soul of a society as it passes from one generation to another.

G. K. Chesterton *The Observer*, 'Sayings of the Week', 6 July 1924

12 Headmasters have powers at their disposal with which Prime Ministers have never yet been invested.

Winston Churchill (1874–1965) British statesman. *My Early Life*, Ch. 2

13 The ape-like virtues without which no one can enjoy a public school.

Cyril Connolly (1903–74) British journalist. *Enemies of Promise*, Ch. 1

14 When he has learnt that bottinney means a knowledge of plants, he goes and knows 'em. That's our system, Nickleby; what do you think of it?

Charles Dickens (1812–70) British novelist. Said by Mr Squeers. *Nicholas Nickleby*, Ch. 8

15 I pay the schoolmaster, but 'tis the schoolboys that educate my son.

Ralph Waldo Emerson (1803–82) US poet and essayist. *Journal*

16 Public schools are the nurseries of all vice and immorality.

Henry Fielding (1707–54) British novelist. *Joseph Andrews*, Bk. III, Ch. 5

17 It is not that the Englishman can't feel – it is that he is afraid to feel. He has been taught at his public school that feeling is bad form. He must not express great joy or sorrow, or even open his mouth too wide when he talks – his pipe might fall out if he did.

E. M. Forster (1879–1970) British novelist. *Abinger Harvest*, 'Notes on the English character'

18 They go forth into it with well-developed bodies, fairly developed minds, and undeveloped hearts.

E. M. Forster Referring to public schoolboys going into the world. *Abinger Harvest*, 'Notes on the English Character'

19 Spoon feeding in the long run teaches us nothing but the shape of the spoon.

E. M. Forster *The Observer*, 'Sayings of the Week', 7 Oct 1951

20 To the University of Oxford I acknowledge no obligation; and she will as cheerfully renounce me for a son, as I am willing to disclaim her for a mother. I spent fourteen months at Magdalen College: they proved the fourteen months the most idle and unprofitable of my whole life.

Edward Gibbon (1737–94) British historian. *Autobiography*

21 Education made us what we are.

Claude-Adrien Helvétius (1715–71) French philosopher. *Discours* XXX, Ch. 30

22 And seek for truth in the groves of Academe.

Horace (Quintus Horatius Flaccus; 65–8 BC) Roman poet. *Epistles*, II

23 You sought the last resort of feeble minds with classical educations. You became a schoolmaster.

Aldous Huxley (1894–1964) British novelist. *Antic Hay*

24 Some experience of popular lecturing had convinced me that the necessity of making things plain to uninstructed people was one of the very best means of clearing up the obscure corners in one's own mind.

T. H. Huxley (1825–95) British biologist. *Man's Place in Nature*, Preface

25 Any attempt to reform the university without attending to the system of which it is an integral part is like trying to do urban renewal in New York City from the twelfth storey up.

Ivan Illich (1926–) Austrian sociologist. *Deschooling Society*, Ch. 3

26 It is no matter what you teach them first, any more than what leg you shall put into your breeches first.

Samuel Johnson (1709–84) British lexicographer. *Life of Johnson* (J. Boswell), Vol. I

27 There is now less flogging in our great schools than formerly, but then less is learned there; so that what the boys get at one end they lose at the other.

Samuel Johnson *Life of Johnson* (J. Boswell), Vol. II

28 I find the three major administrative problems on a campus are sex for the students, athletics for the alumni and parking for the faculty.

Clark Kerr (1911–) US educator. *Time*, 17 Nov 1958

29 Nothing would more effectively further the development of education than for all flogging pedagogues to learn to educate with the head instead of with the hand.

Ellen Key (Karolina Sofia Key; 1849–1926) Swedish writer. *The Century of the Child*, Ch. 3

30 If every day in the life of a school could be the last day but one, there would be little fault to find with it.

Stephen Leacock (1869–1944) English-born Canadian economist and humorist. *College Days*, 'Memories and Miseries of a Schoolmaster'

31 Four times, under our educational rules, the human pack is shuffled and cut – at eleven-plus, sixteen-plus, eighteen-plus and twenty-plus – and happy is he who comes top of the deck on each occasion, but especially the last. This is called Finals, the very name of which implies that nothing of importance can happen after it. The British postgraduate student is a lonely forlorn soul…for whom nothing has been real since the Big Push.

David Lodge (1935–) British author. *Changing Places*, Ch. 1

32 Universities are the cathedrals of the modern age. They shouldn't have to justify their existence by utilitarian criteria.

David Lodge *Nice Work IV*

33 If you educate a man you educate a person, but if you educate a woman you educate a family.

Ruby Manikan (20th century) Indian Church leader. *The Observer*, 'Sayings of the Week', 30 Mar 1947

34 A gentleman need not know Latin, but he should at least have forgotten it.

Brander Matthews (1852–1929) US writer. Attrib.

35 A whale ship was my Yale College and my Harvard.

Herman Melville (1819–91) US novelist. *Moby Dick*, Ch. 24

36 One tongue is sufficient for a woman.

John Milton (1608–74) English poet. On being asked whether he would allow his daughters to learn foreign languages. Attrib.

37 And if education is always to be conceived along the same antiquated lines of a mere transmission of knowledge, there is little to be hoped from it in the bettering of man's future. For what is the use of transmitting knowledge if the individual's total development lags behind?

Maria Montessori (1870–1952) Italian doctor and educationalist. *The Absorbent Mind*

38 We teachers can only help the work going on, as servants wait upon a master.

Maria Montessori *The Absorbent Mind*

39 Discussion in class, which means letting twenty young blockheads and two cocky neurotics discuss something that neither their teacher nor they know.

Vladimir Nabokov (1899–1977) Russian-born US novelist. *Pnin*, Ch. 6

40 Every schoolmaster after the age of 49 is inclined to flatulence, is apt to swallow frequently, and to puff.

Harold Nicolson (1886–1968) British writer. *The Old School*

41 The schoolteacher is certainly underpaid as a childminder, but ludicrously overpaid as an educator.

John Osborne (1929–94) British dramatist. *The Observer*, 'Sayings of the Week', 21 July 1985

42 School yourself to demureness and patience. Learn to innure yourself to drudgery in science. Learn, compare, collect the facts.

Ivan Pavlov (1849–1936) Russian physiologist. *Bequest to the Academic Youth of Soviet Russia*, 27 Feb 1936

43 He was sent, as usual, to a public school, where a little learning was painfully beaten into him, and from thence to the university, where it was carefully taken out of him.

Thomas Love Peacock (1785–1866) British novelist. *Nightmare Abbey*, Ch. 1

44 'Tis education forms the common mind,
Just as the twig is bent, the tree's inclined.

Alexander Pope (1688–1744) British poet. *Moral Essays*, I

45 Girls and boys grow up more normally together than apart.

Daphne Rae Wife of the Head Master of Westminster School. Remark, May 1988

46 A man who has never gone to school may steal from a freight car, but if he has a university education he may steal the whole railroad.

Franklin D. Roosevelt (1882–1945) US Democratic president. Attrib.

47 But, good gracious, you've got to educate him first.
You can't expect a boy to be vicious till he's been to a good school.

Saki (Hector Hugh Munro; 1870–1916) British writer. *Reginald in Russia*

48 For every person wishing to teach there are thirty not wanting to be taught.

W. C. Sellar (1898–1951) British humorous writer. *And Now All This*

49 No profit grows where is no pleasure ta'en;
In brief, sir, study what you most affect.

William Shakespeare (1564–1616) English dramatist. *The Taming of the Shrew*, I:1

50 A learned man is an idler who kills time by study.

George Bernard Shaw (1856–1950) Irish dramatist and critic. *Man and Superman*

51 There is nothing on earth intended for innocent people so horrible as a school. It is in some respects more cruel than a prison. In a prison, for example, you are not forced to read books written by the warders and the governor.

George Bernard Shaw *Parents and Children*

52 He who can, does. He who cannot, teaches.

George Bernard Shaw *Man and Superman*, 'Maxims for Revolutionists'

53 Indeed one of the ultimate advantages of an education is simply coming to the end of it.

B. F. Skinner (1904–90) US psychologist. *The Technology of Teaching*

54 Education is what survives when what has been learnt has been forgotten.

B. F. Skinner *New Scientist*, 21 May 1964, 'Education in 1984'

55 To me education is a leading out of what is already there in the pupil's soul. To Miss Mackay it is a putting in of something that is not there, and that is not what I call education, I call it intrusion....

Muriel Spark (1918–) British novelist. *The Prime of Miss Jean Brodie*, Ch. 2

56 Soap and education are not as sudden as a massacre, but they are more deadly in the long run.

Mark Twain (Samuel Langhorne Clemens; 1835–1910) US writer. *The Facts concerning the Recent Resignation*

57 People at the top of the tree are those without qualifications to detain them at the bottom.

Peter Ustinov (1921–) British actor. Attrib.

58 I expect you'll be becoming a schoolmaster sir. That's what most of the gentlemen does sir, that gets sent down for indecent behaviour.

Evelyn Waugh (1903–66) British novelist. *Decline and Fall*, Prelude

59 We class schools you see, into four grades: Leading School, First-rate School, Good School, and School.

Evelyn Waugh *Decline and Fall*, Pt. I, Ch. 1

60 We schoolmasters must temper discretion with deceit.

Evelyn Waugh *Decline and Fall*, Pt. I, Ch. 1

61 That's the public-school system all over. They may kick you out, but they never let you down.

Evelyn Waugh *Decline and Fall*, Pt. I, Ch. 3

62 Anyone who has been to an English public school will always feel comparatively at home in prison.

Evelyn Waugh *Decline and Fall*, Pt. III, Ch. 4

63 Assistant masters came and went.... Some liked little boys too little and some too much.

Evelyn Waugh *A Little Learning*

64 The battle of Waterloo was won on the playing fields of Eton.

Duke of Wellington (1769–1852) British general and statesman. Attrib.

65 A very large part of English middle-class education is devoted to the training of servants...In so far as it is, by definition, the training of upper servants, it includes, of course, the instilling of that kind of confidence which will enable the upper servants to supervise and direct the lower servants.

Raymond Henry Williams (1921–88) British academic and writer. *Culture and Society*, Ch. 3

EFFORT

See also work

1 If a job's worth doing, it's worth doing well.

Proverb

2 Energy is Eternal Delight.

William Blake (1757–1827) British poet. *The Marriage of Heaven and Hell*, 'The Voice of the Devil'

3 I have nothing to offer but blood, toil, tears and sweat.

Winston Churchill (1874–1965) British statesman. On becoming prime minister. Speech, House of Commons, 13 May 1940

4 A world where nothing is had for nothing.

Arthur Hugh Clough (1819–61) British poet. *The Bothie of Tober-na-Vuolich*, Bk. VIII, Ch. 5

5 As is the case in all branches of art, success depends in a very large measure upon individual initiative and exertion, and cannot be achieved except by dint of hard work.

Anna Pavlova (1881–1931) Russian ballet dancer. *Pavlova: A Biography* (ed. A. H. Franks), 'Pages of My Life'

6 And here is the lesson I learned in the army. If you want to do a thing badly, you have to work at it as though you want to do it well.

Peter Ustinov (1921–) British actor. *Dear Me*, Ch. 8

7 Please do not shoot the pianist. He is doing his best.

Oscar Wilde (1854–1900) Irish-born British dramatist. *Impressions of America*, 'Leadville'

EGOTISM

See also arrogance, conceit, pride, selfishness

1 Against whom?

Alfred Adler (1870–1937) Austrian psychiatrist. Said when he heard that an egocentric had fallen in love. *Some of My Best Friends* (J. Bishop), 'Exponent of the Soul'

2 No poet or novelist wishes he were the only one who ever lived, but most of them wish they were the only one alive, and quite a number fondly believe their wish has been granted.

W. H. Auden (1907–73) British poet. *The Dyer's Hand*, 'Writing'

3 *Egotist*, n. A person of low taste, more interested in himself than in me.

Ambrose Bierce (1842–?1914) US writer and journalist. *The Devil's Dictionary*

4 Someone said of a very great egotist: 'He would burn your house down to cook himself a couple of eggs.

Nicolas Chamfort (1741–94) French writer. *Caractères et anecdotes*

5 An author who speaks about his own books is almost as bad as a mother who talks about her own children.

Benjamin Disraeli (1804–81) British statesman. Speech in Glasgow, 19 Nov 1873

6 If the Almighty himself played the violin, the credits would still read 'Rubinstein, God, and Piatigorsky', in that order.

Jascha Heifetz (1901–87) Russian-born US violinist. Whenever Heifetz played in trios with Arthur Rubinstein (piano) and Gregor Piatigorsky (cello), Rubinstein always got top billing. *Los Angeles Times*, 29 Aug 1982

7 One had rather malign oneself than not speak of oneself at all.

Duc de la Rochefoucauld (1613–80) French writer. *Maximes*, 138

8 As who should say 'I am Sir Oracle,
And when I ope my lips let no dog bark'.

William Shakespeare (1564–1616) English dramatist. *The Merchant of Venice*, I:1

9 A pompous woman of his acquaintance, complaining that the head-waiter of a restaurant had not shown her and her husband immediately to a table, said, 'We had to tell him who we were.'

Gerald, interested, enquired, 'And who were you?'

Edith Sitwell (1887–1964) British poet and writer. *Taken Care Of*, Ch. 15

10 No man thinks there is much ado about nothing when the ado is about himself.

Anthony Trollope (1815–82) British novelist. *The Bertrams*, Ch. 27

11 I am the only person in the world I should like to know thoroughly.

Oscar Wilde (1854–1900) Irish-born British dramatist. *Lady Windermere's Fan*, II

EMBARRASSMENT

1 The question about everything was, would it bring a blush to the cheek of a young person?

Charles Dickens (1812–70) British novelist. Pondered by Mr Podsnap. *Our Mutual Friend*, Bk. I, Ch. 11

2 Man is the only animal that blushes.
Or needs to.

Mark Twain (Samuel Langhorne Clemens; 1835–1910) US writer. *Following the Equator*, heading of Ch. 27

EMOTION

See also passion, sentimentality

1 There is a road from the eye to the heart that does not go through the intellect.

G. K. Chesterton (1874–1936) British writer. *The Defendant*

2 'There are strings', said Mr Tappertit, 'in the human heart that had better not be wibrated.'

Charles Dickens (1812–70) British novelist. *Barnaby Rudge*, Ch. 22

3 Grief and disappointment give rise to anger, anger to envy, envy to malice, and malice to grief again, till the whole circle be completed.

David Hume (1711–76) Scottish philosopher. *A Treatise of Human Nature*

4 The intellect is always fooled by the heart.

Duc de la Rochefoucauld (1613–80) French writer. *Maximes*, 102

5 Light breaks where no sun shines;
Where no sea runs, the waters of the heart
Push in their tides.

Dylan Thomas (1914–53) Welsh poet. *Light breaks where no sun shines*

6 Pure and complete sorrow is as impossible as pure and complete joy.

Leo Tolstoy (1828–1910) Russian writer. *War and Peace*, Bk. XV, Ch. 1

ENDING

1 All good things must come to an end.

Proverb

2 All's well that ends well.

Proverb

3 This is the way the world ends
Not with a bang but a whimper.

T. S. Eliot (1888–1965) US-born British poet and dramatist. *The Hollow Men*

4 We'll to the woods no more,
The laurels all are cut.

A. E. Housman (1859–1936) British scholar and poet. *Last Poems*, Introductory

5 That but this blow
Might be the be-all and the end-all here –
But here upon this bank and shoal of time –
We'd jump the life to come.

William Shakespeare (1564–1616) English dramatist. *Macbeth*, I:7

6 The bright day is done,
And we are for the dark.

William Shakespeare *Antony and Cleopatra*, V:2

7 Ring out, wild bells, to the wild sky,
The flying cloud, the frosty light:
The year is dying in the night;
Ring out, wild bells, and let him die.

Alfred, Lord Tennyson (1809–92) British poet. *In Memoriam A.H.H.*, CVI

ENDURANCE

See also comfort, courage, determination, misfortune, suffering

1 Even a worm will turn.

Proverb

2 The last straw breaks the camel's back.

Proverb

3 What can't be cured, must be endured.

Proverb

4 Nothing happens to any man that he is not formed by nature to bear.

Marcus Aurelius (121–180 AD) Roman emperor. *Meditations*, Bk. V, Ch. 18

5 Through the night of doubt and sorrow
Onward goes the pilgrim band,
Singing songs of expectation,
Marching to the Promised Land.

Sabine Baring-Gould (1834–1924) British author and hymn writer. *Through the Night of Doubt and Sorrow*

6 In the fell clutch of circumstance,
I have not winced nor cried aloud;
Under the bludgeonings of chance
My head is bloody, but unbowed.

William Ernest Henley (1849–1903) British writer. *Echoes*, IV, 'Invictus. In Mem. R.T.H.B.'

7 ...we could never learn to be brave and patient, if there were only joy in the world.

Helen Keller (1880–1968) US writer and lecturer. *Atlantic Monthly* (May 1890)

8 Job endured everything – until his friends

came to comfort him, then he grew impatient.

Søren Kierkegaard (1813–55) Danish philosopher. *Journal*

9 Sorrow and silence are strong, and patient endurance is godlike.

Henry Wadsworth Longfellow (1807–82) US poet. *Evangeline*

10 Know how sublime a thing it is
To suffer and be strong.

Henry Wadsworth Longfellow *The Light of Stars*

11 The weariest nights, the longest days, sooner or later must perforce come to an end.

Baroness Orczy (1865–1947) British novelist. *The Scarlet Pimpernel*, Ch. 22

12 No pain, no palm; no thorns, no throne; no gall, no glory; no cross, no crown.

William Penn (1644–1718) English preacher. *No Cross, No Crown*

13 The Muse but serv'd to ease some friend, not Wife,
To help me through this long disease, my life.

Alexander Pope (1688–1744) British poet. *Epistle to Dr. Arbuthnot*

14 The pain passes, but the beauty remains.

Pierre Auguste Renoir (1841–1919) French impressionist painter. Explaining why he still painted when his hands were twisted with arthritis. Attrib.

15 Does the road wind up-hill all the way?
Yes, to the very end.
Will the day's journey take the whole long day?
From morn to night, my friend.

Christina Rossetti (1830–74) British poet. *Up-Hill*

16 Had we lived, I should have had a tale to tell of the hardihood, endurance, and courage of my companions which would have stirred the heart of every Englishman. These rough notes and our dead bodies must tell the tale.

Captain Robert Falcon Scott (1868–1912) British explorer. *Message to the Public*

17 Men must endure
Their going hence, even as their coming hither:
Ripeness is all.

William Shakespeare (1564–1616) English dramatist. *King Lear*, V:2

18 For there was never yet philosopher
That could endure the toothache patiently.

William Shakespeare *Much Ado About Nothing*, V:1

19 Let's talk sense to the American people. Let's tell them the truth, that there are no gains without pains.

Adlai Stevenson (1900–65) US statesman. Speech, Chicago, 26 July 1952

20 If you can't stand the heat, get out of the kitchen.

Harry S. Truman (1884–1972) US statesman. Perhaps proverbial in origin, possibly echoes the expression 'kitchen cabinet'. *Mr Citizen*, Ch. 15

21 O you who have borne even heavier things,
God will grant an end to these too.

Virgil (Publius Vergilius Maro; 70–19 BC) Roman poet. *Aeneid*, Bk. I

22 Maybe one day we shall be glad to remember even these hardships.

Virgil *Aeneid*, Bk. I

23 I sing of arms and the man who first from the shores
of Troy came destined an exile to Italy and the Lavinian beaches, much buffeted he on land and on
the deep by force of the gods because of fierce Juno's never-forgetting anger.

Virgil Referring to Aeneas. *Aeneid*, Bk. I

24 Much in sorrow, oft in woe,
Onward, Christians, onward go.

Henry Kirke White (1785–1806) British poet. A hymn, better known in its later form, 'Oft in danger, oft in woe'

ENEMIES

1 Better a thousand enemies outside the house than one inside.

Arabic proverb

2 But I say unto you, That ye resist not evil: but whosoever shall smite thee on thy right cheek, turn to him the other also.
And if any man will sue thee at the law, and take away thy coat, let him have thy cloke also.
And whosoever shall compel thee to go a mile, go with him twain.

Bible: Matthew 5:39–41

3 But I say unto you, Love your enemies, bless them that curse you, do good to them that hate you, and pray for them which despitefully use you, and persecute you;
That ye may be the children of your Father which is in heaven: for he maketh his sun to rise on the evil and on the good, and sendeth rain on the just and on the unjust.
For if ye love them which love you, what reward have ye? do not even the publicans the same?

Bible: Matthew 5:44–46

4 Even a paranoid can have enemies.

Henry Kissinger (1923–) German-born US politician and diplomat. *Time*, 24 Jan 1977

5 They made peace between us; we embraced, and we have been mortal enemies ever since.

Alain-René Lesage (1668–1747) French writer. *Le Diable boiteux*, Ch. 3

6 You must hate a Frenchman as you hate the devil.

Lord Nelson (1758–1805) British admiral. *Life of Nelson* (Southey), Ch. 3

7 The only good Indians I ever saw were dead.

Philip H. Sheridan (1831–88) US general. *The People's Almanac 2* (D. Wallechinsky)

8 He makes no friend who never made a foe.

Alfred, Lord Tennyson (1809–92) British poet. *Idylls of the King*, 'Lancelot and Elaine'

9 I should be like a lion in a cave of savage Daniels.

Oscar Wilde (1854–1900) Irish-born British dramatist. Explaining why he would not be attending a function at a club whose members were hostile to him. Attrib.

ENGLAND

See also Britain, Cambridge, English, London, Oxford, patriotism

1 Oh! who can ever be tired of Bath?

Jane Austen (1775–1817) British novelist. *Northanger Abbey*, Ch. 10

2 One has no great hopes from Birmingham. I always say there is something direful in the sound.

Jane Austen *Emma*, Ch. 36

3 When you think about the defence of England you no longer think of the chalk cliffs of Dover. You think of the Rhine. That is where our frontier lies to-day.

Stanley Baldwin (1867–1947) British statesman. Speech, House of Commons, 30 July 1934

4 Come, friendly bombs, and fall on Slough
It isn't fit for humans now.
There isn't grass to graze a cow
Swarm over, Death!
...
Come, friendly bombs, and fall on Slough
To get it ready for the plough.
The cabbages are coming now:
The earth exhales.

John Betjeman (1906–84) British poet. *Slough*

5 And did those feet in ancient time
Walk upon England's mountains green?
And was the holy lamb of God
On England's pleasant pastures seen?
...
I will not cease from mental fight,
Nor shall my sword sleep in my hand,
Till we have built Jerusalem
In England's green and pleasant land.

William Blake (1757–1827) British poet. Better known as the hymn 'Jerusalem', with music by Sir Hubert Parry; not to be confused with Blake's longer poem *Jerusalem*. *Milton*, Preface

6 England is the mother of parliaments.

John Bright (1811–89) British radical politician. Speech, Birmingham, 18 Jan 1865

7 For England's the one land, I know,
Where men with Splendid Hearts may go;
And Cambridgeshire, of all England,
The shire for Men who Understand.

Rupert Brooke (1887–1915) British poet. *The Old Vicarage, Grantchester*

8 Oh, to be in England
Now that April's there.

Robert Browning (1812–89) British poet. *Home Thoughts from Abroad*

9 Without class differences, England would cease to be the living theatre it is.

Anthony Burgess (John Burgess Wilson; 1917–93) British novelist. *The Observer*, 'Sayings of the Week', 26 May 1985

10 In England there are sixty different religions, and only one sauce.

Domenico Caracciolo (1715–89) Governor of Sicily. Attrib.

11 This could have occurred nowhere but in England, where men and sea interpenetrate, so to speak.

Joseph Conrad (Teodor Josef Konrad Korzeniowski; 1857–1924) Polish-born British novelist. *Youth*

12 Very flat, Norfolk.

Noël Coward (1899–1973) British dramatist. *Private Lives*

13 Regions Caesar never knew
Thy posterity shall sway,
Where his eagles never flew,
None invincible as they.

William Cowper (1731–1800) British poet. *Boadicea*

14 There are many things in life more worthwhile than money. One is to be brought up in this our England which is still the envy of less happy lands.

Lord Denning (1899–1989) British judge. *The Observer*, 'Sayings of the Week', 4 Aug 1968

15 Kent, sir – everybody knows Kent – apples, cherries, hops and women.

Charles Dickens (1812–70) British novelist. *Pickwick Papers*, Ch. 2

16 The Continent will not suffer England to be the workshop of the world.

Benjamin Disraeli (1804–81) British statesman. Speech, House of Commons, 15 Mar 1838

17 England is the paradise of women, the purgatory of men, and the hell of horses.

John Florio (c. 1553–1625) English lexicographer. *Second Fruits*

18 Living in England, provincial England, must be like being married to a stupid but exquisitely beautiful wife.

Margaret Halsey (1910–) US writer. *With Malice Toward Some*

19 All of Stratford, in fact, suggests powdered history – add hot water and stir and you have a delicious, nourishing Shakespeare.

Margaret Halsey *With Malice Toward Some*

20 Dr Johnson's morality was as English an article as a beefsteak.

Nathaniel Hawthorne (1804–64) US novelist and writer. *Our Old Home*, 'Lichfield and Uttoxeter'

21 Pass a law to give every single wingeing bloody Pommie his fare home to England. Back to the smoke and the sun shining ten days a year and shit in the streets. Yer can have it.

Thomas Keneally (1935–) Australian novelist. *The Chant of Jimmy Blacksmith*

22 Winds of the World, give answer! They are whimpering to and fro –
And what should they know of England who only England know?

Rudyard Kipling (1865–1936) Indian-born British writer. *The English Flag*

23 It was one of those places where the spirit of aboriginal England still lingers, the old savage England, whose last blood flows still in a few Englishmen, Welshmen, Cornishmen.

D. H. Lawrence (1885–1930) British novelist. *St Mawr*

24 And suddenly she craved again for the more absolute silence of America. English stillness was so soft, like an inaudible murmur of voices, of presences.

D. H. Lawrence *St Mawr*

25 In an English ship, they say, it is poor grub, poor pay, and easy work; in an American ship, good grub, good pay, and hard work. And this is applicable to the working populations of both countries.

Jack London (1876–1916) US novelist. *The People of the Abyss*, Ch. 20

26 In no country, I believe, are the marriage laws so iniquitous as in England, and the conjugal relation, in consequence, so impaired.

Harriet Martineau (1802–76) British writer. *Society in America*, Vol. III, 'Marriage'

27 In England there is only silence or scandal.

André Maurois (Émile Herzog; 1885–1967) French writer. Attrib.

28 When people say England, they sometimes mean Great Britain, sometimes the United Kingdom, sometimes the British Isles, – but never England.

George Mikes (1912–87) Hungarian-born British writer. *How to be an Alien*

29 It was twenty-one years ago that England and I first set foot on each other. I came for a fortnight; I have stayed ever since.

George Mikes *How to be Inimitable*

30 A family with the wrong members in control – that, perhaps, is as near as one can come to describing England in a phrase.

George Orwell (Eric Blair; 1903–50) British novelist. *The Lion and the Unicorn*, 'The Ruling Class'

31 There can hardly be a town in the South of England where you could throw a brick without hitting the niece of a bishop.

George Orwell *The Road to Wigan Pier*, Ch. 7

32 Damn you, England. You're rotting now, and quite soon you'll disappear.

John Osborne (1929–94) British dramatist. Letter in *Tribune*, Aug 1961

33 There'll always be an England
While there's a country lane,
Wherever there's a cottage small
Beside a field of grain.

Clarke Ross Parker (1914–74) British songwriter. *There'll Always Be an England*

34 The real fact is that I could no longer stand their eternal cold mutton.

Cecil Rhodes (1853–1902) South African statesman. Explaining why he had left his friends in England and come to South Africa. *Cecil Rhodes* (G. le Sueur)

35 England is the paradise of individuality, eccentricity, heresy, anomalies, hobbies, and humours.

George Santayana (1863–1952) US philosopher. *Soliloquies in England*, 'The British Character'

36 This royal throne of kings, this sceptred isle,
This earth of majesty, this seat of Mars,
This other Eden, demi-paradise,
This fortress built by Nature for herself
Against infection and the hand of war,
This happy breed of men, this little world,
This precious stone set in the silver sea,
Which serves it in the office of a wall,
Or as a moat defensive to a house,
Against the envy of less happier lands;
This blessed plot, this earth, this realm, this England,
This nurse, this teeming womb of royal kings,
Fear'd by their breed, and famous by their birth.

William Shakespeare (1564–1616) English dramatist. *Richard II*, II:1

37 Well, I cannot last ever; but it was always yet the trick of our English nation, if they have a good thing, to make it too common.

William Shakespeare *Henry IV, Part Two*, I:2

38 The English take their pleasures sadly after the fashion of their country.

Duc de Sully (1560–1641) French statesman. *Memoirs*

39 They say that men become attached even to Widnes.

A. J. P. Taylor (1906–90) British historian. *The Observer*, 15 Sept 1963

40 Yes. I remember Adlestrop –
The name, because one afternoon
Of heat the express train drew up there
Unwontedly. It was late June.

Edward Thomas (1878–1917) British poet. *Adlestrop*

41 You never find an Englishman among the underdogs – except in England of course.

Evelyn Waugh (1903–66) British novelist. *The Loved One*

ENGLISH

See also British, nationality

1 An Englishman's home is his castle.

Proverb

2 An Englishman's word is his bond.

Proverb

3 That typically English characteristic for which

there is no English name – *esprit de corps.*

Frank Ezra Adcock (1886–1968) British classicist. Presidential address

4 The English instinctively admire any man who has no talent and is modest about it.

James Agate (1877–1947) British theatre critic. Attrib.

5 But of all nations in the world the English are perhaps the least a nation of pure philosophers.

Walter Bagehot (1826–77) British economist and journalist. *The English Constitution*, 'The Monarchy'

6 I like the English. They have the most rigid code of immorality in the world.

Malcolm Bradbury (1932–) British academic and novelist. *Eating People is Wrong*, Ch. 5

7 The wish to spread those opinions that we hold conducive to our own welfare is so deeply rooted in the English character that few of us can escape its influence.

Samuel Butler (1835–1902) British writer. *Erewhon*, Ch. 20

8 The most dangerous thing in the world is to make a friend of an Englishman, because he'll come sleep in your closet rather than spend 10s on a hotel.

Truman Capote (1924–84) US novelist. *The Observer*, 'Sayings of the Week', 24 Mar 1968

9 Thirty millions, mostly fools.

Thomas Carlyle (1795–1881) Scottish historian and essayist. When asked what the population of England was. Attrib.

10 He's an Anglo-Saxon Messenger – and those are Anglo-Saxon attitudes.

Lewis Carroll (Charles Lutwidge Dodgson; 1832–98) British writer. *Through the Looking-Glass*, Ch. 7

11 All the faces here this evening seem to be bloody Poms.

Charles, Prince of Wales (1948–) Eldest son of Elizabeth II. Remark at Australia Day dinner, 1973

12 Smile at us, pay us, pass us; but do not quite forget.
For we are the people of England, that never have spoken yet.

G. K. Chesterton (1874–1936) British writer. *The Secret People*

13 It is said, I believe, that to behold the Englishman at his *best* one should watch him play tip-and-run.

Ronald Firbank (1886–1926) British novelist. *The Flower Beneath the Foot*, Ch. 14

14 *Non Angli sed Angeli*
Not Angles, but angels.

Gregory I (540–604) Pope and saint. Attrib.

15 ...it takes a great deal to produce ennui in an Englishman and if you do, he only takes it as convincing proof that you are well-bred.

Margaret Halsey (1910–) US writer. *With Malice Toward Some*

16 The attitude of the English...toward English history reminds one a good deal of the attitude of a Hollywood director toward love.

Margaret Halsey *With Malice Toward Some*

17 ...the English think of an opinion as something which a decent person, if he has the misfortune to have one, does all he can to hide.

Margaret Halsey *With Malice Toward Some*

18 The English (it must be owned) are rather a foul-mouthed nation.

William Hazlitt (1778–1830) British essayist. *On Criticism*

19 The Englishman never enjoys himself except for a noble purpose.

A. P. Herbert (1890–1971) British writer and politician. *Uncommon Law*

20 When two Englishmen meet, their first talk is of the weather.

Samuel Johnson (1709–84) British lexicographer. *The Idler*

21 The English people on the whole are surely the *nicest* people in the world, and everyone makes everything so easy for everybody else, that there is almost nothing to resist at all.

D. H. Lawrence (1885–1930) British novelist. *Dull London*

22 England is...a country infested with people who love to tell us what to do, but who very rarely seem to know what's going on.

Colin MacInnes (1914–76) British novelist. *England, Half English*, 'Pop Songs and Teenagers'

23 An Englishman, even if he is alone, forms an orderly queue of one.

George Mikes (1912–87) Hungarian-born British writer. *How to be an Alien*

24 Continental people have sex life; the English have hot-water bottles.

George Mikes *How to be an Alien*

25 English women are elegant until they are ten years old, and perfect on grand occasions.

Nancy Mitford (1904–73) British writer. *The Wit of Women* (L. and M. Cowan)

26 The English are busy; they don't have time to be polite.

Baron de Montesquieu (1689–1755) French writer. *Pensées diverses*

27 It has to be admitted that we English have sex on the brain, which is a very unsatisfactory place to have it.

Malcolm Muggeridge (1903–90) British writer. *The Observer*, 'Sayings of the Decade', 1964

28 England is a nation of shopkeepers.

Napoleon I (Napoleon Bonaparte; 1769–1821) French emperor. Attrib.

29 To be an Englishman is to belong to the most exclusive club there is.

Ogden Nash (1902–71) US poet. *England Expects*

30 But Lord! to see the absurd nature of Englishmen, that cannot forbear laughing and jeering at everything that looks strange.

Samuel Pepys (1633–1703) English diarist. *Diary*, 27 Nov 1662

31 Remember that you are an Englishman, and have consequently won first prize in the lottery of life.

Cecil Rhodes (1853–1902) South African statesman. *Dear Me* (Peter Ustinov), Ch. 4

32 The English have no respect for their language, and will not teach their children to speak it...It is impossible for an Englishman to open his mouth, without making some other Englishman despise him.

George Bernard Shaw (1856–1950) Irish dramatist and critic. *Pygmalion*, Preface

33 I think for my part one half of the nation is mad – and the other not very sound.

Tobias Smollett (1721–71) British novelist. *The Adventures of Sir Launcelot Greaves*, Ch. 6

34 I cannot but conclude the bulk of your natives to be the most pernicious race of little odious vermin that nature ever suffered to crawl upon the surface of the earth.

Jonathan Swift (1667–1745) Irish-born Anglican priest and writer. *Gulliver's Travels*, 'Voyage to Brobdingnag', Ch. 6

35 The national sport of England is obstacle-racing. People fill their rooms with useless and cumbersome furniture, and spend the rest of their lives in trying to dodge it.

Herbert Beerbohm Tree (1853–1917) British actor and theatre manager. *Beerbohm Tree* (Hesketh Pearson)

ENTHUSIASM

1 How can I take an interest in my work when I don't like it?

Francis Bacon (1909–92) British painter. *Francis Bacon* (Sir John Rothenstein)

2 It is unfortunate, considering that enthusiasm moves the world, that so few enthusiasts can be trusted to speak the truth.

Arthur Balfour (1848–1930) British statesman. Letter to Mrs Drew, 1918

3 Nothing is so contagious as enthusiasm....It is the genius of sincerity and truth accomplishes no victories without it.

Edward Bulwer-Lytton (1803–73) British novelist and politician. *Dale Carnegie's Scrapbook*

4 Nothing great was ever achieved without enthusiasm.

Ralph Waldo Emerson (1803–82) US poet and essayist. *Essays*, 'Circles'

5 The love of life is necessary to the vigorous prosecution of any undertaking.

Samuel Johnson (1709–84) British lexicographer. *The Rambler*

6 Don't clap too hard – it's a very old building.

John Osborne (1929–94) British dramatist. *The Entertainer*

7 Every man loves what he is good at.

Thomas Shadwell (1642–92) English dramatist. *A True Widow*, V:1

8 To business that we love we rise betime,
And go to't with delight.

William Shakespeare (1564–1616) English dramatist. *Antony and Cleopatra*, IV:4

ENVIRONMENT

See also conservation, ecology

1 One cannot assess in terms of cash or exports and imports an imponderable thing like the turn of a lane or an inn or a church tower or a familiar skyline.

John Betjeman (1906–84) British poet. On siting a new London airport at Wing. *The Observer*, 'Sayings of the Week', 20 July 1969

2 They improvidentially piped growing volumes of sewage into the sea, the healing virtues of which were advertised on every railway station.

Robert Cecil (1913–94) British writer. Referring to seaside resorts. *Life in Edwardian England*

3 If sunbeams were weapons of war, we would have had solar energy long ago.

George Porter (1920–) British chemist. *The Observer*, 'Sayings of the Week', 26 Aug 1973

4 The work is going well, but it looks like the end of the world.

Sherry Rowland (Frank Sherwood R.; 1927–) US chemist. Referring to his research into the destruction of the ozone layer

5 The emergence of intelligence, I am convinced, tends to unbalance the ecology. In other words, intelligence is the great polluter. It is not until a creature begins to manage its environment that nature is thrown into disorder.

Clifford D. Simak (1904–88) US journalist. *Shakespeare's Planet*

ENVY

See also discontent, jealousy

1 Better be envied than pitied.

Proverb

2 The rich man has his motor car,
His country and his town estate.
He smokes a fifty-cent cigar
And jeers at Fate.

F. P. Adams (1881–1960) US journalist. *The Rich Man*

3 Yet though my lamp burns low and dim,
Though I must slave for livelihood –
Think you that I would change with him?
You bet I would!

F. P. Adams *The Rich Man*

4 I am sure the grapes are sour.

Aesop (6th century BC) Reputed Greek writer of fables. *Fables*, 'The Fox and the Grapes'

5 Nearly every man in the city wants a farm until he gets it.

Jacob M. Braude

6 Fools may our scorn, not envy raise,
For envy is a kind of praise.

John Gay (1685–1732) English poet and dramatist. *Fables*

7 The man with toothache thinks everyone happy whose teeth are sound.

George Bernard Shaw (1856–1950) Irish dramatist and critic. *Man and Superman*

8 Whenever a friend succeeds, a little something in me dies.

Gore Vidal (1925–) US novelist. *The Sunday Times Magazine*, 16 Sept 1973

9 Never having been able to succeed in the world, he took his revenge by speaking ill of it.

Voltaire (François-Marie Arouet; 1694–1778) French writer. *Zadig*, Ch. 4

EPITAPHS

See also memorials, obituaries

1 She sleeps alone at last.

Robert Benchley (1889–1945) US humorist. Suggested epitaph for an actress. Attrib.

2 Their name, their year, spelt by the unlettered muse,
The place of fame and elegy supply:
On many a holy text around she strews,
That teach the rustic moralist to die.

Thomas Gray (1716–71) British poet. *Elegy Written in a Country Churchyard*

3 In lapidary inscriptions a man is not upon oath.

Samuel Johnson (1709–84) British lexicographer. *Life of Johnson* (J. Boswell), Vol. II

4 Nowhere probably is there more true feeling, and nowhere worse taste, than in a churchyard – both as regards the monuments and the inscriptions. Scarcely a word of true poetry anywhere.

Benjamin Jowett (1817–93) British theologian. *Letters of B. Jowett* (Abbott and Campbell)

Some actual and literary examples

5 Hereabouts died a very gallant gentleman, Captain L. E. G. Oates of the Inniskilling Dragoons. In March 1912, returning from the Pole, he walked willingly to his death in a blizzard, to try and save his comrades, beset by hardships.

E. L. Atkinson (1882–1929) British naval officer. Epitaph on memorial in the Antarctic.

6 I've played everything but the harp.

Lionel Barrymore (1848–1954) US actor. When asked what words he would like engraved on his tombstone. Attrib.

7 When Sir Joshua Reynolds died
All Nature was degraded;
The King dropped a tear in the Queen's ear,
And all his pictures faded.

William Blake (1757–1827) British poet. *On Art and Artists*

8 With death doomed to grapple,
Beneath this cold slab, he
Who lied in the chapel
Now lies in the Abbey.

Lord Byron (1788–1824) British poet. *Epitaph for William Pitt*

9 Here Skugg
Lies snug
As a bug
In a rug.

Benjamin Franklin (1706–90) US scientist and statesman. An epitaph for a squirrel, 'skugg' being a dialect name for the animal. Letter to Georgiana Shipley, 26 Sept 1772

10 The body of
Benjamin Franklin, printer,
(Like the cover of an old book,
Its contents worn out,
And stript of its lettering and gilding)
Lies here, food for worms!
Yet the work itself shall not be lost,
For it will, as he believed, appear once more
In a new
And more beautiful edition,
Corrected and amended
By its Author!

Benjamin Franklin Suggestion for his own epitaph.

11 Here rests his head upon the lap of Earth
A youth to fortune and to fame unknown.
Fair Science frown'd not on his humble birth,
And Melancholy mark'd him for her own.

Thomas Gray (1716–71) British poet. *Elegy Written in a Country Churchyard*

12 He gave to Mis'ry all he had, a tear,
He gain'd from Heav'n ('twas all he wish'd) a friend.

Thomas Gray *Elegy Written in a Country Churchyard*

13 John Brown's body lies a-mouldering in the grave,
His soul is marching on!

Charles Sprague Hall (19th century) US songwriter. The song commemorates the American hero who died in the cause of abolishing slavery. *John Brown's Body*

14 To Oliver Goldsmith, A Poet, Naturalist, and Historian, who left scarcely any style of writing untouched, and touched none that he did not adorn.

Samuel Johnson (1709–84) British lexicographer. Epitaph on Goldsmith. *Life of Johnson* (J. Boswell), Vol. III

15 Over my dead body!

George S. Kaufman (1889–1961) US dramatist. On being asked to suggest his own epitaph. *The Algonquin Wits* (R. Drennan)

16 Here lies one whose name was writ in water.

John Keats (1795–1821) British poet. Suggesting his own epitaph (recalling a line from *Philaster* by Beaumont and Fletcher). *Life of Keats* (Lord Houghton), Ch. 2

17 'There is a report that Piso is dead; it is a great loss; he was an honest man, who deserved to live longer; he was intelligent and agreeable, resolute and courageous, to be depended upon, generous and faithful.' Add: 'provided

he is really dead'.

Jean de La Bruyère (1645–96) French satirist. *Les Caractères*

18 Go, stranger, and tell the Lacedaemonians that here we lie, obedient to their commands.

Leonidas (d. 480 BC) King of Sparta. Epitaph over the tomb in which he and his followers were buried after their defeat at Thermopylae.

19 Malcolm Lowry
Late of the Bowery
His prose was flowery
And often glowery
He lived, nightly, and drank, daily,
And died playing the ukulele.

Malcolm Lowry (1909–57) British novelist. *Epitaph*

20 Beneath this slab
John Brown is stowed.
He watched the ads
And not the road.

Ogden Nash (1902–71) US poet. *Lather as You Go*

21 For all the Brothers were valiant, and all the Sisters virtuous.

Margaret, Duchess of Newcastle (1624–74) Second wife of William Cavendish. Epitaph in Westminster Abbey

22 He lies below, correct in cypress wood,
And entertains the most exclusive worms.

Dorothy Parker (1893–1967) US writer. *Epitaph for a Very Rich Man*

23 The poor son-of-a-bitch!

Dorothy Parker Quoting from *The Great Gatsby* on paying her last respects to F. Scott Fitzgerald. *Thalberg: Life and Legend* (B. Thomas)

24 In wit a man; simplicity a child.

Alexander Pope (1688–1744) British poet. *Epitaph on Mr. Gay*

25 At last God caught his eye.

Harry Secombe (1921–) Welsh singer, actor, and comedian. Suggested epitaph for a head waiter. In *Punch*, May 1962

26 Alas, poor Yorick! I knew him, Horatio: a fellow of infinite jest, of most excellent fancy.

William Shakespeare (1564–1616) English dramatist. *Hamlet*, V:1

27 *Si monumentum requiris, circumspice.*
If you seek my monument, look around you.

Sir Christopher Wren (1632–1723) English architect. Inscription in St Paul's Cathedral, London

28 Under bare Ben Bulben's head
In Drumcliff churchyard Yeats is laid…
On limestone quarried near the spot
By his command these words are cut:

W. B. Yeats (1865–1939) Irish poet. *Under Ben Bulben*, VI

Some anonymous examples

29 All who come my grave to see
Avoid damp beds and think of me.

Epitaph of Lydia Eason, St Michael's, Stoke

30 Beneath this stone, in hope of Zion,
Doth lie the landlord of the 'Lion'.
His son keeps on the business still,
Resign'd unto the Heavenly will.

Epitaph, Upton-on-Severn churchyard

31 Here lie I and my four daughters,
Killed by drinking Cheltenham waters.
Had we but stick to Epsom salts,
We wouldn't have been in these here vaults.

Cheltenham Waters

32 Here lie I by the chancel door;
They put me here because I was poor.
The further in, the more you pay,
But here lie I as snug as they.

Epitaph, Devon churchyard

33 Here lies a man who was killed by lightning;
He died when his prospects seemed to be brightening.
He might have cut a flash in this world of trouble,
But the flash cut him, and he lies in the stubble.

Epitaph, Torrington, Devon

34 Here lies a valiant warrior
Who never drew a sword;
Here lies a noble courtier
Who never kept his word;
Here lies the Earl of Leicester
Who governed the estates
Whom the earth could never living love,
And the just heaven now hates.

Attrib. to Ben Jonson in *Collection of Epitaphs* (Tissington), 1857.

35 Here lies father and mother and sister and I,
We all died within the space of one short year;
They all be buried at Wimble, except I,
And I be buried here.

Epitaph, Staffordshire churchyard

36 Here lies Fred,
Who was alive and is dead:
Had it been his father,
I had much rather;
Had it been his brother,
Still better than another;
Had it been his sister,
No one would have missed her;
Had it been the whole generation,
Still better for the nation:
But since 'tis only Fred,
Who was alive and is dead, –
There's no more to be said.

Referring to Frederick, Prince of Wales (d. 1751), eldest son of George II and father of George III. Memoirs of George II (Horace Walpole)

37 Here lies my wife,
Here lies she;
Hallelujah!
Hallelujee!

Epitaph, Leeds churchyard

38 Here lies the body of Mary Ann Lowder,
She burst while drinking a seidlitz powder.
Called from the world to her heavenly rest,
She should have waited till it effervesced.

Epitaph

39 Here lies the body of Richard Hind,
Who was neither ingenious, sober, nor kind.
Epitaph

40 Here lies Will Smith – and, what's something rarish,
He was born, bred, and hanged, all in the same parish.
Epitaph

41 Mary Ann has gone to rest,
Safe at last on Abraham's breast,
Which may be nuts for Mary Ann,
But is certainly rough on Abraham.
Epitaph

42 My sledge and anvil lie declined
My bellows too have lost their wind
My fire's extinct, my forge decayed,
And in the Dust my Vice is laid
My coals are spent, my iron's gone
My Nails are Drove, My Work is done.
An epitaph to William Strange, blacksmith, died 6 June 1746 and buried in Nettlebed churchyard.

43 Sacred to the memory of
Captain Anthony Wedgwood
Accidentally shot by his gamekeeper
Whilst out shooting
"Well done thou good and faithful servant"
Epitaph

44 Stranger! Approach this spot with gravity!
John Brown is filling his last cavity.
Epitaph of a dentist

45 This the grave of Mike O'Day
Who died maintaining his right of way.
His right was clear, his will was strong.
But he's just as dead as if he'd been wrong.
Epitaph

46 Warm summer sun shine kindly here:
Warm summer wind blow softly here:
Green sod above lie light, lie light:
Good-night, Dear Heart: good-night, good-night.
Memorial to Clorinda Haywood, St Bartholomew's, Edgbaston

EQUALITY

See also class, feminism, human rights

1 A cat may look at a king.
Proverb

2 All cats are grey in the dark.
Proverb

3 The Prophet Mohamed wanted equality for women. But when Islam went from the desert to the palaces, men put in certain loopholes.
Zeenat Ali Islamic historian. *The Independent*, 16 Sept 1993

3 Equality may perhaps be a right, but no power on earth can ever turn it into a fact.
Honoré de Balzac (1799–1850) French novelist. *La Duchesse de Langeais*

4 From the point of view of sexual morality the aeroplane is valuable in war in that it destroys men and women in equal numbers.
Ernest William Barnes (1874–1953) British clergyman and mathematician. *Rise of Christianity*

5 What makes equality such a difficult business is that we only want it with our superiors.
Henry Becque (1837–99) French dramatist. *Querelles littéraires*

6 All service ranks the same with God –
With God, whose puppets, best and worst,
Are we: there is no last or first.
Robert Browning (1812–89) British poet. *Pippa Passes*, Pt. I

7 The terrorist and the policeman both come from the same basket.
Joseph Conrad (Teodor Josef Konrad Korzeniowski; 1857–1924) Polish-born British novelist. *The Secret Agent*, Ch. 4

8 The majestic egalitarianism of the law, which forbids rich and poor alike to sleep under bridges, to beg in the streets, and to steal bread.
Anatole France (Jacques Anatole François Thibault; 1844–1924) French writer. *The Red Lily*, Ch. 7

9 Men are made by nature unequal. It is vain, therefore, to treat them as if they were equal.
J. A. Froude (1818–94) British historian. *Short Studies on Great Subjects*, 'Party Politics'

10 That all men are equal is a proposition to which, at ordinary times, no sane individual has ever given his assent.
Aldous Huxley (1894–1964) British novelist. *Proper Studies*

11 A just society would be one in which liberty for one person is constrained only by the demands created by equal liberty for another.
Ivan Illich (1926–) Austrian sociologist. *Tools for Conviviality*

12 His foreparents came to America in immigrant ships. My foreparents came to America in slave ships. But whatever the original ships, we are both in the same boat tonight.
Jesse Jackson (1941–) US statesman. Speech, July 1988

13 Your levellers wish to level *down* as far as themselves; but they cannot bear levelling *up* to themselves.
Samuel Johnson (1709–84) British lexicographer. *Life of Johnson* (J. Boswell), Vol. I

14 It is better that some should be unhappy than that none should be happy, which would be the case in a general state of equality.
Samuel Johnson *Life of Johnson* (J. Boswell), Vol. III

15 I have a dream that one day this nation will rise up, live out the true meaning of its creed: we hold these truths to be self-evident, that all men are created equal.
Martin Luther King (1929–68) US Black civil-rights leader. He used the words 'I have a dream' in a number of speeches. Speech, Washington, 27 Aug 1963

16 Never descend to the ways of those

above you.

George Mallaby (1902–78) British diplomat and writer. *From My Level*

17 The cry of equality pulls everyone down.

Iris Murdoch (1919–) Irish-born British novelist. Remark, Sept 1987

18 All animals are equal but some animals are more equal than others.

George Orwell (Eric Blair; 1903–50) British novelist. *Animal Farm*, Ch. 10

19 EQUALITY...is the thing. It is the only true and central premise from which constructive ideas can radiate freely and be operated without prejudice.

Mervyn Peake (1911–68) British novelist. *Titus Groan*, 'The Sun goes down'

20 In America everybody is of the opinion that he has no social superiors, since all men are equal, but he does not admit that he has no social inferiors.

Bertrand Russell (1872–1970) British philosopher. *Unpopular Essays*

21 I think the King is but a man as I am: the violet smells to him as it doth to me.

William Shakespeare (1564–1616) English dramatist. *Henry V*, IV:1

22 Hath not a Jew eyes? Hath not a Jew hands, organs, dimensions, senses, affections, passions, fed with the same food, hurt with the same weapons, subject to the same diseases, healed by the same means, warmed and cooled by the same winter and summer, as a Christian is? If you prick us, do we not bleed? If you tickle us, do we not laugh? If you poison us, do we not die? And if you wrong us, shall we not revenge?

William Shakespeare *The Merchant of Venice*, III:1

23 This is a movie, not a lifeboat.

Spencer Tracy (1900–67) US film star. Defending his demand for equal billing with Katherine Hepburn. Attrib.

24 Everybody should have an equal chance – but they shouldn't have a flying start.

Harold Wilson (1916–95) British politician and prime minister. *The Observer*, 'Sayings of the Year', 1963

25 Whatever women do, they must do it twice as well as men to be thought half as good. Luckily, this is not difficult.

Charlotte Witton Attrib.

Equality in death

See also death

26 It comes equally to us all, and makes us all equal when it comes. The ashes of an Oak in the Chimney, are no epitaph of that Oak, to tell me how high or how large that was; It tells me not what flocks it sheltered while it stood, nor what men it hurt when it fell. The dust of great persons' graves is speechless too, it says nothing, it distinguishes nothing.

John Donne (1573–1631) English poet. *Sermons*, XV

27 Now at last our child is just like all children.

Charles De Gaulle (1890–1970) French general and statesman. On the death of his retarded daughter Anne. *Ten First Ladies of the World* (Pauline Frederick)

28 Pale Death kicks his way equally into the cottages of the poor and the castles of kings.

Horace (Quintus Horatius Flaccus; 65–8 BC) Roman poet. *Odes*, I

29 A heap of dust alone remains of thee;
'Tis all thou art, and all the proud shall be!

Alexander Pope (1688–1744) British poet. *Elegy to the Memory of an Unfortunate Lady*

ESCAPE

1 I bet you a hundred bucks he ain't in here.

Charles Bancroft Dillingham (1868–1934) US theatrical manager. Referring to the escapologist Harry Houdini; said at his funeral, while carrying his coffin. Attrib.

2 He can run, but he can't hide.

Joe Louis (Joseph Louis Barrow; 1914–81) US boxer. Referring to the speed for which his coming opponent, Billy Conn, was renowned. Attrib.

ETERNITY

See also immortality, time

1 Kiss till the cow comes home.

Francis Beaumont (1584–1616) English dramatist. *Scornful Lady*, II:2

2 As it was in the beginning, is now, and ever shall be: world without end.

The Book of Common Prayer *Morning Prayer, Gloria*

3 Thou, silent form, dost tease us out of thought
As doth eternity: Cold Pastoral!

John Keats (1795–1821) British poet. *Ode on a Grecian Urn*

4 Eternity's a terrible thought. I mean, where's it going to end?

Tom Stoppard (1937–) Czech-born British dramatist. *Rosencrantz and Guildenstern Are Dead*, II

ETIQUETTE

See also manners

1 Phone for the fish knives Norman,
As Cook is a little unnerved;
You kiddies have crumpled the serviettes
And I must have things daintily served.

John Betjeman (1906–84) British poet. *How to get on in Society*

2 It is necessary to clean the teeth frequently, more especially after meals, but not on any account with a pin, or the point of a penknife, and it must never be done at table.

St Jean Baptiste de la Salle (1651–1719) *The Rules of Christian Manners and Civility*, I

3 'It is very pleasant dining with a bachelor,' said Miss Matty, softly, as we settled ourselves in the counting-house. 'I only hope it is not improper; so many pleasant things are!'

Elizabeth Gaskell (1810–65) British novelist. *Cranford*, Ch. 4

4 It's all right, Arthur, the white wine came up with the fish.

Herman J. Mankiewicz (1897–1953) US journalist and screenwriter. After vomiting at the table of a fastidious host. Attrib.

5 We could not lead a pleasant life,
And 'twould be finished soon,
If peas were eaten with the knife,
And gravy with the spoon.
Eat slowly: only men in rags
And gluttons old in sin
Mistake themselves for carpet bags
And tumble victuals in.

Walter Raleigh (1861–1922) British scholar. *Laughter from a Cloud*, 'Stans puer ad mensam'

6 'How did you think I managed at dinner, Clarence?' 'Capitally!' 'I had a knife and two forks left at the end,' she said regretfully.

William Pett Ridge (1860–1930) British novelist. *Love at Paddington Green*, Ch. 6

7 I think she must have been very strictly brought up, she's so desperately anxious to do the wrong thing correctly.

Saki (Hector Hugh Munro; 1870–1916) British writer. *Reginald on Worries*

EUROPE

See also Bosnia and Hercegovina, Britain, England, France, Germany, Ireland, Russia, Scotland, Switzerland, Venice, Wales

1 Rome's just a city like anywhere else. A vastly overrated city, I'd say. It trades on belief just as Stratford trades on Shakespeare.

Anthony Burgess (John Burgess Wilson; 1917–93) British novelist. *Mr Enderby*, Pt. II, Ch. 2

2 But the age of chivalry is gone. That of sophisters, economists, and calculators, has succeeded; and the glory of Europe is extinguished for ever.

Edmund Burke (1729–97) British politician. *Reflections on the Revolution in France*

3 The isles of Greece, the isles of Greece!
Where burning Sappho loved and sung,
Where grew the arts of war and peace,
Where Delos rose, and Phoebus sprung!
Eternal summer gilds them yet,
But all, except their sun, is set.

Lord Byron (1788–1824) British poet. *Don Juan*, III

4 The mountains look on Marathon –
And Marathon looks on the sea:
And musing there an hour alone,
I dream'd that Greece might still be free.

Lord Byron *Don Juan*, III

5 While stands the Coliseum, Rome shall stand;
When falls the Coliseum, Rome shall fall;
And when Rome falls – the World.

Lord Byron *Childe Harold's Pilgrimage*, IV

6 We must build a kind of United States of Europe.

Winston Churchill (1874–1965) British statesman. Speech, Zurich, 19 Sept 1946

7 I have never read it. You should not waste your time.

Kenneth Clarke (1940–) British politician. Referring to the Maastricht Treaty. *The Independent*, 17 Mar 1995

8 Apart from cheese and tulips, the main product of the country is advocaat, a drink made from lawyers.

Alan Coren (1938–) British humorist and writer. Referring to Holland. *The Sanity Inspector*, 'All You Need to Know about Europe'

9 Europe is not just about material results, it is about spirit. Europe is a state of mind.

Jacques Delors (1925–) French politician and European statesman. *The Independent*, 19 May 1994

10 Brussels is a madness. I will fight it from within.

James Goldsmith (1933–) British businessman. *The Times*, 10 June 1994

8 Holland…lies so low they're only saved by being dammed.

Thomas Hood (1799–1845) British poet. *Up the Rhine*

11 It's not enough to be Hungarian, you must have talent too.

Alexander Korda (Sandor Kellner; 1893–1956) Hungarian-born British film director. *Alexander Korda* (K. Kulik)

12 In Western Europe there are now only small countries – those that know it and those that don't know it yet.

Théo Lefèvre (1914–73) Belgian prime minister. *The Observer*, 'Sayings of the Year', 1963

13 I am inclined to notice the ruin in things, perhaps because I was born in Italy.

Arthur Miller (1915–) US dramatist. *A View from the Bridge*, I

14 Austria is Switzerland speaking pure German and with history added.

J. E. Morpurgo (1918–) British writer and academic. *The Road to Athens*

15 Providence has given to the French the empire of the land, to the English that of the sea, and to the Germans that of the air.

Jean Paul Richter (Johann Paul Friedrich Richter; 1763–1825) German novelist. Quoted by Thomas Carlyle

16 The people of Crete unfortunately make more history than they can consume locally.

Saki (Hector Hugh Munro; 1870–1916) British writer. *The Jesting of Arlington Stringham*

17 We are part of the community of Europe and

we must do our duty as such.

Marquess of Salisbury (1830–1903) British statesman. Speech, Caernarvon, 11 Apr 1888

18 We're from Madeira, but perfectly respectable, so far.

George Bernard Shaw (1856–1950) Irish dramatist and critic. *You Never Can Tell*, I

19 Let there be light! said Liberty,
And like sunrise from the sea,
Athens arose!

Percy Bysshe Shelley (1792–1822) British poet. *Hellas*, I

20 This going into Europe will not turn out to be the thrilling mutual exchange supposed. It is more like nine middle-aged couples with failing marriages meeting in a darkened bedroom in a Brussels hotel for a Group Grope.

E. P. Thompson (1924–93) British historian. On the Europe debate, *Sunday Times*, 27 Apr 1975

21 Every place I look at I work out the cubic feet, and I say it will make a good warehouse or it won't. Can't help myself. One of the best warehouses I ever see was the Vatican in Rome.

Arnold Wesker (1932–) British dramatist. *Chips with Everything*, I:6

22 That Europe's nothin' on earth but a great big auction, that's all it is.

Tennessee Williams (1911–83) US dramatist. *Cat on a Hot Tin Roof*, I

EVIL

See also good and evil, sin, vice

1 *Honi soit qui mal y pense.*
Evil be to him who evil thinks.

Anonymous Motto for the Order of the Garter

2 It takes a certain courage and a certain greatness even to be truly base.

Jean Anouilh (1910–87) French dramatist. *Ardele*

3 Wherefore I praised the dead which are already dead more than the living which are yet alive.
Yea, better is he than both they, which hath not yet been, who hath not seen the evil work that is done under the sun.

Bible: Ecclesiastes 4:2–3

4 But evil men and seducers shall wax worse and worse, deceiving, and being deceived.

Bible: II Timothy 3:13

5 And this is the condemnation, that light is come into the world, and men loved darkness rather than light, because their deeds were evil.

Bible: John 3:19

6 I never saw a brute I hated so;
He must be wicked to deserve such pain.

Robert Browning (1812–89) British poet. *Childe Roland to the Dark Tower Came*, XIV

7 The belief in a supernatural source of evil is not necessary; men alone are quite capable of every wickedness.

Joseph Conrad (Teodor Josef Konrad Korzeniowski; 1857–1924) Polish-born British novelist. *Under Western Eyes*, Part 2

8 There's a young man hid with me, in comparison with which young man I am a Angel. That young man hears the words I speak. That young man has a secret way pecooliar to himself, of getting at a boy, and at his heart, and at his liver.

Charles Dickens (1812–70) British novelist. Said by Magwitch. *Great Expectations*, Ch. 1

9 Something nasty in the woodshed.

Stella Gibbons (1902–89) British poet and novelist. *Cold Comfort Farm*

10 But evil is wrought by want of thought,
As well as want of heart!

Thomas Hood (1799–1845) British poet. *The Lady's Dream*

11 He who passively accepts evil is as much involved in it as he who helps to perpetrate it.

Martin Luther King (1929–68) US Black civil-rights leader. *Stride Towards Freedom*

12 Farewell remorse! All good to me is lost;
Evil, be thou my Good.

John Milton (1608–74) English poet. *Paradise Lost*, Bk. IV

13 Take thy beak from out my heart, and take thy form from off my door!
Quoth the Raven, 'Nevermore.'

Edgar Allan Poe (1809–49) US poet and writer. *The Raven*

14 There is scarcely a single man sufficiently aware to know all the evil he does.

Duc de la Rochefoucauld (1613–80) French writer. *Maximes*, 269

15 She is a smart old broad. It is a pity she is so nefarious.

Damon Runyon (1884–1946) US writer. *Runyon à la carte*, 'Broadway Incident'

16 Friends, Romans, countrymen, lend me your ears
I come to bury Caesar, not to praise him.
The evil that men do lives after them;
The good is oft interred with their bones.

William Shakespeare (1564–1616) English dramatist. *Julius Caesar*, III:2

17 Evil visited us yesterday.

Ron Taylor British headteacher of Dunblane Primary School. Referring to the killing of 16 children and their teacher by a gunman. 14 March 1996

EVOLUTION

See also survival

1 Descended from the apes? My dear, we will hope it is not true. But if it is, let us pray that it may not become generally known.

Anonymous Remark by the wife of a canon of Worcester Cathedral. *Man's Most Dangerous Myth, The Fallacy of Race* (F. Ashley Montagu)

2 From an evolutionary point of view, man has stopped moving, if he ever did move.

Pierre Teilhard de Chardin (1881–1955) French Jesuit and palaeontologist. *The Phenomenon of Man*, Postscript

3 Man is developed from an ovule, about the 125th of an inch in diameter, which differs in no respect from the ovules of other animals.

Charles Darwin (1809–82) British life scientist. *The Descent of Man*, Ch. 1

4 We must, however, acknowledge, as it seems to me, that man with all his noble qualities, still bears in his bodily frame the indelible stamp of his lowly origin.

Charles Darwin Closing words. *Descent of Man*, Ch. 21

5 We will now discuss in a little more detail the struggle for existence.

Charles Darwin *Origin of Species*, Ch. 3

6 I have called this principle, by which each slight variation, if useful, is preserved, by the term of Natural Selection.

Charles Darwin *Origin of Species*, Ch. 3

7 The expression often used by Mr Herbert Spencer of the Survival of the Fittest is more accurate, and is sometimes equally convenient.

Charles Darwin *Origin of Species*, Ch. 3

8 The question is this: Is man an ape or an angel? I, my lord, am on the side of the angels.

Benjamin Disraeli (1804–81) British statesman. Speech, 25 Nov 1864

9 Philip is a living example of natural selection. He was as fitted to survive in this modern world as a tapeworm in an intestine.

William Golding (1911–93) British novelist. *Free Fall*, Ch. 2

10 I asserted – and I repeat – that a man has no reason to be ashamed of having an ape for his grandfather. If there were an ancestor whom I should feel shame in recalling it would rather be a *man* – a man of restless and versatile intellect – who, not content with an equivocal success in his own sphere of activity, plunges into scientific questions with which he has no real acquaintance, only to obscure them by an aimless rhetoric, and distract the attention of his hearers from the real point at issue by eloquent digressions and skilled appeals to religious prejudice.

T. H. Huxley (1825–95) British biologist. Replying to Bishop WILBERFORCE in the debate on Darwin's theory of evolution at the meeting of the British Association at Oxford. No transcript was taken at the time; the version above is commonly quoted. After hearing Wilberforce's speech, and before rising himself, Huxley is said to have remarked, 'The Lord has delivered him into my hands!'. Speech, 30 June 1860

11 And, in conclusion, I would like to ask the gentleman...whether the ape from which he is descended was on his grandmother's or his grandfather's side of the family.

Samuel Wilberforce (1805–73) British churchman. *See* T. H. HUXLEY. Speech, 30 June 1860

EXAMINATIONS

See also education

1 Examinations are formidable even to the best prepared, for the greatest fool may ask more than the wisest man can answer.

Charles Caleb Colton (?1780–1832) British clergyman and writer. *Lacon*, Vol. II

2 Do not on any account attempt to write on both sides of the paper at once.

W. C. Sellar (1898–1951) British humorous writer. *1066 And All That*, Test Paper 5

3 If silicon had been a gas I should have been a major-general.

James Whistler (1834–1903) US painter. Referring to his failure in a West Point chemistry examination. *English Wits* (L. Russell)

EXAMPLE

1 Practise what you preach.

Proverb

2 Example is the school of mankind, and they will learn at no other.

Edmund Burke (1729–97) British politician. *Letters on a Regicide Peace*, letter 1

3 Do as you would be done by is the surest method that I know of pleasing.

Earl of Chesterfield (1694–1773) English statesman. Letter to his son, 16 Oct 1747

4 What you do not want done to yourself, do not do to others.

Confucius (K'ung Fu-tzu; 551–479 BC) Chinese philosopher. *Analects*

5 Men are not hanged for stealing horses, but that horses may not be stolen.

George Saville (1633–95) English statesman. *Political, Moral and Miscellaneous Thoughts and Reflections*

6 A precedent embalms a principle.

William Scott (1745–1836) British jurist. An opinion given while Advocate-General. Attrib.; also quoted by Benjamin Disraeli (1848)

7 Preachers say, Do as I say, not as I do. But if the physician had the same disease upon him that I have, and he should bid me do one thing, and himself do quite another, could I believe him?

John Selden (1584–1654) English historian. *Table Talk*

8 Do not, as some ungracious pastors do,
Show me the steep and thorny way to heaven,
Whiles, like a puff'd and reckless libertine,
Himself the primrose path of dalliance treads
And recks not his own rede.

William Shakespeare (1564–1616) English dramatist. *Hamlet*, I:3

9 *Dans ce pays-ci, il est bon de tuer de temps en temps un amiral pour encourager les autres.*
In this country it is good to kill an admiral from

time to time, to encourage the others.

Voltaire (François-Marie Arouet; 1694–1778) French writer. Referring to England: Admiral Byng was executed for failing to defeat the French at Minorca (1757). *Candide*, Ch. 23

EXCELLENCE

See also superiority

1 Whatever is worth doing at all is worth doing well.

Earl of Chesterfield (1694–1773) English statesman. Letter to his son, 10 Mar 1746

2 The danger chiefly lies in acting well,
No crime's so great as daring to excel.

Charles Churchill (1731–64) British poet. *Epistle to William Hogarth*

3 If you had been mine when you were seven you would have been the crème de la crème.

Muriel Spark (1918–) British novelist. *The Prime of Miss Jean Brodie*, Ch. 2

4 The best is the enemy of the good.

Voltaire (François-Marie Arouet; 1694–1778) French writer. *Dictionnaire philosophique*, 'Art dramatique'

EXCESS

See also extravagance, moderation

1 *L'embarras des richesses.*
A superfluity of good things.

Abbé Lénor Jean d'Allainval (1700–53) French dramatist. Play title

2 What fun it would be to be poor, as long as one was *excessively* poor! Anything in excess is most exhilarating.

Jean Anouilh (1910–87) French dramatist. *Ring Round the Moon*

3 The road of excess leads to the palace of Wisdom.

William Blake (1757–1827) British poet. *The Marriage of Heaven and Hell*, 'Proverbs of Hell'

4 I would remind you that extremism in the defence of liberty is no vice. And let me remind you also that moderation in the pursuit of justice is no virtue!

Barry Goldwater (1909–) US politician. Speech, San Francisco, 17 July 1964

5 No part of the walls is left undecorated. From everywhere the praise of the Lord is drummed into you.

Nikolaus Pevsner (Bernhard Leon; 1902–83) German-born British art historian. *London, except the Cities of London and Westminster*

6 In baiting a mouse-trap with cheese, always leave room for the mouse.

Saki (Hector Hugh Munro; 1870–1916) British writer. *The Square Egg*

7 'Tis not the drinking that is to be blamed, but the excess.

John Selden (1584–1654) English historian. *Table Talk*

8 The lady doth protest too much, methinks.

William Shakespeare (1564–1616) English dramatist. *Hamlet*, III:2

9 Well said; that was laid on with a trowel.

William Shakespeare *As You Like It*, I:2

10 To gild refined gold, to paint the lily,
To throw a perfume on the violet,
To smooth the ice, or add another hue
Unto the rainbow, or with taper-light
To seek the beauteous eye of heaven to garnish,
Is wasteful and ridiculous excess.

William Shakespeare *King John*, IV:2

11 Heat not a furnace for your foe so hot
That it do singe yourself. We may outrun
By violent swiftness that which we run at,
And lose by over-running.

William Shakespeare *Henry VIII*, I:1

12 It out-herods Herod.

William Shakespeare *Hamlet*, III:2

13 Extreme *busyness*, whether at school or college, kirk or market, is a symptom of deficient vitality.

Robert Louis Stevenson (1850–94) Scottish writer. *Virginibus Puerisque*

14 Battering the gates of heaven with storms of prayer.

Alfred, Lord Tennyson (1809–92) British poet. *St Simeon Stylites*

15 Moderation is a fatal thing, Lady Hunstanton. Nothing succeeds like excess.

Oscar Wilde (1854–1900) Irish-born British dramatist. *A Woman of No Importance*, III

EXECUTION

See also last words, martyrdom, punishment

1 It's time for me to enjoy another pinch of snuff. Tomorrow my hands will be bound, so as to make it impossible.

Jean Sylvain Bailly (1736–93) French astronomer. Said on the evening before his execution. *Anekdotenschatz* (H. Hoffmeister)

2 And almost all things are by the law purged with blood; and without shedding of blood is no remission.

Bible: Hebrews 9:22

3 And when they were come to the place, which is called Calvary, there they crucified him, and the malefactors, one on the right hand, and the other on the left.

Bible: Luke 23:33

4 I die a Christian, according to the Profession of the Church of England, as I found it left me by my Father.

Charles I (1600–49) King of England. Speech on the scaffold, 30 Jan 1649

5 Thou wilt show my head to the people: it is worth showing.

Georges Jacques Danton (1759–94) French political activist. Said as he mounted the scaffold, 5 Apr 1794. *French Revolution* (Carlyle), Bk. VI, Ch. 2

6 It is a far, far, better thing that I do, than I have ever done; it is a far, far, better rest that I go to, than I have ever known.

Charles Dickens (1812–70) British novelist. Said by Sydney Carton. *A Tale of Two Cities*, Bk. II, Ch. 15

7 To die for faction is a common evil,
But to be hanged for nonsense is the Devil.

John Dryden (1631–1700) British poet and dramatist. *Absalom and Achitophel*, II

8 Son of Saint Louis, ascend to heaven.

Abbé Edgeworth de Firmont (1745–1807) Irish-born confessor to Louis XVI. Said to Louis XVI as he climbed up to the guillotine. Attrib.

9 Let them bestow on every airth a limb;
Then open all my veins, that I may swim
To thee, my Maker! in that crimson lake;
Then place my parboiled head upon a stake –
Scatter my ashes – strew them in the air; –
Lord! since thou know'st where all these atoms are,
I'm hopeful thou'lt recover once my dust,
And confident thou'lt raise me with the just.

James Graham (1612–50) Scottish general. Lines written on the window of his jail the night before his execution.

10 And have they fixed the where and when?
And shall Trelawny die?
Here's twenty thousand Cornish men
Will know the reason why!

R. S. Hawker (1803–75) British poet. Referring to the imprisonment (1688) of Trelawny, Bishop of Bristol, by James II. *Song of the Western Men*

11 They hang us now in Shrewsbury jail:
The whistles blow forlorn,
And trains all night groan on the rail
To men that die at morn.

A. E. Housman (1859–1936) British scholar and poet. *A Shropshire Lad*, 'Reveillé'

12 Depend upon it, Sir, when a man knows he is to be hanged in a fortnight, it concentrates his mind wonderfully.

Samuel Johnson (1709–84) British lexicographer. *Life of Johnson* (J. Boswell), Vol. III

13 If we are to abolish the death penalty, I should like to see the first step taken by our friends the murderers.

Alphonse Karr (1808–90) French writer. *Les Guêpes*, Jan 1849

14 'For they're hangin' Danny Deever, you can hear the Dead March play,
The Regiment's in 'ollow square – they're hangin' 'im to-day;
They've taken of 'is buttons off an' cut 'is stripes away,
An' they're hangin' Danny Deever in the mornin'.'

Rudyard Kipling (1865–1936) Indian-born British writer. *Danny Deever*

15 Be of good comfort, Master Ridley, and play the man; we shall this day light such a candle, by God's grace, in England as I trust shall never be put out.

Hugh Latimer (1485–1555) English churchman. Said to Nicholas Ridley as they were about to be burnt at the stake for heresy. *Famous Last Words* (B. Conrad)

16 He nothing common did or mean
Upon that memorable scene,
But with his keener eye
The axe's edge did try.

Andrew Marvell (1621–78) English poet. Referring to the execution of Charles I. *An Horatian Ode upon Cromwell's Return from Ireland*

17 Do not hack me as you did my Lord Russell.

Duke of Monmouth (1649–85) An illegitimate son of Charles II. Said to the headsman before his execution. *History of England* (Macaulay), Vol. I, Ch. 5

18 I pray you, Master Lieutenant, see me safe up, and for coming down let me shift for myself.

Thomas More (1478–1535) English lawyer and scholar. On climbing onto the scaffold prior to his execution. *Life of Sir Thomas More* (William Roper)

19 Pluck up thy spirits, man, and be not afraid to do thine office; my neck is very short; take heed therefore thou strike not awry, for saving of thine honesty.

Thomas More Said to the headsman. *Life of Sir Thomas More* (Roper)

20 This hath not offended the king.

Thomas More Said as he drew his beard aside before putting his head on the block

21 The sight of it gave me infinite pleasure, as it proved that I was in a civilized society.

Mungo Park (1771–1806) Scottish explorer. Remark on finding a gibbet in an unexplored part of Africa. Attrib.

22 I went out to Charing Cross, to see Major-general Harrison hanged, drawn, and quartered; which was done there, he looking as cheerful as any man could do in that condition.

Samuel Pepys (1633–1703) English diarist. *Diary*, 13 Oct 1660

23 The world itself is but a large prison, out of which some are daily led to execution.

Walter Raleigh (1554–1618) English explorer. Said after his trial for treason, 1603. Attrib.

24 So the heart be right, it is no matter which way the head lies.

Walter Raleigh On laying his head on the executioner's block. Attrib.

25 Tis a sharp remedy, but a sure one for all ills.

Walter Raleigh Referring to the executioner's axe just before he was beheaded. Attrib.

26 If you give me six lines written by the most honest man, I will find something in them to hang him.

Cardinal Richelieu (1585–1642) French statesman. Exact wording uncertain. Attrib.

27 *'O liberté! O liberté! Que de crimes on commet en ton nom!'*
Oh liberty! Oh liberty! What crimes are committed in thy name!

Madame Roland (1754–93) French revolutionary. Said as she mounted the steps of the guillotine. Attrib.

28 Then, with that faint fleeting smile playing about his lips, he faced the firing squad; erect and motionless, proud and disdainful, Walter Mitty, the undefeated, inscrutable to the last.

James Thurber (1894–1961) US humorist. *My World and Welcome to It*, 'The Secret Life of Walter Mitty'

EXISTENCE

1 Dear Sir, Your astonishment's odd:
I am always about in the Quad.
And that's why the tree
Will continue to be,
Since observed by Yours faithfully, God.

Anonymous The response to KNOX's limerick

2 Let us be moral. Let us contemplate existence.

Charles Dickens (1812–70) British novelist. *Martin Chuzzlewit*, Ch. 10

3 As far as we can discern, the sole purpose of human existence is to kindle a light in the darkness of mere being.

Carl Gustav Jung (1875–1961) Swiss psychoanalyst. *Memories, Dreams, Reflections*, Ch. 11

4 There once was a man who said 'God
Must think it exceedingly odd
If he find that this tree
Continues to be
When there's no one about in the Quad.'

Ronald Knox (1888–1957) British Roman Catholic priest. For a reply, *see* ANONYMOUS. Attrib.

5 I know perfectly well that I don't want to do anything; to do something is to create existence – and there's quite enough existence as it is.

Jean-Paul Sartre (1905–80) French writer. *Nausea*

EXPECTATION

See also anticipation, disappointment, hope

1 When the seagulls are following a trawler, it's because they think sardines are going to be thrown into the sea.

Eric Cantona (1966–) French football player. Remark made after he kicked a fan who taunted him during a match. *The Independent*, 27 Jan 1995

2 As I know more of mankind I expect less of them, and am ready now to call a man *a good man*, upon easier terms than I was formerly.

Samuel Johnson (1709–84) British lexicographer. *Life of Johnson* (J. Boswell), Vol. IV

3 Dear Mary, We all knew you had it in you.

Dorothy Parker (1893–1967) US writer. Telegram sent to a friend on the successful outcome of her much-publicized pregnancy

4 'Blessed is the man who expects nothing, for he shall never be disappointed' was the ninth beatitude.

Alexander Pope (1688–1744) British poet. Letter to Fortescue, 23 Sept 1725

5 See yon pale stripling! when a boy,
A mother's pride, a father's joy!

Walter Scott (1771–1832) Scottish novelist. *Rokeby*, III

6 Gomer Owen who kissed her once by the pigsty when she wasn't looking and never kissed her again although she was looking all the time.

Dylan Thomas (1914–53) Welsh poet. *Under Milk Wood*

7 This suspense is terrible. I hope it will last.

Oscar Wilde (1854–1900) Irish-born British dramatist. *The Importance of Being Earnest*, III

EXPEDIENCY

1 And my parents finally realize that I'm kidnapped and they snap into action immediately: they rent out my room.

Woody Allen (Allen Stewart Konigsberg; 1935–) US film actor. *Woody Allen and His Comedy* (E. Lax)

2 I would rather be an opportunist and float than go to the bottom with my principles round my neck.

Stanley Baldwin (1867–1947) British statesman. Attrib.

3 Nobody is forgotten when it is convenient to remember him.

Benjamin Disraeli (1804–81) British statesman. Attrib.

4 You can't learn too soon that the most useful thing about a principle is that it can always be sacrificed to expediency.

W. Somerset Maugham (1874–1965) British novelist. *The Circle*, III

5 Death and taxes and childbirth! There's never any convenient time for any of them!

Margaret Mitchell (1909–49) US novelist. *Gone with the Wind*

6 No man is justified in doing evil on the ground of expediency.

Theodore Roosevelt (1858–1919) US Republican president. *The Strenuous Life*

7 Well, a widow, I see, is a kind of sinecure.

William Wycherley (1640–1716) English dramatist. *The Plain Dealer*, V:3

EXPERIENCE

See also history, past

1 A young physician fattens the churchyard.

Proverb

2 Experience is the best teacher.
Proverb

3 Experience is the mother of wisdom.
Proverb

4 Live and learn.
Proverb

5 Practice makes perfect.
Proverb

6 Experience is a good teacher, but she sends in terrific bills.
Minna Antrim (b. 1861) US writer. *Naked Truth and Veiled Allusions*

7 One should try everything once, except incest and folk-dancing.
Arnold Bax (1883–1953) British composer. *Farewell to My Youth*

8 You will think me lamentably crude: my experience of life has been drawn from life itself.
Max Beerbohm (1872–1956) British writer. *Zuleika Dobson*, Ch. 7

9 Experience isn't interesting till it begins to repeat itself – in fact, till it does that, it hardly *is* experience.
Elizabeth Bowen (1899–1973) Irish novelist. *The Death of the Heart*, Pt. I, Ch. 1

10 When all is said and done, no literature can outdo the cynicism of real life; you won't intoxicate with one glass someone who has already drunk up a whole barrel.
Anton Chekhov (1860–1904) Russian dramatist. Letter, 1887

11 If men could learn from history, what lessons it might teach us! But passion and party blind our eyes and the light which experience gives is a lantern on the stern, which shines only on the waves behind us!
Samuel Taylor Coleridge (1772–1834) British poet. *Recollections* (Allsop)

12 An experience of women which extends over many nations and three continents.
Arthur Conan Doyle (1856–1930) British writer. *The Sign of Four*

13 How many roads must a man walk down
Before you call him a man?
Bob Dylan (Robert Allen Zimmerman; 1941–) US popular singer. *Blowin' in the Wind*

14 What experience and history teach is this – that people and governments never have learned anything from history, or acted on principles deduced from it.
Hegel (1770–1831) German philosopher. *Philosophy of History*, Introduction

15 A moment's insight is sometimes worth a life's experience.
Oliver Wendell Holmes (1809–94) US writer. *The Professor at the Breakfast Table*, Ch. 10

16 Experience is never limited, and it is never complete; it is an immense sensibility, a kind of huge spider-web of the finest silken threads suspended in the chamber of consciousness, and catching every air-borne particle in its tissue.
Henry James (1843–1916) US novelist. *Partial Portraits*, 'The Art of Fiction'

17 Nothing ever becomes real till it is experienced – even a proverb is no proverb to you till your life has illustrated it.
John Keats (1795–1821) British poet. Letter to George and Georgiana Keats, 19 Mar 1819

18 He was what I often think is a dangerous thing for a statesman to be – a student of history; and like most of those who study history, he learned from the mistakes of the past how to make new ones.
A. J. P. Taylor (1906–90) British historian. Referring to Napoleon III. *The Listener*, 6 June 1963

19 Nourishing a youth sublime
With the fairy tales of science, and the long result of Time.
Alfred, Lord Tennyson (1809–92) British poet. *Locksley Hall*

20 All experience is an arch wherethro'
Gleams that untravelled world, whose margin fades
For ever and for ever when I move.
Alfred, Lord Tennyson *Ulysses*

21 You don't set a fox to watching the chickens just because he has a lot of experience in the hen house.
Harry S. Truman (1884–1972) US statesman. Referring to Vice-President Nixon's nomination for President. Speech, 30 Oct 1960

22 I have learned
To look on nature, not as in the hour
Of thoughtless youth; but hearing often-times
The still, sad music of humanity.
William Wordsworth (1770–1850) British poet. *Lines composed a few miles above Tintern Abbey*

EXPERTS

1 By studying the masters – not their pupils.
Niels Henrik Abel (1809–29) Norwegian mathematician. When asked how he had become a great mathematician so quickly. *Men of Mathematics* (E. T. Bell)

2 An expert is a man who has made all the mistakes, which can be made, in a very narrow field.
Niels Bohr (1885–1962) Danish physicist. Attrib.

3 An expert is someone who knows some of the worst mistakes that can be made in his subject, and how to avoid them.
Werner Heisenberg (1901–76) German physicist. *Physics and Beyond*

4 An accomplished man to his finger-tips.
Horace (Quintus Horatius Flaccus; 65–8 BC) Roman poet. *Satires*, I

5 Specialist – A man who knows more and more

about less and less.

William James Mayo (1861–1934) US surgeon. Also attributed to Nicholas Butler

6 The trouble with specialists is that they tend to think in grooves.

Elaine Morgan (1920–) British writer. *The Descent of Woman*, Ch. 1

EXPLANATIONS

1 I am one of those unfortunates to whom death is less hideous than explanations.

Wyndham Lewis (1891–1969) British journalist and writer. *Welcome to All This*

2 There is occasions and causes why and wherefore in all things.

William Shakespeare (1564–1616) English dramatist. *Henry V*, V:1

EXPLOITATION

1 Thus the devil played at chess with me, and yielding a pawn, thought to gain a queen of me, taking advantage of my honest endeavours.

Thomas Browne (1605–82) English physician and writer. *Religio Medici*, Pt. I

2 Mortals, whose pleasures are their only care,
First wish to be imposed on, and then are.

William Cowper (1731–1800) British poet. *The Progress of Error*

3 I should be trading on the blood of my men.

Robert E. Lee (1807–70) US general. Refusing to write his memoirs. *Nobody Said It Better* (M. Ringo)

4 I am confident that the English legal system will not support Mr Justice Parker's decision or uphold what is effectively professional slavery.

George Michael (1963–) British pop singer. Referring to his court action against Sony, who refused to release him from a recording contract he signed in his youth. *The Times*, 22 June 1994

EXPLORATION

See also discovery

1 The fair breeze blew, the white foam flew,
The furrow followed free;
We were the first that ever burst
Into that silent sea.

Samuel Taylor Coleridge (1772–1834) British poet. *The Rime of the Ancient Mariner*, II

2 Go West, young man, and grow up with the country.

Horace Greeley (1811–72) US politician and journalist. Also attributed to the US writer John Soule (1815–91), *Terre Haute* (Indiana) *Express*, 1851. *Hints toward Reform*

3 Nothing easier. One step beyond the pole, you see, and the north wind becomes a south one.

Robert Edwin Peary (1856–1920) US explorer. Explaining how he knew he had reached the North Pole. Attrib.

EXTRAVAGANCE

See also excess, luxury, money, ostentation, thrift, waste

1 Riches are for spending.

Francis Bacon (1561–1626) English philosopher. *Essays*, 'Of Expense'

2 All progress is based upon a universal innate desire on the part of every organism to live beyond its income.

Samuel Butler (1835–1902) British writer. *Notebooks*

3 He sometimes forgets that he is Caesar, but I always remember that I am Caesar's daughter.

Julia (39 BC–14 AD) Daughter of Augustus. Replying to suggestions that she should live in the simple style of her father, which contrasted with her own extravagance. *Saturnalia* (Macrobius)

4 All decent people live beyond their incomes nowadays, and those who aren't respectable live beyond other people's. A few gifted individuals manage to do both.

Saki (Hector Hugh Munro; 1870–1916) British writer. *The Match-Maker*

5 I suppose that I shall have to die beyond my means.

Oscar Wilde (1854–1900) Irish-born British dramatist. When told that an operation would be expensive. He is also believed to have said 'I am dying beyond my means' on accepting a glass of champagne as he lay on his deathbed. *Life of Wilde* (Sherard)

EYES

See also appearance

1 It needs no dictionary of quotations to remind me that the eyes are the windows of the soul.

Max Beerbohm (1872–1956) British writer. *Zuleika Dobson*, Ch. 4

2 Jeepers Creepers – where'd you get them peepers?

Johnny Mercer (1909–76) US lyricist and composer. *Jeepers Creepers*

3 Out vile jelly!
Where is thy lustre now?

William Shakespeare (1564–1616) English dramatist. Spoken by Cornwall as he puts out Gloucester's remaining eye. *King Lear*, III:7

F

FACTS

See also truth

1 Now, what I want is Facts...Facts alone are wanted in life.

Charles Dickens (1812–70) British novelist. *Hard Times,* Bk. I, Ch. 1

2 Facts do not cease to exist because they are ignored.

Aldous Huxley (1894–1964) British novelist. *Proper Studies*

3 Facts speak louder than statistics.

Geoffrey Streatfield (1897–1978) British lawyer. *The Observer,* 'Sayings of the Week', 19 Mar 1950

FAILURE

See also success

1 A miss is as good as a mile.

Proverb

2 She knows there's no success like failure
And that failure's no success at all.

Bob Dylan (Robert Allen Zimmerman; 1941–) US popular singer. *Love Minus Zero No Limit*

3 It doesn't hurt to lose my crown, it hurts to lose.

Steffi Graf (1969–) German tennis player. *The Independent,* 22 June 1994

4 Here lies Joseph, who failed in everything he undertook.

Joseph II (1741–90) Holy Roman Emperor. Suggesting his own epitaph when reflecting upon the disappointment of his hopes for reform. Attrib.

5 Show me a good and gracious loser and I'll show you a failure.

Knute Rockne (1888–1931) US football coach. Attrib.

6 Like a dull actor now
I have forgot my part and I am out,
Even to a full disgrace.

William Shakespeare (1564–1616) English dramatist. *Coriolanus,* V:3

FAIRIES

See also supernatural

1 Every time a child says 'I don't believe in fairies' there is a little fairy somewhere that falls down dead.

J. M. Barrie (1860–1937) British novelist and dramatist. *Peter Pan,* I

2 When the first baby laughed for the first time, the laugh broke into a thousand pieces and they all went skipping about, and that was the beginning of fairies.

J. M. Barrie

3 There are fairies at the bottom of our garden.

Rose Fyleman (1877–1957) British writer. *Fairies and Chimneys*

FAITH

See also belief, faithfulness, God, religion, trust

1 Faith will move mountains.

Proverb

2 By faith the walls of Jericho fell down, after they were compassed about seven days.

Bible: Hebrews 11:30

3 Now faith is the substance of things hoped for, the evidence of things not seen.

Bible: Hebrews 11:1

4 These all died in faith, not having received the promises, but having seen them afar off, and were persuaded of them, and embraced them, and confessed that they were strangers and pilgrims on the earth.

Bible: Hebrews 11:13

5 For we walk by faith, not by sight.

Bible: II Corinthians 5:7

6 For I am now ready to be offered, and the time of my departure is at hand.
I have fought a good fight, I have finished my course, I have kept the faith:
Henceforth there is laid up for me a crown of righteousness, which the Lord, the righteous judge, shall give me at that day: and not to me only, but unto all them also that love his appearing.

Bible: II Timothy 4:6–8

7 Even so faith, if it hath not works, is dead, being alone.

Bible: James 2:17

8 And Jesus said unto them, I am the bread of life: he that cometh to me shall never hunger; and he that believeth on me shall never thirst.

Bible: John 6:35

9 I feel no need for any other faith than my faith in human beings.

Pearl Buck (1892–1973) US novelist. *I Believe*

10 The prayer that reforms the sinner andheals the sick is an absolute faith that all things are possible to God – a spiritual understanding of Him, an unselfed love.

Mary Baker Eddy (1821–1910) US religious leader. *Science and Health, with Key to the Scriptures*

11 And I said to the man who stood at the gate of the year: 'Give me a light that I may tread safely into the unknown'. And he replied: 'Go out into the darkness and put your hand into the hand of God. That shall be to you better than light and safer than a known way.'

Minnie Louise Haskins (1875–1957) US writer. Remembered because it was quoted by George VI in his Christmas broadcast, 1939. *The Desert*, Introduction

12 My dear child, you must believe in God in spite of what the clergy tell you.

Benjamin Jowett (1817–93) British theologian. *Autobiography* (Asquith), Ch. 8

13 Booth died blind and still by faith he trod,
Eyes still dazzled by the ways of God.

Vachel Lindsay (1879–1931) US poet. *General William Booth Enters Heaven*

14 Faith may be defined briefly as an illogical belief in the occurrence of the improbable.

H. L. Mencken (1880–1956) US journalist. *Prejudices*, 'Types of Men'

15 It takes a long while for a naturally trustful person to reconcile himself to the idea that after all God will not help him.

H. L. Mencken *Notebooks*, 'Minority Report'

16 Lead, kindly Light, amid the encircling gloom,
Lead thou me on;
The night is dark, and I am far from home,
Lead thou me on.

Cardinal Newman (1801–90) British theologian. *Lead Kindly Light*

17 Even such is Time, that takes in trust
Our youth, our joys, our all we have,
And pays us but with age and dust;
Who in the dark and silent grave,
When we have wandered all our ways,
Shuts up the story of our days;
But from this earth, this grave, this dust,
My God shall raise me up, I trust.

Walter Raleigh (1554–1618) English explorer. Written on the night before his execution. Attrib.

18 'Tis not the dying for a faith that's so hard, Master Harry – every man of every nation has done that – 'tis the living up to it that is difficult.

William Makepeace Thackeray (1811–63) British novelist. *Henry Esmond*, Ch. 6

19 Faith consists in believing when it is beyond the power of reason to believe. It is not enough that a thing be possible for it to be believed.

Voltaire (François-Marie Arouet; 1694–1778) French writer. *Questions sur l'encyclopédie*

FAITHFULNESS

See also loyalty

1 It is better to be unfaithful than faithful without wanting to be.

Brigitte Bardot (1934–) French film actress. *The Observer*, 'Sayings of the Week', 18 Feb 1968

2 Through perils both of wind and limb,
Through thick and thin she follow'd him.

Samuel Butler (1612–80) English satirist. *Hudibras*, Pt. II

3 I have been faithful to thee, Cynara! in my fashion.

Ernest Dowson (1867–1900) British lyric poet. *Non Sum Qualis Eram Bonae Sub Regno Cynarae*

4 We only part to meet again.
Change, as ye list, ye winds; my heart shall be
The faithful compass that still points to thee.

John Gay (1685–1732) English poet and dramatist. *Sweet William's Farewell*

5 But I'm always true to you, darlin', in my fashion,
Yes, I'm always true to you, darlin', in my way.

Cole Porter (1893–1964) US songwriter. *Kiss Me, Kate*, 'Always True to You in My Fashion'

FAME

See also popularity, posterity, reputation

1 A celebrity is a person who works hard all his life to become known, then wears dark glasses to avoid being recognized.

Fred Allen (1894–1956) US comedian. *Treadmill to Oblivion*

2 Fame is like a river, that beareth up things light and swollen, and drowns things weighty and solid.

Francis Bacon (1561–1626) English philosopher. *Essays*, 'Of Praise'

3 I should like one of these days to be so well known, so popular, so celebrated, so famous, that it would permit me…to break wind in society, and society would think it a most natural thing.

Honoré de Balzac (1799–1850) French novelist. Attrib.

4 The celebrity is a person who is known for his well-knownness.

Daniel J. Boorstin (1914–) US writer. *The Image*, 'From Hero to Celebrity: The Human Pseudo-event'

5 A best-seller was a book which somehow sold well simply because it was selling well.

Daniel J. Boorstin *The Image*, 'From Shapes to Shadows: Dissolving Forms'

6 I awoke one morning and found myself famous.

Lord Byron (1788–1824) British poet. Remark made after the publication of *Childe Harold's Pilgrimage* (1812). Entry in Memoranda

7 Being a star has made it possible for me to get insulted in places where the average Negro could never hope to get insulted.

Sammy Davis Jnr (1925–90) US singer. *Yes I Can*

8 If a man make a better mouse-trap than his neighbour, though he build his house in the woods, the world will make a beaten path to his door.

Ralph Waldo Emerson (1803–82) US poet and essayist. Attrib.

9 A big man has no time really to do anything but just sit and be big.

F. Scott Fitzgerald (1896–1940) US novelist. *This Side of Paradise*, Bk. III, Ch. 2

10 Fame is sometimes like unto a kind of mushroom, which Pliny recounts to be the greatest miracle in nature, because growing and having no root.

Thomas Fuller (1608–61) English historian. *The Holy State and the Profane State*

11 Fame is a powerful aphrodisiac.

Graham Greene (1904–91) British novelist. *Radio Times*, 10 Sept 1964

12 Every man has a lurking wish to appear considerable in his native place.

Samuel Johnson (1709–84) British lexicographer. Letter to Sir Joshua Reynolds. *Life of Johnson* (J. Boswell), Vol. II

13 One of the drawbacks of Fame is that one can never escape from it.

Nellie Melba (Helen Porter Mitchell; 1861–1931) Australian soprano. *Melodies and Memories*

14 Fame is the spur that the clear spirit doth raise
(That last infirmity of noble mind)
To scorn delights, and live laborious days.

John Milton (1608–74) English poet. *Lycidas*

15 'What are you famous *for*?'
'For nothing. I am just famous.'

Iris Murdoch (1919–) Irish-born British novelist. *The Flight from the Enchanter*

16 I'm never going to be famous…I don't do anything. Not one single thing. I used to bite my nails, but I don't even do that any more.

Dorothy Parker (1893–1967) US writer. *The Little Hours*

17 If you have to tell them who you are, you aren't anybody.

Gregory Peck (1916–) US film star. Remarking upon the failure of anyone in a crowded restaurant to recognize him. *Pieces of Eight* (S. Harris)

18 The more you are talked about, the more you will wish to be talked about. The condemned murderer who is allowed to see the account of his trial in the Press is indignant if he finds a newspaper which has reported it inadequately.…Politicians and literary men are in the same case.

Bertrand Russell (1872–1970) British philosopher. *Human Society in Ethics and Politics*

19 Love of fame is the last thing even learned men can bear to be parted from.

Tacitus (c. 55–c. 120 AD) Roman historian. *Histories*, IV, 6

20 To famous men all the earth is a sepulchre.

Thucydides (c. 460–c. 400 BC) Greek historian and general. *History of the Peloponnesian War*, Bk. II, Ch. 43

21 The only man who wasn't spoilt by being lionized was Daniel.

Herbert Beerbohm Tree (1853–1917) British actor and theatre manager. *Beerbohm Tree* (Hesketh Pearson)

22 When I pass my name in such large letters I blush, but at the same time instinctively raise my hat.

Herbert Beerbohm Tree *Beerbohm Tree* (Hesketh Pearson)

23 In the future, everyone will be famous for 15 minutes.

Andy Warhol (Andrew Warhola; 1926–87) US pop artist. Attrib.

24 There is only one thing in the world worse than being talked about, and that is not being talked about.

Oscar Wilde (1854–1900) Irish-born British dramatist. *The Picture of Dorian Gray*, Ch. 1

FAMILIARITY

1 Familiarity breeds contempt.

Proverb

2 No man is a hero to his valet.

Anne-Marie Bigot de Cornuel (1605–94) French society hostess. *Lettres de Mlle Aissé*, 13 Aug 1728

3 I've grown accustomed to the trace
Of something in the air,
Accustomed to her face.

Alan Jay Lerner (1918–86) US songwriter. *My Fair Lady*, II:6

4 I have been here before.
But when or how I cannot tell:
I know the grass beyond the door,
The sweet keen smell,
The sighing sound, the lights around the shore.

Dante Gabriel Rossetti (1828–82) British painter and poet. *Sudden Light*

5 I like familiarity. In me it does not breed contempt. Only more familiarity.

Gertrude Stein (1874–1946) US writer. *Dale Carnegie's Scrapbook*

6 He began to think the tramp a fine, brotherly, generous fellow. He was also growing accustomed to something – shall I call it an olfactory bar – that had hitherto kept them apart.

H. G. Wells (1866–1946) British writer. *Bealby*, Pt. VI, Ch. 3

FAMILY

See also ancestry, babies, birth, children, fathers, marriage, motherhood, pregnancy

1 Blood is thicker than water.

Proverb

2 Every family has a skeleton in the cupboard.

Proverb

3 The family that prays together stays together.

Proverb

4 There's a black sheep in every flock.

Proverb

5 He that hath wife and children hath given

hostages to fortune; for they are impediments to great enterprises, either of virtue or mischief.

Francis Bacon (1561–1626) English philosopher. *See also* LUCAN. *Essays*, 'Of Marriage and Single Life'

6 The joys of parents are secret, and so are their griefs and fears.

Francis Bacon *Essays*, 'Of Parents and Children'

7 Behold, every one that useth proverbs shall use this proverb against thee, saying, As is the mother, so is her daughter.

Bible: Ezekiel 16:44–45

8 If one is not going to take the necessary precautions to avoid having parents one must undertake to bring them up.

Quentin Crisp (?1910–) Model, publicist, and writer. *The Naked Civil Servant*

9 Fate chooses your relations, you choose your friends.

Jacques Delille (1738–1813) French abbé and poet. *Malheur et pitié*, I

10 It is a melancholy truth that even great men have their poor relations.

Charles Dickens (1812–70) British novelist. *Bleak House*, Ch. 28

11 Problem children tend to grow up into problem adults and problem adults tend to produce more problem children.

David Farrington (1944–) British criminal psychologist. *The Times*, 19 May 1994

12 What a marvellous place to drop one's mother-in-law!

Marshal Foch (1851–1929) French soldier. Remark on being shown the Grand Canyon. Attrib.

13 My father was frightened of his mother. I was frightened of my father, and I'm damned well going to make sure that my children are frightened of me.

George V (1865–1936) King of the United Kingdom. Attrib.

14 And so do his sisters, and his cousins and his aunts!
His sisters and his cousins,
Whom he reckons up by dozens,
And his aunts!

W. S. Gilbert (1836–1911) British dramatist. *HMS Pinafore*, I

15 A person may be indebted for a nose or an eye, for a graceful carriage or a voluble discourse, to a great-aunt or uncle, whose existence he has scarcely heard of.

William Hazlitt (1778–1830) British essayist. *On Personal Character*

16 Good families are generally worse than any others.

Anthony Hope (Sir Anthony Hope Hawkins; 1863–1933) British novelist. *The Prisoner of Zenda*, Ch. 1

17 But there, everything has its drawbacks, as the man said when his mother-in-law died, and they came down upon him for the funeral expenses.

Jerome K. Jerome (1859–1927) British humorist. *Three Men in a Boat*, Ch. 3

18 A poor relation – is the most irrelevant thing in nature.

Charles Lamb (1775–1834) British essayist. *Last Essays of Elia*, 'Poor Relations'

19 They fuck you up, your mum and dad.
They may not mean to, but they do.
They fill you with the faults they had
And add some extra, just for you.

Philip Larkin (1922–85) British poet. *This be the Verse*

20 Far from being the basis of the good society, the family, with its narrow privacy and tawdry secrets, is the source of all our discontents.

Edmund Leach (1910–89) British social anthropologist. In the BBC Reith Lectures for 1967. Lecture reprinted in *The Listener*

21 I have a wife, I have sons: all of them hostages given to fate.

Lucan (Marcus Annaeus Lucanus; 39–65 AD) Roman poet. *See also* BACON. *Works*, VII

22 A group of closely related persons living under one roof; it is a convenience, often a necessity, sometimes a pleasure, sometimes the reverse; but who first exalted it as admirable, an almost religious ideal?

Rose Macaulay (1889–1958) British writer. *The World My Wilderness*, Ch. 20

23 You're a disgrace to our family name of Wagstaff, if such a thing is possible.

Groucho Marx (Julius Marx; 1895–1977) US comedian. *Horse Feathers*

24 The sink is the great symbol of the bloodiness of family life. All life is bad, but family life is worse.

Julian Mitchell (1935–) British writer. *As Far as You Can Go*, Pt. I, Ch. 1

25 I cumber you goode Margaret muche, but I woulde be sorye, if it shoulde be any lenger than to morrowe, for it is S. Thomas evin and the vtas of Sainte Peter and therefore to morowe longe I to goe to God, it were a daye very meete and conveniente for me. I neuer liked your maner towarde me better then when you kissed me laste for I loue when doughterly loue and deere charitie hathe no laisor to looke to worldely curtesye. Fare well my deere childe and praye for me, and I shall for you and all your friendes that we maie merily meete in heaven.

Thomas More (1478–1535) English lawyer and scholar. Last letter to Margaret Roper, his daughter, on the eve of his execution on 6 July 1535

26 Children aren't happy with nothing to ignore,
And that's what parents were created for.

Ogden Nash (1902–71) US poet. *The Parents*

27 Parents are sometimes a bit of a disappointment to their children. They don't fulfil the promise of their early years.

Anthony Powell (1905–) British novelist. *A Buyer's Market*

28 All men are brothers, but, thank God, they aren't all brothers-in-law.

Anthony Powell *A Dance to the Music of Time: At Lady Molly's*, Ch. 4

29 For there is no friend like a sister
In calm or stormy weather;
To cheer one on the tedious way,
To fetch one if one goes astray,
To lift one if one totters down,
To strengthen whilst one stands.

Christina Rossetti (1830–74) British poet. *Goblin Market*

30 Two mothers-in-law.

Lord John Russell (1792–1878) British statesman. His answer when asked what he would consider a proper punishment for bigamy. *Anekdotenschatz* (H. Hoffmeister)

31 That dear octopus from whose tentacles we never quite escape, nor in our innermost hearts never quite wish to.

Dodie Smith (1896–1990) British dramatist and novelist. *Dear Octopus*

32 I wish either my father or my mother, or indeed both of them, as they were in duty both equally bound to it, had minded what they were about when they begot me.

Laurence Sterne (1713–68) Irish-born British writer. *Tristram Shandy*

33 If a man's character is to be abused, say what you will, there's nobody like a relation to do the business.

William Makepeace Thackeray (1811–63) British novelist. *Vanity Fair*, Ch. 19

34 All happy families resemble one another, each unhappy family is unhappy in its own way.

Leo Tolstoy (1828–1910) Russian writer. *Anna Karenina*, Pt. I, Ch. 1

35 Parents are the bones on which children sharpen their teeth.

Peter Ustinov (1921–) British actor. *Dear Me*

36 Don't hold your parents up to contempt. After all, you are their son, and it is just possible that you may take after them.

Evelyn Waugh (1903–66) British novelist. *The Tablet*, 9 May 1951

37 The thing that impresses me most about America is the way parents obey their children.

Duke of Windsor (1894–1972) King of the United Kingdom; abdicated 1936. *Look Magazine*, 5 Mar 1957

38 It is no use telling me that there are bad aunts and good aunts. At the core they are all alike. Sooner or later, out pops the cloven hoof.

P. G. Wodehouse (1881–1975) British humorous novelist. *The Code of the Woosters*

FANATICISM

1 Defined in psychological terms, a fanatic is a man who consciously over-compensates a secret doubt.

Aldous Huxley (1894–1964) British novelist. *Vulgarity in Literature*, Ch. 4

2 Fanatics have their dreams, wherewith they weave
A paradise for a sect.

John Keats (1795–1821) British poet. *The Fall of Hyperion*, I

3 You are never dedicated to something you have complete confidence in. No one is fanatically shouting that the sun is going to rise tomorrow. They *know* it's going to rise tomorrow. When people are fanatically dedicated to political or religious faiths or any other kind of dogmas or goals, it's always because these dogmas or goals are in doubt.

Robert T. Pirsig (1928–) US writer. *Zen and the Art of Motorcycle Maintenance*, Pt. II, Ch. 13

FASCISM

See also Hitler, Nazism

1 I should be pleased, I suppose, that Hitler has carried out a revolution on our lines. But they are Germans. So they will end by ruining our idea.

Benito Mussolini (1883–1945) Italian dictator. *Benito Mussolini* (C. Hibbert), Pt. II, Ch. 1

2 Fascism is a religion; the twentieth century will be known in history as the century of Fascism.

Benito Mussolini On Hitler's seizing power. *Sawdust Caesar* (George Seldes), Ch. 24

3 Fascism is not an article for export.

Benito Mussolini Report in the German press, 1932

4 Today in Britain, a fascist has won an election. Can you imagine how we feel? I am a proud and loyal man, madam. We had so much faith in this country. In the war, I thought it is time to help Britain to save democracy and fight fascism. They don't remember what we did, three million of us fought as volunteers remember – in the desert, in Burma. It makes me so sad.

Rajinder Singh British soldier. Referring to the election of a neo-Nazi British National Party councillor. *The Independent*, 22 Nov 1993

5 Every communist has a fascist frown, every fascist a communist smile.

Muriel Spark (1918–) British novelist. *The Girls of Slender Means*, Ch. 4

6 Fascism means war.

John St Loe Strachey (1901–63) British politician. Slogan, 1930s

FASHION

See also clothes

1 Fashion is architecture: it is a matter of proportions.

Coco Chanel (1883–1971) French dress designer. *Coco Chanel, Her Life, Her Secrets* (Marcel Haedrich)

2 One had as good be out of the world, as out of the fashion.

Colley Cibber (1671–1757) British actor and dramatist. *Love's Last Shift*, II

3 I walk down the Strand
With my gloves on my hand,
And I walk down again
With them off.

W. F. Hargreaves (1846–1919) British songwriter. *Burlington Bertie*

4 There are few who would not rather be taken in adultery than in provincialism.

Aldous Huxley (1894–1964) British novelist. *Antic Hay*, Ch. 10

5 A baseball cap is just as valid as a felt hat was 20 years ago.

Stephen Jones (1957–) British milliner. *The Observer*, 'Sayings of the Week', 17 Apr 1994

6 Her frocks are built in Paris but she wears them with a strong English accent.

Saki (Hector Hugh Munro; 1870–1916) British writer. *Reginald on Women*

7 For an idea ever to be fashionable is ominous, since it must afterwards be always old-fashioned.

George Santayana (1863–1952) US philosopher. *Winds of Doctrine*, 'Modernism and Christianity'

8 Fashions, after all, are only induced epidemics.

George Bernard Shaw (1856–1950) Irish dramatist and critic. *Doctor's Dilemma*, Preface

9 A love of fashion makes the economy go round.

Liz Tilberis (1947–) Editor of Vogue. Remark, Aug 1987

FATHERS

See also babies, children, family, motherhood

1 Like father, like son.

Proverb

2 Sir Walter, being strangely surprised and put out of his countenance at so great a table, gives his son a damned blow over the face. His son, as rude as he was, would not strike his father, but strikes over the face the gentleman that sat next to him and said 'Box about: 'twill come to my father anon'.

John Aubrey (1626–97) English antiquary. *Brief Lives*, 'Sir Walter Raleigh'

3 Fathers, provoke not your children to anger, lest they be discouraged.

Bible: Colossians 3:21

4 LEONTINE. An only son, sir, might expect more indulgence.
CROAKER. An only father, sir, might expect more obedience.

Oliver Goldsmith (1728–74) Irish-born British writer. *The Good-Natured Man*, I

5 Men are generally more careful of the breed of their horses and dogs than of their children.

William Penn (1644–1718) English preacher. *Some Fruits of Solitude, in Reflections and Maxims relating to the conduct of Humane Life*, Pt. I, No 52

6 It is a wise father that knows his own child.

William Shakespeare (1564–1616) English dramatist. *The Merchant of Venice*, II:2

7 No man is responsible for his father. That is entirely his mother's affair.

Margaret Turnbull (fl. 1920s–1942) US writer. *Alabaster Lamps*

FEAR

1 It is a miserable state of mind to have few things to desire and many things to fear.

Francis Bacon (1561–1626) English philosopher. *Essays*, 'Of Empire'

2 For God hath not given us the spirit of fear; but of power, and of love, and of a sound mind.

Bible: II Timothy 1:7

3 There is no fear in love; but perfect love casteth out fear: because fear hath torment. He that feareth is not made perfect in love.

Bible: I John 4:18

4 Fear has many eyes and can see things underground.

Miguel de Cervantes (1547–1616) Spanish novelist. *Don Quixote*, Pt. I, Ch. 20

5 You may take the most gallant sailor, the most intrepid airman, or the most audacious soldier, put them at a table together – what do you get? *The sum of their fears.*

Winston Churchill (1874–1965) British statesman. Talking about the Chiefs of Staffs system, 16 Nov 1943. *The Blast of War* (H. Macmillan), Ch. 16

6 Like one, that on a lonesome road
Doth walk in fear and dread,
And having once turned round walks on,
And turns no more his head;
Because he knows, a frightful fiend
Doth close behind him tread.

Samuel Taylor Coleridge (1772–1834) British poet. *The Rime of the Ancient Mariner*, VI

7 I'm not frightened of the darkness outside. It's the darkness inside houses I don't like.

Shelagh Delaney (1939–) British dramatist. *A Taste of Honey*, I:1

8 I wants to make your flesh creep.

Charles Dickens (1812–70) British novelist. *Pickwick Papers*, Ch. 8

9 And I will show you something different from either
Your shadow at morning striding behind you,
Or your shadow at evening rising to meet you
I will show you fear in a handful of dust.

T. S. Eliot (1888–1965) US-born British poet and dramatist. *The Waste Land*, 'The Burial of the Dead'

10 Let me assert my firm belief that the only thing we have to fear is fear itself.

Franklin D. Roosevelt (1882–1945) US Democratic president. First Inaugural Address, 4 Mar 1933

11 I had else been perfect,
Whole as the marble, founded as the rock,
As broad and general as the casing air,
But now I am cabin'd, cribb'd, confin'd, bound in
To saucy doubts and fears.

William Shakespeare (1564–1616) English dramatist. *Macbeth*, II:4

12 A lion among ladies is a most dreadful thing; for there is not a more fearful wild-fowl than your lion living.

William Shakespeare *A Midsummer Night's Dream*, III:1

13 Fear lent wings to his feet.

Virgil (Publius Vergilius Maro; 70–19 BC) Roman poet. *Aeneid*, Bk. VIII

14 He had one peculiar weakness; he had faced death in many forms but he had never faced a dentist. The thought of dentists gave him just the same sick horror as the thought of Socialism.

H. G. Wells (1866–1946) British writer. *Bealby*, Pt. VIII, Ch. 1

15 By night an atheist half believes a God.

Edward Young (1683–1765) British poet. *Night Thoughts*

FEMINISM

See also equality, sexes, woman's role, women

Supporters

1 Old-fashioned ways which no longer apply to changed conditions are a snare in which the feet of women have always become readily entangled.

Jane Addams (1860–1935) US social worker. In *Newer Ideals of Peace*, 'Utilization of Women in City Government'

2 Men their rights and nothing more; women their rights and nothing less.

Susan B. Anthony (1820–1906) US editor. *The Revolution*, Motto

3 ...there never will be complete equality until women themselves help to make laws and elect lawmakers.

Susan B. Anthony In *The Arena*, (May 1897) 'The Status of Women, Past, Present and Future'

4 From a timid, shy girl I had become a woman of resolute character, who could not longer be frightened by the struggle with troubles.

Anna Dostoevsky (1846–1918) Russian diarist and writer. *Dostoevsky Portrayed by His Wife*

5 The extension of women's rights is the basic principle of all social progress.

Charles Fourier (1772–1837) French social reformer. *Théorie des Quatre Mouvements*

6 Where young boys plan for what they will achieve and attain, young girls plan for whom they will achieve and attain.

Charlotte Perkins Gilman (1860–1935) US writer. *Women and Economics*, Ch. 5

7 A woman needs a man like a fish needs a bicycle.

Graffiti

8 Mother is the dead heart of the family, spending father's earnings on consumer goods to enhance the environment in which he eats, sleeps and watches the television.

Germaine Greer (1939–) Australian-born British writer and feminist. *The Female Eunuch*

9 Women fail to understand how much men hate them.

Germaine Greer *The Female Eunuch*

10 I know you do not make the laws but I also know that you are the wives and mothers, the sisters and daughters of those who do.

Angelina Grimké (1805–79) US writer and reformer. *The Anti-Slavery Examiner* (Sep 1836), 'Appeal to the Christian Women of the South'

11 ...the emancipation of women is practically the greatest egoistic movement of the nineteenth century, and the most intense affirmation of the right of the self that history has yet seen...

Ellen Key (Karolina Sofia Key; 1849–1926) Swedish writer. *The Century of the Child*, Ch. 2

12 Can anything be more absurd than keeping women in a state of ignorance, and yet so vehemently to insist on their resisting temptation?

Vicesimus Knox (1752–1821) British essayist. *Liberal Education*, Vol. I, 'On the Literary Education of Women'

13 It is ironic that the wife who made Britain great again, and who is the leader of the Western World, has to get her husband to sign her tax form.

Jacqui Lait Referring to Margaret Thatcher. Speech, Oct 1987

14 Other books have been written by men physicians...One would suppose in reading them that women possess but one class of physical organs, and that these are always diseased. Such teaching is pestiferous, and tends to cause and perpetuate the very evils it professes to remedy.

Mary Ashton Livermore (c. 1820–1905) US writer. *What Shall We Do with Our Daughters?*, Ch. 2

15 I'm furious about the Women's Liberationists. They keep getting up on soapboxes and proclaiming that women are brighter than men. That's true, but it should be kept very quiet or it ruins the whole racket.

Anita Loos (1891–1981) US novelist. *The Observer*, 'Sayings of the Year', 30 Dec 1973

16 ...is it to be understood that the principles of the Declaration of Independence bear no relation to half of the human race?

Harriet Martineau (1802–76) British writer. *Society in America*, Vol. III, 'Marriage'

17 The most important thing women have to do

is to stir up the zeal of women themselves.

John Stuart Mill (1806–73) British philosopher. Letter to Alexander Bain, 14 July 1869

18 ...the rumblings of women's liberation are only one pointer to the fact that you already have a discontented work force. And if conditions continue to lag so far behind the industrial norm and the discomfort increases, you will find...that you will end up with an inferior product.

Elaine Morgan (1920–) British writer. *The Descent of Woman*, Ch. 11

19 No *man*, not even a doctor, ever gives any other definition of what a nurse should be than this – "devoted and obedient." This definition would do just as well for a porter. It might even do for a horse. It would not do for a policeman.

Florence Nightingale (1820–1910) British nurse. *Notes on Nursing*

20 The vote, I thought, means nothing to women. We should be armed.

Edna O'Brien (1936–) Irish novelist. Quoted as epigraph to *Fear of Flying* (Erica Jong), Ch. 16

21 ...if civilisation is to advance at all in the future, it must be through the help of women, women freed of their political shackles, women with full power to work their will in society. It was rapidly becoming clear to my mind that men regarded women as a servant class in the community, and that women were going to remain in the servant class until they lifted themselves out of it.

Emmeline Pankhurst (1858–1928) British suffragette. *My Own Story*

22 Women had always fought for men, and for their children. Now they were ready to fight for their own human rights. Our militant movement was established.

Emmeline Pankhurst *My Own Story*

23 We have taken this action, because as women...we realize that the condition of our sex is so deplorable that it is our duty even to break the law in order to call attention to the reasons why we do so.

Emmeline Pankhurst Speech in court, 21 Oct 1908. *Shoulder to Shoulder* (ed. Midge Mackenzie)

24 The prolonged slavery of women is the darkest page in human history.

Elizabeth Stanton (1815–1902) US suffragette. *History of Woman Suffrage* (with Susan B. Anthony and Mathilda Gage), Vol. I

25 Womanhood is the great fact in her life; wifehood and motherhood are but incidental relations.

Elizabeth Stanton *History of Woman Suffrage* (with Susan B. Anthony and Mathilda Gage), Vol. I

26 *Declaration of Sentiments:*...We hold these truths to be self-evident: that all men and women are created equal...

Elizabeth Stanton *History of Woman Suffrage* (with Susan B. Anthony and Mathilda Gage), Vol. I

27 People call me a feminist whenever I express sentiments that differentiate me from a doormat or a prostitute.

Rebecca West (Cicely Isabel Fairfield; 1892–1983) British novelist and journalist. Attrib.

28 Women have always been the guardians of wisdom and humanity which makes them natural, but usually secret, rulers. The time has come for them to rule openly, but together with and not against men.

Charlotte Wolff (1904–86) German-born British writer. *Bisexuality: A Study*, Ch. 2

29 Women have served all these centuries as looking-glasses possessing the magic and delicious power of reflecting the figure of man at twice its natural size.

Virginia Woolf (1882–1941) British novelist. *A Room of One's Own*

30 The *divine right* of husbands, like the divine right of kings, may, it is hoped, in this enlightened age, be contested without danger.

Mary Wollstonecraft 1759–97) British writer. *A Vindication of the Rights of Woman*, Ch. 3

31 I do not wish them to have power over men; but over themselves.

Mary Wollstonecraft Referring to women. *A Vindication of the Rights of Woman*, Ch. 4

Opponents

32 There is a tide in the affairs of women, Which, taken at the flood, leads – God knows where.

Lord Byron (1788–1824) British poet. *Don Juan*, VI

33 Nothing would induce me to vote for giving women the franchise. I am not going to be henpecked into a question of such importance.

Winston Churchill (1874–1965) British statesman. R*The Amazing Mr Churchill* (Robert Lewis Taylor)

34 The great question...which I have not been able to answer, despite my thirty years of research into the feminine soul, is 'What does a woman want'?

Sigmund Freud (1856–1939) Austrian psychoanalyst. *Psychiatry in American Life* (Charles Rolo)

35 The First Blast of the Trumpet Against the Monstrous Regiment of Women.

John Knox (c. 1514–72) Scottish religious reformer. Title of Pamphlet, 1558

36 Women's Liberation is just a lot of foolishness. It's the men who are discriminated against. They can't bear children. And no one's likely to do anything about that.

Golda Meir (1898–1978) Russian-born Israeli stateswoman. Attrib.

37 The only good thing about Hammerfall, women's lib was dead milliseconds after Hammerstrike.

Larry Niven (1938–) US science-fiction writer. 'Hammerfall' was a fictional collision in the late 1970s between the Earth and a large comet that destroyed civilization. *Lucifer's Hammer*, Pt. III (with Jerry Pournelle)

38 Give women the vote, and in five years there will be a crushing tax on bachelors.

George Bernard Shaw (1856–1950) Irish dramatist and critic. *Man and Superman*, Preface

39 The Queen is most anxious to enlist every one who can speak or write to join in checking this mad, wicked folly of 'Woman's Rights', with all its attendant horrors, on which her poor feeble sex is bent, forgetting every sense of womanly feeling and propriety.

Victoria (1819–1901) Queen of the United Kingdom. Letter to Sir Theodore Martin, 29 May 1870

40 The thought could not be avoided that the best home for a feminist was in another person's lab.

James Dewey Watson (1928–) US geneticist. *The Double Helix*, Ch. 2

Lastly

41 The battle for women's rights has been largely won.

Margaret Thatcher (1925–) British politician and prime minister. *The Guardian*, 1982

42 I do, and I also wash and iron them.

Denis Thatcher (1915–) British businessman married to Margaret Thatcher. Replying to the question "Who wears the pants in this house?". *Times* (Los Angeles), 21 Apr 1981

43 WOMEN'S RIGHTS NOW!

Followed by.
Yes Dear

Exchange of graffiti

FICTION

See also books, literature, novels, writing

1 Science fiction is no more written for scientists than ghost stories are written for ghosts.

Brian Aldiss (1925–) British science-fiction writer. *Penguin Science Fiction*, Introduction

2 Sometimes I don't know whether Zelda and I are real or whether we are characters in one of my novels.

F. Scott Fitzgerald (1896–1940) US novelist. Said of himself and his wife. *A Second Flowering* (Malcolm Cowley)

3 There are many reasons why novelists write, but they all have one thing in common – a need to create an alternative world.

John Fowles (1926–) British novelist. *The Sunday Times Magazine*, 2 Oct 1977

4 Casting my mind's eye over the whole of fiction, the only absolutely original creation I can think of is Don Quixote.

W. Somerset Maugham (1874–1965) British novelist. *10 Novels and Their Authors*, Ch. 1

5 Contentment and fulfilment don't make for very good fiction.

Joanna Trollope (1943–) British writer. *The Times*, 25 June 1994

FIRE

1 All things, oh priests, are on fire…The eye is on fire; forms are on fire; eye-consciousness is on fire; impressions received by the eye are on fire.

Buddha (Gautama Siddhartha; c. 563–c. 483 BC) Indian religious teacher. *The Fire Sermon*

2 Billy, in one of his nice new sashes,
Fell in the fire and was burnt to ashes;
Now, although the room grows chilly,
I haven't the heart to poke poor Billy.

Harry Graham (1874–1936) British writer. *Ruthless Rhymes for Heartless Homes*, 'Tender-Heartedness'

3 Whatsoever might be the extent of the private calamity, I hope it will not interfere with the public business of the country.

Richard Brinsley Sheridan (1751–1816) British dramatist. On learning, whilst in the House of Commons, that his Drury Lane Theatre was on fire. *Memoirs of the Life of the Rt. Hon. Richard Brinsley Sheridan* (T. Moore)

4 A man may surely be allowed to take a glass of wine by his own fireside.

Richard Brinsley Sheridan As he sat in a coffeehouse watching his theatre burn down. *Memoirs of the Life of the Rt. Hon. Richard Brinsley Sheridan* (T. Moore)

5 Arson, after all, is an artificial crime…A large number of houses deserve to be burnt.

H. G. Wells (1866–1946) British writer. *The History of Mr Polly*, Pt. X, Ch. 1

FIRST IMPRESSIONS

1 First impressions are the most lasting.

Proverb

2 There is a lady sweet and kind,
Was never face so pleased my mind;
I did but see her passing by,
And yet I love her till I die.

Anonymous *Passing By*

3 Harris, I am not well; pray get me a glass of brandy.

George IV (1762–1830) King of the United Kingdom. On seeing Caroline of Brunswick for the first time. *Diaries* (Earl of Malmesbury)

4 You have sent me a Flanders mare.

Henry VIII (1491–1547) King of England. Said on meeting his fourth wife, Anne of Cleves, for the first time. Attrib.

5 First feelings are always the most natural.

Louis XIV (1638–1715) French king. Repeated by Mme de Sévigné

6 Who ever loved, that loved not at first sight?

Christopher Marlowe (1564–93) English dramatist. *Hero and Leander*, I

7 Mistrust first impulses; they are nearly always good.

Talleyrand (Charles Maurice de Talleyrand-Périgord; 1754–1838) French politician. Sometimes attrib. to Count Montrond. Attrib.

FISHING

See also sport and games

1 Fly fishing may be a very pleasant amusement; but angling or float fishing I can only compare to a stick and a string, with a worm at one end and a fool at the other.

Samuel Johnson (1709–84) British lexicographer. Attrib. in *Instructions to Young Sportsmen* (Hawker)

2 Angling is somewhat like poetry, men are to be born so.

Izaak Walton *The Compleat Angler*, Ch. 1

3 Let the blessing of St Peter's Master be... upon all that are lovers of virtue; and dare trust in His providence; and be quiet; and go a-Angling.

Izaak Walton *The Compleat Angler*, Ch. 21

4 Angling may be said to be so like the mathematics, that it can never be fully learnt.

Izaak Walton *The Compleat Angler*, Epistle to the Reader

5 We may say of angling as Dr Boteler said of strawberries, 'Doubtless God could have made a better berry, but doubtless God never did.'

Izaak Walton *The Compleat Angler*, Ch. 5

FLATTERY

See also compliments, insincerity, praise, servility

1 Imitation is the sincerest form of flattery.

Proverb

2 It is happy for you that you possess the talent of flattering with delicacy. May I ask whether these pleasing attentions proceed from the impulse of the moment, or are the result of previous study?

Jane Austen (1775–1817) British novelist. *Pride and Prejudice*, Ch. 14

3 A rich man's joke is always funny.

Thomas Edward Brown (1830–97) British poet. *The Doctor*

4 Every woman is infallibly to be gained by every sort of flattery, and every man by one sort or other.

Earl of Chesterfield (1694–1773) English statesman. Letter to his son, 16 Mar 1752

5 Madam, before you flatter a man so grossly to his face, you should consider whether or not your flattery is worth his having.

Samuel Johnson (1709–84) British lexicographer. *Diary and Letters* (Mme D'Arblay), Vol. I, Ch. 2

6 Be advised that all flatterers live at the expense of those who listen to them.

Jean de La Fontaine (1621–95) French poet. *Fables*, I, 'Le Corbeau et le Renard'

7 I will praise any man that will praise me.

William Shakespeare (1564–1616) English dramatist. *Antony and Cleopatra*, II:6

8 Flattery is all right so long as you don't inhale.

Adlai Stevenson (1900–65) US statesman. Attrib.

9 'Tis an old maxim in the schools,
That flattery's the food of fools;
Yet now and then your men of wit
Will condescend to take a bit.

Jonathan Swift (1667–1745) Irish-born Anglican priest and writer. *Cadenus and Vanessa*

FLOWERS

See also gardens

1 She wore a wreath of roses,
The night that first we met.

Thomas Haynes Bayly (1797–1839) British writer. *She Wore a Wreath of Roses*

2 Just now the lilac is in bloom
All before my little room.

Rupert Brooke (1887–1915) British poet. *The Old Vicarage, Grantchester*

3 Tiptoe through the tulips with me.

Al Dubin (20th century) US songwriter. From the musical, *Gold Diggers of Broadway. Tiptoe Through the Tulips*

4 I sometimes think that never blows so red
The Rose as where some buried Caesar bled;
That every Hyacinth the Garden wears
Dropt in her Lap from some once lovely Head.

Edward Fitzgerald (1809–83) British poet. *The Rubáiyát of Omar Khayyám* (1st edn.), XVIII

5 Their smiles,
Wan as primroses gather'd at midnight
By chilly finger'd spring.

John Keats (1795–1821) British poet. *Endymion*, IV

6 Good God, I forgot the violets!

Walter Savage Landor (1775–1864) British poet and writer. Having thrown his cook out of an open window onto the flowerbed below. *Irreverent Social History* (F. Muir)

7 And I will make thee beds of roses
And a thousand fragrant posies.

Christopher Marlowe (1564–93) English dramatist. *The Passionate Shepherd to his Love*

8 Gather the flowers, but spare the buds.

Andrew Marvell (1621–78) English poet. *The Picture of Little T.C. in a Prospect of Flowers*

9 'Tis the last rose of summer
Left blooming alone;
All her lovely companions
Are faded and gone.

Thomas Moore (1779–1852) Irish poet. *Irish Melodies*, 'Tis the Last Rose'

10 Say it with flowers.

Patrick O'Keefe (1872–1934) US advertising agent. Slogan for Society of American Florists

11 They are for prima donnas or corpses – I am neither.

Arturo Toscanini (1867–1957) Italian conductor. Refusing a floral wreath at the end of a performance. *The Elephant that Swallowed a Nightingale* (C. Galtey)

12 But as we went along there were more and yet more and there at last under the boughs of the trees, we saw that there was a long belt of them along the shore, about the breadth of a country turnpike road. I never saw daffodils so beautiful they grew among the mossy stones about and about them, some rested their heads upon these stones as on pillow for weariness and the rest tossed and reeled and danced and seemed as if they verily laughed with the wind that blew upon them over the lake.

Dorothy Wordsworth (1771–1855) British diarist and sister of William Wordsworth. *The Grasmere Journals*, 15 Apr 1802

13 Thou unassuming common-place
Of Nature.

William Wordsworth (1770–1850) British poet. *To the Daisy*

14 I wandered lonely as a cloud
That floats on high o'er vales and hills,
When all at once I saw a crowd,
A host, of golden daffodils.

William Wordsworth *I Wandered Lonely as a Cloud*

FLYING

See also travel

1 Had I been a man I might have explored the Poles or climbed Mount Everest, but as it was my spirit found outlet in the air....

Amy Johnson (1903–41) British flyer. *Myself When Young* (ed. Margot Asquith)

2 I feel about airplanes the way I feel about diets. It seems to me that they are wonderful things for other people to go on.

Jean Kerr (1923–) US dramatist. *The Snake Has All the Lines*, 'Mirror, Mirror, on the Wall'

3 There are only two emotions in a plane: boredom and terror.

Orson Welles (1915–85) US film actor. *The Observer*, 'Sayings of the Week', 12 May 1985

4 Nor law, nor duty bade me fight,
Nor public men, nor cheering crowds,
A lonely impulse of delight
Drove to this tumult in the clouds;
I balanced all, brought all to mind,
The years to come seemed waste of breath,
A waste of breath the years behind
In balance with this life, this death.

W. B. Yeats (1865–1939) Irish poet. *An Irish Airman Foresees his Death*

FOOD

See also etiquette, greed, obesity

1 A meal without flesh is like feeding on grass.

Proverb

2 An apple-pie without some cheese is like a kiss without a squeeze.

Proverb

3 Bread is the staff of life.

Proverb

4 Eat to live and not live to eat.

Proverb

5 The nearer the bone, the sweeter the flesh.

Proverb

6 I always eat peas with honey
I've done it all my life,
They do taste kind of funny,
But it keeps them on the knife.

Anonymous *Peas*

7 'Oh, my Friends, be warned by me,
That Breakfast, Dinner, Lunch and Tea
Are all the Human Frame requires...'
With that the Wretched Child expires.

Hilaire Belloc (1870–1953) French-born British poet. *Cautionary Tales*, 'Henry King'

8 The Chief Defect of Henry King
Was chewing little bits of String.

Hilaire Belloc *Cautionary Tales*, 'Henry King'

9 I know what I wanted to ask you;
Is trifle sufficient for sweet?

John Betjeman (1906–84) British poet. *How to get on in Society*

10 I'm a man
More dined against than dining.

Maurice Bowra (1898–1971) British scholar. *Summoned by Bells* (J. Betjeman)

11 Some hae meat, and canna eat,
And some wad eat that want it,
But we hae meat and we can eat,
And sae the Lord be thankit.

Robert Burns (1759–96) Scottish poet. *The Selkirk Grace*

12 The Queen of Hearts, she made some tarts,
All on a summer day:
The Knave of Hearts, he stole those tarts,
And took them quite away!

Lewis Carroll (Charles Lutwidge Dodgson; 1832–98) British writer. *Alice's Adventures in Wonderland*, Ch. 11

13 Soup of the evening, beautiful Soup!

Lewis Carroll Said by the Mock Turtle. *Alice's Adventures in Wonderland*, Ch. 10

14 The right diet directs sexual energy into the parts that matter.

Barbara Cartland (1902–) British romantic novelist. Remark, Jan 1981

15 Don't eat too many almonds; they add weight to the breasts

Colette (1873–1954) French novelist. *Gigi*

16 As the low-fat diet unfolded, I really felt that God was showing me the way.

Rosemary Conley *The Observer*, 27 June 1993

17 Do you *know* what breakfast cereal is made of? It's made of all those little curly wooden shavings you find in pencil sharpeners!

Roald Dahl (1916–90) British writer. *Charlie and the Chocolate Factory*, Ch. 27

18 Eating disorders, whether it be anorexia or bulimia, show how individuals can turn the nourishment of the body into a painful attack on themselves and they have at the core a far deeper problem than mere vanity.

Diana, Princess of Wales (1961–) *The Times*, 28 Apr 1993

19 Bouillabaisse is only good because cooked by the French, who, if they cared to try, could produce an excellent and nutritious substitute out of cigar stumps and empty matchboxes.

Norman Douglas (1868–1952) British novelist. *Siren Land*, 'Rain on the Hills'

20 The winter evening settles down
With smell of steaks in passageways.

T. S. Eliot (1888–1965) US-born British poet and dramatist. *Preludes*

21 You have a situation where girls of eight want to lose weight and at 12 they can tell you the fat content of an avocado...but they don't know what constitutes a healthy meal.

Mary Evans Young Chairwoman of Dietbreakers *The Observer*, 1 May 1994

22 The way to a man's heart is through his stomach.

Fanny Fern (1811–72) US writer. *Willis Parton*

23 Oh! The roast beef of England.
And old England's roast beef.

Henry Fielding (1707–54) British novelist. *The Grub Street Opera*, III:3

24 With my little stick of Blackpool rock,
Along the Promenade I stroll.
It may be sticky but I never complain,
It's nice to have a nibble at it now and again.

George Formby (1905–61) British comedian. *With My Little Stick of Blackpool Rock*

25 Take your hare when it is cased...

Hannah Glasse (18th century) English writer. Often misquoted as, 'First catch your hare'. *The Art of Cookery Made Plain and Easy*, Ch. 1

26 The best number for a dinner party is two – myself and a dam' good head waiter.

Nubar Gulbenkian (1896–1972) Turkish oil magnate. Attrib.

27 But one day, one cold winter's day,
He screamed out, 'Take the soup away!'

Heinrich Hoffman (1809–74) German writer. *Struwwelpeter*, 'Augustus'

28 The British hamburger thus symbolised, with savage neatness, the country's failure to provide its ordinary people with food which did anything more for them than sustain life.

Clive James (1939–) Writer and broadcaster, born in Australia. *Falling Towards England*, Ch.17

29 This was a good dinner enough, to be sure; but it was not a dinner to *ask* a man to.

Samuel Johnson (1709–84) British lexicographer. *Life of Johnson* (J. Boswell), Vol. I

30 It is as bad as bad can be: it is ill-fed, ill-killed, ill-kept, and ill-drest.

Samuel Johnson About the roast mutton at an inn. *Life of Johnson* (J. Boswell), Vol. IV

31 A cucumber should be well sliced, and dressed with pepper and vinegar, and then thrown out, as good for nothing.

Samuel Johnson *Tour to the Hebrides* (J. Boswell)

32 I hate a man who swallows it, affecting not to know what he is eating. I suspect his taste in higher matters.

Charles Lamb (1775–1834) British essayist. Referring to food. *Essays of Elia*, 'Grace before Meat'

33 Any two meals at a boarding-house are together less than two square meals.

Stephen Leacock (1869–1944) English-born Canadian economist and humorist. *Literary Lapses*, 'Boarding-House Geometry'

34 They dined on mince, and slices of quince,
Which they ate with a runcible spoon;
And hand in hand, on the edge of the sand,
They danced by the light of the moon.

Edward Lear (1812–88) British artist and writer. *The Owl and the Pussy-Cat*

35 Food is an important part of a balanced diet.

Fran Lebowitz (1950–) US writer. *Metropolitan Life*, 'Food for Thought and Vice Versa'

36 This piece of cod passes all understanding.

Edwin Lutyens (1869–1944) British architect. Comment made in a restaurant. Attrib.

37 It's a very odd thing –
As odd as can be –
That whatever Miss T eats
Turns into Miss T.

Walter De La Mare (1873–1956) British poet. *Miss T*

38 Many children are suffering from muesli-belt malnutrition.

Professor Vincent Marks British nutritionist. Remark, June 1986

39 To eat well in England you should have breakfast three times a day.

W. Somerset Maugham (1874–1965) British novelist. Attrib.

40 Kissing don't last: cookery do!

George Meredith (1828–1909) British novelist. *The Ordeal of Richard Feverel*, Ch. 28

41 One should eat to live, not live to eat.

Molière (Jean Baptiste Poquelin; 1622–73) French dramatist. *L'Avare*, III:2

42 Some breakfast food manufacturer hit upon the simple notion of emptying out the leavings of carthorse nosebags, adding a few other things like unconsumed portions of chicken layer's mash, and the sweepings of racing stables, packing the mixture in little bags and selling them in health food shops.

Frank Muir (1920–) British writer and broadcaster. *Upon My Word!*

43 An army marches on its stomach.

Napoleon I (Napoleon Bonaparte; 1769–1821) French emperor. Attrib.

44 I think I could eat one of Bellamy's veal pies.

William Pitt the Younger (1759–1806) British statesman. Last words. Attrib.

45 The vulgar boil, the learned roast an egg.

Alexander Pope (1688–1744) British poet. *Satires and Epistles of Horace Imitated*, Bk II

46 To the old saying that man built the house but woman made of it a 'home' might be added the modern supplement that woman accepted cooking as a chore but man has made of it a recreation.

Emily Post (1873–1960) US writer. *Etiquette*, Ch. 34

47 Dinner at the Huntercombes' possessed 'only two dramatic features – the wine was a farce and the food a tragedy'.

Anthony Powell (1905–) British novelist. *A Dance to the Music of Time: The Acceptance World*, Ch. 4

48 Great restaurants are, of course, nothing but mouth-brothels. There is no point in going to them if one intends to keep one's belt buckled.

Frederic Raphael (1931–) British author. *The Sunday Times Magazine*, 25 Sep 1977

49 The thought of two thousand people crunching celery at the same time horrified me.

George Bernard Shaw (1856–1950) Irish dramatist and critic. Explaining why he had turned down an invitation to a vegetarian gala dinner. *The Greatest Laughs of All Time* (G. Lieberman)

50 Food is for eating, and good food is to be enjoyed...I think food is, actually, very beautiful in itself.

Delia Smith British cookery writer and broadcaster. *The Times*, 17 Oct 1990

51 Yes, cider and tinned salmon are the staple diet of the agricultural classes.

Evelyn Waugh (1903–66) British novelist. *Scoop*, Bk. I, Ch. 1

52 I saw him even now going the way of all flesh, that is to say towards the kitchen.

John Webster (1580–1625) English dramatist. *Westward Hoe*, II:2

53 You breed babies and you eat chips with everything.

Arnold Wesker (1932–) British dramatist. *Chips with Everything*, I:2

54 If I had the choice between smoked salmon and tinned salmon, I'd have it tinned. With vinegar.

Harold Wilson (1916–95) British politician and prime minister. *The Observer*, 'Sayings of the Week,' 11 Nov 1962

FOOLISHNESS

See also gullibility, ignorance, stupidity, wisdom and foolishness

1 A fool and his money are soon parted.

Proverb

2 A fool at forty is a fool indeed.

Proverb

3 A fool believes everything.

Proverb

4 Better be a fool than a knave.

Proverb

5 Empty vessels make the greatest sound.

Proverb

6 Fools build houses, and wise men buy them.

Proverb

7 Fools live poor to die rich.

Proverb

8 There's no fool like an old fool.

Proverb

9 Give not that which is holy unto the dogs, neither cast ye your pearls before swine, lest they trample them under their feet, and turn again and rend you.

Bible: Matthew 7:6

10 Answer a fool according to his folly, lest he be wise in his own conceit.

Bible: Proverbs 26:5

11 The world is made up for the most part of fools and knaves.

Duke of Buckingham (1628–87) English politician. *To Mr Clifford, on his Humane Reason*

12 He's a muddle-headed fool, with frequent lucid intervals.

Miguel de Cervantes (1547–1616) Spanish novelist. Sancho Panza describing Don Quixote. *Don Quixote*, Pt. II, Ch. 18

13 The wisest fool in Christendom.

Henri IV (1553–1610) King of France. Referring to James I of England. Attrib.

14 Mix a little foolishness with your serious plans: it's lovely to be silly at the right moment.

Horace (Quintus Horatius Flaccus; 65–8 BC) Roman poet. *Odes*, IV

15 Fools are in a terrible, overwhelming majority, all the wide world over.

Henrik Ibsen (1828–1906) Norwegian dramatist. *An Enemy of the People*, IV

16 You cannot fashion a wit out of two half-wits.

Neil Kinnock (1942–) British politician. *The Times*, 1983

17 No creature smarts so little as a fool.

Alexander Pope (1688–1744) British poet. *Epistle to Dr. Arbuthnot*

18 Lord, what fools these mortals be!

William Shakespeare (1564–1616) English dramatist. *A Midsummer Night's Dream*, III:2

19 He was a bold man that first eat an oyster.

Jonathan Swift (1667–1745) Irish-born writer. Polite conversation, Dialogue 2

FOOTBALL

See also sport and games

1 Professional football is no longer a game. It's a war. And it brings out the same primitive instincts that go back thousands of years.

Malcolm Allison British football manager. *The Observer*, 'Sayings of the Week', 14 Mar 1973

2 I do love cricket – it's so very English.

Sarah Bernhardt (Sarah Henriette Rosine Bernard; 1844–1923) French actress. On seeing a game of football. *Nijinsky* (R. Buckle)

3 The quest for spontaneity is fundamental in art and football expresses it best.

Eric Cantona (1966–) French football player. *The Independent*, 27 Jan 1995

4 The goal stands up, the keeper
Stands up to keep the goal.

A. E. Housman (1859–1936) British scholar and poet. *A Shropshire Lad*, 'Bredon Hill'

5 I loathed the game...it was very difficult for me to show courage at it. Football, it seemed to me, is not really played for the pleasure of kicking a ball about, but is a species of fighting.

George Orwell (Eric Blair; 1903–50) British novelist. *Such, Such Were The Joys*

6 The streets were full of footballs.

Samuel Pepys (1633–1703) English diarist. *Diary*, 2 Jan 1665

7 A man who had missed the last home match of 't 'United' had to enter social life on tiptoe in Bruddersford.

J. B. Priestley (1894–1984) British novelist. *The Good Companions*

8 Football isn't a matter of life and death – it's much more important than that.

Bill Shankly (1914–81) British football manager. Attrib.

9 Footeball...causeth fighting, brawling, contention, quarrel picking, murder, homicide and great effusion of bloode, as daily experience teacheth.

Philip Stubbes (fl. 1583–91) English puritan pamphleteer. *Anatomie of Abuses*

10 I will not permit thirty men to travel four hundred miles to agitate a bag of wind.

Andrew Dickson White (1832–1918) US educationalist. Refusing to allow the Cornell American football team to visit Michigan to play a match. *The People's Almanac* (D. Wallechinsky)

FORCE

See also oppression, power politics, violence

1 Force is not a remedy.

John Bright (1811–89) British radical politician. Speech, Birmingham, 16 Nov 1880

2 The use of force alone is but *temporary*. It may subdue for a moment; but it does not remove the necessity of subduing again: and a nation is not governed, which is perpetually to be conquered.

Edmund Burke (1729–97) British politician. *Speech on Conciliation with America* (House of Commons, 22 Mar 1775)

FORGIVENESS

1 Forgive and forget.

Proverb

2 Let bygones be bygones.

Proverb

3 Even if someone throws a stone at you, respond with food.

Kazakh proverb *The Independent*, 29 Nov 1993

4 Come now, and let us reason together, saith the Lord: though your sins be as scarlet, they shall be as white as snow; though they be red like crimson, they shall be as wool.

Bible: Isaiah 1:18

5 Then said Jesus, Father, forgive them; for they know not what they do. And they parted his raiment, and cast lots.

Bible: Luke 23:34

6 Wherefore I say unto thee, Her sins, which are many, are forgiven; for she loved much: but to whom little is forgiven, the same loveth little.

Bible: Luke 7:47

7 Then came Peter to him, and said, Lord, how oft shall my brother sin against me, and I forgive him? till seven times?
Jesus saith unto him, I say not unto thee, Until seven times: but, Until seventy times seven.

Bible: Matthew 18:21–22

8 The cut worm forgives the plough.

William Blake (1757–1827) British poet. *The Marriage of Heaven and Hell*, 'Proverbs of Hell'

9 The women pardoned all except her face.

Lord Byron (1788–1824) British poet. *Don Juan*, V

10 It is the government that should ask me for a pardon.

Eugene Victor Debs (1855–1926) US trade unionist, socialist, and pacifist. When released from prison (1921) on the orders of President Harding after being jailed for sedition (1918). *The People's Almanac* (D. Wallechinsky)

11 Once a woman has forgiven her man, she must not reheat his sins for breakfast.

Marlene Dietrich (Maria Magdalene von Losch; 1901–92) German-born film star. *Marlene Dietrich's ABC*

12 God may pardon you, but I never can.

Elizabeth I (1533–1603) Queen of England. To the

Countess of Nottingham. *History of England under the House of Tudor* (Hume), Vol. II, Ch. 7

13 Only lies and evil come from letting people off…

Iris Murdoch (1919–) Irish-born British novelist. *A Severed Head*

14 To err is human, to forgive, divine.

Alexander Pope (1688–1744) British poet. *An Essay on Criticism*

15 Beware of the man who does not return your blow: he neither forgives you nor allows you to forgive yourself.

George Bernard Shaw (1856–1950) Irish dramatist and critic. *Man and Superman*, 'Maxims for Revolutionists'

16 The stupid neither forgive nor forget; the naive forgive and forget; the wise forgive but do not forget.

Thomas Szasz (1920–) US psychiatrist. *The Second Sin*

17 I bear no ill-will against those responsible for this. That sort of talk will not bring her back to life. I know there has to be a plan even though we might not understand it. God is good and we shall meet again.

Gordon Wilson Retired businessman. Speaking of the murder of his daughter, Marie Wilson, in an IRA bombing at the Enniskillen Remembrance Day service, 8 Nov 1987

FRANCE

See also Europe, French Revolution, Paris

1 All Gaul is divided into three parts.

Julius Caesar (100–44 BC) Roman general and statesman. *De Bello Gallico*, Vol. I, Ch. 1

2 France was a long despotism tempered by epigrams.

Thomas Carlyle (1795–1881) Scottish historian and essayist. *History of the French Revolution*, Pt. I, Bk. I, Ch. 1

3 They are short, blue-vested people who carry their own onions when cycling abroad, and have a yard which is 3.37 inches longer than other people's.

Alan Coren (1938–) British humorist and writer. *The Sanity Inspector*, 'All You Need to Know about Europe'

4 There's always something fishy about the French.

Noël Coward (1899–1973) British dramatist. *Conversation Piece*, I:6

5 Bouillabaisse is only good because cooked by the French, who, if they cared to try, could produce an excellent and nutritious substitute out of cigar stumps and empty matchboxes.

Norman Douglas (1868–1952) British novelist. *Siren Land*, 'Rain on the Hills'

6 The French will only be united under the threat of danger. Nobody can simply bring together a country that has 265 kinds of cheese.

Charles De Gaulle (1890–1970) French general and statesman. Speech, 1951

7 I hate the French because they are all slaves, and wear wooden shoes.

Oliver Goldsmith (1728–74) Irish-born British writer. *Essays*, 'Distresses of a Common Soldier'

8 The best thing I know between France and England is – the sea.

Douglas William Jerrold (1803–57) British dramatist. *Wit and Opinions of Douglas Jerrold*, 'The Anglo-French Alliance'

9 A Frenchman must be always talking, whether he knows anything of the matter or not; an Englishman is content to say nothing, when he has nothing to say.

Samuel Johnson (1709–84) British lexicographer. *Life of Johnson* (J. Boswell), Vol. IV

10 *Allons, enfants, de la patrie,*
Le jour de gloire est arrivé.
Come, children of our native land,
The day of glory has arrived.

Rouget de Lisle (Claude Joseph Rouget de Lisle; 1760–1836) French military engineer and composer. *La Marseillaise* (French national anthem)

11 Yet, who can help loving the land that has taught us
Six hundred and eighty-five ways to dress eggs?

Thomas Moore (1779–1852) Irish poet. *The Fudge Family in Paris*

12 There's something Vichy about the French.

Ivor Novello (David Ivor Davies; 1893–1951) British actor, composer, and dramatist. *Ambrosia and Small Beer* (Edward Marsh), Ch. 4

13 A mademoiselle from Armenteers,
She hasn't been kissed for forty years,
Hinky, dinky, par-lee-voo.

Edward Rowland (20th century) British songwriter. Armentières was completely destroyed (1918) in World War I. *Mademoiselle from Armentières* (song)

14 They are a loyal, a gallant, a generous, an ingenious, and good-temper'd people as is under heaven – if they have a fault, they are too *serious*.

Laurence Sterne (1713–68) Irish-born British writer. *A Sentimental Journey*, 'The Character. Versailles'

15 I do not dislike the French from the vulgar antipathy between neighbouring nations, but for their insolent and unfounded airs of superiority.

Horace Walpole (1717–97) British writer. Letter to Hannah More, 14 Oct 1787

16 France is a country where the money falls apart in your hands and you can't tear the toilet paper.

Billy Wilder (Samuel Wilder; 1906–) Austrian-born US film director. Attrib.

FRANKNESS

See also honesty, sincerity, truth

1 But of all plagues, good Heaven, thy wrath can send,

Save me, oh, save me, from the candid friend.

George Canning (1770–1827) British statesman. *New Morality*

2 I have two very cogent reasons for not printing any list of subscribers; – one, that I have lost all the names, – the other, that I have spent all the money.

Samuel Johnson (1709–84) British lexicographer. Referring to subscribers to his *Dictionary of the English Language. Life of Johnson* (J. Boswell), Vol. IV

3 The great consolation in life is to say what one thinks.

Voltaire (François-Marie Arouet; 1694–1778) French writer. Letter, 1765

4 On an occasion of this kind it becomes more than a moral duty to speak one's mind. It becomes a pleasure.

Oscar Wilde (1854–1900) Irish-born British dramatist. *The Importance of Being Earnest*, II

FREEDOM

See also human rights, imprisonment

1 I'll have a fling.

Francis Beaumont (1584–1616) English dramatist. *Rule a Wife and have a Wife*, III:5

2 My policy is to be able to take a ticket at Victoria Station and go anywhere I damn well please.

Ernest Bevin (1881–1951) British trade-union leader and politician. *The Spectator*, 20 Apr 1951

3 Conscience, I say, not thine own, but of the other: for why is my liberty judged of another man's conscience?

Bible: I Corinthians 10:29

4 So free we seem, so fettered fast we are!

Robert Browning (1812–89) British poet. *Andrea del Sarto*

5 Liberty, too, must be limited in order to be possessed.

Edmund Burke (1729–97) British politician. Letter to the Sheriffs of Bristol, 1777

6 Hereditary bondsmen! know ye not
Who would be free themselves must strike the blow?

Lord Byron (1788–1824) British poet. *Childe Harold's Pilgrimage*, I

7 England may as well dam up the waters from the Nile with bulrushes as to fetter the step of Freedom, more proud and firm in this youthful land.

Lydia M. Child (1802–80) US abolitionist campaigner. *The Rebels*, Ch. 4

8 But what is Freedom? Rightly understood,
A universal licence to be good.

Hartley Coleridge (1796–1849) British poet. *Liberty*

9 The condition upon which God hath given liberty to man is eternal vigilance.

John Philpot Curran (1750–1817) Irish judge. Speech on the Right of Election of Lord Mayor of Dublin, 10 July 1790

10 Yes, 'n' how many years can some people exist
Before they're allowed to be free?
Yes, 'n' how many times can a man turn his head,
Pretending he just doesn't see?
The answer, my friend, is blowin' in the wind.

Bob Dylan (Robert Allen Zimmerman; 1941–) US popular singer. *Blowin' in the Wind*

11 My people and I have come to an agreement which satisfies us both. They are to say what they please, and I am to do what I please.

Frederick the Great (1712–86) King of Prussia. Attrib.

12 This is Liberty-Hall, gentlemen.

Oliver Goldsmith (1728–74) Irish-born British writer. *She Stoops to Conquer*, II

13 *Laissez faire, laissez passer.*
Liberty of action, liberty of movement.

Jean Claude Vincent de Gournay (1712–59) French economist. Speech, Sept 1758

14 Power is so apt to be insolent and Liberty to be saucy, that they are seldom upon good Terms.

Lord Halifax (1633–95) English statesman. *Political, Moral, and Miscellaneous Thoughts and Reflections*

15 The love of liberty is the love of others; the love of power is the love of ourselves.

William Hazlitt (1778–1830) British essayist. *The Times*, 1819

16 I know not what course others may take; but as for me, give me liberty or give me death.

Patrick Henry (1736–99) US statesman. Speech, Virginia Convention, 23 Mar 1775

17 I struck the board, and cried, 'No more;
I will abroad.'
What, shall I ever sigh and pine?
My lines and life are free; free as the road,
Loose as the wind, as large as store.

George Herbert (1593–1633) English poet. *The Collar*

18 'Painters and poets alike have always had licence to dare anything.' We know that, and we both claim and allow to others in their turn this indulgence.

Horace (Quintus Horatius Flaccus; 65–8 BC) Roman poet. *Ars Poetica*

19 *Nullius addictus iurare in verba magistri,*
Quo me cumque rapit tempestas, deferor hospes.
Not bound to swear allegiance to any master, wherever the wind takes me I travel as a visitor.

Horace *Nullius in verba* is the motto of the Royal Society. *Epistles*, I

20 A man should never put on his best trousers when he goes out to battle for freedom and truth.

Henrik Ibsen (1828–1906) Norwegian dramatist. *An Enemy of the People*, V

21 The tree of liberty must be refreshed from time to time with the blood of patriots and tyrants. It is its natural manure.

Thomas Jefferson (1743–1826) US statesman. Letter to W. S. Smith, 13 Nov 1787

22 I have got no further than this: Every man has a right to utter what he thinks truth, and every other man has a right to knock him down for it. Martyrdom is the test.

Samuel Johnson (1709–84) British lexicographer. *Life of Johnson* (J. Boswell), Vol. IV

23 The Liberty of the press is the *Palladium* of all the civil, political and religious rights of an Englishman.

Junius An unidentified writer of letters (1769–72) to the *London Public Advertiser*. *Letters*, 'Dedication'

24 It's often safer to be in chains than to be free.

Franz Kafka (1883–1924) Czech novelist. *The Trial*, Ch. 8

25 One of the few remaining freedoms we have is the blank page. No one can prescribe how we should fill it.

James Kelman (1946–) Scottish writer. *The Guardian*, 12 Oct 1994

26 Freedom's just another word for nothing left to lose.

Kris Kristofferson (1936–) US film actor and folk musician. *Me and Bobby McGee*

27 It is true that liberty is precious – so precious that it must be rationed.

Lenin (Vladimir Ilich Ulyanov; 1870–1924) Russian revolutionary leader. Attrib.

28 I intend no modification of my oft-expressed personal wish that all men everywhere could be free.

Abraham Lincoln (1809–65) US statesman. Letter to Horace Greeley, 22 Aug 1862

29 Those who deny freedom to others, deserve it not for themselves.

Abraham Lincoln Speech, 19 May 1856

30 Many politicians of our time are in the habit of laying it down as a self-evident proposition, that no people ought to be free till they are fit to use their freedom. The maxim is worthy of the fool in the old story, who resolved not to go into the water till he had learnt to swim. If men are to wait for liberty till they become wise and good in slavery, they may indeed wait for ever.

Lord Macaulay (1800–59) British historian. *Literary Essays Contributed to the 'Edinburgh Review'*, 'Milton',

31 It would be better that England should be free than that England should be compulsorily sober.

William Connor Magee (1821–91) British clergyman. Speech on the Intoxicating Liquor Bill, House of Lords, 2 May 1872

32 I cannot and will not give any undertaking at a time when I, and you, the people, are not free. Your freedom and mine cannot be separated.

Nelson Mandela (1918–) South African lawyer and politician. Message read by his daughter to a rally in Soweto, 10 Feb 1985

33 Letting a hundred flowers blossom and a hundred schools of thought contend is the policy for promoting the progress of the arts and the sciences.

Mao Tse-Tung (1893–1976) Chinese communist leader. *Quotations from Chairman Mao Tse-Tung*, Ch. 32

34 The liberty of the individual must be thus far limited; he must not make himself a nuisance to other people.

John Stuart Mill (1806–73) British philosopher. *On Liberty*, Ch. 3

35 None can love freedom heartily, but good men; the rest love not freedom, but licence.

John Milton (1608–74) English poet. *Tenure of Kings and Magistrates*

36 Liberty is the right to do everything which the laws allow.

Baron de Montesquieu (1689–1755) French writer. *L'Esprit des lois*

37 Before the organization of the Blackshirt movement free speech did not exist in this country.

Oswald Mosley (1896–1980) British politician. Selections from the *New Statesman, This England*, Pt. I

38 My government will protect all liberties but one – the liberty to do away with other liberties.

Gustavo Diaz Ordaz (1911–79) President of Mexico (1964–1970). Inaugural speech

39 Freedom is the right to tell people what they do not want to hear.

George Orwell (Eric Blair; 1903–50) British novelist. *The Road to Wigan Pier*

40 I sometimes think that the price of liberty is not so much eternal vigilance as eternal dirt.

George Orwell *The Road to Wigan Pier*, Ch. 4

41 We must plan for freedom, and not only for security, if for no other reason than that only freedom can make security secure.

Karl Popper (1902–94) Austrian-born British philosopher. *The Open Society and Its Enemies*

42 Now: heaven knows, anything goes.

Cole Porter (1893–1964) US songwriter. *Anything Goes*, title song

43 *Laissez faire, laissez passer.*
Let it be, let it pass.

François Quesnay (1694–1774) French economist. Attrib.

44 In their rules there was only one clause: Do what you will.

François Rabelais (1483–1553) French satirist. Referring to the fictional Abbey of Thélème. *Gargantua*, Bk. I, Ch. 57

45 *'O liberté! O liberté! Que de crimes on commet en ton nom!'*
Oh liberty! Oh liberty! What crimes are committed in thy name!

Madame Roland (1754–93) French revolutionary. Said as she mounted the steps of the guillotine at her execution. Attrib.

46 Man was born free and everywhere

he is in chains.

Jean Jacques Rousseau (1712–78) French philosopher. *Du contrat social*, Ch. 1

47 No human being, however great, or powerful, was ever so free as a fish.

John Ruskin (1819–1900) British art critic and writer. *The Two Paths*, Lecture V

48 Man is condemned to be free.

Jean-Paul Sartre (1905–80) French writer. *Existentialism is a Humanism*

49 You took my freedom away a long time ago and you can't give it back because you haven't got it yourself.

Alexander Solzhenitsyn (1918–) Soviet novelist. *The First Circle*, Ch. 17

50 My definition of a free society is a society where it is safe to be unpopular.

Adlai Stevenson (1900–65) US statesman. Speech, Detroit, Oct 1952

51 It is by the goodness of God that in our country we have those three unspeakably precious things: freedom of speech, freedom of conscience, and the prudence never to practise either of them.

Mark Twain (Samuel Langhorne Clemens; 1835–1910) US writer. *Following the Equator*, heading of Ch. 20

52 I disapprove of what you say, but I will defend to the death your right to say it.

Voltaire (François-Marie Arouet; 1694–1778) French writer. Attrib.

53 Me this unchartered freedom tires;
I feel the weight of chance-desires:
My hopes no more must change their name,
I long for a repose that ever is the same.

William Wordsworth (1770–1850) British poet. *Ode to Duty*

54 We must be free or die, who speak the tongue
That Shakespeare spake; the faith and morals hold
Which Milton held.

William Wordsworth *Sonnets*, 'It is not to be thought of'

55 Two voices are there; one is of the sea,
One of the mountains; each a mighty voice:
In both from age to age thou didst rejoice,
They were thy chosen music, Liberty!

William Wordsworth *Sonnets*, 'Two voices are there'

FRENCH REVOLUTION

See also France, revolution

1 It was the best of times, it was the worst of times, it was the age of wisdom, it was the age of foolishness, it was the epoch of belief, it was the epoch of incredulity, it was the season of Light, it was the season of Darkness, it was the spring of hope, it was the winter of despair, we had everything before us, we had nothing before us, we were all going direct to Heaven, we were all going direct the other way.

Charles Dickens (1812–70) British novelist. The opening words of the book. *A Tale of Two Cities*, Bk. I, Ch. 1

2 How much the greatest event it is that ever happened in the world! and how much the best!

Charles James Fox (1749–1806) British Whig politician. Referring to the fall of the Bastille, 14 July 1789. Letter to Fitzpatrick, 30 July 1789

3 Bliss was it in that dawn to be alive,
But to be young was very heaven!

William Wordsworth (1770–1850) British poet. *The Prelude*, XI

4 That which sets
...The budding rose above the rose full blown.

William Wordsworth *The Prelude*, XI

5 Not in Utopia, – subterranean fields, –
Or some secreted island, Heaven knows where!
But in the very world, which is the world
Of all of us, – the place where, in the end,
We find our happiness, or not at all!

William Wordsworth *The Prelude*, XI

FRIENDS

See also enemies, friendship

1 Books and friends should be few but good.

Proverb

2 Forsake not an old friend; for the new is not comparable to him: a new friend is as new wine; when it is old, thou shalt drink it with pleasure.

Bible: Ecclesiasticus 9:10

3 Cost his enemies a long repentance,
And made him a good friend, but bad acquaintance.

Lord Byron (1788–1824) British poet. *Don Juan*, III

4 Tell me what company thou keepest, and I'll tell thee what thou art.

Miguel de Cervantes (1547–1616) Spanish novelist. *Don Quixote*, Pt. II, Ch. 23

5 Have no friends not equal to yourself.

Confucius (K'ung Fu-tzu; 551–479 BC) Chinese philosopher. *Analects*

6 Fate chooses your relations, you choose your friends.

Jacques Delille (1738–1813) French abbé and poet. *Malheur et pitié*, I

7 A Friend may well be reckoned the masterpiece of Nature.

Ralph Waldo Emerson (1803–82) US poet and essayist. *Essays*, 'Friendship'

8 *Changez vos amis.*
Change your friends.

Charles De Gaulle (1890–1970) French general and statesman. Replying to the complaint by Jacques Soustelle that he was being attacked by his own friends. Attrib.

9 If a man does not make new acquaintance as he advances through life, he will soon find himself left alone. A man, Sir, should keep his friendship in constant repair.

Samuel Johnson (1709–84) British lexicographer. *Life of Johnson* (J. Boswell), Vol. I

10 I get by with a little help from my friends.

John Lennon (1940–80) British rock musician. *With a Little Help from My Friends* (with Paul McCartney)

11 He's an oul' butty o' mine – oh, he's a darlin' man, a daarlin' man.

Sean O'Casey (1884–1964) Irish dramatist. *Juno and the Paycock*, I

12 It is more shameful to distrust one's friends than to be deceived by them.

Duc de la Rochefoucauld (1613–80) French writer. *Maximes*, 84

13 A friend should bear his friend's infirmities,
But Brutus makes mine greater than they are.

William Shakespeare (1564–1616) English dramatist. *Julius Caesar*, IV:3

14 If it is abuse – why one is always sure to hear of it from one damned good-natured friend or other!

Richard Brinsley Sheridan (1751–1816) British dramatist. *The Critic*, I

15 Associate yourself with men of good quality if you esteem your own reputation; for 'tis better to be alone than in bad company.

George Washington (1732–99) US statesman. *Rules of Civility*

FRIENDSHIP

See also friends, love and friendship

1 A friend in need is a friend indeed.

Proverb

2 A good friend is my nearest relation.

Proverb

3 A hedge between keeps friendship green.

Proverb

4 God defend me from my friends; from my enemies I can defend myself.

Proverb

5 Love is blind; friendship closes its eyes.

Proverb

6 The best of friends must part.

Proverb

7 There is no such thing as a free lunch.

Anonymous Often attributed to Milton Friedman.

8 Two are better than one; because they have a good reward for their labour.
For if they fall, the one will lift up his fellow: but woe to him that is alone when he falleth; for he hath not another to help him up.

Bible: Ecclesiastes 4:9–10

9 Saul and Jonathan were lovely and pleasant in their lives, and in their death they were not divided: they were swifter than eagles, they were stronger than lions.

Bible: II Samuel 1:23–24

10 I've noticed your hostility towards him…I ought to have guessed you were friends.

Malcolm Bradbury (1932–) British academic and novelist. *The History Man*, Ch. 7

11 I don't trust him. We're friends.

Bertolt Brecht (1898–1956) German dramatist. *Mother Courage*, III

12 Should auld acquaintance be forgot,
And never brought to min'?

Robert Burns (1759–96) Scottish poet. *Auld Lang Syne*

13 We'll tak a cup o' kindness yet,
For auld lang syne.

Robert Burns *Auld Lang Syne*

14 Two may talk together under the same roof for many years, yet never really meet; and two others at first speech are old friends.

Mary Catherwood (1847–1901) US writer. *Mackinac and Lake Stories*, 'Marianson'

15 A woman can become a man's friend only in the following stages – first an acquaintance, next a mistress, and only then a friend.

Anton Chekhov (1860–1904) Russian dramatist. *Uncle Vanya*, II

16 There is nothing in the world I wouldn't do for Hope, and there is nothing he wouldn't do for me…We spend our lives doing nothing for each other.

Bing Crosby (Harry Lillis; 1904–77) US singer. Referring to Bob Hope. *The Observer*, 'Sayings of the Week', 7 May 1950

17 It is not so much our friends' help that helps us as the confident knowledge that they will help us.

Epicurus (341–270 BC) Greek philosopher.

18 These are called the pious frauds of friendship.

Henry Fielding (1707–54) British novelist. *Amelia*, Bk. III, Ch. 4

19 Always, Sir, set a high value on spontaneous kindness. He whose inclination prompts him to cultivate your friendship of his own accord, will love you more than one whom you have been at pains to attach to you.

Samuel Johnson (1709–84) British lexicographer. *Life of Johnson* (J. Boswell), Vol. IV

20 Sir, I look upon every day to be lost, in which I do not make a new acquaintance.

Samuel Johnson *Life of Johnson* (J. Boswell), Vol. IV

21 Greater love than this, he said, no man hath that a man lay down his wife for a friend. Go thou and do likewise. Thus, or words to that effect, saith Zarathustra, sometime regius professor of French letters to the University of Oxtail.

James Joyce (1882–1941) Irish novelist. *Ulysses*

22 Friendship is unnecessary, like philosophy, like art.... It has no survival value; rather it is one of those things that give value to survival.

C. S. Lewis (1898–1963) British academic and writer. *The Four Loves, Friendship*

23 That the world will never be quite – what a cliché – the same again
Is what we only learn by the event
When a friend dies out on us and is not there
To share the periphery of a remembered scent.

Louis MacNiece (1907–63) Irish-born British poet. *Tam Cari Capitis*

24 Two buttocks of one bum.

T. Sturge Moore (1870–1944) British poet and illustrator. Referring to Hilaire Belloc and G. K. Chesterton.

25 A true bond of friendship is usually only possible between people of roughly equal status. This equality is demonstrated in many indirect ways, but it is reinforced in face-to-face encounters by a matching of the posture of relaxation or alertness.

Desmond Morris (1928–) British biologist. *Manwatching*, 'Postural Echo'

26 To like and dislike the same things, that is indeed true friendship.

Sallust (Gaius Sallustius Crispus; c. 86–c. 34 BC) Roman historian and politician. *Bellum Catilinae*

27 I might give my life for my friend, but he had better not ask me to do up a parcel.

Logan Pearsall Smith (1865–1946) US writer. *Trivia*

FUNERALS

See also death

1 Most of the people who will walk after me will be children, so make the beat keep time with short steps.

Hans Christian Andersen (1805–75) Danish writer. Planning the music for his funeral. *Hans Christian Andersen* (R. Godden)

2 This is the last time that I will take part as an amateur.

Daniel-François-Esprit Auber (1782–1871) French composer. Said at a funeral. *Das Buch des Lachens* (W. Scholz)

3 When we attend the funerals of our friends we grieve for them, but when we go to those of other people it is chiefly our own deaths that we mourn for.

Gerald Brenan (Edward Fitzgerald Brenan; 1894–1987) British writer. *Thoughts in a Dry Season*, 'Death'

4 'If you don't go to other men's funerals,' he told Father stiffly, 'they won't go to yours.'

Clarence Shepard Day (1874–1935) US writer. *Life With Father*, 'Father plans'

5 I bet you a hundred bucks he ain't in here.

Charles Bancroft Dillingham (1868–1934) US theatrical manager. Referring to the escapologist Harry Houdini; said at his funeral, while carrying his coffin. Attrib.

6 When I die I want to decompose in a barrel of porter and have it served in all the pubs in Dublin.

J. P. Donleavy (1926–) US novelist. *The Ginger Man*

7 Why should I go? She won't be there.

Arthur Miller (1915–) US dramatist. When asked if he would attend Marilyn Monroe's funeral. Attrib.

8 It proves what they say, give the public what they want to see and they'll come out for it.

Red Skelton (Richard Bernard Skelton; 1913–) US actor and comedian. Said while attending the funeral in 1958 of Hollywood producer Harry Cohn. It has also been attributed to Samuel Goldwyn while attending Louis B. Mayer's funeral in 1957.

9 How Henry would have loved it!

Ellen Terry (1847–1928) British actress. Referring to Sir Henry Irving's funeral. *Yesterdays* (Robert Hitchens)

10 Not a drum was heard, not a funeral note,
As his corse to the rampart we hurried.

Charles Wolfe (1791–1823) Irish poet. *The Burial of Sir John Moore at Corunna*, I

11 We carved not a line, and we raised not a stone –
But we left him alone with his glory.

Charles Wolfe *The Burial of Sir John Moore at Corunna*, VIII

FUTILITY

See also purpose

1 Why buy a cow when milk is so cheap?

Proverb

2 Why keep a dog and bark yourself?

Proverb

3 You can't get blood out of a stone.

Proverb

4 Don't curse the darkness – light a candle.

Chinese Proverb

5 Mock on, mock on, Voltaire, Rousseau;
Mock on, mock on; 'tis all in vain!
You throw the sand against the wind,
And the wind blows it back again.

William Blake (1757–1827) British poet. *Mock on, mock on, Voltaire, Rousseau*

6 It's but little good you'll do a-watering the last year's crop.

George Eliot (Mary Ann Evans; 1819–80) British novelist. *Adam Bede*

7 He is very fond of making things which he does not want, and then giving them to people who have no use for them.

Anthony Hope (Sir Anthony Hope Hawkins; 1863–1933) British novelist. *The Dolly Dialogues*

8 He's a real Nowhere Man,
Sitting in his Nowhere Land,
Making all his nowhere plans for nobody.
Doesn't have a point of view,

Knows not where he's going to,
Isn't he a bit like you and me?

John Lennon (1940–80) British rock musician. *Nowhere Man* (with Paul McCartney)

9 'Tis not necessary to light a candle to the sun.

Algernon Sidney (1622–83) English statesman. *Discourses concerning Government*, Ch. 2

10 People talking without speaking,
People listening without hearing,
People writing songs that voices never shared.

Paul Simon (1942–) US singer. *Sound of Silence*

11 All dressed up, with nowhere to go.

William Allen White (1868–1944) US writer. Referring to the Progressive Party, after Theodore Roosevelt's withdrawal from the 1916 US Presidential election

FUTURE

See also past, present, promises, prophecy, time

1 Years hence, perhaps, may dawn an age,
More fortunate, alas! than we,
Which without hardness will be sage,
And gay without frivolity.

Matthew Arnold (1822–88) British poet and critic. *The Grande Chartreuse*

2 I have a vision of the future, chum.
The workers' flats in fields of soya beans
Tower up like silver pencils.

John Betjeman (1906–84) British poet.

3 Boast not thyself of tomorrow; for thou knowest not what a day may bring forth.

Bible: Proverbs 27:1

4 *Future*, n That period of time in which our affairs prosper, our friends are true and our happiness is assured.

Ambrose Bierce (1842–?1914) US writer and journalist. *The Devil's Dictionary*

5 Not a future. At least not in Europe. America's different, of course, but America's really only a kind of Russia. You've no idea how pleasant it is not to have any future. It's like having a totally efficient contraceptive.

Anthony Burgess (John Burgess Wilson; 1917–93) British novelist. *Honey for the Bears*, Pt. II, Ch. 6

6 I never think of the future. It comes soon enough.

Albert Einstein (1879–1955) German-born US physicist. Interview, 1930

7 I have seen the future and it works.

Lincoln Steffens (1866–1936) US journalist. Speaking to Bernard Baruch after visiting the Soviet Union, 1919. *Autobiography*, Ch. 18

8 The future is made of the same stuff as the present.

Simone Weil (1909–43) French philosopher. *On Science, Necessity, and the Love of God* (ed. Richard Rees), 'Some Thoughts on the Love of God'

G

GARDENS

See also flowers

1 Mary, Mary, quite contrary,
How does your garden grow?
With silver bells and cockle shells,
And pretty maids all in a row.

Anonymous *Tommy Thumb's Pretty Song Book*

2 God Almighty first planted a garden. And indeed it is the purest of human pleasures.

Francis Bacon (1561–1626) English philosopher. *Essays*, 'Of Gardens'

3 But there went up a mist from the earth, and watered the whole face of the ground.
And the Lord God formed man of the dust of the ground, and breathed into his nostrils the breath of life; and man became a living soul.
And the Lord God planted a garden eastward in Eden; and there he put the man whom he had formed.
And out of the ground made the Lord God to grow every tree that is pleasant to the sight, and good for food; the tree of life also in the midst of the garden, and the tree of knowledge of good and evil.
And a river went out of Eden to water the garden.

Bible: Genesis 2:6–10

4 A garden is a lovesome thing, God wot!

Thomas Edward Brown (1830–97) British poet. *My Garden*

5 To get the best results you must talk to your vegetables.

Charles, Prince of Wales (1948–) Eldest son of Elizabeth II. *The Observer*, 'Sayings of the Week', 28 Sept 1986

6 God the first garden made, and the first city Cain.

Abraham Cowley (1618–67) English poet. *The Garden*

7 The kiss of sun for pardon,
The song of the birds for mirth –
One is nearer God's Heart in a garden
Than anywhere else on earth.

Dorothy Gurney (1858–1932) British poet. *The Lord God Planted a Garden*

8 Oh, Adam was a gardener, and God who made him sees
That half a proper gardener's work is done upon his knees,
So when your work is finished, you can wash your hands and pray
For the Glory of the Garden, that it may not pass away!

Rudyard Kipling (1865–1936) Indian-born British writer. *The Glory of the Garden*

9 A little thin, flowery border, round, neat, not gaudy.

Charles Lamb (1775–1834) British essayist. Letter to Wordsworth, June 1806

10 I have a garden of my own,
But so with roses overgrown,
And lilies, that you would it guess
To be a little wilderness.

Andrew Marvell (1621–78) English poet. *The Nymph Complaining for the Death of her Fawn*

GENERALIZATIONS

See also classification

1 To generalize is to be an idiot.

William Blake (1757–1827) British poet. *Life of Blake* (Gilchrist)

2 All generalizations are dangerous, even this one.

Alexandre Dumas, fils (1824–95) French writer. Attrib.

3 Any general statement is like a cheque drawn on a bank. Its value depends on what is there to meet it.

Ezra Pound (1885–1972) US poet. *ABC of Reading*, Ch. 2

GENEROSITY

See also charity, gifts, kindness, parasites

1 A bit of fragrance always clings to the hand that gives you roses.

Chinese Proverb

2 Every man according as he purposeth in his heart, so let him give; not grudgingly, or of necessity: for God loveth a cheerful giver.

Bible: II Corinthians 9:7

3 Heal the sick, cleanse the lepers, raise the dead, cast out devils: freely ye have received, freely give.

Bible: Matthew 10:8

4 Experience was to be taken as showing that one might get a five-pound note as one got a light for a cigarette; but one had to check the friendly impulse to ask for it in the same way.

Henry James (1843–1916) US novelist. *The Awkward Age*

5 In the first place, I have only five guineas in my pocket; and in the second, they are very much at your service.

Lord Peterborough (1658–1735) English military and naval commander. Persuading an angry mob that he was not the Duke of Marlborough, notorious for his meanness. *Dictionary of National Biography*

GENIUS

See also talent, talent and genius

1 Genius is an infinite capacity for taking pains.

Proverb

2 Genius (which means transcendent capacity of taking trouble, first of all).

Thomas Carlyle (1795–1881) Scottish historian and essayist. *Frederick the Great*, Vol. IV, Ch. 3

3 I'm going to live forever. Geniuses don't die.

Salvador Dali (1904–89) Spanish painter. Remark, July 1986

4 Great Wits are sure to Madness near alli'd
And thin Partitions do their Bounds divide.

John Dryden (1631–1700) British poet and dramatist. *Absalom and Achitophel*, I

5 Genius is one per cent inspiration and ninety-nine per cent perspiration.

Thomas Edison (1847–1931) US inventor. Attrib.

6 True genius walks along a line, and, perhaps, our greatest pleasure is in seeing it so often near falling, without being ever actually down.

Oliver Goldsmith (1728–74) Irish-born British writer. *The Bee*, 'The Characteristics of Greatness'

7 The true genius is a mind of large general powers, accidentally determined to some particular direction.

Samuel Johnson (1709–84) British lexicographer. *Lives of the English Poets*, 'Cowley'

8 A genius! For thirty-seven years I've practiced fourteen hours a day, and now they call me a genius!

Pablo Sarasate (1844–1908) Spanish violinist and composer. On being hailed as a genius by a critic. Attrib.

9 When a true genius appears in the world, you may know him by this sign, that the dunces are all in confederacy against him.

Jonathan Swift (1667–1745) Irish-born Anglican priest and writer. *Thoughts on Various Subjects*

GERMANY

See also Europe, Hitler, Nazism, World War I, World War II

1 Hamelin Town's in Brunswick,
By famous Hanover city;
The river Weser, deep and wide,
Washes its wall on the southern side;
A pleasanter spot you never spied.

Robert Browning (1812–89) British poet. *The Pied Piper of Hamelin*

2 Don't let's be beastly to the Germans.

Noël Coward (1899–1973) British dramatist. *Title of song*

3 *Deutschland, Deutschland über alles.*
Germany, Germany before all else.

Heinrich Hoffmann von Fallersleben (1798–1876) German poet. German national anthem

4 Germany will be either a world power or will not be at all.

Adolf Hitler (1889–1945) German dictator. *Mein Kampf*, Ch. 14

5 How appallingly thorough these Germans always managed to be, how emphatic! In sex no less than in war – in scholarship, in science. Diving deeper than anyone else and coming up muddier.

Aldous Huxley (1894–1964) British novelist.

6 All free men, wherever they may live, are citizens of Berlin. And therefore, as a free man, I take pride in the words *Ich bin ein Berliner.*

John Fitzgerald Kennedy (1917–63) US statesman. Speech, City Hall, West Berlin, 26 June 1963

7 Germany is our fatherland, the united Europe our future.

Helmut Kohl (1930–) German statesman. On the unification of the two Germanies. *The Times*, Oct 1990

8 This is a day of jubilation, a day of remembrance and gratitude. Our common task now is to establish a new European order.

Hans-Dietrich Genscher (1927–) German politician. Referring to the conclusion of the agreement to reunite East and West Germany. *The Independent*, 10 Sept 1990

9 America...is the prize amateur nation of the world. Germany is the prize professional nation.

Woodrow Wilson (1856–1925) US statesman. Speech, Aug 1917. *Mr Wilson's War* (John Dos Passos), Pt. III, Ch. 13

10 It was still a time for open trust, for innocence and illusions.

Christa Wolf (1929–) German writer. Referring to the first few months after the reunification of Germany. *Im Dialog*

GIFTS

See also generosity, materialism

1 Every good gift and every perfect gift is from above, and cometh down from the Father of lights, with whom is no variableness, neither shadow of turning.

Bible: James 1:17

2 Heal the sick, cleanse the lepers, raise the dead, cast out devils: freely ye have received, freely give.

Bible: Matthew 10:8

3 'They gave it me,' Humpty Dumpty continued thoughtfully...'for an un-birthday present.'

Lewis Carroll (Charles Lutwidge Dodgson; 1832–98) British writer. *Through the Looking-Glass*, Ch. 6

4 The manner of giving is worth more than the gift.

Pierre Corneille (1606–84) French dramatist. *Le Menteur*, I:1

5 If one doesn't get birthday presents it can remobilize very painfully the persecutory anxiety which usually follows birth.

Henry Reed (1914–86) British poet and dramatist. *The Primal Scene, as it were*

GLORY

1 Fools! For I also had my hour;
One far fierce hour and sweet;

There was a shout about my ears,
And palms before my feet.

G. K. Chesterton (1874–1936) British writer. *The Donkey*

2 May God deny you peace but give you glory!

Miguel de Unamuno y Jugo (1864–1936) Spanish writer. Closing words. *The Tragic Sense of Life*

3 *Sic transit gloria mundi.*
Thus the glory of the world passes away.

Thomas à Kempis (Thomas Hemmerken; c. 1380–1471) German monk. *The Imitation of Christ*, I

4 Wi' a hundred pipers an' a', an' a'.

Carolina Nairne (1766–1845) Scottish songwriter. A romantic glorification of the 1745 Jacobite Rebellion. *The Hundred Pipers*

5 'Hurrah! hurrah! we bring the Jubilee!
Hurrah! hurrah! the flag that makes you free!'
So we sang the chorus from Atlanta to the sea
As we were marching through Georgia.

Henry Clay Work (1832–84) US songwriter. Commemorating the march (Nov–Dec 1864) by a Union army under General Sherman through Confederate Georgia. *Marching Through Georgia*

GOD

See also atheism, creation, faith, prayer, religion

1 God be in my head,
And in my understanding;
God be in my eyes,
And in my looking;
God be in my mouth,
And in my speaking;
God be in my heart,
And in my thinking;
God be at my end,
And at my departing.

Anonymous *Sarum Missal*

2 Every man thinks God is on his side. The rich and powerful know that he is.

Jean Anouilh (1910–87) French dramatist. *The Lark*

3 It were better to have no opinion of God at all, than such an opinion as is unworthy of him.

Francis Bacon (1561–1626) English philosopher. *Essays*, 'Of Superstition'

4 Then Peter opened his mouth, and said,
Of a truth I perceive that God is no respecter of persons.

Bible: Acts 10:34

5 For in him we live, and move, and have our being; as certain also of your own poets have said, For we are also his offspring.

Bible: Acts 17:28

6 Seek him that maketh the seven stars and Orion, and turneth the shadow of death into the morning, and maketh the day dark with night: that calleth for the waters of the sea, and poureth them out upon the face of the earth: The Lord is his name.

Bible: Amos 5:8

7 And he changeth the times and the seasons: he removeth kings, and setteth up kings: he giveth wisdom unto the wise, and knowledge to them that know understanding:
He revealeth the deep and secret things: he knoweth what is in the darkness, and the light dwelleth with him.

Bible: Daniel 2:21–22

8 Be strong and of a good courage, fear not, nor be afraid of them: for the Lord thy God, he it is that doth go with thee; he will not fail thee, nor forsake thee.

Bible: Deuteronomy 31:6

9 Let us hear the conclusion of the whole matter: Fear God, and keep his commandments: for this is the whole duty of man.

Bible: Ecclesiastes 12:13

10 I am the Lord thy God, which have brought thee out of the land of Egypt, out of the house of bondage.
Thou shalt have no other gods before me.
Thou shalt not make unto thee any graven image, or any likeness of any thing that is in heaven above, or that is in the earth beneath, or that is in the water under the earth:
Thou shalt not bow down thyself to them, nor serve them: for Lord thy God am a jealous God, visiting the iniquity of the fathers upon the children unto the third and fourth generation of them that hate me;
And shewing mercy unto thousands of them that love me, and keep my commandments.
Thou shalt not take the name of the Lord thy God in vain; for the Lord will not hold him guiltless that taketh his name in vain.
Remember the sabbath day, to keep it holy.
Six days shalt thou labour, and do all thy work:
But the seventh day is the sabbath of the Lord thy God: in it thou shalt not do any work, thou, nor thy son, nor thy daughter, thy manservant, nor thy maidservant, nor thy cattle, nor thy stranger that is within thy gates:
For in six days the Lord made heaven and earth, the sea, and all that in them is, and rested the seventh day: wherefore the Lord blessed the sabbath day, and hallowed it.
Honour thy father and thy mother: that thy days may be long upon the land which the Lord thy God giveth thee.
Thou shalt not kill.
Thou shalt not commit adultery.
Thou shalt not steal.
Thou shalt not bear false witness against thy neighbour.
Thou shalt not covet thy neighbour's house, thou shalt not covet thy neighbour's wife, nor his manservant, nor his maidservant, nor his ox, nor his ass, nor any thing that is thy neighbour's.

Bible: Exodus 20:2–17

11 And he said, Thou canst not see my face: for there shall no man see me, and live.

Bible: Exodus 33:20

12 For the kingdom of God is not in word, but in

power.

Bible: I Corinthians 4:20

13 And he said, Go forth, and stand upon the mount before the Lord. And, behold, the Lord passed by, and a great and strong wind rent the mountains, and brake in pieces the rocks before the Lord; but the Lord was not in the wind: and after the wind an earthquake; but the Lord was not in the earthquake:
And after the earthquake a fire; but the Lord was not in the fire: and after the fire a still small voice.

Bible: I Kings 19:11–12

14 Man has learned to cope with all questions of importance without recourse to God as a working hypothesis.

Dietrich Bonhoeffer (1906–45) German theologian. *Letters and Papers from Prison*, 8 June 1944

15 A God who let us prove his existence would be an idol.

Dietrich Bonhoeffer *No Rusty Swords*

16 God's gifts put man's best gifts to shame.

Elizabeth Barrett Browning (1806–61) British poet. *Sonnets from the Portuguese*, XXVI

17 Thou shalt have one God only; who
Would be at the expense of two?

Arthur Hugh Clough (1819–61) British poet. *The Latest Decalogue*, 1

18 God moves in a mysterious way
His wonders to perform;
He plants his footsteps in the sea,
And rides upon the storm.

William Cowper (1731–1800) British poet. *Olney Hymns*, 35

19 It is the final proof of God's omnipotence that he need not exist in order to save us.

Peter De Vries (1910–93) US novelist. *The Mackerel Plaza*, Ch. 2

20 What sort of God are we portraying and believing in if we insist on what I will nickname 'the divine laser beam' type of miracle as the heart and basis of the Incarnation and Resurrection?

Bishop of Durham (1925–) British churchman. Speech, July 1986

21 God is subtle but he is not malicious.

Albert Einstein (1879–1955) German-born US physicist. Inscribed over the fireplace in the Mathematical Institute, Princeton. It refers to Einstein's objection to the quantum theory. *Albert Einstein* (Carl Seelig), Ch. 8

22 At bottom God is nothing more than an exalted father.

Sigmund Freud (1856–1939) Austrian psychoanalyst. *Totem and Taboo*

23 O worship the King, all glorious above!
O gratefully sing his power and his love!
Our Shield and Defender – the Ancient of Days,
Pavilioned in splendour, and girded with praise.

Robert Grant (1779–1838) British hymn writer. Hymn

24 Holy, holy, holy, Lord God Almighty!
Early in the morning our song shall rise to thee.

Reginald Heber (1783–1826) British bishop and hymn writer. *Holy, Holy, Holy*

25 The world is charged with the grandeur of God.

Gerard Manley Hopkins (1844–99) British Jesuit and poet. *God's Grandeur*

26 Mine eyes have seen the glory of the coming of the Lord:
He is trampling out the vintage where the grapes of wrath are stored.

Julia Ward Howe (1819–1910) US writer. *Battle Hymn of the American Republic*

27 Operationally, God is beginning to resemble not a ruler but the last fading smile of a cosmic Cheshire cat.

Julian Huxley (1887–1975) British biologist. *Religion without Revelation*

28 The chess-board is the world; the pieces are the phenomena of the universe; the rules of the game are what we call the laws of Nature. The player on the other side is hidden from us. We know that his play is always fair, just, and patient. But also we know, to our cost, that he never overlooks a mistake, or makes the smallest allowance for ignorance.

T. H. Huxley (1825–95) British biologist. *Lay Sermons*, 'A Liberal Education'

29 An honest God is the noblest work of man.

Robert G. Ingersoll (1833–99) US lawyer and agnostic. *Gods*

30 Man proposes but God disposes.

Thomas à Kempis (Thomas Hemmerken; c. 1380–1471) German monk. *The Imitation of Christ*, I

31 A man with God is always in the majority.

John Knox (c. 1514–72) Scottish religious reformer. Inscription, Reformation Monument, Geneva, Switzerland

32 What God does, He does well.

Jean de La Fontaine (1621–95) French poet. *Fables*, IX, 'Le Gland et la Citrouille'

33 I have no need of that hypothesis.

Marquis de Laplace (1749–1827) French mathematician and astronomer. On being asked by Napoleon why he had made no mention of God in his book about the universe, *Mécanique céleste*. *Men of Mathematics* (E. Bell)

34 Though the mills of God grind slowly, yet they grind exceeding small;
Though with patience He stands waiting, with exactness grinds He all.

Friedrich von Logau (1604–55) German poet and writer. *Sinngedichte*, III

35 God is the immemorial refuge of the incompetent, the helpless, the miserable. They find not only sanctuary in His arms, but also a kind of superiority, soothing to their macerated egos; He will set them above their betters.

H. L. Mencken (1880–1956) US journalist. *Notebooks*, 'Minority Report'

36 There's a Friend for little children

Above the bright blue sky,
A Friend who never changes,
Whose love will never die.

Albert Midlane (1825–1909) British hymn writer. Hymn

37 Let us with a gladsome mind
Praise the Lord, for he is kind,
For his mercies ay endure,
Ever faithful, ever sure.

John Milton (1608–74) English poet. *Psalm*

38 What in me is dark
Illumine, what is low raise and support;
That, to the height of this great argument,
I may assert Eternal Providence,
And justify the ways of God to men.

John Milton *Paradise Lost*, Bk. I

39 God is dead: but considering the state the species Man is in, there will perhaps be caves, for ages yet, in which his shadow will be shown.

Friedrich Wilhelm Nietzsche (1844–1900) German philosopher. *Die Fröhliche Wissenschaft*, Bk. III

40 God is a gentleman. He prefers blondes.

Joe Orton (1933–67) British dramatist. *Loot*, II

41 One on God's side is a majority.

Wendell Phillips (1811–84) US reformer. Speech, Brooklyn, 1 Nov 1859

42 God is really only another artist. He invented the giraffe, the elephant, and the cat. He has no real style, He just goes on trying other things.

Pablo Picasso (1881–1973) Spanish painter. *Life with Picasso* Ch. 1 (Françoise Gilot and Carlton Lake),

43 God can stand being told by Professor Ayer and Marghanita Laski that He doesn't exist.

J. B. Priestley (1894–1984) British novelist. *The Listener*, 1 July 1965, 'The BBC's Duty to Society'

44 Write down that they hope they serve God; and write God first; for God defend but God should go before such villains!

William Shakespeare (1564–1616) English dramatist. *Much Ado About Nothing*, IV:2

45 But already it is time to depart, for me to die, for you to go on living; which of us takes the better course, is concealed from anyone except God.

Socrates (469–399 BC) Athenian philosopher. *Apology* (Plato)

46 In the days of my youth I remembered my God!
And He hath not forgotten my age.

Robert Southey (1774–1843) British poet. *The Old Man's Comforts, and how he Gained them*

47 Yet her conception of God was certainly not orthodox. She felt towards Him as she might have felt towards a glorified sanitary engineer; and in some of her speculations she seems hardly to distinguish between the Deity and the Drains.

Lytton Strachey (1880–1932) British writer. *Eminent Victorians*, 'Florence Nightingale'

48 It is a mistake to assume that God is interested only, or even chiefly, in religion.

William Temple (1881–1944) British churchman. Attrib.

49 If God did not exist, it would be necessary to invent Him.

Voltaire (François-Marie Arouet; 1694–1778) French writer. *Épîtres*, 'À l'auteur du livre des trois Imposteurs'

50 If God made us in His image, we have certainly returned the compliment.

Voltaire *Le Sottisier*

GOLDWYNISMS

Sayings attributed to Samuel Goldwyn (Samuel Goldfish; 1882–1974). Most are apocryphal. *See also* cinema, mixed metaphors

1 Let's have some new clichés.

The Observer, 'Sayings of the Week', 24 Oct 1948

2 Too caustic? To hell with cost; we'll make the picture anyway.

3 We're overpaying him but he's worth it.

4 What we want is a story that starts with an earthquake and works its way up to a climax.

5 I am willing to admit that I may not always be right, but I am never wrong.

6 I don't care if it doesn't make a nickel, I just want every man, woman, and child in America to see it!

Referring to his film *The Best Years of Our Lives.*

7 A wide screen just makes a bad film twice as bad.

8 For years I have been known for saying 'Include me out'; but today I am giving it up for ever.

Address, Balliol College, Oxford, 1 Mar 1945

9 In two words: im - possible.

Attrib.

10 Anybody who goes to see a psychiatrist ought to have his head examined.

11 Every director bites the hand that lays the golden egg.

12 I'll give you a definite maybe.

13 A verbal contract isn't worth the paper it's written on.

14 You ought to take the bull between the teeth.

15 We have all passed a lot of water since then.

16 I read part of it all the way through.

17 If Roosevelt were alive he'd turn in his grave.

18 It's more than magnificent – it's mediocre.

19 'Why only twelve?' 'That's the original number.' 'Well, go out and get thousands.'

Referring to the number of disciples whilst filming a scene for *The Last Supper.*

20 Yes, I'm going to have a bust made of them.
Replying to an admiring comment about his wife's hands.

21 Tell me, how did you love my picture?

22 I don't want any yes-men around me. I want everybody to tell me the truth even if it costs them their jobs.

GOLF

See also sport and games

1 It's not in support of cricket but as an earnest protest against golf.
Max Beerbohm (1872–1956) British writer. Said when giving a shilling towards W. G. Grace's testimonial. *Carr's Dictionary of Extraordinary English Cricketers*

2 Golf may be played on Sunday, not being a game within the view of the law, but being a form of moral effort.
Stephen Leacock (1869–1944) English-born Canadian economist and humorist. *Other Fancies*, 'Why I refuse to play Golf'

3 All I've got against it is that it takes you so far from the club house.
Eric Linklater (1889–1974) Scottish novelist. Referring to golf. *Poet's Pub*, Ch. 3

GOOD

See also good and evil, righteousness, virtue

1 Men have never been good, they are not good, they never will be good.
Karl Barth (1886–1968) Swiss Protestant theologian. *Time*, 12 Apr 1954

2 He who would do good to another must do it in Minute Particulars.
General Good is the plea of the scoundrel, hypocrite, and flatterer.
William Blake (1757–1827) British poet. *Jerusalem*

3 *Summum bonum.*
The greatest good.
Cicero (106–43 BC) Roman orator and statesman. *De Officiis*, I

4 Nice guys finish last.
Leo Durocher (1905–91) US baseball player. Attrib.

5 What is a weed? A plant whose virtues have not been discovered.
Ralph Waldo Emerson (1803–82) US poet and essayist. *Fortune of the Republic*

6 Would to God that we might spend a single day really well!
Thomas à Kempis (Thomas Hemmerken; c. 1380–1471) German monk. *The Imitation of Christ*, I

7 Teach us delight in simple things,
And mirth that has no bitter springs;
Forgiveness free of evil done,
And love to all men 'neath the sun!
Rudyard Kipling (1865–1936) Indian-born British writer. *The Children's Song*

8 The greatest pleasure I know, is to do a good action by stealth, and to have it found out by accident.
Charles Lamb (1775–1834) British essayist. *The Athenaeum*, 'Table Talk by the late Elia', 4 Jan 1834

9 Goodness does not more certainly make men happy than happiness makes them good.
Walter Savage Landor (1775–1864) British poet and writer. *Imaginary Conversations*, 'Lord Brooke and Sir Philip Sidney'

10 Dowel, Dobet and Dobest.
William Langland (c. 1330–c. 1400) English poet. Do well, Do better, and Do Best: three concepts central to the search for Truth in *Piers Plowman*, in which they appear as allegorical characters. *The Vision of Piers Plowman*

11 Much benevolence of the passive order may be traced to a disinclination to inflict pain upon oneself.
George Meredith (1828–1909) British novelist. *Vittoria*, Ch. 42

12 Abashed the devil stood,
And felt how awful goodness is.
John Milton (1608–74) English poet. *Paradise Lost*, Bk. IV

13 The good is the beautiful.
Plato (429–347 BC) Greek philosopher. *Lysis*

14 Do good by stealth, and blush to find it fame.
Alexander Pope (1688–1744) British poet. *Epilogue to the Satires*, Dialogue I

15 How far that little candle throws his beams!
So shines a good deed in a naughty world.
William Shakespeare (1564–1616) English dramatist. *The Merchant of Venice*, V:1

16 Nothing can harm a good man, either in life or after death.
Socrates (469–399 BC) Athenian philosopher. *Apology* (Plato)

17 – My goodness those diamonds are lovely!
Goodness had nothing whatever to do with it.
Mae West (1892–1980) US actress. Used in 1959 as the title of the first volume of her autobiography. *Diamond Lil*, film 1932

18 You shouldn't say it is not good. You should say you do not like it; and then, you know, you're perfectly safe.
James Whistler (1834–1903) US painter. *Whistler Stories* (D. Seitz)

GOOD AND EVIL

See also evil, good, virtue and vice

1 There is so much good in the worst of us,
And so much bad in the best of us,
That it hardly becomes any of us
To talk about the rest of us.
Anonymous *Good and Bad*

2 Evil comes at leisure like the disease; good comes in a hurry like the doctor.

G. K. Chesterton (1874–1936) British writer. *The Man who was Orthodox*

3 The good die early, and the bad die late.

Daniel Defoe (1660–1731) British journalist and writer. *Character of the late Dr. Annesley*

4 The web of our life is of a mingled yarn, good and ill together.

William Shakespeare (1564–1616) English dramatist. *All's Well that Ends Well*, IV:3

5 The good die first,
And they whose hearts are dry as summer dust
Burn to the socket.

William Wordsworth (1770–1850) British poet. *The Excursion*

GOSSIP

See also secrecy

1 A tale never loses in the telling.

Proverb

2 Don't wash your dirty linen in public.

Proverb

3 No names, no pack-drill.

Proverb

4 There's no smoke without fire.

Proverb

5 Throw dirt enough, and some will stick.

Proverb

6 Walls have ears.

Proverb

7 How these curiosities would be quite forgot, did not such idle fellows as I am put them down.

John Aubrey (1626–97) English antiquary. *Brief Lives*, 'Venetia Digby'

8 No one gossips about other people's secret virtues.

Bertrand Russell (1872–1970) British philosopher. *On Education*

9 Her first economic drive will be to replace X-ray by hearsay.

Gwyn Thomas (1913–81) British writer. *The Keep*, II

10 I remember that a wise friend of mine did usually say, 'that which is everybody's business is nobody's business'.

Izaak Walton (1593–1683) English writer. *The Compleat Angler*, Ch. 2

GOVERNMENT

See also democracy, Houses of Parliament, monarchy, opposition, politicians, politics

1 I will undoubtedly have to seek what is happily known as gainful employment, which I am glad to say does not describe holding public office.

Dean Acheson (1893–1971) US lawyer and statesman. Remark made on leaving his post as secretary of state, 1952; he subsequently returned to private legal practice

2 The danger is not that a particular class is unfit to govern. Every class is unfit to govern.

Lord Acton (1834–1902) British historian. Letter to Mary Gladstone, 1881

3 Whose Finger do you want on the Trigger When the World Situation Is So Delicate?

Anonymous Headline from the *Daily Mirror* on the day before the General Election, Oct 1951. *Publish and Be Damned* (Hugh Cudlipp), 1953

4 Where some people are very wealthy and others have nothing, the result will be either extreme democracy or absolute oligarchy, or despotism will come from either of those excesses.

Aristotle (384–322 BC) Greek philosopher. *Politics*, Bk. IV

5 One to mislead the public, another to mislead the Cabinet, and the third to mislead itself.

Herbert Henry Asquith (1852–1928) British statesman. Explaining why the War Office kept three sets of figures. *The Price of Glory* (Alastair Horne), Ch. 2

6 The object of government in peace and in war is not the glory of rulers or of races, but the happiness of the common man.

Lord Beveridge (1879–1963) British economist. *Social Insurance*

7 Too bad all the people who know how to run the country are busy driving cabs and cutting hair.

George Burns (1896–1996) US comedian.

8 A small acquaintance with history shows that all Governments are selfish and the French Governments more selfish than most.

David Eccles (1904–) British politician. *The Observer*, 'Sayings of the Year', 29 Dec 1962

9 He was uniformly of an opinion which, though not a popular one, he was ready to aver, that the right of governing was not property but a trust.

Charles James Fox (1749–1806) British Whig politician. Referring to William Pitt's plans for parliamentary reform. *C.J. Fox* (J. L. Hammond)

10 The principles of a free constitution are irrecoverably lost, when the legislative power is nominated by the executive.

Edward Gibbon (1737–94) British historian. *Decline and Fall of the Roman Empire*, Ch. 3

11 A government that is big enough to give you all you want is big enough to take it all away.

Barry Goldwater (1909–) US politician. *Bachman's Book of Freedom Quotations* (M. Ivens and R. Dunstan)

12 They that are discontented under *monarchy*, call it *tyranny*; and they that are displeased with *aristocracy*, call it *oligarchy*: so also, they which find themselves grieved under a *democracy*, call it *anarchy*, which signifies the want of government; and yet I think no man believes, that want of government, is any new kind of government.

Thomas Hobbes (1588–1679) English philosopher. *Leviathan*, Pt. II, Ch. 19

13 I would not give half a guinea to live under one form of government rather than another. It is of no moment to the happiness of an individual.

Samuel Johnson (1709–84) British lexicographer. *Life of Johnson* (J. Boswell), Vol. II

14 We give the impression of being in office but not in power.

Norman Lamont (1942–) British Conservative politician. *The Observer*, 13 June 1993

15 Any cook should be able to run the country.

Lenin (Vladimir Ilich Ulyanov; 1870–1924) Russian revolutionary leader. *The First Circle* (Alexander Solzhenitsyn)

16 What is our task? To make Britain a fit country for heroes to live in.

David Lloyd George (1863–1945) British Liberal statesman. Speech, 24 Nov 1918

17 The Commons, faithful to their system, remained in a wise and masterly inactivity.

James Mackintosh (1765–1832) Scottish lawyer, philosopher, and historian. *Vindiciae Gallicae*

18 Every country has the government it deserves.

Joseph de Maistre (1753–1821) French monarchist. *Lettres et Opuscules Inédits*, 15 Aug 1811

19 The worst government is the most moral. One composed of cynics is often very tolerant and human. But when fanatics are on top there is no limit to oppression.

H. L. Mencken (1880–1956) US journalist. *Notebooks*, 'Minority Report'

20 One day the don't-knows will get in, and then where will we be?

Spike Milligan (1918–) British comic actor and author. Attributed remark made about a pre-election poll

21 Do you not know, my son, with how little wisdom the world is governed?

Axel Oxenstierna (1583–1654) Swedish statesman. Letter to his son, 1648

22 Government, even in its best state, is but a necessary evil; in its worst state, an intolerable one.

Thomas Paine (1737–1809) British writer. *Common Sense*, Ch. 1

23 As to religion, I hold it to be the indispensable duty of government to protect all conscientious professors thereof, and I know of no other business which government hath to do therewith.

Thomas Paine *Common Sense*, Ch. 4

24 We live under a government of men and morning newspapers.

Wendell Phillips (1811–84) US reformer. *Address: The Press*

25 I don't make jokes – I just watch the government and report the facts.

Will Rogers (1879–1935) US actor and humorist. *Saturday Review*, 'A Rogers Thesaurus', 25 Aug 1962

26 Hansard is history's ear, already listening.

Herbert Samuel (1870–1963) British Liberal statesman. *The Observer*, 'Sayings of the Week', 18 Dec 1949

27 Parliament is the longest running farce in the West End.

Cyril Smith (1928–93) British Liberal politician. *The Times*, 23 Sept 1977

28 It would be desirable if every government, when it comes to power, should have its old speeches burned.

Philip Snowden (1864–1937) British politician. *Biography* (C. E. Bechafer Roberts)

29 Accidentally.

Talleyrand (Charles Maurice de Talleyrand-Périgord; 1754–1838) French politician. Replying, during the reign of Louis Philippe, to the query 'How do you think this government will end?'. *The Wheat and the Chaff* (F. Mitterand)

30 People are not willing to be governed by those who do not speak their language.

Norman Tebbit (1931–) British politician. *The Observer*, 24 Nov 1991

31 Governments needs to have both shepherds and butchers.

Voltaire (François-Marie Arouet; 1694–1778) French writer. *Notebooks*

32 Many people consider the things which government does for them to be social progress, but they consider the things government does for others as socialism.

Earl Warren (1891–1971) US lawyer. *Peter's Quotations* (Laurence J. Peter)

33 The people's government, made for the people, made by the people, and answerable to the people.

Daniel Webster (1782–1852) US statesman. Second speech on Foote's resolution, 26 Jan 1830

34 If people behaved in the way nations do they would all be put in straitjackets.

Tennessee Williams (1911–83) US dramatist. BBC interview

GRAMMAR

See also language, words

1 'Whom are you?' said he, for he had been to night school.

George Ade (1866–1944) US dramatist and humorist. *Bang! Bang!: The Steel Box*

2 When I split an infinitive, god damn it, I split it so it stays split.

Raymond Chandler (1888–1959) US novelist. Letter to his English publisher

3 By being so long in the lowest form I gained an immense advantage over the cleverest boys...I got into my bones the essential structure of the normal British sentence – which is a noble thing.

Winston Churchill (1874–1965) British statesman. *My Early Life*, Ch. 2

4 This is the sort of English up with which I will not put.

Winston Churchill The story is that Churchill wrote the comment in the margin of a report in which a Civil Servant had used an awkward construction to avoid ending a sentence with a preposition. An alternative version substitutes 'bloody nonsense' for 'English'. *Plain Words* (E. Gowers), Ch. 9

5 I will not go down to posterity talking bad grammar.

Benjamin Disraeli (1804–81) British statesman. Remark made when correcting proofs of his last parliamentary speech, 31 Mar 1881. *Disraeli* (Blake), Ch. 32

6 Grammar, which can govern even kings.

Molière (Jean Baptiste Poquelin; 1622–73) French dramatist. *Les Femmes savantes*, II:6

7 I am the Roman Emperor, and am above grammar.

Sigismund (1368–1437) Holy Roman Emperor. Responding to criticism of his Latin. Attrib.

8 Why care for grammar as long as we are good?

Artemus Ward (Charles Farrar Browne; 1834–67) US humorous writer. *Pyrotechny*

9 Subjunctive to the last, he preferred to ask, 'And that, sir, would be the Hippodrome?'

Alexander Woollcott (1887–1943) US journalist. *While Rome Burns*, 'Our Mrs Parker'

GRATITUDE

1 There are minds so impatient of inferiority that their gratitude is a species of revenge, and they return benefits, not because recompense is a pleasure, but because obligation is a pain.

Samuel Johnson (1709–84) British lexicographer. *The Rambler*

2 When the messenger who carried the last sheet to Millar returned, Johnson asked him, 'Well, what did he say?' – 'Sir (answered the messenger), he said, thank God I have done with him.' – 'I am glad (replied Johnson, with a smile) that he thanks God for anything.'

Samuel Johnson After the final page of his *Dictionary* had been delivered. *Life of Johnson* (J. Boswell)

3 I am not going to thank anybody – because I did it all myself.

Spike Milligan (1918–) British comic actor and author. On receiving the British Comedy Award for Lifetime Achievement in 1994

4 Thank me no thankings, nor proud me no prouds.

William Shakespeare (1564-1616) English dramatist. *Romeo and Juliet*, III:5

GREATNESS

1 A truly great man never puts away the simplicity of a child.

Chinese proverb

2 The dullard's envy of brilliant men is always assuaged by the suspicion that they will come to a bad end.

Max Beerbohm (1872–1956) British writer. *Zuleika Dobson*

3 Great men are but life-sized. Most of them, indeed, are rather short.

Max Beerbohm *And Even Now*

4 Great things are done when men and mountains meet;
This is not done by jostling in the street.

William Blake (1757–1827) British poet. *Gnomic Verses*

5 Nothing grows well in the shade of a big tree.

Constantin Brancusi (1876–1957) Romanian sculptor. Refusing Rodin's invitation to work in his studio. *Compton's Encyclopedia*

6 No great man lives in vain. The history of the world is but the biography of great men.

Thomas Carlyle (1795–1881) Scottish historian and essayist. *Heroes and Hero-Worship*, 'The Hero as Divinity'

7 To be great is to be misunderstood.

Ralph Waldo Emerson (1803–82) US poet and essayist. *Essays*, 'Self-Reliance'

8 The world's great men have not commonly been great scholars, nor great scholars great men.

Oliver Wendell Holmes (1809–94) US writer. *The Autocrat of the Breakfast Table*, Ch. 6

9 If I am a great man, then a good many of the great men of history are frauds.

Bonar Law (1858–1923) British statesman. Attrib.

10 You are one of the forces of nature.

Jules Michelet (1798–1874) French historian. From a letter received by Dumas. *Memoirs*, Vol. VI, Ch. 138 (Alexandre Dumas)

11 To be alone is the fate of all great minds – a fate deplored at times, but still always chosen as the less grievous of two evils.

Arthur Schopenhauer (1788–1860) German philosopher. *Aphorismen zur Lebensweisheit*

12 Some are born great, some achieve greatness, and some have greatness thrust upon 'em.

William Shakespeare (1564–1616) English dramatist. *Twelfth Night*, II:5

13 'My name is Ozymandias, king of kings:
Look on my works, ye Mighty, and despair!'

Percy Bysshe Shelley (1792–1822) British poet. *Ozymandias*

14 Oh, Vanity of vanities!
How wayward the decrees of Fate are;
How very weak the very wise,

How very small the very great are!

William Makepeace Thackeray (1811–63) British novelist. *Vanitas Vanitatum*

15 A great city is that which has the greatest men and women.

Walt Whitman (1819–92) US poet. *Song of the Broad-Axe*, 5

GREED

See also food, materialism, obesity

1 Give him an inch and he'll take a yard.

Proverb

2 Kill not the goose that lays the golden egg.

Proverb

3 The eye is bigger than the belly.

Proverb

4 Beware that you do not lose the substance by grasping at the shadow.

Aesop (6th century BC) Reputed Greek writer of fables. *Fables*, 'The Dog and the Shadow'

5 But answer came there none –
And this was scarcely odd because
They'd eaten every one.

Lewis Carroll (Charles Lutwidge Dodgson; 1832–98) British writer. *Through the Looking-Glass*, Ch. 4

6 Gluttony is an emotional escape, a sign something is eating us.

Peter De Vries (1910–93) US novelist. *Comfort me with Apples*, Ch. 7

7 The mountain sheep are sweeter,
But the valley sheep are fatter;
We therefore deemed it meeter
To carry off the latter.

Thomas Love Peacock (1785–1866) British novelist. *The Misfortunes of Elphin*, Ch. 11, 'The War-Song of Dinas Vawr'

8 These citizens are always willing to bet that what Nicely-Nicely dies of will be over-feeding and never anything small like pneumonia, for Nicely-Nicely is known far and wide as a character who dearly loves to commit eating.

Damon Runyon (1884–1946) US writer. *Take it Easy*, 'Lonely Heart'

9 Wealth is like sea-water; the more we drink, the thirstier we become; and the same is true of fame.

Arthur Schopenhauer (1788–1860) German philosopher. *Parerga and Paralipomena*

10 People will swim through shit if you put a few bob in it.

Peter Sellers (1925–80) British comic actor. *Halliwell's Filmgoer's and Video Viewer's Companion*

11 He hath eaten me out of house and home.

William Shakespeare (1564–1616) English dramatist. *Henry IV, Part Two*, II:1

GREETINGS

1 *Atque in perpetuum, frater, ave atque vale.*
And for ever, brother, hail and farewell!

Catullus (c. 84–c. 54 BC) Roman poet. *Carmina*, CI

2 Wery glad to see you indeed, and hope our acquaintance may be a long 'un, as the gen'l'm'n said to the fi' pun' note.

Charles Dickens (1812–70) British novelist. *Pickwick Papers*, Ch. 25

3 Dr Livingstone, I presume?

Henry Morton Stanley (1841–1904) British explorer. On finding David Livingstone at Ujiji on Lake Tanganyika, Nov 1871. *How I found Livingstone*, Ch. 11

4 Lafayette, we are here!

C. E. Stanton (1859–1933) US colonel. The Marquis de Lafayette (1757–1834) aided the colonists in the US War of Independence. Address at Lafayette's grave, Paris, 4 July 1917

GUIDANCE

See also leadership

1 Everyman, I will go with thee, and be thy guide.
In thy most need to go by thy side.

Anonymous *Everyman* Pt. 1

2 Wandering in a vast forest at night, I have only a faint light to guide me. A stranger appears and says to me: 'My friend, you should blow out your candle in order to find your way more clearly.' This stranger is a theologian.

Denis Diderot (1713–84) French writer. *Addition aux Pensées philosophiques*

3 A little onward lend thy guiding hand
To these dark steps, a little further on.

John Milton (1608–74) English poet. *Samson Agonistes*

GUILT

See also conscience, regret

1 It is quite gratifying to feel guilty if you haven't done anything wrong: how noble! Whereas it is rather hard and certainly depressing to admit guilt and to repent.

Hannah Arendt (1906–75) German-born US philosopher and historian. *Eichmann in Jerusalem*, Ch. 15

2 Alone, alone, about the dreadful wood
Of conscious evil runs a lost mankind,
Dreading to find its Father.

W. H. Auden (1907–73) British poet. *For the Time Being*, 'Chorus'

3 When Pilate saw that he could prevail nothing, but that rather a tumult was made, he took water, and washed his hands before the multitude, saying, I am innocent of the blood of this just person: see ye to it.
Then answered all the people, and said, His blood

be on us, and on our children.
Bible: Matthew 27:24–25

4 The many men, so beautiful!
And they all dead did lie:
And a thousand thousand slimy things
Lived on; and so did I.
Samuel Taylor Coleridge (1772–1834) British poet. *The Rime of the Ancient Mariner*, IV

5 Love bade me welcome; yet my soul drew back,
Guilty of dust and sin.
George Herbert (1593–1633) English poet. *Love*

6 You will put on a dress of guilt
and shoes with broken high ideals.
Roger McGough (1937–) British poet. *Comeclose and Sleepnow*

7 I am in blood
Stepp'd in so far that, should I wade no more,
Returning were as tedious as go o'er.
William Shakespeare (1564–1616) English dramatist. *Macbeth*, III:4

8 Out, damned spot! out, I say!
William Shakespeare *Macbeth*, V:1

9 Here's the smell of the blood still. All the perfumes of Arabia will not sweeten this little hand.
William Shakespeare *Macbeth*, V:1

GULLIBILITY

See also foolishness, impressionability

1 There's a sucker born every minute.
Phineas Taylor Barnum (1810–91) US showman. Attrib.

2 When lovely woman stoops to folly,
And finds too late that men betray,
What charm can soothe her melancholy,
What art can wash her guilt away?
Oliver Goldsmith (1728–74) Irish-born British writer. *The Vicar of Wakefield*, Ch. 9

H

HABIT

See also custom

1 Old habits die hard.
Proverb

2 Habit is a great deadener.
Samuel Beckett (1906–89) Irish novelist and dramatist. *Waiting for Godot*, III

3 Curious things, habits. People themselves never knew they had them.
Agatha Christie (1891–1976) British detective-story writer. *Witness for the Prosecution*

4 Men's natures are alike; it is their habits that carry them far apart.
Confucius (K'ung Fu-tzu; 551–479 BC) Chinese philosopher. *Analects*

5 Cultivate only the habits that you are willing should master you.
Elbert Hubbard (1856–1915) US writer. Attrib.

6 They do those little personal things people sometimes do when they think they are alone in railway carriages; things like smelling their own armpits.
Jonathan Miller (1934–) British doctor and television and stage director. *Beyond the Fringe*

HALF MEASURES

1 Two half-truths do not make a truth, and two half-cultures do not make a culture.
Arthur Koestler (1905–83) Hungarian-born British writer. *The Ghost in the Machine*, Preface

2 I'm not really a Jew; just Jew-ish, not the whole hog.
Jonathan Miller (1934–) British doctor and television and stage director. *Beyond the Fringe*

HAPPINESS

See also contentment, laughter, pleasure

1 One joy scatters a hundred griefs.
Chinese proverb

2 If you haven't been happy very young, you can still be happy later on, but it's much harder. You need more luck.
Simone de Beauvoir (1908–86) French writer. *The Observer*, 'Sayings of the Week', 19 May 1975

3 The greatest happiness of the greatest number is the foundation of morals and legislation.
Jeremy Bentham (1748–1832) British philosopher. *The Commonplace Book*

4 There was a jolly miller once,
Lived on the river Dee;
He worked and sang from morn till night;
No lark more blithe than he.
Isaac Bickerstaffe (c. 1735–c. 1812) Irish dramatist. *Love in a Village*, I

5 When the green woods laugh with
the voice of joy.
William Blake (1757–1827) British poet. *Songs of Innocence*, 'Laughing song'

6 In every adversity of fortune, to have been happy is the most unhappy kind of misfortune.
Boethius (c. 480–524) Roman statesman, philosopher, and scholar. *The Consolation of Philosophy*

7 Happiness is a mystery like religion, and should never be rationalized.
G. K. Chesterton (1874–1936) British writer. *Heretics*, Ch. 7

8 To marvel at nothing is just about the one and only thing, Numicius, that can make a man happy and keep him that way.
Horace (Quintus Horatius Flaccus; 65–8 BC) Roman poet. *Epistles*, I

9 Not the owner of many possessions will you be right to call happy: he more rightly deserves the name of happy who knows how to use the gods' gifts wisely and to put up with rough poverty, and who fears dishonour more than death.
Horace *Odes*, IV

10 That action is best, which procures the greatest happiness for the greatest numbers.
Francis Hutcheson (1694–1746) Scottish philosopher. *Inquiry into the Original of our Ideas of Beauty and Virtue*, Treatise II, 'Concerning Moral Good and Evil'

11 Happiness is like coke – something you get as a by-product in the process of making something else.
Aldous Huxley (1894–1964) British novelist. *Point Counter Point*

12 That all who are happy, are equally happy, is not true. A peasant and a philosopher may be equally *satisfied*, but not equally *happy*. Happiness consists in the multiplicity of agreeable consciousness.
Samuel Johnson (1709–84) British lexicographer. *Life of Johnson* (J. Boswell), Vol. II

13 ...because happiness is not an ideal of reason but of imagination.
Immanuel Kant (1724–1804) German philosopher. *Grundlegung zur Metaphysik der Sitten*, II

14 Ask yourself whether you are happy, and you cease to be so.
John Stuart Mill (1806–73) British philosopher. *Autobiography*, Ch. 5

15 When a small child...I thought that success spelled happiness. I was wrong. Happiness is like a butterfly which appears and delights us for one brief moment, but soon flits away.

Anna Pavlova (1881–1931) Russian ballet dancer. *Pavlova: A Biography* (ed. A. H. Franks), 'Pages of My Life'

16 And we suddenly know, what heaven we're in,
When they begin the beguine.

Cole Porter (1893–1964) US songwriter. *Jubilee*, 'Begin the Beguine'

17 We are never so happy nor so unhappy as we imagine.

Duc de la Rochefoucauld (1613–80) French writer. *Maximes*, 49

18 Happiness is not best achieved by those who seek it directly.

Bertrand Russell (1872–1970) British philosopher. *Mysticism and Logic*

19 Every time I talk to a savant I feel quite sure that happiness is no longer a possibility. Yet when I talk with my gardener, I'm convinced of the opposite.

Bertrand Russell Attrib.

20 To be without some of the things you want is an indispensable part of happiness.

Bertrand Russell Attrib.

21 One is happy as a result of one's own efforts, once one knows the necessary ingredients of happiness – simple tastes, a certain degree of courage, self denial to a point, love of work, and, above all, a clear conscience. Happiness is no vague dream, of that I now feel certain.

George Sand (Aurore Dupin, Baronne Dudevant; 1804–76) French novelist. *Correspondence*, Vol. V

22 Happiness is the only sanction of life; where happiness fails, existence remains a mad and lamentable experiment.

George Santayana (1863–1952) US philosopher. *The Life of Reason*

23 Happiness? That's nothing more than health and a poor memory.

Albert Schweitzer (1875–1965) French Protestant theologian, philosopher, physician and musician. Attrib.

24 A lifetime of happiness: no man alive could bear it: it would be hell on earth.

George Bernard Shaw (1856–1950) Irish dramatist and critic. *Man and Superman*, I

25 Mankind are always happy for having been happy, so that if you make them happy now, you make them happy twenty years hence by the memory of it.

Sydney Smith (1771–1845) British clergyman and essayist. *Elementary Sketches of Moral Philosophy*

26 A man is happy so long as he choose to be happy and nothing can stop him.

Alexander Solzhenitsyn (1918–) Soviet novelist. *Cancer Ward*

27 There is no duty we so much underrate as the duty of being happy.

Robert Louis Stevenson (1850–94) Scottish writer. *Virginibus Puerisque*

28 Happiness is an imaginary condition, formerly often attributed by the living to the dead, now usually attributed by adults to children, and by children to adults.

Thomas Szasz (1920–) US psychiatrist. *The Second Sin*

29 If you want to be happy, be.

Leo Tolstoy (1828–1910) Russian writer. *Kosma Prutkov*

30 Happiness is no laughing matter.

Richard Whately (1787–1863) British churchman. *Apohthegms*

31 Happy Days Are Here Again.

Jack Yellen (b. 1892) US lyricist. Used by Roosevelt as a campaign song in 1932. Song title

32 For the good are always the merry,
Save by an evil chance,
And the merry love the fiddle,
And the merry love to dance

W. B. Yeats (1865–1939) Irish poet. *The Fiddler of Dooney*

33 The hell with it. Who never knew the price of happiness will not be happy.

Yevgeny Yevtushenko (1933–) Soviet poet. *Lies*

HASTE

See also impetuosity

1 Don't throw the baby out with the bathwater.

Proverb

2 First come, first served.

Proverb

3 Haste makes waste.

Proverb

4 More haste, less speed.

Proverb

5 'Will you walk a little faster?' said a whiting to a snail,
'There's a porpoise close behind us, and he's treading on my tail.'

Lewis Carroll (Charles Lutwidge Dodgson; 1832–98) British writer. *Alice's Adventures in Wonderland*, Ch. 10

6 In skating over thin ice, our safety is in our speed.

Ralph Waldo Emerson (1803–82) US poet and essayist. *Essays*, 'Prudence'

7 Slow and steady wins the race.

Robert Lloyd (1733–64) British poet. *The Hare and the Tortoise*

8 For fools rush in where angels fear to tread.

Alexander Pope (1688–1744) British poet. *An Essay on Criticism*

9 Never before have we had so little time in which to do so much.

Franklin D. Roosevelt (1882–1945) US Democratic president. Radio address, 23 Feb 1942

10 If it were done when 'tis done, then 'twere well

It were done quickly.

William Shakespeare (1564–1616) English dramatist. *Macbeth*, I:7

11 Wisely and slow; they stumble that run fast.

William Shakespeare *Romeo and Juliet*, II:3

12 Hurry! I never hurry. I have no time to hurry.

Igor Stravinsky (1882–1971) Russian-born US composer. Responding to his publisher's request that he hurry his completion of a composition. Attrib.

HATE

See also bitterness, love and hate

1 I do not love thee, Doctor Fell,
The reason why I cannot tell;
But this alone I know full well,
I do not love thee, Doctor Fell.

Thomas Brown (1663–1704) English satirist. Translation of Martial's *Epigrams*

2 Gr-r-r- there go, my heart's abhorrence!
Water your damned flower-pots, do!

Robert Browning (1812–89) British poet. *Soliloquy of the Spanish Cloister*

3 I am free of all prejudice. I hate everyone equally.

W. C. Fields (1880–1946) US actor. Attrib.

4 We can scarcely hate any one that we know.

William Hazlitt (1778–1830) British essayist. *On Criticism*

5 If you hate a person, you hate something in him that is part of yourself. What isn't part of ourselves doesn't disturb us.

Hermann Hesse (1877–1962) German novelist and poet. *Demian*, Ch. 6

6 With a heavy step Sir Matthew left the room and spent the morning designing mausoleums for his enemies.

Eric Linklater (1889–1974) Scottish novelist. *Juan in America*, Prologue

7 Few people can be happy unless they hate some other person, nation or creed.

Bertrand Russell (1872–1970) British philosopher. Attrib.

8 An intellectual hatred is the worst.

W. B. Yeats (1865–1939) Irish poet. *A Prayer for My Daughter*

HEALTH AND HEALTHY LIVING

See also doctors, illness, medicine, remedies

1 An apple a day keeps the doctor away.

Proverb

2 Health is better than wealth.

Proverb

3 It is a fact that not once in all my life have I gone out for a walk. I have been taken out for walks; but that is another matter.

Max Beerbohm (1872–1956) British writer. *Going Out of a Walk*

4 I answer 20 000 letters a year and so many couples are having problems because they are not getting the right proteins and vitamins.

Barbara Cartland (1902–) British romantic novelist. *The Observer*, 'Sayings of the Week', 31 Aug 1986

5 The strongest possible piece of advice I would give to any young woman is: Don't screw around, and don't smoke.

Edwina Currie (1946–) British politician. *The Observer*, 'Sayings of the Week', 3 Apr 1988

6 Exercise is bunk. If you are healthy, you don't need it: if you are sick you shouldn't take it.

Henry Ford (1863–1947) US car manufacturer. Attrib.

7 I have the body of a man half my age. Unfortunately, he's in terrible shape.

George Foreman (1948–) US boxer. . *The Guardian Weekend*, 28 Dec 1996

8 A wise man ought to realize that health is his most valuable possession.

Hippocrates (c. 460 –c. 377 BC) Greek physician. *A Regimen for Health*, 9

9 One swears by wholemeal bread, one by sour milk; vegetarianism is the only road to salvation of some, others insist not only on vegetables alone, but on eating those raw. At one time the only thing that matters is calories; at another time they are crazy about vitamins or about roughage. The scientific truth may be put quite briefly; eat moderately, having an ordinary mixed diet, and don't worry.

Robert Hutchison (1871–1960) *Newcastle Medical Journal*, Vol. 12, 1932

10 Vegetarianism is harmless enough, though it is apt to fill a man with wind and self righteousness.

Robert Hutchison Attrib.

11 *Orandum est ut sit mens sana in corpore sano.* Your prayer must be for a sound mind in a sound body.

Juvenal (Decimus Junius Juvenalis; 60–130 AD) Roman satirist. *Satires*, X

12 Look to your health: and if you have it, praise God, and value it next to a good conscience; for health is the second blessing that we mortals are capable of; a blessing that money cannot buy.

Izaak Walton (1593–1683) English writer. *The Compleat Angler*, Pt. I, Ch. 21

HEAVEN

See also afterlife

1 And he dreamed, and behold a ladder set up on the earth, and the top of it reached to heaven: and behold the angels of God ascending and descending on it.

Bible: Genesis 28:12

2 And Jacob awaked out of his sleep, and he said, Surely the Lord is in this place; and I knew it not.
And he was afraid, and said, How dreadful is this place! this is none other but the house of God, and this is the gate of heaven.
Bible: Genesis 28:16–17

3 In my Father's house are many mansions: if it were not so, I would have told you. I go to prepare a place for you.
Bible: John 14:2

4 Then let him receive the new knowledge and wait us,
Pardoned in heaven, the first by the throne!
Robert Browning (1812–89) British poet. *The Lost Leader*

5 Probably no invention came more easily to man than Heaven.
Georg Christoph Lichtenberg (1742–99) German physicist and writer. *Aphorisms*

6 A heav'n on earth.
John Milton (1608–74) English poet. *Paradise Lost*, Bk. IV

7 Glorious things of thee are spoken,
Zion, city of our God.
John Newton (1725–1807) British hymn writer. *Glorious Things*

8 It may be only glory that we seek here, but I persuade myself that, as long as we remain here, that is right. Another glory awaits us in heaven and he who reaches there will not wish even to think of earthly fame.
Petrarch (Francesco Petrarca; 1304–74) Italian poet. *Secretum*

9 For observe, that to hope for Paradise is to live in Paradise, a very different thing from actually getting there.
Vita Sackville-West (Victoria Sackville-West; 1892–1962) British poet and novelist. *Passenger to Tehran*, Ch. 1

10 I expect no very violent transition.
Catharine Maria Sedgwick (1789–1867) US writer. Comparing heaven with her home-town of Stockbridge, Massachussetts. *Edie* (Jean Stein)

11 If you go to Heaven without being naturally qualified for it you will not enjoy yourself there.
George Bernard Shaw (1856–1950) Irish dramatist and critic. *Man and Superman*

12 Heaven, as conventionally conceived, is a place so inane, so dull, so useless, so miserable, that nobody has ever ventured to describe a whole day in heaven, though plenty of people have described a day at the seaside.
George Bernard Shaw *Misalliance*, Preface

13 Shall shine the traffic of Jacob's ladder
Pitched between Heaven and Charing Cross.
Francis Thompson (1859–1907) British poet. *The Kingdom of God*

14 Grant me paradise in this world; I'm not so sure I'll reach it in the next.
Tintoretto (Jacopo Robusti; 1518–94) Venetian painter. Arguing that he be allowed to paint the *Paradiso* at the doge's palace in Venice, despite his advanced age. Attrib.

15 There is a happy land,
Far, far away,
Where saints in glory stand,
Bright, bright as day.
Andrew John Young (1885–1971) Scottish poet. *There is a Happy Land*

HELL

See also damnation, devil

1 Every wolf's and lion's howl
Raises from Hell a human soul.
William Blake (1757–1827) British poet. *Auguries of Innocence*

2 Abandon hope, all ye who enter here.
Dante (1265–1321) Italian poet. The inscription at the entrance to Hell. *Divine Comedy, Inferno*, III

3 Hell is oneself;
Hell is alone, the other figures in it
Merely projections. There is nothing to escape from
And nothing to escape to. One is always alone.
T. S. Eliot (1888–1965) US-born British poet and dramatist. *The Cocktail Party*, I:3

4 Long is the way
And hard, that out of hell leads up to light.
John Milton (1608–74) English poet. *Paradise Lost*, Bk. II

5 Which way I fly is Hell; myself am Hell;
And, in the lowest deep, a lower deep
Still threat'ning to devour me opens wide,
To which the Hell I suffer seems a Heaven.
John Milton *Paradise Lost*, Bk. IV

6 Hell is other people.
Jean-Paul Sartre (1905–80) French writer. *Huis clos*

7 The way down to Hell is easy.
Virgil (Publius Vergilius Maro; 70–19 BC) Roman poet. *Aeneid*, Bk. VI

HELP

See also charity, support

1 Every little helps.
Proverb

2 Many hands make light work.
Proverb

3 One good turn deserves another.
Proverb

4 Scratch my back and I'll scratch yours.
Proverb

5 Too many cooks spoil the broth.
Proverb

6 Two heads are better than one.
Proverb

7 People must help one another; it is nature's law.
Jean de La Fontaine (1621–95) French poet. *Fables*, VIII, 'L'Âne et le Chien'

HEROISM

See also courage, endurance, patriotism, war

1 Some talk of Alexander, and some of Hercules,
Of Hector and Lysander, and such great names as these;
But of all the world's brave heroes there's none that can compare
With a tow, row, row, row, row, row for the British Grenadier.
Anonymous *The British Grenadiers*

2 They died to save their country and they only saved the world.
Hilaire Belloc (1870–1953) French-born British poet. *The English Graves*

3 ANDREA. Unhappy the land that has no heroes.
GALILEO. No, unhappy the land that needs heroes.
Bertolt Brecht (1898–1956) German dramatist. *Galileo*, 13

4 In short, he was a perfect cavaliero,
And to his very valet seem'd a hero.
Lord Byron (1788–1824) British poet. *Beppo*

5 Every hero becomes a bore at last.
Ralph Waldo Emerson (1803–82) US poet and essayist. *Representative Men*, 'Uses of Great Men'

6 Being a hero is about the shortest-lived profession on earth.
Will Rogers (1879–1935) US actor and humorist. *Saturday Review*, 'A Rogers Thesaurus', 25 Aug 1962

HISTORIANS

See also history

1 A good historian is timeless; although he is a patriot, he will never flatter his country in any respect.
François Fénelon (1651–1715) French writer and prelate. Letter to M. Dacier

2 The historian must have…some conception of how men who are not historians behave. Otherwise he will move in a world of the dead.
E. M. Forster (1879–1970) British novelist. *Abinger Harvest*, 'Captain Edward Gibbon'

3 Great abilities are not requisite for an Historian… Imagination is not required in any high degree.
Samuel Johnson (1709–84) British lexicographer. *Life of Johnson* (J. Boswell), Vol. I

4 History is too serious to be left to historians.
Iain Macleod (1913–70) British politician. *The Observer*, 'Sayings of the Week', 16 July 1961

5 And even I can remember
A day when the historians left blanks in their writings,
I mean for things they didn't know.
Ezra Pound (1885–1972) US poet. *Cantos*, XIII

6 A historian is a prophet in reverse.
Friedrich von Schlegel (1772–1829) German diplomat, writer, and critic. *Das Athenäum*

7 Historians are like deaf people who go on answering questions that no one has asked them.
Leo Tolstoy (1828–1910) Russian writer. *A Discovery of Australia*, 'Being an Historian' (Manning Clark)

HISTORY

See also experience, historians, past

1 History repeats itself.
Proverb

2 History is the sum total of the things that could have been avoided.
Konrad Adenauer (1876–1967) German statesman.

3 Political history is far too criminal and pathological to be a fit subject of study for the young. Children should acquire their heroes and villains from fiction.
W. H. Auden (1907–73) British poet. *A Certain World*

4 Man is a history-making creature who can neither repeat his past nor leave it behind.
W. H. Auden *The Dyer's Hand*, 'D. H. Lawrence'

5 All things from eternity are of like forms and come round in a circle.
Marcus Aurelius (121–180 AD) Roman emperor. *Meditations*, Bk. II, Ch. 14

6 History does not repeat itself. Historians repeat each other.
Arthur Balfour (1848–1930) British statesman. Attrib.

7 History is the essence of innumerable biographies.
Thomas Carlyle (1795–1881) Scottish historian and essayist. *Critical and Miscellaneous Essays*, 'History'

8 No great man lives in vain. The history of the world is but the biography of great men.
Thomas Carlyle *Heroes and Hero-Worship*, 'The Hero as Divinity'

9 The history of every country begins in the heart of a man or woman.
Willa Cather (1873–1947) US writer and poet. *O Pioneers!*, Pt. II, Ch. 4

10 History is philosophy teaching by examples.
Dionysius of Halicarnassus (40–8 BC) Greek historian. *Ars rhetorica*, XI:2

11 History is an endless repetition of the

wrong way of living.

Lawrence Durrell (1912–90) British novelist. *The Listener*, 1978

12 There is properly no history; only biography.

Ralph Waldo Emerson (1803–82) US poet and essayist. *Essays*, 'History'

13 History is more or less bunk. It's tradition. We don't want tradition. We want to live in the present and the only history that is worth a tinker's damn is the history we make today.

Henry Ford (1863–1947) US car manufacturer. *Chicago Tribune*, 25 May 1916

14 There are moments in history when brooding tragedy and its dark shadows can be lightened by recalling great moments of the past.

Indira Gandhi (1917–84) Indian stateswoman. Letter to Richard Nixon, 16 Dec 1971

15 History never looks like history when you are living through it. It always looks confusing and messy, and it always feels uncomfortable.

John W. Gardner (1912–) US writer. *No Easy Victories*

16 His reign is marked by the rare advantage of furnishing very few materials for history; which is, indeed, little more than the register of the crimes, follies, and misfortunes of mankind.

Edward Gibbon (1737–94) British historian. Referring to the reign of Antoninus Pius. *Decline and Fall of the Roman Empire*, Ch. 3

17 What we know of the past is mostly not worth knowing. What is worth knowing is mostly uncertain. Events in the past may roughly be divided into those which probably never happened and those which do not matter.

Dean Inge (1860–1954) British churchman. *Assessments and Anticipations*, 'Prognostications'

18 It takes a great deal of history to produce a little literature.

Henry James (1843–1916) US novelist. *Life of Nathaniel Hawthorne*, Ch. 1

19 'History', Stephen said, 'is a nightmare from which I am trying to awake'.

James Joyce (1882–1941) Irish novelist. *Ulysses*

20 Hegel says somewhere that all great events and personalities in world history reappear in one fashion or another. He forgot to add: the first time as tragedy, the second as farce.

Karl Marx (1818–83) German philosopher and revolutionary. *The Eighteenth Brumaire of Louis Napoleon*

21 It is impossible to write ancient history because we do not have enough sources, and impossible to write modern history because we have far too many.

Charles Pierre Péguy (1873–1914) French writer. *Clio*

22 There is no history of mankind, there are only many histories of all kinds of aspects of human life. And one of these is the history of political power. This is elevated into the history of the world.

Karl Popper (1902–94) Austrian-born British philosopher. *The Open Society and Its Enemies*

23 Progress, far from consisting in change, depends on retentiveness. Those who cannot remember the past are condemned to repeat it.

George Santayana (1863–1952) US philosopher. *The Life of Reason*

24 I have looked upon the face of Agamemnon.

Heinrich Schliemann (1822–90) German archaeologist. On discovering a gold death mask at an excavation in Mycenae. *The Story of Civilization* (W. Durant), Vol. 2

25 History is past politics, and politics present history.

John Robert Seeley (1834–95) British historian. Quoting the historian E. A. Freeman. *The Growth of British Policy*

26 Hindsight is always twenty-twenty.

Billy Wilder (Samuel Wilder; 1906–) Austrian-born US film director. Attrib.

27 The Cavaliers (Wrong but Wromantic) and the Roundheads (Right but Repulsive).

W. C. Sellar (1898–1951) British humorous writer. *1066 And All That*

28 1066 And All That.

W. C. Sellar Book title

29 The Roman Conquest was, however, a *Good Thing*, since the Britons were only natives at the time.

W. C. Sellar *1066 And All That*

30 Napoleon's armies used to march on their stomachs, shouting: 'Vive l'intérieur!'

W. C. Sellar *1066 And All That*

31 America became top nation and history came to a full stop.

W. C. Sellar *1066 And All That*

32 When in the chronicle of wasted time
I see descriptions of the fairest wights.

William Shakespeare (1564–1616) English dramatist. *Sonnet 106*

33 History gets thicker as it approaches recent times.

A. J. P. Taylor (1906–90) British historian. *English History, 1914–1945*, Bibliography

34 All our ancient history, as one of our wits remarked, is no more than accepted fiction.

Voltaire (François-Marie Arouet; 1694–1778) French writer. *Jeannot et Colin*

35 Indeed, history is nothing more than a tableau of crimes and misfortunes.

Voltaire *L'Ingénu*, Ch. 10

36 Anything but history, for history must be false.

Robert Walpole (1676–1745) British statesman. *Walpoliana*

37 The greater part of what passes for diplomatic history is little more than the record of what one clerk said to another clerk.

George Malcolm Young (1882–1959) British historian. *Victorian England: Portrait of an Age*

HITLER

See also fascism, Germany, Nazism, World War II

1 The people Hitler never understood, and whose actions continued to exasperate him to the end of his life, were the British.

Alan Bullock (1914–) British academic and historian. *Hitler, A Study in Tyranny*, Ch. 8

2 Hitler showed surprising loyalty to Mussolini, but it never extended to trusting him.

Alan Bullock *Hitler, A Study in Tyranny*, Ch. 11

3 I have only one purpose, the destruction of Hitler, and my life is much simplified thereby. If Hitler invaded Hell I would make at least a favourable reference to the Devil in the House of Commons.

Winston Churchill (1874–1965) British statesman. *The Grand Alliance*

4 The Italians will laugh at me; every time Hitler occupies a country he sends me a message.

Benito Mussolini (1883–1945) Italian dictator. *Hitler* (Alan Bullock), Ch. 8

5 That garrulous monk.

Benito Mussolini Referring to Hitler. *The Second World War* (W. Churchill)

6 I wouldn't believe Hitler was dead, even if he told me so himself.

Hjalmar Schacht (1877–1970) German banker. Attrib.

7 A racing tipster who only reached Hitler's level of accuracy would not do well for his clients.

A. J. P. Taylor (1906–90) British historian. *The Origins of the Second World War*, Ch. 7

8 Germany was the cause of Hitler just as much as Chicago is responsible for the *Chicago Tribune*.

Alexander Woollcott (1887–1943) US writer and critic. Woollcott died after the broadcast. Radio broadcast, 1943

HOME

See also homesickness, travel

1 East, west, home's best.

Proverb

2 Home is where the heart is.

Proverb

3 Home is home, though it be never so homely.

John Clarke (fl. 1639) English scholar. *Paroemiologia Anglo-Latina*

4 Home is the place where, when you have to go there,
They have to take you in.

Robert Frost (1875–1963) US poet. *The Death of the Hired Man*

5 In fact there was but one thing wrong with the Babbitt house; it was not a home.

Sinclair Lewis (1885–1951) US novelist. *Babbitt*, Ch. 2

6 A man travels the world over in search of what he needs and returns home to find it.

George Moore (1852–1933) Irish writer and art critic. *The Brook Kerith*, Ch. 11

7 Mid pleasures and palaces though we may roam,
Be it ever so humble, there's no place like home;
...
Home, home, sweet, sweet home!
There's no place like home! there's no place like home!

John Howard Payne (1791–1852) US actor and dramatist. *Clari, or the Maid of Milan*

8 Home-keeping youth have ever homely wits.

William Shakespeare (1564–1616) English dramatist. *The Two Gentlemen of Verona*, I:1

9 Seek home for rest,
For home is best.

Thomas Tusser (1524–80) English farmer. *Five Hundred Points of Good Husbandry*, 'Instructions to Housewifery'

HOMESICKNESS

See also home, nostalgia

1 They say there's bread and work for all,
And the sun shines always there:
But I'll not forget old Ireland,
Were it fifty times as fair.

Helen Selina Blackwood (1807–67) British poet. *Lament of the Irish Emigrant*

2 Weep no more, my lady,
Oh! weep no more today!
We will sing one song for the old Kentucky Home,
For the old Kentucky Home far away.

Stephen Foster (1826–64) US composer of popular songs. *My Old Kentucky Home*

3 'Way down upon de Swanee Ribber,
Far, far away,
Dere's where my heart is turning ebber:
Dere's where de old folks stay.
All up and down de whole creation
Sadly I roam,
Still longing for de old plantation,
And for de old folks at home.

Stephen Foster *Old Folks at Home*

4 Oh give me a home where the buffalo roam,
Where the deer and the antelope play,
Where seldom is heard a discouraging word
And the skies are not cloudy all day.

Brewster Higley (19th century) US songwriter. *Home on the Range*

5 The accent of one's birthplace lingers in the

mind and in the heart as it does in one's speech.
Duc de la Rochefoucauld (1613–80) French writer. *Maximes*, 342

6 Breathes there the man, with soul so dead,
Who never to himself hath said,
This is my own, my native land!
Whose heart hath ne'er within him burn'd,
As home his footsteps he hath turn'd
From wandering on a foreign strand!
Walter Scott (1771–1832) Scottish novelist. *The Lay of the Last Minstrel*, VI

7 In home-sickness you must keep moving – it is the only disease that does not require rest.
H. de Vere Stacpoole (1863–1931) Irish-born novelist. *The Bourgeois*

8 Good-bye Piccadilly, Farewell Leicester Square;
It's a long, long way to Tipperary, but my heart's right there!
Harry Williams (1874–1924) British songwriter. Written with Jack Judge (1878–1938). *It's a Long Way to Tipperary*

9 I travelled among unknown men
In lands beyond the sea;
Nor, England! did I know till then
What love I bore to thee.
William Wordsworth (1770–1850) British poet. *I Travelled among Unknown Men*

HOMOSEXUALITY

See also sex

1 But the men of Sodom were wicked and sinners before the Lord exceedingly.
Bible: Genesis 13:13

2 I became one of the stately homos of England.
Quentin Crisp (?1910–) Model, publicist, and writer. *The Naked Civil Servant*

3 The...problem which confronts homosexuals is that they set out to win the love of a 'real' man. If they succeed, they fail. A man who 'goes with' other men is not what they would call a real man.
Quentin Crisp *The Naked Civil Servant*

4 I am the Love that dare not speak its name.
Lord Alfred Douglas (1870–1945) British writer and poet. *Two Loves*

5 The 'homo' is the legitimate child of the 'suffragette'.
Wyndham Lewis (1882–1957) British novelist. *The Art of Being Ruled*, Pt. VIII, Ch. 4

6 Well, he looks like a man.
Abraham Lincoln (1809–65) US statesman. On catching sight of Walt Whitman for the first time. Attrib.

7 If there was a war tomorrow you wouldn't be discriminating against gays and lesbians. You'd be dragging them in, just as you did in 1939.
Eddie Loyden (1923–) British Labour politician. Referring to the ban on homosexual people in the military. *The Guardian Weekend*, 28 Dec 1996

8 Constant conditioning in my youth and social pressure in every department of my life all failed to convert me to heterosexuality.
Ian McKellen (1939–) British actor. *The Times*, 5 Dec 1991

9 This sort of thing may be tolerated by the French, but we are British – thank God.
Lord Montgomery (1887–1976) British field marshal. Comment on a bill to relax the laws against homosexuals. *Daily Mail*, 27 May 1965

10 Wilde's captors were the police. But his persecutors were to be found on the letters page of the *Daily Telegraph*.
Matthew Parris (1949–) British journalist. *The Times*, 7 Apr 1993

11 If Michelangelo had been straight, the Sistine Chapel would have been wallpapered.
Robin Tyler US comedienne. Speech to gay-rights rally, Washington, 9 Jan 1988

HONESTY

See also frankness, integrity, sincerity, truth

1 An honest man's word is as good as his bond.
Proverb

2 Honesty is the best policy.
Proverb

3 It is impossible that a man who is false to his friends and neighbours should be true to the public.
Bishop Berkeley (1685–1753) Irish churchman and philosopher. *Maxims Concerning Patriotism*

4 The worst crime is faking it.
Kurt Cobain (1967–94) US rock musician. *The Observer*, 'Sayings of the Week', 17 Apr 1994

5 You see, I always divide people into two groups. Those who live by what they know to be a lie, and those who live by what they believe, falsely, to be the truth.
Christopher Hampton (1946–) British writer and dramatist. *The Philanthropist*, Sc. 6

6 Though I be poor, I'm honest.
Thomas Middleton (1580–1627) English dramatist. *The Witch*, III:2

7 To make your children *capable of honesty* is the beginning of education.
John Ruskin (1819–1900) British art critic and writer. *Time and Tide*, Letter VIII

8 To be honest, as this world goes, is to be one man pick'd out of ten thousand.
William Shakespeare (1564–1616) English dramatist. *Hamlet*, II:2

9 I thank God I am as honest as any man living that is an old man and no honester than I.
William Shakespeare *Much Ado About Nothing*, III:5

10 Though I am not naturally honest, I am so sometimes by chance.
William Shakespeare *The Winter's Tale*, IV:3

11 Father, I cannot tell a lie. I did it with my little hatchet.

George Washington (1732–99) US statesman. Attrib.

12 Honesty is the best policy; but he who is governed by that maxim is not an honest man.

Richard Whately (1787–1863) British churchman. *Apophthegms*

13 It is a terrible thing for a man to find out suddenly that all his life he has been speaking nothing but the truth.

Oscar Wilde (1854–1900) Irish-born British dramatist. *The Importance of Being Earnest*, III

14 If you do not tell the truth about yourself you cannot tell it about other people.

Virginia Woolf (1882–1941) British novelist. *The Moment and Other Essays*

HONOUR

See also titles

1 And they were offended in him. But Jesus said unto them, A prophet is not without honour, save in his own country, and in his own house.

Bible: Matthew 13:57

2 That chastity of honour, that felt a stain like a wound.

Edmund Burke (1729–97) British politician. *Reflections on the Revolution in France*

3 Remember, men, we're fighting for this woman's honour; which is probably more than she ever did.

Groucho Marx (Julius Marx; 1895–1977) US comedian. *Duck Soup*

4 Honour pricks me on. Yea, but how if honour prick me off when I come on? How then? Can honour set to a leg? No. Or an arm? No. Or take away the grief of a wound? No. Honour hath no skill in surgery, then? No. What is honour? A word. What is in that word? Honour. What is that honour? Air.

William Shakespeare (1564–1616) English dramatist. *Henry IV, Part One*, V:1

5 For Brutus is an honourable man;
So are they all, all honourable men.

William Shakespeare *Julius Caesar*, III:2

6 I once had a sparrow alight upon my shoulder for a moment while I was hoeing in a village garden, and I felt that I was more distinguished by that circumstance than I should have been by any epaulet I could have worn.

Henry David Thoreau (1817–62) US writer. *Walden*, 'Winter Visitors'

7 Brothers all
In honour, as in one community,
Scholars and gentlemen.

William Wordsworth (1770–1850) British poet. *The Prelude*, IX

HOPE

See also ambition, desire, expectation, optimism

1 A drowning man will clutch at a straw.

Proverb

2 Hope for the best.

Proverb

3 It is a long lane that has no turning.

Proverb

4 Still nursing the unconquerable hope,
Still clutching the inviolable shade.

Matthew Arnold (1822–88) British poet and critic. *The Scholar Gipsy*

5 Charity is the power of defending that which we know to be indefensible. Hope is the power of being cheerful in circumstances which we know to be desperate.

G. K. Chesterton (1874–1936) British writer. *Heretics*, Ch. 12

6 While there is life, there's hope,' he cried;
'Then why such haste?' so groaned and died.

John Gay (1685–1732) English poet and dramatist. *Fables*

7 After all, tomorrow is another day.

Margaret Mitchell (1909–49) US novelist. The closing words of the book. *Gone with the Wind*

8 Hope springs eternal in the human breast;
Man never is, but always to be blest.

Alexander Pope (1688–1744) British poet. *An Essay on Man*, I

9 For hope is but the dream of those that wake.

Matthew Prior (1664–1721) British poet. *Solomon*, II

10 The miserable have no other medicine
But only hope.

William Shakespeare (1564–1616) English dramatist. *Measure for Measure*, III:1

HORSES

See also animals, hunting, sport and games

1 When I appear in public people expect me to neigh, grind my teeth, paw the ground and swish my tail – none of which is easy.

Princess Anne (1950–) The Princess Royal, only daughter of Elizabeth II. *The Observer*, 'Sayings of the Week', 22 May 1977

2 I know two things about the horse,
And one of them is rather coarse.

Anonymous *The Horse*

3 I sprang to the stirrup, and Joris, and he;
I galloped, Dirck galloped, we galloped all three.

Robert Browning (1812–89) British poet. *How they brought the Good News from Ghent to Aix*

4 As lene was his hors as is a rake.

Geoffrey Chaucer (c. 1342–1400) English poet. *The Canterbury Tales*, Prologue

5 The blue ribbon of the turf.

Benjamin Disraeli (1804–81) British statesman. Describing the Derby. *Life of Lord George Bentinck*, Ch. 26

6 Gwine to run all night!
Gwine to run all day!
I bet my money on the bob-tail nag.
Somebody bet on the bay.

Stephen Foster (1826–64) US composer of popular songs. *Camptown Races*

7 They say princes learn no art truly, but the art of horsemanship. The reason is, the brave beast is no flatterer. He will throw a prince as soon as his groom.

Ben Jonson (1573–1637) English dramatist. *Timber, or Discoveries made upon Men and Matter*

8 It takes a good deal of physical courage to ride a horse. This, however, I have. I get it at about forty cents a flask, and take it as required.

Stephen Leacock (1869–1944) English-born Canadian economist and humorist. *Literary Lapses*, 'Reflections on Riding'

9 To confess that you are totally Ignorant about the Horse, is social suicide: you will be despised by everybody, especially the horse.

W. C. Sellar (1898–1951) British humorous writer. *Horse Nonsense*

10 A horse! a horse ! my kingdom for a horse.

William Shakespeare (1564–1616) English dramatist. *Richard III*, V:4

11 I have endured the Sandhurst riding-school,
I have galloped for an impetuous general,
I have been steward at regimental races, but
none of these feats have altered my opinion
that the horse, as a means of locomotion, is
obsolete.

E. Œ. Somerville (1858–1949) Irish writer. *Experiences of an Irish R.M.*, 'Great-Uncle McCarthy'

HOSPITALITY

1 A constant guest is never welcome.

Proverb

2 Fish and guests smell in three days.

Proverb

3 The first day a guest, the second day a guest, the third day a calamity.

Indian proverb

4 The guest who outstays his fellow-guests loses his overcoat.

Chinese proverb

5 I'd rather be a host than a guest. As Beerbohm wonderfully observed, a happy host makes a sad guest.

Harold Acton (1904–94) British writer. *The Times*, 18 Apr 1970

6 Let brotherly love continue.
Be not forgetful to entertain strangers: for thereby some have entertained angels unawares.

Bible: Hebrews 13:1–2

HOSTAGES

See also imprisonment

1 We apologise for having captured you. We recognise now that it was the wrong thing to do, that holding hostages achieves no useful, constructive purpose.

Anonymous Lebanese terrorist, on releasing Terry Waite. *The Times*, 19 Nov 1991

2 Sometimes it seems that the adulation, affection and warmth in which I am cocooned by friends and family is a kind of hothouse of obligations, both personal and public. I was unprepared for this…This psychological, emotional and social temperature change – from freezing to boiling point – knocks the personality out of balance and makes difficult any meaningful response to the world.

Brian Keenan (1950–) Irish hostage. *The Times*, 1990

3 He has come out of a black hole into glaring light and he will be overwhelmed by it.

Jill Morrell Friend of John McCarthy, who campaigned for his release. Referring to the release of John McCarthy. *The Times*, 9 Aug 1991

4 My word, Bunyan, you're a lucky fellow. You've got a window out of which you can look, see the sky, and here I am in a dark room.

Terry Waite (1939–) British church envoy. Contemplating a picture postcard, sent to him while in captivity, depicting the author John Bunyan. *The Times*, 21 Nov 1991

HOUSES

See also architecture, home, stately homes

1 Houses are built to live in and not to look on; therefore let use be preferred before uniformity, except where both may be had.

Francis Bacon (1561–1626) English philosopher. *Essays*, 'Of Building'

2 A hundred and fifty accurate reproductions of Anne Hathaway's cottage, each complete with central heating and garage.

Osbert Lancaster (1908–86) British cartoonist. *Pillar to Post*, 'Stockbrokers Tudor'

3 A house is a machine for living in.

Le Corbusier (Charles-Édouard Jeanneret; 1887–1965) Swiss-born French architect. *Towards an Architecture*

4 They're all made out of ticky-tacky, and they all look just the same.

Malvina Reynolds (1900–78) US folksinger and songwriter. Song describing a housing scheme built in the hills south of San Francisco. *Little Boxes*

5 It's 'aving 'ouses built by men, I believe, makes all the work and trouble.

H. G. Wells (1866–1946) British writer. *Kipps*, Bk. III, Ch. 1

HOUSES OF PARLIAMENT

See also aristocracy, government, politics

1 This is a rotten argument, but it should be good enough for their lordships on a hot summer afternoon.

Anonymous A note on a ministerial brief read out by mistake in the House of Lords. *The Way the Wind Blows* (Lord Home), 1976

2 The House of Lords is like a glass of champagne that has stood for five days.

Clement Attlee (1883–1967) British statesman and Labour prime minister. Attrib.

3 A severe though not unfriendly critic of our institutions said that 'the cure for admiring the House of Lords was to go and look at it.'

Walter Bagehot (1826–77) British economist and journalist. *The English Constitution*, 'The House of Lords'

4 A lot of hard-faced men who look as if they had done very well out of the war.

Stanley Baldwin (1867–1947) British statesman. Referring to the first House of Commons elected after World War I (1918). *Economic Consequences of the Peace* (J. M. Keynes), Ch. 5

5 The House of Lords is the British Outer Mongolia for retired politicians.

Tony Benn (1925–) British politician. Speech, 11 Feb 1962

6 Better than a play.

Charles II (1630–85) King of England. Referring to House of Lords debate on the Divorce Bill. Attrib.

7 I think…that it is the best club in London.

Charles Dickens (1812–70) British novelist. Mr Tremlow describing the House of Commons. *Our Mutual Friend*, Bk. II, Ch. 3

8 I am dead: dead, but in the Elysian fields.

Benjamin Disraeli (1804–81) British statesman. Said on his move to the House of Lords. Attrib.

9 The House of Lords is a model of how to care for the elderly.

Frank Field (1942–) British politician. *The Observer*, 24 May 1981

10 The House of Peers, throughout the war,
Did nothing in particular,
And did it very well.

W. S. Gilbert (1836–1911) British dramatist. *Iolanthe*, II

11 I have neither eye to see, nor tongue to speak here, but as the House is pleased to direct me.

William Lenthall (1591–1662) English parliamentarian. Said on 4 Jan 1642 in the House of Commons when asked by Charles I if he had seen five MPs whom the King wished to arrest. It was a succinct restatement of the Speaker's traditional role. *Historical Collections* (Rushworth)

12 Mr Balfour's Poodle.

David Lloyd George (1863–1945) British Liberal statesman. Referring to the House of Lords and its in-built Conservative majority; said in reply to a claim that it was 'the watchdog of the nation'. Remark, House of Commons, 26 June 1907

13 Every man has a House of Lords in his own head. Fears, prejudices, misconceptions – those are the peers, and they are hereditary.

David Lloyd George Speech, Cambridge, 1927

14 The British, being brought up on team games, enter their House of Commons in the spirit of those who would rather be doing something else. If they cannot be playing golf or tennis, they can at least pretend that politics is a game with very similar rules.

Cyril Northcote Parkinson (1919–93) British historian and writer. *Parkinson's Law*, Ch. 2

15 The House of Lords must be the only institution in the world which is kept efficient by the persistent absenteeism of most of its members.

Herbert Samuel (1870–1963) British Liberal statesman. *News Review*, 5 Feb 1948

16 A life peer is like a mule – no pride of ancestry, no hope of posterity.

Lord Shackleton (1911–94) British politician, businessman, and life peer. Attrib.

17 The House of Lords is a perfect eventide home.

Mary Stocks (1891–1975) British politician and writer. *The Observer*, 'Sayings of the Week', 4 Oct 1970

18 The House of Lords, an illusion to which I have never been able to subscribe – responsibility without power, the prerogative of the eunuch throughout the ages.

Tom Stoppard (1937–) Czech-born British dramatist. *Lord Malquist and Mr Moon*, Pt. VI, Ch. 1

19 You must build your House of Parliament upon the river: so…that the populace cannot exact their demands by sitting down round you.

Duke of Wellington (1769–1852) British general and statesman. *Words on Wellington* (Sir William Fraser)

HOUSEWORK

See also woman's role

1 Housekeeping ain't no joke.

Louisa May Alcott (1832–88) US novelist. *Little Women*, Pt. I

2 Our motto: Life is too short to stuff a mushroom.

Shirley Conran (1932–) British designer and journalist. *Superwoman*, Epigraph

3 There was no need to do any housework at all. After the first four years the dirt doesn't get any worse.

Quentin Crisp (?1910–) Model, publicist, and writer. *The Naked Civil Servant*

4 Cleaning your house while your kids are still growing
Is like shoveling the walk before it stops snowing.

Phyllis Diller (1917–) US writer and comedienne. *Phyllis Diller's Housekeeping Hints*

5 I do, and I also wash and iron them.

Denis Thatcher (1915–) British businessman married to

Mrs Margaret Thatcher. Replying to the question 'Who wears the pants in this house?'. *Times* (Los Angeles), 21 Apr 1981

HUMAN CONDITION

See also human nature, life, mankind

1 A wanderer is man from his birth.
He was born in a ship
On the breast of the river of Time.

Matthew Arnold (1822–88) British poet and critic. *The Future*

2 Thou hast created us for Thyself, and our heart is not quiet until it rests in Thee.

St Augustine of Hippo (354–430) Bishop of Hippo. *Confessions*, Bk. I, Ch. 1

3 Man that is born of a woman is of few days, and full of trouble.

Bible: Job 14:1

4 We mortals cross the ocean of this world
Each in his average cabin of a life.

Robert Browning (1812–89) British poet. *Bishop Blougram's Apology*

5 The human race, to which so many of my readers belong.

G. K. Chesterton (1874–1936) British writer. *The Napoleon of Notting Hill*, Vol. I, Ch. 1

6 If God were suddenly condemned to live the life which he has inflicted on men, He would kill Himself.

Alexandre Dumas, fils (1824–95) French writer. *Pensées d'album*

7 Every man is wanted, and no man is wanted much.

Ralph Waldo Emerson (1803–82) US poet and essayist. *Essays*, 'Nominalist and Realist'

8 The world is a beautiful place
to be born into
if you don't mind some people dying
all the time
or maybe only starving
some of the time
which isn't half so bad
if it isn't you.

Laurence Ferlinghetti (1919–) US poet. *Pictures of the Gone World*

9 Oh wearisome condition of humanity!
Born under one law, to another bound.

Fulke Greville (1554–1628) English poet and politician. *Mustapha*, V:6

10 The condition of man...is a condition of war of everyone against everyone.

Thomas Hobbes (1588–1679) English philosopher. *Leviathan*, Pt. I, Ch. 4

11 No arts; no letters; no society; and which is worst of all, continual fear and danger of violent death; and the life of man, solitary, poor, nasty, brutish, and short.

Thomas Hobbes *Leviathan*, Pt. I, Ch. 13

12 Fade far away, dissolve, and quite forget
What thou among the leaves hast never known,
The weariness, the fever, and the fret,
Here, where men sit and hear each other groan.

John Keats (1795–1821) British poet. *Ode to a Nightingale*

13 You come into the world alone, you go out alone. In between it's nice to know a few people, but being alone is a fundamental quality of human life, depressing as that is.

Helen Mirren (1945–) British actress. Remark, Jan 1989

14 Created half to rise, and half to fall;
Great lord of all things, yet a prey to all;
Sole judge of truth, in endless error hurl'd;
The glory, jest, and riddle of the world!

Alexander Pope (1688–1744) British poet. *An Essay on Man*, II

15 Brief and powerless is Man's life; on him and all his race the slow, sure doom falls pitiless and dark.

Bertrand Russell (1872–1970) British philosopher. *Mysticism and Logic*, 'A Free Man's Worship'

16 Farewell, a long farewell, to all my greatness!
This is the state of man: to-day he puts forth
The tender leaves of hopes: to-morrow blossoms
And bears his blushing honours thick upon him;
The third day comes a frost, a killing frost,
And when he thinks, good easy man, full surely
His greatness is a-ripening, nips his root,
And then he falls, as I do.

William Shakespeare (1564–1616) English dramatist. *Henry VIII*, III:2

17 All the world's a stage,
And all the men and women merely players;
They have their exits and their entrances;
And one man in his time plays many parts,
His acts being seven ages.

William Shakespeare *As You Like It*, II:7

18 When we are born, we cry that we are come
To this great stage of fools.

William Shakespeare *King Lear*, IV:6

19 We have to believe in free-will. We've got no choice.

Isaac Bashevis Singer (1904–91) Polish-born US writer. *The Times*, 21 June 1982

20 But what am I?
An infant crying in the night:
An infant crying for the light:
And with no language but a cry.

Alfred, Lord Tennyson (1809–92) British poet. *In Memoriam A.H.H.*, LIV

21 All men should strive to learn before they die
What they are running from, and to, and why.

James Thurber (1894–1961) American humorist. Attrib.

22 For what human ill does not dawn seem to be an alternative?

Thornton Wilder (1897–1975) US novelist and dramatist. *The Bridge of San Luis Rey*

HUMAN NATURE

See also mankind

1 Human nature is so well disposed towards those who are in interesting situations, that a young person, who either marries or dies, is sure to be kindly spoken of.

Jane Austen (1775–1817) British novelist. *Emma*, Ch. 22

2 A man's nature runs either to herbs, or to weeds; therefore let him seasonably water the one, and destroy the other.

Francis Bacon (1561–1626) English philosopher. *Essays*, 'Of Nature in Men'

3 There is in human nature generally more of the fool than of the wise.

Francis Bacon *Essays*, 'Of Boldness'

4 Nature is often hidden, sometimes overcome, seldom extinguished.

Francis Bacon *Essays*, 'Of Nature in Men'

5 Nature, to be commanded, must be obeyed.

Francis Bacon *Novum Organum*

6 Pleasant people are just as real as horrible people.

John Braine (1922–86) British novelist. Remark, Apr 1983

7 When dealing with people, let us remember we are not dealing with creatures of logic. We are dealing with creatures of emotion, creatures bristling with prejudices and motivated by pride and vanity.

Dale Carnegie (1888–1955) US lecturer and writer. *Dale Carnegie's Scrapbook*

8 I got disappointed in human nature as well and gave it up because I found it too much like my own.

J. P. Donleavy (1926–) US novelist. *Fairy Tales of New York*

9 A man so various, that he seem'd to be
Not one, but all Mankind's Epitome.
Stiff in Opinions, always in the wrong;
Was Everything by starts, and Nothing long.

John Dryden (1631–1700) British poet and dramatist. *Absalom and Achitophel*, I

10 A person seldom falls sick, but the bystanders are animated with a faint hope that he will die.

Ralph Waldo Emerson (1803–82) US poet and essayist. *Conduct of Life*, 'Considerations by the Way'

11 Looks like whatever you try to do, somebody jumps up and hollers and raises cain – then the feller next to him jumps up and hollers how much he likes it.

Woody Guthrie (1912–67) US folk singer. *My Beat: An Intimate Volume of Shop Talk* (Howard Taubman)

12 You may drive out nature with a pitchfork, yet she'll be constantly running back.

Horace (Quintus Horatius Flaccus; 65–8 BC) Roman poet. *Epistles*, I

13 Most human beings have an almost infinite capacity for taking things for granted.

Aldous Huxley (1894–1964) British novelist. *Themes and Variations*

14 We need more understanding of human nature, because the only real danger that exists is man himself...We know nothing of man, far too little. His psyche should be studied because we are the origin of all coming evil.

Carl Gustav Jung (1875–1961) Swiss psychoanalyst. BBC television interview

15 Out of the crooked timber of humanity no straight thing can ever be made.

Immanuel Kant (1724–1804) German philosopher. *Idee zu einer allgemeinen Geschichte in weltbürgerlicher Absicht*

16 Scenery is fine – but human nature is finer.

John Keats (1795–1821) British poet. Letter to Benjamin Bailey, 13 Mar 1818

17 Upon the whole I dislike mankind: whatever people on the other side of the question may advance, they cannot deny that they are always surprised at hearing of a good action and never of a bad one.

John Keats Letter, 1820

18 No absolute is going to make the lion lie down with the lamb unless the lamb is inside.

D. H. Lawrence (1885–1930) British novelist. *The Later D. H. Lawrence*

19 Observe diners arriving at any restaurant and you will see them make a bee-line for the wall-seats. No one ever voluntarily selects a centre table in an open space. Open seating positions are only taken when all the wall-seats are already occupied. This dates back to a primeval feeding practice of avoiding sudden attack during the deep concentration involved in consuming food.

Desmond Morris (1928–) British biologist. *Manwatching*, 'Feeding Behaviour'

20 In the misfortune of our best friends we always find something which is not displeasing to us.

Duc de la Rochefoucauld (1613–80) French writer. *Maximes*, 99

21 'Tis the way of all flesh.

Thomas Shadwell (1642–92) English dramatist. *The Sullen Lovers*, V:2

22 It is part of human nature to hate the man you have hurt.

Tacitus (c. 55–c. 120 AD) Roman historian. *Agricola*, 42

23 It is not the ape, nor the tiger in man that I fear, it is the donkey.

William Temple (1881–1944) British churchman. Attrib.

24 ...use thought only to justify their injustices, and speech only to conceal their thoughts.

Voltaire (François-Marie Arouet; 1694–1778) French writer. Referring to men. *Dialogue*, 'Le Chapon et la poularde'

25 The earth does not argue,
Is not pathetic, has no arrangements,
Does not scream, haste, persuade, threaten,

promise,
Makes no discriminations, has no conceivable failures,
Closes nothing, refuses nothing, shuts none out.

Walt Whitman (1819–92) US poet. *To the sayers of words*

HUMAN RIGHTS

See also equality, freedom, race

1 All human beings are born free and equal in dignity and rights.

Anonymous *Universal Declaration of Human Rights* (1948), Article 1

2 *Liberté! Égalité! Fraternité!*
Freedom! Equality! Brotherhood!

Anonymous Motto for French Revolutionaries

3 We hold these truths to be self-evident: that all men are created equal; that they are endowed by their Creator with certain unalienable rights; that among these are life, liberty, and the pursuit of happiness.

Thomas Jefferson (1743–1826) US statesman. Declaration of American Independence, 4 July 1776

4 We look forward to a world founded upon four essential human freedoms. The first is freedom of speech and expression – everywhere in the world. The second is freedom of every person to worship God in his own way – everywhere in the world. The third is freedom from want...everywhere in the world. The fourth is freedom from fear...anywhere in the world.

Franklin D. Roosevelt (1882–1945) US Democratic president. Speech to Congress, 6 Jan 1941

5 Freedom is an indivisible word. If we want to enjoy it, and fight for it, we must be prepared to extend it to everyone, whether they are rich or poor, whether they agree with us or not, no matter what their race or the colour of their skin.

Wendell Lewis Willkie (1892–1944) US lawyer and businessman. *One World*, Ch. 13

HUMILITY

See also service, servility

1 Blessed are the meek: for they shall inherit the earth.

Bible: Matthew 5:5

2 Humility is only doubt,
And does the sun and moon blot out.

William Blake (1757–1827) British poet. *The Everlasting Gospel*

3 I do not consider it an insult but rather a compliment to be called an agnostic. I do not pretend to know where many ignorant men are sure.

Clarence Seward Darrow (1857–1938) US lawyer. Remark during the trial (1925) of John Scopes for teaching the theory of evolution in school.

4 It is difficult to be humble. Even if you aim at humility, there is no guarantee that when you have attained the state you will not be proud of the feat.

Bonamy Dobrée (1891–1974) British scholar and writer. *John Wesley*

5 Less than the dust beneath thy chariot wheel,
Less than the weed that grows beside thy door,
Less than the rust that never stained thy sword,
Less than the need thou hast in life of me,
Even less am I.

Laurence Hope (Mrs M. H. Nicolson; 1804–1905) British poet and songwriter. *The Garden of Kama and other Love Lyrics from India*, 'Less than the Dust'

6 The meek do not inherit the earth unless they are prepared to fight for their meekness.

H. J. Laski (1893–1950) British political theorist. Attrib.

7 The humble and meek are thirsting for blood.

Joe Orton (1933–67) British dramatist. *Funeral Games*, I

8 Because there's no fourth class.

George Santayana (1863–1952) US philosopher. On being asked why he always travelled third class. *Living Biographies of the Great Philosophers* (H. Thomas)

9 I too had thoughts once of being an intellectual, but I found it too difficult.

Albert Schweitzer (1875–1965) French Protestant theologian, philosopher, physician, and musician. Remark made to an African who refused to perform a menial task on the grounds that he was an intellectual. Attrib.

10 Take physic, pomp;
Expose thyself to feel what wretches feel.

William Shakespeare (1564–1616) English dramatist. *King Lear*, III:4

11 We have the highest authority for believing that the meek shall inherit the Earth; though I have never found any particular corroboration of this aphorism in the records of Somerset House.

F. E. Smith (1872–1930) British lawyer and politician. *Contemporary Personalities*, 'Marquess Curzon'

12 This is not for me. The honour is for the poor.

Mother Teresa (Agnes Gonxha Bojaxhui; 1910–) Yugoslavian missionary in Calcutta. Said on receiving the Order of Merit, 24 Nov 1983. *The Sunday Times*, 3 Dec 1989

13 When I survey the wondrous Cross,
On which the Prince of Glory died,
My richest gain I count but loss
And pour contempt on all my pride.

Isaac Watts (1674–1748) English theologian and hymn writer. *When I Survey the Wondrous Cross*

14 Gentle Jesus, meek and mild,
Look upon a little child;
Pity my simplicity,
Suffer me to come to thee.

Charles Wesley (1707–88) British religious leader. *Hymns and Sacred Poems*

HUMOUR

See also laughter, nonsense, puns

On the subject

1 I have a fine sense of the ridiculous, but no sense of humour.

Edward Albee (1928–) US dramatist. *Who's Afraid of Virginia Woolf?*, I

2 The marvellous thing about a joke with a double meaning is that it can only mean one thing.

Ronnie Barker (1929–) British comedian. *Sauce*, 'Daddie's Sauce'

3 The world would not be in such a snarl, had Marx been Groucho instead of Karl.

Irving Berlin (Israel Baline; 1888–1989) US composer. Telegram to Groucho Marx on his seventy-first birthday

4 It's a good deed to forget a poor joke.

Brendan Bracken (1901–58) British newspaper publisher and politician. *The Observer*, 'Sayings of the Week', 17 Oct 1943

5 All I need to make a comedy is a park, a policeman and a pretty girl.

Charlie Chaplin (Sir Charles Spencer C.; 1889–1977) British film actor. *My Autobiography*

6 I remain just one thing, and one thing only – and that is a clown.
It places me on a far higher plane than any politician.

Charlie Chaplin *The Observer*, 'Sayings of the Week', 17 June 1960

7 A joke's a very serious thing.

Charles Churchill (1731–64) British poet. *The Ghost*, Bk. IV

8 Men will confess to treason, murder, arson, false teeth, or a wig. How many of them will own up to a lack of humour?

Frank More Colby (1865–1925) US editor. *Essays*, I

9 No mind is thoroughly well organized that is deficient in a sense of humour.

Samuel Taylor Coleridge (1772–1834) British poet. *Table Talk*

10 Total absence of humour renders life impossible.

Colette (1873–1954) French novelist. *Chance Acquaintances*

11 A different taste in jokes is a great strain on the affections.

George Eliot (Mary Ann Evans; 1819–80) British novelist. *Daniel Deronda*

12 Comedy, like sodomy, is an unnatural act.

Marty Feldman (1933–83) British comedian. *The Times*, 9 June 1969

13 As for the Freudian, it is a very low, Central European sort of humour.

Robert Graves (1895–1985) British poet and novelist. *Occupation: Writer*

14 Funny peculiar, or funny ha-ha?

Ian Hay (John Hay Beith; 1876–1952) British novelist and dramatist. *The Housemaster*, III

15 His foe was folly and his weapon wit.

Anthony Hope (Sir Anthony Hope Hawkins; 1863–1933) British novelist. Written for the inscription on the memorial to W. S. Gilbert, Victoria Embankment, London.

16 Every man has, some time in his life, an ambition to be a wag.

Samuel Johnson (1709–84) British lexicographer. *Diary and Letters* (Mme D'Arblay), Vol. III, Ch. 46

17 The essence of any blue material is timing. If you sit on it, it becomes vulgar.

Danny La Rue (Daniel Patrick Carroll; 1928–) British entertainer. Attrib.

18 The coarse joke proclaims that we have here an animal which finds its own animality either objectionable or funny.

C. S. Lewis (1898–1963) British academic and writer. *Miracles*

19 Impropriety is the soul of wit.

W. Somerset Maugham (1874–1965) British novelist. *The Moon and Sixpence*, Ch. 4

20 It is not for nothing that, in the English language alone, to accuse someone of trying to be funny is highly abusive.

Malcolm Muggeridge (1903–90) British writer. *Tread Softly For You Tread on My Jokes*

21 One always writes comedy at the moment of deepest hysteria.

V. S. Naipaul (1932–) West Indian-born British novelist. *The Observer*, 'Sayings of the Week', 1 May 1994

22 Attic wit.

Pliny the Elder (Gaius Plinius Secundus; 23–79 AD) Roman scholar. *Natural History*, II

23 True wit is nature to advantage dress'd;
What oft was thought, but ne'er so well express'd.

Alexander Pope (1688–1744) British poet. *An Essay on Criticism*

24 Comedy, we may say, is society protecting itself – with a smile.

J. B. Priestley (1894–1984) British novelist. *George Meredith*

25 A comedian can only last till he either takes himself serious or his audience takes him serious.

Will Rogers (1879–1935) US actor and humorist. Newspaper article, 1931

26 Everything is funny, as long as it's happening to somebody else.

Will Rogers *The Illiterate Digest*

27 I am not only witty in myself, but the cause that wit is in other men. I do here walk before thee like a sow that hath overwhelm'd all her litter but one.

William Shakespeare (1564–1616) English dramatist. *Henry IV, Part Two*, I:2

28 A jest's prosperity lies in the ear
Of him that hears it, never in the tongue
Of him that makes it.

William Shakespeare *Love's Labour's Lost*, V:2

29 People no longer need the jokes explained; everyone gets irony nowadays.

John Waters (1946–) US film director. *The Times*, 11 June 1994

30 It's hard to be funny when you have to be clean.

Mae West (1892–1980) US actress. *The Wit and Wisdom of Mae West* (ed. J. Weintraub)

Some examples

31 There's a wonderful family called Stein,
There's Gert and there's Epp and there's Ein;
Gert's poems are bunk,
Epp's statues are junk,
And no one can understand Ein.

Anonymous

32 Little Willy from his mirror
Licked the mercury right off,
Thinking in his childish error,
It would cure the whooping cough.
At the funeral his mother
Smartly said to Mrs Brown:
''Twas a chilly day for Willie
When the mercury went down'.

Anonymous *Willie's Epitaph*

33 There was an old man from Darjeeling,
Who boarded a bus bound for Ealing,
He saw on the door:
'Please don't spit on the floor',
So he stood up and spat on the ceiling.

Anonymous

34 I do most of my work sitting down; that's where I shine.

Robert Benchley (1889–1945) US humorist. Attrib.

35 No visit to Dove Cottage, Grasmere, is complete without examining the outhouse where Hazlitt's father, a Unitarian minister of strong liberal views, attempted to put his hand up Dorothy Wordsworth's skirt.

Alan Coren (1938–) British humorist and writer. *All Except the Bastard*, 'Bohemia'

36 Dear 338171 (May I call you 338?).

Noël Coward (1899–1973) British dramatist. Starting a letter to T. E. Lawrence who had retired from public life to become Aircraftsman Brown, 338171. *Letters to T. E. Lawrence*

37 Miss Bolo rose from the table considerably agitated, and went straight home, in a flood of tears and a Sedan chair.

Charles Dickens (1812–70) British novelist. *Pickwick Papers*, Ch. 35

38 It...was full of dry rot. An unkind visitor said the only reason Menabilly still stood was that the woodworm obligingly held hands.

Daphne Du Maurier (1907–89) British novelist. Interview – referring to her own house in Cornwall upon which Manderley in *Rebecca* was based

39 Wembley, adj. Suffering from a vague *malaise*. 'I feel a bit w. this morning.'

Paul Jennings (1918–89) British humorous writer. *The Jenguin Pennings*, 'Ware, Wye, Watford'

40 The desire of the moth for the star.

James Joyce (1882–1941) Irish novelist. Commenting on the interruption of a music recital when a moth flew into the singer's mouth. *James Joyce* (R. Ellmann)

41 'When I makes tea I makes tea,' as old mother Grogan said. 'And when I makes water I makes water'.

James Joyce *Ulysses*

42 The landlady of a boarding-house is a parallelogram – that is, an oblong angular figure, which cannot be described, but which is equal to anything.

Stephen Leacock (1869–1944) English-born Canadian economist and humorist. *Literary Lapses*, 'Boarding-House Geometry'

43 One morning I shot an elephant in my pajamas.
How he got into my pajamas I'll never know.

Groucho Marx (Julius Marx; 1895–1977) US comedian. *Animal Crackers*

44 I could dance with you till the cows come home. Better still, I'll dance with the cows and *you* come home.

Groucho Marx *Duck Soup*

45 Go – and never darken my towels again.

Groucho Marx *Duck Soup*

46 I don't have a photograph, but you can have my footprints. They are upstairs in my socks.

Groucho Marx *A Night At the Opera*

47 The strains of Verdi will come back to you tonight, and Mrs Claypool's cheque will come back to you in the morning.

Groucho Marx *A Night at the Opera*

48 Please accept my resignation. I don't want to belong to any club that will accept me as a member.

Groucho Marx Resigning from the Friar's Club in Hollywood. Attrib.

49 Dr Strabismus (Whom God Preserve) of Utrecht is carrying out research work with a view to crossing salmon with mosquitoes. He says it will mean a bite every time for fishermen.

J. B. Morton (1893–1979) British journalist. *By the Way*, 'January Tail-piece'

50 Oh, don't worry about Alan...Alan will always land on somebody's feet.

Dorothy Parker (1893–1967) US writer. Said of her husband on the day their divorce became final. *You Might As Well Live* (J. Keats), Pt. IV, Ch. 1

51 He bit his lip in a manner which immediately awakened my maternal sympathy, and I helped him bite it.

S. J. Perelman (1904–79) US humorous writer. *Crazy Like a Fox*, 'The Love Decoy'

52 I have Bright's disease and he has mine.

S. J. Perelman (Bennet Cerf)

53 A case of the tail dogging the wag.

S. J. Perelman Having escaped with some difficulty from the persistent attentions of some prostitutes in the street. *Another Almanac of Words at Play* (W. Epsy)

54 The cook was a good cook, as cooks go; and as cooks go she went.

Saki (Hector Hugh Munro; 1870–1916) British writer. *Reginald on Besetting Sins*

55 Napoleon's armies used to march on their stomachs, shouting: 'Vive l'intérieur!'

W. C. Sellar (1898–1951) British humorous writer. *1066 And All That*

56 You wait here and I'll bring the etchings down.

James Thurber (1894–1961) US humorist. Cartoon caption

57 Wall is the name – Max Wall. My father was the Great Wall of China. He was a brick.

Max Wall (1908–90) British comedian. Opening line of one of his acts

58 He spoke with a certain what-is-it in his voice, and I could see that, if not actually disgruntled, he was far from being gruntled.

P. G. Wodehouse (1881–1975) British humorous novelist. *The Code of the Woosters*

HUNGER

See also desire, food, thirst

1 Hunger is the best sauce.

Proverb

2 Poverty is an anomaly to rich people. It is very difficult to make out why people who want dinner do not ring the bell.

Walter Bagehot (1826–77) British economist and journalist. *Literary Studies*, II

3 When he told men to love their neighbour, their bellies were full. Nowadays things are different.

Bertolt Brecht (1898–1956) German dramatist. *Mother Courage*, II

4 The best sauce in the world is hunger.

Miguel de Cervantes (1547–1616) Spanish novelist. *Don Quixote*, Pt. II, Ch. 5

5 If only it were as easy to banish hunger by rubbing the belly as it is to masturbate.

Diogenes (412–322 BC) Greek philosopher. *Lives and Opinions of Eminent Philosophers* (Diogenes Laertius)

6 They that die by famine die by inches.

Matthew Henry (1662–1714) English nonconformist minister. *Exposition of the Old and New Testaments*

7 The war against hunger is truly mankind's war of liberation.

John Fitzgerald Kennedy (1917–63) US statesman. Speech, World Food Congress, 4 June 1963

8 A hungry stomach has no ears.

Jean de La Fontaine (1621–95) French poet. *Fables*, IX, 'Le Milan et le Rossignol'

9 I came home…hungry as a hunter.

Charles Lamb (1775–1834) British essayist. Letter to Coleridge, Apr 1800

10 Let them eat cake.

Marie-Antoinette (1755–93) Queen of France. On being told that the people had no bread to eat; in fact she was repeating a much older saying. Attrib.

HUNTING

See also sport and games

1 Spirits of well-shot woodcock, partridge, snipe
Flutter and bear him up the Norfolk sky.

John Betjeman (1906–84) British poet. *Death of King George V*

2 Detested sport,
That owes its pleasures to another's pain.

William Cowper (1731–1800) British poet. *The Task*

3 Wild animals never kill for sport. Man is the only one to whom the torture and death of his fellow-creatures is amusing in itself.

J. A. Froude (1818–94) British historian. *Oceana*, Ch. 5

4 D'ye ken John Peel with his coat so gay?
D'ye ken John Peel at the break of the day?
D'ye ken John Peel when he's far far away
With his hounds and his horn in the morning?

'Twas the sound of his horn called me from my bed,
And the cry of his hounds has me oft-times led;
For Peel's view-hollo would waken the dead,
Or a fox from his lair in the morning.

John Woodcock Graves (1795–1886) British poet, huntsman, and songwriter. *John Peel*

5 It is very strange, and very melancholy, that the paucity of human pleasures should persuade us ever to call hunting one of them.

Samuel Johnson (1709–84) British lexicographer. *Johnsonian Miscellanies* (ed. G. B. Hill), Vol. I

6 Hunting people tend to be church-goers on a higher level than ordinary folk. One has a religious experience in the field.

Christopher Seal British churchman. *The Times*, 30 Dec 1993

7 It isn't mere convention. Everyone can see that the people who hunt are the right people and the people who don't are the wrong ones.

George Bernard Shaw (1856–1950) Irish dramatist and critic. *Heartbreak House*

8 But He was never, well,
What I call
A Sportsman;

For forty days
He went out into the desert
– And never shot anything.

Osbert Sitwell (1892–1969) British writer. *Old Fashioned Sportsmen*

9 The English country gentleman galloping after a fox – the unspeakable in full pursuit of the uneatable.

Oscar Wilde (1854–1900) Irish-born British dramatist. *A Woman of No Importance*, I

HURT

See also cruelty, insensitivity, nastiness, suffering

1 Those have most power to hurt us that we love.

Francis Beaumont (1584–1616) English dramatist. *The Maid's Tragedy*, V:6

2 Mrs Montagu has dropt me. Now, Sir, there are people whom one should like very well to drop, but would not wish to be dropped by.

Samuel Johnson (1709–84) British lexicographer. *Life of Johnson* (J. Boswell), Vol. IV

3 It takes your enemy and your friend, working together, to hurt you to the heart; the one to slander you and the other to get the news to you.

Mark Twain (Samuel Langhorne Clemens; 1835–1910) US writer. *Following the Equator*

4 We flatter those we scarcely know,
We please the fleeting guest,
And deal full many a thoughtless blow
To those who love us best.

Ella Wheeler Wilcox (1850–1919) US poet. *Life's Scars*

HYPOCHONDRIA

1 I never read a patent medicine advertisement without being impelled to the conclusion that I am suffering from the particular disease therein dealt with in its most virulent form.

Jerome K. Jerome (1859–1927) British humorist. *Three Men in a Boat*, Ch. 1

2 People who are always taking care of their health are like misers, who are hoarding a treasure which they have never spirit enough to enjoy.

Laurence Sterne (1713–68) Irish-born British writer. Attrib.

3 The imaginary complaints of indestructible old ladies.

Elwyn Brooks White (1899–1985) US journalist and humorist. *Harper's Magazine*, Nov 1941

HYPOCRISY

See also example, insincerity

1 All are not saints that go to church.

Proverb

2 It is the wisdom of the crocodiles, that shed tears when they would devour.

Francis Bacon (1561–1626) English philosopher. *Essays*, 'Of Wisdom for a Man's Self'

3 Woe unto you, scribes and Pharisees, hypocrites! for ye are like unto whited sepulchres, which indeed appear beautiful outward, but are within full of dead men's bones, and of all uncleanness.

Bible: Matthew 23:27

4 Prisons are built with stones of Law, brothels with bricks of Religion.

William Blake (1757–1827) British poet. *The Marriage of Heaven and Hell*, 'Proverbs of Hell'

5 God be thanked, the meanest of his creatures
Boasts two soul-sides, one to face the world with,
One to show a woman when he loves her!

Robert Browning (1812–89) British poet. *One Word More*, XVII

6 Man is the only animal that can remain on friendly terms with the victims he intends to eat until he eats them.

Samuel Butler (1835–1902) British writer. *Notebooks*

7 The smyler with the knyf under the cloke.

Geoffrey Chaucer (c. 1342–1400) English poet. *The Canterbury Tales*, 'The Knight's Tale'

8 We ought to see far enough into a hypocrite to see even his sincerity.

G. K. Chesterton (1874–1936) British writer. *Heretics*, Ch. 5

9 The book written against fame and learning has the author's name on the title-page.

Ralph Waldo Emerson (1803–82) US poet and essayist. *Journal*

10 Man is the only animal that learns by being hypocritical. He pretends to be polite and then, eventually, he *becomes* polite.

Jean Kerr (1923–) US dramatist. *Finishing Touches*

11 Hypocrisy is the most difficult and nerve-racking vice that any man can pursue; it needs an unceasing vigilance and a rare detachment of spirit. It cannot, like adultery or gluttony, be practised at spare moments; it is a whole-time job.

W. Somerset Maugham (1874–1965) British novelist. *Cakes and Ale*, Ch. 1

12 For neither man nor angel can discern
Hypocrisy, the only evil that walks
Invisible, except to God alone.

John Milton (1608–74) English poet. *Paradise Lost*, Bk. III

13 Ancient sculpture is the true school of modesty. But where the Greeks had modesty, we have cant; where they had poetry, we have cant; where they had patriotism, we have cant; where they had anything that exalts, delights, or adorns humanity, we have nothing but cant, cant, cant.

Thomas Love Peacock (1785–1866) British novelist. *Crotchet Castle*, Ch. 7

14 Hypocrisy is the homage paid by

vice to virtue.

Duc de la Rochefoucauld (1613–80) French writer. *Maximes*, 218

15 Well, whiles I am a beggar, I will rail
And say there is no sin but to be rich;
And being rich, my virtue then shall be
To say there is no vice but beggary.

William Shakespeare (1564–1616) English dramatist. *King John*, II:1

16 Come not, when I am dead,
To drop thy foolish tears upon my grave,
To trample round my fallen head,
And vex the unhappy dust thou wouldst not save.

Alfred, Lord Tennyson (1809–92) British poet. *Come Not, When I Am Dead*

17 I sit on a man's back, choking him and making him carry me, and yet assure myself and others that I am very sorry for him and wish to ease his lot by all possible means – except by getting off his back.

Leo Tolstoy (1828–1910) Russian writer. *What Then Must We Do?*, Ch. 16

18 I hope you have not been leading a double life, pretending to be wicked and being really good all the time. That would be hypocrisy.

Oscar Wilde (1854–1900) Irish-born British dramatist. *The Importance of Being Earnest*, II

19 A Christian is a man who feels
Repentance on a Sunday
For what he did on Saturday
And is going to do on Monday.

Thomas Russell Ybarra (b. 1880) Venezuelan-born US writer. *The Christian*

I

IDEALISM

1 If a man hasn't discovered something that he would die for, he isn't fit to live.
Martin Luther King (1929–68) US Black civil-rights leader. Speech, Detroit, 23 June 1963

2 If you can talk with crowds and keep your virtue,
Or walk with Kings – nor lose the common touch,
If neither foes nor loving friends can hurt you,
If all men count with you, but none too much;
If you can fill the unforgiving minute
With sixty seconds' worth of distance run,
Yours is the Earth and everything that's in it,
And – which is more – you'll be a Man my son!
Rudyard Kipling (1865–1936) Indian-born British writer. *If*

3 Ideal mankind would abolish death, multiply itself million upon million, rear up city upon city, save every parasite alive, until the accumulation of mere existence is swollen to a horror.
D. H. Lawrence (1885–1930) British novelist. *St Mawr*

4 An idealist is one who, on noticing that a rose smells better than a cabbage, concludes that it will also make better soup.
H. L. Mencken (1880–1956) US journalist. *Sententiae*

5 Do not despair
For Johnny head-in-air;
He sleeps as sound
As Johnny underground.
John Sleigh Pudney (1909–77) British poet and writer. *For Johnny*

6 A radical is a man with both feet firmly planted in the air.
Franklin D. Roosevelt (1882–1945) US Democratic president. Broadcast, 26 Oct 1939

7 Those who have never dwelt in tents have no idea either of the charm or of the discomfort of a nomadic existence. The charm is purely romantic, and consequently very soon proves to be fallacious.
Vita Sackville-West (Victoria Sackville-West; 1892–1962) British poet and novelist. *Twelve Days*, Ch. 6

IDEAS

See also opinions, theory

1 What was once thought can never be unthought.
Friedrich Dürrenmatt (1921–90) Swiss writer. *The Physicists*

2 A stand can be made against invasion by an army; no stand can be made against invasion by an idea.
Victor Hugo (1802–85) French writer. *Histoire d'un Crime*, 'La Chute'

3 Many ideas grow better when transplanted into another mind than in the one where they sprang up.
Oliver Wendell Holmes Jnr (1841–1935) US jurist.

4 Society goes on and on and on. It is the same with ideas.
Ramsey MacDonald (1866–1937) British statesman and prime minister. Speech, 1935

5 An idea isn't responsible for the people who believe in it.
Don Marquis (1878–1937) US journalist. *New York Sun*

6 A society made up of individuals who were all capable of original thought would probably be unendurable. The pressure of ideas would simply drive it frantic.
H. L. Mencken (1880–1956) US journalist. *Notebooks*, 'Minority Report'

7 If an idea's worth having once, it's worth having twice.
Tom Stoppard (1937–) British writer. *Indian Ink*

IDLENESS

See also bed, laziness, leisure, unemployment

1 The devil finds work for idle hands to do.
Proverb

2 The dreadful burden of having nothing to do.
Nicolas Boileau (1636–1711) French writer. *Épitres*, XI

3 Idleness is only the refuge of weak minds.
Earl of Chesterfield (1694–1773) English statesman. Letter to his son, 20 July 1749

4 What is this life if, full of care,
We have no time to stand and stare?
W. H. Davies (1871–1940) British poet. *Leisure*

5 It is impossible to enjoy idling thoroughly unless one has plenty of work to do.
Jerome K. Jerome (1859–1927) British humorist. *Idle Thoughts of an Idle Fellow*

6 I like work; it fascinates me. I can sit and look at it for hours. I love to keep it by me; the idea of getting rid of it nearly breaks my heart.
Jerome K. Jerome *Three Men in a Boat*, Ch. 15

7 We would all be idle if we could.
Samuel Johnson (1709–84) British lexicographer. *Life of Johnson* (J. Boswell), Vol. III

8 Young people ought not to be idle. It is very bad for them.
Margaret Thatcher (1925–) British politician and prime minister. *The Times*, 1984

9 I am happiest when I am idle. I could live for months without performing any kind of labour, and at the expiration of that time I should feel fresh and vigorous enough to go right on in the same way for numerous more months.

Artemus Ward (Charles Farrar Browne; 1834–67) US humorous writer. *Pyrotechny*

10 For Satan finds some mischief still
For idle hands to do.

Isaac Watts (1674–1748) English theologian and hymn writer. *Divine Songs for Children*, 'Against Idleness and Mischief'

IGNORANCE

See also foolishness, innocence, innocence of childhood, stupidity

1 He that knows little, often repeats it.

Proverb

2 He that knows nothing, doubts nothing.

Proverb

3 What you don't know can't hurt you.

Proverb

4 Happy the hare at morning, for she cannot read
The Hunter's waking thoughts.

W. H. Auden (1907–73) British poet. *The Dog Beneath the Skin* (with Christopher Isherwood)

5 She is an excellent creature, but she never can remember which came first, the Greeks or the Romans.

Benjamin Disraeli (1804–81) British statesman. Referring to his wife. Attrib.

6 To each his suff'rings, all are men,
Condemn'd alike to groan;
The tender for another's pain,
Th' unfeeling for his own.
Yet ah! why should they know their fate?
Since sorrow never comes too late,
And happiness too swiftly flies.
Thought would destroy their paradise.
No more; where ignorance is bliss,
'Tis folly to be wise.

Thomas Gray (1716–71) British poet. *Ode on a Distant Prospect of Eton College*

7 Alas, regardless of their doom,
The little victims play!

Thomas Gray *Ode on a Distant Prospect of Eton College*

8 I wish you would read a little poetry sometimes. Your ignorance cramps my conversation.

Anthony Hope (Sir Anthony Hope Hawkins; 1863–1933) British novelist. *The Dolly Dialogues*

9 Ignorance, madam, pure ignorance.

Samuel Johnson (1709–84) British lexicographer. His reply on being questioned, by a lady reader of his *Dictionary*, why he had incorrectly defined 'pastern' as the 'knee' of a horse. *Life of Johnson* (J. Boswell), Vol. I

10 The ignorant man always adores what he cannot understand.

Cesare Lombroso (1853–1909) Italian criminologist. *The Man of Genius*, Pt. III, Ch. 3

11 I count religion but a childish toy,
And hold there is no sin but ignorance.

Christopher Marlowe (1564–93) English dramatist. *The Jew of Malta*, Prologue

12 From ignorance our comfort flows,
The only wretched are the wise.

Matthew Prior (1664–1721) British poet. *To the Hon. Charles Montague*

13 He hath never fed of the dainties that are bred in a book; he hath not eat paper, as it were; he hath not drunk ink; his intellect is not replenished.

William Shakespeare (1564–1616) English dramatist. *Love's Labour's Lost*, IV:2

14 He that is robb'd, not wanting what is stol'n,
Let him not know't, and he's not robb'd at all.

William Shakespeare *Othello*, III:3

15 What you don't know would make a great book.

Sydney Smith (1771–1845) British clergyman and essayist. *Memoir* (Lady Holland)

16 Somebody else's ignorance is bliss.

Jack Vance (1916–) US writer. *Star King*

17 Ignorance is like a delicate exotic fruit; touch it, and the bloom is gone.

Oscar Wilde (1854–1900) Irish-born British dramatist. *The Importance of Being Earnest*, I

ILLEGITIMACY

1 If you please, ma'am, it was a very little one.

Captain Frederick Marryat (1792–1848) British novelist. Said by the nurse to excuse the fact that she had had an illegitimate baby. *Mr. Midshipman Easy*, Ch. 3

2 There are no illegitimate children – only illegitimate parents.

Léon R. Yankwich US lawyer. Decision, State District Court, Southern District of California, Jun 1928, quoting columnist O. O. McIntyre

ILLNESS

See also disease, doctors, drugs, health and healthy living, medicine, remedies

1 Across the wires the electric message came:
'He is no better, he is much the same.'

Alfred Austin (1835–1913) British poet. Generally attrib. to Austin but there is no definite evidence that he wrote it. *On the Illness of the Prince of Wales*

2 'Ye can call it influenza if ye like,' said Mrs Machin. 'There was no influenza in my young days. We called a cold a cold.'

Arnold Bennett (1867–1931) British novelist. *The Card*, Ch. 8

3 My message to the businessmen of this country when they go abroad on business is that there is one thing above all they can take with them to stop them catching Aids, and that is the wife.

Edwina Currie (1946–) British politician. *The Observer*, 'Sayings of the Week', 15 Feb 1987

4 Much of the world's work, it has been said, is done by men who do not feel quite well. Marx is a case in point.

John Kenneth Galbraith (1908–) US economist. *The Age of Uncertainty*, Ch. 3

5 Every time you sleep with a boy you sleep with all his old girlfriends.

Government-sponsored AIDS advertisement, 1987

6 Hungry Joe collected lists of fatal diseases and arranged them in alphabetical order so that he could put his finger without delay on any one he wanted to worry about.

Joseph Heller (1923–) US novelist. *Catch-22*, Ch. 17

7 For that old enemy the gout
Had taken him in toe!

Thomas Hood (1799–1845) British poet. *Lieutenant Luff*

8 Indigestion is charged by God with enforcing morality on the stomach.

Victor Hugo (1802–85) French writer. *Les Misérables*, 'Fantine', Bk. III, Ch. 7

9 How few of his friends' houses would a man choose to be at when he is sick.

Samuel Johnson (1709–84) British lexicographer. *Life of Johnson* (J. Boswell), Vol. IV

10 Oh what can ail thee, knight at arms
Alone and palely loitering;
The sedge has wither'd from the lake,
And no birds sing.

John Keats (1795–1821) British poet. *La Belle Dame Sans Merci*

11 How sickness enlarges the dimensions of a man's self to himself.

Charles Lamb (1775–1834) British essayist. *Last Essays of Elia*, 'The Convalescent'

12 I am only half there when I am ill, and so there is only half a man to suffer. To suffer in one's whole self is so great a violation, that it is not to be endured.

D. H. Lawrence (1885–1930) British novelist. Letter to Catherine Carswell, 16 Apr 1916

13 Too late for fruit, too soon for flowers.

Walter De La Mare (1873–1956) British poet. On being asked, as he lay seriously ill, whether he would like some fruit or flowers. Attrib.

14 Only do always in health what you have often promised to do when you are sick.

Sigismund (1368–1437) Holy Roman Emperor. His advice on achieving happiness. *Biographiana*, Vol. I

15 Illness is the night-side of life, a more onerous citizenship. Everyone who is born holds dual citizenship, in the kingdom of the well and in the kingdom of the sick. Although we all prefer to use only the good passport, sooner or later each of us is obliged, at least for a spell, to identify ourselves as citizens of that other place.

Susan Sontag (1933–) US novelist and essayist. *Illness as Metaphor*

16 Most of the time we think we're sick, it's all in the mind.

Thomas Wolfe (1900–38) US novelist. *Look Homeward, Angel*, Pt. I, Ch. 1

IMAGINATION

1 The primary imagination I hold to be the living power and prime agent of all human perception, and as a repetition in the finite mind of the eternal act of creation in the infinite I AM.

Samuel Taylor Coleridge (1772–1834) British poet. *Biographia Literaria*, Ch. 13

2 The Fancy is indeed no other than a mode of memory emancipated from the order of time and space.

Samuel Taylor Coleridge *Biographia Literaria*, Ch. 13

3 Art is ruled uniquely by the imagination.

Benedetto Croce (1866–1952) Italian philospher. *Esthetic*, Ch. 1

4 Imagination is more important than knowledge.

Albert Einstein (1879–1955) German-born US physicist. *On Science*

5 She has no imagination and that means no compassion.

Michael Foot (1913–) British Labour politician and journalist. Referring to Margaret Thatcher. Attrib.

6 Were it not for imagination, Sir, a man would be as happy in the arms of a chambermaid as of a Duchess.

Samuel Johnson (1709–84) British lexicographer. *Life of Johnson* (J. Boswell), Vol. III

7 I am certain of nothing but the holiness of the heart's affections and the truth of imagination – what the imagination seizes as beauty must be truth – whether it existed before or not.

John Keats (1795–1821) British poet. Letter to Benjamin Bailey, 22 Nov 1817

8 Picture yourself in a boat on a river with tangerine trees and marmalade skies.
Somebody calls you, you answer quite slowly a girl with kaleidoscope eyes.

John Lennon (1940–80) British rock musician. *Lucy in the Sky with Diamonds* (with Paul McCartney)

9 His imagination resembled the wings of an ostrich. It enabled him to run, though not to soar.

Lord Macaulay (1800–59) British historian. *Essays and Biographies*, 'John Dryden'. *Edinburgh Review*

10 Imagination and fiction make up more than three quarters of our real life.

Simone Weil (1909–43) French philosopher. *Gravity and Grace*

IMITATION

See also originality

1 A lotta cats copy the Mona Lisa, but people still line up to see the original.

Louis Armstrong (1900–71) US jazz trumpeter. When asked whether he objected to people copying his style. Attrib.

2 Imitation is the sincerest form of flattery.

Charles Caleb Colton (?1780–1832) British clergyman and writer. *Lacon*, Vol. I

3 When people are free to do as they please, they usually imitate each other.

Eric Hoffer (1902–83) US writer. *The Passionate State of Mind*

4 A mere copier of nature can never produce anything great.

Joshua Reynolds (1723–92) British portrait painter. Discourse to Students of the Royal Academy, 14 Dec 1770

5 He who resolves never to ransack any mind but his own, will be soon reduced, from mere barrenness, to the poorest of all imitations; he will be obliged to imitate himself, and to repeat what he has before often repeated.

Joshua Reynolds Discourse to Students of the Royal Academy, 10 Dec 1774

6 Of all my verse, like not a single line;
But like my title, for it is not mine.
That title from a better man I stole;
Ah, how much better, had I stol'n the whole!

Robert Louis Stevenson (1850–94) Scottish writer. *Underwoods*, Foreword

7 You will, Oscar, you will.

James Whistler (1834–1903) US painter. Replying to Oscar Wilde's exclamation 'I wish I had said that!'. Attrib.

IMMORTALITY

See also eternity, mortality, posterity

1 I don't want to achieve immortality through my work…I want to achieve it through not dying.

Woody Allen (Allen Stewart Konigsberg; 1935–) US film actor. *Woody Allen and His Comedy* (E. Lax)

2 No young man believes he shall ever die.

William Hazlitt (1778–1830) British essayist. *On the Feeling of Immortality in Youth*

3 He had decided to live for ever or die in the attempt.

Joseph Heller (1923–) US novelist. *Catch-22*, Ch. 3

4 I detest life-insurance agents; they always argue that I shall some day die, which is not so.

Stephen Leacock (1869–1944) English-born Canadian economist and humorist. *Literary Lapses*, 'Insurance. Up to Date'

5 Stuck with placards for 'Deathless', that bitter beer that tastes sweet to its drinkers.

Rainer Maria Rilke (1875–1926) Austrian poet. *Duineser Elegien*, X

6 We feel and know that we are eternal.

Benedict Spinoza (Baruch de Spinoza; 1632–77) Dutch philosopher. *Ethics*

7 A slumber did my spirit seal;
I had no human fears:
She seemed a thing that could not feel
The touch of earthly years.

No motion has she now, no force;
She neither hears nor sees;
Rolled round in earth's diurnal course,
With rocks, and stones, and trees.

William Wordsworth (1770–1850) British poet. *A Slumber did my Spirit seal*

IMPERFECTION

See also mistakes, perfection, weakness

1 Accidents will happen in the best regulated families.

Proverb

2 No man is infallible.

Proverb

3 To err is human.

Proverb

4 Watch and pray, that ye enter not into temptation: the spirit indeed is willing, but the flesh is weak.

Bible: Matthew 26:41

5 He has his talents, his vast and cultivated mind, his vivid imagination, his independence of soul and his high-souled principles of honour. But then – ah, these Buts! Saint Preux never kicked the fireirons, nor made puddings in his tea cup.

Jane Welsh Carlyle (1801–66) The wife of Thomas Carlyle. Referring to her husband, Thomas Carlyle. Letter to a friend, July 1821

6 When you have faults, do not fear to abandon them.

Confucius (K'ung Fu-tzu; 551–479 BC) Chinese philosopher. *Analects*

7 Even imperfection itself may have its ideal or perfect state.

Thomas De Quincey (1785–1859) British writer. *Murder Considered as one of the Fine Arts*

8 We must touch his weaknesses with a delicate hand. There are some faults so nearly allied to excellence, that we can scarce weed out the fault without eradicating the virtue.

Oliver Goldsmith (1728–74) Irish-born British writer. *The Good-Natured Man*, I

9 I'm aggrieved when sometimes even excellent Homer nods.

Horace (Quintus Horatius Flaccus; 65–8 BC) Roman poet. *Ars Poetica*

10 People often say that, by pointing out to a man the faults of his mistress, you succeed only in strengthening his attachment to her, because he does not believe you; yet how much more so if he does!

Marcel Proust (1871–1922) French novelist. *À la recherche du temps perdu: Du côté de chez Swann*

11 We only confess our little faults to persuade people that we have no large ones.

Duc de la Rochefoucauld (1613–80) French writer. *Maximes*, 327

12 If we had no faults of our own, we would not take so much pleasure in noticing those of others.

Duc de la Rochefoucauld *Maximes*, 31

13 Oh. I have got lots of human weaknesses, who hasn't?

Margaret Thatcher (1925–) British politician and prime minister. *The Times*, 1983

14 We are none of us infallible – not even the youngest of us.

William Hepworth Thompson (1810–86) British academic. Referring to G. W. Balfour, who was a junior fellow of Trinity College at the time. *Collections and Recollections* (G. W. E. Russell), Ch. 18

IMPERTINENCE

See also frankness, rudeness

1 He has to learn that petulance is not sarcasm, and that insolence is not invective.

Benjamin Disraeli (1804–81) British statesman. Said of Sir C. Wood. Speech, House of Commons, 16 Dec 1852

2 Must! Is *must* a word to be addressed to princes? Little man, little man! thy father, if he had been alive, durst not have used that word.

Elizabeth I (1533–1603) Queen of England. Said to Robert Cecil, on her death bed. *A Short History of the English People* (J. R. Green), Ch. 7

3 The right people are rude. They can afford to be.

W. Somerset Maugham (1874–1965) British novelist. *Our Betters*, II

4 JUDGE WILLIS. You are extremely offensive, young man.
F. E. SMITH. As a matter of fact, we both are, and the only difference between us is that I am trying to be, and you can't help it.

F. E. Smith (1872–1930) British lawyer and politician. *Frederick Elwin, Earl of Birkenhead* (Lord Birkenhead), Vol. I, Ch. 9

IMPETUOSITY

See also haste, spontaneity

1 In me the need to talk is a primary impulse, and I can't help saying right off what comes to my tongue.

Miguel de Cervantes (1547–1616) Spanish novelist. *Don Quixote*, Pt. I, Ch. 30

2 There are some who speak one moment before they think.

Jean de La Bruyère (1645–96) French satirist. *Les Caractères*

3 Celerity is never more admir'd
Than by the negligent.

William Shakespeare (1564–1616) English dramatist. *Antony and Cleopatra*, III:7

4 A youth to whom was given
So much of earth – so much of heaven,
And such impetuous blood.

William Wordsworth (1770–1850) British poet. *Ruth*

IMPORTANCE

See also triviality

1 Not to be sneezed at.

George Colman, the Younger (1762–1836) British dramatist. *Heir-at-Law*, II:1

2 In heaven an angel is nobody in particular.

George Bernard Shaw (1856–1950) Irish dramatist and critic. *Man and Superman*, 'Maxims for Revolutionists'

3 Art and religion first; then philosophy; lastly science. That is the order of the great subjects of life, that's their order of importance.

Muriel Spark (1918–) British novelist. *The Prime of Miss Jean Brodie*, Ch. 2

IMPOSSIBILITY

See possibility

IMPRESSIONABILITY

See also gullibility

1 She had
A heart – how shall I say? – too soon made glad,
Too easily impressed.

Robert Browning (1812–89) British poet. *My Last Duchess*

2 Like a cushion, he always bore the impress of the last man who sat on him.

David Lloyd George (1863–1945) British Liberal statesman. Referring to Lord Derby. Attrib. in *The Listener*, 7 Sep 1978. This remark is also credited to Earl Haig

3 Give me a girl at an impressionable age, and she is mine for life.

Muriel Spark (1918–) British novelist. *The Prime of Miss Jean Brodie*, Ch. 1

IMPRISONMENT

See also freedom, oppression, slavery

1 A robin redbreast in a cage
Puts all Heaven in a rage.

William Blake (1757–1827) British poet. *Auguries of Innocence*

2 O! dreadful is the check – intense the agony
When the ear begins to hear, and the eye begins to see;
When the pulse begins to throb – the brain to think again –
The soul to feel the flesh, and the flesh to feel the chain.

Emily Brontë (1818–48) British novelist. *The Prisoner*

3 She's only a bird in a gilded cage.

A. J. Lamb (1870–1928) British songwriter. Song title

4 Stone walls do not a prison make,
Nor iron bars a cage.

Richard Lovelace (1618–58) English poet. *To Althea, from Prison*

5 Forget the outside world. Life has different laws in here. This is Campland, an invisible country. It's not in the geography books, or the psychology books or the history books. This is the famous country where ninety-nine men weep while one laughs.

Alexander Solzhenitsyn (1918–) Soviet novelist. *The Love-Girl and the Innocent*, I:3

6 We think caged birds sing, when indeed they cry.

John Webster (1580–1625) English dramatist. *The White Devil*, V:4

7 I never saw a man who looked
With such a wistful eye
Upon that little tent of blue
Which prisoners call the sky.

Oscar Wilde (1854–1900) Irish-born British dramatist. *The Ballad of Reading Gaol*, I:3

8 The Governor was strong upon
The Regulations Act:
The Doctor said that Death was but
A scientific fact:
And twice a day the Chaplain called,
And left a little tract.

Oscar Wilde *The Ballad of Reading Gaol*, III:3

9 Something was dead in each of us,
And what was dead was Hope.

Oscar Wilde *The Ballad of Reading Gaol*, III:31

10 I know not whether Laws be right,
Or whether Laws be wrong;
All that we know who lie in gaol
Is that the wall is strong;
And that each day is like a year,
A year whose days are long.

Oscar Wilde *The Ballad of Reading Gaol*, V:1

11 If this is the way Queen Victoria treats her prisoners, she doesn't deserve to have any.

Oscar Wilde Complaining at having to wait in the rain for transport to take him to prison. Attrib.

IMPROVEMENT

See also progress

1 He so improved the city that he justly boasted that he found it brick and left it marble.

Augustus (63 BC–14 AD) Roman emperor. Referring to Rome. *The Lives of the Caesars* (Suetonius), 'Augustus'

2 I've got to admit it's getting better.
It's a little better all the time.

John Lennon (1940–80) British rock musician. *Getting Better* (with Paul McCartney)

3 It is a stupidity second to none, to busy oneself with the correction of the world.

Molière (Jean Baptiste Poquelin; 1622–73) French dramatist. *Le Misanthrope*, I:1

INATTENTION

1 Thank you for the manuscript; I shall lose no time in reading it.

Benjamin Disraeli (1804–81) British statesman. His customary reply to those who sent him unsolicited manuscripts. *Irreverent Social History* (F. Muir)

2 That should assure us of at least forty-five minutes of undisturbed privacy.

Dorothy Parker (1893–1967) US writer. Pressing a button marked NURSE during a stay in hospital. *The Algonquin Wits* (R. Drennan)

3 Donsmanship…'the art of criticizing without actually listening'.

Stephen Potter (1900–69) British writer. *Lifemanship*, Ch. 6

4 I murdered my grandmother this morning.

Franklin D. Roosevelt (1882–1945) US Democratic president. His habitual greeting to any guest at the White House he suspected of paying no attention to what he said. *Ear on Washington* (D. McClellan)

INCOMPETENCE

1 This island is almost made of coal and surrounded by fish. Only an organizing genius could produce a shortage of coal and fish in Great Britain at the same time.

Aneurin Bevan (1897–1960) British Labour politician. Speech, Blackpool, 18 May 1945

2 The grotesque chaos of a Labour council – a *Labour* council – hiring taxis to scuttle around a city handing out redundancy notices to its own workers.

Neil Kinnock (1942–) British politician. Attacking militant members in Liverpool. Speech, Labour Party Conference, Bournemouth, 1985

3 He really deserves some sort of decoration… a medal inscribed 'For Vaguery in the Field'.

John Osborne (1929–94) British dramatist. *Look Back in Anger*, I

4 Work is accomplished by those employees who have not yet reached their level of incompetence.

Laurence J. Peter (1919–90) Canadian writer. *The Peter Principle*

5 Madame, there you sit with that magnificent

instrument between your legs, and all you can do is *scratch* it!

Arturo Toscanini (1867–1957) Italian conductor. Rebuking an incompetent woman cellist. Attrib.

6 His ideas of first-aid stopped short at squirting soda-water.

P. G. Wodehouse (1881–1975) British humorous novelist. *My Man Jeeves*, 'Doing Clarence a Bit of Good'

INDECISION

See also uncertainty

1 I will have nothing to do with a man who can blow hot and cold with the same breath.

Aesop (6th century BC) Reputed Greek writer of fables. *Fables*, 'The Man and the Satyr'

2 Nothing is so exhausting as indecision, and nothing is so futile.

Bertrand Russell (1872–1970) British philosopher. Attrib.

3 I must have a prodigious quantity of mind; it takes me as much as a week, sometimes, to make it up.

Mark Twain (Samuel Langhorne Clemens; 1835–1910) US writer. *The Innocents Abroad*, Ch. 7

INDEPENDENCE

See also self-reliance, society

1 I'm short enough and ugly enough to succeed on my own.

Woody Allen (Allen Stewart Konigsberg; 1935–) US film actor. *Play It Again Sam*

2 When in the course of human events, it becomes necessary for one people to dissolve the political bonds which have connected them with another, and to assume among the powers of the earth the separate and equal station to which the laws of nature and of Nature's God entitle them, a decent respect to the opinions of mankind requires that they should declare the causes which impel them to the separation.

Thomas Jefferson (1743–1826) US statesman. Declaration of Independence, Preamble bonds

3 I think it much better that...every man paddle his own canoe.

Captain Frederick Marryat (1792–1848) British novelist. *Settlers in Canada*, Ch. 8

INDIFFERENCE

See also insensitivity

1 But what is past my help is past my care.

Francis Beaumont (1584–1616) English dramatist. With John Fletcher. *The Double Marriage*, I:1

2 Nothing is so fatal to religion as indifference, which is, at least, half infidelity.

Edmund Burke (1729–97) British politician. Letter to William Smith, 29 Jan 1795

3 Sir, I view the proposal to hold an international exhibition at San Francisco with an equanimity bordering on indifference.

W. S. Gilbert (1836–1911) British dramatist. *Gilbert, His Life and Strife* (Hesketh Pearson)

4 It's no go the picture palace, it's no go the stadium,
It's no go the country cot with a pot of pink geraniums,
It's no go the Government grants, it's no go the elections,
Sit on your arse for fifty years and hang your hat on a pension.

Louis MacNeice (1907–63) Irish-born British poet. *Bagpipe Music*

5 At length the morn and cold indifference came.

Nicholas Rowe (1674–1718) English dramatist. *The Fair Penitent*, I:1

6 I don't care a twopenny damn what becomes of the ashes of Napoleon Bonaparte.

Duke of Wellington (1769–1852) British general and statesman. Attrib.

7 I hear it was charged against me that I sought to destroy institutions,
But really I am neither for nor against institutions.

Walt Whitman (1819–92) US poet. *I Hear It was Charged against Me*

INDIVIDUALITY

See also difference, opinions, taste

1 Here's tae us wha's like us?
Gey few, and they're a' deid.

Anonymous Scottish toast.

2 Nature made him, and then broke the mould.

Ludovico Ariosto (1474–1533) Italian poet. Referring to Charlemagne's paladin, Roland. *Orlando furioso*

3 We are the party of the individual because we are the party of the community.

Tony Blair (1953–) British Labour politician. *The Independent*, 5 Oct 1994

4 It is the common wonder of all men, how among so many million of faces, there should be none alike.

Thomas Browne (1605–82) English physician and writer. *Religio Medici*, Pt. II

5 We boil at different degrees.

Ralph Waldo Emerson (1803–82) US poet and essayist. *Society and Solitude*, 'Eloquence'

INDOCTRINATION

See also education

1 Their teacher had advised them not to read Tolstoy novels, because they were very long and would easily confuse the clear ideas which they had learned from reading critical studies of him.

Alexander Solzhenitsyn (1918–) Soviet novelist. *The First Circle*, Ch. 40

2 This universal, obligatory force-feeding with lies is now the most agonizing aspect of existence in our country – worse than all our material miseries, worse than any lack of civil liberties.

Alexander Solzhenitsyn *Letter to Soviet Leaders*, 6

3 For us, the tasks of education in socialism were closely integrated with those of fighting. Ideas that enter the mind under fire remain there securely and for ever.

Leon Trotsky (Lev Davidovich Bronstein; 1879–1940) Russian revolutionary. *My Life*, Ch. 35

INDULGENCE

1 Love is a boy, by poets styl'd,
Then spare the rod, and spoil the child.

Samuel Butler (1612–80) English satirist. *Hudibras*, Pt. II

2 Every luxury was lavished on you – atheism, breast-feeding, circumcision. I had to make my own way.

Joe Orton (1933–67) British dramatist. *Loot*, I

INDUSTRIAL RELATIONS

See also diplomacy, strikes

1 British management doesn't seem to understand the importance of the human factor.

Charles, Prince of Wales (1948–) Eldest son of Elizabeth II. Speech, Parliamentary and Scientific Committee lunch, 21 Feb 1979

2 Industrial relations are like sexual relations. It's better between two consenting parties.

Vic Feather (1908–76) British trade-union leader. *Guardian Weekly*, 8 Aug 1976

3 It might be said that it is the ideal of the employer to have production without employees and the ideal of the employee is to have income without work.

E. F. Schumacher (1911–77) German-born economist. *The Observer*, 'Sayings of the Week', 4 May 1975

INFERIORITY

See also equality, mediocrity

1 I just met X in the street, I stopped for a moment to exchange ideas, and now I feel like a complete idiot.

Heinrich Heine (1797–1856) German poet and writer. *Autant en apportent les mots* (Pedrazzini)

2 Wherever an inferiority complex exists, there is a good reason for it. There is always something inferior there, although not just where we persuade ourselves that it is.

Carl Gustav Jung (1875–1961) Swiss psychoanalyst. Interview, 1943

3 It is an infallible sign of the second-rate in nature and intellect to make use of everything and everyone.

Ada Beddington Leverson (1862–1933) British writer. *The Limit*

4 There's no such thing as a bad Picasso, but some are less good than others.

Pablo Picasso (1881–1973) Spanish painter. *Come to Judgment* (A. Whitman)

5 No one can make you feel inferior without your consent.

Eleanor Roosevelt (1884–1962) US writer and lecturer. *This is My Story*

6 A king of shreds and patches.

William Shakespeare (1564–1616) English dramatist. *Hamlet*, III:4

INFINITY

1 The Desire of Man being Infinite, the possession is Infinite, and himself Infinite.

William Blake (1757–1827) British poet. *There is no Natural Religion*

2 I cannot help it; – in spite of myself, infinity torments me.

Alfred de Musset (1810–57) French dramatist and poet. *L'Espoir en Dieu*

INFLEXIBILITY

See also determination, stubbornness

1 Whenever you accept our views we shall be in full agreement with you.

Moshe Dayan (1915–81) Israeli general. Said to Cyrus Vance during Arab-Israeli negotiations. *The Observer*, 'Sayings of the Week', 14 Aug 1977

2 You cannot shake hands with a clenched fist.

Indira Gandhi (1917–84) Indian stateswoman. Remark at a press conference, New Delhi, 19 Oct 1971

3 U-turn if you want to. The lady's not for turning.

Margaret Thatcher (1925–) British politician and prime minister. Speech, Conservative Conference, 1980

4 Minds like beds always made up,
(more stony than a shore)
unwilling or unable.

William Carlos Williams (1883–1963) US poet. *Patterson*, I, Preface

INFLUENCE

See also inspiration, power

1 Though Rome's gross yoke
Drops off, no more to be endured,
Her teaching is not so obscured
By errors and perversities,
That no truth shines athwart the lies.

Robert Browning (1812–89), British poet. *Christmas Eve*, XI

2 How to Win Friends and Influence People.

Dale Carnegie (1888–1955) US lecturer and writer. Book title

3 He who influences the thought of his times, influences all the times that follow. He has made his impress on eternity.

Hypatia (*c.* 370–415) Greek mathematician. *Little Journeys to the Homes of Great Teachers* (Elbert Hubbard)

4 The proper time to influence the character of a child is about a hundred years before he is born.

Dean Inge (1860–1954) British churchman. *The Observer*, 21 June, 1929

5 We have met too late. You are too old for me to have any effect on you.

James Joyce (1882–1941) Irish novelist. On meeting W. B. Yeats. *James Joyce* (R. Ellmann)

6 Practical men, who believe themselves to be quite exempt from any intellectual influences, are usually the slaves of some defunct economist. Madmen in authority, who hear voices in the air, are distilling their frenzy from some academic scribbler of a few years back.

John Maynard Keynes (1883–1946) British economist. *The General Theory of Employment, Interest and Money*, Bk. VI, Ch. 24

7 The great man...walks across his century and leaves the marks of his feet all over it, ripping out the dates on his goloshes as he passes.

Stephen Leacock (1869–1944) English-born Canadian economist and humorist. *Literary Lapses*, 'The Life of John Smith'

8 So you're the little woman who wrote the book that made this great war!

Abraham Lincoln (1809–65) US statesman. Said on meeting Harriet Beecher Stowe, the author of *Uncle Tom's Cabin* (1852), which stimulated opposition to slavery before the US Civil War. *Abraham Lincoln: The War Years* (Carl Sandburg), Vol. II, Ch. 39

9 Athens holds sway over all Greece; I dominate Athens; my wife dominates me; our newborn son dominates her.

Themistocles (c. 528–462 BC) Athenian statesman. Explaining an earlier remark to the effect that his young son ruled all Greece. Attrib.

10 The hand that rocks the cradle
Is the hand that rules the world.

William Ross Wallace (1819–81) US poet and songwriter. *John o'London's Treasure Trove*

11 The man who can dominate a London dinner-table can dominate the world.

Oscar Wilde (1854–1900) Irish-born British dramatist. Attrib. by R. Aldington in his edition of Wilde

INGRATITUDE

1 Never look a gift horse in the mouth.

Proverb

2 And having looked to government for bread, on the very first scarcity they will turn and bite the hand that fed them.

Edmund Burke (1729–97) British politician. *Thoughts and Details on Scarcity*

3 Our gratitude to most benefactors is the same as our feeling for dentists who have pulled our teeth. We acknowledge the good they have done and the evil from which they have delivered us, but we remember the pain they occasioned and do not love them very much.

Nicolas Chamfort (1741–94) French writer. *Maximes et pensées*

4 Blow, blow, thou winter wind,
Thou art not so unkind
As man's ingratitude.

William Shakespeare (1564–1616) English dramatist. *As You Like It*, II:7

5 Ingratitude, thou marble-hearted fiend,
More hideous when thou show'st thee in a child
Than the sea-monster!

William Shakespeare *King Lear* I:4

6 I hate ingratitude more in a man
Than lying, vainness, babbling drunkenness,
Or any taint of vice whose strong corruption
Inhabits our frail blood.

William Shakespeare *Twelfth Night*, III:4

INJUSTICE

1 Give a dog a bad name and hang him.

Proverb

2 Those who have had no share in the good fortunes of the mighty often have a share in their misfortunes.

Bertolt Brecht (1898–1956) German dramatist. *The Caucasian Chalk Circle*

3 When one has been threatened with a great injustice, one accepts a smaller as a favour.

Jane Welsh Carlyle (1801–66) The wife of Thomas Carlyle. *Journal*, 21 Nov 1855

4 'No, no!' said the Queen. 'Sentence first – verdict afterwards.'

Lewis Carroll (Charles Lutwidge Dodgson; 1832–98) British writer. *Alice's Adventures in Wonderland*, Ch. 12

5 I feel as a horse must feel when the beautiful cup is given to the jockey.

Edgar Degas (1834–1917) French artist. On seeing one of his pictures sold at auction. Attrib.

6 To disarm the strong and arm the weak would be to change the social order which it's my job to preserve. Justice is the means by which established injustices are sanctioned.

Anatole France (Jacques Anatole François Thibault; 1844–1924) French writer. *Crainquebille*

7 Undeservedly you will atone for the sins of your fathers.

Horace (Quintus Horatius Flaccus; 65–8 BC) Roman poet. *Odes*, III

8 We was robbed!

Joe Jacobs (1896–1940) US boxing manager. Complaining to the audience when the heavyweight title of Max Schmeling, whom he managed, was passed to Jack Sharkey. Attrib.

9 How could God do this to me after all I have done for him?

Louis XIV (1638–1715) French king. On receiving news of the French army's defeat at the Battle of Blenheim. *Saint-Simon at Versailles* (L. Norton)

10 The government burns down whole cities while the people are forbidden to light lamps.

Mao Tse-Tung (1893–1976) Chinese communist leader. Attrib.

11 That in the captain's but a choleric word
Which in the soldier is flat blasphemy.

William Shakespeare (1564–1616) English dramatist. *Measure for Measure*, II:2

12 I am a man
More sinn'd against than sinning.

William Shakespeare *King Lear*, III:2

13 He was quite sure that he had been wronged. Not to be wronged is to forgo the first privilege of goodness.

H. G. Wells (1866–1946) British writer. *Bealby*, Pt. IV, Ch. 1

14 There is something utterly nauseating about a system of society which pays a harlot 25 times as much as it pays its Prime Minister, 250 times as much as it pays its Members of Parliament, and 500 times as much as it pays some of its ministers of religion.

Harold Wilson (1916–95) British politician and prime minister. Referring to the case of Christine Keeler. Speech, House of Commons, June 1963

INNOCENCE

See also conscience, ignorance

1 Now I am ashamed of confessing that I have nothing to confess.

Fanny Burney (Frances Burney D'Arblay; 1752–1840) British novelist. *Evelina*, Letter 59

2 Now my innocence begins to weigh me down.

Jean Racine (1639–99) French dramatist. *Andromaque*, III:1

Innocence of childhood

See also age, children, ignorance

3 'But the Emperor has nothing on at all!' cried a little child.

Hans Christian Andersen (1805–75) Danish writer. *The Emperor's New Clothes*

4 No, it is not only our fate but our business to lose innocence, and once we have lost that, it is futile to attempt a picnic in Eden.

Elizabeth Bowen (1899–1973) Irish novelist. In *Orion III*, 'Out of a Book'

5 Ralph wept for the end of innocence, the darkness of man's heart, and the fall through the air of the true, wise friend called Piggy.

William Golding (1911–93) British novelist. *Lord of the Flies*, Ch. 12

6 I remember, I remember,
The fir trees dark and high;
I used to think their slender tops
Were close against the sky:
It was a childish ignorance,
But now 'tis little joy
To know I'm farther off from heav'n
Than when I was a boy.

Thomas Hood (1799–1845) British poet. *I Remember*

7 Credulity is the man's weakness, but the child's strength.

Charles Lamb (1775–1834) British essayist. *Essays of Elia*, 'Witches and other Night Fears'

8 I'd the upbringing a nun would envy and that's the truth. Until I was fifteen I was more familiar with Africa than my own body.

Joe Orton (1933–67) British dramatist. *Entertaining Mr Sloane*, I

9 And the wild boys innocent as strawberries.

Dylan Thomas (1914–53) Welsh poet. *The hunchback in the park*

10 We live in our own world,
A world that is too small
For you to stoop and enter
Even on hands and knees,
The adult subterfuge.

R. S. Thomas *Song at the Year's Turning*, 'Children's Song'

11 There was a time when meadow, grove, and stream,
The earth, and every common sight,
To me did seem
Apparelled in celestial light,
The glory and the freshness of a dream.

William Wordsworth (1770–1850) British poet. *Ode. Intimations of Immortality*, I

INNOVATION

See also conservatism, novelty, originality, progress

1 He that will not apply new remedies must expect new evils: for time is the greatest innovator.

Francis Bacon (1561–1626) English philosopher. *Essays*, 'Of Innovations'

2 I once knew a chap who had a system of just hanging the baby on the clothes line to dry and he was greatly admired by his fellow citizens for having discovered a wonderful innovation on changing a diaper.

Damon Runyon (1884–1946) US writer. *Short Takes*, 'Diaper Dexterity'

INNUENDO

See also meaning

1 There was an old man of Boulogne
Who sang a most topical song.
It wasn't the words
That frightened the birds,
But the horrible double-entendre.

Anonymous

2 I'm one of the ruins that Cromwell knocked about a bit.

Marie Lloyd (1870–1922) British music-hall singer. Song title

3 Where more is meant than meets the ear.

John Milton (1608–74) English poet. *Il Penseroso*

INSENSITIVITY

See also hurt, indifference

1 Miss Buss and Miss Beale
Cupid's darts do not feel.
How different from us,
Miss Beale and Miss Buss.

Anonymous Written about the headmistresses of North London Collegiate School and Cheltenham Ladies' College, respectively

2 'There's been an accident' they said,
'Your servant's cut in half; he's dead!'
'Indeed!' said Mr Jones, 'and please
Send me the half that's got my keys.'

Harry Graham (1874–1936) British writer. *Ruthless Rhymes for Heartless Homes*, 'Mr. Jones'

3 Just as the meanest and most vicious deeds require spirit and talent, so even the greatest deeds require a certain insensitiveness which on other occasions is called stupidity.

Georg Christoph Lichtenberg (1742–99) German physicist and writer. *Aphorisms*

4 One would have to have a heart of stone to read the death of Little Nell without laughing.

Oscar Wilde (1854–1900) Irish-born British dramatist. Lecturing upon Dickens. *Lives of the Wits* (H. Pearson)

INSIGNIFICANCE

See also triviality

1 There are some people who leave impressions not so lasting as the imprint of an oar upon the water.

Kate Chopin (1851–1904) US writer. *The Awakening*, Ch. 34

2 She was one of those indispensables of whom one makes the discovery, when they are gone, that one can get on quite as well without them.

Aldous Huxley (1894–1964) British novelist. *Mortal Coils*, 'Nuns at Luncheon'

INSINCERITY

See also hypocrisy

1 Experience teaches you that the man who looks you straight in the eye, particularly if he adds a firm handshake, is hiding something.

Clifton Fadiman (1904–) US writer. *Enter, Conversing*

2 He who praises everybody praises nobody.

Samuel Johnson (1709–84) British lexicographer. *Life of Johnson* (J. Boswell), Vol. III

3 Went to hear Mrs Turner's daughter…play on the harpsichon; but, Lord! it was enough to make any man sick to hear her; yet was I forced to commend her highly.

Samuel Pepys (1633–1703) English diarist. *Diary*, 1 May 1663

4 Most friendship is feigning, most loving mere folly.

William Shakespeare (1564–1616) English dramatist. *As You Like It*, II:7

INSPIRATION

1 A spur in the head is worth two in the heel.

Proverb

2 Ninety per cent of inspiration is perspiration.

Proverb

3 I dare not alter these things; they come to me from above.

Alfred Austin (1835–1913) British poet. When accused of writing ungrammatical verse. *A Number of People* (E. Marsh)

4 That I make poetry and give pleasure (if I give pleasure) are because of you.

Horace (Quintus Horatius Flaccus; 65–8 BC) Roman poet. *Odes*, IV

5 Biting my truant pen, beating myself for spite: 'Fool!' said my Muse to me, 'look in thy heart and write.'

Philip Sidney (1554–86) English poet and courtier. Sonnet, *Astrophel and Stella*

6 I did not write it. God wrote it. I merely did his dictation.

Harriet Beecher Stowe (1811–96) US novelist. Referring to *Uncle Tom's Cabin*. Attrib.

7 The true God, the mighty God, is the God of ideas.

Alfred de Vigny (1797–1863) French writer. *La Bouteille à la mer*

INSULTS

See also actors, criticism, politicians, rudeness

1 Sticks and stones may break my bones, but words will never hurt me.

Proverb

2 I don't want you here – now sod off!

Princess Anne (1950–) The Princess Royal, only daughter of Elizabeth II. Remark, Jan 1987

3 Lloyd George could not see a belt without hitting below it.

Margot Asquith (1865–1945) The second wife of Herbert Asquith. *The Autobiography of Margot Asquith*

4 She was a woman of mean understanding, little information, and uncertain temper.

Jane Austen (1775–1817) British novelist. *Pride and Prejudice*, Ch. 1

5 I have known many an instance of a man writing a letter and forgetting to sign his name, but this is the only instance I have ever known of a man signing his name and forgetting to write the letter.

Henry Ward Beecher (1813–87) US Congregational minister. Said on receiving a note containing the single word: 'Fool'. *The Best Stories in the World* (T. Masson)

6 Of course we all know that Morris was a wonderful all-round man, but the act of walking round him has always tired me.

Max Beerbohm (1872–1956) British writer. Referring to William Morris. *Conversations with Max* (S. N. Behrman)

7 Come in, you Anglo-Saxon swine
And drink of my Algerian wine.
'Twill turn your eyeballs black and blue,
And damn well good enough for you.

Brendan Behan (1923–64) Irish playwright. Painted as an advert on the window of a Paris café (the owner of which could not speak English). *My Life with Brendan* (B. Behan)

8 So boring you fall asleep halfway through her name.

Alan Bennett (1934–) British playwright. Referring to the Greek writer Arianna Stassinopoulos. *The Observer*, 18 Sept 1983

9 I mock thee not, though I by thee am mockèd;
Thou call'st me madman, but I call thee blockhead.

William Blake (1757–1827) British poet. *To Flaxman*

10 If there is anyone here whom I have not insulted, I beg his pardon.

Johannes Brahms (1833–97) German composer. Said on leaving a gathering of friends. *Brahms* (P. Latham)

11 Macaulay is well for a while, but one wouldn't *live* under Niagara.

Thomas Carlyle (1795–1881) Scottish historian and essayist. *Notebook* (R. M. Milnes)

12 An injury is much sooner forgotten than an insult.

Earl of Chesterfield (1694–1773) English statesman. Letter to his son, 9 Oct 1746

13 The only time in his life he ever put up a fight was when we asked him for his resignation.

Georges Clemenceau (1841–1929) French statesman. Referring to Marshal Joffre. *Here I Lie* (A.M. Thomson)

14 The Cat, the Rat, and Lovell our dog
Rule all England under a hog.

William Collingbourne (d. 1484) English landowner. The cat was Sir William Catesby; the rat Sir Richard Ratcliffe; the dog Lord Lovell, who had a dog on his crest. The wild boar refers to the emblem of Richard III. *Chronicles* (R. Holinshed), III

15 Your dexterity seems a happy compound of the smartness of an attorney's clerk and the intrigue of a Greek of the lower empire.

Benjamin Disraeli (1804–81) British statesman. Speaking to Lord Palmerston. Attrib.

16 Good-morning, gentlemen both.

Elizabeth I (1533–1603) Queen of England. When addressing a group of eighteen tailors. *Sayings of Queen Elizabeth* (Chamberlin)

17 A semi-house-trained polecat.

Michael Foot (1913–) British Labour politician and journalist. Referring to Norman Tebbit. Speech, House of Commons

18 Like being savaged by a dead sheep.

Denis Healey (1917–) British Labour politician. Referring to the attack launched by Geoffrey Howe upon his Budget proposals. *The Listener*, 21 Dec 1978

19 Do you call that thing under your hat a head?

Ludwig Holberg (1684–1754) Danish dramatist. Reply to the jibe, 'Do you call that thing on your head a hat?'. *Anekdotenschatz* (H. Hoffmeister)

20 In a disastrous fire in President Reagan's library both books were destroyed. And the real tragedy is that he hadn't finished colouring one.

Jonathan Hunt (1938–) New Zealand politician. *The Observer*, 30 Aug 1981

21 Sir, your wife, under pretence of keeping a bawdy-house, is a receiver of stolen goods.

Samuel Johnson (1709–84) British lexicographer. An example of the customary badinage between travellers on the Thames. *Life of Johnson* (J. Boswell), Vol. IV

22 Calumnies are answered best with silence.

Ben Jonson (1573–1637) English dramatist. *Volpone*, II:2

23 They travel best in gangs, hanging around like clumps of bananas, thick skinned and yellow.

Neil Kinnock (1942–) British politician. Referring to Tory critics. *The Observer*, 'Sayings of the Week', 22 Feb 1987

24 She only went to Venice because somebody told her she could walk down the middle of the street.

Neil Kinnock Referring to Margaret Thatcher who attended a meeting in Venice just before the 1987 election. Speech, Leeds, 9 June 1987

25 Play us a medley of your hit.

Oscar Levant (1906–72) US pianist and actor. Replying to George Gershwin's barb 'If you had it all over again, would you fall in love with yourself?'. Attrib.

26 I'm sure he had a fork in the other.

Ada Beddington Leverson (1862–1933) British writer. Reply when told by Oscar Wilde of a devoted *apache* (Parisian gangster) who used to follow him with a knife in one hand. Attrib.

27 When they circumcised Herbert Samuel they threw away the wrong bit.

David Lloyd George (1863–1945) British Liberal statesman. Attrib. in *The Listener*, 7 Sept 1978

28 The answer is in the plural and they bounce.

Edwin Lutyens (1869–1944) British architect. Attrib.

29 From the moment I picked up your book until I laid it down, I was convulsed with laughter. Some day I intend reading it.

Groucho Marx (Julius Marx; 1895–1977) US comedian. *The Last Laugh* (S. J. Perelman)

30 I have forgotten more law than you ever knew, but allow me to say, I have not forgotten much.

John Maynard (1602–90) English judge. Replying to Judge Jeffreys' suggestion that he was so old he had forgotten the law.

31 And I don't feel the attraction of the Kennedys at all...I don't think they are Christians; they may be Catholics but they are not Christians, in my belief anyway.

Mary McCarthy (1912–89) US novelist. *The Observer*, 14 Oct 1979

32 Peel's smile: like the silver plate on a coffin.

Daniel O'Connell (1775–1847) Irish politician. Referring to Sir Robert Peel; quoting J. P. Curran (1750–1817). *Hansard*, 26 Feb 1835

33 I remember coming across him at the Grand Canyon and finding him peevish, refusing to admire it or even look at it properly. He was jealous of it.

J. B. Priestley (1894–1984) British novelist. Referring to George Bernard Shaw. *Thoughts In the Wilderness*

34 Thou whoreson zed! thou unnecessary letter!

William Shakespeare (1564–1616) English dramatist. *King Lear*, II:2

35 He has occasional flashes of silence, that make his conversation perfectly delightful.

Sydney Smith (1771–1845) British clergyman and essayist. Referring to Lord Macaulay. *Memoir* (Lady Holland)

36 You silly moo.

Johnny Speight (1920–) British television scriptwriter. *Till Death Do Us Part*

37 Okie use' to mean you was from Oklahoma. Now it means you're scum. Don't mean nothing itself, it's the way they say it.

John Steinbeck (1902–68) US novelist. *The Grapes of Wrath*, Ch. 18

38 I dunno. Maybe it's that tally-ho lads attitude. You know, there'll always be an England, all that Empire crap they dish out. But I never could cop Poms.

Jeff Thomson Australian cricketer. Remark, Oct 1987

39 It's too late to apologize.

Arturo Toscanini (1867–1957) Italian conductor. Retort to the insult 'Nuts to you!' shouted at him by a player he had just ordered from the stage during rehearsal. *The Humor of Music* (L. Humphrey)

40 A triumph of the embalmer's art.

Gore Vidal (1925–) US novelist. Referring to Ronald Reagan. *The Observer*, 26 Apr 1981

41 A typical triumph of modern science to find the only part of Randolph that was not malignant and remove it.

Evelyn Waugh (1903–66) British novelist. Remarking upon the news that Randolph Churchill had had a noncancerous lung removed. Attrib.

42 Perhaps not, but then you can't call yourself a great work of nature.

James Whistler (1834–1903) US painter. Responding to a sitter's complaint that his portrait was not a great work of art. *Whistler Stories* (D. Seitz)

43 I do not mind the Liberals, still less do I mind the Country Party, calling me a bastard. In some circumstances I am only doing my job if they do. But I hope you will not publicly call me a bastard, as some bastards in the Caucus have.

Gough Whitlam (1916–) Australian statesman. Speech to the Australian Labor Party, 9 June 1974

44 You have Van Gogh's ear for music.

Billy Wilder (Samuel Wilder; 1906–) Austrian-born US film director. Said to Cliff Osmond. Attrib.

45 I have always said about Tony that he immatures with age.

Harold Wilson (1916–95) British politician and prime minister. Referring to Anthony Wedgwood Benn. *The Chariot of Israel*

46 If I had had to choose between him and a cockroach as a companion for a walking-tour, the cockroach would have had it by a short head.

P. G. Wodehouse (1881–1975) British humorous novelist. *My Man Jeeves*, 'The Spot of Art'

INTEGRITY

See also honesty, morality, principles, righteousness, self, sincerity

1 Be so true to thyself, as thou be not false to others.

Francis Bacon (1561–1626) English philosopher. *Essays*, 'Of Wisdom for a Man's Self'

2 Caesar's wife must be above suspicion.

Julius Caesar (100–44 BC) Roman general and statesman. Said in justification of his divorce from Pompeia, after she was unwittingly involved in a scandal. *Lives*, 'Julius Caesar' (Plutarch)

3 I cannot and will not cut my conscience to fit this year's fashions, even though I long ago came to the conclusion that I was not a political person and could have no comfortable place in any political group.

Lillian Hellman (1905–84) US dramatist. Letter to the US

House of Representatives Committee on Un-American Activities, *The Nation*, 31 May 1952

4 Integrity without knowledge is weak and useless, and knowledge without integrity is dangerous and dreadful.

Samuel Johnson (1709–84) British lexicographer. *Rasselas*, Ch. 41

5 It is necessary to the happiness of man that he be mentally faithful to himself. Infidelity does not consist in believing, or in disbelieving, it consists in professing to believe what one does not believe.

Thomas Paine (1737–1809) British writer. *The Age of Reason*, Pt. I

6 Neither a borrower nor a lender be;
For loan oft loses both itself and friend,
And borrowing dulls the edge of husbandry.
This above all: to thine own self be true,
And it must follow, as the night the day,
Thou canst not then be false to any man.

William Shakespeare (1564–1616) English dramatist. *Hamlet*, I:3

7 My strength is as the strength of ten,
Because my heart is pure.

Alfred, Lord Tennyson (1809–92) British poet. *Sir Galahad*

INTELLECT

See also intelligence, mind, thinking

1 We should take care not to make the intellect our god; it has, of course, powerful muscles, but no personality.

Albert Einstein (1879–1955) German-born US physicist. *Out of My Later Life*, 51

2 The voice of the intellect is a soft one, but it does not rest till it has gained a hearing.

Sigmund Freud (1856–1939) Austrian psychoanalyst. *The Future of an Illusion*

3 Man is an intellectual animal, and therefore an everlasting contradiction to himself. His senses centre in himself, his ideas reach to the ends of the universe; so that he is torn in pieces between the two, without a possibility of its ever being otherwise.

William Hazlitt (1778–1830) British essayist. *Characteristics*

4 We are thinking beings, and we cannot exclude the intellect from participating in any of our functions.

William James (1842–1910) US psychologist and philosopher. *Varieties of Religious Experience*

5 The highest intellects, like the tops of mountains, are the first to catch and to reflect the dawn.

Lord Macaulay (1800–59) British historian. *Historical Essays Contributed to the 'Edinburgh Review'*, 'Sir James Mackintosh'

6 The higher the voice the smaller the intellect.

Ernest Newman (1868–1959) British music critic. Attrib.

7 Intellect is invisible to the man who has none.

Arthur Schopenhauer (1788–1860) German philosopher. *Aphorismen zur Lebensweisheit*

INTELLECTUALS

See also academics

1 An intellectual is a man who doesn't know how to park a bike.

Spiro Agnew (1918–96) US politician. Attrib.

2 To the man-in-the-street, who, I'm sorry to say
Is a keen observer of life,
The word Intellectual suggests straight away
A man who's untrue to his wife.

W. H. Auden (1907–73) British poet. *Note on Intellectuals*

3 I've been called many things, but never an intellectual.

Tallulah Bankhead (1903–68) US actress. *Tallulah*, Ch. 15

4 Intellectuals are people who believe that ideas are of more importance than values. That is to say, their own ideas and other people's values.

Gerald Brenan (Edward Fitzgerald Brenan; 1894–1987) British writer. *Thoughts in a Dry Season*, 'Life'

5 An intellectual is someone whose mind watches itself.

Albert Camus (1913–60) French existentialist writer. *Notebooks*, 1935–42

6 You will hear more good things on the outside of a stagecoach from London to Oxford than if you were to pass a twelvemonth with the undergraduates, or heads of colleges, of that famous university.

William Hazlitt (1778–1830) British essayist. *The Ignorance of the Learned*

7 The trouble with me is, I belong to a vanishing race. I'm one of the intellectuals.

Robert E. Sherwood (1896–1955) US writer and dramatist. *The Petrified Forest*

8 Do you think it pleases a man when he looks into a woman's eyes and sees a reflection of the British Museum Reading Room?

Muriel Spark (1918–) British novelist. *The Wit of Women* (L. and M. Cowan)

9 What is a highbrow? It is a man who has found something more interesting than women.

Edgar Wallace (1875–1932) British thriller writer. Interview

INTELLIGENCE

See also intellect, knowledge, mind, perception, thinking, understanding, wisdom

1 The intelligent are to the intelligentsia what a man is to a gent.

Stanley Baldwin (1867–1947) British statesman. Attrib.

2 I never heard tell of any clever man that came

of entirely stupid people.

Thomas Carlyle (1795–1881) Scottish historian and essayist. Speech, Edinburgh, 2 Apr 1886

3 Intelligence is almost useless to the person whose only quality it is.

Alexis Carrel (1873–1944) French surgeon. *Man, the Unknown*

4 One wants to mutter deeply that apart from having two good legs I also have two good degrees and it is just possible that I do know what I'm talking about.

Edwina Currie (1946–) British politician. Remark, Nov 1986

5 A really intelligent man feels what other men only know.

Baron de Montesquieu (1689–1755) French writer. *Essai sur les causes qui peuvent affecter les esprits et les caractères*

6 The more intelligence one has the more people one finds original. Commonplace people see no difference between men.

Blaise Pascal (1623–62) French philosopher and mathematician. *Pensées*, I

7 The height of cleverness is to be able to conceal it.

Duc de la Rochefoucauld (1613–80) French writer. *Maximes*, 245

8 All the unhappy marriages come from the husbands having brains. What good are brains to a man? They only unsettle him.

P. G. Wodehouse (1881–1975) British humorous novelist. *The Adventures of Sally*

INTERRUPTIONS

1 On awaking he…instantly and eagerly wrote down the lines that are here preserved. At this moment he was unfortunately called out by a person on business from Porlock.

Samuel Taylor Coleridge (1772–1834) British poet. *Kubla Khan* (preliminary note)

2 As I was saying the other day.

Luis Ponce de Léon (1527–91) Spanish monk. Said on resuming a lecture interrupted by five years' imprisonment

3 And now excuse me while I interrupt myself.

Murray Walker British sports commentator. *The Independent*, 22 Dec 1994

4 Mr Wordsworth is never interrupted.

Mary Wordsworth (1770–1850) Wife of William Wordsworth. Rebuking John Keats for interrupting a long monologue by William Wordsworth. Attrib.

INTRIGUE

1 Ay, now the plot thickens very much upon us.

Duke of Buckingham (1628–87) English politician. *The Rehearsal*, III:1

2 Everybody was up to something, especially, of course, those who were up to nothing.

Noël Coward (1899–1973) British dramatist. *Future Indefinite*

INTRODUCTIONS

1 'You look a little shy; let me introduce you to that leg of mutton,' said the Red Queen. 'Alice – Mutton; Mutton – Alice.'

Lewis Carroll (Charles Lutwidge Dodgson; 1832–98) British writer. *Through the Looking-Glass*, Ch. 9

2 Do you suppose I could buy back my introduction to you?

Groucho Marx (Julius Marx; 1895–1977) US comedian. *Monkey Business*

INVITATIONS

See also summons

1 'Will you walk into my parlour?' said a spider to a fly:
''Tis the prettiest little parlour that ever you did spy.'

Mary Howitt (1799–1888) British writer. *The Spider and the Fly*

2 Come into the garden, Maud,
For the black bat, night, has flown,
Come into the garden, Maud,
I am here at the gate alone.

Alfred, Lord Tennyson (1809–92) British poet. *Maud*, I

3 I always did like a man in uniform. And that one fits you grand. Why don't you come up sometime and see me?

Mae West (1892–1980) US actress. Often misquoted as 'Come up and see me some time'. *She Done Him Wrong*, film 1933

IRELAND

See also Britain, Irish

1 It's my view that the peace process will be irreversible and for good.

Gerry Adams (1948–) Irish politician. Referring to John Major's Anglo-Irish peace initiative. *The Times*, 8 Oct 1994

2 I met wid Napper Tandy, and he took me by the hand,
And he said, 'How's poor ould Ireland, and how does she stand?'
She's the most disthressful country that iver yet was seen,
For they're hangin' men an' women there for the wearin' o' the Green.

Anonymous *The Wearin' o' the Green*

3 A bit of shooting takes your mind off your troubles – it makes you forget the cost of living.

Brendan Behan (1923–64) Irish playwright. *The Hostage*

4 Ulster will fight; Ulster will be right.

Lord Randolph Churchill (1849–95) British Conservative politician. Letter, 7 May 1886

5 By yesterday morning British troops were patrolling the streets of Belfast. I fear that once Catholics and Protestants get used to our presence they will hate us more than they hate each other.

Richard Crossman (1907–74) British politician. *Diaries*, 17 Aug 1969

6 Thus you have a starving population, an absentee aristocracy, and an alien Church, and in addition the weakest executive in the world. That is the Irish Question.

Benjamin Disraeli (1804–81) British statesman. Speech, House of Commons, 16 Feb 1844

7 I never met anyone in Ireland who understood the Irish question, except one Englishman who had only been there a week.

Keith Fraser (1867–1935) British politician. Speech, House of Commons, May 1919

8 Worth seeing? yes; but not worth going to see.

Samuel Johnson (1709–84) British lexicographer. Referring to the Giant's Causeway. *Life of Johnson* (J. Boswell), Vol. III

9 Ireland is the old sow that eats her farrow.

James Joyce (1882–1941) Irish novelist. *A Portrait of the Artist as a Young Man*, Ch. 5

10 It is a symbol of Irish art. The cracked looking glass of a servant.

James Joyce *Ulysses*

11 The problem with Ireland is that it's a country full of genius, but with absolutely no talent.

Hugh Leonard (1926–) Irish dramatist. Said during an interview. *The Times*, Aug 1977

12 There is no excuse, no justification and no future for the use of violence in Northern Ireland.

John Major (1943–) British politician and prime minister. Press conference, 15 Dec 1993

13 The harp that once through Tara's halls
The soul of music shed,
Now hangs as mute on Tara's walls
As if that soul were fled. –
So sleeps the pride of former days,
So glory's thrill is o'er;
And hearts, that once beat high for praise,
Now feel that pulse no more.

Thomas Moore (1779–1852) Irish poet. *Irish Melodies*, 'The Harp that Once'

14 It is a city where you can see a sparrow fall to the ground, and God watching it.

Conor Cruise O'Brien (1917–) Irish diplomat and writer. Referring to Dublin. Attrib.

15 You have sold Ulster to buy off the fiendish republican scum. You will learn in a bitter school that all appeasement of these monsters is self-destructive.

Ian Paisley (1926–) Northern Irish politician. Referring to John Major's Anglo-Irish peace initiative. *The Independent*, 16 Dec 1993

16 I will drive a coach and six horses through the Act of Settlement.

Stephen Rice (1637–1715) English politician. *State of the Protestants of Ireland* (W. King), Ch. 3

17 The English should give Ireland home rule – and reserve the motion picture rights.

Will Rogers (1879–1935) US actor and humorist. *Autobiography* (published posthumously)

18 Before Irish Home Rule is conceded by the Imperial Parliament, England as the predominant member of the three kingdoms will have to be convinced of its justice and equity.

Lord Rosebery (1847–1929) British statesman. Speech, House of Lords, 11 Mar 1894

19 The moment the very name of Ireland is mentioned, the English seem to bid adieu to common feeling, common prudence, and common sense, and to act with the barbarity of tyrants, and the fatuity of idiots.

Sydney Smith (1771–1845) British clergyman and essayist. *The Letters of Peter Plymley*

20 I would have liked to go to Ireland, but my grandmother would not let me. Perhaps she thought I wanted to take the little place.

Wilhelm II (1859–1941) King of Prussia and Emperor of Germany. Queen Victoria was his grandmother. *Carson* (H. Montgomery Hyde), Ch. 9

IRISH

See also British, Ireland

1 Put an Irishman on the spit, and you can always get another Irishman to baste him.

Proverb

2 Other people have a nationality. The Irish and the Jews have a psychosis.

Brendan Behan (1923–64) Irish playwright. *Richard's Cork Leg*, I

3 The English and Americans dislike only *some* Irish – the same Irish that the Irish themselves detest, Irish writers – the ones that *think*.

Brendan Behan *Richard's Cork Leg*, I

4 Not in vain is Ireland pouring itself all over the earth...The Irish, with their glowing hearts and reverent credulity, are needed in this cold age of intellect and skepticism.

Lydia M. Child (1802–80) US abolitionist campaigner. *Letters from New York*, Vol. I, No. 33, 8 Dec 1842

5 All races have produced notable economists, with the exception of the Irish who doubtless can protest their devotion to higher arts.

John Kenneth Galbraith (1908–) US economist. *The Age of Uncertainty*, Ch. 1

6 Irish Americans are about as Irish as Black Americans are African.

Bob Geldof (1952–) Irish rock musician. *The Observer*, 'Sayings of the Week', 22 Jun 1986

7 The Irish are a fair people; – they never speak well of one another.

Samuel Johnson (1709–84) British lexicographer. *Life of Johnson* (J. Boswell), Vol. II

8 The Irish don't know what they want and are prepared to fight to the death to get it.

Sidney Littlewood (1895–1967) President of the Law Society. Speech, 13 Apr 1961

IRREVOCABILITY

1 The die is cast.

Julius Caesar (100–44 BC) Roman general and statesman. Said on crossing the Rubicon (49 BC) at the start of his campaign against Pompey. Attrib.

2 The Gods themselves cannot recall their gifts.

Alfred, Lord Tennyson (1809–92) British poet. *Tithonus*

J

JEALOUSY

See also envy

1 For the ear of jealousy heareth all things: and the noise of murmurings is not hid.

Bible: Wisdom 1:10

2 Jealousy is no more than feeling alone among smiling enemies.

Elizabeth Bowen (1899–1973) Irish novelist. *The House in Paris*

3 The others were only my wives. But you, my dear, will be my widow.

Sacha Guitry (1885–1957) French actor and dramatist. Allaying his fifth wife's jealousy of his previous wives. *Speaker's and Toastmaster's Handbook* (J. Brawle)

4 The secret of my success is that no woman has ever been jealous of me.

Elsa Maxwell (1883–1963) US songwriter, broadcaster, and actress. *The Natives were Friendly* (Noël Barber)

5 O, beware, my lord, of jealousy;
It is the green-ey'd monster which doth mock
The meat it feeds on.

William Shakespeare (1564–1616) English dramatist. *Othello*, III:3

6 O curse of marriage,
That we can call these delicate creatures ours,
And not their appetites! I had rather be a toad,
And live upon the vapour of a dungeon,
Than keep a corner in the thing I love
For others' uses.

William Shakespeare *Othello*, III:3

JEWS

See also Nazism, prejudice, racism, religion

1 Other people have a nationality. The Irish and the Jews have a psychosis.

Brendan Behan (1923–64) Irish playwright. *Richard's Cork Leg*, I

2 The gentleman will please remember that when his half-civilized ancestors were hunting the wild boar in Silesia, mine were princes of the earth.

Judah Philip Benjamin (1811–84) US politician. Replying to a senator of Germanic origin who had made an antisemitic remark. Attrib.

3 Now the Lord had said unto Abram, Get thee out of thy country, and from thy kindred, and from thy father's house, unto a land that I will shew thee:
And I will make of thee a great nation, and I will bless thee, and make thy name great; and thou shalt be a blessing:
And I will bless them that bless thee, and curse him that curseth thee: and in thee shall all families of the earth be blessed.

Bible: Genesis 12:1–3

4 How odd
Of God
To choose
The Jews.

William Norman Ewer (1885–1976) British writer. For a reply see Cecil BROWNE. *How Odd*

5 But not so odd
As those who choose
A Jewish God,
But spurn the Jews.

Cecil Browne In reply to EWER (above)

6 It is extremely difficult for a Jew to be converted, for how can he bring himself to believe in the divinity of – another Jew?

Heinrich Heine (1797–1856) German poet and writer. Attrib.

7 For me this is a vital litmus test: no intellectual society can flourish where a Jew feels even slightly uneasy.

Paul Johnson (1928–) British editor. *The Sunday Times Magazine*, 6 Feb 1977

8 The very best that is in the Jewish blood: a faculty for pure disinterestedness, and warm, physically warm love, that seems to make the corpuscles of the blood glow.

D. H. Lawrence (1885–1930) British novelist. *Kangaroo*, Ch. 6

9 Pessimism is a luxury that a Jew never can allow himself.

Golda Meir (1898–1978) Russian-born Israeli stateswoman. *The Observer*, 'Sayings of the Year', 29 Dec 1974

10 There are not enough prisons and concentration camps in Palestine to hold all the Jews who are ready to defend their lives and property.

Golda Meir Speech, 2 May 1940

11 And furthermore did you know that behind the discovery of America there was a Jewish financier?

Mordecai Richler (1931–) Canadian novelist. *Cocksure*, Ch. 24

12 Doctor, my doctor, what do you say – let's put the id back in yid!

Philip Roth (1933–) US novelist. *Portnoy's Complaint*

13 A Jewish man with parents alive is a fifteen-year-old boy, and will remain a fifteen-year-old boy till they die.

Philip Roth *Portnoy's Complaint*

14 I believe that the Jews have made a contribution to the human condition out of all proportion to their numbers: I believe them to be an immense people. Not only have they supplied the world with two leaders of the stature of Jesus Christ and Karl Marx, but they have even indulged in the luxury of following neither one nor the other.

Peter Ustinov (1921–) British actor. *Dear Me*, Ch. 19

15 The law of dislike for the unlike will always prevail. And whereas the unlike is normally situated at a safe distance, the Jews bring the unlike into the heart of *every milieu*, and must there defend a frontier line as large as the world.

Israel Zangwill (1864–1926) British writer. *Speeches, Articles and Letters*, 'The Jewish Race'

JOURNALISM

See also editors, newspapers

1 Have you noticed that life, real honest to goodness life, with murders and catastrophes and fabulous inheritances, happens almost exclusively in newspapers?

Jean Anouilh (1910–87) French dramatist. *The Rehearsal*

2 What the proprietorship of these papers is aiming at is power, and power without responsibility – the prerogative of the harlot through the ages.

Stanley Baldwin (1867–1947) British statesman. Attacking the press barons Lords Rothermere and Beaverbrook. It was first used by KIPLING. *See also* DEVONSHIRE (10th Duke). Speech, election rally, 18 Mar 1931

3 'Christianity, of course but why journalism?'

Arthur Balfour (1848–1930) British statesman. In reply to Frank Harris's remark, '...all the faults of the age come from Christianity and journalism'. *Autobiography* (Margot Asquith), Ch. 10

4 Go out and speak for the inarticulate and the submerged.

Lord Beaverbrook (1879–1964) British newspaper owner and politician. *Somerset Maugham* (E. Morgan)

5 Because he shakes hands with people's hearts.

Lord Beaverbrook On being asked why the sentimental writer Godfrey Winn was paid so much. *Somerset Maugham* (E. Morgan)

6 If you want to make mischief come and work on my papers.

Lord Beaverbrook Inviting Anthony Howard to join his staff. *Radio Times*, 27 June 1981

7 If I rescued a child from drowning, the Press would no doubt headline the story 'Benn grabs child'.

Tony Benn (1925–) British politician. *The Observer*, 'Sayings of the Week', 2 Mar 1975

8 Journalists say a thing that they know isn't true, in the hope that if they keep on saying it long enough it will be true.

Arnold Bennett (1867–1931) British novelist. *The Title*, II

9 No news is good news; no journalists is even better.

Nicolas Bentley (1907–78) British cartoonist and writer. Attrib.

10 I read the newspaper avidly. It is my one form of continuous fiction.

Aneurin Bevan (1897–1960) British Labour politician. *The Observer*, 'Sayings of the Week', 3 Apr 1960

11 When a dog bites a man that is not news, but when a man bites a dog that is news.

John B. Bogart (1845–1920) US journalist. Sometimes attributed to Charles Dana and Amos Cummings. Attrib.

12 Journalism is the only job that requires no degrees, no diplomas and no specialised knowledge of any kind.

Patrick Campbell (1913–80) British humorous writer and editor. *My Life and Easy Times*

13 Journalism largely consists of saying 'Lord Jones is dead' to people who never knew Lord Jones was alive.

G. K. Chesterton (1874–1936) British writer. Attrib.

14 Literature is the art of writing something that will be read twice; journalism what will be grasped at once.

Cyril Connolly (1903–74) British journalist. *Enemies of Promise*, Ch. 3

15 I hesitate to say what the functions of the modern journalist may be; but I imagine that they do not exclude the intelligent anticipation of facts even before they occur.

Lord Curzon (1859–1925) British politician. Speech, House of Commons, 29 Mar 1898

16 Good God, that's done it. He's lost us the tarts' vote.

Duke of Devonshire (1895–1950) Conservative politician. Referring to Stanley BALDWIN's attack on newspaper proprietors; recalled by Harold Macmillan. Attrib.

17 I am myself a gentleman of the Press, and I bear no other scutcheon.

Benjamin Disraeli (1804–81) British statesman. Speech, House of Commons, 18 Feb 1863

18 Blood sport is brought to its ultimate refinement in the gossip columns.

Bernard Ingham (1932–) British journalist. *The Observer*, 'Sayings of the Week', 28 Dec 1986

19 Newspapers always excite curiosity. No one ever lays one down without a feeling of disappointment.

Charles Lamb (1775–1834) British essayist. *Last Essays of Elia*, 'Detached Thoughts on Books and Reading'

20 On the whole I would not say that our Press is obscene. I would say that it trembles on the brink of obscenity.

Lord Longford (1905–) British politician and social reformer. *The Observer*, 'Sayings of the Year', 1963

21 The gallery in which the reporters sit has become a fourth estate of the realm.

Lord Macaulay (1800–59) British historian. Referring to the press gallery in the House of Commons. *Historical Essays Contributed to the 'Edinburgh Review'*, 'Hallam's "Constitutional History"'

22 Once a newspaper touches a story, the facts are lost forever, even to the protagonists.

Norman Mailer (1923–) US writer. *The Presidential Papers*

23 A good newspaper, I suppose, is a nation talking to itself.

Arthur Miller (1915–) US dramatist. *The Observer*, 'Sayings of the Week', 26 Nov 1961

24 SIXTY HORSES WEDGED IN A CHIMNEY
The story to fit this sensational headline has not turned up yet.

J. B. Morton (1893–1979) British journalist. *The Best of Beachcomber*, 'Mr Justice Cocklecarrot: Home Life'

25 A reporter is a man who has renounced everything in life but the world, the flesh, and the devil.

David Murray (1888–1962) British journalist. *The Observer*, 'Sayings of the Week', 5 July 1931

26 We live under a government of men and morning newspapers.

Wendell Phillips (1811–84) US reformer. *Address: The Press*

27 Its primary office is the gathering of news. At the peril of its soul it must see that the supply is not tainted. Neither in what it gives, nor in what it does not give, nor in the mode of presentation, must the unclouded face of truth suffer wrong. Comment is free but facts are sacred.

C. P. Scott (1846–1932) British journalist. *Manchester Guardian*, 6 May 1926

28 He's someone who flies around from hotel to hotel and thinks the most interesting thing about any story is the fact that he has arrived to cover it.

Tom Stoppard (1937–) Czech-born British dramatist. Referring to foreign correspondents. *Night and Day*, I

29 MILNE. No matter how imperfect things are, if you've got a free press everything is correctable, and without it everything is conceivable.
RUTH. I'm with you on the free press. It's the newspapers I can't stand.

Tom Stoppard *Night and Day*, I

30 Freedom of the press in Britain is freedom to print such of the proprietor's prejudices as the advertisers don't object to.

Hannen Swaffer (1879–1962) British journalist. Attrib.

31 Journalism – an ability to meet the challenge of filling the space.

Rebecca West (Cicely Isabel Fairfield; 1892–1983) British novelist and journalist. *The New York Herald Tribune*, 22 April 1956

32 There is much to be said in favour of modern journalism. By giving us the opinions of the uneducated, it keeps us in touch with the ignorance of the community.

Oscar Wilde (1854–1900) Irish-born British dramatist. *The Critic as Artist*, Pt. 2

33 You cannot hope
to bribe or twist,
thank God! the
British journalist.

But, seeing what
the man will do
unbribed, there's
no occasion to.

Humbert Wolfe (1886–1940) British poet. *The Uncelestial City*, Bk. I, 'Over the Fire'

JUDGMENT

1 And this is the writing that was written, MENE, MENE, TEKEL, UPHARSIN.
This is the interpretation of the thing:
MENE; God hath numbered thy kingdom, and finished it.
TEKEL; Thou art weighed in the balances, and art found wanting.
PERES; Thy kingdom is divided, and given to the Medes and Persians.

Bible: Daniel 5:25–28

2 Judge not, that ye be not judged.

Bible: Matthew 7:1

3 And why beholdest thou the mote that is in thy brother's eye, but considerest not the beam that is in thine own eye?

Bible: Matthew 7:3

4 And I saw a great white throne, and him that sat on it, from whose face the earth and the heaven fled away; and there was found no place for them.
And I saw the dead, small and great, stand before God; and the books were opened: and another book was opened, which is the book of life: and the dead were judged out of those things which were written in the books, according to their works.
And the sea gave up the dead which were in it; and death and hell delivered up the dead which were in them: and they were judged every man according to their works.

Bible: Revelations 20:11–13

5 No man can justly censure or condemn another, because indeed no man truly knows another.

Thomas Browne (1605–82) English physician and writer. *Religio Medici*, Pt. II

6 Your representative owes you, not his industry only, but his judgement; and he betrays instead of serving you if he sacrifices it to your opinion.

Edmund Burke (1729–97) British politician. Speech to the electors of Bristol, 3 Nov 1774

7 You shall judge of a man by his foes as well as by his friends.

Joseph Conrad (Teodor Josef Konrad Korzeniowski; 1857–1924) Polish-born British novelist. *Lord Jim*, Ch. 34

8 Judge not the play before the play be done.

John Davies (1569–1626) English jurist. *Respice Finem*

9 Force, if unassisted by judgement, collapses

through its own mass.

Horace (Quintus Horatius Flaccus; 65–8 BC) Roman poet. *Odes*, III

10 Let me remind you of the old maxim: people under suspicion are better moving than at rest, since at rest they may be sitting in the balance without knowing it, being weighed together with their sins.

Franz Kafka (1883–1924) Czech novelist. *The Trial*, Ch. 8

11 Consider what you think justice requires, and decide accordingly. But never give your reasons; for your judgement will probably be right, but your reasons will certainly be wrong.

Lord Mansfield (1705–93) British judge and politician. Advice given to a new colonial governor. *Lives of the Chief Justices* (Campbell), Ch. 40

12 Everyone complains of his memory, but no one complains of his judgement.

Duc de la Rochefoucauld (1613–80) French writer. *Maximes*, 89

JUSTICE

See also injustice, judgment, law, lawyers

1 The place of justice is a hallowed place.

Francis Bacon (1561–1626) English philosopher. *Essays*, 'Of Judicature'

2 When I came back to Dublin, I was court-martialled in my absence and sentenced to death in my absence, so I said they could shoot me in my absence.

Brendan Behan (1923–64) Irish playwright. *The Hostage*, I

3 It is better that ten guilty persons escape than one innocent suffer.

William Blackstone (1723–80) British jurist. *Commentaries on the Laws of England*, Bk. IV, Ch. 27

4 The rain it raineth on the just
And also on the unjust fella:
But chiefly on the just, because
The unjust steals the just's umbrella.

Charles Bowen (1835–94) British judge. *Sands of Time* (Walter Sichel)

5 Trial by jury itself, instead of being a security to persons who are accused, will be a delusion, a mockery, and a snare.

Thomas Denman (1779–1854) British judge. Judgment in O'Connell v The Queen, 4 Sept 1844

6 'It is my duty to warn you that it will be used against you,' cried the Inspector, with the magnificent fair play of the British criminal law.

Arthur Conan Doyle (1856–1930) British writer. *The Dancing Men*

7 Let justice be done, though the world perish.

Ferdinand I (1503–64) Holy Roman Emperor. Attrib.

8 Ah, colonel, all's fair in love and war, you know.

Nathan Bedford Forrest (1821–77) Confederate general. Remark to a captured enemy officer who had been tricked into surrendering. *A Civil War Treasury* (B. Botkin)

9 Let no guilty man escape, if it can be avoided...No personal considerations should stand in the way of performing a public duty.

Ulysses Simpson Grant (1822–85) US general. Referring to the Whiskey Ring. Indorsement of a letter, 29 July 1875

10 Justice should not only be done, but should manifestly and undoubtedly be seen to be done.

Gordon Hewart (1870–1943) British lawyer and politician. *The Chief* (R. Jackson)

11 I have come to regard the law courts not as a cathedral but rather as a casino.

Richard Ingrams (1937–) British editor. *The Guardian*, 30 July 1977

12 Consider, Sir, how should you like, though conscious of your innocence, to be tried before a jury for a capital crime, once a week.

Samuel Johnson (1709–84) British lexicographer. *Life of Johnson* (J. Boswell), Vol. III

13 A lawyer has no business with the justice or injustice of the cause which he undertakes, unless his client asks his opinion, and then he is bound to give it honestly. The justice or injustice of the cause is to be decided by the judge.

Samuel Johnson *Tour to the Hebrides* (J. Boswell)

14 Justice is the constant and perpetual wish to render to every one his due.

Justinian I (482–565 AD) Byzantine emperor. *Institutes*, I

15 Justice is such a fine thing that we cannot pay too dearly for it.

Alain-René Lesage (1668–1747) French writer. *Crispin rival de son maître*, IX

16 I'm arm'd with more than complete steel –
The justice of my quarrel.

Christopher Marlowe (1564–93) English dramatist. Play also attributed to others. *Lust's Dominion*, IV:3

17 In England, Justice is open to all, like the Ritz hotel.

James Mathew (1830–1908) British judge. Also attrib. to Lord Darling. *Miscellany-at-Law* (R. E. Megarry)

18 A judge is not supposed to know anything about the facts of life until they have been presented in evidence and explained to him at least three times.

Hubert Lister Parker (1900–72) Lord Chief Justice of England. *The Observer*, 'Sayings of the Week', 12 Mar 1961

19 The hungry judges soon the sentence sign,
And wretches hang that jury-men may dine.

Alexander Pope (1688–1744) British poet. *The Rape of the Lock*, III

20 The love of justice in most men is simply the fear of suffering injustice.

Duc de la Rochefoucauld (1613–80) French writer. *Maximes*, 78

21 A man who is good enough to shed his blood for the country is good enough to be given a square deal afterwards. More than that no man is entitled to, and less than that no man shall have.

Theodore Roosevelt (1858–1919) US Republican president. Speech at the Lincoln Monument, Springfield, Illinois, 4 June 1903

22 Haste still pays haste, and leisure answers leisure;
Like doth quit like, and Measure still for Measure.

William Shakespeare (1564–1616) English dramatist. *Measure for Measure*, V:1

23 This is a British murder inquiry and some degree of justice must be seen to be more or less done.

Tom Stoppard (1937–) Czech-born British dramatist. *Jumpers*, II

24 Under a government which imprisons any unjustly, the true place for a just man is also a prison.

Henry David Thoreau (1817–62) US writer. *Civil Disobedience*

K

KILLING

See also assassination, death, murder, suicide

1 Euthanasia is a long, smooth-sounding word, and it conceals its danger as long, smooth words do, but the danger is there, nevertheless.

Pearl Buck (1892–1973) US novelist. *The Child Who Never Grew*, Ch. 2

2 Thou shalt not kill; but needst not strive
Officiously to keep alive.

Arthur Hugh Clough (1819–61) British poet. *The Latest Decalogue*, 11

3 To save a man's life against his will is the same as killing him.

Horace (Quintus Horatius Flaccus; 65–8 BC) Roman poet. *Ars Poetica*

4 To kill a human being is, after all, the least injury you can do him.

Henry James (1843–1916) US novelist. *My Friend Bingham*

5 Killing
Is the ultimate simplification of life.

Hugh MacDiarmid (Christopher Murray Grieve; 1892–1978) Scottish poet. *England's Double Knavery*

6 ...there's no difference between one's killing and making decisions that will send others to kill. It's exactly the same thing, or even worse.

Golda Meir (1898–1978) Russian-born Israeli stateswoman. *L'Europeo* (Oriana Fallaci)

7 Kill a man, and you are a murderer. Kill millions of men, and you are a conqueror. Kill everyone, and you are a god.

Jean Rostand (1894–1977) French biologist and writer. *Pensées d'un biologiste*

8 Yet each man kills the thing he loves,
By each let this be heard,
Some do it with a bitter look,
Some with a flattering word.
The coward does it with a kiss,
The brave man with a sword!

Oscar Wilde (1854–1900) Irish-born British dramatist. *The Ballad of Reading Gaol*, I:7

KINDNESS

See also charity, generosity

1 Recompense injury with justice, and recompense kindness with kindness.

Confucius (K'ung Fu-tzu; 551–479 BC) Chinese philosopher. *Analects*

2 I love thee for a heart that's kind –
Not for the knowledge in thy mind.

W. H. Davies (1871–1940) British poet. *Sweet Stay-at-Home*

3 One kind word can warm three winter months.

Japanese Proverb

4 Yet do I fear thy nature;
It is too full o' th' milk of human kindness
To catch the nearest way.

William Shakespeare (1564–1616) English dramatist. *Macbeth*, I:5

5 This is a way to kill a wife with kindness.

William Shakespeare *The Taming of the Shrew*, IV:1

6 So many gods, so many creeds,
So many paths that wind and wind,
While just the art of being kind
Is all the sad world needs.

Ella Wheeler Wilcox (1850–1919) US poet. *The World's Need*

7 That best portion of a good man's life,
His little, nameless, unremembered acts
Of kindness and of love.

William Wordsworth (1770–1850) British poet. *Lines composed a few miles above Tintern Abbey*

KISSING

1 What of soul was left, I wonder, when the kissing had to stop?

Robert Browning (1812–89) British poet. *A Toccata of Galuppi's*

2 Jenny kissed me when we met,
Jumping from the chair she sat in;
Time, you thief, who love to get
Sweets into your list, put that in:
Say I'm weary, say I'm sad,
Say that health and wealth have missed me,
Say I'm growing old, but add,
Jenny kissed me.

Leigh Hunt (1784–1859) British poet. Writing about Jane Carlyle. *Rondeau*

3 Being kissed by a man who didn't wax his moustache was – like eating an egg without salt.

Rudyard Kipling (1865–1936) Indian-born British writer. A similar remark is attributed to the US poet Madison Julius Cawein (1865–1914). *Soldiers Three*, 'The Gadsbys, Poor Dear Mamma'

4 A kiss without a moustache, they said then, is like an egg without salt; I will add to it: and it is like Good without Evil.

Jean-Paul Sartre (1905–80) French writer. *Words*

KNOWLEDGE

See also learning, self-knowledge, wisdom

1 Knowledge is the mother of all virtue; all vice proceeds from ignorance.

Proverb

2 Learning is a treasure which accompanies its owner everywhere.

Chinese proverb

3 *Nam et ipsa scientia potestas est.*
Knowledge itself is power.

Francis Bacon (1561–1626) English philosopher. *Religious Meditations*, 'Of Heresies'

4 I have taken all knowledge to be my province.

Francis Bacon Letter to Lord Burleigh, 1592

5 For all knowledge and wonder (which is the seed of knowledge) is an impression of pleasure in itself.

Francis Bacon *The Advancement of Learning*, Bk. I, Ch. 1

6 For in much wisdom is much grief: and he that increaseth knowledge increaseth sorrow.

Bible: Ecclesiastes 1:18

7 And the Lord God took the man, and put him into the garden of Eden to dress it and to keep it.
And the Lord God commanded the man, saying, Of every tree of the garden thou mayest freely eat:
But of the tree of the knowledge of good and evil, thou shalt not eat of it: for in the day that thou eatest thereof thou shalt surely die.

Bible: Genesis 2:15–17

8 Now as touching things offered unto idols, we know that we all have knowledge. Knowledge puffeth up, but charity edifieth.

Bible: I Corinthians 8:1

9 There goes a woman who knows all the things that can be taught and none of the things that cannot be taught.

Coco Chanel (1883–1971) French dress designer. *Coco Chanel, Her Life, Her Secrets* (Marcel Haedrich)

10 Learning without thought is labour lost; thought without learning is perilous.

Confucius (K'ung Fu-tzu; 551–479 BC) Chinese philosopher. *Analects*

11 Knowledge dwells
In heads replete with thoughts of other men;
Wisdom in minds attentive to their own.

William Cowper (1731–1800) British poet. *The Task*

12 A smattering of everything, and a knowledge of nothing.

Charles Dickens (1812–70) British novelist. *Sketches by Boz*, 'Tales', Ch. 3

13 A man should keep his little brain attic stocked with all the furniture that he is likely to use, and the rest he can put away in the lumber room of his library, where he can get it if he wants it.

Arthur Conan Doyle (1856–1930) British writer. *Five Orange Pips*

14 For lust of knowing what should not be known,
We take the Golden Road to Samarkand.

James Elroy Flecker (1884–1915) British poet. *Hassan*, V:2

15 I now want to know all things under the sun, and the moon, too. For all things are beautiful in themselves, and become more beautiful when known to man. Knowledge is Life with wings.

Kahlil Gibran (1833–1931) Lebanese mystic and poet. *Beloved Prophet* (ed. Virginia Hiln)

16 I am the very model of a modern Major-General,
I've information vegetable, animal and mineral,
I know the kings of England, and I quote the fights historical,
From Marathon to Waterloo, in order categorical.

W. S. Gilbert (1836–1911) British dramatist. *The Pirates of Penzance*, I

17 In arguing too, the parson own'd his skill,
For e'en though vanquish'd, he could argue still;
While words of learned length, and thund'ring sound
Amazed the gazing rustics rang'd around,
And still they gaz'd, and still the wonder grew,
That one small head could carry all he knew.

Oliver Goldsmith (1728–74) Irish-born British writer. *The Deserted Village*

18 The clever men at Oxford
Know all that there is to be knowed.
But they none of them know one half as much
As intelligent Mr Toad.

Kenneth Grahame (1859–1932) Scottish writer. *The Wind in the Willows*, Ch. 10

19 It is the province of knowledge to speak and it is the privilege of wisdom to listen.

Oliver Wendell Holmes (1809–94) US writer. *The Poet at the Breakfast Table*, Ch. 10

20 Knowledge is proportionate to being. ...You know in virtue of what you are.

Aldous Huxley (1894–1964) British novelist. *Time Must Have a Stop*, Ch. 26

21 If a little knowledge is dangerous, where is the man who has so much as to be out of danger?

T. H. Huxley (1825–95) British biologist. *On Elementary Instruction in Physiology*

22 There was never an age in which useless knowledge was more important than in our own.

Cyril Joad (1891–1953) British writer and broadcaster. *The Observer*, 'Sayings of the Week', 30 Sept 1951

23 All knowledge is of itself of some value. There is nothing so minute or inconsiderable, that I would not rather know it than not.

Samuel Johnson (1709–84) British lexicographer. *Life of Johnson* (J. Boswell)

24 Integrity without knowledge is weak and useless, and knowledge without integrity is dangerous and dreadful.

Samuel Johnson *Rasselas*, Ch. 41

25 In my early years I read very hard. It is a sad reflection, but a true one, that I knew almost as much at eighteen as I do now.

Samuel Johnson *Life of Johnson* (J. Boswell), Vol. I

26 Knowledge is of two kinds. We know a subject ourselves, or we know where we can find information upon it.

Samuel Johnson *Life of Johnson* (J. Boswell), Vol. II

27 A study of history shows that civilizations that abandon the quest for knowledge are doomed to disintegration.

Bernard Lovell (1913–) British astronomer and writer. *The Observer*, 'Sayings of the Week', 14 May 1972

28 Knowledge advances by steps, and not by leaps.

Lord Macaulay (1800–59) British historian. *Essays and Biographies*, 'History'. *Edinburgh Review*

29 We have learned the answers, all the answers:
It is the question that we do not know.

Archibald MacLeish (1892–1982) US poet and dramatist. *The Hamlet of A. Macleish*

30 A little learning is a dangerous thing;
Drink deep, or taste not the Pierian spring:
There shallow draughts intoxicate the brain,
And drinking largely sobers us again.

Alexander Pope (1688–1744) British poet. *An Essay on Criticism*

31 Our knowledge can only be finite, while our ignorance must necessarily be infinite.

Karl Popper (1902–94) Austrian-born British philosopher. *Conjectures and Refutations*

32 His had been an intellectual decision founded on his conviction that if a little knowledge was a dangerous thing, a lot was lethal.

Tom Sharpe (1928–) British novelist. *Porterhouse Blue*, Ch. 18

33 These things shall be! A loftier race
Than e'er the world hath known shall rise,
With flame of freedom in their souls,
And light of knowledge in their eyes.

John Addington Symonds (1840–93) British art historian. *Hymn*

34 Beware you be not swallowed up in books! An ounce of love is worth a pound of knowledge.

John Wesley (1703–91) British religious leader. *Life of Wesley* (R. Southey), Ch. 16

35 'I dunno,' Arthur said. 'I forget what I was taught. I only remember what I've learnt.'

Patrick White (1912–90) British-born Australian novelist. *The Solid Mandala*, Ch. 2

36 I have drunk ale from the Country of the Young
And weep because I know all things now.

W. B. Yeats (1865–1939) Irish poet. *He Thinks of his Past Greatness*

L

LANGUAGE

See also class, communication, grammar, Goldwynisms, malapropisms, mixed metaphors, opera, pronunciation, speech, spoonerisms, style, words, writing

1 The Greeks Had a Word for It.

Zoë Akins (1886–1958) US dramatist. Play title

2 Therefore is the name of it called Babel; because the Lord did there confound the language of all the earth: and from thence did the Lord scatter them abroad upon the face of all the earth.

Bible: Genesis 11:9

3 The cliché is dead poetry. English, being the language of an imaginative race, abounds in clichés, so that English literature is always in danger of being poisoned by its own secretions.

Gerald Brenan (Edward Fitzgerald Brenan; 1894–1987) British writer. *Thoughts in a Dry Season*, 'Literature'

4 'Take some more tea,' the March Hare said to Alice, very earnestly.
'I've had nothing yet,' Alice replied in an offended tone, 'so I can't take more.'
'You mean you can't take *less*,' said the Hatter: 'it's very easy to take *more* than nothing.'

Lewis Carroll (Charles Lutwidge Dodgson; 1832–98) British writer. *Alice's Adventures in Wonderland*, Ch. 7

5 A silly remark can be made in Latin as well as in Spanish.

Miguel de Cervantes (1547–1616) Spanish novelist. *The Dialogue of the Dogs*

6 Well, frankly, the problem as I see it at this moment in time is whether I should just lie down under all this hassle and let them walk all over me, or whether I should just say OK, I get the message, and do myself in.
I mean, let's face it, I'm in a no-win situation, and quite honestly, I'm so stuffed up to here with the whole stupid mess that I can tell you I've just got a good mind to take the easy way out. That's the bottom line. The only problem is, what happens if I find, when I've bumped myself off, there's some kind of…ah, you know, all that mystical stuff about when you die, you might find you're still – know what I mean?

Charles, Prince of Wales (1948–) Eldest son of Elizabeth II. At the presentation of the Thomas Cranmer Schools Prize, 1989, suggesting a possible modern English version of Hamlet's soliloquy. The original version is:
To be, or not to be: that is the question:
Whether 'tis nobler in the mind to suffer
The slings and arrows of outrageous fortune,
Or to take arms against a sea of troubles,
And by opposing end them? To die: to sleep;
No more; and, by a sleep to say we end
The heartache and the thousand natural shocks
That flesh is heir to, 'tis a consummation
Devoutly to be wish'd. To die, to sleep;
To sleep: perchance to dream: aye, there's the rub;
For in that sleep of death what dreams may come
When we have shuffled off this mortal coil,
Must give us pause.

7 I speak Spanish to God, Italian to women, French to men, and German to my horse.

Charles V (1500–58) Holy Roman Emperor. Attrib.

8 The one stream of poetry which is continually flowing is slang.

G. K. Chesterton (1874–1936) British writer. *The Defendant*

9 All slang is metaphor, and all metaphor is poetry.

G. K. Chesterton *The Defendant*

10 I don't hold with abroad and think that foreigners speak English when our backs are turned.

Quentin Crisp (?1910–) Model, publicist, and writer. *The Naked Civil Servant*

11 Bring on the empty horses!

Michael Curtiz (1888–1962) Hungarian-born US film director. Said during the filming of *The Charge of the Light Brigade*. Curtiz, who was not noted for his command of the English language, meant 'riderless horses'. When people laughed at his order he became very angry, shouting, 'You think I know fuck-nothing, when I know fuck-all!' David Niven used the remark as the title of his second volume of autobiography about his experiences in the film industry.
Bring on the Empty Horses (David Niven)

12 Imagine the Lord talking French! Aside from a few odd words in Hebrew, I took it completely for granted that God had never spoken anything but the most dignified English.

Clarence Shepard Day (1874–1935) US writer. *Life With Father*, 'Father interferes'

13 What is the prose for God?

Harley Granville-Barker (1877–1946) British actor and dramatist. *Waste*, I

14 I have laboured to refine our language to grammatical purity, and to clear it from colloquial barbarisms, licentious idioms, and irregular combinations.

Samuel Johnson (1709–84) British lexicographer. *The Rambler*

15 I am always sorry when any language is lost, because languages are the pedigree of nations.

Samuel Johnson *Tour to the Hebrides* (J. Boswell)

16 I am not yet so lost in lexicography, as to forget that words are the daughters of earth, and that things are the sons of heaven. Language is only the instrument of science, and words are but the signs of ideas: I wish, however, that the instrument might be less apt to decay, and that signs might be permanent, like the things which they denote.

Samuel Johnson *Dictionary of the English Language*

17 The baby doesn't understand English and the Devil knows Latin.

Ronald Knox (1888–1957) British Roman Catholic priest.

Said when asked to conduct a baptism service in English.
Ronald Knox (Evelyn Waugh), Pt. I, Ch. 5

18 If the English language had been properly organized…then there would be a word which meant both 'he' and 'she', and I could write, 'If John or Mary comes heesh will want to play tennis,' which would save a lot of trouble.

A. A. Milne (1882–1956) British writer. *The Christopher Robin Birthday Book*

19 Most of their discourse was about hunting, in a dialect I understand very little.

Samuel Pepys (1633–1703) English diarist. *Diary*, 22 Nov 1663

20 I include 'pidgin-English'…even though I am referred to in that splendid language as 'Fella belong Mrs Queen'.

Prince Philip (1921–) The consort of Queen Elizabeth II. Speech, English-Speaking Union Conference, Ottawa, 29 Oct 1958

21 Life is too short to learn German.

Richard Porson (1759–1808) British classicist. *Gryll Grange* (T. L. Peacock), Ch. 3

22 Sign language is the equal of speech, lending itself equally to the rigorous and the poetic, to philosophical analysis or to making love.

Oliver Sacks (1933–) British neurologist. *The Times*, 16 June 1994

23 Language grows out of life, out of its needs and experiences…*Language* and *knowledge* are indissolubly connected; they are interdependent. Good work in language presupposes and depends on a real knowledge of things.

Annie Sullivan (1866–1936) US teacher of the handicapped. Speech, American Association to Promote the Teaching of Speech to the Deaf, July 1894

24 A foreign swear-word is practically inoffensive except to the person who has learnt it early in life and knows its social limits.

Paul Theroux (1941–) US-born writer. *Saint Jack*, Ch. 12

25 The most attractive sentences are not perhaps the wisest, but the surest and soundest.

Henry David Thoreau (1817–62) US writer. *Journal*, 1842

26 I am not like a lady at the court of Versailles, who said: 'What a dreadful pity that the bother at the tower of Babel should have got language all mixed up, but for that, everyone would always have spoken French.

Voltaire (François-Marie Arouet; 1694–1778) French writer. Letter to Catherine the Great, Empress of Russia, 26 May 1767

27 We should constantly use the most common, little, easy words (so they are pure and proper) which our language affords.

John Wesley (1703–91) British religious leader. Advice for preaching to 'plain people'. Attrib.

28 We dissect nature along lines laid down by our native language… Language is not simply a reporting device for experience but a defining framework for it.

Benjamin Lee Whorf (1897–1941) US linguist. *New Directions in the Study of Language* (ed. Hoyer), 'Thinking in Primitive Communities'

LAST WORDS

Not always the actual last words said, but including remarks made when dying. Many are apocryphal, hence the fact that some people have more than one set of attributed 'last words'. *See also* death, execution

1 A lot of people, on the verge of death, utter famous last words or stiffen into attitudes, as if the final stiffening in three days' time were not enough; they will have ceased to exist three days' hence, yet they still want to arouse admiration and adopt a pose and tell a lie with their last gasp.

Henry de Montherlant (1896–1972) French novelist. *Explicit Mysterium*

Some examples

2 I inhabit a weak, frail, decayed tenement; battered by the winds and broken in on by the storms, and, from all I can learn, the landlord does not intend to repair.

John Quincy Adams (1767–1848) Sixth president of the USA. Said during his last illness. Attrib.

3 See in what peace a Christian can die.

Joseph Addison (1672–1719) British essayist.

4 *Ave Caesar, morituri te salutant.*
Hail Caesar; those who are about to die salute you.

Anonymous Greeting to the Roman Emperor by gladiators

5 Jakie, is it my birthday or am I dying?

Nancy Astor (1879–1964) American-born British politician. To her son on her death bed. He replied: 'A bit of both, Mum'.

6 How were the receipts today in Madison Square Garden?

Phineas Taylor Barnum (1810–91) US showman.

7 I am ready to die for my Lord, that in my blood the Church may obtain liberty and peace.

Thomas Becket (c. 1118–79) English churchman. One version of his last words. *Vita S. Thomae, Cantuariensis Archiepiscopi et Martyris* (Edward Grim)

8 Thank you, sister. May you be the mother of a bishop!

Brendan Behan (1923–64) Irish playwright. Said to a nun nursing him on his deathbed. Attrib.

9 When Jesus therefore had received the vinegar, he said, It is finished: and he bowed his head, and gave up the ghost.

Bible: John 19:30

10 And when Jesus had cried with a loud voice, he said, Father, into thy hands I commend my spirit: and having said thus, he gave up the ghost.

Bible: Luke 23:46

11 Jesus, when he had cried again with a loud voice, yielded up the ghost.
And, behold, the veil of the temple was rent in twain from the top to the bottom; and the earth

did quake, and the rocks rent;
And the graves were opened; and many bodies of the saints which slept arose.
Bible: Matthew 27:50–52

12 *Et tu, Brute?*
You too, Brutus?
Julius Caesar (100–44 BC) Roman general and statesman.

13 All right, then, I'll say it: Dante makes me sick.
Lope Félix de Vega Carpio (1562–1635) Spanish dramatist and poet. On being informed he was about to die. Attrib.

14 I realize that patriotism is not enough. I must have no hatred or bitterness towards anyone.
Edith Cavell (1865–1915) British nurse. Before her execution by the Germans in 1915.

15 Let not poor Nelly starve.
Charles II (1630–85) King of England. Referring to Nell Gwynne. Said on his death bed

16 Give Dayrolles a chair.
Earl of Chesterfield (1694–1773) English statesman. Said on his deathbed when visited by his godson, Solomon Dayrolles. Last words

17 Nurse, it was I who discovered that leeches have red blood.
Baron Georges Cuvier (1769–1832) French zoologist. On his deathbed when the nurse came to apply leeches. *The Oxford Book of Death* (D. Enright)

18 No, it is better not. She will only ask me to take a message to Albert.
Benjamin Disraeli (1804–81) British statesman. On his deathbed, declining an offer of a visit from Queen Victoria.

19 Shakespeare, I come!
Theodore Dreiser (1871–1945) US novelist. His intended last words. *The Constant Circle* (S. Mayfield)

20 Goodbye, my friends, I go on to glory.
Isadora Duncan (1878–1927) US dancer. She was strangled when her long scarf became entangled in the wheel of a sports car. Attrib.

21 My work is done. Why wait?
George Eastman (1854–1932) US inventor and industrialist. His suicide note

22 All my possessions for a moment of time.
Elizabeth I (1533–1603) Queen of England.

23 I have no pain, dear mother, now;
But oh! I am so dry:
Just moisten poor Jim's lips once more;
And, mother, do not cry!
Edward Farmer (1809–76) British writer. A typical sentimental verse of the time. *The Collier's Dying Child*

24 Now I'll have *eine kleine Pause.*
Kathleen Ferrier (1912–53) British contralto. Said shortly before her death. *Am I Too Loud?* (Gerald Moore)

25 It is high time for me to depart, for at my age I now begin to see things as they really are.
Bernard de Fontenelle (1657–1757) French philosopher. Remark on his deathbed. *Anekdotenschatz* (H. Hoffmeister)

26 I feel nothing, apart from a certain difficulty in continuing to exist.
Bernard de Fontenelle Remark on his deathbed. *Famous Last Words* (B. Conrad)

27 I die happy.
Charles James Fox (1749–1806) British Whig politician. *Life and Times of C. J. Fox* (Russell), Vol. III

28 We are all going to Heaven, and Vandyke is of the company.
Thomas Gainsborough (1727–88) British painter. *Thomas Gainsborough* (Boulton), Ch. 9

29 I don't mind if my life goes in the service of the nation. If I die today every drop of my blood will invigorate the nation.
Indira Gandhi (1917–84) Indian stateswoman. Said the night before she was assassinated by Sikh militants, 30 Oct 1984. *The Sunday Times*, 3 Dec 1989

30 Bugger Bognor.
George V (1865–1936) King of the United Kingdom. His alleged last words, when his doctor promised him he would soon be well enough to visit Bognor Regis.

31 How is the Empire?
George V Last words. *The Times*, 21 Jan 1936

32 We are as near to heaven by sea as by land.
Humphrey Gilbert (c. 1539–83) English navigator. Remark made shortly before he went down with his ship *Squirrel. A Book of Anecdotes* (D. George)

33 *Mehr Licht!*
More light!
Goethe (1749–1832) German poet and dramatist. Attrib. last words. In fact he asked for the second shutter to be opened, to allow more light in.

34 Well, I've had a happy life.
William Hazlitt (1778–1830) British essayist.

35 You might make that a double.
Neville Heath (1917–46) British murderer. Comment made when offered a drink before his execution. Attrib.

36 God will pardon me. It is His trade.
Heinrich Heine (1797–1856) German poet and writer. *Journal* (Edmond and Charles Goncourt), 23 Feb 1863

37 Turn up the lights, I don't want to go home in the dark.
O. Henry (William Sidney Porter; 1862–1910) US short-story writer. Quoting a popular song of the time. *O. Henry* (C. A. Smith), Ch. 9

38 I am about to take my last voyage, a great leap in the dark.
Thomas Hobbes (1588–1679) English philosopher.

39 If heaven had granted me five more years, I could have become a real painter.
Hokusai (1760–1849) Japanese painter. Said on his deathbed. *Famous Last Words* (B. Conrad)

40 On the contrary!
Henrik Ibsen (1828–1906) Norwegian dramatist. His nurse had just remarked that he was feeling a little better. *True Remarkable Occurrences* (J. Train)

41 So it has come at last, the distinguished thing.

Henry James (1843–1916) US novelist. *A Backward Glance* (Edith Wharton), Ch. 14

42 Don't give up the ship.

James Lawrence (1781–1813) US naval officer. As he lay dying in his ship, the US frigate *Chesapeake*, during the battle with the British frigate *Shannon*.

43 It's all been rather lovely.

John Le Mesurier (1912–83) British actor. *The Times*, 15 Nov 1983

44 Why are you weeping? Did you imagine that I was immortal?

Louis XIV (1638–1715) French king. Noticing as he lay on his deathbed that his attendants were crying. *Louis XIV* (V. Cronin)

45 *Tête d'Armée.*
Chief of the Army.

Napoleon I (Napoleon Bonaparte; 1769–1821) French emperor. Last words. Attrib.

46 I do not have to forgive my enemies, I have had them all shot.

Ramón Maria Narváez (1800–68) Spanish general and political leader. Said on his deathbed, when asked by a priest if he forgave his enemies. *Famous Last Words* (B. Conrad)

47 Kiss me, Hardy.

Lord Nelson (1758–1805) British admiral. Spoken to Sir Thomas Hardy, captain of the *Victory*, during the Battle of Trafalgar, 1805.

48 I am just going outside and may be some time.

Captain Lawrence Oates (1880–1912) British soldier and explorer. Before leaving the tent and vanishing into the blizzard on the ill-fated Antarctic expedition (1910–12). Oates was afraid that his lameness would slow down the others. *Journal* (R. F. Scott), 17 Mar 1912

49 Die, my dear Doctor, that's the last thing I shall do!

Lord Palmerston (1784–1865) British statesman.

50 I am curious to see what happens in the next world to one who dies unshriven.

Pietro Perugino (1446–1523) Italian painter. Giving his reasons for refusing to see a priest as he lay dying. Attrib.

51 Oh, my country! How I leave my country!

William Pitt the Younger (1759–1806) British statesman.

52 I think I could eat one of Bellamy's veal pies.

William Pitt the Younger

53 I have not told half of what I saw.

Marco Polo (c. 1254–1324) Venetian traveller. *The Story of Civilization* (W. Durant), Vol. I

54 I owe much; I have nothing; the rest I leave to the poor.

François Rabelais (1483–1553) French satirist.

55 Ring down the curtain, the farce is over.

François Rabelais

56 I am going in search of a great perhaps.

François Rabelais

57 I have a long journey to take, and must bid the company farewell.

Walter Raleigh (1554–1618) English explorer. *Sir Walter Raleigh* (Edward Thompson), Ch. 26

58 So little done, so much to do.

Cecil Rhodes (1853–1902) South African statesman.

59 You can keep the things of bronze and stone and give me one man to remember me just once a year.

Damon Runyon (1884–1946) US writer.

60 Dear World, I am leaving you because I am bored. I am leaving you with your worries. Good luck.

George Sanders (1906–72) British film actor. Suicide note

61 Everybody has got to die, but I have always believed an exception would be made in my case. Now what?

William Saroyan (1908–81) US dramatist. *Time*, 16 Jan 1984

62 At last I am going to be well!

Paul Scarron (1610–60) French poet. As he lay dying. Attrib.

63 Nonsense, they couldn't hit an elephant at this distance

John Sedgwick (1813–64) US general. In response to a suggestion that he should not show himself over the parapet during the Battle of the Wilderness. Attrib.

64 Thank heavens the sun has gone in and I don't have to go out and enjoy it.

Logan Pearsall Smith (1865–1946) US writer.

65 Crito, we owe a cock to Aesculapius; please pay it and don't let it pass.

Socrates (469–399 BC) Athenian philosopher. Before his execution by drinking hemlock. *Phaedo* (Plato), 118

66 Beautifully done.

Stanley Spencer (1891–1959) British artist. Said to the nurse who had injected him, just before he died. *Stanley Spencer, a Biography* (Maurice Collis), Ch. 19

67 If this is dying, I don't think much of it.

Lytton Strachey (1880–1932) British writer. *Lytton Strachey* (Michael Holroyd), Pt. V, Ch. 17

68 Ah, a German and a genius! a prodigy, admit him!

Jonathan Swift (1667–1745) Irish-born Anglican priest and writer. Learning of the arrival of Handel.

69 God bless ... God damn.

James Thurber (1894–1961) US humorist.

70 Even in the valley of the shadow of death, two and two do not make six.

Leo Tolstoy (1828–1910) Russian writer. Refusing to reconcile himself with the Russian Orthodox Church as he lay dying.

71 I have had no real gratification or enjoyment of any sort more than my neighbor on the next block who is worth only half a million.

William Henry Vanderbilt (1821–85) US railway chief. *Famous Last Words* (B. Conrad)

72 Dear me, I believe I am becoming a god. An emperor ought at least to die on his feet.

Vespasian (9–79 AD) Roman emperor. *Lives of the Caesars* (Suetonius)

73 Either that wall paper goes, or I do.

Oscar Wilde (1854–1900) Irish-born British dramatist. As he lay dying in a drab Paris bedroom. *Time*, 16 Jan 1984

74 I expect I shall have to die beyond my means

Oscar Wilde On accepting a glass of champagne on his deathbed.

75 Now God be praised, I will die in peace.

James Wolfe (1727–59) British general. After being mortally wounded at the Battle of Quebec, 1759. *Historical Journal of Campaigns, 1757–60* (J. Knox), Vol. II

LAUGHTER

See also happiness, humour

1 Laugh and grow fat.

Proverb

2 Laugh before breakfast, you'll cry before supper.

Proverb

3 Laughter is the best medicine.

Proverb

4 I make myself laugh at everything, so that I do not weep.

Beaumarchais (1732–99) French dramatist. *Le Barbier de Séville*, I:2

5 I said of laughter, It is mad: and of mirth, What doeth it?

Bible: Ecclesiastes 2:2

6 The most wasted of all days is that on which one has not laughed.

Nicolas Chamfort (1741–94) French writer. *Maximes et pensées*

7 But laughter is weakness, corruption, the foolishness of our flesh.

Umberto Eco (1932–) Italian semiologist and writer. *The Name of the Rose*

8 One must laugh before one is happy, or one may die without ever laughing at all.

Jean de La Bruyère (1645–96) French satirist. *Les Caractères*

9 Laughter is pleasant, but the exertion is too much for me.

Thomas Love Peacock (1785–1866) British novelist. Said by the Hon. Mr Listless. *Nightmare Abbey*, Ch. 5

10 Laugh, and the world laughs with you;
Weep, and you weep alone,
For the sad old earth must borrow its mirth,
But has trouble enough of its own.

Ella Wheeler Wilcox (1850–1919) US poet. *Solitude*

LAW

See also crime, justice, lawyers

1 A judge knows nothing unless it has been explained to him three times.

Proverb

2 Every dog is allowed one bite.

Proverb

3 Every one is innocent until he is proved guilty.

Proverb

4 Possession is nine points of the law.

Proverb

5 The law does not concern itself about trifles.

Proverb

6 One of the Seven was wont to say: 'That laws were like cobwebs; where the small flies were caught, and the great brake through.'

Francis Bacon (1561–1626) English philosopher. *See also* SHENSTONE; SOLON; SWIFT. *Apothegms*

7 The good of the people is the chief law.

Cicero (106–43 BC) Roman orator and statesman. *De Legibus*, III

8 The Law of England is a very strange one; it cannot compel anyone to tell the truth.…But what the Law can do is to give you seven years for not telling the truth.

Lord Darling (1849–1936) British judge. *Lord Darling* (D. Walker-Smith), Ch. 27

9 'If the law supposes that,' said Mr Bumble… 'the law is a ass – a idiot.'

Charles Dickens (1812–70) British novelist. *Oliver Twist*, Ch. 51

10 Although we have some laws which are unfair to women, some women can live their whole lives and not know the law as it affects them.

Taujan Faisal Jordanian politician. *The Times*, 15 June 1994

11 When I went to the Bar as a very young man,
(Said I to myself – said I),
I'll work on a new and original plan,
(Said I to myself – said I).

W. S. Gilbert (1836–1911) British dramatist. *Iolanthe*, I

12 The Law is the true embodiment
Of everything that's excellent.
It has no kind of fault or flaw,
And I, my lords, embody the Law.

W. S. Gilbert *Iolanthe*, I

13 There's no better way of exercising the imagination than the study of law. No poet ever interpreted nature as freely as a lawyer interprets truth.

Jean Giraudoux (1882–1944) French dramatist. *Tiger at the Gates*, I

14 Laws grind the poor, and rich men

rule the law.

Oliver Goldsmith (1728–74) Irish-born British writer. *The Traveller*

15 I know no method to secure the repeal of bad or obnoxious laws so effective as their stringent execution.

Ulysses Simpson Grant (1822–85) US general. Inaugural address, 4 Mar 1869

16 The Common Law of England has been laboriously built about a mythical figure – the figure of 'The Reasonable Man'.

A. P. Herbert (1890–1971) British writer and politician. *Uncommon Law*

17 In *this* country, my Lords,...the individual subject...'has nothing to do with the laws but to obey them.'

Bishop Samuel Horsley (1733–1806) British bishop. House of Lords, 13 Nov 1795

18 Oh, Mr. President, do not let so great an achievement suffer from any taint of legality.

Philander Chase Knox (1853–1921) US lawyer and politician. Responding to Theodore Roosevelt's request for legal justification of his acquisition of the Panama Canal Zone. *Violent Neighbours* (T. Buckley)

19 In university they don't tell you that the greater part of the law is learning to tolerate fools.

Doris Lessing (1919–) British novelist. *Martha Quest*, Pt. III, Ch. 2

20 No brilliance is needed in the law. Nothing but common sense, and relatively clean finger nails.

John Mortimer (1923–) British lawyer and dramatist. *A Voyage Round My Father*, I

21 Laws were made to be broken.

Christopher North (John Wilson; 1785–1854) Scottish writer. *Noctes Ambrosianae*, 24 May 1830

22 Let us consider the reason of the case. For nothing is law that is not reason.

John Powell (1645–1713) English judge. Coggs v. Bernard, 2 Lord Raymond, 911

23 Every law is a contract between the king and the people and therefore to be kept.

John Selden (1584–1654) English historian. *Table Talk*

24 Ignorance of the law excuses no man; not that all men know the law, but because 'tis an excuse every man will plead, and no man can tell how to confute him.

John Selden *Table Talk*

25 Still you keep o' th' windy side of the law.

William Shakespeare (1564–1616) English dramatist. *Twelfth Night*, III:4

26 Laws are generally found to be nets of such a texture, as the little creep through, the great break through, and the middle-sized are alone entangled in.

William Shenstone *See also* BACON; SOLON; SWIFT. *Essays on Men, Manners, and Things*, 'On Politics'

27 Laws are like spider's webs: if some poor weak creature come up against them, it is caught; but a bigger one can break through and get away.

Solon (6th century BC) Athenian statesman. *See also* BACON; SHENSTONE; SWIFT. *Lives of the Eminent Philosophers* (Diogenes Laertius), I

28 Laws are like cobwebs, which may catch small flies, but let wasps and hornets break through.

Jonathan Swift (1667–1745) Irish-born Anglican priest and writer. *See also* BACON; SHENSTONE; SOLON. *A Tritical Essay upon the Faculties of the Mind*

29 It is only those with the deepest pockets who can risk going to law.

Lord Woolf (1933–) British lawyer. *The Times*, 23 June 1994

LAWYERS

See also law

1 He that is his own lawyer has a fool for a client.

Proverb

2 A lawyer never goes to law himself.

Proverb

3 A lawyer's opinion is worth nothing unless paid for.

Proverb

4 Lawyers are the only persons in whom ignorance of the law is not punished.

Jeremy Bentham (1748–1832) British philosopher. Attrib.

5 Woe unto you, lawyers! for ye have taken away the key of knowledge: ye entered not in yourselves, and them that were entering in ye hindered.

Bible: Luke 11:52

6 A client is fain to hire a lawyer to keep from the injury of other lawyers – as Christians that travel in Turkey are forced to hire Janissaries, to protect them from the insolencies of other Turks.

Samuel Butler (1835–1902) British writer. *Prose Observations*

7 I do not care to speak ill of any man behind his back, but I believe the gentleman is an *attorney*.

Samuel Johnson (1709–84) British lexicographer. *Life of Johnson* (J. Boswell), Vol. II

8 It is a very salutary check for a judge to realise that if he does say something silly it is liable to get into the papers.

Mr Justice Templeman (1920–) British judge. *Observer*, 20 Aug 1978

LAZINESS

See also bed, idleness

1 I make no secret of the fact that I would

rather lie on a sofa than sweep beneath it. But you have to be efficient if you're going to be lazy.

Shirley Conran (1932–) British designer and journalist. *Superwoman*, 'The Reason Why'

2 Happy is the man with a wife to tell him what to do and a secretary to do it.

Lord Mancroft (1917–87) British businessman and writer. *The Observer*, 'Sayings of the Week', 18 Dec 1966

3 For one person who dreams of making fifty thousand pounds, a hundred people dream of being left fifty thousand pounds.

A. A. Milne (1882–1956) British writer. *If I May*, 'The Future'

4 It is better to have loafed and lost than never to have loafed at all.

James Thurber (1894–1961) US humorist. *Fables for Our Time*, 'The Courtship of Arthur and Al'

5 'Tis the voice of the sluggard, I heard him complain:
'You have waked me too soon, I must slumber again.'

Isaac Watts (1674–1748) English theologian and hymn writer. *The Sluggard*

LEADERSHIP

See also guidance

1 The trouble in modern democracy is that men do not approach to leadership until they have lost the desire to lead anyone.

Lord Beveridge (1879–1963) British economist. *The Observer*, 'Sayings of the Week', 15 Apr 1934

2 And he shall rule them with a rod of iron; as the vessels of a potter shall they be broken to shivers: even as I received of my Father.

Bible: Revelations 2:27

3 I believe in benevolent dictatorship provided I am the dictator.

Richard Branson (1950–) British entrepreneur. Remark, Nov 1984

4 Captains of industry.

Thomas Carlyle (1795–1881) Scottish historian and essayist. *Past and Present*, Bk. IV, Ch. 4

5 As the Prime Minister put it to me...he saw his role as being that of Moses.

Peter Jay (1937–) British economist and broadcaster. Referring to a conversation with James Callaghan. *Guardian Weekly*, 18 Sept 1977

6 Let me pass, I have to follow them, I am their leader.

Alexandre Auguste Ledru-Rollin (1807–74) French lawyer and politician. Trying to force his way through a mob during the Revolution of 1848, of which he was one of the chief instigators. A similar remark is attributed to Bonar Law. *The Fine Art of Political Wit* (L. Harris)

7 A leader who doesn't hesitate before he sends his nation into battle is not fit to be a leader.

Golda Meir (1898–1978) Russian-born Israeli stateswoman. *As Good as Golda* (ed. Israel and Mary Shenker)

8 No general in the midst of battle has a great discussion about what he is going to do if defeated.

David Owen (1938–) British politician. *The Observer*, 'Sayings of the Week', 6 June 1987

LEARNING

See also education, knowledge

1 What we have to learn to do, we learn by doing.

Aristotle (384–322 BC) Greek philosopher. *Nicomachean Ethics*, Bk. II

2 Miss not the discourse of the elders: for they also learned of their fathers, and of them thou shalt learn understanding, and to give answer as need requireth.

Bible: Ecclesiasticus 8:9

3 Read, mark, learn and inwardly digest.

The Book of Common Prayer *Collect, 2nd Sunday in Advent*

4 An art can only be learned in the workshop of those who are winning their bread by it.

Samuel Butler (1835–1902) British writer. *Erewhon*, Ch. 20

5 LIBOV ANDREEVNA. Are you still a student?
TROFIMOV. I expect I shall be a student to the end of my days.

Anton Chekhov (1860–1904) Russian dramatist. *The Cherry Orchard*, I

6 ...that is what learning is. You suddenly understand something you've understood all your life, but in a new way.

Doris Lessing (1919–) British novelist. *The Four-Gated City*

7 He intended, he said, to devote the rest of his life to learning the remaining twenty-two letters of the alphabet.

George Orwell (Eric Blair; 1903–50) British novelist. *Animal Farm*, Ch. 9

8 For where is any author in the world
Teaches such beauty as a woman's eye?
Learning is but an adjunct to oneself.

William Shakespeare (1564–1616) English dramatist. *Love's Labour's Lost*, IV:3

9 Not with blinded eyesight poring over miserable books.

Alfred, Lord Tennyson (1809–92) British poet. *Locksley Hall*

10 One impulse from a vernal wood
May teach you more of man,
Of moral evil and of good,
Than all the sages can.

William Wordsworth (1770–1850) British poet. *The Tables Turned*

11 Some for renown, on scraps of learning dote,
And think they grow immortal as they quote.

Edward Young (1683–1765) British poet. *Love of Fame*, I

LEISURE

See also idleness, merrymaking, pleasure, rest

1 The wisdom of a learned man cometh by opportunity of leisure: and he that hath little business shall become wise.
How can he get wisdom that holdeth the plough, and that glorieth in the goad, that driveth oxen, and is occupied in their labours, and whose talk is of bullocks?

Bible: Ecclesiasticus 38:24–25

2 God put us on this earth to read *Ulysses* and to try to find the time to get started on *Finnegan's Wake*...He did not intend us to pole-vault or bungy-jump, do aerobics or go white-water rafting.

Malcolm Bradbury (1932–) British novelist.
The Independent Magazine, 'Physicality', 22 May 1993

3 Hey! Mr Tambourine Man, play a song for me.
I'm not sleepy and there is no place I'm going to.

Bob Dylan (Robert Allen Zimmerman; 1941–) US popular singer. *Mr Tambourine Man*

4 If all the year were playing holidays, To sport would be as tedious as to work.

William Shakespeare (1564–1616) English dramatist. *Henry IV, Part One*, I:2

5 Days off.

Spencer Tracy (1900–67) US film star. Explaining what he looked for in a script. Attrib.

LETTER-WRITING

See also communication

1 ...a habit the pleasure of which increases with practise, but becomes more urksome with neglect.

Abigail Adams (1744–1818) US feminist. Letter to her daughter, 8 May 1808

2 When he wrote a letter, he would put that which was most material in the postscript, as if it had been a by-matter.

Francis Bacon (1561–1626) English philosopher. *Essays*, 'Of Cunning'

3 His sayings are generally like women's letters; all the pith is in the postscript.

William Hazlitt (1778–1830) British essayist. Referring to Charles Lamb. *Conversations of Northcote*

LEXICOGRAPHY

1 To finish is both a relief and a release from an extraordinarily pleasant prison.

Robert Burchfield (1923–) New Zealand editor. On completing the supplements to the Oxford English Dictionary. *The Observer*, 'Sayings of the Week', 11 Sept 1986

2 Like Webster's Dictionary
We're Morocco bound.

Johnny Burke (1908–64) US songwriter. Song, 'Road to Morocco' from the film *The Road to Morocco*

3 The responsibility of a dictionary is to record a language, not set its style.

Philip Babcock Gove (1902–72) US dictionary editor. Letter to *Life Magazine*, 17 Nov 1961

4 But these were the dreams of a poet doomed at last to wake a lexicographer.

Samuel Johnson (1709–84) British lexicographer. *Dictionary of the English Language*

5 *Dull.* 8. To make dictionaries is dull work.

Samuel Johnson *Dictionary of the English Language*

6 *Lexicographer.* A writer of dictionaries, a harmless drudge.

Samuel Johnson *Dictionary of the English Language*

7 I've been in *Who's Who*, and I know what's what, but this is the first time I ever made the dictionary.

Mae West (1892–1980) US actress. On having a life-jacket named after her. Attrib.

LIBERALISM

1 To be absolutely honest, what I feel really bad about is that I don't feel worse. There's the ineffectual liberal's problem in a nutshell.

Michael Frayn (1933–) British journalist and writer. *The Observer*, 8 Aug 1965

2 When a liberal is abused, he says: Thank God they didn't beat me. When he is beaten, he thanks God they didn't kill him. When he is killed, he will thank God that his immortal soul has been delivered from its mortal clay.

Lenin (Vladimir Ilich Ulyanov; 1870–1924) Russian revolutionary leader. Lenin heard this characterization at a meeting, and repeated it with approval. *The Government's Falsification of the Duma and the Tasks of the Social-Democrats*, 'Proletary', Dec 1906.

3 A pleasant old buffer, nephew to a lord,
Who believed that the bank was mightier than the sword,
And that an umbrella might pacify barbarians abroad:
Just like an old liberal
Between the wars.

William Plomer (1903–73) South African poet and novelist. *Father and Son: 1939*

LIBERTY

1 It is not our frowning battlements...or the strength of our gallant and disciplined army. These are not our reliance against a resumption of tyranny in our fair land....Our defence is in the preservation of the spirit which prizes liberty as the heritage of all men, in all lands, everywhere.

Abraham Lincoln (1809–65) US statesman. Speech, 11 Sept 1858

2 Liberty means responsibility. That is why most men dread it.

George Bernard Shaw (1856–1950) Irish dramatist and critic.

LIFE

See also afterlife, human condition, life and death, mortality, purpose, time, world-weariness

1 Life begins at forty.

Proverb

2 Life is just a bowl of cherries.

Proverb

3 Life is sweet.

Proverb

4 Is it so small a thing
To have enjoy'd the sun,
To have lived light in the spring,
To have loved, to have thought, to have done?

Matthew Arnold (1822–88) British poet and critic. *Empedocles on Etna*

5 Before this strange disease of modern life,
With its sick hurry, its divided aims.

Matthew Arnold *The Scholar Gipsy*

6 Who saw life steadily, and saw it whole:
The mellow glory of the Attic stage.

Matthew Arnold *Sonnets to a Friend*

7 Remember that no man loses any other life than this which he now lives, nor lives any other than this which he now loses.

Marcus Aurelius (121–180 AD) Roman emperor. *Meditations*, Bk. II, Ch. 14

8 The universe is transformation; our life is what our thoughts make it.

Marcus Aurelius *Meditations*, Bk. IV, Ch. 3

9 The present life of men on earth, O king, as compared with the whole length of time which is unknowable to us, seems to me to be like this: as if, when you are sitting at dinner with your chiefs and ministers in wintertime,...one of the sparrows from outside flew very quickly through the hall; as if it came in one door and soon went out through another. In that actual time it is indoors it is not touched by the winter's storm; but yet the tiny period of calm is over in a moment, and having come out of the winter it soon returns to the winter and slips out of your sight. Man's life appears to be more or less like this; and of what may follow it, or what preceded it, we are absolutely ignorant.

St Bede (The Venerable Bede; c. 673–735 AD) English churchman and historian. *Ecclesiastical History of the English People*, Bk. II, Ch. 13

10 Life is rather like a tin of sardines – we're all of us looking for the key.

Alan Bennett (1934–) British playwright. *Beyond the Fringe*

11 Your whole life is on the other side of the glass. And there is nobody watching.

Alan Bennett *The Old Country*, I

12 Life is the ensemble of functions that resist death.

Marie François Bichat (1771–1802) French pathologist. *Recherches physiologiques sur la vie et la mort*

13 For everything that lives is holy, life delights in life.

William Blake (1757–1827) British poet. *America*

14 At last awake
From life, that insane dream we take
For waking now.

Robert Browning (1812–89) British poet. *Easter-Day*, XIV

15 How good is man's life, the mere living! how fit to employ
All the heart and the soul and the senses for ever in joy!

Robert Browning *Saul*, IX

16 Life is one long process of getting tired.

Samuel Butler (1835–1902) British writer. *Notebooks*

17 Life is the art of drawing sufficient conclusions from insufficient premises.

Samuel Butler *Notebooks*

18 Life is a tragedy when seen in close-up, but a comedy in long-shot.

Charlie Chaplin (Sir Charles Spencer C.; 1889–1977) British film actor. In *The Guardian*, Obituary, 28 Dec 1977

19 Life is a maze in which we take the wrong turning before we have learnt to walk.

Cyril Connolly (1903–74) British journalist. *The Unquiet Grave*

20 Life is an incurable disease.

Abraham Cowley (1618–67) English poet. *To Dr Scarborough*

21 What a fine comedy this world would be if one did not play a part in it!

Denis Diderot (1713–84) French writer. *Letters to Sophie Volland*

22 People do not live nowadays – they get about ten percent out of life.

Isadora Duncan (1878–1927) US dancer. *This Quarter Autumn*, 'Memoirs'

23 'Put your shoes at the door, sleep, prepare for life.'
The last twist of the knife.

T. S. Eliot (1888–1965) US-born British poet and dramatist. *Rhapsody on a Windy Night*

24 I have measured out my life with coffee spoons.

T. S. Eliot *The Love Song of J. Alfred Prufrock*

25 One thing is certain, that Life flies;
One thing is certain, and the Rest is Lies;
The Flower that once has blown for ever dies.

Edward Fitzgerald (1809–83) British poet. *The Rubáiyát of Omar Khayyám* (1st edn.), XXVI

26 Life is a jest; and all things show it.

I thought so once; but now I know it.

John Gay (1685–1732) English poet and dramatist. *My Own Epitaph*

27 Life's Little Ironies.

Thomas Hardy (1840–1928) British novelist. Title of book of stories

28 The world is like a ride in an amusement park…some people have been on the ride for a long time and they begin to question, 'Is this real or is this just a ride?' and other people have remembered and they come back to us and they say 'Hey, don't worry, don't be afraid ever because this is just a ride,' and we kill those people… but it doesn't matter because it's just a ride and we can change it any time we want – it's only a choice…a choice right now between fear and love.

Bill Hicks (1961–94) US comedian. *Revelations*

29 Life is just one damned thing after another.

Elbert Hubbard (1856–1915) US writer. *A Thousand and One Epigrams*

30 Life isn't all beer and skittles.

Thomas Hughes (1822–96) British novelist. *Tom Brown's Schooldays*, Pt. I, Ch. 2

31 Live all you can; it's a mistake not to. It doesn't so much matter what you do in particular, so long as you have your life. If you haven't had that what *have* you had?

Henry James (1843–1916) US novelist. *The Ambassadors*, Bk. V, Ch. 2

32 Life is like a sewer. What you get out of it depends on what you put into it.

Tom Lehrer (1928–) US university teacher and songwriter. *We Will all Go together When We Go*

33 Life is what happens to you while you're busy making other plans.

John Lennon (1940–80) British rock musician. *Beautiful Boy*

34 Our ingress into the world
Was naked and bare;
Our progress through the world
Is trouble and care.

Henry Wadsworth Longfellow (1807–82) US poet. *Tales of A Wayside Inn*, 'The Student's Tale'

35 And thou wilt give thyself relief, if thou doest every act of thy life as if it were the last.

Marcus Aurelius (121–180 AD) Roman emperor. *Meditations*, Bk. II, Ch. 5

36 Life to me is like boarding-house wallpaper. It takes a long time to get used to it, but when you finally do, you never notice that it's there. And then you hear the decorators are arriving.

Derek Marlowe (1938–) British writer. *A Dandy in Aspic*

37 I've looked at life from both sides now
From win and lose and still somehow
It's life's illusions I recall
I really don't know life at all.

Joni Mitchell (1943–) U.S. singer and songwriter. *Both Sides Now*

38 There are three ingredients in the good life: learning, earning and yearning.

Christopher Darlington Morley (1890–1957) US writer. *Parnassus on Wheels*, Ch. 10

39 Our lives are merely strange dark interludes in the electric display of God the Father.

Eugene O'Neill (1888–1953) US dramatist. *Strange Interlude*

40 Most people get a fair amount of fun out of their lives, but on balance life is suffering and only the very young or the very foolish imagine otherwise.

George Orwell (Eric Blair; 1903–50) British novelist. *Shooting an Elephant*

41 The vanity of human life is like a river, constantly passing away, and yet constantly coming on.

Alexander Pope (1688–1744) British poet. *Thoughts on Various Subjects*

42 Life is not a spectacle or a feast; it is a predicament.

George Santayana (1863–1952) US philosopher. *The Perpetual Pessimist* (Sagittarius and George)

43 It is only in the microscope that our life looks so big. It is an indivisible point, drawn out and magnified by the powerful lenses of Time and Space.

Arthur Schopenhauer (1788–1860) German philosopher. *Parerga and Paralipomena*, 'The Vanity of Existence'

44 Life is as tedious as a twice-told tale
Vexing the dull ear of a drowsy man.

William Shakespeare (1564–1616) English dramatist. *King John*, III:4

45 Tomorrow, and tomorrow, and tomorrow,
Creeps in this petty pace from day to day
To the last syllable of recorded time,
And all our yesterdays have lighted fools
The way to dusty death. Out, out, brief candle!
Life's but a walking shadow, a poor player,
That struts and frets his hour upon the stage,
And then is heard no more; it is a tale
Told by an idiot, full of sound and fury,
Signifying nothing.

William Shakespeare *Macbeth*, V:5

46 And so, from hour to hour, we ripe and ripe,
And then, from hour to hour, we rot and rot;
And thereby hangs a tale.

William Shakespeare *As You Like It*, II:7

47 Lift not the painted veil which those who live
Call life.

Percy Bysshe Shelley (1792–1822) British poet. *Lift not the Painted Veil*

48 Life is a gamble, at terrible odds – if it was a bet, you wouldn't take it.

Tom Stoppard (1937–) Czech-born British dramatist. *Rosencrantz and Guildenstern Are Dead*, III

49 As our life is very short, so it is very miserable, and therefore it is well it is short.

Jeremy Taylor (1613–67) English Anglican theologian. *The Rule and Exercise of Holy Dying*, Ch. 1

50 A life that moves to gracious ends
Thro' troops of unrecording friends,
A deedful life, a silent voice.

Alfred, Lord Tennyson (1809–92) British poet. *To –, after reading a Life and Letters*

51 Oh, isn't life a terrible thing, thank God?

Dylan Thomas (1914–53) Welsh poet. *Under Milk Wood*

52 For life is but a dream whose shapes return,
Some frequently, some seldom, some by night
And some by day.

James Thomson (1834–82) British poet. *The City of Dreadful Night*, I

53 The world is a comedy to those who think, a tragedy to those who feel.

Horace Walpole (1717–97) British writer. Letter to Sir Horace Mann, 1769

54 I spent the afternoon musing on Life. If you come to think of it, what a queer thing Life is! So unlike anything else, don't you know, if you see what I mean.

P. G. Wodehouse (1881–1975) British humorous novelist. *My Man Jeeves*, 'Rallying Round Old George'

55 When I think of all the books I have read, and of the wise words I have heard spoken, and of the anxiety I have given to parents and grandparents, and of the hopes that I have had, all life weighed in the scales of my own life seems to me preparation for something that never happens.

W. B. Yeats (1865–1939) Irish poet. *Autobiography*

56 Never to have lived is best, ancient writers say;
Never to have drawn the breath of life,
never to have looked into the eye of day
The second best's a gay goodnight and quickly turn away.

W. B. Yeats *Oedipus at Colonus*

LIFE AND DEATH

See also death, life

1 Every moment dies a man,
Every moment one and one sixteenth is born.

Charles Babbage (1792–1871) British mathematician. A parody of TENNYSON's *Vision of Sin*. Letter to Tennyson

2 I call heaven and earth to record this day against you, that I have set before you life and death, blessing and cursing: therefore choose life, that both thou and thy seed may live.

Bible: Deuteronomy 30:19

3 God has forgotten me.

Jeanne Calment (1875–) French woman, aged 120 years. *The Daily Telegraph*, Oct 1995

4 This world nis but a thurghfare ful of wo,
And we ben pilgrimes, passinge to and fro;
Deeth is an ende of every worldly sore.

Geoffrey Chaucer (c. 1342–1400) English poet. *The Canterbury Tales*, 'The Knight's Tale'

5 Birth, and copulation, and death.
That's all the facts when you come to brass tacks.

T. S. Eliot (1888–1965) US-born British poet and dramatist. *Sweeney Agonistes*, 'Fragment of an Agon'

6 I came like Water, and like Wind I go.

Edward Fitzgerald (1809–83) British poet. *The Rubáiyát of Omar Khayyám* (1st edn.), XXVIII

7 I believe that the struggle against death, the unconditional and self-willed determination to live, is the motive power behind the lives and activities of all outstanding men.

Hermann Hesse (1877–1962) German novelist and poet. *Steppenwolf*, 'Treatise on the Steppenwolf'

8 There are only three events in a man's life; birth, life, and death; he is not conscious of being born, he dies in pain, and he forgets to live.

Jean de La Bruyère (1645–96) French satirist. *Les Caractères*

9 I strove with none; for none was worth my strife;
Nature I loved, and, next to Nature, Art;
I warmed both hands before the fire of life;
It sinks, and I am ready to depart.

Walter Savage Landor (1775–1864) British poet and writer. *I Strove with None*

10 Many men would take the death-sentence without a whimper to escape the life-sentence which fate carries in her other hand.

T. E. Lawrence (1888–1935) British soldier and writer. *The Mint*, Pt. I, Ch. 4

11 Life is a great surprise. I do not see why death should not be an even greater one.

Vladimir Nabokov (1899–1977) Russian-born US novelist. *Pale Fire*, 'Commentary'

12 There is no cure for birth and death save to enjoy the interval.

George Santayana (1863–1952) US philosopher. *Soliloquies in England*, 'War Shrines'

13 He hath awakened from the dream of life –
'Tis we, who lost in stormy visions, keep
With phantoms an unprofitable strife,
And in mad trance, strike with our spirit's knife
Invulnerable nothings.

Percy Bysshe Shelley (1792–1822) British poet. *Adonais*, XXXIX

14 Every moment dies a man,
Every moment one is born.

Alfred, Lord Tennyson (1809–92) British poet. For a parody, *see* BABBAGE. *The Vision of Sin*

15 Because there is no difference.

Thales (c. 624–547 BC) Greek philosopher and astronomer. His reply when asked why he chose to carry on living after saying there was no difference between life and death. *The Story of Civilization* (W. Durant), Vol. 2

LIMERICKS

A small selection

1 There's a wonderful family called Stein,
There's Gert and there's Epp and there's Ein;
Gert's poems are bunk,
Epp's statues are junk,
And no one can understand Ein.

Anonymous

2 There was a faith-healer of Deal,
Who said, 'Although pain isn't real,
If I sit on a pin
And it punctures my skin,
I dislike what I fancy I feel.'

Anonymous

3 There was an old man from Darjeeling,
Who boarded a bus bound for Ealing,
He saw on the door:
'Please don't spit on the floor,'
So he stood up and spat on the ceiling.

Anonymous

4 There was an old man of Boulogne
Who sang a most topical song.
It wasn't the words
That frightened the birds,
But the horrible double-entendre.

Anonymous

5 There was a young lady of Riga,
Who went for a ride on a tiger;
They returned from the ride
With the lady inside,
And a smile on the face of the tiger.

Anonymous

6 There was a young man of Japan
Whose limericks never would scan;
When they said it was so,
He replied, 'Yes, I know,
But I always try to get as many words into the
last line as ever I possibly can.'

Anonymous

7 There once was a man who said 'God
Must think it exceedingly odd
If he find that this tree
Continues to be
When there's no one about in the Quad.'

Ronald Knox (1888–1957) British Roman Catholic priest. For a reply, see below. Atrrib.

8 Dear Sir, Your astonishment's odd:
I am always about in the Quad.
And that's why the tree
Will continue to be,
Since observed by Yours faithfully, God.

Anonymous A reply to KNOX.

9 There was an Old Man with a beard,
Who said, 'It is just as I feared! –
Two Owls and a Hen,
Four Larks and a Wren,
Have all built their nests in my beard!'

Edward Lear (1812–88) British artist and writer. *Book of Nonsense*

LITERACY

See also reading, writing

1 The ratio of literacy to illiteracy is constant, but nowadays the illiterates can read and write.

Alberto Moravia (Alberto Pincherle; 1907–90) Italian novelist. *The Observer*, 14 Oct 1979

2 To be a well-favoured man is the gift of fortune; but to write and read comes by nature.

William Shakespeare (1564–1616) English dramatist. *Much Ado About Nothing*, III:3

LITERATURE

See also arts, books, criticism, fiction, novels, plays, poetry, poetry and prose, poets, prose, reading, theatre, writers, writing

1 Literature is the art of writing something that will be read twice; journalism what will be grasped at once.

Cyril Connolly (1903–74) British journalist. *Enemies of Promise*, Ch. 3

2 A work that aspires, however humbly, to the condition of art should carry its justification in every line.

Joseph Conrad (Teodor Josef Konrad Korzeniowski; 1857–1924) Polish-born British novelist. *The Nigger of the Narcissus*, Preface

3 The reading of all good books is like a conversation with the finest men of past centuries.

René Descartes (1596–1650) French philosopher. *Le Discours de la méthode*

4 Shakespeare is fine for grammar school kids.

Nigel de Gruchy (1943–) British teacher and trade unionist. *The Observer*, 5 July 1992

5 He knew everything about literature except how to enjoy it.

Joseph Heller (1923–) US novelist. *Catch-22*, Ch. 8

6 The proper study of mankind is books.

Aldous Huxley (1894–1964) British novelist. *Chrome Yellow*

7 Literature flourishes best when it is half a trade and half an art.

Dean Inge (1860–1954) British churchman. *The Victorian Age*

8 It takes a great deal of history to produce a little literature.

Henry James (1843–1916) US novelist. *Life of Nathaniel Hawthorne*, Ch. 1

9 Was there ever yet anything written by mere man that was wished longer by its readers, excepting *Don Quixote, Robinson Crusoe,* and the *Pilgrim's Progress*?

Samuel Johnson (1709–84) British lexicographer. *Johnsonian Miscellanies* (ed. G. B. Hill), Vol. I

10 *Sturm und Drang.*
Storm and stress.

Friedrich Maximilian von Klinger (1752–1831) German

dramatist and novelist. Used to designate a late 18th-century literary movement in Germany. Play title

11 Our American professors like their literature clear and cold and pure and very dead.

Sinclair Lewis (1885–1951) US novelist. Speech, on receiving the Nobel Prize, 1930

12 Literature is mostly about having sex and not much about having children; life is the other way round.

David Lodge (1935–) British author. *The British Museum is Falling Down*, Ch. 4

13 You understand *Epipsychidion* best when you are in love; *Don Juan* when anger is subsiding into indifference. Why not Strindberg when you have a temperature?

Desmond MacCarthy (1877–1952) British writer and theatre critic. *Theatre*, 'Miss Julie and the Pariah'

14 Literature and butterflies are the two sweetest passions known to man.

Vladimir Nabokov (1899–1977) Russian-born US novelist. *Radio Times*, Oct 1962

15 Literature is news that STAYS news.

Ezra Pound (1885–1972) US poet. *ABC of Reading*, Ch. 2

16 Great Literature is simply language charged with meaning to the utmost possible degree.

Ezra Pound *How to Read*

17 Romanticism is the art of presenting people with the literary works which are capable of affording them the greatest possible pleasure, in the present state of their customs and beliefs. Classicism, on the other hand, presents them with the literature that gave the greatest possible pleasure to their great-grandfathers.

Stendhal (Henri Beyle; 1783–1842) French novelist. *Racine et Shakespeare*, Ch. 3

18 Something that everybody wants to have read and nobody wants to read.

Mark Twain (Samuel Langhorne Clemens; 1835–1910) US writer. Definition of a classic of literature. Speech at Nineteenth Century Club, New York, 20 Nov 1900

19 '*Language*, man!' roared Parsons; 'why, it's LITERATURE!'

H. G. Wells (1866–1946) British writer. *The History of Mr Polly*, Pt. I, Ch. 3

20 Literature is the orchestration of platitudes.

Thornton Wilder (1897–1975) US novelist and dramatist. *Time* magazine

LOGIC

See also philosophy

1 'Contrariwise,' continued Tweedledee, 'if it was so, it might be; and if it were so, it would be: but as it isn't, it ain't. That's logic.'

Lewis Carroll (Charles Lutwidge Dodgson; 1832–98) British writer. *Through the Looking-Glass*, Ch. 4

2 You can only find truth with logic if you have already found truth without it.

G. K. Chesterton (1874–1936) British writer. *The Man who was Orthodox*

3 Logical consequences are the scarecrows of fools and the beacons of wise men.

T. H. Huxley (1825–95) British biologist. *Science and Culture*, 'On the Hypothesis that Animals are Automata'

4 The world is everything that is the case.

Ludwig Wittgenstein (1889–1951) Austrian philosopher. *Tractatus Logico-Philosophicus*, Ch. 1

5 Logic must take care of itself.

Ludwig Wittgenstein *Tractatus Logico-Philosophicus*, Ch. 5

LONDON

See also England

1 The streets of London are paved with gold.

Proverb

2 Oranges and lemons,
Say the bells of St Clement's.
You owe me five farthings,
Say the bells of St Martin's.
When will you pay me?
Say the bells of Old Bailey.
When I grow rich,
Say the bells of Shoreditch.
When will that be?
Say the bells of Stepney.
I'm sure I don't know,
Says the great bell at Bow.
Here comes a candle to light you to bed,
Here comes a chopper to chop off your head.

Tommy Thumb's Pretty Song Book

3 Nobody is healthy in London, nobody can be.

Jane Austen (1775–1817) British novelist. *Emma*, Ch. 12

4 Let's all go down the Strand.

Harry Castling (19th century) British songwriter. Song title

5 But what is to be the fate of the great wen of all?

William Cobbett (1763–1835) British journalist and writer. A wen is a sebaceous cyst. *Rural Rides*

6 London, that great cesspool into which all the loungers of the Empire are irresistibly drained.

Arthur Conan Doyle (1856–1930) British writer. *A Study in Scarlet*

7 Crowds without company, and dissipation without pleasure.

Edward Gibbon (1737–94) British historian. *Autobiography*

8 The tourists who come to our island take in the Monarchy along with feeding the pigeons in Trafalgar Square.

William Hamilton (1917–) Scottish MP. *My Queen and I*, Ch. 9

9 I think the full tide of human existence is at Charing-Cross.

Samuel Johnson (1709–84) British lexicographer. *Life of Johnson* (J. Boswell), Vol. II

10 When a man is tired of London, he is tired of life; for there is in London all that life can afford.

Samuel Johnson *Life of Johnson* (J. Boswell), Vol. III

11 London, that great sea, whose ebb and flow
At once is deaf and loud, and on the shore
Vomits its wrecks, and still howls on for more.

Percy Bysshe Shelley (1792–1822) British poet. *Letter to Maria Gisborne*, I

12 Hell is a city much like London –
A populous and smoky city.

Percy Bysshe Shelley *Peter Bell the Third*

13 Crossing Piccadilly Circus.

Joseph Thomson (1858–95) Scottish explorer. His reply when asked by J. M. Barrie what was the most hazardous part of his expedition to Africa. *J. M. Barrie* (D. Dunbar)

14 Earth has not anything to show more fair:
Dull would he be of soul who could pass by
A sight so touching in its majesty:
The City now doth, like a garment, wear
The beauty of the morning; silent, bare,
Ships, towers, domes, theatres, and temples lie
Open unto the fields, and to the sky;
All bright and glittering in the smokeless air.

William Wordsworth (1770–1850) British poet. *Sonnets*, 'Composed upon Westminster Bridge'

LONELINESS

See also solitude

1 Oh! why does the wind blow upon me so wild?
– It is because I'm nobody's child?

Phila Henrietta Case (fl. 1864) British poet. *Nobody's Child*

2 A fav'rite has no friend.

Thomas Gray (1716–71) British poet. *Ode on the Death of a Favourite Cat*

3 Pray that your loneliness may spur you into finding something to live for, great enough to die for.

Dag Hammarskjöld (1905–61) Swedish diplomat. *Diaries*, 1951

4 Waits at the window, wearing the face that she keeps in a jar by the door
Who is it for? All the lonely people, where do they all come from?
All the lonely people, where do they all belong?

John Lennon (1940–80) British rock musician. *Eleanor Rigby* (with Paul McCartney)

5 My heart is a lonely hunter that hunts on a lonely hill.

Fiona Macleod (William Sharp; 1856–1905) Scottish poet and writer. *The Lonely Hunter*

6 To be alone is the fate of all great minds – a fate deplored at times, but still always chosen as the less grievous of two evils.

Arthur Schopenhauer (1788–1860) German philosopher. *Aphorismen zur Lebensweisheit*

7 Loneliness and the feeling of being unwanted is the most terrible poverty.

Mother Teresa (Agnes Gonxha Bojaxhui; 1910–) Yugoslavian missionary in Calcutta. *Time*, 'Saints Among Us', 29 Dec 1975

8 The hunchback in the park
A solitary mister
Propped between trees and water.

Dylan Thomas (1914–53) Welsh poet. *The Hunchback in the Park*

9 She dwelt among the untrodden ways
Beside the springs of Dove,
A maid whom there were none to praise
And very few to love...

William Wordsworth (1770–1850) British poet. *She Dwelt Among the Untrodden Ways*

10 The wind blows out of the gates of the day,
The wind blows over the lonely of heart,
And the lonely of heart is withered away.

W. B. Yeats (1865–1939) Irish poet. *The Land of Heart's Desire*

LONGEVITY

See also age, life, old age

1 Aging seems to be the only available way to live a long time.

Daniel-François-Esprit Auber (1782–1871) French composer. *Dictionnaire Encyclopédique* (E. Guérard)

2 Get your room full of good air, then shut up the windows and keep it. It will keep for years. Anyway, don't keep using your lungs all the time. Let them rest.

Stephen Leacock (1869–1944) English-born Canadian economist and humorist. *Literary Lapses*, 'How to Live to be 200'

3 If you live long enough, the venerability factor creeps in; you get accused of things you never did and praised for virtues you never had.

I. F. Stone (1907–89) US writer and publisher. *Peter's Quotations* (Laurence J. Peter)

LOSS

See also defeat, mourning

1 'Tis better to have loved and lost than never to have lost at all.

Samuel Butler (1835–1902) British writer. *The Way of All Flesh*, Ch. 77

2 What's lost upon the roundabouts we pulls up on the swings!

Patrick Reginald Chalmers (1872–1942) British banker and novelist. *Green Days and Blue Days: Roundabouts and Swings*

3 And much more am I sorrier for my good knights' loss than for the loss of my fair queen; for queens I might have enough, but such a fellowship of good knights shall never be together in no company.

Thomas Malory (1400–71) English writer. *Morte d'Arthur*, Bk. XX, Ch. 9

4 There is a ghost
That eats handkerchiefs;
It keeps you company
On all your travels.

Christian Morgenstern (1871–1914) German poet. *Der Gingganz*, 'Gespenst'

5 Where have all the flowers gone?
Young girls picked them every one.

Pete Seeger (1919–) US folksinger and songwriter. *Where Have All the Flowers Gone?*

6 I've lost the only playboy of the western world.

John Millington Synge (1871–1909) Anglo-Irish dramatist. The closing words. *The Playboy of the Western World*, III

7 I've lost one of my children this week.

Joseph Turner (1775–1851) British painter. His customary remark following the sale of one of his paintings. *Sketches of Great Painters* (E. Chubb)

8 To lose one parent, Mr Worthing, may be regarded as a misfortune; to lose both looks like carelessness.

Oscar Wilde (1854–1900) Irish-born British dramatist. *The Importance of Being Earnest*, I

LOVE

See also admiration, love and death, love and friendship, love and hate, love and marriage, lust, passion, sex

1 All is fair in love and war.

Proverb

2 All the world loves a lover.

Proverb

3 Love laughs at locksmiths.

Proverb

4 Love makes the world go round.

Proverb

5 Love me, love my dog.

Proverb

6 Love will find a way.

Proverb

7 Lucky at cards, unlucky in love.

Proverb

8 No love like the first love.

Proverb

9 Salt water and absence wash away love.

Proverb

10 The way to a man's heart is through his stomach.

Proverb

11 True love never grows old.

Proverb

12 When poverty comes in at the door, love flies out of the window.

Proverb

13 In Scarlet town, where I was born,
There was a fair maid dwellin',
Made every youth cry *Well-a-way!*
Her name was Barbara Allen.

All in the merry month of May,
When green buds they were swellin',
Young Jemmy Grove on his death-bed lay,
For love of Barbara Allen.

So slowly, slowly rase she up,
And slowly she came nigh him,
And when she drew the curtain by –
'Young man, I think you're dyin'!'.

Anonymous *Barbara Allen's Cruelty*

14 Greensleeves was all my joy,
Greensleeves was my delight,
Greensleeves was my heart of gold,
And who but Lady Greensleeves.

Anonymous *Greensleeves*

15 There were twa sisters sat in a bour;
Binnorie, O Binnorie!
There came a knight to be their wooer,
By the bonnie milldams o' Binnorie.

Anonymous *Binnorie*

16 Oh, love is real enough, you will find it some day, but it has one arch-enemy – and that is life.

Jean Anouilh (1910–87) French dramatist. *Ardèle*

17 Love is, above all, the gift of oneself.

Jean Anouilh *Ardèle*

18 When it comes, will it come without warning
Just as I'm picking my nose?
Will it knock on my door in the morning,
Or tread in the bus on my toes?
Will it come like a change in the weather?
Will its greeting be courteous or rough?
Will it alter my life altogether?
O tell me the truth about love.

W. H. Auden (1907–73) British poet. *Twelve Songs*, XII

19 Nuptial love maketh mankind; friendly love perfecteth it; but wanton love corrupteth and embaseth it.

Francis Bacon (1561–1626) English philosopher. *Essays*, 'Of Love'

20 Women who love the same man have a kind of bitter freemasonry.

Max Beerbohm (1872–1956) British writer. *Zuleika Dobson*, Ch. 4

21 Love ceases to be a pleasure, when it ceases to be a secret.

Aphra Behn (1640–89) English novelist and dramatist. *The Lover's Watch*, 'Four o'clock'

22 Beloved, let us love one another: for love is of God; and every one that loveth is born of God, and knoweth God.
He that loveth not knoweth not God;

for God is love.
Bible: I John 4:7–8

23 If a man say, I love God, and hateth his brother, he is a liar: for he that loveth not his brother whom he hath seen, how can he love God whom he hath not seen?
Bible: I John 4:20

24 There is no fear in love; but perfect love casteth out fear: because fear hath torment. He that feareth is not made perfect in love.
Bible: I John 4:18

25 Greater love hath no man than this, that a man lay down his life for his friends.
Bible: John 15:13

26 Jesus said unto him, Thou shalt love the Lord thy God with all thy heart, and with all thy soul, and with all thy mind.
This is the first and great commandment.
And the second is like unto it, Thou shalt love thy neighbour as thyself.
On these two commandments hang all the law and the prophets.
Bible: Matthew 22:37–40

27 Love seeketh not itself to please,
Nor for itself hath any care,
But for another gives its ease,
And builds a Heaven in Hell's despair.
William Blake (1757–1827) British poet. *Songs of Experience*, 'The Clod and the Pebble'

28 Love seeketh only Self to please,
To bind another to its delight,
Joys in another's loss of ease,
And builds a Hell in Heaven's despite.
William Blake *Songs of Experience*, 'The Clod and the Pebble'

29 Although love dwells in gorgeous palaces, and sumptuous apartments, more willingly than in miserable and desolate cottages, it cannot be denied but that he sometimes causes his power to be felt in the gloomy recesses of forests, among the most bleak and rugged mountains, and in the dreary caves of a desert...
Giovanni Boccaccio (1313–75) Italian writer and poet. *Decameron*, 'Third Day'

30 I love thee with a love I seemed to lose
With my lost saints – I love thee with the breath,
Smiles, tears, of all my life! – and, if God choose,
I shall but love thee better after death.
Elizabeth Barrett Browning (1806–61) British poet. *Sonnets from the Portuguese*, XLIII

31 Such ever was love's way; to rise, it stoops.
Robert Browning (1812–89) British poet. *A Death in the Desert*

32 Green grow the rashes O,
Green grow the rashes O,
The sweetest hours that e'er I spend,
Are spent amang the lasses O!
Robert Burns (1759–96) Scottish poet. *Green Grow the Rashes*

33 My love is like a red red rose
That's newly sprung in June:
My love is like the melodie
That's sweetly play'd in tune.
Robert Burns *A Red, Red Rose*

34 Gin a body meet a body
Coming through the rye;
Gin a body kiss a body,
Need a body cry?
Robert Burns *Coming through the Rye*

35 God is Love – I dare say. But what a mischievous devil Love is!
Samuel Butler (1835–1902) British writer. *Notebooks*

36 Of all the girls that are so smart
There's none like pretty Sally;
She is the darling of my heart
And she lives in our alley.
Henry Carey (c. 1690–1743) English poet and musician. *Sally in our Alley*

37 There ain't a lady livin' in the land
As I'd swop for my dear old Dutch!
Albert Chevalier (1861–1923) British music-hall artist. *My Old Dutch*

38 Many a man has fallen in love with a girl
in a light so dim he would not have chosen a suit by it.
Maurice Chevalier (1888–1972) French singer and actor. Attrib.

39 To the men and women who own men and women
those of us meant to be lovers
we will not pardon you
for wasting our bodies and time
Leonard Cohen (1934–) Canadian poet. *The Energy of Slaves*

40 Love and a cottage! Eh, Fanny! Ah, give me indifference and a coach and six!
George Colman, the Elder (1732–94) British dramatist. *The Clandestine Marriage*, I:2

41 See how love and murder will out.
William Congreve (1670–1729) British Restoration dramatist. *The Double Dealer*, IV:6

42 Lord, what is a lover that it can give? Why one makes lovers as fast as one pleases, and they live as long as one pleases, and they die as soon as one pleases: and then if one pleases one makes more.
William Congreve *The Way of the World*, II:4

43 Say what you will, 'tis better to be left than never to have been loved.
William Congreve *The Way of the World*, II:1

44 Mad about the boy.
Noël Coward (1899–1973) British dramatist. *Title of song*

45 Love is a sickness full of woes,
All remedies refusing;
A plant that with most cutting grows,
Most barren with best using.
Why so?

More we enjoy it, more it dies;
If not enjoyed, it sighing cries,
Hey ho.

Samuel Daniel (c. 1562–1619) English poet and dramatist. *Hymen's Triumph*, I

46 It has been said that love robs those who have it of their wit, and gives it to those who have none.

Denis Diderot (1713–84) French writer. *Paradoxe sur le comédien*

47 Come live with me, and be my love,
And we will some new pleasures prove
Of golden sands, and crystal brooks,
With silken lines, and silver hooks.

John Donne (1573–1631) English poet. *The Bait*

48 I am two fools, I know,
For loving, and for saying so
In whining Poetry.

John Donne *The Triple Fool*

49 O my America! my new-found-land,
My Kingdom, safeliest when with one man man'd.

John Donne *Elegies*, 19, 'Going To Bed'

50 It seems to me that he has never loved, that he has only imagined that he has loved, that there has been no real love on his part. I even think that he is incapable of love; he is too much occupied with other thoughts and ideas to become strongly attached to anyone earthly.

Anna Dostoevsky (1846–1918) Russian diarist and writer. *Dostoevsky Portrayed by His Wife*

51 And I was desolate and sick of an old passion.

Ernest Dowson (1867–1900) British lyric poet. *Non Sum Qualis Eram Bonae Sub Regno Cynarae*

52 You may not be an angel
'Cause angels are so few,
But until the day that one comes along
I'll string along with you.

Al Dubin (20th century) US songwriter. *Twenty Million Sweethearts*

53 All mankind love a lover.

Ralph Waldo Emerson (1803–82) US poet and essayist. *Essays*, 'Love'

54 Don't you think I was made for you? I feel like you had me ordered – and I was delivered to you – to be worn – I want you to wear me, like a watch-charm or a button hole bouquet – to the world.

Zelda Fitzgerald (1900–48) US writer. Letter to F. Scott Fitzgerald, 1919

55 ...I don't want to live – I want to love first, and live incidentally...

Zelda Fitzgerald Letter to F. Scott Fitzgerald, 1919

56 *Plaisir d'amour ne dure qu'un moment,*
Chagrin d'amour dure toute la vie.
Love's pleasure lasts but a moment; love's sorrow lasts all through life.

Jean-Pierre Claris de Florian (1755–94) French writer of fables. *Celestine*

57 I'm leaning on a lamp-post at the corner of the street,
In case a certain little lady walks by.

George Formby (1905–61) British comedian. *Leaning on a Lamp-post*

58 Try thinking of love, or something.
Amor vincit insomnia.

Christopher Fry (1907–) British dramatist. *A Sleep of Prisoners*

59 If with me you'd fondly stray,
Over the hills and far away.

John Gay (1685–1732) English poet and dramatist. *The Beggar's Opera*

60 She who has never loved has never lived.

John Gay *Captives*

61 Everyone has experienced that truth: that love, like a running brook, is disregarded, taken for granted; but when the brook freezes over, then people begin to remember how it was when it ran, and they want it to run again.

Kahlil Gibran (1833–1931) Lebanese mystic and poet. *Beloved Prophet* (ed. Virginia Hilu)

62 It's a song of a merryman, moping mum,
Whose soul was sad, and whose glance was glum,
Who sipped no sup, and who craved no crumb,
As he sighed for the love of a ladye.

W. S. Gilbert (1836–1911) British dramatist. *The Yeoman of the Guard*, I

63 In love as in sport, the amateur status must be strictly maintained.

Robert Graves (1895–1985) British poet and novelist. *Occupation: Writer*

64 Love, love, love – all the wretched cant of it, masking egotism, lust, masochism, fantasy under a mythology of sentimental postures, a welter of self-induced miseries and joys, blinding and masking the essential personalities in the frozen gestures of courtship, in the kissing and the dating and the desire, the compliments and the quarrels which vivify its barrenness.

Germaine Greer (1939–) Australian-born British writer and feminist. *The Female Eunuch*

65 If you were the only girl in the world,
And I were the only boy.

George Grossmith the Younger (1874–1935) British singer, actor, and songwriter. *The Bing Boys*, 'If you were the Only Girl' (with Fred Thompson; 1884–1949)

66 Hello, Young Lovers, Wherever You Are.

Oscar Hammerstein (1895–1960) US lyricist. From the musical *The King and I*. Song title

67 A lover without indiscretion is no lover at all.

Thomas Hardy (1840–1928) British novelist. *The Hand of Ethelberta*, Ch. 20

68 'You must sit down,' says Love, 'and taste My meat,'
So I did sit and eat.

George Herbert (1593–1633) English poet. *Love*

69 My love she's but a lassie yet.

James Hogg (1770–1835) Scottish poet and writer. Title of song

70 Pale hands I loved beside the Shalimar,
Where are you now? Who lies beneath your spell?

Laurence Hope (Mrs M. H. Nicolson; 1804–1905) British poet and songwriter. *The Garden of Kama and other Love Lyrics from India*, 'Pale Hands I Loved'

71 Look not in my eyes, for fear
They mirror true the sight I see,
And there you find your face too clear
And love it and be lost like me.

A. E. Housman (1859–1936) British scholar and poet. *A Shropshire Lad*, 'March'

72 Love is like the measles; we all have to go through with it.

Jerome K. Jerome (1859–1927) British humorist. *Idle Thoughts of an Idle Fellow*

73 Love's like the measles – all the worse when it comes late in life.

Douglas William Jerrold (1803–57) British dramatist. *Wit and Opinions of Douglas Jerrold*, 'A Philanthropist'

74 Love is the wisdom of the fool and the folly of the wise.

Samuel Johnson (1709–84) British lexicographer. *Johnsonian Miscellanies* (ed. G. B. Hill), Vol. II

75 Drink to me only with thine eyes,
And I will pledge with mine;
Or leave a kiss but in the cup,
And I'll not look for wine.
The thirst that from the soul doth rise
Doth ask a drink divine;
But might I of Jove's nectar sup,
I would not change for thine.

I sent thee late a rosy wreath,
Not so much honouring thee,
As giving it a hope that there
It could not wither'd be.

Ben Jonson (1573–1637) English dramatist. *The Forest, IX*, 'To Celia'

76 Come, my Celia, let us prove,
While we can, the sports of love,
Time will not be ours for ever,
He, at length, our good will sever.

Ben Jonson *Volpone*, III:6

77 Love in a hut, with water and a crust,
Is – Love, forgive us! – cinders, ashes, dust;
Love in a palace is perhaps at last
More grievous torment than a hermit's fast.

John Keats (1795–1821) British poet. *Lamia*, II

78 Soft adorings from their loves receive
Upon the honey'd middle of the night.

John Keats *The Eve of Saint Agnes*, VI

79 I love a lassie.

Harry Lauder (Hugh MacLennon; 1870–1950) Scottish music-hall artist. Song title

80 You must always be a-waggle with LOVE.

D. H. Lawrence (1885–1930) British novelist. *Bibbles*

81 I'm not sure if a mental relation with a woman doesn't make it impossible to love her. To know the *mind* of a woman is to end in hating her. Love means the pre-cognitive flow…it is the honest state before the apple.

D. H. Lawrence Letter to Dr Trigant Burrow, 3 Aug 1927

82 If there's anything that you want,
If there's anything I can do,
Just call on me,
And I'll send it along with love from me to you.

John Lennon (1940–80) British rock musician. *From Me to You* (with Paul McCartney)

83 She loves you, yeh, yeh, yeh,
And with a love like that you know you should be glad.

John Lennon *She Loves You* (with Paul McCartney)

84 Any scientist who has ever been in love knows that he may understand everything about sex hormones but the actual experience is something quite different.

Kathleen Lonsdale (1903–71) British crystallographer. *Universities Quarterly*, No. 17, 1963

85 Two souls with but a single thought,
Two hearts that beat as one.

Maria Lovell (1803–77) British actress and dramatist. *Ingomar the Barbarian*, II (transl. of Friedrich Halm)

86 Time was away and somewhere else,
There were two glasses and two chairs
And two people with one pulse.

Louis MacNeice (1907–63) Irish-born British poet. *Meeting Point*

87 Come live with me, and be my love;
And we will all the pleasures prove
That hills and valleys, dales and fields,
Woods or steepy mountain yields.

Christopher Marlowe (1564–93) English dramatist. *The Passionate Shepherd to his Love*

88 Let us roll all our strength and all
Our sweetness up into one ball,
And tear our pleasures with rough strife
Thorough the iron gates of life:
Thus, though we cannot make our sun
Stand still, yet we will make him run.

Andrew Marvell (1621–78) English poet. *To His Coy Mistress*

89 Send two dozen roses to Room 424 and put 'Emily, I love you' on the back of the bill.

Groucho Marx (Julius Marx; 1895–1977) US comedian. *A Night in Casablanca*

90 Love is based on a view of women that is impossible to those who have had any experience with them.

H. L. Mencken (1880–1956) US journalist.

91 My heart shall be thy garden.

Alice Meynell (1847–1922) British poet. *The Garden*

92 When a man is in love he endures more than

at other times; he submits to everything.

Friedrich Wilhelm Nietzsche (1844–1900) German philosopher. *The Antichrist*

93 I do not love thee! – no! I do not love thee!
And yet when thou art absent I am sad.

Caroline Elizabeth Sarah Norton (1808–77) British poet. *I do Not Love Thee*

94 K-K-Katy, beautiful Katy,
You're the only g-g-g-girl that I adore,
When the m-m-m-moon shines over the cow-shed,
I'll be waiting at the k-k-k-kitchen door.

Geoffrey O'Hara (1882–1967) Canadian-born US songwriter. *K-K-Katy* (song)

95 By the time you swear you're his,
Shivering and sighing,
And he vows his passion is
Infinite, undying –
Lady, make a note of this:
One of you is lying.

Dorothy Parker (1893–1967) US writer. *Unfortunate Coincidence*

96 Every love is the love before
In a duller dress.

Dorothy Parker *Death and Taxes*

97 Love is like quicksilver in the hand. Leave the fingers open and it stays. Clutch it, and it darts away.

Dorothy Parker Attrib.

98 Love's perfect blossom only blows
Where noble manners veil defect.
Angels may be familiar; those
Who err each other must respect.

Coventry Patmore (1823–96) British poet. *The Angel in the House*, Bk. I, Prelude 2

99 Ye gods! annihilate but space and time.
And make two lovers happy.

Alexander Pope (1688–1744) British poet. *The Art of Sinking in Poetry*, 11

100 I've Got You Under My Skin.

Cole Porter (1893–1964) US songwriter. *Born to Dance*, song title

101 Night and day, you are the one,
Only you beneath the moon and under the sun.

Cole Porter *The Gay Divorcee*, 'Night and Day'

102 Let's Do It; Let's Fall in Love.

Cole Porter *Paris*, song title

103 I have sometimes regretted living so close to Marie...because I may be very fond of her, but I am not quite so fond of her company.

Marcel Proust (1871–1922) French novelist. *À la recherche du temps perdu: Sodome et Gomorrhe*

104 There can be no peace of mind in love, since the advantage one has secured is never anything but a fresh starting-point for further desires.

Marcel Proust *À la recherche du temps perdu: À l'ombre des jeunes filles en fleurs*

105 I loved you when you were inconstant. What should I have done if you had been faithful?

Jean Racine (1639–99) French dramatist. *Andromaque*, IV:5

106 If all the world and love were young,
And truth in every shepherd's tongue,
These pretty pleasures might me move
To live with thee, and be thy love.

Walter Raleigh (1554–1618) English explorer. *Answer to Marlow*

107 There are very few people who are not ashamed of having been in love when they no longer love each other.

Duc de la Rochefoucauld (1613–80) French writer. *Maximes*, 71

108 It takes a woman twenty years to make a man of her son, and another woman twenty minutes to make a fool of him.

Helen Rowland (1876–1950) US writer. *Reflections of a Bachelor Girl*

109 To fear love is to fear life, and those who fear life are already three parts dead.

Bertrand Russell (1872–1970) British philosopher. *Marriage and Morals*

110 Of all forms of caution, caution in love is perhaps the most fatal to true happiness.

Bertrand Russell *Marriage and Morals*

111 Every little girl knows about love. It is only her capacity to suffer because of it that increases.

Françoise Sagan (1935–) French writer. *Daily Express*

112 Liszt said to me today that God alone deserves to be loved. It may be true, but when one has loved a man it is very different to love God.

George Sand (Aurore Dupin, Baronne Dudevant; 1804–76) French novelist. *Intimate Journal*

113 True love's the gift which God has given
To man alone beneath the heaven.

Walter Scott (1771–1832) Scottish novelist. *The Lay of the Last Minstrel*, V

114 Therefore love moderately: long love doth so;
Too swift arrives as tardy as too slow.

William Shakespeare (1564–1616) English dramatist. *Romeo and Juliet*, II:6

115 The triple pillar of the world transform'd
Into a strumpet's fool.

William Shakespeare *Antony and Cleopatra*, I:1

116 There's beggary in the love that can be reckon'd.

William Shakespeare *Antony and Cleopatra*, I:1

117 If thou remembr'st not the slightest folly
That ever love did make thee run into,
Thou hast not lov'd.

William Shakespeare *As You Like It*, II:4

118 But love is blind, and lovers cannot see
The pretty follies that themselves commit.

William Shakespeare *The Merchant of Venice*, II:6

119 For aught that I could ever read,
Could ever hear by tale or history,

The course of true love never did run smooth.
William Shakespeare *A Midsummer Night's Dream*, I:1

120 Love looks not with the eyes, but with the mind;
And therefore is wing'd Cupid painted blind.
William Shakespeare *A Midsummer Night's Dream*, I:1

121 The lunatic, the lover, and the poet,
Are of imagination all compact.
William Shakespeare *A Midsummer Night's Dream*, V:1

122 A woman's face, with Nature's own hand painted,
Hast thou, the Master Mistress of my passion.
William Shakespeare *Sonnet 20*

123 Let me not to the marriage of true minds
Admit impediments. Love is not love
Which alters when it alteration finds,
Or bends with the remover to remove.
O, no! it is an ever-fixed mark,
That looks on tempests and is never shaken.
William Shakespeare *Sonnet 116*

124 Love alters not with his brief hours and weeks,
But bears it out even to the edge of doom.
If this be error, and upon me prov'd,
I never writ, nor no man ever lov'd.
William Shakespeare *Sonnet 116*

125 To be wise and love
Exceeds man's might.
William Shakespeare *Troilus and Cressida*, III:2

126 She never told her love,
But let concealment, like a worm i' th' bud,
Feed on her damask cheek. She pin'd in thought;
And with a green and yellow melancholy
She sat like Patience on a monument,
Smiling at grief.
William Shakespeare *Twelfth Night*, II:4

127 Love sought is good, but given unsought is better.
William Shakespeare *Twelfth Night*, III:1

128 Then must you speak
Of one that lov'd not wisely, but too well;
Of one not easily jealous, but, being wrought,
Perplexed in the extreme; of one whose hand,
Like the base Indian, threw a pearl away
Richer than all his tribe.
William Shakespeare *Othello*, V:2

129 Nowadays we don't think much of a man's love for an animal; we laugh at people who are attached to cats. But if we stop loving animals, aren't we bound to stop loving humans too?
Alexander Solzhenitsyn (1918–) Soviet novelist. *Cancer Ward*, Pt. I, Ch. 20

130 A woman despises a man for loving her, unless she returns his love.
Elizabeth Drew Stoddard (1823–1902) US novelist and poet. *Two Men*, Ch. 32

131 I know she likes me,
'Cause she says so.
Eugene Stratton (1861–1918) British music-hall singer. *The Lily of Laguna*

132 I hold it true, whate'er befall;
I feel it, when I sorrow most;
'Tis better to have loved and lost
Than never to have loved at all.
Alfred, Lord Tennyson (1809–92) British poet. *In Memoriam A.H.H.*, XXVII

133 Such a one do I remember, whom to look at was to love.
Alfred, Lord Tennyson *Locksley Hall*

134 The rose was awake all night for your sake,
Knowing your promise to me;
The lilies and roses were all awake,
They sighed for the dawn and thee.
Alfred, Lord Tennyson *Maud*, I

135 O tell her, brief is life but love is long.
Alfred, Lord Tennyson *The Princess*, IV

136 God gives us love. Something to love
He lends us; but, when love is grown
To ripeness that on which it throve
Falls off, and love is left alone.
Alfred, Lord Tennyson *To J.S.*

137 'Tis strange what a man may do, and a woman yet think him an angel.
William Makepeace Thackeray (1811–63) British novelist. *Henry Esmond*, Ch. 7

138 All, everything that I understand, I understand only because I love.
Leo Tolstoy (1828–1910) Russian writer. *War and Peace*, Bk. VII, Ch. 16

139 One can't live on love alone; and I am so stupid that I can do nothing but think of him.
Sophie Tolstoy (1844–1919) Russian writer. *A Diary of Tolstoy's Wife, 1860–1891*

140 Those who have courage to love should have courage to suffer.
Anthony Trollope (1815–82) British novelist. *The Bertrams*, Ch. 27

141 I doubt whether any girl would be satisfied with her lover's mind if she knew the whole of it.
Anthony Trollope *The Small House at Allington*, Ch. 4

142 Walking My Baby Back Home.
Roy Turk (20th century) US songwriter. Title of song

143 Love conquers all things: let us too give in to Love.
Virgil (Publius Vergilius Maro; 70–19 BC) Roman poet. *Eclogue*, Bk. X

144 The boy I love is up in the gallery,
The boy I love is looking now at me.
George Ware (19th century) British songwriter. *The Boy in the Gallery*

145 It is like a cigar. If it goes out, you can light it again but it never tastes quite the same.
Lord Wavell (1883–1950) British field marshall. Attrib.

146 Beware you be not swallowed up in books! An ounce of love is worth a pound of knowledge.

John Wesley (1703–91) British religious leader. *Life of Wesley* (R. Southey), Ch. 16

147 I have found it impossible to carry the heavy burden of responsibility and to discharge my duties as King as I would wish to do without the help and support of the woman I love.

Duke of Windsor (1894–1972) King of the United Kingdom; abdicated 1936. Radio broadcast, 11 Dec 1936

148 'Ah, love, love' he said. 'Is there anything like it? Were you ever in love, Beach?'
'Yes, sir, on one occasion, when I was a young under-footman. But it blew over.'

P. G. Wodehouse (1881–1975) British humorous novelist. *Pigs Have Wings*

149 There is a comfort in the strength of love;
'Twill make a thing endurable, which else
Would overset the brain, or break the heart.

William Wordsworth (1770–1850) British poet. *Michael*, 448

150 Love fled
And paced upon the mountains overhead
And hid his face amid a crowd of stars.

W. B. Yeats (1865–1939) Irish poet. *When you are Old*

151 But Love has pitched his mansion in
The place of excrement.

W. B. Yeats *Crazy Jane Talks with the Bishop*

152 A pity beyond all telling
Is hid in the heart of love.

W. B. Yeats *The Pity of Love*

LOVE AND DEATH

See also death, love

1 And for bonnie Annie Laurie
I'll lay me doun and dee.

William Douglas (1672–1748) Scottish poet. *Annie Laurie*

2 For, Heaven be thanked, we live is such an age,
When no man dies for love, but on the stage.

John Dryden (1631–1700) British poet and dramatist. *Mithridates*, Epilogue

3 Love is my religion – I could die for that.

John Keats (1795–1821) British poet. Letter to Fanny Brawne, 13 Oct 1819

4 How alike are the groans of love to
those of the dying.

Malcolm Lowry (1909–57) British novelist. *Under the Volcano*, Ch. 12

5 It is very rarely that a man loves
And when he does it is nearly always fatal.

Hugh MacDiarmid (Christopher Murray Grieve; 1892–1978) Scottish poet. *The International Brigade*

6 Men have died from time to time, and worms have eaten them, but not for love.

William Shakespeare (1564–1616) English dramatist. *As You Like It*, IV:1

7 'Tis said that some have died for love.

William Wordsworth (1770–1850) British poet. *'Tis Said that some have Died*

LOVE AND FRIENDSHIP

See also friendship, love

1 Love is blind; friendship closes its eyes.

Proverb

2 Friendship is a disinterested commerce between equals; love, an abject intercourse between tyrants and slaves.

Oliver Goldsmith (1728–74) Irish-born British writer. *The Good-Natured Man*, I

3 Friendship is constant in all other things
Save in the office and affairs of love.

William Shakespeare (1564–1616) English dramatist. *Much Ado About Nothing*, II:1

LOVE AND HATE

See also hate, love

1 Now hatred is by far the longest pleasure;
Men love in haste, but they detest at leisure.

Lord Byron (1788–1824) British poet. *Don Juan*, XIII

2 *Odi et amo.*
I hate and love.

Catullus (c. 84–c. 54 BC) Roman poet. *Carmina*, LXXXV

3 Heaven has no rage like love to hatred turned,
Nor hell a fury like a woman scorned.

William Congreve (1670–1729) British Restoration dramatist. *The Mourning Bride*, III

4 Oh, I have loved him too much to feel no hate for him.

Jean Racine (1639–99) French dramatist. *Andromaque*, II:1

5 If one judges love by its visible effects, it looks more like hatred than like friendship.

Duc de la Rochefoucauld (1613–80) French writer. *Maximes*, 72

LOVE AND MARRIAGE

See also love, marriage

1 Love and marriage, love and marriage,
Go together like a horse and carriage.

Sammy Cahn (Samuel Cohen; 1913–93) US songwriter. *Our Town*, 'Love and Marriage'

2 ALMA. I rather suspect her of being in love with him.
MARTIN. Her own husband? Monstrous! What a

selfish woman!

Jennie Jerome Churchill (1854–1921) US-born British hostess and writer. *His Borrowed Plumes*

3 Love is moral even without legal marriage, but marriage is immoral without love.

Ellen Key (Karolina Sofia Key; 1849–1926) Swedish writer. *The Morality of Woman and Other Essays*, 'The Morality of Woman'

4 Any one must see at a glance that if men and women marry those whom they do not love, they must love those whom they do not marry.

Harriet Martineau (1802–76) British writer. *Society in America*, Vol. III, 'Marriage'

5 Can't you read? The score demands *con amore*, and what are you doing? You are playing it like married men!

Arturo Toscanini (1867–1957) Italian conductor. Criticizing the playing of an Austrian orchestra during rehearsal. Attrib.

6 The amount of women in London who flirt with their own husbands is perfectly scandalous. It looks so bad. It is simply washing one's clean linen in public.

Oscar Wilde (1854–1900) Irish-born British dramatist. *The Importance of Being Earnest*, I

LOYALTY

See also betrayal, faithfulness, patriotism, support

1 Dog does not eat dog.

Proverb

2 There is honour among thieves.

Proverb

3 You cannot run with the hare and hunt with the hounds.

Proverb

4 Here's a health unto his Majesty...
Confusion to his enemies...
And he that will not drink his health,
I wish him neither wit nor wealth,
Nor yet a rope to hang himself.

Anonymous *Here's a Health unto his Majesty*

5 And Ruth said, Intreat me not to leave thee, or to return from following after thee: for whither thou goest, I will go; and where thou lodgest, I will lodge: thy people shall be my people, and thy God my God:
Where thou diest, will I die, and there will I be buried: the Lord do so to me, and more also, if ought but death part thee and me.

Bible: Ruth 1:16–17

6 The State, in choosing men to serve it, takes no notice of their opinions. If they be willing faithfully to serve it, that satisfies.

Oliver Cromwell (1599–1658) English soldier and statesman. Said before the Battle of Marston Moor, 2 July 1644

7 We are all the President's men.

Henry Kissinger (1923–) German-born US politician and diplomat. Said regarding the invasion of Cambodia, 1970. *The Sunday Times Magazine*, 4 May 1975

8 A man who will steal *for* me will steal *from* me.

Theodore Roosevelt (1858–1919) US Republican president. Firing a cowboy who had applied Roosevelt's brand to a steer belonging to a neighbouring ranch. *Roosevelt in the Bad Lands* (Herman Hagedorn)

9 If this man is not faithful to his God, how can he be faithful to me, a mere man?

Theodoric (c. 445–526) King of the Ostrogoths. Explaining why he had had a trusted minister, who had said he would adopt his master's religion, beheaded. *Dictionnaire Encyclopédique* (E. Guérard)

10 When I forget my sovereign, may God forget me!

Lord Thurlow (1731–1806) British lawyer. Speech, House of Lords, 15 Dec 1778

11 Had I but served God as diligently as I have served the king, he would not have given me over in my gray hairs.

Cardinal Wolsey (1475–1530) English churchman. Remark to Sir William Kingston. *Negotiations of Thomas Wolsey* (Cavendish)

LUCK

See also chance, superstition

1 A bad penny always turns up.

Proverb

2 A cat has nine lives.

Proverb

3 Finders keepers, losers weepers.

Proverb

4 It is better to be born lucky than rich.

Proverb

5 The devil looks after his own.

Proverb

6 There, but for the grace of God, goes John Bradford.

John Bradford (c. 1510–55) English Protestant martyr. Said on seeing some criminals being led to execution. Attrib.

7 This is the temple of Providence where disciples still hourly mark its ways and note the system of its mysteries. Here is the one God whose worshippers prove their faith by their works and in their destruction still trust in Him.

F. H. Bradley (1846–1924) British philosopher. Referring to Monte Carlo. *Aphorisms*

8 Fortune, that favours fools.

Ben Jonson (1573–1637) English dramatist. *The Alchemist*, Prologue

9 I am a great believer in luck, and I find the harder I work the more I have of it.

Stephen Leacock (1869–1944) English-born Canadian economist and humorist. *Literary Lapses*

10 The Eskimo had his own explanation. Said he: 'The devil is asleep or having trouble with his wife, or we should never have come back so easily.'

Robert Edwin Peary (1856–1920) US explorer. *The North Pole*

11 We need greater virtues to sustain good fortune than bad.

Duc de la Rochefoucauld (1613–80) French writer. *Maximes*, 25

12 'My aunt was suddenly prevented from going a voyage
in a ship what went down – would you call that a case
of Providential interference?'
'Can't tell: didn't know your aunt.'

Frederick Temple (1821–1902) British churchman. *Memoirs of Archbishop Temple* (Sandford), Vol. II

LUST

See also animalism, desire, love, sex

1 Licence my roving hands, and let them go,
Before, behind, between, above, below.

John Donne (1573–1631) English poet. *Elegies*, 18, 'Love's Progress'

2 What is commonly called love, namely the desire of satisfying a voracious appetite with a certain quantity of delicate white human flesh.

Henry Fielding (1707–54) British novelist. *Tom Jones*, Bk. VI, Ch. 1

3 I'll come no more behind your scenes, David; for the silk stockings and white bosoms of your actresses excite my amorous propensities.

Samuel Johnson (1709–84) British lexicographer. Said to the actor-manager David Garrick. *Life of Johnson* (J. Boswell), Vol. I

4 Oh, to be seventy again!

Oliver Wendell Holmes Jnr (1841–1935) US jurist. Said in his eighty-seventh year, while watching a pretty girl. *The American Treasury* (C. Fadiman)

5 Stand close around, ye Stygian set,
With Dirce in one boat conveyed!
Or Charon, seeing, may forget
That he is old and she a shade.

Walter Savage Landor (1775–1864) British poet and writer. In Greek mythology, Dirce, a follower of Dionysius, was killed by her great-nephews Amphion and Zethus because of her mistreatment of their mother Antiope; Charon was the ferryman who transported dead souls across the River Styx to the underworld. *Dirce*

6 Lolita, light of my life, fire of my loins. My sin, my Soul.

Vladimir Nabokov (1899–1977) Russian-born US novelist. *Lolita*

7 Th' expense of spirit in a waste of shame
Is lust in action; and till action, lust
Is perjur'd, murd'rous, bloody, full of blame,
Savage, extreme, rude, cruel, not to trust;
Enjoy'd no sooner but despised straight.

William Shakespeare (1564–1616) English dramatist. *Sonnet 129*

8 Nonconformity and lust stalking hand in hand through the country, wasting and ravaging.

Evelyn Waugh (1903–66) British novelist. *Decline and Fall*, Pt. I, Ch. 5

LUXURY

See also extravagance, wealth

1 It's grand, and ye canna expect to be baith grand and comfortable.

J. M. Barrie (1860–1937) British novelist and dramatist. *The Little Minister*, Ch. 10

2 The saddest thing I can imagine is to get used to luxury.

Charlie Chaplin (Sir Charles Spencer C.; 1889–1977) British film actor. *My Autobiography*

3 In the affluent society no useful distinction can be made between luxuries and necessaries.

John Kenneth Galbraith (1908–) US economist. *The Affluent Society*, Ch. 21

4 Give us the luxuries of life, and we will dispense with its necessities.

John Lothrop Motley (1814–77) US historian and diplomat. Also quoted by Frank Lloyd Wright. *The Autocrat of the Breakfast Table* (O. W. Holmes), Ch. 6

5 How many things I can do without!

Socrates (469–399 BC) Athenian philosopher. Examining the range of goods on sale at a market. *Lives of the Eminent Philosophers* (Diogenes Laertius), II

6 Beulah, peel me a grape.

Mae West (1892–1980) US actress. *I'm No Angel*, film 1933

LYING

See also deception, honesty, truth

1 A liar is worse than a thief.

Proverb

2 The boy cried 'Wolf, wolf!' and the villagers came out to help him.

Aesop (6th century BC) Reputed Greek writer of fables. *Fables*, 'The Shepherd's Boy'

3 It contains a misleading impression, not a lie. I was being economical with the truth.

Robert Armstrong (1913–) British civil servant. Giving evidence on behalf of the British Government in an Australian court case, Nov 1986. Armstrong was, in fact, quoting Edmund Burke (1729–97).

4 Woe unto them that call evil good, and good evil; that put darkness for light, and light for darkness; that put bitter for sweet, and sweet for bitter!

Bible: Isaiah 5:20

5 Nobody speaks the truth when there's something they must have.

Elizabeth Bowen (1899–1973) Irish novelist. *The House in Paris*, Ch. 5

6 A lie can be half-way round the world before

the truth has got its boots on.

James Callaghan (1912–) British politician and prime minister. Speech, 1 Nov 1976

7 It cannot in the opinion of His Majesty's Government be classified as slavery in the extreme acceptance of the word without some risk of terminological inexactitude.

Winston Churchill (1874–1965) British statesman. Speech, House of Commons, 22 Feb 1906

8 The broad mass of a nation...will more easily fall victim to a big lie than to a small one.

Adolf Hitler (1889–1945) German dictator. *Mein Kampf*, Ch. 10

9 She's too crafty a woman to invent a new lie when an old one will serve.

W. Somerset Maugham (1874–1965) British novelist. *The Constant Wife*, II

10 It is hard to believe that a man is telling the truth when you know that you would lie if you were in his place.

H. L. Mencken (1880–1956) US journalist. *Prejudices*

11 Unless a man feels he has a good enough memory, he should never venture to lie.

Michel de Montaigne (1533–92) French essayist. Also quoted in *Le Menteur*, IV:5 by Pierre Corneille (1606–84). *Essais*, I

12 He led a double life. Did that make him a liar? He did not feel a liar. He was a man of two truths.

Iris Murdoch (1919–) Irish-born British novelist. *The Sacred and Profane Love Machine*

13 He who does not need to lie is proud of not being a liar.

Friedrich Wilhelm Nietzsche (1844–1900) German philosopher. *Nachgelassene Fragmente*

14 It has made more liars out of the American people than Golf.

Will Rogers (1879–1935) US actor and humorist. Referring to income tax. *Saturday Review*, 'A Rogers Thesaurus', 25 Aug 1962

15 In our country the lie has become not just a moral category but a pillar of the State.

Alexander Solzhenitsyn (1918–) Soviet novelist. *The Observer*, 'Sayings of the Year', 29 Dec 1974

16 A lie is an abomination unto the Lord and a very present help in trouble.

Adlai Stevenson (1900–65) US statesman. Speech, Jan 1951

17 That a lie which is all a lie may be met and fought with outright,
But a lie which is part a truth is a harder matter to fight.

Alfred, Lord Tennyson (1809–92) British poet. *The Grandmother*

18 There was things which he stretched, but mainly he told the truth.

Mark Twain (Samuel Langhorne Clemens; 1835–1910) US writer. *The Adventures of Huckleberry Finn*, Ch. 1

M

MADNESS

See also psychiatry, psychology

1 We all are born mad. Some remain so.

Samuel Beckett (1906–89) Irish novelist and dramatist. *Waiting for Godot*, II

2 A knight errant who turns mad for a reason deserves neither merit nor thanks. The thing is to do it without cause.

Miguel de Cervantes (1547–1616) Spanish novelist. *Don Quixote*, Pt. I, Ch. 25

3 The madman is not the man who has lost his reason. The madman is the man who has lost everything except his reason.

G. K. Chesterton (1874–1936) British writer. *Orthodoxy*, Ch. 1

4 Those whom God wishes to destroy, he first makes mad.

Euripides (c. 480–406 BC) Greek dramatist. *Fragment*

5 With lack of sleep and too much understanding I grow a little crazy, I think, like all men at sea who live too close to each other and too close thereby to all that is monstrous under the sun and moon.

William Golding (1911–93) British novelist. *Rites of Passage*, '&'

6 Show me a sane man and I will cure him for you.

Carl Gustav Jung (1875–1961) Swiss psychoanalyst. *The Observer*, 19 July 1975

7 Every one is more or less mad on one point.

Rudyard Kipling (1865–1936) Indian-born British writer. *Plain Tales from the Hills*, 'On the Strength of a Likeness'

8 Madness need not be all breakdown. It may also be break-through. It is potential liberation and renewal as well as enslavement and existential death.

R. D. Laing (1927–89) British psychiatrist. *The Politics of Experience*, Ch. 16

9 The world is becoming like a lunatic asylum run by lunatics.

David Lloyd George (1863–1945) British Liberal statesman. *The Observer*, 'Sayings of Our Times', 31 May 1953

10 His father's sister had bats in the belfry and was put away.

Eden Phillpotts (1862–1960) British novelist and dramatist. *Peacock House*, 'My First Murder'

11 A body seriously out of equilibrium, either with itself or with its environment, perishes outright. Not so a mind. Madness and suffering can set themselves no limit.

George Santayana (1863–1952) US philosopher. *The Life of Reason: Reason in Common Sense*, 2

12 Though this be madness, yet there is method in't.

William Shakespeare (1564–1616) English dramatist. *Hamlet*, II:2

13 Madness in great ones must not unwatch'd go.

William Shakespeare *Hamlet*, III:1

14 O, let me not be mad, not mad, sweet heaven!
Keep me in temper; I would not be mad!

William Shakespeare *King Lear*, I:5

15 If you talk to God, you are praying; if God talks to you, you have schizophrenia. If the dead talk to you, you are a spiritualist; if God talks to you, you are a schizophrenic.

Thomas Szasz (1920–) US psychiatrist. *The Second Sin*

16 When we remember that we are all mad, the mysteries disappear and life stands explained.

Mark Twain (Samuel Longhorne Clemens; 1835–1910) US writer.

17 Men will always be mad and those who think they can cure them are the maddest of all.

Voltaire (François-Marie Arouet; 1694–1778) French writer. Letter, 1762

18 I shudder and I sigh to think
That even Cicero
And many-minded Homer were
Mad as the mist and snow.

W. B. Yeats (1865–1939) Irish poet. *Mad as the Mist and Snow*

MAJORITY

See also democracy, minority, public

1 'It's always best on these occasions to do what the mob do.'
'But suppose there are two mobs?' suggested Mr Snodgrass.
'Shout with the largest,' replied Mr Pickwick.

Charles Dickens (1812–70) British novelist. *Pickwick Papers*, Ch. 13

2 A majority is always the best repartee.

Benjamin Disraeli (1804–81) British statesman. *Tancred*, Bk. II, Ch. 14

3 The majority has the might – more's the pity – but it hasn't right...The minority is always right.

Henrik Ibsen (1828–1906) Norwegian dramatist. *An Enemy of the People*, IV

4 The worst enemy of truth and freedom in our society is the compact majority. Yes, the damned, compact, liberal majority.

Henrik Ibsen *An Enemy of the People*, IV

5 It is time for the great silent majority of Americans to stand up and be counted.

Richard Milhous Nixon (1913–94) US president. Election speech, Oct 1970

MALAPROPISMS

Remarks of a type associated with Mrs Malaprop in Sheridan's play *The Rivals.*

1 Our watch, sir, have indeed comprehended two aspicious persons.

William Shakespeare (1564–1616) English dramatist. *Much Ado About Nothing,* III:5

2 Comparisons are odorous.

William Shakespeare *Much Ado About Nothing,* III:5

3 A progeny of learning.

Richard Brinsley Sheridan (1751–1816) British dramatist. *The Rivals,* I

4 Illiterate him, I say, quite from your memory.

Richard Brinsley Sheridan *The Rivals,* II

5 It gives me the hydrostatics to such a degree.

Richard Brinsley Sheridan *The Rivals,* III

6 As headstrong as an allegory on the banks of the Nile.

Richard Brinsley Sheridan *The Rivals,* III

7 He is the very pine-apple of politeness!

Richard Brinsley Sheridan *The Rivals,* III

8 If I reprehend any thing in this world, it is the use of my oracular tongue, and a nice derangement of epitaphs!

Richard Brinsley Sheridan *The Rivals,* III

MANKIND

See also evolution, human condition, human nature, men, misanthropy, philanthropy, public, society, women

1 Pray consider what a figure a man would make in the republic of letters.

Joseph Addison (1672–1719) British essayist. *Ancient Medals*

2 Either a beast or a god.

Aristotle (384–322 BC) Greek philosopher. *Politics,* Bk. I

3 Whatever this is that I am, it is a little flesh and breath, and the ruling part.

Marcus Aurelius (121–180 AD) Roman emperor. *Meditations,* Bk. II, Ch. 2

4 Drinking when we are not thirsty and making love all year round, madam; that is all there is to distinguish us from other animals.

Beaumarchais (1732–99) French dramatist. *Le Mariage de Figaro,* II:21

5 And God said, Let us make man in our image, after our likeness: and let them have dominion over the fish of the sea, and over the fowl of the air, and over the cattle, and over all the earth, and over every creeping thing that creepeth upon the earth.
So God created man in his own image, in the image of God created he him; male and female created he them.
And God blessed them, and God said unto them, Be fruitful, and multiply, and replenish the earth, and subdue it: and have dominion over the fish of the sea, and over the fowl of the air, and over every living thing that moveth upon the earth.

Bible: Genesis 1:26–28

6 For Mercy has a human heart,
Pity a human face,
And Love, the human form divine,
And Peace, the human dress.

William Blake (1757–1827) British poet. *Songs of Innocence,* 'The Divine Image'

7 What is man, when you come to think upon him, but a minutely set, ingenious machine for turning, with infinite artfulness, the red wine of Shiraz into urine?

Karen Blixen (Isak Dinesen; 1885–1962) Danish writer. *Seven Gothic Tales,* 'The Dreamers'

8 Every animal leaves traces of what it was; man alone leaves traces of what he created.

Jacob Bronowski (1908–74) British scientist and writer. *The Ascent of Man,* Ch. 1

9 Man is a noble animal, splendid in ashes, and pompous in the grave.

Thomas Browne (1605–82) English physician and writer. *Urn Burial,* Ch. 5

10 A single sentence will suffice for modern man: he fornicated and read the papers.

Albert Camus (1913–60) French existentialist writer. *The Fall*

11 Carlyle said that men were mostly fools. Christianity, with a surer and more reverend realism, says that they are all fools.

G. K. Chesterton (1874–1936) British writer. *Heretics,* Ch. 12

12 Mankind is not a tribe of animals to which we owe compassion. Mankind is a club to which we owe our subscription.

G. K. Chesterton *Daily News,* 10 Apr 1906

13 The evolution of the human race will not be accomplished in the ten thousand years of tame animals, but in the million years of wild animals, because man is and will always be a wild animal.

Charles Darwin (1887–1962) British life scientist. *The Next Ten Million Years,* Ch. 4

14 On earth there is nothing great but man; in man there is nothing great but mind.

William Hamilton (1788–1856) Scottish philosopher. *Lectures on Metaphysics*

15 The majority of men devote the greater part of their lives to making their remaining years unhappy.

Jean de La Bruyère (1645–96) French satirist. *Les Caractères*

16 The anthropologist respects history, but he does not accord it a special value. He conceives it as a study complementary to his own: one of them unfurls the range of human societies in time, the other in space.

Claude Lévi-Strauss (1908–) French anthropologist. *The Savage Mind*

17 I'll give you my opinion of the human race… Their heart's in the right place, but their head is a thoroughly inefficient organ.

W. Somerset Maugham (1874–1965) British novelist. *The Summing Up*

18 Clearly, then, the city is not a concrete jungle, it is a human zoo.

Desmond Morris (1928–) British biologist and writer. *The Human Zoo*, Introduction

19 There are one hundred and ninety-three living species of monkeys and apes. One hundred and ninety-two of them are covered with hair. The exception is a naked ape self-named *Homo sapiens.*

Desmond Morris *The Naked Ape*, Introduction

20 Man, as he is, is not a genuine article. He is an imitation of something, and a very bad imitation.

P. D. Ouspensky (1878–1947) Russian-born occultist. *The Psychology of Man's Possible Evolution*, Ch. 2

21 The human face is indeed, like the face of the God of some Oriental theogony, a whole cluster of faces, crowded together but on different surfaces so that one does not see them all at once.

Marcel Proust (1871–1922) French novelist. *À la recherche du temps perdu: À l'ombre des jeunes filles en fleurs*

22 I wish I loved the Human Race;
I wish I loved its silly face;
I wish I liked the way it walks;
I wish I liked the way it talks;
And when I'm introduced to one
I wish I thought *What Jolly Fun!*

Walter Raleigh (1861–1922) British scholar. *Laughter from a Cloud*, 'Wishes of an Elderly Man'

23 Everything is good when it leaves the Creator's hands; everything degenerates in the hands of man.

Jean Jacques Rousseau (1712–78) French philosopher. Attrib.

24 I love mankind – it's people I can't stand.

Charles M. Schultz (1922–) US cartoonist. *Go Fly a Kite, Charlie Brown*

25 After all, for mankind as a whole there are no exports. We did not start developing by obtaining foreign exchange from Mars or the moon. Mankind is a closed society.

E. F. Schumacher (1911–77) German-born economist. *Small is Beautiful, A Study of Economics as if People Mattered*, Ch. 14

26 But man, proud man
Dress'd in a little brief authority,
Most ignorant of what he's most assur'd,
His glassy essence, like an angry ape,
Plays such fantastic tricks before high heaven
As makes the angels weep.

William Shakespeare (1564–1616) English dramatist. *Measure for Measure*, II:2

27 What a piece of work is a man! How noble in reason! how infinite in faculties! in form and moving, how express and admirable! in action, how like an angel! in apprehension, how like a god! the beauty of the world! the paragon of animals! And yet, to me, what is this quintessence of dust? Man delights not me – no, nor woman neither.

William Shakespeare *Hamlet*, II:2

28 How beauteous mankind is! O brave new world
That has such people in't!

William Shakespeare *The Tempest*, V:1

29 Physically there is nothing to distinguish human society from the farm-yard except that children are more troublesome and costly than chickens and women are not so completely enslaved as farm stock.

George Bernard Shaw (1856–1950) Irish dramatist and critic. *Getting Married*, Preface

30 Man, unlike any other thing organic or inorganic in the universe, grows beyond his work, walks up the stairs of his concepts, emerges ahead of his accomplishments.

John Steinbeck (1902–68) US novelist. *The Grapes of Wrath*, Ch. 14

31 Glory to Man in the highest! for Man is the master of things.

Algernon Charles Swinburne (1837–1909) British poet. *Hymn of Man*

32 I am a man, I count nothing human foreign to me.

Terence (Publius Terentius Afer; c. 190–159 BC) Roman poet. *Heauton Timorumenos*

33 …he willed that the hearts of Men should seek beyond the world and should find no rest therein; but they should have a virtue to shape their life, amid the powers and chances of the world.

J. R. R. Tolkien (1892–1973) British writer. 'He' is Ilúvatar, the Creator. *The Silmarillion*, Ch. 1

34 The highest wisdom has but one science – the science of the whole – the science explaining the whole creation and man's place in it.

Leo Tolstoy (1828–1910) Russian writer. *War and Peace*, Bk.V, Ch. 2

35 One thousand years more. That's all *Homo sapiens* has before him.

H. G. Wells (1866–1946) British writer. *Diary* (Harold Nicolson)

36 If anything is sacred the human body is sacred.

Walt Whitman (1819–92) US poet. *I Sing the Body Electric*, 8

37 But there comes a moment in everybody's life when he must decide whether he'll live among human beings or not – a fool among fools or a fool alone.

Thornton Wilder (1897–1975) US novelist and dramatist. *The Matchmaker*, IV

38 We're all of us guinea pigs in the laboratory of God. Humanity is just a work in progress.

Tennessee Williams (1911–83) US dramatist. *Camino Real*, 12

39 If this belief from heaven be sent,
If such be Nature's holy plan,
Have I not reason to lament
What man has made of man?

William Wordsworth (1770–1850) British poet. *Lines written in Early Spring*

MANNERS

See also courtesy, etiquette

1 Leave off first for manners' sake: and be not unsatiable, lest thou offend.

Bible: Ecclesiasticus 31:17

2 'Speak when you're spoken to!' the Red Queen sharply interrupted her.

Lewis Carroll (Charles Lutwidge Dodgson; 1832–98) British writer. *Through the Looking-Glass*, Ch. 9

3 To Americans English manners are far more frightening than none at all.

Randall Jarrell (1914–65) US author. *Pictures from an Institution*, Pt. I, Ch. 5

4 On the Continent people have good food; in England people have good table manners.

George Mikes (1912–87) Hungarian-born British writer. *How to be an Alien*

5 Good breeding consists in concealing how much we think of ourselves and how little we think of other persons.

Mark Twain (Samuel Langhorne Clemens; 1835–1910) US writer. *Notebooks*

6 Politeness is organised indifference.

Paul Valéry (1871–1945) French poet and writer. *Tel Quel*

7 Manners are especially the need of the plain. The pretty can get away with anything.

Evelyn Waugh (1903–66) British novelist. *The Observer*, 'Sayings of the Year,' 1962

8 Manners maketh man.

William of Wykeham (1324–1404) English churchman. Motto of Winchester College and New College, Oxford

MARRIAGE

See also adultery, family, love and marriage, unfaithfulness

1 Better be an old man's darling than a young man's slave.

Proverb

2 Marriages are made in heaven.

Proverb

3 Marry in haste, and repent at leisure.

Proverb

4 Marry in Lent, and you'll live to repent.

Proverb

5 Marry in May, rue for aye.

Proverb

6 The first wife is matrimony, the second company, the third heresy.

Proverb

7 I had vaguely supposed that marriage in a registry office, while lacking both sanctity and style, was at least a swift, straightforward business. If not, then what was the use of it, even to the heathen? A few inquiries, however, showed it to be no such thing.

Richard Adams (1920–) British novelist. *The Girl in a Swing*, Ch. 13

8 To marry a man out of pity is folly; and, if you think you are going to influence the kind of fellow who has 'never had a chance, poor devil,' you are profoundly mistaken. One can only influence the strong characters in life, not the weak; and it is the height of vanity to suppose that you can make an honest man of anyone.

Margot Asquith (1865–1945) The second wife of Herbert Asquith. *The Autobiography of Margot Asquith*, Ch. 6

9 I married beneath me – all women do.

Nancy Astor (1879–1964) American-born British politician. *Dictionary of National Biography*

10 It is a truth universally acknowledged, that a single man in possession of a good fortune must be in want of a wife.

Jane Austen (1775–1817) British novelist. The opening words of the book. *Pride and Prejudice*, Ch. 1

11 Happiness in marriage is entirely a matter of chance.

Jane Austen *Pride and Prejudice*, Ch. 6

12 Mrs Hall of Sherbourne was brought to bed yesterday of a dead child, some weeks before she expected, owing to a fright. I suppose she happened unawares to look at her husband.

Jane Austen Letter, 27 Oct 1798

13 Wives are young men's mistresses, companions for middle age, and old men's nurses.

Francis Bacon (1561–1626) English philosopher. *Essays*, 'Of Marriage and Single Life'

14 He was reputed one of the wise men, that made answer to the question, when a man should marry? A young man not yet, an elder man not at all.

Francis Bacon *Essays*, 'Of Marriage and Single Life'

15 I rather think of having a career of my own.

Arthur Balfour (1848–1930) British statesman. When asked whether he was going to marry Margot Tennant. *Autobiography* (Margot Asquith), Ch. 9

16 It is easier to be a lover than a husband, for the same reason that it is more difficult to show a ready wit all day long than to produce an occasional *bon mot*.

Honoré de Balzac (1799–1850) French novelist. Attrib.

17 The majority of husbands remind me of an orangutang trying to play the violin.

Honoré de Balzac *La Physiologie du mariage*

18 No man should marry until he has studied anatomy and dissected at least one woman.

Honoré de Balzac *La Physiologie du mariage*

19 My father argued sair – my mother didna speak,
But she looked in my face till my heart was like to break;
They gied him my hand but my heart was in the sea;
And so auld Robin Gray, he was gudeman to me.

Lady Ann Barnard (1750–1825) British poet. *Auld Robin Gray*

20 I don't like your Christian name. I'd like to change it.

Thomas Beecham ((1879–1961) British conductor. To his future wife. She replied, 'You can't, but you can change my surname.'. Attrib.

21 I think weddings is sadder than funerals, because they remind you of your own wedding. You can't be reminded of your own funeral because it hasn't happened. But weddings always make me cry.

Brendan Behan (1923–64) Irish playwright. *Richard's Cork Leg*, I

22 Being a husband is a whole-time job. That is why so many husbands fail. They cannot give their entire attention to it.

Arnold Bennett (1867–1931) British novelist. *The Title*, I

23 Husbands, love your wives, and be not bitter against them.

Bible: Colossians 3:19

24 Let the husband render unto the wife due benevolence: and likewise also the wife unto the husband.

Bible: I Corinthians 7:3

25 But if they cannot contain, let them marry: for it is better to marry than to burn.

Bible: I Corinthians 7:9

26 But he that is married careth for the things that are of the world, how he may please his wife.

Bible: I Corinthians 7:33

27 Wherefore they are no more twain, but one flesh. What therefore God hath joined together, let not man put asunder.

Bible: Matthew 19:6

28 Even as Sara obeyed Abraham, calling him lord: whose daughters ye are, as long as ye do well, and are not afraid with any amazement. Likewise, ye husbands, dwell with them according to knowledge, giving honour unto the wife, as unto the weaker vessel, and as being heirs together of the grace of life; that your prayers be not hindered.

Bible: I Peter 3:6–7

29 *Marriage*, n. The state or condition of a community consisting of a master, a mistress and two slaves, making in all two.

Ambrose Bierce (1842–?1914) US writer and journalist. *The Devil's Dictionary*

30 To have and to hold from this day forward, for better for worse, for richer for poorer, in sickness and in health, to love and to cherish, till death us do part.

The Book of Common Prayer *Solemnization of Matrimony*

31 'We stay together, but we distrust one another.'
'Ah, yes...but isn't that a definition of marriage?'

Malcolm Bradbury (1932–) British academic and novelist. *The History Man*, Ch. 3

32 Ah, gentle dames! It gars me greet
To think how mony counsels sweet,
How mony lengthen'd sage advices,
The husband frae the wife despises!

Robert Burns (1759–96) Scottish poet. *Tam o' Shanter*

33 Marriage is distinctly and repeatedly excluded from heaven. Is this because it is thought likely to mar the general felicity?

Samuel Butler (1835–1902) British writer. *Notebooks*

34 Wedlock – the deep, deep peace of the double bed after the hurly-burly of the chaise-longue.

Mrs Patrick Campbell (Beatrice Stella Tanner; 1865–1940) British actress. *Jennie* (Ralph G. Martin), Vol. II

35 She was a worthy womman al hir lyve,
Housbondes at chirche-dore she hadde fyve,
Withouten other companye in youthe.

Geoffrey Chaucer (c. 1342–1400) English poet. Referring to the wife of Bath. *The Canterbury Tales*, Prologue

36 An archaeologist is the best husband any woman can have: the older she gets, the more interested he is in her.

Agatha Christie (1891–1976) British detective-story writer. Attrib.

37 The most happy marriage I can picture or imagine to myself would be the union of a deaf man to a blind woman.

Samuel Taylor Coleridge (1772–1834) British poet. *Recollections* (Allsop)

38 SHARPER: Thus grief still treads upon the heels of pleasure:
Marry'd in haste, we may repent at leisure.
SETTER: Some by experience find those words mis-plac'd:
At leisure marry'd, they repent in haste.

William Congreve (1670–1729) British Restoration dramatist. *The Old Bachelor*, V:8

39 Courtship to marriage, as a very witty prologue to a very dull Play.

William Congreve *The Old Bachelor*, V:10

40 I hope you do not think me prone to any iteration of nuptials.

William Congreve *The Way of the World*, IV:12

41 Marriage is a wonderful invention; but then

again so is a bicycle repair kit.

Billy Connolly (1942–) British comedian. *The Authorized Version*

42 Says John, It is my wedding-day,
And all the world would stare,
If wife should dine at Edmonton,
And I should dine at Ware.

William Cowper (1731–1800) British poet. *John Gilpin*

43 To-morrow is our wedding-day,
And we will then repair
Unto the Bell at Edmonton,
All in a chaise and pair.

William Cowper *John Gilpin*

44 Daisy, Daisy, give me your answer, do!
I'm half crazy, all for the love of you!
It won't be a stylish marriage,
I can't afford a carriage,
But you'll look sweet upon the seat
Of a bicycle made for two!

Harry Dacre (19th century) British songwriter. *Daisy Bell*

45 If a man stays away from his wife for seven years, the law presumes the separation to have killed him; yet according to our daily experience, it might well prolong his life.

Lord Darling (1849–1936) British judge. *Scintillae Juris*

46 This man, she reasons, as she looks at her husband, is a poor fish. But he is the nearest I can get to the big one that got away.

Nigel Dennis (1912–89) British writer. *Cards of Identity*

47 'Old girl,' said Mr Bagnet, 'give him my opinion. You know it.'

Charles Dickens (1812–70) British novelist. *Bleak House*, Ch. 27

48 Every woman should marry – and no man.

Benjamin Disraeli (1804–81) British statesman. *Lothair*, Ch. 30

49 It destroys one's nerves to be amiable every day to the same human being.

Benjamin Disraeli *The Young Duke*

50 Now one of the great reasons why so many husbands and wives make shipwreck of their lives together is because a man is always seeking for happiness, while a woman is on a perpetual still hunt for trouble.

Dorothy Dix (Elizabeth Meriwether Gilmer; 1861–1951) US journalist and writer. *Dorothy Dix, Her Book*, Ch. 1

51 The husband was a teetotaller, there was no other woman, and the conduct complained of was that he had drifted into the habit of winding up every meal by taking out his false teeth and hurling them at his wife.

Arthur Conan Doyle (1856–1930) British writer. *A Case of Identity*

52 Here lies my wife; here let her lie!
Now she's at rest, and so am I.

John Dryden (1631–1700) British poet and dramatist. *Epitaph Intended for Dryden's Wife*

53 I am to be married within these three days; married past redemption.

John Dryden *Marriage à la Mode*, I

54 So that ends my first experience with matrimony, which I always thought a highly overrated performance.

Isadora Duncan (1878–1927) US dancer. *The New York Times*, 1923

55 Being an old maid is like death by drowning, a really delightful sensation after you cease to struggle.

Edna Ferber (1887–1968) US writer. *Wit's End* (R. E. Drennan), 'Completing the Circle'

56 His designs were strictly honourable, as the phrase is; that is, to rob a lady of her fortune by way of marriage.

Henry Fielding (1707–54) British novelist. *Tom Jones*, Bk. XI, Ch. 4

57 Composed that monstrous animal a husband and wife.

Henry Fielding *Tom Jones*, Bk. XV, Ch. 9

58 When widows exclaim loudly against second marriages, I would always lay a wager, that the man, if not the wedding-day, is absolutely fixed on.

Henry Fielding *Amelia*, Bk. VI, Ch. 8

59 One fool at least in every married couple.

Henry Fielding *Amelia*, Bk. IX, Ch. 4

60 Most marriages don't add two people together. They subtract one from the other.

Ian Fleming (1908–64) British journalist and author. *Diamonds are Forever*

61 Husbands are like fires. They go out when unattended.

Zsa Zsa Gabor (1919–) Hungarian-born US film star. *Newsweek*, 28 Mar 1960

62 A man in love is incomplete until he has married. Then he's finished.

Zsa Zsa Gabor *Newsweek*, 28 Mar 1960

63 Do you think your mother and I should have liv'd comfortably so long together, if ever we had been married?

John Gay (1685–1732) English poet and dramatist. *The Beggar's Opera*

64 No, I shall have mistresses.

George II (1683–1760) King of Great Britain and Ireland. Reply to Queen Caroline's suggestion, as she lay on her deathbed, that he should marry again after her death. *Memoirs of George the Second* (Hervey), Vol. II

65 I was ever of opinion, that the honest man who married and brought up a large family, did more service than he who continued single and only talked of population.

Oliver Goldsmith (1728–74) Irish-born British writer. *The Vicar of Wakefield*, Ch. 1

66 I...chose my wife, as she did her wedding gown, not for a fine glossy surface, but such qualities as would wear well.

Oliver Goldsmith *The Vicar of Wakefield*, Preface

67 The trouble with my wife is that she is a whore in the kitchen and a cook in bed.

Geoffrey Gorer (1905–85) British writer and anthropologist. *Exploring the English Character*

68 When a woman gets married it is like jumping into a hole in the ice in the middle of winter; you do it once and you remember it the rest of your days.

Maxim Gorky (Aleksei Maksimovich Peshkov; 1868–1936) Russian writer. *The Lower Depths*

69 The concept of two people living together for 25 years without having a cross word suggests a lack of spirit only to be admired in sheep.

A. P. Herbert (1890–1971) British writer and politician. *News Chronicle*, 1940

70 The critical period in matrimony is breakfast-time.

A. P. Herbert *Uncommon Law*

71 Then be not coy, but use your time;
And while ye may, go marry:
For having lost but once your prime,
You may for ever tarry.

Robert Herrick (1591–1674) English poet. *Hesperides*, 'To the Virgins, to Make Much of Time'

72 Marriage has many pains, but celibacy has no pleasures.

Samuel Johnson (1709–84) British lexicographer. *Rasselas*, Ch. 26

73 The triumph of hope over experience.

Samuel Johnson Referring to the hasty remarriage of an acquaintance following the death of his first wife, with whom he had been most unhappy. *Life of Johnson* (J. Boswell), Vol. II

74 It has been discovered experimentally that you can draw laughter from an audience anywhere in the world, of any class or race, simply by walking on to a stage and uttering the words 'I am a married man'.

Ted Kavanagh (1892–1958) British radio scriptwriter. *News Review*, 10 July 1947

75 Nothing is to me more distasteful than that entire complacency and satisfaction which beam in the countenances of a new-married couple.

Charles Lamb (1775–1834) British essayist. *Essays of Elia*, 'A Bachelor's Complaint of Married People'

76 Same old slippers,
Same old rice,
Same old glimpse of
Paradise.

William James Lampton (1859–1917) British writer. *June Weddings*

77 We take the view that the time has now arrived when the law should declare that a rapist remains a rapist and is subject to the criminal law, irrespective of his relationship with his victim.

Lord Lane (1918–) British judge and Lord Chief Justice. Dismissing the appeal of a man who argued, on the 1736 principle of Chief Justice Hale, that he could not be guilty of raping his wife. *The Times*, 15 Mar 1991

78 There was I, waiting at the church,
Waiting at the church, waiting at the church,
When I found he'd left me in the lurch,
Lor', how it did upset me!...
Can't get away to marry you today –
My wife won't let me.

Fred W. Leigh (19th century) British songwriter. *Waiting at the Church*

79 I'm getting married in the morning!
Ding dong! the bells are gonna chime.
Pull out the stopper!
Let's have a whopper!
But get me to the church on time!

Alan Jay Lerner (1918–86) US songwriter. *My Fair Lady*, II:3

80 I am in truth very thankful for not having married at all.

Harriet Martineau (1802–76) British writer. *Harriet Martineau's Autobiography*, Vol. I

81 ...the early marriages of silly children... where...every woman is married before she well knows how serious a matter human life is.

Harriet Martineau *Society in America*, Vol. III, 'Marriage'

82 In no country, I believe, are the marriage laws so iniquitous as in England, and the conjugal relation, in consequence, so impaired.

Harriet Martineau *Society in America*, Vol. III, 'Marriage'

83 When married people don't get on they can separate, but if they're not married it's impossible. It's a tie that only death can sever.

W. Somerset Maugham (1874–1965) British novelist. *The Circle*, III

84 Marriage is like a cage; one sees the birds outside desperate to get in, and those inside equally desperate to get out.

Michel de Montaigne (1533–92) French essayist. *Essais*, III

85 It has been said that a bride's attitude towards her betrothed can be summed up in three words: Aisle. Altar. Hymn.

Frank Muir (1920–) British writer and broadcaster. *Upon My Word!* (Frank Muir and Dennis Norden), 'A Jug of Wine'

86 One doesn't have to get anywhere in a marriage. It's not a public conveyance.

Iris Murdoch (1919–) Irish-born British novelist. *A Severed Head*

87 Writing is like getting married. One should never commit oneself until one is amazed at one's luck.

Iris Murdoch *The Black Prince*, 'Bradley Pearson's Foreword'

88 Marriage is an insult and women shouldn't touch it.

Jenni Murray (1950–) British broadcaster. *The Independent*, 20 June 1992

89 Why have hamburger out when you've got steak at home? That doesn't mean it's always tender.

Paul Newman (1925–) US film actor. Remark, Mar 1984

90 It is now known...that men enter local politics

solely as a result of being unhappily married.

Cyril Northcote Parkinson (1919–93) British historian and writer. *Parkinson's Law*, Ch. 10

91 Marriage may often be a stormy lake, but celibacy is almost always a muddy horse-pond.

Thomas Love Peacock (1785–1866) British novelist. *Melincourt*

92 Sir, I have quarrelled with my wife; and a man who has quarrelled with his wife is absolved from all duty to his country.

Thomas Love Peacock *Nightmare Abbey*, Ch. 11

93 Strange to say what delight we married people have to see these poor fools decoyed into our condition.

Samuel Pepys (1633–1703) English diarist. *Diary*, 25 Dec 1665

94 When a man opens the car door for his wife, it's either a new car or a new wife.

Prince Philip (1921–) The consort of Queen Elizabeth II. Remark, Mar 1988

95 He loved me, and 'twas right that he should, for I had come to him as a girl-bride; we two had made such wise provision in all our love that our two hearts were moved in all things, whether of joy or of sorrow, by a common wish, more united in love than the hearts of brother and sister.

Christine de Pisan (?1363–?1430) Italian poet. *Women of Medieval France* (Pierce Butler)

96 A loving wife will do anything for her husband except stop criticising and trying to improve him.

J. B. Priestley (1894–1984) British novelist. *Rain on Godshill*

97 It doesn't much signify whom one marries, for one is sure to find next morning that it was someone else.

Samuel Rogers (1763–1855) British poet. *Table Talk* (ed. Alexander Dyce)

98 A married couple are well suited when both partners usually feel the need for a quarrel at the same time.

Jean Rostand (1894–1977) French biologist and writer. *Le Mariage*

99 Never feel remorse for what you have thought about your wife; she has thought much worse things about you.

Jean Rostand *Le Mariage*

100 When you see what some girls marry, you realize how they must hate to work for a living.

Helen Rowland (1876–1950) US writer. *Reflections of a Bachelor Girl*

101 The Western custom of one wife and hardly any mistresses.

Saki (Hector Hugh Munro; 1870–1916) British writer. *Reginald in Russia*

102 It takes two to make a marriage a success and only one a failure.

Herbert Samuel (1870–1963) British Liberal statesman. *A Book of Quotations*

103 Marriage is nothing but a civil contract.

John Selden (1584–1654) English historian. *Table Talk*

104 For a light wife doth make a heavy husband.

William Shakespeare (1564–1616) English dramatist. *The Merchant of Venice*, V:1

105 Many a good hanging prevents a bad marriage.

William Shakespeare *Twelfth Night*, I:5

106 Marriage is popular because it combines the maximum of temptation with the maximum of opportunity.

George Bernard Shaw (1856–1950) Irish dramatist and critic. *Man and Superman*

107 It is a woman's business to get married as soon as possible, and a man's to keep unmarried as long as he can.

George Bernard Shaw *Man and Superman*, II

108 Have you not heard
When a man marries, dies, or turns Hindoo,
His best friends hear no more of him?

Percy Bysshe Shelley (1792–1822) British poet. Referring to Thomas Love Peacock, who worked for the East India Company and had recently married. *Letter to Maria Gisborne*, I

109 Married women are kept women, and they are beginning to find it out.

Logan Pearsall Smith (1865–1946) US writer. *Afterthoughts*, 'Other people'

110 My definition of marriage:....it resembles a pair of shears, so joined that they cannot be separated; often moving in opposite directions, yet always punishing anyone who comes between them.

Sydney Smith (1771–1845) British clergyman and essayist. *Memoir* (Lady Holland)

111 A little in drink, but at all times yr faithful husband.

Richard Steele (1672–1729) Dublin-born British essayist. Letter to his wife, 27 Sep 1708

112 Even if we take matrimony at its lowest, even if we regard it as no more than a sort of friendship recognized by the police.

Robert Louis Stevenson (1850–94) Scottish writer. *Virginibus Puerisque*

113 Marriage is a step so grave and decisive that it attracts light-headed, variable men by its very awfulness.

Robert Louis Stevenson *Virginibus Puerisque*

114 Marriage is like life in this – that it is a field of battle, and not a bed of roses.

Robert Louis Stevenson *Virginibus Puerisque*

115 In marriage, a man becomes slack and selfish and undergoes a fatty degeneration of his moral being.

Robert Louis Stevenson *Virginibus Puerisque*

116 Bachelor's fare; bread and cheese,

and kisses.

Jonathan Swift (1667–1745) Irish-born Anglican priest and writer. *Polite Conversation*, Dialogue 1

117 What they do in heaven we are ignorant of; what they do *not* we are told expressly, that they neither marry, nor are given in marriage.

Jonathan Swift *Thoughts on Various Subjects*

118 He that loves not his wife and children, feeds a lioness at home and broods a nest of sorrows.

Jeremy Taylor (1613–67) English Anglican theologian. *Sermons*, 'Married Love'

119 Or when the moon was overhead,
Came two young lovers lately wed;
'I am half sick of shadows,' said
The Lady of Shalott.

Alfred, Lord Tennyson (1809–92) British poet. *The Lady of Shalott*, Pt. II

120 Remember, it is as easy to marry a rich woman as a poor woman.

William Makepeace Thackeray (1811–63) British novelist. *Pendennis*, Ch. 28

121 This I set down as a positive truth. A woman with fair opportunities and without a positive hump, may marry whom she likes.

William Makepeace Thackeray *Vanity Fair*, Ch. 4

122 Every night of her married life she has been late for school.

Dylan Thomas (1914–53) Welsh poet. *Under Milk Wood*

123 It should be a very happy marriage – they are both so much in love with *him.*

Irene Thomas (1920–) British writer. Attrib.

124 Divorce? Never. But murder often!

Sybil Thorndike (1882–1976) British actress. Replying to a query as to whether she had ever considered divorce during her long marriage to Sir Lewis Casson. Attrib.

125 A man should not insult his wife publicly, at parties. He should insult her in the privacy of the home.

James Thurber (1894–1961) US humorist. *Thurber Country*

126 Nearly all marriages, even happy ones, are mistakes: in the sense that almost certainly (in a more perfect world, or even with a little more care in this very imperfect one) both partners might have found more suitable mates. But the real soul-mate is the one you are actually married to.

J. R. R. Tolkien (1892–1973) British writer. Letter to Michael Tolkien, 6–8 Mar 1941

127 Marriage is the only adventure open to the cowardly.

Voltaire (François-Marie Arouet; 1694–1778) French writer. *Thoughts of a Philosopher*

128 Marriage is a great institution, but I'm not ready for an institution, yet.

Mae West (1892–1980) US actress.

129 I think women are basically quite lazy. Marriage is still a woman's best investment, because she can con some man into supporting her for the rest of his life.

Alan Whicker (1925–) British television broadcaster and writer. *The Observer*, 'Sayings of the Week', 10 Sept 1972

130 And what would happen to my illusion that I am a force for order in the home if I wasn't married to the only man north of the Tiber who is even untidier than I am?

Katherine Whitehorn (1926–) British journalist. *Sunday Best*, 'Husband-Swapping'

131 In married life three is company and two is none.

Oscar Wilde (1854–1900) Irish-born British dramatist. *The Importance of Being Earnest*, I

132 Twenty years of romance makes a woman look like a ruin; but twenty years of marriage make her something like a public building.

Oscar Wilde *A Woman of No Importance*, I

133 The best part of married life is the fights. The rest is merely so-so.

Thornton Wilder (1897–1975) US novelist and dramatist. *The Matchmaker*, II

134 Of course, I do have a slight advantage over the rest of you. It helps in a pinch to be able to remind your bride that you gave up a throne for her.

Duke of Windsor (1894–1972) King of the United Kingdom; abdicated 1936. Discussing the maintenance of happy marital relations. Attrib.

135 Judges, as a class, display, in the matter of arranging alimony, that reckless generosity that is found only in men who are giving away somebody else's cash.

P. G. Wodehouse (1881–1975) British humorous novelist. *Louder and Funnier*

136 I can honestly say that I always look on Pauline as one of the nicest girls I was ever engaged to.

P. G. Wodehouse *Thank You Jeeves*, Ch. 6

137 Wondering why one's friends chose to marry the people they did is unprofitable, but recurrent. One could so often have done so much better for them.

John Wyndham (1903–69) British science-fiction writer. *The Kraken Wakes*

MARTYRDOM

See also execution

1 The king has been very good to me. He promoted me from a simple maid to be a marchioness. Then he raised me to be a queen. Now he will raise me to be a martyr.

Anne Boleyn (1507–36) Second wife of Henry VIII. *Notable Women in History* (W. Abbot)

2 'Dying for an idea,' again, sounds well enough, but why not let the idea die instead of you?

Wyndham Lewis (1882–1957) British novelist. *The Art of Being Ruled*, Pt. I, Ch. 1

3 I will burn, but this is a mere incident. We shall continue our discussion in eternity.

Michael Servetus (1511–53) Spanish physician and theologian. Comment to the judges of the Inquisition after being condemned to be burned at the stake as a heretic. *Borges: A Reader* (E. Monegal)

4 And they blest him in their pain, that they were not left to Spain,
To the thumbscrew and the stake, for the glory of the Lord.

Alfred, Lord Tennyson (1809–92) British poet. *The Revenge*, III

5 A thing is not necessarily true because a man dies for it.

Oscar Wilde (1854–1900) Irish-born British dramatist. *Oscariana*

MARXISM

See also Communism, socialism

1 Karl Marx wasn't a Marxist all the time. He got drunk in the Tottenham Court Road.

Michael Foot (1913–) British Labour politician and journalist. *Behind The Image* (Susan Barnes)

2 Marxian Socialism must always remain a portent to the historians of Opinion – how a doctrine so illogical and so dull can have exercised so powerful and enduring an influence over the minds of men, and, through them, the events of history.

John Maynard Keynes (1883–1946) British economist. *The End of Laissez-Faire*, III

3 The workers have nothing to lose but their chains. They have a world to gain. Workers of the world, unite.

Karl Marx (1818–83) German philosopher and revolutionary. *The Communist Manifesto*, 4

4 From each according to his abilities, to each according to his needs.

Karl Marx *Criticism of the Gotha Programme*

5 The dictatorship of the proletariat.

Karl Marx Attrib.

6 And what a prize we have to fight for: no less than the chance to banish from our land the dark divisive clouds of Marxist socialism.

Margaret Thatcher (1925–) British politician and prime minister. Speech, Scottish Conservative Conference, 1983

MASCULINITY

See also men

1 It makes me feel masculine to tell you that I do not answer questions like this without being paid for answering them.

Lillian Hellman (1905–84) US dramatist. When asked by *Harper's* magazine when she felt most masculine; this question had already been asked of several famous men. *Reader's Digest*, July 1977

2 You may have my husband, but not my horse. My husband won't need emasculating, and my horse I won't have you meddle with. I'll preserve one last male thing in the museum of this world, if I can.

D. H. Lawrence (1885–1930) British novelist. *St Mawr*

MATERIALISM

See also greed, money, wealth

1 Benefits make a man a slave.

Arabic proverb. Proverb

2 Thinking to get at once all the gold that the goose could give, he killed it, and opened it only to find – nothing.

Aesop (6th century BC) Reputed Greek writer of fables. *Fables*, 'The Goose with the Golden Eggs'

3 Jesus said unto him, If thou wilt be perfect, go and sell that thou hast, and give to the poor, and thou shalt have treasure in heaven: and come and follow me.
But when the young man heard that saying, he went away sorrowful: for he had great possessions.

Bible: Matthew 19:21–22

4 Maidens, like moths, are ever caught by glare,
And Mammon wins his way where Seraphs might despair.

Lord Byron (1788–1824) British poet. *Childe Harold's Pilgrimage*, I

5 For gold in phisik is a cordial,
Therfore he lovede gold in special.

Geoffrey Chaucer (c. 1342–1400) English poet. Referring to the doctor. *The Canterbury Tales*, Prologue

6 To be clever enough to get all that money, one must be stupid enough to want it.

G. K. Chesterton (1874–1936) British writer. *The Innocence of Father Brown*

7 I never hated a man enough to give him diamonds back.

Zsa Zsa Gabor (1919–) Hungarian-born US film star. *The Observer*, 'Sayings of the Week', 28 Aug 1957

8 What female heart can gold despise?
What cat's averse to fish?

Thomas Gray (1716–71) British poet. *Ode on the Death of a Favourite Cat*

9 Man must choose whether to be rich in things or in the freedom to use them.

Ivan Illich (1926–) Austrian sociologist. *Deschooling Society*, Ch. 4

10 In a consumer society there are inevitably two kinds of slaves: the prisoners of addiction and the prisoners of envy.

Ivan Illich *Tools for Conviviality*

11 The almighty dollar, that great object of universal devotion throughout our land, seems to have no genuine devotees in these peculiar villages.

Washington Irving (1783–1859) US writer. *Wolfert's Roost*, 'The Creole Village'

12 Good morning to the day: and, next, my gold! –
Open the shrine, that I may see my saint.

Ben Jonson (1573–1637) English dramatist. *Volpone*, I:1

13 Kissing your hand may make you feel very very good but a diamond and safire bracelet lasts forever.

Anita Loos (1891–1981) US novelist. *Gentlemen Prefer Blondes*, Ch. 4

14 When an American heiress wants to buy a man, she at once crosses the Atlantic. The only really materialistic people I have ever met have been Europeans.

Mary McCarthy (1912–89) US novelist. *On the Contrary* 1962

15 Years ago a person, he was unhappy, didn't know what to do with himself – he'd go to church, start a revolution – *something*. Today you're unhappy? Can't figure it out? What is the salvation? Go shopping.

Arthur Miller (1915–) US dramatist. *The Price*, I

16 Why is it no one ever sent me yet
One perfect limousine, do you suppose?
Ah no, it's always just my luck to get
One perfect rose.

Dorothy Parker (1893–1967) US writer. *One Perfect Rose*

17 Diamonds Are A Girl's Best Friend.

Leo Robin (1899–1984) US songwriter. *Gentlemen Prefer Blondes*, song title

18 Bell, book, and candle, shall not drive me back,
When gold and silver becks me to come on.

William Shakespeare (1564–1616) English dramatist. *King John*, III:3

19 The want of a thing is perplexing enough, but the possession of it is intolerable.

John Vanbrugh (1664–1726) English architect and dramatist. *The Confederacy*, I:2

20 Conspicuous consumption of valuable goods is a means of reputability to the gentleman of leisure.

Thorstein Bunde Veblen (1857–1929) US social scientist. *The Theory of the Leisure Class*

21 What do you not drive human hearts into, cursed
craving for gold!

Virgil (Publius Vergilius Maro; 70–19 BC) Roman poet. *Aeneid*, Bk. III

22 There's something about a crowd like that that brings a lump to my wallet.

Eli Wallach (1915–) US actor. Remarking upon the long line of people at the box office before one of his performances. Attrib.

23 A gold rush is what happens when a line of chorus girls spot a man with a bank roll.

Mae West (1892–1980) US actress. *Klondike Annie*, film 1936

MATHEMATICS

See also numbers

1 What is algebra exactly; is it those three-cornered things?

J. M. Barrie (1860–1937) British novelist and dramatist. *Quality Street*, II

2 I never could make out what those damned dots meant.

Lord Randolph Churchill (1849–95) British Conservative politician. Referring to decimal points. *Lord Randolph Churchill* (W. S. Churchill)

3 As far as the laws of mathematics refer to reality, they are not certain, and as far as they are certain, they do not refer to reality.

Albert Einstein (1879–1955) German-born US physicist. *The Tao of Physics* (F. Capra), Ch. 2

4 There is no 'royal road' to geometry.

Euclid (c. 300 BC) Greek mathematician. Said to Ptolemy I when asked if there were an easier way to solve theorems. *Comment on Euclid* (Proclus)

5 About binomial theorems I'm teeming with a lot of news,
With many cheerful facts about the square on the hypoteneuse.

W. S. Gilbert (1836–1911) British dramatist. *The Pirates of Penzance*, I

6 MORIARTY. How are you at Mathematics?
HARRY SECOMBE. I speak it like a native.

Spike Milligan (1918–) British comic actor and author. *The Goon Show*

7 The only way I can distinguish proper from improper fractions
Is by their actions.

Ogden Nash (1902–71) US poet. *Ask Daddy, He Won't Know*

8 One geometry cannot be more true than another; it can only be more convenient. Geometry is not true, it is advantageous.

Robert T. Pirsig (1928–) US writer. *Zen and the Art of Motorcycle Maintenance*, Pt. III, Ch. 22

9 Let no one ignorant of mathematics enter here.

Plato (429–347 BC) Greek philosopher. Inscription written over the entrance to the Academy. *Biographical Encyclopedia* (I. Asimov)

10 The true spirit of delight, the exaltation, the sense of being more than Man, which is the touchstone of the highest excellence is to be found in mathematics as surely as in poetry.

Bertrand Russell (1872–1970) British philosopher. *Mysticism and Logic*

11 Mathematics, rightly viewed, possesses not only truth by supreme beauty – a beauty cold and austere like that of sculpture.

Bertrand Russell *Mysticism and Logic*

12 Mathematics may be defined as the subject in which we never know what we are talking about, nor whether what we are saying is true.
Bertrand Russell *Mysticism and Logic*, Ch. 4

13 Pure mathematics consists entirely of assertions to the effect that, if such and such a proposition is true of *anything*, then such and such another proposition is true of that thing. It is essential not to discuss whether the first proposition is really true, and not to mention what the anything is, of which it is supposed to be true.
Bertrand Russell *Mysticism and Logic*, Ch. 5

14 Mathematics possesses not only truth, but supreme beauty – a beauty cold and austere, like that of sculpture.
Bertrand Russell *The Study of Mathematics*

15 Numbers constitute the only universal language.
Nathaniel West (Nathan Weinstein; 1903–40) US novelist. *Miss Lonelyhearts*

MEANING

See also purpose, words

1 'Then you should say what you mean,' the March Hare went on. 'I do,' Alice hastily replied; 'at least – at least I mean what I say – that's the same thing, you know.'
'Not the same thing a bit!' said the Hatter. 'Why, you might just as well say that 'I see what I eat' is the same thing as 'I eat what I see!''
Lewis Carroll (Charles Lutwidge Dodgson; 1832–98) British writer. *Alice's Adventures in Wonderland*, Ch. 7

2 Take care of the sense, and the sounds will take care of themselves.
Lewis Carroll *Alice's Adventures in Wonderland*, Ch. 9

3 'When *I* use a word,' Humpty Dumpty said in rather a scornful tone, 'it means just what I choose it to mean – neither more nor less.'
Lewis Carroll *Through the Looking-Glass*, Ch. 6

4 Where in this small-talking world can I find
A longitude with no platitude?
Christopher Fry (1907–) British dramatist. *The Lady's Not for Burning*, III

5 The least of things with a meaning is worth more in life than the greatest of things without it.
Carl Gustav Jung (1875–1961) Swiss psychoanalyst. *Modern Man in Search of a Soul*

MEDICINE

See also disease, doctors, drugs, health and healthy living, illness, nurses, remedies

1 The prime goal is to alleviate suffering, and not to prolong life. And if your treatment does not alleviate suffering, but only prolongs life, that treatment should be stopped.
Christiaan Barnard (1922–) South African surgeon.

2 Medical men all over the world having merely entered into a tacit agreement to call all sorts of maladies people are liable to, in cold weather, by one name; so that one sort of treatment may serve for all, and their practice thereby be greatly simplified.
Jane Welsh Carlyle (1801–66) The wife of Thomas Carlyle. Letter to John Welsh, 4 Mar 1837

3 A miracle drug is any drug that will do what the label says it will do.
Eric Hodgins (1899–1971) US writer and editor. *Episode*

4 One of the most difficult things to contend with in a hospital is the assumption on the part of the staff that because you have lost your gall bladder you have also lost your mind.
Jean Kerr (1923–) US dramatist. *Please Don't Eat the Daisies*

5 The ultimate indignity is to be given a bedpan by a stranger who calls you by your first name.
Maggie Kuhn (1905–95) US writer and social activist. *The Observer*, 20 Aug 1978

6 The art of medicine is generally a question of time.
Ovid (Publius Ovidius Naso; 43 BC–17 AD) Roman poet. *Remedia Amoris*

7 Not even medicine can master incurable diseases.
Seneca (c. 4 BC–65 AD) Roman author. *Epistulae ad Lucilium*, XCIV

8 Optimistic lies have such immense therapeutic value that a doctor who cannot tell them convincingly has mistaken his profession.
George Bernard Shaw (1856–1950) Irish dramatist and critic. *Misalliance*, Preface

9 I've already had medical attention – a dog licked me when I was on the ground.
Neil Simon (1927–) US playwright. *Only When I Laugh* (screenplay)

10 Formerly, when religion was strong and science weak, men mistook magic for medicine, now, when science is strong and religion weak, men mistake medicine for magic.
Thomas Szasz (1920–) US psychiatrist. *The Second Sin*

11 Human beings, yes, but not surgeons.
Rudolph Virchow (1821–1902) German pathologist. Answering a query as to whether human beings could survive appendectomy, which had recently become a widespread practice. *Anekdotenschatz* (H. Hoffmeister)

12 The art of medicine consists of amusing the patient while Nature cures the disease.
Voltaire (François-Marie Arouet; 1694–1788) French writer. Attrib.

MEDIOCRITY

See also inferiority

1 The most insidious influence on the young is not violence, drugs, tobacco, drink or sexual perversion, but our pursuit of the trivial and our tolerance of the third rate.

Eric Anderson (1936–) British teacher; headmaster of Eton. *The Observer*, 'Sayings of the Week', 12 June 1994

2 Only mediocrity can be trusted to be always at its best.

Max Beerbohm (1872–1956) British writer. *Conversations with Max* (S.N. Behrman)

3 The world is made of people who never quite get into the first team and who just miss the prizes at the flower show.

Jacob Bronowski (1908–74) British scientist and writer. *The Face of Violence*, Ch. 6

4 Mediocrity knows nothing higher than itself, but talent instantly recognizes genius.

Arthur Conan Doyle (1856–1930) British writer. *The Valley of Fear*

5 Some men are born mediocre, some men achieve mediocrity, and some men have mediocrity thrust upon them. With Major Major it had been all three.

Joseph Heller (1923–) US novelist. *Catch-22*, Ch. 9

6 Women want mediocre men, and men are working to be as mediocre as possible.

Margaret Mead (1901–78) US anthropologist. *Quote Magazine*, 15 May 1958

7 With first-rate sherry flowing into second-rate whores,
And third-rate conversation without one single pause:
Just like a couple
Between the wars.

William Plomer (1903–73) South African poet and novelist. *Father and Son: 1939*

8 It isn't evil that is ruining the earth, but mediocrity. The crime is not that Nero played while Rome burned, but that he played badly.

Ned Rorem (1923–) US composer and writer. *The Final Diary*

9 Much of a muchness.

John Vanbrugh (1664–1726) English architect and dramatist. *The Provok'd Husband*, I:1

MELANCHOLY

See also despair, sorrow

1 Nothing's so dainty sweet as lovely melancholy.

Francis Beaumont (1584–1616) English dramatist. *The Nice Valour*, III:3

2 All my joys to this are folly,
Naught so sweet as Melancholy.

Robert Burton (1577–1640) English scholar and explorer. *Anatomy of Melancholy*, Abstract

3 If there is a hell upon earth, it is to be found in a melancholy man's heart.

Robert Burton *Anatomy of Melancholy*, Pt. I

4 Twentieth-Century Blues.

Noël Coward (1899–1973) British dramatist. *Title of song*

5 I am aware of the damp souls of the housemaids
Sprouting despondently at area gates.

T. S. Eliot (1888–1965) US-born British poet and dramatist. *Morning at the Window*

6 I am in that temper that if I were under water I would scarcely kick to come to the top.

John Keats (1795–1821) British poet. Letter to Benjamin Bailey, 21 May 1818

7 My heart aches, and a drowsy numbness pains
My sense.

John Keats *Ode to a Nightingale*

8 Ay, in the very temple of delight
Veil'd Melancholy has her sovran shrine.
Though seen of none save him whose strenuous tongue
Can burst Joy's grape against his palate fine.

John Keats *Ode on Melancholy*

9 Where glowing embers through the room
Teach light to counterfeit a gloom,
Far from all resort of mirth,
Save the cricket on the hearth.

John Milton (1608–74) English poet. *Il Penseroso*

10 Wrapt in a pleasing fit of melancholy.

John Milton *Comus*

11 I was told I am a true cosmopolitan. I am unhappy everywhere.

Stephen Vizinczey (1933–) Hungarian-born British writer. *The Guardian*, 7 Mar 1968

MEMORIALS

See also epitaphs, memory, obituaries, reputation

1 When I am dead, and laid in grave,
And all my bones are rotten,
By this may I remembered be
When I should be forgotten.

Anonymous On a girl's sampler, 1736

2 All your better deeds
Shall be in water writ, but this in marble.

Francis Beaumont (1584–1616) English dramatist. *The Nice Valour*, V:3

3 They shall grow not old, as we that are left grow old:
Age shall not weary them, nor the years condemn.
At the going down of the sun and in the morning
We will remember them.

Laurence Binyon (1869–1943) British poet. *Poems For the Fallen*

4 John Brown's body lies a-mouldering in the grave,
His soul is marching on!

Charles Sprague Hall (19th century) US songwriter. The

song commemorates the American hero who died in the cause of abolishing slavery. *John Brown's Body*

5 I have executed a memorial longer lasting than bronze.

Horace (Quintus Horatius Flaccus; 65–8 BC) Roman poet. *Odes*, III

6 In a larger sense we cannot dedicate, we cannot consecrate, we cannot hallow this ground. The brave men, living and dead, who struggled here, have consecrated it far above our power to add or detract. The world will little note, nor long remember, what we say here, but it can never forget what they did here. It is for us, the living, rather to be dedicated here to the unfinished work which they who fought here have thus far so nobly advanced. It is rather for us to be here dedicated to the great task remaining before us... that we here highly resolve that the dead shall not have died in vain, that this nation, under God, shall have a new birth of freedom; and that government of the people, by the people, and for the people, shall not perish from the earth.

Abraham Lincoln (1809–65) US statesman. Report of Lincoln's address at the dedication (19 Nov 1863) of the national cemetery on the site of the Battle of Gettysburg.

7 The monument sticks like a fishbone
in the city's throat.

Robert Lowell (1917–77) US poet. *For the Union Dead*

8 In Flanders fields the poppies blow
Between the crosses, row on row,
That mark our place.

John McCrae (1872–1918) Canadian poet and doctor. *In Flanders Fields*, 'Ypres Salient', 3 May 1915

9 I was told that the Chinese said they would bury me by the Western Lake and build a shrine to my memory. I have some slight regret that this did not happen, as I might have become a god, which would have been very *chic* for an atheist.

Bertrand Russell (1872–1970) British philosopher. *The Autobiography of Bertrand Russell*, Vol. II, Ch. 3

10 Men's evil manners live in brass: their virtues
We write in water.

William Shakespeare (1564–1616) English dramatist. *Henry VIII*, IV:2

11 I met a traveller from an antique land
Who said: Two vast and trunkless legs of stone
Stand in the desert.

Percy Bysshe Shelley (1792–1822) British poet. Referring to the legs of a broken statue of the Pharaoh Rameses II (1301–1234 BC; Greek name, Ozymandias). *Ozymandias*

12 Move Queen Anne? Most certainly not! Why it might some day be suggested that *my* statue should be moved, which I should much dislike.

Victoria (1819–1901) Queen of the United Kingdom. Said at the time of her Diamond Jubilee (1897), when it was suggested that the statue of Queen Anne should be moved from outside St. Paul's. *Men, Women and Things* (Duke of Portland), Ch. 5

MEMORY

See also memorials, nostalgia, past

1 Memories are hunting horns whose sound dies on the wind.

Guillaume Apollinaire (Wilhelm de Kostrowitzky; 1880–1918) Italian-born French poet. *Cors de Chasse*

2 I have more memories than if I were a thousand years old.

Charles Baudelaire (1821–67) French poet. *Spleen*

3 Time whereof the memory of man runneth not to the contrary.

William Blackstone (1723–80) British jurist. *Commentaries on the Laws of England*, Bk. I, Ch. 18

4 Am in Birmingham. Where ought I to be?

G. K. Chesterton (1874–1936) British writer. Telegram to his wife during a lecture tour. *Portrait of Barrie* (C. Asquith)

5 When I meet a man whose name I can't remember, I give myself two minutes; then, if it is a hopeless case, I always say, And how is the old complaint?

Benjamin Disraeli (1804–81) British statesman. Attrib.

6 I have forgot much, Cynara! gone with the wind,
Flung roses, roses riotously with the throng.

Ernest Dowson (1867–1900) British lyric poet. *Non Sum Qualis Eram Bonae Sub Regno Cynarae*

7 Oh! don't you remember sweet Alice, Ben Bolt,
Sweet Alice, whose hair was so brown,
Who wept with delight when you gave her a smile,
And trembled with fear at your frown?

Thomas Dunn English (1819–1902) US lawyer and writer. *Ben Bolt*

8 To endeavour to forget anyone is a certain way of thinking of nothing else.

Jean de La Bruyère (1645–96) French satirist. *Les Caractères*

9 I never forget a face, but I'll make an exception in your case.

Groucho Marx (Julius Marx; 1895–1977) US comedian. *The Guardian*, 18 June 1965

10 What a strange thing is memory, and hope; one looks backward, the other forward. The one is of today, the other is the Tomorrow. Memory is history recorded in our brain, memory is a painter, it paints pictures of the past and of the day.

Grandma Moses (Anna Mary Robertson Moses; 1860–1961) US primitive painter. *Grandma Moses, My Life's History* (ed. Aotto Kallir), Ch. 1

11 The taste was that of the little crumb of madeleine which on Sunday mornings at Combray..., when I used to say good-day to her in her bedroom, my aunt Léonie used to give me, dipping it first in her own cup of real or of lime-flower tea.

Marcel Proust (1871–1922) French novelist. *À la recherche du temps perdu: Du côté de chez Swann*

12 Thanks For the Memory.

Leo Robin (1899–1984) US songwriter. *Big Broadcast*, song title

13 Remember me when I am gone away,
Gone far away into the silent land.

Christina Rossetti (1830–74) British poet. *Remember*

14 Better by far you should forget and smile
Than that you should remember and be sad.

Christina Rossetti *Remember*

15 To expect a man to retain everything that he has ever read is like expecting him to carry about in his body everything that he has ever eaten.

Arthur Schopenhauer (1788–1860) German philosopher. *Parerga and Paralipomena*

16 Old men forget; yet all shall be forgot,
But he'll remember, with advantages,
What feats he did that day.

William Shakespeare (1564–1616) English dramatist. *Henry V*, IV:3

17 Music, when soft voices die,
Rose leaves, when the rose is dead,
Are heaped for the beloved's bed;
And so thy thoughts, when thou art gone,
Love itself shall slumber on.

Percy Bysshe Shelley (1792–1822) British poet. *To –*

18 As a perfume doth remain
In the folds where it hath lain,
So the thought of you, remaining
Deeply folded in my brain,
Will not leave me: all things leave me:
You remain.

Arthur Symons (1865–1945) British poet. *Memory*

19 I suppose that the high-water mark of my youth in Columbus, Ohio, was the night the bed fell on my father.

James Thurber (1894–1961) US humorist. *My Life and Hard Times*, Ch. 1

MEN

See also mankind, marriage, masculinity, sexes, women

1 One cannot be always laughing at a man without now and then stumbling on something witty.

Jane Austen (1775–1817) British novelist. *Pride and Prejudice*, Ch. 40

2 A man's a man for a' that.

Robert Burns (1759–96) Scottish poet. *For a' that and a' that*

3 It is men who face the biggest problems in the future, adjusting to their new and complicated role.

Anna Ford British newscaster. Remark, Jan 1981

4 All men are rapists and that's all they are. They rape us with their eyes, their laws and their codes.

Marilyn French (1929–) US novelist. *The Women's Room*

5 A man...is *so* in the way in the house!

Elizabeth Gaskell (1810–65) British novelist. *Cranford*, Ch. 1

6 Probably the only place where a man can feel really secure is in a maximum security prison, except for the imminent threat of release.

Germaine Greer (1939–) Australian-born British writer and feminist. *The Female Eunuch*

7 And let her learn through what kind of dust
He has earned his thirst and the right to quench it
And what sweat he has exchanged for his money
And the blood-weight of money. He'll humble her

Ted Hughes (1930–) British poet. *Selected Poems 1957–1981*, 'Her Husband'

8 How beastly the bourgeois is
especially the male of the species.

D. H. Lawrence (1885–1930) British novelist. *How beastly the bourgeois is*

9 One realizes with horror, that the race of men is almost extinct in Europe. Only Christ-like heroes and woman-worshipping Don Juans, and rabid equality-mongrels.

D. H. Lawrence *Sea and Sardinia*, Ch. 3

10 Why can't a woman be more like a man?
Men are so honest, so thoroughly square;
Eternally noble, historically fair.

Alan Jay Lerner (1918–86) US songwriter. *My Fair Lady*, II:4

11 He was formed for the ruin of our sex.

Tobias Smollett (1721–71) British novelist. *Roderick Random*, Ch. 22

12 It is an ancient contention of my wife that I, in common with all other men, in any dispute between a female relative and a tradesman, side with the tradesman, partly from fear, partly from masculine clannishness, and most of all from a desire to stand well with the tradesman.

E. Œ. Somerville (1858–1949) Irish writer. *Experiences of an Irish R.M.*, 'The Pug-nosed Fox'

13 Sometimes I think if there was a third sex men wouldn't get so much as a glance from me.

Amanda Vail (Warren Miller; 1921–66) US writer. *Love Me Little*, Ch. 6

14 A man in the house is worth two in the street.

Mae West (1892–1980) US actress. *Belle of the Nineties*, film 1934

MERCY

1 I seem forsaken and alone,
I hear the lion roar;
And every door is shut but one,
And that is Mercy's door.

William Cowper (1731–1800) British poet. *Olney Hymns*, 33

2 The quality of mercy is not strain'd;

It droppeth as the gentle rain from heaven
Upon the place beneath. It is twice blest;
It blesseth him that gives and him that takes.

William Shakespeare (1564–1616) English dramatist. *The Merchant of Venice*, IV:1

3 And her face so sweet and pleading, yet with sorrow pale and worn,
Touched his heart with sudden pity – lit his eye with misty light;
'Go, your lover lives!' said Cromwell; 'Curfew shall not ring tonight!'

Rose Hartwick Thorpe (1850–1939) US poet and novelist. *Curfew Shall Not Ring Tonight*

MERIT

1 A good dog deserves a good bone.

Proverb

2 I don't deserve this, but I have arthritis, and I don't deserve that either.

Jack Benny (Benjamin Kubelsky; 1894–1974) US actor. Said when accepting an award. Attrib.

3 But many that are first shall be last; and the last shall be first.

Bible: Matthew 19:30

4 GOLDSMITH: Here's such a stir about a fellow that has written one book, and I have written many.
JOHNSON: Ah, Doctor, there go two-and-forty sixpences you know to one guinea.

Samuel Johnson (1709–84) British lexicographer. Referring to Beattie's *Essay on Truth*. *Johnsonian Miscellanies* (ed. G. B. Hill), Vol. I

5 I guess this is the week I earn my salary.

John Fitzgerald Kennedy (1917–63) US statesman. Comment made during the Cuban missile crisis. *Nobody Said It Better* (M. Ringo)

6 Use every man after his desert, and who shall scape whipping?

William Shakespeare (1564–1616) English dramatist. *Hamlet*, II:2

7 I wasn't lucky. I deserved it.

Margaret Thatcher (1925–) British politician and prime minister. Said after receiving school prize, aged nine. Attrib.

8 The Rise of the Meritocracy.

Michael Young (1915–) British political writer. Book title

MERRYMAKING

See also parties, pleasure

1 Come lasses and lads, get leave of your dads,
And away to the Maypole hie,
For every he has got him a she,
And the fiddler's standing by.

Anonymous *Come Lasses and Lads*

2 There was a sound of revelry by night,
And Belgium's capital had gather'd then
Her Beauty and her Chivalry, and bright
The lamps shone o'er fair women and brave men.

Lord Byron (1788–1824) British poet. *Childe Harold's Pilgrimage*, III

3 Dost thou think, because thou art virtuous, there shall be no more cakes and ale?

William Shakespeare (1564–1616) English dramatist. *Twelfth Night*, II:3

4 We have heard the chimes at midnight.

William Shakespeare *Henry IV, Part Two*, III:2

5 You must wake and call me early, call me early, mother dear;
To-morrow 'ill be the happiest time of all the glad New-year;
Of all the glad New-year, mother, the maddest merriest day;
For I'm to be Queen o' the May, mother, I'm to be Queen o' the May.

Alfred, Lord Tennyson (1809–92) British poet. *The May Queen*

6 I love such mirth as does not make friends ashamed to look upon one another next morning.

Izaak Walton (1593–1683) English writer. *The Compleat Angler*, Ch. 5

METAPHYSICS

See also philosophy

1 A blind man in a dark room – looking for a black hat – which isn't there.

Lord Bowen (1835–94) British judge. Characterization of a metaphysician. Attrib.

2 Metaphysics is the finding of bad reasons for what we believe upon instinct; but to find these reasons is no less an instinct.

F. H. Bradley (1846–1924) British philosopher. *Appearance and Reality*, Preface

3 We used to think that if we knew one, we knew two, because one and one are two. We are finding that we must learn a great deal more about 'and'.

Arthur Eddington (1882–1944) British astronomer. *The Harvest of a Quiet Eye* (A. L. Mackay)

4 In other words, apart from the known and the unknown, what else is there?

Harold Pinter (1930–) British dramatist. *The Homecoming*, II

5 Whither is fled the visionary gleam?
Where is it now, the glory and the dream?

Our birth is but a sleep and a forgetting:
The Soul that rises with us, our life's Star,
Hath had elsewhere its setting,
And cometh from afar;
Not in entire forgetfulness,
And not in utter nakedness,
But trailing clouds of glory do we come
From God, who is our home:
Heaven lies about us in our infancy!
Shades of the prison-house begin to close

Upon the growing boy.

William Wordsworth (1770–1850) British poet. *Ode. Intimations of Immortality*, IV

6 Hence in a season of calm weather
Though inland far we be,
Our souls have sight of that immortal sea
Which brought us hither...

William Wordsworth *Ode. Intimations of Immortality*, IX

MIDDLE EAST

See also hostages, Jews

1 The Israelis are now what we call the 'enemy-friends'.

Anonymous adviser to the Palestinian leader Yasser Arafat. *The Independent*, 5 July 1994

2 It's not good enough to have just any old state, a replica of a Third World state, an instrument of Israeli domination.

Hanan Ashrawi (1946–) Palestinian politician. *The Independent*, 31 May 1995

3 The Jews and Arabs should sit down and settle their differences like good Christians.

Warren Austin (1877–1962) US politician and diplomat. Attrib.

4 I will draw a line in the sand.

George Bush (1924–) US politician and president. Referring to the defence of Saudi Arabia by US forces following the Iraqi invasion of Kuwait (1990). Speech, 1990

5 The war wasn't fought about democracy in Kuwait.

George Bush *The Observer*, 14 July 1991 Referring to the Gulf War (1991).

6 Throughout the Middle East, there is a great yearning for the quiet miracle of a normal life.

Bill Clinton (William Jefferson C.; 1946–) US politician and president. Referring to the signing of the Israel–PLO peace agreement. *The Times*, 14 Sept 1993

7 We are not at war with Egypt. We are in an armed conflict.

Anthony Eden (1897–1977) British statesman. Speech, House of Commons, 4 Nov 1956

8 They will drown in their own blood.

Saddam Hussein (1937–) Iraqi ruler. Referring to the coalition forces assembing in Saudi Arabia to expel the Iraqis from Kuwait. Speech, 1990

9 The mother of battles will be our battle of victory and martyrdom.

Saddam Hussein Referring to the imminent Gulf War. Speech, 1991

10 Jerusalem the golden,
With milk and honey blest,
Beneath thy contemplation
Sink heart and voice oppresst.

John Mason Neale (1818–66) British churchman. *Jerusalem the Golden*

11 If Kuwait and Saudi Arabia sold bananas or oranges, the Americans would not go there. They are there because Kuwait is an oil monarchy.

Julius Nyerere (1922–) Tanzanian statesman. Referring to the international response to the Iraqi invasion of Kuwait (Aug 1990). *The Independent*, 28 Sept 1990

12 Peace is made with yesterday's enemies. What is the alternative?

Shimon Peres (1923–) Israeli politician. *The Observer*, 'Sayings of the Week', 16 Oct 1994

13 A brilliant soldier who hated war, he was a man of battle who longed for peace.

Jonathan Sacks (1948–) British rabbi. Referring to Yitzhak Rabin. *The Times Magazine*, 30 Dec 1995

14 A very great man once said you should love your enemies and that's not a bad piece of advice. We can love them but, by God, that doesn't mean we're not going to fight them.

Norman Schwarzkopf (1934–) US general. Referring to the Gulf War (1991). *The Observer*, 14 July 1991

15 I think the Kuwaitis enjoy a crisis now and again. It brings them world attention.

Barzan al-Takriti Iraqi ambassador. *The Times*, 5 Dec 1994

MILTON

1 Malt does more than Milton can,
To justify God's way to man.

A. E. Housman (1859–1936) British scholar and poet. *A Shropshire Lad*

2 Milton, Madam, was a genius that could cut a Colossus from a rock; but could not carve heads upon cherry-stones.

Samuel Johnson (1709–84) British lexicographer. *Life of Johnson* (James Boswell)

3 Milton's Devil as a moral being is far superior to his God....Milton has so far violated the popular creed (if this shall be judged a violation), as to have alleged no superiority of moral virtue to his God over his Devil. And this bold neglect of direct moral purpose is the most decisive proof of Milton's genius.

Percy Bysshe Shelley (1792–1822) British poet. *Defence of Poetry*

4 That mighty orb of song, The divine Milton.

William Wordsworth (1770–1850) British poet. *The Excursion*

MIND

See also intellect, intelligence, thinking

1 *Brain*, n. An apparatus with which we think that we think.

Ambrose Bierce (1842–?1914) US writer and journalist. *The Devil's Dictionary*

2 We know the human brain is a device to keep the ears from grating on one another.

Peter De Vries (1910–93) US novelist. *Comfort me with Apples*, Ch. 1

3 The pendulum of the mind oscillates between

sense and nonsense, not between right and wrong.

Carl Gustav Jung (1875–1961) Swiss psychoanalyst. *Memories, Dreams, Reflections*, Ch. 5

4 A mind not to be changed by place or time.
The mind is its own place, and in itself
Can make a Heaven of Hell, a Hell of Heaven.

John Milton (1608–74) English poet. *Paradise Lost*, Bk. I

5 That's the classical mind at work, runs fine inside but looks dingy on the surface.

Robert T. Pirsig (1928–) US writer. *Zen and the Art of Motorcycle Maintenance*, Pt. III, Ch. 25

6 The dogma of the Ghost in the Machine.

Gilbert Ryle (1900–76) British philosopher. *The Concept of Mind*, Ch. 1

7 If it is for mind that we are seaching the brain, then we are supposing the brain to be much more than a telephone-exchange. We are supposing it a telephone-exchange along with the subscribers as well.

Charles Scott Sherrington (1857–1952) British physiologist. *Man on his Nature*

8 When people will not weed their own minds, they are apt to be overrun with nettles.

Horace Walpole (1717–97) British writer. Letter to Lady Ailesbury, 10 July 1779

9 The mind can also be an erogenous zone.

Raquel Welch (Raquel Tejada; 1940–) US film star. *Colombo's Hollywood* (J. R. Colombo)

10 The mind, once expanded to the dimensions of larger ideas, never returns to its original size.

Oliver Wendell Holmes (1809–94) US writer.

11 Strongest minds
Are often those of whom the noisy world
Hears least.

William Wordsworth (1770–1850) British poet. *The Excursion*

MINORITY

See also majority

1 What's a cult? It just means not enough people to make a minority.

Robert Altman (1922–) US film director. *The Observer*, 1981

2 The majority has the might – more's the pity – but it hasn't right...The minority is always right.

Henrik Ibsen (1828–1906) Norwegian dramatist. *An Enemy of the People*, IV

3 Minorities...are almost always in the right.

Sydney Smith (1771–1845) British clergyman and essayist. *The Smith of Smiths* (H. Pearson), Ch. 9

MISANTHROPY

See also mankind

1 What though the spicy breezes
Blow soft o'er Ceylon's isle;
Though every prospect pleases,
And only man is vile...

Reginald Heber (1783–1826) British bishop and hymn writer. *From Greenland's Icy Mountains*

2 I've always been interested in people, but I've never liked them.

W. Somerset Maugham (1874–1965) British novelist. *The Observer*, 'Sayings of the Week', 28 Aug 1949

3 I love mankind – it's people I can't stand.

Charles M. Schultz (1922–) US cartoonist. *Go Fly a Kite, Charlie Brown*

4 Other people are quite dreadful. The only possible society is oneself.

Oscar Wilde (1854–1900) Irish-born British dramatist. *An Ideal Husband*, III

MISFORTUNE

See also accidents, curses, sorrow, suffering

1 It is easy to bear the misfortunes of others.

Proverb

2 It never rains but it pours.

Proverb

3 Prosperity doth best discover vice; but adversity doth best discover virtue.

Francis Bacon (1561–1626) English philosopher. *Essays*, 'Of Adversity'

4 Calamities are of two kinds. Misfortune to ourselves and good fortune to others.

Ambrose Bierce (1842–?1914) US writer and journalist. *The Devil's Dictionary*

5 There remaineth a rest for the people of God:
And I have had troubles enough, for one.

Robert Browning (1812–89) British poet. *Old Pictures in Florence*, XVII

6 Tragedie is to seyn a certeyn storie,
As olde bokes maken us memorie,
Of him that stood in greet prosperitee
And is y-fallen out of heigh degree
Into miserie, and endeth wrecchedly.

Geoffrey Chaucer (c. 1342–1400) English poet. *The Canterbury Tales*, 'The Monk's Prologue'

7 For of fortunes sharp adversitee
The worst kinde of infortune is this,
A man to have ben in prosperitee,
And it remembren, what is passed is.

Geoffrey Chaucer *Troilus and Criseyde*, 3

8 A chapter of accidents.

Earl of Chesterfield (1694–1773) English statesman. Letter to his son, 16 Feb 1753

9 'I am a lone lorn creetur,' were Mrs Gummidge's words...'and everythink goes contrairy with me.'

Charles Dickens (1812–70) British novelist. *David Copperfield*, Ch. 3

10 Life is mostly froth and bubble;
Two things stand like stone,
Kindness in another's trouble,
Courage in your own.

Adam Lindsay Gordon (1833–70) Australian poet. *Ye Wearie Wayfarer*, Fytte 8

11 Depend upon it that if a man talks of his misfortunes there is something in them that is not disagreeable to him; for where there is nothing but pure misery there never is any recourse to the mention of it.

Samuel Johnson (1709–84) British lexicographer. *Life of Johnson* (J. Boswell), Vol. IV

12 There exist some evils so terrible and some misfortunes so horrible that we dare not think of them, whilst their very aspect makes us shudder; but if they happen to fall on us, we find ourselves stronger than we imagined, we grapple with our ill luck, and behave better than we expected we should.

Jean de La Bruyère (1645–96) French satirist. *Les Caractères*

13 I never knew any man in my life who could not bear another's misfortunes perfectly like a Christian.

Alexander Pope (1688–1744) British poet. *Thoughts on Various Subjects*

14 We are all strong enough to bear the misfortunes of others.

Duc de la Rochefoucauld (1613–80) French writer. *Maximes*, 19

15 In the misfortune of our best friends, we always find something which is not displeasing to us.

Duc de la Rochefoucauld *Maximes*, 99

16 Misery acquaints a man with strange bedfellows.

William Shakespeare (1564–1616) English dramatist. *The Tempest*, II:2

17 When sorrows come, they come not single spies,
But in battalions!

William Shakespeare *Hamlet*, IV:5

18 This is the excellent foppery of the world, that, when we are sick in fortune, often the surfeits of our own behaviour, we make guilty of our disasters the sun, the moon, and stars.

William Shakespeare *King Lear*, I:2

MISOGYNY

See also women

1 The souls of women are so small,
That some believe they've none at all.

Samuel Butler (1612–80) English satirist. *Miscellaneous Thoughts*

2 You have to admit that most women who have done something with their lives have been disliked by almost everyone.

Françoise Gilot Artist and mistress of Picasso. Remark, Oct 1987

3 I'd be equally as willing
For a dentist to be drilling
Than to ever let a woman in my life.

Alan Jay Lerner (1918–86) US songwriter. *My Fair Lady*, I:2

4 There are already so many women in the world! Why then...was I born a woman, to be scorned by men in words and deeds?

Isotta Nogarola (1418–1466) Italian scholar and author. Letter to Guarino Veronese

5 How can I possibly dislike a sex to which Your Majesty belongs?

Cecil Rhodes (1853–1902) South African statesman. Replying to Queen Victoria's suggestion that he disliked women. *Rhodes* (Lockhart)

6 Would you have me speak after my custom, as being a professed tyrant to their sex?

William Shakespeare (1564–1616) English dramatist. *Much Ado About Nothing*, I:1

MISQUOTATIONS

1 Misquotations are the only quotations that are never misquoted.

Hesketh Pearson (1887–1964) British biographer. *Common Misquotations*

2 A widely-read man never quotes accurately... Misquotation is the pride and privilege of the learned.

Hesketh Pearson *Common Misquotations*

Some examples

3 Had I been present at the Creation, I would have given some useful hints for the better ordering of the universe.

Alfonso the Wise (c. 1221–84) King of Castile and Léon. Referring to the complicated Ptolemaic model of the universe. Often quoted as, 'Had I been consulted I would have recommended something simpler'. Attrib.

4 We have ways of making men talk.

Anonymous Film catchphrase, often repeated as 'We have ways of making you talk'. *Lives of a Bengal Lancer*

5 That's one small step for man, one giant leap for mankind.

Neil Armstrong (1930–) US astronaut. Said on stepping onto the moon. Often quoted as, 'small step for a man...' (which is probably what he intended). Remark, 21 July 1969

6 I have seldom spoken with greater regret, for my lips are not yet unsealed. Were these troubles over I would make a case, and I guarantee that not a man would go into the Lobby against us.

Stanley Baldwin (1867–1947) British statesman. Referring to the Abyssinian crisis; usually misquoted as 'My lips are sealed'. Speech, House of Commons, 10 Dec 1935

7 And behold joy and gladness, slaying oxen, and killing sheep, eating flesh, and drinking wine:

let us eat and drink; for tomorrow we shall die.

Bible: Isaiah 22:13 A similar sentiment is expressed in Corinthians 15:32–33. Often misquoted as 'let us eat, drink, and be merry'.

8 So when they continued asking him, he lifted up himself, and said unto them, He that is without sin among you, let him first cast a stone at her.

Bible: John 8:7 Often misquoted as 'cast the first stone'.

9 Then said Jesus unto him, Put up again thy sword into his place: for all they that take the sword shall perish with the sword.

Bible: Matthew 26:52 Often msiquoted as 'They that live by the sword shall die by the sword'.

10 Pride goeth before destruction, and an haughty spirit before a fall.

Bible: Proverbs 16:18 Often misquoted as 'Pride goeth before a fall'.

11 Play it, Sam. Play 'As Time Goes By.'

Humphrey Bogart (1899–1957) US film star. Often misquoted as 'Play it again, Sam'. *Casablanca*

12 You dirty double-crossing rat!

James Cagney (1899–1986) US actor. Usually misquoted by impressionists as 'You dirty rat'. *Blonde Crazy*

13 I have nothing to offer but blood, toil, tears and sweat.

Winston Churchill (1874–1965) British statesman. On becoming prime minister. Often misquoted as 'blood, sweat and tears'. Speech, House of Commons, 13 May 1940

14 War is the continuation of politics by other means.

Karl von Clausewitz (1780–1831) Prussian general. The usual misquotation of 'War is nothing but a continuation of politics with the admixture of other means'. *Vom Kriege*

15 'Excellent!' I cried. 'Elementary,' said he.

Arthur Conan Doyle (1856–1930) British writer. Watson talking to Sherlock Holmes; Holmes's reply is often misquoted as 'Elementary my dear Watson'. *The Crooked Man*

16 I got there fustest with the mostest.

Nathan Bedford Forrest (1821–77) Confederate general. Popular misquotation of his explanation of his success in capturing Murfreesboro; his actual words were, 'I just took the short cut and got there first with the most men'. *A Civil War Treasury* (B. Botkin)

17 I never said, 'I want to be alone.' I only said, 'I want to be *left* alone.' There is all the difference.

Greta Garbo (1905–90) Swedish-born US film star. *Garbo* (John Bainbridge)

18 Take your hare when it is cased...

Hannah Glasse (18th century) English writer. Often misquoted as, 'First catch your hare' and wrongly attributed to Mrs Beaton. *The Art of Cookery Made Plain and Easy*, Ch. 1

19 Once I built a rail-road,
Now it's done.
Brother, can you spare a dime?

E. Y. Harburg (1898–1981) US lyricist. Often quoted as 'Buddy can you spare a dime'. *New Americana*, 'Brother Can You Spare a Dime'.

20 I am happy now that Charles calls on my bedchamber less frequently than of old. As it is, I now endure but two calls a week and when I hear his steps outside my door I lie down on my bed, close my eyes, open my legs and think of England.

Lady Alice Hillingdon (1857–1940) Wife of 2nd Baron Hillingdon. Often mistakenly attributed to Queen Victoria. *Journal* (1912)

21 Jerry Ford is so dumb that he can't fart and chew gum at the same time.

Lyndon B. Johnson (1908–73) US statesman. Sometimes quoted as '...can't walk and chew gum'. *A Ford, Not a Lincoln* (R. Reeves), Ch. 1

22 Alas, poor Yorick! I knew him,
Horatio: a fellow of infinite jest, of most excellent fancy.

William Shakespeare (1564–1616) English dramatist. Often misquoted as 'I knew him well'. *Hamlet*, V:1

23 I always did like a man in uniform. And that one fits you grand. Why don't you come up sometime and see me?

Mae West (1892–1980) US actress. Often misquoted as 'Come up and see me some time'. *She Done Him Wrong*, film 1933

MISTAKES

See also imperfection

1 Two wrongs do not make a right.

Proverb

2 It is worse than immoral, it's a mistake.

Dean Acheson (1893–1971) US lawyer and statesman. Describing the Vietnam war. *See also* BOULAY DE LA MEURTHE. Quoted by Alistair Cooke in his radio programme *Letter from America*

3 The weak have one weapon: the errors of those who think they are strong.

Georges Bidault (1899–1983) French statesman. *The Observer*, 1962

4 It is worse than a crime, it is a blunder.

Antoine Boulay de la Meurthe (1761–1840) French politician. *See also* ACHESON. Referring to the summary execution of the Duc d'Enghien by Napoleon, 1804. Attrib.

5 I guess that'll hold the little bastards.

Don Carney (1897–1954) US broadcaster. Carney was ending a children's radio show and thought that he was off the air. Attrib.

6 I beseech you, in the bowels of Christ, think it possible you may be mistaken.

Oliver Cromwell (1599–1658) English soldier and statesman. Letter to the General Assembly of the Church of Scotland, 3 Aug 1650

7 Better send them a Papal Bull.

Lord Curzon (1859–1925) British politician. Written in the margin of a Foreign Office document. The phrase 'the monks of Mount Athos were violating their vows' had been misprinted as '...violating their cows'. *Life of Lord Curzon* (Ronaldshay), Vol. III, Ch. 15

8 Yes, once – many, many years ago. I thought I

had made a wrong decision. Of course, it turned out that I had been right all along. But I was wrong to have *thought* that I was wrong.

John Foster Dulles (1888–1959) US politician. On being asked whether he had ever been wrong. *Facing the Music* (H. Temianka)

9 Pardon me, madam, but *I* am my brother.

Karl Gustav Jacob Jacobi (1804–51) German mathematician. On being mistaken by a lady for his brother. *Men of Mathematics* (M. H. Jacobi)

10 Erratum. In my article on the Price of Milk, 'Horses' should have read 'Cows' throughout.

J. B. Morton (1893–1979) British journalist. *The Best of Beachcomber*

11 The man who makes no mistakes does not usually make anything.

Edward John Phelps (1822–1900) US lawyer and diplomat. Speech, Mansion House, London, 24 Jan 1899

12 A man should never be ashamed to own he has been in the wrong, which is but saying, in other words, that he is wiser to-day than he was yesterday.

Alexander Pope (1688–1744) British poet. *Thoughts on Various Subjects*

13 To err is human, to forgive, divine.

Alexander Pope *An Essay on Criticism*

14 The follies which a man regrets the most in his life, are those which he didn't commit when he had the opportunity.

Helen Rowland (1876–1950) US writer. *Guide To Men*

15 What time is the next swan?

Leo Slezak (1873–1946) Czechoslovakian-born tenor. When the mechanical swan left the stage without him during a performance of *Lohengrin*. *What Time Is the Next Swan?* (Walter Slezak)

16 We often discover what *will* do, by finding out what will not do; and probably he who never made a mistake never made a discovery.

Samuel Smiles (1812–1904) British writer. *Self-Help*, Ch. 11

17 Human blunders usually do more to shape history than human wickedness.

A. J. P. Taylor (1906–90) British historian. *The Origins of the Second World War*, Ch. 10

18 Well, if I called the wrong number, why did you answer the phone?

James Thurber (1894–1961) US humorist. Cartoon caption

19 If we had more time for discussion we should probably have made a great many more mistakes.

Leon Trotsky (Lev Davidovich Bronstein; 1879–1940) Russian revolutionary. *My Life*

20 The physician can bury his mistakes, but the architect can only advise his client to plant vines.

Frank Lloyd Wright (1869–1959) US architect. *New York Times Magazine*, 4 Oct 1953

MISTRUST

See also suspicion, trust

1 After shaking hands with a Greek, count your fingers.

Proverb

2 While I see many hoof-marks going in, I see none coming out.

Aesop (6th century BC) Reputed Greek writer of fables. *Fables*, 'The Lion, the Fox, and the Beasts'

3 The lion and the calf shall lie down together but the calf won't get much sleep.

Woody Allen (Allen Stewart Konigsberg; 1935–) US film actor. *Without Feathers*, 'The Scrolls'

4 The louder he talked of his honour, the faster we counted our spoons.

Ralph Waldo Emerson (1803–82) US poet and essayist. *Conduct of Life*, 'Worship'

5 Let me remind you what the wary fox said once upon a time to the sick lion: 'Because those footprints scare me, all directed your way, none coming back.'

Horace (Quintus Horatius Flaccus; 65–8 BC) Roman poet. *Epistles*, I back

6 But if he does really think that there is no distinction between virtue and vice, why, Sir, when he leaves our houses let us count our spoons.

Samuel Johnson (1709–84) British lexicographer. *Life of Johnson* (J. Boswell), Vol. I

7 *Quis custodiet ipsos custodes?*
Who is to guard the guards themselves?

Juvenal (Decimus Junius Juvenalis; 60–130 AD) Roman satirist. *Satires*, VI

8 Ye diners-out from whom we guard our spoons.

Lord Macaulay (1800–59) British historian. Letter to Hannah Macaulay, 29 June 1831

9 Let me have men about me that are fat;
Sleek-headed men, and such as sleep o' nights.
Yon Cassius has a lean and hungry look;
He thinks too much. Such men are dangerous.

William Shakespeare (1564–1616) English dramatist. *Julius Caesar*, I:2

10 An ally has to be watched just like an enemy.

Leon Trotsky (Lev Davidovich Bronstein; 1879–1940) Russian revolutionary. *Expansion and Coexistence* (A. Ulam)

11 *Equo ne credite, Teucri.*
Quidquid id est timeo Danaos et dona ferentis.
Do not trust the horse, Trojans. Whatever it is, I fear the Greeks even when they bring gifts.

Virgil (Publius Vergilius Maro; 70–19 BC) Roman poet. *Aeneid*, Bk. II

MIXED METAPHORS

See also Goldwynisms

1 If you open that Pandora's Box you never

know what Trojan 'orses will jump out.
Ernest Bevin (1881–1951) British trade-union leader and politician. Referring to the Council of Europe. *Ernest Bevin and the Foreign Office* (Sir Roderick Barclay)

2 Every director bites the hand that lays the golden egg.
Samuel Goldwyn (Samuel Goldfish; 1882–1974) Polish-born US film producer. Attrib.

3 You ought to take the bull between the teeth.
Samuel Goldwyn Attrib.

4 Mr Speaker, I smell a rat; I see him forming in the air and darkening the sky; but I'll nip him in the bud.
Boyle Roche (1743–1807) British politician. Attrib.

MODERATION

See also excess

1 Moderation in all things.
Proverb

2 You can have too much of a good thing.
Proverb

3 By God, Mr Chairman, at this moment I stand astonished at my own moderation!
Clive of India (1725–74) British soldier and governor of Bengal. Reply during Parliamentary Inquiry, 1773

4 Not too much zeal.
Talleyrand (Charles Maurice de Talleyrand-Périgord; 1754–1838) French politician. Attrib.

5 Moderation is a fatal thing, Lady Hunstanton. Nothing succeeds like excess.
Oscar Wilde (1854–1900) Irish-born British dramatist. *A Woman of No Importance*, III

MODESTY

1 Nurse, take away the candle and spare my blushes.
Henry James (1843–1916) US novelist. On being informed, whilst confined to his bed, that he had been awarded the Order of Merit. *The American Treasury* (C. Fadiman)

2 It was involuntary. They sank my boat.
John Fitzgerald Kennedy (1917–63) US statesman. Responding to praise of his courage whilst serving in the US navy against the Japanese in World War II. *Nobody Said It Better* (M. Ringo)

3 In some remote regions of Islam it is said, a woman caught unveiled by a stranger will raise her skirt to cover her face.
Raymond Mortimer (1895–1980) British literary critic and writer. *Colette*

4 If you want people to think well of you, do not speak well of yourself.
Blaise Pascal (1623–62) French philosopher and mathematician. *Pensées*, I

5 Be modest! It is the kind of pride least likely to offend.
Jules Renard (1894–1910) French writer. *Journal*

6 ...the nuns who never take a bath without wearing a bathrobe all the time. When asked why, since no man can see them, they reply 'Oh, but you forget the good God.'
Bertrand Russell (1872–1970) British philosopher. *The Basic Writings*, Pt. II, Ch. 7

7 I have often wished I had time to cultivate modesty...But I am too busy thinking about myself.
Edith Sitwell (1887–1964) British poet and writer. *The Observer*, 'Sayings of the Week', 30 Apr 1950

MONARCHY

See also royalty

1 The best reason why Monarchy is a strong government is that it is an intelligible government. The mass of mankind understand it, and they hardly anywhere in the world understand any other.
Walter Bagehot (1826–77) British economist and journalist. *The English Constitution*, 'The Monarchy'

2 The Sovereign has, under a constitutional monarchy such as ours, three rights – the right to be consulted, the right to encourage, the right to warn.
Walter Bagehot *The English Constitution*, 'The Monarchy'

3 God grant him peace and happiness but never understanding of what he has lost.
Stanley Baldwin (1867–1947) British statesman. Referring to Edward VIII's abdication.

4 That the king can do no wrong, is a necessary and fundamental principle of the English constitution.
William Blackstone (1723–80) British jurist. *Commentaries on the Laws of England*, Bk. III, Ch. 17

5 The king never dies.
William Blackstone *Commentaries on the Laws of England*, Bk. I, Ch. 7

6 I would rather hew wood than be a king under the conditions of the King of England.
Charles X (1757–1836) King of France. *Encyclopaedia Britannica*

7 There is no middle course between the throne and the scaffold.
Charles X Said to Talleyrand, who is said to have replied 'You are forgetting the postchaise'. Attrib.

8 Loss of the Royal Family's symbolism together with Britain's other problems may have serious outcomes. Those are pre-fascist conditions.
Noam Chomsky (1928–) US philosopher. *The Independent*, 18 Oct 1994

9 Magna Charta is such a fellow, that

he will have no sovereign.

Edward Coke (1552–1634) English lawyer and politician. Speaking on the Lords Amendment to the Petition of Right, 17 May 1628. *Hist. Coll.* (Rushworth), I

10 The influence of the Crown has increased, is increasing, and ought to be diminished.

John Dunning (1731–83) British lawyer and politician. Motion passed by the House of Commons, 1780

11 There will soon be only five kings left – the Kings of England, Diamonds, Hearts, Spades and Clubs.

Farouk I (1920–65) The last king of Egypt. Remark made to Lord Boyd-Orr

12 Kings govern by means of popular assemblies only when they cannot do without them.

Charles James Fox (1749–1806) British Whig politician. Attrib.

13 I will govern according to the common weal, but not according to the common will.

James I (1566–1625) King of England. *History of the English People* (J. R. Green)

14 A constitutional king must learn to stoop.

Leopold II (1835–1909) King of the Belgians. Instructing Prince Albert, the heir apparent, to pick up some papers that had fallen onto the floor. *The Mistress* (Betty Kelen)

15 *L'État c'est moi.*
I am the State.

Louis XIV (1638–1715) French king. Attrib.

16 There is something behind the throne greater than the King himself.

William Pitt the Elder (1708–78) British statesman. Speech, House of Lords, 2 Mar 1770

17 The right divine of kings to govern wrong.

Alexander Pope (1688–1744) British poet. *The Dunciad*, IV

18 A king is a thing men have made for their own sakes, for quietness' sake. Just as if in a family one man is appointed to buy the meat.

John Selden (1584–1654) English historian. *Table Talk*

19 Every subject's duty is the King's; but every subject's soul is his own.

William Shakespeare (1564–1616) English dramatist. *Henry V*, IV:1

20 There's such divinity doth hedge a king
That treason can but peep to what it would.

William Shakespeare *Hamlet*, IV:5

21 Not all the water in the rough rude sea
Can wash the balm from an anointed king;
The breath of worldly men cannot depose
The deputy elected by the Lord.

William Shakespeare *Richard II*, III:2

22 Uneasy lies the head that wears a crown.

William Shakespeare *Henry IV, Part Two*, III:1

23 The king reigns, and the people govern themselves.

Louis Adolphe Thiers (1797–1877) French statesman and historian. In an unsigned article attributed to Thiers. *Le National*, 20 Jan 1830

24 As guardian of His Majesty's conscience.

Lord Thurlow (1731–1806) British lawyer. Speech, House of Lords, 1779

25 The monarchy is a labour-intensive industry.

Harold Wilson (1916–95) British politician and prime minister. *The Observer*, 13 Feb 1977

26 The king reigns, but does not govern.

Jan Zamoyski (1541–1605) Grand chancellor of Poland. Speech, Polish Parliament, 1605

MONEY

See also bribery, economics, extravagance, greed, materialism, thrift, wealth

1 Easy come, easy go.

Proverb

2 Out of debt, out of danger.

Proverb

3 Take care of the pence, and the pounds will take care of themselves.

Proverb

4 I can't afford to waste my time making money.

Jean Louis Rodolphe Agassiz (1807–73) Swiss naturalist. When asked to give a lecture for a fee. Attrib.

5 It does seem to be true that the more you get the more you spend. It is rather like being on a golden treadmill.

Charles Allsop (1940–) Commodities broker. Remark, Dec 1988

6 Business, you know, may bring money, but friendship hardly ever does.

Jane Austen (1775–1817) British novelist. *Emma*, Ch. 34

7 Money is like muck, not good except it be spread.

Francis Bacon (1561–1626) English philosopher. *See also* MURCHISON. *Essays*, 'Of Seditions and Troubles'

8 Money, it turned out, was exactly like sex, you thought of nothing else if you didn't have it and thought of other things if you did.

James Baldwin (1924–87) US writer. *Nobody Knows My Name*

9 I'm tired of Love: I'm still more tired of Rhyme.
But Money gives me pleasure all the Time.

Hilaire Belloc (1870–1953) French-born British poet. *Fatigue*

10 A feast is made for laughter, and wine maketh merry: but money answereth all things.

Bible: Ecclesiastes 10:19

11 For the love of money is the root of all evil: which while some coveted after, they have erred from the faith, and pierced themselves through with many sorrows.

Bible: I Timothy 6:10

12 If it's a good script, I'll do it. And if it's a bad

script, and they pay me enough, I'll do it.

George Burns (1896–1996) US comedian. Remark, Nov 1988

13 Straighteners, managers and cashiers of the Musical Banks.

Samuel Butler (1835–1902) British writer. *Erewhon*, Ch. 9

14 It has been said that the love of money is the root of all evil. The want of money is so quite as truly.

Samuel Butler *Erewhon*, Ch. 20

15 What makes all doctrines plain and clear?
About two hundred pounds a year.

Samuel Butler *Hudibras*, Pt. III

16 It is a kind of spiritual snobbery that makes people think that they can be happy without money.

Albert Camus (1913–60) French existentialist writer. *Notebooks*, 1935–1942

17 Where large sums of money are concerned, it is advisable to trust nobody.

Agatha Christie (1891–1976) British detective-story writer. *Endless Night*, Bk. II, Ch. 15

18 How pleasant it is to have money.

Arthur Hugh Clough (1819–61) British poet. *Dipsychus*, Bk. I

19 But then one is always excited by descriptions of money changing hands. It's much more fundamental than sex.

Nigel Dennis (1912–89) British writer. *Cards of Identity*

20 Buy an annuity cheap, and make your life interesting to yourself and everybody else that watches the speculation.

Charles Dickens (1812–70) British novelist. *Martin Chuzzlewit*, Ch. 18

21 Making money is pretty pointless and it needs constant attention.

Adam Faith (1940–) British pop singer. *The Observer*, 'Sayings of the Week', 8 May 1994

22 Ah, take the Cash in hand and waive the Rest;
Oh, the brave Music of a *distant* Drum!

Edward Fitzgerald (1809–83) British poet. *The Rubáiyát of Omar Khayyám* (1st edn.), XII

23 It is only the poor who pay cash, and that not from virtue, but because they are refused credit.

Anatole France (Jacques Anatole François Thibault; 1844–1924) French writer. *A Cynic's Breviary* (J. R. Solly)

24 Money differs from an automobile, a mistress or cancer in being equally important to those who have it and those who do not.

John Kenneth Galbraith (1908–) US economist. Attrib.

25 If possible honestly, if not, somehow, make money.

Horace (Quintus Horatius Flaccus; 65–8 BC) Roman poet. *Epistles*, I

26 We all know how the size of sums of money appears to vary in a remarkable way according as they are being paid in or paid out.

Julian Huxley (1887–1975) British biologist. *Essays of a Biologist*, 5

27 Money is like manure. If you spread it around it does a lot of good. But if you pile it up in one place it stinks like hell.

Clint Murchison Jnr (1895–1969) US industrialist. Following BACON. *Time Magazine*, 16 June 1961

28 There are few ways in which a man can be more innocently employed than in getting money.

Samuel Johnson (1709–84) British lexicographer. *Life of Johnson* (J. Boswell), Vol. II

29 You don't seem to realize that a poor person who is unhappy is in a better position than a rich person who is unhappy. Because the poor person has hope. He thinks money would help.

Jean Kerr (1923–) US dramatist. *Poor Richard*

30 Clearly money has something to do with life
– In fact, they've a lot in common, if you enquire:
You can't put off being young until you retire.

Philip Larkin (1922–85) British poet. *Money*

31 For I don't care too much for money,
For money can't buy me love.

John Lennon (1940–80) British rock musician. *Can't Buy Me Love* (with Paul McCartney)

32 The working classes are never embarrassed by money – only the absence of it.

Ken Livingstone (1945–) British Labour politician. Speech, Sept 1987

33 What's a thousand dollars? Mere chicken feed. A poultry matter.

Groucho Marx (Julius Marx; 1895–1977) US comedian. *The Cocoanuts*

34 Do they allow tipping on the boat?
– Yes, sir.
Have you got two fives?
– Oh, yes, sir.
Then you won't need the ten cents I was going to give you.

Groucho Marx *A Night at the Opera*

35 Money is like a sixth sense without which you cannot make a complete use of the other five.

W. Somerset Maugham (1874–1965) British novelist. *Of Human Bondage*, Ch. 51

36 Money can't buy friends, but you can get a better class of enemy.

Spike Milligan (1918–) British comic actor and author. *Puckoon*, Ch. 6

37 Some people's money is merited
And other people's is inherited.

Ogden Nash (1902–71) US poet. *The Terrible People*

38 Check enclosed.

Dorothy Parker (1893–1967) US writer. Giving her version of the two most beautiful words in the English language. Attrib.

39 Money is good for bribing yourself through

the inconveniences of life.

Gottfried Reinhardt (1911–94) Austrian film producer. *Picture*, 'Looks Like We're Still in Business' (Lillian Ross)

40 My boy...always try to rub up against money, for if you rub up against money long enough, some of it may rub off on you.

Damon Runyon (1884–1946) US writer. *Furthermore*, 'A Very Honourable Guy'

41 He that wants money, means, and content, is without three good friends.

William Shakespeare (1564–1616) English dramatist. *As You Like It*, III:2

42 I can get no remedy against this consumption of the purse; borrowing only lingers and lingers it out, but the disease is incurable.

William Shakespeare *Henry IV, Part Two*, I:2

43 Put money in thy purse.

William Shakespeare *Othello*, I:3

44 Lack of money is the root of all evil.

George Bernard Shaw (1856–1950) Irish dramatist and critic. *Man and Superman*, 'Maxims for Revolutionists.'

45 The trouble, Mr Goldwyn is that you are only interested in art and I am only interested in money.

George Bernard Shaw Turning down Goldwyn's offer to buy the screen rights of his plays. *The Movie Moguls* (Philip French), Ch. 4

46 Nothing links man to man like the frequent passage from hand to hand of cash.

Walter Richard Sickert (1860–1942) British impressionist painter. *A Certain World* (W. H. Auden)

47 Pieces of eight!

Robert Louis Stevenson (1850–94) Scottish writer. *Treasure Island*, Ch. 10

48 I think I could be a good woman if I had five thousand a year.

William Makepeace Thackeray (1811–63) British novelist. *Vanity Fair*, Ch. 36

49 No one would have remembered the Good Samaritan if he'd only had good intentions. He had money as well.

Margaret Thatcher (1925–) British politician and prime minister. Television interview, 1980

50 The easiest way for your children to learn about money is for you not to have any.

Katherine Whitehorn (1926–) British journalist. *How to Survive Children*

51 You can be young without money but you can't be old without it.

Tennessee Williams (1911–83) US dramatist. *Cat on a Hot Tin Roof*, I

52 All these financiers, all the little gnomes of Zürich and the other financial centres, about whom we keep on hearing.

Harold Wilson (1916–95) British politician and prime minister. Speech, House of Commons, 12 Nov 1956

MONTHS

See also seasons

1 March comes in like a lion and goes out like a lamb.

Proverb

2 Ne'er cast a clout till May be out.

Proverb

3 The cuckoo comes in April, and stays the month of May; sings a song at midsummer, and then goes away.

Proverb

4 Thirty days hath September,
April, June, and November;
All the rest have thirty-one,
Excepting February alone,
And that has twenty-eight days clear
And twenty-nine in each leap year.

Anonymous *See also* GRAFTON. Stevins Manuscript, c. 1555

5 There are twelve months in all the year,
As I hear many men say,
But the merriest month in all the year
Is the merry month of May.

Anonymous *Robin Hood and the Widow's Three Sons*

6 And after April, when May follows,
And the whitethroat builds, and all the swallows!

Robert Browning (1812–89) British poet. *Home Thoughts from Abroad*

7 Whan that Aprille with his shoures sote
The droghte of Marche hath perced to the rote.

Geoffrey Chaucer (c. 1342–1400) English poet. *The Canterbury Tales*, Prologue

8 April is the cruellest month, breeding
Lilacs out of the dead land, mixing
Memory and desire, stirring
Dull roots with spring rain.

T. S. Eliot (1888–1965) US-born British poet and dramatist. *The Waste Land*, 'The Burial of the Dead'

9 Thirty days hath November,
April, June and September,
February hath twenty-eight alone,
And all the rest have thirty-one.

Richard Grafton (d. c. 1572) English chronicler and printer. *Abridgement of the Chronicles of England*, Introduction

10 No warmth, no cheerfulness, no healthful ease,
No comfortable feel in any member –
No shade, no shine, no butterflies, no bees,
No fruits, no flowers, no leaves, no birds, –
November!

Thomas Hood (1799–1845) British poet. *No!*

11 February, fill the dyke
With what thou dost like.

Thomas Tusser (1524–80) English farmer. *Five Hundred Points of Good Husbandry*, 'February's Husbandry'

12 Sweet April showers

Do spring May flowers.

Thomas Tusser *Five Hundred Points of Good Husbandry*, 'April's Husbandry'

MOON

See also astronomy, space, universe

1 I saw the new moon late yestreen
Wi' the auld moon in her arm;
And if we gang to sea master;
I fear we'll come to harm.

Anonymous The 'new moon in the old moon's arms' is generally regarded as a sign of bad weather. Sir Patrick Spens

2 The moving Moon went up the sky,
And no where did abide:
Softly she was going up,
And a star or two beside.

Samuel Taylor Coleridge (1772–1834) British poet. *The Rime of the Ancient Mariner*, IV

3 who knows if the moon's
a balloon, coming out of a keen city
in the sky – filled with pretty people?

e. e. cummings (1894–1962) US poet. Used for the title and epigraph of David Niven's first volume of autobiography, *The Moon's a Balloon*, about his experiences in the film industry.

4 So sicken waning moons too near the sun,
And blunt their crescents on the edge of day.

John Dryden (1631–1700) British poet and dramatist. *Annus Mirabilis*

5 For years politicians have promised the moon, I'm the first one to be able to deliver it.

Richard Milhous Nixon (1913–94) US president. Radio message to astronauts on the moon, 20 Jul 1969

6 Oh! shine on, shine on, harvest moon
Up in the sky.
I ain't had no lovin'
Since April, January, June or July.

Jack Norworth (1879–1959) US vaudeville comedian and songwriter. *Shine On, Harvest Moon* (song)

MORALITY

See also integrity, principles, righteousness

1 In his own way each man must struggle, lest the moral law become a far-off abstraction utterly separated from his active life.

Jane Addams (1860–1935) US social worker. *Twenty Years at Hull House*

2 No morality can be founded on authority, even if the authority were divine.

A. J. Ayer (1910–89) British philosopher. *Essay on Humanism*

3 Morality's not practical. Morality's a gesture. A complicated gesture learnt from books.

Robert Bolt (1924–95) British playwright. *A Man for All Seasons*

4 The propriety of some persons seems to consist in having improper thoughts about their neighbours.

F. H. Bradley (1846–1924) British philosopher. *Aphorisms*

5 And there isn't any way that one can get rid of the guilt of having a nice body by saying that one can serve society with it, because that would end up with oneself as what? There simply doesn't seem to be any moral place for flesh.

Margaret Drabble (1939–) British novelist. *A Summer Bird-Cage*, Ch. 10

6 What is moral is what you feel good after, and what is immoral is what you feel bad after.

Ernest Hemingway (1899–1961) US novelist. *Death in the Afternoon*

7 The quality of moral behaviour varies in inverse ratio to the number of human beings involved.

Aldous Huxley (1894–1964) British novelist. *Grey Eminence*, Ch. 10

8 Finally, there is an imperative which commands a certain conduct immediately...This imperative is Categorical...This imperative may be called that of Morality.

Immanuel Kant (1724–1804) German philosopher. *Grundlegung zur Metaphysik der Sitten*, II

9 Morality which is based on ideas, or on an ideal, is an unmitigated evil.

D. H. Lawrence (1885–1930) British novelist. *Fantasia of the Unconscious*, Ch. 7

10 We know no spectacle so ridiculous as the British public in one of its periodical fits of morality.

Lord Macaulay (1800–59) British historian. *Literary Essays Contributed to the 'Edinburgh Review'*, 'Moore's 'Life of Lord Byron''

11 It is a public scandal that gives offence, and it is no sin to sin in secret.

Molière (Jean Baptiste Poquelin; 1622–73) French dramatist. *Tartuffe*, IV:5

12 Morality in Europe today is herd-morality.

Friedrich Wilhelm Nietzsche (1844–1900) German philosopher. *Jenseits von Gut und Böse*

13 We have, in fact, two kinds of morality side by side; one which we preach but do not practise, and another which we practise but seldom preach.

Bertrand Russell (1872–1970) British philosopher. *Sceptical Essays*

14 All universal moral principles are idle fancies.

Marquis de Sade (1740–1814) French novelist. *The 120 Days of Sodom*

15 Without doubt the greatest injury...was done by basing morals on myth, for sooner or later myth is recognized for what it is, and disappears. Then morality loses the foundation on which it has been built.

Herbert Samuel (1870–1963) British Liberal statesman. Romanes Lecture, 1947

16 Morality consists in suspecting other people

of not being legally married.

George Bernard Shaw (1856–1950) Irish dramatist and critic. *The Doctor's Dilemma*

17 He never does a proper thing without giving an improper reason for it.

George Bernard Shaw *Major Barbara*, III

18 The so-called new morality is too often the old immorality condoned.

Lord Shawcross (1902–) British Labour politician and lawyer. *The Observer*, 17 Nov 1963

19 'Twas Peter's drift
To be a kind of moral eunuch.

Percy Bysshe Shelley (1792–1822) British poet. *Peter Bell the Third*

20 Moral indignation is in most cases 2 percent moral, 48 percent indignation and 50 percent envy.

Vittorio De Sica (1901–74) Italian film director. *The Observer*, 1961

21 If your morals make you dreary, depend upon it, they are wrong.

Robert Louis Stevenson (1850–94) Scottish writer. *Across the Plains*

22 Victorian values…were the values when our country became great.

Margaret Thatcher (1925–) British politician and prime minister. Television interview, 1982

23 Morals are an acquirement – like music, like a foreign language, like piety, poker, paralysis – no man is born with them.

Mark Twain (Samuel Langhorne Clemens; 1835–1910) US writer. *Seventieth Birthday*

MORTALITY

See also death, equality in death, human condition, immortality, life, life and death, time, transience

1 All men are mortal.

Proverb

2 Mortality, behold and fear!
What a change of flesh is here!

Francis Beaumont (1584–1616) English dramatist. *On the Tombs in Westminster Abbey*

3 That lyf so short, the craft so long to lerne,
Th' assay so hard, so sharp the conquerynge.

Geoffrey Chaucer (c. 1342–1400) English poet. *See also* HIPPOCRATES. *The Parliament of Fowls*

4 What argufies pride and ambition?
Soon or late death will take us in tow:
Each bullet has got its commission,
And when our time's come we must go.

Charles Dibdin (1745–1814) British actor and dramatist. *Each Bullet has its Commission*

5 All humane things are subject to decay,
And, when Fate summons, Monarchs must obey.

John Dryden (1631–1700) British poet and dramatist. *Mac Flecknoe*

6 The Wine of Life keeps oozing drop by drop,
The Leaves of Life keep falling one by one.

Edward Fitzgerald (1809–83) British poet. *The Rubáiyát of Omar Khayyám* (4th edn.), VIII

7 Is life a boon?
If so, it must befall
That Death, whene'er he call,
Must call too soon.

W. S. Gilbert (1836–1911) British dramatist. The lines are written on Arthur Sullivan's memorial in the Embankment gardens. *The Yeoman of the Guard*, I

8 I was not unaware that I had begotten a mortal.

Goethe (1749–1832) German poet and dramatist. On learning of his son's death. *The Story of Civilization* (W. Durant), Vol. X

9 Man wants but little here below,
Nor wants that little long.

Oliver Goldsmith (1728–74) Irish-born British writer. *Edwin and Angelina, or the Hermit*

10 The boast of heraldry, the pomp of pow'r,
And all that beauty, all that wealth e'er gave,
Awaits alike th' inevitable hour,
The paths of glory lead but to the grave.

Thomas Gray (1716–71) British poet. *Elegy Written in a Country Churchyard*

11 I expect to pass through this world but once; any good thing therefore that I can do, or any kindness that I can show to any fellow-creature, let me do it now; let me not defer or neglect it, for I shall not pass this way again.

Stephen Grellet (1773–1855) French-born US missionary. Attrib. *Treasure Trove* (John o'London)

12 The life so short, the craft so long to learn.

Hippocrates (c. 460–c. 377 BC) Greek physician. Describing medicine. It is often quoted in Latin as *Ars longa, vita brevis*, and interpreted as 'Art lasts, life is short'. *See also* CHAUCER. *Aphorisms*, I

13 Life's short span forbids us to enter on far-reaching hopes.

Horace (Quintus Horatius Flaccus; 65–8 BC) Roman poet. *Odes*, I

14 Art is long, and Time is fleeting,
And our hearts, though stout and brave,
Still, like muffled drums, are beating
Funeral marches to the grave.

Henry Wadsworth Longfellow (1807–82) US poet. *See also* HIPPOCRATES. *A Psalm of Life*

15 *Inque brevi spatio mutantur saecla animantum*
Et quasi cursores vitai lampada tradunt.
The generations of living things pass in a short time, and like runners hand on the torch of life.

Lucretius (Titus Lucretius Carus; c. 99–55 BC) Roman philosopher. *On the Nature of the Universe*, II

16 Fear no more the heat o' th' sun
Nor the furious winter's rages;
Thou thy worldly task hast done,
Home art gone, and ta'en thy wages.
Golden lads and girls all must,

As chimney-sweepers, come to dust.

William Shakespeare (1564–1616) English dramatist. *Cymbeline*, IV:2

17 Our revels now are ended. These our actors,
As I foretold you, were all spirits, and
Are melted into air, into thin air;
And, like the baseless fabric of this vision,
The cloud-capp'd towers, the gorgeous palaces,
The solemn temples, the great globe itself,
Yea, all which it inherit, shall dissolve,
And, like this insubstantial pageant faded,
Leave not a rack behind. We are such stuff
As dreams are made on; and our little life
Is rounded with a sleep.

William Shakespeare *The Tempest*, IV:1

18 Old and young, we are all on our last cruise.

Robert Louis Stevenson (1850–94) Scottish writer. *Virginibus Puerisque*

19 The woods decay, the woods decay and fall,
The vapours weep their burthen to the ground,
Man comes and tills the field and lies beneath,
And after many a summer dies the swan.

Alfred, Lord Tennyson (1809–92) British poet. *Tithonus*

20 A power is passing from the earth
To breathless Nature's dark abyss;
But when the great and good depart,
What is it more than this –

That Man who is from God sent forth,
Doth yet again to God return? –
Such ebb and flow must ever be,
Then wherefore should we mourn?

William Wordsworth (1770–1850) British poet. Referring to Charles James Fox, the hero of the liberal Whigs, who died in 1806. *Lines on the Expected Dissolution of Mr. Fox*

21 The clouds that gather round the setting sun
Do take a sober colouring from an eye
That hath kept watch o'er man's mortality.

William Wordsworth *Ode. Intimations of Immortality*, XI

22 I am moved to pity, when I think of the brevity of human life, seeing that of all this host of men not one will still be alive in a hundred years' time.

Xerxes (d. 465 BC) King of Persia. On surveying his army.

23 That is no country for old men. The young
In one another's arms, birds in the trees
– Those dying generations – at their song,
The salmon-falls, the mackerel-crowded seas,
Fish, flesh, or fowl, commend all summer long
Whatever is begotten, born, and dies.

W. B. Yeats (1865–1939) Irish poet. *Sailing to Byzantium*, I

24 Man wants but little, nor that little long.

Edward Young (1683–1765) British poet. *Night Thoughts*

MOTHERHOOD

See also babies, birth, children, family, fathers, pregnancy

1 The best thing that could happen to motherhood already has. Fewer women are going into it.

Victoria Billings (1945–) US journalist and writer. *Womansbook*, 'Meeting Your Personal Needs'

2 Women, who are, beyond all doubt, the mothers of all mischief, also nurse that babe to sleep when he is too noisy.

R. D. Blackmore (1825–1900) British writer. *Lorna Doone*

3 Women do not have the right to have a child.

Virginia Bottomley (1948–) British Conservative politician. *The Times*, 28 Dec 1993

4 Womanliness means only motherhood;
All love begins and ends there.

Robert Browning (1812–89) British poet. *The Inn Album*

5 Motherhood meant I have written four fewer books, but I know more about life.

A(ntonia) S(usan) Byatt (1936–) British novelist. *The Sunday Times*, 21 Oct 1990

6 I love all my children, but some of them I don't like.

Lillian Carter (1902–83) The mother of Jimmy Carter. In *Woman*, 9 Apr 1977

7 An author who speaks about his own books is almost as bad as a mother who talks about her own children.

Benjamin Disraeli (1804–81) British statesman. Speech in Glasgow, 19 Nov 1873

8 Claudia...remembered that when she'd had her first baby she had realised with astonishment that the perfect couple consisted of a mother and child and not, as she had always supposed, a man and woman.

Alice Thomas Ellis (1932–) British writer. *The Other Side of the Fire*

9 The mother-child relationship is paradoxical and, in a sense, tragic. It requires the most intense love on the mother's side, yet this very love must help the child grow away from the mother and to become fully independent.

Erich Fromm (1900–80) US psychologist and philosopher.

10 Mother is the dead heart of the family; spending father's earnings on consumer goods to enhance the environment in which he eats, sleeps and watches the television.

Germaine Greer (1939–) Australian-born British writer and feminist. *The Female Eunuch*

11 Now, as always, the most automated appliance in a household is the mother.

Beverly Jones (1927–) US writer and feminist. *The Florida Paper on Women's Liberation*

12 And Her Mother Came Too.

Ivor Novello (David Ivor Davies; 1893–1951) British actor, composer, and dramatist. Title of song

13 Who has not watched a mother stroke her child's cheek or kiss her child *in a certain way* and felt a nervous shudder at the possessive outrage done to a free solitary human soul?

John Cowper Powys (1872–1963) British writer. *The Meaning of Culture*

14 Maternity is on the face of it an unsocial experience. The selfishness that a woman has learned to stifle or to dissemble where she alone is concerned, blooms freely and unashamed on behalf of her offspring.

Emily James Putnam (1865–1944) US educator, writer, and college administrator. First dean of Barnard College, New York. *The Lady*, Introduction

15 No matter how old a mother is she watches her middle-aged children for signs of improvement.

Florida Scott-Maxwell (b. 1883) US-born British writer, psychologist, playwright, suffragette, and actress. *The Measure of My Days*

16 Though motherhood is the most important of all the professions – requiring more knowledge than any other department in human affairs – there was no attention given to preparation for this office.

Elizabeth Cady Stanton (1815–1902) US suffragette and abolitionist. *Eighty Years and More*

17 A mother! What are we worth really? They all grow up whether you look after them or not.

Christina Stead (1902–83) Australian writer. *The Man Who Loved Children*, Ch. 10

MOTIVE

See also purpose

1 Never ascribe to an opponent motives meaner than your own.

J. M. Barrie (1860–1937) British novelist and dramatist. Speech, St Andrews, 3 May 1922

2 The last temptation is the greatest treason:
To do the right deed for the wrong reason.

T. S. Eliot (1888–1965) US-born British poet and dramatist. *Murder in the Cathedral*, I

3 Because it is there.

George Mallory (1886–1924) British mountaineer. Answer to the question 'Why do you want to climb Mt. Everest?'. *George Mallory* (D. Robertson)

4 Nobody ever did anything very foolish except from some strong principle.

Lord Melbourne (1779–1848) British statesman. *The Young Melbourne* (Lord David Cecil)

5 The heart has its reasons which reason does not know.

Blaise Pascal (1623–62) French philosopher and mathematician. *Pensées*, IV

6 Men are rewarded and punished not for what they do, but rather for how their acts are defined. This is why men are more interested in better justifying themselves than in better behaving themselves.

Thomas Szasz (1920–) US psychiatrist. *The Second Sin*

MOUNTAINS

1 Mountains interposed
Make enemies of nations, who had else,
Like kindred drops, been mingled into one.

William Cowper (1731–1800) British poet. *The Task*

2 Separate from the pleasure of your company, I don't much care if I never see another mountain in my life.

Charles Lamb (1775–1834) British essayist. Letter to William Wordsworth, 30 Jan 1801

3 Mountains are the beginning and the end of all natural scenery.

John Ruskin (1819–1900) British art critic and writer. *Modern Painters*, Vol. IV

4 They say that if the Swiss had designed these mountains they'd be rather flatter.

Paul Theroux (1941–) US-born writer. Referring to the Alps. *The Great Railway Bazaar*, Ch. 28

MOURNING

See also death, loss, regret, sorrow

1 We met…Dr Hall in such very deep mourning that either his mother, his wife, or himself must be dead.

Jane Austen (1775–1817) British novelist. Letter to Cassandra Austen, 17 May 1799

2 I am distressed for thee, my brother
Jonathan: very pleasant hast thou been unto me:
thy love to me was wonderful, passing the love of
women.
How are the mighty fallen, and the weapons of
war perished!

Bible: II Samuel 1:26–27

3 With proud thanksgiving, a mother for her children,
England mourns for her dead across the sea.

Laurence Binyon (1869–1943) British poet. In response to the slaughter of World War I. *Poems For the Fallen*

4 MEDVEDENKO. Why do you wear black all the time?
MASHA. I'm in mourning for my life, I'm unhappy.

Anton Chekhov (1860–1904) Russian dramatist. *The Seagull*, I

5 There's a one-eyed yellow idol to the north of Khatmandu,
There's a little marble cross below the town;
There's a broken-hearted woman tends the grave of Mad Carew
And the Yellow God forever gazes down.

J. Milton Hayes (1884–1940) British writer. *The Green Eye of the Yellow God*

6 What we call mourning for our dead is perhaps not so much grief at not being able to call them back as it is grief at not being able to want to do so.

Thomas Mann (1875–1955) German novelist. *The Magic Mountain*

7 In a cavern, in a canyon,
Excavating for a mine
Dwelt a miner, Forty-niner,
And his daughter, Clementine.
Oh, my darling, Oh, my darling, Oh, my darling
Clementine!
Thou art lost and gone for ever, dreadful sorry,
Clementine.

Percy Montrose (19th century) US songwriter. *Clementine*

8 She is far from the land where her young
hero sleeps,
And lovers are round her, sighing:
But coldly she turns from their gaze, and weeps,
For her heart in his grave is lying.

Thomas Moore (1779–1852) Irish poet. *Irish Melodies*, 'She is Far'

9 And my poor fool is hang'd! No, no, no life!
Why should a dog, a horse, a rat have life,
And thou no breath at all? Thou'lt come no more,
Never, never, never, never.

William Shakespeare (1564–1616) English dramatist. *King Lear*, V:3

10 Alas, poor Yorick! I knew him, Horatio: a fellow of infinite jest, of most excellent fancy.

William Shakespeare *Hamlet*, V:1

11 O, wither'd is the garland of the war,
The soldier's pole is fall'n! Young boys and girls
Are level now with men. The odds is gone,
And there is nothing left remarkable
Beneath the visiting moon.

William Shakespeare *Antony and Cleopatra*, IV:13

12 But I have that within which passes show – these but the trappings and the suits of woe.

William Shakespeare *Hamlet*, I:2

13 If thou didst ever hold me in thy heart,
Absent thee from felicity awhile,
And in this harsh world draw thy breath in pain,
To tell my story.

William Shakespeare *Hamlet*, V:2

14 I weep for Adonais – he is dead!
O, weep for Adonais! though our tears
Thaw not the frost which binds so dear a head!

Percy Bysshe Shelley (1792–1822) British poet. Prompted by the death of Keats. *Adonais*, I

15 A lady asked me why, on most occasions, I wore black. 'Are you in mourning?'
'Yes.'
'For whom are you in mourning?'
'For the world.'

Edith Sitwell (1887–1964) British poet and writer. *Taken Care Of*, Ch. 1

16 Home they brought her warrior dead.
She nor swoon'd, nor utter'd cry:
All her maidens, watching said,
'She must weep or she will die.'

Alfred, Lord Tennyson (1809–92) British poet. *The Princess*, VI

MURDER

See also assassination, crime, killing

1 Lizzie Borden took an axe
And gave her mother forty whacks;
When she saw what she had done
She gave her father forty-one!

Anonymous On 4 Aug 1892 in Fall River, Massachusetts, Lizzie Borden was acquitted of the murder of her stepmother and her father.

2 And the Lord said unto Cain, Where is Abel thy brother? And he said, I know not: Am I my brother's keeper?
And he said, What hast thou done? the voice of thy brother's blood crieth unto me from the ground.

Bible: Genesis 4:9–10

3 I've been accused of every death except the casualty list of the World War.

Al Capone (1899–1947) Italian-born US gangster. *The Bootleggers* (Kenneth Allsop), Ch. 11

4 Mordre wol out, that see we day by day.

Geoffrey Chaucer (c. 1342–1400) English poet. *The Canterbury Tales*, 'The Nun's Priest's Tale'

5 See how love and murder will out.

William Congreve (1670–1729) British Restoration dramatist. *The Double Dealer*, IV:6

6 Murder considered as one of the Fine Arts.

Thomas De Quincey (1785–1859) British writer. Essay title

7 I made a remark a long time ago. I said I was very pleased that television was now showing murder stories, because it's bringing murder back into its rightful setting – in the home.

Alfred Hitchcock (1889–1980) British film director. *The Observer*, 'Sayings of the Week', 17 Aug 1969

8 It takes two to make a murder. There are born victims, born to have their throats cut.

Aldous Huxley (1894–1964) British novelist. *Point Counter Point*

9 Murder, like talent, seems occasionally to run in families.

G. H. Lewes (1817–78) British philosopher and writer. *The Physiology of Common Life*, Ch. 12

10 Put out the light, and then put out the light.
If I quench thee, thou flaming minister,
I can again thy former light restore,
Should I repent me; but once put out thy light,
Thou cunning'st pattern of excelling nature,
I know not where is that Promethean heat
That can thy light relume.

William Shakespeare (1564–1616) English dramatist. *Othello*, V:2

11 Murder most foul, as in the best it is;
But this most foul, strange, and unnatural.

William Shakespeare *Hamlet*, I:5

12 I met Murder on the way –
He had a mask like Castlereagh.

Percy Bysshe Shelley (1792–1822) British poet. Viscount

Castlereagh (1769–1822) was British foreign secretary (1812–22); he was highly unpopular and became identified with such controversial events as the Peterloo massacre of 1819. *The Mask of Anarchy*, 5

13 Other sins only speak; murder shrieks out.

John Webster (1580–1625) English dramatist. *The Duchess of Malfi*, IV:2

14 The person by far the most likely to kill you is yourself.

Jock Young British criminologist. *The Observer*, 'Sayings of the Week', 8 May 1994

MUSEUMS

1 The Arab who builds himself a hut out of the marble fragments of a temple in Palmyra is more philosophical than all the curators of the museums in London, Munich or Paris.

Anatole France (Jacques Anatole François Thibault; 1844–1924) French writer. *The Crime of Sylvestre Bonnard*

2 If there was a little room somewhere in the British Museum that contained only about twenty exhibits and good lighting, easy chairs, and a notice imploring you to smoke, I believe I should become a museum man.

J. B. Priestley (1894–1984) British novelist. *Self-Selected Essays*, 'In the British Museum'

3 There is in the British Museum an enormous mind. Consider that Plato is there cheek by jowl with Aristotle; and Shakespeare with Marlowe. This great mind is hoarded beyond the power of any single mind to possess it.

Virginia Woolf (1882–1941) British novelist. *Jacob's Room*, Ch. 9

MUSIC

See also criticism, musicians, opera, singing

1 Music helps not the toothache.

Proverb

2 Nothing is capable of being well set to music that is not nonsense.

Joseph Addison (1672–1719) British essayist. *The Spectator*, 18

3 The music teacher came twice each week to bridge the awful gap between Dorothy and Chopin.

George Ade (1866–1944) US dramatist and humorist. Attrib.

4 Brass bands are all very well in their place – outdoors and several miles away.

Thomas Beecham (1879–1961) British conductor. Attrib.

5 The English may not like music – but they absolutely love the noise it makes.

Thomas Beecham *The Wit of Music* (L. Ayre)

6 The sound of the harpsichord resembles that of a bird-cage played with toasting-forks.

Thomas Beecham Attrib.

7 There are two golden rules for an orchestra: start together and finish together. The public doesn't give a damn what goes on in between.

Thomas Beecham *Beecham Stories* (H. Atkins and A. Newman)

8 A musicologist is a man who can read music but can't hear it.

Thomas Beecham *Beecham Remembered* (H. Procter-Gregg)

9 When I composed that, I was conscious of being inspired by God Almighty. Do you think I can consider your puny little fiddle when He speaks to me?

Ludwig van Beethoven (1770–1827) German composer. Said when a violinist complained that a passage was unplayable. *Music All Around Me* (A. Hopkins)

10 *Fiddle, n.* An instrument to tickle human ears by function of a horse's tail on the entrails of a cat.

Ambrose Bierce (1842–?1914) US writer and journalist. *The Devil's Dictionary*

11 Down South where I come from you don't go around hitting too many white keys.

Eubie Blake (1883–1983) US pianist and ragtime composer. When asked why his compositions contained so many sharps and flats. Attrib.

12 Piping down the valleys wild,
Piping songs of pleasant glee,
On a cloud I saw a child.

William Blake (1757–1827) British poet. *Songs of Innocence*, Introduction

13 'Pipe a song about a Lamb!'
So I piped with merry cheer.

William Blake *Songs of Innocence*, Introduction

14 No one really understood music unless he was a scientist, her father had declared, and not just a scientist, either, oh, no, only the real ones, the theoreticians, whose language was mathematics.

Pearl Buck (1892–1973) US novelist. *The Goddess Abides*, Pt. I

15 Music has charms to soothe a savage breast.

William Congreve (1670–1729) British Restoration dramatist. *The Mourning Bride*, I

16 Strange how potent cheap music is.

Noël Coward (1899–1973) British dramatist. *Private Lives*

17 Music is the arithmetic of sounds as optics is the geometry of light.

Claude Debussy (1862–1918) French composer. Attrib.

18 The century of aeroplanes deserves its own music. As there are no precedents I must create anew.

Claude Debussy Attrib.

19 When I was 25, Bartok needed me, a young man who would get up on the podium, play his music and be whistled at for it.

Antal Dorati (1906–88) US conductor and composer. Remark, Apr 1986

20 Music was invented to confirm human loneliness.

Lawrence Durrell (1912–90) British novelist. *Clea*

21 Beethoven's Fifth Symphony is the most sublime noise that has ever penetrated into the ear of man.

E. M. Forster (1879–1970) British novelist. *Howards End*, Ch. 5

22 The hills are alive with the sound of music
With the songs they have sung
For a thousand years.

Oscar Hammerstein (1895–1960) US lyricist. *The Sound of Music*, title song

23 I do not see any reason why the devil should have all the good tunes.

Rowland Hill (1744–1833) British clergyman. Attrib.

24 Never compose anything unless the not composing of it becomes a positive nuisance to you.

Gustav Holst (1874–1934) British composer. Letter to W. G. Whittaker

25 Since Mozart's day composers have learned the art of making music throatily and palpitatingly sexual.

Aldous Huxley (1894–1964) British novelist. *Along the Road*, 'Popular music'

26 The only sensual pleasure without vice.

Samuel Johnson (1709–84) British lexicographer. Referring to music. *Johnsonian Miscellanies* (ed. G. B. Hill), Vol. II

27 Heard melodies are sweet, but those unheard
Are sweeter; therefore, ye soft pipes, play on.

John Keats (1795–1821) British poet. *Ode on a Grecian Urn*

28 But I can't listen to music too often. It affects your nerves, makes you want to say stupid, nice things, and stroke the heads of people who could create such beauty while living in this vile hell.

Lenin (Vladimir Ilich Ulyanov; 1870–1924) Russian revolutionary leader. *Lenin and the Russian Revolution* (Christopher Hill)

29 There's sure no passion in the human soul,
But finds its food in music.

George Lillo (1693–1739) English dramatist. *Fatal Curiosity*, I:2

30 Music, Maestro, Please.

Herb Magidson (20th century) US songwriter. Song title

31 Music is not written in red, white and blue. It is written in the heart's blood of the composer.

Nellie Melba (Helen Porter Mitchell; 1861–1931) Australian soprano. *Melodies and Memories*

32 Music creates order out of chaos; for rhythm imposes unanimity upon the divergent, melody imposes continuity upon the disjointed, and harmony imposes compatibility upon the incongruous.

Yehudi Menuhin (1916–) US-born British violinist. *The Sunday Times*, 10 Oct 1976

33 The melting voice through mazes running;
Untwisting all the chains that tie
The hidden soul of harmony.

John Milton (1608–74) English poet. *L'Allegro*

34 The song that we hear with our ears is only the song that is sung in our hearts.

Ouida (Marie Louise de la Ramée; 1839–1908) British novelist. *Wisdom, Wit and Pathos*, 'Ariadne'

35 What a terrible revenge by the culture of the Negroes on that of the whites.

Ignacy Paderewski (1860–1941) Polish pianist, composer, and statesman. Referring to jazz. Attrib.

36 Music is your own experience, your thoughts, your wisdom. If you don't live it, it won't come out of your horn.

Charlie Parker (1920–55) US black jazz musician. *Hear Me Talkin' to Ya* (Nat Shapiro and Nat Hentoff)

37 Music and women I cannot but give way to, whatever my business is.

Samuel Pepys (1633–1703) English diarist. *Diary*, 9 Mar 1666

38 The basic difference between classical music and jazz is that in the former the music is always greater than its performance – whereas the way jazz is performed is always more important than what is being played.

André Previn (1929–) German-born conductor. *An Encyclopedia of Quotations about Music* (Nat Shapiro)

39 Seated one day at the organ,
I was weary and ill at ease,
And my fingers wandered idly
Over the noisy keys.
...
But I struck one chord of music,
Like the sound of a great Amen.

Adelaide Anne Procter (1825–64) British poet. Better known in the setting by Sir Arthur Sullivan. *Legends and Lyrics*, 'A Lost Chord'

40 I have already heard it. I had better not go: I will start to get accustomed to it and finally like it.

Nikolai Rimsky-Korsakov (1844–1908) Russian composer. Referring to music by Debussy. *Conversations with Stravinsky* (Robert Craft and Igor Stravinsky)

41 Give me a laundry-list and I'll set it to music.

Gioacchino Rossini (1792–1868) Italian operatic composer. Attrib.

42 To be played with both hands in the pocket.

Erik Satie (1866–1925) French composer. Direction on one of his piano pieces. *The Unimportance of Being Oscar* (O. Levant)

43 The sonatas of Mozart are unique; they are too easy for children, and too difficult for artists.

Artur Schnabel (1882–1951) Austrian concert pianist. *An Encyclopedia of Quotations about Music* (Nat Shapiro)

44 I am never merry when I hear sweet music.

William Shakespeare (1564–1616) English dramatist. *The Merchant of Venice*, V:1

45 The man that hath no music in himself,
Nor is not mov'd with concord of sweet sounds,
Is fit for treasons, stratagems, and spoils.

William Shakespeare *The Merchant of Venice*, V:1

46 If music be the food of love, play on,
Give me excess of it, that, surfeiting,
The appetite may sicken and so die.

William Shakespeare *Twelfth Night*, I:1

47 I wish the Government would put a tax on pianos for the incompetent.

Edith Sitwell (1887–1964) British poet and writer. *Letters, 1916–1964*

48 Jazz will endure just as long as people hear it through their feet instead of their brains.

John Philip Sousa (1854–1932) US composer, conductor, and writer. Attrib.

49 I don't write modern music. I only write good music.

Igor Stravinsky (1882–1971) Russian-born US composer. To journalists on his first visit to America, 1925.

50 My music is best understood by children and animals.

Igor Stravinsky *The Observer*, 'Sayings of the Week', 8 Oct 1961

51 Music that gentlier on the spirit lies,
Than tir'd eyelids upon tir'd eyes.

Alfred, Lord Tennyson (1809–92) British poet. *The Lotos-Eaters*, 'Choric Song'

52 Oh I'm a martyr to music.

Dylan Thomas (1914–53) Welsh poet. *Under Milk Wood*

53 The cello is not one of my favourite instruments. It has such a lugubrious sound, like someone reading a will.

Irene Thomas (1920–) British writer. Attrib.

54 God tells me how he wants this music played – and you get in his way.

Arturo Toscanini (1867–1957) Italian conductor. *Etude* (Howard Tubman)

55 You know, sometimes I don't even like music.

Sir William Walton (1902–83) British composer. Remark, Mar 1982

56 When I play on my fiddle in Dooney,
Folk dance like a wave of the sea.

W. B. Yeats (1865–1939) Irish poet. *The Fiddler of Dooney*

MUSICIANS

See also critics, singers

General quotes

1 Musicians don't retire; they stop when there's no more music in them.

Louis Armstrong (1900–71) US jazz trumpeter. *The Observer*, 'Sayings of the Week', 21 Apr 1968

2 Off with you! You're a happy fellow, for you'll give happiness and joy to many other people. There is nothing better or greater than that!

Ludwig van Beethoven (1770–1827) German composer. Said to Franz Liszt when Liszt, aged 11, had visited Beethoven and played for him. *Beethoven: Letters, Journals and Conversations* (M. Hamburger)

3 The public doesn't want a new music: the main thing it demands of a composer is that he be dead.

Arthur Honegger (1892–1955) French composer. Attrib.

4 Of all musicians, flautists are most obviously the ones who know something we don't know.

Paul Jennings (1918–89) British humorous writer. *The Jenguin Pennings*, 'Flautists Flaunt Afflatus'

5 The conductor has the advantage of not seeing the audience.

André Kostalenetz (1903–80) Russian-born conductor. Attrib.

6 You see, our fingers are circumcised, which gives it a very good dexterity, you know, particularly in the pinky.

Itzhak Perlman (1945–) Israeli violinist. Responding to an observation that many great violinists are Jewish. *Close Encounters* (M. Wallace)

7 Sometimes, I think, not so much am I a pianist, but a vampire. All my life I have lived off the blood of Chopin.

Arthur Rubinstein (1887–1982) Polish-born US pianist. Attrib.

8 The notes I handle no better than many pianists. But the pauses between the notes – ah, that is where the art resides.

Artur Schnabel (1882–1951) Austrian concert pianist. *Chicago Daily News*, 11 June 1958

9 A good composer does not imitate; he steals.

Igor Stravinsky (1882–1971) Russian-born composer. *Twentieth Century Music* (Peter Yates)

Specific quotes

10 A master is dead. Today we sing no more.

Johannes Brahms (1833–97) German composer. Stopping a choral rehearsal on hearing of the death of Wagner. *Brahms* (P. Latham)

11 Bach is like an astronomer who, with the aid of ciphers, finds the most wonderful stars.

Frédéric Chopin (1810–49) Polish composer and pianist. *Letter to Delphine Potocka*

12 Wagner is the Puccini of music.

J. B. Morton (1893–1979) British journalist. Attrib.

13 My dear hands. Farewell, my poor hands.

Sergei Rachmaninov (1873–1943) Russian composer. On being informed that he was dying from cancer. *The Great Pianists* (H. Schonberg)

14 When a piece gets difficult make faces.

Artur Schnabel (1882–1951) Austrian concert pianist. Advice given to the pianist Vladimir Horowitz. *The Unimportance of Being Oscar* (O. Levant)

15 Music owes as much to Bach as religion to its founder.

Robert Schumann (1810–56) German composer. Attrib.

16 Brahms is just like Tennyson, an extraordinary musician with the brains of a third-rate village policeman.

George Bernard Shaw (1856–1950) Irish dramatist and critic. Letter to Packenham Beatty, 4 Apr 1893

17 Unlike many contemporaries, he never writes paper music; everything has first been vividly heard by an inner ear of amazing acuteness. This faculty explains the speed at which he composes. The processes of trial and error take place mostly in the head.

Desmond Shawe-Taylor (1907–95) British music critic. Referring to Benjamin Britten. *Sunday Times*, 17 Nov 1963

18 Walton wrote *Belshazzar's Feast* in that barn out there. He made such a frightful din on the piano we had to banish him from the house.

Sacheverell Sitwell (1897–1980) British writer. *The Times, Profile*, 16 Nov 1982

19 He was the only pianist I have ever seen who did not grimace. That is a great deal.

Igor Stravinsky (1882–1971) Russian-born US composer. Referring to Rachmaninov. *Conversations with Igor Stravinsky* (Igor Stravinsky and Robert Craft)

20 Rachmaninov's immortalizing totality was his scowl. He was a six-and-a-half-foot-tall scowl.

Igor Stravinsky *Conversations with Igor Stravinsky* (Igor Stravinsky and Robert Craft)

21 Ah, a German and a genius! a prodigy, admit him!

Jonathan Swift (1667–1745) Irish-born Anglican priest and writer. Learning of the arrival of Handel: Swift's last words. Attrib.

MYTHS

1 Science must begin with myths, and with the criticism of myths.

Karl Popper (1902–94) Austrian-born British philosopher. *British Philosophy in the Mid-Century* (ed. C. A. Mace)

2 A myth is, of course, not a fairy story. It is the presentation of facts belonging to one category in the idioms appropriate to another. To explode a myth is accordingly not to deny the facts but to re-allocate them.

Gilbert Ryle (1900–76) British philosopher. *The Concept of Mind*, Introduction

N

NAKEDNESS

1 Nakedness is uncomely as well in mind, as body.

Francis Bacon (1561–1626) English philosopher. *Essays*, 'Of Simulation and Dissimulation'

2 Lives there the man that can figure a naked Duke of Windlestraw addressing a naked House of Lords?

Thomas Carlyle (1795–1881) Scottish historian and essayist. *Sartor Resartus*, Bk. I, Ch. 9

3 a pretty girl who naked is
is worth a million statues.

e. e. cummings (1894–1962) US poet. *Collected Poems*, 133

4 No woman so naked as one you can see to be naked underneath her clothes.

Michael Frayn (1933–) British journalist and writer. *Constructions*

5 How idiotic civilization is! Why be given a body if you have to keep it shut up in a case like a rare, rare fiddle?

Katherine Mansfield (1888–1923) New-Zealand-born British writer. *Bliss and Other Stories*, 'Bliss'

6 The part never calls for it. And I've never ever used that excuse. The box office calls for it.

Helen Mirren (1945–) British actress. Referring to nudity. *The Observer*, 'Sayings of the Week', 27 Mar 1994

7 JOURNALIST. Didn't you have anything on?
M. M. I had the radio on.

Marilyn Monroe (Norma-Jean Baker; 1926–62) US film star. Attrib.

NAMES

1 Ball...how very singular.

Thomas Beecham (1879–1961) British conductor. To a man called Ball. *Sir Thomas Beecham* (N. Cardus)

2 Known by the *sobriquet* of 'The artful Dodger.'

Charles Dickens (1812–70) British novelist. *Oliver Twist*, Ch. 8

3 I'm called Little Buttercup – dear Little Buttercup,
Though I could never tell why.

W. S. Gilbert (1836–1911) British dramatist. *HMS Pinafore*, I

4 A nickname is the heaviest stone that the devil can throw at a man.

William Hazlitt (1778–1830) British essayist. *Nicknames*

5 No, Groucho is not my real name. I'm breaking it in for a friend.

Groucho Marx (Julius Marx; 1895–1977) US comedian. Attrib.

6 O Romeo, Romeo! wherefore art thou Romeo?

William Shakespeare (1564–1616) English dramatist. *Romeo and Juliet*, II:2

7 What's in a name? That which we call a rose
By any other name would smell as sweet.

William Shakespeare *Romeo and Juliet*, II:2

8 'It's giving girls names like that', said Buggins, 'that nine times out of ten makes 'em go wrong. It unsettles 'em. If ever I was to have a girl, if ever I was to have a dozen girls, I'd call 'em all Jane.'

H. G. Wells (1866–1946) British writer. Referring to the name Euphemia. *Kipps*, Bk. I, Ch. 4

NASTINESS

See also cruelty, hurt

1 But are they all horrid, are you sure they are all horrid?

Jane Austen (1775–1817) British novelist. *Northanger Abbey*, Ch. 6

2 I do not want people to be very agreeable, as it saves me the trouble of liking them a great deal.

Jane Austen Letter, 24 Dec 1798

3 There is an unseemly exposure of the mind, as well as of the body.

William Hazlitt (1778–1830) British essayist. *On Disagreeable People*

4 Because I am a bastard.

Ernest Hemingway (1899–1961) US novelist. When asked why he had deserted his wife for another woman. *Americans in Paris* (B. Morton)

5 He was one of those born neither to obey nor to command, but to be evil to the commander and the obeyer alike. Perhaps there was nothing in life that he had much wanted to do, except to shoot rabbits and hit his father on the jaw, and both these things he had done.

John Masefield (1878–1967) British poet. *The Bird of Dawning*

6 One of the worst things about life is not how nasty the nasty people are. You know that already. It is how nasty the nice people can be.

Anthony Powell (1905–) British novelist. *A Dance to the Music of Time: The Kindly Ones*, Ch. 4

7 I can't see that she could have found anything nastier to say if she'd thought it out with both hands for a fortnight.

Dorothy L. Sayers (1893–1957) British writer. *Busman's Holiday*, 'Prothalamion'

8 'I grant you that he's not two-faced,' I said. 'But what's the use of that when the one face he has got is so peculiarly unpleasant?'

C. P. Snow (1905–80) British novelist. *The Affair*, Ch. 4

9 Malice is like a game of poker or tennis; you don't play it with anyone who is manifestly inferior to you.

Hilde Spiel (1911–90) Austrian writer. *The Darkened Room*

10 We are all American at puberty; we die French.

Evelyn Waugh (1903–66) British novelist. *Diaries*, 'Irregular Notes', 18 July 1961

NATIONALITY

See also Americans, British

1 He was born an Englishman and remained one for years.

Brendan Behan (1923–64) Irish playwright. *The Hostage*, I

2 PAT. He was an Anglo-Irishman.
MEG. In the blessed name of God, what's that?
PAT. A Protestant with a horse.

Brendan Behan *The Hostage*, I

3 England is a paradise for women, and hell for horses: Italy a paradise for horses, hell for women.

Robert Burton (1577–1640) English scholar and explorer. *Anatomy of Melancholy*, Pt. III

4 The Almighty in His infinite wisdom did not see fit to create Frenchmen in the image of Englishmen.

Winston Churchill (1874–1965) British statesman. Speech, House of Commons, 10 Dec 1942

5 For he might have been a Roosian,
A French, or Turk, or Proosian,
Or perhaps Ital-ian!
But in spite of all temptations
To belong to other nations,
He remains an Englishman!

W. S. Gilbert (1836–1911) British dramatist. *HMS Pinafore*, II

6 The Saxon is not like us Normans. His manners are not so polite.
But he never means anything serious till he talks about justice and right,
When he stands like an ox in the furrow with his sullen set eyes on your own,
And grumbles, 'This isn't fair dealing,' my son, leave the Saxon alone.

Rudyard Kipling (1865–1936) Indian-born British writer. *Norman and Saxon*

7 Great artists have no country.

Alfred de Musset (1810–57) French dramatist and poet. *Lorenzaccio*, I:5

8 I am not an Athenian or a Greek, but a citizen of the world.

Socrates (469–399 BC) Athenian philosopher. *Of Banishment* (Plutarch)

9 Men of England! You wish to kill me because I am a Frenchman. Am I not punished enough in not being born an Englishman?

Voltaire (François-Marie Arouet; 1694–1778) French writer. Addressing an angry London mob who desired to hang him because he was a Frenchman. Attrib.

NATIONS

See also places

1 The day of small nations has long passed away. The day of Empires has come.

Joseph Chamberlain (1836–1914) British politician. Speech, Birmingham, 12 May 1904

2 The nations which have put mankind and posterity most in their debt have been small states – Israel, Athens, Florence, Elizabethan England.

Dean Inge (1860–1954) British churchman. *Wit and Wisdom of Dean Inge* (ed. Marchant)

3 This agglomeration which was called and which still calls itself the Holy Roman Empire was neither holy, nor Roman, nor an empire.

Voltaire (François-Marie Arouet; 1694–1778) French writer. *Essai sur les moeurs et l'esprit des nations*, LXX

NATURE

See also animals, birds, countryside, ecology, flowers, human nature, science

1 All things are artificial, for nature is the art of God.

Thomas Browne (1605–82) English physician and writer. *Religio Medici*, Pt. I

2 Ye banks and braes o' bonnie Doon,
How can ye bloom sae fresh and fair?
How can ye chant, ye little birds,
And I sae weary fu' o' care?

Robert Burns (1759–96) Scottish poet. *Ye Banks and Braes*

3 There is a pleasure in the pathless woods,
There is a rapture on the lonely shore,
There is society, where none intrudes,
By the deep Sea, and music in its roar:
I love not Man the less, but Nature more.

Lord Byron (1788–1824) British poet. *Childe Harold's Pilgrimage*, IV

4 Nature admits no lie.

Thomas Carlyle (1795–1881) Scottish historian and essayist. *Latter-Day Pamphlets*, 5

5 Is ditchwater dull? Naturalists with microscopes have told me that it teems with quiet fun.

G. K. Chesterton (1874–1936) British writer. *The Spice of Life*

6 Nature is but a name for an effect
Whose cause is God.

William Cowper (1731–1800) British poet. *The Task*

7 All my life through, the new sights of Nature made me rejoice like a child.

Marie Curie (1867–1934) Polish chemist. *Pierre Curie*

8 By viewing Nature, Nature's handmaid, art, Makes mighty things from small beginnings grow.

John Dryden (1631–1700) British poet and dramatist. *Annus Mirabilis*

9 All Nature wears one universal grin.

Henry Fielding (1707–54) British novelist. *Tom Thumb the Great*, I:1

10 Natural science does not simply describe and explain nature, it is part of the interplay between nature and ourselves.

Werner Heisenberg (1901–76) German physicist. *Physics and Philosophy*

11 In nature there are neither rewards nor punishments – there are consequences.

Robert G. Ingersoll (1833–99) US lawyer and agnostic. *Lectures & Essays*, 'Some Reasons Why'

12 Nature is very consonant and conformable with herself.

Isaac Newton (1642–1727) British scientist. *Opticks*, Bk. III

13 It is far from easy to determine whether she has proved a kind parent to man or a merciless step-mother.

Pliny the Elder (Gaius Plinius Secundus; 23–79 AD) Roman scholar. *Natural History*, VII

14 Nature abhors a vacuum.

François Rabelais (1483–1553) French satirist. Attrib.

15 Are God and Nature then at strife
That Nature lends such evil dreams?
So careful of the type she seems,
So careless of the single life.

Alfred, Lord Tennyson (1809–92) British poet. *In Memoriam A.H.H.*

16 Nature is usually wrong.

James Whistler (1834–1903) US painter. *The Gentle Art of Making Enemies*

17 After you have exhausted what there is in business, politics, conviviality, and so on – have found that none of these finally satisfy, or permanently wear – what remains? Nature remains.

Walt Whitman (1819–92) US poet. *Specimen Days*, 'New Themes Entered Upon'

18 Nature never did betray
The heart that loved her.

William Wordsworth (1770–1850) British poet. *Lines composed a few miles above Tintern Abbey*

19 Earth fills her lap with pleasures of her own:
Yearnings she hath in her own natural kind.

William Wordsworth *Ode. Intimations of Immortality*, VI

20 Come forth into the light of things,
Let Nature be your Teacher.

William Wordsworth *The Tables Turned*

21 Another race hath been, and other palms are won.
Thanks to the human heart by which we live,
Thanks to its tenderness, its joys and fears,
To me the meanest flower that blows can give
Thoughts that do often lie too deep for tears.

William Wordsworth *Ode. Intimations of Immortality*, IX

22 O chestnut tree, great rooted blossomer,
Are you the leaf, the blossom or the bole?
O body swayed to music; O brightening glance,
How can we know the dancer from the dance?

W. B. Yeats (1865–1939) Irish poet. *Among School Children*

NAVY

See also boats, officers, sea, war

1 Ye Mariners of England
That guard our native seas,
Whose flag has braved, a thousand years,
The battle and the breeze –
Your glorious standard launch again
To match another foe!
And sweep through the deep,
While the stormy winds do blow, –
While the battle rages loud and long,
And the stormy winds do blow.

Thomas Campbell (1777–1844) British poet. *Ye Mariners of England*

2 Don't talk to me about naval tradition. It's nothing but rum, sodomy, and the lash.

Winston Churchill (1874–1965) British statesman. *Former Naval Person* (Sir Peter Gretton), Ch. 1

3 There were gentlemen and there were seamen in the navy of Charles the Second. But the seamen were not gentlemen; and the gentlemen were not seamen.

Lord Macaulay (1800–59) British historian. *History of England*, Vol. I, Ch. 3

4 The Fleet's lit up. It is like fairyland; the ships are covered with fairy lights.

Thomas Woodroofe (1899–1978) British radio broadcaster. Said during commentary at the Coronation Review of the Royal Navy, May 1937

NAZISM

See also fascism, Germany, Hitler, Jews, World War II

1 I herewith commission you to carry out all preparations with regard to...a *total solution* of the Jewish question, in those territories of Europe which are under German influence.

Hermann Goering (1893–1946) German leader. *The Rise and Fall of the Third Reich* (William Shirer)

2 For more than forty years I have selected my collaborators on the basis of their intelligence and their character and not on the basis of their grandmothers, and I am not willing for the rest of my life to change this method which I have found so good.

Fritz Haber (1868–1934) German physical chemist. Letter of resignation over the Nazis' demand that he dismiss his Jewish colleagues at the Kaizer Wilhelm Institute, 30 Apr 1933

3 *Kraft durch Freude.*
Strength through joy.

Robert Ley (1890–1945) German Nazi. German Labour Front slogan

4 The former allies had blundered in the past by offering Germany too little, and offering even that too late, until finally Nazi Germany had become a menace to all mankind.

Allan Nevins (1890–1971) US historian. *Current History*, May 1935

5 In Germany, the Nazis came for the Communists and I didn't speak up because I was not a Communist. Then they came for the Jews and I didn't speak up because I was not a Jew. Then they came for the trade unionists and I didn't speak up because I was not a trade unionist. Then they came for the Catholics and I was a Protestant so I didn't speak up. Then they came for me...By that time there was no one to speak up for anyone.

Martin Niemöller (1892–1984) German pastor. *Concise Dictionary of Religious Quotations* (W. Neil)

NECESSITY

1 Beggars can't be choosers.

Proverb

2 Necessity is the mother of invention.

Proverb

3 Needs must when the devil drives.

Proverb

4 Necessity is the plea for every infringement of human freedom. It is the argument of tyrants; it is the creed of slaves.

William Pitt the Younger (1759–1806) British statesman. Speech, House of Commons, 18 Nov 1783

5 O, reason not the need! Our basest beggars
Are in the poorest thing superfluous.
Allow not nature more than nature needs,
Man's life is cheap as beast's.

William Shakespeare (1564–1616) English dramatist. *King Lear*, II:4

6 Teach thy necessity to reason thus:
There is no virtue like necessity.

William Shakespeare *Richard II*, I:3

7 Necessity knows no law.

Publilius Syrus (1st century BC) Roman dramatist. Attrib.

8 I find no hint throughout the universe
Of good or ill, of blessing or of curse;
I find alone Necessity Supreme.

James Thomson (1834–82) British poet. *The City of Dreadful Night*, XIV

NEGLECT

1 A little neglect may breed mischief,...for want of a nail, the shoe was lost; for want of a shoe the horse was lost; and for want of a horse the rider was lost.

Benjamin Franklin (1706–90) US scientist and statesman. *Poor Richard's Almanack*

2 The general idea, of course, in any first-class laundry is to see that no shirt or collar ever comes back twice.

Stephen Leacock (1869–1944) English-born Canadian economist and humorist. *Winnowed Wisdom*, Ch. 6

3 The dust and silence of the upper shelf.

Lord Macaulay (1800–59) British historian. *Literary Essays Contributed to the 'Edinburgh Review'*, 'Milton'

4 What time he can spare from the adornment of his person he devotes to the neglect of his duties.

William Hepworth Thompson (1810–86) British academic. Referring to the Cambridge Professor of Greek, Sir Richard Jebb. *With Dearest Love to All* (M. R. Bobbit), Ch. 7

NEIGHBOURS

1 Love your neighbour, yet pull not down your hedge.

Proverb

2 Thou shalt love thy neighbour as thy self.

Bible: Matthew 22:39

3 My apple trees will never get across
And eat the cones under his pines, I tell him.
He only says, 'Good fences make good neighbours.'

Robert Frost (1875–1963) US poet. *North of Boston*, 'Mending Wall'

4 For it is your business, when the wall next door catches fire.

Horace (Quintus Horatius Flaccus; 65–8 BC) Roman poet. *Epistles*, I

NEPOTISM

1 I am against government by crony.

Harold L. Ickes (1874–1952) US Republican politician. Comment on his resignation as Secretary of the Interior (1946) after a dispute with President Truman

2 I can't see that it's wrong to give him a little legal experience before he goes out to practice law.

John Fitzgerald Kennedy (1917–63) US statesman. On being criticized for making his brother Robert attorney general. *Nobody Said It Better* (M. Ringo)

NEUROSIS

See also psychiatry, psychology

1 Neurosis has an absolute genius for malingering. There is no illness which it cannot counterfeit perfectly...If it is capable of deceiving the doctor, how should it fail to deceive the patient?

Marcel Proust (1871–1922) French novelist. *À la recherche du temps perdu: Le Côté de Guermantes*

2 Everything great in the world is done by neurotics; they alone founded our religions and created our masterpieces.

Marcel Proust *The Perpetual Pessimist* (Sagittarius and George)

3 Neurosis is the way of avoiding non-being by avoiding being.

Paul Tillich (1886–1965) German-born US theologian. *The Courage to Be*

NEWSPAPERS

See also editors, journalism

1 *The Times* has made many ministries.

Walter Bagehot (1826–77) British economist and journalist. *The English Constitution*, 'The Cabinet'

2 Deleted by French censor.

James Gordon Bennett (1841–1918) US newspaper owner and editor. Used to fill empty spaces in his papers during World War I when news was lacking. *Americans in Paris* (B. Morton)

3 Price of Herald three cents daily. Five cents Sunday. Bennett.

James Gordon Bennett Telegram to William Randolph Hearst, when he heard that Hearst was trying to buy his paper. *The Life and Death of the Press Barons* (P. Brandon)

4 Reading someone else's newspaper is like sleeping with someone else's wife. Nothing seems to be precisely in the right place, and when you find what you are looking for, it is not clear then how to respond to it.

Malcolm Bradbury (1932–) British academic and novelist. *Stepping Westward*, Bk. I, Ch. 1

5 *The Times* is speechless and takes three columns to express its speechlessness.

Winston Churchill (1874–1965) British statesman. Referring to Irish Home Rule. Speech, Dundee, 14 May 1908

6 I believe it has been said that one copy of *The Times* contains more useful information than the whole of the historical works of Thucydides.

Richard Cobden (1804–65) British politician. Speech, Manchester, 27 Dec 1850

7 Nothing is news until it has appeared in *The Times.*

Ralph Deakin (1888–1952) Foreign News Editor of *The Times*. Attrib.

8 And when it's gay priests, even the tabloids suddenly find they have a religious affairs correspondent.

David Hare (1947–) British playwright. *The Sunday Times*, 11 Feb 1990

9 All the news that's fit to print.

Adolph Simon Ochs (1858–1935) US newspaper publisher. The motto of the *New York Times*

10 Well, there are only two posh papers on a Sunday – the one you're reading and this one.

John Osborne (1929–94) British dramatist. *Look Back in Anger*, I

11 Written by office boys for office boys.

Marquess of Salisbury (1830–1903) British statesman. Reaction to the launch of the *Daily Mail*, 1896. *Northcliffe, an Intimate Biography* (Hamilton Fyfe), Ch. 4

12 They have been just as spiteful to me in the American press as the Soviet press was.

Alexander Solzhenitsyn (1918–) Russian novelist. *The Observer*, 'Sayings of the Week', 1 May 1994

13 The *Pall Mall Gazette* is written by gentlemen for gentlemen.

William Makepeace Thackeray (1811–63) British novelist. *Pendennis*, Ch. 32

14 '*The Beast* stands for strong mutually antagonistic governments everywhere', he said. 'Self-sufficiency at home, self-assertion abroad.'

Evelyn Waugh (1903–66) British novelist. *Scoop*, Bk. I, Ch. 1

15 News is what a chap who doesn't care much about anything wants to read. And it's only news until he's read it. After that it's dead.

Evelyn Waugh *Scoop*, Bk. I, Ch. 5

16 They were not so much published as carried screaming into the street.

H. G. Wells (1866–1946) British writer. *War In the Air*

NOBILITY

See also aristocracy, honour

1 There is surely a piece of divinity in us, something that was before the elements, and owes no homage unto the sun.

Thomas Browne (1605–82) English physician and writer. *Religio Medici*, Pt. II

2 *Noblesse oblige.*
Nobility has its own obligations.

Duc de Lévis (1764–1830) French writer and soldier. *Maximes et Réflexions*

3 The high sentiments always win in the end, the leaders who offer blood, toil, tears and sweat always get more out of their followers than those who offer safety and a good time. When it comes to the pinch, human beings are heroic.

George Orwell (Eric Blair; 1903–50) British novelist. *The Art of Donald McGill*

4 This was the noblest Roman of them all.
All the conspirators save only he
Did that they did in envy of great Caesar.

William Shakespeare (1564–1616) English dramatist. *Julius Caesar*, V:5

5 His life was gentle, and the elements
So mixed in him that Nature might stand up
And say to all the world, 'This was a man!'

William Shakespeare *Julius Caesar*, V:5

6 There is
One great society alone on earth:
The noble living and the noble dead.

William Wordsworth (1770–1850) British poet. *The Prelude*, XI

7 Thy soul was like a star, and dwelt apart.

William Wordsworth *Sonnets*, 'Milton! thou shouldst'

NONCOMMITMENT

1 We know what happens to people who stay in the middle of the road. They get run over.

Aneurin Bevan (1897–1960) British Labour politician. *The Observer*, 'Sayings of the Week', 9 Dec 1953

2 Let them eat the lie and swallow it with their bread. Whether the two were lovers or no, they'll have accounted to God for it by now. I have my own fish to fry.

Miguel de Cervantes (1547–1616) Spanish novelist. *Don Quixote*, Pt. I, Ch. 25

3 The Right Hon. gentleman has sat so long on the fence that the iron has entered his soul.

David Lloyd George (1863–1945) British Liberal statesman. Referring to Sir John Simon. Attrib.

NONSENSE

See also humour

1 If all the world were paper,
And all the sea were ink,
And all the trees were bread and cheese,
What should we do for drink?

Anonymous *If All the World were Paper*

2 If ever there was a case of clearer evidence than this of persons acting in concert together, this case is that case.

William Arabin (1773–1841) British judge. *Arabinesque at Law* (Sir R. Megarry)

3 The fleas that tease in the high Pyrenees.

Hilaire Belloc (1870–1953) French-born British poet. *Tarantella*

4 What happens to the hole when the cheese is gone?

Bertolt Brecht (1898–1956) German dramatist. *Mother Courage*, VI

5 Twinkle, twinkle, little bat!
How I wonder what you're at!
Up above the world you fly!
Like a teatray in the sky.

Lewis Carroll (Charles Lutwidge Dodgson; 1832–98) British writer. *Alice's Adventures in Wonderland*, Ch. 7

6 For the Snark *was* a Boojum, you see.

Lewis Carroll *The Hunting of the Snark*

7 'Twas brillig, and the slithy toves
Did gyre and gimble in the wabe;
All mimsy were the borogoves,
And the mome raths outgrabe.

Lewis Carroll *Through the Looking-Glass*, Ch. 1

8 Now, *here*, you see, it takes all the running *you* can do, to keep in the same place. If you want to get somewhere else, you must run at least twice as fast as that!

Lewis Carroll *Through the Looking-Glass*, Ch. 2

9 'The time has come,' the Walrus said,
'To talk of many things:
Of shoes – and ships – and sealing-wax –
Of cabbages – and kings –
And why the sea is boiling hot –
And whether pigs have wings.'

Lewis Carroll *Through the Looking-Glass*, Ch. 4

10 Colourless green ideas sleep furiously.

Noam Chomsky (1928–) US academic linguist. Used by Chomsky to demonstrate that an utterance can be grammatical without having meaning. *Syntactic Structures*

11 Go, and catch a falling star,
Get with child a mandrake root,
Tell me, where all past years are,
Or who cleft the Devil's foot.

John Donne (1573–1631) English poet. *Go and Catch a Falling Star*

12 So she went into the garden to cut a cabbage-leaf; to make an apple-pie; and at the same time a great she-bear, coming up the street, pops its head into the shop. 'What! no soap?' So he died, and she very imprudently married the barber; and there were present the Picninnies, and the Joblillies, and the Garyalies, and the grand Panjandrum himself, with the little round button at top, and they all fell to playing the game of catch as catch can, till the gun powder ran out at the heels of their boots.

Samuel Foote (1720–77) British actor and dramatist. Nonsense composed to test the actor Charles Macklin's claim that he could memorize anything.

13 If the man who turnips cries,
Cry not when his father dies,
'Tis a proof that he had rather
Have a turnip than his father.

Samuel Johnson (1709–84) British lexicographer. *Johnsonian Miscellanies* (ed. G. B. Hill), Vol. I

14 Three quarks for Muster Mark!

James Joyce (1882–1941) Irish novelist. The word quark has since been adopted by physicists for hypothetical elementary particles. *Finnegans Wake*

15 Lord Ronald said nothing; he flung himself from the room, flung himself upon his horse and rode madly off in all directions.

Stephen Leacock (1869–1944) English-born Canadian economist and humorist. *Nonsense Novels*, 'Gertrude the Governess'

16 On the Coast of Coromandel
Where the early pumpkins blow,
In the middle of the woods
Lived the Yonghy-Bonghy-Bò.

Edward Lear (1812–88) British artist and writer. *The Courtship of the Yonghy-Bonghy-Bò*

17 The Dong! – the Dong!
The wandering Dong through the forest goes!
The Dong! – the Dong!
The Dong with a luminous Nose!

Edward Lear *The Dong with a Luminous Nose*

18 Far and few, far and few,
Are the lands where the Jumblies live;
Their heads are green, and their hands are blue,
And they went to sea in a sieve.

Edward Lear *The Jumblies*

19 He has many friends, laymen and clerical.
Old Foss is the name of his cat:
His body is perfectly spherical,
He weareth a runcible hat.

Edward Lear *Nonsense Songs*, preface

20 The Owl and the Pussy-Cat went to sea
In a beautiful pea-green boat,
They took some honey, and plenty of money,
Wrapped up in a five-pound note.

Edward Lear *The Owl and the Pussy-Cat*

21 Serve up in a clean dish, and throw the whole out of the window as fast as possible.

Edward Lear *To make an Amblongus Pie*

22 As I was going up the stair
I met a man who wasn't there.
He wasn't there again to-day.
I wish, I wish he'd stay away.

Hughes Mearns (1875–1965) US writer. *The Psychoed*

23 I'm walking backwards till Christmas.

Spike Milligan (1918–) British comic actor and author. *The Goon Show*

NORMALITY

1 She always says she dislikes the abnormal, it is so obvious. She says the normal is so much more simply complicated and interesting.

Gertrude Stein (1874–1946) US writer. *The Autobiography of Alice B. Toklas*

2 My suit is pale yellow. My nationality is French, and my normality has been often subject to question.

Tennessee Williams (1911–83) US dramatist. *Camino Real*, Block 4

NOSTALGIA

See also homesickness, memory, past, regret

1 Were we closer to the ground as children, or is the grass emptier now?

Alan Bennett (1934–) British playwright. *Forty Years On*

2 Play it, Sam. Play 'As Time Goes By.'

Humphrey Bogart (1899–1957) US film star. Often misquoted as 'Play it again, Sam'. *Casablanca*

3 Stands the Church clock at ten to three?
And is there honey still for tea?

Rupert Brooke (1887–1915) British poet. *The Old Vicarage, Grantchester*

4 John Anderson my jo, John,
When we were first acquent,
Your locks were like the raven,
Your bonnie brow was brent.

Robert Burns (1759–96) Scottish poet. *John Anderson My Jo*

5 The 'good old times' – all times when old are good –
Are gone.

Lord Byron (1788–1824) British poet. *The Age of Bronze*, I

6 Nothing recalls the past so potently as a smell.

Winston Churchill (1874–1965) British statesman. *My Early Life*

7 What peaceful hours I once enjoyed!
How sweet their memory still!
But they have left an aching void
The world can never fill.

William Cowper (1731–1800) British poet. *Olney Hymns*, 1

8 I'm sitting on the stile, Mary,
Where we sat, side by side.

Countess of Dufferin (1807–67) British poet. *Lament of the Irish Emigrant*

9 I remember, I remember,
The house where I was born,
The little window where the sun
Came peeping in at morn;
He never came a wink too soon,
Nor brought too long a day,
But now, I often wish the night
Had borne my breath away!

Thomas Hood (1799–1845) British poet. *I Remember*

10 Into my heart an air that kills
From yon far country blows:
What are those blue remembered hills,
What spires, what farms are those?

A. E. Housman (1859–1936) British scholar and poet. *A Shropshire Lad*, 'The Welsh Marches'

11 With rue my heart is laden
For golden friends I had,
For many a rose-lipt maiden
And many a lightfoot lad.

A. E. Housman *A Shropshire Lad*, 'The Welsh Marches'

12 I have had playmates, I have had companions
In my days of childhood, in my joyful schooldays –
All, all are gone, the old familiar faces.

Charles Lamb (1775–1834) British essayist. *The Old Familiar Faces*

13 For love that time was not as love is nowadays.

Thomas Malory (1400–71) English writer. *Morte d'Arthur*, Bk. XX, Ch. 3

14 Oft in the stilly night,
Ere Slumber's chain has bound me,
Fond Memory brings the light
Of other days around me;
The smiles, the tears,
Of boyhood's years,
The words of love then spoken;
The eyes that shone,
Now dimmed and gone,

The cheerful hearts now broken!

Thomas Moore (1779–1852) Irish poet. *National Airs*, 'Oft in the Stilly Night'

15 Fings Ain't Wot They Used T'Be.

Frank Norman (1931–80) British dramatist and broadcaster. Title of musical

16 Before the war, and especially before the Boer War, it was summer all the year round.

George Orwell (Eric Blair; 1903–50) British novelist. *Coming Up for Air*, Pt. II, Ch. 1

17 They spend their time mostly looking forward to the past.

John Osborne (1929–94) British dramatist. *Look Back in Anger*, II:1

18 Come to me in the silence of the night;
Come in the speaking silence of a dream;
Come with soft rounded cheeks and eyes as bright
As sunlight on a stream;
Come back in tears,
O memory, hope, love of finished years.

Christina Rossetti (1830–74) British poet. *Echo*

19 For now I see the true old times are dead,
When every morning brought a noble chance,
And every chance brought out a noble knight.

Alfred, Lord Tennyson (1809–92) British poet. *Idylls of the King*, 'The Passing of Arthur'

20 Dear as remembered kisses after death,
And sweet as those by hopeless fancy feign'd
On lips that are for others: deep as love,
Deep as first love, and wild with all regret;
O Death in Life, the days that are no more.

Alfred, Lord Tennyson *The Princess*, IV

21 And the stately ships go on
To their haven under the hill;
But O for the touch of a vanish'd hand,
And the sound of a voice that is still!

Alfred, Lord Tennyson *Break, Break, Break*

22 *Mais où sont les neiges d'antan?*
But where are the snows of yesteryear?

François Villon (1431–85) French poet. *Ballade des dames du temps jadis*

23 Where are the boys of the Old Brigade?

Frederic Edward Weatherly (1848–1929) British lawyer and songwriter. *The Old Brigade*

24 Sweet childish days, that were as long
As twenty days are now.

William Wordsworth (1770–1850) British poet. *To a Butterfly, I've Watched you now*

NOTHING

1 Nothing can be created out of nothing.

Lucretius (Titus Lucretius Carus; c. 99–55 BC) Roman philosopher. *On the Nature of the Universe*, I

2 Nothing will come of nothing. Speak again.

William Shakespeare (1564–1616) English dramatist. *King Lear*, I:1

NOVELS

See also books, criticism, fiction, literature, writers, writing

1 My scrofulous French novel
On grey paper with blunt type!

Robert Browning (1812–89) British poet. *Soliloquy of the Spanish Cloister*

2 A good novel tells us the truth about its hero; but a bad novel tells us the truth about its author.

G. K. Chesterton (1874–1936) British writer. *Heretics*, Ch. 15

3 When I want to read a novel I write one.

Benjamin Disraeli (1804–81) British statesman. Attrib.

4 Yes – oh dear, yes – the novel tells a story.

E. M. Forster (1879–1970) British novelist. *Aspects of the Novel*, Ch. 2

5 The romance of *Tom Jones*, that exquisite picture of human manners, will outlive the palace of the Escurial and the imperial eagle of the house of Austria.

Edward Gibbon (1737–94) British historian. *Autobiography*

6 Historians tell the story of the past, novelists the story of the present.

Edmond de Goncourt (1822–96) French novelist. *Journal*

7 The only obligation to which in advance we may hold a novel, without incurring the accusation of being arbitrary, is that it be interesting.

Henry James (1843–1916) US novelist. *Partial Portraits*, 'The Art of Fiction'

8 Far too many relied on the classic formula of a beginning, a muddle, and an end.

Philip Larkin (1922–85) British poet. Referring to modern novels. *New Fiction*, 15 (January 1978)

9 I am a man, and alive...For this reason I am a novelist. And being a novelist, I consider myself superior to the saint, the scientist, the philosopher, and the poet, who are all great masters of different bits of man alive, but never get the whole hog.

D. H. Lawrence (1885–1930) British novelist. *Phoenix*, 'Why the Novel Matters'

10 I would sooner read a time-table or a catalogue than nothing at all. They are much more entertaining than half the novels that are written.

W. Somerset Maugham (1874–1965) British novelist. *The Summing Up*

11 An interviewer asked me what book I thought best represented the modern American woman. All I could think of to answer was: *Madame Bovary*.

Mary McCarthy (1912–89) US novelist. *On the Contrary*

12 People think that because a novel's invented, it isn't true. Exactly the reverse is the case. Biography and memoirs can never be wholly true, since they cannot include every conceivable circumstance of what happened. The novel can do that.

Anthony Powell (1905–) British novelist. *A Dance to the Music of Time: Hearing Secret Harmonies*, Ch. 3

13 The detective novel is the art-for-art's-sake of yawning Philistinism.

V. S. Pritchett (1900–) British short-story writer. *Books in General*, 'The Roots of Detection'

14 It is the sexless novel that should be distinguished: the sex novel is now normal.

George Bernard Shaw (1856–1950) Irish dramatist and critic. *Table-Talk of G.B.S.*

15 A novel is a mirror walking along a main road.

Stendhal (Henri Beyle; 1783–1842) French novelist. *Le Rouge et le noir*, Ch. 49

16 A novel is a static thing that one moves through; a play is a dynamic thing that moves past one.

Kenneth Tynan (1927–80) British theatre critic. *Curtains*

17 The novel being dead, there is no point to writing made-up stories. Look at the French who will not and the Americans who cannot.

Gore Vidal (1925–) US novelist. *Myra Breckinridge*, Ch. 2

NOVELTY

See also conservatism, innovation, progress

1 All the rivers run into the sea; yet the sea is not full; unto the place from whence the rivers come, thither they return again.
All things are full of labour; man cannot utter it: the eye is not satisfied with seeing, nor the ear filled with hearing.
The thing that hath been, it is that which shall be; and that which is done is that which shall be done: and there is no new thing under the sun.

Bible: Ecclesiastes 1:7–9

2 Most of the change we think we see in life
Is due to truths being in and out of favour.

Robert Frost (1875–1963) US poet. *The Black Cottage*

3 There are three things which the public will always clamour for, sooner or later: namely, Novelty, novelty, novelty.

Thomas Hood (1799–1845) British poet. Announcement of *Comic Annual*, 1836

4 It is the customary fate of new truths to begin as heresies and to end as superstitions.

T. H. Huxley (1825–95) British biologist. *The Coming of Age of the Origin of Species*

5 New opinions are always suspected, and usually opposed, without any other reason but because they are not already common.

John Locke (1632–1704) English philosopher. *An Essay Concerning Human Understanding*, dedicatory epistle

6 Rummidge...had lately suffered the mortifying fate of most English universities of its type (civic redbrick): having competed strenuously for fifty years with two universities chiefly valued for being old, it was, at the moment of drawing level, rudely overtaken in popularity and prestige by a batch of universities chiefly valued for being new.

David Lodge (1935–) British author. *Changing Places*, Ch. 1

7 There are no new truths, but only truths that have not been recognized by those who have perceived them without noticing.

Mary McCarthy (1912–89) US novelist. *On the Contrary*

8 There is always something new out of Africa.

Pliny the Elder (Gaius Plinius Secundus; 23–79 AD) Roman scholar. *Natural History*, VIII

9 All great truths begin as blasphemies.

George Bernard Shaw (1856–1950) Irish dramatist and critic. *Annajanska*

10 If we do not find anything pleasant, at least we shall find something new.

Voltaire (François-Marie Arouet; 1694–1778) French writer. *Candide*, Ch. 17

NUCLEAR WEAPONS

See also weapons

1 Now we are all sons of bitches.

Kenneth Bainbridge (1904–) US physicist. After the first atomic test. *The Decision to Drop the Bomb*

2 If you carry this resolution and follow out all its implications and do not run away from it you will send a Foreign Minister, whoever he may be, naked into the conference chamber.

Aneurin Bevan (1897–1960) British Labour politician. Opposing a motion advocating unilateral nuclear disarmament. Speech, Labour Party Conference, 3 Oct 1957

3 The way to win an atomic war is to make certain it never starts.

Omar Nelson Bradley (1893–1981) US general. *The Observer*, 'Sayings of the Week', 20 Apr 1952

4 The Bomb brought peace but man alone can keep that peace.

Winston Churchill (1874–1965) British statesman. Speech, House of Commons, 16 Aug 1945

5 If only I had known, I should have become a watchmaker.

Albert Einstein (1879–1955) German-born US physicist. Reflecting on his role in the development of the atom bomb. *New Statesman*, 16 Apr 1965

6 Surely the right course is to test the Russians, not the bombs.

Hugh Gaitskell (1906–63) British Labour politician. *Observer*, 'Sayings of the Week', 23 June 1957

7 We thus denounce the false and dangerous programme of the arms race, of the secret rivalry between peoples for military superiority.

John Paul II (Karol Wojtyla; 1920–) Polish pope (1978–). *The Observer*, 'Sayings of the Week', 19 Dec 1976

8 Preparing for suicide is not a very intelligent means of defence.

Bruce Kent (1929–) British campaigner for nuclear

disarmament. *The Observer*, 'Sayings of the Week', 10 Aug 1986

9 Hitherto man had to live with the idea of death as an individual; from now onward mankind will have to live with the idea of its death as a species.

Arthur Koestler (1905–83) Hungarian-born British writer. Referring to the development of the atomic bomb. *Peter's Quotations* (Laurence J. Peter)

10 The statesmen of the world who boast and threaten that they have Doomsday weapons are far more dangerous, and far more estranged from 'reality', than many of the people on whom the label 'psychotic' is affixed.

R. D. Laing (1927–89) British psychiatrist. *The Divided Self*, Preface

11 At first it was a giant column that soon took the shape of a supramundane mushroom.

William L. Laurence (1888–1977) US journalist. Referring to the explosion of the first atomic bomb, over Hiroshima, 6 Aug 1945. *The New York Times*, 26 Sept 1945

12 The atom bomb is a paper tiger which the United States reactionaries use to scare people.

Mao Tse-Tung (1893–1976) Chinese communist leader. Interview, Aug 1946

13 As a military man who has given half a century of active service, I say in all sincerity that the nuclear arms race has no military purpose. Wars cannot be fought with nuclear weapons; their existence only adds to our perils because of the illusions which they have generated.

Louis Mountbatten of Burma (1900–79) British admiral and colonial administrator. Speech, Strasbourg, 11 May 1979

14 We knew the world would not be the same.

J. Robert Oppenheimer (1904–67) US physicist. After the first atomic test. *The Decision to Drop the Bomb*

15 It was on this issue, the nuclear defence of Britain, on which I left the Labour Party, and on this issue I am prepared to stake my entire political career.

David Owen (1938–) British politician. *The Observer*, 'Sayings of the Week', 9 Nov 1986

16 To adopt nuclear disarmament would be akin to behaving like a virgin in a brothel.

David Penhaligon (1944–86) British politician. *The Guardian*, 1980

17 You may reasonably expect a man to walk a tightrope safely for ten minutes; it would be unreasonable to do so without accident for two hundred years.

Bertrand Russell (1872–1970) British philosopher. On the subject of nuclear war between the USA and the Soviets. *The Tightrope Men* (D. Bagley)

18 There is no evil in the atom; only in men's souls.

Adlai Stevenson (1900–65) US statesman. Speech, Hartford, Connecticut, 18 Sept 1952

19 For Hon. Members opposite the deterrent is a phallic symbol. It convinces them that they are men.

George Wigg (1900–76) British politician. *The Observer*, 'Sayings of the Week', 8 Mar 1964

NUMBERS

See also mathematics, statistics

1 Round numbers are always false.

Samuel Johnson (1709–84) British lexicographer. *Life of Johnson* (J. Boswell), Vol. III

2 No, I don't know his telephone number. But it was up in the high numbers.

John Maynard Keynes (1883–1946) British economist. Attrib.

3 No, it is a very interesting number, it is the smallest number expressible as a sum of two cubes in two different ways.

Srinivasa Ramanujan (1887–1920) Indian mathematician. The mathematician G. H. Hardy had referred to the number – 1729 as 'dull'. *Collected Papers of Srinivasa Ramanujan*

4 Oh, quite easy! The Septuagint minus the Apostles.

Arthur Woollgar Verrall (1851–1912) British classicist. Reply to a person who thought the number 58 difficult to remember

NURSERY RHYMES

A selection is given here. The form used is that most commonly used today – not the one in the original publication.

1 A frog he would a-wooing go,
Heigh ho! says Rowley,
A frog he would a-wooing go,
Whether his mother would let him or no.
With a rowley, powley, gammon and spinach,
Heigh ho! says Anthony Rowley.

Melismata (Thomas Ravenscroft)

2 All the birds of the air
Fell a-sighing and a-sobbing,
When they heard the bell toll
For poor Cock Robin.

Tommy Thumb's Pretty Song Book

3 As I was going to St Ives,
I met a man with seven wives.
Each wife had seven sacks
Each sack had seven cats,
Each cat had seven kits,
How many were going to St Ives?

Mother Goose's Quarto

4 Baa, baa, black sheep,
Have you any wool?
Yes, sir, yes, sir,
Three bags full;
One for the master,
And one for the dame,
And one for the little boy
Who lives down the lane.

Tommy Thumb's Pretty Song Book

5 Bobby Shafto's gone to sea,

Silver buckles on his knee;
He'll come back and marry me,
Bonny Bobby Shafto!
Songs for the Nursery

6 Boys and girls come out to play,
The moon doth shine as bright as day.
Useful Transactions in Philosophy (William King)

7 Come, let's to bed
Says Sleepy-head;
Tarry a while, says Slow;
Put on the pan;
Says Greedy Nan,
Let's sup before we go.
Gammer Gurton's Garland (R. Christopher)

8 Curly locks, Curly locks,
Wilt thou be mine?
Thou shalt not wash dishes
Nor yet feed the swine,
But sit on a cushion
And sew a fine seam,
And feed upon strawberries,
Sugar and cream
Infant Institutes

9 Ding dong, bell,
Pussy's in the well.
Who put her in?
Little Johnny Green.
Who pulled her out?
Little Tommy Stout.
Mother Goose's Melody

10 Doctor Foster went to Gloucester
In a shower of rain:
He stepped in a puddle,
Right up to his middle,
And never went there again.
The Nursery Rhymes of England (J. O. Halliwell)

11 Eena, meena, mina, mo,
Catch a nigger by his toe;
If he hollers, let him go,
Eena, meena, mina, mo.
Games and Songs of American Children (Newell)

12 Georgie Porgie, pudding and pie,
Kissed the girls and made them cry;
When the boys came out to play,
Georgie Porgie ran away.
The Nursery Rhymes of England (J. O. Halliwell)

13 Goosey, goosey gander,
Whither shall I wander?
Upstairs and downstairs
And in my lady's chamber.
Gammer Gurton' Garland

14 Hey diddle diddle,
The cat and the fiddle,
The cow jumped over the moon;
The little dog laughed
To see such sport,
And the dish ran away with the spoon.
Mother Goose's Melody

15 Hickory, dickory, dock,
The mouse ran up the clock.
The clock struck one,
The mouse ran down,
Hickory, dickory, dock.
Tommy Thumb's Pretty Song Book

16 Hot cross buns!
Hot cross buns!
One a penny, two a penny,
Hot cross buns!
Christmas Box

17 How many miles to Babylon?
Three score miles and ten.
Can I get there by candle-light?
Yes, and back again.
If your heels are nimble and light,
You may get there by candle-light.
Songs for the Nursery

18 Humpty Dumpty sat on a wall,
Humpty Dumpty had a great fall.
All the king's horses,
And all the king's men,
Couldn't put Humpty together again.
Gammer Gurton's Garland

19 Hush-a-bye, baby, on the tree top,
When the wind blows the cradle will rock;
When the bough breaks the cradle will fall,
Down will come baby, cradle, and all.
Mother Goose's Melody

20 I had a little nut tree,
Nothing would it bear
But a silver nutmeg
And a golden pear;
The King of Spain's daughter
Came to visit me,
And all for the sake
Of my little nut tree.
Newest Christmas Box

21 I had a little pony,
His name was Dapple Grey;
I lent him to a lady
To ride a mile away.
She whipped him, she lashed him,
She rode him through the mire;
I would not lend my pony now,
For all the lady's hire.
Poetical Alphabet

22 I love sixpence, jolly little sixpence,
I love sixpence better than my life;
I spent a penny of it, I lent a penny of it,
And I took fourpence home to my wife.
Gammer Gurton's Garland

23 I'm the king of the castle,
Get down you dirty rascal.
Brand's Popular Antiquities

24 Jack and Jill went up the hill
To fetch a pail of water;
Jack fell down and broke his crown,
And Jill came tumbling after.
Mother Goose's Melody

25 Jack Sprat could eat no fat,
His wife could eat no lean,
And so between them both you see,
They licked the platter clean.
Paroemiologia Anglo-Latina (John Clark)

26 Ladybird, ladybird,
Fly away home,
Your house is on fire
And your children all gone.
Tommy Thumb's Pretty Song Book

27 Little Bo-peep has lost her sheep,
And can't tell where to find them;
Leave them alone, and they'll come home,
Bringing their tails behind them.
Gammer Gurton's Garland

28 Little Boy Blue,
Come blow your horn,
The sheep's in the meadow,
The cow's in the corn.
Famous Tommy Thumb's Little Story Book

29 Little Jack Horner
Sat in the corner,
Eating a Christmas pie;
He put in his thumb,
And pulled out a plum,
And said, What a good boy am I!
Namby Pamby (Henry Carey)

30 Little Miss Muffet
Sat on a tuffet,
Eating her curds and whey;
There came a big spider,
Who sat down beside her
And frightened Miss Muffet away.
Songs for the Nursery

31 Little Tommy Tucker,
Sings for his supper:
What shall we give him?
White bread and butter
How shall he cut it
Without a knife?
How will be be married
Without a wife?
Tommy Thumb's Pretty Song Book

32 London Bridge is falling down,
My fair lady.
Namby Pamby (Henry Carey)

33 Mary, Mary, quite contrary,
How does your garden grow?
With silver bells and cockle shells,
And pretty maids all in a row.
Tom Thumb's Pretty Song Book

34 Monday's child is fair of face,
Tuesday's child is full of grace,
Wednesday's child is full of woe,
Thursday's child has far to go,
Friday's child is loving and giving,
Saturday's child works hard for his living,
And the child that is born on the Sabbath day
Is bonny and blithe, and good and gay.
Traditions of Devonshire (A. E. Bray)

35 My mother said that I never should
Play with the gypsies in the wood;
If I did, she would say,
Naughty girl to disobey.
Come Hither (Walter de la Mare)

36 Old Mother Hubbard
Went to the cupboard,
To fetch her poor dog a bone;
But when she got there
The cupboard was bare
And so the poor dog had none.
The Comic Adventures of Old Mother Hubbard and Her Dog

37 One, two,
Buckle my shoe;
Three, four,
Knock at the door.
Songs for the Nursery

38 Pat-a-cake, pat-a-cake, baker's man,
Bake me a cake as fast as you can;
Pat it and prick it, and mark it with B,
Put it in the oven for baby and me.
The Campaigners (Tom D'Urfey)

39 Peter Piper picked a peck of pickled pepper;
A peck of pickled pepper Peter Piper picked;
If Peter Piper picked a peck of pickled pepper,
Where's the peck of pickled pepper Peter Piper picked?
Peter Piper's Practical Principles of Plain and Perfect Pronunciation

40 Polly put the kettle on,
Polly put the kettle on,
Polly put the kettle on,
We'll all have tea.
Sukey take it off again,
Sukey take it off again,
Sukey take it off again,
They've all gone away.
Traditional

41 Pussy cat, pussy cat, where have you been?
I've been to London to look at the queen.
Pussy cat, pussy cat, what did you there?
I frightened a little mouse under her chair.
Songs for the Nursery

42 Ride a cock-horse to Banbury Cross,
To see a fine lady upon a white horse;
Rings on her fingers and bells on her toes,
And she shall have music wherever she goes.
Gammer Gurton's Garland

43 Ring-a-ring o'roses,
A pocket full of posies,
A-tishoo! A-tishoo!
We all fall down.
Mother Goose (Kate Greenaway)

44 Round and round the garden
Like a teddy bear;
One step, two step,
Tickle you under there!
Traditional

45 Rub-a-dub-dub,

Three men in a tub,
And who do you think they be?
The butcher, the baker,
The candlestick-maker,
And they all sailed out to sea.

Christmas Box

46 See-saw, Margery Daw,
Jacky shall have a new master;
Jacky shall have but a penny a day,
Because he can't work any faster.

Mother Goose's Melody

47 Simple Simon met a pieman,
Going to the fair;
Says Simple Simon to the pieman,
Let me taste your ware.
Says the pieman to Simple Simon,
Show me first your penny;
Says Simple Simon to the pieman,
Indeed I have not any.

Simple Simon (Chapbook Advertisement)

48 Sing a song of sixpence,
A pocket full of rye;
Four and twenty blackbirds,
Baked in a pie.
When the pie was opened,
The birds began to sing;
Wasn't that a dainty dish,
To set before the king?

The king was in his counting-house,
Counting out his money;
The queen was in the parlour,
Eating bread and honey.
The maid was in the garden,
Hanging out the clothes,
When down came a blackbird,
And pecked off her nose.

Tommy Thumb's Pretty Song Book

49 Solomon Grundy,
Born on a Monday,
Christened on Tuesday,
Married on Wednesday,
Took ill on Thursday,
Worse on Friday,
Died on Saturday,
Buried on Sunday.
This is the end
Of Solomon Grundy.

The Nursery Rhymes of England (J. O. Halliwell)

50 The lion and the unicorn
Were fighting for the crown;
The lion beat the unicorn
All round about the town.

Useful Transactions in Philosophy (William King)

51 The Queen of Hearts
She made some tarts,
All on a summer's day;
The Knave of Hearts
He stole the tarts,
And took them clean away.

The European Magazine

52 There was a crooked man, and he walked a crooked mile,
He found a crooked sixpence against a crooked stile:
He bought a crooked cat, which caught a crooked mouse,
And they all lived together in a little crooked house.

The Nursery Rhymes of England (J. O. Halliwell)

53 There was an old woman
Lived under a hill,
And if she's not gone
She lives there still.

Academy of Complements

54 There was an old woman who lived in a shoe,
She had so many children she didn't know what to do;
She gave them some broth without any bread;
She whipped them all soundly and put them to bed.

Gammer Gurton's Garland

55 The twelfth day of Christmas,
My true love sent to me
Twelve lords a-leaping,
Eleven ladies dancing,
Ten pipers piping,
Nine drummers drumming,
Eight maids a-milking,
Seven swans a-swimming,
Six geese a-laying,
Five gold rings,
Four colly birds,
Three French hens,
Two turtle doves, and
A partridge in a pear tree.

Mirth without Mischief

56 Thirty days hath September,
April, June, and November;
All the rest have thirty-one,
Excepting February alone
And that has twenty-eight days clear
And twenty-nine in each leap year.

Abridgement of the Chronicles of England (Richard Grafton)

57 This is the farmer sowing his corn,
That kept the cock that crowed in the morn,
That waked the priest all shaven and shorn,
That married the man all tattered and torn,
That kissed the maiden all forlorn,
That milked the cow with the crumpled horn,
That tossed the dog,
That worried the cat,
That killed the rat,
That ate the corn,
That lay in the house that Jack built.

Nurse Truelove's New-Year-Gift

58 This little piggy went to market,
This little piggy stayed at home,
This little piggy had roast beef,
This little piggy had none,
And this little piggy cried, Wee-wee-wee-wee-wee,
I can't find my way home.

The Famous Tommy Thumb's Little Story Book

59 Three blind mice, see how they run!

They all run after the farmer's wife,
Who cut off their tails with a carving knife,
Did you ever see such a thing in your life,
As three blind mice?

Deuteromelia (Thomas Ravenscroft)

60 Tinker,
Tailor,
Soldier,
Sailor,
Rich man,
Poor man,
Beggarman,
Thief.

Popular Rhymes and Nursery Tales (J. O. Halliwell)

61 Tom, he was a piper's son,
He learnt to play when he was young,
And all the tune that he could play
Was 'Over the hills and far away'.

Tom, The Piper's Son

62 Tom, Tom, the piper's son,
Stole a pig and away he run;
The pig was eat
And Tom was beat,
And Tom went howling down the street.

Tom, The Piper's Son

63 Two little dicky birds,
Sitting on a wall;
One named Peter,
The other named Paul,
Fly away, Peter!
Fly away, Paul!
Come back, Peter!
Come back, Paul!

Mother Goose's Melody

64 Wee Willie Winkie runs through the town
upstairs and downstairs and in his nightgown,
Rapping at the window, crying through the lock,
Are the children all in their beds? It's past eight o'clock.

In *Whistle-Binkie* (W. Miller)

65 What are little boys made of?
Frogs and snails
And puppy-dogs' tails,
That's what little boys are made of.
What are little girls made of?
Sugar and spice
And all that's nice,
That's what little girls are made of.

Nursery Rhymes (J. O. Halliwell)

66 Where are you going to, my pretty maid?
I'm going a-milking, sir, she said.

Archaeologia Cornu-Britannica (William Pryce)

67 What is your fortune, my pretty maid?
My face is my fortune, sir, she said.
Then I can't marry you, my pretty maid.
Nobody asked you, sir, she said.

Archaeologia Cornu-Britannica (William Pryce)

68 Who killed Cock Robin?
I, said the Sparrow,
With my bow and arrow,
I killed Cock Robin.
Who saw him die?
I, said the Fly,
With my little eye,
I saw him die.

Tommy Thumb's Pretty Song Book

69 Yankee Doodle came to town,
Riding on a pony;
He stuck a feather in his cap
And called it macaroni.

Gammer Gurton's Garland

O

OBEDIENCE

1 Children, obey your parents in the Lord: for this is right.
Bible: Ephesians 6:1

2 'She still seems to me in her own way a person born to command,' said Luce...
'I wonder if anyone is born to obey,' said Isabel.
'That may be why people command rather badly, that
they have no suitable material to work on.'
Ivy Compton-Burnett (1892–1969) British novelist. *Parents and Children*, Ch. 3

3 It is much safer to obey than to rule.
Thomas à Kempis (Thomas Hemmerken; c. 1380–1471) German monk. *The Imitation of Christ*, I

4 'Forward the Light Brigade!'
Was there a man dismay'd?
Not tho' the soldier knew
Some one had blunder'd:
Their's not to make reply,
Their's not to reason why,
Their's but to do and die:
Into the valley of Death
Rode the six hundred.
Alfred, Lord Tennyson (1809–92) British poet. *The Charge of the Light Brigade*

OBESITY

See also food, greed

1 Outside every fat man there is an even fatter man trying to close in.
Kingsley Amis (1922–95) British novelist. *See also* CONNOLLY, ORWELL. *One Fat Englishman*, Ch. 3

2 Who's your fat friend?
'Beau' Brummel (George Bryan Brummell; 1778–1840) British dandy. Referring to George, Prince of Wales. *Reminiscences* (Gronow)

3 Just the other day in the Underground I enjoyed the pleasure of offering my seat to three ladies.
G. K. Chesterton (1874–1936) British writer. Suggesting that fatness had its consolations. *Das Buch des Lachens* (W. Scholz)

4 I want to reassure you I am not this size, really – dear me no, I'm being amplified by the mike.
G. K. Chesterton At a lecture in Pittsburgh. *The Outline of Sanity: A Life of G. K. Chesterton* (S. D. Dale)

5 Imprisoned in every fat man a thin one is wildly signalling to be let out.
Cyril Connolly (1903–74) British journalist. *See also* AMIS, ORWELL. *The Unquiet Grave*

6 O fat white woman whom nobody loves,
Why do you walk through the fields in gloves...
Missing so much and so much?
F. M. Cornford (1886–1960) British poet. *To a Fat Lady Seen from a Train*

7 I see no objection to stoutness, in moderation.
W. S. Gilbert (1836–1911) British dramatist. *Iolanthe*, I

8 I'm fat, but I'm thin inside. Has it ever struck you that there's a thin man inside every fat man, just as they say there's a statue inside every block of stone?
George Orwell (Eric Blair; 1903–50) British novelist. *See also* AMIS, CONNOLLY. *Coming Up For Air*, Pt. I, Ch. 3

9 My advice if you insist on slimming: Eat as much as you like – just don't swallow it.
Harry Secombe (1921–) Welsh singer, actor, and comedian. *Daily Herald*, 5 Oct 1962

10 Falstaff sweats to death
And lards the lean earth as he walks along.
William Shakespeare (1564–1616) English dramatist. *Henry IV, Part One*, II:2

11 I have more flesh than another man, and therefore more frailty.
William Shakespeare *Henry IV, Part One*, III:3

12 She fitted into my biggest armchair as if it had been built round her by someone who knew they were wearing armchairs tight about the hips that season.
P. G. Wodehouse (1881–1975) British humorous novelist. *My Man Jeeves*, 'Jeeves and the Unbidden Guest'

13 The Right Hon. was a tubby little chap who looked as if he had been poured into his clothes and had forgotten to say 'When!'
P. G. Wodehouse *Very Good Jeeves!*, 'Jeeves and the Impending Doom'

OBITUARIES

See also death, epitaphs, memorials

1 With the newspaper strike on I wouldn't consider it.
Bette Davis (Ruth Elizabeth Davis; 1908–89) US film star. When told that a rumour was spreading that she had died. *Book of Lists* (I. Wallace)

2 I've just read that I am dead. Don't forget to delete me from your list of subscribers.
Rudyard Kipling (1865–1936) Indian-born British writer. Writing to a magazine that had mistakenly published an announcement of his death. *Anekdotenschatz* (H. Hoffmeister)

3 In these days a man is nobody unless his biography is kept so far posted up that it may be ready for the national breakfast-table on the morning after his demise.
Anthony Trollope (1815–82) British novelist. *Doctor Thorne*, Ch. 25

4 Reports of my death are greatly exaggerated.
Mark Twain (Samuel Langhorne Clemens; 1835–1910) US writer. On learning that his obituary had been published. Cable to the Associated Press

OBJECTIVITY

See also perspective, subjectivity

1 *Sir Roger* told them, 'with the air of a man who would not give his judgment rashly, that 'much might be said on both sides'.
Joseph Addison (1672–1719) British essayist. Sir Roger de Coverley was a fictional archetype of the old-fashioned and eccentric country squire. *The Spectator*, 122

2 Thus I live in the world rather as a Spectator of mankind, than as one of the species, by which means I have made myself a speculative statesman, soldier, merchant, and artisan, without ever meddling with any practical part of life.
Joseph Addison *The Spectator*, 1

3 Only reason can convince us of those three fundamental truths without a recognition of which there can be no effective liberty: that what we believe is not necessarily true; that what we like is not necessarily good; and that all questions are open.
Clive Bell (1881–1964) British art critic. *Civilization*, Ch. 5

4 I am a camera with its shutter open, quite passive, recording, not thinking.
Christopher Isherwood (1904–86) British novelist. *Goodbye to Berlin*

5 The man who sees both sides of a question is a man who sees absolutely nothing at all.
Oscar Wilde (1854–1900) Irish-born British dramatist. *The Critic as Artist*, Pt. 2

OBLIGATION

See also duty

1 The debt which cancels all others.
Charles Caleb Colton (?1780–1832) British clergyman and writer. *Lacon*, Vol. II

2 It is the nature of men to be bound by the benefits they confer as much as by those they receive.
Machiavelli (1469–1527) Italian statesman. *The Prince*

OBLIVION

1 Many brave men lived before Agamemnon's time; but they are all, unmourned and unknown, covered by the long night, because they lack their sacred poet.
Horace (Quintus Horatius Flaccus; 65–8 BC) Roman poet. *Odes*, IV

2 No, no, go not to Lethe, neither twist
Wolf's-bane, tight-rooted, for its poisonous wine.
John Keats (1795–1821) British poet. *Ode on Melancholy*

3 Annihilating all that's made
To a green thought in a green shade.
Andrew Marvell (1621–78) English poet. *The Garden*

OBSESSIONS

1 I have three phobias which, could I mute them, would make my life as slick as a sonnet, but as dull as ditch water: I hate to go to bed, I hate to get up, and I hate to be alone.
Tallulah Bankhead (1903–68) US actress. *Tallulah*, Ch. 1

2 *Papyromania* – compulsive accumulation of papers...
Papyrophobia – abnormal desire for 'a clean desk'.
Laurence J. Peter (1919–90) Canadian writer. *The Peter Principle*, Glossary

OBSTRUCTION

1 I'll put a spoke among your wheels.
Francis Beaumont (1584–1616) English dramatist. *The Mad Lover*, III:6

2 If any of you know cause, or just impediment.
The Book of Common Prayer *Solemnization of Matrimony*

3 There was only one catch and that was Catch-22, which specified that a concern for one's own safety in the face of dangers that were real and immediate was the process of a rational mind.
Joseph Heller (1923–) US novelist. *Catch-22*, Ch. 5

OCCUPATIONS

See also doctors, lawyers, police

1 A priest sees people at their best, a lawyer at their worst, but a doctor sees them as they really are.
Proverb

2 Every man to his trade.
Proverb

3 Jack of all trades, master of none.
Proverb

4 Old soldiers never die, they simply fade away.
Proverb

5 Once a parson always a parson.
Proverb

6 Sailors have a port in every storm.
Proverb

7 Doctors bury their mistakes. Lawyers hang them. But journalists put theirs on the front page.
Anonymous

8 The ugliest of trades have their moments of pleasure. Now, if I were a grave-digger, or even a hangman, there are some people I could work for with a great deal of enjoyment.

Douglas William Jerrold (1803–57) British dramatist. *Wit and Opinions of Douglas Jerrold*, 'Ugly Trades'

9 He did not know that a keeper is only a poacher turned outside in, and a poacher a keeper turned inside out.

Charles Kingsley (1819–75) British writer. *The Water Babies*, Ch. 1

10 Under the spreading chestnut tree
The village smithy stands;
The smith, a mighty man is he,
With large and sinewy hands;
And the muscles of his brawny arms
Are strong as iron bands.

Henry Wadsworth Longfellow (1807–82) US poet. *The Village Blacksmith*

11 The trained nurse has given nursing the human, or shall we say, the divine touch, and made the hospital desirable for patients with serious ailments regardless of their home advantages.

Charles H. Mayo (1865–1939) US physician. *Collected Papers of the Mayo Clinic and Mayo Foundation*

12 I have nothing against undertakers personally. It's just that I wouldn't want one to bury my sister.

Jessica Mitford (1917–96) British writer. Attrib. in *Saturday Review*, 1 Feb 1964

13 If I didn't start painting, I would have raised chickens.

Grandma Moses (Anna Mary Robertson Moses; 1860–1961) US primitive painter. *Grandma Moses, My Life's History* (ed. Aotto Kallir), Ch. 3

14 No *man*, not even a doctor, ever gives any other definition of what a nurse should be than this – 'devoted and obedient.' This definition would do just as well for a porter. It might even do for a horse. It would not do for a policeman.

Florence Nightingale (1820–1910) British nurse. *Notes on Nursing*

15 The trained nurse has become one of the great blessings of humanity, taking a place beside the physician and the priest, and not inferior to either in her mission.

William Osler (1849–1919) Canadian physician. *Aequanimitas, with Other Addresses*, 'Nurse and Patient'

16 A doctor who doesn't say too many foolish things is a patient half-cured, just as a critic is a poet who has stopped writing verse and a policeman a burglar who has retired from practice.

Marcel Proust (1871–1922) French novelist. *À la recherche du temps perdu: Le Côté de Guermantes*

17 Everybody hates house-agents because they have everybody at a disadvantage. All other callings have a certain amount of give and take; the house-agent simply takes.

H. G. Wells (1866–1946) British writer. *Kipps*, Bk. III, Ch. 1

18 The best careers advice to give to the young is 'Find out what you like doing best and get someone to pay you for doing it.'

Katherine Whitehorn (1926–) British journalist. *The Observer*, 1975

OFFICERS

See also army, navy, soldiers, war

1 Any officer who shall behave in a scandalous manner, unbecoming the character of an officer and a gentleman shall…be cashiered.

Anonymous The words 'conduct unbecoming the character of an officer' are a direct quotation from the Naval Discipline Act (10 Aug 1860), Article 24. *Articles of War* (1872), *Disgraceful Conduct*, 79

2 If Kitchener was not a great man, he was, at least, a great poster.

Margot Asquith (1865–1945) The second wife of Herbert Asquith. *Kitchener: Portrait of an Imperialist* (Sir Philip Magnus), Ch. 14

3 In defeat unbeatable; in victory unbearable.

Winston Churchill (1874–1965) British statesman. Referring to Viscount Montgomery. *Ambrosia and Small Beer* (E. Marsh), Ch. 5

4 Jellicoe was the only man on either side who could lose the war in an afternoon.

Winston Churchill *The Observer*, 'Sayings of the Week', 13 Feb 1927

5 War is too important to be left to the generals.

Georges Clemenceau (1841–1929) French statesman. A similar remark is attributed to Talleyrand. Attrib.

6 When I was a lad I served a term
As office boy to an Attorney's firm.
I cleaned the windows and I swept the floor,
And I polished up the handle of the big front door.
I polished up that handle so carefullee
That now I am the Ruler of the Queen's Navee!

W. S. Gilbert (1836–1911) British dramatist. *HMS Pinafore*, I

7 Stick close to your desks and never go to sea,
And you all may be Rulers of the Queen's Navee!

W. S. Gilbert *HMS Pinafore*, I

8 LUDENDORFF: The English soldiers fight like lions.
HOFFMANN: True. But don't we know that they are lions led by donkeys.

Max Hoffmann (1869–1927) German general. Referring to the performance of the British army in World War I. *The Donkeys* (A. Clark)

9 I can't spare this man; he fights.

Abraham Lincoln (1809–65) US statesman. Resisting demands for the dismissal of Ulysses Grant. Attrib.

10 The Nelson touch.

Lord Nelson (1758–1805) British admiral. Diary, 9 Oct 1805

11 Nelson, born in a fortunate hour for himself and for his country, was always in his element and always on his element.

George Macaulay Trevelyan (1876–1962) British historian. *History of England*, Bk. V, Ch. 5

12 I didn't fire him because he was a dumb son of a bitch, although he was, but that's not against the law for generals. If it was, half to three-quarters of them would be in gaol.

Harry S. Truman (1884–1972) US statesman. Referring to General MacArthur. *Plain Speaking* (Merle Miller)

13 I don't know what effect these men will have on the enemy, but, by God, they frighten me.

Duke of Wellington (1769–1852) British general and statesman. Referring to his generals. Attrib.

14 It is not the business of generals to shoot one another.

Duke of Wellington Refusing an artillery officer permission to fire upon Napoleon himself during the Battle of Waterloo, 1815. Attrib.

15 Not upon a man from the colonel to the private in a regiment – both inclusive. We may pick up a marshal or two perhaps; but not worth a damn.

Duke of Wellington Said during the Waterloo campaign, when asked whether he anticipated any desertions from Napoleon's army. *Creevey Papers*, Ch. X

16 I used to say of him that his presence on the field made the difference of forty thousand men.

Duke of Wellington Referring to Napoleon. *Notes of Conversations with the Duke of Wellington* (Stanhope), 2 Nov 1831

OLD AGE

See also age, longevity

1 Grey hairs are death's blossoms.

Proverb

2 You can't teach an old dog new tricks.

Proverb

3 When you are forty, half of you belongs to the past...And when you are seventy, nearly all of you.

Jean Anouilh (1910–87) French dramatist.

4 I will never be an old man. To me, old age is always fifteen years older than I am.

Bernard Baruch (1870–1965) US financier and presidential adviser. *The Observer* 'Sayings of the Week', 21 Aug 1955

5 Better is a poor and a wise child than an old and foolish king, who will no more be admonished.

Bible: Ecclesiastes 4:13

6 With the ancient is wisdom; and in length of days understanding.

Bible: Job 12:12

7 To be old is to be part of a huge and ordinary multitude...the reason why old age was venerated in the past was because it was extraordinary.

Ronald Blythe (1922–) British author. *The View in Winter*

8 Old age takes away from us what we have inherited and gives us what we have earned.

Gerald Brenan (Edward Fitzgerald Brenan; 1894–1987) British writer. *Thoughts in a Dry Season*, 'Life'

9 As a white candle
In a holy place,
So is the beauty
Of an aged face.

Joseph Campbell (1879–1944) Irish poet. *The Old Woman*

10 'You are old, Father William,' the young man said,
'And your hair has become very white;
And yet you incessantly stand on your head –
Do you think at your age, it is right?'

Lewis Carroll (Charles Lutwidge Dodgson; 1832–98) British writer. *See also* Robert SOUTHEY. *Alice's Adventures in Wonderland*, Ch. 5

11 Old age is the out-patients' department of purgatory.

Lord Cecil (1869–1956) British politician. *The Cecils of Hatfield House* (David Cecil)

12 I prefer old age to the alternative.

Maurice Chevalier (1888–1972) French singer and actor. Attrib.

13 Old-age, a second child, by Nature curs'd
With more and greater evils than the first,
Weak, sickly, full of pains; in ev'ry breath
Railing at life, and yet afraid of death.

Charles Churchill (1731–64) British poet. *Gotham*, I

14 Oh to be seventy again.

Georges Clemenceau (1841–1929) French statesman. Remark on his eightieth birthday, noticing a pretty girl in the Champs Elysées. *Ego 3* (James Agate)

15 So, perhaps, I may escape otherwise than by death the last humiliation of an aged scholar, when his juniors conspire to print a volume of essays and offer it to him as a sign that they now consider him senile.

Robin George Collingwood (1889–1943) British philosopher and archaeologist. *Autobiography*

16 When a man fell into his anecdotage it was a sign for him to retire from the world.

Benjamin Disraeli (1804–81) British statesman. *Lothair*, Ch. 28

17 I grow old...I grow old...
I shall wear the bottoms of my trousers rolled.

T. S. Eliot (1888–1965) US-born British poet and dramatist. *The Love Song of J. Alfred Prufrock*

18 Shall I part my hair behind? Do I dare to eat a peach?
I shall wear white flannel trousers, and walk upon the beach.
I have heard the mermaids singing, each to each.

T. S. Eliot *The Love Song of J. Alfred Prufrock*

19 Old age brings along with its uglinesses the comfort that you will soon be out of it, – which ought to be a substantial relief to such discontented pendulums as we are.

Ralph Waldo Emerson (1803–82) US poet and essayist. *Journal*

20 He cannot bear old men's jokes. That is not new. But now he begins to think of them himself.

Max Frisch (1911–91) Swiss dramatist and novelist. *Sketchbook 1966–71*

21 Time goes by: reputation increases, ability declines.

Dag Hammarskjöld (1905–61) Swedish diplomat. *Diaries*, 1964

22 And now in age I bud again,
After so many deaths I live and write;
I once more smell the dew and rain,
And relish versing; O, my only Light,
It cannot be
That I am he
On whom Thy tempests fell all night.

George Herbert (1593–1633) English poet. *The Flower*

23 It is so comic to hear oneself called old, even at ninety I suppose!

Alice James (1848–92) US diarist. Letter to William James, 14 June 1889. *The Diary of Alice James* (ed. Leon Edel)

24 There is a wicked inclination in most people to suppose an old man decayed in his intellects. If a young or middle-aged man, when leaving a company, does not recollect where he laid his hat, it is nothing; but if the same inattention is discovered in an old man, people will shrug up their shoulders, and say, 'His memory is going.'

Samuel Johnson (1709–84) British lexicographer. *Life of Johnson* (J. Boswell), Vol. IV

25 Perhaps being old is having lighted rooms
Inside your head, and people in them, acting.
People you know, yet can't quite name.

Philip Larkin (1922–85) British poet. *The Old Fools*

26 A 'Grand Old Man'. That means on our continent any one with snow white hair who has kept out of jail till eighty.

Stephen Leacock (1869–1944) English-born Canadian economist and humorist. *The Score and Ten*

27 Old age is woman's hell.

Ninon de Lenclos (1620–1705) French courtesan. Attrib.

28 From the earliest times the old have rubbed it into the young that they are wiser than they, and before the young had discovered what nonsense this was they were old too, and it profited them to carry on the imposture.

W. Somerset Maugham (1874–1965) British novelist. *Cakes and Ale*, Ch. 9

29 Being seventy is not a sin.

Golda Meir (1898–1978) Russian-born Israeli stateswoman. *Reader's Digest* (July 1971), 'The Indestructible Golda Meir'

30 A ready means of being cherished by the English is to adopt the simple expedient of living a long time. I have little doubt that if, say, Oscar Wilde had lived into his nineties, instead of dying in his forties, he would have been considered a benign, distinguished figure suitable to preside at a school prize-giving or to instruct and exhort scoutmasters at their jamborees. He might even have been knighted.

Malcolm Muggeridge (1903–90) British writer. *Tread Softly for you Tread on my Jokes*

31 I prefer to forget both pairs of glasses and pass my declining years saluting strange women and grandfather clocks.

Ogden Nash (1902–71) US poet. *Peekaboo, I Almost See You*

32 Age only matters when one is ageing. Now that I have arrived at a great age, I might just as well be twenty.

Pablo Picasso (1881–1973) Spanish painter. *The Observer, Shouts and Murmurs*, 'Picasso in Private' (John Richardson)

33 See how the world its veterans rewards!
A youth of frolics, an old age of cards.

Alexander Pope (1688–1744) British poet. *Moral Essays*, II

34 Growing old is like being increasingly penalized for a crime you haven't committed.

Anthony Powell (1905–) British novelist. *A Dance to the Music of Time: Temporary Kings*, Ch. 1

35 Darling, I am growing old,
Silver threads among the gold.

Eben Rexford (1848–1916) British songwriter. *Silver Threads Among the Gold*

36 Age seldom arrives smoothly or quickly. It's more often a succession of jerks.

Jean Rhys (1894–1979) Dominican-born British novelist. *The Observer*, 'Sayings of the Week', 25 May 1975

37 As I grow older and older,
And totter towards the tomb,
I find that I care less and less
Who goes to bed with whom.

Dorothy L. Sayers (1893–1957) British writer. *That's Why I Never Read Modern Novels*

38 Last scene of all,
That ends this strange eventful history,
Is second childishness and mere oblivion;
Sans teeth, sans eyes, sans taste, sans every thing.

William Shakespeare (1564–1616) English dramatist. *As You Like It*, II:7

39 I have liv'd long enough.
My way of life
Is fall'n into the sear, the yellow leaf;
And that which should accompany old age,
As honour, love, obedience, troops of friends,
I must not look to have.

William Shakespeare *Macbeth*, V:3

40 That time of year thou mayst in me behold
When yellow leaves, or none, or few, do hang
Upon those boughs which shake against the cold,
Bare ruin'd choirs, where late the sweet birds sang.

William Shakespeare *Sonnet 73*

41 Old men are dangerous; it doesn't matter to them what is going to happen to the world.

George Bernard Shaw (1856–1950) Irish dramatist and critic. *Heartbreak House*

42 You are old, Father William, the young man

cried,
The few locks which are left you are grey;
You are hale, Father William, a hearty old man,
Now tell me the reason, I pray.

Robert Southey (1774–1843) British poet. *See also* Lewis CARROLL. *The Old Man's Comforts, and how he Gained them*

43 Being over seventy is like being engaged in a war. All our friends are going or gone and we survive amongst the dead and the dying as on a battlefield.

Muriel Spark (1918–) British novelist. *Memento Mori*, Ch. 4

44 There are so few who can grow old with a good grace.

Richard Steele (1672–1729) Dublin-born British essayist. *The Spectator*, 263

45 The greatest problem about old age is the fear that it may go on too long.

A. J. P. Taylor (1906–90) British historian. *Observer* 'Sayings of the Week', 1 Nov 1981

46 Sleeping as quiet as death, side by wrinkled side, toothless, salt and brown, like two old kippers in a box.

Dylan Thomas (1914–53) Welsh poet. *Under Milk Wood*

47 Old age is the most unexpected of all the things that happen to a man.

Leon Trotsky (Lev Davidovich Bronstein; 1879–1940) Russian revolutionary. *Diary in Exile*, 8 May 1935

48 There is nothing funny or commendable about old age. It is a miserable affliction which brings a sort of imbecility to those who suffer from it and distresses everyone else.

Auberon Waugh (1939–) British novelist. *The Diaries of Auberon Waugh 1976–1985*, 'July 21, 1982'

49 The gods bestowed on Max the gift of perpetual old age.

Oscar Wilde (1854–1900) Irish-born British dramatist. Referring to Max Beerbohm. Attrib.

50 It is a terrible thing for an old woman to outlive her dogs.

Tennessee Williams (1911–83) US dramatist. *Camino Real*

51 He was either a man of about a hundred and fifty who was rather young for his years or a man of about a hundred and ten who had been aged by trouble.

P. G. Wodehouse (1881–1975) British humorous novelist. *Wodehouse at Work to the End* (Richard Usborne), Ch. 6

52 The wiser mind
Mourns less for what age takes away
Than what it leaves behind.

William Wordsworth (1770–1850) British poet. *The Fountain*

53 Provoke
The years to bring the inevitable yoke.

William Wordsworth *Ode. Intimations of Immortality*, VIII

54 When you are old and gray and full of sleep,
And nodding by the fire, take down this book,
And slowly read, and dream of the soft look
Your eyes had once, and of their shadows deep...

W. B. Yeats (1865–1939) Irish poet. *When you are Old*

ONE-UPMANSHIP

See also snobbery, superiority

1 Keeping up with the Joneses was a full-time job with my mother and father. It was not until many years later when I lived alone that I realized how much cheaper it was to drag the Joneses down to my level.

Quentin Crisp (?1910–) Model, publicist, and writer. *The Naked Civil Servant*

2 There is no doubt that basic weekendmanship should contain some reference to Important Person Play.

Stephen Potter (1900–69) British writer. *Lifemanship*, Ch. 2

3 *How to be one up* – how to make the other man feel that something has gone wrong, however slightly.

Stephen Potter *Lifemanship*, Introduction

OPERA

See also music, singing

1 I do not mind what language an opera is sung in so long as it is a language I don't understand.

Edward Appleton (1892–1965) British physicist. *The Observer*, 'Sayings of the Week,' 28 Aug 1955

2 No good opera plot can be sensible, for people do not sing when they are feeling sensible.

W. H. Auden (1907–73) British poet. *Time*, 29 Dec 1961

3 The opera isn't over till the fat lady sings.

Dan Cook US journalist. *Washington Post*, 13 June 1978

4 People are wrong when they say the opera isn't what it used to be. It is what it used to be. That's what's wrong with it.

Noël Coward (1899–1973) British dramatist. *Design for Living*

5 Opera in English, is, in the main, just about as sensible as baseball in Italian.

H. L. Mencken (1880–1956) US journalist. *The Frank Muir Book* (Frank Muir)

6 I sometimes wonder which would be nicer – an opera without an interval, or an interval without an opera.

Ernest Newman (1868–1959) British music critic. *Berlioz, Romantic and Classic*, (ed. Peter Heyworth)

7 His vocal cords were kissed by God.

Harold Schoenberg (1915–) US music critic. Referring to Luciano Pavarotti. *The Times*, 30 June 1981

8 Tenors are noble, pure and heroic and get the soprano. But baritones are born villains in opera. Always the heavy and never the hero.

Leonard Warren (1911–60) US baritone singer. *The New York World Telegram*, 13 Feb 1957

9 Like German opera, too long and too loud.
Evelyn Waugh (1903–66) British novelist. Giving his opinions of warfare after the Battle of Crete, 1941. Attrib.

10 An unalterable and unquestioned law of the musical world required that the German text of French operas sung by Swedish artists should be translated into Italian for the clearer understanding of English speaking audiences.
Edith Wharton (1862–1937) US novelist. *The Age of Innocence*, Bk. I, Ch. 1

OPINIONS

See also ideas

1 We must say that the same opinions have arisen among men in cycles, not once, twice, nor a few times, but infinitely often.
Aristotle (384–322 BC) Greek philosopher. *Meteorologica*

2 They that approve a private opinion, call it opinion; but they that mislike it, heresy: and yet heresy signifies no more than private opinion.
Thomas Hobbes (1588–1679) English philosopher. *Leviathan*, Pt. I, Ch. 11

3 The superiority of one man's opinion over another's is never so great as when the opinion is about a woman.
Henry James (1843–1916) US novelist. *The Tragic Muse*, Ch. 9

4 'Tis with our judgments as our watches, none
Go just alike, yet each believes his own.
Alexander Pope (1688–1744) British poet. *An Essay on Criticism*

5 The fact that an opinion has been widely held is no evidence whatever that it is not utterly absurd.
Bertrand Russell (1872–1970) British philosopher. Attrib.

6 It is folly of too many to mistake the echo of a London coffee-house for the voice of the kingdom.
Jonathan Swift (1667–1745) Irish-born Anglican priest and writer. *The Conduct of the Allies*

7 So many men, so many opinions.
Terence (Publius Terentius Afer; c. 190–159 BC) Roman poet. *Phormio*

8 I agree with no man's opinion. I have some of my own.
Ivan Turgenev (1818–83) Russian novelist. *Fathers and Sons*, Ch. 13

OPPORTUNITY

See also chance, present

1 All's grist that comes to the mill.
Proverb

2 Every dog has his day.
Proverb

3 Hoist your sail when the wind is fair.
Proverb

4 Make hay while the sun shines.
Proverb

5 Nothing ventured, nothing gained.
Proverb

6 Opportunity seldom knocks twice.
Proverb

7 Strike while the iron is hot.
Proverb

8 Whenever you fall, pick up something.
Oswald Theodore Avery (1877–1955) Canadian bacteriologist. Attrib.

9 A wise man will make more opportunities than he finds.
Francis Bacon (1561–1626) English philosopher. *Essays*, 'Of Ceremonies and Respects'

10 Cast thy bread upon the waters: for thou shalt find it after many days.
Bible: Ecclesiastes 11:1

11 Let him now speak, or else hereafter for ever hold his peace.
The Book of Common Prayer *Solemnization of Matrimony*

12 Opportunities are usually disguised as hard work, so most people don't recognise them.
Ann Landers (1918–) US journalist. Attrib.

13 One can present people with opportunities. One cannot make them equal to them.
Rosamond Lehmann (1901–90) British novelist. *The Ballad and the Source*

14 Equality of opportunity means equal opportunity to be unequal.
Iain Macleod (1913–70) British politician. *Way Of Life* (John Boyd Carpenter)

15 Grab a chance and you won't be sorry for a might have been.
Arthur Ransome (1884–1967) British novelist. *We Didn't Mean to Go to Sea*

16 There is a tide in the affairs of men
Which, taken at the flood, leads on to fortune;
Omitted, all the voyage of their life
Is bound in shallows and in miseries.
On such a full sea are we now afloat,
And we must take the current when it serves,
Or lose our ventures.
William Shakespeare (1564–1616) English dramatist. *Julius Caesar*, IV:3

17 Why, then the world's mine oyster,
Which I with sword will open.
William Shakespeare *The Merry Wives of Windsor*, II:2

18 I missed the chance of a lifetime, too. Fifty lovelies in the rude and I'd left my Bunsen burner home.
Dylan Thomas (1914–53) Welsh poet. *Portrait of the Artist as a Young Dog*, 'One Warm Saturday'

OPPOSITES

See also conflict, difference

1 It takes all sorts to make a world.
Proverb

2 Fish die belly-upward and rise to the surface; it is their way of falling.
André Gide (1869–1951) French novelist. *Journals*

3 The poet and the dreamer are distinct,
Diverse, sheer opposite, antipodes.
The one pours out a balm upon the world,
The other vexes it.
John Keats (1795–1821) British poet. *The Fall of Hyperion*, I

4 Oh, East is East, and West is West, and never the twain shall meet.
Rudyard Kipling (1865–1936) Indian-born British writer. *The Ballad of East and West*

5 War is Peace, Freedom is Slavery, Ignorance is Strength.
George Orwell (Eric Blair; 1903–50) British novelist. *Nineteen Eighty-Four*

6 Doublethink means the power of holding two contradictory beliefs in one's mind simultaneously, and accepting both of them.
George Orwell *Nineteen Eighty-Four*

7 The sublime and the ridiculous are often so nearly related that it is difficult to class them separately. One step above the sublime makes the ridiculous; and one step above the ridiculous makes the sublime again.
Thomas Paine (1737–1809) British writer. *The Age of Reason*, Pt. 2

OPPOSITION

See also government, politics

1 It has been said that England invented the phrase, 'Her Majesty's Opposition'.
Walter Bagehot (1826–77) British economist and journalist. *See* HOBHOUSE. *The English Constitution*, 'The Monarchy'

2 The duty of an opposition is to oppose.
Lord Randolph Churchill (1849–95) British Conservative politician. *Lord Randolph Churchill* (W. S. Churchill)

3 When I invented the phrase 'His Majesty's Opposition' he paid me a compliment on the fortunate hit.
John Cam Hobhouse (1786–1869) British politician. Speaking about Canning. *Recollections of a Long Life*, II, Ch. 12

4 One fifth of the people are against everything all the time.
Robert Kennedy (1925–68) US politician. *The Observer*, 'Sayings of the Week', 10 May 1964

5 ...I have spent many years of my life in opposition and I rather like the role.
Eleanor Roosevelt (1884–1962) US writer and lecturer. Letter to Bernard Baruch, 18 Nov 1952

OPPRESSION

See also imprisonment, indoctrination, power politics, slavery, tyranny

1 When Israel was in Egypt land,
Let my people go,
Oppressed so hard they could not stand,
Let my people go.
Go down, Moses,
Way-down in Egypt land,
Tell old Pharaoh
To let my people go.
Anonymous Negro spiritual

2 To the capitalist governors Timor's petroleum smells better than Timorese blood and tears.
Anonymous priest *Distant Voices* (John Pilger; 1994)

3 Christ in this country would quite likely have been arrested under the Suppression of Communism Act.
Joost de Blank (1908–68) Dutch-born British churchman. Referring to South Africa. *The Observer*, 'Sayings of the Week', 27 Oct 1963

4 The enemies of Freedom do not argue; they shout and they shoot.
Dean Inge (1860–1954) British churchman. *The End of an Age*, Ch. 4

5 All the government gives us is charity at election time...Afterwards, death returns to our homes.
Marcos Mexican rebel leader. *The Independent*, 12 Jan 1994

6 If you want a picture of the future, imagine a boot stamping on a human face – for ever.
George Orwell (Eric Blair; 1903–50) British novelist. *Nineteen Eighty-Four*

7 In the first days of the revolt you must kill: to shoot down a European is to kill two birds with one stone, to destroy an oppressor and the man he oppresses at the same time: there remain a dead man, and a free man.
Jean-Paul Sartre (1905–80) French writer. *The Wretched of the Earth* (F. Fanon), Preface

OPTIMISM

See also hope

1 After a storm comes a calm.
Proverb

2 Every cloud has a silver lining.
Proverb

3 It's an ill wind that blows nobody any good.
Proverb

4 It will all come right in the wash.
Proverb

5 Look on the bright side.
Proverb

6 No news is good news.
Proverb

7 Nothing so bad but it might have been worse.
Proverb

8 The darkest hour is just before the dawn.
Proverb

9 Tomorrow is another day.
Proverb

10 When one door shuts, another opens.
Proverb

11 While there's life there's hope.
Proverb

12 Are we downhearted? No!
Anonymous A favourite expression of the British soldiers during World War I. Attrib.

13 What's the use of worrying?
It never was worth while,
So, pack up your troubles in your old kit-bag,
And smile, smile, smile.
George Asaf (George H. Powell; 1880–1951) US songwriter. *Pack up Your Troubles in Your Old Kit-bag*

14 Let other pens dwell on guilt and misery.
Jane Austen (1775–1817) British novelist. *Mansfield Park*, Ch. 48

15 *Future,* n. That period of time in which our affairs prosper, our friends are true and our happiness is assured.
Ambrose Bierce (1842–?1914) US writer and journalist. *The Devil's Dictionary*

16 My sun sets to rise again.
Robert Browning (1812–89) British poet. *At the 'Mermaid'*

17 No, at noonday in the bustle of man's work-time
Greet the unseen with a cheer!
Robert Browning *Epilogue to Asolando*

18 Don't you know each cloud contains
Pennies from Heaven?
Johnny Burke (1908–64) US songwriter. *Pennies from Heaven*

19 The optimist proclaims we live in the best of all possible worlds; and the pessimist fears this is true.
James Cabell (1879–1958) US novelist and journalist. *The Silver Stallion*

20 The place where optimism most flourishes is the lunatic asylum.
Havelock Ellis (1859–1939) British sexologist. *The Dance of Life*

21 Two men look out through the same bars:
One sees the mud, and one the stars.
Frederick Langbridge (1849–1923) British religious writer. *A Cluster of Quiet Thoughts*

22 The worst is not
So long as we can say 'This is the worst'.
William Shakespeare (1564–1616) English dramatist. *King Lear*, IV:1

23 Now is the winter of our discontent
Made glorious summer by this sun of York.
William Shakespeare *Richard III*, I:1

24 Life may change, but it may fly not;
Hope may vanish, but can die not;
Truth be veiled, but still it burneth;
Love repulsed, – but it returneth!
Percy Bysshe Shelley (1792–1822) British poet. *Hellas*, I

25 The latest definition of an optimist is one who fills up his crossword puzzle in ink.
Clement King Shorter (1857–1926) British journalist and critic. *The Observer*, 'Sayings of the Week', 22 Feb 1925

26 I am an optimist, unrepentant and militant. After all, in order not to be a fool an optimist must know how sad a place the world can be. It is only the pessimist who finds this out anew every day.
Peter Ustinov (1921–) British actor. *Dear Me*, Ch. 9

27 All is for the best in the best of possible worlds.
Voltaire (François-Marie Arouet; 1694–1778) French writer. *Candide*, Ch. 30

28 We are all in the gutter, but some of us are looking at the stars.
Oscar Wilde (1854–1900) Irish-born British dramatist. *Lady Windermere's Fan*, III

29 Nor greetings where no kindness is, nor all
The dreary intercourse of daily life,
Shall e'er prevail against us, or disturb
Our cheerful faith, that all which we behold
Is full of blessings.
William Wordsworth (1770–1850) British poet. *Lines composed a few miles above Tintern Abbey*

ORDER

1 I am an orderly man. I say this with no sense of false modesty, or of conceit....Being orderly, as a matter of fact, can be excessively tiresome and it often irritates me greatly, but I cannot pull away.
Dirk Bogarde (1921–) British actor and writer. *An Orderly Man*, Ch.1

2 'Where shall I begin, please your Majesty?' he asked.
'Begin at the beginning' the King said, gravely, 'and go on till you come to the end: then stop.'
Lewis Carroll (Charles Lutwidge Dodgson; 1832–98) British writer. *Alice's Adventures in Wonderland*, Ch. 11

3 Order is heaven's first law.
Alexander Pope (1688–1744) British poet. *An Essay on Man*, IV

4 O, when degree is shak'd,
Which is the ladder of all high designs,

The enterprise is sick!

William Shakespeare (1564–1616) English dramatist. *Troilus and Cressida*, I:3

5 How sour sweet music is
When time is broke and no proportion kept!
So is it in the music of men's lives.

William Shakespeare *Richard II*, V:5

6 A place for everything, and everything in its place.

Samuel Smiles (1812–1904) British writer. *Thrift*, Ch. 5

ORIGINALITY

See also imitation, innovation

1 Anything that is worth doing has been done frequently. Things hitherto undone should be given, I suspect, a wide berth.

Max Beerbohm (1872–1956) British writer. *Mainly on the Air*

2 An original writer is not one who imitates nobody, but one whom nobody can imitate.

Vicomte de Chateaubriand (1768–1848) French diplomat and writer. *Génie du Christianisme*

3 A thought is often original, though you have uttered it a hundred times.

Oliver Wendell Holmes (1809–94) US writer. *The Autocrat of the Breakfast Table*, Ch. 1

4 All good things which exist are the fruits of originality.

John Stuart Mill (1806–73) British philosopher. *On Liberty*, Ch. 3

5 Nothing has yet been said that's not been said before.

Terence (Publius Terentius Afer; c. 190–159 BC) Roman poet. *Eunuchus*, Prologue

6 The notion of doing something impossibly new usually turns out to be an illusion.

Twyla Tharp (1941–) US choreographer. *The Independent*, 8 Dec 1995

7 Another unsettling element in modern art is that common symptom of immaturity, the dread of doing what has been done before.

Edith Wharton (1862–1937) US novelist. *The Writing of Fiction*, Ch. 1

ORTHODOXY

See also conformity

1 The difference between Orthodoxy or Mydoxy and Heterodoxy or Thy-doxy.

Thomas Carlyle (1795–1881) Scottish historian and essayist. A similar remark is attributed to the British churchman William Warburton (1698–1779). *History of the French Revolution*, Pt. II, Bk. IV, Ch. 2

2 The word 'orthodoxy' not only no longer means being right; it practically means being wrong.

G. K. Chesterton (1874–1936) British writer. *Heretics*, Ch. 1

3 Worldly wisdom teaches that it is better for the reputation to fail conventionally than to succeed unconventionally.

John Maynard Keynes (1883–1946) British economist. *The General Theory of Employment, Interest and Money*, Bk. IV, Ch. 12

OSTENTATION

See also affectation

1 That's it, baby, if you've got it, flaunt it.

Mel Brooks (Melvyn Kaminsky; 1926–) US film director. *The Producers*

2 The possession of a book becomes a substitute for reading it.

Anthony Burgess (John Burgess Wilson; 1917–93) British novelist. *New York Times Book Review*

3 Wealth has never been a sufficient source of honour in itself. It must be advertised, and the normal medium is obtrusively expensive goods.

John Kenneth Galbraith (1908–) US economist. *The Affluent Society*, Ch. 7

4 When I meet those remarkable people whose company is coveted, I often wish they would show off a little more.

Desmond MacCarthy (1877–1952) British writer and theatre critic. *Theatre*, 'Good Talk'

5 She's like the old line about justice – not only must be done but must be seen to be done.

John Osborne (1929–94) British dramatist. *Time Present*, I

6 With the great part of rich people, the chief employment of riches consists in the parade of riches.

Adam Smith (1723–90) Scottish economist. *The Wealth of Nations*

OXFORD

See also Cambridge, education, England

1 Home of lost causes, and forsaken beliefs, and unpopular names, and impossible loyalties!

Matthew Arnold (1822–88) British poet and critic. *Essays in Criticism*, First Series, Preface

2 That sweet City with her dreaming spires
She needs not June for beauty's heightening.

Matthew Arnold *Thyrsis*

3 Oxford is on the whole more attractive than Cambridge to the ordinary visitor; and the traveller is therefore recommended to visit Cambridge first, or to omit it altogether if he cannot visit both.

Karl Baedeker (1801–59) German publisher. *Baedeker's Great Britain*, 'From London to Oxford'

4 The King to Oxford sent a troop of horse,
For Tories own no argument but force:

With equal skill to Cambridge books he sent,
For Whigs admit no force but argument.

William Browne (1692–1774) English physician. A reply to TRAPP. *Literary Anecdotes* (Nichols), Vol. III

5 Very nice sort of place, Oxford, I should think, for people that like that sort of place.

George Bernard Shaw (1856–1950) Irish dramatist and critic. *Man and Superman*, II

6 The King, observing with judicious eyes
The state of both his universities,
To Oxford sent a troop of horse, and why?
That learned body wanted loyalty;
To Cambridge books, as very well discerning
How much that loyal body wanted learning.

Joseph Trapp (1679–1747) English churchman and academic. Written after George I donated the Bishop of Ely's library to Cambridge; for reply see BROWNE. *Literary Anecdotes* (Nichols), Vol. III

7 Oxford is, and always has been, full of cliques, full of factions, and full of a particular non-social snobbiness.

Mary Warnock (1924–) British philosopher and educationalist. *The Observer*, 2 Nov 1980

P

PAINTING

See also art, artists

1 Buy old masters. They fetch a better price than old mistresses.

Lord Beaverbrook (1879–1964) British newspaper owner and politician. Attrib.

2 *Painting, n.* The art of protecting flat surfaces from the weather and exposing them to the critic.

Ambrose Bierce (1842–?1914) US writer and journalist. *The Devil's Dictionary*

3 Good painters imitate nature, bad ones spew it up.

Miguel de Cervantes (1547–1616) Spanish novelist. *El Licenciado Vidriera*

4 It's either easy or impossible.

Salvador Dali (1904–89) Spanish painter. Reply when asked if he found it hard to paint a picture. Attrib.

5 Never mind about my soul, just make sure you get my tie right.

James Joyce (1882–1941) Irish novelist. Responding to the painter Patrick Tuohy's assertion that he wished to capture Joyce's soul in his portrait of him. *James Joyce* (R. Ellmann)

6 If people only knew as much about painting as I do, they would never buy my pictures.

Edwin Landseer (1802–73) British painter and sculptor. Said to W. P. Frith. *Landseer the Victorian Paragon* (Campbell Lennie), Ch. 12

7 I mix them with my brains, sir.

John Opie (1761–1807) British painter. When asked what he mixed his colours with. *Self-Help* (Samuel Smiles), Ch. 4

8 A picture has been said to be something between a thing and a thought.

Samuel Palmer (1805–81) British landscape painter. *Life of Blake* (Arthur Symons)

9 If I like it, I say it's mine. If I don't I say it's a fake.

Pablo Picasso (1881–1973) Spanish painter. When asked how he knew which paintings were his. *The Sunday Times*, 10 Oct 1965

10 I paint objects as I think them, not as I see them.

Pablo Picasso Attrib.

11 Painting is a blind man's profession. He paints not what he sees, but what he feels, what he tells himself about what he has seen.

Pablo Picasso *Journals* (Jean Cocteau), 'Childhood'

12 It's better like that, if you want to kill a picture all you have to do is to hang it beautifully on a nail and soon you will see nothing of it but the frame. When it's out of place you see it better.

Pablo Picasso Explaining why a Renoir in his apartment was hung crooked. *Picasso: His Life and Work* (Ronald Penrose)

13 It is bad enough to be condemned to drag around this image in which nature has imprisoned me. Why should I consent to the perpetuation of the image of this image?

Plotinus (205–270 AD) Egyptian-born Greek philosopher. Refusing to have his portrait painted. Attrib.

14 I just keep painting till I feel like pinching. Then I know it's right.

Pierre Auguste Renoir (1841–1919) French impressionist painter. Explaining how he achieved such lifelike flesh tones in his nudes. Attrib.

15 Every time I paint a portrait I lose a friend.

John Singer Sargent (1856–1925) US portrait painter. Attrib.

16 Portraits of famous bards and preachers, all fur and wool from the squint to the kneecaps.

Dylan Thomas (1914–53) Welsh poet. *Under Milk Wood*

17 My business is to paint not what I know, but what I see.

Joseph Turner (1775–1851) British painter. Responding to a criticism of the fact that he had painted no portholes on the ships in a view of Plymouth. *Proust: The Early Years* (G. Painter)

PARASITES

1 Many a man who thinks to found a home discovers that he has merely opened a tavern for his friends.

Norman Douglas (1868–1952) British novelist. *South Wind*, Ch. 24

2 A free-loader is a confirmed guest. He is the man who is always willing to come to dinner.

Damon Runyon (1884–1946) US writer. *Short Takes*, 'Free-Loading Ethics'

3 So, naturalist observe, a flea
Hath smaller fleas that on him prey,
And these have smaller fleas to bite 'em.
And so proceed *ad infinitum*.

Jonathan Swift (1667–1745) Irish-born Anglican priest and writer. *On Poetry*

4 But was there ever dog that praised his fleas?

W. B. Yeats (1865–1939) Irish poet. *To a Poet, who would have me Praise certain Bad Poets, Imitators of His and Mine*

PARIS

See also France

1 If you are lucky enough to have lived in Paris as a young man, then wherever you go for the rest of your life, it stays with you, for Paris is a moveable feast.

Ernest Hemingway (1899–1961) US novelist. *A Moveable Feast*, Epigraph

2 Paris is worth a mass.

Henri IV (1553–1610) King of France. Said on entering Paris (March 1594), having secured its submission to his authority by becoming a Roman Catholic. Attrib.

3 Is Paris burning?

Adolf Hitler (1889–1945) German dictator. Referring to the liberation of Paris, 1944

4 As an artist, a man has no home in Europe save in Paris.

Friedrich Wilhelm Nietzsche (1844–1900) German philosopher. *Ecce Homo*

5 I love Paris in the springtime.

Cole Porter (1893–1964) US songwriter. *Can-Can*, 'I Love Paris'

PAROCHIALISM

See also self-interest, selfishness

1 This fellow did not see further than his own nose.

Jean de La Fontaine (1621–95) French poet. *Fables*, III, 'Le Renard et le Bouc'

2 A broken head in Cold Bath Fields produces a greater sensation among us than three pitched battles in India.

Lord Macaulay (1800–59) British historian. Speech, 10 July 1833

3 'That is well said,' replied Candide, 'but we must cultivate our garden.'

Voltaire (François-Marie Arouet; 1694–1778) French writer. *Candide*, Ch. 30

PARTIES

See also society

1 The sooner every party breaks up the better.

Jane Austen (1775–1817) British novelist. *Emma*, Ch. 25

2 And bring hither the fatted calf, and kill it; and let us eat, and be merry:
For this my son was dead, and is alive again; he was lost, and is found. And they began to be merry.

Bible: Luke 15:23–24

3 I entertained on a cruising trip that was so much fun that I had to sink my yacht to make my guests go home.

F. Scott Fitzgerald (1896–1940) US novelist. *The Crack-Up*, 'Notebooks, K'

4 I was one of the few guests who had actually been invited. People were not invited – they went there.

F. Scott Fitzgerald *The Great Gatsby*, Ch. 3

5 HE. Have you heard it's in the stars
Next July we collide with Mars?
SHE. Well, did you evah! What a swell
party this is.

Cole Porter (1893–1964) US songwriter. *High Society* 'Well, Did You Evah!'

6 Certainly, there is nothing else here to enjoy.

George Bernard Shaw (1856–1950) Irish dramatist and critic. Said at a party when his hostess asked him whether he was enjoying himself. *Pass the Port* (Oxfam)

7 'So like one's first parties' said Miss Runcible 'being sick with other people singing.'

Evelyn Waugh (1903–66) British novelist. *Vile Bodies*

8 She had heard someone say something about an Independent Labour Party, and was furious that she had not been asked.

Evelyn Waugh *Vile Bodies*

9 The Life and Soul, the man who will never go home while there is one man, woman or glass of anything not yet drunk.

Katherine Whitehorn (1926–) British journalist. *Sunday Best*, 'Husband-Swapping'

PARTING

See also departure, greetings, separation

1 Adieu, adieu, kind friends, adieu, adieu, adieu,
I can no longer stay with you, stay with you.
I'll hang my harp on a weeping willow-tree.
And may the world go well with thee.

Anonymous *There is a Tavern in the Town*

2 There is a tavern in the town,
And there my dear love sits him down,
And drinks his wine 'mid laughter free,
And never, never thinks of me.

Fare thee well, for I must leave thee,
Do not let this parting grieve thee,
And remember that the best of friends must part.

Anonymous *There is a Tavern in the Town*

3 Farewell and adieu to you,
Fair Spanish Ladies
Farewell and adieu to you, Ladies of Spain.

Anonymous *Spanish Ladies*

4 Forty years on, when afar and asunder
Parted are those who are singing to-day.

E. E. Bowen (1836–1901) British writer. *Forty Years On* (the Harrow school song)

5 Parting is all we know of heaven,
And all we need of hell.

Emily Dickinson (1830–86) US poet. *My Life Closed Twice Before its Close*

6 Since there's no help, come let us kiss and part –
Nay, I have done, you get no more of me;
And I am glad, yea glad with all my heart
That thus so cleanly I myself can free.

Michael Drayton (1563–1631) English poet. *Sonnets*, 61

7 But tha mun dress thysen, an' go back to thy stately homes of England, how beautiful they stand. Time's up! Time's up for Sir John, an' for little Lady Jane! Put thy shimmy on, Lady Chatterley!

D. H. Lawrence (1885–1930) British novelist. *Lady Chatterley's Lover*, Ch. 15

8 It was not like your great and gracious ways!
Do you, that have nought other to lament,
Never, my Love, repent
Of how, that July afternoon,
You went,
With sudden, unintelligible phrase, – And frightened eye,
Upon your journey of so many days,
Without a single kiss or a good-bye?

Coventry Patmore (1823–96) British poet. *The Unknown Eros*, Bk. I, 'Departure'

9 It is seldom indeed that one parts on good terms, because if one were on good terms one would not part.

Marcel Proust (1871–1922) French novelist. *À la recherche du temps perdu: La Prisonnière*

10 Good night, good night! Parting is such sweet sorrow
That I shall say good night till it be morrow.

William Shakespeare (1564–1616) English dramatist. *Romeo and Juliet*, II:2

11 Farewell! thou art too dear for my possessing,
And like enough thou know'st thy estimate:
The charter of thy worth gives thee releasing;
My bonds in thee are all determinate.

William Shakespeare *Sonnet 87*

12 Good-by-ee! – good-bye-ee!
Wipe the tear, baby dear, from your eye-ee.
Tho' it's hard to part, I know,
I'll be tickled to death to go.
Don't cry-ee! – don't sigh-ee!
There's a silver lining in the sky-ee! –
Bonsoir, old thing! cheerio! chin-chin!
Nahpoo! Toodle-oo! Good-bye-ee!

R. P. Weston (20th century) British songwriter. *Good-byee!* (with Bert Lee)

PASSION

See also emotion, love

1 The man who is master of his passions is Reason's slave.

Cyril Connolly (1903–74) British journalist. *Turnstile One* (ed. V. S. Pritchett)

2 A man who has not passed through the inferno of his passions has never overcome them.

Carl Gustav Jung (1875–1961) Swiss psychoanalyst. *Memories, Dreams, Reflections*, Ch. 9

3 For ever warm and still to be enjoy'd,
For ever panting and for ever young;
All breathing human passion far above,
That leaves a heart high-sorrowful and cloy'd,
A burning forehead, and a parching tongue.

John Keats (1795–1821) British poet. *Ode on a Grecian Urn*

4 It is with our passions as it is with fire and water, they are good servants, but bad masters.

Roger L'Estrange (1616–1704) English journalist and writer. *Aesop's Fables*, 38

5 And hence one master-passion in the breast,
Like Aaron's serpent,
swallows up the rest.

Alexander Pope (1688–1744) British poet. *An Essay on Man*, II

6 The ruling passion, be it what it will
The ruling passion conquers reason still.

Alexander Pope *Moral Essays*, III

7 Passion, you see, can be destroyed by a doctor. It cannot be created.

Peter Shaffer (1926–) British dramatist. *Equus*, II:35

8 So I triumphed ere my passion, sweeping thro' me, left me dry,
Left me with the palsied heart, and left me with the jaundiced eye.

Alfred, Lord Tennyson (1809–92) British poet. *Locksley Hall*

9 Strange fits of passion have I known:
And I will dare to tell,
But in the lover's ear alone,
What once to me befell.

William Wordsworth (1770–1850) British poet. *Strange Fits of Passion*

PAST

See also experience, future, history, memory, nostalgia, present, regret, time

1 Even God cannot change the past.

Agathon (c. 446–401 BC) Athenian poet and playwright. *Nicomachean Ethics* (Aristotle), VI

2 There is always something rather absurd about the past.

Max Beerbohm (1872–1956) British writer. *1880*

3 A king lived long ago,
In the morning of the world,
When earth was nigher heaven than now.

Robert Browning (1812–89) British poet. *Pippa Passes*, Pt. I

4 Study the past, if you would divine the future.

Confucius (K'ung Fu-tzu; 551–479 BC) Chinese philosopher. *Analects*

5 The past is a foreign country: they do things differently there.

L. P. Hartley (1895–1972) British novelist. *The Go-Between*

6 Look back, and smile at perils past.

Walter Scott (1771–1832) Scottish novelist. *The Bridal of Triermain*, Introduction

7 The past is the only dead thing that smells sweet.

Edward Thomas (1878–1917) British poet. *Early One Morning*

8 Keep off your thoughts from things that are past and done;

For thinking of the past wakes regret and pain.

Arthur Waley (1889–1966) British poet and translator. Translation from the Chinese of Po-Chü-I. *Resignation*

9 The past, at least, is secure.

Daniel Webster (1782–1852) US statesman. Speech, US Senate, 26 Jan 1830

PATIENCE

See also endurance, persistence

1 A watched pot never boils.

Proverb

2 Everything comes to him who waits.

Proverb

3 First things first.

Proverb

4 Patience is a virtue.

Proverb

5 Rome was not built in a day.

Proverb

6 We must learn to walk before we can run.

Proverb

7 Wait and see.

Herbert Henry Asquith (1852–1928) British statesman. In various speeches, 1910

8 *Patience*, n. A minor form of despair, disguised as a virtue.

Ambrose Bierce (1842–?1914) US writer and journalist. *The Devil's Dictionary*

9 The bud may have a bitter taste,
But sweet will be the flower.

William Cowper (1731–1800) British poet. *Olney Hymns*, 35

10 Beware the Fury of a Patient Man.

John Dryden (1631–1700) British poet and dramatist. *Absalom and Achitophel*, I

11 Patience and passage of time do more than strength and fury.

Jean de La Fontaine (1621–95) French poet. *Fables*, II, 'Le Lion et le Rat'

12 Though patience be a tired mare, yet she will plod.

William Shakespeare (1564–1616) English dramatist. *Henry V*, II:1

13 It is very strange…that the years teach us patience; that the shorter our time, the greater our capacity for waiting.

Elizabeth Taylor (1912–75) British writer. *A Wreath of Roses*, Ch. 10

PATIENTS

1 Keep a watch also on the faults of the patients, which often make them lie about the taking of things prescribed.

Hippocrates (c. 460–c. 377 BC) Greek physician. *Decorum*, 14

2 The sick man is a parasite of society. In certain cases it is indecent to go on living. To continue to vegetate in a state of cowardly dependence upon doctors and special treatments, once the meaning of life, the right to life has been lost, ought to be regarded with the greatest contempt by society.

Friedrich Wilhelm Nietzsche (1844–1900) German philosopher. *The Twilight of the Idols*, 'Skirmishes in a War with the Age'

PATRIOTISM

See also homesickness, loyalty, war

1 What pity is it
That we can die but once to serve our country!

Joseph Addison (1672–1719) British essayist. *Cato*, IV:4

2 Speak for England.

Leopold Amery (1873–1955) British statesman. Shouted to Arthur Greenwood, Labour Party spokesman, before he began to speak in a House of Commons debate immediately preceding the declaration of war, 2 Sept 1939

3 That this house will in no circumstances fight for its King and country.

Anonymous Motion passed at the Oxford Union, 9 Feb 1933

4 Patriotism is seen not only as the last refuge of the scoundrel but as the first bolt-hole of the hypocrite.

Melvyn Bragg (1939–) British author and television presenter. *Speak for England*, Introduction

5 'My country, right or wrong' is a thing that no patriot would think of saying, except in a desperate case. It is like saying 'My mother, drunk or sober.'

G. K. Chesterton (1874–1936) British writer. *The Defendant*

6 Be England what she will,
With all her faults, she is my country still.

Charles Churchill (1731–64) British poet. *The Farewell*

7 England, with all thy faults, I love thee still,
My country.

William Cowper (1731–1800) British poet. *The Task*

8 Our country! In her intercourse with foreign nations, may she always be in the right; but our country, right or wrong.

Stephen Decatur (1779–1820) US naval officer. Speech, Norfolk, Virginia, Apr 1816

9 Nationalism is an infantile disease. It is the measles of mankind.

Albert Einstein (1879–1955) German-born US physicist. *Einstein: A Study in Simplicity* (Edwin Muller)

10 I have never understood why one's affections must be confined, as once with women, to a single country.

John Kenneth Galbraith (1908–) US economist. *A Life in our Times*

11 Anyone who wants to carry on the war against the outsiders, come with me. I can't offer you either honours or wages; I offer you hunger, thirst, forced marches, battles and death. Anyone who loves his country, follow me.

Giuseppe Garibaldi (1807–82) Italian general and political leader. *Garibaldi* (Guerzoni)

12 That kind of patriotism which consists in hating all other nations.

Elizabeth Gaskell (1810–65) British novelist. *Sylvia's Lovers*, Ch. 1

13 I only regret that I have but one life to lose for my country.

Nathan Hale (1755–76) US revolutionary hero. Speech before his execution, 22 Sept 1776

14 Unlike so many who find success, she remained a 'dinkum hard-swearing Aussie' to the end.

Arnold Haskell (1903–80) English writer on ballet. Referring to Dame Nellie Melba. *Waltzing Matilda*

15 *Dulce et decorum est pro patria mori.*
It is a sweet and seemly thing to die for one's country.

Horace (Quintus Horatius Flaccus; 65–8 BC) Roman poet. Odes, III

16 We don't want to fight, but, by jingo if we do,
We've got the ships, we've got the men, we've got the money too.
We've fought the Bear before, and while Britons shall be true,
The Russians shall not have Constantinople.

George William Hunt (c. 1829–1904) British writer. *We Don't Want to Fight*

17 Patriotism is the last refuge of a scoundrel.

Samuel Johnson (1709–84) British lexicographer. *Life of Johnson* (J. Boswell), Vol. II

18 And so, my fellow Americans: ask not what your country can do for you – ask what you can do for your country. My fellow citizens of the world: ask not what America will do for you, but what together we can do for the freedom of man.

John Fitzgerald Kennedy (1917–63) US statesman. Inaugural address, 20 Jan 1961

19 Those who prate about Blimpish patriotism in the mode of Margaret Thatcher are also the ones who will take millions off the caring services of this country.

Neil Kinnock (1942–) British politician. Speech, Labour Party Conference, Brighton, 1983

20 I would die for my country...but I would not let my country die for me.

Neil Kinnock Speech on nuclear disarmament, 1987

21 'Take my drum to England, hang et by the shore,
Strike et when your powder's runnin' low;
If the Dons sight Devon, I'll quit the port o' Heaven,
An' drum them up the Channel as we drummed them long ago.'

Henry John Newbolt (1862–1938) British poet. *Drake's Drum*

22 But cared greatly to serve God and the King,
And keep the Nelson touch.

Henry John Newbolt *Minora Sidera*

23 The old Lie: *Dulce et decorum est*
Pro patria mori.

Wilfred Owen (1893–1918) British poet. *Dulce et decorum est*

24 If I were an American, as I am an Englishman, while a foreign troop was landed in my country, I never would lay down my arms, – never – never – never!

William Pitt the Elder (1708–78) British statesman. Speech, House of Lords, 18 Nov 1777

25 There is no room in this country for hyphenated Americanism.

Theodore Roosevelt (1858–1919) US Republican president. Speech, New York, 12 Oct 1915

26 There can be no fifty-fifty Americanism in this country. There is room here for only one hundred per cent Americanism.

Theodore Roosevelt Speech, Saratoga, 19 July 1918

27 Patriots always talk of dying for their country and never of killing for their country.

Bertrand Russell (1872–1970) British philosopher. *The Autobiography of Bertrand Russell*

28 Not that I lov'd Caesar less, but that I lov'd Rome more.

William Shakespeare (1564–1616) English dramatist. *Julius Caesar*, III:2

29 True patriotism is of no party.

Tobias Smollett (1721–71) British novelist. *The Adventures of Sir Launcelote Greaves*

30 Patriotism to the Soviet State is a revolutionary duty, whereas patriotism to a bourgeois State is treachery.

Leon Trotsky (Lev Davidovich Bronstein; 1879–1940) Russian revolutionary. *Disputed Barricade* (Fitzroy Maclean)

31 I was born an American; I will live an American; I shall die an American.

Daniel Webster (1782–1852) US statesman. Speech, US Senate, 17 July 1850

32 'Shoot, if you must, this old gray head,
But spare your country's flag,' she said.

A shade of sadness, a blush of shame,
Over the face of the leader came.

John Greenleaf Whittier (1807–92) US poet. *Barbara Frietchie*

33 There is one certain means by which I can be sure never to see my country's ruin; I will die in the last ditch.

William III (1650–1702) King of England. *History of England* (Hume)

PATRONAGE

See also promotion

1 *Patron.* Commonly a wretch who supports with insolence, and is paid with flattery.

Samuel Johnson (1709–84) British lexicographer. *Dictionary of the English Language*

2 Is not a Patron, my Lord, one who looks with unconcern on a man struggling for life in the water, and, when he has reached ground, encumbers him with help? The notice which you have been pleased to take of my labours, had it been early, had been kind; but it has been delayed till I am indifferent, and cannot enjoy it; till I am solitary, and cannot impart it; till I am known, and do not want it.

Samuel Johnson Letter to Lord Chesterfield, 7 Feb 1755. *Life of Johnson* (J. Boswell), Vol. I

PEACE

See also war and peace

1 The wolf also shall dwell with the lamb, and the leopard shall lie down with the kid; and the calf and the young lion and the fatling together: and a little child shall lead them.
And the cow and the bear shall feed; their young ones shall lie down together: and the lion shall eat straw like the ox.
And the sucking child shall play on the hole of the asp, and the weaned child shall put his hand on the cockatrice' den.
They shall not hurt nor destroy in all my holy mountain: for the earth shall be full of the knowledge of the Lord, as the waters cover the sea.

Bible: Isaiah 11:6–9

2 Peace I leave with you, my peace I give unto you: not as the world giveth, give I unto you. Let not your heart be troubled, neither let it be afraid.

Bible: John 14:27

3 *Peace,* n. In international affairs, a period of cheating between two periods of fighting.

Ambrose Bierce (1842–?1914) US writer and journalist. *The Devil's Dictionary*

4 Give peace in our time, O Lord.

The Book of Common Prayer *Morning Prayer,* Versicles

5 Don't tell me peace has broken out.

Bertolt Brecht (1898–1956) German dramatist. *Mother Courage,* VIII

6 I believe it is peace for our time...peace with honour.

Neville Chamberlain (1869–1940) British statesman. Broadcast after Munich Agreement, 1 Oct 1938

7 Anythin' for a quiet life, as the man said wen he took the sitivation at the lighthouse.

Charles Dickens (1812–70) British novelist. *Pickwick Papers,* Ch. 43

8 Lord Salisbury and myself have brought you back peace – but a peace I hope with honour.

Benjamin Disraeli (1804–81) British statesman. Speech, House of Commons, 16 July 1878

9 Let us have peace.

Ulysses Simpson Grant (1822–85) US general. On accepting nomination. Letter, 29 May 1868

10 Arms alone are not enough to keep the peace – it must be kept by men.

John Fitzgerald Kennedy (1917–63) US statesman. *The Observer,* 'Sayings of the Decade', 1962

11 And who will bring white peace
That he may sleep upon his hill again?

Vachel Lindsay (1879–1931) US poet. *Abraham Lincoln Walks at Midnight*

12 The issues are the same. We wanted peace on earth, love, and understanding between everyone around the world. We have learned that change comes slowly.

Paul McCartney (1943–) British rock musician. *The Observer,* 'Sayings of the Week', 7 June 1987

13 Roll up that map: it will not be wanted these ten years.

William Pitt the Younger (1759–1806) British statesman. On learning that Napoleon had won the Battle of Austerlitz. Attrib.

14 Nation shall speak peace unto nation.

Montague John Rendall (1862–1950) British schoolmaster. Motto of BBC, 1927

15 Here, where the world is quiet;
Here, where all trouble seems
Dead winds' and spent waves' riot
In doubtful dreams of dreams.

Algernon Charles Swinburne (1837–1909) British poet. *The Garden of Proserpine*

16 We are the true peace movement.

Margaret Thatcher (1925–) British politician and prime minister. *The Times,* 1983

17 And I shall have some peace there, for peace comes dropping slow,
Dropping from the veils of the morning to where the cricket sings.

W. B. Yeats (1865–1939) Irish poet. *The Lake Isle of Innisfree*

PERCEPTION

1 If the doors of perception were cleansed everything would appear to man as it is, infinite.

William Blake (1757–1827) British poet. *The Marriage of Heaven and Hell,* 'A Memorable Fancy'

2 Man's Desires are limited by his Perceptions; none can desire what he has not perceived.

William Blake *There is no Natural Religion*

3 'What,' it will be questioned, 'when the sun rises, do you not see a round disc of fire somewhat like a guinea?' 'O no, no, I see an innumerable company of the heavenly host crying, 'Holy,

Holy, Holy is the Lord God Almighty!"

William Blake *Descriptive Catalogue*, 'The Vision of Judgment'

4 I saw it, but I did not realize it.

Elizabeth Peabody (1804–94) US educationalist. Giving a Transcendentalist explanation for her accidentally walking into a tree. *The Peabody Sisters of Salem* (L. Tharp)

PERFECTION

See also imperfection

1 The pursuit of perfection, then, is the pursuit of sweetness and light...He who works for sweetness and light united, works to make reason and the will of God prevail.

Matthew Arnold (1822–88) British poet and critic. *Culture and Anarchy*, Ch. 1

2 The year's at the spring,
And day's at the morn;
Morning's at seven;
The hill-side's dew-pearled;
The lark's on the wing;
The snail's on the thorn;
God's in His heaven –
All's right with the world.

Robert Browning (1812–89) British poet. *Pippa Passes*, Pt. I

3 What's come to perfection perishes.
Things learned on earth, we shall practise in heaven.
Works done least rapidly, Art most cherishes.

Robert Browning *Old Pictures in Florence*, XVII

4 You would attain to the divine perfection,
And yet not turn your back upon the world.

Henry Wadsworth Longfellow (1807–82) US poet. *Michael Angelo*

5 Perfection has one grave defect; it is apt to be dull.

W. Somerset Maugham (1874–1965) British novelist. *The Summing Up*

6 Whoever thinks a faultless piece to see,
Thinks what ne'er was, nor is, nor e'er shall be.

Alexander Pope (1688–1744) British poet. *An Essay on Criticism*

7 Oysters are more beautiful than any religion...There's nothing in Christianity or Buddhism that quite matches the sympathetic unselfishness of an oyster.

Saki (Hector Hugh Munro; 1870–1916) British writer. *The Match-Maker*

8 Everything's Coming Up Roses.

Stephen Sondheim (1930–) US composer and lyricist. Song title

9 Finality is death. Perfection is finality. Nothing is perfect. There are lumps in it.

James Stephens (1882–1950) Irish novelist. *The Crock of Gold*

PERSISTENCE

See also determination, endurance, patience

1 If the mountain will not come to Mahomet, Mahomet must go to the mountain.

Proverb

2 Never say die.

Proverb

3 Slow but sure wins the race.

Proverb

4 And ye shall be hated of all men for my name's sake: but he that endureth to the end shall be saved.

Bible: Matthew 10:22

5 If at first you don't succeed,
Try, try again.

William Edward Hickson (1803–70) British educationalist. *Try and Try Again*

6 A man may write at any time, if he will set himself doggedly to it.

Samuel Johnson (1709–84) British lexicographer. *Life of Johnson* (J. Boswell), Vol. I

7 The drop of rain maketh a hole in the stone, not by violence, but by oft falling.

Hugh Latimer (1485–1555) English churchman. *See also* LUCRETIUS; OVID. Sermon preached before Edward VI

8 Keep right on to the end of the road.

Harry Lauder (Hugh MacLennon; 1870–1950) Scottish music-hall artist. Song title

9 You persisted for a certain number of years like a stammer. You were a *stammer*, if you like, of Space-Time.

Wyndham Lewis (1882–1957) British novelist. *The Human Age*, 'The Childermass'

10 Constant dripping hollows out a stone.

Lucretius (Titus Lucretius Carus; c. 99–55 BC) Roman philosopher. *On the Nature of the Universe*, I. *See also* LATIMER; OVID

11 Dripping water hollows out a stone, a ring is worn away by use.

Ovid (Publius Ovidius Naso; 43 BC–17 AD) Roman poet. *See also* LATIMER; LUCRETIUS. *Epistulae Ex Ponto*, Bk. IV

12 I am a kind of burr; I shall stick.

William Shakespeare (1564–1616) English dramatist. *Measure for Measure*, IV:3

PERSPECTIVE

See also objectivity

1 'Tis distance lends enchantment to the view,
And robes the mountain in its azure hue.

Thomas Campbell (1777–1844) British poet. *Pleasures of Hope*, I

2 One sees great things from the valley;

only small things from the peak.

G. K. Chesterton (1874–1936) British writer. *The Hammer of God*

3 Fleas know not whether they are upon the body of a giant or upon one of ordinary size.

Walter Savage Landor (1775–1864) British poet and writer. *Imaginary Conversations*, 'Southey and Porson'

4 Everything must be taken seriously, nothing tragically.

Louis Adolphe Thiers (1797–1877) French statesman and historian. Speech, French National Assembly, 24 May 1873

PERSUASION

1 They will conquer, but they will not convince.

Miguel de Unamuno y Jugo (1864–1936) Spanish writer. Referring to the Franco rebels. Attrib.

2 There is a holy, mistaken zeal in politics, as well as religion. By persuading others we convince ourselves.

Junius An unidentified writer of letters (1769–72) to the *London Public Advertiser*. Letter, 19 Dec 1769

3 For a priest to turn a man when he lies a-dying, is just like one that has a long time solicited a woman, and cannot obtain his end; at length makes her drunk, and so lies with her.

John Selden (1584–1654) English historian. *Table Talk*

4 The President spends most of his time kissing people on the cheek in order to get them to do what they ought to do without getting kissed.

Harry S. Truman (1884–1972) US statesman. *The Observer*, 'Sayings of the Week', 6 Feb 1949

PERVERSITY

See also petulance, stubbornness

1 If it's heaven for climate, it's hell for company.

J. M. Barrie (1860–1937) British novelist and dramatist. *The Little Minister*, Ch. 3

2 Never the time and the place
And the loved one all together!

Robert Browning (1812–89) British poet. *Never the Time and the Place*

3 For 'tis a truth well known to most,
That whatsoever thing is lost –
We seek it, ere it come to light,
In every cranny but the right.

William Cowper (1731–1800) British poet. *The Retired Cat*

4 Let's find out what everyone is doing,
And then stop everyone from doing it.

A. P. Herbert (1890–1971) British writer and politician. *Let's Stop Somebody*

5 I had never had a piece of toast
Particularly long and wide,
But fell upon the sanded floor,
And always on the buttered side.

James Payn (1830–98) British writer and editor. *Chambers's Journal*, 2 Feb 1884

6 Adam was but human – this explains it all. He did not want the apple for the apple's sake, he wanted it only because it was forbidden.

Mark Twain (Samuel Langhorne Clemens; 1835–1910) US writer. *Pudd'nhead Wilson's Calendar*, Ch. 2

PESSIMISM

1 Pessimism, when you get used to it, is just as agreeable as optimism.

Arnold Bennett (1867–1931) British novelist. *Things that have Interested Me*, 'The Slump in Pessimism'

2 Scratch a pessimist, and you find often a defender of privilege.

Lord Beveridge (1879–1963) British economist. *The Observer*, 'Sayings of the Week', 17 Dec 1943

3 The optimist proclaims we live in the best of all possible worlds; and the pessimist fears this is true.

James Cabell (1879–1958) US novelist and journalist. *The Silver Stallion*

4 He who despairs over an event is a coward, but he who holds hopes for the human condition is a fool.

Albert Camus (1913–60) French existentialist writer. *The Rebel*

5 A Hard Rain's A-Gonna Fall.

Bob Dylan (Robert Allen Zimmerman; 1941–) US popular singer. Song title

6 Sleep is good, death is better; but of course, the best thing would be never to have been born at all.

Heinrich Heine (1797–1856) German poet and writer. *Morphine*

7 Nothing to do but work,
Nothing to eat but food,
Nothing to wear but clothes,
To keep one from going nude.

Benjamin Franklin King (1857–94) American humorist. *The Pessimist*

8 If we see light at the end of the tunnel it is the light of an oncoming train.

Robert Lowell (1917–77) US poet. *Day by Day*

9 How many pessimists end up by desiring the things they fear, in order to prove that they are right.

Robert Mallet (1915–) French writer. *Apostilles*

10 A pessimist is a man who looks both ways before crossing a one-way street.

Laurence J. Peter (1919–90) Canadian writer. *Peter's Quotations*

11 It is not, nor it cannot come to good.

William Shakespeare (1564–1616) English dramatist. *Hamlet*, I:2

PETULANCE

See also perversity, stubbornness

1 She refused to begin the 'Beguine'
Tho' they besought her to
And with language profane and obscene
She curs'd the man who taught her to
She curs'd Cole Porter too!

Noël Coward (1899–1973) British dramatist. *Sigh No More*, 'Nina'

2 He has to learn that petulance is not sarcasm, and that insolence is not invective.

Benjamin Disraeli (1804–81) British statesman. Said of Sir C. Wood. Speech, House of Commons, 16 Dec 1852

3 I am the emperor, and I want dumplings.

Ferdinand I (1793–1875) Emperor of Austria. *The Fall of the House of Habsburg* (E. Crankshaw)

4 I hate a fellow whom pride, or cowardice, or laziness drives into a corner, and who does nothing when he is there but sit and *growl*; let him come out as I do, and *bark*.

Samuel Johnson (1709–84) British lexicographer. *Life of Johnson* (J. Boswell), Vol. IV

PHILISTINISM

See also arts, books, culture

1 For this class we have a designation which now has become pretty well known, and which we may as well still keep for them, the designation of Philistines.

Matthew Arnold (1822–88) British poet and critic. Referring to the middle class. *Culture and Anarchy*, Ch. 3

2 The great apostle of the Philistines, Lord Macaulay.

Matthew Arnold *Joubert*

3 The finest collection of frames I ever saw.

Humphry Davy (1778–1829) British chemist. When asked what he thought of the Paris art galleries. Attrib.

4 When I hear anyone talk of Culture, I reach for my revolver.

Hermann Goering (1893–1946) German leader. Attrib. to Goering but probably said by Hanns Johst

5 I've never been in there...but there are only three things to see, and I've seen colour reproductions of all of them.

Harold W. Ross (1892–1951) US journalist. Referring to the Louvre. *A Farewell to Arms* (Ernest Hemingway)

6 All my wife has ever taken from the Mediterranean – from that whole vast intuitive culture – are four bottles of Chianti to make into lamps, and two china condiment donkeys labelled Sally and Peppy.

Peter Shaffer (1926–) British dramatist. *Equus*, I:18

7 Particularly against books the Home Secretary is. If we can't stamp out literature in the country, we can at least stop it being brought in from outside.

Evelyn Waugh (1903–66) British novelist. *Vile Bodies*, Ch. 2

8 Listen! There never was an artistic period. There never was an Art-loving nation.

James Whistler (1834–1903) US painter. Attrib.

PHILOSOPHERS

See also philosophy

1 All are lunatics, but he who can analyze his delusion is called a philosopher.

Ambrose Bierce (1842–?1914) US writer and journalist. *Epigrams*

2 There is nothing so absurd but some philosopher has said it.

Cicero (106–43 BC) Roman orator and statesman. *De Divinatione*, II

3 To a philosopher no circumstance, however trifling, is too minute.

Oliver Goldsmith (1728–74) Irish-born British writer. *The Citizen of the World*

4 Philosophers never balance between profit and honesty, because their decisions are general, and neither their passions nor imaginations are interested in the objects.

David Hume (1711–76) Scottish philosopher. *A Treatise of Human Nature*

5 I doubt if the philosopher lives, or ever has lived, who could know himself to be heartily despised by a street boy without some irritation.

T. H. Huxley (1825–95) British biologist. *Evolution and Ethics*

6 In the philosopher there is nothing whatever impersonal; and, above all, his morality bears decided and decisive testimony to *who he is* – that is to say, to the order of rank in which the innermost drives of his nature stand in relation to one another.

Friedrich Wilhelm Nietzsche (1844–1900) German philosopher. *Jenseits von Gut und Böse*

7 Not to care for philosophy is to be a true philosopher.

Blaise Pascal (1623–62) French philosopher and mathematician. *Pensées*, I

8 Three passions, simple but overwhelmingly strong, have governed my life: the longing for love, the search for knowledge, and unbearable pity for the suffering of mankind.

Bertrand Russell (1872–1970) British philosopher. *The Autobiography of Bertrand Russell*, Prologue

9 Philosophers are as jealous as women. Each wants a monopoly of praise.

George Santayana (1863–1952) US philosopher. *Dialogues In Limbo*

10 There are now-a-days professors of philosophy but not philosophers.

Henry David Thoreau (1817–62) US writer. *Walden*, 'Economy'

PHILOSOPHY

See also logic, metaphysics, philosophers, thinking

1 The principles of logic and metaphysics are true simply because we never allow them to be anything else.

A. J. Ayer (1910–89) British philosopher. *Language, Truth and Logic*

2 The formula 'Two and two make five' is not without its attractions.

Fedor Mikhailovich Dostoevsky (1821–81) Russian novelist. *Notes from the Underground*

3 If we take in our hand any volume; of divinity or school metaphysics, for instance; let us ask, *Does it contain any abstract reasoning concerning quantity or number?* No. *Does it contain any experimental reasoning, concerning matter of fact and existence?* No. Commit it then to the flames: for it can contain nothing but sophistry and illusion.

David Hume (1711–76) Scottish philosopher. *An Enquiry Concerning Human Understanding*

4 We are perpetually moralists, but we are geometricians only by chance. Our intercourse with intellectual nature is necessary; our speculations upon matter are voluntary, and at leisure.

Samuel Johnson (1709–84) British lexicographer. *Lives of the English Poets*, 'Milton'

5 I refute it *thus.*

Samuel Johnson Replying to Boswell's contention that they were unable to refute Bishop Berkeley's theory of matter, by kicking a large stone with his foot. *Life of Johnson* (J. Boswell), Vol. I

6 There are innumerable questions to which the inquisitive mind can in this state receive no answer: Why do you and I exist? Why was this world created? Since it was to be created, why was it not created sooner?

Samuel Johnson *Life of Johnson* (J. Boswell), Vol. III

7 Do not all charms fly
At the mere touch of cold philosophy?

John Keats (1795–1821) British poet. *Lamia*, II

8 Axioms in philosophy are not axioms until they are proved upon our pulses; we read fine things but never feel them to the full until we have gone the same steps as the author.

John Keats Letter to J. H. Reynolds, 3 May 1818

9 There will be no end to the troubles of states, or indeed, my dear Glaucon, of humanity itself, till philosophers become kings in this world, or till those we now call kings and rulers really and truly become philosophers.

Plato (429–347 BC) Greek philosopher. *Republic*, Bk. 5

10 We thought philosophy ought to be patient and unravel people's mental blocks. Trouble with doing that is, once you've unravelled them, their heads fall off.

Frederic Raphael (1931–) British author. *The Glittering Prizes: A Double Life*, III:2

11 Matter…a convenient formula for describing what happens where it isn't.

Bertrand Russell (1872–1970) British philosopher. *An Outline of Philosophy*

12 Philosophy is the replacement of category-habits by category-disciplines.

Gilbert Ryle (1900–76) British philosopher. *The Concept of Mind*, Introduction

13 It is a great advantage for a system of philosophy to be substantially true.

George Santayana (1863–1952) US philosopher. *The Unknowable*

14 Philosophy is the product of wonder.

A. N. Whitehead (1861–1947) British philosopher. *Nature and Life*, Ch. 1

15 The history of Western philosophy is, after all, no more than a series of footnotes to Plato's philosophy.

A. N. Whitehead Attrib.

16 My advice to you is not to inquire why or whither, but just enjoy your ice-cream while it's on your plate, – that's my philosophy.

Thornton Wilder (1897–1975) US novelist and dramatist. *The Skin of Our Teeth*, I

17 Philosophy, as we use the word, is a fight against the fascination which forms of expression exert upon us.

Ludwig Wittgenstein (1889–1951) Austrian philosopher. *The Blue Book*

18 Philosophy is not a theory but an activity.

Ludwig Wittgenstein *Tractatus Logico-Philosophicus*, Ch. 4

PHOTOGRAPHY

1 Photography can never grow up if it imitates some other medium. It has to walk alone; it has to be itself.

Berenice Abbott (1898–1991) US photographer. *Infinity*, 'It Has to Walk Alone'

2 Most things in life are moments of pleasure and a lifetime of embarrassment; photography is a moment of embarrassment and a lifetime of pleasure.

Tony Benn (1925–) British politician. *The Sunday Times*, 31 Dec 1989

3 In a portrait, I'm looking for the silence in somebody.

Henri Cartier-Bresson (1908–) French photographer. *The Observer*, 'Sayings of the Week', 15 May 1994

4 The camera cannot lie. But it can be an accessory to untruth.

Harold Evans (1928–) British journalist. *Pictures on a Page*

5 As far as I knew, he had never taken a photograph before, and the summit of Everest was hardly the place to show him how.

Edmund Hillary (1919–) New Zealand mountaineer. Referring to Tenzing Norgay, his companion on the conquest of Mt Everest (1953). *High Adventure*

6 The modern pantheist not only sees the god in everything, he takes photographs of it.

D. H. Lawrence (1885–1930) British novelist. *St Mawr*

7 I have for instance among my purchases... several original Mona Lisas and all painted (according to the Signature) by the great artist Kodak.

Spike Milligan (1918–) British comic actor and author. *A Dustbin of Milligan*, 'Letters to Harry Secombe'

8 A photograph is not only an image (as a painting is an image), an interpretation of the real; it is also a trace, something directly stencilled off the real, like a footprint or a death mask.

Susan Sontag (1933–) US novelist and essayist. *On Photography*

PLACES

See also Britain, China, Europe, Ireland, Middle East, South Africa

1 The shortest way out of Manchester is notoriously a bottle of Gordon's gin.

William Bolitho (1890–1930) British writer. Attrib.

2 India is a geographical term. It is no more a united nation than the Equator.

Winston Churchill (1874–1965) British statesman. Speech, Royal Albert Hall, 18 Mar 1931

3 There are few virtues which the Poles do not possess and there are few errors they have ever avoided.

Winston Churchill Speech, House of Commons, 1945

4 Latins are tenderly enthusiastic. In Brazil they throw flowers at you. In Argentina they throw themselves.

Marlene Dietrich (Maria Magdalene von Losch; 1901–92) German-born film star. *Newsweek*, 24 Aug 1959

5 I find it hard to say, because when I was there it seemed to be shut.

Clement Freud (1924–) British Liberal politician and broadcaster. On being asked for his opinion of New Zealand. Similar remarks have been attributed to others. BBC radio, 12 Apr 1978

6 From Greenland's icy mountains,
From India's coral strand,
Where Afric's sunny fountains
Roll down their golden sand.

Reginald Heber (1783–1826) British bishop and hymn writer. *From Greenland's Icy Mountains*

7 Dublin, though a place much worse than London, is not so bad as Iceland.

Samuel Johnson (1709–84) British lexicographer. Letter to Mrs Christopher Smart. *Life of Johnson* (J. Boswell), Vol. IV

8 Asia is not going to be civilized after the methods of the West. There is too much Asia and she is too old.

Rudyard Kipling (1865–1936) Indian-born British writer. *Life's Handicap*, 'The Man Who Was'

9 On the road to Mandalay
Where the flyin'-fishes play.

Rudyard Kipling *The Road to Mandalay*

10 And all lying mysteriously within the Australian underdark, that peculiar, lost weary aloofness of Australia. There was the vast town of Sydney. And it didn't seem to be real, it seemed to be sprinkled on the surface of a darkness into which it never penetrated.

D. H. Lawrence (1885–1930) British novelist. *Kangaroo*, Ch. 1

11 So you're going to Australia! Well, I made twenty thousand pounds on my tour there, but of course *that* will never be done again. Still, it's a wonderful country, and you'll have a good time. What are you going to sing? All I can say is – sing 'em muck! It's all they can understand!

Nellie Melba (Helen Porter Mitchell; 1861–1931) Australian soprano. Speaking to Clara Butt. *Clara Butt: Her Life Story* (W. H. Ponder)

12 Once a jolly swagman camped by a billy-bong,
Under the shade of a coolibah tree,
And he sang as he sat and waited for his billy-boil,
'You'll come a-waltzing, Matilda, with me.'

Andrew Barton Paterson (1864–1941) Australian journalist and poet. *Waltzing Matilda*

13 Great God! this is an awful place.

Captain Robert Falcon Scott (1868–1912) British explorer. Referring to the South Pole. *Journal*, 17 Jan 1912

14 Cusins is a very nice fellow, certainly: nobody would ever guess that he was born in Australia.

George Bernard Shaw (1856–1950) Irish dramatist and critic. *Major Barbara*, I

15 The Japanese have perfected good manners and made them indistinguishable from rudeness.

Paul Theroux (1941–) US-born writer. *The Great Railway Bazaar*, Ch. 2

16 I'm Charley's aunt from Brazil, where the nuts come from.

Brandon Thomas (1856–1914) British actor and dramatist. *Charley's Aunt*, I

PLAYS

See also acting, actors, criticism, literature, Shakespeare, theatre, writers, writing

1 Now a whole is that which has a beginning, a middle, and an end.

Aristotle (384–322 BC) Greek philosopher. Referring specifically to the dramatic form of tragedy. *Poetics*, Ch. 7

2 One of Edward's Mistresses was Jane Shore, who has had a play written about her, but it is a tragedy and therefore not worth reading.

Jane Austen (1775–1817) British novelist. *The History of England*

3 In the theatre the audience want to be surprised – but by things that they expect.

Tristan Bernard (1866–1947) French dramatist. *Contes, Repliques et Bon Mots*

4 Prologues precede the piece – in mournful verse;
As undertakers – walk before the hearse.

David Garrick (1717–79) British actor and manager. *Apprentice*, Prologue

5 He always hurries to the main event and whisks his audience into the middle of things as though they knew already.

Horace (Quintus Horatius Flaccus; 65–8 BC) Roman poet. *Ars Poetica*

6 I think you would have been very glad if I had written it.

Alexis Piron (1689–1773) French poet and dramatist. Discussing Voltaire's *Sémiramis* with him after its poor reception on the first night. *Cyclopaedia of Anecdotes* (K. Arvine)

7 Depending upon shock tactics is easy, whereas writing a good play is difficult. Pubic hair is no substitute for wit.

J. B. Priestley (1894–1984) British novelist. *Outcries and Asides*

8 My soul; sit thou a patient looker-on;
Judge not the play before the play is done:
Her plot hath many changes, every day
Speaks a new scene; the last act crowns the play.

Francis Quarles (1592–1644) English poet. *Epigram, Respice Finem*

9 Rehearsing a play is making the word flesh. Publishing a play is reversing the process.

Peter Shaffer (1926–) British dramatist. *Equus*, Note

10 If it be true that good wine needs no bush, 'tis true that a good play needs no epilogue.

William Shakespeare (1564–1616) English dramatist. *As You Like It*, Epilogue

11 The play's the thing
Wherein I'll catch the conscience of the King.

William Shakespeare *Hamlet*, II:2

12 A good many inconveniences attend play-going in any large city, but the greatest of them is usually the play itself.

Kenneth Tynan (1927–80) British theatre critic. *New York Herald Tribune*

13 A novel is a static thing that one moves through; a play is a dynamic thing that moves past one.

Kenneth Tynan *Curtains*

14 The play was a great success, but the audience was a disaster.

Oscar Wilde (1854–1900) Irish-born British dramatist. Referring to a play that had recently failed. Attrib.

PLEASURE

See also debauchery, happiness, leisure, merrymaking

1 No pleasure without pain.

Proverb

2 And if the following day, he chance to find
A new repast, or an untasted spring,
Blesses his stars, and thinks it luxury.

Joseph Addison (1672–1719) British essayist. *Cato*, I:4

3 One half of the world cannot understand the pleasures of the other.

Jane Austen (1775–1817) British novelist. *Emma*, Ch. 9

4 Then I commended mirth, because a man hath no better thing under the sun, than to eat, and to drink, and to be merry: for that shall abide with him of his labour the days of his life, which God giveth him under the sun.

Bible: Ecclesiastes 8:15

5 He who bends to himself a Joy
Doth the wingèd life destroy;
But he who kisses the Joy as it flies
Lives in Eternity's sunrise.

William Blake (1757–1827) British poet. *Gnomic Verses*

6 Pleasure after all is a safer guide than either right or duty.

Samuel Butler (1835–1902) British writer. *The Way of All Flesh*, Ch. 19

7 Though sages may pour out their wisdom's treasure,
There is no sterner moralist than Pleasure.

Lord Byron (1788–1824) British poet. *Don Juan*, III

8 In Xanadu did Kubla Khan
A stately pleasure-dome decree:
Where Alph, the sacred river, ran
Through caverns measureless to man
Down to a sunless sea.

Samuel Taylor Coleridge (1772–1834) British poet. *Kubla Khan*

9 It was a miracle of rare device,
A sunny pleasure-dome with caves of ice!

Samuel Taylor Coleridge *Kubla Khan*

10 Nothing can permanently please, which does not contain in itself the reason why it is so, and not otherwise.

Samuel Taylor Coleridge *Biographia Literaria*, Ch. 14

11 For present joys are more to flesh and blood
Than a dull prospect of a distant good.

John Dryden (1631–1700) British poet and dramatist. *The Hind and the Panther*, III

12 The art of pleasing consists in being pleased.

William Hazlitt (1778–1830) British essayist. *On Manner*

13 People must not do things for fun. We are not here for fun. There is no reference to fun in any Act of Parliament.

A. P. Herbert (1890–1971) British writer and politician. *Uncommon Law*

14 Pleasure is very seldom found where it is sought; our brightest blazes of gladness are commonly kindled by unexpected sparks.

Samuel Johnson (1709–84) British lexicographer. *The Idler*

15 No man is a hypocrite in his pleasures.

Samuel Johnson *Life of Johnson* (J. Boswell), Vol. IV

16 If I had no duties, and no reference to futurity, I would spend my life in driving briskly in a post-chaise with a pretty woman.

Samuel Johnson *Life of Johnson* (J. Boswell), Vol. III

17 Give me books, fruit, French wine and fine weather and a little music out of doors, played by somebody I do not know.

John Keats (1795–1821) British poet. Letter to Fanny Keats, 29 Aug 1819

18 Life would be tolerable, were it not for its amusements.

George Cornewall Lewis (1806–63) British statesman and writer. *The Perpetual Pessimist* (Sagittarius and George)

19 A little of what you fancy does you good.

Marie Lloyd (1870–1922) British music-hall singer. Song title

20 Who loves not wine, woman and song,
Remains a fool his whole life long.

Martin Luther (1483–1546) German Protestant. Attrib.

21 My candle burns at both ends;
It will not last the night;
But ah, my foes, and oh my friends –
It gives a lovely light!

Edna St Vincent Millay (1892–1950) US poet. *A Few Figs from Thistles*, 'First Fig'

22 To sport with Amaryllis in the shade,
Or with the tangles of Neaera's hair.

John Milton (1608–74) English poet. *Lycidas*

23 Hence, vain deluding Joys,
The brood of Folly without father bred!

John Milton *Il Penseroso*

24 Great lords have their pleasures, but the people have fun.

Baron de Montesquieu (1689–1755) French writer. *Pensées diverses*

25 I wish thee as much pleasure in the reading, as I had in the writing.

Francis Quarles (1592–1644) English poet. *Emblems*, 'To the Reader'

26 Pleasures are all alike simply considered in themselves...He that takes pleasure to hear sermons enjoys himself as much as he that hears plays.

John Selden (1584–1654) English historian. *Table Talk*

27 Pleasure is nothing else but the intermission of pain.

John Selden *Table Talk*

28 A Good Time Was Had by All.

Stevie Smith (Florence Margaret Smith; 1902–71) British poet. Book title

29 This is the best moment of my life, since my Granny caught her tit in the mangle.

Daley Thompson (Francis Morgan T.; 1958–) British decathlete. On winning the decathlon at the Olympics *The Guardian*, 1984

30 Everyone is dragged on by their favourite pleasure.

Virgil (Publius Vergilius Maro; 70–19 BC) Roman poet. *Eclogue*, Bk. II

31 All the things I really like to do are either immoral, illegal, or fattening.

Alexander Woollcott (1887–1943) US journalist. Attrib.

32 Pleasures newly found are sweet
When they lie about our feet.

William Wordsworth (1770–1850) British poet. *To the Small Celandine*

POETRY

See also criticism, inspiration, literature, poetry and prose, poets

1 For this reason poetry is something more philosophical and more worthy of serious attention than history.

Aristotle (384–322 BC) Greek philosopher. *Poetics*, Ch. 9

2 A criticism of life under the conditions fixed for such a criticism by the laws of poetic truth and poetic beauty.

Matthew Arnold (1822–88) British poet and critic. *Essays in Criticism*, Second Series, 'The Study of Poetry'

3 I think it will be found that the grand style arises in poetry, when a noble nature, poetically gifted, treats with simplicity or with severity a serious subject.

Matthew Arnold Closing words. *On Translating Homer*

4 The difference between genuine poetry and the poetry of Dryden, Pope, and all their school, is briefly this: their poetry is conceived and composed in their wits, genuine poetry is conceived and composed in the soul.

Matthew Arnold *Thomas Gray*

5 Now Ireland has her madness and her weather still,
For poetry makes nothing happen.

W. H. Auden (1907–73) British poet. *In Memory of W. B. Yeats*, II

6 Too many people in the modern world view poetry as a luxury, not a necessity like petrol. But to me it's the oil of life.

John Betjeman (1906–84) British poet. *The Observer*, 'Sayings of the Year', 1974

7 Poetry is as much a part of the universe as mathematics and physics. It is not a cleverer device or recreation, unless the Eternal is clever.

Edmund Blunden (1896–1974) British poet. Speech on his election as Professor of Poetry at Oxford University, 1966

8 Nothing so difficult as a beginning
In poesy, unless perhaps the end.

Lord Byron (1788–1824) British poet. *Don Juan*, IV

9 I have nothing to say, I am saying it, and that is poetry.

John Cage (1912–92) US composer. In *The Sunday Times* (quoted by Cyril Connolly), 10 Sept 1972

10 For the godly poet must be chaste himself, but there is no need for his verses to be so.

Catullus (c. 84–c. 54 BC) Roman poet. *Carmina*, XVI

11 That willing suspension of disbelief for the moment, which constitutes poetic faith.

Samuel Taylor Coleridge (1772–1834) British poet. *Biographia Literaria*, Ch. 14

12 Poetry's unnat'ral; no man ever talked poetry 'cept a beadle on boxin' day.

Charles Dickens (1812–70) British novelist. *Pickwick Papers*, Ch. 33

13 I am afeered that werges on the poetical, Sammy.

Charles Dickens Said by Sam Weller. *Pickwick Papers*, Ch. 33

14 Poetry is not a turning loose of emotion, but an escape from emotion; it is not the expression of personality, but an escape from personality.

T. S. Eliot (1888–1965) US-born British poet and dramatist. *Tradition and the Individual Talent*

15 All one's inventions are true, you can be sure of that. Poetry is as exact a science as geometry.

Gustave Flaubert (1821–80) French novelist. Letter to Louise Colet, 14 Aug 1853

16 We all write poems; it is simply that poets are the ones who write in words.

John Fowles (1926–) British novelist. *The French Lieutenant's Woman*, Ch. 19

17 Writing free verse is like playing tennis with the net down.

Robert Frost (1875–1963) US poet. Speech, Milton Academy, 17 May 1935

18 Rightly thought of there is poetry in peaches...even when they are canned.

Harley Granville-Barker (1877–1946) British actor and dramatist. *The Madras House*, I

19 If Galileo had said in verse that the world moved, the Inquisition might have let him alone.

Thomas Hardy (1840–1928) British novelist. *The Later Years of Thomas Hardy* (F. E. Hardy)

20 Even when poetry has a meaning, as it usually has, it may be inadvisable to draw it out...Perfect understanding will sometimes almost extinguish pleasure.

A. E. Housman (1859–1936) British scholar and poet. *The Name and Nature of Poetry*

21 'Why Sir, it is much easier to say what it is not. We all *know* what light is; but it is not easy to *tell* what it is.'

Samuel Johnson (1709–84) British lexicographer. When asked, 'What is poetry'. *Life of Johnson* (J. Boswell), Vol. III

22 A drainless shower
Of light is poesy; 'tis the supreme of power;
'Tis might half slumb'ring on its own right arm.

John Keats (1795–1821) British poet. *Sleep and Poetry*

23 A long poem is a test of invention which I take to be the Polar star of poetry, as fancy is the sails, and imagination the rudder.

John Keats Letter to Benjamin Bailey, 8 Oct 1817

24 We hate poetry that has a palpable design upon us – and if we do not agree, seems to put its hand in its breeches pocket. Poetry should be great and unobtrusive, a thing which enters into one's soul, and does not startle or amaze it with itself, but with its subject.

John Keats Letter to J. H. Reynolds, 3 Feb 1818

25 If poetry comes not as naturally as leaves to a tree it had better not come at all.

John Keats Letter to John Taylor, 27 Feb 1818

26 When power narrows the areas of man's concern, poetry reminds him of the richness and diversity of his existence.

John Fitzgerald Kennedy (1917–63) US statesman. Address at Dedication of the Robert Frost Library, 26 Oct 1963

27 Perhaps no person can be a poet, or can even enjoy poetry, without a certain unsoundness of mind.

Lord Macaulay (1800–59) British historian. *Literary Essays Contributed to the 'Edinburgh Review'*, 'Milton'

28 Poem me no poems.

Rose Macaulay (1889–1958) British writer. *Poetry Review*, Autumn 1963

29 Poetry is a comforting piece of fiction set to more or less lascivious music.

H. L. Mencken (1880–1956) US journalist. *Prejudices*, 'The Poet and his Art'

30 Blest pair of Sirens, pledges of Heaven's joy,
Sphere-born harmonious sisters, Voice and Verse.

John Milton (1608–74) English poet. *At a Solemn Music*

31 Rhyme being no necessary adjunct or true ornament of poem or good verse, in longer works especially, but the invention of a barbarous age, to set off wretched matter and lame metre.

John Milton *Paradise Lost*, The Verse. Preface to 1668 ed.

32 The troublesome and modern bondage of Rhyming.

John Milton *Paradise Lost*, The Verse. Preface to 1668 ed.

33 ...poetry, 'The Cinderella of the Arts.'

Harriet Monroe (1860–1936) US poet and editor. *Famous American Women* (Hope Stoddard), 'Harriet Monroe'

34 Above all I am not concerned with Poetry. My subject is War, and the pity of War. The Poetry is in the pity.

Wilfred Owen (1893–1918) British poet. *Poems*, Preface

35 Curst be the verse, how well so'er it flow,
That tends to make one worthy man my foe.

Alexander Pope (1688–1744) British poet. *Epistle to Dr. Arbuthnot*

36 For three years, out of key with his time,
He strove to resuscitate the dead art
Of poetry to maintain 'the sublime'

In the old sense. Wrong from the start.

Ezra Pound (1885–1972) US poet. *Pour l'élection de son sépulcre*

37 It is a perfectly possible means of overcoming chaos.

I. A. Richards (1893–1979) British critic. *Science and Poetry*

38 A sonnet is a moment's monument, –
Memorial from the Soul's eternity
To one dead deathless hour.

Dante Gabriel Rossetti (1828–82) British painter and poet. *The House of Life*, Introduction

39 What is poetry? The suggestion, by the imagination, of noble grounds for the noble emotions.

John Ruskin (1819–1900) British art critic and writer. *Modern Painters*, Vol. III

40 The truest poetry is the most feigning.

William Shakespeare (1564–1616) English dramatist. *As You Like It*, III:3

41 The poet's eye, in a fine frenzy rolling,
Doth glance from heaven to earth, from earth to heaven;
And as imagination bodies forth
The forms of things unknown, the poet's pen
Turns them to shapes, and gives to airy nothing
A local habitation and a name.

William Shakespeare *A Midsummer Night's Dream*, V:1

42 Not marble, nor the gilded monuments
Of princes, shall outlive this powerful rhyme.

William Shakespeare *Sonnet 55*

43 The lunatic, the lover, and the poet,
Are of imagination all compact.

William Shakespeare *A Midsummer Night's Dream*, V:1

44 Poetry is the record of the best and happiest moments of the happiest and best minds.

Percy Bysshe Shelley (1792–1822) British poet. *A Defence of Poetry*

45 One of the purposes of poetry is to show the dimensions of man that are, as Sir Arthur Eddington said 'midway in scale between the atom and the star.'

Edith Sitwell (1887–1964) British poet and writer. *Rhyme and Reason*

46 My poems are hymns of praise to the glory of life.

Edith Sitwell *Collected Poems*, 'Some Notes on My Poetry'

47 A man does not write poems about what he knows, but about what he does not know.

Robin Skelton (1925–) British academic. *Teach Yourself Poetry*

48 These poems, with all their crudities, doubts, and confusions, are written for the love of Man and in praise of God, and I'd be a damn' fool if they weren't.

Dylan Thomas (1914–53) Welsh poet. *Collected Poems*, Note

49 What was it Chaucer
Said once about the long toil
That goes like blood to the poem's making?
Leave it to nature and the verse sprawls,
Limp as bindweed, if it break at all
Life's iron crust.

R. S. Thomas (1913–) Welsh poet. *Poetry for Supper*

50 Having verse set to music is like looking at a painting through a stained glass window.

Paul Valéry (1871–1945) French poet and writer. Attrib.

51 Hence no force however great can stretch a cord however fine into an horizontal line which is accurately straight: there will always be a bending downwards.

William Whewell (1794–1866) British philosopher and mathematician. An example of unintentional versification. *Elementary Treatise on Mechanics* (1819 edition), Ch. 4

52 No one will ever get at my verses who insists upon viewing them as a literary performance.

Walt Whitman (1819–92) US poet. *A Backward Glance O'er Travel'd Roads*

53 I would rather have written those lines than take Quebec.

James Wolfe (1727–59) British general. Referring to Gray's Elegy, on the eve of the Battle of Quebec, 1759. Attrib.

54 Poetry is the spontaneous overflow of powerful feelings: it takes its origin from emotion recollected in tranquillity.

William Wordsworth (1770–1850) British poet. *Lyrics Ballads*, Preface

55 Out of the quarrel with others we make rhetoric; out of the quarrel with ourselves we make poetry.

W. B. Yeats (1865–1939) Irish poet. *Essay*

POETRY AND PROSE

See also poetry, prose

1 Poetry is not the proper antithesis to prose, but to science. Poetry is opposed to science, and prose to metre.

Samuel Taylor Coleridge (1772–1834) British poet. *Lectures and Notes of 1818*, I

2 I wish our clever young poets would remember my homely definitions of prose and poetry; that is, prose = words in their best order; – poetry = the best words in the best order.

Samuel Taylor Coleridge *Table Talk*

3 Prose on certain occasions can bear a great deal of poetry: on the other hand, poetry sinks and swoons under a moderate weight of prose.

Walter Savage Landor (1775–1864) British poet and writer. *Imaginary Conversations*, 'Archdeacon Hare and Walter Landor'

4 For to write good prose is an affair of good manners. It is, unlike verse, a civil art.... Poetry is baroque.

W. Somerset Maugham (1874–1965) British novelist. *The Summing Up*

5 Poetry is to prose as dancing is to walking.

John Wain (1925–94) British novelist and poet. Talk, BBC radio, 13 Jan 1976

6 The poet gives us his essence, but prose takes the mould of the body and mind entire.

Virginia Woolf (1882–1941) British novelist. *The Captain's Death Bed*, 'Reading'

7 There neither is, nor can be, any *essential* difference between the language of prose and metrical composition.

William Wordsworth (1770–1850) British poet. *Lyrical Ballads*, Preface

8 O'CONNOR. How are you?
W.B.Y. Not very well, I can only write prose today.

W. B. Yeats (1865–1939) Irish poet. Attrib.

POETS

See also Chaucer, criticism, Milton, poetry, Shakespeare, writers

General quotes

1 Poets and painters are outside the class system, or rather they constitute a special class of their own, like the circus people and the gipsies.

Gerald Brenan (Edward Fitzgerald Brenan; 1894–1987) British writer. *Thoughts in a Dry Season*, 'Writing'

2 The Fleshly School of Poetry.

Robert Williams Buchanan (1841–1901) British poet and writer. Referring to Swinburne, William Morris, D. G. Rossetti, etc. Title of article in the *Contemporary Review*, Oct 1871

3 A poet without love were a physical and metaphysical impossibility.

Thomas Carlyle (1795–1881) Scottish historian and essayist. *Critical and Miscellaneous Essays*, 'Burns'

4 A true poet does not bother to be poetical. Nor does a nursery gardener scent his roses.

Jean Cocteau (1889–1963) French poet and artist. *Professional Secrets*

5 Immature poets imitate; mature poets steal.

T. S. Eliot (1888–1965) US-born British poet and dramatist. *Philip Massinger*

6 To be a poet is a condition rather than a profession.

Robert Graves (1895–1985) British poet and novelist. *Horizon*

7 Shelley and Keats were the last English poets who were at all up to date in their chemical knowledge.

J. B. S. Haldane (1892–1964) British geneticist. *Daedalus or Science and the Future*

8 Not gods, nor men, nor even booksellers have put up with poets' being second-rate.

Horace (Quintus Horatius Flaccus; 65–8 BC) Roman poet. *Ars Poetica*

9 Sir, there is no settling the point of precedency between a louse and a flea.

Samuel Johnson (1709–84) British lexicographer. When Maurice Morgann asked him who he considered to be the better poet – Smart or Derrick. *Life of Johnson* (J. Boswell), Vol. IV

10 For ne'er
Was flattery lost on poet's ear:
A simple race! they waste their toil
For the vain tribute of a smile.

Walter Scott (1771–1832) Scottish novelist. *The Lay of the Last Minstrel*, IV

11 There have been many most excellent poets that have never versified, and now swarm many versifiers that need never answer to the name of poets.

Philip Sidney (1554–86) English poet and courtier. *The Defence of Poesy*

12 I hate the whole race...There is no believing a word they say – your professional poets, I mean – there never existed a more worthless set than Byron and his friends for example.

Duke of Wellington (1769–1852) British general and statesman. Lady Salisbury's diary, 26 Oct 1833

Specific quotes

13 Reader! I am to let thee know,
Donne's Body only, lyes below:
For, could the grave his Soul comprize,
Earth would be richer than the skies.

Anonymous Epitaph, written on the wall above Donne's grave the day after his burial

14 It always seems to me that the right sphere for Shelley's genius was the sphere of music, not of poetry.

Matthew Arnold (1822–88) British poet and critic. *Maurice de Guérin*, Footnote

15 When Byron's eyes were shut in death,
We bow'd our head and held our breath.
He taught us little: but our soul
Had *felt* him like the thunder's roll.

Matthew Arnold *Memorial Verses*

16 He spoke, and loos'd our heart in tears.
He laid us as we lay at birth
On the cool flowery lap of earth.

Matthew Arnold Referring to Wordsworth. *Memorial Verses*

17 Time may restore us in his course
Goethe's sage mind and Byron's force:
But where will Europe's latter hour
Again find Wordsworth's healing power?

Matthew Arnold *Memorial Verses*

18 Earth, receive an honoured guest:
William Yeats is laid to rest.
Let the Irish vessel lie
Emptied of its poetry.

W. H. Auden (1907–73) British poet. *In Memory of W. B. Yeats*, III

19 So long as Byron tried to write Poetry with a capital P, to express deep emotions and profound thoughts, his work deserved that epithet he most dreaded, *una seccatura*...His attempts to write satirical heroic couplets were less unsuccessful, but aside from the impossibility of equaling Dryden and Pope in their medium, Byron was really a comedian, not a satirist.

W. H. Auden *The Dyer's Hand*

20 He was the one English love poet who was not afraid to acknowledge that he was composed of body, soul, and mind; and who faithfully recorded all the pitched battles, alarms, treaties, sieges, and fanfares of that extraordinary triangular warfare.

Rupert Brooke (1887–1915) British poet. Referring to John Donne. *John Donne*

21 The great Metaquizzical poet.

Lord Byron (1788–1824) British poet. Said of Wordsworth. Letter to John Murray, 19 Jan 1821

22 Here is Johnny Keats piss-a-bed poetry. No more Keats, I entreat.

Lord Byron Letter to the publisher John Murray, 12 Oct 1821

23 If they had said the sun and the moon was gone out of the heavens it could not have struck me with the idea of a more awful and dreary blank in the creation than the words: Byron is dead.

Jane Welsh Carlyle (1801–66) The wife of Thomas Carlyle. Letter to Thomas Carlyle, 1824

24 A weak, diffusive, weltering, ineffectual man.

Thomas Carlyle (1795–1881) Scottish historian and essayist. Referring to Coleridge. Attrib.

25 How great a possibility; how small a realized result.

Thomas Carlyle Referring to Coleridge. Letter to Ralph Waldo Emerson, 12 Aug 1834

26 A gifted Byron rises in his wrath; and feeling too surely that he for his part is not 'happy', declares the same in very violent language, as a piece of news that may be interesting. It evidently has surprised him much. One dislikes to see a man and poet reduced to proclaim on the streets such tidings.

Thomas Carlyle *Past and Present*

27 He could not think up to the height of his own towering style.

G. K. Chesterton (1874–1936) British writer. Speaking of Tennyson. *The Victorian Age in Literature*, Ch. 3

28 With Donne, whose muse on dromedary trots,
Wreathe iron pokers into true-love knots.

Samuel Taylor Coleridge (1772–1834) British poet. *On Donne's Poetry*

29 The misfortune is, that he has begun to write verses without very well understanding what metre is.

Samuel Taylor Coleridge Referring to Tennyson. *Table Talk*

30 The world is rid of Lord Byron, but the deadly slime of his touch still remains.

John Constable (1776–1837) British landscape painter. Letter to John Fisher, three weeks after Byron's death.

31 Few writers have shown a more extraordinary compass of powers than Donne; for he combined what no other man has ever done – the last sublimation of subtlety with the most impassioned majesty.

Thomas De Quincey (1785–1859) British writer. Referring to John Donne. *Blackwood's Magazine*, Dec 1828

32 This illustrious man, the largest and most spacious intellect, the subtlest and the most comprehensive, in my judgement, that has yet existed amongst men.

Thomas De Quincey Talking of Coleridge. *Recollections of the Lake Poets*

33 He seems to me the most *vulgar-minded* genius that ever produced a great effect in literature.

George Eliot (Mary Ann Evans; 1819–80) British novelist. Referring to Byron. Letter, 21 Sept 1869

34 Blake...knew what interested him, and he therefore presents only the essential, only, in fact, what can be presented, and need not be explained...He approached everything with a mind unclouded by current opinions. There was nothing of the superior person about him. This makes him terrifying.

T. S. Eliot (1888–1965) US-born British poet and dramatist. *The Sacred Wood*

35 Blake is damned good to steal from!

Henry Fuseli (1741–1825) Swiss artist. *Life of Blake* (Alexander Gilchrist)

36 *Hugo – hélas!*

André Gide (1869–1951) French novelist. Replying to an inquiry as to whom he considered the finest poet of the 19th century. *André Gide–Paul Valéry Correspondence 1890–1942*

37 He has no sense of the ludicrous, and, as to God, a worm crawling in a privy is as worthy an object as any other, all being to him indifferent. So to Blake the Chimney Sweeper etc. He is ruined by vain struggles to get rid of what presses on his brain – he attempts impossibles.

William Hazlitt (1778–1830) British essayist. Referring to Blake. *Diary* (Henry Crabb Robinson)

38 He talked on for ever; and you wished him to talk on for ever.

William Hazlitt Referring to Coleridge. *Lectures on the English Poets*, Lecture VIII, 'On the Living Poets'

39 His thoughts did not seem to come with labour and effort; but as if borne on the gusts of genius, and as if the wings of his imagination lifted him from off his feet.

William Hazlitt Referring to Coleridge. *Lectures on the English Poets*, Lecture VIII, 'On the Living Poets'

40 He had a fire in his eye, a fever in his blood, a maggot in his brain, a hectic flutter in his speech, which mark out the philosophic fanatic.

William Hazlitt Referring to Shelley. *Table Talk*

41 The most original poet now living, and the

one whose writings could the least be spared; for they have no substitutes elsewhere.

William Hazlitt Referring to Wordsworth. *The Spirit of the Age*

42 Dr Donne's verses are like the peace of God; they pass all understanding.

James I (1566–1625) King of England. Attrib.

43 He was dull in a new way, and that made many people think him *great*.

Samuel Johnson (1709–84) British lexicographer. Referring to the poet Thomas Gray. *Life of Johnson* (J. Boswell), Vol. II

44 Milton, Madam, was a genius that could cut a Colossus from a rock; but could not carve heads upon cherry-stones.

Samuel Johnson When Miss Hannah More had wondered why Milton could write the epic *Paradise Lost* but only very poor sonnets. *Life of Johnson* (J. Boswell), Vol. IV

45 For Shelley's nature is utterly womanish. Not merely his weak points, but his strong ones, are those of a woman. Tender and pitiful as a woman; and yet, when angry, shrieking, railing, hysterical as a woman...The nature of a woman looks out of that wild, beautiful, girlish face – the nature: but not the spirit.

Charles Kingsley (1819–75) British writer. *Thoughts on Shelley and Byron*

46 Mad, bad, and dangerous to know.

Lady Caroline Lamb (1785–1828) The wife of William Lamb. Said of Byron in her journal. *Journal*

47 Separate from the pleasure of your company, I don't much care if I never see another mountain in my life.

Charles Lamb (1775–1834) British essayist. Letter to Wordsworth, 30 Jan 1801

48 His face when he repeats his verses hath its ancient glory, an Archangel a little damaged.

Charles Lamb Referring to Coleridge. Letter, 26 Apr 1816

49 Keats, at a time when the phrase had not yet been invented, practised the theory of art for art's sake. He is the type, not of the poet, but of the artist. He was not a great personality, his work comes to us as a greater thing than his personality. When we read his verse, we think of the verse, not of John Keats.

F. R. Leavis (1895–1978) British literary critic. *Revaluation*

50 Walt Whitman who laid end to end words never seen in each other's company before outside of a dictionary.

David Lodge (1935–) British author. *Changing Places*, Ch. 5

51 Your works will be read after Shakespeare and Milton are fogotten – and not till then.

Richard Porson (1759–1808) British classicist. Giving his opinion of the poems of Robert Southey. *Quotable Anecdotes* (L. Meissen)

52 Mr Wordsworth, a stupid man, with a decided gift for portraying nature in vignettes, never yet ruined anyone's morals, unless, perhaps, he has driven some susceptible persons to crime in a very fury of boredom.

Ezra Pound (1885–1972) US poet. *Future*, Nov 1917

53 I weep for Adonais – he is dead!
O, weep for Adonais! though our tears
Thaw not the frost which binds so dear a head!
And thou, sad Hour, selected from all years
To mourn our loss, rouse thy obscure compeers,
And teach them thine own sorrow, say: 'With me
Died Adonais; till the Future dares
Forget the Past, his fate and fame shall be
An echo and a light unto eternity!'

Percy Bysshe Shelley (1792–1822) British poet. Written on the death of Keats. *Adonais*

54 People sometimes divide others into those you laugh at and those you laugh with. The young Auden was someone you could laugh-at-with.

Stephen Spender (1909–95) British poet. Address, W. H. Auden's memorial service, Oxford 27 Oct 1973

55 Blake, in the hierarchy of the inspired, stands very high indeed. If one could strike an average among poets, it would probably be true to say that, as far as inspiration is concerned, Blake is to the average poet, as the average poet is to the man in the street. All poetry, to be poetry at all, must have the power of making one, now and then, involuntarily ejaculate: 'What made him think of that?' With Blake, one is asking the question all the time.

Lytton Strachey (1880–1932) British writer. *Books and Characters*

56 Blake is the only poet who sees all temporal things under a form of eternity...Where other poets use reality as a spring-board into space, he uses it as a foothold on his return from flight.

Arthur Symons (1865–1945) British poet. *William Blake*

57 Wordsworth was a tea-time bore, the great Frost of literature, the verbose, the humourless, the platitudinary reporter of Nature in her dullest moods. Open him at any page: and there lies the English language not, as George Moore said of Pater, in a glass coffin, but in a large, sultry, and unhygienic box.

Dylan Thomas (1914–53) Welsh poet. Letter to Pamela Hansford Johnson, 1933

58 The Poet of Immortal Youth.

Henry Van Dyke *Keats*

59 He found in stones the sermons he had already hidden there.

Oscar Wilde (1854–1900) Irish-born British dramatist. Referring to Wordsworth. *The Decay of Lying*

60 There is no doubt that this poor man was mad, but there is something in the madness of this man which interests me more than the sanity of Lord Byron and Walter Scott.

William Wordsworth (1770–1850) British poet. Talking of Blake. *Reminiscences* (Henry Crabb Robinson)

61 I see a schoolboy when I think of him
With face and nose pressed to a

sweetshop window.

W. B. Yeats (1865–1939) Irish poet. Referring to Keats. Attrib.

62 That William Blake
Who beat upon the wall
Till Truth obeyed his call.

W. B. Yeats *An Acre of Grass*

POLICE

1 When constabulary duty's to be done –
A policeman's lot is not a happy one.

W. S. Gilbert (1836–1911) British dramatist. *The Pirates of Penzance*, II

2 The police are the only 24-hour social service in the country.

Commander Alex Marnoch Remark, Feb 1983

3 Policemen are numbered in case they get lost.

Spike Milligan (1918–) British comic actor and author. *The Last Goon Show of All*

4 A thing of duty is a boy for ever.

Flann O'Brien (Brian O'Nolan; 1911–66) Irish novelist and journalist. About policemen always seeming to be young-looking. *The Listener*, 24 Feb 1977

5 Reading isn't an occupation we encourage among police officers. We try to keep the paper work down to a minimum.

Joe Orton (1933–67) British dramatist. *Loot*, II

6 My father didn't create you to arrest me.

Lord Peel (1829–1912) British politician. Protesting against his arrest by the police, recently established by his father. Attrib.

7 One always has the air of someone who is lying when one speaks to a policeman.

Charles-Louis Philippe (1874–1909) French novelist. *Les Chroniques du canard sauvage*

POLITICAL CORRECTNESS

1 Anyone who pushes for equality, or criticises the male Anglo-Saxon world, is declared "PC" and thereby discredited and silenced. McCarthyism to counteract imagined totalitarianism. Where have we seen that before?

Jasmin Alibhai-Brown British writer and broadcaster. *The Independent*, 11 Aug 1993

2 Where is the Proust of Papua? When the Zulus have a Tolstoy, we will read him.

Saul Bellow (1915–) US writer. *Harpers Magazine*, Nov 1994

3 There shouldn't be opposition between the classical Canon and the multicultural cause. Historically, things have always changed.

James Fenton (1949–) British poet. *The Independent*, 21 Nov 1994

4 Political correctness is a really inane concept. It automatically gives the impression that left-wing ideas are about toeing some line, it makes people think that being left-wing means being a Stalinist. I find the idea of PC petty. Plus it makes the racists look like the rebels.

Mark Thomas British comedian. Comment, Feb 1993

5 But they underestimate the cumulative effect of always hearing Stone-Age man, postman, chairman; of the different reactions you have to 'landlord' and 'landlady' or 'a bit of a bitch' and 'a bit of a dog'.

Katherine Whitehorn (1926–) British journalist. *The Observer*, 18 Aug 1991

POLITICIANS

See also Churchill, compliments, government, Hitler, Houses of Parliament, insults, politics

General quotes

1 No man has come so near our definition of a constitutional statesman – the powers of a first-rate man and the creed of a second-rate man.

Walter Bagehot (1826–77) British economist and journalist. *Historical Essays*, 'The Character of Sir Robert Peel'

2 Politics and the fate of mankind are shaped by men without ideas and without greatness. Men who have greatness within them don't go in for politics.

Albert Camus (1913–60) French existentialist writer. *Notebooks*, 1935–42

3 a politician is an arse upon which everyone has sat except a man.

e. e. cummings (1894–1962) US poet. *A Politician*

4 When I was a boy I was told that anybody could become President of the United States. I am beginning to believe it.

Clarence Seward Darrow (1857–1938) US lawyer. Attrib.

5 There are two problems in my life. The political ones are insoluble and the economic ones are incomprehensible.

Alec Douglas-Home (1903–95) British statesman. Speech, Jan 1964

6 For Politicians neither love nor hate.

John Dryden (1631–1700) British poet and dramatist. *Absalom and Achitophel*, I

7 Since a politician never believes what he says, he is surprised when others believe him.

Charles De Gaulle (1890–1970) French general and statesman. Attrib.

8 In order to become the master, the politician poses as the servant.

Charles De Gaulle Attrib.

9 I have come to the conclusion that politics are too serious a matter to be left to the politicians.

Charles De Gaulle Attrib.

10 I always voted at my party's call,

And I never thought of thinking for myself at all.

W. S. Gilbert (1836–1911) British dramatist. *HMS Pinafore*, I

11 The prospect of a lot
Of dull MPs in close proximity,
All thinking for themselves is what
No man can face with equanimity.

W. S. Gilbert *Iolanthe*, I

12 You need to rent an MP just like you rent a London taxi.

Ian Greer British parliamentary lobbyist, involved in the 'cash-for-questions' scandal. *The Observer*, 'Sayings of the Week', 23 Oct 1994

13 'Do you pray for the senators, Dr Hale?' 'No, I look at the senators and I pray for the country.'

Edward Everett Hale (1822–1909) US author and clergyman. *New England Indian Summer* (Van Wyck Brooks)

14 Politicians are the same everywhere. They promise to build bridges even where there are no rivers.

Nikita Khrushchev (1894–1971) Soviet statesman. Attrib., Oct 1960

15 Political renegades always start their career of treachery as 'the best men of all parties' and end up in the Tory knackery.

Neil Kinnock (1942–) British politician. Speech, Welsh Labour Party Conference, 1985

16 A politician is a person with whose politics you don't agree; if you agree with him he is a statesman.

David Lloyd George (1863–1945) British Liberal statesman. Attrib.

17 When you're abroad you're a statesman: when you're at home you're just a politician.

Harold Macmillan (1894–1986) British politician and prime minister. Speech, 1958

18 It is very unfair to expect a politician to live in private up to the statements he makes in public.

W. Somerset Maugham (1874–1965) British novelist. *The Circle*

19 A statesman is a politician who places himself at the service of the nation. A politician is a statesman who places the nation at his service.

Georges Pompidou (1911–74) French statesman. *The Observer*, 'Sayings of the Year', 30 Dec 1973

20 All political lives, unless they are cut off in mid-stream at a happy juncture, end in failure.

Enoch Powell (1912–) British politician. *Sunday Times*, 6 Nov 1977

21 Above any other position of eminence, that of Prime Minister is filled by fluke.

Enoch Powell *The Observer*, 'Sayings of the Week', 8 Mar 1987

22 A number of anxious dwarfs trying to grill a whale.

J. B. Priestley (1894–1984) British novelist. *Outcries and Asides*

23 Get thee glass eyes,
And, like a scurvy politician, seem
To see the things thou dost not.

William Shakespeare (1564–1616) English dramatist. *King Lear*, IV:6

24 He knows nothing; and he thinks he knows everything. That points clearly to a political career.

George Bernard Shaw (1856–1950) Irish dramatist and critic. *Major Barbara*, III

25 All politicians have vanity. Some wear it more gently than others.

David Steel (1938–) British politician. *The Observer*, 'Sayings of the Week', 14 July 1985

26 A politician is a statesman who approaches every question with an open mouth.

Adlai Stevenson Also attrib. to Arthur Goldberg. *The Fine Art of Political Wit* (L. Harris)

27 Whoever could make two ears of corn or two blades of grass to grow upon a spot of ground where only one grew before would deserve better of mankind and do more essential service to his country than the whole race of politicians put together.

Jonathan Swift (1667–1745) Irish-born Anglican priest and writer. *Gulliver's Travels*, 'Voyage to Brobdingnag', Ch. 7

28 In politics, if you want anything said, ask a man; if you want anything done, ask a woman.

Margaret Thatcher (1925–) British politician and prime minister. *The Changing Anatomy of Britain* (Anthony Sampson)

29 A politician is a man who understands government, and it takes a politician to run a government. A statesman is a politician who's been dead ten or fifteen years.

Harry S. Truman (1884–1972) US statesman. *New York World Telegram and Sun*, 12 Apr 1958

30 Politicians can forgive almost anything in the way of abuse; they can forgive subversion, revolution, being contradicted, exposed as liars, even ridiculed, but they can never forgive being ignored.

Auberon Waugh (1939–) British novelist and critic. *The Observer*, 11 Oct 1981

31 It is a pity, as my husband says, that more politicians are not bastards by birth instead of vocation.

Katherine Whitehorn (1926–) British journalist. *The Observer*, 1964

Specific quotes

32 The only man who has ever run away from the circus to become an accountant.

Anonymous Referring to John Major's background – his father had once been a trapeze artist

33 Paddy Ashdown is the first trained killer to be a party leader…Mrs Thatcher being self-taught.

Gilbert Archer President of Edinburgh Chamber of Commerce. Remark, 1992

34 It is fitting that we should have buried the Unknown Prime Minister by the side of the Unknown Soldier.

Herbert Henry Asquith (1852–1928) British statesman. Said at Bonar Law's funeral, 5 Nov 1923. Attrib.

35 He believes, with all his heart and soul and strength, that there *is* such a thing as truth; he has the soul of a martyr with the intellect of an advocate.

Walter Bagehot Referring to Gladstone. *Historical Essays*, 'Mr Gladstone'

36 If I rescued a child from drowning, the Press would no doubt headline the story 'Benn grabs child'.

Tony Benn (1925–) British politician. *The Observer*, 'Sayings of the Week', 2 Mar 1975

37 A dessicated calculating machine.

Aneurin Bevan (1897–1960) British Labour politician. Referring to Hugh Gaitskell. *Hugh Gaitskell* (W. T. Rodgers)

38 There is no reason to attack the monkey when the organ-grinder is present.

Aneurin Bevan The 'monkey' was Selwyn Lloyd; the 'organ-grinder' was Harold Macmillan. Speech, House of Commons

39 She is trying to wear the trousers of Winston Churchill.

Leonid Brezhnev (1906–82) Soviet statesman. Referring to Margaret Thatcher. Speech, 1979

40 He was not merely a chip off the old block, but the old block itself.

Edmund Burke (1729–97) British politician. Referring to William Pitt the Younger's first speech in the House of Commons, 26 Feb 1781. Attrib.

41 Mr Macmillan is the best prime minister we have.

R. A. Butler (1902–82) British Conservative politician. Often quoted in the form above. In fact, Butler simply answered 'Yes' to the question 'Would you say that this is the best prime minister we have?'. Interview, London Airport, Dec 1955

42 Pitt is to Addington
As London is to Paddington.

George Canning (1770–1827) British statesman. *The Oracle*

43 The seagreen Incorruptible.

Thomas Carlyle (1795–1881) Scottish historian and essayist. Referring to Robespierre. *History of the French Revolution*, Pt. II, Bk. IV, Ch. 4

44 She is clearly the best man among them.

Barbara Castle (1910–) British politician. Referring to Margaret Thatcher. *The Castle Diaries*

45 An old man in a hurry.

Lord Randolph Churchill (1849–95) British Conservative politician. Referring to Gladstone. Speech, June 1886

46 I remember, when I was a child, being taken to the celebrated Barnum's circus, which contained an exhibition of freaks and monstrosities, but the exhibit...which I most desired to see was the one described as 'The Boneless Wonder'. My parents judged that that spectacle would be too revolting and demoralising for my youthful eyes, and I have waited 50 years to see the boneless wonder sitting on the Treasury Bench.

Winston Churchill (1874–1965) British statesman. Referring to Ramsey MacDonald. Speech, House of Commons, 28 Jan 1931

47 I have never seen a human being who more perfectly represented the modern conception of a robot.

Winston Churchill Referring to the Soviet statesman Molotov. *The Second World War*

48 In Franklin Roosevelt there died the greatest American friend we have ever known and the greatest champion of freedom who has ever brought help and comfort from the New World to the Old.

Winston Churchill *The Second World War*

49 In private conversation he tries on speeches like a man trying on ties in his bedroom to see how he would look in them.

Lionel Curtis (1872–1955) British writer. Referring to Winston Churchill. Letter to Nancy Astor, 1912

50 Not even a public figure. A man of no experience. And of the utmost insignificance.

Lord Curzon (1859–1925) British politician. Referring to Stanley Baldwin on his appointment as Prime Minister. *Curzon: The Last Phase* (Harold Nicolson)

51 If a traveller were informed that such a man was leader of the House of Commons, he may well begin to comprehend how the Egyptians worshipped an insect.

Benjamin Disraeli (1804–81) British statesman. Referring to Lord John Russell. Attrib.

52 He is used to dealing with estate workers. I cannot see how anyone can say he is out of touch.

Lady Caroline Douglas-Home (1937–) Daughter of Alec Douglas-Home. Referring to her father's suitability to his new role as prime minister. *Daily Herald*, 21 Oct 1963 (Jon Akass)

53 For the past few months she has been charging about like some bargain-basement Boadicea.

Denis Healey (1917–) British Labour politician. Referring to Margaret Thatcher. *The Observer*, 'Sayings of the Week', 7 Nov 1982

54 I am the Gromyko of the Labour party.

Denis Healey Alluding to Andrei Gromyko (1909–89), Soviet statesman who was foreign minister from 1957 to 1985. Attrib.

55 He would rather follow public opinion than lead it.

Harry Hopkins (1890–1946) US politician. Referring to Roosevelt. Attrib.

56 If a man were to go by chance at the same time with Burke under a shed, to shun a shower, he would say – 'this is an extraordinary man.'

Samuel Johnson (1709–84) British lexicographer. Referring to Edmund Burke. *Life of Johnson* (J. Boswell), Vol. IV

57 Do you realize the responsibility I carry? I'm the only person standing between Nixon and the White House.

John Fitzgerald Kennedy (1917–63) US statesman. Said to

Arthur Schlesinger, 13 Oct 1960; Richard Nixon was the Republican candidate in the 1960 US Presidential election. *A Thousand Days* (Arthur M. Schlesinger, Jnr)

58 This goat-footed bard, this half-human visitor to our age from the hag-ridden magic and enchanted woods of Celtic antiquity.

John Maynard Keynes (1883–1946) British economist. Referring to Lloyd George. *Essays and Sketches in Biography*

59 We have heard of people being thrown to the wolves, but never before have we heard of a man being thrown to the wolves with a bargain on the part of the wolves that they would not eat him.

Bonar Law (1858–1923) British statesman. Referring to the fact that the then war minister, Col Seely, had offered his resignation. Speech, House of Common, Mar 1914

60 Look at that man's eyes. You will hear more of him later.

Bonar Law Referring to Mussolini. Attrib.

61 Poor Bonar can't bear being called a liar. Now I don't mind.

David Lloyd George (1863–1945) British Liberal statesman. Referring to Bonar Law, prime minister 1922–23. *Stanley Baldwin* (G. M. Young)

62 He saw foreign policy through the wrong end of a municipal drainpipe.

David Lloyd George Referring to Neville Chamberlain. *The Fine Art of Political Wit* (Harris), Ch. 6

63 So restless Cromwell could not cease
In the inglorious arts of peace.

Andrew Marvell (1621–78) English poet. *An Horatian Ode upon Cromwell's Return from Ireland*

64 Sit down, man. You're a bloody tragedy.

James Maxton (1885–1946) Scottish Labour leader. Said to Ramsay MacDonald when he made his last speech in Parliament. Attrib.

65 The rogue elephant among British prime ministers.

Kenneth Morgan (1934–) British historian. Referring to Lloyd George. *Life of David Lloyd George*

66 I am not and never have been, a man of the right. My position was on the left and is now in the centre of politics.

Oswald Mosley (1896–1980) British politician. *The Times*, 26 Apr 1968

67 Argue as you please, you are nowhere, that grand old man, the Prime Minister, insists on the other thing.

Lord Northcote (1818–87) British statesman. Referring to Gladstone; the phrase, and its acronym GOM, became his nickname – temporarily reversed to MOG ('Murderer of Gordon') in 1885, after the death of General Gordon at Khartoum. Speech, Liverpool, 12 Apr 1882

68 How could they tell?

Dorothy Parker (1893–1967) US writer. Reaction to news of the death of Calvin Coolidge, US President 1923–29; also attributed to H. L. Mencken. *You Might As Well Live* (J. Keats)

69 Coolidge is a better example of evolution than either Bryan or Darrow, for he knows when not to talk, which is the biggest asset the monkey possesses over the human.

Will Rogers (1879–1935) US actor and humorist. *Saturday Review*, 'A Rogers Thesaurus', 25 Aug 1962

70 Stalin hates the guts of all your top people. He thinks he likes me better, and I hope he will continue to do so.

Franklin D. Roosevelt (1882–1945) US Democratic president. *The Hinge of Fate* (Winston S. Churchill), Ch. 11

71 I will not accept if nominated, and will not serve if elected.

General William Sherman (1820–91) US general. Replying to a request that he accept the Republican presidential nomination. Attrib.

72 He was the Messiah of the new age, and his crucifixion was yet to come.

George Edward Slocombe (1894–1963) British journalist. Referring to Woodrow Wilson and his visit to the Versailles conference. *Mirror to Geneva*

73 Nixon is the kind of politician who would cut down a redwood tree, then mount the stump for a conservation speech.

Adlai Stevenson (1900–65) US statesman. Attrib.

74 I hope Mrs Thatcher will go until the turn of the century looking like Queen Victoria.

Norman Tebbit (1931–) British Conservative politician. *The Observer*, 'Sayings of the Week', 17 May 1987

75 If a woman like Eva Peron with no ideals can get that far, think how far I can go with all the ideals that I have.

Margaret Thatcher (1925–) British politician and prime minister. *The Sunday Times*, 1980

76 Introducing Super-Mac.

Vicky (Victor Weisz; 1913–66) German-born British cartoonist. Cartoon caption depicting Harold Macmillan as Superman. *Evening Standard*, 6 Nov 1958

77 The danger to the country, to Europe, to her vast Empire, which is involved in having all these great interests entrusted to the shaking hand of an old, wild, and incomprehensible man of 82½, is very great!

Victoria (1819–1901) Queen of the United Kingdom. Reaction to Gladstone's fourth and last appointment as prime minister, 1892. Letter to Lord Lansdowne, 12 Aug 1892

78 He speaks to Me as if I was a public meeting.

Victoria Referring to Gladstone. *Collections and Recollections* (G. W. E. Russell), Ch. 14

POLITICS

See also Communism, democracy, diplomacy, government, Houses of Parliament, monarchy, opposition, politicians, power politics, socialism

1 Politics, as a practice, whatever its professions, has always been the systematic organisation of hatreds.

Henry Brooks Adams (1838–1918) US historian. *The Education of Henry Adams*

2 He warns the heads of parties against

believing their own lies.

John Arbuthnot (1667–1735) Scottish writer and physician. *The Art of Political Lying*

3 Man is by nature a political animal.

Aristotle (384–322 BC) Greek philosopher. *Politics*, Bk. I

4 The accursed power which stands on Privilege
(And goes with Women, and Champagne, and Bridge)
Broke – and Democracy resumed her reign:
(Which goes with Bridge, and Women and Champagne).

Hilaire Belloc (1870–1953) French-born British poet. *Epigrams*, 'On a Great Election'

5 Every Briton is at heart a Tory – especially every British Liberal.

Arnold Bennett (1867–1931) British novelist. *Journal*

6 Politics is a blood sport.

Aneurin Bevan (1897–1960) British Labour politician. *My Life with Nye* (Jennie Lee)

7 No attempt at ethical or social seduction can eradicate from my heart a deep burning hatred for the Tory Party...So far as I am concerned they are lower than vermin.

Aneurin Bevan Speech, Manchester, 4 July 1949

8 Politics is not an exact science.

Bismarck (1815–98) German statesman. Speech, Prussian Chamber, 18 Dec 1863

9 Politics is not a science...but an art.

Bismarck Speech, Reichstag, 15 Mar 1884

10 Good temper and moderation are the characteristics of parliamentary language.

Betty Boothroyd (1929–) British politician and Speaker of the House of Commons. *The Independent*, 9 Feb 1995

11 Politics are usually the executive expression of human immaturity.

Vera Brittain (1893–1970) British writer and feminist. *The Rebel Passion*

12 Party loyalty lowers the greatest of men to the petty level of the masses.

Jean de La Bruyère (1645–96) French satirist. *Les Caractères*

13 Politics is the art of the possible.

R. A. Butler (1902–82) British Conservative politician. Often attrib. to Butler but used earlier by others, including Bismarck. *The Art of the Possible*, Epigraph

14 The healthy stomach is nothing if not conservative. Few radicals have good digestions.

Samuel Butler (1835–1902) British writer. *Notebooks*

15 I am not made for politics because I am incapable of wishing for, or accepting the death of my adversary.

Albert Camus (1913–60) French existentialist writer. *The Rebel*

16 Detente is like the race in 'Alice in Wonderland' where everyone had to have a prize.

Lord Carrington (1919–) British politician. Speech, Mar 1980

17 What a genius the Labour Party has for cutting itself in half and letting the two parts writhe in public.

Cassandra (William Neil Cannon; 1910–67) Irish journalist. *The Daily Mirror*

18 Labour is not fit to govern.

Winston Churchill (1874–1965) British statesman. Election speech, 1920

19 The disastrous element in the Labour party is its intellectuals.

George Norman Clark (1890–1979) British historian. *A Man of the Thirties* (A. L. Rowse)

20 We now are, as we always have been, decidedly and conscientiously attached to what is called the Tory, and which might with more propriety be called the Conservative, party.

John Wilson Croker (1780–1857) British Tory politician. The first use of the term 'Conservative Party'. In *Quarterly Review*, Jan 1830

21 A Conservative government is an organized hypocrisy.

Benjamin Disraeli (1804–81) British statesman. Speech, 17 Mar 1845

22 The right honourable gentleman caught the Whigs bathing, and walked away with their clothes.

Benjamin Disraeli Referring to Sir Robert Peel. Speech, House of Commons, 28 Feb 1845

23 During the last few weeks I have felt that the Suez Canal was flowing through my drawing room.

Clarissa Eden (1920–85) Wife of Anthony Eden. Said during the Suez crisis of 1956. Attrib.

24 All terrorists, at the invitation of the Government, end up with drinks at the Dorchester.

Hugh Gaitskell (1906–63) British Labour politician. Letter to *The Guardian*, 23 Aug 1977 (Dora Gaitskell)

25 There are some of us...who will fight, fight, fight, and fight again to save the party we love.

Hugh Gaitskell After his policy for a nuclear deterrent had been defeated. Speech, Labour Party conference, Scarborough, 3 Oct 1960

26 There are times in politics when you must be on the right side and lose.

John Kenneth Galbraith (1908–) US economist. *The Observer*, 'Sayings of the Week', 11 Feb 1968

27 Few things are as immutable as the addiction of political groups to the ideas by which they have once won office.

John Kenneth Galbraith *The Affluent Society*, Ch. 13

28 There is just one rule for politicians all over the world. Don't say in Power what you say in Opposition: if you do you only have to carry out what the other fellows have found impossible.

John Galsworthy (1867–1933) British novelist. *Maid in Waiting*

29 It isn't worth a pitcher of warm spit.

John Nance Garner (1868–1937) US Democratic vice-president. Referring to the Vice-Presidency; sometimes 'piss' is substituted for 'spit'. Attrib.

30 I myself have become a Gaullist only little by little.

Charles De Gaulle (1890–1970) French general and statesman. *The Observer*, 'Sayings of the Year', 29 Dec 1963

31 I often think it's comical
How Nature always does contrive
That every boy and every gal
That's born into the world alive
Is either a little Liberal
Or else a little Conservative!

W. S. Gilbert (1836–1911) British dramatist. *Iolanthe*, II

32 If the British public falls for this, I say it will be stark, staring bonkers.

Lord Hailsham (1907–) British Conservative politician. Referring to Labour policy in the 1964 general-election campaign. Press conference, Conservative Central Office, 12 Oct 1964

33 A great party is not to be brought down because of a scandal by a woman of easy virtue and a proved liar.

Lord Hailsham Referring to the Profumo affair, in BBC interview, 13 June 1963. *The Pendulum Years*, Ch. 3 (Bernard Levin)

34 Their Europeanism is nothing but imperialism with an inferiority complex.

Denis Healey (1917–) British Labour politician. Referring to the policies of the Conservative party. *The Observer*, 'Sayings of the Week', 7 Oct 1962

35 I don't think that modesty is the oustanding characteristic of contemporary politics, do you?

Edward Heath (1916–) British politician and prime minister. Remark, Dec 1988

36 The essential thing is the formation of the political will of the nation: that is the starting point for political action.

Adolf Hitler (1889–1945) German dictator. Speech, Düsseldorf, 27 Jan 1932

37 A little rebellion, now and then, is a good thing, and as necessary in the political world as storms in the physical.

Thomas Jefferson (1743–1826) US statesman.

38 If you're in politics and you can't tell when you walk into a room who's for you and who's against you, then you're in the wrong line of work.

Lyndon B. Johnson (1908–73) US statesman. *The Lyndon Johnson Story* (B. Mooney)

39 Sir, I perceive you are a vile Whig.

Samuel Johnson (1709–84) British lexicographer. Speaking to Sir Adam Fergusson. *Life of Johnson* (J. Boswell), Vol. II

40 Why, Sir, most schemes of political improvement are very laughable things.

Samuel Johnson *Life of Johnson* (J. Boswell), Vol. II

41 Politics are now nothing more than a means of rising in the world.

Samuel Johnson *Life of Johnson* (J. Boswell), Vol. II

42 The idea that there is a model Labour voter, a blue-collar council house tenant who belongs to a union and has 2.4 children, a five-year-old car and a holiday in Blackpool, is patronizing and politically immature.

Neil Kinnock (1942–) British politician. Speech, 1986

43 Proportional Representation, I think, is fundamentally counter-democratic.

Neil Kinnock *Marxism Today*, 1983

44 States, like men, have their growth, their manhood, their decrepitude, their decay.

Walter Savage Landor (1775–1864) British poet and writer. *Imaginary Conversations*, 'Pollio and Calvus'

45 If it were necessary to give the briefest possible definition of imperialism we should have to say that imperialism is the monopoly stage of capitalism.

Lenin (Vladimir Ilich Ulyanov; 1870–1924) Russian revolutionary leader. *Imperialism, the Highest Stage of Capitalism*, Ch. 7

46 In every age the vilest specimens of human nature are to be found among demagogues.

Lord Macaulay (1800–59) British historian. *History of England*, Vol. I, Ch. 5

47 I thought the best thing to do was to settle up these little local difficulties, and then turn to the wider vision of the Commonwealth.

Harold Macmillan (1894–1986) British politician and prime minister. Referring to resignation of ministers. Attrib., London Airport, 7 Jan 1958

48 There are three groups that no prime minister should provoke: the Treasury, the Vatican, and the National Union of Mineworkers.

Harold Macmillan First used by Stanley Baldwin. Attrib.

49 First of all the Georgian silver goes, and then that nice furniture that used to be in the saloon. Then the Canalettos go.

Harold Macmillan Referring to privatization of profitable nationalized industries. Speech, House of Lords, 1985

50 In politics, as in grammar, one should be able to tell the substantives from the adjectives. Hitler was a substantive; Mussolini only an adjective. Hitler was a nuisance. Mussolini was bloody. Together a bloody nuisance.

Salvador de Madariaga y Rogo (1886–1978) Spanish diplomat and writer. Attrib.

51 It is time to get back to basics: to self-discipline and respect for the law, to consideration for others, to accepting responsibility for yourself and your family, and not shuffling it off on the state.

John Major (1943–) British politician and prime minister. Speech, Conservative party conference, Blackpool, 8 Oct 1993

52 Every intellectual attitude is latently political.

Thomas Mann (1875–1955) German novelist. *The Observer*, 11 Aug 1974

53 All reactionaries are paper tigers.

Mao Tse-Tung (1893–1976) Chinese communist leader. *Quotations from Chairman Mao Tse-Tung*, Ch. 6

54 McCarthyism is Americanism with its sleeves rolled.

Joseph R. McCarthy (1908–57) US senator. Speech, 1952

55 The expression 'positive neutrality' is a contradiction in terms. There can be no more positive neutrality than there can be a vegetarian tiger.

V. K. Krishna Menon (1896–1974) Indian barrister and writer. *The New York Times*, 18 Oct 1960

56 We cannot change our policy now. After all, we are not political whores.

Benito Mussolini (1883–1945) Italian dictator. *Hitler* (Alan Bullock), Ch. 8

57 I still love you, but in politics there is no heart, only head.

Napoleon I (Napoleon Bonaparte; 1769–1821) French emperor. Referring to his divorce, for reasons of state, from the Empress Josephine (1809). *Bonaparte* (C. Barnett)

58 In our time, political speech and writing are largely the defence of the indefensible.

George Orwell (Eric Blair; 1903–50) British novelist. *Politics and the English Language*

59 I used to say that politics was the second lowest profession and I have come to know that it bears a great similarity to the first.

Ronald Reagan (1911–) US politician and president. *The Observer*, 13 May 1979

60 Please assure me that you are all Republicans!

Ronald Reagan Addressing the surgeons on being wheeled into the operating theatre for an emergency operation after an assassination attempt. *Presidential Anecdotes* (P. Boller)

61 Remember this, Griffin. The revolution eats its own. Capitalism re-creates itself.

Mordecai Richler (1931–) Canadian novelist. *Cocksure*, Ch. 22

62 The more you read about politics, you got to admit that each party is worse than the other.

Will Rogers (1879–1935) US actor and humorist. *Saturday Review*, 'A Rogers Thesaurus', 25 Aug 1962

63 England elects a Labour Government. When a man goes in for politics over here, he has no time to labour, and any man that labours has no time to fool with politics. Over there politics is an obligation; over here it's a business.

Will Rogers *Autobiography*, Ch. 14

64 You have to clean your plate.

Lord Rosebery (1847–1929) British statesman. Said to the Liberal Party. Speech, Chesterfield, 16 Dec 1901

65 The collection of prejudices which is called political philosophy is useful provided that it is not called philosophy.

Bertrand Russell (1872–1970) British philosopher. *The Observer*, 'Sayings of the Year', 1962

66 History is past politics, and politics present history.

John Robert Seeley (1834–95) British historian. Quoting the historian E. A. Freeman. *The Growth of British Policy*

67 Most Conservatives believe that a creche is something that happens between two Range Rovers in Tunbridge Wells.

Caroline Shorten Liberal spokesperson *The Independent*, 22 Sept 1993

68 If ever there's any emergence of a fourth party in this country, the task of the Liberal party is to strangle it at birth.

Cyril Smith (1928–93) British Liberal politician. *The Guardian*, 1981

69 If Her Majesty stood for Parliament – if the Tory Party had any sense and made Her its leader instead of that grammar school twit Heath – us Tories, mate, would win every election we went in for.

Johnny Speight (1920–) British television scriptwriter. *Till Death Do Us Part*

70 The Republican form of Government is the highest form of government; but because of this it requires the highest type of human nature – a type nowhere at present existing.

Herbert Spencer (1820–1903) British philosopher. *Essays*, 'The Americans'

71 The tasks of the party are...to be cautious and not allow our country to be drawn into conflicts by warmongers who are accustomed to have others pull the chestnuts out of the fire for them.

Joseph Stalin (J. Dzhugashvili; 1879–1953) Soviet statesman. Speech, 8th Congress of the Communist Party, 6 Jan 1941

72 Disdain is the wrong word, but perhaps affection is too strong a word

David Steel (1938–) British politician. Referring to his attitude to the Liberal party. *The Observer*, 'Sayings of the Week', 22 Sept 1985

73 Go back to your constituencies and prepare for government!

David Steel Speech to party conference, 1985

74 I sense that the British electorate is now itching to break out once and for all from the discredited straight-jacket of the past.

David Steel *The Times*, 2 June 1987

75 An independent is a guy who wants to take the politics out of politics.

Adlai Stevenson (1900–65) US statesman. *The Art Of Politics.*

76 Politics is perhaps the only profession for which no preparation is thought necessary.

Robert Louis Stevenson (1850–94) Scottish writer. *Familiar Studies of Men and Books*, 'Yoshida-Torajiro'

77 Socialists treat their servants with respect and then wonder why they vote Conservative.

Tom Stoppard (1937–) Czech-born British dramatist. *Lord Malquist and Mr Moon*, Pt. V, Ch. 1

78 Revolts, republics, revolutions, most

No graver than a schoolboy's barring out.

Alfred, Lord Tennyson (1809–92) British poet. *The Princess*, Conclusion

79 Any woman who understands the problems of running a home will be nearer to understanding the problems of running a country.

Margaret Thatcher (1925–) British politician and prime minister. *The Observer*, 8 May 1979

80 I can trust my husband not to fall asleep on a public platform and he usually claps in the right places.

Margaret Thatcher *Observer*, 20 Aug 1978

81 Britain is no longer in the politics of the pendulum, but of the ratchet.

Margaret Thatcher Speech, Institute of Public Relations, 1977

82 Politics is the art of preventing people from taking part in affairs which properly concern them.

Paul Valéry (1871–1945) French poet and writer. *Tel quel*

83 Any American who is prepared to run for President should automatically, by definition, be disqualified from ever doing so.

Gore Vidal (1925–) US novelist. Attrib.

84 Politics come from man. Mercy, compassion and justice come from God.

Terry Waite (1939–) British churchman. *The Observer*, 'Sayings of the Week', 13 Jan 1985

85 The hungry hare has no frontiers and doesn't follow ideologies. The hungry hare goes where it finds the food. And the other hares don't block its passage with the tanks.

Lech Walesa (1943–) Polish trade unionist. Interview, 1981

86 A writer of crook stories ought never to stop seeking new material.

Edgar Wallace (1875–1932) British thriller writer. Said when a candidate for Parliament. *The Long Weekend* (Alan Hodge)

87 He stood twice for Parliament, but so diffidently that his candidature passed almost unnoticed.

Evelyn Waugh (1903–66) British novelist. *Decline and Fall*, Pt. III, Ch. 1

88 Pappenhacker says that every time you are polite to a proletarian you are helping to bolster up the capitalist system.

Evelyn Waugh *Scoop*, Bk. I, Ch. 5

89 The Labour Party is going about the country stirring up apathy.

William Whitelaw (1918–) British politician. Attrib.

90 The Labour party is like a stage-coach. If you rattle along at great speed everybody inside is too exhilarated or too seasick to cause any trouble. But if you stop everybody gets out and argues about where to go next.

Harold Wilson (1916–95) British politician and prime minister. *Harold Wilson, The Authentic Portrait* (Leslie Smith)

91 Hence the practised performances of latter-day politicians in the game of musical daggers: never be left holding the dagger when the music stops.

Harold Wilson *The Governance of Britain*, Ch. 2

92 A week is a long time in politics.

Harold Wilson First said in 1965 or 1966, and repeated on several occasions. Attrib.

POLLUTION

See conservation, ecology, environment

POP MUSIC

1 Rock'n'roll is part of a pest to undermine the morals of the youth of our nation. It...brings people of both races together.

Anonymous Statement by the North Alabama Citizens' Council in the 1950s

2 Give me that rock'n'roll music,
Any old way you choose it,
It's got to be rock'n'roll music,
If you want to dance with me.

The Beatles British pop group. *Rock'n'roll music*

3 Listen kid, take my advice, never hate a song that has sold half a million copies.

Irving Berlin (Israel Baline; 1888–1989) Russian-born US composer. Giving advice to Cole Porter. Attrib.

4 Roll Over Beethoven.

Chuck Berry (1931–) US rock-and-roll musician. Song title.

5 Hail, hail rock'n'roll'.
Deliver me from the days of old.

Chuck Berry *Hail, hail, rock'n'roll*

6 Do they merit vitriol, even a drop of it? Yes, because they corrupt the young, persuading them that the mature world, which produced Beethoven and Schweitzer, sets an even higher value on the transient anodynes of youth than does youth itself...They are the Hollow Men. They are electronic lice.

Anthony Burgess (1917–93) British novelist. Referring to disc jockeys. *Punch*, 20 Sept 1967

7 Canned music is like audible wallpaper.

Alistair Cooke (1908–) British broadcaster. Attrib.

8 Sounds like a gameboy down a well.

Elvis Costello (Declan McManus; 1954–) British singer and songwriter. Referring to techno music. BBC TV programme, *The O Zone*, 9 Jan 1995

9 Strange how potent cheap music is.

Noël Coward (1899–1973) British dramatist. *Private Lives*

10 I think popular music in this country is one of the few things in the twentieth century that have made giant strides in reverse.

Bing Crosby (Harry Lillis Crosby; 1904–77) US singer. Interview in *This Week*

11 Yea, some of them are about ten minutes long, others five or six.

Bob Dylan (Robert Allen Zimmerman; 1941–) US songwriter. On being asked in an interview, to say something about his songs. Attrib.

12 In Manchester, you either become a musician, a footballer, a drugs dealer or work in a factory. And there aren't a lot of factories left, y'know.

Noel Gallagher (1967–) British pop musician in the group Oasis. *The Guardian Weekend*, 4 Jan 1997

13 Rock Around the Clock.

Bill Haley and The Comets US rock-and-roll band. Song title

14 We're more popular than Jesus Christ now. I don't know which will go first, Rock and Roll or Christianity.

John Lennon (1940–80) British rock musician. *The Beatles Illustrated Lyrics*

15 What a terrible revenge by the culture of the Negroes on that of the Whites.

Ignacy Paderewski (1860–1941) Polish pianist. Referring to jazz. Attrib.

16 Every popular song has at least one line or sentence that is perfectly clear – the line that fits the music.

Ezra Pound (1885–1972) US poet and critic. Attrib.

17 It's only rock and roll
But I like it.

The Rolling Stones British rock band. *It's Only Rock and Roll*

18 Jazz will endure just as long as people hear it through their feet instead of their brains.

John Philip Sousa (1854–1932) US composer, conductor, and writer. Attrib.

19 We don't get groupies. We get teenagers who want to read us their poetry.

Michael Stipe US singer with the group REM. *Q*, 1 Sept 1994

POPULARITY

See also fame

1 Do not let that trouble Your Excellency; perhaps the greetings are intended for me.

Ludwig van Beethoven (1770–1827) German composer. Said when walking with Goethe, when Goethe complained about greetings from passers-by. *Thayer's Life of Beethoven* (E. Forbes)

2 Everybody hates me because I'm so universally liked.

Peter De Vries (1910–93) US novelist. *The Vale of Laughter*, Pt. I

3 Popularity is a crime from the moment it is sought; it is only a virtue where men have it whether they will or no.

Lord Halifax (1633–95) English statesman. *Political, Moral and Miscellaneous Thoughts and Reflections*

4 Popularity? It's glory's small change.

Victor Hugo (1802–85) French writer. *Ruy Blas*, III

5 The worse I do, the more popular I get.

John Fitzgerald Kennedy (1917–63) US statesman. Referring to his popularity following the failure of the US invasion of Cuba. *The People's Almanac* (D. Wallechinsky)

6 We're more popular than Jesus Christ now. I don't know which will go first. Rock and roll or Christianity.

John Lennon (1940–80) British rock musician. *The Beatles Illustrated Lyrics*

7 He's liked, but he's not well liked.

Arthur Miller (1915–) US dramatist. *Death of a Salesman*, I

8 I don't resent his popularity or anything else. Good Lord, I co-starred with Errol Flynn once.

Ronald Reagan (1911–) US politician and president. Remark, Dec 1987

9 He hasn't an enemy in the world, and none of his friends like him.

Oscar Wilde (1854–1900) Irish-born British dramatist. Said of G. B. Shaw. *Sixteen Self Sketches* (Shaw), Ch. 17

PORNOGRAPHY

See also censorship, prudery, sex

1 This is the kind of show that gives pornography a bad name.

Clive Barnes (1927–) British-born theatre and ballet critic. Reviewing *Oh, Calcutta!*. Attrib.

2 I don't think pornography is very harmful, but it is terribly, terribly boring.

Noël Coward (1899–1973) British dramatist. *The Observer*, 'Sayings of the Week', 24 Sept 1972

3 Pornography is the attempt to insult sex, to do dirt on it.

D. H. Lawrence (1885–1930) British novelist. *Phoenix*, 'Pornography and Obscenity'

4 Its avowed purpose is to excite sexual desire, which, I should have thought, is unnecessary in the case of the young, inconvenient in the case of the middle aged, and unseemly in the old.

Malcolm Muggeridge (1903–90) British writer. *Tread Softly For You Tread On My Jokes*, 1966

5 *Lady Chatterley's Lover* is a book that all Christians might read with profit.

John Robinson (1919–83) Bishop of Woolwich. Said in the court case against Penguin Books. Attrib.

6 Don't be daft. You don't get any pornography on there, not on the telly. Get filth, that's all. The only place you get pornography is in yer Sunday papers.

Johnny Speight (1920–) British television scriptwriter. *Till Death Do Us Part*

POSSIBILITY

1 The grand Perhaps!

Robert Browning (1812–89) British poet. *Bishop Blougram's Apology*

2 However, one cannot put a quart in a pint cup.
Charlotte Perkins Gilman (1860–1935) US writer. *The Living of Charlotte Perkins Gilman*

3 Your If is the only peace-maker; much virtue in If.
William Shakespeare (1564–1616) English dramatist. *As You Like It*, V:4

POSTERITY

See also death, fame, future, immortality, reputation

1 Think of your forefathers! Think of your posterity!
John Quincy Adams (1767–1848) Sixth president of the USA. Speech, Plymouth, Massachusetts, 22 Dec 1802

2 We are always doing something for posterity, but I would fain see posterity do something for us.
Joseph Addison (1672–1719) British essayist. *The Spectator*, 583

3 Let us honour if we can
The vertical man
Though we value none
But the horizontal one.
W. H. Auden (1907–73) British poet. *Epigraph for Poems*

4 When a man is in doubt about this or that in his writing, it will often guide him if he asks himself how it will tell a hundred years hence.
Samuel Butler (1835–1902) British writer. *Notebooks*

5 I think I shall be among the English Poets after my death.
John Keats (1795–1821) British poet. Letter to George and Georgiana Keats, 14 Oct 1818

6 A writer's ambition should be to trade a hundred contemporary readers for ten readers in ten years' time and for one reader in a hundred years' time.
Arthur Koestler (1905–83) Hungarian-born British writer. *New York Times Book Review*, 1 Apr 1951

7 Damn the age. I'll write for antiquity.
Charles Lamb (1775–1834) British essayist. Referring to his lack of payment for the *Essays of Elia*. *English Wits* (L. Russell)

8 Now I'm dead in the grave with my lips moving
And every schoolboy repeating my words by heart.
Osip Mandelstam (1891–1938) Russian poet. *Poems*, No. 306

9 My time has not yet come either; some are born posthumously.
Friedrich Wilhelm Nietzsche (1844–1900) German philosopher. *Ecce Homo*

POVERTY

See also hunger, poverty and wealth

1 From clogs to clogs in three generations.
Proverb

2 Poverty is not a crime.
Proverb

3 To some extent, if you've seen one city slum you've seen them all.
Spiro Agnew (1918–96) US politician. Election speech, Detroit, 18 Oct 1968

4 To be poor and independent is very nearly an impossibility.
William Cobbett (1763–1835) British journalist and writer. *Advice to Young Men*

5 He found it inconvenient to be poor.
William Cowper (1731–1800) British poet. *Charity*

6 Poverty and oysters always seem to go together.
Charles Dickens (1812–70) British novelist. *Pickwick Papers*, Ch. 22

7 Poverty, therefore, was comparative. One measured it by a sliding scale. One was always poor, in terms of those who were richer.
Margaret Drabble (1939–) British novelist. *The Radiant Way*

8 There's no scandal like rags, nor any crime so shameful as poverty.
George Farquhar (1678–1707) Irish dramatist. *The Beaux' Strategem*, I:1

9 The very poor are unthinkable and only to be approached by the statistician and the poet.
E. M. Forster (1879–1970) British novelist. *Howards End*

10 It is only the poor who are forbidden to beg.
Anatole France (Jacques Anatole François Thibault; 1844–1924) French writer. *Crainquebille*

11 No sir, tho' I was born and bred in England, I can dare to be poor, which is the only thing nowa-days men are asham'd of.
John Gay (1685–1732) English poet and dramatist. *Polly*

12 Is it possible that my people live in such awful conditions?...I tell you, Mr Wheatley, that if I had to live in conditions like that I would be a revolutionary myself.
George V (1865–1936) King of the United Kingdom. On being told Mr Wheatley's life story. *The Tragedy of Ramsay MacDonald* (L. MacNeill Weir), Ch. 16

13 Let not Ambition mock their useful toil,
Their homely joys, and destiny obscure;
Nor Grandeur hear with a disdainful smile,
The short and simple annals of the poor.
Thomas Gray (1716–71) British poet. *Elegy Written in a Country Churchyard*

14 People who are much too sensitive to demand of cripples that they run races ask of the poor that they get up and act just like everyone else in society.
Michael Harrington (1928–89) US socialist and writer. *The Other America*

15 I want there to be no peasant in my kingdom

so poor that he is unable to have a chicken in his pot every Sunday.

Henri IV (1553–1610) King of France. *Hist. de Henry le Grand* (Hardouin de Péréfixe)

16 Seven cities warr'd for Homer, being dead,
Who, living, had no roof to shroud his head.

Thomas Heywood (c. 1574–1641) English dramatist. *The Hierarchy of the Blessed Angels*

17 Oh! God! that bread should be so dear,
And flesh and blood so cheap!

Thomas Hood (1799–1845) British poet. *The Song of the Shirt*

18 Hard to train to accept being poor.

Horace (Quintus Horatius Flaccus; 65–8 BC) Roman poet. *Odes*, I

19 It is easy enough to say that poverty is no crime. No; if it were men wouldn't be ashamed of it. It is a blunder, though, and is punished as such. A poor man is despised the whole world over.

Jerome K. Jerome (1859–1927) British humorist. *Idle Thoughts of an Idle Fellow*

20 Resolve not to be poor: whatever you have, spend less. Poverty is a great enemy to human happiness; it certainly destroys liberty, and it makes some virtues impracticable and others extremely difficult.

Samuel Johnson (1709–84) British lexicographer. *Life of Johnson* (J. Boswell), Vol. IV

21 The misfortunes of poverty carry with them nothing harder to bear than that it exposes men to ridicule.

Juvenal (Decimus Junius Juvenalis; 60–130 AD) Roman satirist. *Satires*, III

22 It's not easy for people to rise out of obscurity when they have to face straitened circumstances at home.

Juvenal *Satires*, III

23 We're really all of us bottomly broke.
I haven't had time to work in weeks.

Jack Kerouac (1922–69) US novelist. *On the Road*, Pt. I

24 Few, save the poor, feel for the poor.

Letitia Landon (1802–38) British poet and novelist. *The Poor*

25 'The Workhouse' – always a word of shame, grey shadow falling on the close of life, most feared by the old (even when called The Infirmary); abhorred more than debt, or prison, or beggary, or even the stain of madness.

Laurie Lee (1914–) British novelist and poet. *Cider with Rosie*

26 Look at me: I worked my way up from nothing to a state of extreme poverty.

Groucho Marx (Julius Marx; 1895–1977) US comedian. *Monkey Business*

27 The forgotten man at the bottom of the economic pyramid.

Franklin D. Roosevelt (1882–1945) US Democratic president. Speech on radio, 7 Apr 1932

28 The poor don't know that their function in life is to exercise our generosity.

Jean-Paul Sartre (1905–80) French writer. *Words*

29 The heart of the matter, as I see it, is the stark fact that world poverty is primarily a problem of two million villages, and thus a problem of two thousand million villagers.

E. F. Schumacher (1911–77) German-born economist. *Small is Beautiful, A Study of Economics as if People Mattered*, Ch. 13

30 CUSINS. Do you call poverty a crime?
UNDERSHAFT. The worst of all crimes. All the other crimes are virtues beside it.

George Bernard Shaw (1856–1950) Irish dramatist and critic. *Major Barbara*, IV

31 ...the poor are our brothers and sisters....people in the world who need love, who need care, who have to be wanted.

Mother Teresa (Agnes Gonxha Bojaxhui; 1910–) Yugoslavian missionary in Calcutta. *Time*, 'Saints Among Us', 29 Dec 1975

32 There were times my pants were so thin I could sit on a dime and tell if it was heads or tails.

Spencer Tracy (1900–67) US film star. *Spencer Tracy* (L. Swindell)

33 As for the virtuous poor, one can pity them, of course, but one cannot possibly admire them.

Oscar Wilde (1854–1900) Irish-born British dramatist. *The Soul of Man under Socialism*

34 But I, being poor, have only my dreams;
I have spread my dreams under your feet;
Tread softly because you tread on my dreams.

W. B. Yeats (1865–1939) Irish poet. *He Wishes for the Cloths of Heaven*

POVERTY AND WEALTH

See also money, poverty, wealth

1 She was poor but she was honest
Victim of a rich man's game.
First he loved her, then he left her,
And she lost her maiden name.

See her on the bridge at midnight,
Saying 'Farewell, blighted love.'
Then a scream, a splash and goodness,
What is she a-doin' of?

It's the same the whole world over,
It's the poor wot gets the blame,
It's the rich wot gets the gravy.
Ain't it all a bleedin' shame?

Anonymous *She was Poor but she was Honest*

2 There was a certain rich man, which was clothed in purple and fine linen, and fared sumptuously every day:
And there was a certain beggar named Lazarus, which was laid at his gate, full of sores,
And desiring to be fed with the crumbs which fell from the rich man's table: moreover the dogs

came and licked his sores.
And it came to pass, that the beggar died, and was carried by the angels into Abraham's bosom: the rich man also died, and was buried;
And in hell he lift up his eyes, being in torments, and seeth Abraham afar off, and Lazarus in his bosom.

Bible: Luke 16:19–23

3 There are only two families in the world, my old grandmother used to say, The *Haves* and the *Have-Nots.*

Miguel de Cervantes (1547–1616) Spanish novelist. *Don Quixote*, Pt. II, Ch. 20

4 'Two nations; between whom there is no intercourse and no sympathy; who are as ignorant of each other's habits, thoughts, and feelings, as if they were dwellers in different zones, or inhabitants of different planets; who are formed by a different breeding, are fed by a different food, are ordered by different manners, and are not governed by the same laws.'
'You speak of –' said Egremont, hesitatingly
'THE RICH AND THE POOR.'

Benjamin Disraeli (1804–81) British statesman. *Sybil*, Bk. II, Ch. 5

5 Errors look so very ugly in persons of small means – one feels they are taking quite a liberty in going astray; whereas people of fortune may naturally indulge in a few delinquencies.

George Eliot (Mary Ann Evans; 1819–80) British novelist. *Janet's Repentance*, Ch. 25

6 Whereas it has long been known and declared that the poor have no right to the property of the rich, I wish it also to be known and declared that the rich have no right to the property of the poor.

John Ruskin (1819–1900) British art critic and writer. *Unto this Last*, Essay III

7 When the rich wage war it is the poor who die.

Jean-Paul Sartre (1905–80) French writer. *The Devil and the Good Lord*

8 As long as men are men, a poor society cannot be too poor to find a right order of life, nor a rich society too rich to have need to seek it.

R. H. Tawney (1880–1962) British economist and historian. *The Acquisitive Society*

POWER

See also influence, leadership, responsibility

1 Divide and rule.

Proverb

2 He who pays the piper calls the tune.

Proverb

3 Power tends to corrupt, and absolute power corrupts absolutely. Great men are almost always bad men...There is no worse heresy than that the office sanctifies the holder of it.

Lord Acton (1834–1902) British historian. Often misquoted as 'Power corrupts...'. Letter to Bishop Mandell Creighton, 5 Apr 1887

4 A friend in power is a friend lost.

Henry Brooks Adams (1838–1918) US historian. *The Education of Henry Adams*

5 Nothing destroyeth authority so much as the unequal and untimely interchange of power pressed too far, and relaxed too much.

Francis Bacon (1561–1626) English philosopher. *Essays*, 'Of Empire'

6 He did not care in which direction the car was travelling, so long as he remained in the driver's seat.

Lord Beaverbrook (1879–1964) British newspaper owner and politician. Referring to Lloyd George. *New Statesman*, 14 June 1963

7 The strongest poison ever known
Came from Caesar's laurel crown.

William Blake (1757–1827) British poet. *Auguries of Innocence*

8 The greater the power, the more dangerous the abuse.

Edmund Burke (1729–97) British politician. Speech, House of Commons, 7 Feb 1771

9 If you think you have someone eating out of your hand, it's a good idea to count your fingers.

Martin Buxbaume Attrib.

10 There is one thing about being President – nobody can tell you when to sit down.

Dwight D. Eisenhower (1890–1969) US general and statesman. *The Observer*, 'Sayings of the Week', 9 Aug 1953

11 Men of power have not time to read; yet men who do not read are unfit for power.

Michael Foot (1913–) British Labour politician and journalist. *Debts Of Honour*

12 Power is so apt to be insolent and Liberty to be saucy, that they are seldom upon good Terms.

Lord Halifax (1633–95) English statesman. *Political, Moral, and Miscellaneous Thoughts and Reflections*

13 It was a symptom of Britain's post-war condition that anyone given power before his hair turned white was called a whizz-kid.

Clive James (1939–) Writer and broadcaster, born in Australia. *Falling Towards England*, Ch. 18

14 Power is the ultimate aphrodisiac.

Henry Kissinger (1923–) German-born US politician and diplomat. *The Guardian*, 28 Nov 1976

15 Power? It's like a dead sea fruit; when you achieve it, there's nothing there.

Harold Macmillan (1894–1986) British politician and prime minister. Attrib.

16 It could never be a correct justification that, because the whites oppressed us yesterday when they had power, that the blacks must oppress them today because they have power.

Robert Mugabe (1925–) Zimbabwe politician and president. Speech, Mar 1980

17 To reign is worth ambition, though in Hell:

Better to reign in Hell than serve in Heaven.

John Milton (1608–74) English poet. *Paradise Lost*, Bk. I

18 Who controls the past controls the future. Who controls the present controls the past.

George Orwell (Eric Blair; 1903–50) British novelist. *Nineteen Eighty-Four*

19 Unlimited power is apt to corrupt the minds of those who possess it.

William Pitt the Elder (1708–78) British statesman. *See also* Lord ACTON. Speech, House of Lords, 9 Jan 1770

20 The megalomaniac differs from the narcissist by the fact that he wishes to be powerful rather than charming, and seeks to be feared rather than loved. To this type belong many lunatics and most of the great men of history.

Bertrand Russell (1872–1970) British philosopher. *The Conquest of Happiness*

21 We are the masters at the moment – and not only for the moment, but for a very long time to come.

Lord Shawcross (1902–) British Labour politician and lawyer. Sometimes quoted as, 'We are the masters now!'. House of Commons, 2 Apr 1946

22 The official world, the corridors of power, the dilemmas of conscience and egotism – she disliked them all.

C. P. Snow (1905–80) British novelist. *Homecomings*, Ch. 22

23 You only have power over people so long as you don't take *everything* away from them. But when you've robbed a man of everything he's no longer in your power – he's free again.

Alexander Solzhenitsyn (1918–) Soviet novelist. *The First Circle*, Ch. 17

24 Power corrupts, but lack of power corrupts absolutely.

Adlai Stevenson (1900–65) US statesman. *The Observer*, Jan 1963

25 He aspired to power instead of influence, and as a result forfeited both.

A. J. P. Taylor (1906–90) British historian. Referring to Lord Northcliffe. *English History, 1914–1945*, Ch. 1

26 One Ring to rule them all, One Ring to find them,
One Ring to bring them all and in the darkness bind them.

J. R. R. Tolkien (1892–1973) British writer. *The Lord of the Rings*, Pt. I: *The Fellowship of the Ring*, Ch. 2

27 The balance of power.

Robert Walpole (1676–1745) British statesman. Speech, House of Commons

28 The good old rule
Sufficeth them, the simple plan,
That they should take, who have the power,
And they should keep who can.

William Wordsworth (1770–1850) British poet. *Rob Roy's Grave*

29 The wrong sort of people are always in power because they would not be in power if they were not the wrong sort of people.

Jon Wynne-Tyson (1924–) British humorous writer. *Times Literary Supplement*

POWER POLITICS

See also force, oppression, violence, weapons

1 Whatever happens, we have got
The Maxim Gun, and they have not.

Hilaire Belloc (1870–1953) French-born British poet. Referring to African natives. *The Modern Traveller*

2 The great questions of our day cannot be solved by speeches and majority votes...but by iron and blood.

Bismarck (1815–98) German statesman. Usually misquoted as 'blood and iron' – a form Bismarck himself used in 1886. Speech, Prussian Chamber, 30 Sept 1862

3 Guns will make us powerful; butter will only make us fat.

Hermann Goering (1893–1946) German leader. Radio broadcast, 1936

4 A man may build himself a throne of bayonets, but he cannot sit on it.

Dean Inge (1860–1954) British churchman. *Wit and Wisdom of Dean Inge* (ed. Marchant)

5 Every Communist must grasp the truth, 'Political power grows out of the barrel of a gun.'

Mao Tse-Tung (1893–1976) Chinese communist leader. *Selected Works*, Vol II, 'Problems of War and Strategy', 6 Nov 1938

6 There is a homely adage which runs 'Speak softly and carry a big stick, you will go far'.

Theodore Roosevelt (1858–1919) US Republican president. Speech, Minnesota State Fair, 2 Sept 1901

7 God is always on the side of the big battalions.

Vicomte de Turenne (1611–75) French marshal. Attrib.

8 God is on the side not of the heavy battalions, but of the best shots.

Voltaire (François-Marie Arouet; 1694–1778) French writer. *Notebooks*

PRACTICALITY

1 I have no dress except the one I wear every day. If you are going to be kind enough to give me one, please let it be practical and dark so that I can put it on afterwards to go to the laboratory.

Marie Curie (1867–1934) Polish chemist. Referring to a wedding dress. Letter to a friend

2 What would you do with it? It is full of leprosy.

Father Damien (Joseph de Veuster; 1840–89) Belgian Roman Catholic missionary. When asked on his deathbed whether he would leave another priest his mantle, like Elijah. *Memoirs of an Aesthete* (H. Acton)

3 The Arab who builds himself a hut out of the marble fragments of a temple in Palmyra is more philosophical than all the curators of the museums in London, Munich or Paris.

Anatole France (Jacques Anatole François Thibault; 1844–1924) French writer. *The Crime of Sylvestre Bonnard*

4 I'm really an experimentalist. I used to say "I think with my hands." I just like manipulation.

Dorothy Crowfoot Hodgkin (1910–94) British chemist. *A Passion for Science* (L. Wolpert and A. Richards)

5 Talk to him of Jacob's ladder, and he would ask the number of the steps.

Douglas William Jerrold (1803–57) British dramatist. *Wit and Opinions of Douglas Jerrold*, 'A Matter-of-fact Man'

6 Don't carry away that arm till I have taken off my ring.

Lord Raglan (1788–1855) British field marshal. Request immediately after his arm had been amputated following the battle of Waterloo. *Dictionary of National Biography*

7 Very well, then I shall not take off my boots.

Duke of Wellington (1769–1852) British general and statesman. Responding to the news, as he was going to bed, that the ship in which he was travelling seemed about to sink. Attrib.

PRAISE

See also admiration, boasts, compliments, flattery

1 Self-praise is no recommendation.

Proverb

2 Just as it is always said of slander that something always sticks when people boldly slander, so it might be said of self-praise (if it is not entirely shameful and ridiculous) that if we praise ourselves fearlessly, something will always stick.

Francis Bacon (1561–1626) English philosopher. *The Advancement of Learning*

3 Let us now praise famous men, and our fathers that begat us.

Bible: Ecclesiasticus 44:1

4 The advantage of doing one's praising for oneself is that one can lay it on so thick and exactly in the right places.

Samuel Butler (1835–1902) British writer. *The Way of All Flesh*, Ch. 34

5 Fondly we think we honour merit then,
When we but praise ourselves in other men.

Alexander Pope (1688–1744) British poet. *An Essay on Criticism*

6 To refuse praise reveals a desire to be praised twice over.

Duc de la Rochefoucauld (1613–80) French writer. *Maximes*, 149

PRAYER

See also Christianity, faith, God, religion

1 Hail Mary, full of grace, the Lord is with thee: Blessed art thou among women, and blessed is the fruit of thy womb, Jesus.

Anonymous *Ave Maria*, 11th century

2 From ghoulies and ghosties and long-leggety beasties
And things that go bump in the night,
Good Lord, deliver us!

Anonymous Cornish

3 O Lord! thou knowest how busy I must be this day: if I forget thee, do not thou forget me.

Lord Astley (1579–1652) English Royalist general. Prayer before taking part in the Battle of Edgehill. *Memoires* (Sir Philip Warwick)

4 But when ye pray, use not vain repetitions, as the heathen do: for they think that they shall be heard for their much speaking.
Be not ye therefore like unto them: for your Father knoweth what things ye have need of, before ye ask him.
After this manner therefore pray ye: Our Father which art in heaven, Hallowed be thy name.
Thy kingdom come. Thy will be done in earth, as it is in heaven.
Give us this day our daily bread.
And forgive us our debts, as we forgive our debtors.
And lead us not into temptation, but deliver us from evil: For thine is the kingdom, and the power, and the glory, for ever. Amen.

Bible: Matthew 6:7–13

5 To Mercy, Pity, Peace, and Love
All pray in their distress.

William Blake (1757–1827) British poet. *Songs of Innocence*, 'The Divine Image'

6 When two or three are gathered together in thy Name thou wilt grant their requests.

The Book of Common Prayer *Morning Prayer, Prayer of St Chrysostom*

7 A leap over the hedge is better than good men's prayers.

Miguel de Cervantes (1547–1616) Spanish novelist. *Don Quixote*, Pt. I, Ch. 21

8 He prayeth well, who loveth well
Both man and bird and beast.

Samuel Taylor Coleridge (1772–1834) British poet. *The Rime of the Ancient Mariner*, VII

9 He prayeth best, who loveth best
All things both great and small;
For the dear God who loveth us,
He made and loveth all.

Samuel Taylor Coleridge *The Rime of the Ancient Mariner*, VII

10 Prayer makes the Christian's armour bright;
And Satan trembles when he sees
The weakest saint upon his knees.

William Cowper (1731–1800) British poet. *Olney Hymns*, 29

11 The idea that He would take his attention away from the universe in order to give me a bicycle with three speeds is just so unlikely

I can't go along with it.

Quentin Crisp (?1910–) Model, publicist, and writer. *The Sunday Times*, 18 Dec 1977

12 Forgive, O Lord, my little jokes on Thee
And I'll forgive Thy great big one on me.

Robert Frost (1875–1963) US poet. *In the clearing*, 'Cluster of Faith'

13 Religion's in the heart, not in the knees.

Douglas William Jerrold (1803–57) British dramatist. *The Devil's Ducat*, I.2

14 The Beadsman, after thousand aves told,
For aye unsought-for slept among his ashes cold.

John Keats (1795–1821) British poet. *The Eve of Saint Agnes*, I

15 Our dourest parsons, who followed the nonconformist fashion of long extemporary prayers, always seemed to me to be bent on bullying God. After a few 'beseech thees' as a mere politeness, they adopted a sterner tone and told Him what they expected from Him and more than hinted He must attend to His work.

J. B. Priestley (1894–1984) British novelist. *Outcries and Asides*

16 I am just going to pray for you at St Paul's, but with no very lively hope of success.

Sydney Smith (1771–1845) British clergyman and essayist. On meeting an acquaintance. *The Smith of Smiths* (H. Pearson), Ch. 13

17 If thou shouldst never see my face again,
Pray for my soul. More things are wrought by prayer
Than this world dreams of.

Alfred, Lord Tennyson (1809–92) British poet. *Idylls of the King*, 'The Passing of Arthur'

18 Whatever a man prays for, he prays for a miracle. Every prayer reduces itself to this: 'Great God grant that twice two be not four.'

Ivan Turgenev (1818–83) Russian novelist. *Prayer*

PRECOCITY

See also children, youth

1 One of those men who reach such an acute limited excellence at twenty-one that everything afterward savours of anti-climax.

F. Scott Fitzgerald (1896–1940) US novelist. *The Great Gatsby*, Ch. 1

2 Thank you, madam, the agony is abated.

Lord Macaulay (1800–59) British historian. Replying, aged four, to a lady who asked if he had hurt himself. *Life and Letters of Macaulay* (Trevelyan), Ch. 1

PREGNANCY

See also babies, birth, motherhood

1 The baby bounced gently off the wall of her uterus. She opened her dressing gown and put her hands back on her belly. It moved again like a dolphin going through the water; that was the way she imagined it. Are yeh normal? she said.

Roddy Doyle (1958–) Irish novelist and playwright. *The Snapper*

2 It seems an insult to nature and to the Creator to imagine that pregnancy was ever intended to be a sickness...False states of society, false modes of dress, false habits of life, etc., all contribute to bring suffering at this time.

Mrs E. B. Duffey *What Women Should Know*

3 It is the woman who is ultimately held responsible for pregnancy. While not being allowed to have control over her body, she is nevertheless held responsible for its products.

Carol Glassman (c. 1942–) US civil rights activist. *Sisterhood Is Powerful* (ed. Robin Morgan)

4 Dear Mary, We all knew you had it in you.

Dorothy Parker (1893–1967) US writer. Telegram sent to a friend on the successful outcome of her much-publicized pregnancy

PREJUDICE

See also equality, feminism, Jews, objectivity, racism, religion, subjectivity

1 I am a Catholic. As far as possible I go to Mass every day. As far as possible I kneel down and tell these beads every day. If you reject me on account of my religion, I shall thank God that he has spared me the indignity of being your representative.

Hilaire Belloc (1870–1953) French-born British poet. Said in his first election campaign. Speech, Salford, 1906

2 Mother is far too clever to understand anything she does not like.

Arnold Bennett (1867–1931) British novelist. *The Title*

3 Common sense is the collection of prejudices acquired by age eighteen.

Albert Einstein (1879–1955) German-born US physicist. *Scientific American*, Feb 1976

4 Vegetarians have wicked, shifty eyes, and laugh in a cold and calculating manner. They pinch little children, steal stamps, drink water, favour beards...wheeze, squeak, drawl and maunder.

J. B. Morton (1893–1979) British journalist. *By the Way*, '4 June'

5 ...I *too well* know its truth, from experience, that whenever any poor Gipsies are encamped anywhere and crimes and robberies &c. occur, it is invariably laid to their account, which is shocking; and if they are always looked upon as vagabonds, how *can* they become good people?

Victoria (1819–1901) Queen of the United Kingdom. Journal, 29 Dec 1836

6 I do not intend to prejudge the past.

William Whitelaw (1918–) British politician. Said on arriving in Ulster as Minister for Northern Ireland. *The Times*, 3 Dec 1973

7 No Jewish blood runs among my blood,
but I am as bitterly and hardly hated
by every anti-semite
as if I were a Jew. By this
I am a Russian.

Yevgeny Yevtushenko (1933–) Soviet poet. *Babi Yar*

PRESENT

See also future, opportunity, past, time

1 No time like the present.

Proverb

2 The past was nothing to her; offered no lesson which she was willing to heed. The future was a mystery which she never attempted to penetrate. The present alone was significant...

Kate Chopin (1851–1904) US writer. *The Awakening*, Ch. 15

3 I have learned to live each day as it comes, and not to borrow trouble by dreading tomorrow. It is the dark menace of the future that makes cowards of us.

Dorothy Dix (Elizabeth Meriwether Gilmer; 1861–1951) US journalist and writer. *Dorothy Dix, Her Book*, Introduction

4 Happy the Man, and happy he alone,
He who can call today his own:
He who, secure within, can say,
Tomorrow do thy worst, for I have liv'd today.

John Dryden (1631–1700) British poet and dramatist. *Translation of Horace*, III

5 Ah, my Belovéd, fill the Cup that clears
TO-DAY of past Regrets and Future Fears:
To-morrow! – Why, To-morrow I may be
Myself with Yesterday's Sev'n thousand Years.

Edward Fitzgerald (1809–83) British poet. *The Rubáiyát of Omar Khayyám* (1st edn.), XX

6 Gather ye rosebuds while ye may,
Old time is still a-flying:
And this same flower that smiles today
Tomorrow will be dying.

Robert Herrick (1591–1674) English poet. *Hesperides*, 'To the Virgins, to Make Much of Time'

7 *Carpe diem.*
Seize the day.

Horace (Quintus Horatius Flaccus; 65–8 BC) Roman poet. *Odes*, I

8 Drop the question what tomorrow may bring, and count as profit every day that Fate allows you.

Horace *Odes*, I

9 While we're talking, time will have meanly run on: pick today's fruits, not relying on the future in the slightest.

Horace *Odes*, I

10 Believe each day that has dawned is your last. Some hour to which you have not been looking forward will prove lovely. As for me, if you want a good laugh, you will come and find me fat and sleek, in excellent condition, one of Epicurus' herd of pigs.

Horace *Epistles*, I

11 We live in stirring times – tea-stirring times.

Christopher Isherwood (1904–86) British novelist. *Mr Norris Changes Trains*

12 Redeem thy mis-spent time that's past;
Live this day, as if 'twere thy last.

Thomas Ken (1637–1711) English bishop. *A Morning Hymn*

13 What is love? 'Tis not hereafter;
Present mirth hath present laughter;
What's to come is still unsure.
In delay there lies no plenty,
Then come kiss me, sweet and twenty;
Youth's a stuff will not endure.

William Shakespeare (1564–1616) English dramatist. *Twelfth Night*, II:3

PRIDE

See also arrogance, conceit, egotism, self-respect

1 Pride goeth before destruction, and an haughty spirit before a fall.

Bible: Proverbs 16:18

2 He that is down needs fear no fall;
He that is low, no pride.

John Bunyan (1628–88) English writer. *The Pilgrim's Progress*, 'Shepherd Boy's Song'

3 I know of no case where a man added to his dignity by standing on it.

Winston Churchill (1874–1965) British politician. Attrib.

4 When the Lord sent me forth into the world, He forbade me to put off my hat to any high or low.

George Fox (1624–91) English religious leader. *Journal*

5 And if you include me among the lyric poets, I'll hold my head so high it'll strike the stars.

Horace (Quintus Horatius Flaccus; 65–8 BC) Roman poet. *Odes*, I

6 We are not ashamed of what we have done, because, when you have a great cause to fight for, the moment of greatest humiliation is the moment when the spirit is proudest.

Christabel Pankhurst (1880–1958) British suffragette. Speech, Albert Hall, London, 19 Mar 1908

7 Yes; I am proud, I must be proud to see
Men not afraid of God, afraid of me.

Alexander Pope (1688–1744) British poet. *Epilogue to the Satires*, Dialogue II

8 Of all the causes which conspire to blind
Man's erring judgment, and misguide the mind,
What the weak head with strongest bias rules,
Is Pride, the never-failing vice of fools.

Alexander Pope *An Essay on Criticism*

9 There is false modesty, but there is
no false pride.

Jules Renard (1894–1910) French writer. *Journal*

10 I am proud to have a son who died doing the job he loved for the country he loved.

Harry Taylor Father of soldier killed in Falklands war. Remark, May 1982

11 The French want no-one to be their *superior.* The English want *inferiors.* The Frenchman constantly raises his eyes above him with anxiety. The Englishman lowers his beneath him with satisfaction. On either side it is pride, but understood in a different way.

Alexis de Tocqueville (1805–59) French writer, historian, and politician. *Voyage en Angleterre et en Irlande de 1835*, 18 May

12 We cannot bring ourselves to believe it possible that a foreigner should in any respect be wiser than ourselves. If any such point out to us our follies, we at once claim those follies as the special evidences of our wisdom.

Anthony Trollope (1815–82) British novelist. *Orley Farm*, Ch. 18

PRINCIPLES

See also integrity, morality

1 It is easier to fight for one's principles than to live up to them.

Alfred Adler (1870–1937) Austrian psychiatrist. *Alfred Adler* (P. Bottome)

2 If one sticks too rigidly to one's principles one would hardly see anybody.

Agatha Christie (1891–1976) British detective-story writer. *Towards Zero*, I

3 Whenever two good people argue over principles, they are both right.

Marie Ebner von Eschenbach (1830–1916) Austrian writer. *Aphorism*

4 Well, sir, you never can tell. That's a principle in life with me, sir, if you'll excuse my having such a thing, sir.

George Bernard Shaw (1856–1950) Irish dramatist and critic. *You Never Can Tell*, II

PRIVACY

1 The house of every one is to him as his castle and fortress.

Edward Coke (1552–1634) English lawyer and politician. *Semayne's Case*

2 I never said, 'I want to be alone.' I only said, 'I want to be *left* alone.' There is all the difference.

Greta Garbo (1905–90) Swedish-born US film star. *Garbo* (John Bainbridge)

3 Isn't it amazing that there's no copyright on your own life?

Sarah Miles (1941–) British actress. *The Observer*, 'Sayings of the Week', 2 Feb 1994

4 The poorest man may in his cottage bid defiance to all the forces of the Crown. It may be frail – its roof may shake – the wind may blow through it – the storm may enter – the rain may enter – but the King of England cannot enter! – all his force dares not cross the threshold of the ruined tenement!

William Pitt the Elder (1708–78) British statesman. *Statesmen in the Time of George III* (Lord Brougham), Vol. I

5 This is a free country, madam. We have a right to share your privacy in a public place.

Peter Ustinov (1921–) British actor. *Romanoff and Juliet*, I

PROCRASTINATION

1 Never put off till tomorrow what you can do today.

Proverb

2 Put off the evil hour as long as you can.

Proverb

3 The road to hell is paved with good intentions.

Proverb

4 Give me chastity and continence, but not yet.

St Augustine of Hippo (354–430) Bishop of Hippo. *Confessions*, Bk. VIII, Ch. 7

5 Procrastination is the thief of time.

Edward Young (1683–1765) British poet. *Night Thoughts*

PROGRESS

See also change, conservatism, improvement, innovation, novelty, technology

1 The people who live in the past must yield to the people who live in the future. Otherwise the world would begin to turn the other way round.

Arnold Bennett (1867–1931) British novelist. *Milestones*

2 All progress is based upon a universal innate desire on the part of every organism to live beyond its income.

Samuel Butler (1835–1902) British writer. *Notebooks*

3 As enunciated today, 'progress' is simply a comparative of which we have not settled the superlative.

G. K. Chesterton (1874–1936) British writer. *Heretics*, Ch. 2

4 New roads: new ruts.

G. K. Chesterton Attrib.

5 What we call progress is the exchange of one nuisance for another nuisance.

Havelock Ellis (1859–1939) British sexologist. Attrib.

6 All that is human must retrograde if it does not advance.

Edward Gibbon (1737–94) British historian. *Decline and Fall of the Roman Empire*, Ch. 71

7 You cannot fight against the future.

Time is on our side.

William Ewart Gladstone (1809–98) British statesman. Advocating parliamentary reform. Speech, 1866

8 One step forward, two steps back…It happens in the lives of individuals, and it happens in the history of nations and in the development of parties.

Lenin (Vladimir Ilich Ulyanov; 1870–1924) Russian revolutionary leader. *One Step Forward, Two Steps Back*

9 If I have seen further it is by standing on the shoulders of giants.

Isaac Newton (1642–1727) British scientist. Letter to Robert Hooke, 5 Feb 1675

10 You can't say civilization don't advance, however, for in every war they kill you a new way.

Will Rogers (1879–1935) US actor and humorist. *Autobiography*, Ch. 12

11 Organic life, we are told, has developed gradually from the protozoon to the philosopher, and this development, we are assured, is indubitably an advance. Unfortunately it is the philosopher, not the protozoon, who gives us this assurance.

Bertrand Russell (1872–1970) British philosopher. *Mysticism and Logic*, Ch. 6

12 Man's 'progress' is but a gradual discovery that his questions have no meaning.

Antoine de Saint-Exupéry (1900–44) French novelist and aviator. *The Wisdom of the Sands*

PROMISCUITY

See also sex

1 I see – she's the original good time that was had by all.

Bette Davis (Ruth Elizabeth Davis; 1908–89) US film star. Referring to a starlet of the time. *The Filmgoer's Book of Quotes* (Leslie Halliwell)

2 Lady Capricorn, he understood, was still keeping open bed.

Aldous Huxley (1894–1964) British novelist. *Antic Hay*, Ch. 21

3 The woman's a whore, and there's an end on't.

Samuel Johnson (1709–84) British lexicographer. Referring to Lady Diana Beauclerk. *Life of Johnson* (J. Boswell), Vol. II

4 You were born with your legs apart. They'll send you to the grave in a Y-shaped coffin.

Joe Orton (1933–67) British dramatist. *What the Butler Saw*, I

5 You know, she speaks eighteen languages. And she can't say 'No' in any of them.

Dorothy Parker (1893–1967) US writer. Speaking of an acquaintance. Attrib.

6 I'm glad you like my Catherine. I like her too. She ruled thirty million people and had three thousand lovers. I do the best I can in two hours.

Mae West (1892–1980) US actress. After her performance in *Catherine the Great*. Speech from the stage

PROMISES

1 Better is it that thou shouldest not vow, than that thou shouldest vow and not pay.

Bible: Ecclesiastes 5:5

2 I do set my bow in the cloud, and it shall be for a token of a covenant between me and the earth.

Bible: Genesis 9:13

3 The rule is, jam tomorrow and jam yesterday – but never jam today.

Lewis Carroll (Charles Lutwidge Dodgson; 1832–98) British writer. *Through the Looking-Glass*, Ch. 5

4 If you feed people just with revolutionary slogans they will listen today, they will listen tomorrow, they will listen the day after tomorrow, but on the fourth day they will say 'To hell with you!'

Nikita Khrushchev (1894–1971) Soviet statesman. Attrib.

5 A promise made is a debt unpaid.

Robert William Service (1874–1958) Canadian poet. *The Cremation of Sam McGee*

6 Jam today, and men aren't at their most exciting: Jam tomorrow, and one often sees them at their noblest.

C. P. Snow (1905–80) British novelist. *The Two Cultures and the Scientific Revolution*, 4

7 Promises and pie-crust are made to be broken.

Jonathan Swift (1667–1745) Irish-born Anglican priest and writer. *Polite Conversation*, Dialogue 1

PROMOTION

See also patronage

1 Tired of knocking at Preferment's door.

Matthew Arnold (1822–88) British poet and critic. *The Scholar Gipsy*

2 He had said he had known many kicked down stairs, but he never knew any kicked up stairs before.

Lord Halifax (1633–95) English statesman. *Original Memoirs* (Burnet)

PROMPTNESS

1 Liberality lies less in giving liberally than in the timeliness of the gift.

Jean de La Bruyère (1645–96) French satirist. *Les Caractères*

2 Punctuality is the politeness of kings.

Louis XVIII (1755–1824) French king. Attrib.

3 Better never than late.

George Bernard Shaw (1856–1950) Irish dramatist and critic. Responding to an offer by a producer to present one of Shaw's plays, having earlier rejected it. *The Unimportance of Being Oscar* (Oscar Levant)

4 He gives twice who gives promptly.

Publilius Syrus (1st century BC) Roman dramatist. Attrib.

5 Punctuality is the virtue of the bored.

Evelyn Waugh (1903–66) British novelist. *Diaries*, 'Irregular Notes', 26 Mar 1962

PRONUNCIATION

See also class, language, speech, spelling

1 Everybody has a right to pronounce foreign names as he chooses.

Winston Churchill (1874–1965) British statesman. *The Observer*, 'Sayings of the Week', 5 Aug 1951

2 Oh my God! Remember you're in Egypt. The *skay* is only seen in Kensington.

Herbert Beerbohm Tree (1853–1917) British actor and theatre manager. To a leading lady. *Beerbohm Tree* (Hesketh Pearson)

3 They spell it Vinci and pronounce it Vinchy; foreigners always spell better than they pronounce.

Mark Twain (Samuel Langhorne Clemens; 1835–1910) US writer. *The Innocents Abroad*, Ch. 19

PROOF

1 One swallow does not make a summer.

Proverb

2 What is now proved was once only imagined.

William Blake (1757–1827) British poet. *The Marriage of Heaven and Hell*, 'Proverbs of Hell'

3 If a man could pass through Paradise in a dream, and have a flower presented to him as a pledge that his soul had really been there, and if he found that flower in his hand when he awoke – Aye, and what then?

Samuel Taylor Coleridge (1772–1834) British poet. *Anima Poetae*

4 Of course, before we *know* he is a saint, there will have to be miracles.

Graham Greene (1904–91) British novelist. *The Power and the Glory*, Pt. IV

5 If only I could get down to Sidcup! I've been waiting for the weather to break. He's got my papers, this man I left them with, it's got it all down there, I could prove everything.

Harold Pinter (1930–) British dramatist. *The Caretaker*, I

6 Some circumstantial evidence is very strong, as when you find a trout in the milk.

Henry David Thoreau (1817–62) US writer. *Journal*, 1850

PROPAGANDA

1 Propaganda is that branch of the art of lying which consists in nearly deceiving your friends without quite deceiving your enemies.

F. M. Cornford (1886–1960) British poet. *New Statesman*, 15 Sept 1978

2 The greater the lie, the greater the chance that it will be believed.

Adolf Hitler (1889–1945) German dictator. *Mein Kampf*

3 I wonder if we could contrive...some magnificent myth that would in itself carry conviction to our whole community.

Plato (429–347 BC) Greek philosopher. *Republic*, Bk. 5

PROPHECY

See also beginning, future

1 'I saw the new moon late yestreen
Wi' the auld moon in her arm;
And if we gang to sea master,
I fear we'll come to harm.'

Anonymous *Sir Patrick Spens*

2 And there arose not a prophet since in Israel like unto Moses, whom the Lord knew face to face.

Bible: Deuteronomy 34:10

3 I am signing my death warrant.

Michael Collins (1890–1922) Irish nationalist. Said on signing the agreement with Great Britain, 1921, that established the Irish Free State. He was assassinated in an ambush some months later. *Peace by Ordeal* (Longford), Pt. 6, Ch. 1

4 I will sit down now, but the time will come when you will hear me.

Benjamin Disraeli (1804–81) British statesman. Maiden Speech, House of Commons, 7 Dec 1837

5 The lamps are going out over all Europe; we shall not see them lit again in our lifetime.

Lord Grey (1862–1933) British statesman. Remark made on 3 Aug 1914, the eve of World War I.

6 You ain't heard nothin' yet, folks.

Al Jolson (Asa Yoelson; 1886–1950) US actor and singer. In the film *The Jazz Singer*, July 1927.

7 For not wanting to consent to the divorce, which then afterwards will be recognized as unworthy, the King of the islands will be forced to flee, and one put in his place who has no sign of kingship.

Nostradamus (1503–66) French astrologer. Thought to refer to the abdication of Edward VIII. *The Prophecies of Nostradamus*, Century X, 22

8 At night they will think they have seen the sun, when they see the half pig man: Noise, screams, battles seen fought in the skies. The brute beasts will be heard to speak.

Nostradamus Thought to prophecy a 20th-century air-battle. *The Prophecies of Nostradamus*, Century I, 64

9 The blood of the just will be demanded of London burnt by fire in three times twenty plus six. The ancient lady will fall from her high position, and many of the same denomination will be killed.

Nostradamus Believed to refer to the Great Fire of London, 1666. The 'ancient lady' is interpreted as the Cathedral of St. Paul's, which was destroyed in the fire. *The Prophecies of Nostradamus*, Century II, 51

10 *Après nous le déluge.*
After us the deluge.

Madame de Pompadour (1721–64) The mistress of Louis XV of France. After the Battle of Rossbach, 1757

11 As I look ahead, I am filled with foreboding. Like the Roman, I seem to see 'the River Tiber foaming with much blood'.

Enoch Powell (1912–) British politician. Talking about immigration. Speech in Birmingham, 20 Apr 1968

12 Beware the ides of March.

William Shakespeare (1564–1616) English dramatist. *Julius Caesar*, I:2

13 Mr Turnbull had predicted evil consequences…and was now doing the best in his power to bring about the verification of his own prophecies.

Anthony Trollope (1815–82) British novelist. *Phineas Finn*, Ch. 25

14 I see wars, horrible wars, and the Tiber foaming with
much blood.

Virgil (Publius Vergilius Maro; 70–19 BC) Roman poet. Part of the Sibyl's prophecy to Aeneas, foretelling his difficulties in winning a home in Italy. *Aeneid*, Bk. VI

15 When the Paris Exhibition closes, electric light will close with it and no more will be heard of it.

Erasmus Wilson

PROSE

See also books, criticism, fiction, literature, novels, poetry and prose, writing

1 Yet no one hears his own remarks as prose.

W. H. Auden (1907–73) British poet. *At a Party*

2 Men will forgive a man anything except bad prose.

Winston Churchill (1874–1965) British statesman. Election speech, Manchester, 1906

3 Good heavens! I have been talking prose for over forty years without realizing it.

Molière (Jean Baptiste Poquelin; 1622–73) French dramatist. *Le Bourgeois Gentilhomme*, II:4

PROTESTANTISM

See also Catholicism, Christianity, religion

1 The chief contribution of Protestantism to human thought is its massive proof that God is a bore.

H. L. Mencken (1880–1956) US journalist. *Notebooks*, 'Minority Report'

2 'You're a Christian?' 'Church of England,' said Mr Polly. 'Mm,' said the employer, a little checked. 'For good all round business work, I should have preferred a Baptist.'

H. G. Wells (1866–1946) British writer. *The History of Mr Polly*, Pt. III, Ch. 1

3 Take heed of thinking. *The farther you go from the church of Rome, the nearer you are to God.*

Henry Wotton (1568–1639) English poet and diplomat. *Reliquiae Wottonianae* (Izaak Walton)

PROVOCATION

1 My wife hath something in her gizzard, that only waits an opportunity of being provoked to bring up.

Samuel Pepys (1633–1703) English diarist. *Diary*, 17 June 1668

2 Ask you what provocation I have had?
The strong antipathy of good to bad.

Alexander Pope (1688–1744) British poet. *Epilogue to the Satires*, Dialogue II

PRUDENCE

See also caution, wisdom

1 A bird in the hand is worth two in the bush.

Proverb

2 Forewarned is forearmed.

Proverb

3 For want of a nail the shoe was lost; for want of a shoe the horse was lost; for want of a horse the rider was lost.

Proverb

4 Prevention is better than cure.

Proverb

5 It is always good
When a man has two irons in the fire.

Francis Beaumont (1584–1616) English dramatist. *The Faithful Friends*, I:2

6 Put your trust in God, my boys, and keep your powder dry.

Valentine Blacker (1778–1823) British soldier. *Oliver Cromwell's Advice*

7 I'd much rather have that fellow inside my tent pissing out, than outside my tent pissing in.

Lyndon B. Johnson (1908–73) US statesman. When asked why he retained J. Edgar Hoover at the FBI. *Guardian Weekly*, 18 Dec 1971

8 One should oblige everyone to the extent of one's ability. One often needs someone smaller than oneself.

Jean de La Fontaine (1621–95) French poet. *Fables*, II, 'Le Lion et le Rat'

9 Any girl who was a lady would not even think of having such a good time that she did not remember to hang on to her jewelry.

Anita Loos (1891–1981) US novelist. *Gentlemen Prefer Blondes*, Ch. 4

10 Be nice to people on your way up because you'll meet 'em on your way down.

Wilson Mizner (1876–1933) US writer and wit. Also attributed to Jimmy Durante. *A Dictionary of Catch Phrases* (Eric Partridge)

PRUDERY

See also censorship, pornography, puritanism

1 Would you allow your wife or your servant to read this book?

Mervyn Griffith-Jones (1909–78) British lawyer. As counsel for the prosecution in the *Lady Chatterley's Lover* trial

2 Age will bring all things, and everyone knows, Madame, that twenty is no age to be a prude.

Molière (Jean Baptiste Poquelin; 1622–73) French dramatist. *Le Misanthrope*, III:4

3 An orgy looks particularly alluring seen through the mists of righteous indignation.

Malcolm Muggeridge (1903–90) British writer. *The Most of Malcolm Muggeridge*, 'Dolce Vita in a Cold Climate'

4 Obscenity is what happens to shock some elderly and ignorant magistrate.

Bertrand Russell (1872–1970) British philosopher. *Look* magazine

PSYCHIATRY

See also madness, neurosis, psychology

1 To us he is no more a person
Now but a climate of opinion.

W. H. Auden (1907–73) British poet. *In Memory of Sigmund Freud*

2 The trouble with Freud is that he never played the Glasgow Empire Saturday night.

Ken Dodd (1931–) British comedian. TV interview, 1965

3 The psychic development of the individual is a short repetition of the course of development of the race.

Sigmund Freud (1856–1939) Austrian psychoanalyst. *Leonardo da Vinci*

4 Anybody who goes to see a psychiatrist ought to have his head examined.

Samuel Goldwyn (Samuel Goldfish; 1882–1974) Polish-born US film producer. Attrib.

5 Schizophrenic behaviour is a special strategy that a person invents in order to live in an unlivable situation.

R. D. Laing (1927–89) British psychiatrist. *The Politics of Experience*

6 Schizophrenia cannot be understood without understanding despair.

R. D. Laing *The Divided Self*, Ch. 2

7 The mystic sees the ineffable, and the psychopathologist the unspeakable.

W. Somerset Maugham (1874–1965) British novelist. *The Moon and Sixpence*, Ch. 1

8 If the nineteenth century was the age of the editorial chair, ours is the century of the psychiatrist's couch.

Marshall McLuhan (1911–81) Canadian sociologist. *Understanding Media*, Introduction

9 A psychiatrist is a man who goes to the Folies-Bergère and looks at the audience.

Mervyn Stockwood (1913–95) British churchman. *The Observer*, 'Sayings of the Week', 15 Oct 1961

10 Psychiatrists classify a person as neurotic if he suffers from his problems in living, and a psychotic if he makes others suffer.

Thomas Szasz (1920–) US psychiatrist. *The Second Sin*

11 A neurotic is the man who builds a castle in the air. A psychotic is the man who lives in it. And a psychiatrist is the man who collects the rent.

Lord Robert Webb-Johnstone (b. 1879) *Collected Papers*

12 He was meddling too much in my private life.

Tennessee Williams (1911–83) US dramatist. Explaining why he had given up visiting his psychoanalyst. Attrib.

13 He is always called a nerve specialist because it sounds better, but everyone knows he's a sort of janitor in a looney bin.

P. G. Wodehouse (1881–1975) British humorous novelist. *The Inimitable Jeeves*

PSYCHOLOGY

See also mind, psychiatry

1 What progress we are making. In the Middle Ages they would have burned me. Now they are content with burning my books.

Sigmund Freud (1856–1939) Austrian psychoanalyst. Referring to the public burning of his books in Berlin. Letter to Ernest Jones, 1933

2 I don't think the profession of historian fits a man for psychological analysis. In our work we have to deal only with simple feelings to which we give generic names such as Ambition and Interest.

Jean-Paul Sartre (1905–80) French writer. *Nausea*

PUBLIC

See also class, majority

1 *Vox populi, vox dei.*
The voice of the people is the voice of God.

Alcuin (c. 735–804) English theologian. Letter to Charlemagne

2 But that vast portion, lastly, of the working-class which, raw and half-developed, has long lain half-hidden amidst its poverty and squalor, and is now issuing from its hiding-place to assert an Englishman's heaven-born privilege of doing as he likes, and is beginning to perplex us by marching where it likes, meeting where it likes, bawling what it likes, breaking what it likes – to this vast residuum we may with great propriety give the name of Populace.

Matthew Arnold (1822–88) British poet and critic. *Culture and Anarchy*, Ch. 3

3 Our researchers into Public Opinion are content
That he held the proper opinions for the time of year;
When there was peace, he was for peace; when there was war, he went.

W. H. Auden (1907–73) British poet. *The Unknown Citizen*

4 You cannot make a man by standing a sheep on its hind legs. But by standing a flock of sheep in that position you can make a crowd of men.

Max Beerbohm (1872–1956) British writer. *Zuleika Dobson*, Ch. 9

5 The great Unwashed.

Henry Peter Brougham (1778–1868) Scottish lawyer and politician. Attrib.

6 The people are the masters.

Edmund Burke (1729–97) British politician. *Speech on the Economical Reform* (House of Commons, 11 Feb 1780)

7 The public buys its opinions as it buys its meat, or takes in its milk, on the principle that it is cheaper to do this than to keep a cow. So it is, but the milk is more likely to be watered.

Samuel Butler (1835–1902) British writer. *Notebooks*

8 The Public is an old woman. Let her maunder and mumble.

Thomas Carlyle (1795–1881) Scottish historian and essayist. *Journal*, 1835

9 The people would be just as noisy if they were going to see me hanged.

Oliver Cromwell (1599–1658) English soldier and statesman. Referring to a cheering crowd.

10 If by the people you understand the multitude, the *hoi polloi*, 'tis no matter what they think; they are sometimes in the right, sometimes in the wrong; their judgement is a mere lottery.

John Dryden (1631–1700) British poet and dramatist. *Essay of Dramatic Poesy*

11 Nor is the Peoples Judgment always true:
The Most may err as grosly as the Few.

John Dryden *Absalom and Achitophel*, I

12 Ill fares the land, to hast'ning ills a prey,
Where wealth accumulates, and men decay;
Princes and lords may flourish, or may fade;
A breath can make them, as a breath has made;
But a bold peasantry, their country's pride,
When once destroy'd, can never be supplied.

Oliver Goldsmith (1728–74) Irish-born British writer. *The Deserted Village*

13 There is not a more mean, stupid, dastardly, pitiful, selfish, spiteful, envious, ungrateful animal than the public. It is the greatest of cowards, for it is afraid of itself.

William Hazlitt (1778–1830) British essayist. *On Living to Oneself*

14 Only constant repetition will finally succeed in imprinting an idea on the memory of the crowd.

Adolf Hitler (1889–1945) German dictator. *Mein Kampf*, Ch. 6

15 The people long eagerly for just two things – bread and circuses.

Juvenal (Decimus Junius Juvenalis; 60–130 AD) Roman satirist. *Satires*, X

16 They are only ten.

Lord Northcliffe (1865–1922) Irish-born British newspaper proprietor. Rumoured to have been a notice to remind his staff of his opinion of the mental age of the general public. Attrib.

17 The multitude is always in the wrong.

Earl of Roscommon (1633–85) Irish-born English poet. *Essay on Translated Verse*

18 Once the people begin to reason, all is lost.

Voltaire (François-Marie Arouet; 1694–1778) French writer. Letter to Damilaville, 1 Apr 1766

19 The century on which we are entering – the century which will come out of this war – can be and must be the century of the common man.

Henry Wallace (1888–1965) US economist and politician. Speech, 'The Price of Free World Victory', 8 May 1942

20 Our supreme governors, the mob.

Horace Walpole (1717–97) British writer. Letter to Sir Horace Mann, 7 Sept 1743

21 I have no concern for the common man except that he should not be so common.

Angus Wilson (1913–91) British novelist. *No Laughing Matter*

PUBLIC HOUSES

See also alcohol, drunkenness

1 A tavern chair is the throne of human felicity.

Samuel Johnson (1709–84) British lexicographer. *Johnsonian Miscellanies* (ed. G. B. Hill), Vol. II

2 There is nothing which has yet been contrived by man, by which so much happiness is produced as by a good tavern or inn.

Samuel Johnson *Life of Johnson* (J. Boswell), Vol. II

3 Souls of poets dead and gone,
What Elysium have ye known,
Happy field or mossy cavern,
Choicer than the Mermaid Tavern?
Have ye tippled drink more fine
Than mine host's Canary wine?

John Keats (1795–1821) British poet. *Lines on the Mermaid Tavern*

4 The hands of the clock have stayed still at half past eleven for fifty years. It is always opening time in the Sailors Arms.

Dylan Thomas (1914–53) Welsh poet. *Under Milk Wood*

5 Come, Come, Come and have a drink with me
Down at the old 'Bull and Bush'.

Harry Tilzer (Albert von Tilzer; 1878–1956) British songwriter. *The Old Bull and Bush*

PUBLISHING

See also books, editors

1 Publication is the male equivalent of childbirth.

Richard Acland (1906–90) British politician and writer. *The Observer*, 'Sayings of the Week', 19 May 1974

2 If I had been someone not very clever, I would have done an easier job like publishing. That's the easiest job I can think of.

A. J. Ayer (1910–89) British philosopher. Remark, Sept 1984

3 I'll publish, right or wrong:
Fools are my theme, let satire be my song.

Lord Byron (1788–1824) British poet. *English Bards and Scotch Reviewers*

4 Now Barabbas was a publisher.

Thomas Campbell (1777–1844) British poet. Attrib.

5 Gentlemen, you must not mistake me. I admit that he is the sworn foe of our nation, and, if you will, of the whole human race. But, gentlemen, we must be just to our enemy. We must not forget that he once shot a bookseller.

Thomas Campbell Excusing himself in proposing a toast to Napoleon at a literary dinner. *The Life and Letters of Lord Macaulay* (G. O. Trevelyan)

6 As repressed sadists are supposed to become policemen or butchers so those with irrational fear of life become publishers.

Cyril Connolly (1903–74) British journalist. *Enemies of Promise*, Ch. 3

7 Let it be kept till the ninth year, the manuscript put away at home: you may destroy whatever you haven't published; once out, what you've said can't be stopped.

Horace (Quintus Horatius Flaccus; 65–8 BC) Roman poet. *Ars Poetica*

8 My own motto is publish and be sued.

Richard Ingrams (1937–) British editor. Referring to his editorship of *Private Eye*. BBC radio broadcast, 4 May 1977

9 The booksellers are generous liberal-minded men.

Samuel Johnson (1709–84) British lexicographer. *Life of Johnson* (J. Boswell), Vol. I

10 I don't mind your thinking slowly: I mind your publishing faster than you think.

Wolfgang Pauli (1900–58) Austrian-born Swiss physicist. *A Dictionary of Scientific Quotations* (A. L. Mackay; 1991)

11 Publish and be damned!

Duke of Wellington (1769–1852) British general and statesman. On being offered the chance to avoid mention in the memoirs of Harriette Wilson by giving her money. Attrib.

PUNISHMENT

See also education, execution, imprisonment, retribution

1 Wherefore putting away lying, speak every man truth with his neighbour: for we are members one of another.
Be ye angry, and sin not: let not the sun go down upon your wrath:
Neither give place to the devil.
Let him that stole steal no more: but rather let him labour, working with his hands the thing which is good, that he may have to give to him that needeth.

Bible: Ephesians 4:25–28

2 When thou tillest the ground, it shall not henceforth yield unto thee her strength; a fugitive and a vagabond shalt thou be in the earth.
And Cain said unto the Lord, My punishment is greater than I can bear.

Bible: Genesis 4:12–13

3 Then the Lord rained upon Sodom and upon Gomorrah brimstone and fire from the Lord out of heaven.

Bible: Genesis 19:24

4 And surely your blood of your lives will I require; at the hand of every beast will I require it, and at the hand of man; at the hand of every man's brother will I require the life of man.
Whoso sheddeth man's blood, by man shall his blood be shed: for in the image of God made he man.

Bible: Genesis 9:5–6

5 There is no peace, saith the Lord, unto the wicked.

Bible: Isaiah 48:22

6 Love is a boy, by poets styl'd,
Then spare the rod, and spoil the child.

Samuel Butler (1612–80) English satirist. *Hudibras*, Pt. II

7 Quoth he, 'The man hath penance done,
And penance more will do.'

Samuel Taylor Coleridge (1772–1834) British poet. *The Rime of the Ancient Mariner*, V

8 Punishment is not for revenge, but to lessen crime and reform the criminal.

Elizabeth Fry (1780–1845) British prison reformer. *Biography of Distinguished Women* (Sarah Josepha Hale)

9 As some day it may happen that a victim must be found
I've got a little list – I've got a little list
Of society offenders who might well be underground,
And who never would be missed – who never would be missed!

W. S. Gilbert (1836–1911) British dramatist. *The Mikado*, I

10 My object all sublime
I shall achieve in time –
To let the punishment fit the crime –
The punishment fit the crime.

W. S. Gilbert *The Mikado*, II

11 The billiard sharp whom any one catches,
His doom's extremely hard –
He's made to dwell –
In a dungeon cell
On a spot that's always barred.
And there he plays extravagant matches
In fitless finger-stalls
On a cloth untrue
With a twisted cue
And elliptical billiard balls.

W. S. Gilbert *The Mikado*, II

12 The door flew open, in he ran,
The great, long, red-legged scissor-man.

Heinrich Hoffman (1809–74) German writer. *Struwwelpeter*, 'The Little Suck-a-Thumb'

13 Corporal punishment is as humiliating for him who gives it as for him who receives it; it is ineffective besides. Neither shame nor physical pain have any other effect than a hardening one…

Ellen Key (Karolina Sofia Key; 1849–1926) Swedish writer. *The Century of the Child*, Ch. 8

14 The refined punishments of the spiritual mode are usually much more indecent and dangerous than a good smack.

D. H. Lawrence (1885–1930) British novelist. *Fantasia of the Unconscious*, Ch. 4

15 He must have known me had he seen me as he was wont to see me, for he was in the habit of flogging me constantly. Perhaps he did not recognize me by my face.

Anthony Trollope (1815–82) British novelist. *Autobiography*, Ch. 1

16 I'm all for bringing back the birch, but only between consenting adults.

Gore Vidal (1925–) US novelist. Said when asked by David Frost in a TV interview for his views about corporal punishment.

PUNS

See also humour

1 When I am dead, I hope it may be said:
'His sins were scarlet, but his books were read.'

Hilaire Belloc (1870–1953) French-born British poet. *Epigrams*, 'On His Books'

2 VISITOR. Ah, Bottomley, sewing?
BOTTOMLEY. No, reaping.

Horatio William Bottomley (1860–1933) British newspaper editor. When found sewing mail bags. *Horatio Bottomley* (Julian Symons)

3 A man who could make so vile a pun would not scruple to pick a pocket.

John Dennis (1657–1734) British critic and dramatist. *The Gentleman's Magazine*, 1781

4 Any stigma will do to beat a dogma.

Philip Guedalla (1889–1944) British writer. Attrib.

5 His death, which happen'd in his berth,
At forty-odd befell:
They went and told the sexton, and
The sexton toll'd the bell.

Thomas Hood (1799–1845) British poet. *Faithless Sally Brown*

6 For that old enemy the gout
Had taken him in toe!

Thomas Hood *Lieutenant Luff*

7 The love that loves a scarlet coat
Should be more uniform.

Thomas Hood *Faithless Nelly Gray*

8 Ben Battle was a soldier bold,
And used to war's alarms:
But a cannon-ball took off his legs,
So he laid down his arms!

Thomas Hood *Faithless Nelly Gray*

9 For here I leave my second leg,
And the Forty-second Foot!

Thomas Hood *Faithless Nelly Gray*

10 It is a pistol let off at the ear; not a feather to tickle the intellect.

Charles Lamb (1775–1834) British essayist. Referring to the nature of a pun. *Last Essays of Elia*, 'Popular Fallacies'

11 Thou canst not serve both cod and salmon.

Ada Beddington Leverson (1862–1933) British writer. Reply when offered a choice of fish at dinner. *The Times*, 7 Nov 1970

12 You know it's hard to hear what a bearded man is saying. He can't speak above a whisker.

Herman J. Mankiewicz (1897–1953) US journalist and screenwriter. *Wit's End* (R. E. Drennan)

13 What's a thousand dollars? Mere chicken feed. A poultry matter.

Groucho Marx (Julius Marx; 1895–1977) US comedian. *The Cocoanuts*

14 It has been said that a bride's attitude towards her betrothed can be summed up in three words: Aisle. Altar. Hymn.

Frank Muir (1920–) British writer and broadcaster. *Upon My Word!* (Frank Muir and Dennis Norden), 'A Jug of Wine'

15 A thing of duty is a boy for ever.

Flann O'Brien (Brian O'Nolan; 1911–66) Irish novelist and journalist. About policemen always seeming to be young-looking. *The Listener*, 24 Feb 1977

16 You can lead a whore to culture but you can't make her think.

Dorothy Parker (1893–1967) US writer. Speech to American Horticultural Society

17 You can't teach an old dogma new tricks.

Dorothy Parker *Wit's End* (R. E. Drennan)

18 I tried to resist his overtures, but he plied me with symphonies, quartettes, chamber music and cantatas.

S. J. Perelman (1904–79) US humorous writer. *Crazy Like a Fox*, 'The Love Decoy'

19 Mother always told me my day was coming, but I never realized that I'd end up being the shortest knight of the year.

Gordon Richards (1904–86) British champion jockey.

Referring to his diminutive size, on learning of his knighthood. Attrib.

20 Private Means is dead,
God rest his soul,
Officers and fellow-rankers said.

Stevie Smith (Florence Margaret Smith; 1902–71) British poet. *Private Means is Dead*

21 That's right. 'Taint yours, and 'taint mine.

Mark Twain (Samuel Langhorne Clemens; 1835–1910) US writer. Agreeing with a friend's comment that the money of a particular rich industrialist was 'tainted'. Attrib.

22 To me Adler will always be Jung.

Max Wall (1908–90) British comedian. Telegram to Larry Adler on his 60th birthday

PURITANISM

See also prudery

1 A puritan's a person who pours righteous indignation into the wrong things.

G. K. Chesterton (1874–1936) British writer. Attrib.

2 To the Puritan all things are impure, as somebody says.

D. H. Lawrence (1885–1930) British novelist. *Etruscan Places*, 'Cerveteri'

3 The Puritan hated bear-baiting, not because it gave pain to the bear, but because it gave pleasure to the spectators.

Lord Macaulay (1800–59) British historian. *History of England*, Vol. I, Ch. 2

4 Puritanism – The haunting fear that someone, somewhere, may be happy.

H. L. Mencken (1880–1956) US journalist. *A Book of Burlesques*

PURITY

1 Caesar's wife must be above suspicion.

Proverb

2 I'm as pure as the driven slush.

Tallulah Bankhead (1903–68) US actress. *The Observer*, 'Sayings of the Week', 24 Feb 1957

3 A simple maiden in her flower
Is worth a hundred coats-of-arms.

Alfred, Lord Tennyson (1809–92) British poet. *Lady Clara Vere de Vere*, II

4 It is one of the superstitions of the human mind to have imagined that virginity could be a virtue.

Voltaire (François-Marie Arouet; 1694–1778) French writer. *Notebooks*

5 Age cannot wither her, nor custom stale her infinite virginity.

Daniel Webster (1782–1852) US statesman. Paraphrasing a line from Shakespeare's *Antony and Cleopatra* on hearing of Andrew Jackson's steadfast maintenance that his friend Peggy Eaton did not deserve her scandalous reputation. *Presidential Anecdotes* (P. Boller)

6 I used to be Snow White...but I drifted.

Mae West (1892–1980) US actress. *The Wit and Wisdom of Mae West* (ed. J. Weintraub)

PURPOSE

See also futility, motive

1 Everything's got a moral, if only you can find it.

Lewis Carroll (Charles Lutwidge Dodgson; 1832–98) British writer. *Alice's Adventures in Wonderland*, Ch. 9

2 What is the use of a new-born child?

Benjamin Franklin (1706–90) US scientist and statesman. Response when asked the same question of a new invention. *Life and Times of Benjamin Franklin* (J. Parton), Pt. IV

3 A useless life is an early death.

Goethe (1749–1832) German poet and dramatist. *Iphegenie*, I:2

4 Fortunately, in her kindness and patience, Nature has never put the fatal question as to the meaning of their lives into the mouths of most people. And where no one asks, no one needs to answer.

Carl Gustav Jung (1875–1961) Swiss psychoanalyst. *The Development of Personality*

5 I go among the fields and catch a glimpse of a stoat or a fieldmouse peeping out of the withered grass – the creature hath a purpose and its eyes are bright with it. I go amongst the buildings of a city and I see a man hurrying along – to what? the Creature has a purpose and his eyes are bright with it.

John Keats (1795–1821) British poet. Letter, 1819

6 Riddle of destiny, who can show
What thy short visit meant, or know
What thy errand here below?

Charles Lamb (1775–1834) British essayist. *On an Infant Dying as soon as Born*

7 Yes there is a meaning; at least for me, there is one thing that matters – to set a chime of words tinkling in the minds of a few fastidious people.

Logan Pearsall Smith (1865–1946) US writer. Attrib.

8 It should not merely be useful and ornamental; it should preach a high moral lesson.

Lytton Strachey (1880–1932) British writer. Referring to Prince Albert's plans for the Great Exhibition. *Queen Victoria*, Ch. 4

Q

QUOTATIONS

See also misquotation

1 It is a good thing for an uneducated man to read books of quotations.

Winston Churchill (1874–1965) British statesman. *My Early Life*, Ch. 9

2 We prefer to believe that the absence of inverted commas guarantees the originality of a thought, whereas it may be merely that the utterer has forgotten its source.

Clifton Fadiman (1904–) US writer. *Any Number Can Play*

3 When a thing has been said and said well, have no scruple. Take it and copy it.

Anatole France (Jacques Anatole François Thibault; 1844–1924) French writer. In *The Routledge Dictionary of Quotations* (Robert Andrews)

4 Classical quotation is the *parole* of literary men all over the world.

Samuel Johnson (1709–84) British lexicographer. *Life of Johnson* (J. Boswell), Vol. IV

5 Every quotation contributes something to the stability or enlargement of the language.

Samuel Johnson *Dictionary of the English Language*

6 To be amused at what you read – that is the great spring of happy quotation.

C. E. Montague (1867–1928) British editor and writer. *A Writer's Notes on his Trade*

7 If with the literate I am
Impelled to try an epigram
I never seek to take the credit
We all assume that Oscar said it.

Dorothy Parker (1893–1967) US writer. *Oscar Wilde*

8 I might repeat to myself...a list of quotations from minds profound – if I can remember any of the damn things.

Dorothy Parker *The Little Hours*

9 A book that furnishes no quotations is, *me judice*, no book – it is a plaything.

Thomas Love Peacock (1785–1866) British novelist. *Crotchet Castle*, Ch. 9

10 It is gentlemanly to get one's quotations very slightly wrong. In that way one unprigs oneself and allows the company to correct one.

Lord Ribblesdale (1854–1925) British aristocrat. *The Light of Common Day* (Lady D. Cooper)

11 To say that anything was a quotation was an excellent method, in Eleanor's eyes, for withdrawing it from discussion.

Saki (Hector Hugh Munro; 1870–1916) British writer. *The Jesting of Arlington Stringham*

12 The devil can cite Scripture for his purpose.

William Shakespeare (1564–1616) English dramatist. *The Merchant of Venice*, I:3

13 It's better to be quotable than to be honest.

Tom Stoppard (1937–) Czech-born British dramatist. *The Guardian*

14 In the dying world I come from quotation is a national vice. It used to be the classics, now it's lyric verse.

Evelyn Waugh (1903–66) British novelist. *The Loved One*

15 The nicest thing about quotes is that they give us a nodding acquaintance with the originator which is often socially impressive.

Kenneth Williams (1926–88) British comic actor. *Acid Drops*

R

RABBITS

See also animals

1 The rabbit has a charming face;
Its private life is a disgrace.

Anonymous *The Rabbit*

2 I shall tell you a tale of four little rabbits whose names were Flopsy, Mopsy, Cottontail and Peter.

Beatrix Potter (1866–1943) British children's writer. *The Tale of Peter Rabbit*

RACISM

See also equality, freedom, human rights, Jews, oppression, prejudice, slavery, South Africa

1 There was a young woman called Starkie,
Who had an affair with a darky.
The result of her sins
Was quadruplets, not twins –
One black, and one white, and two khaki.

Anonymous

2 It is a great shock at the age of five or six to find that in a world of Gary Coopers you are the Indian.

James Baldwin (1924–87) US writer. Speech, Cambridge Union, 17 Feb 1965

3 The future is...black.

James Baldwin *The Observer*, 'Sayings of the Week', 25 Aug 1963

4 Down South where I come from you don't go around hitting too many white keys.

Eubie Blake (1883–1983) US pianist and ragtime composer. When asked why his compositions contained so many sharps and flats. Attrib.

5 My mother bore me in the southern wild.
And I am black, but O! my soul is white;
White as an angel is the English child,
But I am black, as if bereav'd of light.

William Blake (1757–1827) British poet. *Songs of Innocence*, 'The Little Black Boy'

6 People think we do not understand our black and coloured countrymen. But there is a special relationship between us.

Elize Botha Wife of South African President, P. W. Botha. Remark, May 1987

7 Black people are doing what they have been told and bettering themselves, but it is not getting them anywhere.

Donna Covey British trade union official. *The Independent*, 7 Sept 1993

8 To like an individual because he's black is just as insulting as to dislike him because he isn't white.

e. e. cummings (1894–1962) US poet. Attrib.

9 I suffer from an incurable disease – colour blindness.

Joost de Blank (1908–68) Dutch-born British churchman. Attrib.

10 I'm a coloured, one-eyed Jew.

Sammy Davis Jnr (1925–90) US singer. When asked what his handicap was during a game of golf. Attrib.

11 The so-called white races are really pinko-gray.

E. M. Forster (1879–1970) British novelist. *A Passage to India*, Ch. 7

12 When the white man came we had the land and they had the Bibles; now they have the land and we have the Bibles.

Dan George (1899–1982) Canadian Indian chief. Attrib.

13 All those who are not racially pure are mere chaff.

Adolf Hitler (1889–1945) German dictator. *Mein Kampf*, Ch. 2

14 I want to be the white man's brother, not his brother-in-law.

Martin Luther King (1929–68) US Black civil-rights leader. *New York Journal-American*, 10 Sept 1962

15 Take up the White Man's burden –
And reap his old reward:
The blame of those ye better,
The hate of those ye guard.

Rudyard Kipling (1865–1936) Indian-born British writer. *The White Man's Burden*

16 So 'ere's to you, Fuzzy-Wuzzy, at your 'ome in the Soudan;
You're a pore benighted 'eathen but a first-class fightin' man;
An' 'ere's to you, Fuzzy-Wuzzy, with your 'ayrick 'ead of 'air –
You big black boundin' beggar – for you broke a British square!

Rudyard Kipling *Fuzzy-Wuzzy*

17 When old settlers say 'One has to understand the country', what they mean is, 'You have to get used to our ideas about the native.' They are saying, in effect, 'Learn our ideas, or otherwise get out; we don't want you.'

Doris Lessing (1919–) British novelist. Referring specifically to South Africa. *The Grass is Singing*, Ch. 1

18 When a white man in Africa by accident looks into the eyes of a native and sees the human being (which it is his chief preoccupation to avoid), his sense of guilt, which he denies, fumes up in resentment and he brings down the whip.

Doris Lessing *The Grass is Singing*, Ch. 8

19 A coloured man can tell, in five seconds dead, whether a white man likes him or not. If the white man *says* he does, he is instantly – and usually quite rightly – mistrusted.

Colin MacInnes (1914–76) British novelist. *England, Half English*, 'A Short Guide for Jumbles'

20 It's just like when you've got some coffee that's too black, which means it's too strong. What do you do? You integrate it with cream, you make it weak...It used to wake you up, now it puts you to sleep.

Malcolm X (1925–65) US Black leader. Referring to Black Power and the Civil Rights movement. *Malcolm X Speaks*, Ch. 14

21 The soil of our country is destined to be the scene of the fiercest fight and the sharpest struggles to rid our continent of the last vestiges of white minority rule.

Nelson Mandela (1918–) South African lawyer and politician. Referring to South Africa. Remark, June 1980

22 I have cherished the ideal of a democratic and free society in which all persons live together in harmony and with equal opportunites...if needs be, it is an ideal for which I am prepared to die.

Nelson Mandela Speech, 11 Feb 1990, after his release from prison. Mandela was reiterating his words at his trial in 1964

23 One of the things that makes a Negro unpleasant to white folk is the fact that he suffers from their injustice. He is thus a standing rebuke to them.

H. L. Mencken (1880–1956) US journalist. *Notebooks*, 'Minority Report'

24 He's really awfully fond of coloured people. Well, he says himself, he wouldn't have white servants.

Dorothy Parker (1893–1967) US writer. *Arrangements in Black and White*

25 If you stay much longer you will go back with slitty eyes.

Prince Philip (1921–) The consort of Queen Elizabeth II. Said to English students on a visit to China. Remark, Oct 1986

26 As I look ahead, I am filled with foreboding. Like the Roman, I seem to see 'the River Tiber foaming with much blood'.

Enoch Powell (1912–) British politician. Talking about immigration. Speech in Birmingham, 20 Apr 1968

27 He liked to patronise coloured people and treated them as equals because he was quite sure they were not.

Bertrand Russell (1872–1970) British philosopher. *The Autobiography of Bertrand Russell*

28 I don't believe in black majority rule ever in Rhodesia...not in a thousand years.

Ian Smith (1919–) Rhodesian (Zimbabwe) politician. Speech, Mar 1976

29 We don't want apartheid liberalized. We want it dismantled. You can't improve something that is intrinsically evil.

Desmond Tutu (1931–) South African clergyman. *The Observer*, 'Sayings of the Week', 10 Mar 1985

30 It seems that the British Government sees black people as expendable.

Bishop Desmond Tutu Speech, June 1986

31 There are two kinds of blood, the blood that flows in the veins and the blood that flows out of them.

Julian Tuwim (1894–1954) Polish writer and poet. *We, the Polish Jews*

READING

See also books, criticism, fiction, literacy, literature, novels, writing

1 Reading maketh a full man; conference a ready man; and writing an exact man.

Francis Bacon (1561–1626) English philosopher. *Essays*, 'Of Studies'

2 He has only half learned the art of reading who has not added to it the even more refined accomplishments of skipping and skimming.

Arthur Balfour (1848–1930) British statesman. *Mr. Balfour* (E. T. Raymond)

3 I read, much of the night, and go south in the winter.

T. S. Eliot (1888–1965) US-born British poet and dramatist. *The Waste Land*, 'The Burial of the Dead'

4 A lonesome man on a rainy day who does not know how to read.

Benjamin Franklin (1706–90) US scientist and statesman. On being asked what condition of man he considered the most pitiable. *Wit, Wisdom, and Foibles of the Great* (C. Shriner)

5 As writers become more numerous, it is natural for readers to become more indolent.

Oliver Goldsmith (1728–74) Irish-born British writer. *The Bee*, 'Upon Unfortunate Merit'

6 Reading is sometimes an ingenious device for avoiding thought.

Arthur Helps (1813–75) British historian. *Friends in Council*

7 ELPHINSTON. What, have you not read it through?...
JOHNSON. No, Sir, do *you* read books *through*?

Samuel Johnson (1709–84) British lexicographer. *Life of Johnson* (J. Boswell), Vol. II

8 A man ought to read just as inclination leads him; for what he reads as a task will do him little good.

Samuel Johnson *Life of Johnson* (J. Boswell), Vol. I

9 I love to lose myself in other men's minds. When I am not walking, I am reading; I cannot sit and think. Books think for me.

Charles Lamb (1775–1834) British essayist. *Last Essays of Elia*, 'Detached Thoughts on Books and Reading'

10 I'm re-reading it with a slow deliberate carelessness.

T. E. Lawrence (1888–1935) British soldier and writer. Letter to Edward Marsh, 18 Apr 1929

11 To read too many books is harmful.

Mao Tse-Tung (1893–1976) Chinese communist leader. *The New Yorker*, 7 Mar 1977

12 I have only read one book in my life and that is *White Fang*. It's so frightfully good I've never bothered to read another.

Nancy Mitford (1904–73) British writer. *The Pursuit Of Love*

13 There are two motives for reading a book: one, that you enjoy it, the other that you can boast about it.

Bertrand Russell (1872–1970) British philosopher. *The Conquest of Happiness*

14 People say that life is the thing, but I prefer reading.

Logan Pearsall Smith (1865–1946) US writer. *Afterthoughts*, 'Myself'

15 Reading is to the mind what exercise is to the body.

Richard Steele (1672–1729) Dublin-born British essayist. *The Tatler*, 147

16 Education…has produced a vast population able to read but unable to distinguish what is worth reading.

George Macaulay Trevelyan (1876–1962) British historian. *English Social History*, Ch. 18

17 I have led a life of business so long that I have lost my taste for reading, and now – what shall I do?

Horace Walpole (1717–97) British writer. *Thraliana* (K. Balderston)

18 Lady Peabury was in the morning room reading a novel; early training gave a guilty spice to this recreation, for she had been brought up to believe that to read a novel before luncheon was one of the gravest sins it was possible for a gentlewoman to commit.

Evelyn Waugh (1903–66) British novelist. *Work Suspended*, 'An Englishman's Home'

19 As in the sexual experience, there are never more than two persons present in the act of reading – the writer who is the impregnator, and the reader who is the respondent.

Elwyn Brooks White (1899–1985) US journalist and humorist. *The Second Tree from the Corner*

REALISM

1 Mr Lely, I desire you would use all your skill to paint my picture truly like me, and not flatter me at all; but remark all these roughnesses, pimples, warts, and everything as you see me, otherwise I will never pay a farthing for it.

Oliver Cromwell (1599–1658) English soldier and statesman. The origin of the expression 'warts and all'. *Anecdotes of Painting* (Horace Walpole), Ch. 12

2 If at first you don't succeed, try, try again. Then quit. No use being a damn fool about it.

W. C. Fields (1880–1946) US actor.

3 We must rediscover the distinction between hope and expectation.

Ivan Illich (1926–) Austrian sociologist. *Deschooling Society*, Ch. 7

4 Better by far
For Johnny-the-bright-star,
To keep your head
And see his children fed.

John Sleigh Pudney (1909–77) British poet and writer. *For Johnny*

REALITY

1 There are no things, only processes.

David Bohm (1917–92) US physicist.

2 For I see now that I am asleep that I dream when I am awake.

Pedro Calderón de la Barca (1600–81) Spanish dramatist. *La Vida es Sueño*, II

3 Human kind
Cannot bear very much reality.

T. S. Eliot (1888–1965) US-born British poet and dramatist. *Four Quartets*, 'Burnt Norton'

4 Dear friend, theory is all grey,
And the golden tree of life is green.

Goethe (1749–1832) German poet and dramatist. *Faust*, Pt. I

5 I fancy, for myself, that they are rather out of touch with reality; by reality I mean shops like Selfridges, and motor buses, and the *Daily Express*.

T. E. Lawrence (1888–1935) British soldier and writer. Referring to expatriate authors living in Paris, such as James Joyce. Letter to W. Hurley, 1 Apr 1929

6 If this were play'd upon a stage now, I could condemn it as an improbable fiction.

William Shakespeare (1564–1616) English dramatist. *Twelfth Night*, III:4

REASON

See also motive

1 Some who had received a liberal education at the Colleges of Unreason, and taken the highest degrees in hypothetics, which are their principal study.

Samuel Butler (1835–1902) British writer. *Erewhon*, Ch. 9

2 Reason is itself a matter of faith. It is an act of faith to assert that our thoughts have any relation to reality at all.

G. K. Chesterton (1874–1936) British writer. *Orthodoxy*, Ch. 3

3 My dear friend, clear your *mind* of cant… You may *talk* in this manner; it is a mode of talking in Society: but don't *think* foolishly.

Samuel Johnson (1709–84) British lexicographer. *Life of Johnson* (J. Boswell), Vol. IV

4 A man who does not lose his reason over

certain things has none to lose.

Gotthold Ephraim Lessing (1729–81) German dramatist. *Emilia Galotti*, IV:7

REBELLION

See also revolution

1 The defiance of established authority, religious and secular, social and political, as a world-wide phenomenon may well one day be accounted the outstanding event of the last decade.

Hannah Arendt (1906–75) German-born US philosopher and historian. *Crises of the Republic*, 'Civil Disobedience'

2 What is a rebel? A man who says no.

Albert Camus (1913–60) French existentialist writer. *The Rebel*

3 No one can go on being a rebel too long without turning into an autocrat.

Lawrence Durrell (1912–90) British novelist. *Balthazar*, II

4 When the People contend for their Liberty, they seldom get anything by their Victory but new masters.

Lord Halifax (1633–95) English statesman. *Political, Moral, and Miscellaneous Thoughts and Reflections*

5 A little rebellion now and then is a good thing.

Thomas Jefferson (1743–1826) US statesman. Letter to James Madison, 30 Jan 1787

6 A riot is at bottom the language of the unheard.

Martin Luther King (1929–68) US Black civil-rights leader. *Chaos or Community*, Ch. 4

7 Angry Young Man.

Leslie Paul (1905–85) British writer. Book title

REGRET

See also apologies, memory, mourning, nostalgia, past, sorrow

1 It is no use crying over spilt milk.

Proverb

2 It's too late to shut the stable door after the horse has bolted.

Proverb

3 What's done cannot be undone.

Proverb

4 One doesn't recognize in one's life the really important moments – not until it's too late.

Agatha Christie (1891–1976) British detective-story writer. *Endless Night*, Bk. II, Ch. 14

5 This hand hath offended.

Thomas Cranmer (1489–1556) English churchman. *Memorials of Cranmer* (Strype)

6 Were it not better to forget
Than but remember and regret?

Letitia Landon (1802–38) British poet and novelist. *Despondency*

7 We might have been – These are but common words,
And yet they make the sum of life's bewailing.

Letitia Landon *Three Extracts from the Diary of a Week*

8 And so, I missed my chance with one of the lords
Of life.
And I have something to expiate;
A pettiness.

D. H. Lawrence (1885–1930) British novelist. *Snake*

9 Make it a rule of life never to regret and never to look back. Regret is an appalling waste of energy; you can't build on it; it's only good for wallowing in.

Katherine Mansfield (1888–1923) New Zealand-born British writer. Attrib.

10 Maybe it would have been better if neither of us had been born.

Napoleon I (Napoleon Bonaparte; 1769–1821) French emperor. Said while looking at the tomb of the philosopher Jean-Jacques Rousseau, whose theories had influenced the French Revolution. *The Story of Civilization* (W. Durant), Vol. II

11 Good-bye, I've barely said a word to you, it is always like that at parties, we never see the people, we never say the things we should like to say, but it is the same everywhere in this life. Let us hope that when we are dead things will be better arranged.

Marcel Proust (1871–1922) French novelist. *À la recherche du temps perdu: Sodome et Gomorrhe*

12 The follies which a man regrets most in his life are those which he didn't commit when he had the opportunity.

Helen Rowland (1876–1950) US writer. *Reflections of a Bachelor Girl*

13 But with the morning cool repentance came.

Walter Scott (1771–1832) Scottish novelist. *Rob Roy*, Ch. 12

14 Things sweet to taste prove in digestion sour.

William Shakespeare (1564–1616) English dramatist. *Richard II*, I:3

15 What's gone and what's past help
Should be past grief.

William Shakespeare *The Winter's Tale*, III:2

16 O, pardon me, thou bleeding piece of earth,
That I am meek and gentle with these butchers!
Thou art the ruins of the noblest man
That ever lived in the tide of times.

William Shakespeare *Julius Caesar*, III:1

17 To mourn a mischief that is past and gone
Is the next way to draw new mischief on.

William Shakespeare *Othello*, I:3

18 When to the sessions of sweet silent thought
I summon up remembrance of things past,
I sigh the lack of many a thing I sought,

And with old woes new wail my dear time's waste.

William Shakespeare *Sonnet 30*

19 Had I but serv'd my God with half the zeal
I serv'd my King, he would not in mine age
Have left me naked to mine enemies.

William Shakespeare *Henry VIII*, III:2

20 The bitterest tears shed over graves are for words left unsaid and deeds left undone.

Harriet Beecher Stowe (1811–96) US novelist. *Little Foxes*, Ch. 3

21 I never wonder to see men wicked, but I often wonder to see them not ashamed.

Jonathan Swift (1667–1745) Irish-born Anglican priest and writer. *Thoughts on Various Subjects*

22 Though nothing can bring back the hour
Of splendour in the grass, of glory in the flower;
We will grieve not, rather find
Strength in what remains behind...

William Wordsworth (1770–1850) British poet. *Ode. Intimations of Immortality*, IX

23 Men are we, and must grieve when even the shade
Of that which once was great is passed away.

William Wordsworth *Sonnets*, 'Once did she hold'

RELIGION

See also atheism, belief, Bible, Catholicism, Christianity, Christmas, Church, damnation, devil, doomsday, faith, God, heaven, hell, Jews, martyrdom, prayer, Protestantism, Sunday

1 Karin needed nothing from God. He just had the power to kill her that's all; to destroy her flesh and blood, the tools without which she could not work.

Richard Adams (1920–) British novelist. *The Girl in a Swing*, Ch. 28

2 Nearer, my God, to thee,
Nearer to thee!

Sarah F. Adams (1805–48) British poet and hymn writer. *Nearer My God to Thee*

3 There is no salvation outside the church.

St Augustine of Hippo (354–430) Bishop of Hippo. *De Bapt.*, IV

4 [INDIGESTION], n. A disease which the patient and his friends frequently mistake for deep religious conviction and concern for the salvation of mankind. As the simple Red Man of the western wild put it, with, it must be confessed, a certain force: 'Plenty well, no pray; big bellyache, heap God.'

Ambrose Bierce (1842–?1914) US writer and journalist. *The Devil's Dictionary*

5 If the concept of God has any validity or use, it can only be to make us larger, freer, and more loving. If God cannot do this, then it is time we got rid of Him.

James Baldwin (1924–87) US writer. *The Fire next Time*

6 If I really believed that the Church of England came out of the loins of Henry VIII I could be as free as I liked about making changes, but I do not believe that.

Canon Peter Boulton British clergyman. Remark, Mar 1987

7 Every day people are straying away from the church and going back to God. Really.

Lenny Bruce (1925–66) US comedian. *The Essential Lenny Bruce* (ed. J. Cohen), 'Religions Inc.'

8 This Ariyan Eightfold Path, that is to say: Right view, right aim, right speech, right action, right living, right effort, right mindfulness, right contemplation.

Buddha (Gautama Siddhartha; c. 563–c. 483 BC) Indian religious teacher. *Some Sayings of the Buddha* (F. L. Woodward)

9 Man is by his constitution a religious animal.

Edmund Burke (1729–97) British politician. *Reflections on the Revolution in France*

10 One religion is as true as another.

Robert Burton (1577–1640) English scholar and explorer. *Anatomy of Melancholy*, Pt. III

11 To be at all is to be religious more or less.

Samuel Butler (1835–1902) British writer. *Notebooks*

12 Not a religion for gentlemen.

Charles II (1630–85) King of England. Referring to Presbyterianism. *History of My Own Time* (Burnet), Vol. I, Bk. II, Ch. 2

13 Religion is by no means a proper subject of conversation in a mixed company.

Earl of Chesterfield (1694–1773) English statesman. Letter to his godson

14 When your ladyship's faith has removed them, I will go thither with all my heart.

Earl of Chesterfield Said to his sister, Lady Gertrude Hotham, when she suggested he go to a Methodist seminary in Wales to recuperate, recommending the views of the mountains. Attrib.

15 Talk about the pews and steeples
And the cash that goes therewith!
But the souls of Christian peoples...
Chuck it, Smith!

G. K. Chesterton (1874–1936) British writer. *Antichrist, or the Reunion of Christendom*

16 Men will wrangle for religion; write for it; fight for it; anything but – live for it.

Charles Caleb Colton (?1780–1832) British clergyman and writer. *Lacon*, Vol. I

17 Pray remember, Mr Dean, no dogma, no Dean.

Benjamin Disraeli (1804–81) British statesman. Attrib.

18 'Sensible men are all of the same religion.' 'And pray what is that?' inquired the prince. 'Sensible men never tell.'

Benjamin Disraeli *Endymion*, Bk. I, Ch. 81

19 In pious times, e'r Priest-craft did begin,

Before Polygamy was made a Sin.

John Dryden (1631–1700) British poet and dramatist. *Absalom and Achitophel*, I

20 Christian Science explains all cause and effect as mental, not physical.

Mary Baker Eddy (1821–1910) US religious leader. *Science and Health, with Key to the Scriptures*

21 Sickness, sin and death, being inharmonious, do not originate in God, nor belong to His government.

Mary Baker Eddy *Science and Health, with Key to the Scriptures*

22 Science without religion is lame, religion without science is blind.

Albert Einstein (1879–1955) German-born US physicist. *Out of My Later Years*

23 The religions we call false were once true.

Ralph Waldo Emerson (1803–82) US poet and essayist. *Essays*, 'Character'

24 Religion is an illusion and it derives its strength from the fact that it falls in with our instinctual desires.

Sigmund Freud (1856–1939) Austrian psychoanalyst. *New Introductory Lectures on Psychoanalysis*, 'A Philosophy of Life'

25 Religion
Has made an honest woman of the supernatural,
And we won't have it kicking over the traces again.

Christopher Fry (1907–) British dramatist. *The Lady's Not for Burning*, II

26 There exists no politician in India daring enough to attempt to explain to the masses that cows can be eaten.

Indira Gandhi (1917–84) Indian stateswoman. *New York Review of Books*, 'Indira's Coup' (Oriana Fallaci)

27 The various modes of worship, which prevailed in the Roman world, were all considered by the people as equally true; by the philosopher, as equally false; and by the magistrate, as equally useful. And thus toleration produced not only mutual indulgence, but even religious concord.

Edward Gibbon (1737–94) British historian. *Decline and Fall of the Roman Empire*, Ch. 2

28 As I take my shoes from the shoemaker, and my coat from the tailor, so I take my religion from the priest.

Oliver Goldsmith (1728–74) Irish-born British writer. *Life of Johnson* (J. Boswell)

29 Those who marry God...can become domesticated too – it's just as humdrum a marriage as all the others.

Graham Greene (1904–91) British novelist. *A Burnt-Out Case*, Ch. 1

30 Pray, good people, be civil. I am the Protestant whore.

Nell Gwyn (1650–87) English actress. On being surrounded in her coach by an angry mob in Oxford at the time of the Popish Plot. *Nell Gwyn* (Bevan), Ch. 13

31 But as I rav'd and grew more fierce and wild
At every word,
Methought I heard one calling, 'Child';
And I replied, 'My Lord.'

George Herbert (1593–1633) English poet. *The Collar*

32 The sedate, sober, silent, serious, sad-coloured sect.

Thomas Hood (1799–1845) British poet. Referring to the Quakers. *The Doves and the Crows*

33 To become a popular religion, it is only necessary for a superstition to enslave a philosophy.

Dean Inge (1860–1954) British churchman. *Outspoken Essays*

34 Many people believe that they are attracted by God, or by Nature, when they are only repelled by man.

Dean Inge *More Lay Thoughts of a Dean*

35 Many people think they have religion when they are troubled with dyspepsia.

Robert G. Ingersoll (1833–99) US lawyer and agnostic. *Liberty of Man, Woman and Child*, Section 3

36 Among all my patients in the second half of life...there has not been one whose problem in the last resort was not that of finding a religious outlook on life.

Carl Gustav Jung (1875–1961) Swiss psychoanalyst. *Modern Man in Search of a Soul*

37 The author of the Satanic Verses book, which is against Islam, the Prophet and the Koran, and all those involved in its publication who were aware of its content, are sentenced to death. I ask all Moslems to execute them wherever they find them.

Ayatollah Ruholla Khomeini (1900–89) Iranian Shiite Muslim leader. Speech, 14 Feb 1989

38 The month of Ramadan shall ye fast, in which the Koran was sent down from heaven, a direction unto men, and declarations of direction, and the distinction between good and evil.

Koran Ch. II

39 But I suppose even God was born
too late to trust the old religion –
all those setting out
that never left the ground,
beginning in wisdom, dying in doubt.

Robert Lowell (1917–77) US poet. *Tenth Muse*

40 Here stand I. I can do no other. God help me. Amen.

Martin Luther (1483–1546) German Protestant. Speech at the Diet of Worms, 18 Apr 1521

41 Abide with me; fast falls the eventide;
The darkness deepens; Lord, with me abide;
When other helpers fail, and comforts flee,
Help of the helpless, O, abide with me.

Henry Francis Lyte (1793–1847) British hymn writer. *Abide with Me*

42 Religion...is the opium of the people.

Karl Marx (1818–83) German philosopher and revolutionary. *Criticism of the Hegelian Philosophy of Right*, Introduction

43 Things have come to a pretty pass when religion is allowed to invade the sphere of private life.

Lord Melbourne (1779–1848) British statesman. Attrib.

44 There are many who stay away from church these days because you hardly ever mention God any more.

Arthur Miller (1915–) US dramatist. *The Crucible*, I

45 New Presbyter is but old Priest writ large.

John Milton (1608–74) English poet. *Sonnet*: 'On the New Forcers of Conscience under the Long Parliament'

46 Man is quite insane. He wouldn't know how to create a maggot and he creates Gods by the dozen.

Michel de Montaigne (1533–92) French essayist. *Essais*, II

47 There is a very good saying that if triangles invented a god, they would make him three-sided.

Baron de Montesquieu (1689–1755) French writer. *Lettres persanes*

48 There's no reason to bring religion into it. I think we ought to have as great a regard for religion as we can, so as to keep it out of as many things as possible.

Sean O'Casey (1884–1964) Irish dramatist. *The Plough and the Stars*, I

49 Organized religion is making Christianity political rather than making politics Christian.

Laurens Van der Post (1906–96) South African novelist. *The Observer*, 'Sayings of the Week', 9 Nov 1986

50 Religion has always been the wound, not the bandage.

Dennis Potter (1935–94) British dramatist. *The Observer*, 'Sayings of the Week', 10 Apr 1994

51 Unlike Christianity, which preached a peace that it never achieved, Islam unashamedly came with a sword.

Steven Runciman (1903–) British academic and diplomat. *A History of the Crusades*, 'The First Crusade'

52 I call upon the intellectual community in this country and abroad to stand up for freedom of the imagination, an issue much larger than my book or indeed my life.

Salman Rushdie (1947–) Indian-born British novelist. Press statement, 14 Feb 1989

53 I have been into many of the ancient cathedrals – grand, wonderful, mysterious. But I always leave them with a feeling of indignation because of the generations of human beings who have struggled in poverty to build these altars to the unknown god.

Elizabeth Cady Stanton (1815–1902) US suffragette. *Diary*

54 Whenever a man talks loudly against religion, – always suspect that it is not his reason, but his passions which have got the better of his creed.

Laurence Sterne (1713–68) Irish-born British writer. *Tristram Shandy*

55 I believe in the Church, One Holy, Catholic and Apostolic, and I regret that it nowhere exists.

William Temple (1881–1944) British churchman. Attrib.

56 Alas, O Lord, to what a state dost Thou bring those who love Thee!

St Teresa of Ávila (1515–82) Spanish mystic. *The Interior Castle*, VI

57 It is spring, moonless night in the small town, starless and bible-black.

Dylan Thomas (1914–53) Welsh poet. *Under Milk Wood*

58 I fled Him, down the nights and down the days;
I fled Him, down the arches of the years;
I fled Him, down the labyrinthine ways
Of my own mind; and in the mist of tears
I hid from Him, and under running laughter.

Francis Thompson (1859–1907) British poet. *The Hound of Heaven*

59 Rock of ages, cleft for me,
Let me hide myself in Thee.

Augustus Montague Toplady (1740–78) British hymn writer. *Rock of Ages*

60 Beware when you take on the Church of God. Others have tried and have bitten the dust.

Desmond Tutu (1931–) South African clergyman. Speech, Apr 1987

61 In general the churches, visited by me too often on weekdays... bore for me the same relation to God that billboards did to Coca-Cola: they promoted thirst without quenching it.

John Updike (1932–) US novelist. *A Month of Sundays*, Ch. 2

62 Jesus loves me – this I know,
For the Bible tells me so.

Susan Warner (1819–85) US novelist. *The Love of Jesus*

63 Lord, I ascribe it to Thy grace,
And not to chance, as others do,
That I was born of Christian race,
And not a Heathen, or a Jew.

Isaac Watts (1674–1748) English theologian and hymn writer. *Divine Songs for Children*, 'Praise for the Gospel'

64 Our God, our help in ages past,
Our hope for years to come,
Our shelter from the stormy blast,
And our eternal home.

Isaac Watts *Our God, Our Help in Ages Past*

65 I have noticed again and again since I have been in the Church that lay interest in ecclesiastical matters is often a prelude to insanity.

Evelyn Waugh (1903–66) British novelist. *Decline and Fall*, Pt. I, Ch. 8

66 There is a species of person called a 'Modern Churchman' who draws the full salary of a beneficed clergyman and need not commit himself to any religious belief.

Evelyn Waugh *Decline and Fall*, Pt. II, Ch. 4

67 Religion is love; in no case is it logic.

Beatrice Webb (1858–1943) British economist and writer. *My Apprenticeship*, Ch. 2

68 I look upon all the world as my parish.

John Wesley (1703–91) British religious leader. *Journal*, 11 June 1739

69 Why do born-again people so often make you wish they'd never been born the first time?

Katherine Whitehorn (1926–) British journalist. *The Observer*, 20 May 1979

70 So many gods, so many creeds,
So many paths that wind and wind,
While just the art of being kind
Is all the sad world needs.

Ella Wheeler Wilcox (1850–1919) US poet. *The World's Need*

71 The itch of disputing will prove the scab of churches.

Henry Wotton (1568–1639) English poet and diplomat. *A Panegyric to King Charles*

72 The Ethiopians say that their gods are snub-nosed and black, the Thracians that theirs have light blue eyes and red hair.

Xenophanes (c. 560–c. 478 BC) Greek poet and philosopher. *Fragment 15*

73 No Jew was ever fool enough to turn Christian unless he was a clever man.

Israel Zangwill (1864–1926) British writer. *Children of the Ghetto*, Ch. 1

REMEDIES

See also doctors, drugs, health and healthy living, illness, medicine

1 Cure the disease and kill the patient.

Francis Bacon (1561–1626) English philosopher. *Essays*, 'Of Friendship'

2 The remedy is worse than the disease.

Francis Bacon *Essays*, 'Of Seditions and Troubles'

3 Then Peter said, Silver and gold have I none; but such as I have give I thee: In the name of Jesus Christ of Nazareth rise up and walk.

Bible: Acts 3:6

4 And besought him that they might only touch the hem of his garment: and as many as touched were made perfectly whole.

Bible: Matthew 14:36

5 My father invented a cure for which there was no disease and unfortunately my mother caught it and died of it.

Victor Borge (1909–) Danish-born US composer, actor, and musical comedian. *In Concert*

6 Well, now, there's a remedy for everything except death.

Miguel de Cervantes (1547–1616) Spanish novelist. *Don Quixote*, Pt. II, Ch. 10

7 When a lot of remedies are suggested for a disease, that means it can't be cured.

Anton Chekhov (1860–1904) Russian dramatist. *The Cherry Orchard*, II

8 Every day, in every way, I am getting better and better.

Émile Coué (1857–1920) French doctor. Formula for a cure by autosuggestion

9 His *Majestie* began first to Touch for the Evil according to costome; Thus, his Majestie sitting under his State in the *Banqueting* house: The *Chirurgeons* cause the sick to be brought or led up to the throne, who kneeling, the King strokes their faces or cheekes with both his hands at once: at which instant a *Chaplaine* in his formalities, says, *He put his hands upon them, & he healed them.*

John Evelyn (1620–1706) English diarist. *Diary*, 6 July 1660

10 Extreme remedies are most appropriate for extreme diseases.

Hippocrates (c. 460–c. 377 BC) Greek physician. *Aphorisms*, I

11 As soon as he ceased to be mad he became merely stupid. There are maladies we must not seek to cure because they alone protect us from others that are more serious.

Marcel Proust (1871–1922) French novelist. *À la recherche du temps perdu: Le Côté de Guermantes*

12 They all thought she was dead; but my father he kept ladling gin down her throat till she came to so sudden that she bit the bowl off the spoon.

George Bernard Shaw (1856–1950) Irish dramatist and critic. *Pygmalion*, III

13 Our body is a machine for living. It is organized for that, it is its nature. Let life go on in it unhindered and let it defend itself, it will do more than if you paralyse it by encumbering it with remedies.

Leo Tolstoy (1828–1910) Russian writer. *War and Peace*, Bk. X, Ch. 29

14 Sparrowhawks, Ma'am.

Duke of Wellington (1769–1852) British general and statesman. Advice when asked by Queen Victoria how to remove sparrows from the Crystal Palace. Attrib.

15 There is only one cure for grey hair. It was invented by a Frenchman. It is called the guillotine.

P. G. Wodehouse (1881–1975) British humorous novelist. *The Old Reliable*

RENUNCIATION

See also dismissal

1 Renounce the devil and all his works.

The Book of Common Prayer *Publick Baptism of Infants*

2 I would rather be a brilliant memory than a curiosity.

Emma Eames (1865–1952) US opera singer. Referring to her retirement at the age of 47. *The Elephant that Swallowed a Nightingale* (C. Galtey)

3 You won't have Nixon to kick around any more, gentlemen. This is my last Press Conference.

Richard Milhous Nixon (1913–94) US president. Press

conference, after losing the election for the governorship of California, 2 Nov 1962

4 I'll break my staff,
Bury it certain fathoms in the earth,
And deeper than did ever plummet sound
I'll drown my book.

William Shakespeare (1564–1616) English dramatist. *The Tempest*, V:1

5 It is very simple. The artists retired. The British remained.

James Whistler (1834–1903) US painter. Explaining his resignation as president of the Royal Society of British Artists. *Whistler Stories* (D. Seitz)

REPARTEE

1 This is very true: for my words are my own, and my actions are my ministers'.

Charles II (1630–85) King of England. Replying to Lord Rochester's suggested epitaph. *King Charles II* (A. Bryant)

2 Stand a little less between me and the sun.

Diogenes (412–322 BC) Greek philosopher. When Alexander the Great asked if there was anything he wanted. *Life of Alexander* (Plutarch)

3 Oh! he is mad, is he? Then I wish he would bite some other of my generals.

George II (1683–1760) King of Great Britain and Ireland. Replying to advisors who told him that General James Wolfe was mad. Attrib.

4 JUDGE WILLIS. What do you suppose I am on the Bench for, Mr Smith?
SMITH. It is not for me to attempt to fathom the inscrutable workings of Providence.

F. E. Smith (1872–1930) British lawyer and politician. *Frederick Elwin, Earl of Birkenhead* (Lord Birkenhead), Vol. I, Ch. 9

5 LORD SANDWICH. You will die either on the gallows, or of the pox.
WILKES. That must depend on whether I embrace your lordship's principles or your mistress.

John Wilkes (1725–97) British politician. Sometimes attrib. to Samuel Foote. *Portrait of a Patriot* (Charles Chenevix-Trench), Ch. 3

REPRESENTATION

1 Taxation without representation is tyranny.

James Otis (1725–83) US political activist. As 'No taxation without representation' this became the principal slogan of the American Revolution. Attrib.

2 No annihilation without representation.

Arnold Toynbee (1889–1975) British historian. Urging the need for a greater British influence in the UN 1947

REPUBLIC

See also democracy, State

1 Our object in the construction of the state is the greatest happiness of the whole, and not that of any one class.

Plato (429–347 BC) Greek philosopher. *Republic*, Bk. 4

2 As there was no form of government common to the peoples thus segregated, nor tie of language, history, habit, or belief, they were called a Republic.

Evelyn Waugh (1903–66) British novelist. *Scoop*, Bk. II, Ch. 1

REPUTATION

See also fame, posterity

1 For my name and memory, I leave it to men's charitable speeches, and to foreign nations, and the next ages.

Francis Bacon (1561–1626) English philosopher. Will, 19 Dec 1625

2 I hold it as certain, that no man was ever written out of reputation but by himself.

Richard Bentley (1662–1742) English academic. *The Works of Alexander Pope* (W. Warburton), Vol. IV

3 Reputation is a bubble which bursts when a man tries to blow it up for himself.

Emma Carleton Attrib.

4 Die when I may, I want it said of me by those who know me best, that I have always plucked a thistle and planted a flower where I thought a flower would grow.

Abraham Lincoln (1809–65) US statesman. *Presidential Anecdotes* (P. Boller)

5 Until you've lost your reputation, you never realize what a burden it was or what freedom really is.

Margaret Mitchell (1909–49) US novelist. *Gone with the Wind*

6 Seventeen years of reputation doesn't really matter to a media that sniffs blood.

Anita Roddick (1942–) British business executive, chief executive of *The Body Shop plc*. *The Independent*, 7 Oct 1994

7 Reputation, reputation, reputation! O, I have lost my reputation! I have lost the immortal part of myself, and what remains is bestial.

William Shakespeare (1564–1616) English dramatist. *Othello*, II:3

8 Good name in man and woman, dear my lord,
Is the immediate jewel of their souls:
Who steals my purse steals trash; 'tis something, nothing;
'Twas mine, 'tis his, and has been slave to thousands;
But he that filches from me my good name
Robs me of that which not enriches him
And makes me poor indeed.

William Shakespeare *Othello*, III:3

9 The purest treasure mortal times afford
Is spotless reputation; that away,
Men are but gilded loam or painted clay.

William Shakespeare *Richard II*, I:1

10 I'm called away by particular business. But I leave my character behind me.

Richard Brinsley Sheridan (1751–1816) British dramatist. *The School for Scandal*, II

11 Everything.

Mae West (1892–1980) US actress. When asked what she wanted to be remembered for. Attrib.

RESEARCH

1 O speculator concerning this machine of ours let it not distress you that you impart knowledge of it through another's death, but rejoice that our Creator has ordained the intellect to such excellence of perception.

Leonardo da Vinci (1452–1519) Italian artist. *Quaderni d'Anatomia*, Vol. II

2 Research! A mere excuse for idleness; it has never achieved, and will never achieve any results of the slightest value.

Benjamin Jowett (1817–93) British theologian. *Unforgotten Years* (Logan Pearsall Smith)

3 The aim of research is the discovery of the equations which subsist between the elements of phenomena.

Ernst Mach (1838–1916) Austrian physicist and philosopher. *Popular Scientific Lectures*

4 Always verify your references.

Martin Joseph Routh (1755–1854) British scholar. Attrib.

5 We haven't the money, so we've got to think.

Ernest Rutherford (1871–1937) British physicist. Attrib.

6 The outcome of any serious research can only be to make two questions grow where only one grew before.

Thorstein Bunde Veblen (1857–1929) US social scientist. *The Place of Science in Modern Civilization*

RESPECT

See also courtesy, self-respect

1 Let them hate, so long as they fear.

Lucius Accius (170–c. 85 BC) Roman tragic playwright. *Atreus*, 'Seneca'

2 One does not arrest Voltaire.

Charles De Gaulle (1890–1970) French general and statesman. Explaining why he had not arrested Jean-Paul Sartre for urging French soldiers in Algeria to desert. Attrib.

3 I hate victims who respect their executioners.

Jean-Paul Sartre (1905–80) French writer. *Altona*

4 We owe respect to the living; to the dead we owe only truth.

Voltaire (François-Marie Arouet; 1694–1778) French writer. *Oeuvres*, 'Première lettre sur Oedipe'

5 The old-fashioned respect for the young is fast dying out.

Oscar Wilde (1854–1900) Irish-born British dramatist. *The Importance of Being Earnest*, I

RESPECTABILITY

1 Since when was genius found respectable?

Elizabeth Barrett Browning (1806–61) British poet. *Aurora Leigh*, Bk. VI

2 Let them cant about decorum
Who have characters to lose.

Robert Burns (1759–96) Scottish poet. *The Jolly Beggars*

3 Respectable means rich, and decent means poor. I should die if I heard my family called decent.

Thomas Love Peacock (1785–1866) British novelist. *Crotchet Castle*, Ch. 3

4 So live that you wouldn't be ashamed to sell the family parrot to the town gossip.

Will Rogers (1879–1935) US actor and humorist. Attrib.

RESPONSIBILITY

See also accusation

1 A bad workman always blames his tools.

Proverb

2 What the proprietorship of these papers is aiming at is power, and power without responsibility – the prerogative of the harlot through the ages.

Stanley Baldwin (1867–1947) British statesman. Attacking the press barons Lords Rothermere and Beaverbrook. It was first used by KIPLING. *See also* DUKE OF DEVONSHIRE; STOPPARD. Speech, election rally, 18 Mar 1931

3 Each man the architect of his own fate.

Appius Caecus (4th–3rd century BC) Roman statesman. *De Civitate* (Sallust), Bk. I

4 Everyone threw the blame on me. I have noticed that they nearly always do. I suppose it is because they think I shall be able to bear it best.

Winston Churchill (1874–1965) British statesman. *My Early Life*, Ch. 17

5 Perhaps it is better to be irresponsible and right than to be responsible and wrong.

Winston Churchill Party Political Broadcast, London, 26 Aug 1950

6 Good God, that's done it. He's lost us the tarts' vote.

Duke of Devonshire (1895–1950) Conservative politician. Referring to Stanley BALDWIN's attack on newspaper proprietors; recalled by Harold Macmillan. Attrib.

7 What a man does defiles him, not what is done by others.

William Golding (1911–93) British novelist. *Rites of Passage*, 'Next Day'

8 It matters not how strait the gate,
How charged with punishments the scroll,
I am the master of my fate:
I am the captain of my soul.

William Ernest Henley (1849–1903) British writer. *Echoes*, IV, 'Invictus. In Mem. R.T.H.B.'

9 Power without responsibility – the prerogative of the harlot throughout the ages.

Rudyard Kipling (1865–1936) Indian-born British writer. Better known for its subsequent use by BALDWIN. Attrib.

10 Accuse not Nature, she hath done her part; Do thou but thine.

John Milton (1608–74) English poet. *Paradise Lost*, Bk. VIII

11 *We can believe what we choose.* We are answerable for what we choose to believe.

Cardinal Newman (1801–90) British theologian. Letter to Mrs Froude, 27 June 1848

12 You become responsible, forever, for what you have tamed. You are responsible for your rose.

Antoine de Saint-Exupéry (1900–44) French novelist and aviator. *The Little Prince*, Ch. 21

13 The salvation of mankind lies only in making everything the concern of all.

Alexander Solzhenitsyn (1918–) Soviet novelist. Nobel Lecture, 1970

14 The House of Lords, an illusion to which I have never been able to subscribe – responsibility without power, the prerogative of the eunuch throughout the ages.

Tom Stoppard (1937–) Czech-born British dramatist. *See also* BALDWIN. *Lord Malquist and Mr Moon*, Pt. VI, Ch. 1

15 For man is man and master of his fate.

Alfred, Lord Tennyson (1809–92) British poet. *Idylls of the King*, 'The Marriage of Geraint'

16 The buck stops here.

Harry S. Truman (1884–1972) US statesman. Sign kept on his desk during his term as president. *Presidential Anecdotes* (P. Boller)

17 In dreams begins responsibility.

W. B. Yeats (1865–1939) Irish poet. *Old Play, Epigraph, Responsibilities*

REST

See also bed, idleness, leisure, sleep

1 Will there be beds for me and all who seek?
Yea, beds for all who come.

Christina Rossetti (1830–74) British poet. *Up-Hill*

2 Unarm, Eros; the long day's task is done,
And we must sleep.

William Shakespeare (1564–1616) English dramatist. *Antony and Cleopatra*, IV:12

3 It is well to lie fallow for a while.

Martin Farquhar Tupper (1810–89) British writer. *Proverbial Philosophy*, 'Of Recreation'

RESULTS

1 Desperate cuts must have desperate cures.

Proverb

2 The little bit (two inches wide) of ivory on which I work with so fine a brush as produces little effect after much labour.

Jane Austen (1775–1817) British novelist. Letter, 16 Dec 1816

3 Ye shall know them by their fruits. Do men gather grapes of thorns, or figs of thistles?
Even so every good tree bringeth forth good fruit; but a corrupt tree bringeth forth evil fruit.
A good tree cannot bring forth evil fruit, neither can a corrupt tree bring forth good fruit.
Every tree that bringeth not forth good fruit is hewn down, and cast into the fire.
Wherefore by their fruits ye shall know them.

Bible: Matthew 7:16–20

4 Our love of what is beautiful does not lead to extravagance; our love of the things of the mind does not make us soft.

Pericles (c. 495–429 BC) Greek statesman. Part of the funeral oration, 430 BC, for the dead of the first year of the Peloponnesian War. Attrib. in *Histories* Bk. II, Ch. 40 (Thucydides)

5 What dire offence from am'rous causes springs,
What mighty contests rise from trivial things.

Alexander Pope (1688–1744) British poet. *The Rape of the Lock*, I

RETRIBUTION

See also punishment, revenge

1 Give a thief enough rope and he'll hang himself.

Proverb

2 *Nemo me impune lacessit.*
No one provokes me with impunity.

Anonymous Motto of the Crown of Scotland

3 And if any mischief follow, then thou shalt give life for life,
Eye for eye, tooth for tooth, hand for hand, foot for foot,
Burning for burning, wound for wound, stripe for stripe.

Bible: Exodus 21:23–25

4 Be not deceived: God is not mocked: for whatsoever a man soweth, that shall he also reap.
For he that soweth to his flesh shall of the flesh reap corruption; but he that soweth to the Spirit shall of the Spirit reap life everlasting.
And let us not be weary in well doing: for in due season we shall reap, if we faint not.

Bible: Galatians 6:7–9

5 For they have sown the wind, and they shall reap the whirlwind: it hath no stalk: the bud shall yield no meal: if so be it yield, the strangers shall swallow it up.

Bible: Hosea 8:7

6 For I say unto you, That except your righteousness shall exceed the righteousness of the scribes and Pharisees, ye shall in no case enter

into the kingdom of heaven.
Bible: Matthew 5:20

7 And if thy right eye offend thee, pluck it out, and cast it from thee: for it is profitable for thee that one of thy members should perish, and not that thy whole body should be cast into hell.
Bible: Matthew 5:29

8 For thou shalt heap coals of fire upon his head, and the Lord shall reward thee.
Bible: Proverbs 25:22

9 But men never violate the laws of God without suffering the consequences, sooner or later.
Lydia M. Child (1802–80) US abolitionist campaigner. *The Freedmen's Book*, 'Toussaint L'Ouverture'

10 The Germans, if this Government is returned, are going to pay every penny; they are going to be squeezed, as a lemon is squeezed – until the pips squeak. My only doubt is not whether we can squeeze hard enough, but whether there is enough juice.
Eric Campbell Geddes (1875–1937) British politician. Speech, Cambridge, 10 Dec 1918

RETURN

1 Poor wandering one!
Though thou hast surely strayed,
Take heart of grace,
Thy steps retrace,
Poor wandering one!
W. S. Gilbert (1836–1911) British dramatist. *The Pirates of Penzance*, I

2 Ten o'clock...and back he'll come. I can just see him.
With vine leaves in his hair. Flushed and confident.
Henrik Ibsen (1828–1906) Norwegian dramatist. *Hedda Gabler*, II

3 Better lo'ed ye canna be,
Will ye no come back again?
Carolina Nairne (1766–1845) Scottish songwriter. Referring to Bonnie Prince Charlie. *Bonnie Charlie's now awa!*

REVENGE

See also retribution

1 Don't cut off your nose to spite your face.
Proverb

2 Revenge is a dish that tastes better cold.
Proverb

3 Revenge is sweet.
Proverb

4 Revenge is a kind of wild justice; which the more man's nature runs to, the more ought law to weed it out.
Francis Bacon (1561–1626) English philosopher. *Essays*, 'Of Revenge'

5 A man that studieth revenge keeps his own wounds green.
Francis Bacon *Essays*, 'Of Revenge'

6 Perish the Universe, provided I have my revenge.
Cyrano de Bergerac (1619–55) French writer. *La Mort d'Agrippine*, IV

7 And the Lord said unto him, Therefore whosoever slayeth Cain, vengeance shall be taken on him sevenfold. And the Lord set a mark upon Cain, lest any finding him should kill him. And Cain went out from the presence of the Lord, and dwelt in the land of Nod, on the east of Eden.
Bible: Genesis 4:15–16

8 I make war on the living, not on the dead.
Charles V (1500–58) Holy Roman Emperor. After the death of Martin Luther, when it was suggested that he hang the corpse on a gallows. Attrib.

9 Rome shall perish – write that word
In the blood that she has spilt.
William Cowper (1731–1800) British poet. *Boadicea*

10 Wisdom has taught us to be calm and meek,
To take one blow, and turn the other cheek;
It is not written what a man shall do
If the rude caitiff smite the other too!
Oliver Wendell Holmes (1809–94) US writer. *Non-Resistance*

11 No one delights more in vengeance than a woman.
Juvenal (Decimus Junius Juvenalis; 60–130 AD) Roman satirist. *Satires*, XIII

12 We had no use for the policy of the Gospels: if someone slaps you, just turn the other cheek. We had shown that anyone who slapped us on our cheek would get his head kicked off.
Nikita Khrushchev (1894–1971) Soviet statesman. *Khrushchev Remembers*, Vol. II

13 Revenge, at first though sweet,
Bitter ere long back on itself recoils.
John Milton (1608–74) English poet. *Paradise Lost*, Bk. IX

14 Those who offend us are generally punished for the offence they give; but we so frequently miss the satisfaction of knowing that we are avenged!
Anthony Trollope (1815–82) British novelist. *The Small House at Allington*, Ch. 50

REVOLUTION

See also French Revolution, rebellion, Russian Revolution

1 Inferiors revolt in order that they may be equal and equals that they may be superior. Such is the state of mind which creates revolutions.
Aristotle (384–322 BC) Greek philosopher. *Politics*, Bk. V

2 All modern revolutions have ended in a reinforcement of the power of the State.

Albert Camus (1913–60) French existentialist writer. *The Rebel*

3 The uprising of the masses implies a fabulous increase of vital possibilities; quite the contrary of what we hear so often about the decadence of Europe.

José Ortega y Gasset (1883–1955) Spanish philosopher. *The Revolt of the Masses*, Ch. 2

4 Revolution is not the uprising against preexisting order, but the setting-up of a new order contradictory to the traditional one.

José Ortega y Gasset *The Revolt of the Masses*, Ch. 6

5 We are dancing on a volcano.

Comte de Salvandy (1795–1856) French nobleman. A remark made before the July Revolution in 1830.

6 Insurrection is an art, and like all arts it has its laws.

Leon Trotsky (Lev Davidovich Bronstein; 1879–1940) Russian revolutionary. *History of the Russian Revolution*, Pt. III, Ch. 6

7 Revolutions are always verbose.

Leon Trotsky *History of the Russian Revolution*, Pt. II, Ch. 12

8 The fundamental premise of a revolution is that the existing social structure has become incapable of solving the urgent problems of development of the nation.

Leon Trotsky *History of the Russian Revolution*, Pt. III, Ch. 6

9 Revolution by its very nature is sometimes compelled to take in more territory than it is capable of holding. Retreats are possible – when there is territory to retreat from.

Leon Trotsky *Diary in Exile*, 15 Feb 1935

10 The word 'revolution' is a word for which you kill, for which you die, for which you send the labouring masses to their death, but which does not possess any content.

Simone Weil (1909–43) French philosopher. *Oppression and Liberty*, 'Reflections Concerning the Causes of Liberty and Social Oppression'

11 We invented the Revolution
but we don't know how to run it.

Peter Weiss (1916–82) German novelist and dramatist. *Marat Sade*, 15

12 Where the populace rise at once against the never-ending audacity of elected persons.

Walt Whitman (1819–92) US poet. *Song of the Broad Axe*, 5

RIDICULE

See also contempt, satire

1 For what do we live, but to make sport for our neighbours, and laugh at them in our turn?

Jane Austen (1775–1817) British novelist. *Pride and Prejudice*, Ch. 57

2 Few women care to be laughed at and men not at all, except for large sums of money.

Alan Ayckbourn (1939–) British dramatist. *The Norman Conquests*, Preface

3 It often happens, that he who endeavours to ridicule other people, especially in things of a serious nature, becomes himself a jest, and frequently to his great cost.

Giovanni Boccaccio (1313–75) Italian writer and poet. *Decameron*, 'Second Day'

4 Ridicule often checks what is absurd, and fully as often smothers that which is noble.

Walter Scott (1771–1832) Scottish novelist. *Quentin Durward*

RIGHT

1 This the grave of Mike O'Day
Who died maintaining his right of way.
His right was clear, his will was strong.
But he's just as dead as if he'd been wrong.

Anonymous Epitaph

2 A child becomes an adult when he realizes that he has a right not only to be right but also to be wrong.

Thomas Szasz (1920–) US psychiatrist. *The Second Sin*

3 While I'd rather be right than president, at any time I'm ready to be both.

Norman M. Thomas (1884–1968) US politician. Referring to his lack of success in presidential campaigns. The expression 'I'd rather be right than president' is also attributed to the US politician Henry Clay (1777–1852). *Come to Judgment* (A. Whitman)

4 Right is more precious than peace.

Woodrow Wilson (1856–1925) US statesman. *Radio Times*, 10 Sept 1964

RIGHTEOUSNESS

See also good, integrity, morality, virtue

1 The eternal *not ourselves* that makes for righteousness.

Matthew Arnold (1822–88) British poet and critic. *Literature and Dogma*, Ch. 8

2 Righteous people terrify me...Virtue is its own punishment.

Aneurin Bevan (1897–1960) British Labour politician. *Aneurin Bevan 1897–1945* (Michael Foot)

3 Ye must leave righteous ways behind, not to speak of unrighteous ways.

Buddha (Gautama Siddhartha; c. 563–c. 483 BC) Indian religious teacher. *Some Sayings of the Buddha* (F. L. Woodward)

4 The man of life upright,
Whose guiltless heart is free
From all dishonest deeds
Or thought of vanity.

Thomas Campion (1567–1620) English poet. *The Man of Life Upright*

5 Good thoughts his only friends,
His wealth a well-spent age,
The earth his sober inn
And quiet pilgrimage.

Thomas Campion *The Man of Life Upright*

6 Perhaps it is better to be irresponsible and right than to be responsible and wrong.

Winston Churchill (1874–1965) British statesman. Party Political Broadcast, London, 26 Aug 1950

7 Looks the whole world in the face,
For he owes not any man.

Henry Wadsworth Longfellow (1807–82) US poet. *The Village Blacksmith*

8 Live among men as if God beheld you; speak to God as if men were listening.

Seneca (c. 4 BC–65 AD) Roman author. *Epistles*

RIVERS

1 I have seen the Mississippi. That is muddy water. I have seen the St Lawrence. That is crystal water. But the Thames is liquid history.

John Burns (1858–1943) British Labour politician. Attrib.

2 Ol' man river, dat ol' man river,
He must know sumpin', but don't say nothin',
He just keeps rollin', he keeps on rollin' along.

Oscar Hammerstein (1895–1960) US lyricist. From the musical *Show Boat. Ol' Man River*

3 What is there to make so much of in the Thames? I am quite tired of it. Flow, flow, flow, always the same.

Duke of Queensberry (1724–1810) British peer. *Century of Anecdote* (J. Timbs)

4 *Die Wacht am Rhein.*
The Watch on the Rhine.

Max Schneckenburger (1819–49) German poet. Song title

5 Sweet Thames! run softly, till I end my Song.

Edmund Spenser (1552–99) English poet. *Prothalamion*, 18

6 I come from haunts of coot and hern,
I make a sudden sally
And sparkle out among the fern,
To bicker down a valley.

Alfred, Lord Tennyson (1809–92) British poet. *The Brook*

ROYALTY

See also monarchy

1 The King over the Water.

Anonymous Jacobite toast

2 'How different, how very different from the home life of our own dear Queen!'

Anonymous Remark about the character of Cleopatra as performed by Sarah Bernhardt

3 Here lies Fred,
Who was alive and is dead:
Had it been his father,
I had much rather;
Had it been his brother,
Still better than another;
Had it been his sister,
No one would have missed her;
Had it been the whole generation,
Still better for the nation:
But since 'tis only Fred,
Who was alive and is dead, –
There's no more to be said.

Anonymous Referring to Frederick, Prince of Wales, eldest son of George II and father of George III. *Memoirs of George II* (Horace Walpole)

4 The house is well, but it is you, Your Majesty, who have made me too great for my house.

Francis Bacon (1561–1626) English philosopher. Reply when Elizabeth I remarked on the smallness of his house. *After-dinner Stories and Anecdotes* (L. Meissen)

5 Speed, bonny boat, like a bird on the wing;
'Onward', the sailors cry;
Carry the lad that's born to be king
Over the sea to Skye.

H. E. Boulton (1859–1935) Scottish songwriter. Referring to Bonnie Prince Charlie. *Skye Boat Song*

6 Such grace had kings when the world begun!

Robert Browning (1812–89) British poet. *Pippa Passes*, Pt. I

7 Kings are naturally lovers of low company.

Edmund Burke (1729–97) British politician. *Speech on the Economical Reform* (House of Commons, 11 Feb 1780)

8 A better farmer ne'er brushed dew from lawn,
A worse king never left a realm undone!

Lord Byron (1788–1824) British poet. Referring to George III. *The Vision of Judgment*, VIII

9 Conquering kings their titles take.

John Chandler (1806–76) British clergyman and writer. Poem title

10 Brother, I am too old to go again to my travels.

Charles II (1630–85) King of England. Referring to his exile, 1651–60. *History of Great Britain (Hume)*, Vol. II, Ch. 7

11 The monarchy is the oldest profession in the world.

Charles, Prince of Wales (1948–) Eldest son of Elizabeth II. Attrib.

12 Her Majesty is not a subject.

Benjamin Disraeli (1804–81) British statesman. Responding to Gladstone's taunt that Disraeli could make a joke out of any subject, including Queen Victoria. Attrib.

13 I know I have the body of a weak and feeble woman, but I have the heart and stomach of a King, and of a King of England too.

Elizabeth I (1533–1603) Queen of England. Speech at Tilbury on the approach of the Spanish Armada

14 Though God hath raised me high, yet this I count the glory of my crown: that I have reigned with your loves.

Elizabeth I *The Golden Speech*, 1601

15 I will make you shorter by a head.

Elizabeth I *Sayings of Queen Elizabeth* (Chamberlin)

16 I should like to be a horse.

Elizabeth II (1926–) Queen of the United Kingdom. When asked about her ambitions when a child. Attrib.

17 I think that everyone will conceed that – today of all days – I should begin by saying, 'My husband and I'.

Elizabeth II On her silver-wedding. Speech, Guildhall, 1972

18 1992 is not a year I shall look back on with undiluted pleasure. In the words of one of my more sympathetic correspondents, it has turned out to be an 'annus horribilis'.

Elizabeth II Alluding to *Annus Mirabilis*, a poem by John Dryden.

19 We're not a family; we're a firm.

George VI (1895–1952) King of the United Kingdom. *Our Future King* (Peter Lane)

20 I'm prepared to take advice on leisure from Prince Philip. He's a world expert on leisure. He's been practising for most of his adult life.

Neil Kinnock (1942–) British politician. *Western Mail*, 1981

21 I don't mind your being killed, but I object to your being taken prisoner.

Lord Kitchener (1850–1916) British field marshal. Said to the Prince of Wales (later Edward VIII) when he asked to go to the Front. *Journal* (Viscount Esher), 18 Dec 1914

22 When it comes to culture, you'll find more on a month-old carton of yoghurt than between the ears of the Princess of Wales.

Richard Littlejohn *The Sun*, 1993

23 Ah, if I were not king, I should lose my temper.

Louis XIV (1638–1715) French king. Attrib.

24 For God's sake, ma'am, let's have no more of that. If you get the English people into the way of making kings, you'll get them into the way of *un*making them.

Lord Melbourne (1779–1848) British statesman. Advising Queen Victoria against granting Prince Albert the title of King Consort. *Lord M.* (Lord David Cecil)

25 You can divide my life into two. During the first part of my life I was an ordinary conventional naval officer, trying not to be different in the sense of being royal trying not to show myself off as being rich and ostentatious – like always using a small car to drive to the dockyard instead of my Rolls Royce.

Louis Mountbatten of Burma (1900–79) British admiral and colonial administrator. *Mountbatten, Hero of Our Time*, Ch. 9 (Richard Hough)

26 He will go from resort to resort getting more tanned and more tired.

Westbrook Pegler (1894–1969) US journalist. On the abdication of Edward VIII. *Six Men* (Alistair Cooke), Pt. II

27 I'm self-employed.

Prince Philip (1921–) The consort of Queen Elizabeth II. Answering a query as to what nature of work he did. Attrib.

28 Not least among the qualities in a great King is a capacity to permit his ministers to serve him.

Cardinal Richelieu (1585–1642) French statesman. *Testament Politique*, Maxims

29 Kings and such like are just as funny as politicians.

Theodore Roosevelt (1858–1919) US Republican president. *Mr Wilson's War* (John Dos Passos), Ch. 1

30 The sun does not set in my dominions.

Friedrich von Schiller (1759–1805) German dramatist. Said by Philip II. *Don Carlos*, I:6

31 Kings are earth's gods; in vice their law's their will.

William Shakespeare (1564–1616) English dramatist. *Pericles*, I:1

32 For God's sake let us sit upon the ground
And tell sad stories of the death of kings:
How some have been depos'd, some slain in war,
Some haunted by the ghosts they have depos'd,
Some poison'd by their wives, some sleeping kill'd,
All murder'd – for within the hollow crown
That rounds the mortal temples of a king
Keeps Death his court.

William Shakespeare *Richard II*, III:2

33 Ay, every inch a king.

William Shakespeare *King Lear*, IV:6

34 I would not be a queen
For all the world.

William Shakespeare *Henry VIII*, II:3

35 Albert was merely a young foreigner, who suffered from having no vices, and whose only claim to distinction was that he had happened to marry the Queen of England.

Lytton Strachey (1880–1932) British writer. *Queen Victoria*, Ch. 5

36 Authority forgets a dying king.

Alfred, Lord Tennyson (1809–92) British poet. *Idylls of the King*, 'The Passing of Arthur'

37 We are not amused!

Victoria (1819–1901) Queen of the United Kingdom. Attrib.

38 I sat between the King and Queen. We left supper soon. My health was drunk. I then danced one more quadrille with Lord Paget....I was *very* much amused.

Victoria Journal, 16 June 1833

39 It has none, your Highness. Its history dates from today.

James Whistler (1834–1903) US painter. Replying to a query from the Prince of Wales about the history of the Society of British Artists, which he was visiting for the first time. *Whistler Stories* (D. Seitz)

40 Now what do I do with *this*?

Duke of Windsor (1894–1972) King of the United Kingdom; abdicated 1936. On being handed the bill after a lengthy stay in a luxury hotel. Attrib.

RUDENESS

See impertinence, insults

RULES

See also conformity, rebellion

1 The exception proves the rule.
Proverb

2 Rules and models destroy genius and art.
William Hazlitt (1778–1830) British essayist. *On Taste*

3 The golden rule is that there are no golden rules.
George Bernard Shaw (1856–1950) Irish dramatist and critic. *Man and Superman*, 'Maxims for Revolutionists'

RUSSIA

See also Cold War, Communism, Russian Revolution

1 Reforms mean you can have a big car if you're in the mafia. Reforms mean hard-currency shops for a handful of people who have it. I'm a factory worker. I'll never have a big car or dollars, so reform for me will be when the milk isn't sour, that's all.
Anonymous Remark by a Russian woman while queuing for food. *The Times*, 25 Nov 1992

2 The Chechens are especially disappointed that England has not helped us in our struggle for freedom, because our legends say that we are descended from the same race as the English, and that one day an English king will come to rule over us.
Hassan Bibulatov Chechen army officer. *The Times*, 17 Dec 1994

3 I cannot forecast to you the action of Russia. It is a riddle wrapped in a mystery inside an enigma.
Winston Churchill (1874–1965) British statesman. Broadcast talk, 1 Oct 1939

4 Russia will certainly inherit the future. What we already call the greatness of Russia is only her pre-natal struggling.
D. H. Lawrence (1885–1930) British novelist. *Phoenix*, Preface

5 Neither can you expect a revolution, because there is no new baby in the womb of our society. Russia is a collapse, not a revolution.
D. H. Lawrence *Phoenix*, 'The Good Man'

6 Scratch the Russian and you will find the Tartar.
Joseph de Maistre (1753–1821) French monarchist. Attributed also to Napoleon and Prince de Ligne

7 Absolutism tempered by assassination.
Ernst Friedrich Herbert Münster (1766–1839) Hanoverian statesman. Referring to the Russian Constitution. Letter

8 Yeltsin got where he is by slogans. He is an old party communist and has the old mentality. He is good at leading from the top of a tank.
Zianon Pozniak Belarussian politician. *The Times*, 4 Feb 1995

9 The people are not masters in their own house and therefore there is no democracy in Russia.
Alexander Solzhenitsyn (1918–) Russian novelist. *The Independent*, 22 July 1994

10 It was the supreme expression of the mediocrity of the apparatus that Stalin himself rose to his position.
Leon Trotsky (Lev Davidovich Bronstein; 1879–1940) Russian revolutionary. *My Life*, Ch. 40

11 From being a patriotic myth, the Russian people have become an awful reality.
Leon Trotsky *History of the Russian Revolution*, Pt. III, Ch. 7

12 America has brought us McDonald's and horror movies. The West is trying to tell us how to live.
Vladimir Zhirinovsky (1946–) Russian politician. *The Sunday Times*, 3 Apr 1994

RUSSIAN REVOLUTION

See also revolution, Russia

1 Our hand will not tremble.
Joseph Stalin (J. Dzhugashvili; 1879–1953) Soviet statesman. Reply to a telegraph from Lenin at the start of the Red Terror (1918) urging him to be merciless against the Bolsheviks' enemies

2 The 23rd of February was International Woman's Day…It had not occurred to anyone that it might become the first day of the revolution.
Leon Trotsky (Lev Davidovich Bronstein; 1879–1940) Russian revolutionary. *History of the Russian Revolution*, Pt. I, Ch. 7

3 The revolution does not choose its paths: it made its first steps towards victory under the belly of a Cossack's horse.
Leon Trotsky *History of the Russian Revolution*, Pt. I, Ch. 7

RUTHLESSNESS

See also cruelty

1 Would that the Roman people had but one neck!
Caligula (Gaius Caesar; 12–41 AD) Roman Emperor. *Life of Caligula* (Suetonius), Ch. 30

2 What millions died – that Caesar might be great!
Thomas Campbell (1777–1844) British poet. *Pleasures of Hope*, II

3 Exterminate all brutes.

Joseph Conrad (Teodor Josef Konrad Korzeniowski; 1857–1924) Polish-born British novelist. *Heart of Darkness*

4 I do not have to forgive my enemies, I have had them all shot.

Ramón Maria Narváez (1800–68) Spanish general and political leader. Said on his deathbed, when asked by a priest if he forgave his enemies. *Famous Last Words* (B. Conrad)

5 3RD FISHERMAN. Master, I marvel how the fishes live in the sea.
1ST FISHERMAN. Why, as men do a-land –
the great ones eat up the little ones.

William Shakespeare (1564–1616) English dramatist. *Pericles*, II:1

6 The world continues to offer glittering prizes to those who have stout hearts and sharp swords.

F. E. Smith (1872–1930) British lawyer and politician. Speech, Glasgow University, 7 Nov 1923

7 It is not enough to succeed. Others must fail.

Gore Vidal (1925–) US novelist. *Antipanegyric for Tom Driberg* (G. Irvine)

S

SARCASM

1 Sarcasm I now see to be, in general, the language of the devil.

Thomas Carlyle (1795–1881) Scottish historian and essayist. *Sartor Resartus*, Bk. II, Ch. 4

2 If you don't want to use the army, I should like to borrow it for a while. Yours respectfully, A. Lincoln.

Abraham Lincoln (1809–65) US statesman. Letter to General George B. McClellan, whose lack of activity during the US Civil War irritated Lincoln.

SATIRE

See also ridicule, sarcasm

1 It's hard not to write satire.

Juvenal (Decimus Junius Juvenalis; 60–130 AD) Roman satirist. *Satires*, I

2 Satire should, like a polished razor keen,
Wound with a touch that's scarcely felt or seen.

Lady Mary Wortley Montagu (1689–1762) English writer. *To the Imitator of the First Satire of Horace*, Bk. II

3 Satire is a sort of glass, wherein beholders do generally discover everybody's face but their own.

Jonathan Swift (1667–1745) Irish-born Anglican priest and writer. *The Battle of the Books*, 'Preface'

SATISFACTION

See also contentment

1 Youth will be served, every dog has his day, and mine has been a fine one.

George Henry Borrow (1803–81) British writer. *Lavengro*, Ch. 92

2 I wasna fou, but just had plenty.

Robert Burns (1759–96) Scottish poet. *Death and Doctor Hornbrook*

3 The reward of a thing well done is to have done it.

Ralph Waldo Emerson (1803–82) US poet and essayist. *Essays*, 'New England Reformers'

SAYINGS

See also quotations

1 A platitude is simply a truth repeated till people get tired of hearing it.

Stanley Baldwin (1867–1947) British statesman. Attrib.

2 The hunter for aphorisms on human nature has to fish in muddy water, and he is even condemned to find much of his own mind.

F. H. Bradley (1846–1924) British philosopher. *Aphorisms*

3 The great writers of aphorisms read as if they had all known each other well.

Elias Canetti (1905–94) Bulgarian-born novelist. *The Human Province*

4 A proverb is much matter decorated into few words.

Thomas Fuller (1608–61) English historian. *The History of the Worthies of England*, Ch. 2

5 A new maxim is often a brilliant error.

Chrétien Guillaume de Lamoignonde Malesherbes (1721–94) French statesman. *Pensées et maximes*

6 A proverb is one man's wit and all men's wisdom.

Lord John Russell (1792–1878) British statesman. Attrib.

7 A truism is on that account none the less true.

Herbert Samuel (1870–1963) British Liberal statesman. *A Book of Quotations*

SCEPTICISM

See also doubt, proof

1 We don't believe in rheumatism and true love until after the first attack.

Marie Ebner von Eschenbach (1830–1916) Austrian writer. *Aphorism*

2 I am too much of a sceptic to deny the possibility of anything.

T. H. Huxley (1825–95) British biologist. Letter to Herbert Spencer, 22 Mar 1886

3 Truth, Sir, is a cow, which will yield such people no more milk, and so they are gone to milk the bull.

Samuel Johnson (1709–84) British lexicographer. Referring to sceptics. *Life of Johnson* (J. Boswell), Vol. I

4 It is undesirable to believe a proposition when there is no ground whatever for supposing it true.

Bertrand Russell (1872–1970) British philosopher. *Sceptical Essays*

5 She believed in nothing; only her scepticism kept her from being an atheist.

Jean-Paul Sartre (1905–80) French writer. *Words*

6 The temerity to believe in nothing.

Ivan Turgenev (1818–83) Russian novelist. *Fathers and Sons*, Ch. 14

SCIENCE

See also discovery, mathematics, Nature, progress, research, scientists, technology

1 That is the essence of science: ask an impertinent question, and you are on the way to the pertinent answer.

Jacob Bronowski (1908–74) British scientist and writer. *The Ascent of Man*, Ch. 4

2 Physics becomes in those years the greatest collective work of science – no, more than that, the great collective work of art of the twentieth century.

Jacob Bronowski Referring to the period around the turn of the century marked by the elucidation of atomic structure and the development of the quantum theory. *The Ascent of Man*, Ch. 10

3 There was a young lady named Bright,
Whose speed was far faster than light;
She set out one day
In a relative way,
And returned home the previous night.

Arthur Henry Reginald Buller (1874–1944) British botanist. *Limerick*

4 That is how the atom is split. But what does it mean? To us who think in terms of practical use it means – Nothing!

Ritchie Calder (1898–1976) US engineer and sculptor. *The Daily Herald*, 27 June 1932

5 It is, of course, a bit of a drawback that science was invented after I left school.

Lord Carrington (1919–) British statesman. *The Observer*, 23 Jan 1983

6 When a distinguished but elderly scientist states that something is possible, he is almost certainly right. When he states that something is impossible, he is very probably wrong.

Arthur C. Clarke (1917–) British science-fiction writer. *Profiles of the Future*

7 We have discovered the secret of life!

Francis Crick (1916–) British biophysicist. Excitedly bursting into a Cambridge pub with James Watson to celebrate the fact that they had unravelled the structure of DNA. *The Double Helix* (J. D. Watson)

8 After all, science is essentially international, and it is only through lack of the historical sense that national qualities have been attributed to it.

Marie Curie (1867–1934) Polish chemist. *Memorandum*, 'Intellectual Co-operation'

9 And new Philosophy calls all in doubt,
The Element of fire is quite put out;
The Sun is lost, and th' earth, and no man's wit
Can well direct him where to look for it.

John Donne (1573–1631) English poet. *An Anatomy of the World*, 205

10 Electrical force is defined as something which causes motion of electrical charge; an electrical charge is something which exerts electric force.

Arthur Eddington (1882–1944) British astronomer. *The Nature of the Physical World*

11 Man is slightly nearer to the atom than the stars. From his central position he can survey the grandest works of Nature with the astronomer, or the minutest works with the physicist.

Arthur Eddington *Stars and Atoms*

12 When you are courting a nice girl an hour seems like a second. When you sit on a red-hot cinder a second seems like an hour. That's relativity.

Albert Einstein (1879–1955) German-born US physicist. *News Chronicle*, 14 Mar 1949

13 The whole of science is nothing more than a refinement of everyday thinking.

Albert Einstein *Out of My Later Years*

14 Science without religion is lame, religion without science is blind.

Albert Einstein *Out of My Later Years*

15 God does not play dice.

Albert Einstein Einstein's objection to the quantum theory, in which physical events can only be known in terms of probabilities. It is sometimes quoted as 'God does not play dice with the Universe'. *Albert Einstein, Creator and Rebel* (B. Hoffman), Ch. 10

16 A vacuum can only exist, I imagine, by the things which enclose it.

Zelda Fitzgerald (1900–48) US writer. Journal, 1932

17 Shelley and Keats were the last English poets who were at all up to date in their chemical knowledge.

J. B. S. Haldane (1892–1964) British geneticist. *Daedalus or Science and the Future*

18 MASTER: They split the atom by firing particles at it, at 5,500 miles a second.
BOY: Good heavens. And they only split it?

Will Hay (1888–1949) British comedian. *The Fourth Form at St Michael's*

19 Science has 'explained' nothing; the more we know the more fantastic the world becomes and the profounder the surrounding darkness.

Aldous Huxley (1894–1964) British novelist. *Views Of Holland*

20 Science is nothing but trained and organized common sense, differing from the latter only as a veteran may differ from a raw recruit: and its methods differ from those of common sense only as far as the guardsman's cut and thrust differ from the manner in which a savage wields his club.

T. H. Huxley (1825–95) British biologist. *Collected Essays*, 'The Method of Zadig'

21 The great tragedy of Science – the slaying of a beautiful hypothesis by an ugly fact.

T. H. Huxley *Collected Essays*, 'Biogenesis and Abiogenesis'

22 Reason, Observation, and Experience – the Holy Trinity of Science.

Robert G. Ingersoll (1833–99) US lawyer and agnostic. *The Gods*

23 Life exists in the universe only because the carbon atom possesses certain exceptional properties.

James Jeans (1877–1946) British scientist. *The Mysterious Universe*, Ch. 1

24 Science should leave off making pronouncements: the river of knowledge has too often turned back on itself.

James Jeans *The Mysterious Universe*, Ch. 5

25 We have genuflected before the god of science only to find that it has given us the atomic bomb, producing fears and anxieties that science can never mitigate.

Martin Luther King (1929–68) US Black civil-rights leader. *Strength through Love*, Ch. 13

26 'In everything that relates to science, I am a whole Encyclopaedia behind the rest of the world.

Charles Lamb (1775–1834) British essayist. *Essays of Elia*, 'The Old and the New Schoolmaster'

27 Water is H_2O, hydrogen two parts, oxygen one,
but there is also a third thing, that makes it water
and nobody knows what that is.

D. H. Lawrence (1885–1930) British novelist. *Pansies*, 'The Third Thing'

28 You don't destroy the mystery of a rainbow by understanding the light processes that form it.

Anne McLaren (1927–) British geneticist. *The Independent*, 5 Sept 1994

29 Scientific discovery is a private event, and the delight that accompanies it, or the despair of finding it illusory does not travel.

Peter Medawar (1915–87) British immunologist. *Hypothesis and Imagination*

30 *Laboratorium est oratorium.* The place where we do our scientific work is a place of prayer.

Joseph Needham (1900–95) British biochemist. *The Harvest of a Quiet Eye* (A. L. Mackay)

31 Do you really believe that the sciences would ever have originated and grown if the way had not been prepared by magicians, alchemists, astrologers and witches whose promises and pretensions first had to create a thirst, a hunger, a taste for *hidden* and *forbidden* powers? Indeed, infinitely more had to be *promised* than could ever be fulfilled in order that anything at all might be fulfilled in the realms of knowledge.

Friedrich Wilhelm Nietzsche (1844–1900) German philosopher. *The Gay Science*

32 There are no such things as applied sciences, only applications of science.

Louis Pasteur (1822–95) French scientist. Address, 11 Sept 1872

33 Traditional scientific method has always been at the very *best*, 20-20 hindsight. It's good for seeing where you've been.

Robert T. Pirsig (1928–) US writer. *Zen and the Art of Motorcycle Maintenance*, Pt. III, Ch. 24

34 Science must begin with myths, and with the criticism of myths.

Karl Popper (1902–94) Austrian-born British philosopher. *British Philosophy in the Mid-Century* (ed. C. A. Mace)

35 Should we force science down the throats of those that have no taste for it? Is it our duty to drag them kicking and screaming into the twenty-first century? I am afraid that it is.

George Porter (1920–) British chemist. Speech, Sept 1986

36 Science without conscience is the death of the soul.

François Rabelais (1483–1553) French satirist.

37 The simplest schoolboy is now familiar with truths for which Archimedes would have sacrified his life.

Ernest Renan (1823–92) French philosopher and theologian. *Souvenirs d'enfance et de jeunesse*

38 If all the arts aspire to the condition of music, all the sciences aspire to the condition of mathematics.

George Santayana (1863–1952) US philosopher. *The Observer*, 'Sayings of the Week', 4 Mar 1928

39 People must understand that science is inherently neither a potential for good nor for evil. It is a potential to be harnessed by man to do his bidding.

Glenn T. Seaborg (1912–) US physicist. Associated Press interview with Alton Blakeslee, 29 Sept 1964

40 Science is the great antidote to the poison of enthusiasm and superstition.

Adam Smith (1723–90) Scottish economist. *The Wealth of Nations*, Bk. V, Ch. 1

41 Her own mother lived the latter years of her life in the horrible suspicion that electricity was dripping invisibly all over the house.

James Thurber (1894–1961) US humorist. *My Life and Hard Times*, Ch. 2

42 Modern Physics is an instrument of Jewry for the destruction of Nordic science...True physics is the creation of the German spirit.

Rudolphe Tomaschek (20th century) German scientist. *The Rise and Fall of the Third Reich* (W. L. Shirer), Ch. 8

43 Science robs men of wisdom and usually converts them into phantom beings loaded up with facts.

Miguel de Unamuno y Jugo (1864–36) Spanish writer. *Essays and Soliloquies*

44 The term Science should not be given to anything but the aggregate of the recipes that are always successful. All the rest is literature.

Paul Valéry (1871–1945) French poet and writer. *Moralités*

45 Classical physics has been superseded by quantum theory: quantum theory is verified by experiments. Experiments must be described in terms of classical physics.

C. F. von Weizsäcker (1912–) German physicist and philosopher. Attrib.

46 A science which hesitates to forget its founders is lost.

A. N. Whitehead (1861–1947) British philosopher. Attrib.

47 The airplane stays up because it doesn't have the time to fall.

Orville Wright (1871–1948) US aviator. Explaining the principles of powered flight. Attrib.

SCIENCE FICTION

1 Far out in the uncharted backwaters of the unfashionable end of the Western Spiral arm of the Galaxy lies a small unregarded yellow sun. Orbiting this at a distance of roughly ninety-two million miles is an utterly insignificant little blue green planet whose ape-descended life forms are so amazingly primitive that they still think digital watches are a pretty neat idea.

Douglas Adams (1952–) British writer. *The Hitch Hiker's Guide to the Galaxy*, Introduction

2 Science fiction is the search for a definition of mankind and his status in the universe which will stand in our advanced but confused state of knowledge (science), and is characteristically cast in the Gothic or post-Gothic mode.

Brian Aldiss (1925–) British science-fiction writer. *Trillion Year Spree*, Ch. 1

3 *Star Maker* is really the one great grey holy book of science fiction...

Brian Aldiss Referring to Olaf Stapledon's novel *Star Maker*. *Trillion Year Spree*, Ch. 8

SCIENTISTS

See also science

General quotes

1 When I find myself in the company of scientists, I feel like a shabby curate who has strayed by mistake into a drawing-room full of dukes.

W. H. Auden (1907–73) British poet. *The Dyer's Hand*

2 The true men of action in our time, those who transform the world, are not the politicians and statesmen, but the scientists. Unfortunately, poetry cannot celebrate them, because their deeds are concerned with things, not persons and are, therefore, speechless.

W. H. Auden *The Dyer's Hand*

3 If you want to find out anything from the theoretical physicists about the methods they use, I advise you to stick closely to one principle: Don't listen to their words fix your attention on their deeds.

Albert Einstein (1879–1955) German-born US physicist. *The World As I See It*

4 Scientists are treated like gods handing down new commandments. People tend to assume that religion has been disproved by science. But the scientist may tell us how the world works, not why it works, not how we should live our lives, not how we face death or make moral decisions.

Susan Howatch (1940–) British writer. *The Observer*, 8 May 1994

5 The physicists have known sin; and this is a knowledge which they cannot lose.

J. Robert Oppenheimer (1904–67) US physicist. Lecture, Massachusetts Institute of Technology, 25 Nov 1947

6 He doubted the existence of the Deity but accepted Carnot's cycle, and he had read Shakespeare and found him weak in chemistry.

H. G. Wells (1866–1946) British writer. *Short Stories*, 'The Lord of the Dynamos'

Specific quotes

7 Sir Humphry Davy
Abominated gravy.
He lived in the odium
Of having discovered Sodium.

Edmund Clerihew Bentley (1875–1956) British writer. *Biography for Beginners*

8 Edison, whose inventions did as much as any to add to our material convenience, wasn't what we would call a scientist at all, but a supreme 'do-it-yourself' man – the successor to Benjamin Franklin.

Kenneth Clark (1903–83) British art historian. *Civilisation*

9 I believe the souls of five hundred Sir Isaac Newtons would go to the making up of a Shakespeare or a Milton.

Samuel Taylor Coleridge (1772–1834) British poet. Letter to Thomas Poole, 23 Mar 1801

10 I went to the Society where were divers experiments in Mr Boyle's Pneumatic Engine. We put in a snake but could not kill it by exhausting the air, only making it extremely sick, but a chick died of convulsions in a short space.

John Evelyn (1620–1706) English diarist. *Diary*, 22 Apr 1661

11 Einstein – the greatest Jew since Jesus. I have no doubt that Einstein's name will still be remembered and revered when Lloyd George, Foch and William Hohenzollern share with Charlie Chaplin that uneluctable oblivion which awaits the uncreative mind.

J. B. S. Haldane (1892–1964) British geneticist. *Daedalus or Science and the Future*

12 Bacon discovered the art of making reading-glasses...and various other mathematical and astronomical instruments....That the ingredients of gunpowder and the art of making it were known to him is now undeniable; but the ***humane philosopher*** dreading the consequences of communicating the discovery to the world, transposed the letters of the Latin words which signify charcoal, which made the whole obscure.

Robert Henry *History of England*

13 Had he not been an untidy man and apt to leave his cultures exposed on the laboratory table the spore of hyssop mould, the ***penicillin notatum***, might never have floated in from Praed Street and settled on his dish of staphylococci.

André Maurois (Émile Herzog; 1885–1967) French writer. *Life of Alexander Fleming*

14 Nature, and Nature's laws lay hid in night:
God said, Let *Newton be!* and all was light.

Alexander Pope (1688–1744) British poet. For a reply, *see* John Collings SQUIRE. *Epitaphs*, 'Intended for Sir Isaac Newton'

15 It did not last: the Devil howling 'Ho!

Let Einstein be!' restored the status quo.

John Collings Squire (1884–1958) British journalist. Answer to POPE's Epitaph for Newton. *Epigrams*, 'The Dilemma'

16 He snatched the lightning shaft from heaven, and the sceptre from tyrants.

Anne-Robert-Jacques Turgot (1727–81) French economist. An inscription for a bust of Benjamin Franklin, alluding both to Franklin's invention of the lightning conductor and to his role in the American Revolution. *Vie de Turgot* (A. N. de Condorcet)

17 Already for thirty-five years he had not stopped talking and almost nothing of fundamental value had emerged.

James Dewey Watson (1928–) US geneticist. Referring to Francis Crick. *The Double Helix*, Ch. 8

SCOTLAND

See also Britain, Scots

1 O ye'll tak' the high road, and I'll tak' the low road,
And I'll be in Scotland afore ye,
But me and my true love will never meet again,
On the bonnie, bonnie banks o' Loch Lomon'.

Anonymous *The Bonnie Banks o' Loch Lomon'*

2 My heart's in the Highlands, my heart is not here;
My heart's in the Highlands a-chasing the deer;
Chasing the wild deer, and following the roe,
My heart's in the Highlands, wherever I go.

Robert Burns (1759–96) Scottish poet. *My Heart's in the Highlands*

3 *Oats.* A grain, which in England is generally given to horses, but in Scotland supports the people.

Samuel Johnson (1709–84) British lexicographer. *Dictionary of the English Language*

4 Norway, too, has noble wild prospects; and Lapland is remarkable for prodigious noble wild prospects. But, Sir, let me tell you, the noblest prospect which a Scotchman ever sees, is the high road that leads him to England!

Samuel Johnson *Life of Johnson* (J. Boswell), Vol. I

5 Seeing Scotland, Madam, is only seeing a worse England.

Samuel Johnson *Life of Johnson* (J. Boswell), Vol. III

6 Roamin' in the gloamin',
By the bonny banks of Clyde.

Harry Lauder (Hugh MacLennon; 1870–1950) Scottish music-hall artist. Song

7 O Caledonia! stern and wild,
Meet nurse for a poetic child!
Land of brown heath and shaggy wood,
Land of the mountain and the flood,
Land of my sires! what mortal hand
Can e'er untie the filial band
That knits me to thy rugged strand!

Walter Scott (1771–1832) Scottish novelist. *The Lay of the Last Minstrel*, VI

8 That knuckle-end of England – that land of Calvin, oat-cakes, and sulphur.

Sydney Smith (1771–1845) British clergyman and essayist. *Memoir* (Lady Holland)

SCOTS

See also British, Scotland

1 You've forgotten the grandest moral attribute of a Scotsman, Maggie, that he'll do nothing which might damage his career.

J. M. Barrie (1860–1937) British novelist and dramatist. *What Every Woman Knows*, II

2 There are few more impressive sights in the world than a Scotsman on the make.

J. M. Barrie *What Every Woman Knows*, II

3 A Scotchman must be a very sturdy moralist who does not love Scotland better than truth.

Samuel Johnson (1709–84) British lexicographer. *Journey to the Western Islands of Scotland*, 'Col'

4 BOSWELL. I do indeed come from Scotland, but I cannot help it...
JOHNSON. That, Sir, I find, is what a very great many of your countrymen cannot help.

Samuel Johnson *Life of Johnson* (J. Boswell), Vol. I

5 Much may be made of a Scotchman, if he be *caught* young.

Samuel Johnson Referring to Lord Mansfield. *Life of Johnson* (J. Boswell), Vol. II

6 Their learning is like bread in a besieged town: every man gets a little, but no man gets a full meal.

Samuel Johnson Referring to education in Scotland. *Life of Johnson* (J. Boswell), Vol. II

7 I have been trying all my life to like Scotchmen, and am obliged to desist from the experiment in despair.

Charles Lamb (1775–1834) British essayist. *Essays of Elia*, 'Imperfect Sympathies'

8 In all my travels I never met with any one Scotchman but what was a man of sense. I believe everybody of that country that has any, leaves it as fast as they can.

Francis Lockier (1667–1740) English writer. *Anecdotes* (Joseph Spence)

9 Join a Highland regiment, me boy. The kilt is an unrivalled garment for fornication and diarrhoea.

John Masters (1914–83) British writer. *Bugles and a Tiger*

10 It's ill taking the breeks aff a wild Highlandman.

Walter Scott (1771–1832) Scottish novelist. *The Fair Maid of Perth*, Ch. 5

11 It is never difficult to distinguish between a Scotsman with a grievance and a ray of sunshine.

P. G. Wodehouse (1881–1975) British humorous novelist. *Wodehouse at Work to the End* (Richard Usborne), Ch. 8

SCULPTURE

See art, artists

SEA

See also boats, Navy, seaside

1 The sea is calm to-night,
The tide is full, the moon lies fair
Upon the Straits.

Matthew Arnold (1822–88) British poet and critic. *Dover Beach*

2 For all at last return to the sea – to Oceanus, the ocean river, like the ever-flowing stream of time, the beginning and the end.

Rachel Carson (1907–64) US biologist. The closing words of the book. *The Sea Around Us*

3 The voice of the sea speaks to the soul. The touch of the sea is sensuous, enfolding the body in its soft, close embrace.

Kate Chopin (1851–1904) US writer. *The Awakening*, Ch. 6

4 The ice was here, the ice was there,
The ice was all around:
It cracked and growled, and roared and howled,
Like noises in a swound!

Samuel Taylor Coleridge (1772–1834) British poet. *The Rime of the Ancient Mariner*, I

5 We are as near to heaven by sea as by land.

Humphrey Gilbert (c. 1539–83) English navigator. Remark made shortly before he went down with his ship *Squirrel. A Book of Anecdotes* (D. George)

6 When men come to like a sea-life, they are not fit to live on land.

Samuel Johnson (1709–84) British lexicographer. *Life of Johnson* (J. Boswell), Vol. II

7 The snotgreen sea. The scrotumtightening sea.

James Joyce (1882–1941) Irish novelist. *Ulysses*

8 It keeps eternal whisperings around
Desolate shores, and with its mighty swell
Gluts twice ten thousand Caverns.

John Keats (1795–1821) British poet. *On the Sea*

9 'Wouldst thou' – so the helmsman answered–
'Learn the secret of the sea?
Only those who brave its dangers
Comprehend its mystery!'

Henry Wadsworth Longfellow (1807–82) US poet. *The Secret of the Sea*

10 I must down to the seas again, to the lonely sea and the sky,
And all I ask is a tall ship and a star to steer her by,
And the wheel's kick and the wind's song and the white sail's shaking,
And a grey mist on the sea's face and a grey dawn breaking.

John Masefield (1878–1967) British poet. Often quoted using 'sea' rather than 'seas', and 'I must go down' rather than 'I must down'. *Sea Fever*

11 Rocked in the cradle of the deep.

Emma Millard (1787–1870) British songwriter. Song

12 ...the sea, trembling with a long line of radiance, and showing in the clear distance the sails of vessels stealing in every direction along its surface.

Ann Radcliffe (1764–1823) British novelist. *The Italian*

13 A life on the ocean wave,
A home on the rolling deep.

Epes Sargent (1813–80) US writer and dramatist. *A Life on the Ocean Wave*

14 O hear us when we cry to Thee
For those in peril on the sea.

William Whiting (1825–78) British hymn writer. *Eternal Father Strong to Save*

15 The sea! the sea!

Xenophon (430–354 BC) Greek historian. *Anabasis*, IV:7

SEASIDE

See also sea

1 The Walrus and the Carpenter
Were walking close at hand;
They wept like anything to see
Such quantities of sand:
'If this were only cleared away,'
They said, 'it *would* be grand!'

Lewis Carroll (Charles Lutwidge Dodgson; 1832–98) British writer. *Through the Looking-Glass*, Ch. 4

2 It is the drawback of all sea-side places that half the landscape is unavailable for purposes of human locomotion, being covered by useless water.

Norman Douglas (1868–1952) British novelist. *Alone*, 'Mentone'

3 I do Like to be Beside the Seaside.

John A. Glover-Kind (19th century) US songwriter. Song title

SEASONS

See also months

1 Sumer is icumen in,
Lhude sing cuccu!
Groweth sed, and bloweth med,
And springth the wude nu.

Anonymous *Cuckoo Song*

2 Many human beings say that they enjoy the winter, but what they really enjoy is feeling proof against it.

Richard Adams (1920–) British novelist. *Watership Down*, Ch. 50

3 All the live murmur of a summer's day.

Matthew Arnold (1882–88) British poet and critic. *The Scholar Gipsy*

4 It is time for the destruction of error.
The chairs are being brought in from the garden.

The summer talk stopped on that savage coast
Before the storms.

W. H. Auden (1907–73) British poet. *It is time*

5 My beloved spake, and said unto me, Rise up, my love, my fair one, and come away. For, lo, the winter is past, the rain is over and gone;
The flowers appear on the earth; the time of the singing of birds is come, and the voice of the turtle is heard in our land.

Bible: Song of Solomon 2:10–12

6 Now Spring, sweet laxative of Georgian strains,
Quickens the ink in literary veins,
The Stately Homes of England ope their doors
To piping Nancy-boys and Crashing Bores.

Roy Campbell (1901–57) South African poet. *The Georgiad*

7 Summer has set in with its usual severity.

Samuel Taylor Coleridge (1772–1834) British poet. Quoted in Lamb's letter to V. Novello, 9 May 1826

8 Summer afternoon – summer afternoon; to me those have always been the two most beautiful words in the English language.

Henry James (1843–1916) US novelist. *A Backward Glance* (Edith Wharton), Ch. 10

9 St Agnes Eve – Ah, bitter chill it was!
The owl, for all his feathers, was a-cold;
The hare limp'd trembling through the frozen grass,
And silent was the flock in woolly fold.

John Keats (1795–1821) British poet. *The Eve of Saint Agnes*, I

10 Four seasons fill the measure of the year;
There are four seasons in the mind of men.

John Keats *Four Seasons*

11 Where are the songs of Spring? Ay, where are they?

John Keats *To Autumn*

12 Season of mists and mellow fruitfulness,
Close bosom-friend of the maturing sun;
Conspiring with him how to load and bless
With fruit the vines that round the thatch-eaves run.

John Keats *To Autumn*

13 No one thinks of winter when the grass is green!

Rudyard Kipling (1865–1936) Indian-born British writer. *A St Helena Lullaby*

14 In a somer season, when soft was the sonne.

William Langland (c. 1330–c. 1400) English poet. *The Vision of Piers Plowman*, Prologue

15 Russia has two generals in whom she can confide – Generals Janvier and Février.

Nicholas I (1796–1855) Tsar of Russia. Referring to the Russian winter. Nicholas himself succumbed to a February cold in 1855 – the subject of the famous *Punch* Cartoon, 'General Février turned traitor', 10 Mar 1855. Attrib.

16 Winter is icummen in,
Lhude sing Goddamm,
Raineth drop and staineth slop
And how the wind doth ramm!
Sing: Goddamm.

Ezra Pound (1885–1972) US poet. *Ancient Music*

17 Spring has returned. The earth is like a child that knows poems.

Rainer Maria Rilke (1875–1926) Austrian poet. *Die Sonette an Orpheus*, I, 21

18 In the bleak mid-winter
Frosty wind made moan,
Earth stood hard as iron,
Water like a stone;
Snow had fallen, snow on snow,
Snow on snow,
In the bleak mid-winter,
Long ago.

Christina Rossetti (1830–74) British poet. *Mid-Winter*

19 The country habit has me by the heart,
For he's bewitched for ever who has seen,
Not with his eyes but with his vision, Spring
Flow down the woods and stipple leaves with sun.

Vita Sackville-West (Victoria Sackville-West; 1892–1962) British poet and novelist. *The Land*, 'Winter'

20 When icicles hang by the wall,
And Dick the shepherd blows his nail,
And Tom bears logs into the hall,
And milk comes frozen home in pail,
When blood is nipp'd, and ways be foul,
Then nightly sings the staring owl:
'Tu-who;
Tu-whit, Tu-who' – A merry note.
While greasy Joan doth keel the pot.

William Shakespeare (1564–1616) English dramatist. *Love's Labour's Lost*, V:2

21 If Winter comes, can Spring be far behind?

Percy Bysshe Shelley (1792–1822) British poet. *Ode to the West Wind*

22 When the hounds of spring are on winter's traces,
The mother of months in meadow or plain
Fills the shadows and windy places
With lisp of leaves and ripple of rain…

Algernon Charles Swinburne (1837–1909) British poet. *Atlanta in Calydon*

23 The moans of doves in immemorial elms,
And murmuring of innumerable bees.

Alfred, Lord Tennyson (1809–92) British poet. *The Princess*, VII

24 In the Spring a young man's fancy lightly turns to thoughts of love.

Alfred, Lord Tennyson *Locksley Hall*

25 It is a winter's tale
That the snow blind twilight ferries over the lakes
And floating fields from the farm in the cup of the vales.

Dylan Thomas (1914–53) Welsh poet. *A Winter's Tale*

26 Spring is come home with her world-wandering feet.
And all the things are made young

with young desires.

Francis Thompson (1859–1907) British poet. *The Night of Forebeing*, 'Ode to Easter'

27 The comic almanacs give us dreadful pictures of January and February; but, in truth, the months which should be made to look gloomy in England are March and April. Let no man boast himself that he has got through the perils of winter till at least the seventh of May.

Anthony Trollope (1815–82) British novelist. *Doctor Thorne*, Ch. 47

28 Like an army defeated
The snow hath retreated.

William Wordsworth (1770–1850) British poet. *Written in March*

SECRECY

See also gossip

1 Only the nose knows
Where the nose goes
When the door close.

Muhammad Ali (Cassius Clay; 1942–) US boxer. When asked whether a boxer should have sex before a big fight. Remark, reported by Al Silverman

2 I have seldom spoken with greater regret, for my lips are not yet unsealed. Were these troubles over I would make a case, and I guarantee that not a man would go into the Lobby against us.

Stanley Baldwin (1867–1947) British statesman. Referring to the Abyssinian crisis; usually misquoted as 'My lips are sealed'. Speech, House of Commons, 10 Dec 1935

3 Curse not the king, no not in thy thought; and curse not the rich in thy bedchamber: for a bird of the air shall carry the voice, and that which hath wings shall tell the matter.

Bible: Ecclesiastes 10:20

4 If thou hast heard a word, let it die with thee; and be bold, it will not burst thee.

Bible: Ecclesiasticus 19:10

5 Stolen waters are sweet, and bread eaten in secret is pleasant.

Bible: Proverbs 9:17

6 Mum's the word.

George Colman, the Younger (1762–1836) British dramatist. *The Battle of Hexham*, II:1

7 O fie miss, you must not kiss and tell.

William Congreve (1670–1729) British Restoration dramatist. *Love for Love*, II:10

8 I know that's a secret, for it's whispered every where.

William Congreve *Love for Love*, III:3

9 Three may keep a secret, if two of them are dead.

Benjamin Franklin (1706–90) US scientist and statesman. *Poor Richard's Almanack*

10 It is a secret in the Oxford sense: you may tell it to only one person at a time.

Oliver Franks (1905–92) British philosopher and administrator. *Sunday Telegraph*, 30 Jan 1977

SELF

See also self-confidence, etc.

1 Every man is his own worst enemy.

Proverb

2 God helps them that help themselves.

Proverb

3 He helps little that helps not himself.

Proverb

4 He travels fastest who travels alone.

Proverb

5 Lord, deliver me from myself.

Thomas Browne (1605–82) English physician and writer. *Religio Medici*, Pt. II

6 I have always disliked myself at any given moment; the total of such moments is my life.

Cyril Connolly (1903–74) British journalist. *Enemies of Promise*, Ch. 18

7 But I do nothing upon myself, and yet I am mine own Executioner.

John Donne (1573–1631) English poet. *Devotions*, 12

8 We never remark any passion or principle in others, of which, in some degree or other, we may not find a parallel in ourselves.

David Hume (1711–76) Scottish philosopher. *A Treatise of Human Nature*

9 Whenever I look inside myself I am afraid.

Cyril Joad (1891–1953) British writer and broadcaster. *The Observer*, 'Sayings of the Week', 8 Nov 1942

10 All censure of a man's self is oblique praise. It is in order to shew how much he can spare.

Samuel Johnson (1709–84) British lexicographer. *Life of Johnson* (J. Boswell), Vol. III

11 One should examine oneself for a very long time before thinking of condemning others.

Molière (Jean Baptiste Poquelin; 1622–73) French dramatist. *Le Misanthrope*, III:4

12 Self-love seems so often unrequited.

Anthony Powell (1905–) British novelist. *The Acceptance World*

13 Do not love your neighbour as yourself. If you are on good terms with yourself it is an impertinence; if on bad, an injury.

George Bernard Shaw (1856–1950) Irish dramatist and critic. *Man and Superman*, 'Maxims for Revolutionists'

14 The unexamined life is not worth living.

Socrates (469–399 BC) Athenian philosopher. *Apology* (Plato)

15 I am always with myself, and it is I

who am my tormentor.

Leo Tolstoy (1828–1910) Russian writer. *Memoirs of a Madman*

16 Meanwhile you will write an essay on 'self-indulgence'. There will be a prize of half a crown for the longest essay, irrespective of any possible merit.

Evelyn Waugh (1903–66) British novelist. *Decline and Fall*, Pt. I, Ch. 5

17 I can't quite explain it, but I don't believe one can ever be unhappy for long provided one does just exactly what one wants to and when one wants to.

Evelyn Waugh *Decline and Fall*, Pt. I, Ch. 5

18 I celebrate myself, and sing myself,
And what I assume you shall assume.

Walt Whitman (1819–92) US poet. *Song of Myself*, 1

19 Behold, I do not give lectures or a little charity,
When I give I give myself.

Walt Whitman *Song of Myself*, 40

20 I have said that the soul is not more than the body,
And I have said that the body is not more than the soul,
And nothing, but God, is greater to one than one's self is.

Walt Whitman *Song of Myself*, 48

21 Do I contradict myself?
Very well then I contradict myself,
(I am large, I contain multitudes).

Walt Whitman *Song of Myself*, 51

SELF-CONFIDENCE

See also shyness

1 Those who believe that they are exclusively in the right are generally those who achieve something.

Aldous Huxley (1894–1964) British novelist. *Proper Studies*

2 I can honestly say that I was never affected by the question of the success of an undertaking. If I felt it was the right thing to do, I was for it regardless of the possible outcome.

Golda Meir (1898–1978) Russian-born Israeli stateswoman. *Golda Meir: Woman with a Cause* (Marie Syrkin)

3 I wish I was as cocksure of anything as Tom Macaulay is of everything.

Lord Melbourne (1779–1848) British statesman. *Preface to Lord Melbourne's Papers* (Earl Cowper)

4 'Tis an ill cook that cannot lick his own fingers.

William Shakespeare (1564–1616) English dramatist. *Romeo and Juliet*, IV:2

5 'Are you not,' a Rugby master had asked him in discussing one of his essays, 'a little out of your depth here?' 'Perhaps, Sir,' was the confident reply, 'but I can swim.'

William Temple (1881–1944) British churchman. *William Temple* (F. A. Iremonger)

6 I am certain that we will win the election with a good majority. Not that I am ever over-confident.

Margaret Thatcher (1925–) British politician and prime minister. *Evening Standard*, 1987

7 If I ever felt inclined to be timid as I was going into a room full of people, I would say to myself, 'You're the cleverest member of one of the cleverest families in the cleverest class of the cleverest nation in the world, why should you be frightened?'

Beatrice Webb (1858–1943) British economist and writer. *Portraits from Memory* (Bertrand Russell), 'Sidney and Beatrice Webb'

SELF-CONTROL

1 He that is slow to anger is better than the mighty; and he that ruleth his spirit than he that taketh a city.

Bible: Proverbs 16:32

2 No one who cannot limit himself has ever been able to write.

Nicolas Boileau (1636–1711) French writer. *L'Art poétique*, I

3 The highest possible stage in moral culture is when we recognize that we ought to control our thoughts.

Charles Darwin (1809–82) British life scientist. *Descent of Man*, Ch. 4

4 When things are steep, remember to stay level-headed.

Horace (Quintus Horatius Flaccus; 65–8 BC) Roman poet. *Odes*, II

5 If you can keep your head when all about you
Are losing theirs and blaming it on you.

Rudyard Kipling (1865–1936) Indian-born British writer. *If*

6 He that would govern others, first should be
The master of himself.

Philip Massinger (1583–1640) English dramatist. *The Bondman*, I

7 Never lose your temper with the Press or the public is a major rule of political life.

Christabel Pankhurst (1880–1958) British suffragette. *Unshackled*

SELF-DENIAL

See also abstinence, selflessness

1 Self-denial is not a virtue; it is only the effect of prudence on rascality.

George Bernard Shaw (1856–1950) Irish dramatist and critic. *Man and Superman*, 'Maxims for Revolutionists'

2 Thy need is yet greater than mine.

Philip Sidney (1554–86) English poet and courtier. Giving his own water bottle to a humble wounded soldier after he had himself been wounded. Attrib.

SELF-INTEREST

See also parochialism, selfishness

1 Every man for himself, and the devil take the hindmost.

Proverb

2 The land self-interest groans from shore to shore,
For fear that plenty should attain the poor.

Lord Byron (1788–1824) British poet. *The Age of Bronze*, XIV

3 Anyone informed that the universe is expanding and contracting in pulsations of eighty billion years has a right to ask, 'What's in it for me?'

Peter De Vries (1910–93) US novelist. *The Glory of the Hummingbird*, Ch. 1

4 The least pain in our little finger gives us more concern and uneasiness than the destruction of millions of our fellow-beings.

William Hazlitt (1778–1830) British essayist. *American Literature*, 'Dr Channing'

5 It is difficult to love mankind unless one has a reasonable private income and when one has a reasonable private income one has better things to do than loving mankind.

Hugh Kingsmill (1889–1949) British writer. *God's Apology* (R. Ingrams)

6 Self-interest speaks all sorts of tongues, and plays all sorts of roles, even that of disinterestedness.

Duc de la Rochefoucauld (1613–80) French writer. *Maximes*, 39

SELFISHNESS

See also egotism, self-interest

1 I have been a selfish being all my life, in practice, though not in principle.

Jane Austen (1775–1817) British novelist. *Pride and Prejudice*, Ch. 58

2 And this the burthen of his song,
For ever us'd to be,
I care for nobody, not I,
If no one cares for me.

Isaac Bickerstaffe (c. 1735–c. 1812) Irish dramatist. *Love in a Village*, I

3 It's 'Damn you, Jack – I'm all right!' with you chaps.

David Bone (1874–1959) British sea captain and writer. *The Brassbounder*, Ch. 3

4 The proud, the cold untroubled heart of stone,
That never mused on sorrow but its own.

Thomas Campbell (1777–1844) British poet. *Pleasures of Hope*, I

SELF-KNOWLEDGE

1 Resolve to be thyself: and know, that he
Who finds himself, loses his misery.

Matthew Arnold (1822–88) British poet and critic. *Self-Dependence*

2 We confess our bad qualities to others out of fear of appearing naive or ridiculous by not being aware of them.

Gerald Brenan (Edward Fitzgerald Brenan; 1894–1987) British writer. *Thoughts in a Dry Season*

3 'I know myself,' he cried, 'but that is all.'

F. Scott Fitzgerald (1896–1940) US novelist. *This Side of Paradise*, Bk. II, Ch. 5

4 I do not know myself, and God forbid that I should.

Goethe (1749–1832) German poet and dramatist. *Conversations with Eckermann*, 10 Apr 1829

5 Know then thyself, presume not God to scan,
The proper study of Mankind is Man.

Alexander Pope (1688–1744) British poet. *An Essay on Man*, II

6 That true self-love and social are the same;
That virtue only makes our bliss below;
And all our knowledge is, ourselves to know.

Alexander Pope *An Essay on Man*, IV

SELFLESSNESS

See also charity, self-denial

1 The way to get things done is not to mind who gets the credit of doing them.

Benjamin Jowett (1817–93) British theologian. Attrib.

2 To give and not to count the cost;
To fight and not to heed the wounds;
To toil and not to seek for rest;
To labour and not ask for any reward
Save that of knowing that we do Thy will.

St Ignatius Loyola (1491–1556) Spanish priest. *Prayer for Generosity*

3 There is nothing in Christianity or Buddhism that quite matches the sympathetic unselfishness of an oyster.

Saki (Hector Hugh Munro; 1870–1916) British writer. *Chronicles of Clovis*

SELF-MADE MEN

1 I know he is, and he adores his maker.

Benjamin Disraeli (1804–81) British statesman. Replying to a remark made in defence of John Bright that he was a self-made man. *The Fine Art of Political Wit* (L. Harris)

2 He was a self-made man who owed his

lack of success to nobody.
Joseph Heller (1923–) US novelist. *Catch-22*, Ch. 3

3 A self-made man is one who believes in luck and sends his son to Oxford.
Christina Stead (1902–83) Australian novelist. *House of All Nations*, 'Credo'

SELF-PRESERVATION

See also survival

1 Look after number one.
Proverb

2 He that fights and runs away
May live to fight another day.
Anonymous *Musarum Deliciae*

3 This animal is very bad; when attacked it defends itself.
Anonymous *La Ménagerie* (P. K. Théodore), 1828

4 In good King Charles's golden days,
When loyalty no harm meant,
A zealous High Churchman was I,
And so I got preferment.

And this is law, that I'll maintain,
Unto my dying day, Sir,
That whatsoever King shall reign,
I'll be the Vicar of Bray, Sir.
Anonymous *The Vicar of Bray*

5 There was only one catch and that was Catch-22, which specified that a concern for one's own safety in the face of dangers that were real and immediate was the process of a rational mind.
Joseph Heller (1923–) US novelist. *Catch-22*, Ch. 5

6 If a madman were to come into this room with a stick in his hand, no doubt we should pity the state of his mind; but our primary consideration would be to take care of ourselves. We should knock him down first, and pity him afterwards.
Samuel Johnson (1709–84) British lexicographer. *Life of Johnson* (J. Boswell), Vol. III

7 We intend to remain alive. Our neighbors want to see us dead. This is not a question that leaves much room for compromise.
Golda Meir (1898–1978) Russian-born Israeli stateswoman. *Reader's Digest* (July 1971), 'The Indestructible Golda Meir'

8 The better part of valour is discretion; in the which better part I have saved my life.
William Shakespeare (1564–1616) English dramatist. *Henry IV, Part One*, V:4

9 *J'ai vécu.*
I survived.
Abbé de Sieyès (1748–1836) French churchman. Replying to an enquiry concerning what he had done during the Terror. *Dictionnaire Encyclopédique* (E. Guérard)

10 Greater love hath no man than this, that he lay down his friends for his life.
Jeremy Thorpe (1929–) British politician. After Macmillan's 1962 Cabinet reshuffle. *The Pendulum Years* (Bernard Levin), Ch. 12

11 Scheherazade is the classical example of a woman saving her head by using it.
Esme Wynne-Tyson (1898–) British writer. Attrib.

SELF-RELIANCE

See also independence

1 If you want a thing well done, do it yourself.
Proverb

2 The gods help them that help themselves.
Aesop (6th century BC) Reputed Greek writer of fables. *Fables*, 'Hercules and the Waggoner'

3 They do most by Books, who could do much without them, and he that chiefly owes himself unto himself, is the substantial Man.
Thomas Browne (1605–82) English physician and writer. *Christian Morals*, Pt. II

4 I'm not very good at ordinary socialising. I prefer to be thinking or reading.
A(ntonia) S(usan) Byatt (1936–) British novelist. *The Sunday Times*, 21 Oct 1990

5 Let the boy win his spurs.
Edward III (1312–77) King of England. Replying to a suggestion that he should send reinforcements to his son, the Black Prince, during the Battle of Crécy, 1346. Attrib.

6 The first rule in opera is the first rule in life: see to everything yourself.
Nellie Melba (Helen Porter Mitchell; 1861–1931) Australian soprano. *Melodies and Memories*

7 The greatest thing in the world is to know how to be self-sufficient.
Michel de Montaigne (1533–92) French essayist. *Essais*, I

8 Our remedies oft in ourselves do lie,
Which we ascribe to heaven.
William Shakespeare (1564–1616) English dramatist. *All's Well that Ends Well*, I:1

SELF-RESPECT

See also pride, respect

1 It is better to die on your feet than to live on your knees.
Dolores Ibarruri (1895–1989) Spanish politician. Speech, Paris, 1936

2 As for conceit, what man will do any good who is not conceited? Nobody holds a good opinion of a man who has a low opinion of himself.
Anthony Trollope (1815–82) British novelist. *Orley Farm*, Ch. 22

3 And, above all things, never think that you're not good enough yourself. A man should never think that. My belief is that in life people will take you very much at your own reckoning.
Anthony Trollope *The Small House at Allington*, Ch. 32

4 When people do not respect us we are sharply offended; yet deep down in his heart no man much respects himself.

Mark Twain (Samuel Langhorne Clemens; 1835–1910) US writer. *Notebooks*

SENSATION

1 O for a life of sensations rather than of thoughts!

John Keats (1795–1821) British poet. Letter to Benjamin Bailey, 22 Nov 1817

2 'The story is like the wind', the Bushman prisoner said. 'It comes from a far off place, and we feel it.'

Laurens Van der Post (1906–96) South African novelist. *A Story Like the Wind*

SENTIMENTALITY

See also emotion

1 They had been corrupted by money, and he had been corrupted by sentiment. Sentiment was the more dangerous, because you couldn't name its price. A man open to bribes was to be relied upon below a certain figure, but sentiment might uncoil in the heart at a name, a photograph, even a smell remembered.

Graham Greene (1904–91) British novelist. *The Heart of the Matter*

2 Sentimentality is a superstructure covering brutality.

Carl Gustav Jung (1875–1961) Swiss psychoanalyst. *Reflections*

3 One may not regard the world as a sort of metaphysical brothel for emotions.

Arthur Koestler (1905–83) Hungarian-born British writer. *Darkness at Noon*, 'The Second Hearing'

4 Sentimentality is only sentiment that rubs you up the wrong way.

W. Somerset Maugham (1874–1965) British novelist. *A Writer's Notebook*

5 She likes stories that make her cry – I think we all do, it's so nice to feel sad when you've nothing particular to be sad about.

Annie Sullivan (1866–1936) US teacher of the handicapped. Referring to Helen Keller. Letter, 12 Dec 1887

SEPARATION

See also absence, parting

1 My Bonnie lies over the ocean,
My Bonnie lies over the sea,
My Bonnie lies over the ocean,
Oh, bring back my Bonnie to me.

Anonymous *My Bonnie*

2 If I should meet thee
After long years,
How should I greet thee? –
With silence and tears.

Lord Byron (1788–1824) British poet. *When we two parted*

3 Absence from whom we love is worse than death.

William Cowper (1731–1800) British poet. *'Hope, like the Short-lived Ray'*

4 As it will be the right of all, so it will be the duty of some, definitely to prepare for a separation, amicably if they can, violently if they must.

Josiah Quincy (1772–1864) US statesman. *Abridgement of Debates of Congress*, Vol. IV, 14 Jan 1811

5 Every parting gives a foretaste of death; every coming together again a foretaste of the resurrection.

Arthur Schopenhauer (1788–1860) German philosopher. *Gedanken über vielerlei Gegenstände*, XXVI

6 I do desire we may be better strangers.

William Shakespeare (1564–1616) English dramatist. *As You Like It*, III:2

SERIOUSNESS

1 Angels can fly because they take themselves lightly.

G. K. Chesterton (1874–1936) British writer. *Orthodoxy*, Ch. 7

2 Though this may be play to you, 'tis death to us.

Roger L'Estrange (1616–1704) English journalist and writer. *Aesop's Fables*, 398

3 You must not think me necessarily foolish because I am facetious, nor will I consider you necessarily wise because you are grave.

Sydney Smith (1771–1845) British clergyman and essayist. Letter to Bishop Blomfield

4 He rose by gravity; I sank by levity.

Sydney Smith Comparing his career with that of his brother, Robert Percy Smith. Attrib.

SERMONS

See also brevity, speeches, verbosity

1 They are written as if sin were to be taken out of man like Eve out of Adam – by putting him to sleep.

Sydney Smith (1771–1845) British clergyman and essayist. Referring to boring sermons. *Anecdotes of the Clergy* (J. Larwood)

2 I never quite forgave Mahaffy for getting himself suspended from preaching in the College Chapel. Ever since his sermons were discontinued, I suffer from insomnia in church.

George Tyrrell (1861–1909) Irish Catholic theologian. *As I Was Going Down Sackville Street* (Oliver St John Gogarty), Ch. 25

3 Yes, about ten minutes.

Duke of Wellington (1769–1852) British general and

statesman. Responding to a vicar's query as to whether there was anything he would like his forthcoming sermon to be about. Attrib.

SERVICE

See also help

1 His lord said unto him, Well done, thou good and faithful servant: thou hast been faithful over a few things, I will make thee ruler over many things: enter thou into the joy of thy lord.

Bible: Matthew 25:21

2 Oh that I were an orange-tree,
That busy plant!
Then I should ever laden be,
And never want
Some fruit for Him that dressed me.

George Herbert (1593–1633) English poet. *Employment*

3 All English shop assistants are Miltonists. All Miltonists firmly believe that 'they serve who only stand and wait.'

George Mikes (1912–87) Hungarian-born British writer. *How to be Inimitable*

4 God doth not need
Either man's work or his own gifts. Who best
Bear his mild yoke, they serve him best: his state
Is kingly; thousands at his bidding speed,
And post o'er land and ocean without rest;
They also serve who only stand and wait.

John Milton (1608–74) English poet. *Sonnet*: 'On his Blindness'

5 Small service is true service, while it lasts.

William Wordsworth (1770–1850) British poet. *To a Child, Written in her Album*

SERVILITY

See also flattery, humility

1 Fine words and an insinuating appearance are seldom associated with true virtue.

Confucius (K'ung Fu-tzu; 551–479 BC) Chinese philosopher. *Analects*

2 I am well aware that I am the 'umblest person going....My mother is likewise a very 'umble person. We live in a numble abode.

Charles Dickens (1812–70) British novelist. Said by Uriah Heep. *David Copperfield*, Ch. 16

3 Uriah, with his long hands slowly twining over one another, made a ghastly writhe from the waist upwards.

Charles Dickens *David Copperfield*, Ch. 17

4 A pious man is one who would be an atheist if the king were.

Jean de La Bruyère (1645–96) French satirist. *Les Caractères*

5 Wit that can creep, and pride that
licks the dust.

Alexander Pope (1688–1744) British poet. *Epistle to Dr. Arbuthnot*

6 You know that nobody is strongminded around a President...it is always: 'yes sir', 'no sir' (the 'no sir' comes when he asks whether you're dissatisfied).

George Edward Reedy (1917–) US government official. *The White House* (ed. R. Gordon Hoxie)

7 Whenever he met a great man he grovelled before him, and my-lorded him as only a free-born Briton can do.

William Makepeace Thackeray (1811–63) British novelist. *Vanity Fair*, Ch. 13

SEX

See also abstinence, adultery, animalism, contraception, debauchery, illegitimacy, lust, pornography, promiscuity, prudery, purity, sexes

1 Is sex dirty? Only if it's done right.

Woody Allen (Allen Stewart Konigsberg; 1935–) US film actor. *All You've Ever Wanted to Know About Sex*

2 It was the most fun I ever had without laughing.

Woody Allen *Annie Hall*

3 Don't knock it, it's sex with someone you love.

Woody Allen Referring to masturbation. *Annie Hall*

4 She sighed, she cried, she damned near died: she said 'What shall I do?'
So I took her into bed and covered up her head
Just to save her from the foggy, foggy dew.

Anonymous *Weaver's Song*

5 It is called in our schools 'beastliness', and this is about the best name for it...should it become a habit it quickly destroys both health and spirits; he becomes feeble in body and mind, and often ends in a lunatic asylum.

Robert Baden-Powell (1857–1941) British soldier and founder of the Boy Scouts. Referring to masturbation. *Scouting for Boys*

6 The great and terrible step was taken. What else could you expect from a girl so expectant? 'Sex,' said Frank Harris, 'is the gateway to life.' So I went through the gateway in an upper room in the Cafe Royal.

Enid Bagnold (1889–1981) British playwright. *Enid Bagnold's Autobiography*

7 Money, it turned out, was exactly like sex, you thought of nothing else if you didn't have it and thought of other things if you did.

James Baldwin (1924–87) US writer. *Nobody Knows My Name*

8 If God had meant us to have group sex, I guess he'd have given us all more organs.

Malcolm Bradbury (1932–) British academic and novelist. *Who Do You Think You Are?*, 'A Very Hospitable Person'

9 It doesn't matter what you do in the bedroom

as long as you don't do it in the street and frighten the horses.

Mrs Patrick Campbell (Beatrice Stella Tanner; 1865–1940) British actress. *The Duchess of Jermyn Street* (Daphne Fielding), Ch. 2

10 The Summer hath his joys,
And Winter his delights.
Though Love and all his pleasures are but toys,
They shorten tedious nights.

Thomas Campion (1567–1620) English poet. *Now Winter Nights Enlarge*

11 I'll wager you that in 10 years it will be fashionable again to be a virgin.

Barbara Cartland (1902–) British romantic novelist. *The Observer*, 'Sayings of the Week', 20 June 1976

12 I answer 20 000 letters a year and so many couples are having problems because they are not getting the right proteins and vitamins.

Barbara Cartland *The Observer*, 'Sayings of the Week', 31 Aug 1986

13 I said 10 years ago that in 10 years time it would be smart to be a virgin. Now everyone is back to virgins again.

Barbara Cartland *The Observer*, 'Sayings of the Week', 12 July 1987

14 Have you not as yet observed that pleasure, which is undeniably the sole motive force behind the union of the sexes, is nevertheless not enough to form a bond between them? And that, if it is preceded by desire which impels, it is succeeded by disgust which repels? That is a law of nature which love alone can alter.

Pierre Choderlos de Laclos (1741–1803) French novelist. *Les Liaisons Dangereuses*, Letter 131

15 She gave me a smile I could feel in my hip pocket.

Raymond Chandler (1888–1959) US novelist. *Farewell, My Lovely*, Ch. 18

16 When she raises her eyelids it's as if she were taking off all her clothes.

Colette (1873–1954) French novelist. *Claudine and Annie*

17 No more about sex, it's too boring.

Lawrence Durrell (1912–90) British novelist. *Tunc*

18 We're all wankers underneath...Once we acknowledge everyone's a wanker it'll be easy – suddenly all authority figures disappear.

Ben Elton (1959–) British comedian. BBC TV programme, *The Man from Auntie*, 1990

19 He in a few minutes ravished this fair creature, or at least would have ravished her, if she had not, by a timely compliance, prevented him.

Henry Fielding (1707–54) British novelist. *Jonathan Wild*, Bk. III, Ch. 7

20 Older women are best because they always think they may be doing it for the last time.

Ian Fleming (1908–64) British journalist and author. *Life of Ian Fleming* (John Pearson)

21 Personally I know nothing about sex because I've always been married.

Zsa Zsa Gabor (1919–) Hungarian-born US film star. *The Observer*, 'Sayings of the Week', 16 Aug 1987

22 I think God is a callous bitch not making me a lesbian. I'm deeply disappointed by my sexual interest in men.

Diamanda Galas (1955–) US singer. *The Independent*, 27 Oct 1994

23 Prostitution gives her an opportunity to meet people. It provides fresh air and wholesome exercise, and it keeps her out of trouble.

Joseph Heller (1923–) US novelist. *Catch-22*, Ch. 33

24 But did thee feel the earth move?

Ernest Hemingway (1899–1961) US novelist. *For Whom the Bell Tolls*, Ch. 13

25 My life with girls has ended, though till lately I was up to it and soldiered on not ingloriously; now on this wall will hang my weapons and my lyre, discharged from the war.

Horace (Quintus Horatius Flaccus; 65–8 BC) Roman poet. *Odes*, III

26 People will insist...on treating the *mons Veneris* as though it were Mount Everest.

Aldous Huxley (1894–1964) British novelist. *Eyeless in Gaza*, Ch. 30

27 A million million spermatozoa,
All of them alive:
Out of their cataclysm but one poor Noah
Dare hope to survive.

Aldous Huxley *Fifth Philosopher's Song*

28 'Bed,' as the Italian proverb succinctly puts it, 'is the poor man's opera.'

Aldous Huxley *Heaven and Hell*

29 Sexual intercourse began
In nineteen sixty-three
(Which was rather late for me) –
Between the end of the *Chatterley* ban
And the Beatles' first LP.

Philip Larkin (1922–85) British poet. *High Windows*, 'Annus Mirabilis'

30 When Eve ate this particular apple, she became aware of her own womanhood, mentally. And mentally she began to experiment with it. She has been experimenting ever since. So has man. To the rage and horror of both of them.

D. H. Lawrence (1885–1930) British novelist. *Fantasia of the Unconscious*, Ch. 7

31 Making love is the sovereign remedy for anguish.

Frédérick Leboyer (1918–) French obstetrician. *Birth without Violence*

32 There was sex of course, but although both of them were extremely interested in sex, and enjoyed nothing better than discussing it, neither of them, if the truth be told, was quite so interested in actually having it, or at any rate in having it very frequently.

David Lodge (1935–) British author. *Nice Work*, I

33 No sex without responsibility.

Lord Longford (1905–) British politician and social reformer. *The Observer*, 'Sayings of the Week', 3 May 1954

34 The Duke returned from the wars today and did pleasure me in his top-boots.

Sarah, Duchess of Marlborough (1660–1744) Wife of John Churchill, 1st Duke of Marlborough. Attributed to her in various forms; a more ambitious version goes '...pleasure me three times in his top-boots'.

35 FRIAR BARNARDINE. Thou hast committed –
BARABAS. Fornication: but that was in another country;
And beside the wench is dead.

Christopher Marlowe (1564–93) English dramatist. *The Jew of Malta*, IV:1

36 Whoever named it necking was a poor judge of anatomy.

Groucho Marx (Julius Marx; 1895–1977) US comedian. Attrib.

37 If sex is such a natural phenomenon, how come there are so many books on how to?

Bette Midler (1944–) US actress and comedienne.

38 Sex is one of the nine reasons for reincarnation...The other eight are unimportant.

Henry Miller (1891–1980) US novelist. *Big Sur and the Oranges of Hieronymus Bosch*

39 There was a little girl
Who had a little curl
Right in the middle of her forehead,
When she was good she was very very good
And when she was bad she was very very popular.

Max Miller (Harold Sargent; 1895–1963) British music-hall comedian. *The Max Miller Blue Book*

40 The daughter-in-law of Pythagoras said that a woman who goes to bed with a man ought to lay aside her modesty with her skirt, and put it on again with her petticoat.

Michel de Montaigne (1533–92) French essayist. *Essais*, I

41 Why do they put the Gideon Bibles only in the bedrooms where it's usually too late?

Christopher Darlington Morley (1890–1957) US writer. *Quotations for Speakers and Writers*

42 The orgasm has replaced the Cross as the focus of longing and the image of fulfilment.

Malcolm Muggeridge (1903–90) British writer. *The Most of Malcolm Muggeridge*, 'Down with Sex'

43 It has to be admitted that we English have sex on the brain, which is a very unsatisfactory place to have it.

Malcolm Muggeridge *The Observer*, 'Sayings of the Decade', 1964

44 It's all any reasonable child can expect if the dad is present at the conception.

Joe Orton (1933–67) British dramatist. *Entertaining Mr Sloane*, III

45 If all the young ladies who attended the Yale promenade dance were laid end to end, no one would be the least surprised.

Dorothy Parker (1893–1967) US writer. *While Rome Burns* (Alexander Woollcott)

46 I know it does make people happy but to me it is just like having a cup of tea.

Cynthia Payne (1934–) London housewife After her acquittal on a charge of controlling prostitutes in a famous 'sex-for-luncheon-vouchers' case, 8 Nov 1987

47 Love is not the dying moan of a distant violin – it's the triumphant twang of a bedspring.

S. J. Perelman (1904–79) US humorous writer. *Quotations for Speakers and Writers* (A. Andrews)

48 On a sofa upholstered in panther skin
Mona did researches in original sin.

William Plomer (1903–73) South African poet and novelist. *Mews Flat Mona*

49 A PUSHING LADY. What are your views on love?
MME LEROI. Love? I make it constantly but I never talk about it.

Marcel Proust (1871–1922) French novelist. *À la recherche du temps perdu: Le Côté de Guermantes*

50 The Christian view of sex is that it is, indeed, a form of holy communion.

John Robinson (1919–83) Bishop of Woolwich. Giving evidence in the prosecution of Penguin Books for publishing *Lady Chatterly's Lover*.

51 Sex is something I really don't understand too hot. You never know *where* the hell you are. I keep making up these sex rules for myself, and then I break them right away.

J. D. Salinger (1919–) US novelist. *The Catcher in the Rye*, Ch. 9

52 Is it not strange that desire should so many years outlive performance?

William Shakespeare (1564–1616) English dramatist. *Henry IV, Part Two*, II:4

53 Lechery, lechery! Still wars and lechery!
Nothing else holds fashion.

William Shakespeare *Troilus and Cressida*, V:2

54 Someone asked Sophocles, 'How do you feel now about sex? Are you still able to have a woman?' He replied, 'Hush, man; most gladly indeed am I rid of it all, as though I had escaped from a mad and savage master.'

Sophocles (c. 496–406 BC) Greek dramatist. *Republic* (Plato), Bk. I

55 Masturbation: the primary sexual activity of mankind. In the nineteenth century it was a disease; in the twentieth, it's a cure.

Thomas Szasz (1920–) US psychiatrist. *The Second Sin*

56 Traditionally, sex has been a very private, secretive activity. Herein perhaps lies its powerful force for uniting people in a strong bond. As we make sex less secretive, we may rob it of its power to hold men and women together.

Thomas Szasz *The Second Sin*

57 Chasing the naughty couples down the grassgreen gooseberried double bed of the wood.

Dylan Thomas (1914–53) Welsh poet. *Under Milk Wood*

58 Old Nat Burge sat...He was...watching the moon come up lazily out of the old cemetery in which nine of his daughters were lying, and only two of them were dead.

James Thurber (1894–1961) US humorist. *Let Your Mind Alone*, 'Bateman Comes Home'

59 Surely you don't mean by unartificial insemination!

James Thurber On being accosted at a party by a drunk woman who claimed she would like to have a baby by him. Attrib.

60 Familiarity breeds contempt – and children.

Mark Twain (Samuel Langhorne Clemens; 1835–1910) US writer. *Notebooks*

61 Sex is the biggest nothing of all time.

Andy Warhol (Andrew Warhola; 1926–87) US pop artist. *Halliwell's Filmgoer's and Video Viewer's Companion*

62 All this fuss about sleeping together. For physical pleasure I'd sooner go to my dentist any day.

Evelyn Waugh (1903–66) British novelist. *Vile Bodies*, Ch. 6

63 When women go wrong, men go right after them.

Mae West (1892–1980) US actress. *The Wit and Wisdom of Mae West* (ed. J. Weintraub)

64 It's not the men in my life that count; it's the life in my men.

Mae West Attrib.

65 When I'm good I'm very good, but when I'm bad I'm better.

Mae West Attrib.

66 I shall not say why and how I became, at the age of fifteen, the mistress of the Earl of Craven.

Harriette Wilson (1789–1846) British writer and courtesan. *Memoirs*, Opening

67 A mistress should be like a little country retreat near the town, not to dwell in constantly, but only for a night and away.

William Wycherley (1640–1716) English dramatist. *The Country Wife*, I:1

SEXES

See also feminism, marriage, men, sex, woman's role, women

1 As men
Do walk a mile, women should talk an hour,
After supper. 'Tis their exercise.

Francis Beaumont (1584–1616) English dramatist. *Philaster*, II:4

2 And the man said, The woman whom thou gavest to be with me, she gave me of the tree, and I did eat.
And the Lord God said unto the woman, What is this that thou hast done? And the woman said, The serpent beguiled me, and I did eat.
And the Lord God said unto the serpent, Because thou hast done this, thou art cursed above all cattle, and above every beast of the field; upon thy belly shalt thou go, and dust shalt thou eat all the days of thy life:
And I will put enmity between thee and the woman, and between thy seed and her seed; it shall bruise thy head, and thou shalt bruise his heel.
Unto the woman he said, I will greatly multiply thy sorrow and thy conception; in sorrow thou shalt bring forth children; and thy desire shall be to thy husband, and he shall rule over thee.
And unto Adam he said, Because thou hast hearkened unto the voice of thy wife, and has eaten of the tree, of which I commanded thee, saying, Thou shalt not eat of it: cursed is the ground for thy sake; in sorrow shalt thou eat of it all the days of thy life.

Bible: Genesis 3:12–17

3 Mr. Darwin...has failed to hold definitely before his mind the principle that the difference of sex, whatever it may consist in, must itself be subject to natural selection and to evolution.

Antoinette Brown Blackwell (1825–1921) US feminist writer. *The Sexes Throughout Nature*

4 Man's love is of man's life a thing apart,
'Tis woman's whole existence.

Lord Byron (1788–1824) British poet. *Don Juan*, I

5 There is more difference within the sexes than between them.

Ivy Compton-Burnett (1892–1969) British novelist. *Mother and Son*

6 In the sex-war thoughtlessness is the weapon of the male, vindictiveness of the female.

Cyril Connolly (1903–74) British journalist. *The Unquiet Grave*

7 The average man is more interested in a woman who is interested in him than he is in a woman – any woman – with beautiful legs.

Marlene Dietrich (Maria Magdalene von Losch; 1901–92) German-born film star. News item, 13 Dec 1954

8 The reason that husbands and wives do not understand each other is because they belong to different sexes.

Dorothy Dix (Elizabeth Meriwether Gilmer; 1861–1951) US journalist and writer. News item

9 I don't think men and women were meant to live together. They are totally different animals.

Diana Dors (1931–84) British actress. Remark, May 1988

10 Where young boys plan for what they will achieve and attain, young girls plan for whom they will achieve and attain.

Charlotte Perkins Gilman (1860–1935) US writer. *Women and Economics*, Ch. 5

11 Man has his will, – but woman has her way.

Oliver Wendell Holmes (1809–94) US writer. *The Autocrat of the Breakfast Table*, Prologue

12 Boys will be boys –'
'And even that...wouldn't matter if we could only prevent girls from being girls.'

Anthony Hope (Anthony Hope Hawkins; 1863–1933) British novelist. *The Dolly Dialogues*

13 Christ called as his Apostles only men. He did this in a totally free and sovereign way.

John Paul II (Karol Wotjyla; 1920–) Polish pope. Speech, Sept 1988

14 For men must work, and women must weep,
And there's little to earn, and many to keep,
Though the harbour bar be moaning.

Charles Kingsley (1819–75) British writer. *The Three Fishers*

15 The silliest woman can manage a clever man; but it needs a very clever woman to manage a fool.

Rudyard Kipling (1865–1936) Indian-born British writer. *Plain Tales from the Hills*, 'Three and – an Extra'

16 Men are boring to women because there's only about 12 types of us, and they know all the keys. And they're bored by the fact we never escape our types.

Jack Nicholson (1937–) US actor. *The Observer*, 'Sayings of the Week', 21 Aug 1994

17 Perhaps at fourteen every boy should be in love with some ideal woman to put on a pedestal and worship. As he grows up, of course, he will put her on a pedestal the better to view her legs.

Barry Norman (1933–) British cinema critic and broadcaster. *The Listener*

18 The seldom female in a world of males!

Ruth Pitter (1897–1992) British poet. *The Kitten's Eclogue*, IV

19 Women have smaller brains than men.

Hojatolislam Rafsanjani Iranian politician. Remark, July 1986

20 I often want to cry. That is the only advantage women have over men – at least they can cry.

Jean Rhys (1894–1979) Dominican-born British novelist. *Good Morning, Midnight*, Pt. II

21 Woman's virtue is man's greatest invention.

Cornelia Otis Skinner (1901–79) US stage actress. Attrib.

22 Man is a creature who lives not upon bread alone, but principally by catchwords; and the little rift between the sexes is astonishingly widened by simply teaching one set of catchwords to the girls and another to the boys.

Robert Louis Stevenson (1850–94) Scottish writer. *Virginibus Puerisque*

23 Man is the hunter; woman is his game:
The sleek and shining creatures of the chase,
We hunt them for the beauty of their skins.

Alfred, Lord Tennyson (1809–92) British poet. *The Princess*, V

24 Man for the field and woman for the hearth:
Man for the sword and for the needle she:
Man with the head and woman with the heart:
Man to command and woman to obey;
All else confusion.

Alfred, Lord Tennyson *The Princess*, V

25 There are some meannesses which are too mean even for man – woman, lovely woman alone, can venture to commit them.

William Makepeace Thackeray (1811–63) British novelist. *A Shabby-Genteel Story*, Ch. 3

26 The War between Men and Women.

James Thurber (1894–1961) US humorist. Title of a series of cartoons

27 When a man confronts catastrophe on the road, he looks in his purse – but a woman looks in her mirror.

Margaret Turnbull (fl. 1920s–1942) US writer. *The Left Lady*

28 There is no essential sexuality. Maleness and femaleness are something we are dressed in.

Naomi Wallace US writer. *The Times*, 2 Aug 1994

29 Instead of this absurd division into sexes they ought to class people as static and dynamic.

Evelyn Waugh (1903–66) British novelist. *Decline and Fall*, Pt. III, Ch. 7

30 All women become like their mothers. That is their tragedy. No man does. That's his.

Oscar Wilde (1854–1900) Irish-born British dramatist. *The Importance of Being Earnest*, I

31 Women represent the triumph of matter over mind, just as men represent the triumph of mind over morals.

Oscar Wilde *The Picture of Dorian Gray*, Ch. 4

32 Can the fact that Our Lord chose men as his Twelve Apostles be lightly dismissed?

Bishop of Winchester (1926–) British churchman. Remark, July 1988

33 Why are women...so much more interesting to men than men are to women?

Virginia Woolf (1882–1941) British novelist. *A Room of One's Own*

SHAKESPEARE

See also criticism, poets, writers

1 Others abide our question, Thou art free,
We ask and ask: Thou smilest and art still,
Out-topping knowledge.

Matthew Arnold (1822–88) British poet and critic. *Shakespeare*

2 When he killed a calf he would do it in a high style, and make a speech.

John Aubrey (1626–1697) English antiquary. *Brief Lives*, 'William Shakespeare'

3 Our myriad-minded Shakespeare.

Samuel Taylor Coleridge (1772–1834) British poet. *Biographia Literaria*, Ch. 15

4 I have tried lately to read Shakespeare, and found it so intolerably dull that it nauseated me.

Charles Darwin (1809–82) British life scientist. *Autobiography*

5 He was the man who of all modern, and perhaps ancient poets had the largest and most comprehensive soul.

John Dryden (1631–1700) British poet and dramatist. *Essay of Dramatic Poesy*

6 He was naturally learned; he needed not the spectacles of books to read nature; he looked inwards, and found her there.

John Dryden *Essay of Dramatic Poesy*

7 We can say of Shakespeare, that never has a man turned so little knowledge to such great account.

T. S. Eliot (1888–1965) US-born British poet and dramatist. *The Classics and the Man of Letters* (lecture)

8 The remarkable thing about Shakespeare is that he is really very good – in spite of all the people who say he is very good.

Robert Graves (1895–1985) British poet and novelist. *The Observer*, 'Sayings of the Week', 6 Dec 1964

9 Shakespeare never had six lines together without a fault. Perhaps you may find seven, but this does not refute my general assertion.

Samuel Johnson (1709–84) British lexicographer. *Life of Johnson* (J. Boswell), Vol. II

10 He was not of an age, but for all time!

Ben Jonson (1573–1637) English dramatist. *To the Memory of William Shakespeare*

11 Sweet Swan of Avon!

Ben Jonson *To the Memory of William Shakespeare*

12 When I read Shakespeare I am struck with wonder
That such trivial people should muse and thunder
In such lovely language.

D. H. Lawrence (1885–1930) British novelist. *When I Read Shakespeare*

13 Or sweetest Shakespeare, Fancy's child,
Warble his native wood-notes wild.

John Milton (1608–74) English poet. *L'Allegro*

14 Shakespeare – the nearest thing in incarnation to the eye of God.

Laurence Olivier (1907–89) British actor. *Kenneth Harris Talking To*, 'Sir Laurence Olivier'

15 A man can be forgiven a lot if he can quote Shakespeare in an economic crisis.

Prince Philip (1921–) The consort of Queen Elizabeth II. Attrib.

16 With the single exception of Homer, there is no eminent writer, not even Sir Walter Scott, whom I can despise so entirely as I despise Shakespeare when I measure my mind against his...It would positively be a relief to me to dig him up and throw stones at him.

George Bernard Shaw (1856–1950) Irish dramatist and critic. *Dramatic Opinions and Essays*, Vol. 2

17 Wonderful women! Have you ever thought how much we all, and women especially, owe to Shakespeare for his vindication of women in these fearless, high-spirited, resolute and intelligent heroines?

Ellen Terry (1847–1928) British actress. *Four Lectures on Shakespeare*, 'The Triumphant Women'

18 One of the greatest geniuses that ever existed, Shakespeare, undoubtedly wanted taste.

Horace Walpole (1717–97) British writer. Letter to Wren, 9 Aug 1764

SHYNESS

See also self-confidence

1 I'm really a timid person – I was beaten up by Quakers.

Woody Allen (Allen Stewart Konigsberg; 1935–) US film actor. *Sleeper*

2 A timid question will always receive a confident answer.

Lord Darling (1849–1936) British judge. *Scintillae Juris*

3 Why so shy, my pretty Thomasina?
Thomasin, O Thomasin,
Once you were so promisin'.

Christopher Fry (1907–) British dramatist. *The Dark Is Light Enough*, II

4 Shyness is just egotism out of its depth.

Penelope Keith British actress. Remark, July 1988

5 Had we but world enough, and time,
This coyness, lady, were no crime.

Andrew Marvell (1621–78) English poet. *To His Coy Mistress*

6 Shyness is *common*....Self-consciousness it was always called when I was young, and that is what it is. To imagine that it shows a sense of modesty is absurd. *Modesty.* Why, I have never known a *truly* modest person to be the least bit shy.

Elizabeth Taylor (1912–75) British writer. *The Bush*, 'You'll Enjoy It When You Get There'

SIGNATURES

1 Never sign a walentine with your own name.

Charles Dickens (1812–70) British novelist. Said by Sam Weller. *Pickwick Papers*, Ch. 33

2 There, I guess King George will be able to read that.

John Hancock (1737–93) US revolutionary. Referring to his signature, written in a bold hand, on the US Declaration of Independence. *The American Treasury* (C. Fadiman)

3 The hand that signed the treaty bred a fever,
And famine grew, and locusts came;
Great is the hand that holds dominion over
Man by a scribbled name.

Dylan Thomas (1914–53) Welsh poet. *The Hand that Signed the Paper*

SILENCE

See also speech

1 A still tongue makes a wise head.

Proverb

2 Speech is silver, silence is golden.
Proverb

3 No voice; but oh! the silence sank
Like music on my heart.
Samuel Taylor Coleridge (1772–1834) British poet. *The Rime of the Ancient Mariner*, VI

4 When you have nothing to say, say nothing.
Charles Caleb Colton (?1780–1832) British clergyman and writer. *Lacon*, Vol. I

5 For God's sake hold your tongue and let me love.
John Donne (1573–1631) English poet. *The Canonization*

6 Silence is become his mother tongue.
Oliver Goldsmith (1728–74) Irish-born British writer. *The Good-Natured Man*, II

7 That man's silence is wonderful to listen to.
Thomas Hardy (1840–1928) British novelist. *Under the Greenwood Tree*, Ch. 14

8 Silence is as full of potential wisdom and wit as the unhewn marble of great sculpture.
Aldous Huxley (1894–1964) British novelist. *Point Counter Point*

9 Thou still unravish'd bride of quietness,
Thou foster-child of silence and slow time.
John Keats (1795–1821) British poet. *Ode on a Grecian Urn*

10 Silence is the best tactic for him who distrusts himself.
Duc de la Rochefoucauld (1613–80) French writer. *Maximes*, 79

11 You get the impression that their normal condition is silence and that speech is a slight fever which attacks them now and then.
Jean-Paul Sartre (1905–80) French writer. *Nausea*

12 Silence is the perfectest herald of joy: I were but little happy if I could say how much.
William Shakespeare (1564–1616) English dramatist. *Much Ado About Nothing*, II:1

13 Silence is the most perfect expression of scorn.
George Bernard Shaw (1856–1950) Irish dramatist and critic. *Back to Methuselah*

14 The cruellest lies are often told in silence.
Robert Louis Stevenson (1850–94) Scottish writer. *Virginibus Puerisque*

15 Whereof one cannot speak, thereon one must remain silent.
Ludwig Wittgenstein (1889–1951) Austrian philosopher. *Tractatus Logico-Philosophicus*, Ch. 7

SIMILARITY

See also analogy, difference

1 Birds of a feather flock together.
Proverbs

2 Great minds think alike.
Proverb

3 Like breeds like.
Proverb

4 Never mind, dear, we're all made the same, though some more than others.
Noël Coward (1899–1973) British dramatist. *The Café de la Paix*

5 I never knows the children. It's just six of one and half-a-dozen of the other.
Captain Frederick Marryat (1792–1848) British novelist. *The Pirate*, Ch. 4

SIMPLICITY

1 'Excellent!' I cried. 'Elementary,' said he.
Arthur Conan Doyle (1856–1930) British writer. Watson talking to Sherlock Holmes; Holmes's reply is often misquoted as 'Elementary my dear Watson'. *The Crooked Man*

2 The ability to simplify means to eliminate the unnecessary so that the necessary may speak.
Hans Hofmann (1880–1966) German-born US painter. *Search for the Real*

3 O holy simplicity!
John Huss (Jan Hus; c. 1369–1415) Bohemian religious reformer. On noticing a peasant adding a faggot to the pile at his execution. *Apophthegmata* (Zincgreff-Weidner), Pt. III

4 The trivial round, the common task,
Would furnish all we ought to ask;
Room to deny ourselves; a road
To bring us, daily, nearer God.
John Keble (1792–1866) British poet and clergyman. *The Christian Year*, 'Morning'

5 A child of five would understand this.
Send somebody to fetch a child of five.
Groucho Marx (Julius Marx; 1895–1977) US comedian. *Duck Soup*

6 Entities should not be multiplied unnecessarily.
No more things should be presumed to exist than are absolutely necessary.
William of Okham (c. 1280–1349) English philosopher. 'Okham's Razor'. Despite its attribution to William of Okham, it was in fact a repetition of an ancient philosophical maxim.

7 Anybody can shock a baby, or a television audience. But it's too easy, and the effect is disproportionate to the effort.
Richard G. Stern (1928–) US writer. *Golk*, Ch. 4

8 Our life is frittered away by detail...Simplify, simplify.
Henry David Thoreau (1817–62) US writer. *Walden*, 'Where I lived, and What I Lived For'

SIN

See also evil, vice

1 Old sins cast long shadows.
Proverb

2 All sin tends to be addictive, and the terminal point of addiction is what is called damnation.
W. H. Auden (1907–73) British poet. *A Certain World*

3 Wherefore putting away lying, speak every man truth with his neighbour: for we are members one of another.
Be ye angry, and sin not: let not the sun go down upon your wrath:
Neither give place to the devil.
Let him that stole steal no more: but rather let him labour, working with his hands the thing which is good, that he may have to give to him that needeth.
Bible: Ephesians 4:25–28

4 So when they continued asking him, he lifted up himself, and said unto them, He that is without sin among you, let him first cast a stone at her.
Bible: John 8:7

5 If we say that we have no sin, we deceive ourselves, and the truth is not in us.
If we confess our sins, he is faithful and just to forgive us our sins, and to cleanse us from all unrighteousness.
Bible: I John 1:8–9

6 Wherefore I say unto thee, Her sins, which are many, are forgiven; for she loved much: but to whom little is forgiven, the same loveth little.
Bible: Luke 7:47

7 But if ye will not do so, behold, ye have sinned against the Lord: and be sure your sin will find you out.
Bible: Numbers 32:23

8 We have erred, and strayed from thy ways like lost sheep.
The Book of Common Prayer *Morning Prayer, General Confession*

9 We have left undone those things which we ought to have done; and we have done those things we ought not to have done.
The Book of Common Prayer *Morning Prayer, General Confession*

10 A private sin is not so prejudicial in the world as a public indecency.
Miguel de Cervantes (1547–1616) Spanish novelist. *Don Quixote*, Pt. II, Ch. 22

11 He said he was against it.
Calvin Coolidge (1872–1933) US president. Reply when asked what a clergyman had said regarding sin in his sermon. Attrib.

12 It is my belief, Watson, founded upon my experience, that the lowest and vilest alleys of London do not present a more dreadful record of sin than does the smiling and beautiful countryside.
Arthur Conan Doyle (1856–1930) British writer. *Copper Beeches*

13 Did wisely from Expensive Sins refrain,
And never broke the Sabbath, but for Gain.
John Dryden (1631–1700) British poet and dramatist. *Absalom and Achitophel*, I

14 Sin brought death, and death will disappear with the disappearance of sin.
Mary Baker Eddy (1821–1910) US religious leader. *Science and Health, with Key to the Scriptures*

15 There's nothing so artificial as sinning nowadays. I suppose it once was real.
D. H. Lawrence (1885–1930) British novelist. *St Mawr*

16 Of Man's first disobedience, and the fruit
Of that forbidden tree, whose mortal taste
Brought death into the World, and all our woe…
John Milton (1608–74) English poet. *Paradise Lost*, Bk. I

17 The only people who should really sin
Are the people who can sin with a grin.
Ogden Nash (1902–71) US poet. *I'm a Stranger Here Myself*

18 She holds that it were better for sun and moon to drop from heaven, for the earth to fail, and for all the many millions who are upon it to die of starvation in extremest agony, as far as temporal affliction goes, than that one soul, I will not say, should be lost, but should commit one single venial sin, should tell one wilful untruth… or steal one poor farthing without excuse.
Cardinal Newman (1801–90) British theologian. Referring to the Roman Catholic Church. *Lectures on Anglican Difficulties*, VIII

19 At such an hour the sinners are still in bed resting up from their sinning of the night before, so they will be in good shape for more sinning a little later on.
Damon Runyon (1884–1946) US writer. *Runyon à la carte*, 'The Idyll of Miss Sarah Brown'

20 Were't not for gold and women, there would be no damnation.
Cyril Tourneur (1575–1626) English dramatist. *The Revenger's Tragedy*, II:1

SINCERITY

See also frankness, honesty, integrity

1 Best be yourself, imperial, plain and true!
Robert Browning (1812–89) British poet. *Bishop Blougram's Apology*

2 What comes from the heart, goes to the heart.
Samuel Taylor Coleridge (1772–1834) British poet. *Table Talk*

3 Some of the worst men in the world are sincere and the more sincere they are the worse they are.
Lord Hailsham (1907–) British Conservative politician. *The Observer*, 'Sayings of the Week', 7 Jan 1968

4 I'm afraid of losing my obscurity. Genuineness only thrives in the dark. Like celery.

Aldous Huxley (1894–1964) British novelist. *Those Barren Leaves*, Pt. I, Ch. 1

5 What's a man's first duty? The answer's brief:
To be himself.

Henrik Ibsen (1828–1906) Norwegian dramatist. *Peer Gynt*, IV:1

6 A little sincerity is a dangerous thing, and a great deal of it is absolutely fatal.

Oscar Wilde (1854–1900) Irish-born British dramatist. *The Critic as Artist*, Pt. 2

SINGERS

See also musicians, singing

1 Swans sing before they die – 'twere no bad thing,
Did certain persons die before they sing.

Samuel Taylor Coleridge (1772–1834) British poet. *Epigram on a Volunteer Singer*

2 A wandering minstrel I –
A thing of shreds and patches,
Of ballads, songs and snatches,
And dreamy lullaby!

W. S. Gilbert (1836–1911) British dramatist. *The Mikado*, I

3 The Last of the Red-Hot Mamas.

Sophie Tucker (Sophia Abuza; 1884–1966) Russian-born US singer. Description of herself. *Dictionary of Biographical Quotation* (J. Wintle and R. Kenin)

SINGING

See also music, opera, singers

1 You know whatta you do when you shit?
Singing, it's the same thing, only up!

Enrico Caruso (1873–1921) Italian tenor. *Whose Little Boy Are You?* (H. Brown)

2 I have a song to sing O!
Sing me your song, O!

W. S. Gilbert (1836–1911) British dramatist. *The Yeoman of the Guard*, I

3 Just a little more reverence, please, and not so much astonishment.

Malcolm Sargent (1895–1967) British conductor. Rehearsing the female chorus in 'For Unto Us a Child is Born' from Handel's *Messiah. 2500 Anecdotes* (E. Fuller)

SLAVERY

See also imprisonment, oppression, racism

1 The future is the only kind of property that the masters willingly concede to slaves.

Albert Camus (1913–60) French existentialist writer. *The Rebel*

2 There they are cutting each other's throats, because one half of them prefer hiring their servants for life, and the other by the hour.

Thomas Carlyle (1795–1881) Scottish historian and essayist. Referring to the American Civil War. Attrib.

3 Slaves cannot breathe in England; if their lungs
Receive our air, that moment they are free;
They touch our country, and their shackles fall.

William Cowper (1731–1800) British poet. A situation resulting from a judicial decision in 1772. *The Task*

4 The compact which exists between the North and the South is a covenant with death and an agreement with hell.

William Lloyd Garrison (1805–79) US abolitionist. Resolution, Massachusetts Anti-Slavery Society, 27 Jan 1843

5 The whole commerce between master and slave is a perpetual exercise of the most boisterous passions, the most unremitting despotism on the one part, and degrading submissions on the other.

Thomas Jefferson (1743–1826) US statesman. *Notes on the State of Virginia*

SLEEP

See also bed, dreams

1 One hour's sleep before midnight, is worth two after.

Proverb

2 Now I lay me down to sleep,
I pray the Lord my soul to keep.
If I should die before I wake,
I pray the Lord my soul to take.

Anonymous *New England Primer*, 1781

3 Lay your sleeping head, my love,
Human on my faithless arm.

W. H. Auden (1907–73) British poet. *Lullaby*

4 Rock-a-bye baby on the tree top,
When the wind blows the cradle will rock,
When the bough bends the cradle will fall,
Down comes the baby, cradle and all.

Charles Dupee Blake (1846–1903) British writer of nursery rhymes. Attrib.

5 Laugh and the world laughs with you; snore and you sleep alone.

Anthony Burgess (John Burgess Wilson; 1917–93) British novelist. *Inside Mr. Enderby*

6 Oh sleep! it is a gentle thing,
Beloved from pole to pole!

Samuel Taylor Coleridge (1772–1834) British poet. *The Rime of the Ancient Mariner*, V

7 Golden slumbers kiss your eyes,
Smiles awake you when you rise.

Thomas Dekker (c. 1572–1632) English dramatist. *Patient Grissil*, IV:2

8 It appears that every man's insomnia is as different from his neighbor's as are their daytime hopes and aspirations.

F. Scott Fitzgerald (1896–1940) US novelist. *The Crack-up*, 'Sleeping and Waking'

9 Try thinking of love, or something.
Amor vincit insomnia.

Christopher Fry (1907–) British dramatist. *A Sleep of Prisoners*

10 He's a wicked man that comes after children when they won't go to bed and throws handfuls of sand in their eyes.

Ernst Hoffmann (1776–1822) German composer. *The Sandman*

11 The amount of sleep required by the average person is about five minutes more.

Max Kauffmann Attrib.

12 O soft embalmer of the still midnight.

John Keats (1795–1821) British poet. *To Sleep*

13 Turn the key deftly in the oiled wards,
And seal the hushed casket of my soul.

John Keats *To Sleep*

14 How do people go to sleep? I'm afraid I've lost the knack. I might try busting myself smartly over the temple with the nightlight. I might repeat to myself, slowly and soothingly, a list of quotations beautiful from minds profound; if I can remember any of the damn things.

Dorothy Parker (1893–1967) US writer. *The Little Hours*

15 Sleep that knits up the ravell'd sleave of care,
The death of each day's life, sore labour's bath,
Balm of hurt minds, great nature's second course,
Chief nourisher in life's feast.

William Shakespeare (1564–1616) English dramatist. *Macbeth*, II:2

16 Sleep, Death's twin-brother, knows not Death,
Nor can I dream of thee as dead.

Alfred, Lord Tennyson (1809–92) British poet. *In Memoriam A.H.H.*, LXVIII

17 There ain't no way to find out why a snorer can't hear himself snore.

Mark Twain (Samuel Langhorne Clemens; 1835–1910) US writer. *Tom Sawyer Abroad*, Ch. 10

18 It was the time when first sleep begins for weary
mortals and by the gift of the gods creeps over them
most welcomely.

Virgil (Publius Vergilius Maro; 70–19 BC) Roman poet. *Aeneid*, Bk. II

19 I haven't been to sleep for over a year. That's why I go to bed early. One needs more rest if one doesn't sleep.

Evelyn Waugh (1903–66) British novelist. *Decline and Fall*, Pt. II, Ch. 3

20 I believe the greatest asset a head of state can have is the ability to get a good night's sleep.

Harold Wilson (1916–95) British politician and prime minister. *The World Tonight*, BBC Radio, 16 Apr 1975

21 Dear God! the very houses seem asleep;
And all that mighty heart is lying still!

William Wordsworth (1770–1850) British poet. *Sonnets*, 'Composed upon Westminster Bridge'

SMALLNESS

See also triviality

1 The best things come in small parcels.

Proverb

2 The Microbe is so very small
You cannot make him out at all.

Hilaire Belloc (1870–1953) French-born British poet. *More Beasts for Worse Children*, 'The Microbe'

3 One cubic foot less of space and it would have constituted adultery.

Robert Benchley (1889–1945) US humorist. Describing an office shared with Dorothy Parker. Attrib.

4 Small is beautiful.

E. F. Schumacher (1911–77) German-born economist. Title of book

SMOKING

See also abstinence

1 Certainly not – if you don't object if I'm sick.

Thomas Beecham (1879–1961) British conductor. When asked whether he minded if someone smoked in a non-smoking compartment. Attrib.

2 Tobacco, divine, rare, superexcellent tobacco, which goes far beyond all their panaceas, potable gold, and philosopher's stones, a sovereign remedy to all diseases.

Robert Burton (1577–1640) English scholar and explorer. *Anatomy of Melancholy*

3 Jones – (who, I'm glad to say,
Asked leave of Mrs J. –)
Daily absorbs a clay
After his labours.

C. S. Calverley (1831–84) British poet. *Ode to Tobacco*

4 I must point out that my rule of life prescribed as an absolutely sacred rite smoking cigars and also the drinking of alcohol before, after, and if need be during all meals and in the intervals between them.

Winston Churchill (1874–1965) British statesman. Said during a lunch with the Arab leader Ibn Saud, when he heard that the king's religion forbade smoking and alcohol. *The Second World War*

5 It is quite a three-pipe problem.

Arthur Conan Doyle (1856–1930) British writer. *The Red-Headed League*

6 What a blessing this smoking is! perhaps the greatest that we owe to the discovery of America.

Arthur Helps (1813–75) British historian. *Friends in Council*

7 A custom loathsome to the eye, hateful to the

nose, harmful to the brain, dangerous to the lungs, and in the black, stinking fume thereof, nearest resembling the horrible Stygian smoke of the pit that is bottomless.

James I (1566–1625) King of England. *A Counterblast to Tobacco*

8 Neither do thou lust after that tawney weed tobacco.

Ben Jonson (1573–1637) English dramatist. *Bartholomew Fair*, II:6

9 Ods me, I marvel what pleasure or felicity they have in taking their roguish tobacco. It is good for nothing but to choke a man, and fill him full of smoke and embers.

Ben Jonson *Every Man in His Humour*, III:5

10 This very night I am going to leave off tobacco! Surely there must be some other world in which this unconquerable purpose shall be realized. The soul hath not her generous aspirings implanted in her in vain.

Charles Lamb (1775–1834) British essayist. Letter to Thomas Manning, 26 Dec 1815

11 Dr Parr...asked him, how he had acquired his power of smoking at such a rate? Lamb replied, 'I toiled after it, sir, as some men toil after virtue.'

Charles Lamb *Memoirs of Charles Lamb* (Talfourd)

12 He who lives without tobacco is not worthy to live.

Molière (Jean Baptiste Poquelin; 1622–73) French dramatist. *Don Juan*, I:1

13 The very act of smoking a cigarette is, for many, a major source of Displacement Activities...They are stress-smokers, not drug-smokers, and in that capacity at least, smoking can play a valuable role in a society full of minute-by-minute tensions and pressures. It is so much more than a question of inhaling smoke.

Desmond Morris (1928–) British biologist. *Manwatching*, 'Displacement Activities'

14 This vice brings in one hundred million francs in taxes every year. I will certainly forbid it at once – as soon as you can name a virtue that brings in as much revenue.

Napoleon III (1808–73) French emperor. Reply when asked to ban smoking. *Anekdotenschatz* (H. Hoffmeister)

15 My doctor has always told me to smoke. He even explains himself: 'Smoke, my friend. Otherwise someone else will smoke in your place.'

Erik Satie (1866–1925) French composer. *Mémoires d'un amnésique*

16 I have every sympathy with the American who was so horrified by what he had read of the effects of smoking that he gave up reading.

Henry G. Strauss *Quotations for Speakers and Writers* (A. Andrews)

17 I asked a coughing friend of mine why he doesn't stop smoking. 'In this town it wouldn't do any good,' he explained. 'I happen to be a chain breather.'

Robert Sylvester (1907–75) US writer. *Bartlett's Unfamiliar Quotations* (Leonard Louis Levinson)

18 We shall not refuse tobacco the credit of being sometimes medical, when used temperately, though an acknowledged poison.

Jesse Torrey (1787–1834) *The Moral Instructor*, Pt. IV

19 When I was young, I kissed my first woman, and smoked my first cigarette on the same day. Believe me, never since have I wasted any more time on tobacco.

Arturo Toscanini (1867–1957) Italian conductor. Attrib.

20 There are people who strictly deprive themselves of each and every eatable, drinkable and smokable which has in any way acquired a shady reputation. They pay this price for health. And health is all they get for it.

Mark Twain (Samuel Langhorne Clemens; 1835–1910) US writer.

21 I've done it a hundred times!

Mark Twain Referring to giving up smoking. Attrib.

22 Tobacco drieth the brain, dimmeth the sight, vitiateth the smell, hurteth the stomach, destroyeth the concoction, disturbeth the humors and spirits, corrupteth the breath, induceth a trembling of the limbs, exsiccateth the windpipe, lungs, and liver, annoyeth the milt, scorcheth the heart, and causeth the blood to be adjusted.

Tobias Venner (1577–1660) *Via Recta ad Vitam Longam*

23 A cigarette is the perfect type of a perfect pleasure. It is exquisite, and it leaves one unsatisfied. What more can one want?

Oscar Wilde (1854–1900) Irish-born British dramatist. *The Picture of Dorian Gray*, Ch. 6

SNOBBERY

See also aristocracy, class, one-upmanship

1 In our way we were both snobs, and no snob welcomes another who has risen with him.

Cecil Beaton (1904–80) British photographer. Referring to Evelyn Waugh. Attrib.

2 And this is good old Boston,
The home of the bean and the cod,
Where the Lowells talk only to Cabots,
And the Cabots talk only to God.

John Collins Bossidy (1860–1928) US writer. Toast at Holy Cross Alumni dinner, 1910

3 Of course they have, or I wouldn't be sitting here talking to someone like you.

Barbara Cartland (1902–) British romantic novelist. When asked in a radio interview whether she thought that British class barriers had broken down. *Class* (J. Cooper)

4 I've danced with a man, who's danced with a girl, who's danced with the Prince of Wales.

Herbert Farjeon (1887–1945) British writer. *Picnic*

5 His hatred of snobs was a derivative of his snobbishness, but made the simpletons (in other words, everyone) believe that he was immune from snobbishness.

Marcel Proust (1871–1922) French novelist. *À la recherche du temps perdu: Le Côté de Guermantes*

6 I mustn't go on singling out names. One must not be a name-dropper, as Her Majesty remarked to me yesterday.

Norman St John Stevas (1929–) British politician. Speech, Museum of the Year luncheon, 20 June 1979

7 He who meanly admires mean things is a Snob.

William Makepeace Thackeray (1811–63) British novelist. *The Book of Snobs*, Ch. 2

8 It is impossible, in our condition of society, not to be sometimes a Snob.

William Makepeace Thackeray *The Book of Snobs*, Ch. 3

9 She was – but I assure you that she was a very bad cook.

Louis Adolphe Thiers (1797–1877) French statesman and historian. Defending his social status after someone had remarked that his mother had been a cook. Attrib.

10 My dear – the people we should have been seen dead with.

Rebecca West (Cicely Isabel Fairfield; 1892–1983) British novelist and journalist. Cable sent to Noël Coward after learning they had both been on a Nazi death list. *Times Literary Supplement*, 1 Oct 1982

11 CECILY: When I see a spade I call it a spade.
GWENDOLEN: I am glad to say I have never seen a spade. It is obvious that our social spheres have been widely different.

Oscar Wilde (1854–1900) Irish-born British dramatist. *The Importance of Being Earnest*, II

12 Never speak disrespectfully of Society, Algernon. Only people who can't get into it do that.

Oscar Wilde *The Importance of Being Earnest*, III

SOCIALISM

See also Communism, Marxism

1 Why is it always the intelligent people who are socialists?

Alan Bennett (1934–) British playwright. *Forty Years On*

2 The language of priorities is the religion of Socialism.

Aneurin Bevan (1897–1960) British Labour politician. *Aneurin Bevan* (Vincent Brome), Ch. 1

3 The people's flag is deepest red;
It shrouded oft our martyred dead,
And ere their limbs grew stiff and cold,
Their heart's blood dyed its every fold.
Then raise the scarlet standard high!
Within its shade we'll live or die.
Tho' cowards flinch and traitors sneer,
We'll keep the red flag flying here.

James Connell (1852–1929) British socialist. Traditionally sung at the close of annual conferences of the British Labour Party. *The Red Flag*, in *Songs that made History* (H. E. Piggot), Ch. 6

4 Socialism can only arrive by bicycle.

José Antonio Viera Gallo (1943–) Chilean politician. *Energy and Equity* (Ivan Illich)

5 Only socialism would put up with it for so long. Capitalism would have gone bankrupt years ago.

Mikhail Gorbachov (1931–) Soviet statesman. Talking of sub-standard workmanship in the Soviet Union. TV documentary, 23 March 1987

6 Well, what are you socialists going to do about me?

George V (1865–1936) King of the United Kingdom. To Ramsay MacDonald at his first meeting as prime minister. Attrib.

7 We are all Socialists now.

William Harcourt (1827–1904) British statesman. Attrib.

8 Compassion is not a sloppy, sentimental feeling for people who are underprivileged or sick… it is an absolutely practical belief that, regardless of a person's background, ability or ability to pay, he should be provided with the best that society has to offer.

Neil Kinnock (1942–) British politician. Maiden speech, House of Commons, 1970

9 It is inconceivable that we could transform this society without a major extension of public ownership.

Neil Kinnock *Marxism Today*, 1983

10 Under socialism *all* will govern in turn and will soon become accustomed to no one governing.

Lenin (Vladimir Ilich Ulyanov; 1870–1924) Russian revolutionary leader. *The State and Revolution*, Ch. 6

11 As with the Christian religion, the worst advertisement for Socialism is its adherents.

George Orwell (Eric Blair; 1903–50) British novelist. *The Road to Wigan Pier*, Ch. 11

12 To the ordinary working man, the sort you would meet in any pub on Saturday night, Socialism does not mean much more than better wages and shorter hours and nobody bossing you about.

George Orwell *The Road to Wigan Pier*, Ch. 11

13 The higher-water mark, so to speak, of Socialist literature is W. H. Auden, a sort of gutless Kipling.

George Orwell *The Road to Wigan Pier*, Ch. 11

14 State socialism is totally alien to the British character.

Margaret Thatcher (1925–) British politician and prime minister. *The Times*, 1983

15 We are redefining and we are restating our socialism in terms of the scientific revolution…the Britain that is going to be forged in the white heat of this revolution will be no place for restrictive practices or out-dated methods on either side of industry.

Harold Wilson (1916–95) British politician and prime minister. Speech, Labour Party Conference, 1 Oct 1963

SOCIETY

See also mankind

1 A characteristic of Thatcherism is a reversion to the idea of nature, irreparable in its forces. Poverty and sickness are seen as part of an order.

Howard Barker (1946–) British playwright. *The Times*, 3 Jan 1990

2 I am a sociable worker.

Brendan Behan (1923–64) Irish playwright. *The Hostage*, II

3 Man was formed for society.

William Blackstone (1723–80) British jurist. *Commentaries on the Laws of England*, Introduction

4 No man is an Island, entire of itself; every man is a piece of the Continent, a part of the main.

John Donne (1573–1631) English poet. *Devotions*, 17

5 People who need people are the luckiest people in the world.

Bob Merrill (Robert Merrill; 1890–1977) US lyricist and composer. *People Who Need People*

6 Our civilization…has not yet fully recovered from the shock of its birth – the transition from the tribal or 'closed society', with its submission to magical forces, to the 'open society' which sets free the critical powers of man.

Karl Popper (1902–94) Austrian-born British philosopher. *The Open Society and Its Enemies*

7 Man is not a solitary animal, and so long as social life survives, self-realization cannot be the supreme principle of ethics.

Bertrand Russell (1872–1970) British philosopher. *History of Western Philosophy*, 'Romanticism'

8 Society is no comfort
To one not sociable.

William Shakespeare (1564–1616) English dramatist. *Cymbeline*, IV:2

9 Man is a social animal.

Benedict Spinoza (Baruch de Spinoza; 1632–77) Dutch philosopher. *Ethics*

10 What men call social virtues, good fellowship, is commonly but the virtue of pigs in a litter, which lie close together to keep each other warm. It brings men together in crowds and mobs in bar-rooms and elsewhere, but it does not deserve the name of virtue.

Henry David Thoreau (1817–62) US writer. *Journal*, 1852

SOLDIERS

See also army, officers, war

1 It's Tommy this, an' Tommy that, an' 'Chuck him out, the brute!'
But it's 'Saviour of 'is country' when the guns begin to shoot.

Rudyard Kipling (1865–1936) Indian-born British writer. *Tommy*

2 Oh, it's Tommy this, an' Tommy that, an' 'Tommy, go away';
But it's 'Thank you, Mister Atkins,' when the band begins to play.

Rudyard Kipling *Tommy*

3 They're changing guard at Buckingham Palace
Christopher Robin went down with Alice.
Alice is marrying one of the guard.
'A soldier's life is terrible hard,'
Says Alice.

A. A. Milne (1882–1956) British writer. *When We Were Very Young*, 'Buckingham Palace'

4 Volunteers usually fall into two groups. There are the genuinely courageous who are itching to get at the throat of the enemy, and the restless who will volunteer for anything in order to escape from the boredom of what they are presently doing.

David Niven (1909–83) British film actor. *The Moon's a Balloon*, Ch. 12

5 Soldiers are citizens of death's grey land,
Drawing no dividend from time's tomorrows.

Siegfried Sassoon (1886–1967) British poet. *Dreamers*

6 You are a very poor soldier: a chocolate cream soldier!

George Bernard Shaw (1856–1950) Irish dramatist and critic. *Arms and the Man*, I

7 I never expect a soldier to think.

George Bernard Shaw *The Devil's Disciple*, III

8 They're overpaid, overfed, oversexed and over here.

Tommy Trinder (1909–89) British entertainer. Referring to the G.I.s. Attrib.

9 He (the recruiting officer) asked me 'Why tanks?' I replied that I preferred to go into battle sitting down.

Peter Ustinov (1921–) British actor. *Dear Me*

10 It all depends upon that article there.

Duke of Wellington (1769–1852) British general and statesman. Indicating a passing infantryman when asked if he would be able to defeat Napoleon. *The Age of Elegance* (A. Bryant)

SOLITUDE

See also loneliness

1 Whosoever is delighted in solitude is either a wild beast or a god.

Francis Bacon (1561–1626) English philosopher. *Essays*, 'Of Friendship'

2 Alone, alone, all, all alone,
Alone on a wide wide sea!
And never a saint took pity on
My soul in agony.

Samuel Taylor Coleridge (1772–1834) British poet. *The Rime of the Ancient Mariner*, IV

3 Oh for a lodge in some vast wilderness,

Some boundless contiguity of shade,
Where rumour of oppression and deceit,
Of unsuccessful or successful war,
Might never reach me more!

William Cowper (1731–1800) British poet. *The Task*

4 Society, friendship, and love,
Divinely bestowed upon man,
Oh, had I the wings of a dove,
How soon would I taste you again!

William Cowper *Verses supposed to be written by Alexander Selkirk*

5 I am monarch of all I survey,
My right there is none to dispute;
From the centre all round to the sea
I am lord of the fowl and the brute.
Oh, solitude! where are the charms
That sages have seen in thy face?
Better dwell in the midst of alarms,
Than reign in this horrible place.

William Cowper *Verses supposed to be written by Alexander Selkirk*

6 I want to be alone.

Greta Garbo (1905–90) Swedish-born US film star. Words spoken by Garbo in the film *Grand Hotel*, and associated with her for the rest of her career.

7 Far from the madding crowd's ignoble strife,
Their sober wishes never learn'd to stray;
Along the cool sequester'd vale of life
They kept the noiseless tenor of their way.

Thomas Gray (1716–71) British poet. *Elegy Written in a Country Churchyard*

8 One of the pleasantest things in the world is going on a journey; but I like to go by myself.

William Hazlitt (1778–1830) British essayist. *On Going a Journey*

9 It is a fine thing to be out on the hills alone. A man can hardly be a beast or a fool alone on a great mountain.

Francis Kilvert (1840–79) British diarist and clergyman. *Diary*, 29 May 1871

10 In solitude
What happiness? who can enjoy alone,
Or, all enjoying, what contentment find?

John Milton (1608–74) English poet. *Paradise Lost*, Bk. VIII

11 I want to be a movement
But there's no one on my side.

Adrian Mitchell (1932–) British writer and dramatist. *Loose Leaf Poem*

12 A man must keep a little back shop where he can be himself without reserve. In solitude alone can he know true freedom.

Michel de Montaigne (1533–92) French essayist. *Essais*, I

13 I never found the companion that was so companionable as solitude.

Henry David Thoreau (1817–62) US writer. *Walden*, 'Solitude'

14 Alas, Lord, I am powerful but alone. Let me sleep the sleep of the earth.

Alfred de Vigny (1797–1863) French writer. *Moise*

15 For oft, when on my couch I lie
In vacant or in pensive mood,
They flash upon that inward eye
Which is the bliss of solitude.

William Wordsworth (1770–1850) British poet. *I Wandered Lonely as a Cloud*

16 Behold her, single in the field,
Yon solitary Highland lass!

William Wordsworth *The Solitary Reaper*

17 I will arise and go now, and go to Innisfree,
And a small cabin build there, of clay and wattles made;
Nine bean rows will I have there, a hive for the honey bee,
And live alone in the bee-loud glade.

W. B. Yeats (1865–1939) Irish poet. *The Lake Isle of Innisfree*

SORROW

See also despair, melancholy, mourning, regret

1 Every tear from every eye
Becomes a babe in Eternity.

William Blake (1757–1827) British poet. *Auguries of Innocence*

2 Do you hear the children weeping, O my brothers,
Ere the sorrow comes with years?

Elizabeth Barrett Browning (1806–61) British poet. *The Cry of the Children*

3 Follow thy fair sun, unhappy shadow.

Thomas Campion (1567–1620) English poet. *Follow Thy Fair Sun*

4 One often calms one's grief by recounting it.

Pierre Corneille (1606–84) French dramatist. *Polyeucte*, I:3

5 Tears were to me what glass beads are to African traders.

Quentin Crisp (?1910–) Model, publicist, and writer. *The Naked Civil Servant*

6 There is no greater sorrow than to recall a time of happiness when in misery.

Dante (1265–1321) Italian poet. *Divine Comedy, Inferno*, V

7 *Adieu tristesse*
Bonjour tristesse
Tu es inscrite dans les lignes du plafond.
Farewell sadness
Good day sadness
You are written in the lines of the ceiling.

Paul Éluard (Eugène Grindel; 1895–1952) French surrealist poet. *La Vie immédiate*

8 A moment of time may make us unhappy for ever.

John Gay (1685–1732) English poet and dramatist. *The Beggar's Opera*

9 Sadness is almost never anything but a form of fatigue.

André Gide (1869–1951) French novelist. *Journals*, 1922

10 They say my verse is sad: no wonder;
Its narrow measure spans
Tears of eternity, and sorrow,
Not mine, but man's.

A. E. Housman (1859–1936) British scholar and poet. *Last Poems*, 'Fancy's Knell'

11 Then Sir Launcelot saw her visage, but he wept not greatly, but sighed!

Thomas Malory (1400–71) English writer. *Morte d'Arthur*, Bk. XXI, Ch. 11

12 Tears such as angels weep, burst forth.

John Milton (1608–74) English poet. *Paradise Lost*, Bk. I

13 Art thou weary, art thou languid,
Art thou sore distressed?

John Mason Neale (1818–66) British churchman. *Art thou Weary?*

14 Sorrow is tranquillity remembered in emotion.

Dorothy Parker (1893–1967) US writer. *Sentiment*

15 Line after line my gushing eyes o'erflow,
Led through a sad variety of woe.

Alexander Pope (1688–1744) British poet. *Eloisa to Abelard*

16 Not louder shrieks to pitying heav'n are cast,
When husbands, or when lap-dogs breathe their last.

Alexander Pope *The Rape of the Lock*, III

17 As soon as one is unhappy one becomes moral.

Marcel Proust (1871–1922) French novelist. *À la recherche du temps perdu: À l'ombre des jeunes filles en fleurs*

18 Happiness is beneficial for the body, but it is grief that develops the powers of the mind.

Marcel Proust *À la recherche du temps perdu: Le Temps retrouvé*

19 It is such a secret place, the land of tears.

Antoine de Saint-Exupéry (1900–44) French novelist and aviator. *The Little Prince*, Ch. 7

20 He's simply got the instinct for being unhappy highly developed.

Saki (Hector Hugh Munro; 1870–1916) British writer. *The Match-Maker*

21 If you have tears, prepare to shed them now.

William Shakespeare (1564–1616) English dramatist. *Julius Caesar*, III:2

22 Down, thou climbing sorrow,
Thy element's below.

William Shakespeare *King Lear*, II:4

23 The secret of being miserable is to have leisure to bother about whether you are happy or not.

George Bernard Shaw (1856–1950) Irish dramatist and critic. *Misalliance*, Preface

24 'Tis held that sorrow makes us wise.

Alfred, Lord Tennyson (1809–92) British poet. *In Memoriam A.H.H.*, CXIII

25 My regret
Becomes an April violet,
And buds and blossoms like the rest.

Alfred, Lord Tennyson *In Memoriam A.H.H.*, CXV

26 Tears, idle tears, I know not what they mean,
Tears from the depth of some divine despair.

Alfred, Lord Tennyson *The Princess*, IV

27 A grief too much to be told, O queen, you bid me renew.

Virgil (Publius Vergilius Maro; 70–19 BC) Roman poet. The opening words of Aeneas' account to Dido of the fall of Troy. *Aeneid*, Bk. II

SOUL

1 The eyes are the window of the soul.

Proverb

2 We cannot kindle when we will
The fire which in the heart resides,
The spirit bloweth and is still,
In mystery our soul abides.

Matthew Arnold (1822–88) British poet and critic. *Morality*

3 And see all sights from pole to pole,
And glance, and nod, and bustle by;
And never once possess our soul
Before we die.

Matthew Arnold *A Southern Night*

4 Man has no Body distinct from his Soul; for that called Body is a portion of Soul discerned by the five Senses, the chief inlets of Soul in this age.

William Blake (1757–1827) British poet. *The Marriage of Heaven and Hell*, 'The Voice of the Devil'

5 Leave the flesh to the fate it was fit for! the spirit be thine!

Robert Browning (1812–89) British poet. *Saul*, XIII

6 In the real dark night of the soul it is always three o'clock in the morning.

F. Scott Fitzgerald (1896–1940) US novelist. *See* ST JOHN OF THE CROSS. *The Crack-Up*

7 That night, that year
Of now done darkness I wretch lay wrestling with (my God!) my God.

Gerard Manley Hopkins (1844–99) British Jesuit and poet. *Carrion Comfort*

8 The dark night of the soul.

St John of the Cross (Juan de Yepes y Alvarez; 1542–91) Spanish churchman and poet. English translation of *Noche obscura del alma*, the title of a poem; *see also* F. SCOTT FITZGERALD

9 Nor let the beetle, nor the death-moth be
Your mournful Psyche.

John Keats (1795–1821) British poet. *Ode on Melancholy*

10 And looks commercing with the skies,
Thy rapt soul sitting in thine eyes.

John Milton (1608–74) English poet. *Il Penseroso*

11 I am positive I have a soul; nor can all the books with which materialists have pestered the world ever convince me of the contrary.

Laurence Sterne (1713–68) Irish-born British writer. *A Sentimental Journey*, 'Maria, Moulines'

12 Fair seed-time had my soul, and I grew up
Fostered alike by beauty and by fear.

William Wordsworth (1770–1850) British poet. *The Prelude*, I

SOUTH AFRICA

1 South Africa will not allow the double standards and hypocrisy of the Western world, even in the application of legal principles, to stand in the way of our responsibility to protect our country.

P. W. Botha (1916–) South African politician and president. Speech, May 1986

2 You won't force South Africans to commit national suicide.

P. W. Botha Speech, Aug 1986

3 My feelings are that for the first time we are participating in an election that will have legitimacy. Now we can go to the polling booth without a bad conscience.

P. W. Botha *The Independent*, 28 Apr 1994

4 South Africa, renowned both far and wide
For politics and little else beside.

Roy Campbell (1901–57) South African poet. *The Wayzgoose*

5 Today we have closed the book on apartheid.

F. W. de Klerk (1936–) South African politician and president. Remark after a referendum of white South Africans had endorsed his government's reform programme. *The Independent*, 19 Mar 1992

6 Mr Mandela has walked a long road and now stands at the top of the hill. A traveller would sit down and admire the view. But a man of destiny knows that beyond this hill lies another and another.

F. W. de Klerk Speech, 2 May 1994

7 I've a bad case of the Buthelezi Blues, or is it post-Natal depression?

Graffiti

8 I have fought against white domination, and I have fought against black domination. I have cherished the ideal of a democratic and free society in which all persons will live together in harmony and with equal opportunities. It is an ideal which I hope to live for and achieve. But, if needs be, it is an ideal for which I am prepared to die.

Nelson Mandela (1918–) South African lawyer, human rights activist, and president. Speech from the dock, having been charged with treason, 20 Apr 1964 The closing words of his defence statement.

9 Only free men can negotiate; prisoners cannot enter into contracts.

Nelson Mandela Statement from prison, 10 Feb 1985 Replying to an offer to release him if he renounced violence.

10 My fellow South Africans, today we are entering a new era for our country and its people. Today we celebrate not the victory of a party, but a victory for all the people of South Africa.

Nelson Mandela Speech, Cape Town, 9 May 1994 Following his election to the presidency.

11 The task at hand will not be easy, but you have mandated us to change South Africa from a land in which the majority lived with little hope, to one in which they can live and work with dignity, with a sense of self-esteem and confidence in the future.

Nelson Mandela Speech at his presidential inauguration, 10 May 1994

12 The South African Police would leave no stone unturned to see that nothing disturbed the even terror of their lives.

Tom Sharpe (1928–) British novelist. *Indecent Exposure*, Ch. 1

13 It is an incredible feeling, like falling in love.

Desmond Tutu (1931–) South African clergyman. Referring to voting in the first multiracial elections in South Africa. *The Independent*, 27 Apr 1994

14 Improbable as it is, unlikely as it is, we are being set up as a beacon of hope for the world.

Desmond Tutu *The Times*, 11 Oct 1994

15 The paradox in South Africa is that after all these years of white racism, oppression and injustice there is hardly any anti-white feeling.

Desmond Tutu *Black Sash: The Beginning Of A Bridge in South Africa*, Foreword

SPACE

See also astronomy, discovery, exploration, moon, science, stars, sun, technology, universe

1 That's one small step for man, one giant leap for mankind.

Neil Armstrong (1930–) US astronaut. Said on stepping onto the moon. Often quoted as, 'small step for a man...' (which is probably what he intended). Remark, 21 July 1969

2 Outer space is no place for a person of breeding.

Violet Bonham Carter (1887–1969) British politician. *The New Yorker*

3 I am a passenger on the spaceship, Earth.

Richard Buckminster Fuller (1895–1983) US architect and inventor. *Operating Manual for Spaceship Earth*

4 The Earth is just too small and fragile a basket for the human race to keep all its eggs in.

Robert Heinlein (1907–88) US science-fiction writer. Speech

5 Space isn't remote at all. It's only an hour's drive away if your car could go straight upwards.

Fred Hoyle (1915–) British astronomer. *The Observer*, 9 Sept 1979

6 This is the greatest week in the history of the world since the creation.

Richard Milhous Nixon (1913–94) US president. Said when men first landed on the moon. Attrib., 24 July 1969

7 Space is almost infinite. As a matter of fact we think it *is* infinite.
Dan Quayle (James Danforth Q.; 1946–) US statesman. *The Sunday Times*, 31 Dec 1989

8 The astronauts!...Rotarians in outer space.
Gore Vidal (1925–) US novelist. *Two Sisters*

SPECULATION

1 While to deny the existence of an unseen kingdom is bad, to pretend that we know more about it than its bare existence is no better.
Samuel Butler (1835–1902) British writer. *Erewhon*, Ch. 15

2 If the world were good for nothing else, it is a fine subject for speculation.
William Hazlitt (1778–1830) British essayist. *Characteristics*

3 I think the primary notion back of most gambling is the excitement of it. While gamblers naturally want to win, the majority of them derive pleasure even if they lose. The desire to win, rather than the excitement involved, seems to me the compelling force behind speculation.
Joseph Kennedy (1888–1969) US businessman. *The Kennedys*, Ch. 2 (Peter Collier and David Horowitz)

SPEECH

See also silence, speeches, verbosity, words

1 Save your breath to cool your porridge.
Proverb

2 Speak when you are spoken to.
Proverb

3 Let your speech be alway with grace, seasoned with salt, that ye may know how ye ought to answer every man.
Bible: Colossians 4:6

4 Let thy speech be short, comprehending much in few words; be as one that knoweth and yet holdeth his tongue.
Bible: Ecclesiasticus 32:8

5 Even so the tongue is a little member, and boasteth great things. Behold, how great a matter a little fire kindleth!
Bible: James 3:5

6 But the tongue can no man tame; it is an unruly evil, full of deadly poison.
Bible: James 3:8

7 To know how to say what others only know how to think is what makes men poets or sages; and to dare to say what others only dare to think makes men martyrs or reformers – or both.
Elizabeth Charles (1828–96) British writer. *Chronicle of the Schönberg-Cotta Family*

8 No, Sir, because I have time to think before I speak, and don't ask impertinent questions.
Erasmus Darwin (1731–1802) British physician, biologist, and poet. Reply when asked whether he found his stammer inconvenient. *Reminiscences of My Father's Everyday Life* (Sir Francis Darwin)

9 The true use of speech is not so much to express our wants as to conceal them.
Oliver Goldsmith (1728–74) Irish-born British writer. *Essays*, 'The Use of Language'

10 Most men make little use of their speech than to give evidence against their own understanding.
Lord Halifax (1633–95) English statesman. *Political, Moral, and Miscellaneous Thoughts and Reflections*

11 Talking and eloquence are not the same: to speak, and to speak well, are two things.
Ben Jonson (1573–1637) English dramatist. *Timber, or Discoveries made upon Men and Matter*

12 The thoughtless are rarely wordless.
Howard W. Newton Attrib.

13 The most precious things in speech are pauses.
Ralph Richardson (1902–83) British actor. Attrib.

14 But words once spoke can never be recall'd.
Earl of Roscommon (1633–85) Irish-born English poet. *Art of Poetry*

15 Words may be false and full of art,
Sighs are the natural language of the heart.
Thomas Shadwell (1642–92) English dramatist. *Psyche*, III

16 Speech was given to man to disguise his thoughts.
Talleyrand (Charles Maurice de Talleyrand-Périgord; 1754–1838) French politician. Attrib.

SPEECHES

See also brevity, sermons, verbosity

1 I take the view, and always have done, that if you cannot say what you have to say in twenty minutes, you should go away and write a book about it.
Lord Brabazon of Tara (1910–74) British businessman and Conservative politician. Attrib.

2 An after-dinner speech should be like a lady's dress – long enough to cover the subject and short enough to be interesting.
R. A. Butler (1902–82) British Conservative politician. Remark made at an Anglo-Jewish dinner

3 He is one of those orators of whom it was well said, 'Before they get up they do not know what they are going to say; when they are speaking, they do not know what they are saying; and when they sit down, they do not know what they have said'.
Winston Churchill (1874–1965) British statesman. Referring to Lord Charles Beresford. Speech, House of Commons, 20 Dec 1912

4 I dreamt that I was making a speech in the House. I woke up, and by Jove I was!
Duke of Devonshire (1833–1908) Conservative politician. *Thought and Adventures* (W. S. Churchill)

5 For I have neither wit, nor words, nor worth,
Action, nor utterance, nor the power of speech,
To stir men's blood; I only speak right on.

William Shakespeare (1564–1616) English dramatist. *Julius Caesar*, III:2

6 Don't quote Latin; say what you have to say, and then sit down.

Duke of Wellington (1769–1852) British general and statesman. Advice to a new Member of Parliament. Attrib.

SPELLING

See also language, pronunciation, words, writing

1 Put it down a we, my lord, put it down a we!

Charles Dickens (1812–70) British novelist. *Pickwick Papers*, Ch. 34

2 They spell it Vinci and pronounce it Vinchy; foreigners always spell better than they pronounce.

Mark Twain (Samuel Langhorne Clemens; 1835–1910) US writer. *The Innocents Abroad*, Ch. 19

SPONTANEITY

See also impetuosity

1 Spontaneity is only a term for man's ignorance of the gods.

Samuel Butler (1835–1902) British writer. *Erewhon*, Ch. 25

2 *L'acte gratuite.*
The unmotivated action.

André Gide (1869–1951) French novelist. *Les Caves du Vatican*

3 Away with all ideals. Let each individual act spontaneously from the for ever incalculable prompting of the creative wellhead within him. There is no universal law.

D. H. Lawrence (1885–1930) British novelist. *Phoenix*, Preface to 'All Things are Possible' by Leo Shostov

4 Nothing prevents us from being natural so much as the desire to appear so.

Duc de la Rochefoucauld (1613–80) French writer. *Maximes*, 431

SPOONERISMS

Sayings associated with the Oxford clergyman and academic William Archibald Spooner (1844–1930).

1 You will find as you grow older that the weight of rages will press harder and harder on the employer.

Spooner (Sir W. Hayter), Ch. 6

2 I remember your name perfectly, but I just can't think of your face.

3 Kinquering Congs their titles take.

A scrambled announcement of the hymn in New College Chapel (probably apocryphal)

4 Let us drink to the queer old Dean.

5 Sir, you have tasted two whole worms; you have hissed all my mystery lectures and have been caught fighting a liar in the quad; you will leave Oxford by the town drain.

SPORT AND GAMES

See also cricket, fishing, football, golf, horses, hunting

1 Float like a butterfly
Sting like a bee.

Muhammad Ali (Cassius Clay; 1942–) US boxer. Describing his boxing style. Remark

2 Follow up! Follow up! Follow up! Follow up! Follow up!
Till the field ring again and again,
With the tramp of the twenty-two men,
Follow up!

E. E. Bowen (1836–1901) British writer. *Forty Years On* (the Harrow school song)

3 Life's too short for chess.

Henry James Byron (1834–84) British dramatist and actor. *Our Boys*, I

4 I'm old, but I'm not cold.

Linford Christie (1960–) British athlete. Referring to his victory in the 100 m at the Weltklasse Grand Prix, Zurich. *The Independent*, 18 Aug 1994

5 There is plenty of time to win this game, and to thrash the Spaniards too.

Francis Drake (1540–96) British navigator and admiral. Referring to the sighting of the Armada during a game of bowls, 20 July 1588. Attrib.

6 Any boxer who says he loves boxing is either a liar or a fool. I'm not looking for glory…I'm looking for money. I'm looking for readies.

Chris Eubank (1966–) British boxer. *The Times*, 30 Dec 1993

7 Exercise is bunk. If you are healthy, you don't need it: if you are sick, you shouldn't take it.

Henry Ford (1863–1947) US car manufacturer. Attrib.

8 Bullfighting is the only art in which the artist is in danger of death and in which the degree of brilliance in the performance is left to the fighter's honour.

Ernest Hemingway (1899–1961) US novelist. *Death in the Afternoon*, Ch. 9

9 When in doubt, win the trick.

Edmond Hoyle (1672–1769) English writer on card games. *Hoyle's Games*, 'Whist, Twenty-four Short Rules for Learners'

10 The only athletic sport I ever mastered was backgammon.

Douglas William Jerrold (1803–57) British dramatist. *Douglas Jerrold* (W. Jerrold), Vol. I, Ch. 1

11 It is unbecoming for a cardinal to ski badly.

John Paul II (Karol Wojtyla; 1920–) Polish pope (1978–). Replying to the suggestion that it was inappropriate for him, a cardinal, to ski. *John Paul II*

12 I am sorry I have not learned to play at cards. It is very useful in life: it generates kindness and consolidates society.

Samuel Johnson (1709–84) British lexicographer. *Tour to the Hebrides* (J. Boswell)

13 At what time does the dissipation of energy begin?

Lord Kelvin (1824–1907) British physicist. On realizing that his wife was planning an afternoon excursion. *Memories of a Scientific Life* (A. Fleming)

14 Man is a gaming animal. He must always be trying to get the better in something or other.

Charles Lamb (1775–1834) British essayist. *Essays of Elia*, 'Mrs Battle's Opinions on Whist'

15 O, he flies through the air with the greatest of ease,
This daring young man on the flying trapeze.

George Leybourne (d. 1884) British songwriter. *The Man on the Flying Trapeze*

16 It is a major tragedy of the struggle against doping that the atmosphere has been poisoned in this way.

Professor Arne Ljungqvist Head of medical commission of the International Amateur Athletic Federation. *The Times*, 15 Sept 1993

17 I don't like this game.

Spike Milligan (1918–) British comic actor and author. *The Goon Show*

18 Serious sport has nothing to do with fair play. It is bound up with hatred, jealousy, boastfulness, disregard of all rules and sadistic pleasure in witnessing violence; in other words it is war minus the shooting.

George Orwell (Eric Blair; 1903–50) British novelist. *The Sporting Spirit*

19 Gamesmanship or The Art of Winning Games Without Actually Cheating.

Stephen Potter (1900–69) British writer. Book title

20 For when the One Great Scorer comes
To write against your name,
He marks – not that you won or lost –
But how you played the game.

Grantland Rice (1880–1954) US sportswriter. *Alumnus Football*

21 I came from a world of stolen Cortinas; this was taxed and insured Volvo country.

Oliver Skeete (1956–) British showjumper. *The Independent*, 24 May 1995

22 It was remarked to me by the late Mr Charles Roupell…that to play billiards well was a sign of an ill-spent youth.

Herbert Spencer (1820–1903) British philosopher. *Life and Letters of Spencer* (Duncan), Ch. 20

23 I wanted a play that would paint the full face of sensuality, rebellion and revivalism. In South Wales these three phenomena have played second fiddle only to the Rugby Union which is a distillation of all three.

Gwyn Thomas (1913–81) British writer. *Jackie the Jumper* (Introduction), 'Plays and Players' 19 Jan 1963

24 There's no secret. You just press the accelerator to the floor and steer left.

Bill Vukovich (1918–55) US motor-racing driver. Explaining his success in the Indianapolis 500. Attrib.

SPRING

See months, seasons

STARING

1 It is better to be looked over than overlooked.

Mae West (1892–1980) US actress. *The Wit and Wisdom of Mae West* (ed. J. Weintraub)

2 Don't go on looking at me like that, because you'll wear your eyes out.

Émile Zola (1840–1902) French novelist. *La Bête Humaine*, Ch. 5

STARS

See also astronomy, moon, space, sun, universe

1 …things called Stars appeared, which robbed men of their souls and left them unreasoning brutes, so that they destroyed the civilization they themselves had built up.

Isaac Asimov (1920–92) US science-fiction writer. On the fictional world of Lagash night comes once every 2049 years. *Nightfall*

2 And God made two great lights: the greater light to rule the day, and the lesser light to rule the night: he made the stars also.

Bible: Genesis 1:16

3 Look at the stars! look, look up at the skies!
O look at all the fire-folk sitting in the air!
The bright boroughs, the circle-citadels there!

Gerard Manley Hopkins (1844–99) British Jesuit and poet. *The Starlight Night*

4 Bright star, would I were steadfast as thou art.

John Keats (1795–1821) British poet. *Bright Star*

5 Twinkle, twinkle, little star,
How I wonder what you are!
Up above the world so high,
Like a diamond in the sky!

Jane Taylor (1783–1824) British writer. *Rhymes for the Nursery* (with Ann Taylor), 'The Star'

6 For still I looked on that same star,
That fitful, fiery Lucifer,
Watching with mind as quiet as moss
Its light nailed to a burning cross.

Andrew John Young (1885–1971) Scottish poet. *The Evening Star*

7 Stars lay like yellow pollen
That from a flower has fallen;
And single stars I saw
Crossing themselves in awe;
Some stars in sudden fear

Fell like a falling tear.
Andrew John Young *The Stars*

STATE

See also democracy, government, republic

1 The only way to erect such a common power, as may be able to defend them from the invasion of foreigners, and the injuries of one another...is, to confer all their power and strength upon one man, or upon one assembly of men, that may reduce all their wills, by plurality of voices, unto one will...This is the generation of that great Leviathan, or rather (to speak more reverently) of that *Mortal God*, to which we owe under the *Immortal God*, our peace and defence.
Thomas Hobbes (1588–1679) English philosopher. *Leviathan*, Pt. II, Ch. 17

2 So long as the state exists there is no freedom. When there is freedom there will be no state.
Lenin (Vladimir Ilich Ulyanov; 1870–1924) Russian revolutionary leader. *The State and Revolution*, Ch. 5

3 In a free society the state does not administer the affairs of men. It administers justice among men who conduct their own affairs.
Walter Lippman (1889–1974) US editor and writer. *An Enquiry into the Principles of a Good Society*

4 The worth of a State in the long run is the worth of the individuals composing it.
John Stuart Mill (1806–73) British philosopher. *On Liberty*, Ch. 5

5 The state is an instrument in the hands of the ruling class for suppressing the resistance of its class enemies.
Joseph Stalin (J. Dzhugashvili; 1879–1953) Soviet statesman. *Stalin's Kampf* (ed. M. R. Werner)

STATELY HOMES

See also architecture, aristocracy, houses

1 Now Spring, sweet laxative of Georgian strains,
Quickens the ink in literary veins,
The Stately Homes of England ope their doors
To piping Nancy-boys and Crashing Bores.
Roy Campbell (1901–57) South African poet. *The Georgiad*

2 The Stately Homes of England
How beautiful they stand,
To prove the upper classes
Have still the upper hand.
Noël Coward (1899–1973) British dramatist. *Operette*, 'The Stately Homes of England'

3 And though the Van Dycks have to go
And we pawn the Bechstein grand,
We'll stand by the Stately Homes of England.
Noël Coward *Operette*, The Stately Homes of England

4 The stately homes of England,
How beautiful they stand!
Amidst their tall ancestral trees,
O'er all the pleasant land.
Felicia Dorothea Hemans (1793–1835) British poet. *The Homes of England*

5 Those comfortably padded lunatic asylums which are known, euphemistically, as the stately homes of England.
Virginia Woolf (1882–1941) British novelist. *The Common Reader*, 'Lady Dorothy Nevill'

STATISTICS

1 A witty statesman said, you might prove anything by figures.
Thomas Carlyle (1795–1881) Scottish historian and essayist. *Critical and Miscellaneous Essays*, 'Chartism'

2 There are three kinds of lies: lies, damned lies and statistics.
Benjamin Disraeli (1804–81) British statesman. *Autobiography* (Mark Twain)

3 We are just statistics, born to consume resources.
Horace (Quintus Horatius Flaccus; 65–8 BC) Roman poet. *Epistles*, I

4 He uses statistics as a drunken man uses lamp-posts – for support rather than illumination.
Andrew Lang (1844–1912) Scottish writer and poet. *Treasury of Humorous Quotations*

5 You cannot feed the hungry on statistics.
David Lloyd George (1863–1945) British Liberal statesman. Advocating Tariff Reform. Speech, 1904

6 Statistics will prove anything, even the truth.
Noël Moynihan (1916–94) British doctor and writer. Attrib.

7 To understand God's thoughts we must study statistics, for these are the measure of his purpose.
Florence Nightingale (1820–1910) British nurse. *Life...of Francis Galton* (K. Pearson), Vol. II, Ch. 13

8 I am one of the unpraised, unrewarded millions without whom Statistics would be a bankrupt science. It is we who are born, who marry, who die, in constant ratios.
Logan Pearsall Smith (1865–1946) US writer. *Trivia*

9 A single death is a tragedy; a million is a statistic.
Joseph Stalin (J. Dzhugashvili; 1879–1953) Soviet statesman. Attrib.

10 There are two kinds of statistics, the kind you look up and the kind you make up.
Rex Todhunter Stout (1886–1975) US writer. *Death of a Doxy*, Ch. 9

11 Facts speak louder than statistics.
Geoffrey Streatfield (1897–1978) British lawyer. *The Observer*, 'Sayings of the Week', 19 Mar 1950

STRIKES

See also industrial relations

1 Not a penny off the pay; not a minute on the day.

A. J. Cook (1885–1931) British trade-union leader. Slogan used in the miners' strike, 1926

2 There is no right to strike against the public safety by anybody, anywhere, any time.

Calvin Coolidge (1872–1933) US president. Referring to the Boston police strike. Remark, 14 Sept 1919

3 The trouble with employers is that they only like ballots so long as you lose them.

Jimmy Knapp (1940–) General Secretary of the National Union of Railwaymen. Referring to British Rail's decision to go to court following a ballot solidly in favour of strike action. *The Guardian*, 1989

4 Another fact of life that will not have escaped you is that, in this country, the twenty-four-hour strike is like the twenty-four-hour flu. You have to reckon on it lasting at least five days.

Frank Muir (1920–) British writer and broadcaster. *You Can't Have Your Kayak and Heat It* (Frank Muir and Dennis Norden), 'Great Expectations'

5 Have you noticed, the last four strikes we've had, it's pissed down? It wouldn't be a bad idea to check the weather reports before they pull us out next time.

Johnny Speight (1920–) British television scriptwriter. *Till Death Do Us Part*

STUBBORNNESS

See also determination, inflexibility, petulance

1 You can lead a horse to the water, but you can't make him drink.

Proverb

2 Obstinate people can be divided into the opinionated, the ignorant, and the boorish.

Aristotle (384–322 BC) Greek philosopher. *Nicomachean Ethics*, Bk. VII

3 'Tis known by the name of perseverance in a good cause, – and of obstinacy in a bad one.

Laurence Sterne (1713–68) Irish-born British writer. *Tristram Shandy*

STUPIDITY

See also foolishness, ignorance

1 His mind is open; yes, it is so open that nothing is retained; ideas simply pass through him.

F. H. Bradley (1846–1924) British philosopher. Attrib.

2 He'd be sharper than a serpent's tooth, if he wasn't as dull as ditch water.

Charles Dickens (1812–70) British novelist. *Our Mutual Friend*, Bk. III, Ch. 10

3 He is not only dull in himself, but the cause of dullness in others.

Samuel Foote (1720–77) British actor and dramatist. Parody of a line from Shakespeare's *Henry IV, Part 2*. *Life of Johnson* (J. Boswell)

4 The trouble with Senator Long is that he is suffering from halitosis of the intellect. That's presuming Emperor Long has an intellect.

Harold L. Ickes (1874–1952) US Republican politician. *The Politics of Upheaval* (A. M. Schlesinger Jnr), Pt. II, Ch. 14

5 Jerry Ford is so dumb that he can't fart and chew gum at the same time.

Lyndon B. Johnson (1908–73) US statesman. Sometimes quoted as '...can't walk and chew gum'. *A Ford, Not a Lincoln* (R. Reeves), Ch. 1

6 That fellow seems to me to possess but one idea, and that is a wrong one.

Samuel Johnson (1709–84) British lexicographer. *Life of Johnson* (J. Boswell), Vol. II

7 I've been married six months. She looks like a million dollars, but she only knows a hundred and twenty words and she's only got two ideas in her head. The other one's hats.

Eric Linklater (1889–1974) Scottish novelist. *Juan in America*, Pt. II, Ch. 5

8 You've got the brain of a four-year-old boy, and I bet he was glad to get rid of it.

Groucho Marx (Julius Marx; 1895–1977) US comedian. *Horse Feathers*

9 Music-hall songs provide the dull with wit, just as proverbs provide them with wisdom.

W. Somerset Maugham (1874–1965) British novelist. *A Writer's Notebook*

10 Stupidity does not consist in being without ideas. Such stupidity would be the sweet, blissful stupidity of animals, molluscs and the gods. Human Stupidity consists in having lots of ideas, but stupid ones.

Henry de Montherlant (1896–1972) French novelist. *Notebooks*

11 She has a Rolls body and a Balham mind.

J. B. Morton (1893–1979) British journalist. *The Best of Beachcomber*, 'A Foul Innuendo'

12 I've examined your son's head, Mr Glum, and there's nothing there.

Frank Muir (1920–) British writer and broadcaster. *Take It from Here* (Frank Muir and Dennis Norden), 1957

13 You beat your pate, and fancy wit will come;
Knock as you please, there's nobody at home.

Alexander Pope (1688–1744) British poet. *Epigram*

14 Against stupidity the gods themselves struggle in vain.

Friedrich von Schiller (1759–1805) German dramatist. *Die Jungfrau von Orleans*, III:6

15 There is no sin except stupidity.

Oscar Wilde (1854–1900) Irish-born British dramatist. *The Critic as Artist*, Pt. 2

STYLE

See also fashion, taste

1 Style is the man himself.

Comte de Buffon (1707–88) French naturalist. *Discours sur le style*

2 Style, like sheer silk, too often hides eczema.

Albert Camus (1913–60) French existentialist writer. *The Fall*

3 An author arrives at a good style when his language performs what is required of it without shyness.

Cyril Connolly (1903–74) British journalist. *Enemies of Promise*, Ch. 3

4 He has never been known to use a word that might send the reader to the dictionary.

William Faulkner (1897–1962) US novelist. Referring to Ernest HEMINGWAY. Attrib.

5 Poor Faulkner. Does he really think big emotions come from big words? He thinks I don't know the ten-dollar words. I know them all right. But there are older and simpler and better words, and those are the ones I use.

Ernest Hemingway (1899–1961) US novelist. In response to a jibe by William FAULKNER. Attrib.

6 All styles are good except the tiresome sort.

Voltaire (François-Marie Arouet; 1694–1778) French writer. *L'Enfant prodigue*, Preface

7 In matters of grave importance, style, not sincerity, is the vital thing.

Oscar Wilde (1854–1900) Irish-born British dramatist. *The Importance of Being Earnest*, III

SUBJECTIVITY

See also objectivity, prejudice

1 She was one of the people who say, 'I don't know anything about music really, but I know what I like'.

Max Beerbohm (1872–1956) British writer. *Zuleika Dobson*, Ch. 16

2 An apology for the Devil – it must be remembered that we have only heard one side of the case. God has written all the books.

Samuel Butler (1835–1902) British writer. *Notebooks*

3 It is a general mistake to think the men we like are good for everything, and those we do not, good for nothing.

Lord Halifax (1633–95) English statesman. *Political, Moral and Miscellaneous Thoughts and Reflections*

4 He who knows only his own side of the case knows little of that.

John Stuart Mill (1806–73) British philosopher. *On Liberty*, Ch. 2

5 All the world is queer save thee and me, and even thou art a little queer.

Robert Owen (1771–1858) British social reformer. Referring to William Allen, his partner in business. Attrib., 1828

6 To observations which ourselves we make
We grow more partial for th' observer's sake.

Alexander Pope (1688–1744) British poet. *Moral Essays*, I

7 Partisanship is our great curse. We too readily assume that everything has two sides and that it is our duty to be on one or the other.

James Harvey Robinson (1863–1936) US historian and educator. *The Mind in the Making*

SUBURBIA

1 I come from suburbia, Dan, personally, I don't ever want to go back. It's the one place in the world that's further away than anywhere else.

Frederic Raphael (1931–) British author. *The Glittering Prizes: A Sex Life*, I:3

2 She was more than ever proud of the position of the bungalow, so almost in the country.

Angus Wilson (1913–91) British novelist. *A Bit Off the Map*, 'A Flat Country Christmas'

SUCCESS

See also achievement, failure, victory

1 Nothing succeeds like success.

Proverb

2 Nothing is harder on your laurels than resting on them.

Anonymous

3 'Tis not in mortals to command success,
But we'll do more, Sempronius; we'll deserve it.

Joseph Addison (1672–1719) British essayist. *Cato*, I:2

4 The penalty of success is to be bored by people who used to snub you.

Nancy Astor (1879–1964) American-born British politician. *Sunday Express*, 12 Jan 1956

5 One's religion is whatever he is most interested in, and yours is Success.

J. M. Barrie (1860–1937) British novelist and dramatist. *The Twelve-Pound Look*

6 All I think about is winning that bleedin' title.

Frank Bruno (1961–) British boxer. Remark, Jan 1989

7 The only infallible criterion of wisdom to vulgar minds – success.

Edmund Burke (1729–97) British politician. *Letter to a Member of the National Assembly*

8 Success is counted sweetest
By those who ne'er succeed.

Emily Dickinson (1830–86) US poet. *Success is Counted Sweetest*

9 The moral flabbiness born of the bitch-goddess Success.

William James (1842–1910) US psychologist and philosopher. Letter to H. G. Wells, 11 Sept 1906

10 Victory has a thousand fathers but defeat is an orphan.

John Fitzgerald Kennedy (1917–63) US statesman. Attrib.

11 The shortest and best way to make your fortune is to let people see clearly that it is in their interests to promote yours.

Jean de La Bruyère (1645–96) French satirist. *Les Caractères*

12 Sweet Smell of Success.

Ernest Lehman (1920–) US screenwriter. Novel and film title

13 As is the case in all branches of art, success depends in a very large measure upon individual initiative and exertion, and cannot be achieved except by dint of hard work.

Anna Pavlova (1881–1931) Russian ballet dancer. *Pavlova: A Biography* (ed. A. H. Franks), 'Pages of My Life'

14 To succeed in the world, we do everything we can to appear successful.

Duc de la Rochefoucauld (1613–80) French writer. *Maximes*, 50

15 The only place where success comes before work is a dictionary.

Vidal Sassoon (1928–) British hair stylist. Quoting one of his teachers in a BBC radio broadcast

16 There are no gains without pains.

Adlai Stevenson (1900–65) US statesman. Speech, Chicago, 26 July 1952

SUFFERING

1 He that lives long suffers much.

Proverb

2 Who has never tasted what is bitter does not know what is sweet.

German proverb

3 There was a faith-healer of Deal,
Who said, 'Although pain isn't real,
If I sit on a pin
And it punctures my skin,
I dislike what I fancy I feel.'

Anonymous

4 One does not love a place the less for having suffered in it unless it has all been suffering, nothing but suffering.

Jane Austen (1775–1817) British novelist. *Persuasion*, Ch. 20

5 Once drinking deep of that divinest anguish,
How could I seek the empty world again?

Emily Brontë (1818–48) British novelist. *Remembrance*

6 I am convinced that we have a degree of delight, and that no small one, in the real misfortunes and pains of others.

Edmund Burke (1729–97) British politician. *On the Sublime and Beautiful*, Pt. I

7 Pain – has an Element of Blank –
It cannot recollect
When it begun – or if there were
A time when it was not –.

Emily Dickinson (1830–86) US poet. Poem

8 If suffer we must, let's suffer on the heights.

Victor Hugo (1802–85) French writer. *Contemplations*, 'Les Malheureux'

9 The music, yearning like a God in pain.

John Keats (1795–1821) British poet. *The Eve of Saint Agnes*, VII

10 Rather suffer than die is man's motto.

Jean de La Fontaine (1621–95) French poet. *Fables*, I, 'La Mort et le Bûcheron'

11 A man who fears suffering is already suffering from what he fears.

Michel de Montaigne (1533–92) French essayist. *Essais*, III

12 Every reformation must have its victims. You can't expect the fatted calf to share the enthusiasm of the angels over the prodigal's return.

Saki (Hector Hugh Munro; 1870–1916) British writer. *Reginald on the Academy*

13 Remember that pain has this most excellent quality: if prolonged it cannot be severe, and if severe it cannot be prolonged.

Seneca (c. 4 BC–65 AD) Roman author. *Epistulae ad Lucilium*, XCIV

14 Thou art a soul in bliss; but I am bound
Upon a wheel of fire, that mine own tears
Do scald like molten lead.

William Shakespeare (1564–1616) English dramatist. *King Lear*, IV:7

15 I know, by sad experience, with what difficulty a mind, weakened by long and uninterrupted suffering, admits hope, much less assurance.

Sarah Siddons (1755–1831) English actress. Letter to Mrs. FitzHugh, 14 July 1801

SUICIDE

See also death

1 If you must commit suicide…always contrive to do it as decorously as possible; the decencies, whether of life or of death, should never be lost sight of.

George Henry Borrow (1803–81) British writer. *Lavengro*, Ch. 23

2 The strangest whim has seized me…After all I think I will not hang myself today.

G. K. Chesterton (1874–1936) British writer. *A Ballade of Suicide*

3 Not only is suicide a sin, it is the sin. It is the ultimate and absolute evil, the refusal to take the oath of loyalty to life. The man who kills a man, kills a man. The man who kills himself kills all men; as far as he is concerned he wipes out the world.

G. K. Chesterton *Orthodoxy*

4 Suicide is the worst form of murder, because it leaves no opportunity for repentance.

John Churton Collins (1848–1908) *Life and Memoirs of John Churton Collins* (L. C. Collins), Appendix VII

5 There are many who dare not kill themselves for fear of what the neighbours might say.

Cyril Connolly (1903–74) British journalist. *The Unquiet Grave*

6 The thought of suicide is a great source of comfort: with it a calm passage is to be made across many a bad night.

Friedrich Wilhelm Nietzsche (1844–1900) German philosopher. *Jenseits von Gut und Böse*

7 Razors pain you
Rivers are damp;
Acids stain you;
And drugs cause cramp.
Guns aren't lawful;
Nooses give;
Gas smells awful;
You might as well live.

Dorothy Parker (1893–1967) US writer. *Enough Rope*, 'Resumé'

8 When you're between any sort of devil and the deep blue sea, the deep blue sea sometimes looks very inviting.

Terence Rattigan (1911–77) British dramatist. *The Deep Blue Sea*

9 Next week, or next month, or next year I'll kill myself. But I might as well last out my month's rent, which has been paid up, and my credit for breakfast in the morning.

Jean Rhys (1894–1979) Dominican-born British novelist. *Good Morning, Midnight*, Pt. II

10 It is against the law to commit suicide in this man's town ... although what the law can do to a guy who commits suicide I am never able to figure out.

Damon Runyon (1884–1946) US writer. *Guys and Dolls*

11 Dost thou not see my baby at my breast
That sucks the nurse asleep?

William Shakespeare (1564–1616) English dramatist. Holding the asp to her breast. *Antony and Cleopatra*, V:2

12 To be, or not to be – that is the question;
Whether 'tis nobler in the mind to suffer
The slings and arrows of outrageous fortune,
Or to take arms against a sea of troubles,
And by opposing end them? To die, to sleep –
No more; and by a sleep to say we end
The heart-ache and the thousand natural shocks
That flesh is heir to, 'tis a consummation
Devoutly to be wish'd. To die, to sleep;
To sleep, perchance to dream. Ay, there's the rub;
For in that sleep of death what dreams may come,
When we have shuffled off this mortal coil,
Must give us pause.

William Shakespeare *Hamlet*, III:1

13 A still small voice spake unto me,
'Thou art so full of misery,
Were it not better not to be?'

Alfred, Lord Tennyson (1809–92) British poet. *The Two Voices*

14 Never murder a man who is committing suicide.

Woodrow Wilson (1856–1925) US statesman. *Mr Wilson's War* (John Dos Passos), Pt. II, Ch. 10

SUITABILITY

1 In seed time learn, in harvest teach, in winter enjoy.

William Blake (1757–1827) British poet. *The Marriage of Heaven and Hell*, 'Proverbs of Hell'

2 A cow is a very good animal in the field; but we turn her out of a garden.

Samuel Johnson (1709–84) British lexicographer. Responding to Boswell's objections to the expulsion of six Methodists from Oxford University. *The Personal History of Samuel Johnson* (C. Hibbert)

3 Today I dressed to meet my father's eyes; yesterday it was for my husband's.

Julia (39 BC–14 AD) Daughter of Augustus. On being complimented by her father, the emperor Augustus, on her choice of a more modest dress than the one she had worn the previous day. *Saturnalia* (Macrobius)

4 At Christmas I no more desire a rose
Than wish a snow in May's newfangled shows.

William Shakespeare (1564–1616) English dramatist. *Love's Labour's Lost*, I:1

SUMMER

See months, seasons

SUMMONS

See also invitations

1 Go, for they call you, Shepherd, from the hill.

Matthew Arnold (1822–88) British poet and critic. *The Scholar Gipsy*

2 Whistle and she'll come to you.

Francis Beaumont (1584–1616) English dramatist. *Wit Without Money*, IV:4

3 Mr Watson, come here; I want you.

Alexander Graham Bell (1847–1922) Scottish scientist. The first telephone conversation, 10 Mar 1876, in Boston. Attrib.

4 Dauntless the slug-horn to my lips I set,
And blew. *Childe Roland to the Dark Tower came.*

Robert Browning (1812–89) British poet. *Childe Roland to the Dark Tower Came*, XXXIV

SUN

See also weather

1 The Sun came up upon the left,
Out of the sea came he!
And he shone bright, and on the right
Went down into the sea.

Samuel Taylor Coleridge (1772–1834) British poet. *The Rime of the Ancient Mariner*, I

2 Busy old fool, unruly Sun,
Why dost thou thus,
Through windows and through curtains call on us?

John Donne (1573–1631) English poet. *The Sun Rising*

3 I have a horror of sunsets, they're so romantic, so operatic.

Marcel Proust (1871–1922) French novelist. *À la recherche du temps perdu: Sodome et Gomorrhe*

4 ...twentieth-century woman appears to regard sunlight as a kind of cosmetic effulgence with a light aphrodisiac content – which makes it a funny thing that none of her female ancestors are recorded as seeing it the same way. Men, of course, just go on sweating in it from century to century.

John Wyndham (1903–69) British science-fiction writer. *The Kraken Wakes*

SUNDAY

1 And on the seventh day God ended his work which he had made; and he rested on the seventh day from all his work which he had made.

Bible: Genesis 2:2

2 And he said unto them, The sabbath was made for man, and not man for the sabbath: Therefore the Son of man is Lord also of the sabbath.

Bible: Mark 2:27–28

3 Of all the days that's in the week
I dearly love but one day –
And that's the day that comes betwixt
A Saturday and Monday.

Henry Carey (c. 1690–1743) English poet and musician. *Sally in our Alley*

4 The better day, the worse deed.

Matthew Henry (1662–1714) English nonconformist minister. *Exposition of the Old and New Testaments*

5 The feeling of Sunday is the same everywhere, heavy, melancholy, standing still. Like when they say, 'As it was in the beginning, is now, and ever shall be, world without end.'

Jean Rhys (1894–1979) Dominican-born British novelist. *Voyage in the Dark*, Ch. 4

SUPERIORITY

See also equality, excellence, one-upmanship, snobbery

1 My name is George Nathaniel Curzon,
I am a most superior person.
My face is pink, my hair is sleek,
I dine at Blenheim once a week.

Anonymous *The Masque of Balliol*

2 The superior man is satisfied and composed; the mean man is always full of distress.

Confucius (K'ung Fu-tzu; 551–479 BC) Chinese philosopher. *Analects*

3 The superior man is distressed by his want of ability.

Confucius *Analects*

4 When you meet someone better than yourself, turn your thoughts to becoming his equal. When you meet someone not as good as you are, look within and examine your own self.

Confucius *Analects*

5 And lo! Ben Adhem's name led all the rest.

Leigh Hunt (1784–1859) British poet. *Abou Ben Adhem and the Angel*

6 Though I've belted you an' flayed you,
By the livin' Gawd that made you,
You're a better man than I am, Gunga Din!

Rudyard Kipling (1865–1936) Indian-born British writer. *Gunga Din*

7 Sir, you have the advantage of me.
– Not yet I haven't, but wait till I get you outside.

Groucho Marx (Julius Marx; 1895–1977) US comedian. *Monkey Business*

8 Above the vulgar flight of common souls.

Arthur Murphy (1727–1805) Irish dramatist, writer, and actor. *Zenobia*, V

9 I teach you the Superman. Man is something that is to be surpassed.

Friedrich Wilhelm Nietzsche (1844–1900) German philosopher. *Thus Spake Zarathustra*

10 It is brought home to you...that it is only because miners sweat their guts out that superior persons can remain superior.

George Orwell (Eric Blair; 1903–50) British novelist. *The Road to Wigan Pier*, Ch. 2

11 'I believe I take precedence,' he said coldly; 'you are merely the club Bore: I am the club Liar.'

Saki (Hector Hugh Munro; 1870–1916) British writer. *A Defensive Diamond*

12 In the Country of the Blind the One-eyed Man is King.

H. G. Wells (1866–1946) British writer. *The Country of the Blind*

SUPERNATURAL

See also fairies

1 From ghoulies and ghosties and long-leggety beasties
And things that go bump in the night,

Good Lord, deliver us!
Anonymous Cornish prayer

2 Open Sesame!
The Arabian Nights (c. 1500) A collection of tales from the East. *The History of Ali Baba*

3 Thou shalt not suffer a witch to live.
Bible: Exodus 22:18

4 For my part, I have ever believed, and do now know, that there are witches.
Thomas Browne (1605–82) English physician and writer. *Religio Medici*, Pt. I

5 This time it vanished quite slowly, beginning with the end of the tail, and ending with the grin, which remained some time after the rest of it had gone.
Lewis Carroll (Charles Lutwidge Dodgson; 1832–98) British writer. Describing the Cheshire Cat. *Alice's Adventures in Wonderland*, Ch. 6

6 A savage place! as holy and enchanted
As e'er beneath a waning moon was haunted
By woman wailing for her demon-lover!
Samuel Taylor Coleridge (1772–1834) British poet. *Kubla Khan*

7 The girl is lost; she is burnt flesh.
Umberto Eco (1932–) Italian semiologist and writer. Referring to a suspected witch. *The Name of the Rose*

8 Religion
Has made an honest woman of the supernatural,
And we won't have it kicking over the traces again.
Christopher Fry (1907–) British dramatist. *The Lady's Not for Burning*, II

9 All argument is against it; but all belief is for it.
Samuel Johnson (1709–84) British lexicographer. Of the ghost of a dead person. *Life of Johnson* (J. Boswell), Vol. III

10 'La belle Dame sans Merci
Hath thee in thrall!'
John Keats (1795–1821) British poet. *La Belle Dame Sans Merci*

11 That old black magic has me in its spell.
Johnny Mercer (1909–76) US lyricist and composer. *That Old Black Magic*

12 Once upon a midnight dreary, while I pondered, weak and weary,
Over many a quaint and curious volume of forgotten lore,
While I nodded, nearly napping, suddenly there came a tapping,
As of some one gently rapping, rapping at my chamber door.
Edgar Allan Poe (1809–49) US poet and writer. *The Raven*

13 There are more things in heaven and earth, Horatio,
Than are dreamt of in your philosophy.
William Shakespeare (1564–1616) English dramatist. *Hamlet*, I:5

14 This supernatural soliciting
Cannot be ill; cannot be good.
William Shakespeare *Macbeth*, I:3

15 His face was a strong – a very strong – aquiline, with high bridge of the thin nose and peculiarly arched nostrils...The mouth...was fixed and rather cruel-looking, with peculiarly sharp white teeth; these protruded over the lips, whose remarkable ruddiness showed astonishing vitality in a man of his years.
Bram Stoker (1847–1912) Irish novelist. Referring to Count Dracula. *Dracula*, Ch. 2

16 His eyes flamed red with devilish passion; the great nostrils of the white aquiline nose opened wide and quivered at the edges; and the white sharp teeth, behind the full lips of the blood-dripping mouth, champed together like those of a wild beast.
Bram Stoker *Dracula*, Ch. 21

SUPERSTITION

See also luck

1 A dimple in the chin, a devil within.
Proverb

2 Meet on the stairs and you won't meet in heaven.
Proverb

3 One for sorrow, two for mirth; three for a wedding, four for a birth; five for silver, six for gold; seven for a secret, not to be told; eight for heaven, nine for hell; and ten for the devil's own sel.
Proverb. Referring to magpies or crows; there are numerous variants.

4 See a pin and pick it up, all the day you'll have good luck; see a pin and let it lie, you'll want a pin before you die.
Proverb

5 Third time lucky.
Proverb

6 Of course I don't believe in it. But I understand that it brings you luck whether you believe in it or not.
Niels Bohr (1885–1962) Danish physicist. When asked why he had a horseshoe on his wall. Attrib.

7 Superstition is the religion of feeble minds.
Edmund Burke (1729–97) British politician. *Reflections on the Revolution in France*

8 Superstition is the poetry of life.
Goethe (1749–1832) German poet and dramatist. *Sprüche in Prosa*, III

9 And some of the bigger bears try to pretend
That they came round the corner to look for a friend;
And they'll try to pretend that nobody cares
Whether you walk on the lines or the squares.
A. A. Milne (1882–1956) British writer. *When We Were Very Young*, 'Lines and Squares'

10 They say there is divinity in odd numbers, either in nativity, chance, or death.

William Shakespeare (1564–1616) English dramatist. *The Merry Wives of Windsor*, V:1

11 Superstition sets the whole world in flames; philosophy quenches them.

Voltaire (François-Marie Arouet; 1694–1778) French writer. *Dictionnaire philosophique*, 'Superstition'

SUPPORT

See also loyalty

1 He found him in a desert land, and in the waste howling wilderness; he led him about, he instructed him, he kept him as the apple of his eye.

Bible: Deuteronomy 32:10

2 The finest plans have always been spoiled by the littleness of those that should carry them out. Even emperors can't do it all by themselves.

Bertolt Brecht (1898–1956) German dramatist. *Mother Courage*, VI

3 Either back us or sack us.

James Callaghan (1912–) British politician and prime minister. Speech, Labour Party Conference, Brighton, 5 Oct 1977

4 What I want is men who will support me when I am in the wrong.

Lord Melbourne (1779–1848) British statesman. Replying to someone who said he would support Melbourne as long as he was in the right. *Lord M.* (Lord David Cecil)

5 While I cannot be regarded as a pillar, I must be regarded as a buttress of the church, because I support it from the outside.

Lord Melbourne Attrib.

6 Ladies and gentleman, it takes more than one to make a ballet.

Ninette de Valois (Edris Stannus; 1898–) British ballet dancer and choreographer. *New Yorker*

SURVIVAL

See also evolution, self-preservation

1 I haven't asked you to make me young again. All I want is to go on getting older.

Konrad Adenauer (1876–1967) German statesman. Replying to his doctor. Attrib.

2 We are survival machines – robot vehicles blindly programmed to preserve the selfish molecules known as genes. This is a truth which still fills me with astonishment.

Richard Dawkins (1941–) British ethologist. *The Selfish Gene*

3 The perpetual struggle for room and food.

Thomas Robert Malthus (1766–1834) British clergyman and economist. *Essays on the Principle of Population*

4 Our loyalties are to the species and the planet. We speak for Earth. Our obligation to survive is owed not just to ourselves but also to that cosmos, ancient and vast, from which we spring.

Carl Sagan (1934–96) US astronomer. *Cosmos*

5 The thing-in-itself, the will-to-live, exists whole and undivided in every being, even in the tiniest; it is present as completely as in all that ever were, are, and will be, taken together.

Arthur Schopenhauer (1788–1860) German philosopher. *Parerga and Paralipomena*

6 This is the Law of the Yukon, that only the strong shall thrive;
That surely the weak shall perish, and only the Fit survive.

Robert William Service (1874–1958) Canadian poet. *The Law of the Yukon*

SUSPICION

See also mistrust

1 Suspicions amongst thoughts are
like bats amongst birds, they ever fly by twilight.

Francis Bacon (1561–1626) English philosopher. *Essays*, 'Of Suspicion'

SWITZERLAND

See also Europe

1 Since both its national products, snow and chocolate, melt, the cuckoo clock was invented solely in order to give tourists something solid to remember it by.

Alan Coren (1938–) British humorist and writer. *The Sanity Inspector*, 'And Though They Do Their Best'

2 The Swiss who are not a people so much as a neat clean quite solvent business.

William Faulkner (1897–1962) US novelist. *Intruder in the Dust*, Ch. 7

3 I look upon Switzerland as an inferior sort of Scotland.

Sydney Smith (1771–1845) British clergyman and essayist. Letter to Lord Holland, 1815

4 They say that if the Swiss had designed these mountains they'd be rather flatter.

Paul Theroux (1941–) US-born writer. Referring to the Alps. *The Great Railway Bazaar*, Ch. 28

5 In Italy for thirty years under the Borgias they had warfare, terror, murder, bloodshed – they produced Michelangelo, Leonardo da Vinci and the Renaissance. In Switzerland they had brotherly love, five hundred years of democracy and peace, and what did they produce…? The cuckoo clock.

Orson Welles (1915–85) US film actor. *The Third Man*

SYMPATHY

See also comfort

1 Sympathy – for all these people, for being foreigners – lay over the gathering like a woolly blanket; and no one was enjoying it at all.

Malcolm Bradbury (1932–) British academic and novelist. *Eating People is Wrong*, Ch. 2

2 To be sympathetic without discrimination is so very debilitating.

Ronald Firbank (1886–1926) British novelist. *Vainglory*

3 She was a machine-gun riddling her hostess with sympathy.

Aldous Huxley (1894–1964) British novelist. *Mortal Coils*, 'The Gioconda Smile'

4 I can sympathize with people's pains,
but not with their pleasures. There is something curiously boring about somebody else's happiness.

Aldous Huxley *Limbo*, 'Cynthia'

5 To show pity is felt as a sign of contempt because one has clearly ceased to be an object of *fear* as soon as one is pitied.

Friedrich Wilhelm Nietzsche (1844–1900) German philosopher. *The Wanderer and His Shadow*

6 I can sympathize with everything, except suffering.

Oscar Wilde (1854–1900) Irish-born British dramatist. *The Picture of Dorian Gray*, Ch. 3

T

TACT

See also diplomacy

1 Leave well alone.
Proverb

2 Let sleeping dogs lie.
Proverb

3 Social tact is making your company feel at home, even though you wish they were.
Anonymous

4 One shouldn't talk of halters in the hanged man's house.
Miguel de Cervantes (1547–1616) Spanish novelist. *Don Quixote*, Pt. I, Ch. 25

5 Tact consists in knowing how far we may go too far.
Jean Cocteau (1889–1963) French poet and artist. In *Treasury of Humorous Quotations*

6 My advice was delicately poised between the cliché and the indiscretion.
Robert Runcie (1921–) British churchman (Archbishop of Canterbury). Comment to the press concerning his advice to the Prince of Wales and Lady Diana Spencer on their approaching wedding, 13 July 1981

TALENT

See also genius, talent and genius

1 Whom the gods wish to destroy they first call promising.
Cyril Connolly (1903–74) British journalist. *Enemies of Promise*, Ch. 3

2 Talent develops in quiet places, character in the full current of human life.
Goethe (1749–1832) German poet and dramatist. *Torquato Tasso*, I

3 Middle age snuffs out more talent than even wars or sudden deaths do.
Richard Hughes (1900–76) British writer. *The Fox in the Attic*

4 There is no substitute for talent. Industry and all the virtues are of no avail.
Aldous Huxley (1894–1964) British novelist. *Point Counter Point*

5 I think it's the most extraordinary collection of talent, of human knowledge, that has ever been gathered together at the White House – with the possible exception of when Thomas Jefferson dined alone.
John Fitzgerald Kennedy (1917–63) US statesman. Said at a dinner for Nobel Prizewinners, 29 Apr 1962.

6 It's not enough to be Hungarian, you must have talent too.
Alexander Korda (Sandor Kellner; 1893–1956) Hungarian-born British film director. *Alexander Korda* (K. Kulik)

7 Let our children grow tall, and some taller than others if they have it in them to do so.
Margaret Thatcher (1925–) British politician and prime minister. Speech, US tour, 1975

TALENT AND GENIUS

See also genius, talent

1 It takes people a long time to learn the difference between talent and genius, especially ambitious young men and women.
Louisa May Alcott (1832–88) US novelist. *Little Women*, Pt. II

2 Mediocrity knows nothing higher than itself, but talent instantly recognizes genius.
Arthur Conan Doyle (1856–1930) British writer. *The Valley of Fear*

3 Genius does what it must, and Talent does what it can.
Owen Meredith (Robert Bulwer-Lytton, 1st Earl of Lytton; 1831–91) British statesman and poet. *Last Words of a Sensitive Second-rate Poet*

TASTE

See also difference, individuality

1 Good taste is better than bad taste, but bad taste is better than no taste.
Arnold Bennett (1867–1931) British novelist. *The Observer*, 'Sayings of the Week', 24 Aug 1930

2 It's better to have something real than fancy poncy rubbish.
Jarvis Cocker British pop singer with the group Pulp. *The Guardian*, 22 Feb 1996

3 Taste is the feminine of genius.
Edward Fitzgerald (1809–83) British poet. Letter to J. R. Lowell, Oct 1877

4 Our tastes greatly alter. The lad does not care for the child's rattle, and the old man does not care for the young man's whore.
Samuel Johnson (1709–84) British lexicographer. *Life of Johnson* (J. Boswell), Vol. II

5 What is food to one man is bitter poison to others.
Lucretius (Titus Lucretius Carus; c. 99–55 BC) Roman philosopher. *On the Nature of the Universe*, IV

6 The kind of people who always go on about whether a thing is in good taste invariably have very bad taste.
Joe Orton (1933–67) British dramatist. Attrib.

7 The play, I remember, pleas'd not the million; 'twas caviare to the general.

William Shakespeare (1564–1616) English dramatist. *Hamlet*, II:2

8 You had no taste when you married me.

Richard Brinsley Sheridan (1751–1816) British dramatist. *The School for Scandal*, I

TAXATION

1 The Congress will push me to raise taxes and I'll say no, and they'll push, and I'll say no, and they'll push again. And I'll say to them, read my lips, no new taxes.

George Bush (1924–) US politician and president. Often misquoted as 'Watch my lips'. Speech, Republican Party Convention, New Orleans, 19 Aug 1988

2 They can't collect legal taxes from illegal money.

Al Capone (1899–1947) Italian-born US gangster. Objecting to the US Bureau of Internal Revenue claiming large sums in unpaid back tax. *Capone* (J. Kobler)

3 The hardest thing in the world to understand is income tax.

Albert Einstein (1879–1955) German-born US physicist. Attrib.

4 The greatest harm that cometh of a king's poverty is, that he shall by necessity be forced to find exquisite means of getting goods, as to put in default some of his subjects that be innocent, and upon the rich men more than the poor, because they may the better pay.

John Fortescue (c. 1394–1476) English jurist. *The Governance of England*

5 In this world nothing is certain but death and taxes.

Benjamin Franklin (1706–90) US scientist and statesman. Letter to Jean-Baptiste Leroy, 13 Nov 1789

6 *Excise.* A hateful tax levied upon commodities.

Samuel Johnson (1709–84) British lexicographer. *Dictionary of the English Language*

7 Sir, I now pay you this exorbitant charge, but I must ask you to explain to her Majesty that she must not in future look upon me as a source of income.

Charles Kemble (1775–1854) British actor. On being obliged to hand over his income tax to the tax collector. *Humour in the Theatre* (J. Aye)

8 The avoidance of taxes is the only pursuit that still carries any reward.

John Maynard Keynes (1883–1946) British economist. Attrib.

9 The Chancellor of the Exchequer is a man whose duties make him more or less of a taxing machine. He is intrusted with a certain amount of misery which it is his duty to distribute as fairly as he can.

Robert Lowe (1811–92) British lawyer and politician. Speech, House of Commons, 11 Apr 1870

10 The taxpayer is someone who works for the federal government but doesn't have to take a civil service examination.

Ronald Reagan (1911–) US politician and president. Attrib.

11 There is no art which one government sooner learns of another than that of draining money from the pockets of the people.

Adam Smith (1723–90) Scottish economist. *The Wealth of Nations*

12 For God's sake, madam, don't say that in England for if you do, they will surely tax it.

Jonathan Swift (1667–1745) Irish-born Anglican priest and writer. Responding to Lady Carteret's admiration for the quality of the air in Ireland. *Lives of the Wits* (H. Pearson)

TECHNOLOGY

See also computers, progress, science, television and radio

1 Give me a firm place to stand, and I will move the earth.

Archimedes (c. 287–212 BC) Greek mathematician. *On the Lever*

2 Man is a tool-using animal.

Thomas Carlyle (1795–1881) Scottish historian and essayist. *Sartor Resartus*, Bk. I, Ch. 5

3 Any sufficiently advanced technology is indistinguishable from magic.

Arthur C. Clarke (1917–) British science-fiction writer. *The Lost Worlds of 2001*

4 Man is a tool-making animal.

Benjamin Franklin (1706–90) US scientist and statesman. *Life of Johnson* (J. Boswell), 7 Apr 1778

5 One machine can do the work of fifty ordinary men. No machine can do the work of one extraordinary man.

Elbert Hubbard (1856–1915) US writer. *Roycroft Dictionary and Book of Epigrams*

6 That plastic Buddha jars out a Karate screech

Before the soft words with their spores
The cosmetic breath of the gravestone

Death invented the phone it looks like the altar of death

Ted Hughes (1930–) British poet. *Selected Poems 1957–1981*, 'Do not Pick up the Telephone'

7 Have strong suspicions that Crippen London cellar murderer and accomplice are amongst saloon passengers moustache taken off growing beard accomplice dressed as boy voice manner and build undoubtedly a girl both travelling as Mr and Master Robinson

Captain Kendall This was the first time a wireless telegraphy message from a ship at sea led to the arrest of criminals. Telegram to Scotland Yard, 22 July 1910

8 It was difficult to decide whether the system that produced the kettle was a miracle of human ingenuity and co-operation or a colossal waste of resources, human and natural. Would we all be better off boiling our water in a pot hung over an open fire? Or was it the facility to do such things at the touch of a button that freed men, and more particularly women, from servile labour and made it possible for them to become literary critics?

David Lodge (1935–) British author. *Nice Work*, V

9 The new electronic interdependence recreates the world in the image of a global village.

Marshall McLuhan (1911–81) Canadian sociologist. *The Gutenberg Galaxy*

10 For tribal man space was the uncontrollable mystery. For technological man it is time that occupies the same role.

Marshall McLuhan *The Mechanical Bride*, 'Magic that Changes Mood'

11 Marconi's most cherished possession was a gold tablet presented to him by 600 survivors of the *Titanic* who had been saved by the fact that the ship's wireless transmitter had been able to call ships from hundreds of miles away to pick up survivors.

Marchese Guglielmo Marconi (1874–1937) Italian electrical engineer. *The Daily Herald*, 21 July 1937

12 The machine threatens all achievement.

Rainer Maria Rilke (1875–1926) Austrian poet. *Die Sonette an Orpheus*, II, 10

13 Pylons, those pillars
Bare like nude giant girls that have no secret.

Stephen Spender (1909–95) British poet. *The Pylons*

14 No man...who has wrestled with a self-adjusting card table can ever quite be the man he once was.

James Thurber (1894–1961) US humorist. *Let Your Mind Alone*, 'Sex ex Machina'

TEETH

1 For years I have let dentists ride roughshod over my teeth: I have been sawed, hacked, chopped, whittled, bewitched, bewildered, tattooed, and signed on again; but this is cuspid's last stand.

S. J. Perelman (1904–79) US humorous writer. *Crazy Like a Fox*, 'Nothing but the Tooth'

2 I'll dispose of my teeth as I see fit, and after they've gone, I'll get along. I started off living on gruel, and by God, I can always go back to it again.

S. J. Perelman *Crazy Like a Fox*, 'Nothing but the Tooth'

3 Certain people are born with natural false teeth.

Robert Robinson (1927–) British writer and broadcaster. BBC radio programme, *Stop the Week*, 1977

4 Adam and Eve had many advantages, but the principal one was that they escaped teething.

Mark Twain (Samuel Langhorne Clemens; 1835–1910) US writer. *The Tragedy of Pudd'nhead Wilson*, Ch. 4

5 To lose a lover or even a husband or two during the course of one's life can be vexing. But to lose one's teeth is a catastrophe.

Hugh Wheeler (1912–87) British-born US writer. *A Little Night Music*

TELEGRAMS

1 To hell with you. Offensive letter follows.

Anonymous Telegram to Sir Alec Douglas-Home

2 Winston's back.

Anonymous Signal to all ships of the Royal Navy from the Admiralty when Churchill was reappointed First Sea Lord, 3 Sept 1939

3 Streets full of water. Please advise.

Robert Benchley (1889–1945) US humorist. Telegram sent to his editor on arriving in Venice. Attrib.

4 Price of Herald three cents daily.

James Gordon Bennett (1841–1918) US editor. Telegram to William Randolph Hearst, when he heard that Hearst was trying to buy his paper. *The Life and Death of the Press Barons* (P. Brandon)

5 Nothing to be fixed except your performance.

Noël Coward (1899–1973) British dramatist. Replying to a telegram from the actress Gertrude Lawrence – 'Nothing wrong that can't be fixed' – referring to her part in Coward's play *Private Lives*. *Noël Coward and his Friends*

6 Dear Mrs A., hooray hooray,
At last you are deflowered
On this as every other day
I love you. Noël Coward.

Noël Coward Telegram to Gertrude Lawrence on her marriage to Richard S. Aldrich

7 'Old Cary Grant fine. How you?'

Cary Grant (Archibald Leach; 1904–86) British-born US film star. Replying to a telegram sent to his agent inquiring: 'How old Cary Grant?'. *The Filmgoer's Book of Quotes* (Leslie Halliwell)

8 ?

Victor Hugo (1802–85) French writer. The entire contents of a telegram sent to his publishers asking how *Les Misérables* was selling the reply was '!'. *The Literary Life* (R. Hendrickson)

9 Have strong suspicions that Crippen London cellar murderer and accomplice are amongst saloon passengers moustache taken off growing beard accomplice dressed as boy voice manner and build undoubtedly a girl both travelling as Mr and Master Robinson.

Captain Kendall This was the first time a wireless telegraphy message from a ship at sea led to the arrest of criminals. Telegram to Scotland Yard, 22 July 1910

10 We have finished the job, what shall we do with the tools?

Haile Selassie (1892–1975) Emperor of Ethiopia. Telegram sent to Winston Churchill, mimicking his 'Give us the tools, and we will finish the job'. *Ambrosia and Small Beer*, Ch. 4 (Edward Marsh)

11 Reports of my death are greatly exaggerated.

Mark Twain (Samuel Langhorne Clemens; 1835–1910) US writer. On learning that his obituary had been published. Cable to the Associated Press

12 Nurse unupblown.

Evelyn Waugh (1903–66) British novelist. Cable sent after he had failed, while a journalist serving in Ethiopia, to substantiate a rumour that an English nurse had been blown up in an Italian air raid. *Our Marvelous Native Tongue* (R. Claiborne)

13 No, no, Oscar, you forget. When you and I are together we never talk about anything except me.

James Whistler (1834–1903) US painter. Cable replying to Oscar Wilde's message: 'When you and I are together we never talk about anything except ourselves'. *The Gentle Art of Making Enemies*

TELEVISION AND RADIO

See also journalism

1 What do we want? Radio 4! Where do we want it? Long wave! And what do we say? Please!

Anonymous Chanted by protesters who opposed the BBC's plans to broadcast Radio 4 on FM only. *The Guardian*, 5 Apr 1993

2 Television is more interesting than people. If it were not, we should have people standing in the corners of our rooms.

Alan Coren (1938–) British humorist and writer. In *The Times*

3 If any reader of this book is in the grip of some habit of which he is deeply ashamed, I advise him not to give way to it in secret but to do it on television. No-one will pass him with averted gaze on the other side of the street. People will cross the road at the risk of losing their own lives in order to say 'We saw you on the telly'.

Quentin Crisp (?1910–) Model, publicist, and writer. *How to Become a Virgin*

4 Television is an invention that permits you to be entertained in your living room by people you wouldn't have in your home.

David Frost (1939–) British television personality. Attrib., CBS television, 1971 your home

5 Television brought the brutality of war into the comfort of the living room. Vietnam was lost in the living rooms of America – not on the battlefields of Vietnam.

Marshall McLuhan (1911–81) Canadian sociologist. Montreal *Gazette*, 16 May 1975

6 Television? No good will come of this device. The word is half Greek and half Latin.

C. P. Scott (1846–1932) British journalist. Attrib.

7 Television – the drug of the nation
Breeding ignorance and feeding radiation.

The Disposable Heroes of Hiphoprisy US rap band. 'Television, the Drug of the Nation'

TEMPTATION

1 Forbidden fruit is sweet.

Proverb

2 If you can't be good, be careful.

Proverb

3 I am not over-fond of resisting temptation.

William Beckford (1759–1844) British writer. *Vathek*

4 Blessed is the man that endureth temptation: for when he is tried, he shall receive the crown of life, which the Lord hath promised to them that love him.

Bible: James 1:12

5 All the deceits of the world, the flesh, and the devil.

The Book of Common Prayer *Morning Prayer, Prayer of St Chrysostom*

6 Not all that tempts your wand'ring eyes
And heedless hearts, is lawful prize;
Nor all, that glisters, gold.

Thomas Gray (1716–71) British poet. *Ode on the Death of a Favourite Cat*

7 'You oughtn't to yield to temptation.'
'Well, somebody must, or the thing becomes absurd.'

Anthony Hope (Sir Anthony Hope Hawkins; 1863–1933) British novelist. *The Dolly Dialogues*

8 ...with peaches and women, it's only the side next the sun that's tempting.

Ouida (Marie Louise de la Ramée; 1839–1908) British novelist. *Strathmore*

9 I never resist temptation because I have found that things that are bad for me never tempt me.

George Bernard Shaw (1856–1950) Irish dramatist and critic. *The Apple Cart*

10 I can resist everything except temptation.

Oscar Wilde (1854–1900) Irish-born British dramatist. *Lady Windermere's Fan*, I

11 The only way to get rid of a temptation is to yield to it.

Oscar Wilde Repeating a similar sentiment expressed by Clementina Stirling Graham (1782–1877). *The Picture of Dorian Gray*, Ch. 2

THEATRE

See also acting, actors, audiences, criticism, literature, plays, Shakespeare

1 The reason why Absurdist plays take place in No Man's Land with only two characters is primarily financial.

Arthur Adamov (1908–70) Russian-born French dramatist. Said at the Edinburgh International Drama Conference, 13 Sept 1963

2 It's one of the tragic ironies of the theatre that only one man in it can count on steady work – the night watchman.

Tallulah Bankhead (1903–68) US actress. *Tallulah*, Ch. 1

3 The complexities of poetry are destroyed by the media. In the theatre, spoken language can be defended and expanded.

Howard Barker (1946–) British playwright. *The Times*, 3 Jan 1990

4 Drama is the back-stairs of the intellect. Philosophers and historians go in by the front door, but playwrights and novelists sneak up the back stairs with their more disreputable luggage.

Alan Bennett (1934–) British playwright. *The Sunday Times*, 24 Nov 1991

5 Tragedy is if I cut my finger. Comedy is if I walk into an open sewer and die.

Mel Brooks (Melvyn Kaminsky; 1926–) US film director. *New Yorker*, 30 Oct 1978

6 All tragedies are finish'd by a death,
All comedies are ended by a marriage.

Lord Byron (1788–1824) British poet. *Don Juan*, III

7 You know, I go to the theatre to be entertained...I don't want to see plays about rape, sodomy and drug addiction...I can get all that at home.

Peter Cook (1937–95) British writer and entertainer. *The Observer*, caption to cartoon, 8 July 1962

8 Don't put your daughter on the stage, Mrs Worthington.

Noël Coward (1899–1973) British dramatist. *Title of song*

9 Farce is the essential theatre. Farce refined becomes high comedy: farce brutalized becomes tragedy.

Gordon Craig (1872–1966) British actor. *The Story of my Days, Index*

10 We participate in a tragedy; at a comedy we only look.

Aldous Huxley (1894–1964) British novelist. *The Devils of Loudon*, Ch. 11

11 Drama never changed anybody's mind about anything.

David Mamet (1947–) US playwright. *The Times*, 15 Sept 1993

12 I never deliberately set out to shock, but when people don't walk out of my plays I think there is something wrong.

John Osborne (1929–94) British dramatist. *The Observer*, 'Sayings of the Week', 19 Jan 1975

13 I depict men as they ought to be, but Euripides portrays them as they are.

Sophocles (c. 496–406 BC) Greek dramatist. *Poetics* (Aristotle)

14 The bad end unhappily, the good unluckily. That is what tragedy means.

Tom Stoppard (1937–) Czech-born British dramatist. *Rosencrantz and Guildenstern Are Dead*, II

15 I would just like to mention Robert Houdin who in the eighteenth century invented the vanishing bird-cage trick and the theater matinée – may he rot and perish. Good afternoon.

Orson Welles (1915–85) US film actor. Addressing the audience at the end of a matinée performance. *Great Theatrical Disasters* (G. Brandreth)

THEFT

See also crime

1 The fault is great in man or woman
Who steals a goose from off a common;
But what can plead that man's excuse
Who steals a common from a goose?

Anonymous *The Tickler Magazine*, 1 Feb 1821

2 They will steal the very teeth out of your mouth as you walk through the streets. I know it from experience.

William Arabin (1773–1841) British judge. Referring to the people of Uxbridge. *Arabinesque at Law* (Sir R. Megarry)

3 Prisoner, God has given you good abilities, instead of which you go about the country stealing ducks.

William Arabin *Arabinesque at Law* (Sir R. Megarry)

4 I am laughing to think what risks you take to try to find money in a desk by night where the legal owner can never find any by day.

Honoré de Balzac (1799–1850) French novelist. Said on waking to find a burglar in the room. Attrib.

5 Stolen sweets are best.

Colley Cibber (1671–1757) British actor and dramatist. *The Rival Fools*, I

6 Travel light and you can sing in the robber's face.

Juvenal (Decimus Junius Juvenalis; 60–130 AD) Roman satirist. *Satires*, X

7 Stolen sweets are always sweeter,
Stolen kisses much completer,
Stolen looks are nice in chapels,
Stolen, stolen, be your apples.

Hunt Leigh (1784–1859) British poet. *Song of Fairies Robbing an Orchard*

THEORY

See also ideas

1 A thing may look specious in theory, and yet be ruinous in practice; a thing may look evil in theory, and yet be in practice excellent.

Edmund Burke (1729–97) British politician. Impeachment of Warren Hastings, 19 Feb 1788

2 A theory can be proved by experiment; but no path leads from experiment to the birth of a theory.

Albert Einstein (1879–1955) German-born US physicist. *The Sunday Times*, 18 July 1976

3 For hundreds of pages the closely-reasoned arguments unroll, axioms and theorems interlock. And what remains with us in the end? A general sense that the world can be expressed in closely-reasoned arguments, in interlocking axioms and theorems.

Michael Frayn (1933–) British journalist and writer. *Constructions*

4 Dear friend, theory is all grey,
And the golden tree of life is green.

Goethe (1749–1832) German poet and dramatist. *Faust*, Pt. I

5 You know very well that unless you're a scientist, it's much more important for a theory to be shapely, than for it to be true.

Christopher Hampton (1946–) British writer and dramatist. *The Philanthropist*, Sc. 1

6 It is a good morning exercise for a research scientist to discard a pet hypothesis every day before breakfast. It keeps him young.

Konrad Lorenz (1903–89) Austrian zoologist. *On Aggression*, Ch. 2

7 When the torrent sweeps a man against a boulder, you must expect him to scream, and you need not be surprised if the scream is sometimes a theory.

Robert Louis Stevenson (1850–94) Scottish writer. *Virginibus Puerisque*

THINKING

See also belief, ideas, intellect, intelligence, mind, philosophy

1 I have always found that the man whose second thoughts are good is worth watching.

J. M. Barrie (1860–1937) British novelist and dramatist. *What Every Woman Knows*, III

2 Mirrors should think longer before they reflect.

Jean Cocteau (1889–1963) French poet and artist. *The Sunday Times*, 20 Oct 1963

3 *Cogito, ergo sum.*
I think, therefore I am.

René Descartes (1596–1650) French philosopher. *Le Discours de la méthode*

4 The most fluent talkers or most plausible reasoners are not always the justest thinkers.

William Hazlitt (1778–1830) British essayist. *On Prejudice*

5 Most of one's life...is one prolonged effort to prevent oneself thinking.

Aldous Huxley (1894–1964) British novelist. *Mortal Coils*, 'Green Tunnels'

6 You can't think rationally on an empty stomach, and a whole lot of people can't do it on a full one either.

Lord Reith (1889–1971) British administrator. Attrib.

7 People don't seem to realize that it takes time and effort and preparation to think. Statesmen are far too busy making speeches to think.

Bertrand Russell (1872–1970) British philosopher. *Kenneth Harris Talking To:* 'Bertrand Russell' (Kenneth Harris)

8 Many people would sooner die than think. In fact they do.

Bertrand Russell *Thinking About Thinking* (A. Flew)

9 My thought is *me*: that is why I can't stop. I exist by what I think...and I can't prevent myself from thinking.

Jean-Paul Sartre (1905–80) French writer. *Nausea*

10 There is nothing either good or bad, but thinking makes it so.

William Shakespeare (1564–1616) English dramatist. *Hamlet*, II:2

11 Thinking is to me the greatest fatigue in the world.

John Vanbrugh (1664–1726) English architect and dramatist. *The Relapse*, II:1

12 Great thoughts come from the heart.

Marquis de Vauvenargues (1715–47) French soldier and writer. *Réflexions et maximes*

13 In order to draw a limit to thinking, we should have to be able to think both sides of this limit.

Ludwig Wittgenstein (1889–1951) Austrian philosopher. *Tractatus Logico-Philosophicus*, Preface

THIRST

See also alcohol, desire, drinks, hunger

1 There are two reasons for drinking; one is, when you are thirsty, to cure it; the other, when you are not thirsty, to prevent it...Prevention is better than cure.

Thomas Love Peacock (1785–1866) British novelist. *Melincourt*

2 I drink for the thirst to come.

François Rabelais (1483–1553) French satirist. *Gargantua*, Bk. I, Ch. 5

3 As pants the hart for cooling streams
When heated in the chase.

Nahum Tate (1652–1715) Irish-born English poet. *New Version of the Psalms*, 'As Pants the Hart'

THREATS

1 Violet Elizabeth dried her tears. She saw that they were useless and she did not believe in wasting her effects. 'All right,' she said calmly, 'I'll thcream then. I'll thcream, an' thcream, an' thcream till I'm thick.'

Richmal Crompton (Richmal Crompton Lamburn; 1890–1969) British writer. Violet Elizabeth Bott, a character in the *William* books, had both a lisp and an exceptional ability to get her own way. *Just William*

2 If you start throwing hedgehogs under me, I shall throw two porcupines under you.

Nikita Khrushchev (1894–1971) Soviet statesman. *The Observer*, 'Sayings of the Week', 10 Nov 1963

3 After I die, I shall return to earth as a gatekeeper of a bordello and I won't let any of you –

not a one of you – enter!

Arturo Toscanini (1867–1957) Italian conductor. Rebuking an incompetent orchestra. *The Maestro: The Life of Arturo Toscanini* (Howard Taubman)

THRIFT

See also extravagance, money

1 A penny saved is a penny earned.

Proverb

2 Keep something for a rainy day.

Proverb

3 Penny wise, pound foolish.

Proverb

4 I knew once a very covetous, sordid fellow, who used to say, 'Take care of the pence, for the pounds will take care of themselves.'

Earl of Chesterfield (1694–1773) English statesman. Possibly referring to William Lowndes. Letter to his son, 6 Nov 1747

5 ...we owe something to extravagance, for thrift and adventure seldom go hand in hand.

Jennie Jerome Churchill (1854–1921) US-born British hostess and writer. *Pearson's*, 'Extravagance'

6 Thrift has nearly killed her on several occasions, through the agency of old sausages, slow-punctured tyres, rusty blades.

Margaret Drabble (1939–) British novelist. *The Radiant Way*

7 Everybody is always in favour of general economy and particular expenditure.

Anthony Eden (1897–1977) British statesman. *The Observer*, 'Sayings of the Week', 17 June 1956

8 Economy is going without something you do want in case you should, some day, want something you probably won't want.

Anthony Hope (Sir Anthony Hope Hawkins; 1863–1933) British novelist. *The Dolly Dialogues*

9 What! Can't a fellow even enjoy a biscuit any more?

Duke of Portland (1857–1943) British peer. On being informed that as one of several measures to reduce his own expenses he would have to dispense with one of his two Italian pastry cooks. *Their Noble Lordships* (S. Winchester)

10 A hole is the accident of a day, while a darn is premeditated poverty.

Edward Shuter (1728–76) British actor. Explaining why he did not mend the holes in his stocking. *Dictionary of National Biography*

11 Beware of all enterprises that require new clothes.

Henry David Thoreau (1817–62) US writer. *Walden*, 'Economy'

TIME

See also eternity, future, life, past, present, transience

1 An hour in the morning is worth two in the evening.

Proverb

2 There are only twenty-four hours in the day.

Proverb

3 There is a time and place for everything.

Proverb

4 Time and tide wait for no man.

Proverb

5 Time is a great healer.

Proverb

6 Time will tell.

Proverb

7 Except Time all other things are created. Time is the creator; and Time has no limit, neither top nor bottom.

The Persian Rivayat

8 To choose time is to save time.

Francis Bacon (1561–1626) English philosopher. *Essays*, 'Of Dispatch'

9 VLADIMIR. That passed the time.
ESTRAGON. It would have passed in any case.
VLADIMIR. Yes, but not so rapidly.

Samuel Beckett (1906–89) Irish novelist and dramatist. *Waiting for Godot*, I

10 I believe the twenty-four hour day has come to stay.

Max Beerbohm (1872–1956) British writer. *A Christmas Garland*, 'Perkins and Mankind'

11 Time is a great teacher, but unfortunately it kills all its pupils.

Hector Berlioz (1803–69) French composer. *Almanach des lettres françaises*

12 To every thing there is a season, and a time to every purpose under the heaven:
A time to be born, and a time to die; a time to plant, and a time to pluck up that which is planted;
A time to kill, and a time to heal; a time to break down, and a time to build up;
A time to weep, and a time to laugh; a time to mourn, and a time to dance;
A time to cast away stones, and a time to gather stones together; a time to embrace, and a time to refrain from embracing;
A time to get, and a time to lose; a time to keep, and a time to cast away;
A time to rend, and a time to sew; a time to keep silence, and a time to speak;
A time to love, and a time to hate; a time of war, and a time of peace.

Bible: Ecclesiastes 3:1–8

13 Men talk of killing time, while time quietly kills them.

Dion Boucicault (Dionysius Lardner Boursiquot; 1820–90) Irish-born US actor and dramatist. *London Assurance*, II:1

14 Time, like a loan from the bank, is something you're only given when you possess so much that you don't need it.

John Braine (1922–86) British novelist. *Room at the Top*, Ch. 15

15 I recommend you to take care of the minutes: for hours will take care of themselves.

Earl of Chesterfield (1694–1773) English statesman. Letter to his son, 6 Nov 1747

16 Time present and time past
Are both perhaps present in time future
And time future contained in time past.

T. S. Eliot (1888–1965) US-born British poet and dramatist. *Four Quartets*

17 Come, fill the Cup, and in the Fire of Spring
The Winter Garment of Repentance fling:
The Bird of Time has but a little way
To fly – and Lo! the Bird is on the Wing.

Edward Fitzgerald (1809–83) British poet. *The Rubáiyát of Omar Khayyám*

18 Ah, fill the Cup: – what boots it to repeat
How Time is slipping underneath our Feet:
Unborn TOMORROW, and dead YESTERDAY,
Why fret about them if TODAY be sweet!

Edward Fitzgerald *The Rubáiyát of Omar Khayyám*

19 Dost thou love life? Then do not squander time, for that's the stuff life is made of.

Benjamin Franklin (1706–90) US scientist and statesman. *Poor Richard's Almanack*

20 You must remember this;
A kiss is just a kiss,
A sigh is just a sigh –
The fundamental things apply
As time goes by.

Herman Hupfeld (20th century) US songwriter. From the film *Casablanca. As Time Goes By*

21 O aching time! O moments big as years!

John Keats (1795–1821) British poet. *Hyperion*, I

22 We must use time as a tool, not as a couch.

John Fitzgerald Kennedy (1917–63) US statesman. *The Observer*, 'Sayings of the Week', 10 Dec 1961

23 They shut the road through the woods
Seventy years ago.
Weather and rain have undone it again,
And now you would never know
There was once a road through the woods.

Rudyard Kipling (1865–1936) Indian-born British writer. *The Way Through the Woods*

24 The Future is something which everyone reaches at the rate of sixty minutes an hour, whatever he does, whoever he is.

C. S. Lewis (1898–1963) British academic and writer. *The Screwtape Letters*

25 I stood on the bridge at midnight,
As the clocks were striking the hour.

Henry Wadsworth Longfellow (1807–82) US poet. *The Bridge*

26 The man is killing time – there's nothing else.

Robert Lowell (1917–77) US poet. *The Drinker*

27 Time wounds all heels.

Groucho Marx (Julius Marx; 1895–1977) US comedian. Attrib.

28 A physician can sometimes parry the
scythe of death, but has no power over
the sand in the hourglass.

Hester Lynch Piozzi (Mrs. Henry Thrale; 1741–1821) British writer. Letter to Fanny Burney, 22 Nov 1781

29 It is only time that weighs upon our hands.
It is only time, and that is not material.

Sylvia Plath (1932–63) British poet. *Winter Trees*, 'The Three Women'

30 They do that to pass the time, nothing more. But Time is too large, it refuses to let itself be filled up.

Jean-Paul Sartre (1905–80) French writer. *Nausea*

31 Ah! the clock is always slow;
It is later than you think.

Robert William Service (1874–1958) Canadian poet. *It is Later than You Think*

32 Come what come may,
Time and the hour runs through the roughest day.

William Shakespeare (1564–1616) English dramatist. *Macbeth*, I:3

33 Th' inaudible and noiseless foot of Time.

William Shakespeare *All's Well that Ends Well*, V:3

34 Like as the waves make towards the pebbled shore,
So do our minutes hasten to their end.

William Shakespeare *Sonnet 60*

35 Time hath, my lord, a wallet at his back,
Wherein he puts alms for oblivion,
A great-siz'd monster of ingratitudes.

William Shakespeare *Troilus and Cressida*, III:3

36 In reality, *killing time*
Is only the name for another of the multifarious ways
By which Time kills us.

Osbert Sitwell (1892–1969) British writer. *Milordo Inglese*

37 Time driveth onward fast,
And in a little while our lips are dumb.
Let us alone. What is it that will last?
All things are taken from us, and become
Portions and parcels of the dreadful Past.

Alfred, Lord Tennyson (1809–92) British poet. *The Lotos-Eaters*, 'Choric Song'

38 Time is but the stream I go a-fishing in.

Henry David Thoreau (1817–62) US writer. *Walden*, 'Where I Lived, and What I Lived For'

39 As if you could kill time without injuring eternity.

Henry David Thoreau *Walden*, 'Economy'

40 But meanwhile it is flying, irretrievable time is flying.

Virgil (Publius Vergilius Maro; 70–19 BC) Roman poet. *Georgics*, Bk. III

41 Time is what prevents everything from happening at once.

John Archibald Wheeler (1911–) US theoretical physicist. *American Journal of Physics, 1978*

42 Time drops in decay,
Like a candle burnt out.

W. B. Yeats (1865–1939) Irish poet. *The Moods*

43 The bell strikes one. We take no note of time
But from its loss.

Edward Young (1683–1765) British poet. *Night Thoughts*

44 Time flies, death urges, knells call, heaven invites,
Hell threatens.

Edward Young *Night Thoughts*

TITLES

See also aristocracy, courtesy, honour, nobility

1 As far as the 14th Earl is concerned, I suppose Mr Wilson, when you come to think of it, is the 14th Mr Wilson.

Alec Douglas-Home (1903–95) British statesman. On renouncing his peerage (as 14th Earl of Home) to become prime minister. TV interview, 21 Oct 1963

2 Madam I may not call you; mistress I am ashamed to call you; and so I know not what to call you; but howsoever, I thank you.

Elizabeth I (1533–1603) Queen of England. Writing to the wife of the Archbishop of Canterbury, expressing her disapproval of married clergy. *Brief View of the State of the Church* (Harington)

3 Tyndall, I must remain plain Michael Faraday to the last; and let me now tell you, that if I accepted the honour which the Royal Society desires to confer upon me, I would not answer for the integrity of my intellect for a single year.

Michael Faraday (1791–1867) British scientist. Said when Faraday was offered the Presidency of the Royal Society. *Faraday as a Discoverer* (J. Tyndall), 'Illustrations of Character'

4 Pooh-Bah (Lord High Everything Else)

W. S. Gilbert (1836–1911) British dramatist. *The Mikado, Dramatis Personae*

5 I like the Garter; there is no damned merit in it.

Lord Melbourne (1779–1848) British statesman. *Lord Melbourne* (H. Dunckley), 'On the Order of the Garter'

6 When I want a peerage, I shall buy one like an honest man.

Lord Northcliffe (1865–1922) Irish-born British newspaper proprietor. Attrib.

7 Call me madame.

Francis Perkins (1882–1965) US social worker and politician. Deciding the term of address she would prefer when made the first woman to hold a cabinet office in the USA. *Familiar Quotations* (J. Bartlett)

8 Mother always told me my day was coming, but I never realized that I'd end up being the shortest knight of the year.

Gordon Richards (1904–86) British champion jockey. Referring to his diminutive size, on learning of his knighthood. Attrib.

9 Members rise from CMG (known sometimes in Whitehall as 'Call me God') to the KCMG ('Kindly Call me God') to...The GCMG ('God Calls me God').

Anthony Sampson (1926–) British writer and journalist. *Anatomy of Britain*, Ch. 18

10 Titles distinguish the mediocre, embarrass the superior, and are disgraced by the inferior.

George Bernard Shaw (1856–1950) Irish dramatist and critic. *Man and Superman*, 'Maxims for Revolutionists'

11 I've been offered titles, but I think they get one into disreputable company.

George Bernard Shaw *Gossip* (A. Barrow)

12 After half a century of democratic advance, the whole process has ground to a halt with a 14th Earl.

Harold Wilson (1916–95) British politician and prime minister. Speech, Manchester, 19 Oct 1963

TOLERANCE

1 There is, however, a limit at which forbearance ceases to be a virtue.

Edmund Burke (1729–97) British politician. *Observations on a Publication, 'The Present State of the Nation'*

2 No party has a monopoly over what is right.

Mikhail Gorbachov (1931–) Soviet statesman. Speech, Mar 1986

3 It is flattering some men to endure them.

Lord Halifax (1633–95) English statesman. *Political, Moral and Miscellaneous Thoughts and Reflections*

4 If you cannot mould yourself as you would wish, how can you expect other people to be entirely to your liking?

Thomas à Kempis (Thomas Hemmerken; c. 1380–1471) German monk. *The Imitation of Christ*, I

5 We must respect the other fellow's religion, but only in the sense and to the extent that we respect his theory that his wife is beautiful and his children smart.

H. L. Mencken (1880–1956) US journalist. *Notebooks*, 'Minority Report'

6 Steven's mind was so tolerant that he could have attended a lynching every day without becoming critical.

Thorne Smith (1892–1934) US humorist. *The Jovial Ghosts*, Ch. 11

7 So long as a man rides his hobby-horse peaceably and quietly along the king's highway, and neither compels you or me to get up behind him, – pray, Sir, what have either you or I to do with it?

Laurence Sterne (1713–68) Irish-born British writer. *Tristram Shandy*

8 It is because we put up with bad things that

hotel-keepers continue to give them to us.

Anthony Trollope (1815–82) British novelist. *Orley Farm*, Ch. 18

TRAINS

See also travel

1 Rumbling under blackened girders, Midland, bound for Cricklewood,
Puffed its sulphur to the sunset where the Land of Laundries stood.
Rumble under, thunder over, train and tram alternate go.

John Betjeman (1906–84) British poet. *Parliament Hill Fields*

2 The only way to be sure of catching a train is to miss the one before it.

G. K. Chesterton *Vacances à tous prix*, 'Le Supplice de l'heure' (P. Daninos)

3 It's a tremendous achievement, but it isn't easy to work with British Rail. They're never exactly *against* anything, but they're never in favour of anything either. And they always find ways of putting a spanner in the works.

Jean French senior manager with SNCF. Referring to the Channel tunnel. *The Observer*, 1 May 1994

4 Mr Stephenson having taken me on the bench of the engine with him, we started at about ten miles an hour. You cannot imagine how strange it seemed to be journeying on thus, without any visible cause of progressing other than that magical machine, with its flying white breath, and rhythmical unwearying pace.

Fanny Kemble (1809–93) British actress and writer. *Record of a Girlhood*

5 Oh, mister porter, what shall I do?
I wanted to go to Birmingham, but they've carried me on to Crewe.

Marie Lloyd (1870–1922) British music-hall singer. *Oh, Mister Porter*

6 Commuter – one who spends his life
In riding to and from his wife;
A man who shaves and takes a train,
And then rides back to shave again.

Elwyn Brooks White (1899–1985) US journalist and humorist. *The Commuter*

7 I see no reason to suppose that these machines will ever force themselves into general use.

Duke of Wellington (1769–1852) British general and statesman. Referring to steam locomotives. *Geoffrey Madan's Notebooks* (J. Gere)

8 It was the wrong kind of snow.

Terry Worrall British railway manager. Explaining why British Rail's anti-snow measures had not worked. *The Observer*, 17 Feb 1991

TRANSIENCE

See also life, mortality, time

1 Everything is only for a day, both that which remembers and that which is remembered.

Marcus Aurelius (121–180 AD) Roman emperor. *Meditations*, Bk. IV, Ch. 35

2 Time is like a river made up of the events which happen, and its current is strong; no sooner does anything appear than it is swept away, and another comes in its place, and will be swept away too.

Marcus Aurelius *Meditations*, Bk. IV, Ch. 43

3 Faith, Sir, we are here to-day, and gone tomorrow.

Aphra Behn (1640–89) English novelist and dramatist. *The Lucky Chance*, IV

4 What profit hath a man of all his labour which he taketh under the sun?
One generation passeth away, and another generation cometh: but the earth abideth for ever.

Bible: Ecclesiastes 1:2–4

5 I have seen all the works that are done under the sun; and, behold, all is vanity and vexation of spirit.

Bible: Ecclesiastes 1:13–14

6 Whatsoever thy hand findeth to do, do it with thy might; for there is no work, nor device, nor knowledge, nor wisdom, in the grave, whither thou goest.

Bible: Ecclesiastes 9:10

7 And behold joy and gladness, slaying oxen, and killing sheep, eating flesh, and drinking wine: let us eat and drink; for tomorrow we shall die.

Bible: Isaiah A similar sentiment is expressed in Corinthians 15:32–33. 22:13

8 Heaven and earth shall pass away, but my words shall not pass away.

Bible: Matthew 24:35

9 Suddenly, as rare things will, it vanished.

Robert Browning (1812–89) British poet. *One Word More*, IV

10 Now the peak of summer's past, the sky is overcast
And the love we swore would last for an age seems deceit.

C. Day Lewis (1904–72) British poet. *Hornpipe*

11 They are not long, the days of wine and roses.

Ernest Dowson (1867–1900) British lyric poet. *Vitae Summa Brevis Spem Nos Vetat Incohare Longam*

12 A little rule, a little sway,
A sunbeam in a winter's day,
Is all the proud and mighty have
Between the cradle and the grave.

John Dyer (1700–58) British poet. *Grongar Hill*

13 The Worldly Hope men set their Hearts upon
Turns Ashes – or it prospers; and anon,
Like Snow upon the Desert's dusty face,
Lighting a little Hour or two – is gone.

Edward Fitzgerald (1809–83) British poet. *The Rubáiyát of Omar Khayyám*, XIV

14 Fair daffodils, we weep to see
You haste away so soon:
As yet the early-rising sun
Has not attain'd his noon.
Stay, stay,
Until the hasting day
Has run
But to the even-song;
And, having pray'd together, we
Will go with you along.

We have short time to stay, as you,
We have as short a Spring;
As quick a growth to meet decay,
As you or any thing.

Robert Herrick (1591–1674) English poet. *Hesperides*, 'To Daffodils'

15 Not to hope for things to last for ever, is what the year teaches and even the hour which snatches a nice day away.

Horace (Quintus Horatius Flaccus; 65–8 BC) Roman poet. *Odes*, IV

16 Ships that pass in the night, and speak each other in passing;
Only a signal shown and a distant voice in the darkness;
So on the ocean of life we pass and speak one another,
Only a look and a voice; then darkness again and a silence.

Henry Wadsworth Longfellow (1807–82) US poet. *Tales of a Wayside Inn*, 'The Theologian's Tale. Elizabeth'

17 But she was of the world where the fairest things have the worst fate. Like a rose, she has lived as long as roses live, the space of one morning.

François de Malherbe (1555–1628) French poet. *Consolation à M. du Périer*

18 Our little systems have their day;
They have their day and cease to be.

Alfred, Lord Tennyson (1809–92) British poet. *In Memoriam A.H.H.*, Prologue

TRANSLATION

1 The original is unfaithful to the translation.

Jorge Luis Borges (1899–1986) Argentinian writer. Referring to Henley's translation of Beckford's *Vathek. Sobre el 'Vathek' de William Beckford*

2 Translations (like wives) are seldom faithful if they are in the least attractive.

Roy Campbell (1901–57) South African poet. *Poetry Review*

3 Poetry is what gets lost in translation.

Robert Frost (1875–1963) US poet. Attrib.

4 An idea does not pass from one language to another without change.

Miguel de Unamuno y Jugo (1864–1936) Spanish writer. *The Tragic Sense of Life*

5 Humour is the first of the gifts to perish in a foreign tongue.

Virginia Woolf (1882–1941) British novelist. *The Common Reader*

TRAVEL

See also boats, cars, flying, trains

1 Travel broadens the mind.

Proverb

2 Travel, in the younger sort, is a part of education; in the elder, a part of experience.

Francis Bacon (1561–1626) English philosopher. *Essays*, 'Of Travel'

3 I have recently been all round the world and have formed a very poor opinion of it.

Thomas Beecham (1879–1961) British conductor. Speech at the Savoy. *The News Review*, 22 Aug 1946

4 I thought it was quite simple walking from one point to another, but people kept asking me, 'Why?'

Ffyona Campbell (1967–) British long-distance walker. *The Observer Review*, 10 Nov 1996

5 Before the Roman came to Rye or out to Severn strode,
The rolling English drunkard made the rolling English road.

G. K. Chesterton (1874–1936) British writer. *The Rolling English Road*

6 Travelling is almost like talking with men of other centuries.

René Descartes (1596–1650) French philosopher. *Le Discours de la méthode*

7 How does it feel
To be without a home
Like a complete unknown
Like a rolling stone?

Bob Dylan (Robert Allen Zimmerman; 1941–) US popular singer. *Like a Rolling Stone*

8 I read, much of the night, and go south in the winter.

T. S. Eliot (1888–1965) US-born British poet and dramatist. *The Waste Land*, 'The Burial of the Dead'

9 The woods are lovely, dark, and deep,
But I have promises to keep,
And miles to go before I sleep,
And miles to go before I sleep.

Robert Frost (1875–1963) US poet. *Stopping by Woods on a Snowy Evening*

10 He gave the impression that very many cities had rubbed him smooth.

Graham Greene (1904–91) British novelist. *A Gun for Sale*, Ch. 4

11 One of the pleasantest things in the world is going on a journey; but I like to go by myself.

William Hazlitt (1778–1830) British essayist. *On Going a Journey*

12 They change their clime, not their frame of mind, who rush across the sea. We work hard at doing nothing: we look for happiness in boats and carriage rides. What you are looking for is here, is at Ulubrae, if only peace of mind doesn't desert you.

Horace (Quintus Horatius Flaccus; 65–8 BC) Roman poet. *Epistles*, I

13 A man who has not been in Italy, is always conscious of an inferiority, from his not having seen what it is expected a man should see. The grand object of travelling is to see the shores of the Mediterranean.

Samuel Johnson (1709–84) British lexicographer. *Life of Johnson* (J. Boswell), Vol. III

14 Much have I travell'd in the realms of gold,
And many goodly states and kingdoms seen.

John Keats (1795–1821) British poet. *On first looking into Chapman's Homer*

15 Like Brighton pier, all right as far as it goes, but inadequate for getting to France.

Neil Kinnock (1942–) British politician. Speech, House of Commons, 1981

16 The great and recurrent question about abroad is, is it worth getting there?

Rose Macaulay (1889–1958) British writer. Attrib.

17 Whenever I prepare for a journey I prepare as though for death. Should I never return, all is in order. This is what life has taught me.

Katherine Mansfield (1888–1923) New-Zealand-born British writer. *The Journal of Katherine Mansfield*, 1922

18 *Rush hour:* that hour when traffic is almost at a standstill.

J. B. Morton (1893–1979) British journalist. *Morton's Folly*

19 Travel is the most private of pleasures. There is no greater bore than the travel bore. We do not in the least want to hear what he has seen in Hong-Kong.

Vita Sackville-West (Victoria Sackville-West; 1892–1962) British poet and novelist. *Passenger to Tehran*, Ch. 1

20 A man should know something of his own country, too, before he goes abroad.

Laurence Sterne (1713–68) Irish-born British writer. *Tristram Shandy*

21 Wealth I ask not; hope nor love,
Nor a friend to know me;
All I seek, the heaven above
And the road below me.

Robert Louis Stevenson (1850–94) Scottish writer. *Songs of Travel*, 'The Vagabond'

22 For my part, I travel not to go anywhere, but to go. I travel for travel's sake. The great affair is to move.

Robert Louis Stevenson *Travels with a Donkey*, 'Cheylard and Luc'

23 Travel is glamorous only in retrospect.

Paul Theroux (1941–) US-born writer. *The Observer*, 'Sayings of the Week', 7 Oct 1979

24 Yes – around Concord.

Henry David Thoreau (1817–62) US writer. On being asked whether he had travelled much. Attrib.

25 Commuter – one who spends his life
In riding to and from his wife;
A man who shaves and takes a train,
And then rides back to shave again.

Elwyn Brooks White (1899–1985) US journalist and humorist. *The Commuter*

26 The Victorians had not been anxious to go away for the weekend. The Edwardians, on the contrary, were nomadic.

T. H. White (1906–64) British novelist. *Farewell Victoria*, Ch. 4

TREASON

See also betrayal

1 Please to remember the Fifth of November,
Gunpowder Treason and Plot.
We know no reason why gunpowder treason
Should ever be forgot.

Anonymous Traditional

2 During his Office, Treason was no Crime.
The Sons of Belial had a Glorious Time.

John Dryden (1631–1700) British poet and dramatist. *Absalom and Achitophel*, I

3 Treason doth never prosper: what's the reason?
For if it prosper, none dare call it treason.

John Harington (1561–1612) English writer. *Epigrams*, 'Of Treason'

4 Caesar had his Brutus – Charles the First, his Cromwell – and George the Third – ('Treason,' cried the Speaker)...*may profit by their example*. If *this* be treason, make the most of it.

Patrick Henry (1736–99) US statesman. Speech, Virginia Convention, May 1765

TREES

See also countryside, Nature

1 And the Lord God took the man, and put him into the garden of Eden to dress it and to keep it.
And the Lord God commanded the man, saying, Of every tree of the garden thou mayest freely eat:
But of the tree of the knowledge of good and evil, thou shalt not eat of it: for in the day that thou eatest thereof thou shalt surely die.

Bible: Genesis 2:15–17

2 O leave this barren spot to me!
Spare, woodman, spare the beechen tree.

Thomas Campbell (1777–1844) British poet. *The Beech-Tree's Petition*

3 The poplars are felled, farewell to the shade,
And the whispering sound of the cool colonnade!

William Cowper (1731–1800) British poet. *The Poplar Field*

4 On Wenlock Edge the wood's in trouble;
His forest fleece the Wrekin heaves;
The gale, it plies the saplings double,

And thick on Severn snow the leaves.

A. E. Housman (1859–1936) British scholar and poet. *A Shropshire Lad*, 'The Welsh Marches'

5 Loveliest of trees, the cherry now
Is hung with bloom along the bough,
And stands about the woodland ride
Wearing white for Eastertide.

A. E. Housman *A Shropshire Lad*, '1887'

6 I'm replacing some of the timber used up by my books. Books are just trees with squiggles on them.

Hammond Innes (1913–) British novelist. Interview in *Radio Times*, 18 Aug 1984

7 As when, upon a trancèd summer-night,
Those green-rob'd senators of mighty woods,
Tall oaks, branch-charmèd by the earnest stars,
Dream, and so dream all night without a stir.

John Keats (1795–1821) British poet. *Hyperion*, I

8 I think that I shall never see
A poem lovely as a tree.

Alfred Joyce Kilmer (1886–1918) US poet. *Trees*

9 Poems are made by fools like me,
But only God can make a tree.

Alfred Joyce Kilmer *Trees*

10 Yet once more, O ye laurels, and once more,
Ye myrtles brown, with ivy never sere,
I come to pluck your berries harsh and crude,
And with forced fingers rude
Shatter your leaves before the mellowing year.

John Milton (1608–74) English poet. *Lycidas*

11 Woodman, spare that tree!
Touch not a single bough!
In youth it sheltered me,
And I'll protect it now.

George Pope Morris (1802–64) US journalist. *Woodman, Spare That Tree*

12 I think that I shall never see
A billboard lovely as a tree.
Perhaps unless the billboards fall,
I'll never see a tree at all.

Ogden Nash (1902–71) US poet. *Song of the Open Road*

13 The difference between a gun and a tree is a difference of tempo. The tree explodes every spring.

Ezra Pound (1885–1972) US poet. *Criterion*, July 1937

TRIVIALITY

See also insignificance

1 Nothing matters very much, and very few things matter at all.

Arthur Balfour (1848–1930) British statesman. Attrib.

2 A Storm in a Teacup.

W. B. Bernard (1807–75) British dramatist. Play title

3 As she frequently remarked when she made any such mistake, it would be all the same a hundred years hence.

Charles Dickens (1812–70) British novelist. Said by Mrs Squeers. *Martin Chuzzlewit*, Ch. 9

4 Little things affect little minds.

Benjamin Disraeli (1804–81) British statesman. *Sybil*, Bk. III, Ch. 2

5 You know my method. It is founded upon the observance of trifles.

Arthur Conan Doyle (1856–1930) British writer. *The Boscombe Valley Mystery*

6 It has long been an axiom of mine that the little things are infinitely the most important.

Arthur Conan Doyle *A Case of Identity*

7 Depend upon it, there is nothing so unnatural as the commonplace.

Arthur Conan Doyle *A Case of Identity*

8 'Is there any point to which you would wish to draw my attention?'
'To the curious incident of the dog in the night-time.'
'The dog did nothing in the night-time.'
'That was the curious incident,' remarked Sherlock Holmes.

Arthur Conan Doyle *The Silver Blaze*

9 To great evils we submit; we resent little provocations.

William Hazlitt (1778–1830) British essayist. *On Great and Little Things*

10 Little minds are interested in the extraordinary; great minds in the commonplace.

Elbert Hubbard (1856–1915) US writer. *Roycroft Dictionary and Book of Epigrams*

11 What should I do? I think the best thing is to order a new stamp to be made with my face on it.

Charles (1887–1922) Emperor of Austria. On hearing of his accession to emperor. *Anekdotenschatz* (H. Hoffmeister)

12 To suckle fools and chronicle small beer.

William Shakespeare (1564–1616) English dramatist. *Othello*, II:1

13 It's deadly commonplace, but, after all, the commonplaces are the great poetic truths.

Robert Louis Stevenson (1850–94) Scottish writer. *Weir of Hermiston*, Ch. 6

14 Ah God! the petty fools of rhyme
That shriek and sweat in pigmy wars.

Alfred, Lord Tennyson (1809–92) British poet. *Literary Squabbles*

TRUST

See also faith, mistrust

1 Trust ye not in a friend, put ye not confidence in a guide: keep the doors of thy mouth from her that lieth in thy bosom.

Bible: Micah 7:5

2 Never trust the man who hath reason to

suspect that you know he hath injured you.
Henry Fielding (1707–54) British novelist. *Jonathan Wild*, Bk III, Ch. 4

3 We are inclined to believe those whom we do not know because they have never deceived us.
Samuel Johnson (1709–84) British lexicographer. *The Idler*

4 Never trust a husband too far, nor a bachelor too near.
Helen Rowland (1876–1950) US writer. *The Rubaiyat of a Bachelor*

5 Would you buy a second-hand car from this man?
Mort Sahl (1927–) US political comedian. Referring to President Nixon. Attrib.

TRUTH

See also facts, frankness, honesty, lying, sincerity

1 Better a lie that heals than a truth that wounds.
Proverb

2 Many a true word is spoken in jest.
Proverb

3 Tell the truth and shame the devil.
Proverb

4 Truth fears no trial.
Proverb

5 Truth is stranger than fiction.
Proverb

6 Truth will out.
Proverb

7 The truth that makes men free is for the most part the truth which men prefer not to hear.
Herbert Sebastian Agar (1897–1980) US writer. *A Time for Greatness*

8 Plato is dear to me, but dearer still is truth.
Aristotle (384–322 BC) Greek philosopher. Attrib.

9 Truth sits upon the lips of dying men.
Matthew Arnold (1822–88) British poet and critic. *Sohrab and Rustum*

10 What is truth? said jesting Pilate, and would not stay for an answer.
Francis Bacon (1561–1626) English philosopher. *Essays*, 'Of Truth'

11 I am a witness. In the church in which I was raised you were supposed to be a witness to the truth.
James Baldwin (1924–87) US writer. *The Times*, review of a biography, 16 June 1994

12 And ye shall know the truth, and the truth shall make you free.
Bible: John 8:32

13 Pilate saith unto him, What is truth? And when he had said this, he went out again unto the Jews, and saith unto them, I find in him no fault at all.
Bible: John 18:38

14 A truth that's told with bad intent
Beats all the lies you can invent.
William Blake (1757–1827) British poet. *Auguries of Innocence*

15 To treat your facts with imagination is one thing, to imagine your facts is another.
John Burroughs (1837–1921) US naturalist. *The Heart of Burroughs Journals*

16 Some men love truth so much that they seem to be in continual fear lest she should catch a cold on overexposure.
Samuel Butler (1835–1902) British writer. *Notebooks*

17 Agree to a short armistice with truth.
Lord Byron (1788–1824) British poet. *Don Juan*, III

18 'Tis strange – but true; for truth is always strange;
Stranger than fiction: if it could be told,
How much would novels gain by the exchange!
Lord Byron *Don Juan*, XIV

19 You can only find truth with logic if you have already found truth without it.
G. K. Chesterton (1874–1936) British writer. *The Man who was Orthodox*

20 Truth is so seldom the sudden light that shows new order and beauty; more often, truth is the uncharted rock that sinks his ship in the dark.
John Cornforth (1917–) Australian chemist. Referring to scientists. Nobel Prize address, 1975

21 Much truth is spoken, that more may be concealed.
Lord Darling (1849–1936) British judge. *Scintillae Juris*

22 Perjury is often bold and open. It is truth that is shamefaced – as, indeed, in many cases is no more than decent.
Lord Darling *Scintillae Juris*

23 It is an old maxim of mine that when you have excluded the impossible, whatever remains, however improbable, must be the truth.
Arthur Conan Doyle (1856–1930) British writer. *The Beryl Coronet*

24 Errors, like Straws, upon the surface flow;
He who would search for Pearls must dive below.
John Dryden (1631–1700) British poet and dramatist. *All for Love*, Prologue

25 A man is to be cheated into passion, but to be reasoned into truth.
John Dryden *Religio Laici*, Preface

26 I do not want to use the word 'true'. There are only opinions, some of which are preferable to others. One cannot say: 'Ah. If it is just a matter of preference to hell with it'...One can die for an opinion which is only preferable.

Umberto Eco (1932–) Italian semiologist and writer. *Index on Censorship*, Vol. 23, May/June 1994

27 Ethical axioms are found and tested not very differently from the axioms of science. Truth is what stands the test of experience.

Albert Einstein (1879–1955) German-born US physicist. *Out of My Later Years*

28 Truth, like a torch, the more it's shook it shines.

William Hamilton (1788–1856) Scottish philosopher. *Discussions on Philosophy*, title page

29 True and False are attributes of speech, not of things. And where speech is not, there is neither Truth nor Falsehood.

Thomas Hobbes (1588–1679) English philosopher. *Leviathan*, Pt. I, Ch. 4

30 It's easy to make a man confess the lies he tells to himself; it's far harder to make him confess the truth.

Geoffrey Household (1900–88) British writer. *Rogue Male*

31 I am certain of nothing but the holiness of the heart's affections and the truth of imagination – what the imagination seizes as beauty must be truth – whether it existed before or not.

John Keats (1795–1821) British poet. Letter to Benjamin Bailey, 22 Nov 1817

32 I never can feel certain of any truth but from a clear perception of its beauty.

John Keats Letter to George and Georgiana Keats, 16 Dec 1818–4 Jan 1819

33 'Beauty is truth, truth beauty,' – that is all
Ye know on earth, and all ye need to know.

John Keats *Ode on a Grecian Urn*

34 It is one thing to show a man that he is in an error, and another to put him in possession of truth.

John Locke (1632–1704) English philosopher. *An Essay Concerning Human Understanding*, Bk. IV, Ch. 7

35 It is hard to believe that a man is telling the truth when you know that you would lie if you were in his place.

H. L. Mencken (1880–1956) US journalist.

36 Let her and Falsehood grapple; who ever knew Truth put to the worse, in a free and open encounter?

John Milton (1608–74) English poet. *Areopagitica*

37 There can be no whitewash at the White House.

Richard Milhous Nixon (1913–94) US president. Referring to the Watergate scandal. *The Observer*, 'Sayings of the Week', 30 Dec 1973

38 Let us begin by committing ourselves to the truth, to see it like it is and to tell it like it is, to find the truth, to speak the truth and live with the truth. That's what we'll do.

Richard Milhous Nixon Nomination acceptance speech, Miami, 8 Aug 1968

39 Truth has no special time of its own. Its hour is now – always.

Albert Schweitzer (1875–1965) French Protestant theologian, philosopher, physician, and musician. *Out of My Life and Thought*

40 Truth telling is not compatible with the defence of the realm.

George Bernard Shaw (1856–1950) Irish dramatist and critic. *Heartbreak House*

41 My way of joking is to tell the truth. It's the funniest joke in the world.

George Bernard Shaw *John Bull's Other Island*, II

42 When truth is discovered by someone else, it loses something of its attractiveness.

Alexander Solzhenitsyn (1918–) Soviet novelist. *Candle in the Wind*, 3

43 THE TRUTH IS OUT THERE

The X Files BBC TV programme

44 It takes two to speak the truth – one to speak, and another to hear.

Henry David Thoreau (1817–62) US writer. *A Week on the Concord and Merrimack Rivers*

45 The only truths which are universal are those gross enough to be thought so.

Paul Valéry (1871–1945) French poet and writer. *Mauvaises Pensées et autres*

46 But not even Marx is more precious to us than the truth.

Simone Weil (1909–43) French philosopher. *Oppression and Liberty*, 'Revolution Proletarienne'

47 There are no whole truths; all truths are half-truths. It is trying to treat them as whole truths that plays the devil.

A. N. Whitehead (1861–1947) British philosopher. *Dialogues*, 16

48 I believe that in the end the truth will conquer.

John Wycliffe (1329–84) English religious reformer. Said to John of Gaunt, Duke of Lancaster, 1381. *Short History of the English People* (J. R. Green)

49 Truth is on the march; nothing can stop it now.

Émile Zola (1840–1902) French novelist. Referring to the Dreyfus scandal. Attrib.

TYRANNY

See also authoritarianism, oppression

1 Nature has left this tincture in the blood,
That all men would be tyrants if they could.

Daniel Defoe (1660–1731) British journalist and writer. *The Kentish Petition*, Addenda

2 'Twixt kings and tyrants there's this difference known;
Kings seek their subjects' good: tyrants their own.

Robert Herrick (1591–1674) English poet. *Hesperides*, 'Kings and Tyrants'

3 A country governed by a despot is an inverted cone.

Samuel Johnson (1709–84) British lexicographer. *Life of Johnson* (J. Boswell), Vol. III

4 It is better that a man should tyrannize over his bank balance than over his fellow citizens.

John Maynard Keynes (1883–1946) British economist. *The General Theory of Employment, Interest and Money*, Bk. VI, Ch. 24

5 ...whenever kingship approaches tyranny it is near its end, for by this it becomes ripe for division, change of dynasty, or total destruction, especially in a temperate climate...where men are habitually, morally and naturally free.

Nicholas of Oresme (c. 1320–82) Chaplain to Charles V of France. *De Moneta*

6 Where laws end, tyranny begins.

William Pitt the Elder (1708–78) British statesman. Speech, House of Lords, referring to the Wilkes case, 9 Jan 1770

U

UNCERTAINTY

See also doubt, indecision

1 If ifs and ans were pots and pans, there'd be no trade for tinkers.
Proverb

2 I have known uncertainty: a state unknown to the Greeks.
Jorge Luis Borges (1899–1986) Argentinian writer. *Ficciones*, 'The Babylonian Lottery'

3 Of course not. After all, I may be wrong.
Bertrand Russell (1872–1970) British philosopher. On being asked whether he would be prepared to die for his beliefs. Attrib.

UNDERSTANDING

See also intelligence, wisdom

1 You never understand everything. When one understands everything, one has gone crazy.
Philip W. Anderson (1923–95) US physicist.

2 And come hither, and I shall light a candle of understanding in thine heart, which shall not be put out, till the things be performed which thou shalt begin to write.
Bible: II Esdras 14:25

3 It is good to know what a man is, and also what the world takes him for. But you do not understand him until you have learnt how he understands himself.
F. H. Bradley (1846–1924) British philosopher. *Aphorisms*

4 The people may be made to follow a course of action, but they may not be made to understand it.
Confucius (K'ung Fu-tzu; 551–479 BC) Chinese philosopher. *Analects*

5 Should I refuse a good dinner simply because I do not understand the process of digestion?
Oliver Heaviside (1850–1925) British electronic engineer and physicist. On being criticized for using formal mathematical manipulations, without understanding how they worked

6 Only one man ever understood me....And he didn't understand me.
Hegel (1770–1831) German philosopher. Said on his deathbed. *Famous Last Words* (B. Conrad)

7 Even when poetry has a meaning, as it usually has, it may be inadvisable to draw it out...Perfect understanding will sometimes almost extinguish pleasure.
A. E. Housman (1859–1936) British scholar and poet. *The Name and Nature of Poetry*

8 Thought must be divided against itself before it can come to any knowledge of itself.
Aldous Huxley (1894–1964) British novelist. *Do What You Will*

9 She did her work with the thoroughness of a mind that reveres details and never quite understands them.
Sinclair Lewis (1885–1951) US novelist. *Babbitt*, Ch. 18

10 I used to tell my husband that, if he could make *me* understand something, it would be clear to all the other people in the country.
Eleanor Roosevelt (1884–1962) US writer and lecturer. Newspaper column, 'My Day', 12 Feb 1947

11 I have striven not to laugh at human actions, not to weep at them, nor to hate them, but to understand them.
Benedict Spinoza (Baruch de Spinoza; 1632–77) Dutch philosopher. *Tractatus Theologico-Politicus*, Ch. 1

12 All, everything that I understand, I understand only because I love.
Leo Tolstoy (1828–1910) Russian writer. *War and Peace*, Bk. VII, Ch. 16

UNEMPLOYMENT

See also idleness, work

1 Rising unemployment and the recession have been the price that we've had to pay to get inflation down: that is a price well worth paying.
Norman Lamont (1942–) British Conservative politician. *The Observer*, 19 May 1991

2 My father did not wait around...he got on his bike and went out looking for work.
Norman Tebbit (1931–) British Conservative politician. Speech, Conservative Party conference, 1981

3 It's a recession when your neighbour loses his job; it's a depression when you lose your own.
Harry S. Truman (1884–1972) US statesman. *The Observer*, 'Sayings of the Week', 6 Apr 1958

4 Something must be done.
Duke of Windsor (1894–1972) King of the United Kingdom; abdicated 1936. Said while visiting areas of high unemployment in South Wales during the 1930s. Attrib.

UNFAITHFULNESS

See also adultery

1 Early one morning, just as the sun was rising,
I heard a maiden singing in the valley below:
'Oh, don't deceive me; Oh, never leave me!
How could you use a poor maiden so?'
Anonymous *Early One Morning*

2 Swore to be true to each other, true as the stars above;

He was her man, but he done her wrong.

Anonymous *Frankie and Johnny*

3 ...today I was driving a little more slowly because of the rain, but that was the only difference between yesterday and today.
My wife had been unfaithful to me but there was still the same number of traffic lights to obey...

John Braine (1922–86) British novelist. *Life at the Top*, Ch. 16

4 But I kissed her little sister,
And forgot my Clementine.

Percy Montrose (19th century) US songwriter. *Clementine*

5 O, swear not by the moon, th' inconstant moon,
That monthly changes in her circled orb,
Lest that thy love prove likewise variable.

William Shakespeare (1564–1616) English dramatist. *Romeo and Juliet*, II:2

6 His honour rooted in dishonour stood,
And faith unfaithful kept him falsely true.

Alfred, Lord Tennyson (1809–92) British poet. *Idylls of the King*, 'Lancelot and Elaine'

7 No man worth having is true to his wife, or can be true to his wife, or ever was, or ever will be so.

John Vanbrugh (1664–1726) English architect and dramatist. *The Relapse*, III:2

8 Why should marriage bring only tears?
All I wanted was a man
With a single heart,
And we would stay together
As our hair turned white,
Not somebody always after wriggling fish
With his big bamboo rod.

Chuo Wên-chün (?179–117 BC) Chinese poet. *Orchid Boat, Women Poets of China* (Kenneth Rexroth and Ling Chung)

UNITY

1 A chain is no stronger than its weakest link.

Proverb

2 Union is strength.

Proverb

3 United we stand, divided we fall.

Proverb

4 That typically English characteristic for which there is no English name – *esprit de corps*.

Frank Ezra Adcock (1886–1968) British classicist. Presidential address

5 And if one prevail against him, two shall withstand him; and a threefold cord is not quickly broken.

Bible: Ecclesiastes 4:12

6 And the whole earth was of one language, and of one speech.

Bible: Genesis 11:1

7 When bad men combine, the good must associate; else they will fall one by one, an unpitied sacrifice in a contemptible struggle.

Edmund Burke (1729–97) British politician. *Thoughts on the Cause of the Present Discontents*

8 All for one, and one for all.

Alexandre Dumas, père (1802–70) French novelist and dramatist. *The Three Musketeers*

9 We must indeed all hang together, or most assuredly, we shall all hang separately.

Benjamin Franklin (1706–90) US scientist and statesman. Remark on signing the Declaration of Independence, 4 July 1776

10 No human relation gives one possession in another – every two souls are absolutely different. In friendship or in love, the two side by side raise hands together to find what one cannot reach alone.

Kahlil Gibran (1833–1931) Lebanese mystic and poet. *Beloved Prophet* (ed. Virginia Hilu)

11 Everyone has observed how much more dogs are animated when they hunt in a pack, than when they pursue their game apart. We might, perhaps, be at a loss to explain this phenomenon, if we had not experience of a similar in ourselves.

David Hume (1711–76) Scottish philosopher. *A Treatise of Human Nature*

12 Now, is it to lower the price of corn, or isn't it? It is not much matter which we say, but mind, we must all say *the same*.

Lord Melbourne (1779–1848) British statesman. Said at a cabinet meeting. *The English Constitution* (Bagehot), Ch. 1

UNIVERSE

See also astronomy, moon, space, stars, sun, world

1 Had I been present at the Creation, I would have given some useful hints for the better ordering of the universe.

Alfonso the Wise (c. 1221–84) King of Castile and Léon. Referring to the complicated Ptolemaic model of the universe. Often quoted as, 'Had I been consulted I would have recommended something simpler'. Attrib.

2 The visible universe was an illusion or, more precisely, a sophism. Mirrors and fatherhood are abominable because they multiply it and extend it.

Jorge Luis Borges (1899–1986) Argentinian writer. *Ficciones*, 'Tlön, Uqbar, Orbis Tertius'

3 I don't pretend to understand the Universe – it's a great deal bigger than I am...People ought to be modester.

Thomas Carlyle (1795–1881) Scottish historian and essayist. Attrib.

4 MARGARET FULLER. I accept the universe.
CARLYLE. Gad! she'd better!

Thomas Carlyle Attrib.

5 The cosmos is about the smallest hole that a

man can hide his head in.

G. K. Chesterton (1874–1936) British writer. *Orthodoxy*, Ch. 1

6 I am very interested in the Universe – I am specializing in the universe and all that surrounds it.

Peter Cook (1937–95) British writer and entertainer. *Beyond the Fringe*

7 My own suspicion is that the universe is not only queerer than we suppose, but queerer than we *can* suppose.

J. B. S. Haldane (1892–1964) British geneticist. *Possible Worlds*, 'On Being the Right Size'

8 Why does the universe go to all the bother of existing? Is the unified theory so compelling that it brings about it's own existence? Or does it need a creator, and, if so, does he have any other effect on the universe? And who created him?

Stephen Hawking (1942–) British theoretical physicist and cosmologist. *A Brief History of Time*

9 The universe is not hostile, nor yet is it friendly. It is simply indifferent.

John Haynes Holmes (1879–1964) US clergyman. *A Sensible Man's View of Religion*

10 The universe begins to look more like a great thought than like a great machine.

James Jeans (1877–1946) British scientist. *The Mysterious Universe*

11 The universe ought to be presumed too vast to have any character.

C. S. Peirce (1839–1914) US physicist. *Collected Papers*, VI

12 We now have direct evidence of the birth of the Universe and its evolution…ripples in space–time laid down earlier than the first billionth of a second. If you're religious, it's like seeing God.

George Smoot (1945–) US astrophysicist. *Wrinkles in Time*

13 Fifty-five crystal spheres geared to God's crankshaft is my idea of a satisfying universe. I can't think of anything more trivial than quarks, quasars, big bangs and black holes.

Tom Stoppard (1937–) Czech-born British dramatist. *The Observer*, 'Sayings of the Week', 22 May 1994

V

VENICE

See also Europe

1 Streets full of water. Please advise.

Robert Benchley (1889–1945) US humorist. Telegram sent to his editor on arriving in Venice. Attrib.

2 Venice is like eating an entire box of chocolate liqueurs at one go.

Truman Capote (1924–84) US novelist. *The Observer*, 'Sayings of the Week', 26 Nov 1961

3 Venice, the eldest Child of Liberty.
She was a maiden City, bright and free.

William Wordsworth (1770–1850) British poet. Venice, a republic since the Middle Ages, was conquered by Napoleon in 1797 and absorbed into his Kingdom of Italy in 1805. *Sonnets*, 'Once did she hold'

4 Once did she hold the gorgeous east in fee;
And was the safeguard of the west.

William Wordsworth *Sonnets*, 'Once did she hold'

5 When she took unto herself a mate,
She must espouse the everlasting sea.

William Wordsworth *Sonnets*, 'Once did she hold'

VERBOSITY

See also brevity, sermons, speech, speeches, writing

1 There was a young man of Japan
Whose limericks never would scan;
When they said it was so,
He replied, 'Yes, I know,
But I always try to get as many words into the last line as ever I possibly can.'

Anonymous

2 A sophistical rhetorician inebriated with the exuberance of his own verbosity.

Benjamin Disraeli (1804–81) British statesman. Referring to Gladstone. Speech, 27 July 1878

3 But far more numerous was the Herd of such,
Who think too little, and who talk too much.

John Dryden (1631–1700) British poet and dramatist. *Absalom and Achitophel*, I

4 Nothing is more despicable than a professional talker who uses his words as a quack uses his remedies.

François Fénelon (1651–1715) French writer and prelate. Letter to M. Dacier

5 I have made this letter longer than usual, only because I have not had the time to make it shorter.

Blaise Pascal (1623–62) French philosopher and mathematician. *Lettres provinciales*, XVI

6 Words are like leaves; and where they most abound,
Much fruit of sense beneath is rarely found.

Alexander Pope (1688–1744) British poet. *An Essay on Criticism*

VICE

See also crime, evil, sin, virtue and vice

1 When vice prevails, and impious men bear sway,
The post of honour is a private station.

Joseph Addison (1672–1719) British essayist. *Cato*, IV:1

2 We make ourselves a ladder out of our vices if we trample the vices themselves underfoot.

St Augustine of Hippo (354–430) Bishop of Hippo. *Sermons*, Bk. III, 'De Ascensione'

3 Often the fear of one evil leads us into a worse.

Nicolas Boileau (1636–1711) French writer. *L'Art poétique*, I

4 The wickedness of the world is so great you have to run your legs off to avoid having them stolen from under you.

Bertolt Brecht (1898–1956) German dramatist. *The Threepenny Opera*, I:3

5 Vice itself lost half its evil, by losing all its grossness.

Edmund Burke (1729–97) British politician. *Reflections on the Revolution in France*

6 Vice is its own reward.

Quentin Crisp (?1910–) Model, publicist, and writer. *The Naked Civil Servant*

7 In my time, the follies of the town crept slowly among us, but now they travel faster than a stagecoach.

Oliver Goldsmith (1728–74) Irish-born British writer. *She Stoops to Conquer*, I

8 Wrongdoing can only be avoided if those who are not wronged feel the same indignation at it as those who are.

Solon (6th century BC) Athenian statesman. *Greek Wit* (F. Paley)

9 Whenever I'm caught between two evils, I take the one I've never tried.

Mae West (1892–1980) US actress. Attrib.

10 Never support two weaknesses at the same time. It's your combination sinners – your lecherous liars and your miserly drunkards – who dishonour the vices and bring them into bad repute.

Thornton Wilder (1897–1975) US novelist and dramatist. *The Matchmaker*, III

VICTORY

See also war

1 *Veni, vidi, vici.*
I came, I saw, I conquered.

Julius Caesar (100–44 BC) Roman general and statesman. *The Twelve Caesars* (Suetonius)

2 Victory at all costs, victory in spite of all terror, victory however long and hard the road may be; for without victory there is no survival.

Winston Churchill (1874–1965) British statesman. Speech, House of Commons, 13 May 1940

3 We triumph without glory when we conquer without danger.

Pierre Corneille (1606–84) French dramatist. *Le Cid*, II:2

4 The most important thing in the Olympic Games is not winning but taking part...The essential thing in life is not conquering but fighting well.

Pierre de Coubertin (1863–1937) French educator and sportsman. Speech, Banquet to Officials of Olympic Games, London, 24 July 1908

5 A game which a sharper once played with a dupe, entitled 'Heads I win, tails you lose.'

John Wilson Croker (1780–1857) British Tory politician. *Croker Papers*

6 The happy state of getting the victor's palm without the dust of racing.

Horace (Quintus Horatius Flaccus; 65–8 BC) Roman poet. *Epistles*, I

7 We've got no place in this outfit for good losers. We want tough hombres who will go in there and *win*!

Jonas Ingram US admiral. Remark, 1926

8 They talk about who won and who lost. Human reason won. Mankind won.

Nikita Khrushchev (1894–1971) Soviet statesman. Referring to the Cuban missiles crisis. *The Observer*, 'Sayings of the Week', 11 Nov 1962

9 Winning isn't everything, but wanting to win is.

Vince Lombardi (1913–70) US football coach.

10 How vainly men themselves amaze
To win the palm, the oak, or bays.

Andrew Marvell (1621–78) English poet. *The Garden*

11 Who overcomes
By force, hath overcome but half his foe.

John Milton (1608–74) English poet. *Paradise Lost*, Bk. I

12 See, the conquering hero comes!
Sound the trumpets, beat the drums!

Thomas Morell (1703–84) British classicist. The libretto for Handel's oratorio. *Joshua*, Pt. III

13 We have met the enemy, and they are ours.

Oliver Hazard Perry (1785–1819) US naval officer. Message sent reporting his victory in a naval battle on Lake Erie. *Familiar Quotations* (J. Bartlett)

14 Such another victory and we are ruined.

Pyrrhus (319–272 BC) King of Epirus. Commenting upon the costliness of his victory at the Battle of Asculum, 279 BC. *Life of Pyrrhus* (Plutarch)

15 For when the One Great Scorer comes
To write against your name,
He marks – not that you won or lost –
But how you played the game.

Grantland Rice (1880–1954) US sportswriter. *Alumnus Football*

16 I came; I saw; God conquered.

John III Sobieski (1624–96) King of Poland. Announcing his victory over the Turks at Vienna to the pope (paraphrasing Caesar's 'veni, vidi, vici'). Attrib.

17 'And everybody praised the Duke,
Who this great fight did win.'
'But what good came of it at last?'
Quoth little Peterkin.
'Why that I cannot tell,' said he,
'But 'twas a famous victory.'

Robert Southey (1774–1843) British poet. *The Battle of Blenheim*

18 The next greatest misfortune to losing a battle is to gain such a victory as this.

Duke of Wellington (1769–1852) British general and statesman. *Recollections* (S. Rogers)

19 I always say that, next to a battle lost, the greatest misery is a battle gained.

Duke of Wellington *Diary* (Frances, Lady Shelley)

20 By the splendour of God I have taken possession of my realm; the earth of England is in my two hands.

William the Conqueror (1027–87) King of England. Said after falling over when coming ashore at Pevensey with his army of invasion. Attrib.

VIOLENCE

See also cruelty, force, war, weapons

1 A bit of shooting takes your mind off your troubles – it makes you forget the cost of living.

Brendan Behan (1923–64) Irish playwright. *The Hostage*

2 I would be quite happy for men to hit women if there was a law saying that women could carry guns. Because then, if a man hit you, you could shoot him.

Jo Brand (1958–) British comic. *Q*, June 1994

3 So soon as the man overtook me, he was but a word and a blow.

John Bunyan (1628–88) English writer. *The Pilgrim's Progress*, Pt. I

4 Two lovely black eyes,
Oh, what a surprise!
Only for telling a man he was wrong.
Two lovely black eyes!

Charles Coborn (1852–1945) US songwriter. *Two Lovely Black Eyes*

5 It's possible to disagree with someone about

the ethics of non-violence without wanting to kick his face in.

Christopher Hampton (1946–) British writer and dramatist. *Treats*, Sc. 4

6 We are effectively destroying ourselves by violence masquerading as love.

R. D. Laing (1927–89) British psychiatrist. *The Politics of Experience*, Ch. 13

7 If you strike a child, take care that you strike it in anger, even at the risk of maiming it for life. A blow in cold blood neither can nor should be forgiven.

George Bernard Shaw (1856–1950) Irish dramatist and critic. *Man and Superman*, 'Maxims for Revolutionists'

8 The only difference is that the stress and the violence is worse at home, because it happens younger, it happens at the hands of someone you love and there is no recognition that this is the enemy.

Gloria Steinem (1934–) US writer and feminist. Referring to similarities between the trauma suffered by men who have fought in wars and women and girls who have been victims of recurrent domestic violence. *The Observer Life Magazine*, 15 May 1994

9 Not a historical document, but a metaphorical truth that represents a decade of aggression, a culture that worships aggression and makes money from it.

Oliver Stone (1946–) US film director. Referring to his film *Natural Born Killers*. *The Independent*, 21 Feb 1995

10 Violence in real life is terrible; violence in the movies can be cool. It's just another colour to work with.

Quentin Tarantino (1963–) US film director. *The Observer*, 'Sayings of the Week', 16 Oct 1994

VIRTUE

See also good, morality, purity, righteousness, virtue and vice

1 Virtue is like a rich stone, best plain set.

Francis Bacon (1561–1626) English philosopher. *Essays*, 'Of Beauty'

2 As in nature things move violently to their place and calmly in their place, so virtue in ambition is violent, in authority settled and calm.

Francis Bacon *Essays*, 'Of Great Place'

3 A good name is better than precious ointment; and the day of death than the day of one's birth.
It is better to go to the house of mourning, than to go to the house of feasting: for that is the end of all men; and the living will lay it to his heart.

Bible: Ecclesiastes 7:1–2

4 Finally, brethren, whatsoever things are true, whatsoever things are honest, whatsoever things are just, whatsoever things are pure, whatsoever things are lovely, whatsoever things are of good report; if there be any virtue; and if there be any praise, think on these things.

Bible: Philippians 4:8

5 Virtue consisted in avoiding scandal and venereal disease.

Robert Cecil (1913–94) British writer. *Life in Edwardian England*

6 My virtue's still far too small, I don't trot it out and about yet.

Colette (1873–1954) French novelist. *Claudine at School*

7 To be able to practise five things everywhere under heaven constitutes perfect virtue...gravity, generosity of soul, sincerity, earnestness, and kindness.

Confucius (K'ung Fu-tzu; 551–479 BC) Chinese philosopher. *Analects*

8 How next to impossible is the exercise of virtue! It requires a constant watchfulness, constant guard.

William Golding (1911–93) British novelist. *Rites of Passage*, 'Colley's Letter'

9 Good, but not religious-good.

Thomas Hardy (1840–1928) British novelist. *Under the Greenwood Tree*, Ch. 2

10 The greatest offence against virtue is to speak ill of it.

William Hazlitt (1778–1830) British essayist. *On Cant and Hypocrisy*

11 Only a sweet and virtuous soul,
Like season'd timber, never gives;
But though the whole world turn to coal,
Then chiefly lives.

George Herbert (1593–1633) English poet. *Virtue*

12 Be good, sweet maid, and let who can be clever;
Do lovely things, not dream them, all day long;
And so make Life, and Death, and that For Ever,
One grand sweet song.

Charles Kingsley (1819–75) British writer. *A Farewell. To C. E. G.*

13 To be discontented with the divine discontent, and to be ashamed with the noble shame, is the very germ and first upgrowth of all virtue.

Charles Kingsley *Health and Education*

14 Most men admire
Virtue, who follow not her lore.

John Milton (1608–74) English poet. *Paradise Regained*, Bk. I

15 When men grow virtuous in their old age, they only make a sacrifice to God of the devil's leavings.

Alexander Pope (1688–1744) British poet. *Thoughts on Various Subjects*

VIRTUE AND VICE

See also good and evil, vice, virtue

1 Our virtues and vices couple with one another, and get children that resemble both their parents.

Lord Halifax (1633–95) English statesman. *Political, Moral and Miscellaneous Thoughts and Reflections*

2 Most usually our virtues are only vices in disguise.

Duc de la Rochefoucauld (1613–80) French writer. *Maximes*, added to the 4th edition

3 Vice and virtues are products like sulphuric acid and sugar.

Hippolyte Adolphe Taine (1828–93) French writer and philosopher. *Histoire de la littérature anglaise*, Introduction

VULGARITY

See also humour

1 You gotta have a swine to show you where the truffles are.

Edward Albee (1928–) US dramatist. *Who's Afraid of Virginia Woolf?*, I

2 The aristocratic pleasure of displeasing is not the only delight that bad taste can yield. One can love a certain kind of vulgarity for its own sake.

Aldous Huxley (1894–1964) British novelist. *Vulgarity in Literature*, Ch. 4

3 That fellow would vulgarize the day of judgment.

Douglas William Jerrold (1803–57) British dramatist. *Wit and Opinions of Douglas Jerrold*, 'A Comic Author'

4 It is disgusting to pick your teeth. What is vulgar is to use a gold toothpick.

Louis Kronenberger (1904–80) US writer and literary critic. *The Cat and the Horse*

5 With our James vulgarity begins at home, and should be allowed to stay there.

Oscar Wilde (1854–1900) Irish-born British dramatist. Referring to the artist James Whistler. Letter to the *World*

6 I can't stand a naked light bulb, any more than I can a rude remark or a vulgar action.

Tennessee Williams (1911–83) US dramatist. *A Streetcar Named Desire*, II:3

W

WALES

See also Britain, Welsh

1 The thing I value about Wales and Welsh background is that it has always been a genuinely more classless society than many people present England as being.

Geoffrey Howe (1926–) British politician. *The Observer*, 'Sayings of the Week', 9 Nov 1986

2 The land of my fathers. My fathers can have it.

Dylan Thomas (1914–53) Welsh poet. Referring to Wales. *Dylan Thomas* (John Ackerman)

3 Too many of the artists of Wales spend too much time about the position of the artist of Wales. There is only one position for an artist anywhere: and that is, upright.

Dylan Thomas *New Statesman*, 18 Dec 1964

4 Make me content
With some sweetness
From Wales
Whose nightingales
Have no wings.

Edward Thomas (1878–1917) British poet. *Words*

5 We can trace almost all the disasters of English history to the influence of Wales.

Evelyn Waugh (1903–66) British novelist. *Decline and Fall*, Pt. I, Ch. 8

WAR

See also army, Cold War, defeat, navy, nuclear weapons, officers, patriotism, soldiers, victory, war and peace, weapons, World War II

1 Give them the cold steel, boys!

Lewis Addison Arminstead (1817–63) US general. Exhortation given to his troops during the US Civil War. Attrib.

2 And we are here as on a darkling plain
Swept with confused alarms of struggle and flight,
Where ignorant armies clash by night.

Matthew Arnold (1822–88) British poet and critic. *Dover Beach*

3 To save your world you asked this man to die:
Would this man, could he see you now, ask why?

W. H. Auden (1907–73) British poet. *Epitaph for an Unknown Soldier*

4 Well, if you knows of a better 'ole, go to it.

Bruce Bairnsfather (1888–1959) British cartoonist. *Fragments from France*

5 The only defence is in offence, which means that you have to kill more women and children more quickly than the enemy if you want to save yourselves.

Stanley Baldwin (1867–1947) British statesman. Speech, Nov 1932

6 I think it is well also for the man in the street to realise that there is no power on earth that can protect him from being bombed. Whatever people may tell him, the bomber will always get through, and it is very easy to understand that, if you realise the area of space.

Stanley Baldwin Speech, House of Commons, 10 Nov 1932

7 It takes twenty years or more of peace to make a man, it takes only twenty seconds of war to destroy him.

Baudouin I (1930–93) King of Belgium. Addressing US Congress, 12 May 1959

8 I have never understood this liking for war. It panders to instincts already catered for within the scope of any respectable domestic establishment.

Alan Bennett (1934–) British playwright. *Forty Years On*, I

9 And ye shall hear of wars and rumours of wars: see that ye be not troubled: for all these things must come to pass, but the end is not yet. For nation shall rise against nation, and kingdom against kingdom: and there shall be famines, and pestilences, and earthquakes, in divers places. All these are the beginning of sorrows.

Bible: Matthew 24:6–8

10 Then said Jesus unto him, Put up again thy sword into his place: for all they that take the sword shall perish with the sword.

Bible: Matthew 26:52

11 If there is ever another war in Europe, it will come out of some damned silly thing in the Balkans.

Bismarck (1815–98) German statesman. Remark to Ballen, shortly before Bismarck's death

12 *C'est magnifique, mais ce n'est pas la guerre.*
It is magnificent, but it is not war.

Pierre Bosquet (1810–61) French marshal. Referring to the Charge of the Light Brigade at the Battle of Balaclava, 25 Oct 1854. Attrib.

13 The wrong war, at the wrong place, at the wrong time, and with the wrong enemy.

Omar Nelson Bradley (1893–1981) US general. Said in evidence to a Senate inquiry, May 1951, over a proposal by MacArthur that the Korean war should be extended into China

14 What they could do with round here is a good war.

Bertolt Brecht (1898–1956) German dramatist. *Mother Courage*, I

15 A war of which we could say it left nothing to be desired will probably never exist.

Bertolt Brecht *Mother Courage*, VI

16 War is like love, it always finds a way.
Bertolt Brecht *Mother Courage*, VI

17 The Angel of Death has been abroad throughout the land: you may almost hear the beating of his wings.
John Bright (1811–89) British radical politician. Referring to the Crimean War. Speech, House of Commons, 23 Feb 1855

18 If I should die, think only this of me:
That there's some corner of a foreign field
That is forever England.
Rupert Brooke (1887–1915) British poet. *The Soldier*

19 War knows no power. Safe shall be my going,
Secretly armed against all death's endeavour;
Safe though all safety's lost; safe where men fall;
And if these poor limbs die, safest of all.
Rupert Brooke *Safety*

20 Scots, wha hae wi' Wallace bled,
Scots, wham Bruce has aften led,
Welcome to your gory bed,
Or to victorie.
Robert Burns (1759–96) Scottish poet. *Scots, Wha Hae*

21 When civil fury first grew high,
And men fell out they knew not why.
Samuel Butler (1612–80) English satirist. *Hudibras*, Pt. I

22 War, war is still the cry, 'War even to the knife!'
Lord Byron (1788–1824) British poet. *Childe Harold's Pilgrimage*, I

23 Tweedledum and Tweedledee
Agreed to have a battle;
For Tweedledum said Tweedledee
Had spoiled his nice new rattle.
Lewis Carroll (Charles Lutwidge Dodgson; 1832–98) British writer. *Through the Looking-Glass*, Ch. 4

24 Carthage must be destroyed.
Cato the Elder (Marcius Porcius C.; 234–149 BC) Roman statesman. *Life of Cato* (Plutarch)

25 In war, whichever side may call itself the victor, there are no winners, but all are losers.
Neville Chamberlain (1869–1940) British statesman. Speech, Kettering, 3 July 1938

26 Wars, conflict, it's all business. One murder makes a villain. Millions a hero. Numbers sanctify.
Charlie Chaplin (Sir Charles Spencer C.; 1889–1977) British film actor. *Monsieur Verdoux*

27 The redress of the grievances of the vanquished should precede the disarmament of the victors.
Winston Churchill (1874–1965) British statesman. *The Gathering Storm*, Ch. 3

28 I said that the world must be made safe for at least fifty years. If it was only for fifteen to twenty years then we should have betrayed our soldiers.
Winston Churchill *Closing the Ring*, Ch. 20

29 No one can guarantee success in war, but only deserve it.
Winston Churchill *Their Finest Hour*

30 War is the continuation of politics by other means.
Karl von Clausewitz (1780–1831) Prussian general. The usual misquotation of 'War is nothing but a continuation of politics with the admixture of other means'. *Vom Kriege*

31 Now, gentlemen, let us do something today which the world may talk of hereafter.
Lord Collingwood (1750–1810) British admiral. Said before Trafalgar, 21 Oct 1805. *Correspondence and Memoir of Lord Collingwood* (G. L. Newnham; ed. Collingwood)

32 Come on, you sons of bitches! Do you want to live for ever?
Dan Daly (20th century) Sergeant in the US Marines. Remark during Allied resistance at Belleau Wood, June 1918. *See also* FREDERICK THE GREAT. Attrib.

33 If we lose this war, I'll start another in my wife's name.
Moshe Dayan (1915–81) Israeli general. Attrib.

34 There is plenty of time to win this game, and to thrash the Spaniards too.
Francis Drake (1540–96) British navigator and admiral. Referring to the sighting of the Armada during a game of bowls, 20 July 1588. Attrib.

35 I have singed the Spanish king's beard.
Francis Drake Referring to the raid on Cadiz harbour, 1587. Attrib.

36 My centre is giving way, my right is in retreat; situation excellent. I shall attack.
Marshal Foch (1851–1929) French soldier. Message sent during the second battle of the Marne, 1918. *Biography of Foch* (Aston), Ch. 13

37 Praise the Lord and pass the ammunition!
Howell Maurice Forgy (1908–83) US naval lieutenant. Remark made during the Japanese attack on Pearl Harbor, 7 Dec 1941. Attrib. in *The Los Angeles Times*

38 I got there fustest with the mostest.
Nathan Bedford Forrest (1821–77) Confederate general. Popular misquotation of his explanation of his success in capturing Murfreesboro; his actual words were, 'I just took the short cut and got there first with the most men'. *A Civil War Treasury* (B. Botkin)

39 Rascals, would you live for ever?
Frederick the Great (1712–86) King of Prussia. Addressed to reluctant soldiers at the Battle of Kolin, 18 June 1757. *See also* DALY.

40 Madam, I am the civilization they are fighting to defend.
Heathcote William Garrod (1878–1960) British classical scholar. Replying to criticism that he was not fighting to defend civilization, during World War I. *Oxford Now and Then* (D. Balsdon)

41 I have many times asked myself whether there can be more potent advocates of peace upon earth through the years to come than this massed multitude of silent witnesses to the desolation of war.
George V (1865–1936) King of the United Kingdom.

Referring to the massed World War I graves in Flanders, 1922. *Silent Cities* (ed. Gavin Stamp)

42 You've got to forget about this civilian. Whenever you drop bombs, you're going to hit civilians.

Barry Goldwater (1909–) US politician. Speech, New York, 23 Jan 1967

43 No terms except unconditional and immediate surrender can be accepted. I propose to move immediately upon your works.

Ulysses Simpson Grant (1822–85) US general. Message to opposing commander, Simon Bolivar Buckner, during siege of Fort Donelson, 16 Feb 1862.

44 Every position must be held to the last man: there must be no retirement. With our backs to the wall, and believing in the justice of our cause, each one of us must fight on to the end.

Douglas Haig (1861–1928) British general. Order to the British Army, 12 Apr 1918

45 Gentlemen of the French Guard, fire first!

Lord Charles Hay (d. 1760) British soldier. Said at the Battle of Fontenoy, 1745. Attrib.

46 I'd like to see the government get out of war altogether and leave the whole feud to private industry.

Joseph Heller (1923–) US novelist. *Catch 22*

47 In starting and waging a war it is not right that matters, but victory.

Adolf Hitler (1889–1945) German dictator. *The Rise and Fall of the Third Reich* (W. L. Shirer), Ch. 16

48 War? War is an organized bore.

Oliver Wendell Holmes Jnr (1841–1935) US jurist. *Yankee from Olympus* (C. Bowen)

49 Older men declare war. But it is youth that must fight and die.

Herbert Clark Hoover (1874–1964) US statesman. Speech, Republican National Convention, Chicago, 27 June 1944

50 East and west on fields forgotten
Bleach the bones of comrades slain,
Lovely lads and dead and rotten;
None that go return again.

A. E. Housman (1859–1936) British scholar and poet. *A Shropshire Lad*, 'The Welsh Marches'

51 Elevate them guns a little lower.

Andrew Jackson (1767–1845) US statesman. Order given whilst watching the effect of the US artillery upon the British lines at the Battle of New Orleans. Attrib.

52 I had always to remember that I could have lost the war in an afternoon.

Lord Jellicoe (1859–1935) British admiral. Referring to the Battle of Jutland

53 The first casualty when war comes is truth.

Hiram Warren Johnson (1866–1945) US politician. Speech, U.S. Senate, 1917

54 Formerly, a nation that broke the peace did not trouble to try and prove to the world that it was done solely from higher motives...*Now war has a bad conscience.* Now every nation assures us that it is bleeding for a human cause, the fate of which hangs in the balance of its victory.... No nation dares to admit the guilt of blood before the world.

Ellen Key (Karolina Sofia Key; 1849–1926) Swedish writer. *War, Peace, and the Future*, Preface

55 Everything, everything in war is barbaric... But the worst barbarity of war is that it forces men collectively to commit acts against which individually they would revolt with their whole being.

Ellen Key *War, Peace, and the Future*, Ch. 6

56 Our scientific power has outrun our spiritual power. We have guided missiles and misguided men.

Martin Luther King (1929–68) US Black civil-rights leader. *Strength to Love*

57 The conventional army loses if it does not win. The guerrilla wins if he does not lose.

Henry Kissinger (1923–) German-born US politician and diplomat. *Foreign Affairs*, XIII (Jan 1969), 'The Vietnam Negotiations'

58 The most persistent sound which reverberates through men's history is the beating of war drums.

Arthur Koestler (1905–83) Hungarian-born British writer. *Janus: A Summing Up*, Prologue

59 If, therefore, war should ever come between these two countries, which Heaven forbid! it will not, I think, be due to irresistible natural laws, it will be due to the want of human wisdom.

Bonar Law (1858–1923) British statesman. Referring to the UK and Germany. Speech, House of Commons, 27 Nov 1911

60 We have all lost the war. All Europe.

D. H. Lawrence (1885–1930) British novelist. *The Ladybird*, 'The Ladybird'

61 It is well that war is so terrible; else we would grow too fond of it.

Robert E. Lee (1807–70) US general. Speaking to another general during the battle of Fredericksburg. *The American Treasury* (C. Fadiman)

62 This war, like the next war, is a war to end war.

David Lloyd George (1863–1945) British Liberal statesman. Referring to the popular opinion that World War I would be the last major war.

63 'War is the continuation of politics'. In this sense war is politics and war itself is a political action.

Mao Tse-Tung (1893–1976) Chinese communist leader. *See also* CLAUSEWITZ. *Quotations from Chairman Mao Tse-Tung*, Ch. 5

64 We are advocates of the abolition of war, we do not want war; but war can only be abolished through war, and in order to get rid of the gun it is necessary to take up the gun.

Mao Tse-Tung *Quotations from Chairman Mao Tse-Tung*, Ch. 5

65 Television brought the brutality of war into the comfort of the living room. Vietnam was lost in the living rooms of America – not on the battlefields of Vietnam.

Marshall McLuhan (1911–81) Canadian sociologist. Montreal *Gazette*, 16 May 1975

66 War will never cease until babies begin to come into the world with larger cerebrums and smaller adrenal glands.

H. L. Mencken (1880–1956) US journalist. *Notebooks*, 'Minority Report'

67 War is the national industry of Prussia.

Comte de Mirabeau (1749–91) French statesman. Attrib.

68 Fighting is like champagne. It goes to the heads of cowards as quickly as of heroes. Any fool can be brave on a battle field when it's be brave or else be killed.

Margaret Mitchell (1909–49) US novelist. *Gone with the Wind*

69 War hath no fury like a non-combatant.

C. E. Montague (1867–1928) British editor and writer. *Disenchantment*, Ch. 15

70 An empire founded by war has to maintain itself by war.

Baron de Montesquieu (1689–1755) French writer. *Considérations sur les causes de la grandeur et de la décadence des romains*, Ch. 8

71 The U.S. has broken the second rule of war. That is, don't go fighting with your land army on the mainland of Asia. Rule One is don't march on Moscow. I developed these two rules myself.

Lord Montgomery (1887–1976) British field marshal. Referring to the Vietnam war. *Montgomery of Alamein* (Chalfont)

72 The Minstrel Boy to the war has gone,
In the ranks of death you'll find him;
His father's sword he has girded on,
And his wild harp slung behind him.

Thomas Moore (1779–1852) Irish poet. *Irish Melodies*, 'The Minstrel Boy'

73 It's the most beautiful battlefield I've ever seen.

Napoleon I (Napoleon Bonaparte; 1769–1821) French emperor. Referring to carnage on the field of Borodino, near Moscow, after the battle (7 Sept 1812). Attrib.

74 There rises the sun of Austerlitz.

Napoleon I Said at the Battle of Borodino (7 Sept 1812), near Moscow; the Battle of Austerlitz (2 Dec 1805) was Napoleon's great victory over the Russians and Austrians.

75 I don't care for war, there's far too much luck in it for my liking.

Napoleon III (1808–73) French emperor. Said after the narrow but bloody French victory at Solferino (24 June 1859). *The Fall of the House of Habsburg* (E. Crankshaw)

76 The sand of the desert is sodden red, –
Red with the wreck of a square that broke; –
The gatling's jammed and the colonel dead,
And the regiment blind with the dust and smoke.
The river of death has brimmed its banks
And England's far and honour a name.
But the voice of a schoolboy rallies the ranks:
'Play up! play up! and play the game!'

Henry John Newbolt (1862–1938) British poet. *Vitaï Lampada*

77 Drake he's in his hammock till the great Armadas come.
(Capten, art tha sleepin' there below?)
Slung atween the round shot, listenin' for the drum,
An dreamin' arl the time o' Plymouth Hoe.

Henry John Newbolt *Drake's Drum*

78 War is war. The only good human being is a dead one.

George Orwell (Eric Blair; 1903–50) British novelist. *Animal Farm*, Ch. 4

79 Probably the Battle of Waterloo *was* won on the playing-fields of Eton, but the opening battles of all subsequent wars have been lost there.

George Orwell *The Lion and the Unicorn*, 'England, Your England'

80 The quickest way of ending a war is to lose it.

George Orwell *Second Thoughts on James Burnham*

81 The pallor of girls' brows shall be their pall;
Their flowers the tenderness of patient minds,
And each slow dusk a drawing-down of blinds.

Wilfred Owen (1893–1918) British poet. *Anthem for Doomed Youth*

82 Red lips are not so red
As the stained stones kissed by the English dead.

Wilfred Owen *Greater Love*

83 I could not give my name to aid the slaughter in this war, fought on both sides for grossly material ends, which did not justify the sacrifice of a single mother's son. Clearly I must continue to oppose it, and expose it, to all whom I could reach with voice or pen.

Sylvia Pankhurst (1882–1960) British suffragette. *The Home Front*, Ch. 25

84 Stand your ground. Don't fire unless fired upon, but if they mean to have a war, let it begin here!

John Parker (1729–75) US general. Command given at the start of the Battle of Lexington. *Familiar Quotations* (J. Bartlett)

85 War should belong to the tragic past, to history: it should find no place on humanity's agenda for the future.

John Paul II (Karol Wojtyla; 1920–) Polish pope (1978–). Speech, 1982

86 Don't cheer, boys; the poor devils are dying.

John Woodward Philip (1840–1900) US naval officer. Restraining his victorious crew during the naval battle off Santiago in the Spanish-American War. Attrib.

87 Don't fire until you see the whites of their eyes.

William Prescott (1726–95) US revolutionary soldier. Command given at the Battle of Bunker Hill

88 War is, after all, the universal perversion. We are all tainted: if we cannot experience our perversion at first hand we spend our time reading war stories, the pornography of war; or seeing war films, the blue films of war; or titillating our senses with the imagination of great deeds, the masturbation of war.

John Rae (1931–) British schoolmaster and writer. *The Custard Boys*, Ch. 6

89 In a civil war, a general must know – and I'm afraid it's a thing rather of instinct than of practice – he must know exactly when to move over to the other side.

Henry Reed (1914–86) British poet and dramatist. *Not a Drum was Heard: The War Memoirs of General Gland*

90 And the various holds and rolls and throws and breakfalls
Somehow or other I always seemed to put
In the wrong place. And as for war, my wars
Were global from the start.

Henry Reed *A Map of Verona*, 'Lessons of the War', III

91 All Quiet on the Western Front.

Erich Maria Remarque (1898–1970) German novelist. Title of novel

92 All wars are planned by old men
In council rooms apart.

Grantland Rice (1880–1954) US sportswriter. *Two Sides of War*

93 (Fire – without hatred.)

Antonio Rivera (d. 1936) Spanish Nationalist hero. Giving the order to open fire at the siege of the Alcázar. *The Siege of the Alcázar* (C. Eby)

94 More than an end to war, we want an end to the beginnings of all wars.

Franklin D. Roosevelt (1882–1945) US Democratic president. Speech broadcast on the day after his death (13 Apr 1945)

95 They dashed on towards that *thin red line tipped with steel.*

William Howard Russell (1820–1907) British journalist. Description of the Russian charge against the British at the Battle of Balaclava, 1854. *The British Expedition to the Crimea*

96 War is not an adventure. It is a disease. It is like typhus.

Antoine de Saint-Exupéry (1900–44) French novelist and aviator. *Flight to Arras*

97 Sometime they'll give a war and nobody will come.

Carl Sandburg (1878–1967) US author and poet. *The People, Yes*

98 Man, it seemed, had been created to jab the life out of Germans.

Siegfried Sassoon (1886–1967) British poet. *Memoirs of an Infantry Officer*, Pt. I, Ch. 1

99 Safe with his wound, a citizen of life,
He hobbled blithely through the garden gate,
And thought: 'Thank God they had to amputate!'

Siegfried Sassoon *The One-Legged Man*

100 If I were fierce and bald and short of breath,
I'd live with scarlet Majors at the Base,
And speed glum heroes up the line to death.

Siegfried Sassoon *Base Details*

101 And when the war is done and youth stone dead
I'd toddle safely home and die – in bed.

Siegfried Sassoon *Base Details*

102 'Good morning; good morning!' the general said
When we met him last week on our way to the line.
Now the soldiers he smiled at are most of 'em dead,
And we're cursing his staff for incompetent swine.

Siegfried Sassoon *The General*

103 I am making this statement as a wilful defiance of military authority because I believe that the War is being deliberately prolonged by those who have the power to end it.

Siegfried Sassoon *Memoirs of an Infantry Officer*, Pt. X, Ch. 3

104 All wars are popular for the first thirty days.

Arthur Schlesinger Jnr (1917–) US historian, educator, and author. Attrib.

105 When you march into France, let the last man on the right brush the Channel with his sleeve.

Alfred Graf von Schlieffen (1833–1913) German general. Referring to the Schlieffen plan. *August 1914* (Barbara Tuchman), Ch. 2

106 When we, the Workers, all demand: 'What are we fighting for?...
Then, then we'll end that stupid crime, that devil's madness – War.

Robert William Service (1874–1958) Canadian poet. *Michael*

107 Cry 'Havoc!' and let slip the dogs of war.

William Shakespeare (1564–1616) English dramatist. *Julius Caesar*, III:1

108 Farewell the neighing steed and the shrill trump,
The spirit-stirring drum, th'ear piercing fife,
The royal banner, and all quality,
Pride, pomp, and circumstance, of glorious war!

William Shakespeare *Othello*, III:3

109 The British soldier can stand up to anything except the British War Office.

George Bernard Shaw (1856–1950) Irish dramatist and critic. *The Devil's Disciple*, II

110 I am tired and sick of war. Its glory is all moonshine... War is hell.

General William Sherman (1820–91) US general. Attrib. in address, Michigan Military Academy, 19 June 1879

111 Who live under the shadow of a war,
What can I do that matters?

Stephen Spender (1909–95) British poet. *Who live under the Shadow*

112 To win in Vietnam, we will have to exterminate a nation.

Dr Benjamin Spock (1903–) US paediatrician and psychiatrist. *Dr Spock on Vietnam*, Ch.7

113 Yonder are the Hessians. They were bought for seven pounds and tenpence a man. Are you worth more? Prove it. Tonight the American flag floats from yonder hill or Molly Stark sleeps a widow!

John Stark (1728–1822) US general. Urging on his troops at the Battle of Bennington in 1777. *The American Treasury* (C. Fadiman)

114 That's what you are. That's what you all are. All of you young people who served in the war. You are a lost generation.

Gertrude Stein (1874–1946) US writer. *A Moveable Feast* (E. Hemingway)

115 War is capitalism with the gloves off.

Tom Stoppard (1937–) Czech-born British dramatist. *Travesties*

116 Most sorts of diversion in men, children, and other animals, are an imitation of fighting.

Jonathan Swift (1667–1745) Irish-born Anglican priest and writer. *Thoughts on Various Subjects*

117 The guerrilla fights the war of the flea, and his military enemy suffers the dog's disadvantages: too much to defend; too small, ubiquitous, and agile an enemy to come to grips with.

Robert Taber (20th century) US writer. *The War of the Flea*, Ch. 2

118 They make a wilderness and call it peace.

Tacitus (c. 55–c. 120 AD) Roman historian. *Agricola*, 30

119 Now all roads lead to France
And heavy is the tread
Of the living; but the dead
Returning lightly dance.

Edward Thomas (1878–1917) British poet. *Roads*

120 Dead battles, like dead generals, hold the military mind in their dead grip.

Barbara W. Tuchman (1912–89) US editor and writer. *August 1914*, Ch. 2

121 They now *ring* the bells, but they will soon *wring* their hands.

Robert Walpole (1676–1745) British statesman. Said when war was declared in 1739 with Spain, against Walpole's wishes. *Memoirs of Sir Robert Walpole* (W. Coxe)

122 I heard the bullets whistle, and believe me, there is something charming in the sound.

George Washington (1732–99) US statesman. Referring to a recent skirmish in the French and Indian War. *Presidential Anecdotes* (P. Boller)

123 When the war broke out she took down the signed photograph of the Kaiser and, with some solemnity, hung it in the menservants' lavatory; it was her one combative action.

Evelyn Waugh (1903–66) British novelist. *Vile Bodies*, Ch. 3

124 Like German opera, too long and too loud.

Evelyn Waugh Giving his opinions of warfare after the Battle of Crete, 1941. Attrib.

125 It has been a damned serious business – Blücher and I have lost 30,000 men. It has been a damned nice thing – the nearest run thing you ever saw in your life...By God! I don't think it would have done if I had not been there.

Duke of Wellington (1769–1852) British general and statesman. Referring to the Battle of Waterloo. *Creevey Papers*, Ch. X

126 Yes, and they went down very well too.

Duke of Wellington Replying to the observation that the French cavalry had come up very well during the Battle of Waterloo. *The Age of Elegance* (A. Bryant)

127 A battle of giants.

Duke of Wellington Referring to the Battle of Waterloo; said to Samuel Rogers. Attrib.

128 Up, Guards, and at 'em.

Duke of Wellington Order given at the battle of Waterloo, 18 June 1815. Attrib.

129 The military don't start wars. The politicians start wars.

William Westmorland (1914–) US army officer. Attrib.

130 As long as war is regarded as wicked, it will always have its fascination. When it is looked upon as vulgar, it will cease to be popular.

Oscar Wilde (1854–1900) Irish-born British dramatist. *The Critic as Artist*, Pt. 2

131 You will be home before the leaves have fallen from the trees.

Wilhelm II (1859–1941) King of Prussia and Emperor of Germany. Said to troops leaving for the Front, Aug 1914. *August 1914* (Barbara Tuchman), Ch. 9

132 It is my Royal and Imperial Command that you...exterminate first the treacherous English, and...walk over General French's contemptible little Army.

Wilhelm II Referring to the British Expeditionary Force; veterans of this force became known as 'Old Contemptibles'. *The Times*, 1 Oct 1914

133 There is such a thing as a man being too proud to fight.

Woodrow Wilson (1856–1925) US statesman. Address to foreign-born citizens, 10 May 1915

134 The war we have just been through, though it was shot through with terror, is not to be compared with the war we would have to face next time.

Woodrow Wilson *Mr Wilson's War* (John Dos Passos), Pt. V, Ch. 22

135 Once lead this people into war and they'll forget there ever was such a thing as tolerance.

Woodrow Wilson *Mr Wilson's War* (John Dos Passos), Pt. III, Ch. 2

WAR AND PEACE

See also peace, war

1 Since wars begin in the minds of men, it is in the minds of men that the defences of peace must be constructed.

Anonymous Constitution of UNESCO

2 And he shall judge among the nations, and shall rebuke many people: and they shall beat

their swords into plowshares, and their spears into pruning-hooks: nation shall not lift up sword against nation, neither shall they learn war any more.
Bible: Isaiah 2:4

3 In war, resolution; in defeat, defiance; in victory, magnanimity; in peace, goodwill.
Winston Churchill (1874–1965) British statesman. Epigram used by Sir Edward Marsh after World War II; used as 'a moral of the work' in Churchill's book. *The Second World War*

4 Those who can win a war well can rarely make a good peace and those who could make a good peace would never have won the war.
Winston Churchill *My Early Life*, Ch. 26

5 My pacifism is not based on any intellectual theory but on a deep antipathy to every form of cruelty and hatred.
Albert Einstein (1879–1955) German-born US physicist. Said on the outbreak of World War I. Attrib.

6 There never was a good war or a bad peace.
Benjamin Franklin (1706–90) US scientist and statesman. Letter to Josiah Quincy, 11 Sept 1783

7 My argument is that War makes rattling good history; but Peace is poor reading.
Thomas Hardy (1840–1928) British novelist. *The Dynasts*, II:5

8 He that makes a good war makes a good peace.
George Herbert (1593–1633) English poet. *Outlandish Proverbs*, 420

9 The war ended, the explosions stopped.
The men surrendered their weapons
And hung around limply.
Peace took them all prisoner.
Ted Hughes (1930–) British poet. *Selected Poems 1957–1981*, 'A Motorbike'

10 The statistics of suicide show that, for non-combatants at least, life is more interesting in war than in peace.
Dean Inge (1860–1954) British churchman. *The End of an Age*

11 Peace hath her victories
No less renowned than war.
John Milton (1608–74) English poet. *Sonnet*: 'To the Lord General Cromwell, May 1652'

12 Peace is not only better than war, but infinitely more arduous.
George Bernard Shaw (1856–1950) Irish dramatist and critic. *Heartbreak House* (Preface)

13 Let him who desires peace, prepare for war.
Vegetius (Flavius Vegetius Renatus; 4th century AD) Roman writer. *Epitoma Rei Militaris*, 3, 'Prologue'

14 When you're at war you think about a better life; when you're at peace you think about a more comfortable one.
Thornton Wilder (1897–1975) US novelist and dramatist. *The Skin of Our Teeth*, III

15 Foreigners fooling about in others' civil wars are a menace. They excite baseless hope of a fair, lasting peace.
Woodrow Wyatt (1918–) British journalist and writer. *News of the World*, June 1993

WASTE

See also extravagance

1 Waste not, want not.
Proverb

2 Full many a gem of purest ray serene,
The dark unfathom'd caves of ocean bear:
Full many a flower is born to blush unseen,
And waste its sweetness on the desert air.
Thomas Gray (1716–71) British poet. *Elegy Written in a Country Churchyard*

3 The world is too much with us; late and soon,
Getting and spending, we lay waste our powers:
Little we see in Nature that is ours.
William Wordsworth (1770–1850) British poet. *Sonnets*, 'The world is too much with us'

WATER

See also drinks

1 Well, the principle seems the same. The water still keeps falling over.
Winston Churchill (1874–1965) British statesman. When asked whether the Niagara Falls looked the same as when he first saw them. *Closing the Ring*, Ch. 5

2 Water, water, every where,
And all the boards did shrink;
Water, water, every where,
Nor any drop to drink.
Samuel Taylor Coleridge (1772–1834) British poet. *The Rime of the Ancient Mariner*, II

3 Instead of drinking Coca Colas, turn on the tap and drink what the good Lord gave us.
Edwina Currie (1946–) British politician. Speech, Nov 1988

4 Fish fuck in it.
W. C. Fields (1880–1946) US actor. His reason for not drinking water. Attrib.

5 For any ceremonial purposes the otherwise excellent liquid, water, is unsuitable in colour and other respects.
A. P. Herbert (1890–1971) British writer and politician. *Uncommon Law*

6 If you believe Cratinus from days of old, Maecenas, (as you must know) no verse can give pleasure for long, nor last, that is written by drinkers of water.
Horace (Quintus Horatius Flaccus; 65–8 BC) Roman poet. *Epistles*, I

7 The biggest waste of water in the country by

far. You spend half a pint and flush two gallons.

Prince Philip (1921–) The consort of Queen Elizabeth II. Speech, 1965

8 Human beings were invented by water as a device for transporting itself from one place to another.

Tom Robbins (1936–) US novelist. *Another Roadside Attraction*

9 He who drinks a tumbler of London water has literally in his stomach more animated beings than there are men, women and children on the face of the globe.

Sydney Smith (1771–1845) British clergyman and essayist. Letter

WEAKNESS

See also imperfection, yielding

1 The weakest goes to the wall.

Proverb

2 Oh, your precious 'lame ducks'!

John Galsworthy (1867–1933) British novelist. *The Man of Property*, Pt. II, Ch. 12

3 A sheep in sheep's clothing.

Edmund Gosse (1849–1928) British writer and critic. Referring to T. Sturge Moore. Sometimes attributed to Winston Churchill, referring to Clement Attlee. *Under the Bridge* (Ferris Greenslet), Ch. 12

4 Frailty, thy name is woman!

William Shakespeare (1564–1616) English dramatist. *Hamlet*, I:2

WEALTH

See also capitalism, extravagance, materialism, money, ostentation, poverty and wealth

1 The best things in life are free.

Proverb

2 You can't take it with you when you go.

Proverb

3 Rich men's houses are seldom beautiful, rarely comfortable, and never original. It is a constant source of surprise to people of moderate means to observe how little a big fortune contributes to Beauty.

Margot Asquith (1865–1945) The second wife of Herbert Asquith. *The Autobiography of Margot Asquith*, Ch. 17

4 A man who has a million dollars is as well off as if he were rich.

John Jacob Astor (1763–1848) US millionaire. Attrib.

5 For the Lord thy God bringeth thee into a good land, a land of brooks of water, of fountains and depths that spring out of valleys and hills;
A land of wheat, and barley, and vines, and fig trees, and pomegranates; a land of oil olive, and honey;
A land wherein thou shalt eat bread without scarceness, thou shalt not lack any thing in it; a land whose stones are iron, and out of whose hills thou mayest dig brass.
When thou hast eaten and art full, then thou shalt bless the Lord thy God for the good land which he hath given thee.

Bible: Deuteronomy 8:7–10

6 For what shall it profit a man, if he shall gain the whole world, and lose his own soul? Or what shall a man give in exchange for his soul?

Bible: Mark 8:36–37

7 Lay not up for yourselves treasures upon earth, where moth and rust doth corrupt, and where thieves break through and steal:
But lay up for yourselves treasures in heaven, where neither moth nor rust doth corrupt, and where thieves do not break through nor steal:
For where your treasure is, there will your heart be also.

Bible: Matthew 6:19–21

8 Then said Jesus unto his disciples, Verily I say unto you, That a rich man shall hardly enter into the kingdom of heaven.
And again I say unto you, It is easier for a camel to go through the eye of a needle, than for a rich man to enter into the kingdom of God.

Bible: Matthew 19:23–24

9 The rich are the scum of the earth in every country.

G. K. Chesterton (1874–1936) British writer. *The Flying Inn*

10 Poor Little Rich Girl.

Noël Coward (1899–1973) British dramatist. *Title of song*

11 Riches have wings, and grandeur is a dream.

William Cowper (1731–1800) British poet. *The Task*

12 FITZGERALD. The rich are different from us.
HEMINGWAY. Yes, they have more money.

F. Scott Fitzgerald (1896–1940) US novelist. *The Crack-Up*, 'Notebooks, E'

13 Wealth is not without its advantages, and the case to the contrary, although it has often been made, has never proved widely persuasive.

John Kenneth Galbraith (1908–) US economist. *The Affluent Society*, Ch. 1

14 The meek shall inherit the earth but not the mineral rights.

J. Paul Getty (1892–1976) US oil magnate. Attrib.

15 If you can actually count your money you are not really a rich man.

J. Paul Getty *Gossip* (A. Barrow)

16 As I walk along the Bois Bou-long,
With an independent air,
You can hear the girls declare,
'He must be a millionaire',
You can hear them sigh and wish to die,
You can see them wink the other eye
At the man who broke the Bank at Monte Carlo.

Fred Gilbert (1850–1903) British songwriter. The Bois de Boulogne was a fashionable recreational area on the outskirts of Paris. *The Man who Broke the Bank at Monte Carlo* (song)

17 Sir, the insolence of wealth will creep out.

Samuel Johnson (1709–84) British lexicographer. *Life of Johnson* (J. Boswell), Vol. III

18 Most of our people have never had it so good.

Harold Macmillan (1894–1986) British politician and prime minister. Speech, Bedford Football Ground, 20 July 1957

19 And, as their wealth increaseth, so inclose
Infinite riches in a little room.

Christopher Marlowe (1564–93) English dramatist. *The Jew of Malta*, I:1

20 He must have killed a lot of men to have made so much money.

Molière (Jean Baptiste Poquelin; 1622–73) French dramatist. *Le Malade imaginaire*, I:5

21 I am rich beyond the dreams of avarice.

Edward Moore (1712–57) British dramatist. *The Gamester*, II

22 God shows his contempt for wealth by the kind of person he selects to receive it.

Austin O'Malley (1858–1932) US writer.

23 Who Wants to Be a Millionaire? I don't.

Cole Porter (1893–1964) US songwriter. *Who Wants to be a Millionaire?*, title song

24 I am a millionaire. That is my religion.

George Bernard Shaw (1856–1950) Irish dramatist and critic. *Major Barbara*

25 With the great part of rich people, the chief employment of riches consists in the parade of riches.

Adam Smith (1723–90) Scottish economist. *The Wealth of Nations*

26 It is the wretchedness of being rich that you have to live with rich people.

Logan Pearsall Smith (1865–1946) US writer. *Afterthoughts*, 'In the World'

27 If Heaven had looked upon riches to be a valuable thing, it would not have given them to such a scoundrel.

Jonathan Swift (1667–1745) Irish-born Anglican priest and writer. Letter to Miss Vanhomrigh, 12–13 Aug 1720

28 I have had no real gratification or enjoyment of any sort more than my neighbor on the next block who is worth only half a million.

William Henry Vanderbilt (1821–85) US railway chief. *Famous Last Words* (B. Conrad)

29 One can never be too thin or too rich.

Duchess of Windsor (Wallis Warfield Simpson; 1896–1986) The wife of the Duke of Windsor (formerly Edward VIII). Attrib.

30 Just what God would have done if he had the money.

Alexander Woollcott (1887–1943) US journalist. On being shown round Moss Hart's elegant country house and grounds. Attrib.

WEAPONS

See also nuclear weapons, power politics, war

1 If you carry this resolution and follow out all its implications and do not run away from it, you will send a Foreign Secretary, whoever he may be, naked into the conference chamber.

Aneurin Bevan (1897–1960) British Labour politician. Referring to unilateral disarmament. Speech, Labour Party Conference, 2 Oct 1957

2 It was very successful, but it fell on the wrong planet.

Wernher von Braun (1912–77) German rocket engineer. Referring to the first V2 rocket to hit London during World War II. Attrib.

3 We may find in the long run that tinned food is a deadlier weapon than the machine-gun.

George Orwell (Eric Blair; 1903–50) British novelist. *The Road to Wigan Pier*, Ch. 6

4 Arms control so easily becomes an incantation rather than policy.

Richard Perle US politician. Remark, Mar 1987

5 A gun is the ideal weapon of the detached, the reticent, the almost autistic. It is the opposite of a relationship.

Libby Purves (1950–) British writer and broadcaster. *The Times*, 29 Dec 1994

6 Today we have naming of parts. Yesterday,
We had daily cleaning. And tomorrow morning
We shall have what to do after firing. But today,
Today we have naming of parts.

Henry Reed (1914–86) British poet and dramatist. *Naming of Parts*

7 They call it easing the Spring: it is perfectly easy
If you have any strength in your thumb: like the bolt,
And the breech, and the cocking-piece, and the point of balance,
Which in our case we have not got.

Henry Reed *Naming of Parts*

8 But do you value life less than sport?

Pamela Ross British mother of Joanna, who was killed when a gunman opened fire in Dunblane Primary School, 13 Mar 1996. Referring to the government's subsequent decision not to ban all handguns. *The Independent*, 1 Aug 1996

9 Though loaded firearms were strictly forbidden at St Trinian's to all but Sixth-Formers...one or two of them carried automatics acquired in the holidays, generally the gift of some indulgent relative.

Ronald Searle (1920–) British cartoonist. *The Terror of St Trinian's*, Ch. 3

10 But bombs *are* unbelievable until they actually fall.

Patrick White (1912–90) British-born Australian novelist. *Riders in the Chariot*, I:4

WEATHER

See also sun

1 Mackerel sky and mares' tails make lofty ships carry low sails.
Proverb

2 Rain before seven: fine before eleven.
Proverb

3 Rain, rain, go away, come again another day.
Proverb

4 Red sky at night, shepherd's delight; red sky in the morning, shepherd's warning.
Proverb

5 St. Swithin's Day, if thou dost rain, for forty days it will remain; St. Swithin's Day, if thou be fair, for forty days 'twill rain no more.
Proverb

6 The north wind does blow, and we shall have snow.
Proverb

7 What dreadful hot weather we have! It keeps me in a continual state of inelegance.
Jane Austen (1775–1817) British novelist. Letter, 18 Sept 1796

8 I like the weather, when it is not rainy,
That is, I like two months of every year.
Lord Byron (1788–1824) British poet. *Beppo*

9 This is a London particular...A fog, miss.
Charles Dickens (1812–70) British novelist. *Bleak House*, Ch. 3

10 It ain't a fit night out for man or beast.
W. C. Fields (1880–1946) US actor. *The Fatal Glass of Beer*

11 A woman rang to say she heard there was a hurricane on the way. Well don't worry, there isn't.
Michael Fish (1944–) British weatherman. Announcement just before a major hurricane. BBC TV programme, 15 Oct 1987

12 I'm singing in the rain, just singing in the rain;
What a wonderful feeling, I'm happy again.
Arthur Freed (1894–1973) US film producer and songwriter. From the musical, *Hollywood Revue of 1929. Singing in the Rain*

13 This is the weather the cuckoo likes,
And so do I;
When showers betumble the chestnut spikes,
And nestlings fly:
And the little brown nightingale bills his best,
And they sit outside at 'The Travellers' Rest'.
Thomas Hardy (1840–1928) British novelist. *Weathers*

14 This is the weather the shepherd shuns,
And so do I.
Thomas Hardy *Weathers*

15 When two Englishmen meet, their first talk is of the weather.
Samuel Johnson (1709–84) British lexicographer. *The Idler*

16 A snake came to my water-trough
On a hot, hot day, and I in pyjamas for the heat,
To drink there.
D. H. Lawrence (1885–1930) British novelist. *Snake*

17 The British, he thought, must be gluttons for satire: even the weather forecast seemed to be some kind of spoof, predicting every possible combination of weather for the next twenty-four hours without actually committing itself to anything specific.
David Lodge (1935–) British author. *Changing Places*, Ch. 2

18 Who has seen the wind?
Neither you nor I:
But when the trees bow down their heads,
The wind is passing by.
Christina Rossetti (1830–74) British poet. *Who Has Seen the Wind?*

19 Blow, winds, and crack your cheeks; rage, blow.
You cataracts and hurricanoes, spout
Till you have drench'd our steeples, drown'd the cocks.
William Shakespeare (1564–1616) English dramatist. *King Lear*, III:2

20 Rumble thy bellyful. Spit, fire; spout rain.
Nor rain, wind, thunder, fire, are my daughters
I tax not you, you elements, with unkindness.
William Shakespeare *King Lear*, III:2

21 Poor naked wretches, wheresoe'er you are,
That bide the pelting of this pitiless storm,
How shall your houseless heads and unfed sides,
Your loop'd and window'd raggedness, defend you
From seasons such as these?
William Shakespeare *King Lear*, III:4

22 So foul and fair a day I have not seen.
William Shakespeare *Macbeth*, I:3

23 I am the daughter of Earth and Water,
And the nursling of the Sky;
I pass through the pores of the ocean and shores;
I change, but I cannot die,
For after the rain when with never a stain
The pavilion of Heaven is bare,
And the winds and sunbeams with their convex gleams
Build up the blue dome of air,
I silently laugh at my own cenotaph,
And out of the caverns of rain,
Like a child from the womb, like a ghost from the tomb,
I arise and unbuild it again.
Percy Bysshe Shelley (1792–1822) British poet. *The Cloud*

24 I wield the flail of the lashing hail,
And whiten the green plains under,
And then again I dissolve it in rain,
And laugh as I pass in thunder.
Percy Bysshe Shelley *The Cloud*

25 O Wild West Wind, thou breath of Autumn's being,
Thou, from whose unseen presence the leaves dead
Are driven, like ghosts from an enchanter fleeing,
Yellow, and black, and pale, and hectic red,
Pestilence-stricken multitudes.

Percy Bysshe Shelley *Ode to the West Wind*

26 Heat, madam! It was so dreadful that I found there was nothing for it but to take off my flesh and sit in my bones.

Sydney Smith (1771–1845) British clergyman and essayist. Discussing the hot weather with a lady acquaintance. *Lives of the Wits* (H. Pearson)

27 Willows whiten, aspens quiver,
Little breezes dusk and shiver.

Alfred, Lord Tennyson (1809–92) British poet. *The Lady of Shalott*, Pt. I

WELSH

See also British, Wales

1 Eddy was a tremendously tolerant person, but he wouldn't put up with the Welsh. He always said, surely there's enough English to go round.

John Mortimer (1923–) British lawyer and dramatist. *Two Stars for Comfort*, I:2

2 There are still parts of Wales where the only concession to gaiety is a striped shroud.

Gwyn Thomas (1913–81) British writer. *Punch*, 18 June 1958

3 ...an impotent people,
Sick with inbreeding,
Worrying the carcase of an old song.

R. S. Thomas (1913–) Welsh poet. *Welsh Landscape*

4 'The Welsh,' said the Doctor, 'are the only nation in the world that has produced no graphic or plastic art, no architecture, no drama. They just sing,' he said with disgust, sing and blow down wind instruments of plated silver.'

Evelyn Waugh (1903–66) British novelist. *Decline and Fall*, Pt. I, Ch. 8

WHISTLING

See also fear

1 The schoolboy, with his satchel in his hand,
Whistling aloud to bear his courage up.

Robert Blair (1699–1746) Scottish poet. *The Grave*

2 I Whistle a Happy Tune.

Oscar Hammerstein (1895–1960) US lyricist. From the musical *The King and I*. Song title

WINTER

See months, seasons

WISDOM

See also intelligence, knowledge, prudence, wisdom and foolishness

1 It is easy to be wise after the event.

Proverb

2 For in much wisdom is much grief: and he that increaseth knowledge increaseth sorrow.

Bible: Ecclesiastes 1:18

3 The words of wise men are heard in quiet more than the cry of him that ruleth among fools.

Bible: Ecclesiastes 9:17

4 The wisdom of a learned man cometh by opportunity of leisure: and he that hath little business shall become wise.
How can he get wisdom that holdeth the plough, and that glorieth in the goad, that driveth oxen, and is occupied in their labours, and whose talk is of bullocks?

Bible: Ecclesiasticus 38:24–25

5 With the ancient is wisdom; and in length of days understanding.

Bible: Job 12:12

6 No mention shall be made of coral, or of pearls: for the price of wisdom is above rubies.

Bible: Job 28:18

7 A wise man will hear, and will increase learning; and a man of understanding shall attain unto wise counsels:
To understand a proverb, and the interpretation; the words of the wise, and their dark sayings.
The fear of the Lord is the beginning of knowledge: but fools despise wisdom and instruction.

Bible: Proverbs 1:5–7

8 Wisdom is the principal thing; therefore get wisdom: and with all thy getting get understanding.

Bible: Proverbs 4:7

9 Wisdom reacheth from one end to another mightily: and sweetly doth she order all things.

Bible: Wisdom 8:1

10 Does the Eagle know what is in the pit
Or wilt thou go ask the Mole?
Can Wisdom be put in a silver rod,
Or love in a golden bowl?

William Blake (1757–1827) British poet. *The Book of Thel*, 'Thel's Motto'

11 I care not whether a man is Good or Evil; all that I care
Is whether he is a Wise Man or a Fool. Go! put off Holiness,
And put on Intellect.

William Blake *Jerusalem*

12 Be wiser than other people if you can, but do not tell them so.

Earl of Chesterfield (1694–1773) English statesman. Letter to his son, 19 Nov 1745

13 A sadder and a wiser man,
He rose the morrow morn.

Samuel Taylor Coleridge (1772–1834) British poet. *The Rime of the Ancient Mariner*, VII

14 If one is too lazy to think, too vain to do a thing badly, too cowardly to admit it, one will never attain wisdom.

Cyril Connolly (1903–74) British journalist. *The Unquiet Grave*

15 Knowledge dwells
In heads replete with thoughts of other men;
Wisdom in minds attentive to their own.

William Cowper (1731–1800) British poet. *The Task*

16 Some are weather-wise, some are otherwise.

Benjamin Franklin (1706–90) US scientist and statesman. *Poor Richard's Almanack*

17 Knowledge can be communicated but not wisdom.

Hermann Hesse (1877–1962) German novelist and poet. *Siddhartha*

18 It is the province of knowledge to speak and it is the privilege of wisdom to listen.

Oliver Wendell Holmes (1809–94) US writer. *The Poet at the Breakfast Table*, Ch. 10

19 Vain wisdom all, and false philosophy.

John Milton (1608–74) English poet. *Paradise Lost*, Bk. II

20 The young man who has not wept is a savage, and the old man who will not laugh is a fool.

George Santayana (1863–1952) US philosopher. *Dialogues in Limbo*, Ch. 3

21 Some folk are wise, and some are otherwise.

Tobias Smollett (1721–71) British novelist. *Roderick Random*, Ch. 6

22 An ounce of a man's own wit is worth a ton of other people's.

Laurence Sterne (1713–68) Irish-born British writer. *Tristram Shandy*

23 Oh, Vanity of vanities!
How wayward the decrees of Fate are;
How very weak the very wise,
How very small the very great are!

William Makepeace Thackeray (1811–63) British novelist. *Vanitas Vanitatum*

24 It is never wise to try to appear to be more clever than you are. It is sometimes wise to appear slightly less so.

William Whitelaw (1918–) British politician. *The Observer*, 'Sayings of the Year', 1975

WISDOM AND FOOLISHNESS

1 A wise man makes his own decisions, an ignorant man follows the public opinion.

Chinese Proverb

2 Then I saw that wisdom excelleth folly, as far as light excelleth darkness.
The wise man's eyes are in his head; but the fool walketh in darkness: and I myself perceived also that one event happeneth to them all.

Bible: Ecclesiastes 2:13–14

3 But God hath chosen the foolish things of the world to confound the wise; and God hath chosen the weak things of the world to confound the things which are mighty.

Bible: I Corinthians 1:27

4 For ye suffer fools gladly, seeing ye yourselves are wise.

Bible: II Corinthians 11:19

5 A fool sees not the same tree that a wise man sees.

William Blake (1757–1827) British poet. *The Marriage of Heaven and Hell*, 'Proverbs of Hell'

6 Many have been the wise speeches of fools, though not so many as the foolish speeches of wise men.

Thomas Fuller (1608–61) English historian. *The Holy State and the Profane State*

7 Give me the young man who has brains enough to make a fool of himself!

Robert Louis Stevenson (1850–94) Scottish writer. *Virginibus Puerisque*

WOMAN'S ROLE

See also feminism, housework, marriage, women, sexes

1 Whoever rightly considers the order of things may plainly see the whole race of woman-kind is by nature, custom, and the laws, made subject to man, to be governed according to his discretion: therefore it is the duty of every one of us that desires to have ease, comfort, and repose, with those men to whom we belong, to be humble, patient, and obedient, as well as chaste…

Giovanni Boccaccio (1313–75) Italian writer and poet. *Decameron*, 'Ninth Day'

2 Mother is the dead heart of the family, spending father's earnings on consumer goods to enhance the environment in which he eats, sleeps and watches the television.

Germaine Greer (1939–) Australian-born British writer and feminist. *The Female Eunuch*

3 These are rare attainments for a damsel, but pray tell me, can she spin?

James I (1566–1625) King of England. On being introduced to a young girl proficient in Latin, Greek, and Hebrew. Attrib.

4 A man is in general better pleased when he has a good dinner upon his table, than when his wife talks Greek.

Samuel Johnson (1709–84) British lexicographer. *Johnsonian Miscellanies* (ed. G. B. Hill), Vol. II

5 Women exist in the main solely for the propagation of the species.

Arthur Schopenhauer (1788–1860) German philosopher.

WOMEN

See also feminism, men, sexes, woman's role

1 A man of straw is worth a woman of gold.
Proverb

2 A woman's place is in the home.
Proverb

3 A woman's work is never done.
Proverb

4 The hand that rocks the cradle rules the world.
Proverb

5 Old-fashioned ways which no longer apply to changed conditions are a snare in which the feet of women have always become readily entangled.
Jane Addams (1860–1935) US social worker. In *Newer Ideals of Peace*, 'Utilization of Women in City Government'

6 The woman that deliberates is lost.
Joseph Addison (1672–1719) British essayist. *Cato*, IV:1

7 A woman seldom asks advice until she has bought her wedding clothes.
Joseph Addison *The Spectator*, 475

8 ...girls are so queer you never know what they mean. They say No when they mean Yes, and drive a man out of his wits for the fun of it...
Louisa May Alcott (1832–88) US novelist. *Little Women*, Pt. II

9 Next to being married, a girl likes to be crossed in love a little now and then.
Jane Austen (1775–1817) British novelist. *Pride and Prejudice*, Ch. 24

10 A woman, especially if she have the misfortune of knowing anything, should conceal it as well as she can.
Jane Austen *Northanger Abbey*, Ch. 14

11 A lady's imagination is very rapid; it jumps from admiration to love, from love to matrimony in a moment.
Jane Austen *Pride and Prejudice*, Ch. 6

12 Women – one half the human race at least – care fifty times more for a marriage than a ministry.
Walter Bagehot (1826–77) British economist and journalist. *The English Constitution*, 'The Monarchy'

13 One is not born a woman, one becomes one.
Simone de Beauvoir (1908–86) French writer. *Le Deuxième Sexe* (trans. The Second Sex)

14 You will find that the woman who is really kind to dogs is always one who has failed to inspire sympathy in men.
Max Beerbohm (1872–1956) British writer. *Zuleika Dobson*, Ch. 6

15 And the Lord God caused a deep sleep to fall upon Adam, and he slept: and he took one of his ribs, and closed up the flesh instead thereof;
And the rib, which the Lord God had taken from man, made he a woman, and brought her unto the man.
And Adam said, This is now bone of my bones, and flesh of my flesh: she shall be called Woman, because she was taken out of Man.
Therefore shall a man leave his father and his mother, and shall cleave unto his wife: and they shall be one flesh.
And they were both naked, the man and his wife, and were not ashamed.
Bible: Genesis 2:21–25

16 For the lips of a strange woman drop as an honeycomb, and her mouth is smoother than oil:
But her end is bitter as wormwood, sharp as a two-edged sword.
Bible: Proverbs 5:3–4

17 Who can find a virtuous woman? for her price is far above rubies
The heart of her husband doth safely trust in her, so that he shall have no need of spoil.
She will do him good and not evil all the days of her life.
Bible: Proverbs 31:10–12

18 Why need the other women know so much?
Robert Browning (1812–89) British poet. *Any Wife to any Husband*

19 Brigands demand your money or your life; women require both.
Samuel Butler (1612–80) English satirist. Attrib.

20 I thought it would appear
That there had been a lady in the case.
Lord Byron (1788–1824) British poet. *Don Juan*, V

21 Do you know why God withheld the sense of humour from women?
That we may love you instead of laughing at you.
Mrs Patrick Campbell (1865–1940) British actress. To a man. *The Life of Mrs Pat* (M. Peters)

22 Women are much more like each other than men: they have, in truth, but two passions, vanity and love; these are their universal characteristics.
Earl of Chesterfield (1694–1773) English statesman. Letter to his son, 19 Dec 1749

23 How lucky we are that women defend themselves so poorly! We should, otherwise, be no more to them than timid slaves.
Pierre Choderlos de Laclos (1741–1803) French novelist. *Les Liaisons Dangereuses*, Letter 4

24 There is no fury like an ex-wife searching for a new lover.
Cyril Connolly (1903–74) British journalist. *The Unquiet Grave*

25 Certain women should be struck regularly, like gongs.
Noël Coward (1899–1973) British dramatist. *Private Lives*

26 Women never have young minds. They are born three thousand years old.
Shelagh Delaney (1939–) British dramatist. *A Taste of Honey*, I:1

27 'She's the sort of woman now,' said Mould,... 'one would almost feel disposed to bury for nothing: and do it neatly, too!'

Charles Dickens (1812–70) British novelist. *Martin Chuzzlewit*, Ch. 25 nothing

28 It is only the women whose eyes have been washed clear with tears who get the broad vision that makes them little sisters to all the world.

Dorothy Dix (Elizabeth Meriwether Gilmer; 1861–1951) US journalist and writer. *Dorothy Dix, Her Book*, Introduction

29 She takes just like a woman, yes, she does
She makes love just like a woman, yes, she does
And she aches just like a woman
But she breaks just like a little girl.

Bob Dylan (Robert Allen Zimmerman; 1941–) US popular singer. *Just Like a Woman*

30 I should like to know what is the proper function of women, if it is not to make reasons for husbands to stay at home, and still stronger reasons for bachelors to go out.

George Eliot (Mary Ann Evans; 1819–80) British novelist. *The Mill on the Floss*, Ch. 6

31 In the room the women come and go
Talking of Michelangelo.

T. S. Eliot (1888–1965) US-born British poet and dramatist. *The Love Song of J. Alfred Prufrock*

32 When a woman behaves like a man, why doesn't she behave like a nice man?

Edith Evans (1888–1976) British actress. *The Observer*, 'Sayings of the Week', 30 Sept 1956

33 The great question...which I have not been able to answer, despite my thirty years of research into the feminine soul, is 'What does a woman want'?

Sigmund Freud (1856–1939) Austrian psychoanalyst. *Psychiatry in American Life* (Charles Rolo)

34 How, like a moth, the simple maid
Still plays about the flame!

John Gay (1685–1732) English poet and dramatist. *The Beggar's Opera*

35 You have to admit that most women who have done something with their lives have been disliked by almost everyone.

Françoise Gilot Artist and mistress of Picasso. Remark, Oct 1987

36 Fighting is essentially a masculine idea; a woman's weapon is her tongue.

Hermione Gingold (1897–1987) British actress. Attrib.

37 I know you do not make the laws but I also know that you are the wives and mothers, the sisters and daughters of those who do...

Angelina Grimké (1805–79) US writer and reformer. *The Anti-Slavery Examiner* (Sep 1836), 'Appeal to the Christian Women of the South'

38 My mother said it was simple to keep a man, you must be a maid in the living room, a cook in the kitchen and a whore in the bedroom. I said I'd hire the other two and take care of the bedroom bit.

Jerry Hall US model and actress. Remark, Oct 1985

39 If men knew how women pass their time when they are alone, they'd never marry.

O. Henry (William Sidney Porter; 1862–1910) US short-story writer. *The Four Million Memoirs of a Yellow Dog*

40 O! men with sisters dear,
O! men with mothers and wives!
It is not linen you're wearing out,
But human creatures' lives!

Thomas Hood (1799–1845) British poet. *The Song of the Shirt*

41 A woman's preaching is like a dog's walking on his hinder legs. It is not done well; but you are surprised to find it done at all.

Samuel Johnson (1709–84) British lexicographer. *Life of Johnson* (J. Boswell), Vol. I

42 No one delights more in vengeance than a woman.

Juvenal (Decimus Junius Juvenalis; 60–130 AD) Roman satirist. *Satires*, XIII

43 When the Himalayan peasant meets the he-bear in his pride,
He shouts to scare the monster, who will often turn aside.
But the she-bear thus accosted rends the peasant tooth and nail
For the female of the species is more deadly than the male.

Rudyard Kipling (1865–1936) Indian-born British writer. *The Female of the Species*

44 And a woman is only a woman, but a good cigar is a smoke.

Rudyard Kipling *The Betrothed*

45 The First Blast of the Trumpet Against the Monstrous Regiment of Women.

John Knox (c. 1514–72) Scottish religious reformer. Title of Pamphlet, 1558

46 Women run to extremes; they are either better or worse than men.

Jean de La Bruyère (1645–96) French satirist. *Les Caractères*

47 So this gentleman said a girl with brains ought to do something else with them besides think.

Anita Loos (1891–1981) US novelist. *Gentlemen Prefer Blondes*, Ch. 1

48 Women do not find it difficult nowadays to behave like men; but they often find it extremely difficult to behave like gentlemen.

Compton Mackenzie (1883–1972) British writer. *On Moral Courage*

49 The Professor of Gynaecology began his course of lectures as follows: Gentlemen, woman is an animal that micturates once a day, defecates once a week, menstruates once a month, parturates once a year and copulates whenever she has the opportunity.

W. Somerset Maugham (1874–1965) British novelist. *A Writer's Notebook*

50 A woman will always sacrifice herself if you give her the opportunity. It is her favourite form of self-indulgence.

W. Somerset Maugham *The Circle*, III

51 Because women can do nothing except love, they've given it a ridiculous importance.

W. Somerset Maugham *The Moon and Sixpence*, Ch. 41

52 I expect that Woman will be the last thing civilized by Man.

George Meredith (1828–1909) British novelist. *The Ordeal of Richard Feverel*, Ch. 1

53 One tongue is sufficient for a woman.

John Milton (1608–74) English poet. On being asked whether he would allow his daughters to learn foreign languages. Attrib.

54 Women would rather be right than reasonable.

Ogden Nash (1902–71) US poet. *Frailty, Thy Name Is a Misnomer*

55 God created woman. And boredom did indeed cease from that moment – but many other things ceased as well! Woman was God's *second* mistake.

Friedrich Wilhelm Nietzsche (1844–1900) German philosopher. *The Antichrist*

56 When a woman becomes a scholar there is usually something wrong with her sexual organs.

Friedrich Wilhelm Nietzsche *Bartlett's Unfamiliar Quotations* (Leonard Louis Levinson)

57 If women didn't exist, all the money in the world would have no meaning.

Aristotle Onassis (1906–75) Greek businessman. Attrib.

58 Whether a pretty woman grants or withholds her favours, she always likes to be asked for them.

Ovid (Publius Ovidius Naso; 43 BC–17 AD) Roman poet. *Ars Amatoria*

59 Most good women are hidden treasures who are only safe because nobody looks for them.

Dorothy Parker (1893–1967) US writer. Obituary, *The New York Times*, 8 June 1967

60 My wife, who, poor wretch, is troubled with her lonely life.

Samuel Pepys (1633–1703) English diarist. *Diary*, 19 Dec 1662

61 I don't think a prostitute is more moral than a wife, but they are doing the same thing.

Prince Philip (1921–) The consort of Queen Elizabeth II. Remark, Dec 1988

62 There are two kinds of women – goddesses and doormats.

Pablo Picasso (1881–1973) Spanish painter. Attrib.

63 Most women have no characters at all.

Alexander Pope (1688–1744) British poet. *Moral Essays*, II

64 Men, some to business, some to pleasure take;
But every woman is at heart a rake.

Alexander Pope *Moral Essays*, II

65 Woman's at best a contradiction still.

Alexander Pope *Moral Essays*, II

66 Bah! I have sung women in three cities,
But it is all the same;
And I will sing of the sun.

Ezra Pound (1885–1972) US poet. *Cino*

67 She really is a woman just like my mum.

Cliff Richard (1940–) British pop singer. Remark, Aug 1988

68 The fundamental fault of the female character is that it has no sense of justice.

Arthur Schopenhauer (1788–1860) German philosopher. *Gedanken über vielerlei Gegenstände*, XXVII

69 Do you not know I am a woman? When I think, I must speak.

William Shakespeare (1564–1616) English dramatist. *As You Like It*, III:2

70 Frailty, thy name is woman!

William Shakespeare *Hamlet*, I:2

71 I have no other but a woman's reason:
I think him so, because I think him so.

William Shakespeare *The Two Gentlemen of Verona*, I:2

72 This Englishwoman is so refined
She has no bosom and no behind.

Stevie Smith (Florence Margaret Smith; 1902–71) British poet. *This Englishwoman*

73 Womanhood is the great fact in her life; wifehood and motherhood are but incidental relations.

Elizabeth Cady Stanton (1815–1902) US suffragette. *History of Woman Suffrage* (with Susan B. Anthony and Mathilda Gage), Vol. I

74 The really original woman is the one who first imitates a man.

Italo Svevo (Ettore Schmitz; 1861–1928) Italian writer. *A Life*, Ch. 8

75 God made the woman for the man,
And for the good and increase of the world.

Alfred, Lord Tennyson (1809–92) British poet. *Edwin Morris*

76 How sweet are looks that ladies bend
On whom their favours fall!

Alfred, Lord Tennyson *Sir Galahad*

77 I've got a woman's ability to stick to a job and get on with it when everyone else walks off and leaves it.

Margaret Thatcher (1925–) British politician and prime minister. *The Observer*, 'Sayings of the Week', 16 Feb 1975

78 It is a great glory in a woman to show no more weakness than is natural to her sex, and not be talked of, either for good or evil by men.

Thucydides (c. 460–c. 400 BC) Greek historian and general. *History of the Peloponnesian War*, Bk. II, Ch. 45

79 I was seized by the stern hand of Compulsion, that dark, unseasonable Urge that impels women to clean house in the middle of the night.
James Thurber (1894–1961) US humorist. *Alarms and Diversions*, 'There's a Time for Flags'

80 I am a source of satisfaction to him, a nurse, a piece of furniture, a *woman* – nothing more.
Sophie Tolstoy (1844–1919) Russian writer. *A Diary of Tolstoy's Wife, 1860–1891*

81 With many women I doubt whether there be any more effectual way of touching their hearts than ill-using them and then confessing it. If you wish to get the sweetest fragrance from the herb at your feet, tread on it and bruise it.
Anthony Trollope (1815–82) British novelist. *Miss Mackenzie*, Ch. 10

82 Scarce, sir. Mighty scarce.
Mark Twain (Samuel Langhorne Clemens; 1835–1910) US writer. Responding to the question 'In a world without women what would men become?'. Attrib.

83 Woman is unrivaled as a wet nurse.
Mark Twain Attrib.

84 As if a woman of education bought things because she wanted 'em.
John Vanbrugh (1664–1726) English architect and dramatist. *The Confederacy*, II:1

85 Once a woman has given you her heart you can never get rid of the rest of her.
John Vanbrugh *The Relapse*, II:1

86 Woman is always fickle and changing.
Virgil (Publius Vergilius Maro; 70–19 BC) Roman poet. *Aeneid*, Bk. IV

87 I have often observed in women of her type a tendency to regard all athletics as inferior forms of fox-hunting.
Evelyn Waugh (1903–66) British novelist. *Decline and Fall*, Pt. I, Ch. 10

88 'I will not stand for being called a woman in my own house,' she said.
Evelyn Waugh *Scoop*, Bk. I, Ch. 5

89 There is nothing in the whole world so unbecoming to a woman as a Nonconformist conscience.
Oscar Wilde (1854–1900) Irish-born British dramatist. *Lady Windermere's Fan*, III

90 The question of the rights of women to hold secular office is a quite separate matter and should not in any way be connected to or paralleled with the question of women's ordination.
Cardinal Willebrands (1909–) Dutch ecclesiastic. Remark, June 1986

91 I would venture to guess that Anon, who wrote so many poems without signing them, was often a woman.
Virginia Woolf (1882–1941) British novelist. *A Room of One's Own*

92 Women have served all these centuries as looking-glasses possessing the magic and delicious power of reflecting the figure of man at twice its natural size.
Virginia Woolf *A Room of One's Own*

WONDER

See also admiration, curiosity

1 For all knowledge and wonder (which is the seed of knowledge) is an impression of pleasure in itself.
Francis Bacon (1561–1626) English philosopher. *The Advancement of Learning*, Bk. I, Ch. 1

2 To see a World in a grain of sand,
And a Heaven in a wild flower,
Hold Infinity in the palm of your hand,
And Eternity in an hour.
William Blake (1757–1827) British poet. *Auguries of Innocence*

3 Two things fill the mind with ever new and increasing wonder and awe, the more often and the more seriously reflection concentrates upon them: the starry heaven above me and the moral law within me.
Immanuel Kant (1724–1804) German philosopher. *Critique of Practical Reason*, Conclusion

4 Philosophy is the product of wonder.
A. N. Whitehead (1861–1947) British philosopher. *Nature and Life*, Ch. 1

WORDS

See also language, speech, verbosity

1 In the beginning was the Word, and the Word was with God, and the Word was God.
Bible: John 1:1

2 Actions speak louder than words.
Proverb

3 He said true things, but called them by wrong names.
Robert Browning (1812–89) British poet. *Bishop Blougram's Apology*

4 Oaths are but words, and words but wind.
Samuel Butler (1612–80) English satirist. *Hudibras*, Pt. II

5 Be not the slave of Words.
Thomas Carlyle (1795–1881) Scottish historian and essayist. *Sartor Resartus*, Bk. I, Ch. 8

6 We must have a better word than 'prefabricated'. Why not 'ready-made'?
Winston Churchill (1874–1965) British statesman. *Closing the Ring*, Appendix C

7 Words as is well known, are great foes of reality.
Joseph Conrad (Teodor Josef Konrad Korzeniowski; 1857–1924) Polish-born British novelist. *Under Western Eyes*

8 You can stroke people with words.
F. Scott Fitzgerald (1896–1940) US novelist. *The Crack-up*

9 It was in the barbarous, gothic times when words had a meaning; in those days, writers expressed thoughts.

Anatole France (Jacques Anatole François Thibault; 1844–1924) French writer. *The Literary Life*, 'M. Charles Morice'

10 Many terms which have now dropped out of favour, will be revived, and those that are at present respectable will drop out, if usage so choose, with whom resides the decision and the judgement and the code of speech.

Horace (Quintus Horatius Flaccus; 65–8 BC) Roman poet. *Ars Poetica*

11 Thanks to words, we have been able to rise above the brutes; and thanks to words, we have often sunk to the level of the demons.

Aldous Huxley (1894–1964) British novelist. *Adonis and the Alphabet of the demons*

12 *Net.* Anything reticulated or decussated at equal distances, with interstices between the intersections.

Samuel Johnson (1709–84) British lexicographer. *Dictionary of the English Language*

13 Words are, of course, the most powerful drug used by mankind.

Rudyard Kipling (1865–1936) Indian-born British writer. Speech, 14 Feb 1923

14 Words are men's daughters, but God's sons are things.

Samuel Madden (1686–1765) Irish writer. *Boulter's Monument*

15 Until we learn the use of living words
we shall continue to be waxworks inhabited by gramophones.

Walter De La Mare (1873–1956) British poet. *The Observer*, 'Sayings of the Week', 12 May 1929

16 I am a Bear of Very Little Brain, and long words Bother me.

A. A. Milne (1882–1956) British writer. *Winnie-the-Pooh*, Ch. 4

17 It is an important general rule always to refer to your friend's country establishment as a 'cottage'.

Stephen Potter (1900–69) British writer. *Lifemanship*, Ch. 2

18 There is a Southern proverb, – fine words butter no parsnips.

Walter Scott (1771–1832) Scottish novelist. *The Legend of Montrose*, Ch. 3

19 Man does not live by words alone, despite the fact that sometimes he has to eat them.

Adlai Stevenson (1900–65) US statesman. Attrib.

20 She shrank from words, thinking of the scars they leave, which she would be left to tend when he had gone. If he spoke the truth, she could not bear it; if he tried to muffle it with tenderness, she would look upon it as pity.

Elizabeth Taylor (1912–75) British writer. *The Blush*, 'The Letter Writers'

21 For words, like Nature, half reveal
And half conceal the Soul within.

Alfred, Lord Tennyson (1809–92) British poet. *In Memoriam A.H.H.*, V

22 No, my dear, it is *I* who am surprised; you are merely astonished.

Noah Webster (1758–1843) US lexicographer. Responding to his wife's comment that she had been surprised to find him embracing their maid. Attrib.

WORK

See also effort, unemployment

1 All work and no play makes Jack a dull boy.

Proverb

2 No bees, no honey; no work, no money.

Proverb

3 Whatsoever thy hand findeth to do, do it with thy might; for there is no work, nor device, nor knowledge, nor wisdom, in the grave, whither thou goest.

Bible: Ecclesiastes 9:10

4 For even when we were with you, this we commanded you, that if any would not work, neither should he eat.

Bible: II Thessalonians 3:10

5 There is dignity in work only when it is work freely accepted.

Albert Camus (1913–60) French existentialist writer. *Notebooks*, 1935–42

6 Work is the grand cure of all the maladies and miseries that ever beset mankind.

Thomas Carlyle (1795–1881) Scottish historian and essayist. Speech, Edinburgh, 2 Apr 1886

7 Work is much more fun than fun.

Noël Coward (1899–1973) British dramatist. *The Observer*, 'Sayings of the Week', 21 June 1963

8 By working faithfully eight hours a day you may eventually get to be a boss and work twelve hours a day.

Robert Frost (1875–1963) US poet. Attrib.

9 When work is a pleasure, life is a joy! When work is a duty, life is slavery.

Maxim Gorky (Aleksei Maksimovich Peshkov; 1868–1936) Russian writer. *The Lower Depths*

10 That one must do some work seriously and must be independent and not merely amuse oneself in life – this our mother has told us always, but never that science was the only career worth following.

Iréne Joliot-Curie (1897–1956) French scientist. Recalling the advice of her mother, Marie Curie. *A Long Way from Missouri* (Mary Margaret McBride), Ch. 10

11 Horny-handed sons of toil.

Denis Kearney (1847–1907) US Labor leader. Speech, San Francisco, c. 1878

12 It's been a hard day's night.

John Lennon (1940–80) British rock musician. *A Hard Day's Night* (with Paul McCartney)

13 Life is too short to do anything for oneself that one can pay others to do for one.

W. Somerset Maugham (1874–1965) British novelist. *The Summing Up*

14 The rise in the total of those employed is governed by Parkinson's Law and would be much the same whether the volume of work were to increase, diminish or even disappear.

Cyril Northcote Parkinson (1919–93) British historian and writer. *Parkinson's Law*, Ch. 1

15 Work expands so as to fill the time available for its completion.

Cyril Northcote Parkinson *Parkinson's Law*, Ch. 1

16 Work is necessary for man. Man invented the alarm clock.

Pablo Picasso (1881–1973) Spanish painter. Attrib.

17 The harder you work, the luckier you get.

Gary Player (1935–) South African golfer. Attrib.

18 They say hard work never hurt anybody, but I figure why take the chance.

Ronald Reagan (1911–) US politician and president. Attrib.

19 If you have great talents, industry will improve them: if you have but moderate abilities, industry will supply their deficiency.

Joshua Reynolds (1723–92) British portrait painter. Discourse to Students of the Royal Academy, 11 Dec 1769

20 I wish to preach, not the doctrine of ignoble ease, but the doctrine of the strenuous life.

Theodore Roosevelt (1858–1919) US Republican president. Speech, Chicago, 10 Apr 1899

21 One of the symptoms of approaching nervous breakdown is the belief that one's work is terribly important. If I were a medical man, I should prescribe a holiday to any patient who considered his work important.

Bertrand Russell (1872–1970) British philosopher. *The Autobiography of Bertrand Russell*, Vol. II, Ch. 5

22 The only place where success comes before work is a dictionary.

Vidal Sassoon (1928–) British hair stylist. Quoting one of his teachers in a BBC radio broadcast

23 Pennies do not come from heaven. They have to be earned here on earth.

Margaret Thatcher (1925–) British politician and prime minister. *Sunday Telegraph*, 1982

24 Work banishes those three great evils, boredom, vice, and poverty.

Voltaire (François-Marie Arouet; 1694–1778) French writer. *Candide*, Ch. 30

25 How doth the little busy bee
Improve each shining hour,
And gather honey all the day
From every opening flower!

Isaac Watts (1674–1748) English theologian and hymn writer. *Divine Songs for Children*, 'Against Idleness and Mischief'

26 Work is the curse of the drinking classes.

Oscar Wilde (1854–1900) Irish-born British dramatist. Attrib.

27 I haven't got time to be tired.

Wilhelm I (1797–1888) King of Prussia and Emperor of Germany. Said during his last illness

WORLD

See also confusion

1 For the world, I count it not an inn, but an hospital, and a place, not to live, but to die in.

Thomas Browne (1605–82) English physician and writer. *Religio Medici*, Pt. II

2 As I walked through the wilderness of this world.

John Bunyan (1628–88) English writer. *The Pilgrim's Progress*, Pt. I

3 The world degenerates and grows worse every day....The calamities inflicted on Adam... were light in comparison with those inflicted on us.

Martin Luther (1483–1546) German Protestant. Commentary on the Book of Genesis

WORLD WAR I

1 Belgium put the kibosh on the Kaiser,
Europe took a stick and made him sore;
And if Turkey makes a stand
She'll get ghurka'd and japanned,
And it won't be Hoch the Kaiser any more.

Anonymous Song of World War I

2 Six million young men lie in premature graves, and four old men sit in Paris partitioning the earth.

Anonymous *New York Nation*, 1919

3 Just for the word 'neutrality', a word which in wartime has so often been disregarded – just for a scrap of paper, Great Britain is going to make war on a kindred nation who desires nothing better than to be friends with her.

Theobald von Bethmann-Hollweg (1856–1921) German statesman. Letter to Sir Edward Goschen, 4 Aug 1914

4 The battlefield is fearful. One is overcome by a peculiar sour, heavy and penetrating smell of corpses....The legs of an Englishman, still encased in puttees, stick out of a trench, the corpse being built into the parapet; a soldier hangs his rifle on them.

Rudolph Binding *A Fatalist At War*

5 The effects of the successful gas attack were horrible. I am not pleased with the idea of poisoning men. Of course the entire world will rage about it first and then imitate us. All the dead lie on their backs with clenched fists; the whole field is yellow.

Rudolph Binding *A Fatalist At War*

6 What did you do in the Great War, Daddy?

British Recruiting Poster

7 I shall fight before Paris, I shall fight in Paris, I shall fight behind Paris.

Georges Clemenceau (1841–1929) French statesman. Speech, June 1918

8 We'll be over, we're coming over,
And we won't come back till it's over, over there.

George M. Cohan (1878–1942) US comedian. American song of World War I

9 My centre is giving way, my right is in retreat; situation excellent. I shall attack.

Marshal Foch (1851–1929) French soldier. Message sent during the second battle of the Marne, 1918. *Biography of Foch* (Aston), Ch. 13

10 This is not peace: it is an armistice for twenty years.

Marshal Foch Attrib.

11 Please God – let there be victory, before the Americans arrive.

Douglas Haig Diary, 1917

12 Every position must be held to the last man: there must be no retirement. With our backs to the wall, and believing in the justice of our cause, each one of us must fight on to the end.

Douglas Haig (1861–1928) British general. Order to the British Army, 12 Apr 1918

13 If any question why we died,
Tell them because our fathers lied.

Rudyard Kipling (1865–1936) Indian-born British writer. *Epitaphs of War*

14 I cannot get any sense of an enemy – only of a disaster.

D. H. Lawrence (1885–1930) British novelist. Letter to Edward Marsh, Oct 1914

15 This war, like the next war, is a war to end war.

David Lloyd George (1863–1945) British Liberal statesman.

16 We travelled miles of trenches to reach the point we occupy. Some of the places we passed were liquid mud up to our knees. The town we passed through was an absolute ruin, not a house that is not blown to bits. I never saw the like of it, not a soul anywhere. I can't describe the look it has. It made me shiver – wooden crosses on the roadside and in places in the town marking the heroes' death – what devastation – a day of judgement more like. Man builds and then builds machines to destroy, well he seems to have made a better job of destroying this town.

Peter McGregor (1871–1916) Private soldier. Letter to his wife, 21 June 1916

17 I feel my own life all the more precious and more dear in the presence of this deflowering of Europe. While it is true that the guns will effect a little useful weeding, I am furious with chagrin to think that the Minds, which were to have excelled the civilization of two thousand years, are being annihilated – and bodies, the product of aeons of Natural Selection, melted down to pay for political statues.

Wilfred Owen (1893–1918) British poet. Letter, 28 Aug 1914

18 What passing-bells for these who die as cattle?
Only the monstrous anger of the guns,
Only the stuttering rifles' rapid rattle
Can patter out their hasty orisons.

Wilfred Owen *Anthem for Doomed Youth*

19 Man, it seemed, had been created to jab the life out of Germans.

Siegfried Sassoon (1886–1967) British poet. *Memoirs of an Infantry Officer*, Pt. I, Ch. 1

20 ...The lecturer's voice still battered on my brain. 'The bullet and the bayonet are brother and sister.' 'If you don't kill him, he'll kill you.' 'Stick him between the eyes, in the throat, in the chest.' 'Don't waste good steel. Six inches are enough. What's the use of a foot of steel sticking out at the back of a man's neck? Three inches will do for him; when he coughs, go and look for another.'

Siegfried Sassoon *Memoirs of an Infantry Officer*

21 On St Paul's steps I watched a recruiting meeting for some time. There was a tremendous crowd round and a soldier who looked like a Colonial was letting out for all he was worth. He had a number of men in uniform with him and every little while stopped and pointed his finger at some man in the crowd and shouted 'Why haven't you joined?' Of course everyone looked at the victim who felt called upon to make an excuse if he could, and one of the assistants pushed through the crowd to tackle the one singled out.

Robert Saunders Headmaster. Letter to his son, 31 May 1915

22 When you march into France, let the last man on the right brush the Channel with his sleeve.

Alfred Graf von Schlieffen (1833–1913) German general. Referring to the Schlieffen plan. *August 1914* (Barbara Tuchman), Ch. 2

23 We drove the Boche across the Rhine,
The Kaiser from his throne.
Oh, Lafayette, we've paid our debt,
For Christ's sake, send us home.

US Army song

24 You will be home before the leaves have fallen from the trees.

Wilhelm II (1859–1941) King of Prussia and Emperor of Germany. Said to troops leaving for the Front, Aug 1914. *August 1914* (Barbara Tuchman), Ch. 9

25 It is my Royal and Imperial Command that you...exterminate first the treacherous English, and...walk over General French's contemptible little Army.

Wilhelm II Referring to the British Expeditionary Force; veterans of this force became known as 'Old Contemptibles'. *The Times*, 1 Oct 1914

26 There is such a thing as a man being too proud to fight.

Woodrow Wilson (1856–1925) US statesman. Address to foreign-born citizens, 10 May 1915

27 My message today was a message of death for our young men. How strange it seems to applaud that.

Woodrow Wilson Remark after his speech to Congress asking for a declaration of war, Apr 1917

28 There is a price which is too great to pay for peace, and that price can be put into one word. One cannot pay the price of self-respect.

Woodrow Wilson Speech, Des Moines, Iowa, 1 Feb 1916

WORLD WAR II

See also Churchill, Germany, Hitler, Nazism, war

1 How horrible, fantastic, incredible, it is that we should be digging trenches and trying on gas-masks here because of a quarrel in a far-away country between people of whom we know nothing.

Neville Chamberlain (1869–1940) British statesman. Referring to Germany's annexation of the Sudetenland. Radio broadcast, 27 Sept 1938

2 Hitler has missed the bus.

Neville Chamberlain Speech, House of Commons, 4 Apr 1940

3 We have sustained a defeat without a war.

Winston Churchill (1874–1965) Speech, House of Commons, 5 Oct 1938

4 We shall not flag or fail. We shall fight in France, we shall fight on the seas and oceans, we shall fight with growing confidence and growing strength in the air, we shall defend our island, whatever the cost may be, we shall fight on the beaches, we shall fight on the landing grounds, we shall fight in the fields and in the streets, we shall fight in the hills; we shall never surrender.

Winston Churchill Speech, House of Commons, 4 June 1940

5 Let us therefore brace ourselves to our duties, and so bear ourselves that, if the British Empire and its Commonwealth last for a thousand years, men will still say: 'This was their finest hour'.

Winston Churchill Referring to the forthcoming Battle of Britain. Speech, House of Commons, 18 June 1940

6 The battle of Britain is about to begin.

Winston Churchill Speech, House of Commons, 18 June 1940

7 Never in the field of human conflict was so much owed by so many to so few.

Winston Churchill Referring to the Battle of Britain pilots. Speech, House of Commons, 20 Aug 1940

8 We are waiting for the long-promised invasion. So are the fishes.

Winston Churchill Radio broadcast to the French people, 21 Oct 1940

9 Give us the tools, and we will finish the job.

Winston Churchill Referring to Lend-lease, which was being legislated in the USA. Radio broadcast, 9 Feb 1941

10 You do your worst, and we will do our best.

Winston Churchill Addressed to Hitler. Speech, 14 July 1941

11 Do not let us speak of darker days; let us rather speak of sterner days. These are not dark days: these are great days – the greatest days our country has ever lived.

Winston Churchill Address, Harrow School, 29 Oct 1941

12 When I warned them that Britain would fight on alone whatever they did, their Generals told their Prime Minister and his divided Cabinet: 'In three weeks England will have her neck wrung like a chicken.'
Some chicken! Some neck!

Winston Churchill Referring to the French Government; see WEYGAND. Speech, Canadian Parliament, 30 Dec 1941

13 This is not the end. It is not even the beginning of the end. But it is, perhaps, the end of the beginning.

Winston Churchill Referring to the Battle of Egypt. Speech, Mansion House, 10 Nov 1942

14 Wars are not won by evacuations.

Winston Churchill Referring to Dunkirk. *Their Finest Hour*

15 Before Alamein we never had a victory. After Alamein we never had a defeat.

Winston Churchill *The Hinge of Fate*, Ch. 33

16 Peace with Germany and Japan on our terms will not bring much rest...As I observed last time, when the war of the giants is over the wars of the pygmies will begin.

Winston Churchill *Triumph and Tragedy*, Ch. 25

17 Now we can look the East End in the face.

Elizabeth the Queen Mother (1900–) The widow of King George VI. Surveying the damage caused to Buckingham Palace by a bomb during the Blitz in World War II. Attrib.

18 This was the Angel of History! We felt its wings flutter through the room. Was that not the fortune we awaited so anxiously?

Joseph Goebbels (1897–1945) German politician. Referring to Roosevelt's death. *Diary*

19 They entered the war to prevent us from going into the East, not to have the East come to the Atlantic.

Hermann Goering (1893–1946) German leader. Referring to the war aims of the British in World War II. *Nuremberg Diary* (G. M. Gilbert)

20 The little ships, the unforgotten Homeric catalogue of *Mary Jane* and *Peggy IV*, of *Folkestone Belle*, *Boy Billy*, and *Ethel Maud*, of *Lady Haig* and *Skylark*...the little ships of England brought the Army home.

Philip Guedalla (1889–1944) British writer. Referring to the evacuation of Dunkirk. *Mr. Churchill*

21 When Barbarossa commences, the world will hold its breath and make no comment.

Adolf Hitler (1889–1945) German dictator. Referring to the planned invasion of the USSR, Operation Barbarossa, which began on 22 June 1941. Attrib.

22 If we are going in without the help of Russia we are walking into a trap.

David Lloyd George (1863–1945) British Liberal statesman. Speech, House of Commons, 3 Apr 1939

23 Dear Ike, Today I spat in the Seine.

General George Patton (1885–1945) US general. Message sent to Eisenhower reporting his crossing of the Seine in World War II. *The American Treasury* (C. Fadiman)

24 To make a union with Great Britain would be fusion with a corpse.

Marshal Pétain (1856–1951) French marshal. On hearing Churchill's suggestion for an Anglo-French union, 1940. *Their Finest Hour* (Winston S. Churchill), Ch. 10

25 Our great-grandchildren, when they learn how we began this war by snatching glory out of defeat...may also learn how the little holiday steamers made an excursion to hell and came back glorious.

J. B. Priestley (1894–1984) British novelist. Referring to the British Expeditionary Force's evacuation from Dunkirk. Broadcast, 5 June 1940

26 The best immediate defence of the United States is the success of Great Britain defending itself.

Franklin D. Roosevelt (1882–1945) US Democratic president. At press conference, 17 Dec 1940. *Their Finest Hour* (Winston S. Churchill), Ch. 28

27 Defeat of Germany means the defeat of Japan, probably without firing a shot or losing a life.

Franklin D. Roosevelt *The Hinge of Fate* (Winston S. Churchill), Ch. 25

28 We have finished the job, what shall we do with the tools?

Haile Selassie (1892–1975) Emperor of Ethiopia. Telegram sent to Winston Churchill, mimicking his 'Give us the tools, and we will finish the job'. *Ambrosia and Small Beer*, Ch. 4 (Edward Marsh)

29 If we see that Germany is winning the war we ought to help Russia, and if Russia is winning we ought to help Germany, and in that way let them kill as many as possible.

Harry S. Truman (1884–1972) US statesman. *New York Times*, 24 July 1941, when Russia was invaded by Germany

30 In three weeks England will have her neck wrung like a chicken.

Maxime Weygand (1867–1965) French general. Said at the fall of France; see CHURCHILL. *Their Finest Hour* (Winston S. Churchill)

31 I fear we have only awakened a sleeping giant, and his reaction will be terrible.

Isoroku Yamamoto (1884–1943) Japanese admiral. Said after the Japanese attack on Pearl Harbor, 1941.

WORLD-WEARINESS

1 Bankrupt of Life, yet Prodigal of Ease.

John Dryden (1631–1700) British poet and dramatist. *Absalom and Achitophel*, I

2 Spare all I have, and take my life.

George Farquhar (1678–1707) Irish dramatist. *The Beaux' Strategem*, V:2

3 Death is a delightful hiding-place for weary men.

Herodotus (c. 484–c. 424 BC) Greek historian. *Histories*, VII, 46

4 I am sick of this way of life. The weariness and sadness of old age make it intolerable. I have walked with death in hand, and death's own hand is warmer than my own. I don't wish to live any longer.

W. Somerset Maugham (1874–1965) British novelist. Said on his ninetieth birthday. *Familiar Medical Quotations* (M. B. Strauss)

5 Stop the World, I Want to Get Off.

Anthony Newley (1931–) British actor, composer, singer, and comedian. With Leslie Bricusse. Title of musical

6 How weary, stale, flat, and unprofitable,
Seem to me all the uses of this world!

William Shakespeare (1564–1616) English dramatist. *Hamlet*, I:2

7 I have supp'd full with horrors.

William Shakespeare *Macbeth*, V:5

8 I gin to be aweary of the sun,
And wish th' estate o' th' world were now undone.

William Shakespeare *Macbeth*, V:5

9 Death is not the greatest of ills; it is worse to want to die, and not be able to.

Sophocles (c. 496–406 BC) Greek dramatist. *Electra*, 1007

WORRY

See also misfortune

1 A trouble shared is a trouble halved.

Proverb

2 Don't meet troubles half-way.

Proverb

3 It will be all the same in a hundred years.

Proverb

4 Take things as they come.

Proverb

5 Begone, dull care! I prithee begone from me!
Begone, dull care, you and I shall never agree.

Anonymous *Begone Dull Care*

6 Behold the fowls of the air: for they sow not, neither do they reap, nor gather into barns; yet your heavenly Father feedeth them. Are ye not much better than they?
Which of you by taking thought can add one cubit unto his stature?
And why take ye thought for raiment? Consider the lilies of the field, how they grow; they toil not, neither do they spin:
And yet I say unto you, That even Solomon in all his glory was not arrayed like one of these.

Wherefore, if God so clothe the grass of the field, which today is, and tomorrow is cast into the oven, shall he not much more clothe you, O ye of little faith?
Therefore take no thought, saying, What shall we eat? or, What shall we drink? or, Wherewithal shall we be clothed?

Bible: Matthew 6:26–31

7 But seek ye first the kingdom of God, and his righteousness; and all these things shall be added unto you.
Take therefore no thought for the morrow: for the morrow shall take thought for the things of itself. Sufficient unto the day is the evil thereof.

Bible: Matthew 6:33–34

8 Just when we are safest, there's a sunset-touch,
A fancy from a flower-bell, some one's death,
A chorus-ending from Euripides, –
And that's enough for fifty hopes and fears
As old and new at once as Nature's self,
To rap and knock and enter in our soul.

Robert Browning (1812–89) British poet. *Bishop Blougram's Apology*

9 Before the cherry orchard was sold everybody was worried and upset, but as soon as it was all settled finally and once for all, everybody calmed down, and felt quite cheerful.

Anton Chekhov (1860–1904) Russian dramatist. *The Cherry Orchard*, IV

10 When I look back on all these worries I remember the story of the old man who said on his deathbed that he had had a lot of trouble in his life, most of which had never happened.

Winston Churchill (1874–1965) British statesman. *Their Finest Hour*

11 Care
Sat on his faded cheek.

John Milton (1608–74) English poet. *Paradise Lost*, Bk. I

12 Worrying is the most natural and spontaneous of all human functions. It is time to acknowledge this, perhaps even to learn to do it better.

Lewis Thomas (1913–90) US pathologist. *More Notes of a Biology Watcher*, 'The Medusa and the Snail'

WRITERS

See also Chaucer, criticism, Dickens, Milton, poets, Shakespeare, writing

General quotes

1 A reader seldom peruses a book with pleasure until he knows whether the writer of it be a black man or a fair man, of a mild or choleric disposition, married or a bachelor.

Joseph Addison (1672–1719) British essayist. *The Spectator*, 1

2 Writers, like teeth, are divided into incisors and grinders.

Walter Bagehot (1826–77) British economist and journalist. *Estimates of some Englishmen and Scotchmen*, 'The First Edinburgh Reviewers

3 The idea that it is necessary to go to a university in order to become a successful writer, or even a man or woman of letters (which is by no means the same thing), is one of those phantasies that surround authorship.

Vera Brittain (1893–1970) British writer and feminist. *On Being an Author*, Ch. 2

4 Literary men are...a perpetual priesthood.

Thomas Carlyle (1795–1881) Scottish historian and essayist. *Critical and Miscellaneous Essays*, 'The State of German Literature'

5 I believe the souls of five hundred Sir Isaac Newtons would go to the making up of a Shakespeare or a Milton.

Samuel Taylor Coleridge (1772–1834) British poet. Letter to Thomas Poole, 23 Mar 1801

6 The faults of great authors are generally excellences carried to an excess.

Samuel Taylor Coleridge *Miscellanies*, 149

7 A great writer creates a world of his own and his readers are proud to live in it. A lesser writer may entice them in for a moment, but soon he will watch them filing out.

Cyril Connolly (1903–74) British journalist. *Enemies of Promise*, Ch. 1

8 The only way for writers to meet is to share a quick pee over a common lamp-post.

Cyril Connolly *The Unquiet Grave*

9 Talent alone cannot make a writer. There must be a man behind the book.

Ralph Waldo Emerson (1803–82) US poet and essayist. *Goethe*

10 Creative writers are always greater than the causes that they represent.

E. M. Forster (1879–1970) British novelist. *Gide and George*

11 The reciprocal civility of authors is one of the most risible scenes in the farce of life.

Samuel Johnson (1709–84) British lexicographer. *Life of Sir Thomas Browne*

12 Authors are easy to get on with – if you're fond of children.

Michael Joseph (1897–1958) British publisher. *The Observer*, 1949

13 One man is as good as another until he has written a book.

Benjamin Jowett (1817–93) British theologian. *Letters of B. Jowett* (Abbott and Campbell)

14 Our principal writers have nearly all been fortunate in escaping regular education.

Hugh MacDiarmid (Christopher Murray Grieve; 1892–1978) Scottish poet. *The Observer*, 'Sayings of the Week', 29 Mar 1953

15 The trouble with our younger authors is that

they are all in the sixties.

W. Somerset Maugham (1874–1965) British novelist. *The Observer*, 'Sayings of the Week', 14 Oct 1951

16 A novelist is, like all mortals, more fully at home on the surface of the present than in the ooze of the past.

Vladimir Nabokov (1899–1977) Russian-born US novelist. *Strong Opinions*, Ch. 20

17 I think that if a third of all the novelists and maybe two-thirds of all the poets now writing dropped dead suddenly, the loss to literature would not be great.

Charles Osborne (1927–) Author, critic, and Director of Arts Council. Remark, Nov 1985

18 A list of authors who have made themselves most beloved and therefore, most comfortable financially, shows that it is our national joy to mistake for the first-rate, the fecund rate.

Dorothy Parker (1893–1967) US writer. *Wit's End* (R. E. Drennan)

19 A novelist who writes nothing for 10 years finds his reputation rising. Because I keep on producing books they say there must be something wrong with this fellow.

J. B. Priestley (1894–1984) British novelist. *The Observer*, 'Sayings of the Week', 21 Sept 1969

20 Everybody writes a book too many.

Mordecai Richler (1931–) Canadian novelist. *The Observer*, 'Sayings of the Week', 9 Jan 1985

21 Among the many problems which beset the novelist, not the least weighty is the choice of the moment at which to begin his novel.

Vita Sackville-West (Victoria Sackville-West; 1892–1962) British poet and novelist. *The Edwardians*, Ch. 1

22 When I was a little boy they called me a liar but now that I am a grown up they call me a writer.

Isaac Bashevis Singer (1904–91) US novelist and short-story writer. Remark, July 1983

23 No regime has ever loved great writers, only minor ones.

Alexander Solzhenitsyn (1918–) Soviet novelist. *The First Circle*, Ch. 57

24 It is a sad feature of modern life that only women for the most part have time to write novels, and they seldom have much to write about.

Auberon Waugh (1939–) British novelist and critic. Remark, June 1981

25 In my situation as Chancellor of the University of Oxford, I have been much exposed to authors.

Duke of Wellington (1769–1852) British general and statesman. *Collections and Recollections* (G. W. E. Russell)

26 I think it's good for a writer to think he's dying; he works harder.

Tennessee Williams (1911–83) US dramatist. *The Observer*, 'Sayings of the Week', 31 Oct 1976

27 Literature is strewn with the wreckage of men who have minded beyond reason the opinions of others.

Virginia Woolf (1882–1941) British novelist. *A Room of One's Own*

28 It's not a writer's business to hold opinions.

W. B. Yeats (1865–1939) Irish poet. Speaking to playwright, Denis Johnston. *The Guardian*, 5 May 1977

Specific quotes

29 More can be learnt from Miss Austen about the nature of the novel than from almost any other writer.

Walter Allen (1911–95) British author and literary journalist. *The English Novel*

30 From the beginning Wilde performed his life and continued to do so even after fate had taken the plot out of his hands.

W. H. Auden (1907–73) British poet. *Forewords and Afterwords*

31 Shaw's judgements are often scatterbrained, but at least he has brains to scatter.

Max Beerbohm (1872–1956) British writer. *Conversation With Max* (S. N. Behrens)

32 I have been told by hospital authorites that more copies of my works are left behind by departing patients than those of any other author.

Robert Benchley (1889–1945) US humorist. *Chips off the Old Benchley*, 'Why Does Nobody Collect Me?'

33 He sipped at a weak hock and seltzer,
As he gazed at the London skies
Through the Nottingham lace of the curtains
Or was it his bees-winged eyes?

John Betjeman (1906–84) British poet. *The Arrest of Oscar Wilde at the Cadogan Hotel*

34 That sovereign of insufferables.

Ambrose Bierce (1842–?1914) US writer and journalist. Referring to Oscar Wilde. *Wasp* (San Francisco), 1882

35 Miller is not really a writer but a non-stop talker to whom someone has given a typewriter.

Gerald Brenan (Edward Fitzgerald Brenan; 1894–1987) British writer. Referring to Henry Miller. *Thoughts in a Dry Season*, 'Literature'

36 I had not seen *Pride and Prejudice* till I read that sentence of yours, and then I got the book. And what did I find? An accurate daguerreotyped portrait of a commonplace face; a carefully fenced, highly cultivated garden, with neat borders and delicate flowers; but no glance of a bright, vivid physiognomy, no open country, no fresh air, no blue hill, no bonny beck. I should hardly like to live with her ladies and gentlemen, in their elegant but confined houses.

Charlotte Brontë (1816–55) British novelist. Letter to G. H. Lewes, 12 Jan 1848

37 A budding young anthologist sought to include a Shaw piece in a new collection. 'I hope you understand', he wrote to Shaw, 'that I cannot afford to pay your usual fee as I am a very young man.' Shaw replied 'I'll wait for you to grow up.'

Bennett Cerf (1898–1971) US publisher, editor and writer. *Shake Well Before Using*

38 G.B.S. looked aged and feeble and was dressed in very dark tweeds and a black overcoat. His white whiskers and pink face looked like an enamelled portrait, and had that pink lifeless quality of the very old.

Henry Channon (1897–1958) Politician and writer. Diary, 26 Feb 1944

39 Mr Shaw is (I suspect) the only man on earth who has never written any poetry.

G. K. Chesterton (1874–1936) British writer. Referring to George Bernard Shaw. *Orthodoxy*, Ch. 3

40 His gaze was constantly fixed on himself; yet not on himself, but on his reflection in the looking-glass...Introspection of the genuine kind he never achieved...Wilde grew into a Pierrot who liked to play the prophet.

Harold Child Writing of Oscar Wilde. *Times Literary Supplement*, 18 June 1908

41 ...Old dread-death and dread-evil Johnson, that teacher of moping and melancholy...If the writings of this time-serving, mean, dastardly old pensioner had got a firm hold of the minds of the people at large, the people would have been bereft of their very souls.

William Cobbett (1763–1835) British journalist and writer.

42 Shaw relished every opportunity to have himself painted, sketched, photographed or carved, because each likeness provided him with a new extension of himself.

Peter Conrad *The Observer*, Multitude of Shaws, 7 Oct 1979

43 Wilde's voice was of the brown velvet order – mellifluous – rounded – in a sense giving it a plummy quality – rather on the adenotic side – but practically pure cello – and very pleasing.

Franklin Dyall *Life of Oscar Wilde* (Hesketh Pearson)

44 A dangerous person to disagree with.

T. S. Eliot (1888–1965) US-born British poet and dramatist. Referring to Samuel Johnson. *The Metaphysical Poets*

45 I am at a loss to understand why people hold Miss Austen's novels at so high a rate, which seem to me vulgar in tone, sterile in artistic invention, imprisoned in the wretched conventions of English society, without genius, wit, or knowledge of the world. Never was life so pinched and narrow. The one problem in the mind of the writer in both the stories I have read...is marriageableness.

Ralph Waldo Emerson (1803–82) US poet and essayist. *Journal*, 1861

46 This pictorial account of the day-to-day life of an English gamekeeper is full of considerable interest to outdoor minded readers, as it contains many passages on pheasant-raising, the apprehending of poachers, ways to control vermin, and other chores and duties of the professional gamekeeper. Unfortunately, one is obliged to wade through many pages of extraneous material in order to discover and savour those sidelights on the management of a midland shooting estate, and in this reviewer's opinion the book cannot take the place of J. R. Miller's *Practical Gamekeeping*.

Review of *Lady Chatterley's Lover*. *Field and Stream*

47 Lawrence himself is, as far as I know, the only prophetic novelist writing today – all the rest are fantasists or preachers: the only living novelist in whom the song predominates, who has the rapt bardic quality, and whom it is idle to criticize.... Nothing is more disconcerting than to sit down, so to speak, before your prophet, and then suddenly to receive his boot in the pit of your stomach.

E. M. Forster (1879–1970) British novelist. *Aspects of the Novel*

48 Scott misunderstood it when he congratulated her for painting on a square of ivory. She is a miniaturist, but never two-dimensional. All her characters are round, or capable of rotundity.

E. M. Forster Referring to Jane Austen. *Aspects of the Novel*

49 It's not good enough to spend time and ink in describing the penultimate sensations and physical movements of people getting into a state of rut...The body's never worthwhile, and the sooner Lawrence recognizes that, the better – the men we swear by – Tolstoy, Turgenev, Chekov, Maupassant, Flaubert, France – knew that great truth, they only use the body, and that sparingly, to reveal the soul.

John Galsworthy (1867–1933) British novelist. Letter to Edward Garnett, 13 Apr 1914

50 Lunched with Pinker to meet D. H. Lawrence, that provincial genius. Interesting, but a type I could not get on with. Obsessed with self. Dead eyes, and a red beard, long pale narrow face. A strange bird.

John Galsworthy *Life and Letters of John Galsworthy* (H. V. Marrot)

51 There is no arguing with Johnson; for when his pistol misses fire, he knocks you down with the butt end of it.

Oliver Goldsmith (1728–74) Irish-born British writer. *Life of Johnson* (J. Boswell)

52 ...But Mr Hardy's women are moulded of the same flesh as his men; they are liable to flutterings and tremblings; they are not always constant even when they are 'quite nice'; and some of them are actually 'of a coming-on disposition'.

Edmund Gosse (1849–1928) British writer and critic. *Speaker*, 13 Sept 1890

53 Oscar Wilde did not dive very deeply below the surface of human nature, but found, to a certain extent rightly, that there is more on the surface of life than is seen by the eyes of most people.

J. T. Grein *Sunday Special*, 9 Dec 1900

54 The work of Henry James has always seemed divisible by a simple dynastic arrangement into three reigns: James I, James II, and the Old Pretender.

Philip Guedalla (1889–1944) British writer. *Collected Essays*, 'Men of Letters: Mr. Henry James'

55 His worst is better than any other

person's best.

William Hazlitt (1778–1830) British essayist. Referring to Walter Scott. *English Literature*, Ch. XIV, 'Sir Walter Scott'

56 He writes as fast as they can read, and he does not write himself down.

William Hazlitt Referring to Walter Scott. *English Literature*, CH. XIV, 'Sir Walter Scott'

57 Dr Johnson's sayings would not appear so extraordinary, were it not for his *bow-wow way*.

Henry Herbert (1734–94) British general. *Life of Johnson* (J. Boswell)

58 He identified genius with immunity from the cravings and turpitudes which make us human. Hence his regime of sexual continence which so confused and dismayed the women he persisted in loving, and hence too his abstinent diet of grated vegetables.

Michael Holroyd (1935–) British writer. Referring to Shaw. *The Genius of Shaw*

59 To be with Lawrence was a kind of adventure, a voyage of discovery into newness and otherness...For Lawrence, existence was one continuous convalescence; it was as though he were newly re-born from a mortal illness every day of his life.

Aldous Huxley (1894–1964) British novelist. *The Letters of D. H. Lawrence*, Introduction

60 He was unperfect, unfinished, inartistic; he was worse than provincial – he was parochial.

Henry James (1843–1916) US novelist. Referring to Thoreau. *Life of Nathaniel Hawthorne*, Ch. 4

61 He is the richest author that ever grazed the common of literature.

Samuel Johnson (1709–84) British lexicographer. Referring to Dr John Campbell. *Life of Johnson* (J. Boswell), Vol. I

62 What a commonplace genius he has, or a genius for the commonplace, I don't know which. He doesn't rank so terribly high, really. But better than Bernard Shaw, even then.

D. H. Lawrence (1885–1930) British novelist. Referring to Hardy. Letter to Martin Secker, 24 July 1928

63 Charlotte Brontë, one cannot but feel after comparing her early work with modern best-sellers, was only unlike them in being fortunate in her circumstances, which gave her a cultured background, and in the age in which she lived, which did not get between her and her spontaneities.

Q. D. Leavis (1906–81) British writer. *Fiction and the Reading Public*

64 A good man fallen among Fabians.

Lenin (Vladimir Ilich Ulyanov; 1870–1924) Russian revolutionary leader. Referring to Bernard Shaw. Attrib.

65 The last gentleman in Europe.

Ada Beddington Leverson (1862–1933) British writer. Said of Oscar Wilde. *Letters to the Sphinx* (Wilde), 'Reminiscences', 2

66 I ask you, is anything in life or literature, past or present, in earth, heaven or hell, anything more devastatingly tedious than D.H.L.'s interest in the human genitalia.

G. W. Lyttelton Referring to D. H. Lawrence. *The Lyttelton Hart-Davis Letters*, 29 Mar 1956

67 In the foreground is that strange figure which is as familiar to us as the figures of those among whom we have been brought up, the gigantic body, the huge massy face, seamed with the scars of disease, the brown coat, the black worsted stockings, the grey wig with the scorched foretop, the dirty hands, the nails bitten and pared to the quick.

Lord Macaulay (1800–59) British historian. Describing Samuel Johnson. *Essays:* 'Boswell's Life of Johnson'

68 Nothing very much happens in her books, and yet, when you come to the bottom of a page, you eagerly turn it to learn what will happen next. Nothing very much does and again you eagerly turn the page. The novelist who has the power to achieve this has the most precious gift a novelist can possess.

W. Somerset Maugham (1874–1965) British novelist. Referring to Jane Austen. *Ten Novels and Their Authors*

69 I have discovered that our great favourite, Miss Austen, is my countrywoman...with whom mamma before her marriage was acquainted. Mamma says that she was then the prettiest, silliest, most affected, husband-hunting butterfly she ever remembers.

Mary Russell Mitford (1787–1855) British writer. Referring to Jane Austen. Letter to Sir William Elford, 3 Apr 1815

70 English literature's performing flea.

Sean O'Casey (1884–1964) Irish dramatist. Referring to P. G. Wodehouse. Attrib.

71 He is pretty certain to come back into favour. One of the surest signs of his genius is that women dislike his books.

George Orwell (Eric Blair; 1903–50) British novelist. Referring to Conrad. *New English Weekly*, 23 July 1936

72 The foaming denouncers of the bourgeoisie, and the more-water-in-your-beer reformers of whom Shaw is the prototype.

George Orwell *The Road to Wigan Pier*

73 If with the literate I am
Impelled to try an epigram
I never seek to take the credit
We all assume that Oscar said it.

Dorothy Parker (1893–1967) US writer. Referring to Oscar Wilde. Attrib.

74 The poor son-of-a-bitch!

Dorothy Parker Quoting from *The Great Gatsby* on paying her last respects to F. Scott Fitzgerald. *Thalberg: Life and Legend* (B. Thomas)

75 Now that the old lion is dead, every ass thinks he may kick at him.

Samuel Parr (1747–1825) British writer and scholar. Referring to Dr Johnson. *Life of Johnson* (J. Boswell)

76 Even when conversing he could not keep still: jumping up and down, crossing and uncrossing his legs, shoving his hands in his pockets and pulling them out, sitting straight up or lying right back in his chair, bending forward, stretching backward, never remaining in one position for two minutes together.

Hesketh Pearson (1887–1964) British biographer. *Bernard Shaw*

77 Undeterred…,Mr Lawrence has penned another novel, *Women in Love*, which justly merits the fate of its predecessor. I do not claim to be a literary critic, but I know dirt when I smell it and here it is in heaps – festering, putrid heaps which smell to high Heaven.

W. Charles Pilley Critic. Review of *Women in Love. John Bull*, 17 Sept 1921

78 Detestable person but needs watching. I think he learned the proper treatment of modern subjects before I did.

Ezra Pound (1885–1972) US poet. Referring to D. H. Lawrence. Letter to Harriet Monroe, Mar 1913

79 Waldo is one of those people who would be enormously improved by death.

Saki (Hector Hugh Munro; 1870–1916) British writer. Referring to Ralph Waldo Emerson. *The Feast of Nemesis*

80 Sherard Blaw, the dramatist who had discovered himself, and who had given so ungrudgingly of his discovery to the world.

Saki *The Unbearable Bassington*, Ch. 13

81 The Big Bow-Wow strain I can do myself like any now going; but the exquisite touch, which renders ordinary commonplace things and characters interesting, from the truth of the description and the sentiment, is denied to me.

Walter Scott (1771–1832) Scottish novelist. In praise of Jane Austen. *Journal*, 14 Mar 1826

82 That young lady has a talent for describing the involvements and feelings and characters of ordinary life which is to me the most wonderful thing I ever met with.

Walter Scott Referring to Jane Austen. *Journals*, 14 Mar 1826

83 I enjoyed talking to her, but thought *nothing* of her writing. I considered her 'a beautiful little knitter'.

Edith Sitwell (1887–1964) British poet and writer. Referring to Virginia Woolf. Letter to G. Singleton

84 That great Cham of literature, Samuel Johnson.

Tobias Smollett (1721–71) British novelist. Letter to John Wilkes, 16 Mar 1759

85 I wish you had not sent me Jane Eyre. It interested me so much that I have lost (or won if you like) a whole day in reading it at the busiest period, with the printers I know waiting for copy. Who the author can be I can't guess – if a woman she knows her language better than most ladies do, or has had a 'classical' education. It is a fine book though – the man & woman capital – the style very generous and upright so to speak. I thought it was Kinglake for some time.

William Makepeace Thackeray (1811–63) British novelist. Referring to Charlotte Brontë. Letter to W. S. Williams, 23 Oct 1847

86 The poor little woman of genius! the fiery little eager brave tremulous homely-faced creature!…But you see she is a little bit of a creature without a penny worth of good looks, thirty years old I should think, buried in the country, and eating up her own heart there.

William Makepeace Thackeray Referring to Charlotte Brontë. Letter to Lucy Baxter, 11 Mar 1853

87 George Too Shaw To Be Good.

Dylan Thomas (1914–53) Welsh poet. Letter to Pamela Hansford Johnson, Oct 1933

88 William Congreve is the only sophisticated playwright England has produced; and like Shaw, Sheridan, and Wilde, his nearest rivals, he was brought up in Ireland.

Kenneth Tynan (1927–80) British theatre critic. *Curtains*, 'The Way of the World'

89 Jane Austen's books, too, are absent from this library. Just that one omission alone would make a fairly good library out of a library that hadn't a book in it.

Mark Twain (Samuel Langhorne Clemens; 1835–1910) US writer. *Following the Equator*, Pt. II

90 I wouldn't give up writing about God at this stage, if I was you. It would be like P. G. Wodehouse dropping Jeeves half-way through the Wooster series.

Evelyn Waugh (1903–66) British novelist. Said to Graham Greene, who proposed to write a political novel. *Evelyn Waugh* (Christopher Sykes)

91 He was over-dressed, pompous, snobbish, sentimental and vain. But he had an indeniable *flair* for the possibilities of commercial theatre.

Evelyn Waugh Referring to Oscar Wilde. *Harper's Bazaar*, Nov 1930

92 Mr Bernard Shaw has no enemies but is intensely disliked by all his friends.

Oscar Wilde (1854–1900) Irish-born British dramatist. *Autobiographies* (W. B. Yeats)

93 Of all the great Victorian writers, he was probably the most antagonistic to the Victorian age itself.

Edmund Wilson (1895–1972) US critic and writer. Referring to Dickens. *The Wound and the Bow*, 'The Two Scrooges'

94 No one has written worse English than Mr Hardy in some of his novels – cumbrous, stilted, ugly, and inexpressive – yes, but at the same time so strangely expressive of something attractive to us in Mr Hardy himself that we would not change it for the perfection of Sterne at his best. It becomes coloured by its surroundings; it becomes literature.

Virginia Woolf (1882–1941) British novelist. *The Moment*

95 I agree about Shaw – he is haunted by the mystery he flouts. He is an atheist who trembles in the haunted corridor.

W. B. Yeats (1865–1939) Irish poet. Writing of Shaw. Letter to George Russell, 1 July 1921

WRITING

See also books, criticism, fiction, inspiration, letter-writing, literacy, literature, novels, plays, poetry, poetry and prose, prose, reading, style, writers

1 Every book must be chewed to get out its juice.

Chinese proverb

2 The style is the man.

Proverb

3 Beneath the rule of men entirely great,
The pen is mightier than the sword.

Edward Bulwer-Lytton (1803–73) British novelist and politician. *Richelieu*, II:2

4 From this it is clear how much more cruel the pen is than the sword.

Robert Burton (1577–1640) English scholar and explorer. *Anatomy of Melancholy*, Pt. I

5 NINA. Your play's hard to act, there are no living people in it.
TREPLEV. Living people! We should show life neither as it is nor as it ought to be, but as we see it in our dreams.

Anton Chekhov (1860–1904) Russian dramatist. *The Seagull*, I

6 Better to write for yourself and have no public, than write for the public and have no self.

Cyril Connolly (1903–74) British journalist. *Turnstile One* (ed. V. S. Pritchett)

7 All good writing is *swimming under water* and holding your breath.

F. Scott Fitzgerald (1896–1940) US novelist. Letter to Frances Scott Fitzgerald

8 No tears in the writer, no tears in the reader.

Robert Frost (1875–1963) US poet. *Collected Poems*, Preface

9 Another damned, thick, square book! Always scribble, scribble, scribble! Eh! Mr Gibbon?

William, Duke of Gloucester (1743–1805) The brother of George III. Addressing Edward Gibbon, author of *The History of the Decline and Fall of the Roman Empire. Literary Memorials* (Best)

10 You must write for children in the same way as you do for adults, only better.

Maxim Gorky (Aleksei Maksimovich Peshkov; 1868–1936) Russian writer. Attrib.

11 You will have written exceptionally well if, by skilful arrangement of your words, you have made an ordinary one seem original.

Horace (Quintus Horatius Flaccus; 65–8 BC) Roman poet. *Ars Poetica*

12 A bad book is as much a labour to write as a good one; it comes as sincerely from the author's soul.

Aldous Huxley (1894–1964) British novelist. *Point Counter Point*

13 A man will turn over half a library to make one book.

Samuel Johnson (1709–84) British lexicographer. *Life of Johnson* (J. Boswell), Vol. II

14 What is written without effort is in general read without pleasure.

Samuel Johnson *Johnsonian Miscellanies* (ed. G. B. Hill), Vol. II

15 Read over your compositions, and where ever you meet with a passage which you think is particularly fine, strike it out.

Samuel Johnson Recalling the advice of a college tutor. *Life of Johnson* (J. Boswell), Vol. II

16 No man but a blockhead ever wrote, except for money.

Samuel Johnson *Life of Johnson* (J. Boswell), Vol. III

17 Many suffer from the incurable disease of writing, and it becomes chronic in their sick minds.

Juvenal (Decimus Junius Juvenalis; 60–130 AD) Roman satirist. *Satires*, VII

18 Clear writers, like clear fountains, do not seem so deep as they are; the turbid look the most profound.

Walter Savage Landor (1775–1864) British poet and writer. *Imaginary Conversations*, 'Southey and Porson'

19 I like to write when I feel spiteful: it's like having a good sneeze.

D. H. Lawrence (1885–1930) British novelist. Letter to Lady Cynthia Asquith, Nov 1913

20 When once the itch of literature comes over a man, nothing can cure it but the scratching of a pen.

Samuel Lover (1797–1868) Irish novelist. *Handy Andy*, Ch. 36

21 I shall not be satisfied unless I produce something that shall for a few days supersede the last fashionable novel on the tables of young ladies.

Lord Macaulay (1800–59) British historian. Letter to Macvey Napier, 5 Nov 1841

22 There is an impression abroad that everyone has it in him to write one book; but if by this is implied a good book the impression is false.

W. Somerset Maugham (1874–1965) British novelist. *The Summing Up*

23 I suffer from the disease of writing books and being ashamed of them when they are finished.

Baron de Montesquieu (1689–1755) French writer. *Pensées diverses*

24 Writing is like getting married. One should never commit oneself until one is amazed at one's luck.

Iris Murdoch (1919–) Irish-born British novelist. *The Black Prince*, 'Bradley Pearson's Foreword'

25 Poor Knight! he really had two periods, the first – a dull man writing broken English, the second – a broken man writing dull English.

Vladimir Nabokov (1899–1977) Russian-born US novelist. *The Real Life of Sebastian Knight*, Ch. 1

26 True ease in writing comes from art, not chance,
As those move easiest who have learn'd to dance.
'Tis not enough no harshness gives offence,
The sound must seem an echo to the sense.

Alexander Pope (1688–1744) British poet. *An Essay on Criticism*

27 Make 'em laugh; make 'em cry; make 'em wait.

Charles Reade (1814–84) British novelist and dramatist. Advice to an aspiring writer. Attrib.

28 The profession of letters is, after all, the only one in which one can make no money without being ridiculous.

Jules Renard (1894–1910) French writer. *Journal*

29 My scribbling pays me zero francs per line – not including the white spaces.

Marquis de Rochefort (1830–1913) French journalist. Referring to his salary as a writer. *Autant en apportent les mots* (Pedrazzini)

30 No, this right hand shall work it all off.

Walter Scott (1771–1832) Scottish novelist. Refusing offers of help following his bankruptcy in 1826. *Century of Anecdote* (J. Timbs)

31 Writing, when properly managed, (as you may be sure I think mine is) is but a different name for conversation.

Laurence Sterne (1713–68) Irish-born British writer. *Tristram Shandy*

32 Whatever sentence will bear to be read twice, we may be sure was thought twice.

Henry David Thoreau (1817–62) US writer. *Journal*, 1842

33 Not that the story need be long, but it will take a long while to make it short.

Henry David Thoreau Letter, 16 Nov 1867

34 Three hours a day will produce as much as a man ought to write.

Anthony Trollope (1815–82) British novelist. *Autobiography*, Ch. 15

35 I put the words down and push them a bit.

Evelyn Waugh (1903–66) British novelist. Obituary, *New York Times*, 11 Apr 1966

36 All my novels are an accumulation of detail. I'm a bit of a bower-bird.

Patrick White (1912–90) British-born Australian novelist. *Southerly*, 139

37 Every great and original writer, in proportion as he is great and original, must himself create the taste by which he is to be relished.

William Wordsworth (1770–1850) British poet. *Lyrical Ballads*, Preface

Y

YIELDING

See also determination, weakness

1 The concessions of the weak are the concessions of fear.

Edmund Burke (1729–97) British politician. *Speech on Conciliation with America* (House of Commons, 22 Mar 1775)

2 He that complies against his will,
Is of his own opinion still.

Samuel Butler (1612–80) English satirist. *Hudibras*, Pt. III

YOUTH

See also age, children

1 Better is a poor and a wise child than an old and foolish king, who will no more be admonished.

Bible: Ecclesiastes 4:13

2 It is good for a man that he bear the yoke in his youth.

Bible: Lamentations 3:27

3 Youth is something very new: twenty years ago no one mentioned it.

Coco Chanel (1883–1971) French dress designer. *Coco Chanel, Her Life, Her Secrets* (Marcel Haedrich)

4 I remember my youth and the feeling that will never come back any more – the feeling that I could last for ever, outlast the sea, the earth, and all men; the deceitful feeling that lures us on to perils, to love, to vain effort – to death…

Joseph Conrad (Teodor Josef Konrad Korzeniowski; 1857–1924) Polish-born British novelist. *Youth*

5 The young always have the same problem – how to rebel and conform at the same time. They have now solved this by defying their parents and copying one another.

Quentin Crisp (?1910–) Model, publicist, and writer. *The Naked Civil Servant*

6 Almost everything that is great has been done by youth.

Benjamin Disraeli (1804–81) British statesman. *Coningsby*, Bk. III, Ch. 1

7 I never dared be radical when young, for fear it would make me conservative when old.

Robert Frost (1875–1963) US poet. *Precaution*

8 *Les enfants terribles.*
The embarrassing young.

Paul Gavarni (1801–66) French illustrator. Title of a series of prints

9 It is the malady of our age that the young are so busy teaching us that they have no time left to learn.

Eric Hoffer (1902–83) US writer.

10 Youth will come here and beat on my door, and force its way in.

Henrik Ibsen (1828–1906) Norwegian dramatist. *The Master Builder*, I

11 Young men make great mistakes in life; for one thing, they idealize love too much.

Benjamin Jowett (1817–93) British theologian. *Letters of B. Jowett* (Abbott and Campbell)

12 When all the world is young, lad,
And all the trees are green;
And every goose a swan, lad,
And every lass a queen;
Then hey for boot and horse, lad,
And round the world away:
Young blood must have its course, lad,
And every dog his day.

Charles Kingsley (1819–75) British writer. *Songs from The Water Babies*, 'Young and Old'

13 Youth is a malady of which one becomes cured a little every day.

Benito Mussolini (1883–1945) Italian dictator. Said on his 50th birthday.

14 The atrocious crime of being a young man…I shall neither attempt to palliate nor deny.

William Pitt the Elder (1708–78) British statesman. Speech, House of Commons, 27 Jan 1741

15 My salad days,
When I was green in judgment, cold in blood,
To say as I said then!

William Shakespeare (1564–1616) English dramatist. *Antony and Cleopatra*, I:5

16 I would there were no age between ten and three and twenty, or that youth would sleep out the rest; for there is nothing in the between but getting wenches with child, wronging the ancientry, stealing, fighting.

William Shakespeare *The Winter's Tale*, III:3

17 Far too good to waste on children.

George Bernard Shaw (1856–1950) Irish dramatist and critic. *10,000 Jokes, Toasts, and Stories* (L. Copeland)

18 Live as long as you may, the first twenty years are the longest half of your life.

Robert Southey (1774–1843) British poet. *The Doctor*, Ch. 130

APPENDIX

List of Themes 443

List of Names 449

Keyword Index 489

LIST OF THEMES

A
Ability
Abortion
Absence
Abstinence
Academics
Accidents
Accusation
Achievement
Acting
Action
Actors
Adaptability
Addiction
Addresses
Admiration
Adultery
Advertising
Advice
Affectation
Afterlife
Age
Aggravation
Agreement
Agriculture
Aids
Alcohol
Ambition
America
Americans
Analogy
Ancestry
Anger
Animalism
Animals
Anticipation
Apologies
Appearance
Appearances
Architecture
Arguments
Aristocracy
Army
Arrogance
Art
Arthurian Legend
Artists
Arts
Assassination
Astronomy
Atheism
Audiences
Authoritarianism
Autumn

B
Babies
Beauty
Bed
Beginning
Belief
Bequests
Betrayal
Bible
Biography
Birds
Birth
Bitterness
Blessing
Blindness
Boasts
Boats
Boldness
Books
Book, Song, and Play Titles
Boredom
Bores
Borrowing
Bosnia and Hercegovina
Brevity
Bribery
Britain
British
British Empire
Bureaucracy
Business

C
Cambridge
Cannibalism
Capitalism
Cars
Catholicism
Cats
Caution
Censorship
Certainty
Chance
Change
Character
Charity
Charm
Chaucer
Children
China
Chivalry
Choice
Christianity
Christmas
Church
Churchill
Cinema
Civilization
Clarity
Class
Classics
Classification
Cleanness
Clergy
Clocks
Clothes
Cold War
Comfort
Commercialism
Commitment
Communication
Communism
Complaints
Compliments
Composers
Compromise

Computers
Conceit
Conflict
Conformity
Confusion
Conscience
Conservation
Conservatism
Constancy
Contempt
Contentment
Contraception
Conversation
Corruption
Cosmetics
Countryside
Courage
Courtesy
Cowardice
Creation
Cricket
Crime
Criticism
Critics
Cruelty
Culture
Curiosity
Curses
Custom
Cynicism

D

Damnation
Dancing
Danger
Day
Death
Debauchery
Deception
Decision
Decline
Defeat
Delusion
Democracy
Denial
Departure
Design
Desire
Despair
Destiny
Determination
Devil
Diaries
Dickens
Difference
Diplomacy
Disability
Disappointment
Disaster
Discontent
Discovery
Disease
Disillusion
Dismissal
Doctors
Dogs
Doomsday
Doubt
Dreams
Drinks
Drowning
Drugs
Drunkenness
Duty

E

Ecology
Economics
Editors
Education
Effort
Egotism
Embarrassment
Emotion
Ending
Endurance
Enemies
England
English
Enthusiasm
Environment
Envy
Epitaphs
Equality
Escape
Eternity
Etiquette
Europe
Evil
Evolution
Examinations
Example
Excellence
Excess
Execution
Existence
Expectation
Expediency
Experience
Experts
Explanations
Exploitation
Exploration
Extravagance
Eyes

F

Facts
Failure
Fairies
Faith
Faithfulness
Fame
Familiarity
Family
Fanaticism
Fascism
Fashion
Fathers
Fear
Feminism
Fiction
Fire
First Impressions
Fishing
Flattery
Flowers
Flying
Food
Foolishness
Football
Force
Forgiveness
France
Frankness
Freedom
French Revolution
Friends
Friendship
Funerals
Futility
Future

G

Gardens
Generalizations

Generosity
Genius
Germany
Gifts
Glory
God
Goldwynisms
Golf
Good
Good and Evil
Gossip
Government
Grammar
Gratitude
Greatness
Greed
Greetings
Guidance
Guilt
Gullibility

H

Habit
Half Measures
Happiness
Haste
Hate
Health and Healthy Living
Heaven
Hell
Help
Heroism
Historians
History
Hitler
Home
Homesickness
Homosexuality
Honesty
Honour
Hope
Horses
Hospitality
Hostages
Houses
Houses Of Parliament
Housework
Human Condition
Human Nature
Human Rights
Humility
Humour
Hunger
Hunting
Hurt
Hypochondria
Hypocrisy

I

Idealism
Ideas
Idleness
Ignorance
Illegitimacy
Illness
Imagination
Imitation
Immortality
Imperfection
Impertinence
Impetuosity
Importance
Impossibility
Impressionability
Imprisonment
Improvement
Inattention
Incompetence
Indecision
Independence
Indifference
Individuality
Indoctrination
Indulgence
Industrial Relations
Inferiority
Infinity
Inflexibility
Influence
Ingratitude
Injustice
Innocence
Innovation
Innuendo
Insensitivity
Insignificance
Insincerity
Inspiration
Insults
Integrity
Intellect
Intellectuals
Intelligence
Interruptions
Intrigue
Introductions
Invitations
Ireland
Irish
Irrevocability

J

Jealousy
Jews
Journalism
Judgment
Justice

K

Killing
Kindness
Kissing
Knowledge

L

Language
Last Words
Laughter
Law
Lawyers
Laziness
Leadership
Learning
Leisure
Letter-writing
Lexicography
Liberalism
Liberty
Life
Life and Death
Limericks
Literacy
Literature
Logic
London
Loneliness
Longevity
Loss
Love
Love and Death
Love and Friendship
Love and Hate
Love and Marriage
Loyalty
Luck
Lust

Luxury
Lying

M

Madness
Majority
Malapropisms
Mankind
Manners
Marriage
Martyrdom
Marxism
Masculinity
Materialism
Mathematics
Meaning
Medicine
Mediocrity
Melancholy
Memorials
Memory
Men
Mercy
Merit
Merrymaking
Metaphysics
Middle East
Milton
Mind
Minority
Misanthropy
Misfortune
Misogyny
Misquotations
Mistakes
Mistrust
Mixed Metaphors
Moderation
Modesty
Monarchy
Money
Months
Moon
Morality
Mortality
Motherhood
Motive
Mountains
Mourning
Murder
Museums
Music
Musicians
Myths

N

Nakedness
Names
Nastiness
Nationality
Nations
Nature
Navy
Nazism
Necessity
Neglect
Neighbours
Nepotism
Neurosis
Newspapers
Nobility
Noncommitment
Nonsense
Normality
Nostalgia
Nothing
Novels
Novelty
Nuclear Weapons
Numbers
Nursery Rhymes

O

Obedience
Obesity
Obituaries
Objectivity
Obligation
Oblivion
Obsessions
Obstruction
Occupations
Officers
Old Age
One-upmanship
Opera
Opinions
Opportunity
Opposites
Opposition
Oppression
Optimism
Order
Originality
Orthodoxy
Ostentation
Oxford

P

Painting
Parasites
Paris
Parochialism
Parties
Parting
Passion
Past
Patience
Patients
Patriotism
Patronage
Peace
Perception
Perfection
Persistence
Perspective
Persuasion
Perversity
Pessimism
Petulance
Philistinism
Philosophers
Philosophy
Photography
Places
Plays
Pleasure
Poetry
Poetry and Prose
Poets
Police
Political Correctness
Politicians
Politics
Pollution
Pop Music
Popularity
Pornography
Possibility
Posterity
Poverty
Poverty and Wealth
Power
Power Politics
Practicality
Praise

Prayer
Precocity
Pregnancy
Prejudice
Present
Pride
Principles
Privacy
Procrastination
Progress
Promiscuity
Promises
Promotion
Promptness
Pronunciation
Proof
Propaganda
Prophecy
Prose
Protestantism
Provocation
Prudence
Prudery
Psychiatry
Psychology
Public
Public Houses
Publishing
Punishment
Puns
Puritanism
Purity
Purpose

Q
Quotations

R
Rabbits
Racism
Reading
Realism
Reality
Reason
Rebellion
Regret
Religion
Remedies
Renunciation
Repartee
Representation
Republic
Reputation
Research
Respect
Respectability
Responsibility
Rest
Results
Retribution
Return
Revenge
Revolution
Ridicule
Right
Righteousness
Rivers
Royalty
Rudeness
Rules
Russia
Russian Revolution
Ruthlessness

S
Sarcasm
Satire
Satisfaction
Sayings
Scepticism
Science
Science Fiction
Scientists
Scotland
Scots
Sculpture
Sea
Seaside
Seasons
Secrecy
Self
Self-confidence
Self-control
Self-denial
Self-interest
Selfishness
Self-knowledge
Selflessness
Self-made Men
Self-preservation
Self-reliance
Self-respect
Sensation
Sentimentality
Separation
Seriousness
Sermons
Service
Servility
Sex
Sexes
Shakespeare
Shyness
Signatures
Silence
Similarity
Simplicity
Sin
Sincerity
Singers
Singing
Slavery
Sleep
Smallness
Smoking
Snobbery
Socialism
Society
Soldiers
Solitude
Sorrow
Soul
South Africa
Space
Speculation
Speech
Speeches
Spelling
Spontaneity
Spoonerisms
Sport and Games
Spring
Staring
Stars
State
Stately Homes
Statistics
Strikes
Stubbornness
Stupidity
Style
Subjectivity
Suburbia
Success
Suffering
Suicide

Suitability
Summer
Summons
Sun
Sunday
Superiority
Supernatural
Superstition
Support
Survival
Suspicion
Switzerland
Sympathy

T

Tact
Talent
Talent and Genius
Taste
Taxation
Technology
Teeth
Telegrams
Television and Radio
Temptation
Theatre
Theft
Theory
Thinking
Thirst
Threats
Thrift
Time
Titles
Tolerance
Trains
Transience
Translation
Travel
Treason
Trees
Triviality
Trust
Truth
Tyranny

U

Uncertainty
Understanding
Unemployment
Unfaithfulness
Unity
Universe

V

Venice
Verbosity
Vice
Victory
Violence
Virtue
Virtue and Vice
Vulgarity

W

Wales
War
War and Peace
Waste
Water
Weakness
Wealth
Weapons
Weather
Welsh
Whistling
Winter
Wisdom
Wisdom and Foolishness
Woman's Role
Women
Wonder
Words
Work
World
World War I
World War II
World-weariness
Worry
Writers
Writing

Y

Yielding
Youth

LIST OF NAMES

A

Abbott, Berenice
PHOTOGRAPHY, 1

Abel, Niels Henrik
EXPERTS, 1

Abernethy, John
DISEASE, 2

Accius, Lucius
RESPECT, 1

Acheson, Dean
BRITAIN, 1
BUREAUCRACY, 1
CHURCHILL, 1
GOVERNMENT, 1
MISTAKES, 2

Acland, Richard
PUBLISHING, 1

Acton, Lord
GOVERNMENT, 2
POWER, 3

Acton, Harold
HOSPITALITY, 5

Adamov, Arthur
THEATRE, 1

Adams, Abigail
LETTER-WRITING, 1

Adams, Douglas
SCIENCE FICTION, 1

Adams, F. P.
ENVY, 2, 3

Adams, Gerry
IRELAND, 1

Adams, Henry Brooks
POLITICS, 1
POWER, 4

Adams, John Quincy
LAST WORDS, 2
POSTERITY, 1

Adams, Richard
MARRIAGE, 7
RELIGION, 1
SEASONS, 2

Adams, Samuel
BRITAIN, 2

Adams, Sarah F.
RELIGION, 2

Adcock, Frank Ezra
ENGLISH, 3
UNITY, 4

Addams, Jane
CIVILIZATION, 1
FEMINISM, 1
MORALITY, 1
WOMEN, 5

Addison, Joseph
CHRISTMAS, 1
CONVERSATION, 2
CREATION, 1
DRINKS, 1
LAST WORDS, 3
MANKIND, 1
MUSIC, 2
OBJECTIVITY, 1, 2
PATRIOTISM, 1
PLEASURE, 2
POSTERITY, 2
SUCCESS, 3
VICE, 1
WOMEN, 6, 7
WRITERS, 1

Ade, George
GRAMMAR, 1
MUSIC, 3

Adenauer, Konrad
HISTORY, 2
SURVIVAL, 1

Adler, Alfred
EGOTISM, 1
PRINCIPLES, 1

Adler, Larry
CONTRACEPTION, 1

Ady, Thomas
BLESSING, 1

Aesop
ANTICIPATION, 4
APPEARANCES, 8
CLOTHES, 1
ENVY, 4
GREED, 4
INDECISION, 1
LYING, 2
MATERIALISM, 2
MISTRUST, 2
SELF-RELIANCE, 2

Agar, Herbert Sebastian
TRUTH, 7

Agassiz, Jean Louis Rodolphe
MONEY, 4

Agate, James
ACTING, 1
AUDIENCES, 1
ENGLISH, 4

Agathon
PAST, 1

Agnew, Spiro
INTELLECTUALS, 1
POVERTY, 3

Aimee, Anouk
BEAUTY, 6

Akins, Zoë
LANGUAGE, 1

Albee, Edward
BOOK, SONG, AND PLAY TITLES, 1
HUMOUR, 1
VULGARITY, 1

Albert, Prince
ART, 1

Alcott, Louisa May
HOUSEWORK, 1
TALENT AND GENIUS, 1
WOMEN, 8

Alcuin
PUBLIC, 1

Aldiss, Brian
FICTION, 1
SCIENCE FICTION, 2, 3

Aldrich, Dean
ALCOHOL, 8

Alençon, Duchesse d'
COURAGE, 2

Alexander, C. F.
CHRISTIANITY, 1
CHRISTMAS, 2

Alexander the Great
DOCTORS, 1

Alfonso XIII
CLASS, 2

Alfonso the Wise
MISQUOTATIONS, 3
UNIVERSE, 1

Ali, Muhammad
CONCEIT, 1
SECRECY, 1
SPORT AND GAMES, 1

Ali, Zeenat
EQUALITY, 3

Alibhai-Brown, Jasmin
POLITICAL CORRECTNESS, 1

Allainval, Abbé Lénor Jean d'
EXCESS, 1

Allbutt, Sir Clifford
DISEASE, 3

Allen, Fred
CHIVALRY, 1
EDITORS, 1
FAME, 1

Allen, Walter
WRITERS, 29

Allen, Woody
ANIMALISM, 1
CONTRACEPTION, 2
DEATH, 13
EXPEDIENCY, 1
IMMORTALITY, 1
INDEPENDENCE, 1
MISTRUST, 3
SEX, 1, 2, 3

SHYNESS, 1

Alliluyeva, Svetlana
DEATH, 14

Allison, Malcolm
FOOTBALL, 1

Allsop, Charles
MONEY, 5

Altman, Robert
MINORITY, 1

Ambrose, St
CONFORMITY, 2

Amery, Leopold
DISMISSAL, 1
PATRIOTISM, 2

Amis, Kingsley
BOOK, SONG, AND PLAY TITLES, 2
CHILDREN, 3
DRUNKENNESS, 2
OBESITY, 1

Amr Ibn Al-As
DEATH, 15

Andersen, Hans Christian
BOOK, SONG, AND PLAY TITLES, 3
FUNERALS, 1
INNOCENCE, 3

Anderson, Eric
MEDIOCRITY, 1

Anderson, Philip W.
UNDERSTANDING, 1

Anderton, James
AIDS, 1

Anne, Princess
AIDS, 2
HORSES, 1
INSULTS, 2

Anonymous
ACTORS, 8, 9
ADVERTISING, 2
ADVICE, 5
ALCOHOL, 9
AMBITION, 2
ANIMALS, 1
ARMY, 1, 2
BEAUTY, 5
BLESSING, 3
BOSNIA AND HERCEGOVINA, 1
BUREAUCRACY, 2
BUSINESS, 1, 2
CATHOLICISM, 2
CHRISTMAS, 3, 4, 5
COURAGE, 1
DEATH, 16, 17
DISEASE, 4, 5
DRUGS, 1, 2
DRUNKENNESS, 3, 4, 5
ECONOMICS, 2
EVIL, 1
EVOLUTION, 1
EXISTENCE, 1
FIRST IMPRESSIONS, 2
FOOD, 6
FRIENDSHIP, 7
GARDENS, 1
GOD, 1
GOOD AND EVIL, 1
GOVERNMENT, 3
GUIDANCE, 1
HEROISM, 1
HORSES, 2
HOSTAGES, 1
HOUSES OF PARLIAMENT, 1
HUMAN RIGHTS, 1, 2
HUMOUR, 31, 32, 33
INDIVIDUALITY, 1
INNUENDO, 1
INSENSITIVITY, 1
IRELAND, 2
LAST WORDS, 4
LIMERICKS, 1, 2, 3, 4, 5, 6, 8
LOVE, 13, 14, 15
LOYALTY, 4
MEMORIALS, 1
MERRYMAKING, 1
MIDDLE EAST, 1
MISQUOTATIONS, 4
MONTHS, 4, 5
MOON, 1
MURDER, 1
NONSENSE, 1
OCCUPATIONS, 7
OFFICERS, 1
OPPRESSION, 1, 2
OPTIMISM, 12
PARTING, 1, 2, 3
PATRIOTISM, 3
POETS, 13
POLITICIANS, 32
POP MUSIC, 1
POVERTY AND WEALTH, 1
PRAYER, 1, 2
PROPHECY, 1
RABBITS, 1
RACISM, 1
RETRIBUTION, 2
RIGHT, 1
ROYALTY, 1, 2, 3
RUSSIA, 1
SCOTLAND, 1
SEASONS, 1
SELF-PRESERVATION, 2, 3, 4
SEPARATION, 1
SEX, 4
SLEEP, 2
SUCCESS, 2
SUFFERING, 3
SUPERIORITY, 1
SUPERNATURAL, 1
TACT, 3
TELEGRAMS, 1, 2
TELEVISION AND RADIO, 1
THEFT, 1
TREASON, 1
UNFAITHFULNESS, 1, 2
VERBOSITY, 1
WAR AND PEACE, 1
WORLD WAR I, 1, 2
WORRY, 5

Anouilh, Jean
AGE, 3
ART, 2
EVIL, 2
EXCESS, 2
GOD, 2
JOURNALISM, 1
LOVE, 16, 17
OLD AGE, 3

Antall, Jożsef
COLD WAR, 1

Anthony, Susan B.
FEMINISM, 2, 3

Antrim, Minna
APPEARANCE, 3
DEBAUCHERY, 1
EXPERIENCE, 6

Apollinaire, Guillaume
MEMORY, 1

Appleton, Edward
BRITAIN, 3
OPERA, 1

Appleton, Thomas Gold
AMERICANS, 1, 2

Arabin, William
NONSENSE, 2
THEFT, 2, 3

Arbuthnot, John
POLITICS, 2

Archer, Gilbert
POLITICIANS, 33

Archilochus
ANIMALS, 2

Archimedes
DISCOVERY, 1
TECHNOLOGY, 1

Arendt, Hannah
GUILT, 1
REBELLION, 1

Ariosto, Ludovico
INDIVIDUALITY, 2

Aristotle
ANGER, 1
GOVERNMENT, 4
LEARNING, 1
MANKIND, 2
OPINIONS, 1
PLAYS, 1
POETRY, 1
POLITICS, 3
REVOLUTION, 1
STUBBORNNESS, 2
TRUTH, 8

Arminstead, Lewis Addison
WAR, 1

Armstrong, Louis
IMITATION, 1
MUSICIANS, 1

Armstrong, Neil
MISQUOTATIONS, 5
SPACE, 1

Armstrong, Robert
LYING, 3

Arnold, George
CHARITY, 2

Arnold, Matthew
AGE, 4
AMERICA, 1
ARISTOCRACY, 1
BIBLE, 1
CATS, 1
CLASS, 3
CRITICISM, 1
CULTURE, 1, 2
DEATH, 19
DEPARTURE, 1, 2
DISCONTENT, 1
DISEASE, 6
FUTURE, 1
HOPE, 4
HUMAN CONDITION, 1
LIFE, 4, 5, 6
OXFORD, 1, 2
PERFECTION, 1
PHILISTINISM, 1, 2
POETRY, 2, 3, 4
POETS, 14, 15, 16, 17
PROMOTION, 1
PUBLIC, 2
RIGHTEOUSNESS, 1
SEA, 1
SEASONS, 3
SELF-KNOWLEDGE, 1
SHAKESPEARE, 1
SOUL, 2, 3
SUMMONS, 1
TRUTH, 9
WAR, 2

Arnold, Thomas
EDUCATION, 2, 3

Asaf, George
OPTIMISM, 13

Ashrawi, Hanan
MIDDLE EAST, 2

Asimov, Isaac
STARS, 1

Asquith, Herbert Henry
GOVERNMENT, 5
PATIENCE, 7
POLITICIANS, 34

Asquith, Margot
INSULTS, 3
MARRIAGE, 8
OFFICERS, 2
WEALTH, 3

Astley, Lord
PRAYER, 3

Astor, John Jacob
WEALTH, 4

Astor, Nancy
AGE, 5
APPEARANCE, 4
DRUNKENNESS, 6
LAST WORDS, 5
MARRIAGE, 9
SUCCESS, 4

Atkinson, E. L.
EPITAPHS, 5

Attlee, Clement
DEMOCRACY, 1
HOUSES OF PARLIAMENT, 2

Auber, Daniel-François-Esprit
FUNERALS, 2
LONGEVITY, 1

Aubrey, John
FATHERS, 2
GOSSIP, 7
SHAKESPEARE, 2

Auden, W. H.
ACADEMICS, 1
AMERICA, 2
BOOKS, 2
CHILDREN, 4
DISABILITY, 1
DISCOVERY, 2
DISEASE, 7
EGOTISM, 2
GUILT, 2
HISTORY, 3, 4
IGNORANCE, 4
INTELLECTUALS, 2
LOVE, 18
OPERA, 2
POETRY, 5
POETS, 18, 19
POSTERITY, 3
PROSE, 1
PSYCHIATRY, 1
PUBLIC, 3
SCIENTISTS, 1, 2

SEASONS, 4
SIN, 2
SLEEP, 3
WAR, 3
WRITERS, 30

Augustine of Hippo, St
AUTHORITARIANISM, 1
HUMAN CONDITION, 2
PROCRASTINATION, 4
RELIGION, 3
VICE, 2

Augustus
IMPROVEMENT, 1

Aurelius, Marcus
ADAPTABILITY, 1
CONTENTMENT, 1
DESTINY, 2, 3
ENDURANCE, 4
HISTORY, 5
LIFE, 7, 8, 35
MANKIND, 3
TRANSIENCE, 1, 2

Austen, Jane
CONCEIT, 2
CONTEMPT, 1
DISMISSAL, 2
ENGLAND, 1, 2
FLATTERY, 2
HUMAN NATURE, 1
INSULTS, 4
LONDON, 3
MARRIAGE, 10, 11, 12
MEN, 1
MONEY, 6
MOURNING, 1
NASTINESS, 1, 2
OPTIMISM, 14
PARTIES, 1
PLAYS, 2
PLEASURE, 3
RESULTS, 2
RIDICULE, 1
SELFISHNESS, 1
SUFFERING, 4
WEATHER, 7
WOMEN, 9, 10, 11

Austin, Alfred
ILLNESS, 1
INSPIRATION, 3

Austin, Warren
DIPLOMACY, 1
MIDDLE EAST, 3

Avery, Oswald Theodore
OPPORTUNITY, 8

Ayckbourn, Alan
RIDICULE, 2

Ayer, A. J.
MORALITY, 2
PHILOSOPHY, 1
PUBLISHING, 2

B

Babbage, Charles
LIFE AND DEATH, 1

Bacall, Lauren
AGE, 6

Bacon, Francis
ADAPTABILITY, 2
AGE, 7, 8
APPEARANCES, 9
ATHEISM, 2, 3
BEAUTY, 7
BOOKS, 3, 4
CERTAINTY, 1
CHARITY, 3
CHILDREN, 5
CONCEIT, 3
COURTESY, 2
DEATH, 20, 21, 22, 23
DIARIES, 1
DIFFERENCE, 7
DISCOVERY, 3
DISEASE, 8, 9
DOUBT, 1
DREAMS, 1
EDUCATION, 4, 5
ENTHUSIASM, 1
EXTRAVAGANCE, 1
FAME, 2
FAMILY, 5, 6
FEAR, 1
GARDENS, 2
GOD, 3
HOUSES, 1
HUMAN NATURE, 2, 3, 4, 5
HYPOCRISY, 2
INNOVATION, 1
INTEGRITY, 1
JUSTICE, 1
KNOWLEDGE, 3, 4, 5
LAW, 6
LETTER-WRITING, 2
LOVE, 19
MARRIAGE, 13, 14
MISFORTUNE, 3
MONEY, 7
NAKEDNESS, 1
OPPORTUNITY, 9
POWER, 5
PRAISE, 2
READING, 1
REMEDIES, 1, 2
REPUTATION, 1
REVENGE, 4, 5
ROYALTY, 4
SOLITUDE, 1
SUSPICION, 1
TIME, 8
TRAVEL, 2
TRUTH, 10
VIRTUE, 1, 2
WONDER, 1

Baden-Powell, Robert
SEX, 5

Bader, Douglas
DETERMINATION, 3

Baedeker, Karl
CAMBRIDGE, 1
OXFORD, 3

Bagehot, Walter
ENGLISH, 5
HOUSES OF PARLIAMENT, 3
HUNGER, 2
MONARCHY, 1, 2
NEWSPAPERS, 1
OPPOSITION, 1
POLITICIANS, 1, 35
WOMEN, 12
WRITERS, 2

Bagnold, Enid
SEX, 6

Bailly, Jean Sylvain
EXECUTION, 1

Bainbridge, Kenneth
NUCLEAR WEAPONS, 1

Bairnsfather, Bruce
WAR, 4

Baldwin, James
CHILDREN, 6
DISILLUSION, 1
MONEY, 8
RACISM, 2, 3
RELIGION, 5
SEX, 7
TRUTH, 11

Baldwin, Stanley
CHURCHILL, 2
DEPARTURE, 3
DIPLOMACY, 2
ENGLAND, 3
EXPEDIENCY, 2
HOUSES OF PARLIAMENT, 4
INTELLIGENCE, 1
JOURNALISM, 2
MISQUOTATIONS, 6
MONARCHY, 3
RESPONSIBILITY, 2
SAYINGS, 1
SECRECY, 2
WAR, 5, 6

Balfour, Arthur
CHRISTIANITY, 2
CHURCHILL, 3
ENTHUSIASM, 2
HISTORY, 6
JOURNALISM, 3
MARRIAGE, 15
READING, 2
TRIVIALITY, 1

Ball, John
CLASS, 4

Balzac, Honoré de
DETERMINATION, 4
EQUALITY, 3
FAME, 3
MARRIAGE, 16, 17, 18
THEFT, 4

Banda, Hastings
CIVILIZATION, 2

Bangs, Edward
AMERICA, 3

Bankhead, Tallulah
ADDICTION, 1
AGE, 9
CHARITY, 5
CRITICISM, 2
DIARIES, 2
INTELLECTUALS, 3
OBSESSIONS, 1
PURITY, 2
THEATRE, 2

Barca, Pedro Calderón de la
BIRTH, 4
REALITY, 2

Bardot, Brigitte
CONSERVATION, 1
FAITHFULNESS, 1

Baring-Gould, Sabine
CHRISTIANITY, 3
DAY, 1
ENDURANCE, 5

Barker, Howard
SOCIETY, 1
THEATRE, 3

Barker, Ronnie
HUMOUR, 2

Barnard, Lady Ann
MARRIAGE, 19

Barnard, Christiaan
MEDICINE, 1

Barnes, Clive
PORNOGRAPHY, 1

Barnes, Ernest William
EQUALITY, 4

Barnum, Phineas Taylor
GULLIBILITY, 1
LAST WORDS, 6

Barrie, J. M.
BOOKS, 5
BRITISH, 1
CHARM, 1
DEATH, 24
FAIRIES, 1, 2
LUXURY, 1
MATHEMATICS, 1
MOTIVE, 1
PERVERSITY, 1
SCOTS, 1, 2
SUCCESS, 5
THINKING, 1

Barrymore, John
ABSTINENCE, 1

Barrymore, Lionel
EPITAPHS, 6

Barth, Karl
GOOD, 1

Barthes, Roland
CARS, 1

Baruch, Bernard
COLD WAR, 2
OLD AGE, 4

Bates, Katharine Lee
AMERICA, 4

Bath and Wells, Bishop of
DEATH, 25

Baudelaire, Charles
BEGINNING, 6
MEMORY, 2

Baudouin I
WAR, 7

Bax, Arnold
EXPERIENCE, 7

Bayly, Thomas Haynes
ABSENCE, 4
DREAMS, 2
FLOWERS, 1

Beaton, Cecil
SNOBBERY, 1

Beatty, Earl
BOATS, 1

Beaumarchais
LAUGHTER, 4
MANKIND, 4

Beaumont, Francis
ACTION, 6
ETERNITY, 1
FREEDOM, 1
HURT, 1
INDIFFERENCE, 1
MELANCHOLY, 1
MEMORIALS, 2

MORTALITY, 2
OBSTRUCTION, 1
PRUDENCE, 5
SEXES, 1
SUMMONS, 2

Beauvoir, Simone de
AGE, 10
DISILLUSION, 2
HAPPINESS, 2
WOMEN, 13

Beaverbrook, Lord
DIARIES, 3
JOURNALISM, 4, 5, 6
PAINTING, 1
POWER, 6

Becket, Thomas
LAST WORDS, 7

Beckett, Samuel
AFTERLIFE, 1
BOREDOM, 1
HABIT, 2
MADNESS, 1
TIME, 9

Beckford, William
TEMPTATION, 3

Becon, Thomas
DRUNKENNESS, 7

Becque, Henry
EQUALITY, 5

Bede, St
LIFE, 9

Bee, Barnard Elliot
DETERMINATION, 5

Beecham, Thomas
CRITICISM, 3
MARRIAGE, 20
MUSIC, 4, 5, 6, 7, 8
NAMES, 1
SMOKING, 1
TRAVEL, 3

Beecher, Henry Ward
INSULTS, 5

Beeching, H. C.
ACADEMICS, 2

Beerbohm, Max
ART, 3
ARTHURIAN LEGEND, 1
BEAUTY, 8
CLASSICS, 1
CONCEIT, 4
COSMETICS, 1
CRICKET, 1
DOGS, 2
EDUCATION, 6
EXPERIENCE, 8
EYES, 1
GOLF, 1
GREATNESS, 2, 3
HEALTH AND HEALTHY LIVING, 3
INSULTS, 6
LOVE, 20
MEDIOCRITY, 1
ORIGINALITY, 1
PAST, 2
PUBLIC, 4
SUBJECTIVITY, 1
TIME, 10
WOMEN, 14
WRITERS, 31

Beethoven, Ludwig van
MUSIC, 9

MUSICIANS, 2
POPULARITY, 1

Behan, Brendan
BLESSING, 3
CHILDREN, 7, 8
INSULTS, 7
IRELAND, 3
IRISH, 2, 3
JEWS, 1
JUSTICE, 2
LAST WORDS, 8
MARRIAGE, 21
NATIONALITY, 1, 2
SOCIETY, 2
VIOLENCE, 1

Behn, Aphra
LOVE, 21
TRANSIENCE, 3

Bell, Alexander Graham
SUMMONS, 3

Bell, Clive
ART, 4
CRITICS, 1
OBJECTIVITY, 3

Belloc, Hilaire
ARISTOCRACY, 2
BIBLE, 2
BOOKS, 6, 7
CHILDREN, 9, 10
CLERGY, 1
CRITICISM, 4
FOOD, 7, 8
HEROISM, 2
MONEY, 9
NONSENSE, 3
POLITICS, 4
POWER POLITICS, 1
PREJUDICE, 1
PUNS, 1
SMALLNESS, 2

Bellow, Saul
POLITICAL CORRECTNESS, 2

Benchley, Robert
ALCOHOL, 10
BORROWING, 2
CHIVALRY, 2
CRITICISM, 5
DEBAUCHERY, 2
EPITAPHS, 1
HUMOUR, 34
SMALLNESS, 3
TELEGRAMS, 3
VENICE, 1
WRITERS, 32

Benjamin, Judah Philip
JEWS, 2

Benn, Tony
HOUSES OF PARLIAMENT, 5
JOURNALISM, 7
PHOTOGRAPHY, 2
POLITICIANS, 36

Bennett, Alan
DICKENS, 1
DOGS, 3
INSULTS, 8
LIFE, 10, 11
NOSTALGIA, 1
SOCIALISM, 1
THEATRE, 4
WAR, 8

Bennett, Arnold
CONFUSION, 1
ILLNESS, 2

JOURNALISM, 8
MARRIAGE, 22
PESSIMISM, 1
POLITICS, 5
PREJUDICE, 2
PROGRESS, 1
TASTE, 1

Bennett, James Gordon
NEWSPAPERS, 2, 3
TELEGRAMS, 4

Benny, Jack
DESIRE, 1
MERIT, 2

Benson, A. C.
BRITAIN, 4

Bentham, Jeremy
HAPPINESS, 3
LAWYERS, 4

Bentley, Edmund Clerihew
ARCHITECTURE, 1
BIOGRAPHY, 1
BRIBERY, 1
DEATH, 26
ECONOMICS, 3
SCIENTISTS, 7

Bentley, Nicolas
JOURNALISM, 9

Bentley, Richard
ALCOHOL, 11
REPUTATION, 2

Beresford, Charles
APOLOGIES, 1

Berger, John
ARTISTS, 10

Bergerac, Cyrano de
REVENGE, 6

Bergman, Ingrid
ACTING, 2

Berkeley, Bishop
COMPLAINTS, 1
HONESTY, 3

Berlin, Irving
HUMOUR, 3
POP MUSIC, 3

Berlioz, Hector
TIME, 11

Bernard, Tristan
PLAYS, 3

Bernard, W. B.
TRIVIALITY, 2

Bernhardt, Sarah
ACTING, 4
CRICKET, 2
FOOTBALL, 2

Berry, Chuck
POP MUSIC, 4, 5

Bethmann-Hollweg, Theobald von
WORLD WAR I, 3

Betjeman, John
ADMIRATION, 1
BUSINESS, 4
EDUCATION, 7
ENGLAND, 4
ENVIRONMENT, 1
ETIQUETTE, 1
FOOD, 9

FUTURE, 2
HUNTING, 1
POETRY, 6
TRAINS, 1
WRITERS, 33

Bevan, Aneurin
CHURCHILL, 4
COMMUNISM, 1
COMPROMISE, 2
INCOMPETENCE, 1
JOURNALISM, 10
NONCOMMITMENT, 1
NUCLEAR WEAPONS, 2
POLITICIANS, 37, 38
POLITICS, 6, 7
RIGHTEOUSNESS, 2
SOCIALISM, 2
WEAPONS, 1

Beveridge, Lord
GOVERNMENT, 6
LEADERSHIP, 1
PESSIMISM, 2

Bevin, Ernest
FREEDOM, 2
MIXED METAPHORS, 1

Bibulatov, Hassan
RUSSIA, 2

Bichat, Marie François
LIFE, 12

Bickerstaffe, Isaac
HAPPINESS, 4
SELFISHNESS, 2

Bidault, Georges
MISTAKES, 3

Bierce, Ambrose
BORES, 1
DEBAUCHERY, 3
DISEASE, 10
EGOTISM, 3
FUTURE, 4
MARRIAGE, 29
MIND, 1
MISFORTUNE, 4
MUSIC, 10
OPTIMISM, 15
PAINTING, 2
PATIENCE, 8
PEACE, 3
PHILOSOPHERS, 1
RELIGION, 4
WRITERS, 34

Billings, Victoria
MOTHERHOOD, 1

Binding, Rudolph
WORLD WAR I, 4, 5

Binyon, Laurence
MEMORIALS, 3
MOURNING, 3

Bismarck
BOSNIA AND HERCEGOVINA, 2
CHILDREN, 16
DETERMINATION, 6
DIPLOMACY, 3, 4
POLITICS, 8, 9
POWER POLITICS, 2
WAR, 11

Blacker, Valentine
PRUDENCE, 6

Blackmore, R. D.
MOTHERHOOD, 2

Blackstone, William
JUSTICE, 3
MEMORY, 3
MONARCHY, 4, 5
SOCIETY, 3

Blackwell, Antoinette Brown
SEXES, 3

Blackwood, Helen Selina
HOMESICKNESS, 1

Blair, Robert
DEATH, 32
WHISTLING, 1

Blair, Tony
INDIVIDUALITY, 3

Blake, Charles Dupee
SLEEP, 4

Blake, Eubie
MUSIC, 11
RACISM, 4

Blake, William
ACTION, 7
ANIMALS, 4
ARTISTS, 11
BEAUTY, 9
BIRTH, 3
CHILDREN, 17
CONFLICT, 4
CREATION, 7, 8
DESIRE, 2, 3, 4
DOUBT, 3
EFFORT, 2
ENGLAND, 5
EPITAPHS, 7
EXCESS, 3
FORGIVENESS, 8
FUTILITY, 5
GENERALIZATIONS, 1
GOOD, 2
GREATNESS, 4
HAPPINESS, 5
HELL, 1
HUMILITY, 2
HYPOCRISY, 4
IMPRISONMENT, 1
INFINITY, 1
INSULTS, 9
LIFE, 13
LOVE, 27, 28
MANKIND, 6
MUSIC, 12, 13
PERCEPTION, 1, 2, 3
PLEASURE, 5
POWER, 7
PRAYER, 5
PROOF, 2
RACISM, 5
SORROW, 1
SOUL, 4
SUITABILITY, 1
TRUTH, 14
WISDOM, 10, 11
WISDOM AND FOOLISHNESS, 5
WONDER, 2

Blank, Joost de
OPPRESSION, 3
RACISM, 9

Blixen, Karen
MANKIND, 7

Blunden, Edmund
POETRY, 7

Blythe, Ronald
AGE, 13
CLERGY, 3
OLD AGE, 7

Boccaccio, Giovanni
LOVE, 29
RIDICULE, 3
WOMAN'S ROLE, 1

Boethius
HAPPINESS, 6

Boff, Leonardo
CHURCH, 3

Bogarde, Dirk
ORDER, 1

Bogart, Humphrey
ADMIRATION, 2
MISQUOTATIONS, 11
NOSTALGIA, 2

Bogart, John B.
JOURNALISM, 11

Bohm, David
REALITY, 1

Bohr, Niels
EXPERTS, 2
SUPERSTITION, 6

Boileau, Nicolas
ADMIRATION, 3
IDLENESS, 2
SELF-CONTROL, 2
VICE, 3

Boleyn, Anne
MARTYRDOM, 1

Bolitho, William
PLACES, 1

Bolt, Robert
ARISTOCRACY, 3
MORALITY, 3

Bone, David
SELFISHNESS, 3

Bone, James
EDITORS, 2

Bonhoeffer, Dietrich
GOD, 14, 15

Bono, Edward de
DISAPPOINTMENT, 1

Boone, Daniel
CONFUSION, 2

Boorstin, Daniel J.
FAME, 4, 5

Boothroyd, Betty
POLITICS, 10

Borge, Victor
REMEDIES, 5

Borges, Jorge Luis
TRANSLATION, 1
UNCERTAINTY, 2
UNIVERSE, 2

Borrow, George
BRITISH, 2
SATISFACTION, 1
SUICIDE, 1

Bosquet, Pierre
WAR, 12

Bossidy, John Collins
SNOBBERY, 2

Boswell, James
ACTORS, 11
CONVERSATION, 3

Botha, Elize
RACISM, 6

Botha, P. W.
SOUTH AFRICA, 1, 2, 3

Bottomley, Horatio William
PUNS, 2

Bottomley, Virginia
MOTHERHOOD, 3

Boucicault, Dion
TIME, 13

Boulay de la Meurthe, Antoine
MISTAKES, 4

Boulton, Canon Peter
RELIGION, 6

Boulton, H. E.
ROYALTY, 5

Bowen, Lord
METAPHYSICS, 1

Bowen, Charles
JUSTICE, 4

Bowen, E. E.
PARTING, 4
SPORT AND GAMES, 2

Bowen, Elizabeth
ART, 5
EXPERIENCE, 9
INNOCENCE, 4
JEALOUSY, 2
LYING, 5

Bowra, Maurice
DEATH, 34
FOOD, 10

Brabazon of Tara, Lord
SPEECHES, 1

Bracken, Brendan
HUMOUR, 4

Bradbury, Malcolm
BOOK, SONG, AND PLAY TITLES, 4
COURTESY, 3
ENGLISH, 6
FRIENDSHIP, 10
LEISURE, 2
MARRIAGE, 31
NEWSPAPERS, 4
SEX, 8
SYMPATHY, 1

Bradford, John
LUCK, 6

Bradley, F. H.
LUCK, 7
METAPHYSICS, 2
MORALITY, 4
SAYINGS, 2
STUPIDITY, 1
UNDERSTANDING, 3

Bradley, Omar Nelson
NUCLEAR WEAPONS, 3
WAR, 13

Bragg, Melvyn
PATRIOTISM, 4

Brahms, Johannes
INSULTS, 10
MUSICIANS, 10

Braine, John
BOOK, SONG, AND PLAY TITLES, 5
HUMAN NATURE, 6
TIME, 14
UNFAITHFULNESS, 3

Brancusi, Constantin
GREATNESS, 5

Brand, Jo
VIOLENCE, 2

Brando, Marlon
ACTING, 3
ACTORS, 1

Branson, Richard
LEADERSHIP, 3

Braude, Jacob M.
ENVY, 5

Braun, Wernher von
WEAPONS, 2

Brecht, Bertolt
FRIENDSHIP, 11
HEROISM, 3
HUNGER, 3
INJUSTICE, 2
NONSENSE, 4
PEACE, 5
SUPPORT, 2
VICE, 4
WAR, 14, 15, 16

Brenan, Gerald
ARTISTS, 1
FUNERALS, 3
INTELLECTUALS, 4
LANGUAGE, 3
OLD AGE, 8
POETS, 1
SELF-KNOWLEDGE, 2
WRITERS, 35

Brezhnev, Leonid
POLITICIANS, 39

Bridges, Robert
BEAUTY, 10, 11
DAY, 2

Brien, Alan
BOASTS, 1

Bright, John
ENGLAND, 6
FORCE, 1
WAR, 17

Brittain, Vera
POLITICS, 11
WRITERS, 3

Bronowski, Jacob
CRUELTY, 1
MANKIND, 8
MEDIOCRITY, 2
SCIENCE, 1, 2

Brontë, Charlotte
WRITERS, 36

Brontë, Emily
BELIEF, 3
COURAGE, 3
IMPRISONMENT, 2
SUFFERING, 5

Brooke, Rupert
CAMBRIDGE, 2

ENGLAND, 7
FLOWERS, 2
NOSTALGIA, 3
POETS, 20
WAR, 18, 19

Brooks, Mel
OSTENTATION, 1
THEATRE, 5

Brooks, Phillips
CHRISTMAS, 11

Brougham, Henry Peter
PUBLIC, 5

Brown, Thomas
HATE, 1

Brown, Thomas Edward
FLATTERY, 3
GARDENS, 4

Browne, Cecil
JEWS, 5

Browne, Thomas
CHARITY, 10
CRITICISM, 7
EXPLOITATION, 1
INDIVIDUALITY, 4
JUDGMENT, 5
MANKIND, 9
NATURE, 1
NOBILITY, 1
SELF, 5
SELF-RELIANCE, 3
SUPERNATURAL, 4
WORLD, 1

Browne, William
CAMBRIDGE, 3
OXFORD, 4

Browning, Elizabeth Barrett
GOD, 16
LOVE, 30
RESPECTABILITY, 1
SORROW, 2

Browning, Robert
ABSENCE, 5
AGE, 15
AMBITION, 3, 4
ANIMALS, 5, 6
BEGINNING, 7
BETRAYAL, 2
BIBLE, 3
BIRDS, 1
CHRISTIANITY, 20
CONFLICT, 5
CONTEMPT, 2
DAMNATION, 1
DAY, 3
DEATH, 35
DOOMSDAY, 3
DOUBT, 4
DRINKS, 2
ENGLAND, 8
EQUALITY, 6
EVIL, 6
FREEDOM, 4
GERMANY, 1
HATE, 2
HEAVEN, 4
HORSES, 3
HUMAN CONDITION, 4
HYPOCRISY, 5
IMPRESSIONABILITY, 1
INFLUENCE, 1
KISSING, 1
LIFE, 14, 15
LOVE, 31
MISFORTUNE, 5
MONTHS, 6
MOTHERHOOD, 4
NOVELS, 1
OPTIMISM, 16, 17
PAST, 3
PERFECTION, 2, 3
PERVERSITY, 2
POSSIBILITY, 1
ROYALTY, 6
SINCERITY, 1
SOUL, 5
SUMMONS, 4
TRANSIENCE, 9
WOMEN, 18
WORDS, 3
WORRY, 8

Bruce, Lenny
CHRISTIANITY, 21
RELIGION, 7

Brummel, 'Beau'
OBESITY, 2

Bruno, Frank
SUCCESS, 6

Bruno, Giordano
COURAGE, 4

Bruyère, Jean de La
ADMIRATION, 6
ALCOHOL, 17
AMBITION, 11
CRIME, 5
CRITICISM, 26
EPITAPHS, 17
IMPETUOSITY, 2
LAUGHTER, 8
LIFE AND DEATH, 8
MANKIND, 15
MEMORY, 8
MISFORTUNE, 12
POLITICS, 12
PROMPTNESS, 1
SERVILITY, 4
SUCCESS, 11
WOMEN, 46

Buchanan, Robert Williams
CLOTHES, 2
POETS, 2

Buck, Pearl
AGE, 16
BEAUTY, 12
CHINA, 1
FAITH, 9
KILLING, 1
MUSIC, 14

Buckingham, Duke of
FOOLISHNESS, 11
INTRIGUE, 1

Buddha
FIRE, 1
RELIGION, 8
RIGHTEOUSNESS, 3

Buffon, Comte de
STYLE, 1

Buller, Arthur Henry Reginald
SCIENCE, 3

Bullock, Alan
HITLER, 1, 2

Bulmer-Thomas, Ivor
CONCEIT, 5

Bulwer-Lytton, Edward
ENTHUSIASM, 3
WRITING, 3

Buñuel, Luis
ATHEISM, 4

Bunyan, John
ARCHITECTURE, 2
DESPAIR, 2, 3
DREAMS, 3
PRIDE, 2
VIOLENCE, 3
WORLD, 2

Burchfield, Robert
LEXICOGRAPHY, 1

Burgess, Anthony
CLEANNESS, 1
ENGLAND, 9
EUROPE, 1
FUTURE, 5
OSTENTATION, 2
POP MUSIC, 6
SLEEP, 5

Burke, Edmund
ACCUSATION, 1
BEAUTY, 13
CHIVALRY, 3
COMPROMISE, 4
CORRUPTION, 1
DANGER, 4
EUROPE, 2
EXAMPLE, 2
FORCE, 2
FREEDOM, 5
HONOUR, 2
INDIFFERENCE, 2
INGRATITUDE, 2
JUDGMENT, 6
POLITICIANS, 40
POWER, 8
PUBLIC, 6
RELIGION, 9
ROYALTY, 7
SUCCESS, 7
SUFFERING, 6
SUPERSTITION, 7
THEORY, 1
TOLERANCE, 1
UNITY, 7
VICE, 5
YIELDING, 1

Burke, Johnny
LEXICOGRAPHY, 2
OPTIMISM, 18

Burney, Fanny
INNOCENCE, 1

Burns, George
GOVERNMENT, 7
MONEY, 12

Burns, John
RIVERS, 1

Burns, Robert
ACTION, 8
ANIMALS, 7
CRUELTY, 2
DELUSION, 1
DEVIL, 6
DISAPPOINTMENT, 2
FOOD, 11
FRIENDSHIP, 12, 13
LOVE, 32, 33, 34
MARRIAGE, 32
MEN, 2
NATURE, 2
NOSTALGIA, 4
RESPECTABILITY, 2
SATISFACTION, 2
SCOTLAND, 2
WAR, 20

Burroughs, John
TRUTH, 15

Burton, Richard
ACTORS, 2

Burton, Robert
DISEASE, 11
MELANCHOLY, 2, 3
NATIONALITY, 3
RELIGION, 10
SMOKING, 2
WRITING, 4

Bush, George
MIDDLE EAST, 4, 5
TAXATION, 1

Bussy-Rabutin
ABSENCE, 6

Butler, Joseph
AFTERLIFE, 2

Butler, R. A.
POLITICIANS, 41
POLITICS, 13
SPEECHES, 2

Butler, Samuel
ANALOGY, 1
ANTICIPATION, 5
ARGUMENTS, 3
ARTS, 1
BEQUESTS, 1
BOOKS, 9
DOGS, 4
ENGLISH, 7
EXTRAVAGANCE, 2
FAITHFULNESS, 2
HYPOCRISY, 6
INDULGENCE, 1
LAWYERS, 6
LEARNING, 4
LIFE, 16, 17
LOSS, 1
LOVE, 35
MARRIAGE, 33
MISOGYNY, 1
MONEY, 13, 14, 15
PLEASURE, 6
POLITICS, 14
POSTERITY, 4
PRAISE, 4
PROGRESS, 2
PUBLIC, 7
PUNISHMENT, 6
REASON, 1
RELIGION, 11
SPECULATION, 1
SPONTANEITY, 1
SUBJECTIVITY, 2
TRUTH, 16
WAR, 21
WOMEN, 19
WORDS, 4
YIELDING, 2

Butz, Earl
CONTRACEPTION, 3

Buxbaume, Martin
POWER, 9

Byatt, A. S.
COMPUTERS, 1
MOTHERHOOD, 5
SELF-RELIANCE, 4

Byrom, John
CHRISTMAS, 12

Byron, Lord
ADULTERY, 1
AGE, 17
BEAUTY, 14
BOOKS, 10
BORES, 2
CHAUCER, 1
CRITICS, 2
DANCING, 1
DEBAUCHERY, 4
DEPARTURE, 4, 5
DETERMINATION, 7
DOGS, 5
DRUNKENNESS, 10
EPITAPHS, 8
EUROPE, 3, 4, 5
FAME, 6
FEMINISM, 32
FORGIVENESS, 9
FREEDOM, 6
FRIENDS, 3
HEROISM, 4
LOVE AND HATE, 1
MATERIALISM, 4
MERRYMAKING, 2
NATURE, 3
NOSTALGIA, 5
PLEASURE, 7
POETRY, 8
POETS, 21, 22
PUBLISHING, 3
ROYALTY, 8
SELF-INTEREST, 2
SEPARATION, 2
SEXES, 4
THEATRE, 6
TRUTH, 17, 18
WAR, 22
WEATHER, 8
WOMEN, 20

Byron, Henry James
SPORT AND GAMES, 3

C

Cabell, James
DRINKS, 3
OPTIMISM, 19
PESSIMISM, 3

Caecus, Appius
RESPONSIBILITY, 3

Caesar, Julius
FRANCE, 1
INTEGRITY, 2
IRREVOCABILITY, 1
LAST WORDS, 12
VICTORY, 1

Cage, John
POETRY, 9

Cagney, James
MISQUOTATIONS, 12

Cahn, Sammy
LOVE AND MARRIAGE, 1

Calder, Ritchie
SCIENCE, 4

Caligula
RUTHLESSNESS, 1

Callaghan, James
BRITAIN, 5
LYING, 6
SUPPORT, 3

Calment, Jeanne
LIFE AND DEATH, 3

Calverley, C. S.
ALCOHOL, 18
CLASS, 5
SMOKING, 3

Campbell, Ffyona
TRAVEL, 4

Campbell, Jane Montgomery
AGRICULTURE, 1

Campbell, Joseph
OLD AGE, 9

Campbell, Mrs Patrick
MARRIAGE, 34
SEX, 9
WOMEN, 21

Campbell, Patrick
JOURNALISM, 12

Campbell, Roy
SEASONS, 6
SOUTH AFRICA, 4
STATELY HOMES, 1
TRANSLATION, 2

Campbell, Thomas
NAVY, 1
PERSPECTIVE, 1
PUBLISHING, 4, 5
RUTHLESSNESS, 2
SELFISHNESS, 4
TREES, 2

Campion, Thomas
ADMIRATION, 4
RIGHTEOUSNESS, 4, 5
SEX, 10
SORROW, 3

Camus, Albert
APPEARANCE, 6
ARROGANCE, 1
COMMITMENT, 3
CRIME, 2
DOOMSDAY, 4
INTELLECTUALS, 5
MANKIND, 10
MONEY, 16
PESSIMISM, 4
POLITICIANS, 2
POLITICS, 15
REBELLION, 2
REVOLUTION, 2
SLAVERY, 1
STYLE, 2
WORK, 5

Canetti, Elias
ANIMALS, 8
DEATH, 36
SAYINGS, 3

Canning, George
AMERICA, 5
FRANKNESS, 1
POLITICIANS, 42

Cantona, Eric
EXPECTATION, 1
FOOTBALL, 3

Capone, Al
AMERICA, 6
MURDER, 3
TAXATION, 2

Capote, Truman
ENGLISH, 8
VENICE, 2

Caracciolo, Domenico
ENGLAND, 10

Carey, George
CHURCH, 4
CLERGY, 4
COMMERCIALISM, 1

Carey, Henry
BRITAIN, 6
LOVE, 36
SUNDAY, 3

Carleton, Emma
REPUTATION, 3

Carlyle, Jane Welsh
IMPERFECTION, 5
INJUSTICE, 3
MEDICINE, 2
POETS, 23

Carlyle, Thomas
BELIEF, 4
BIOGRAPHY, 2, 3
BOOKS, 11
BRIBERY, 2
CHANGE, 2
CIVILIZATION, 3
COMFORT, 1
ECONOMICS, 4
EDUCATION, 8
ENGLISH, 9
FRANCE, 2
GENIUS, 2
GREATNESS, 6
HISTORY, 7, 8
INSULTS, 11
INTELLIGENCE, 2
LEADERSHIP, 4
NAKEDNESS, 2
NATURE, 4
ORTHODOXY, 1
POETS, 3, 24, 25, 26
POLITICIANS, 43
PUBLIC, 8
SARCASM, 1
SLAVERY, 2
STATISTICS, 1
TECHNOLOGY, 2
UNIVERSE, 3, 4
WORDS, 5
WORK, 6
WRITERS, 4

Carnegie, Dale
ARGUMENTS, 4
HUMAN NATURE, 7
INFLUENCE, 2

Carney, Don
MISTAKES, 5

Carpio, Lope Félix de Vega
LAST WORDS, 13

Carrel, Alexis
INTELLIGENCE, 3

Carrington, Lord
POLITICS, 16
SCIENCE, 5

Carroll, Lewis
BOOKS, 12
CONFUSION, 3
CURIOSITY, 4
DANCING, 2
EDUCATION, 9
ENGLISH, 10
FOOD, 12, 13
GERMANY, 13
GREED, 5
HASTE, 5
INJUSTICE, 4
INTRODUCTIONS, 1
LANGUAGE, 4
LOGIC, 1
MANNERS, 2
MEANING, 1, 2, 3
NONSENSE, 5, 6, 7, 8, 9
OLD AGE, 10
ORDER, 2
PROMISES, 3
PURPOSE, 1
SEASIDE, 1
SUPERNATURAL, 5
WAR, 23

Carson, Rachel
ECOLOGY, 1, 2
SEA, 2

Carter, Jimmy
ADULTERY, 2
BUREAUCRACY, 3

Carter, Lillian
MOTHERHOOD, 6

Carter, Violet Bonham
SPACE, 2

Cartier-Bresson, Henri
PHOTOGRAPHY, 3

Cartland, Barbara
FOOD, 14
HEALTH AND HEALTHY LIVING, 4
SEX, 11, 12, 13
SNOBBERY, 3

Cartwright, John
DEMOCRACY, 2

Caruso, Enrico
SINGING, 1

Cary, Joyce
ADULTERY, 3
ARTISTS, 2

Cary, Phoebe
COURAGE, 5

Case, Phila Henrietta
LONELINESS, 1

Cassandra
POLITICS, 17

Casson, Hugh
BRITISH, 3

Castle, Barbara
POLITICIANS, 44

Castling, Harry
LONDON, 4

Caswall, Edward
DEATH, 37

Cather, Willa
HISTORY, 9

Catherwood, Mary
FRIENDSHIP, 14

Cato the Elder
WAR, 24

Catullus
GREETINGS, 1
LOVE AND HATE, 2
POETRY, 10

Causley, Charles
APPEARANCE, 7

Cavell, Edith
LAST WORDS, 14

Cecil, Lord
DICKENS, 2

OLD AGE, 11

Cecil, Robert
ENVIRONMENT, 2
VIRTUE, 5

Cerf, Bennett
WRITERS, 37

Cervantes, Miguel de
ACTORS, 3
CHARACTER, 3
CHARITY, 11
COMPLIMENTS, 1
DELUSION, 2, 3
FEAR, 4
FOOLISHNESS, 12
FRIENDS, 4
HUNGER, 4
IMPETUOSITY, 1
LANGUAGE, 5
MADNESS, 2
NONCOMMITMENT, 2
PAINTING, 3
POVERTY AND WEALTH, 3
PRAYER, 7
REMEDIES, 6
SIN, 10
TACT, 4

Chalmers, Patrick Reginald
LOSS, 2

Chamberlain, Joseph
ECONOMICS, 5
NATIONS, 1

Chamberlain, Neville
PEACE, 6
WAR, 25
WORLD WAR II, 1, 2

Chamfort, Nicolas
EGOTISM, 4
INGRATITUDE, 3
LAUGHTER, 6

Chandler, John
ROYALTY, 9

Chandler, Raymond
ALCOHOL, 19
APPEARANCE, 8
CINEMA, 1
COURAGE, 6
GRAMMAR, 2
SEX, 15

Chanel, Coco
COSMETICS, 2
FASHION, 1
KNOWLEDGE, 9
YOUTH, 3

Channon, Henry
WRITERS, 38

Channon, Paul
CONSERVATION, 2

Chaplin, Charlie
HUMOUR, 5, 6
LIFE, 18
LUXURY, 2
WAR, 26

Chardin, Pierre Teilhard de
EVOLUTION, 2

Charles
TRIVIALITY, 11

Charles, Prince of Wales
ADULTERY, 4
ARCHITECTURE, 3, 4
INDUSTRIAL RELATIONS, 1
LANGUAGE 6
ROYALTY, 11

Charles I
ACCUSATION, 2
EXECUTION, 4

Charles II
ARROGANCE, 2
DEATH, 38
HOUSES OF PARLIAMENT, 6
LAST WORDS, 15
RELIGION, 12
REPARTEE, 1
ROYALTY, 10

Charles V
AGREEMENT, 1
LANGUAGE, 7
REVENGE, 8

Charles X
MONARCHY, 6, 7

Charles, Elizabeth
SPEECH, 7

Chateaubriand, Vicomte de
CYNICISM, 1
ORIGINALITY, 2

Chaucer, Geoffrey
ALCOHOL, 20
APPEARANCES, 10
BOOKS, 13
CHARACTER, 4, 5
CHIVALRY, 4
CREATION, 9
HORSES, 4
HYPOCRISY, 7
LIFE AND DEATH, 4
MARRIAGE, 35
MATERIALISM, 5
MISFORTUNE, 6, 7
MONTHS, 7
MORTALITY, 3
MURDER, 4

Chekhov, Anton
BEAUTY, 15
CHANGE, 3
ECOLOGY, 3
EXPERIENCE, 10
FRIENDSHIP, 15
LEARNING, 5
MOURNING, 4
REMEDIES, 7
WORRY, 9
WRITING, 5

Chesterfield, Earl of
ADVICE, 6
ARISTOCRACY, 4
BOOKS, 14
BRITISH, 4
CLERGY, 5
CONFORMITY, 3
EXAMPLE, 3
EXCELLENCE, 1
FLATTERY, 4
IDLENESS, 3
INSULTS, 12
LAST WORDS, 16
MISFORTUNE, 8
RELIGION, 13, 14
THRIFT, 4
TIME, 15
WISDOM, 12
WOMEN, 22

Chesterton, G. K.
AMERICA, 7
AMERICANS, 3
ANIMALS, 9
ARISTOCRACY, 5
ARTS, 2
CHARITY, 12
CIVILIZATION, 4
COMPROMISE, 5
CONSERVATISM, 1
CRITICISM, 8
CURIOSITY, 5
DEMOCRACY, 3
DISEASE, 12
EDUCATION, 10, 11
EMOTION, 1
ENGLISH, 12
GLORY, 1
GOOD AND EVIL, 2
HAPPINESS, 7
HOPE, 5
HUMAN CONDITION, 5
HYPOCRISY, 8
JOURNALISM, 13
LANGUAGE, 8, 9
LOGIC, 2
MADNESS, 3
MANKIND, 11, 12
MATERIALISM, 6
MEMORY, 4
NATURE, 5
NOVELS, 2
OBESITY, 3, 4
ORTHODOXY, 2
PATRIOTISM, 5
PERSPECTIVE, 2
POETS, 27
PROGRESS, 3, 4
PURITANISM, 1
REASON, 2
RELIGION, 15
SERIOUSNESS, 1
SUICIDE, 2, 3
TRAINS, 2
TRAVEL, 5
TRUTH, 19
UNIVERSE, 5
WEALTH, 9
WRITERS, 39

Chevalier, Albert
LOVE, 37

Chevalier, Maurice
LOVE, 38
OLD AGE, 12

Child, Harold
WRITERS, 40

Child, Lydia M.
FREEDOM, 7
IRISH, 4
RETRIBUTION, 9

Chirac, Jacques
ECONOMICS, 6

Chomsky, Noam
MONARCHY, 8
NONSENSE, 10

Chopin, Frédéric
MUSICIANS, 11

Chopin, Kate
INSIGNIFICANCE, 1
PRESENT, 2
SEA, 3

Christie, Agatha
HABIT, 3
MARRIAGE, 36
MONEY, 17
PRINCIPLES, 2
REGRET, 4

Christie, Linford
DRUGS, 3
SPORT AND GAMES, 4

Christine de Pisan
MARRIAGE, 95

Chuang Tse
DREAMS, 4

Churchill, Charles
APPEARANCES, 11
EXCELLENCE, 2
HUMOUR, 7
OLD AGE, 13
PATRIOTISM, 6

Churchill, Jennie Jerome
AMBITION, 5
LOVE AND MARRIAGE, 2
THRIFT, 5

Churchill, Lord Randolph
IRELAND, 4
MATHEMATICS, 2
OPPOSITION, 2
POLITICIANS, 45

Churchill, Randolph
CATHOLICISM, 3

Churchill, Winston
ALCOHOL, 21
AUTHORITARIANISM, 3
BRITISH, 5, 6
BRITISH EMPIRE, 1, 2
CHILDREN, 18
CHURCHILL, 5
CLASSICS, 2
COLD WAR, 3
DESTINY, 4, 5
DIPLOMACY, 5, 6, 7
EDUCATION, 12
EFFORT, 3
EUROPE, 6
FEAR, 5
FEMINISM, 33
GRAMMAR, 3, 4
HITLER, 3
LYING, 7
MISQUOTATIONS, 13
NATIONALITY, 4
NAVY, 2
NEWSPAPERS, 5
NOSTALGIA, 6
NUCLEAR WEAPONS, 4
OFFICERS, 3, 4
PLACES, 2, 3
POLITICIANS, 46, 47, 48
POLITICS, 18
PRIDE, 3
PRONUNCIATION, 1
PROSE, 2
QUOTATIONS, 1
RESPONSIBILITY, 4, 5
RIGHTEOUSNESS, 6
RUSSIA, 3
SMOKING, 4
SPEECHES, 3
VICTORY, 2
WAR, 27, 28, 29
WAR AND PEACE, 3, 4
WATER, 1
WORDS, 6
WORLD WAR II, 3, 4, 5, 6, 7, 8, 9, 10, 11, 12, 13, 14, 15, 16
WORRY, 10

Cibber, Colley
FASHION, 2
THEFT, 5

Cicero
CUSTOM, 1
GOOD, 3
LAW, 7
PHILOSOPHERS, 2

Clark, George Norman
POLITICS, 19

Clark, Kenneth
ARTISTS, 12
SCIENTISTS, 8

Clarke, Arthur C.
SCIENCE, 6
TECHNOLOGY, 3

Clarke, John
HOME, 3

Clarke, Kenneth
EUROPE, 7

Clausewitz, Karl von
MISQUOTATIONS, 14
WAR, 30

Clemenceau, Georges
AMERICA, 8
INSULTS, 13
OFFICERS, 5
OLD AGE, 14
WORLD WAR I, 7

Clinton, Bill
COLD WAR, 4
MIDDLE EAST, 6

Clinton, Hillary
CONFUSION, 4

Clive of India
MODERATION, 3

Clough, Arthur Hugh
BELIEF, 5
CONFUSION, 5
DEFEAT, 1
EFFORT, 4
GOD, 17
KILLING, 2
MONEY, 18

Cobain, Kurt
HONESTY, 4

Cobbett, William
DUTY, 1
LONDON, 5
POVERTY, 4
WRITERS, 41

Cobden, Richard
NEWSPAPERS, 6

Coborn, Charles
VIOLENCE, 4

Cocker, Jarvis
TASTE, 2

Cocks, Barnett
BUREAUCRACY, 4

Cocteau, Jean
POETS, 4
TACT, 5
THINKING, 2

Cohan, George M.
WORLD WAR I, 8

Cohen, Leonard
LOVE, 39

Coke, Desmond
BOATS, 2

Coke, Edward
MONARCHY, 9
PRIVACY, 1

Colby, Frank More
AMBITION, 6
HUMOUR, 8

Coleridge, Hartley
FREEDOM, 8

Coleridge, Samuel Taylor
APPEARANCES, 12
BIRDS, 2
BIRTH, 5
BOATS, 3
CAUTION, 9
CHRISTIANITY, 22
CRITICISM, 9
CRITICS, 3
DESIRE, 5
EXPERIENCE, 11
EXPLORATION, 1
FEAR, 6
GUILT, 4
HUMOUR, 9
IMAGINATION, 1, 2
INTERRUPTIONS, 1
MARRIAGE, 37
MOON, 2
PLEASURE, 8, 9, 10
POETRY, 11
POETRY AND PROSE, 1, 2
POETS, 28, 29
PRAYER, 8, 9
PROOF, 3
PUNISHMENT, 7
SCIENTISTS, 9
SEA, 4
SEASONS, 7
SHAKESPEARE, 3
SILENCE, 3
SINCERITY, 2
SINGERS, 1
SLEEP, 6
SOLITUDE, 2
SUN, 1
SUPERNATURAL, 6
WATER, 2
WISDOM, 13
WRITERS, 5, 6

Colette
CLASS, 6
FOOD, 15
HUMOUR, 10
SEX, 16
VIRTUE, 6

Collingbourne, William
INSULTS, 14

Collings, Jesse
AGRICULTURE, 2

Collingwood, Lord
WAR, 31

Collingwood, Robin George
OLD AGE, 15

Collins, John Churton
SUICIDE, 4

Collins, Michael
PROPHECY, 3

Collins, Mortimer
AGE, 18

Colman, the Elder, George
LOVE, 40

Colman, the Younger, George
IMPORTANCE, 1
SECRECY, 6

Colton, Charles Caleb
EXAMINATIONS, 1
IMITATION, 2
OBLIGATION, 1
RELIGION, 16
SILENCE, 4

Compton-Burnett, Ivy
APPEARANCES, 13
OBEDIENCE, 2
SEXES, 5

Confucius
ABILITY, 1
ACHIEVEMENT, 3
CAUTION, 10
EXAMPLE, 4
FRIENDS, 5
HABIT, 4
IMPERFECTION, 6
KINDNESS, 1
KNOWLEDGE, 10
PAST, 4
SERVILITY, 1
SUPERIORITY, 2, 3, 4
UNDERSTANDING, 4
VIRTUE, 7

Congreve, William
AGREEMENT, 2
COUNTRYSIDE, 1
DEATH, 39
DESIRE, 6
LOVE, 41, 42, 43
LOVE AND HATE, 3
MARRIAGE, 38, 39, 40
MURDER, 5
MUSIC, 15
SECRECY, 7, 8

Conley, Rosemary
FOOD, 16

Connell, James
SOCIALISM, 3

Connolly, Billy
MARRIAGE, 41

Connolly, Cyril
BABIES, 1
CAPITALISM, 1
CHARM, 2
CHILDREN, 19
EDUCATION, 13
JOURNALISM, 14
LIFE, 19
LITERATURE, 1
OBESITY, 5
PASSION, 1
PUBLISHING, 6
SELF, 6
SEXES, 6
STYLE, 3
SUICIDE, 5
TALENT, 1
WISDOM, 14
WOMEN, 24
WRITERS, 7, 8
WRITING, 6

Conrad, Joseph
CONCEIT, 6
ENGLAND, 11
EQUALITY, 7
EVIL, 7
JUDGMENT, 7
LITERATURE, 2
RUTHLESSNESS, 3
WORDS, 7
YOUTH, 4

Conrad, Peter
WRITERS, 42

Conran, Shirley
HOUSEWORK, 2
LAZINESS, 1

Constable, John
BEAUTY, 16
POETS, 30

Cook, A. J.
STRIKES, 1

Cook, Dan
OPERA, 3

Cook, Peter
THEATRE, 7
UNIVERSE, 6

Cooke, Alistair
POP MUSIC, 7

Coolidge, Calvin
AMERICA, 9, 10
SIN, 11
STRIKES, 2

Cooper, Lady Diana
CLASS, 7

Copley, John Singleton
BIOGRAPHY, 4

Corbusier, Le
DESIGN, 1, 2
HOUSES, 3

Coren, Alan
ACCIDENTS, 1
ALCOHOL, 22
EUROPE, 8
FRANCE, 3
HUMOUR, 35
SWITZERLAND, 1
TELEVISION AND RADIO, 2

Corneille, Pierre
DUTY, 2
GERMANY, 14
SORROW, 4
VICTORY, 3

Cornford, F. M.
OBESITY, 6
PROPAGANDA, 1

Cornforth, John
TRUTH, 20

Cornuel, Anne-Marie Bigot de
FAMILIARITY, 2

Cory, William Johnson
BOATS, 4

Costello, Elvis
POP MUSIC, 8

Coubertin, Pierre de
VICTORY, 4

Coué, Émile
REMEDIES, 8

Cousin, Victor
ART, 6

Cousteau, Jacques
CONSERVATION, 3

Covey, Donna
RACISM, 7

Coward, Noël
AFTERLIFE, 3
APPEARANCE, 9
ARISTOCRACY, 6
CRITICISM, 10
DANCING, 3
DEBAUCHERY, 5
DECLINE, 1
ENGLAND, 12
FRANCE, 4
GERMANY, 2
HUMOUR, 36
INTRIGUE, 2
LOVE, 44
MELANCHOLY, 4
MUSIC, 16
OPERA, 4
PETULANCE, 1
POP MUSIC, 9
PORNOGRAPHY, 2
SIMILARITY, 4
STATELY HOMES, 2, 3
TELEGRAMS, 5, 6
THEATRE, 8
WEALTH, 10
WOMEN, 25
WORK, 7

Cowley, Abraham
DISEASE, 13
GARDENS, 6
LIFE, 20

Cowper, William
BRITAIN, 7
CHANGE, 4
COUNTRYSIDE, 2
DEATH, 40
DRINKS, 4
ENGLAND, 13
EXPLOITATION, 2
GOD, 18
HUNTING, 2
KNOWLEDGE, 11
MARRIAGE, 42, 43
MERCY, 1
MOUNTAINS, 1
NATURE, 6
NOSTALGIA, 7
PATIENCE, 9
PATRIOTISM, 7
PERVERSITY, 3
POVERTY, 5
PRAYER, 10
REVENGE, 9
SEPARATION, 3
SLAVERY, 3
SOLITUDE, 3, 4, 5
TREES, 3
WEALTH, 11
WISDOM, 15

Cox, David
AIDS, 3

Crabbe, George
APPEARANCE, 10
BOOKS, 15
CLARITY, 1

Craig, Gordon
THEATRE, 9

Crane, Stephen
COURAGE, 7

Cranmer, Thomas
REGRET, 5

Creighton, Mandell
CHARITY, 13

Crick, Francis
SCIENCE, 7

Crisp, Quentin
FAMILY, 8
HOMOSEXUALITY, 2, 3
HOUSEWORK, 3
LANGUAGE, 10
ONE-UPMANSHIP, 1
PRAYER, 11
SORROW, 5
TELEVISION AND RADIO, 3
VICE, 6
YOUTH, 5

Croce, Benedetto
IMAGINATION, 3

Croker, John Wilson
POLITICS, 20
VICTORY, 5

Crompton, Richmal
THREATS, 1

Cromwell, Oliver
DISMISSAL, 3, 4
LOYALTY, 6
MISTAKES, 6
PUBLIC, 9
REALISM, 1

Crosby, Bing
FRIENDSHIP, 16
POP MUSIC, 10

Crossman, Richard
IRELAND, 5

Cukor, George
ACTORS, 10

cummings, e. e.
MOON, 3
NAKEDNESS, 3
POLITICIANS, 3
RACISM, 8

Curie, Marie
ACHIEVEMENT, 4
NATURE, 7
PRACTICALITY, 1
SCIENCE, 8

Curran, John Philpot
FREEDOM, 9

Currie, Edwina
ABSTINENCE, 2
AIDS, 4
HEALTH AND HEALTHY LIVING, 5
ILLNESS, 3
INTELLIGENCE, 4
WATER, 3

Curtis, Lionel
POLITICIANS, 49

Curtiz, Michael
LANGUAGE, 11

Curzon, Lord
BRITISH EMPIRE, 3
JOURNALISM, 15
MISTAKES, 7
POLITICIANS, 50

Cuvier, Baron Georges
LAST WORDS, 17

D

d'Abrantes, Duc
ANCESTRY, 1

Dacre, Harry
MARRIAGE, 44

Dahl, Roald
FOOD, 17

Dali, Salvador
ARTISTS, 13
GENIUS, 3
PAINTING, 4

Dalton, John
CRITICISM, 11

Daly, Dan
WAR, 32

Damien, Father
PRACTICALITY, 2

Daniel, Samuel
LOVE, 45

Daniels, R. G.
APPEARANCE, 11

Dante
HELL, 2
SORROW, 6

Danton, Georges Jacques
COURAGE, 8
EXECUTION, 5

Darling, Lord
LAW, 8
MARRIAGE, 45
SHYNESS, 2
TRUTH, 21, 22

Darrow, Clarence Seward
CLOTHES, 3
HUMILITY, 3
POLITICIANS, 4

Darwin, Charles
EVOLUTION, 3, 4, 5, 6, 7
MANKIND, 13
SELF-CONTROL, 3
SHAKESPEARE, 4

Darwin, Erasmus
SPEECH, 8

Davies, John
JUDGMENT, 8

Davies, W. H.
ABSTINENCE, 3
BIRDS, 3
CONTENTMENT, 2
IDLENESS, 4
KINDNESS, 2

Davis, Bette
ACTING, 5
OBITUARIES, 1
PROMISCUITY, 1

Davis Jnr, Sammy
DISABILITY, 2
FAME, 7
RACISM, 10

Davy, Humphry
PHILISTINISM, 3

Dawkins, Richard
SURVIVAL, 2

Day, Clarence Shepard
FUNERALS, 4
LANGUAGE, 12

Dayan, Moshe
INFLEXIBILITY, 1
WAR, 33

Deakin, Ralph
NEWSPAPERS, 7

Debs, Eugene Victor
FORGIVENESS, 10

Debussy, Claude
MUSIC, 17, 18

Decatur, Stephen
PATRIOTISM, 8

Deffand, Marquise du
BEGINNING, 8

Defoe, Daniel
CHURCH, 5
CLASS, 8
DEVIL, 7
GOOD AND EVIL, 3
TYRANNY, 1

Degas, Edgar
INJUSTICE, 5

De Gaulle, Charles
ACTION, 9
ASSASSINATION, 1
POLITICIANS, 7, 8, 9
POLITICS, 30
RESPECT, 2

Dekker, Thomas
SLEEP, 7

de Klerk, F. W.
SOUTH AFRICA, 5, 6

De La Mare, Walter
FOOD, 37
ILLNESS, 13
WORDS, 15

Delaney, Shelagh
FEAR, 7
WOMEN, 26

de la Salle, St Jean Baptiste
ETIQUETTE, 2

Delille, Jacques
FAMILY, 9
FRIENDS, 6

Delors, Jacques
DEMOCRACY, 4
EUROPE, 9

Deng Xiaoping
CHINA, 2

Denman, Thomas
JUSTICE, 5

Denning, Lord
ENGLAND, 14

Dennis, John
PUNS, 3

Dennis, Nigel
MARRIAGE, 46
MONEY, 19

De Quincey, Thomas
BOOKS, 16
DRUGS, 4
IMPERFECTION, 7
MURDER, 6
POETS, 31, 32

Descartes, René
LITERATURE, 3
THINKING, 3
TRAVEL, 6

Devonshire, Duke of
JOURNALISM, 16
RESPONSIBILITY, 6
SPEECHES, 4

De Vries, Peter
BOREDOM, 2
COWARDICE, 1
DISASTER, 2
GOD, 19
GREED, 6
MIND, 2
POPULARITY, 2
SELF-INTEREST, 3

Diana, Princess of Wales
ABILITY, 2
ADULTERY, 5
BIRTH, 6
FOOD, 18

Díaz, Porfirio
AMERICA, 11

Dibdin, Charles
ALCOHOL, 23
MORTALITY, 4

Dickens, Charles
ACCIDENTS, 2
ALCOHOL, 24
APPEARANCE, 12, 13
BABIES, 2
BLESSING, 6
BUREAUCRACY, 5
BUSINESS, 5
CAUTION, 11
CLASS, 9
COURAGE, 9
DEATH, 41
DISEASE, 14
DRUNKENNESS, 11
ECONOMICS, 7
EDUCATION, 14
EMBARRASSMENT, 1
EMOTION, 2
ENGLAND, 15
EVIL, 8
EXECUTION, 6
EXISTENCE, 2
FACTS, 1
FAMILY, 10
FEAR, 8
FRENCH REVOLUTION, 1
GREETINGS, 2
HOUSES OF PARLIAMENT, 7
HUMOUR, 37
KNOWLEDGE, 12
LAW, 9
MAJORITY, 1
MARRIAGE, 47
MISFORTUNE, 9
MONEY, 20
NAMES, 2
PEACE, 7
POETRY, 12, 13
POVERTY, 6
SERVILITY, 2, 3
SIGNATURES, 1
SPELLING, 1
STUPIDITY, 2
TRIVIALITY, 3
WEATHER, 9
WOMEN, 27

Dickinson, Emily
DEATH, 42, 43
PARTING, 5
SUCCESS, 8
SUFFERING, 7

Diderot, Denis
GUIDANCE, 2
LIFE, 21
LOVE, 46

Dietrich, Marlene
CHANGE, 5
FORGIVENESS, 11
PLACES, 4
SEXES, 7

Diller, Phyllis
ANGER, 3
HOUSEWORK, 4

Dillingham, Charles Bancroft
ESCAPE, 1
FUNERALS, 5

Diogenes
HUNGER, 5
REPARTEE, 2

Dionysius of Halicarnassus
HISTORY, 10

Disraeli, Benjamin
AGE, 19
AGREEMENT, 3
ASSASSINATION, 2
CHRISTIANITY, 23
CONCEIT, 7
EGOTISM, 5
ENGLAND, 16
EVOLUTION, 8
EXPEDIENCY, 3
GRAMMAR, 5
HORSES, 5
HOUSES OF PARLIAMENT, 8
IGNORANCE, 5
IMPERTINENCE, 1
INATTENTION, 1
INSULTS, 15
IRELAND, 6
JOURNALISM, 17
LAST WORDS, 18
MAJORITY, 2
MARRIAGE, 48, 49
MEMORY, 5
MOTHERHOOD, 7
NOVELS, 3
OLD AGE, 16
PEACE, 8
PETULANCE, 2
POLITICIANS, 51
POLITICS, 21, 22
POVERTY AND WEALTH, 4
PROPHECY, 4
RELIGION, 17, 18
ROYALTY, 12
SELF-MADE MEN, 1
STATISTICS, 2
TRIVIALITY, 4
VERBOSITY, 2
YOUTH, 6

Dix, Dom Gregory
CLERGY, 6

Dix, Dorothy
MARRIAGE, 50
PRESENT, 3
SEXES, 8
WOMEN, 28

Dobrée, Bonamy
HUMILITY, 4

Dodd, Ken
PSYCHIATRY, 2

Donleavy, J. P.
FUNERALS, 6
HUMAN NATURE, 8

Donne, John
ANALOGY, 2
BEAUTY, 17
DEATH, 44, 45
EQUALITY, 26
LOVE, 47, 48, 49
LUST, 1
NONSENSE, 11
SCIENCE, 9
SELF, 7
SILENCE, 5
SOCIETY, 4
SUN, 2

Dorati, Antal
MUSIC, 19

Dors, Diana
SEXES, 9

Dostoevsky, Anna
CHARACTER, 6
FEMINISM, 4
LOVE, 50

Dostoevsky, Fedor Mikhailovich
PHILOSOPHY, 2

Douglas, Lord Alfred
HOMOSEXUALITY, 4

Douglas, Archibald
COURAGE, 10

Douglas, Norman
FOOD, 19
FRANCE, 5
PARASITES, 1
SEASIDE, 2

Douglas, William
LOVE AND DEATH, 1

Douglas-Home, Alec
POLITICIANS, 5
TITLES, 1

Douglas-Home, Lady Caroline
POLITICIANS, 52

Dow, Lorenzo
DAMNATION, 2

Dowson, Ernest
FAITHFULNESS, 3
LOVE, 51
MEMORY, 6
TRANSIENCE, 11

Doyle, Arthur Conan
CRIME, 3
EXPERIENCE, 12
JUSTICE, 6
KNOWLEDGE, 13
LONDON, 6
MARRIAGE, 51
MEDIOCRITY, 3
MISQUOTATIONS, 15
SIMPLICITY, 1
SIN, 12
SMOKING, 5
TALENT AND GENIUS, 2
TRIVIALITY, 5, 6, 7, 8
TRUTH, 23

Doyle, Roddy
CINEMA, 2
PREGNANCY, 1

Drabble, Margaret
MORALITY, 5
POVERTY, 7
THRIFT, 6

Drake, Francis
SPORT AND GAMES, 5
WAR, 34, 35

Draper, John
CHURCH, 6

Drayton, Michael
BOATS, 5
PARTING, 6

Dreiser, Theodore
LAST WORDS, 19

Drucker, Peter F.
BUSINESS, 6

Drummond, Thomas
CAPITALISM, 2

Dryden, John
AGE, 20, 21
CHARACTER, 7
CHAUCER, 2
COURAGE, 11
DREAMS, 5
EXECUTION, 7
GENIUS, 4
HUMAN NATURE, 9
LOVE AND DEATH, 2
MARRIAGE, 52, 53
MOON, 4
MORTALITY, 5
NATURE, 8
PATIENCE, 10
PLEASURE, 11
POLITICIANS, 6
PRESENT, 4
PUBLIC, 10, 11
RELIGION, 19
SHAKESPEARE, 5, 6
SIN, 13
TREASON, 2
TRUTH, 24, 25
VERBOSITY, 3
WORLD-WEARINESS, 1

Dubček, Alexander
COMMUNISM, 2

Dubin, Al
FLOWERS, 3
LOVE, 52

Dubos, René and Jean
DISEASE, 15

Dufferin, Countess of
NOSTALGIA, 8

Duffey, Mrs E. B.
PREGNANCY, 2

Duhamel, Georges
COURTESY, 4

Dulles, John Foster
MISTAKES, 8

Dumas, fils, Alexandre
CHILDREN, 20
GENERALIZATIONS, 2
HUMAN CONDITION, 6

Dumas, père, Alexandre
UNITY, 8

Du Maurier, Daphne
DREAMS, 6
HUMOUR, 38

Duncan, Isadora
DANCING, 4
DIPLOMACY, 8
LAST WORDS, 20
LIFE, 22
MARRIAGE, 54

Dunning, John
MONARCHY, 10

Dunstan, Eric
ACTORS, 12

Durham, Bishop of
GOD, 20

Durocher, Leo
GOOD, 4

Durrell, Lawrence
HISTORY, 11
MUSIC, 20
REBELLION, 3
SEX, 17

Dürrenmatt, Friedrich
IDEAS, 1

Dyall, Franklin
WRITERS, 43

Dyer, John
COUNTRYSIDE, 3
TRANSIENCE, 12

Dylan, Bob
CHANGE, 6
EXPERIENCE, 13
FAILURE, 2
FREEDOM, 10
LEISURE, 3
PESSIMISM, 5
POP MUSIC, 11
TRAVEL, 7
WOMEN, 29

E

Eames, Emma
RENUNCIATION, 2

Earhart, Amelia
COURAGE, 12
DANGER, 5

Eastman, George
LAST WORDS, 21

Eaton, Hal
BUSINESS, 7

Eccles, David
GOVERNMENT, 8

Eco, Umberto
LAUGHTER, 7
SUPERNATURAL, 7
TRUTH, 26

Eddington, Arthur
METAPHYSICS, 3
SCIENCE, 10, 11

Eddy, Mary Baker
DEATH, 46
DISEASE, 16
FAITH, 10
RELIGION, 20, 21
SIN, 14

Eden, Anthony
DIPLOMACY, 9
MIDDLE EAST, 7
THRIFT, 7

Eden, Clarissa
POLITICS, 23

Edgeworth, Maria
DRUGS, 5

Edison, Thomas
GENIUS, 5

Edward III
SELF-RELIANCE, 5

Edward VII
ACCIDENTS, 3

Edwards, Ruth Dudley
COMPUTERS, 2

Einstein, Albert
FUTURE, 6
GOD, 21
IMAGINATION, 4
INTELLECT, 1
MATHEMATICS, 3
NUCLEAR WEAPONS, 5
PATRIOTISM, 9
PREJUDICE, 3
RELIGION, 22
SCIENCE, 12, 13, 14, 15
SCIENTISTS, 3
TAXATION, 3
THEORY, 2
TRUTH, 27
WAR AND PEACE, 5

Eisenhower, Dwight D.
ADVICE, 7
AMERICA, 12
POWER, 10

Ekland, Britt
ADULTERY, 6

Eliot, George
ANIMALS, 10
ARROGANCE, 3
CHARACTER, 8
FUTILITY, 6
HUMOUR, 11
POETS, 33
POVERTY AND WEALTH, 5
WOMEN, 30

Eliot, T. S.
AGE, 22, 23
ARTS, 3
BOOKS, 17
CATS, 2
DEPARTURE, 6
ENDING, 3
FEAR, 9
FOOD, 20
HELL, 3
LIFE, 23, 24
LIFE AND DEATH, 5
MELANCHOLY, 5
MONTHS, 8
MOTIVE, 2
OLD AGE, 17, 18
POETRY, 14
POETS, 5, 34
READING, 3
REALITY, 3
SHAKESPEARE, 7
TIME, 16
TRAVEL, 8
WOMEN, 31
WRITERS, 44

Elizabeth I
AMBITION, 7
FORGIVENESS, 12
IMPERTINENCE, 2
INSULTS, 16
LAST WORDS, 22
ROYALTY, 13, 14, 15
TITLES, 2

Elizabeth II
BABIES, 3
ROYALTY, 16, 17, 18

Elizabeth the Queen Mother
WORLD WAR II, 17

Ellerton, John
DAY, 4

Ellis, Alice Thomas
MOTHERHOOD, 8

Ellis, Bill
COMPUTERS, 3

Ellis, Havelock
OPTIMISM, 20
PROGRESS, 5

Ellwanger, George Herman
DISEASE, 17

Elton, Ben
SEX, 18

Éluard, Paul
SORROW, 7

Emerson, Ralph Waldo
AMBITION, 8
AMERICA, 13
ART, 7
BIOGRAPHY, 5
CONFORMITY, 4
CONSTANCY, 1
EDUCATION, 15
ENTHUSIASM, 4
FAME, 8
FRIENDS, 7
GOOD, 5
GREATNESS, 7
HASTE, 6
HEROISM, 5
HISTORY, 12
HUMAN CONDITION, 7
HUMAN NATURE, 10
HYPOCRISY, 9
INDIVIDUALITY, 5
LOVE, 53
MISTRUST, 4
OLD AGE, 19
RELIGION, 23
SATISFACTION, 3
WRITERS, 9, 45

English, Thomas Dunn
MEMORY, 7

Epictetus
CRITICISM, 12

Epicurus
DEATH, 47
FRIENDSHIP, 17

Erasmus
CATHOLICISM, 4

Eschenbach, Marie Ebner von
CLOTHES, 4
CONCEIT, 8
PRINCIPLES, 3
SCEPTICISM, 1

Estienne, Henri
AGE, 24

Eubank, Chris
SPORT AND GAMES, 6

Euclid
MATHEMATICS, 4

Euripides
MADNESS, 4

Evans, Edith
DEATH, 48
WOMEN, 32

Evans, Harold
PHOTOGRAPHY, 4

Evarts, William M.
ABSTINENCE, 4

Evelyn, John
REMEDIES, 9
SCIENTISTS, 10

Ewer, William Norman
JEWS, 4

Eyre, Richard
COMMERCIALISM, 2

F

Fadiman, Clifton
INSINCERITY, 1
QUOTATIONS, 2

Faisal, Taujan
LAW, 10

Faith, Adam
MONEY, 21

Fallersleben, Heinrich Hoffmann von
GERMANY, 3

Faraday, Michael
TITLES, 3

Farjeon, Herbert
SNOBBERY, 4

Farmer, Edward
LAST WORDS, 23

Farnham Lee, Hannah
DISEASE, 18

Farouk I
MONARCHY, 11

Farquhar, George
POVERTY, 8
WORLD-WEARINESS, 2

Farrington, David
FAMILY, 11

Faulkner, William
STYLE, 4
SWITZERLAND, 2

Feather, Vic
INDUSTRIAL RELATIONS, 2

Feiffer, Jules
AGE, 25

Feldman, Marty
HUMOUR, 12

Femina, Jerry Della
ADVERTISING, 3

Fénelon, François
HISTORIANS, 1
VERBOSITY, 4

Fenton, James
POLITICAL CORRECTNESS, 3

Ferber, Edna
MARRIAGE, 55

Ferdinand I
JUSTICE, 7
PETULANCE, 3

Ferlinghetti, Laurence
HUMAN CONDITION, 8

Fermi, Enrico
DESTINY, 6

Fern, Fanny
FOOD, 22

Ferrier, Kathleen
LAST WORDS, 24

Field, Eugene
CRITICISM, 13

Field, Frank
HOUSES OF PARLIAMENT, 9

Fielding, Henry
CLERGY, 7
DEATH, 49
DRUNKENNESS, 12
EDUCATION, 16
FOOD, 23
FRIENDSHIP, 18
LUST, 2
MARRIAGE, 56, 57, 58, 59
NATURE, 9
SEX, 19
TRUST, 2

Fields, W. C.
BIBLE, 5
CHILDREN, 21
DOGS, 6
HATE, 3
REALISM, 2
WATER, 4
WEATHER, 10

Firbank, Ronald
COMPLAINTS, 2
ENGLISH, 13
SYMPATHY, 2

Firmont, Abbé Edgeworth de
EXECUTION, 8

Fischer, Martin H.
DISEASE, 19
DRUGS, 6, 7

Fish, Michael
WEATHER, 11

Fitzgerald, Edward
CONTENTMENT, 3
CREATION, 10
DAY, 5
DEATH, 50
DESTINY, 7, 8, 9, 10
FLOWERS, 4
LIFE, 25
LIFE AND DEATH, 6
MONEY, 22
MORTALITY, 6
PRESENT, 5
TASTE, 3
TIME, 17, 18
TRANSIENCE, 13

Fitzgerald, F. Scott
AGE, 26
ALCOHOL, 25
ARTISTS, 3
BEAUTY, 18
BOOK, SONG, AND PLAY TITLES, 6
CLASS, 10
FAME, 9
FICTION, 2
PARTIES, 3, 4
PRECOCITY, 1
SELF-KNOWLEDGE, 3
SLEEP, 8
SOUL, 6
WEALTH, 12
WORDS, 8
WRITING, 7

Fitzgerald, Zelda
LOVE, 54, 55
SCIENCE, 16

FitzGibbon, Constantine
BOOK, SONG, AND PLAY TITLES, 7

Flanagan, Bud
DREAMS, 7

Flanders, Michael
CANNIBALISM, 1

Flaubert, Gustave
BOOKS, 18
POETRY, 15

Flecker, James Elroy
KNOWLEDGE, 14

Fleming, Ian
BOOK, SONG, AND PLAY TITLES, 8
MARRIAGE, 60
SEX, 20

Fletcher, John
ALCOHOL, 26, 27

Florian, Jean-Pierre Claris de
LOVE, 56

Florio, John
ENGLAND, 17

Foch, Marshal
COWARDICE, 2
FAMILY, 12
WAR, 36
WORLD WAR I, 9, 10

Fontaine, Jean de La
ABILITY, 3
ANTICIPATION, 6
BREVITY, 4
DISAPPOINTMENT, 4
FLATTERY, 6
GOD, 32
HELP, 7
HUNGER, 8
PAROCHIALISM, 1
PATIENCE, 11
PRUDENCE, 8
SUFFERING, 10

Fontenelle, Bernard de
LAST WORDS, 25, 26

Foot, Michael
BUREAUCRACY, 6
IMAGINATION, 5
INSULTS, 17
MARXISM, 1
POWER, 11

Foote, Samuel
NONSENSE, 12
STUPIDITY, 3

Forbes, C. F.
CLOTHES, 5

Ford, Anna
MEN, 3

Ford, Henry
BUSINESS, 8
CHOICE, 1
HEALTH AND HEALTHY LIVING, 6
HISTORY, 13
SPORT AND GAMES, 7

Ford, John
ACTING, 6
BOOK, SONG, AND PLAY TITLES, 9
DEATH, 51
DESTINY, 11

Foreman, George
HEALTH AND HEALTHY LIVING, 7

Forgy, Howell Maurice
WAR, 37

Formby, George
FOOD, 24
LOVE, 57

Forrest, Nathan Bedford
JUSTICE, 8
MISQUOTATIONS, 16
WAR, 38

Forster, E. M.
ART, 8
BETRAYAL, 3
COMMUNICATION, 1
DEATH, 52
EDUCATION, 17, 18, 19
HISTORIANS, 2
MUSIC, 21
NOVELS, 4
POVERTY, 9
RACISM, 11
WRITERS, 10, 47, 48

Fortescue, John
TAXATION, 4

Fosdick, Harry Emerson
ATHEISM, 5

Foster, Stephen
DEATH, 53
HOMESICKNESS, 2, 3
HORSES, 6

Fourier, Charles
FEMINISM, 5

Fowles, John
CIVILIZATION, 5
FICTION, 3
POETRY, 16

Fox, Charles James
APPEARANCES, 14
FRENCH REVOLUTION, 2
GOVERNMENT, 9
LAST WORDS, 27
MONARCHY, 12

Fox, George
PRIDE, 4

Fox, Henry
DEATH, 54

Fox, Henry Stephen
APPEARANCE, 14

France, Anatole
CHANGE, 7, 8
CHRISTIANITY, 24
CRITICS, 5
EQUALITY, 8
INJUSTICE, 6
MONEY, 23
MUSEUMS, 1
POVERTY, 10
PRACTICALITY, 3
QUOTATIONS, 3
WORDS, 9

Francis I
DEFEAT, 2

Franklin, Benjamin
AGE, 27
ARGUMENTS, 5
BUSINESS, 9, 10
EPITAPHS, 9, 10
NEGLECT, 1
PURPOSE, 2
READING, 4
SECRECY, 9
TAXATION, 5
TECHNOLOGY, 4
TIME, 19
UNITY, 9
WAR AND PEACE, 6
WISDOM, 16

Franks, Oliver
SECRECY, 10

Fraser, Keith
IRELAND, 7

Frayn, Michael
LIBERALISM, 1
NAKEDNESS, 4
THEORY, 3

Frederick the Great
FREEDOM, 11
WAR, 39

Freed, Arthur
WEATHER, 12

French, Marilyn
MEN, 4

Freud, Clement
ABSTINENCE, 5
PLACES, 5

Freud, Sigmund
CONSCIENCE, 2
FEMINISM, 34
GOD, 22
INTELLECT, 2
PSYCHIATRY, 3
PSYCHOLOGY, 1
RELIGION, 24
WOMEN, 33

Friedman, Milton
ECONOMICS, 8

Frisch, Max
OLD AGE, 20

Fromm, Erich
MOTHERHOOD, 9

Frost, David
TELEVISION AND RADIO, 4

Frost, Robert
AGE, 28
CHOICE, 2
HOME, 4
NEIGHBOURS, 3
NOVELTY, 2
POETRY, 17

PRAYER, 12
TRANSLATION, 3
TRAVEL, 9
WORK, 8
WRITING, 8
YOUTH, 7

Froude, J. A.
CRUELTY, 3
EQUALITY, 9
HUNTING, 3

Fry, Christopher
CRITICS, 6
LOVE, 58
MEANING, 4
RELIGION, 25
SHYNESS, 3
SLEEP, 9
SUPERNATURAL, 8

Fry, Elizabeth
PUNISHMENT, 8

Fuller, Richard Buckminster
SPACE, 3

Fuller, Thomas
ANGER, 4
APPEARANCE, 15
BOOKS, 19
FAME, 10
SAYINGS, 4
WISDOM AND FOOLISHNESS, 6

Furber, Douglas
DANCING, 5

Fuseli, Henry
POETS, 35

Fyleman, Rose
FAIRIES, 3

G

Gable, Clark
ACTORS, 13

Gabor, Zsa Zsa
MARRIAGE, 61, 62
MATERIALISM, 7
SEX, 21

Gainsborough, Thomas
LAST WORDS, 28

Gaisford, Thomas
CLASSICS, 3

Gaitskell, Hugh
NUCLEAR WEAPONS, 6
POLITICS, 24, 25

Galas, Diamanda
SEX, 22

Galbraith, John Kenneth
BUSINESS, 11
ILLNESS, 4
IRISH, 5
LUXURY, 3
MONEY, 24
OSTENTATION, 3
PATRIOTISM, 10
POLITICS, 26, 27
WEALTH, 13

Galilei, Galileo
ASTRONOMY, 2, 3

Gallagher, Noel
CRIME, 4
POP MUSIC, 12

Gallo, José Antonio Viera
SOCIALISM, 4

Galsworthy, John
ARTISTS, 14
CRITICISM, 14
POLITICS, 28
WEAKNESS, 2
WRITERS, 49, 50

Gandhi, Indira
CHILDREN, 22
HISTORY, 14
INFLEXIBILITY, 2
LAST WORDS, 29
RELIGION, 26

Gandhi, Mahatma
CIVILIZATION, 6

Garbo, Greta
MISQUOTATIONS, 17
PRIVACY, 2
SOLITUDE, 6

Gardner, John W.
HISTORY, 15

Garfield, James A.
ASSASSINATION, 3

Garibaldi, Giuseppe
PATRIOTISM, 11

Garland, Judy
CINEMA, 3

Garner, John Nance
POLITICS, 29

Garrick, David
COURAGE, 13
PLAYS, 4

Garrison, William Lloyd
AMERICA, 14
SLAVERY, 4

Garrod, Heathcote William
WAR, 40

Gaskell, Elizabeth
ETIQUETTE, 3
MEN, 5
PATRIOTISM, 12

Gasset, José Ortega y
REVOLUTION, 3, 4

Gautier, Théophile
ARTS, 4
CHARACTER, 9

Gavarni, Paul
YOUTH, 8

Gay, John
ARGUMENTS, 6
ENVY, 6
FAITHFULNESS, 4
HOPE, 6
LIFE, 26
LOVE, 59, 60
MARRIAGE, 63
POVERTY, 11
SORROW, 8
WOMEN, 34

Geddes, Eric Campbell
RETRIBUTION, 10

Geldof, Bob
CHARITY, 14
IRISH, 6

Genscher, Hans-Dietrich
GERMANY, 8

George II
MARRIAGE, 64
REPARTEE, 3

George IV
FIRST IMPRESSIONS, 3

George V
BRITISH EMPIRE, 4
FAMILY, 13
LAST WORDS, 30, 31
POVERTY, 12
SOCIALISM, 6
WAR, 41

George VI
ROYALTY, 19

George, Dan
RACISM, 12

Getty, J. Paul
WEALTH, 14, 15

Gibbon, Edward
CORRUPTION, 2
EDUCATION, 20
GOVERNMENT, 10
HISTORY, 16
LONDON, 7
NOVELS, 5
PROGRESS, 6
RELIGION, 27

Gibbons, Stella
EVIL, 9

Gibran, Kahlil
CONSERVATION, 4
KNOWLEDGE, 15
LOVE, 61
UNITY, 10

Gide, André
OPPOSITES, 2
POETS, 36
SORROW, 9
SPONTANEITY, 2

Gielgud, John
ACTORS, 14
AGE, 29

Gilbert, Fred
WEALTH, 16

Gilbert, Humphrey
LAST WORDS, 32
SEA, 5

Gilbert, W. S.
AGE, 30
ALCOHOL, 28
ANCESTRY, 2
APPEARANCE, 16
APPEARANCES, 15
ARROGANCE, 4
BIRDS, 4
BOASTS, 2
BOATS, 6
CERTAINTY, 2
CHILDREN, 23
CLASS, 11, 12, 13
CONCEIT, 9, 10
COWARDICE, 3, 4
CRITICISM, 15, 16
DEATH, 55
DISCONTENT, 2
ECONOMICS, 9
FAMILY, 14
HOUSES OF PARLIAMENT, 10
INDIFFERENCE, 3
KNOWLEDGE, 16
LAW, 11, 12
LOVE, 62
MATHEMATICS, 5
MORTALITY, 7
NAMES, 3
NATIONALITY, 5
OBESITY, 7
OFFICERS, 6, 7
POLICE, 1
POLITICIANS, 10, 11
POLITICS, 31
PUNISHMENT, 9, 10, 11
RETURN, 1
SINGERS, 2
SINGING, 2
TITLES, 4

Gilman, Charlotte Perkins
AMERICA, 15
FEMINISM, 6
POSSIBILITY, 2
SEXES, 10

Gilot, Françoise
MISOGYNY, 2
WOMEN, 35

Gingold, Hermione
WOMEN, 36

Giraudoux, Jean
CLARITY, 2
LAW, 13

Gladstone, William Ewart
CLASS, 14
PROGRESS, 7

Glasse, Hannah
FOOD, 25
MISQUOTATIONS, 18

Glassman, Carol
PREGNANCY, 3

Gloucester, William, Duke of
WRITING, 9

Glover, Jonathan
CHARACTER, 10

Glover-Kind, John A.
SEASIDE, 3

Godard, Jean-Luc
CINEMA, 4, 5

Goddard, Robert
DREAMS, 8

Goebbels, Joseph
WORLD WAR II, 18

Goering, Hermann
NAZISM, 1
PHILISTINISM, 4
POWER POLITICS, 3
WORLD WAR II, 19

Goethe
BEGINNING, 9
CHARACTER, 11
CONFLICT, 6
DENIAL, 1
DISCOVERY, 4
LAST WORDS, 33
MORTALITY, 8
PURPOSE, 3

REALITY, 4
SELF-KNOWLEDGE, 4
SUPERSTITION, 8
TALENT, 2
THEORY, 4

Golding, William
EVOLUTION, 9
INNOCENCE, 5
MADNESS, 5
RESPONSIBILITY, 7
VIRTUE, 8

Goldsmith, James
EUROPE, 10

Goldsmith, Oliver
ALCOHOL, 29
BOOKS, 20
BUSINESS, 12
CONSCIENCE, 3
CONSERVATISM, 2
DEATH, 56
DOCTORS, 3
DOGS, 7, 8
FATHERS, 4
FRANCE, 7
FREEDOM, 12
GENIUS, 6
GULLIBILITY, 2
IMPERFECTION, 8
KNOWLEDGE, 17
LAW, 14
LOVE AND FRIENDSHIP, 2
MARRIAGE, 65, 66
MORTALITY, 9
PHILOSOPHERS, 3
PUBLIC, 12
READING, 5
RELIGION, 28
SILENCE, 6
SPEECH, 9
VICE, 7
WRITERS, 51

Goldwater, Barry
EXCESS, 4
GOVERNMENT, 11
WAR, 42

Goldwyn, Samuel
ACTORS, 15
CINEMA, 6, 7
MIXED METAPHORS, 2, 3
PSYCHIATRY, 4

Goncourt, Edmond de
NOVELS, 6

Gorbachov, Mikhail
DEMOCRACY, 5
SOCIALISM, 5
TOLERANCE, 2

Gordon, Adam Lindsay
MISFORTUNE, 10

Gorer, Geoffrey
MARRIAGE, 67

Gorky, Maxim
MARRIAGE, 68
WORK, 9
WRITING, 10

Gosse, Edmund
CRITICISM, 17
WEAKNESS, 3
WRITERS, 52

Gournay, Jean Claude Vincent de
FREEDOM, 13

Gove, Philip Babcock
LEXICOGRAPHY, 3

Grace, W. G.
CRICKET, 3

Gracián, Baltasar
BREVITY, 1

Grade, Lew
BOASTS, 3
CHRISTIANITY, 25
CONCEIT, 11

Graf, Steffi
FAILURE, 3

Grafton, Richard
MONTHS, 9

Graham, Harry
FIRE, 2
INSENSITIVITY, 2

Graham, James
EXECUTION, 9

Grahame, Kenneth
BOATS, 7
KNOWLEDGE, 18

Grant, Cary
AGE, 31
TELEGRAMS, 7

Grant, Robert
GOD, 23

Grant, Ulysses Simpson
DETERMINATION, 8
JUSTICE, 9
LAW, 15
PEACE, 9
WAR, 43

Granville-Barker, Harley
ANIMALISM, 2
LANGUAGE, 13
POETRY, 18

Graves, John Woodcock
HUNTING, 4

Graves, Robert
BOOK, SONG, AND PLAY TITLES, 10
HUMOUR, 13
LOVE, 63
POETS, 6
SHAKESPEARE, 8

Gray, Thomas
DAY, 6
DEATH, 57, 58
EPITAPHS, 2, 11, 12
IGNORANCE, 6, 7
LONELINESS, 2
MATERIALISM, 8
MORTALITY, 10
POVERTY, 13
SOLITUDE, 7
TEMPTATION, 6
WASTE, 2

Greeley, Horace
EXPLORATION, 2

Greene, Graham
ATHEISM, 6
BEAUTY, 19
BRIBERY, 3
CLERGY, 8
COMMITMENT, 4
FAME, 11
PROOF, 4
RELIGION, 29

SENTIMENTALITY, 1
TRAVEL, 10

Greer, Germaine
FEMINISM, 8, 9
LOVE, 64
MEN, 6
MOTHERHOOD, 10
WOMAN'S ROLE, 2

Greer, Ian
POLITICIANS, 12

Gregory I
ENGLISH, 14

Grein, J. T.
WRITERS, 53

Grellet, Stephen
MORTALITY, 11

Greville, Fulke
HUMAN CONDITION, 9

Grey, Lord
AMERICA, 16
PROPHECY, 5

Griffith-Jones, Mervyn
PRUDERY, 1

Grimké, Angelina
FEMINISM, 10
WOMEN, 37

Grossmith, George
ABSENCE, 7

Grossmith the Younger, George
LOVE, 65

Gruchy, Nigel de
LITERATURE, 4

Guedalla, Philip
BOATS, 8
PUNS, 4
WORLD WAR II, 20
WRITERS, 54

Guitry, Sacha
JEALOUSY, 3

Gulbenkian, Nubar
FOOD, 26

Gummer, John Selwyn
CARS, 2

Gurney, Dorothy
GARDENS, 7

Guthrie, Woody
HUMAN NATURE, 11

Gwenn, Edmund
ACTING, 7

Gwyn, Nell
RELIGION, 30

H

Haber, Fritz
NAZISM, 2

Haig, Douglas
WAR, 44
WORLD WAR I, 11, 12

Hailsham, Lord
AMERICANS, 4
BOREDOM, 3
POLITICS, 32, 33
SINCERITY, 3

Haldane, J. B. S.
ARISTOCRACY, 7
DISEASE, 20
POETS, 7
SCIENCE, 17
SCIENTISTS, 11
UNIVERSE, 7

Hale, Edward Everett
POLITICIANS, 13

Hale, Matthew
CHRISTIANITY, 26

Hale, Nathan
PATRIOTISM, 13

Hale, Sarah Josepha
ANIMALS, 11

Halifax, Lord
FREEDOM, 14
POPULARITY, 3
POWER, 12
PROMOTION, 2
REBELLION, 4
SPEECH, 10
SUBJECTIVITY, 3
TOLERANCE, 3
VIRTUE AND VICE, 1

Hall, Charles Sprague
EPITAPHS, 13
MEMORIALS, 4

Hall, Jerry
WOMEN, 38

Halsey, Margaret
ENGLAND, 18, 19
ENGLISH, 15, 16, 17

Hamilton, William
BRITAIN, 8
LONDON, 8
MANKIND, 14
TRUTH, 28

Hammarskjöld, Dag
LONELINESS, 3
OLD AGE, 21

Hammerstein, Oscar
DAY, 7
LOVE, 66
MUSIC, 22
RIVERS, 2
WHISTLING, 2

Hampton, Christopher
CAPITALISM, 3
CRITICS, 7
HONESTY, 5
THEORY, 5
VIOLENCE, 5

Hancock, John
SIGNATURES, 2

Hankey, Katherine
CHRISTIANITY, 27

Harback, Otto
DRINKS, 5

Harbord, James Guthrie
DIPLOMACY, 11

Harburg, E. Y.
DESIRE, 7, 8
MISQUOTATIONS, 19

Harcourt, William
SOCIALISM, 7

Hardwicke, Lord
DOUBT, 5

Hardy, Thomas
CHRISTIANITY, 28
CLASS, 15
LIFE, 27
LOVE, 67
POETRY, 19
SILENCE, 7
VIRTUE, 9
WAR AND PEACE, 7
WEATHER, 13, 14

Hare, David
NEWSPAPERS, 8

Hargreaves, W. F.
BED, 3
FASHION, 3

Harington, John
TREASON, 3

Harrington, Michael
POVERTY, 14

Harris, George
ADVICE, 8

Hart, Lorenz
CONFUSION, 6
DECLINE, 2

Hartley, L. P.
CARS, 3
CONFORMITY, 5
PAST, 5

Haskell, Arnold
PATRIOTISM, 14

Haskins, Minnie Louise
FAITH, 11

Hastings, Lady Flora
DEATH, 59

Hawker, R. S.
EXECUTION, 10

Hawking, Stephen
UNIVERSE, 8

Hawthorne, Nathaniel
AFTERLIFE, 4
DISEASE, 21
ENGLAND, 20

Hay, Lord Charles
WAR, 45

Hay, Ian
HUMOUR, 14

Hay, Will
SCIENCE, 18

Hayes, J. Milton
MOURNING, 5

Hazlitt, William
ACHIEVEMENT, 5
ANGER, 5
ARTISTS, 15
BITTERNESS, 1
CLOTHES, 6
COUNTRYSIDE, 4, 5
DISCONTENT, 3
ENGLISH, 18
FAMILY, 15
FREEDOM, 15
HATE, 4
IMMORTALITY, 2
INTELLECT, 3
INTELLECTUALS, 6
LAST WORDS, 34
LETTER-WRITING, 3
NAMES, 4
NASTINESS, 3
PLEASURE, 12
POETS, 37, 38, 39, 40, 41
PUBLIC, 13
RULES, 2
SELF-INTEREST, 4
SOLITUDE, 8
SPECULATION, 2
THINKING, 4
TRAVEL, 11
TRIVIALITY, 9
VIRTUE, 10
WRITERS, 55, 56

Healey, Denis
ADVICE, 9
INSULTS, 18
POLITICIANS, 53, 54
POLITICS, 34

Hearst, William Randolph
DOGS, 9

Heath, Edward
BRITAIN, 9
CAPITALISM, 4
POLITICS, 35

Heath, Neville
LAST WORDS, 35

Heaviside, Oliver
UNDERSTANDING, 5

Heber, Reginald
GOD, 24
MISANTHROPY, 1
PLACES, 6

Hegel
EXPERIENCE, 14
UNDERSTANDING, 6

Heifetz, Jascha
EGOTISM, 6

Heine, Heinrich
CENSORSHIP, 1
INFERIORITY, 1
JEWS, 6
LAST WORDS, 36
PESSIMISM, 6

Heinlein, Robert
DEMOCRACY, 6
SPACE, 4

Heisenberg, Werner
EXPERTS, 3
NATURE, 10

Heller, Joseph
ILLNESS, 6
IMMORTALITY, 3
LITERATURE, 5
MEDIOCRITY, 4
OBSTRUCTION, 3
SELF-MADE MEN, 2
SELF-PRESERVATION, 5
SEX, 23
WAR, 46

Hellman, Lillian
CYNICISM, 2
INTEGRITY, 3
MASCULINITY, 1

Helps, Arthur
READING, 6
SMOKING, 6

Helvétius, Claude-Adrien
EDUCATION, 21

Hemans, Felicia Dorothea
COURAGE, 14
STATELY HOMES, 4

Hemingway, Ernest
DEFEAT, 3
MORALITY, 6
NASTINESS, 4
PARIS, 1
SEX, 24
SPORT AND GAMES, 8
STYLE, 5

Henderson, Leon
ECONOMICS, 10

Henley, William Ernest
ENDURANCE, 6
RESPONSIBILITY, 8

Henri IV
FOOLISHNESS, 13
PARIS, 2
POVERTY, 15

Henry II
ASSASSINATION, 4

Henry VIII
FIRST IMPRESSIONS, 4

Henry, Matthew
HUNGER, 6
SUNDAY, 4

Henry, O.
LAST WORDS, 37
WOMEN, 39

Henry, Patrick
FREEDOM, 16
TREASON, 4

Henry, Robert
SCIENTISTS, 12

Hepworth, Barbara
ART, 9

Heraclitus
CHANGE, 9, 10

Herbert, A. P.
BABIES, 4
DISASTER, 3
ENGLISH, 19
LAW, 16
MARRIAGE, 69, 70
PERVERSITY, 4
PLEASURE, 13
WATER, 5

Herbert, George
ALCOHOL, 30
DAY, 8
DEATH, 60
FREEDOM, 17
GUILT, 5
LOVE, 68
OLD AGE, 22
RELIGION, 31
SERVICE, 2
VIRTUE, 11
WAR AND PEACE, 8

Herbert, Henry
WRITERS, 57

Herford, Oliver
AMBITION, 9

Herodotus
WORLD-WEARINESS, 3

Herrick, Robert
BUSINESS, 13
CLOTHES, 7, 8
MARRIAGE, 71
PRESENT, 6
TRANSIENCE, 14
TYRANNY, 2

Hesse, Hermann
HATE, 5
LIFE AND DEATH, 7
WISDOM, 17

Hewart, Gordon
JUSTICE, 10

Hewitt, James
ADVICE, 10

Heywood, Thomas
BOOK, SONG, AND PLAY TITLES, 11
POVERTY, 16

Hicks, Bill
LIFE, 28

Hicks, Seymour
AGE, 32

Hickson, William Edward
PERSISTENCE, 5

Higley, Brewster
HOMESICKNESS, 4

Hill, Aaron
DECISION, 1

Hill, Geoffrey
CHRISTMAS, 13

Hill, Rowland
MUSIC, 23

Hillary, Edmund
CIVILIZATION, 7
PHOTOGRAPHY, 5

Hillingdon, Lady Alice
MISQUOTATIONS, 20

Hilton, James
DEATH, 61

Hippocrates
HEALTH AND HEALTHY LIVING, 8
MORTALITY, 12
PATIENTS, 1
REMEDIES, 10

Hirst, Damien
ART, 10

Hitchcock, Alfred
ACTORS, 5, 16
MURDER, 7

Hitler, Adolf
DESTINY, 12
GERMANY, 4
LYING, 8
PARIS, 3
POLITICS, 36
PROPAGANDA, 2
PUBLIC, 14
RACISM, 13
WAR, 47
WORLD WAR II, 21

Hobbes, Thomas
CATHOLICISM, 5

GOVERNMENT, 12
HUMAN CONDITION, 10, 11
LAST WORDS, 38
OPINIONS, 2
STATE, 1
TRUTH, 29

Hobhouse, John Cam
OPPOSITION, 3

Hobson, Harold
AMERICA, 17

Hockney, David
ART, 11

Hodgins, Eric
MEDICINE, 3

Hodgkin, Dorothy Crowfoot
PRACTICALITY, 4

Hodgson, Ralph
ANIMALS, 12

Hoff, Marcian
COMPUTERS, 4

Hoffer, Eric
IMITATION, 3
YOUTH, 9

Hoffman, Heinrich
CHILDREN, 24, 25
FOOD, 27
PUNISHMENT, 12

Hoffmann, Ernst
SLEEP, 10

Hoffmann, Max
OFFICERS, 8

Hofmann, Hans
SIMPLICITY, 2

Hogg, James
LOVE, 69

Hokusai
LAST WORDS, 39

Holberg, Ludwig
INSULTS, 19

Holland, Henry Scott
AFTERLIFE, 5

Holloway, David
CHILDREN, 26

Holmes, John Haynes
UNIVERSE, 9

Holmes, Oliver Wendell
EXPERIENCE, 15
GREATNESS, 8
KNOWLEDGE, 19
MIND, 10
ORIGINALITY, 3
REVENGE, 10
SEXES, 11
WISDOM, 18

Holmes Jnr, Oliver Wendell
IDEAS, 3
LUST, 4
WAR, 48

Holroyd, Michael
WRITERS, 58

Holst, Gustav
MUSIC, 24

Honegger, Arthur
MUSICIANS, 3

Hood, Thomas
CRITICS, 8
EUROPE, 8
EVIL, 10
ILLNESS, 7
INNOCENCE, 6
MONTHS, 10
NOSTALGIA, 9
NOVELTY, 3
POVERTY, 17
PUNS, 5, 6, 7, 8, 9
RELIGION, 32
WOMEN, 40

Hooker, Richard
CHANGE, 11

Hoover, Herbert Clark
AMERICA, 18
WAR, 49

Hope, Anthony
CLASS, 16
COMMUNICATION, 2
FAMILY, 16
FUTILITY, 7
HUMOUR, 15
IGNORANCE, 8
SEXES, 12
TEMPTATION, 7
THRIFT, 8

Hope, Laurence
HUMILITY, 5
LOVE, 70

Hopkins, Anthony
AMERICA, 19

Hopkins, Gerard Manley
BEAUTY, 20
DESPAIR, 4
GOD, 25
SOUL, 7
STARS, 3

Hopkins, Harry
POLITICIANS, 55

Hopper, Hedda
ACTORS, 6

Horace
AGE, 33
ARGUMENTS, 7
BREVITY, 2
CHARACTER, 12
CLASSICS, 4
DESTINY, 13
DISAPPOINTMENT, 3
DISCONTENT, 4
EDUCATION, 22
EQUALITY, 28
EXPERTS, 4
FOOLISHNESS, 14
FREEDOM, 18, 19
HAPPINESS, 8, 9
HUMAN NATURE, 12
IMPERFECTION, 9
INJUSTICE, 7
INSPIRATION, 4
JUDGMENT, 9
KILLING, 3
MEMORIALS, 5
MISTRUST, 5
MONEY, 25
MORTALITY, 13
NEIGHBOURS, 4
OBLIVION, 1
PATRIOTISM, 15
PLAYS, 5
POETS, 8
POVERTY, 18
PRESENT, 7, 8, 9, 10
PRIDE, 5
PUBLISHING, 7
SELF-CONTROL, 4
SEX, 25
STATISTICS, 3
TRANSIENCE, 15
TRAVEL, 12
VICTORY, 6
WATER, 6
WORDS, 10
WRITING, 11

Horne, Richard Henry
BEGINNING, 10

Horsley, Bishop Samuel
LAW, 17

Hourmann, Georges
AGRICULTURE, 3

Household, Geoffrey
CATS, 3
TRUTH, 30

Housman, A. E.
AGRICULTURE, 4
ALCOHOL, 31
COUNTRYSIDE, 6
DAY, 9
ENDING, 4
EXECUTION, 11
FOOTBALL, 4
LOVE, 71
MILTON, 1
NOSTALGIA, 10, 11
POETRY, 20
SORROW, 10
TREES, 4, 5
UNDERSTANDING, 7
WAR, 50

Howatch, Susan
SCIENTISTS, 4

Howe, Geoffrey
WALES, 1

Howe, Julia Ward
GOD, 26

Howitt, Mary
INVITATIONS, 1

Hoyle, Edmond
SPORT AND GAMES, 9

Hoyle, Fred
SPACE, 5

Hubbard, Elbert
HABIT, 5
LIFE, 29
TECHNOLOGY, 5
TRIVIALITY, 10

Hubbard, Frank (Kin)
DISEASE, 22

Huchard, Henri
DISEASE, 23

Hughes, Richard
TALENT, 3

Hughes, Ted
MEN, 7
TECHNOLOGY, 6
WAR AND PEACE, 9

Hughes, Thomas
CRICKET, 4
LIFE, 30

Hughes, William Morris
BETRAYAL, 4

Hugo, Victor
BOREDOM, 4
BREVITY, 3
IDEAS, 2
ILLNESS, 8
POPULARITY, 4
SUFFERING, 8
TELEGRAMS, 8

Hume, David
BEAUTY, 21
CHRISTIANITY, 29
CUSTOM, 2
EMOTION, 3
PHILOSOPHERS, 4
PHILOSOPHY, 3
SELF, 8
UNITY, 11

Hungerford, Margaret Wolfe
BEAUTY, 22

Hunt, George William
PATRIOTISM, 16

Hunt, Jonathan
INSULTS, 20

Hunt, Leigh
DREAMS, 12
KISSING, 2
SUPERIORITY, 5

Hupfeld, Herman
TIME, 20

Hurst, Gerald
BORROWING, 4

Huss, John
SIMPLICITY, 3

Hussein, Saddam
MIDDLE EAST, 8, 9

Hutcheson, Francis
HAPPINESS, 10

Hutchison, Robert
HEALTH AND HEALTHY LIVING, 9, 10

Huxley, Aldous
ABSTINENCE, 6
ARGUMENTS, 8
CHRISTIANITY, 30
CONSTANCY, 2
DEATH, 62
DIPLOMACY, 12
DRUGS, 8
EDUCATION, 23
EQUALITY, 10
FACTS, 2
FANATICISM, 1
FASHION, 4
GERMANY, 5
HAPPINESS, 11
HUMAN NATURE, 13
INSIGNIFICANCE, 2
KNOWLEDGE, 20
LITERATURE, 6
MORALITY, 7
MURDER, 8
MUSIC, 25
PROMISCUITY, 2
SCIENCE, 19
SELF-CONFIDENCE, 1
SEX, 26, 27, 28
SILENCE, 8
SINCERITY, 4

SYMPATHY, 3, 4
TALENT, 4
THEATRE, 10
THINKING, 5
UNDERSTANDING, 8
VULGARITY, 2
WORDS, 11
WRITERS, 59
WRITING, 12

Huxley, Julian
GOD, 27
MONEY, 26

Huxley, T. H.
CLASSIFICATION, 1
EDUCATION, 24
EVOLUTION, 10
GOD, 28
KNOWLEDGE, 21
LOGIC, 3
NOVELTY, 4
PHILOSOPHERS, 5
SCEPTICISM, 2
SCIENCE, 20, 21

Hypatia
INFLUENCE, 3

I

Ibarruri, Dolores
COURAGE, 15
SELF-RESPECT, 1

Ibsen, Henrik
DELUSION, 4
DREAMS, 9
FOOLISHNESS, 15
FREEDOM, 20
LAST WORDS, 40
MAJORITY, 3, 4
MINORITY, 2
RETURN, 2
SINCERITY, 5
YOUTH, 10

Icke, David
CONSERVATION, 5

Ickes, Harold L.
NEPOTISM, 1
STUPIDITY, 4

Ignatius Loyola, St
SELFLESSNESS, 2

Illich, Ivan
EDUCATION, 25
EQUALITY, 11
MATERIALISM, 9, 10
REALISM, 3

Inge, Dean
ARGUMENTS, 9
BOREDOM, 5
CONTRACEPTION, 4
DEMOCRACY, 7
HISTORY, 17
INFLUENCE, 4
LITERATURE, 7
NATIONS, 2
OPPRESSION, 4
POWER POLITICS, 4
RELIGION, 33, 34
WAR AND PEACE, 10

Ingersoll, Robert G.
GOD, 29
NATURE, 11
RELIGION, 35
SCIENCE, 22

Ingham, Bernard
JOURNALISM, 18

Ingram, Jonas
VICTORY, 7

Ingrams, Richard
JUSTICE, 11
PUBLISHING, 8

Innes, Hammond
TREES, 6

Ionesco, Eugène
DELUSION, 5

Iphicrates
ANCESTRY, 3

Irving, Washington
AGE, 34
CHANGE, 12
CHARACTER, 13
MATERIALISM, 11

Isherwood, Christopher
OBJECTIVITY, 4
PRESENT, 11

Izetbegovic, Alija
BOSNIA AND HERCEGOVINA, 3

J

Jackson, Andrew
WAR, 51

Jackson, F. J. Foakes
ACADEMICS, 3

Jackson, Jesse
EQUALITY, 12

Jacobi, Karl Gustav Jacob
MISTAKES, 9

Jacobs, Joe
INJUSTICE, 8

James I
DRUNKENNESS, 14
MONARCHY, 13
POETS, 42
SMOKING, 7
WOMAN'S ROLE, 3

James, Alice
CONTENTMENT, 4
DOCTORS, 4
OLD AGE, 23

James, Clive
FOOD, 28
POWER, 13

James, Henry
CHARACTER, 14
EXPERIENCE, 16
GENEROSITY, 4
HISTORY, 18
KILLING, 4
LAST WORDS, 41
LIFE, 31
LITERATURE, 8
MODESTY, 1
NOVELS, 7
OPINIONS, 3
SEASONS, 8
WRITERS, 60

James, William
DEATH, 63
DRUNKENNESS, 13
INTELLECT, 4
SUCCESS, 9

Jarrell, Randall
ADAPTABILITY, 3
CHILDREN, 27
MANNERS, 3

Jarry, Alfred
CHIVALRY, 5

Jay, Peter
LEADERSHIP, 5

Jean
TRAINS, 3

Jeans, James
SCIENCE, 23, 24
UNIVERSE, 10

Jefferson, Thomas
FREEDOM, 21
HUMAN RIGHTS, 3
INDEPENDENCE, 2
POLITICS, 37
REBELLION, 5
SLAVERY, 5

Jellicoe, Lord
WAR, 52

Jennings, Elizabeth
CRITICS, 9
DEATH, 64

Jennings, Paul
HUMOUR, 39
MUSICIANS, 4

Jerome, Jerome K.
COMPLAINTS, 3
CONCEIT, 12
FAMILY, 17
HYPOCHONDRIA, 1
IDLENESS, 5, 6
LOVE, 72
POVERTY, 19

Jerrold, Douglas William
BORES, 3
FRANCE, 8
LOVE, 73
OCCUPATIONS, 8
PRACTICALITY, 5
PRAYER, 13
SPORT AND GAMES, 10
VULGARITY, 3

Jewel, John
CLERGY, 9

Joad, Cyril
ECOLOGY, 4
KNOWLEDGE, 22
SELF, 9

John III Sobieski
VICTORY, 16

John XXIII, Pope
DEATH, 67

John of the Cross, St
DEATH, 65
SOUL, 8

John Paul II
CHILDREN, 28
NUCLEAR WEAPONS, 7
SEXES, 13
SPORT AND GAMES, 11
WAR, 85

Johnson, Amy
FLYING, 1

Johnson, Hiram Warren
WAR, 53

Johnson, Ladybird
DISILLUSION, 3

Johnson, Lyndon B.
AMBITION, 10
DEMOCRACY, 8
MISQUOTATIONS, 21
POLITICS, 38
PRUDENCE, 7
STUPIDITY, 5

Johnson, Paul
JEWS, 7

Johnson, Samuel
ALCOHOL, 32, 33, 34
AMERICANS, 5
ARGUMENTS, 10
BED, 4
BOATS, 9
BRITAIN, 10
CATHOLICISM, 6
CATS, 4
CHARACTER, 15, 16
CLERGY, 10
CLOTHES, 9
COMPLAINTS, 4
CONVERSATION, 4, 5
CRITICISM, 18, 19, 20, 21, 22, 23, 24, 25
CRITICS, 10, 11
DEATH, 66
DECEPTION, 3
DETERMINATION, 9
DISILLUSION, 4
DOCTORS, 5
DRUNKENNESS, 15
EDUCATION, 26, 27
ENGLISH, 20
ENTHUSIASM, 5
EPITAPHS, 3, 14
EQUALITY, 13, 14
EXECUTION, 12
EXPECTATION, 2
FAME, 12
FISHING, 1
FLATTERY, 5
FOOD, 29, 30, 31
FRANCE, 9
FRANKNESS, 2
FREEDOM, 22
FRIENDS, 9
FRIENDSHIP, 19, 20
GENIUS, 7
GOVERNMENT, 13
GRATITUDE, 1, 2
HAPPINESS, 12
HISTORIANS, 3
HUMOUR, 16
HUNTING, 5
HURT, 2
IDLENESS, 7
IGNORANCE, 9
ILLNESS, 9
IMAGINATION, 6
INSINCERITY, 2
INSULTS, 21
INTEGRITY, 4
IRELAND, 8
IRISH, 7
JUSTICE, 12, 13
KNOWLEDGE, 23, 24, 25, 26
LANGUAGE, 14, 15, 16
LAWYERS, 7
LEXICOGRAPHY, 4, 5, 6
LITERATURE, 9
LONDON, 9, 10
LOVE, 74
LUST, 3
MARRIAGE, 72, 73
MERIT, 4

MILTON, 2
MISFORTUNE, 11
MISTRUST, 6
MONEY, 28
MUSIC, 26
NONSENSE, 13
NUMBERS, 1
OLD AGE, 24
PATRIOTISM, 17
PATRONAGE, 1, 2
PERSISTENCE, 6
PETULANCE, 4
PHILOSOPHY, 4, 5, 6
PLACES, 7
PLEASURE, 14, 15, 16
POETRY, 21
POETS, 9, 43, 44
POLITICIANS, 56
POLITICS, 39, 40, 41
POVERTY, 20
PROMISCUITY, 3
PUBLIC HOUSES, 1, 2
PUBLISHING, 9
QUOTATIONS, 4, 5
READING, 7, 8
REASON, 3
SCEPTICISM, 3
SCOTLAND, 3, 4, 5
SCOTS, 3, 4, 5, 6
SEA, 6
SELF, 10
SELF-PRESERVATION, 6
SHAKESPEARE, 9
SPORT AND GAMES, 12
STUPIDITY, 6
SUITABILITY, 2
SUPERNATURAL, 9
TASTE, 4
TAXATION, 6
TRAVEL, 13
TRUST, 3
TYRANNY, 3
WEALTH, 17
WEATHER, 15
WOMAN'S ROLE, 4
WOMEN, 41
WORDS, 12
WRITERS, 11, 61
WRITING, 13, 14, 15, 16

Joliot-Curie, Iréne
WORK, 10

Jolson, Al
PROPHECY, 6

Jones, Beverly
MOTHERHOOD, 11

Jones, John Paul
DETERMINATION, 10

Jones, Stephen
FASHION, 5

Jonson, Ben
CLASSICS, 5
COMPLIMENTS, 2
DREAMS, 10
HORSES, 7
INSULTS, 22
LOVE, 75, 76
LUCK, 8
MATERIALISM, 12
SHAKESPEARE, 10, 11
SMOKING, 8, 9
SPEECH, 11

Joseph II
FAILURE, 4

Joseph, Keith
BRITAIN, 11

Joseph, Michael
WRITERS, 12

Jowett, Benjamin
ATHEISM, 7
EPITAPHS, 4
FAITH, 12
RESEARCH, 2
SELFLESSNESS, 1
WRITERS, 13
YOUTH, 11

Joyce, James
FRIENDSHIP, 21
HISTORY, 19
HUMOUR, 40, 41
INFLUENCE, 5
IRELAND, 9, 10
NONSENSE, 14
PAINTING, 5
SEA, 7

Juang-zu
DEATH, 68

Jugo, Miguel de Unamuno y
DEATH, 69
GLORY, 2
PERSUASION, 1
SCIENCE, 43
TRANSLATION, 4

Julia
EXTRAVAGANCE, 3
SUITABILITY, 3

Jung, Carl Gustav
ADDICTION, 2
EXISTENCE, 3
HUMAN NATURE, 14
INFERIORITY, 2
MADNESS, 6
MEANING, 5
MIND, 3
PASSION, 2
PURPOSE, 4
RELIGION, 36
SENTIMENTALITY, 2

Jung Chang
CHINA, 3, 4

Junius
FREEDOM, 23
PERSUASION, 2

Justinian I
JUSTICE, 14

Juvenal
AUTHORITARIANISM, 4
CHILDREN, 29
DEBAUCHERY, 6
HEALTH AND HEALTHY LIVING, 11
MISTRUST, 7
POVERTY, 21, 22
PUBLIC, 15
REVENGE, 11
SATIRE, 1
THEFT, 6
WOMEN, 42
WRITING, 17

K

Kafka, Franz
DESPAIR, 5
FREEDOM, 24
JUDGMENT, 10

Kant, Immanuel
HAPPINESS, 13
HUMAN NATURE, 15
MORALITY, 8
WONDER, 3

Karr, Alphonse
CONSTANCY, 3
EXECUTION, 13

Kauffmann, Max
SLEEP, 11

Kaufman, George S.
EPITAPHS, 15

Kavanagh, Ted
MARRIAGE, 74

Kearney, Denis
WORK, 11

Keats, John
ADMIRATION, 5
AFTERLIFE, 6
ALCOHOL, 35, 36, 37
APPEARANCE, 17
ARGUMENTS, 11
ARTS, 5
BEAUTY, 23, 24
BEGINNING, 11
BIRDS, 5
DEATH, 70, 71
DEPARTURE, 7
DISCONTENT, 5
DISCOVERY, 5
DOUBT, 6
EPITAPHS, 16
ETERNITY, 3
EXPERIENCE, 17
FANATICISM, 2
FLOWERS, 5
HUMAN CONDITION, 12
HUMAN NATURE, 16, 17
ILLNESS, 10
IMAGINATION, 7
LOVE, 77, 78
LOVE AND DEATH, 3
MELANCHOLY, 6, 7, 8
MUSIC, 27
OBLIVION, 2
OPPOSITES, 3
PASSION, 3
PHILOSOPHY, 7, 8
PLEASURE, 17
POETRY, 22, 23, 24, 25
POSTERITY, 5
PRAYER, 14
PUBLIC HOUSES, 3
PURPOSE, 5
SEA, 8
SEASONS, 9, 10, 11, 12
SENSATION, 1
SILENCE, 9
SLEEP, 12, 13
SOUL, 9
STARS, 4
SUFFERING, 9
SUPERNATURAL, 10
TIME, 21
TRAVEL, 14
TREES, 7
TRUTH, 31, 32, 33

Keble, John
SIMPLICITY, 4

Keenan, Brian
HOSTAGES, 2

Keith, Penelope
SHYNESS, 4

Keller, Helen
BLINDNESS, 2
CAPITALISM, 5
ENDURANCE, 7

Kelman, James
FREEDOM, 25

Kelvin, Lord
SPORT AND GAMES, 13

Kemble, Charles
TAXATION, 7

Kemble, Fanny
TRAINS, 4

Kemble, John Philip
AUDIENCES, 2

Kempis, Thomas à
GLORY, 3
GOD, 30
GOOD, 6
OBEDIENCE, 3
TOLERANCE, 4

Ken, Thomas
DEATH, 72
PRESENT, 12

Kendall, Captain
TECHNOLOGY, 7
TELEGRAMS, 9

Keneally, Thomas
ENGLAND, 21

Kennedy, Anthony
CLERGY, 11

Kennedy, Florynce R.
ABORTION, 1

Kennedy, John Fitzgerald
AMERICA, 20
ART, 12
BEGINNING, 12
DIFFERENCE, 8
GERMANY, 6
HUNGER, 7
MERIT, 5
MODESTY, 2
NEPOTISM, 2
PATRIOTISM, 18
PEACE, 10
POETRY, 26
POLITICIANS, 57
POPULARITY, 5
SUCCESS, 10
TALENT, 5
TIME, 22

Kennedy, Joseph
SPECULATION, 3

Kennedy, Robert
OPPOSITION, 4

Kent, Bruce
NUCLEAR WEAPONS, 8

Kerouac, Jack
CONFUSION, 7
CONSERVATISM, 3
POVERTY, 23

Kerr, Clark
EDUCATION, 28

Kerr, Jean
ALCOHOL, 38
CHILDREN, 30
FLYING, 2
HYPOCRISY, 10
MEDICINE, 4
MONEY, 29

Key, Ellen
CHILDREN, 31
EDUCATION, 29

FEMINISM, 11
LOVE AND MARRIAGE, 3
PUNISHMENT, 13
WAR, 54, 55

Key, Francis Scott
AMERICA, 21

Keynes, John Maynard
AMERICANS, 6
CONSERVATISM, 4
DEATH, 73
ECONOMICS, 11
INFLUENCE, 6
MARXISM, 2
NUMBERS, 2
ORTHODOXY, 3
POLITICIANS, 58
TAXATION, 8
TYRANNY, 4

Khomeini, Ayatollah Ruholla
RELIGION, 37

Khrushchev, Nikita
BUSINESS, 14
COMMUNISM, 3
ECONOMICS, 12
POLITICIANS, 14
PROMISES, 4
REVENGE, 12
THREATS, 2
VICTORY, 8

Kierkegaard, Søren
DEATH, 74
ENDURANCE, 8

Kilmer, Alfred Joyce
TREES, 8, 9

Kilvert, Francis
BRITISH, 7
SOLITUDE, 9

King, Benjamin Franklin
PESSIMISM, 7

King, Martin Luther
EQUALITY, 15
EVIL, 11
IDEALISM, 1
RACISM, 14
REBELLION, 6
SCIENCE, 25
WAR, 56

Kingsley, Charles
AGRICULTURE, 5
BIBLE, 6
CHIVALRY, 6
CHOICE, 3
DROWNING, 1
OCCUPATIONS, 9
POETS, 45
SEXES, 14
VIRTUE, 12, 13
YOUTH, 12

Kingsmill, Hugh
SELF-INTEREST, 5

Kinnock, Neil
CAPITALISM, 6
FOOLISHNESS, 16
INCOMPETENCE, 2
INSULTS, 23, 24
PATRIOTISM, 19, 20
POLITICIANS, 15
POLITICS, 42, 43
ROYALTY, 20
SOCIALISM, 8, 9
TRAVEL, 15

Kipling, Rudyard
APPEARANCES, 16
ART, 13
BOASTS, 4
BOOK, SONG, AND PLAY TITLES, 12
CLOTHES, 10
DEBAUCHERY, 7
DESIRE, 9
DISCONTENT, 6
ENGLAND, 22
EXECUTION, 14
GARDENS, 8
GOOD, 7
IDEALISM, 2
KISSING, 3
MADNESS, 7
NATIONALITY, 6
OBITUARIES, 2
OPPOSITES, 4
PLACES, 8, 9
RACISM, 15, 16
RESPONSIBILITY, 9
SEASONS, 13
SELF-CONTROL, 5
SEXES, 15
SOLDIERS, 1, 2
SUPERIORITY, 6
TIME, 23
WOMEN, 43, 44
WORDS, 13
WORLD WAR I, 13

Kissinger, Henry
ENEMIES, 4
LOYALTY, 7
POWER, 14
WAR, 57

Kitchener, Lord
ROYALTY, 21

Klinger, Friedrich Maximilian von
LITERATURE, 10

Knapp, Jimmy
STRIKES, 3

Knox, John
FEMINISM, 35
GOD, 31
WOMEN, 45

Knox, Philander Chase
LAW, 18

Knox, Ronald
BABIES, 5
DEVIL, 8
EXISTENCE, 4
LANGUAGE, 17
LIMERICKS, 7

Knox, Vicesimus
FEMINISM, 12

Koestler, Arthur
COURAGE, 16
HALF MEASURES, 1
NUCLEAR WEAPONS, 9
POSTERITY, 6
SENTIMENTALITY, 3
WAR, 58

Kohl, Helmut
GERMANY, 7

Kollwitz, Käthe
ACHIEVEMENT, 6

Koran
RELIGION, 38

Korda, Alexander
EUROPE, 11
TALENT, 6

Kostalenetz, André
MUSICIANS, 5

Kramer, Larry
AIDS, 6
DISEASE, 24

Kristofferson, Kris
FREEDOM, 26

Kronenberger, Louis
VULGARITY, 4

Kubrick, Stanley
CINEMA, 8
DIPLOMACY, 13

Kuhn, Maggie
MEDICINE, 5

Kyi, Aung San Suu
DEMOCRACY, 20

L

Laclos, Pierre Choderlos de
SEX, 14
WOMEN, 23

Lai, Chou En
DIPLOMACY, 14

Laing, R. D.
BOOKS, 21
MADNESS, 8
NUCLEAR WEAPONS, 10
PSYCHIATRY, 5, 6
VIOLENCE, 6

Lait, Jacqui
FEMINISM, 13

Lamb, A. J.
IMPRISONMENT, 3

Lamb, Lady Caroline
POETS, 46

Lamb, Charles
BORROWING, 5, 6
CHILDREN, 32
FAMILY, 18
FOOD, 32
GARDENS, 9
GOOD, 8
HUNGER, 9
ILLNESS, 11
INNOCENCE, 7
JOURNALISM, 19
MARRIAGE, 75
MOUNTAINS, 2
NOSTALGIA, 12
POETS, 47, 48
POSTERITY, 7
PUNS, 10
PURPOSE, 6
READING, 9
SCIENCE, 26
SCOTS, 7
SMOKING, 10, 11
SPORT AND GAMES, 14

Lamb, Mary
CHILDREN, 33

Lamont, Norman
ECONOMICS, 13
GOVERNMENT, 14
UNEMPLOYMENT, 1

Lampton, William James
MARRIAGE, 76

Lancaster, Osbert
ARCHITECTURE, 5
HOUSES, 2

Lanchester, Elsa
ACTORS, 17

Landers, Ann
OPPORTUNITY, 12

Landon, Letitia
POVERTY, 24
REGRET, 6, 7

Landor, Walter Savage
FLOWERS, 6
GOOD, 9
LIFE AND DEATH, 9
LUST, 5
PERSPECTIVE, 3
POETRY AND PROSE, 3
POLITICS, 44
WRITING, 18

Landseer, Edwin
PAINTING, 6

Lane, Lord
MARRIAGE, 77

Lang, Andrew
STATISTICS, 4

Lang, Julia S.
BEGINNING, 13

Langbridge, Frederick
OPTIMISM, 21

Langland, William
GOOD, 10
SEASONS, 14

Laplace, Marquis de
GOD, 33

Lardner Jnr, Ring
ALCOHOL, 39
CLOTHES, 11
CONTEMPT, 3

Larkin, Philip
BOOKS, 22
FAMILY, 19
MONEY, 30
NOVELS, 8
OLD AGE, 25
SEX, 29

Laski, H. J.
HUMILITY, 6

Latimer, Hugh
EXECUTION, 15
PERSISTENCE, 7

Lauder, Harry
BED, 5
LOVE, 79
PERSISTENCE, 8
SCOTLAND, 6

Laurence, William L.
NUCLEAR WEAPONS, 11

Law, Bonar
GREATNESS, 9
POLITICIANS, 59, 60
WAR, 59

Lawrence, D. H.
ANIMALISM, 3, 4
APPEARANCE, 18

BOOKS, 23
CATHOLICISM, 7
CLASS, 17
CLASSIFICATION, 2
CRITICISM, 27
DEATH, 75, 76
DEVIL, 9
ENGLAND, 23, 24
ENGLISH, 21
HUMAN NATURE, 18
IDEALISM, 3
ILLNESS, 12
JEWS, 8
LOVE, 80, 81
MASCULINITY, 2
MEN, 8, 9
MORALITY, 9
NOVELS, 9
PARTING, 7
PHOTOGRAPHY, 6
PLACES, 10
PORNOGRAPHY, 3
PUNISHMENT, 14
PURITANISM, 2
REGRET, 8
RUSSIA, 4, 5
SCIENCE, 27
SEX, 30
SHAKESPEARE, 12
SIN, 15
SPONTANEITY, 3
WAR, 60
WEATHER, 16
WORLD WAR I, 14
WRITERS, 62
WRITING, 19

Lawrence, James
LAST WORDS, 42

Lawrence, T. E.
DREAMS, 11
LIFE AND DEATH, 10
READING, 10
REALITY, 5

Lawson, Nigel
BRITISH, 8

Lazarus, Emma
AMERICA, 22

Leach, Edmund
FAMILY, 20

Leach, Penelope
CHILDREN, 34

Leacock, Stephen
ALCOHOL, 40
ASTRONOMY, 4
CLASSICS, 6
DEATH, 77
EDUCATION, 30
FOOD, 33
GOLF, 2
HORSES, 8
HUMOUR, 42
IMMORTALITY, 4
INFLUENCE, 7
LONGEVITY, 2
LUCK, 9
NEGLECT, 2
NONSENSE, 15
OLD AGE, 26

Lear, Edward
APPEARANCE, 19
FOOD, 34
LIMERICKS, 9
NONSENSE, 16, 17, 18, 19, 20, 21

Leary, Timothy
DEATH, 78

Leavis, F. R.
CRITICISM, 28
POETS, 49

Leavis, Q. D.
WRITERS, 63

Lebowitz, Fran
BOOKS, 24
FOOD, 35

Leboyer, Frédérick
BIRTH, 7
SEX, 31

Ledru-Rollin, Alexandre Auguste
LEADERSHIP, 6

Lee, Harper
ANCESTRY, 4
BOOK, SONG, AND PLAY TITLES, 13

Lee, Laurie
POVERTY, 25

Lee, Robert E.
ABSTINENCE, 7
EXPLOITATION, 3
WAR, 61

Lefèvre, Théo
EUROPE, 12

Lehman, Ernest
SUCCESS, 12

Lehmann, Rosamond
OPPORTUNITY, 13

Lehrer, Tom
AGE, 35
LIFE, 32

Lei Feng
CHINA, 5

Leigh, Fred W.
MARRIAGE, 78

Leigh, Hunt
THEFT, 7

Le Mesurier, John
LAST WORDS, 43

Lenclos, Ninon de
OLD AGE, 27

Lenin
CAPITALISM, 7
CLASS, 18
COMMUNISM, 4
FREEDOM, 27
GOVERNMENT, 15
LIBERALISM, 2
MUSIC, 28
POLITICS, 45
PROGRESS, 8
SOCIALISM, 10
STATE, 2
WRITERS, 64

Lennon, John
BOOK, SONG, AND PLAY TITLES, 14
DEPARTURE, 8
FRIENDS, 10
FUTILITY, 8
IMAGINATION, 8
IMPROVEMENT, 2
LIFE, 33
LONELINESS, 4
LOVE, 82, 83
MONEY, 31
POP MUSIC, 14

POPULARITY, 6
WORK, 12

Lenthall, William
HOUSES OF PARLIAMENT, 11

Léon, Luis Ponce de
INTERRUPTIONS, 2

Leonard, Hugh
IRELAND, 11

Leonardo da Vinci
RESEARCH, 1

Leonidas
EPITAPHS, 18

Leopold II
MONARCHY, 14

Leo X
CATHOLICISM, 8

Lerner, Alan Jay
CHARM, 3
CLASS, 19
DESIRE, 10
FAMILIARITY, 3
MARRIAGE, 79
MEN, 10
MISOGYNY, 3

Lerner, Max
DRUGS, 9

Lesage, Alain-René
ENEMIES, 5
JUSTICE, 15

Lessing, Doris
ARTISTS, 16
CATS, 5
LAW, 19
LEARNING, 6
RACISM, 17, 18

Lessing, Gotthold Ephraim
REASON, 4

L'Estrange, Roger
PASSION, 4
SERIOUSNESS, 2

Lethaby, W. R.
ART, 14

Levant, Oscar
APPEARANCES, 17
INSULTS, 25

Leverhulme, Viscount
ADVERTISING, 4

Leverson, Ada Beddington
INFERIORITY, 3
INSULTS, 26
PUNS, 11
WRITERS, 65

Levin, Bernard
ARCHITECTURE, 6
BRITAIN, 12
ECONOMICS, 14

Lévis, Duc de
NOBILITY, 2

Lévi-Strauss, Claude
MANKIND, 16

Lewes, G. H.
MURDER, 9

Lewis, C. Day
DECLINE, 3

TRANSIENCE, 10

Lewis, C. S.
CHARITY, 15
CHRISTIANITY, 31
DESIRE, 11
FRIENDSHIP, 22
HUMOUR, 18
TIME, 24

Lewis, George Cornewall
PLEASURE, 18

Lewis, John Llewellyn
CLASS, 20

Lewis, Sinclair
AMERICA, 23
APPEARANCE, 20
HOME, 5
LITERATURE, 11
UNDERSTANDING, 9

Lewis, Wyndham
ANIMALISM, 5
EXPLANATIONS, 1
HOMOSEXUALITY, 5
MARTYRDOM, 2
PERSISTENCE, 9

Ley, Robert
NAZISM, 3

Leybourne, George
SPORT AND GAMES, 15

Liberace
CRITICISM, 29

Lichtenberg, Georg Christoph
BOOKS, 25
HEAVEN, 5
INSENSITIVITY, 3

Lie, Trygve
COLD WAR, 5

Liebermann, Max
BOASTS, 5

Lillie, Beatrice
ACCIDENTS, 4
BIRTH, 8

Lillo, George
MUSIC, 29

Lin, Maya
ARCHITECTURE, 7

Lincoln, Abraham
ANCESTRY, 5
APPEARANCE, 21
CHANGE, 13
CONSERVATISM, 5
CRITICISM, 30
DECEPTION, 4
DEMOCRACY, 9, 10, 11, 12
FREEDOM, 28, 29
HOMOSEXUALITY, 6
INFLUENCE, 8
LIBERTY, 1
MEMORIALS, 6
OFFICERS, 9
REPUTATION, 4
SARCASM, 2

Lindsay, Vachel
FAITH, 13
PEACE, 11

Linklater, Eric
AMERICANS, 7
GOLF, 3
HATE, 6

STUPIDITY, 7

Linton, W. J.
CHIVALRY, 7

Lin Yutang
CHINA, 6

Li Peng
CHINA, 7

Lippman, Walter
STATE, 3

Lisle, Rouget de
FRANCE, 10

Littlejohn, Richard
ROYALTY, 22

Littlewood, Sidney
IRISH, 8

Livermore, Mary Ashton
FEMINISM, 14

Livingstone, Ken
MONEY, 32

Livy
DEFEAT, 4

Ljungqvist, Professor Arne
SPORT AND GAMES, 16

Llewellyn, Richard
BOOK, SONG, AND PLAY TITLES, 15

Lloyd, Harold
AGE, 36

Lloyd, Marie
INNUENDO, 2
PLEASURE, 19
TRAINS, 5

Lloyd, Robert
HASTE, 7

Lloyd George, David
ARISTOCRACY, 8, 9
CHANGE, 14
GOVERNMENT, 16
HOUSES OF PARLIAMENT, 12, 13
IMPRESSIONABILITY, 2
INSULTS, 27
MADNESS, 9
NONCOMMITMENT, 3
POLITICIANS, 16, 61, 62
STATISTICS, 5
WAR, 62
WORLD WAR I, 15
WORLD WAR II, 22

Locke, John
NOVELTY, 5
TRUTH, 34

Lockier, Francis
SCOTS, 8

Lodge, David
EDUCATION, 31, 32
LITERATURE, 12
NOVELTY, 6
POETS, 50
SEX, 32
TECHNOLOGY, 8
WEATHER, 17

Loesser, Frank
BOATS, 10

Logau, Friedrich von
GOD, 34

Logue, Christopher
CLASS, 21

Lombardi, Vince
VICTORY, 9

Lombroso, Cesare
IGNORANCE, 10

London, Jack
AMERICA, 24
ENGLAND, 25

Longfellow, Henry Wadsworth
AMBITION, 12, 13
BOATS, 11
CHANCE, 3
DEATH, 79
ENDURANCE, 9, 10
LIFE, 34
MORTALITY, 14
OCCUPATIONS, 10
PERFECTION, 4
RIGHTEOUSNESS, 7
SEA, 9
TIME, 25
TRANSIENCE, 16

Longford, Lord
JOURNALISM, 20
SEX, 33

Longworth, Alice Roosevelt
APPEARANCE, 22

Lonsdale, Kathleen
LOVE, 84

Loos, Anita
APPEARANCE, 23
FEMINISM, 15
MATERIALISM, 13
PRUDENCE, 9
WOMEN, 47

Lorenz, Konrad
THEORY, 6

Louis XIV
FIRST IMPRESSIONS, 5
INJUSTICE, 9
LAST WORDS, 44
MONARCHY, 15
ROYALTY, 23

Louis XVIII
PROMPTNESS, 2

Louis, Joe
ESCAPE, 2

Louis Philippe
DIPLOMACY, 15

Lovelace, Richard
IMPRISONMENT, 4

Lovell, Bernard
KNOWLEDGE, 27

Lovell, Maria
LOVE, 85

Lover, Samuel
WRITING, 20

Low, David
ART, 15

Lowe, Robert
TAXATION, 9

Lowell, Robert
MEMORIALS, 7
PESSIMISM, 8
RELIGION, 39
TIME, 26

Lowry, Malcolm
CHILDREN, 35
EPITAPHS, 19
LOVE AND DEATH, 4

Loyden, Eddie
HOMOSEXUALITY, 7

Lucan
FAMILY, 21

Lucretius
MORTALITY, 15
NOTHING, 1
PERSISTENCE, 10
TASTE, 5

Luther, Martin
PLEASURE, 20
RELIGION, 40
WORLD, 3

Lutyens, Edwin
FOOD, 36
INSULTS, 28

Lyte, Henry Francis
RELIGION, 41

Lyttelton, G. W.
WRITERS, 66

Lytton, Lady Constance
CHURCHILL, 6

M

Macarthur, Douglas
DETERMINATION, 11

Macaulay, Lord
BETRAYAL, 5
BIBLE, 7
CIVILIZATION, 8
COURAGE, 17
CRITICISM, 31
DIPLOMACY, 16
FREEDOM, 30
IMAGINATION, 9
INTELLECT, 5
JOURNALISM, 21
KNOWLEDGE, 28
MISTRUST, 8
MORALITY, 10
NAVY, 3
NEGLECT, 3
PAROCHIALISM, 2
POETRY, 27
POLITICS, 46
PRECOCITY, 2
PURITANISM, 3
WRITERS, 67
WRITING, 21

Macaulay, Rose
CLASSIFICATION, 3
CRITICISM, 32
FAMILY, 22
POETRY, 28
TRAVEL, 16

MacCarthy, Desmond
ARTS, 6
LITERATURE, 13
OSTENTATION, 4

McCarthy, Joseph R.
POLITICS, 54

McCarthy, Mary
AMERICA, 27
DECISION, 3
INSULTS, 31
MATERIALISM, 14
NOVELS, 11
NOVELTY, 7

McCartney, Paul
PEACE, 12

McCrae, John
MEMORIALS, 8

McCullers, Carson
BOOK, SONG, AND PLAY TITLES, 18

MacDiarmid, Hugh
KILLING, 5
LOVE AND DEATH, 5
WRITERS, 14

MacDonald, Betty
APPEARANCE, 24

MacDonald, Ramsey
DIPLOMACY, 17
IDEAS, 4

McGonagall, William
DEATH, 86
DISASTER, 4

McGough, Roger
GUILT, 6

McGregor, Peter
WORLD WAR I, 16

Mach, Ernst
RESEARCH, 3

Machiavelli
OBLIGATION, 2

MacInnes, Colin
ART, 16
ENGLISH, 22
RACISM, 19

McKellen, Ian
HOMOSEXUALITY, 8

Mackenzie, Compton
WOMEN, 48

Mackintosh, James
GOVERNMENT, 17

McLaren, Anne
SCIENCE, 28

MacLeish, Archibald
KNOWLEDGE, 29

Macleod, Fiona
LONELINESS, 5

Macleod, Iain
HISTORIANS, 4
OPPORTUNITY, 14

McLuhan, Marshall
CARS, 4
COMMUNICATION, 3
PSYCHIATRY, 8
TECHNOLOGY, 9, 10
TELEVISION AND RADIO, 5
WAR, 65

Macmillan, Harold
CHANGE, 15
ECONOMICS, 15
POLITICIANS, 17
POLITICS, 47, 48, 49
POWER, 15
WEALTH, 18

MacNally, Leonard
ADMIRATION, 7

MacNeice, Louis
FRIENDSHIP, 23
INDIFFERENCE, 4
LOVE, 86

Madariaga y Rogo, Salvador de
AMERICA, 25
POLITICS, 50

Madden, Samuel
WORDS, 14

Magee, William Connor
FREEDOM, 31

Magidson, Herb
MUSIC, 30

Mahbubani, Kishore
DEMOCRACY, 13

Mailer, Norman
AGE, 37
JOURNALISM, 22

Maistre, Joseph de
GOVERNMENT, 18
RUSSIA, 6

Major, John
IRELAND, 12
POLITICS, 51

Malamud, Bernard
DISAPPOINTMENT, 5

Malcolm X
RACISM, 20

Malesherbes, Chrétien
SAYINGS, 5

Malherbe, François de
TRANSIENCE, 17

Mallaby, George
EQUALITY, 16

Mallet, Robert
PESSIMISM, 9

Mallory, George
MOTIVE, 3

Malory, Thomas
ACHIEVEMENT, 7
LOSS, 3
NOSTALGIA, 13
SORROW, 11

Malthus, Thomas Robert
ECONOMICS, 16
SURVIVAL, 3

Mamet, David
THEATRE, 11

Mancroft, Lord
LAZINESS, 2

Mandela, Nelson
FREEDOM, 32
RACISM, 21, 22
SOUTH AFRICA, 8, 9, 10, 11

Mandelstam, Osip
DENIAL, 2
POSTERITY, 8

Manikan, Ruby
EDUCATION, 33

Mankiewicz, Herman J.
ARROGANCE, 5
DEATH, 80
DISEASE, 25
ETIQUETTE, 4
PUNS, 12

Mann, Thomas
MOURNING, 6
POLITICS, 52

Mansfield, Lord
JUDGMENT, 11

Mansfield, Katherine
NAKEDNESS, 5
REGRET, 9
TRAVEL, 17

Mao Tse-Tung
CHINA, 8
FREEDOM, 33
INJUSTICE, 10
NUCLEAR WEAPONS, 12
POLITICS, 53
POWER POLITICS, 5
READING, 11
WAR, 63, 64

Map, Walter
ALCOHOL, 41

Marconi, Marchese Guglielmo
TECHNOLOGY, 11

Marcos
OPPRESSION, 5

Marcuse, Herbert
CAPITALISM, 8

Marie-Antoinette
HUNGER, 10

Marks, Professor Vincent
FOOD, 38

Marlborough, Sarah, Duchess of
SEX, 34

Marlowe, Christopher
BEAUTY, 25, 26
DAMNATION, 3, 4
DANCING, 6
DEATH, 81
DOOMSDAY, 5
FIRST IMPRESSIONS, 6
FLOWERS, 7
IGNORANCE, 11
JUSTICE, 16
LOVE, 87
SEX, 35
WEALTH, 19

Marlowe, Derek
LIFE, 36

Marnoch, Commander Alex
POLICE, 2

Marquis, Don
IDEAS, 5

Marryat, Captain Frederick
ILLEGITIMACY, 1
INDEPENDENCE, 3
SIMILARITY, 5

Marsh, Edward Howard
CRITICS, 12

Martineau, Harriet
AMERICA, 26
ENGLAND, 26
FEMINISM, 16
LOVE AND MARRIAGE, 4
MARRIAGE, 80, 81, 82

Marvell, Andrew
AGE, 38
BIRDS, 6
DEATH, 82
DESTINY, 14
EXECUTION, 16
FLOWERS, 8
GARDENS, 10
LOVE, 88
OBLIVION, 3
POLITICIANS, 63
SHYNESS, 5
VICTORY, 10

Marx, Groucho
AGE, 39
APPEARANCE, 25
BEAUTY, 27
COMPLAINTS, 5
COMPLIMENTS, 3
CRITICISM, 33
DEATH, 83, 84
DISMISSAL, 5
FAMILY, 23
HONOUR, 3
HUMOUR, 43, 44, 45, 46, 47, 48
INSULTS, 29
INTRODUCTIONS, 2
LOVE, 89
MEMORY, 9
MONEY, 33, 34
NAMES, 5
POVERTY, 26
PUNS, 13
SEX, 36
SIMPLICITY, 5
STUPIDITY, 8
SUPERIORITY, 7
TIME, 27

Marx, Karl
CAPITALISM, 9
CLASS, 22
HISTORY, 20
MARXISM, 3, 4, 5
RELIGION, 42

Mary I
DEFEAT, 5

Maschwitz, Eric
BIRDS, 7

Masefield, John
ANIMALS, 13
BOATS, 12, 13
NASTINESS, 5
SEA, 10

Masor, Nathan
ALCOHOL, 42

Massinger, Philip
SELF-CONTROL, 6

Masters, John
SCOTS, 9

Mathew, James
JUSTICE, 17

Matthews, Brander
EDUCATION, 34

Maudling, Reginald
DISMISSAL, 6

Maugham, W. Somerset
ADULTERY, 7
BED, 6
BOOK, SONG, AND PLAY TITLES, 16, 17
CHARACTER, 17
CIVILIZATION, 9
CRITICISM, 34
DEATH, 85
DECISION, 2
EXPEDIENCY, 4
FICTION, 4
FOOD, 39
HUMOUR, 19
HYPOCRISY, 11
IMPERTINENCE, 3
LYING, 9
MANKIND, 17
MARRIAGE, 83
MISANTHROPY, 2
MONEY, 35
NOVELS, 10
OLD AGE, 28
PERFECTION, 5
POETRY AND PROSE, 4
POLITICIANS, 18
PSYCHIATRY, 7
SENTIMENTALITY, 4
STUPIDITY, 9
WOMEN, 49, 50, 51
WORK, 13
WORLD-WEARINESS, 4
WRITERS, 15, 68
WRITING, 22

Maurois, André
ENGLAND, 27
SCIENTISTS, 13

Maxton, James
POLITICIANS, 64

Maxwell, Elsa
JEALOUSY, 4

Mayakovsky, Vladimir
ART, 17

Mayer, Louis B.
BIBLE, 8

Maynard, John
INSULTS, 30

Mayo, Charles H.
DISEASE, 26
OCCUPATIONS, 11

Mayo, William James
EXPERTS, 5

Mead, Margaret
ECOLOGY, 5
MEDIOCRITY, 5

Mearns, Hughes
NONSENSE, 22

Medawar, Peter
SCIENCE, 29

Meir, Golda
FEMINISM, 36
JEWS, 9, 10
KILLING, 6
LEADERSHIP, 7
OLD AGE, 29
SELF-CONFIDENCE, 2
SELF-PRESERVATION, 7

Melba, Nellie
FAME, 13
MUSIC, 31
PLACES, 11

SELF-RELIANCE, 6

Melbourne, Lord
CLERGY, 12
MOTIVE, 4
RELIGION, 43
ROYALTY, 24
SELF-CONFIDENCE, 3
SUPPORT, 4, 5
TITLES, 5
UNITY, 12

Mellon, Andrew William
ECONOMICS, 17

Melville, Herman
DRUNKENNESS, 16
EDUCATION, 35

Menander
DEATH, 87

Mencken, H. L.
ALCOHOL, 43, 44
BUSINESS, 15
CONSCIENCE, 4
CONTRACEPTION, 5
CYNICISM, 3
FAITH, 14, 15
GOD, 35
GOVERNMENT, 19
IDEALISM, 4
IDEAS, 6
LOVE, 90
LYING, 10
OPERA, 5
POETRY, 29
PROTESTANTISM, 1
PURITANISM, 4
RACISM, 23
TOLERANCE, 5
TRUTH, 35
WAR, 66

Menon, V. K. Krishna
POLITICS, 55

Menuhin, Yehudi
MUSIC, 32

Mercer, Johnny
EYES, 2
SUPERNATURAL, 11

Meredith, George
FOOD, 40
GOOD, 11
WOMEN, 52

Meredith, Owen
TALENT AND GENIUS, 3

Merrill, Bob
SOCIETY, 5

Meynell, Alice
LOVE, 91

Michael, George
EXPLOITATION, 4

Michelet, Jules
GREATNESS, 10

Middleton, Thomas
HONESTY, 6

Midlane, Albert
GOD, 36

Midler, Bette
SEX, 37

Mikes, George
CLASS, 23
ENGLAND, 28, 29
ENGLISH, 23, 24
MANNERS, 4
SERVICE, 3

Miles, Sarah
PRIVACY, 3

Mill, John Stuart
FEMINISM, 17
FREEDOM, 34
HAPPINESS, 14
ORIGINALITY, 4
STATE, 4
SUBJECTIVITY, 4

Millard, Emma
SEA, 11

Millay, Edna St Vincent
PLEASURE, 21

Mille, Cecil B. de
ACTORS, 4
CRITICS, 4

Miller, Arthur
EUROPE, 13
FUNERALS, 7
JOURNALISM, 23
MATERIALISM, 15
POPULARITY, 7
RELIGION, 44

Miller, Henry
BOOKS, 26
CLASSICS, 7
SEX, 38

Miller, Jonathan
HABIT, 6
HALF MEASURES, 2

Miller, Max
SEX, 39

Milligan, Spike
ANIMALISM, 6
CLASS, 24
CONTRACEPTION, 6
GOVERNMENT, 20
GRATITUDE, 3
MATHEMATICS, 6
MONEY, 36
NONSENSE, 23
PHOTOGRAPHY, 7
POLICE, 3
SPORT AND GAMES, 17

Mills, Hugh
ART, 18

Milman, Henry Hart
CHRISTIANITY, 32

Milne, A. A.
AGE, 40
LANGUAGE, 18
LAZINESS, 3
SOLDIERS, 3
SUPERSTITION, 9
WORDS, 16

Milton, John
AGE, 41
ALCOHOL, 45
BEAUTY, 28
BIRDS, 8, 9
BLINDNESS, 3, 4, 5
BOOKS, 27, 28
CHANGE, 16
CORRUPTION, 3, 4
DANCING, 7
DAY, 10, 11, 12
DECLINE, 4
DETERMINATION, 12
DEVIL, 10
DISEASE, 27
EDUCATION, 36
EVIL, 12
FAME, 14
FREEDOM, 35
GOD, 37, 38
GOOD, 12
GUIDANCE, 3
HEAVEN, 6
HELL, 4, 5
HYPOCRISY, 12
INNUENDO, 3
MELANCHOLY, 9, 10
MIND, 4
MUSIC, 33
PLEASURE, 22, 23
POETRY, 30, 31, 32
POWER, 17
RELIGION, 45
RESPONSIBILITY, 10
REVENGE, 13
SERVICE, 4
SHAKESPEARE, 13
SIN, 16
SOLITUDE, 10
SORROW, 12
SOUL, 10
TREES, 10
TRUTH, 36
VICTORY, 11
VIRTUE, 14
WAR AND PEACE, 11
WISDOM, 19
WOMEN, 53
WORRY, 11

Mirabeau, Comte de
WAR, 67

Mirren, Helen
HUMAN CONDITION, 13
NAKEDNESS, 6

Mitchell, Adrian
SOLITUDE, 11

Mitchell, Joni
LIFE, 37

Mitchell, Julian
FAMILY, 24

Mitchell, Margaret
BOOK, SONG, AND PLAY TITLES, 19
EXPEDIENCY, 5
HOPE, 7
REPUTATION, 5
WAR, 68

Mitford, Jessica
OCCUPATIONS, 12

Mitford, Mary Russell
WRITERS, 69

Mitford, Nancy
ARISTOCRACY, 10
ENGLISH, 25
READING, 12

Mizner, Wilson
PRUDENCE, 10

Molière
DEATH, 88
FOOD, 41
GRAMMAR, 6
IMPROVEMENT, 3
MORALITY, 11
PROSE, 3
PRUDERY, 2
SELF, 11
SMOKING, 12
WEALTH, 20

Monmouth, Duke of
EXECUTION, 17

Monroe, Harriet
POETRY, 33

Monroe, Marilyn
NAKEDNESS, 7

Monsell, John
CHRISTIANITY, 33

Montagu, Lady Mary Wortley
SATIRE, 2

Montague, C. E.
QUOTATIONS, 6
WAR, 69

Montaigne, Michel de
ADMIRATION, 8
CATS, 6
CURIOSITY, 6
LYING, 11
MARRIAGE, 84
RELIGION, 46
SELF-RELIANCE, 7
SEX, 40
SOLITUDE, 12
SUFFERING, 11

Montesquieu, Baron de
CHRISTIANITY, 34
ENGLISH, 26
FREEDOM, 36
INTELLIGENCE, 5
PLEASURE, 24
RELIGION, 47
WAR, 70
WRITING, 23

Montessori, Maria
EDUCATION, 37, 38

Montgomery, Lord
HOMOSEXUALITY, 9
WAR, 71

Montherlant, Henry de
LAST WORDS, 1
STUPIDITY, 10

Montrose, Percy
MOURNING, 7
UNFAITHFULNESS, 4

Moore, Clement Clarke
CHRISTMAS, 14

Moore, Edward
AGGRAVATION, 1
WEALTH, 21

Moore, George
ACTING, 8
ART, 19
HOME, 6

Moore, Thomas
ANIMALS, 14
FLOWERS, 9
FRANCE, 11
IRELAND, 13
MOURNING, 8
NOSTALGIA, 14
WAR, 72

Moore, T. Sturge
FRIENDSHIP, 24

Moravia, Alberto
LITERACY, 1

More, Thomas
CRITICISM, 35
EXECUTION, 18, 19, 20

FAMILY, 25

Morell, Thomas
VICTORY, 12

Morgan, Elaine
EXPERTS, 6
FEMINISM, 18

Morgan, Kenneth
POLITICIANS, 65

Morgenstern, Christian
LOSS, 4

Morley, Christopher Darlington
LIFE, 38
SEX, 41

Morley, Robert
COMMUNISM, 5
CONVERSATION, 6

Morpurgo, J. E.
EUROPE, 14

Morrell, Jill
HOSTAGES, 3

Morris, Desmond
FRIENDSHIP, 25
HUMAN NATURE, 19
MANKIND, 18, 19
SMOKING, 13

Morris, George Pope
TREES, 11

Morris, William
DESIGN, 3, 4, 5

Mortimer, John
LAW, 20
WELSH, 1

Mortimer, Raymond
MODESTY, 3

Morton, J. B.
CARS, 5
HUMOUR, 49
JOURNALISM, 24
MISTAKES, 10
MUSICIANS, 12
PREJUDICE, 4
STUPIDITY, 11
TRAVEL, 18

Moses, Grandma
ARTISTS, 4
MEMORY, 10
OCCUPATIONS, 13

Mosley, Oswald
BRITISH EMPIRE, 5
FREEDOM, 37
POLITICIANS, 66

Motley, John Lothrop
LUXURY, 4

Mountbatten of Burma, Louis
NUCLEAR WEAPONS, 13
ROYALTY, 25

Moynihan, Noël
STATISTICS, 6

Mugabe, Robert
POWER, 16

Muggeridge, Malcolm
BORES, 4
DECLINE, 5
DRUGS, 10
ENGLISH, 27
HUMOUR, 20
OLD AGE, 30
PORNOGRAPHY, 4
PRUDERY, 3
SEX, 42, 43

Muir, Frank
ANIMALS, 15
FOOD, 42
MARRIAGE, 85
PUNS, 14
STRIKES, 4
STUPIDITY, 12

Münster, Ernst Friedrich Herbert
RUSSIA, 7

Murchison Jnr, Clint
MONEY, 27

Murdoch, Iris
ART, 20
EQUALITY, 17
FAME, 15
FORGIVENESS, 13
LYING, 12
MARRIAGE, 86, 87
WRITING, 24

Murphy, Arthur
SUPERIORITY, 8

Murphy, C. W.
ABSENCE, 8

Murray, David
JOURNALISM, 25

Murray, Jenni
MARRIAGE, 88

Musset, Alfred de
INFINITY, 2
NATIONALITY, 7

Mussolini, Benito
FASCISM, 1, 2, 3
HITLER, 4, 5
POLITICS, 56
YOUTH, 13

N

Nabokov, Vladimir
ACADEMICS, 4
CAMBRIDGE, 4
EDUCATION, 39
LIFE AND DEATH, 11
LITERATURE, 14
LUST, 6
WRITERS, 16
WRITING, 25

Naipaul, V. S.
HUMOUR, 21

Nairne, Carolina
ADMIRATION, 9
GLORY, 4
RETURN, 3

Napoleon I
ARROGANCE, 6
DEATH, 89
DECLINE, 6
ENGLISH, 28
FOOD, 43
LAST WORDS, 45
POLITICS, 57
REGRET, 10
WAR, 73, 74

Napoleon III
SMOKING, 14
WAR, 75

Narváez, Ramón Maria
LAST WORDS, 46
RUTHLESSNESS, 4

Nash, Ogden
AGE, 42
ANIMALS, 16
DEBAUCHERY, 8
DOGS, 10
ENGLISH, 29
EPITAPHS, 20
FAMILY, 26
MATHEMATICS, 7
MONEY, 37
OLD AGE, 31
SIN, 17
TREES, 12
WOMEN, 54

Neale, John Mason
CHRISTMAS, 15
MIDDLE EAST, 10
SORROW, 13

Needham, Joseph
SCIENCE, 30

Nelson, Lord
DUTY, 3
ENEMIES, 6
LAST WORDS, 47
OFFICERS, 10

Nevins, Allan
NAZISM, 4

Newbolt, Henry John
BLINDNESS, 6
BOATS, 14
CRICKET, 5
PATRIOTISM, 21, 22
WAR, 76, 77

Newcastle, Margaret, Duchess of
EPITAPHS, 21

Newley, Anthony
WORLD-WEARINESS, 5

Newman, Cardinal
ARGUMENTS, 12
BITTERNESS, 2
CHIVALRY, 8
FAITH, 16
RESPONSIBILITY, 11
SIN, 18

Newman, Ernest
INTELLECT, 6
OPERA, 6

Newman, Paul
MARRIAGE, 89

Newton, Howard W.
SPEECH, 12

Newton, Isaac
ACCIDENTS, 5
DISCOVERY, 6
NATURE, 12
PROGRESS, 9

Newton, John
HEAVEN, 7

Nicholas I
DECLINE, 7
SEASONS, 15

Nicholas of Oresme
TYRANNY, 5

Nicholson, Jack
SEXES, 16

Nicolson, Harold
EDUCATION, 40

Niebuhr, Reinhold
DEMOCRACY, 14

Niemöller, Martin
NAZISM, 5

Nietzsche, Friedrich Wilhelm
AFTERLIFE, 7
BOREDOM, 6
CHRISTIANITY, 35
CRITICS, 13
DANGER, 6
DRUGS, 11
GOD, 39
LOVE, 92
LYING, 13
MORALITY, 12
PARIS, 4
PATIENTS, 2
PHILOSOPHERS, 6
POSTERITY, 9
SCIENCE, 31
SUICIDE, 6
SUPERIORITY, 9
SYMPATHY, 5
WOMEN, 55, 56

Nightingale, Florence
FEMINISM, 19
OCCUPATIONS, 14
STATISTICS, 7

Niven, David
BOOK, SONG, AND PLAY TITLES, 20
SOLDIERS, 4

Niven, Larry
ADVICE, 11
FEMINISM, 37

Nixon, Richard Milhous
BETRAYAL, 6
DENIAL, 3
MAJORITY, 5
MOON, 5
RENUNCIATION, 3
SPACE, 6
TRUTH, 37, 38

Nogarola, Isotta
MISOGYNY, 4

Norman, Barry
SEXES, 17

Norman, Frank
NOSTALGIA, 15

Norris, Steven
CARS, 6

North, Christopher
BRITISH EMPIRE, 6
LAW, 21

Northcliffe, Lord
PUBLIC, 16
TITLES, 6

Northcote, Lord
POLITICIANS, 67

Norton, Caroline Elizabeth Sarah
LOVE, 93

Norworth, Jack
MOON, 6

Nostradamus
PROPHECY, 7, 8, 9

Novello, Ivor
FRANCE, 12
MOTHERHOOD, 12

Noyes, Alfred
DETERMINATION, 13

Nyerere, Julius
MIDDLE EAST, 11

O

Oakeley, Frederick
CHRISTMAS, 16

Oates, Captain Lawrence
LAST WORDS, 48

O'Brien, Conor Cruise
DOCTORS, 6
IRELAND, 14

O'Brien, Edna
APPEARANCE, 26
FEMINISM, 20

O'Brien, Flann
POLICE, 4
PUNS, 15

O'Casey, Sean
CURIOSITY, 7
FRIENDS, 11
RELIGION, 48
WRITERS, 70

Ochs, Adolph Simon
NEWSPAPERS, 9

O'Connell, Daniel
INSULTS, 32

O'Hara, Geoffrey
LOVE, 94

O'Keefe, Patrick
FLOWERS, 10

Olivier, Laurence
SHAKESPEARE, 14

O'Malley, Austin
WEALTH, 22

Onassis, Aristotle
WOMEN, 57

O'Neill, Eugene
LIFE, 39

Opie, John
PAINTING, 7

Oppenheimer, J. Robert
NUCLEAR WEAPONS, 14
SCIENTISTS, 5

Orczy, Baroness
ABSENCE, 9
ENDURANCE, 11

Ordaz, Gustavo Diaz
FREEDOM, 38

O'Rourke, P. J.
BOSNIA AND HERCEGOVINA, 4

Orton, Joe
GOD, 40
HUMILITY, 7
INDULGENCE, 2
INNOCENCE, 8
POLICE, 5
PROMISCUITY, 4
SEX, 44
TASTE, 6

Orwell, George
AGE, 43, 44
ATHEISM, 8
AUTHORITARIANISM, 5
BOOKS, 29
CAPITALISM, 10
CHILDREN, 36
CLASS, 25
COWARDICE, 5
CRITICISM, 36
ENGLAND, 30, 31
EQUALITY, 18
FOOTBALL, 5
FREEDOM, 39, 40
LEARNING, 7
LIFE, 40
NOBILITY, 3
NOSTALGIA, 16
OBESITY, 8
OPPOSITES, 5, 6
OPPRESSION, 6
POLITICS, 58
POWER, 18
SOCIALISM, 11, 12, 13
SPORT AND GAMES, 18
SUPERIORITY, 10
WAR, 78, 79, 80
WEAPONS, 3
WRITERS, 71, 72

Osborne, Charles
WRITERS, 17

Osborne, John
CHANGE, 17
CLASS, 26
EDUCATION, 41
ENGLAND, 32
ENTHUSIASM, 6
INCOMPETENCE, 3
NEWSPAPERS, 10
NOSTALGIA, 17
OSTENTATION, 5
THEATRE, 12

Osler, William
DRUGS, 12
OCCUPATIONS, 15

O'Sullivan, John L.
ALCOHOL, 46

Otis, James
REPRESENTATION, 1

Ouida
CHRISTIANITY, 36
CRUELTY, 4
MUSIC, 34
TEMPTATION, 8

Ouspensky, P. D.
MANKIND, 20

Overbury, Thomas
DISCONTENT, 7

Ovid
CORRUPTION, 5
DECLINE, 8
MEDICINE, 6
PERSISTENCE, 11
WOMEN, 58

Owen, David
LEADERSHIP, 8
NUCLEAR WEAPONS, 15

Owen, Robert
SUBJECTIVITY, 5

Owen, Wilfred
DEATH, 90
PATRIOTISM, 23
POETRY, 34
WAR, 81, 82
WORLD WAR I, 17, 18

Oxenstierna, Axel
GOVERNMENT, 21

P

Paderewski, Ignacy
MUSIC, 35
POP MUSIC, 15

Paine, Thomas
COWARDICE, 6
GOVERNMENT, 22, 23
INTEGRITY, 5
OPPOSITES, 7

Paisley, Ian
IRELAND, 15

Palmer, Samuel
PAINTING, 8

Palmerston, Lord
CHANCE, 4
LAST WORDS, 49

Pankhurst, Christabel
PRIDE, 6
SELF-CONTROL, 7

Pankhurst, Emmeline
FEMINISM, 21, 22, 23

Pankhurst, Sylvia
CAPITALISM, 11
WAR, 83

Papanek, Victor
DESIGN, 6

Park, Mungo
EXECUTION, 21

Parker, Charlie
MUSIC, 36

Parker, Clarke Ross
ENGLAND, 33

Parker, Dorothy
ABORTION, 2
APPEARANCE, 27, 28
BREVITY, 5
CATHOLICISM, 9
CLOTHES, 12
CONSERVATISM, 6
CRITICISM, 37, 38
DEATH, 91
EPITAPHS, 22, 23
EXPECTATION, 3
FAME, 16
HUMOUR, 50
INATTENTION, 2
LOVE, 95, 96, 97
MATERIALISM, 16
MONEY, 38
POLITICIANS, 68
PREGNANCY, 4
PROMISCUITY, 5
PUNS, 16, 17
QUOTATIONS, 7, 8
RACISM, 24
SEX, 45
SLEEP, 14
SORROW, 14
SUICIDE, 7
WOMEN, 59
WRITERS, 18, 73, 74

Parker, Henry Taylor
AUDIENCES, 3

Parker, Hubert Lister
JUSTICE, 18

Parker, John
WAR, 84

Parkinson, Cecil
ECOLOGY, 6

Parkinson, Cyril Northcote
HOUSES OF PARLIAMENT, 14
MARRIAGE, 90
WORK, 14, 15

Parr, Samuel
WRITERS, 75

Parris, Matthew
HOMOSEXUALITY, 10

Pascal, Blaise
APPEARANCE, 29
CREATION, 11
INTELLIGENCE, 6
MODESTY, 4
MOTIVE, 5
PHILOSOPHERS, 7
VERBOSITY, 5

Pasternak, Boris
DESTINY, 15

Pasteur, Louis
SCIENCE, 32

Pater, Walter
ART, 21

Paterson, Andrew Barton
PLACES, 12

Patmore, Coventry
LOVE, 98
PARTING, 8

Patton, General George
WORLD WAR II, 23

Paul, Leslie
REBELLION, 7

Pauli, Wolfgang
PUBLISHING, 10

Pavese, Cesare
DISILLUSION, 5

Pavlov, Ivan
EDUCATION, 42

Pavlova, Anna
DANCING, 8
EFFORT, 5
HAPPINESS, 15
SUCCESS, 13

Payn, James
PERVERSITY, 5

Payne, Cynthia
SEX, 46

Payne, John Howard
HOME, 7

Paz, Octavio
COMMERCIALISM, 3

Peabody, Elizabeth
PERCEPTION, 4

Peacock, Thomas Love
ANIMALS, 17
EDUCATION, 43
GREED, 7
HYPOCRISY, 13
LAUGHTER, 9
MARRIAGE, 91, 92
QUOTATIONS, 9
RESPECTABILITY, 3
THIRST, 1

Peake, Mervyn
EQUALITY, 19

Pearson, Hesketh
MISQUOTATIONS, 1, 2
WRITERS, 76

Peary, Robert Edwin
EXPLORATION, 3
LUCK, 10

Peck, Gregory
FAME, 17

Peel, Lord
POLICE, 6

Pegler, Westbrook
ROYALTY, 26

Péguy, Charles Pierre
HISTORY, 21

Peirce, C. S.
UNIVERSE, 11

Penhaligon, David
NUCLEAR WEAPONS, 16

Penn, William
ENDURANCE, 12
FATHERS, 5

Pepys, Samuel
APPEARANCE, 30
BED, 7
BLINDNESS, 7
ENGLISH, 30
EXECUTION, 22
FOOTBALL, 6
INSINCERITY, 3
LANGUAGE, 19
MARRIAGE, 93
MUSIC, 37
PROVOCATION, 1
WOMEN, 60

Perelman, S. J.
DISEASE, 28
HUMOUR, 51, 52, 53
PUNS, 18
SEX, 47
TEETH, 1, 2

Peres, Shimon
MIDDLE EAST, 12

Pericles
RESULTS, 4

Perkins, Francis
TITLES, 7

Perle, Richard
WEAPONS, 4

Perlman, Itzhak
MUSICIANS, 6

Perón, Juan
CONTENTMENT, 5

Perronet, Edward
CHRISTIANITY, 37

Perry, Oliver Hazard
VICTORY, 13

Perugino, Pietro
LAST WORDS, 50

Pétain, Marshal
DETERMINATION, 14
WORLD WAR II, 24

Peter, Laurence J.
INCOMPETENCE, 4
OBSESSIONS, 2
PESSIMISM, 10

Peterborough, Lord
GENEROSITY, 5

Petrarch
DEATH, 92
HEAVEN, 8

Petronius Arbiter
DEATH, 18
DOGS, 1

Pevsner, Nikolaus
EXCESS, 5

Phelps, Edward John
MISTAKES, 11

Philip, Prince
ARCHITECTURE, 8
CONSERVATION, 6, 7
ECONOMICS, 18
LANGUAGE, 20
MARRIAGE, 94
RACISM, 25
ROYALTY, 27
SHAKESPEARE, 15
WATER, 7
WOMEN, 61

Philip, John Woodward
WAR, 86

Philippe, Charles-Louis
POLICE, 7

Phillips, Wendell
DEFEAT, 6
GOD, 41
GOVERNMENT, 24
JOURNALISM, 26

Phillpotts, Eden
MADNESS, 10

Picasso, Pablo
ART, 22
ARTISTS, 17
BEAUTY, 29
GOD, 42
INFERIORITY, 4
OLD AGE, 32
PAINTING, 9, 10, 11, 12
WOMEN, 62
WORK, 16

Pilley, W. Charles
WRITERS, 77

Pinero, Arthur
AGE, 45

Pinter, Harold
AMERICA, 28
CRICKET, 6
METAPHYSICS, 4
PROOF, 5

Piozzi, Hester Lynch
TIME, 28

Piron, Alexis
PLAYS, 6

Pirsig, Robert T.
FANATICISM, 3

MATHEMATICS, 8
MIND, 5
SCIENCE, 33

Pitter, Ruth
SEXES, 18

Pitts, William Ewart
CARS, 7

Pitt the Elder, William
MONARCHY, 16
PATRIOTISM, 24
POWER, 19
PRIVACY, 4
TYRANNY, 6
YOUTH, 14

Pitt the Younger, William
FOOD, 44
LAST WORDS, 51, 52
NECESSITY, 4
PEACE, 13

Plath, Sylvia
DEATH, 93
TIME, 29

Plato
DEMOCRACY, 15
GOOD, 13
MATHEMATICS, 9
PHILOSOPHY, 9
PROPAGANDA, 3
REPUBLIC, 1

Player, Gary
WORK, 17

Pliny the Elder
ALCOHOL, 47
HUMOUR, 22
NATURE, 13
NOVELTY, 8

Plomer, William
LIBERALISM, 3
MEDIOCRITY, 6
SEX, 48

Plotinus
PAINTING, 13

Poe, Edgar Allan
EVIL, 13
SUPERNATURAL, 12

Polo, Marco
LAST WORDS, 53

Pompadour, Madame de
PROPHECY, 10

Pompidou, Georges
POLITICIANS, 19

Pope, Alexander
ADMIRATION, 10, 11
CHARACTER, 18
CHAUCER, 3
CLARITY, 3
CRITICISM, 39, 40
CRITICS, 14
DEATH, 94, 95, 96
DISEASE, 29
DOCTORS, 7
DOGS, 11
DRINKS, 6, 7
EDUCATION, 44
ENDURANCE, 13
EPITAPHS, 24
EQUALITY, 29
EXPECTATION, 4
FOOD, 45
FOOLISHNESS, 17
FORGIVENESS, 14
GOOD, 14
HASTE, 8
HOPE, 8
HUMAN CONDITION, 14
HUMOUR, 23
JUSTICE, 19
KNOWLEDGE, 30
LIFE, 41
LOVE, 99
MISFORTUNE, 13
MISTAKES, 12, 13
MONARCHY, 17
OLD AGE, 33
OPINIONS, 4
ORDER, 3
PASSION, 5, 6
PERFECTION, 6
POETRY, 35
PRAISE, 5
PRIDE, 7, 8
PROVOCATION, 2
RESULTS, 5
SCIENTISTS, 14
SELF-KNOWLEDGE, 5, 6
SERVILITY, 5
SORROW, 15, 16
STUPIDITY, 13
SUBJECTIVITY, 6
VERBOSITY, 6
VIRTUE, 15
WOMEN, 63, 64, 65
WRITING, 26

Popper, Karl
DESTINY, 16
FREEDOM, 41
HISTORY, 22
KNOWLEDGE, 31
MYTHS, 1
SCIENCE, 34
SOCIETY, 6

Porson, Richard
LANGUAGE, 21
POETS, 51

Porter, Cole
APOLOGIES, 2
FAITHFULNESS, 5
FREEDOM, 42
HAPPINESS, 16
LOVE, 100, 101, 102
PARIS, 5
PARTIES, 5
WEALTH, 23

Porter, George
ENVIRONMENT, 3
SCIENCE, 35

Portland, Duke of
THRIFT, 9

Post, Emily
CONVERSATION, 7
FOOD, 46

Post, Laurens Van der
RELIGION, 49
SENSATION, 2

Potter, Beatrix
CAUTION, 12
RABBITS, 2

Potter, Dennis
RELIGION, 50

Potter, Stephen
ALCOHOL, 48, 49
INATTENTION, 3
ONE-UPMANSHIP, 2, 3

SPORT AND GAMES, 19
WORDS, 17

Pound, Ezra
AGE, 46
ARTS, 7
BOOKS, 30
GENERALIZATIONS, 3
HISTORIANS, 5
LITERATURE, 15, 16
POETRY, 36
POETS, 52
POP MUSIC, 16
SEASONS, 16
TREES, 13
WOMEN, 66
WRITERS, 78

Powell, Anthony
BOOK, SONG, AND PLAY TITLES, 21
CONCEIT, 13
COUNTRYSIDE, 7
FAMILY, 27, 28
FOOD, 47
NASTINESS, 6
NOVELS, 12
OLD AGE, 34
SELF, 12

Powell, Enoch
DIARIES, 4
POLITICIANS, 20, 21
PROPHECY, 11
RACISM, 26

Powell, John
LAW, 22

Powys, John Cowper
MOTHERHOOD, 13

Pozniak, Zianon
RUSSIA, 8

Prescott, William
WAR, 87

Previn, André
MUSIC, 38

Priestley, J. B.
CHURCH, 7
CRITICS, 15, 16
DRINKS, 8
FOOTBALL, 7
GOD, 43
HUMOUR, 24
INSULTS, 33
MARRIAGE, 96
MUSEUMS, 2
PLAYS, 7
POLITICIANS, 22
PRAYER, 15
WORLD WAR II, 25
WRITERS, 19

Prior, Matthew
DISEASE, 30
DOCTORS, 8
HOPE, 9
IGNORANCE, 12

Pritchett, V. S.
NOVELS, 13

Procter, Adelaide Anne
MUSIC, 39

Proudhon, Pierre Joseph
CAPITALISM, 12

Proust, Marcel
ATHEISM, 9
DESIRE, 12
IMPERFECTION, 10
LOVE, 103, 104
MANKIND, 21
MEMORY, 11
NEUROSIS, 1, 2
OCCUPATIONS, 16
PARTING, 9
REGRET, 11
REMEDIES, 11
SEX, 49
SNOBBERY, 5
SORROW, 17, 18
SUN, 3

Pryce-Jones, David
BOREDOM, 7

Pudney, John Sleigh
IDEALISM, 5
REALISM, 4

Purves, Libby
WEAPONS, 5

Putnam, Emily James
MOTHERHOOD, 14

Pyke, Magnus
CAUTION, 13
ECOLOGY, 7

Pyrrhus
VICTORY, 14

Q

Quarles, Francis
PLAYS, 8
PLEASURE, 25

Quayle, Dan
SPACE, 7

Queensberry, Duke of
RIVERS, 3

Quesnay, François
FREEDOM, 43

Quincy, Josiah
SEPARATION, 4

R

Rabelais, François
BORROWING, 7
DESIRE, 13
DESTINY, 17
FREEDOM, 44
LAST WORDS, 54, 55, 56
NATURE, 14
SCIENCE, 36
THIRST, 2

Rachmaninov, Sergei
MUSICIANS, 13

Racine, Jean
CRIME, 6
INNOCENCE, 2
LOVE, 105
LOVE AND HATE, 4

Radcliffe, Ann
DESTINY, 18
SEA, 12

Rae, Daphne
EDUCATION, 45

Rae, John
WAR, 88

Rafsanjani, Hojatolislam
SEXES, 19

Raglan, Lord
PRACTICALITY, 6

Raleigh, Walter
AMBITION, 14
BOOKS, 31
ETIQUETTE, 5
EXECUTION, 23, 24, 25
FAITH, 17
LAST WORDS, 57
LOVE, 106
MANKIND, 22

Ramanujan, Srinivasa
NUMBERS, 3

Ransome, Arthur
OPPORTUNITY, 15

Raphael, Frederic
CAMBRIDGE, 5
FOOD, 48
PHILOSOPHY, 10
SUBURBIA, 1

Rattigan, Terence
AUDIENCES, 4
CLASS, 27
SUICIDE, 8

Ray, John
DISEASE, 31

Reade, Charles
WRITING, 27

Reagan, Ronald
AGE, 47
AMERICANS, 8
ECONOMICS, 19
POLITICS, 59, 60
POPULARITY, 8
TAXATION, 10
WORK, 18

Reed, Henry
BOOKS, 32
GERMANY, 15
WAR, 89, 90
WEAPONS, 6, 7

Reed, Rex
CINEMA, 9

Reedy, George Edward
SERVILITY, 6

Reich, Wilhelm
ABSTINENCE, 8

Reinhardt, Gottfried
MONEY, 39

Reith, Lord
THINKING, 6

Remarque, Erich Maria
WAR, 91

Renan, Ernest
SCIENCE, 37

Renard, Jules
MODESTY, 5
PRIDE, 9
WRITING, 28

Rendall, Montague John
PEACE, 14

Renoir, Pierre Auguste
ENDURANCE, 14
PAINTING, 14

Revson, Charles
COSMETICS, 3

Rexford, Eben
OLD AGE, 35

Reynolds, Joshua
ARTISTS, 18
IMITATION, 4, 5
WORK, 19

Reynolds, Malvina
HOUSES, 4

Rhodes, Cecil
ENGLAND, 34
ENGLISH, 31
LAST WORDS, 58
MISOGYNY, 5

Rhys, Jean
OLD AGE, 36
SEXES, 20
SUICIDE, 9
SUNDAY, 5

Ribblesdale, Lord
QUOTATIONS, 10

Rice, Grantland
SPORT AND GAMES, 20
VICTORY, 15
WAR, 92

Rice, Stephen
IRELAND, 16

Rice-Davies, Mandy
DENIAL, 4

Richard, Cliff
CHILDREN, 37
WOMEN, 67

Richards, Gordon
PUNS, 19
TITLES, 8

Richards, I. A.
POETRY, 37

Richardson, Ralph
ACTING, 9, 10
SPEECH, 13

Richelieu, Cardinal
EXECUTION, 26
ROYALTY, 28

Richelieu, Duc de
ADULTERY, 8

Richler, Mordecai
JEWS, 11
POLITICS, 61
WRITERS, 20

Richter, Jean Paul
EUROPE, 15

Ridge, William Pett
CHANCE, 5
ETIQUETTE, 6

Ridley, Nicholas
CONSERVATION, 8

Rilke, Rainer Maria
CRITICISM, 41
DEATH, 97
IMMORTALITY, 5
SEASONS, 17
TECHNOLOGY, 12

Rimsky-Korsakov, Nikolai
MUSIC, 40

Ripley, R. L.
BELIEF, 6

Rivarol, Antoine de
CRITICISM, 42

Rivera, Antonio
WAR, 93

Robbins, Tom
WATER, 8

Robespierre
CORRUPTION, 6

Robin, Leo
MATERIALISM, 17
MEMORY, 12

Robinson, Edwin Arlington
DEATH, 98

Robinson, James Harvey
SUBJECTIVITY, 7

Robinson, John
PORNOGRAPHY, 5
SEX, 50

Robinson, Robert
AMERICA, 29
TEETH, 3

Roche, Boyle
MIXED METAPHORS, 4

Rochefort, Marquis de
WRITING, 29

Rochefoucauld, Duc de la
ADVICE, 12
AGREEMENT, 4
ARGUMENTS, 13
CONCEIT, 14
EGOTISM, 7
EMOTION, 4
EVIL, 14
FRIENDS, 12
HAPPINESS, 17
HOMESICKNESS, 5
HUMAN NATURE, 20
HYPOCRISY, 14
IMPERFECTION, 11, 12
INTELLIGENCE, 7
JUDGMENT, 12
JUSTICE, 20
LOVE, 107
LOVE AND HATE, 5
LUCK, 11
MISFORTUNE, 14, 15
PRAISE, 6
SELF-INTEREST, 6
SILENCE, 10
SPONTANEITY, 4
SUCCESS, 14
VIRTUE AND VICE, 2

Rockefeller, John D.
BUSINESS, 16

Rockne, Knute
FAILURE, 5

Roddick, Anita
REPUTATION, 6

Rogers, Samuel
BOOKS, 33
MARRIAGE, 97

Rogers, Will
ARTISTS, 19
COMMUNISM, 6
GOVERNMENT, 25
HEROISM, 6
HUMOUR, 25, 26
IRELAND, 17
LYING, 14
POLITICIANS, 69
POLITICS, 62, 63
PROGRESS, 10
RESPECTABILITY, 4

Roland, Madame
EXECUTION, 27
FREEDOM, 45

Rolleston, Humphrey
DOCTORS, 9

Rolmaz, James
CLOTHES, 13

Roosevelt, Eleanor
DEMOCRACY, 16
INFERIORITY, 5
OPPOSITION, 5
UNDERSTANDING, 10

Roosevelt, Franklin D.
AGE, 48
AMERICA, 30
BOOKS, 34
CHARITY, 16
DEMOCRACY, 17
EDUCATION, 46
FEAR, 10
HASTE, 9
HUMAN RIGHTS, 4
IDEALISM, 6
INATTENTION, 4
POLITICIANS, 70
POVERTY, 27
WAR, 94
WORLD WAR II, 26, 27

Roosevelt, Theodore
EXPEDIENCY, 6
JUSTICE, 21
LOYALTY, 8
PATRIOTISM, 25, 26
POWER POLITICS, 6
ROYALTY, 29
WORK, 20

Rorem, Ned
MEDIOCRITY, 7

Roscommon, Earl of
PUBLIC, 17
SPEECH, 14

Rosebery, Lord
BRITISH, 9
BRITISH EMPIRE, 7
IRELAND, 18
POLITICS, 64

Ross, Alan Strode Campbell
CLASS, 28

Ross, Harold W.
CONFUSION, 8
PHILISTINISM, 5

Ross, Nick
CRIME, 7

Ross, Pamela
WEAPONS, 8

Rossetti, Christina
DEATH, 99
ENDURANCE, 15
FAMILY, 29
MEMORY, 13, 14
NOSTALGIA, 18
REST, 1
SEASONS, 18
WEATHER, 18

Rossetti, Dante Gabriel
CRITICISM, 43
DISAPPOINTMENT, 6
FAMILIARITY, 4
POETRY, 38

Rossini, Gioacchino
CRITICISM, 44
MUSIC, 41

Rostand, Edmond
APPEARANCE, 31

Rostand, Jean
KILLING, 7
MARRIAGE, 98, 99

Roth, Philip
JEWS, 12, 13

Rourke, M. E.
BEAUTY, 30

Rousseau, Jean Jacques
DEATH, 100
FREEDOM, 46
MANKIND, 23

Routh, Martin Joseph
RESEARCH, 4

Rowe, Nicholas
INDIFFERENCE, 5

Rowland, Edward
FRANCE, 13

Rowland, Helen
LOVE, 108
MARRIAGE, 100
MISTAKES, 14
REGRET, 12
TRUST, 4

Rowland, Sherry
ENVIRONMENT, 4

Rowse, A. L.
ART, 23

Rubens, Paul Alfred
DISMISSAL, 7

Rubinstein, Arthur
MUSICIANS, 7

Rubinstein, Helena
AGE, 49
BEAUTY, 31

Rue, Danny La
HUMOUR, 17

Runcie, Robert
TACT, 6

Runciman, Steven
RELIGION, 51

Runciman of Doxford, Lady
CRIME, 8

Runyon, Damon
APPEARANCES, 18
ARISTOCRACY, 11
BEAUTY, 32
EVIL, 15
GREED, 8
INNOVATION, 2
LAST WORDS, 59
MONEY, 40
PARASITES, 2
SIN, 19
SUICIDE, 10

Rushdie, Salman
RELIGION, 52

Ruskin, John
ARCHITECTURE, 9, 10
ART, 24, 25
ARTISTS, 20
BEAUTY, 33
BOOKS, 35, 36, 37
COMMUNICATION, 4
CRITICISM, 45
FREEDOM, 47
HONESTY, 7
MOUNTAINS, 3
POETRY, 39
POVERTY AND WEALTH, 6

Russell, Bertrand
ABSTINENCE, 9
AMERICA, 31
ARGUMENTS, 14
BIBLE, 9
CLOTHES, 14
DOUBT, 7
DRUNKENNESS, 17
EQUALITY, 20
FAME, 18
GOSSIP, 8
HAPPINESS, 18, 19, 20
HATE, 7
HUMAN CONDITION, 15
INDECISION, 2
LOVE, 109, 110
MATHEMATICS, 10, 11, 12, 13, 14
MEMORIALS, 9
MODESTY, 6
MORALITY, 13
NUCLEAR WEAPONS, 17
OPINIONS, 5
PATRIOTISM, 27
PHILOSOPHERS, 8
PHILOSOPHY, 11
POLITICS, 65
POWER, 20
PROGRESS, 11
PRUDERY, 4
RACISM, 27
READING, 13
SCEPTICISM, 4
SOCIETY, 7
THINKING, 7, 8
UNCERTAINTY, 3
WORK, 21

Russell, George William
DRUNKENNESS, 18

Russell, Lord John
FAMILY, 30
SAYINGS, 6

Russell, William Howard
WAR, 95

Rutherford, Ernest
RESEARCH, 5

Ryan, Cornelius
BOOK, SONG, AND PLAY TITLES, 22

Ryle, Gilbert
MIND, 6
MYTHS, 2
PHILOSOPHY, 12

S

Sacks, Jonathan
MIDDLE EAST, 13

Sacks, Oliver
LANGUAGE, 22

Sackville-West, Vita
HEAVEN, 9
IDEALISM, 7
SEASONS, 19
TRAVEL, 19
WRITERS, 21

Sade, Marquis de
MORALITY, 14

Sadleir, Michael
BOOK, SONG, AND PLAY TITLES, 23

Sagan, Carl
SURVIVAL, 4

Sagan, Françoise
LOVE, 111

Sahl, Mort
TRUST, 5

Saint-Exupéry, Antoine de
PROGRESS, 12
RESPONSIBILITY, 12
SORROW, 19
WAR, 96

Saintsbury, George Edward Bateman
ALCOHOL, 50

Saki
ADDRESSES, 1
AGE, 50
ALCOHOL, 51, 52
BEAUTY, 34
CHARACTER, 19
CHINA, 9
CLOTHES, 15
DECLINE, 9
EDUCATION, 47
ETIQUETTE, 7
EUROPE, 16
EXCESS, 6
EXTRAVAGANCE, 4
FASHION, 6
HUMOUR, 54
MARRIAGE, 101
PERFECTION, 7
QUOTATIONS, 11
SELFLESSNESS, 3
SORROW, 20
SUFFERING, 12
SUPERIORITY, 11
WRITERS, 79, 80

Salinger, J. D.
ACTORS, 7
SEX, 51

Salisbury, Marquess of
EUROPE, 17
NEWSPAPERS, 11

Salk, Jonas E.
DISCOVERY, 7

Sallust,
FRIENDSHIP, 26

Salvandy, Comte de
REVOLUTION, 5

Sampson, Anthony
TITLES, 9

Samuel, Herbert
BOOKS, 38
BUREAUCRACY, 7
GOVERNMENT, 26
HOUSES OF PARLIAMENT, 15
MARRIAGE, 102
MORALITY, 15
SAYINGS, 7

Sand, George
HAPPINESS, 21
LOVE, 112

Sandburg, Carl
WAR, 97

Sanders, George
LAST WORDS, 60

Santayana, George
AGE, 51
BIBLE, 10
BREVITY, 6
BUREAUCRACY, 8
DISEASE, 32
ENGLAND, 35
FASHION, 7
HAPPINESS, 22
HISTORY, 23
HUMILITY, 8
LIFE, 42
LIFE AND DEATH, 12
MADNESS, 11
PHILOSOPHERS, 9
PHILOSOPHY, 13
SCIENCE, 38
WISDOM, 20

Sarasate, Pablo
GENIUS, 8

Sargent, Epes
SEA, 13

Sargent, John Singer
PAINTING, 15

Sargent, Malcolm
SINGING, 3

Saroyan, William
LAST WORDS, 61

Sartre, Jean-Paul
AMERICANS, 9
APPEARANCES, 19
CHARACTER, 20
DAY, 13
EXISTENCE, 5
FREEDOM, 48
HELL, 6
KISSING, 4
OPPRESSION, 7
POVERTY, 28
POVERTY AND WEALTH, 7
PSYCHOLOGY, 2
RESPECT, 3
SCEPTICISM, 5
SILENCE, 11
THINKING, 9
TIME, 30

Sassoon, Siegfried
SOLDIERS, 5
WAR, 98, 99, 100, 101, 102, 103
WORLD WAR I, 19, 20

Sassoon, Vidal
SUCCESS, 15
WORK, 22

Satie, Erik
AGE, 52
MUSIC, 42
SMOKING, 15

Saunders, Robert
WORLD WAR I, 21

Saville, George
EXAMPLE, 5

Sayers, Dorothy L.
NASTINESS, 7
OLD AGE, 37

Scarron, Paul
LAST WORDS, 62

Schacht, Hjalmar
HITLER, 6

Schelling, Friedrich Wilhelm Joseph von
ARCHITECTURE, 11

Schiller, Friedrich von
ROYALTY, 30
STUPIDITY, 14

Schlegel, Friedrich von
HISTORIANS, 6

Schlesinger Jnr, Arthur
WAR, 104

Schlieffen, Alfred Graf von
WAR, 105
WORLD WAR I, 22

Schliemann, Heinrich
HISTORY, 24

Schnabel, Artur
AUDIENCES, 5
MUSIC, 43
MUSICIANS, 8, 14

Schneckenburger, Max
RIVERS, 4

Schoenberg, Harold
OPERA, 7

Schopenhauer, Arthur
AFTERLIFE, 8
GREATNESS, 11
GREED, 9
INTELLECT, 7
LIFE, 43
LONELINESS, 6
MEMORY, 15
SEPARATION, 5
SURVIVAL, 5
WOMAN'S ROLE, 5
WOMEN, 68

Schultz, Charles M.
MANKIND, 24
MISANTHROPY, 3

Schumacher, E. F.
INDUSTRIAL RELATIONS, 3
MANKIND, 25
POVERTY, 29
SMALLNESS, 4

Schumann, Robert
MUSICIANS, 15

Schwarzenberg, Prince
DIPLOMACY, 18

Schwarzkopf, Norman
MIDDLE EAST, 14

Schweitzer, Albert
HAPPINESS, 23
HUMILITY, 9
TRUTH, 39

Scott, C. P.
JOURNALISM, 27
TELEVISION AND RADIO, 6

Scott, Captain Robert Falcon
ENDURANCE, 16
PLACES, 13

Scott, Walter
ADMIRATION, 12
CHIVALRY, 9, 10
COUNTRYSIDE, 8
COURAGE, 18
DEATH, 101, 102
EXPECTATION, 5
HOMESICKNESS, 6
LOVE, 113
PAST, 6
POETS, 10
REGRET, 13
RIDICULE, 4
SCOTLAND, 7
SCOTS, 10
WORDS, 18
WRITERS, 81, 82
WRITING, 30

Scott, William
BUSINESS, 17
EXAMPLE, 6

Scott-Maxwell, Florida
MOTHERHOOD, 15

Seaborg, Glenn T.
SCIENCE, 39

Seal, Christopher
HUNTING, 6

Searle, Ronald
APPEARANCE, 32
WEAPONS, 9

Sears, E. H.
CHRISTMAS, 17

Secombe, Harry
EPITAPHS, 25
OBESITY, 9

Sedgwick, Catharine Maria
HEAVEN, 10

Sedgwick, John
LAST WORDS, 63

Seeger, Alan
DEATH, 103

Seeger, Pete
LOSS, 5

Seeley, John Robert
BRITISH EMPIRE, 8
HISTORY, 25
POLITICS, 66

Segal, Erich
APOLOGIES, 3

Seifert, Richard
ARCHITECTURE, 12

Selassie, Haile
TELEGRAMS, 10
WORLD WAR II, 28

Selden, John
DISEASE, 33
EXAMPLE, 7
EXCESS, 7
LAW, 23, 24
MARRIAGE, 103
MONARCHY, 18

PERSUASION, 3
PLEASURE, 26, 27

Selfridge, H. Gordon
BUSINESS, 18

Sellar, W. C.
EDUCATION, 48
EXAMINATIONS, 2
HISTORY, 27, 28, 29, 30, 31
HORSES, 9
HUMOUR, 55

Sellers, Peter
GREED, 10

Seneca
CONVERSATION, 8
DISEASE, 34, 35
MEDICINE, 7
RIGHTEOUSNESS, 8
SUFFERING, 13

Senna, Ayrton
ACCIDENTS, 6

Servetus, Michael
MARTYRDOM, 3

Service, Robert William
PROMISES, 5
SURVIVAL, 6
TIME, 31
WAR, 106

Shackleton, Lord
HOUSES OF PARLIAMENT, 16

Shadwell, Thomas
ENTHUSIASM, 7
HUMAN NATURE, 21
SPEECH, 15

Shaffer, Peter
PASSION, 7
PHILISTINISM, 6
PLAYS, 9

Shah, Idries
CHARACTER, 21

Shahn, Ben
ARTISTS, 5

Shakespeare, William
ACTION, 10, 11
ADMIRATION, 13, 14, 15, 16
AFTERLIFE, 9
AGE, 53, 54, 55
AGREEMENT, 5
ALCOHOL, 53
AMBITION, 15, 16
ANALOGY, 3, 4
ANIMALISM, 7
ANIMALS, 18
APPEARANCES, 20, 21, 22
BEAUTY, 35, 36
BED, 8
BETRAYAL, 7
BIRTH, 9
BORROWING, 8
BREVITY, 7, 8
BRIBERY, 4
BUSINESS, 19
CHARACTER, 22
CHARITY, 17
CLOTHES, 16
COMFORT, 2, 3
COMPLIMENTS, 4
CONFLICT, 7
CONFUSION, 9
CONSCIENCE, 5
CONTENTMENT, 6, 7
CORRUPTION, 7, 8
COUNTRYSIDE, 9
COURAGE, 19
COWARDICE, 7, 8, 9
CRITICISM, 46
CURSES, 1
CUSTOM, 3, 4
DEATH, 104, 105, 106, 107, 108, 109, 110, 111, 112, 113
DECEPTION, 5
DESIRE, 14
DESTINY, 19, 20, 21
DISCONTENT, 8
DISMISSAL, 8
DROWNING, 2
EDUCATION, 49
EGOTISM, 8
ENDING, 5, 6
ENDURANCE, 17, 18
ENGLAND, 36, 37
ENTHUSIASM, 8
EPITAPHS, 26
EQUALITY, 21, 22
EVIL, 16
EXAMPLE, 8
EXCESS, 8, 9, 10, 11, 12
EXPLANATIONS, 2
EYES, 3
FAILURE, 6
FATHERS, 6
FEAR, 11, 12
FLATTERY, 7
FOOLISHNESS, 18
FRIENDS, 13
GOD, 44
GOOD, 15
GOOD AND EVIL, 4
GRATITUDE, 4
GREATNESS, 12
GREED, 11
GUILT, 7, 8, 9
HASTE, 10, 11
HISTORY, 32
HOME, 8
HONESTY, 8, 9, 10
HONOUR, 4, 5
HOPE, 10
HORSES, 10
HUMAN CONDITION, 16, 17, 18
HUMILITY, 10
HUMOUR, 27, 28
HYPOCRISY, 15
IGNORANCE, 13, 14
IMPETUOSITY, 3
INFERIORITY, 6
INGRATITUDE, 4, 5, 6
INJUSTICE, 11, 12
INSINCERITY, 4
INSULTS, 34
INTEGRITY, 6
JEALOUSY, 5, 6
JUSTICE, 22
KINDNESS, 4, 5
LAW, 25
LEARNING, 8
LEISURE, 4
LIFE, 44, 45, 46
LITERACY, 2
LOVE, 114, 115, 116, 117, 118, 119, 120, 121, 122, 123, 124, 125, 126, 127, 128
LOVE AND DEATH, 6
LOVE AND FRIENDSHIP, 3
LUST, 7
MADNESS, 12, 13, 14
MALAPROPISMS, 1, 2
MANKIND, 26, 27, 28
MARRIAGE, 104, 105
MATERIALISM, 18
MEMORIALS, 10
MEMORY, 16
MERCY, 2
MERIT, 6
MERRYMAKING, 3, 4
MISFORTUNE, 16, 17, 18
MISOGYNY, 6
MISQUOTATIONS, 22
MISTRUST, 9
MONARCHY, 19, 20, 21, 22
MONEY, 41, 42, 43
MORTALITY, 16, 17
MOURNING, 9, 10, 11, 12, 13
MURDER, 10, 11
MUSIC, 44, 45, 46
NAMES, 6, 7
NECESSITY, 5, 6
NOBILITY, 4, 5
NOTHING, 2
OBESITY, 10, 11
OLD AGE, 38, 39, 40
OPPORTUNITY, 16, 17
OPTIMISM, 22, 23
ORDER, 4, 5
PARTING, 10, 11
PATIENCE, 12
PATRIOTISM, 28
PERSISTENCE, 12
PESSIMISM, 11
PLAYS, 10, 11
POETRY, 40, 41, 42, 43
POLITICIANS, 23
POSSIBILITY, 3
PRESENT, 13
PROPHECY, 12
QUOTATIONS, 12
REALITY, 6
REGRET, 14, 15, 16, 17, 18, 19
RENUNCIATION, 4
REPUTATION, 7, 8, 9
REST, 2
ROYALTY, 31, 32, 33, 34
RUTHLESSNESS, 5
SEASONS, 20
SELF-CONFIDENCE, 4
SELF-PRESERVATION, 8
SELF-RELIANCE, 8
SEPARATION, 6
SEX, 52, 53
SILENCE, 12
SLEEP, 15
SOCIETY, 8
SORROW, 21, 22
SPEECHES, 5
SUFFERING, 14
SUICIDE, 11, 12
SUITABILITY, 4
SUPERNATURAL, 13, 14
SUPERSTITION, 10
TASTE, 7
THINKING, 10
TIME, 32, 33, 34, 35
TRIVIALITY, 12
UNFAITHFULNESS, 5
WAR, 107, 108
WEAKNESS, 4
WEATHER, 19, 20, 21, 22
WOMEN, 69, 70, 71
WORLD-WEARINESS, 6, 7, 8
YOUTH, 15, 16

Shankly, Bill
FOOTBALL, 8

Sharpe, Tom
CONTRACEPTION, 7
KNOWLEDGE, 32
SOUTH AFRICA, 12

Shaw, George Bernard
AGE, 56, 57
ALCOHOL, 54, 55, 56
APPEARANCE, 33
ART, 26
ASSASSINATION, 5
AUDIENCES, 6
CAPITALISM, 13
CHARACTER, 23
CHRISTIANITY, 38
CLASS, 29, 30, 31
CLASSICS, 8
CRITICISM, 47
DEMOCRACY, 18
DESIRE, 15
DUTY, 4
ECONOMICS, 20
EDUCATION, 50, 51, 52
ENGLISH, 32
ENVY, 7
EUROPE, 18
FASHION, 8
FEMINISM, 38
FOOD, 49
FORGIVENESS, 15
HAPPINESS, 24
HEAVEN, 11, 12
HUNTING, 7
IMPORTANCE, 2
LIBERTY, 2
MANKIND, 29
MARRIAGE, 106, 107
MEDICINE, 8
MONEY, 44, 45
MORALITY, 16, 17
MUSICIANS, 16
NOVELS, 14
NOVELTY, 9
OLD AGE, 41
OXFORD, 5
PARTIES, 6
PLACES, 14
POLITICIANS, 24
POVERTY, 30
PRINCIPLES, 4
PROMPTNESS, 3
REMEDIES, 12
RULES, 3
SELF, 13
SELF-DENIAL, 1
SHAKESPEARE, 16
SILENCE, 13
SOLDIERS, 6, 7
SORROW, 23
TEMPTATION, 9
TITLES, 10, 11
TRUTH, 40, 41
VIOLENCE, 7
WAR, 109
WAR AND PEACE, 12
WEALTH, 24
YOUTH, 17

Shawcross, Lord
MORALITY, 18
POWER, 21

Shawe-Taylor, Desmond
MUSICIANS, 17

Sheen, J. Fulton
BUSINESS, 20

Shelley, Percy Bysshe
BEAUTY, 37
BIRDS, 10
CONVERSATION, 9
DEATH, 114, 115
DEVIL, 11
EUROPE, 19
GREATNESS, 13
LIFE, 47
LIFE AND DEATH, 13
LONDON, 11, 12
MARRIAGE, 108
MEMORIALS, 11
MEMORY, 17
MILTON, 3
MORALITY, 19
MOURNING, 14
MURDER, 12
OPTIMISM, 24

POETRY, 44
POETS, 53
SEASONS, 21
WEATHER, 23, 24, 25

Shenstone, William
LAW, 26

Sheppard, H. R. L.
CHARITY, 18

Sheridan, Philip H.
ENEMIES, 7

Sheridan, Richard Brinsley
ALCOHOL, 57
APOLOGIES, 4
ARROGANCE, 7
BORROWING, 9, 10, 11
COMPLIMENTS, 5
FIRE, 3, 4
FRIENDS, 14
MALAPROPISMS, 3, 4, 5, 6, 7, 8
REPUTATION, 10
TASTE, 8

Sheridan, Tom
BEQUESTS, 2

Sherman, General William
POLITICIANS, 71
WAR, 110

Sherrington, Charles Scott
MIND, 7

Sherwood, Robert E.
CRITICISM, 48
INTELLECTUALS, 7

Shorten, Caroline
POLITICS, 67

Shorter, Clement King
OPTIMISM, 25

Shortt, Edward
CENSORSHIP, 2

Shuter, Edward
THRIFT, 10

Sica, Vittorio De
MORALITY, 20

Sickert, Walter Richard
MONEY, 46

Siddons, Sarah
SUFFERING, 15

Sidney, Algernon
FUTILITY, 9

Sidney, Philip
INSPIRATION, 5
POETS, 11
SELF-DENIAL, 2

Sieyès, Abbé de
SELF-PRESERVATION, 9

Sigerist, Henry E.
DISEASE, 36

Sigismund
GRAMMAR, 7
ILLNESS, 14

Silajdzic, Haris
BOSNIA AND HERCEGOVINA, 5

Simak, Clifford D.
ENVIRONMENT, 5

Simon, Neil
MEDICINE, 9

Simon, Paul
COMFORT, 4
FUTILITY, 10

Simpson, N. F.
ACCIDENTS, 7

Singer, Isaac Bashevis
BOOKS, 39
CHOICE, 4
HUMAN CONDITION, 19
WRITERS, 22

Singh, Rajinder
FASCISM, 4

Sitting Bull
CHARITY, 19

Sitwell, Edith
ALCOHOL, 58
APPEARANCE, 34
CHRISTIANITY, 39
EGOTISM, 9
MODESTY, 7
MOURNING, 15
MUSIC, 47
POETRY, 45, 46
WRITERS, 83

Sitwell, Osbert
ARCHITECTURE, 13
HUNTING, 8
TIME, 36

Sitwell, Sacheverell
MUSICIANS, 18

Skeete, Oliver
SPORT AND GAMES, 21

Skelton, Red
FUNERALS, 8

Skelton, Robin
POETRY, 47

Skinner, B. F.
EDUCATION, 53, 54

Skinner, Cornelia Otis
SEXES, 21

Slezak, Leo
MISTAKES, 15

Slocombe, George Edward
POLITICIANS, 72

Smiles, Samuel
MISTAKES, 16
ORDER, 6

Smith, Adam
BUSINESS, 21
OSTENTATION, 6
SCIENCE, 40
TAXATION, 11
WEALTH, 25

Smith, Cyril
GOVERNMENT, 27
POLITICS, 68

Smith, Delia
FOOD, 50

Smith, Dodie
FAMILY, 31

Smith, F. E.
CHURCHILL, 7
HUMILITY, 11
IMPERTINENCE, 4
REPARTEE, 4
RUTHLESSNESS, 6

Smith, Ian
RACISM, 28

Smith, Joan
ABORTION, 3

Smith, Logan Pearsall
ADVICE, 13
BOOKS, 40
DEATH, 116
FRIENDSHIP, 27
LAST WORDS, 64
MARRIAGE, 109
PURPOSE, 7
READING, 14
STATISTICS, 8
WEALTH, 26

Smith, Stevie
DEATH, 117
DROWNING, 3
PLEASURE, 28
PUNS, 20
WOMEN, 72

Smith, Sydney
BOOKS, 41
BUSINESS, 22
CHARITY, 20
CLERGY, 13
HAPPINESS, 25
IGNORANCE, 15
INSULTS, 35
IRELAND, 19
MARRIAGE, 110
MINORITY, 3
PRAYER, 16
SCOTLAND, 8
SERIOUSNESS, 3, 4
SERMONS, 1
SWITZERLAND, 3
WATER, 9
WEATHER, 26

Smith, Thorne
TOLERANCE, 6

Smollett, Tobias
ENGLISH, 33
MEN, 11
PATRIOTISM, 29
WISDOM, 21
WRITERS, 84

Smoot, George
UNIVERSE, 12

Smythe, Tony
CENSORSHIP, 3

Snow, C. P.
NASTINESS, 8
POWER, 22
PROMISES, 6

Snowden, Philip
GOVERNMENT, 28

Socrates
GOD, 45
GOOD, 16
LAST WORDS, 65
LUXURY, 5
NATIONALITY, 8
SELF, 14

Solon
LAW, 27
VICE, 8

Solzhenitsyn, Alexander
COMMUNISM, 7
DEATH, 118
FREEDOM, 49
HAPPINESS, 26
IMPRISONMENT, 5
INDOCTRINATION, 1, 2
LOVE, 129
LYING, 15
NEWSPAPERS, 12
POWER, 23
RESPONSIBILITY, 13
RUSSIA, 9
TRUTH, 42
WRITERS, 23

Somerville, E.
HORSES, 11
MEN, 12

Sondheim, Stephen
PERFECTION, 8

Sontag, Susan
ILLNESS, 15
PHOTOGRAPHY, 8

Sophocles
SEX, 54
THEATRE, 13
WORLD-WEARINESS, 9

Sousa, John Philip
MUSIC, 48
POP MUSIC, 18

Southey, Robert
CURSES, 2
GOD, 46
OLD AGE, 42
VICTORY, 17
YOUTH, 18

Spaak, Paul Henri
AGREEMENT, 6

Spark, Muriel
AGE, 58
ALCOHOL, 59
APPEARANCE, 35
CHILDREN, 38
COMMUNISM, 8
EDUCATION, 55
EXCELLENCE, 3
FASCISM, 5
IMPORTANCE, 3
IMPRESSIONABILITY, 3
INTELLECTUALS, 8
OLD AGE, 43

Sparrow, John
DOGS, 12

Speight, Johnny
INSULTS, 36
POLITICS, 69
PORNOGRAPHY, 6
STRIKES, 5

Spencer, Herbert
POLITICS, 70
SPORT AND GAMES, 22

Spencer, Stanley
LAST WORDS, 66

Spender, Stephen
POETS, 54
TECHNOLOGY, 13
WAR, 111

Spenser, Edmund
AMBITION, 17
DEATH, 119
RIVERS, 5

Spiel, Hilde
NASTINESS, 9

Spinoza, Benedict
DESIRE, 16
IMMORTALITY, 6
SOCIETY, 9
UNDERSTANDING, 11

Spock, Dr Benjamin
CHILDREN, 39
WAR, 112

Spring-Rice, Cecil Arthur
ACADEMICS, 5

Spyri, Johanna
ANGER, 6
DISAPPOINTMENT, 7

Squire, John Collings
APPEARANCE, 36
DRUNKENNESS, 19
SCIENTISTS, 15

Stacpoole, H. de Vere
HOMESICKNESS, 7

Stalin, Joseph
CATHOLICISM, 10
COMMUNISM, 9
POLITICS, 71
RUSSIAN REVOLUTION, 1
STATE, 5
STATISTICS, 9

Stanley, Henry Morton
GREETINGS, 3

Stanton, C. E.
GREETINGS, 4

Stanton, Elizabeth
CLASS, 32
FEMINISM, 24, 25, 26
MOTHERHOOD, 16
RELIGION, 53
WOMEN, 73

Stanton, Frank L.
BABIES, 6

Stapledon, Olaf
AMERICANS, 10
CREATION, 12

Stark, John
WAR, 113

Stead, Christina
MOTHERHOOD, 17
SELF-MADE MEN, 3

Steel, David
POLITICIANS, 25
POLITICS, 72, 73, 74

Steele, Richard
MARRIAGE, 111
OLD AGE, 44
READING, 15

Steffens, Lincoln
FUTURE, 7

Stein, Gertrude
AMERICA, 32
CONCEIT, 15, 16
FAMILIARITY, 5
NORMALITY, 1
WAR, 114

Steinbeck, John
ADVICE, 14
CHOICE, 5
INSULTS, 37
MANKIND, 30

Steinem, Gloria
VIOLENCE, 8

Steiner, Rudolf
DISEASE, 37

Stekel, Wilhelm
AGE, 59

Stendhal
LITERATURE, 17
NOVELS, 15

Stephens, James
AGE, 60
CURIOSITY, 8
PERFECTION, 9

Stern, Richard G.
SIMPLICITY, 7

Sterne, Laurence
BITTERNESS, 3
FAMILY, 32
FRANCE, 14
HYPOCHONDRIA, 2
RELIGION, 54
SOUL, 11
STUBBORNNESS, 3
TOLERANCE, 7
TRAVEL, 20
WISDOM, 22
WRITING, 31

Stevas, Norman St John
SNOBBERY, 6

Stevenson, Adlai
COMPLIMENTS, 6
DISAPPOINTMENT, 8
EDITORS, 3
ENDURANCE, 19
FLATTERY, 8
FREEDOM, 50
LYING, 16
NUCLEAR WEAPONS, 18
POLITICIANS, 26, 73
POLITICS, 75
POWER, 24
SUCCESS, 16
WORDS, 19

Stevenson, Robert Louis
ABSTINENCE, 10
ALCOHOL, 60
ANTICIPATION, 7
BOOKS, 42
CONCEIT, 17
DEATH, 120
DREAMS, 13
EXCESS, 13
HAPPINESS, 27
IMITATION, 6
MARRIAGE, 112, 113, 114, 115
MONEY, 47
MORALITY, 21
MORTALITY, 18
POLITICS, 76
SEXES, 22
SILENCE, 14
THEORY, 7
TRAVEL, 21, 22
TRIVIALITY, 13
WISDOM AND FOOLISHNESS, 7

Stipe, Michael
POP MUSIC, 19

Stocks, Mary
HOUSES OF PARLIAMENT, 17

Stockwood, Mervyn
PSYCHIATRY, 9

Stoddard, Elizabeth Drew
LOVE, 130

Stoker, Bram
SUPERNATURAL, 15, 16

Stone, I. F.
LONGEVITY, 3

Stone, Oliver
VIOLENCE, 9

Stone, Samuel J.
CHRISTIANITY, 40

Stoppard, Tom
ART, 27
ARTISTS, 6
CRITICS, 17
DEMOCRACY, 19
ETERNITY, 4
HOUSES OF PARLIAMENT, 18
IDEAS, 7
JOURNALISM, 28, 29
JUSTICE, 23
LIFE, 48
POLITICS, 77
QUOTATIONS, 13
RESPONSIBILITY, 14
THEATRE, 14
UNIVERSE, 13
WAR, 115

Stout, Rex Todhunter
AMERICA, 33
STATISTICS, 10

Stowe, Harriet Beecher
CREATION, 13
CRUELTY, 5
INSPIRATION, 6
REGRET, 20

Strachey, John St Loe
CATHOLICISM, 11
FASCISM, 6

Strachey, Lytton
GOD, 47
LAST WORDS, 67
POETS, 55
PURPOSE, 8
ROYALTY, 35

Stratton, Eugene
LOVE, 131

Strauss, Henry G.
SMOKING, 16

Stravinsky, Igor
CRITICS, 18
HASTE, 12
MUSIC, 49, 50
MUSICIANS, 9, 19, 20

Streatfield, Geoffrey
FACTS, 3
STATISTICS, 11

Strindberg, August
DOGS, 13

Stubbes, Philip
FOOTBALL, 9

Sullivan, Annie
ADVICE, 15
LANGUAGE, 23
SENTIMENTALITY, 5

Sully, Duc de
ENGLAND, 38

Svevo, Italo
WOMEN, 74

Swaffer, Hannen
ADVERTISING, 5
JOURNALISM, 30

Swift, Jonathan
BUSINESS, 23
CLERGY, 14
COURAGE, 20
DECLINE, 10
ENGLISH, 34
FLATTERY, 9
FOOLISHNESS, 19
GENIUS, 9
LAST WORDS, 68
LAW, 28
MARRIAGE, 116, 117
MUSICIANS, 21
OPINIONS, 6
PARASITES, 3
POLITICIANS, 27
PROMISES, 7
REGRET, 21
SATIRE, 3
TAXATION, 12
WAR, 116
WEALTH, 27

Swinburne, Algernon Charles
MANKIND, 31
PEACE, 15
SEASONS, 22

Sydenham, Thomas
DISEASE, 38

Sylvester, Robert
BOOKS, 43
SMOKING, 17

Symonds, John Addington
KNOWLEDGE, 33

Symons, Arthur
MEMORY, 18
POETS, 56

Synge, John Millington
LOSS, 6

Syrus, Publilius
NECESSITY, 7
PROMPTNESS, 4

Szasz, Thomas
FORGIVENESS, 16
HAPPINESS, 28
MADNESS, 15
MEDICINE, 10
MOTIVE, 6
PSYCHIATRY, 10
RIGHT, 2
SEX, 55, 56

Szent-Györgyi, Albert
DISCOVERY, 8

T

Taber, Robert
WAR, 117

Tabrar, Joseph
DOGS, 14

Tacitus
FAME, 19
HUMAN NATURE, 22
WAR, 118

Taft, William Howard
DEFEAT, 7

Tagore, Rabindranath
DEATH, 121

Taine, Hippolyte Adolphe
VIRTUE AND VICE, 3

Takriti, Barzan al-
MIDDLE EAST, 15

Talleyrand
AMERICA, 34
CHRISTIANITY, 41
DEFEAT, 8
FIRST IMPRESSIONS, 7
GOVERNMENT, 29
MODERATION, 4
SPEECH, 16

Tarantino, Quentin
VIOLENCE, 10

Tarkington, Booth
ALCOHOL, 61

Tate, Allen
DEATH, 122

Tate, Nahum
CHANGE, 18
CHRISTMAS, 18
THIRST, 3

Taupin, Bernie
ACTORS, 18

Tawney, R. H.
POVERTY AND WEALTH, 8

Taylor, A. J. P.
CAPITALISM, 14
COMMUNISM, 10
ENGLAND, 39
EXPERIENCE, 18
HISTORY, 33
HITLER, 7
MISTAKES, 17
OLD AGE, 45
POWER, 25

Taylor, Bert Leston
BORES, 5

Taylor, Elizabeth
ABSTINENCE, 11
ACTORS, 19
PATIENCE, 13
SHYNESS, 6
WORDS, 20

Taylor, Harry
PRIDE, 10

Taylor, Jane
STARS, 5

Taylor, Jeremy
LIFE, 49
MARRIAGE, 118

Taylor, John
CLOTHES, 17

Taylor, Ron
EVIL, 17

Tebbit, Norman
GOVERNMENT, 30
POLITICIANS, 74
UNEMPLOYMENT, 2

Temple, Frederick
CLERGY, 15
LUCK, 12

Temple, William
CHRISTIANITY, 42
CHURCH, 8
CRICKET, 7
GOD, 48
HUMAN NATURE, 23
RELIGION, 55
SELF-CONFIDENCE, 5

Templeman, Mr Justice
LAWYERS, 8

Tenniel, John
DISMISSAL, 9

Tennyson, Alfred, Lord
ACTION, 12
AFTERLIFE, 10
ARISTOCRACY, 12
ARTHURIAN LEGEND, 2, 3
BEAUTY, 38, 39
CHANGE, 19
CHIVALRY, 11
CHRISTIANITY, 43
CLERGY, 16
CONSTANCY, 4
COURAGE, 21, 22
CURSES, 3, 4
DEATH, 123
DECLINE, 11
DESTINY, 22, 23
DETERMINATION, 15
DREAMS, 14
DUTY, 5
ENDING, 7
ENEMIES, 8
EXCESS, 14
EXPERIENCE, 19, 20
HUMAN CONDITION, 20
HYPOCRISY, 16
INTEGRITY, 7
INVITATIONS, 2
IRREVOCABILITY, 2
LEARNING, 9
LIFE, 50
LIFE AND DEATH, 14
LOVE, 132, 133, 134, 135, 136
LYING, 17
MARRIAGE, 119
MARTYRDOM, 4
MERRYMAKING, 5
MORTALITY, 19
MOURNING, 16
MUSIC, 51
NATURE, 15
NOSTALGIA, 19, 20, 21
OBEDIENCE, 4
PASSION, 8
POLITICS, 78
PRAYER, 17
PURITY, 3
RESPONSIBILITY, 15
RIVERS, 6
ROYALTY, 36
SEASONS, 23, 24
SEXES, 23, 24
SLEEP, 16
SORROW, 24, 25, 26
SUICIDE, 13
TIME, 37
TRANSIENCE, 18
TRIVIALITY, 14
UNFAITHFULNESS, 6
WEATHER, 27
WOMEN, 75, 76
WORDS, 21

Terence
COURAGE, 23
MANKIND, 32
OPINIONS, 7
ORIGINALITY, 5

Teresa, Mother
ABORTION, 4
CHARITY, 21
HUMILITY, 12
LONELINESS, 7
POVERTY, 31

Teresa of Ávila, St
RELIGION, 56

Terry, Ellen
ACTING, 11
ACTORS, 20
DIARIES, 5
FUNERALS, 9
SHAKESPEARE, 17

Tertullian
BELIEF, 7
CHRISTIANITY, 44, 45

Thackeray, William Makepeace
FAITH, 18
FAMILY, 33
GREATNESS, 14
LOVE, 137
MARRIAGE, 120, 121
MONEY, 48
NEWSPAPERS, 13
SERVILITY, 7
SEXES, 25
SNOBBERY, 7, 8
WISDOM, 23
WRITERS, 85, 86

Thales
LIFE AND DEATH, 15

Tharp, Twyla
ORIGINALITY, 6

Thatcher, Denis
FEMINISM, 42
HOUSEWORK, 5

Thatcher, Margaret
AFFECTATION, 1
ARGUMENTS, 15
AUTHORITARIANISM, 6, 7
CHARACTER, 24
CLASS, 33
COMMITMENT, 5
CONCEIT, 18, 19
ECOLOGY, 8
FEMINISM, 41
IDLENESS, 8
IMPERFECTION, 13
INFLEXIBILITY, 3
MARXISM, 6
MERIT, 7
MONEY, 49
MORALITY, 22
PEACE, 16
POLITICIANS, 28, 75
POLITICS, 79, 80, 81
SELF-CONFIDENCE, 6
SOCIALISM, 14
TALENT, 7
WOMEN, 77
WORK, 23

Thayer, W. M.
ACHIEVEMENT, 8

Themistocles
INFLUENCE, 9

Theodoric
LOYALTY, 9

Theroux, Paul
CLASS, 34
LANGUAGE, 24
MOUNTAINS, 4
PLACES, 15
SWITZERLAND, 4
TRAVEL, 23

Thiers, Louis Adolphe
MONARCHY, 23
PERSPECTIVE, 4
SNOBBERY, 9

Thomas, Brandon
PLACES, 16

Thomas, Dylan
AGRICULTURE, 6
APPEARANCE, 37
BORES, 6
CLEANNESS, 2
DEATH, 124, 125, 126
EMOTION, 5
EXPECTATION, 6
INNOCENCE, 9
LIFE, 51
LONELINESS, 8
MARRIAGE, 122
MUSIC, 52
OLD AGE, 46
OPPORTUNITY, 18
PAINTING, 16
POETRY, 48
POETS, 57
PUBLIC HOUSES, 4
RELIGION, 57
SEASONS, 25
SEX, 57
SIGNATURES, 3
WALES, 2, 3
WRITERS, 87

Thomas, Edward
DEATH, 127
ENGLAND, 40
PAST, 7
WALES, 4
WAR, 119

Thomas, Gwyn
BUREAUCRACY, 9
GOSSIP, 9
SPORT AND GAMES, 23
WELSH, 2

Thomas, Irene
CONTRACEPTION, 8
MARRIAGE, 123
MUSIC, 53

Thomas, Lewis
WORRY, 12

Thomas, Lowell
CINEMA, 10

Thomas, Mark
POLITICAL CORRECTNESS, 4

Thomas, Norman M.
RIGHT, 3

Thomas, R. S.
INNOCENCE, 10
POETRY, 49
WELSH, 3

Thompson, Daley
PLEASURE, 29

Thompson, Emma
ACTORS, 21

Thompson, E. P.
EUROPE, 20

Thompson, Francis
HEAVEN, 13
RELIGION, 58
SEASONS, 26

Thompson, William Hepworth
IMPERFECTION, 14
NEGLECT, 4

Thomson, James
BRITAIN, 13
LIFE, 52
NECESSITY, 8

Thomson, Jeff
INSULTS, 38

Thomson, Joseph
LONDON, 13

Thomson of Fleet, Lord
BUSINESS, 24

Thoreau, Henry David
ADVICE, 16
AFTERLIFE, 11
ARGUMENTS, 16
CHARITY, 22
COURAGE, 24
DESPAIR, 6
DISEASE, 39
HONOUR, 6
JUSTICE, 24
LANGUAGE, 25
PHILOSOPHERS, 10
PROOF, 6
SIMPLICITY, 8
SOCIETY, 10
SOLITUDE, 13
THRIFT, 11
TIME, 38, 39
TRAVEL, 24
TRUTH, 44
WRITING, 32, 33

Thorndike, Sybil
MARRIAGE, 124

Thorpe, Jeremy
SELF-PRESERVATION, 10

Thorpe, Rose Hartwick
MERCY, 3

Thucydides
FAME, 20
WOMEN, 78

Thurber, James
ALCOHOL, 62, 63
BED, 9
CONFORMITY, 6
CRITICISM, 49
DECEPTION, 6
DECLINE, 12
EXECUTION, 28
HUMAN CONDITION, 21
HUMOUR, 56
LAST WORDS, 69
LAZINESS, 4
MARRIAGE, 125
MEMORY, 19
MISTAKES, 18
SCIENCE, 41
SEX, 58, 59
SEXES, 26
TECHNOLOGY, 14
WOMEN, 79

Thurlow, Lord
LOYALTY, 10
MONARCHY, 24

Ti, Huang
DRUGS, 13

Tilberis, Liz
FASHION, 9

Tillich, Paul
NEUROSIS, 3

Tilzer, Harry
PUBLIC HOUSES, 5

Tintoretto
HEAVEN, 14

Tocqueville, Alexis de
PRIDE, 11

Tolkien, J. R. R.
MANKIND, 33
MARRIAGE, 126
POWER, 26

Tolstoy, Leo
ARMY, 3
ART, 28
EMOTION, 6
FAMILY, 34
HAPPINESS, 29
HISTORIANS, 7
HYPOCRISY, 17
LAST WORDS, 70
LOVE, 138
MANKIND, 34
REMEDIES, 13
SELF, 15
UNDERSTANDING, 12

Tolstoy, Sophie
CONCEIT, 20
LOVE, 139
WOMEN, 80

Tomaschek, Rudolphe
SCIENCE, 42

Tooke, John Horne
ADULTERY, 9

Toplady, Augustus Montague
RELIGION, 59

Torrey, Jesse
SMOKING, 18

Toscanini, Arturo
FLOWERS, 11
INCOMPETENCE, 5
INSULTS, 39
LOVE AND MARRIAGE, 5
MUSIC, 54
SMOKING, 19
THREATS, 3

Tourneur, Cyril
SIN, 20

Toynbee, Arnold
AMERICA, 35
REPRESENTATION, 2

Tracy, Spencer
EQUALITY, 23
LEISURE, 5
POVERTY, 32

Trapp, Joseph
CAMBRIDGE, 6
OXFORD, 6

Tree, Herbert Beerbohm
ACTING, 12
AGE, 61
BORES, 7
CINEMA, 11
CLOCKS, 1
CRITICS, 19
DEMOCRACY, 21
ENGLISH, 35
FAME, 21, 22
PRONUNCIATION, 2

Trevelyan, George Macaulay
ARISTOCRACY, 13
CRICKET, 8
CURIOSITY, 9
OFFICERS, 11
READING, 16

Trinder, Tommy
SOLDIERS, 8

Trollope, Anthony
ACTION, 13
DICKENS, 3
EGOTISM, 10
LOVE, 140, 141
OBITUARIES, 3
PRIDE, 12
PROPHECY, 13
PUNISHMENT, 15
REVENGE, 14
SEASONS, 27
SELF-RESPECT, 2, 3
TOLERANCE, 8
WOMEN, 81
WRITING, 34

Trollope, Joanna
FICTION, 5

Trotsky, Leon
COMMUNISM, 11
INDOCTRINATION, 3
MISTAKES, 19
MISTRUST, 10
OLD AGE, 47
PATRIOTISM, 30
REVOLUTION, 6, 7, 8, 9
RUSSIA, 10, 11
RUSSIAN REVOLUTION, 2, 3

Truman, Harry S.
ECONOMICS, 21
ENDURANCE, 20
EXPERIENCE, 21
OFFICERS, 12
PERSUASION, 4
POLITICIANS, 29
RESPONSIBILITY, 16
UNEMPLOYMENT, 3
WORLD WAR II, 29

Tuchman, Barbara W.
WAR, 120

Tucker, Sophie
AGE, 62, 63
SINGERS, 3

Tupper, Martin Farquhar
BOOKS, 44
REST, 3

Turenne, Vicomte de
POWER POLITICS, 7

Turgenev, Ivan
DEATH, 128
OPINIONS, 8
PRAYER, 18
SCEPTICISM, 6

Turgot, Anne-Robert-Jacques
SCIENTISTS, 16

Turk, Roy
LOVE, 142

Turnbull, Margaret
FATHERS, 7
SEXES, 27

Turner, Joseph
LOSS, 7
PAINTING, 17

Tusser, Thomas
CHRISTMAS, 19
HOME, 9
MONTHS, 11, 12

Tutu, Desmond
RACISM, 29, 30
RELIGION, 60
SOUTH AFRICA, 13, 14, 15

Tuwim, Julian
RACISM, 31

Twain, Mark
CONSERVATISM, 7
EDUCATION, 56
EMBARRASSMENT, 2
FREEDOM, 51
HURT, 3
INDECISION, 3
LITERATURE, 18
LYING, 18
MADNESS, 16
MANNERS, 5
MORALITY, 23
OBITUARIES, 4
PERVERSITY, 6
PRONUNCIATION, 3
PUNS, 21
SELF-RESPECT, 4
SEX, 60
SLEEP, 17
SMOKING, 20, 21
SPELLING, 2
TEETH, 4
TELEGRAMS, 11
WOMEN, 82, 83
WRITERS, 89

Tyler, Robin
HOMOSEXUALITY, 11

Tynan, Kenneth
COMPLIMENTS, 7
CRITICS, 20, 21
NOVELS, 16
PLAYS, 12, 13
WRITERS, 88

Tyrrell, George
SERMONS, 2

U

Uccello, Paolo
ART, 29

Updike, John
AMERICANS, 11
BORES, 8
CHARACTER, 25
RELIGION, 61

Ure, Mary
CHILDREN, 40

Ussher, James
CREATION, 14

Ustinov, Peter
AGE, 64
ARTISTS, 21
AUTHORITARIANISM, 8
BOOKS, 45
CINEMA, 12
DIPLOMACY, 19
EDUCATION, 57
EFFORT, 6
FAMILY, 35
JEWS, 14

OPTIMISM, 26
PRIVACY, 5
SOLDIERS, 9

V

Vail, Amanda
MEN, 13

Valéry, Paul
ARTISTS, 7
CREATION, 15
MANNERS, 6
POETRY, 50
POLITICS, 82
SCIENCE, 44
TRUTH, 45

Valois, Ninette de
SUPPORT, 6

Vanbrugh, John
MATERIALISM, 19
MEDIOCRITY, 8
THINKING, 11
UNFAITHFULNESS, 7
WOMEN, 84, 85

Vance, Jack
IGNORANCE, 16

Vanderbilt, William Henry
CAPITALISM, 15
LAST WORDS, 71
WEALTH, 28

Van Dyke, Henry
POETS, 58

Vauvenargues, Marquis de
ACHIEVEMENT, 9
THINKING, 12

Veblen, Thorstein Bunde
BUSINESS, 25
MATERIALISM, 20
RESEARCH, 6

Vegetius
WAR AND PEACE, 13

Venner, Tobias
SMOKING, 22

Verrall, Arthur Woollgar
NUMBERS, 4

Vespasian
LAST WORDS, 72

Vicky
POLITICIANS, 76

Victoria
CRITICISM, 50
FEMINISM, 39
MEMORIALS, 12
POLITICIANS, 77, 78
PREJUDICE, 5
ROYALTY, 37, 38

Vidal, Gore
AMERICANS, 12
CHILDREN, 41
ENVY, 8
INSULTS, 40
NOVELS, 17
POLITICS, 83
PUNISHMENT, 16
RUTHLESSNESS, 7
SPACE, 8

Vigny, Alfred de
ARMY, 4
INSPIRATION, 7
SOLITUDE, 14

Villiers, Alan John
BOATS, 15

Villon, François
NOSTALGIA, 22

Vinci, Leonardo da
DEATH, 129

Virchow, Rudolph
MEDICINE, 11

Virgil
ANGER, 7
DANGER, 7
ENDURANCE, 21, 22, 23
FEAR, 13
HELL, 7
LOVE, 143
MATERIALISM, 21
MISTRUST, 11
PLEASURE, 30
PROPHECY, 14
SLEEP, 18
SORROW, 27
TIME, 40
WOMEN, 86

Vizinczey, Stephen
MELANCHOLY, 11

Voltaire
ADMIRATION, 17
ANIMALS, 19
ARTS, 8
BEQUESTS, 3
CRITICISM, 51
DEBAUCHERY, 9
DISEASE, 40
DRINKS, 9
ENVY, 9
EXAMPLE, 9
EXCELLENCE, 4
FAITH, 19
FRANKNESS, 3
FREEDOM, 52
GOD, 49, 50
GOVERNMENT, 31
HISTORY, 34, 35
HUMAN NATURE, 24
LANGUAGE, 26
MADNESS, 17
MARRIAGE, 127
MEDICINE, 12
NATIONALITY, 9
NATIONS, 3
NOVELTY, 10
OPTIMISM, 27
PAROCHIALISM, 3
POWER POLITICS, 8
PUBLIC, 18
PURITY, 4
RESPECT, 4
STYLE, 6
SUPERSTITION, 11
WORK, 24

Vorster, John
CRITICISM, 52

Voznesensky, Andrei
CREATION, 16

Vukovich, Bill
SPORT AND GAMES, 24

W

Wain, John
POETRY AND PROSE, 5

Waite, Terry
HOSTAGES, 4
POLITICS, 84

Waits, Tom
COMMERCIALISM, 4

Wald, George
ACTION, 14

Wałesa, Lech
COMPUTERS, 6
POLITICS, 85

Waley, Arthur
PAST, 8

Walker, Arthur M.
DISEASE, 41

Walker, James J.
CORRUPTION, 9

Walker, Murray
INTERRUPTIONS, 3

Wall, Max
HUMOUR, 57
PUNS, 22

Wallace, Edgar
INTELLECTUALS, 9
POLITICS, 86

Wallace, Henry
PUBLIC, 19

Wallace, Naomi
SEXES, 28

Wallace, William Ross
INFLUENCE, 10

Wallach, Eli
MATERIALISM, 22

Walpole, Horace
AGE, 65
AMERICA, 36
ARGUMENTS, 17
DRUNKENNESS, 20
FRANCE, 15
LIFE, 53
MIND, 8
PUBLIC, 20
READING, 17
SHAKESPEARE, 18

Walpole, Robert
ARISTOCRACY, 14
CORRUPTION, 10
HISTORY, 36
POWER, 27
WAR, 121

Walston, Oliver
ECOLOGY, 9

Walton, Izaak
COMPLIMENTS, 8
FISHING, 2, 3, 4, 5
GOSSIP, 10
HEALTH AND HEALTHY LIVING, 12
MERRYMAKING, 6

Walton, Sir William
MUSIC, 55

Ward, Artemus
ALCOHOL, 64
BORROWING, 12
CHAUCER, 4
GRAMMAR, 8
IDLENESS, 9

Ware, George
LOVE, 144

Warhol, Andy
ARTISTS, 8
DESIRE, 17
FAME, 23
SEX, 61

Warner, Susan
RELIGION, 62

Warnock, Mary
OXFORD, 7

Warren, Earl
GOVERNMENT, 32

Warren, Leonard
OPERA, 8

Washington, George
FRIENDS, 15
HONESTY, 11
WAR, 122

Waters, John
HUMOUR, 29

Watson, James Dewey
FEMINISM, 40
SCIENTISTS, 17

Watts, Isaac
ANIMALS, 20
DEATH, 130
HUMILITY, 13
IDLENESS, 10
LAZINESS, 5
RELIGION, 63, 64
WORK, 25

Waugh, Auberon
CHILDREN, 42
OLD AGE, 48
POLITICIANS, 30
WRITERS, 24

Waugh, Evelyn
ANIMALS, 21
APPEARANCE, 38, 39
ARISTOCRACY, 15
BREVITY, 9
BRITISH, 10
CANNIBALISM, 2
CHARACTER, 26
CHURCHILL, 8
CLASS, 35, 36
CRIME, 9
DEMOCRACY, 22
EDUCATION, 58, 59, 60, 61, 62, 63
ENGLAND, 41
FAMILY, 36
FOOD, 51
INSULTS, 41
LUST, 8
MANNERS, 7
NATIONALITY, 10
NEWSPAPERS, 14, 15
OPERA, 9
PARTIES, 7, 8
PHILISTINISM, 7
POLITICS, 87, 88
PROMPTNESS, 5
QUOTATIONS, 14
READING, 18
RELIGION, 65, 66
REPUBLIC, 2
SELF, 16, 17
SEX, 62
SEXES, 29

SLEEP, 19
TELEGRAMS, 12
WALES, 5
WAR, 123, 124
WELSH, 4
WOMEN, 87, 88
WRITERS, 90, 91
WRITING, 35

Wavell, Lord
LOVE, 145

Wayne, John
CINEMA, 13

Weatherly, Frederic Edward
COMPLIMENTS, 9
NOSTALGIA, 23

Webb, Beatrice
RELIGION, 67
SELF-CONFIDENCE, 7

Webb-Johnstone, Lord Robert
PSYCHIATRY, 11

Webster, Daniel
AMBITION, 18
GOVERNMENT, 33
PAST, 9
PATRIOTISM, 31
PURITY, 5

Webster, John
DESTINY, 24
DOCTORS, 10
FOOD, 52
IMPRISONMENT, 6
MURDER, 13

Webster, Noah
WORDS, 22

Weil, Simone
CULTURE, 3
FUTURE, 8
IMAGINATION, 10
REVOLUTION, 10
TRUTH, 46

Weiss, Peter
REVOLUTION, 11

Weissmuller, Johnny
CINEMA, 14

Weizsäcker, C. F. von
SCIENCE, 45

Welch, Raquel
MIND, 9

Welles, Orson
DECLINE, 13
FLYING, 3
SWITZERLAND, 5
THEATRE, 15

Wellington, Duke of
ARMY, 5
EDUCATION, 64
HOUSES OF PARLIAMENT, 19
INDIFFERENCE, 6
OFFICERS, 13, 14, 15, 16
POETS, 12
PRACTICALITY, 7
PUBLISHING, 11
REMEDIES, 14
SERMONS, 3
SOLDIERS, 10
SPEECHES, 6
TRAINS, 7
VICTORY, 18, 19
WAR, 125, 126, 127, 128

WRITERS, 25

Wells, H. G.
ARMY, 6
BUSINESS, 26
CLASS, 37
CLASSICS, 9
COMMITMENT, 6
CYNICISM, 4
FAMILIARITY, 6
FEAR, 14
FIRE, 5
HOUSES, 5
INJUSTICE, 13
LITERATURE, 19
MANKIND, 35
NAMES, 8
NEWSPAPERS, 16
OCCUPATIONS, 17
PROTESTANTISM, 2
SCIENTISTS, 6
SUPERIORITY, 12

Wên-chün, Chuo
UNFAITHFULNESS, 8

Wenckebach, Karel Frederik
DRUGS, 14

Wesker, Arnold
AFFECTATION, 2
EUROPE, 21
FOOD, 53

Wesley, Charles
HUMILITY, 14

Wesley, John
KNOWLEDGE, 34
LANGUAGE, 27
LOVE, 146
RELIGION, 68

West, Mae
CINEMA, 15
CLOTHES, 18
GOOD, 17
HUMOUR, 30
INVITATIONS, 3
LEXICOGRAPHY, 7
LUXURY, 6
MARRIAGE, 128
MATERIALISM, 23
MEN, 14
MISQUOTATIONS, 23
PROMISCUITY, 6
PURITY, 6
REPUTATION, 11
SEX, 63, 64, 65
STARING, 1
VICE, 9

West, Nathaniel
ADVICE, 17
MATHEMATICS, 15

West, Rebecca
AGGRAVATION, 2
APPEARANCE, 40
ART, 30
BIOGRAPHY, 6
CENSORSHIP, 4
CLASS, 38
CONVERSATION, 10
FEMINISM, 27
JOURNALISM, 31
SNOBBERY, 10

Westmorland, William
WAR, 129

Weston, R. P.
PARTING, 12

Weygand, Maxime
WORLD WAR II, 30

Wharton, Edith
AFFECTATION, 3
CULTURE, 4
OPERA, 10
ORIGINALITY, 7

Whately, Richard
HAPPINESS, 30
HONESTY, 12

Wheeler, Hugh
TEETH, 5

Wheeler, John Archibald
TIME, 41

Whewell, William
POETRY, 51

Whicker, Alan
MARRIAGE, 129

Whistler, James
ARGUMENTS, 18
ARROGANCE, 8, 9
ARTISTS, 22
BIRTH, 10
CONCEIT, 21, 22, 23, 24
EXAMINATIONS, 3
GOOD, 18
IMITATION, 7
INSULTS, 42
NATURE, 16
PHILISTINISM, 8
RENUNCIATION, 5
ROYALTY, 39
TELEGRAMS, 13

White, Andrew Dickson
FOOTBALL, 10

White, Elwyn Brooks
BUSINESS, 27
CHRISTMAS, 20
HYPOCHONDRIA, 3
READING, 19
TRAINS, 6
TRAVEL, 25

White, Henry Kirke
ENDURANCE, 24

White, Patrick
AMBITION, 19
KNOWLEDGE, 35
WEAPONS, 10
WRITING, 36

White, T. H.
TRAVEL, 26

White, William Allen
FUTILITY, 11

Whitehead, A. N.
ABILITY, 4
ART, 31
CATS, 7
PHILOSOPHY, 14, 15
SCIENCE, 46
TRUTH, 47
WONDER, 4

Whitehorn, Katherine
CHILDREN, 43
CLEANNESS, 3
CLOTHES, 19
CONVERSATION, 11
MARRIAGE, 130
MONEY, 50
OCCUPATIONS, 18
PARTIES, 9

POLITICAL CORRECTNESS, 5
POLITICIANS, 31
RELIGION, 69

Whitelaw, William
POLITICS, 89
PREJUDICE, 6
WISDOM, 24

Whiting, William
SEA, 14

Whitlam, Gough
INSULTS, 43

Whitman, Walt
ANIMALS, 22
GREATNESS, 15
HUMAN NATURE, 25
INDIFFERENCE, 7
MANKIND, 36
NATURE, 17
POETRY, 52
REVOLUTION, 12
SELF, 18, 19, 20, 21

Whittier, John Greenleaf
AMERICA, 37
PATRIOTISM, 32

Whittington, Robert
ADAPTABILITY, 4

Whorf, Benjamin Lee
LANGUAGE, 28

Wigg, George
NUCLEAR WEAPONS, 19

Wilberforce, Samuel
CLERGY, 17
EVOLUTION, 11

Wilcox, Ella Wheeler
ARGUMENTS, 19
HURT, 4
KINDNESS, 6
LAUGHTER, 10
RELIGION, 70

Wilde, Oscar
ACTORS, 22
ADDRESSES, 2
AGE, 66, 67
AGREEMENT, 7
AMERICANS, 13
APPEARANCE, 41
APPEARANCES, 23
ART, 32, 33, 34
BIBLE, 11
BOOKS, 46
BORES, 9
CHARM, 4
CLASS, 39
CONCEIT, 25, 26, 27
COUNTRYSIDE, 10
CRICKET, 9
CYNICISM, 5
DEATH, 131
DECEPTION, 7
DEMOCRACY, 23
DIARIES, 6
DICKENS, 4
EFFORT, 7
EGOTISM, 11
ENEMIES, 9
EXCESS, 15
EXPECTATION, 7
EXTRAVAGANCE, 5
FAME, 24
FRANKNESS, 4
HONESTY, 13
HUNTING, 9
HYPOCRISY, 18

IGNORANCE, 17
IMPRISONMENT, 7, 8, 9, 10, 11
INFLUENCE, 11
INSENSITIVITY, 4
JOURNALISM, 32
KILLING, 8
LAST WORDS, 73, 74
LOSS, 8
LOVE AND MARRIAGE, 6
MARRIAGE, 131, 132
MARTYRDOM, 5
MISANTHROPY, 4
MODERATION, 5
OBJECTIVITY, 5
OLD AGE, 49
OPTIMISM, 28
PLAYS, 14
POETS, 59
POPULARITY, 9
POVERTY, 33
RESPECT, 5
SEXES, 30, 31
SINCERITY, 6
SMOKING, 23
SNOBBERY, 11, 12
STUPIDITY, 15
STYLE, 7
SYMPATHY, 6
TEMPTATION, 10, 11
VULGARITY, 5
WAR, 130
WOMEN, 89
WORK, 26
WRITERS, 92

Wilder, Billy
CHARACTER, 27
FRANCE, 16
HISTORY, 26
INSULTS, 44

Wilder, Thornton
ARTISTS, 9
HUMAN CONDITION, 22
LITERATURE, 20
MANKIND, 37
MARRIAGE, 133
PHILOSOPHY, 16
VICE, 10
WAR AND PEACE, 14

Wilhelm I
WORK, 27

Wilhelm II
ARROGANCE, 10
IRELAND, 20
WAR, 131, 132
WORLD WAR I, 24, 25

Wilhelmina
BOASTS, 6

Wilkes, John
ACCIDENTS, 8
REPARTEE, 5

Wilkinson, Ellen Cicely
BRITAIN, 14

Willebrands, Cardinal
WOMEN, 90

William III
DESTINY, 25
PATRIOTISM, 33

William of Okham
SIMPLICITY, 6

William of Wykeham
MANNERS, 8

William the Conqueror
VICTORY, 20

Williams, Harry
HOMESICKNESS, 8

Williams, Kenneth
QUOTATIONS, 15

Williams, Raymond Henry
EDUCATION, 65

Williams, Robin
DRUGS, 15

Williams, Shirley
BUREAUCRACY, 10

Williams, Tennessee
CHARITY, 23
EUROPE, 22
GOVERNMENT, 34
MANKIND, 38
MONEY, 51
NORMALITY, 2
OLD AGE, 50
PSYCHIATRY, 12
VULGARITY, 6
WRITERS, 26

Williams, William Carlos
INFLEXIBILITY, 4

Willkie, Wendell Lewis
AMERICA, 38
CLASS, 40
HUMAN RIGHTS, 5

Wilson, Angus
CATHOLICISM, 12
PUBLIC, 21
SUBURBIA, 2

Wilson, Charles Erwin
BUSINESS, 28

Wilson, Edmund
WRITERS, 93

Wilson, Erasmus
PROPHECY, 15

Wilson, Gordon
FORGIVENESS, 17

Wilson, Harold
ECONOMICS, 22, 23
EQUALITY, 24
FOOD, 54
INJUSTICE, 14
INSULTS, 45
MONARCHY, 25
MONEY, 52
POLITICS, 90, 91, 92
SLEEP, 20
SOCIALISM, 15
TITLES, 12

Wilson, Harriette
SEX, 66

Wilson, Woodrow
AMERICA, 39, 40
BUSINESS, 29
DEMOCRACY, 24
DIPLOMACY, 20
GERMANY, 9
RIGHT, 4
SUICIDE, 14
WAR, 133, 134, 135
WORLD WAR I, 26, 27, 28

Wimperis, Arthur
CRITICISM, 53

Winchell, Walter
CRITICISM, 54

Winchester, Bishop of
SEXES, 32

Windsor, Duchess of
WEALTH, 29

Windsor, Duke of
FAMILY, 37
LOVE, 147
MARRIAGE, 134
ROYALTY, 40
UNEMPLOYMENT, 4

Wittgenstein, Ludwig
BELIEF, 8
LOGIC, 4, 5
PHILOSOPHY, 17, 18
SILENCE, 15
THINKING, 13

Witton, Charlotte
EQUALITY, 25

Wodehouse, P. G.
ALCOHOL, 65, 66
AMERICA, 41
AMERICANS, 14
ANALOGY, 5
APOLOGIES, 5
APPEARANCE, 42, 43
ARISTOCRACY, 16
BORROWING, 13
DISCONTENT, 9
FAMILY, 38
HUMOUR, 58
INCOMPETENCE, 6
INSULTS, 46
INTELLIGENCE, 8
LIFE, 54
LOVE, 148
MARRIAGE, 135, 136
OBESITY, 12, 13
OLD AGE, 51
PSYCHIATRY, 13
REMEDIES, 15
SCOTS, 11

Wolf, Christa
GERMANY, 10

Wolfe, Charles
FUNERALS, 10, 11

Wolfe, Elsie De
ARCHITECTURE, 14

Wolfe, Humbert
JOURNALISM, 33

Wolfe, James
LAST WORDS, 75
POETRY, 53

Wolfe, Thomas
BOOK, SONG, AND PLAY TITLES, 24
ILLNESS, 16

Wolff, Charlotte
FEMINISM, 28

Wolff, Michael
DESIGN, 7

Wollstonecraft, Mary
FEMINISM, 30, 31

Wolsey, Cardinal
LOYALTY, 11

Wood, Mrs Henry
DEATH, 132

Woodroofe, Thomas
NAVY, 4

Woolf, Lord
LAW, 29

Woolf, Virginia
AGE, 68
CHRISTIANITY, 46
CRITICISM, 55, 56
FEMINISM, 29
HONESTY, 14
MUSEUMS, 3
POETRY AND PROSE, 6
SEXES, 33
STATELY HOMES, 5
TRANSLATION, 5
WOMEN, 91, 92
WRITERS, 27, 94

Woollcott, Alexander
ALCOHOL, 67
GRAMMAR, 9
HITLER, 8
PLEASURE, 31
WEALTH, 30

Wordsworth, Dorothy
FLOWERS, 12

Wordsworth, Mary
INTERRUPTIONS, 4

Wordsworth, William
ABSENCE, 10
ADMIRATION, 18
AGE, 69
BIRDS, 11, 12, 13, 14
CONFUSION, 10
CONSTANCY, 5
DEATH, 133, 134
DECLINE, 14, 15
DEFEAT, 9
DISCONTENT, 10
DOUBT, 8
EXPERIENCE, 22
FLOWERS, 13, 14
FREEDOM, 53, 54, 55
FRENCH REVOLUTION, 3, 4, 5
GOOD AND EVIL, 5
HOMESICKNESS, 9
HONOUR, 7
IMMORTALITY, 7
IMPETUOSITY, 4
INNOCENCE, 11
KINDNESS, 7
LEARNING, 10
LONDON, 14
LONELINESS, 9
LOVE, 149
LOVE AND DEATH, 7
MANKIND, 39
METAPHYSICS, 5, 6
MILTON, 4
MIND, 11
MORTALITY, 20, 21
NATURE, 18, 19, 20, 21
NOBILITY, 6, 7
NOSTALGIA, 24
OLD AGE, 52, 53
OPTIMISM, 29
PASSION, 9
PLEASURE, 32
POETRY, 54
POETRY AND PROSE, 7
POETS, 60
POWER, 28
REGRET, 22, 23
SEASONS, 28
SERVICE, 5
SLEEP, 21
SOLITUDE, 15, 16
SOUL, 12
VENICE, 3, 4, 5

WASTE, 3
WRITING, 37

Work, Henry Clay
ALCOHOL, 68
CLOCKS, 2, 3
GLORY, 5

Worrall, Terry
TRAINS, 8

Wotton, Henry
ARCHITECTURE, 15
DIPLOMACY, 21
PROTESTANTISM, 3
RELIGION, 71

Wren, Sir Christopher
EPITAPHS, 27

Wright, Frank Lloyd
DESIGN, 8
MISTAKES, 20

Wright, Orville
SCIENCE, 47

Wyatt, Woodrow
WAR AND PEACE, 15

Wycherley, William
EXPEDIENCY, 7
SEX, 67

Wycliffe, John
TRUTH, 48

Wyndham, John
MARRIAGE, 137
SUN, 4

Wynne-Tyson, Esme
SELF-PRESERVATION, 11

Wynne-Tyson, Jon
POWER, 29

X

Xenophanes
RELIGION, 72

Xenophon
SEA, 15

Xerxes
MORTALITY, 22

Y

Yamamoto, Isoroku
WORLD WAR II, 31

Yankwich, Léon R.
ILLEGITIMACY, 2

Ybarra, Thomas Russell
HYPOCRISY, 19

Yeats, W. B.
AGE, 70, 71, 72, 73
BEAUTY, 40, 41
CRITICISM, 57
DESIRE, 18
DREAMS, 15
EPITAPHS, 28
FLYING, 4
HAPPINESS, 32
HATE, 8
KNOWLEDGE, 36
LIFE, 55, 56
LONELINESS, 10
LOVE, 150, 151, 152
MADNESS, 18
MORTALITY, 23
MUSIC, 56
NATURE, 22
OLD AGE, 54
PARASITES, 4
PEACE, 17
POETRY, 55
POETRY AND PROSE, 8
POETS, 61, 62
POVERTY, 34
RESPONSIBILITY, 17
SOLITUDE, 17
TIME, 42
WRITERS, 28, 95

Yellen, Jack
HAPPINESS, 31

Yeltsin, Boris
COLD WAR, 6

Yevtushenko, Yevgeny
HAPPINESS, 33
PREJUDICE, 7

York and Albany, Duke of
CLOTHES, 20

Young, Andrew John
HEAVEN, 15
STARS, 6, 7

Young, Edward
AGE, 74
ARROGANCE, 11
FEAR, 15
LEARNING, 11
MORTALITY, 24
PROCRASTINATION, 5
TIME, 43, 44

Young, George Malcolm
HISTORY, 37

Young, G. W.
ABSTINENCE, 12

Young, Jock
MURDER, 14

Young, Mary Evans
FOOD, 21

Young, Michael
MERIT, 8

Z

Zamoyski, Jan
MONARCHY, 26

Zangwill, Israel
AMERICA, 42
JEWS, 15
RELIGION, 73

Zanuck, Darryl F.
AGREEMENT, 8

Zhirinovsky, Vladimir
RUSSIA, 12

Zola, Émile
ACCUSATION, 3
STARING, 2
TRUTH, 49

KEYWORD INDEX

A

abandon A. hope, all ye who enter HELL, 2
abashed A. the devil stood GOOD, 12
abated the agony is a. PRECOCITY, 2
Abdul A. the Bulbul Amir COURAGE, 1
abed Not to be a. after midnight BED, 8
abhorrence my heart's a. HATE, 2
abide A. with me; fast falls the eventide RELIGION, 41
abideth now a. faith, hope, charity CHARITY, 6
abilities From each according to his a. MARXISM, 4
Great a. are not requisite for an Historian HISTORIANS, 3
ability a....is capacity to act wisely ABILITY, 4
A young Scotsman of your a. BRITISH, 1
distressed by his want of a. ABILITY, 1; SUPERIORITY, 3
One should oblige everyone to...one's a. ABILITY, 3; PRUDENCE, 8
abnormal she dislikes the a. NORMALITY, 1
abolish Don't be snobbish, we seek to a. CLASS, 21
to a. the death penalty EXECUTION, 13
abolished war can only be a. through war WAR, 64
abortion The greatest destroyer of peace is a. ABORTION, 4
Abou Ben Adhem A. (may his tribe increase!) DREAMS, 12
above they come to me from a. INSPIRATION, 3
Abraham A.'s bosom POVERTY AND WEALTH, 2
abroad an honest man sent to lie a. DIPLOMACY, 21
I don't hold with a. LANGUAGE, 10
know something...before he goes a. TRAVEL, 20
recurrent question about a. is TRAVEL, 16
absence A. from whom we love SEPARATION, 3
A. is to love ABSENCE, 6
A. makes the heart grow fonder ABSENCE, 4
in a fit of a. of mind BRITISH EMPIRE, 8
they could shoot me in my a. JUSTICE, 2
total a. of humour HUMOUR, 10
treacherous air /Of a. ABSENCE, 10
absent Long a. ABSENCE, 1
when thou art a. I am sad LOVE, 93
absolute the more a. silence of America ENGLAND, 24
absolutism A. tempered by assassination RUSSIA, 7
absolved a. from all duty to his country MARRIAGE, 92
abstinence a. from spirituous liquors ABSTINENCE, 7
The few bad poems...created during a. ABSTINENCE, 8
abstract *a. reasoning concerning quantity* PHILOSOPHY, 3
absurd All art deals with the a. ART, 20
something rather a. about the past PAST, 2
There is nothing so a. PHILOSOPHERS, 2
Absurdist why A. plays take place in No Man's Land THEATRE, 1
abuse If it is a. FRIENDS, 14
the more dangerous the a. POWER, 8
Whipping and a. are like laudanum CRUELTY, 5
You *may* a. a tragedy CRITICISM, 20
abusive trying to be funny is highly a. HUMOUR, 20
Academe truth in the groves of A. EDUCATION, 22
Academy I should pronounce in this A. ARTISTS, 18
accelerator press the a. to the floor SPORT AND GAMES, 24
accent a. of one's birthplace lingers HOMESICKNESS, 5
accept I will not a. if nominated POLITICIANS, 71
accessory The camera...an a. to untruth PHOTOGRAPHY, 4
accident A hole is the a. THRIFT, 10
good action...found out by a. GOOD, 8
'There's been an a.' they said INSENSITIVITY, 2
accidental A. and fortuitous concurrence of atoms CHANCE, 4
accidentally A. GOVERNMENT, 29
accidents A. will happen IMPERFECTION, 1
A. will occur ACCIDENTS, 2
chapter of a. MISFORTUNE, 8
chapter of a. is the longest...in the book ACCIDENTS, 8
no small a. on this circuit ACCIDENTS, 6
accomplished An a. man to his finger-tips EXPERTS, 4
accord My cousin Francis and I are in perfect a. AGREEMENT, 1
accountant run away from the circus to become an a. POLITICIANS, 35
accurate a. about her age AGE, 66
accuse A. not Nature RESPONSIBILITY, 10
I a. ACCUSATION, 3
accused A defence...before you be a. ACCUSATION, 2
accustomed A. to her face FAMILIARITY, 3
become a. to no one governing SOCIALISM, 10
I will start to get a. to it MUSIC, 40
ace someone else was about to play the a. CRITICISM, 13
aches My heart a. MELANCHOLY, 7
achieve no man...hath lived...to a. that I have done ACHIEVEMENT, 7
those who a. something SELF-CONFIDENCE, 1
To a. great things ACHIEVEMENT, 9
achieved Nothing great was ever a. ENTHUSIASM, 4
achievement great an a. suffer from...legality LAW, 18
It's a tremendous a. TRAINS, 3
aching an a. void NOSTALGIA, 7
acquaintance a good friend, but bad a. FRIENDS, 3
auld a. be forgot FRIENDSHIP, 12
hope our a. may be a long 'un GREETINGS, 2
act Can't a.. Can't sing ACTORS, 8
last a. crowns the play PLAYS, 8
no reference to fun in any A. of Parliament PLEASURE, 13
The A. of God designation ACCIDENTS, 1
they didn't a. like actors ACTORS, 7
to conceal the fact that the players cannot a. ACTING, 1
acting A. is the expression of a neurotic impulse ACTING, 3
A. is...the lowest of the arts ACTING, 8
The art of a. consists ACTING, 9
The danger chiefly lies in a. well EXCELLENCE, 2
action *A. will furnish belief* BELIEF, 5
Liberty of a. FREEDOM, 13
lust in a. LUST, 7
Suit the a. to the word ACTION, 10
The unmotivated a. SPONTANEITY, 2
thought three times before taking a. CAUTION, 10
true men of a....the scientists SCIENTISTS, 2
actions A. speak louder WORDS, 2
actor a. is something less than a man ACTORS, 2
a.....qualifications, including no money ACTORS, 6
An a.'s a guy who ACTORS, 1
easier to get an a. to be a cowboy ACTING, 6
Like a dull a. now FAILURE, 6
actors A. should be treated like cattle ACTORS, 5
acts And yet the order of the a. is planned DESTINY, 15
He who desires but a. not ACTION, 7
Adam A.'s ale ALCOHOL, 2
A. was but human PERVERSITY, 6
Oh, A. was a gardener GARDENS, 8
When A. delved CLASS, 4
adamant the silvery a. walls of life's exclusive city DEATH, 75
addiction a. of political groups to ideas POLITICS, 27
Every form of a. is bad ADDICTION, 2
prisoners of a. and...prisoners of envy MATERIALISM, 10
the terminal point of a. is...damnation SIN, 2
address Old age is...crossed off names in an a. book AGE, 13
addresses A....conceal our whereabouts ADDRESSES, 1
Three a. always inspire confidence ADDRESSES, 2
adieu a., kind friends, a. PARTING, 1
A.! my native shore DEPARTURE, 4
adjectives tell the substantives from the a. POLITICS, 50

Adler A. will always be Jung PUNS, 22
Adlestrop I remember A. ENGLAND, 40
admiral good to kill an a. EXAMPLE, 9
salutes the A. of the Pacific ARROGANCE, 10
admiration Beauty stands /In the a. BEAUTY, 28
admire a greater fool to a. him ADMIRATION, 3
Not to a. ADMIRATION, 10
one cannot possibly a. them POVERTY, 33
The English instinctively a. ENGLISH, 4
admired Few men have been a. by their servants ADMIRATION, 8
admiring the cure for a. the House of Lords HOUSES OF PARLIAMENT, 3
admit refuse to a. that I am more than fifty-two AGE, 5
ado much a. about nothing when the a. is about himself EGOTISM, 10
adolescence a man suffering from petrified a. CHURCHILL, 4
maturity is only a short break in a. AGE, 25
Adonais I weep for A. – he is dead MOURNING, 14; POETS, 53
adores he a. his maker CONCEIT, 7; SELF-MADE MEN, 1
The ignorant man always a. IGNORANCE, 10
adornment spare from the a. of his person NEGLECT, 4
adrenal larger cerebrums and smaller a. glands WAR, 66
adult A child becomes an a. when RIGHT, 2
The a. subterfuge INNOCENCE, 10
What is an a. AGE, 10
adultery and gods a. ADULTERY, 1
commit a. at one end ADULTERY, 3
I've committed a. in my heart ADULTERY, 2
rather be taken in a. than in provincialism FASHION, 4
the Tasmanians, who never committed a. ADULTERY, 7
thou shalt not commit a. GOD, 10
would have constituted a. SMALLNESS, 3
adults Problem children tend to grow up into problem a. FAMILY, 11
advantage The a. of doing one's praising PRAISE, 4
you have the a. of me SUPERIORITY, 7
advantages Wealth is not without its a. WEALTH, 13
adventure extravagance…thrift and a. THRIFT, 5
Marriage is the only a. open to the cowardly MARRIAGE, 127
To die will be an awfully big a. DEATH, 24
adventures critic…narrates the a. of his mind CRITICS, 5
adversity a. doth best discover virtue MISFORTUNE, 3
advertise It pays to a. ADVERTISING, 2
advertised dosed her children with every specific which was publicly a. DRUGS, 5
Wealth…must be a. OSTENTATION, 3
advertisement the worst a. for Socialism SOCIALISM, 11
advertisers as the a. don't object to JOURNALISM, 30
advertising Half the money I spend on a. ADVERTISING, 4
advice A. is seldom welcome ADVICE, 6
a.…poised between the cliché TACT, 6
A. would be more acceptable ADVICE, 5
earnest a. from my seniors ADVICE, 16
how ready people always are with a. ADVICE, 15
intended to give you some a. ADVICE, 8
No one wants a. ADVICE, 14
nothing so freely as a. ADVICE, 12
woman seldom asks a. WOMEN, 7
advised I a. her on what clothes she should wear ADVICE, 11
advocaat a., a drink made from lawyers ALCOHOL, 22; EUROPE, 8
advocate the soul of a martyr with the intellect of an a. POLITICIANS, 35
aeroplane a. is valuable…destroys men and women EQUALITY, 4
aeroplanes century of a. deserves its own music MUSIC, 18
Aesculapius we owe a cock to A. LAST WORDS, 65
Aesop prettily devised of A. CONCEIT, 3
aesthetic the degree of my a. emotion CRITICS, 1
afar a. and asunder PARTING, 4
affair The great a. is to move TRAVEL, 22
affairs tide in the a. of men OPPORTUNITY, 16
affectation Universities incline wits to sophistry and a. EDUCATION, 4
affection a. is too strong a word POLITICS, 72
affections different taste…strain on the a. HUMOUR, 11
affluent the a. society LUXURY, 3
afford purest treasure mortal times a. REPUTATION, 9
afraid be not a. to do thine office EXECUTION, 19
Englishman…is a. to feel EDUCATION, 17
Men not a. of God, a. of me PRIDE, 7; PRIDE, 7
Whenever I look inside myself I am a. SELF, 9
Afric Where A.'s sunny fountains PLACES, 6
Africa more familiar with A. than my own body INNOCENCE, 8
something new out of A. NOVELTY, 8
When a white man in A. RACISM, 18
after-dinner an a.'s sleep AGE, 53
afterlife that the a. will be any less exasperating AFTERLIFE, 3
after-lives Lazarus was not /Questioned about a. DEATH, 64
afternoon could lose the war in an a. OFFICERS, 4
I could have lost the war in an a. WAR, 52
against A. whom EGOTISM, 1
He said he was a. it SIN, 11
neither for nor a. institutions INDIFFERENCE, 7
who's for you and who's a. you POLITICS, 38
Agamemnon I have looked upon the face of A. HISTORY, 24
Many brave men…before A.'s time OBLIVION, 1
age A child blown up by a. AGE, 10
A. cannot wither her ADMIRATION, 14
A.…nor custom stale her infinite virginity PURITY, 5
a. of chivalry is gone EUROPE, 2
A. only matters when one is ageing OLD AGE, 32
A. seldom arrives smoothly or quickly OLD AGE, 36
A. shall not weary them MEMORIALS, 3
A. will bring all things PRUDERY, 2
A. will not be defied AGE, 7
an a. in which useless knowledge KNOWLEDGE, 22
And now in a. I bud again OLD AGE, 22
an old a. of cards OLD AGE, 33
A tart temper never mellows with a. CHARACTER, 13
At twenty years of a. AGE, 27
Cool'd a long a. in the deep-delved earth ALCOHOL, 36
Crabbed a. and youth AGE, 55
Damn the a.. I'll write for antiquity POSTERITY, 7
Do you think at your a., it is right OLD AGE, 10
gift of perpetual old a. OLD AGE, 49
He hath not forgotten my a. GOD, 46
I prefer old a. to the alternative OLD AGE, 12
I summon a. /To grant youth's heritage AGE, 15
It is…at my a. I now begin to see things LAST WORDS, 25
lady of a certain a. AGE, 17
no a. between ten and three and twenty YOUTH, 16
nothing in thy youth, how canst thou find any thing in thine a. AGE, 11
not of an a., but for all time SHAKESPEARE, 10
No woman should ever be quite accurate about her a. AGE, 66
Old-a., a second child OLD AGE, 13
Old a.…gives us what we have earned OLD AGE, 8
old a. is…older than I am OLD AGE, 4
Old a. is the most unexpected OLD AGE, 47
Old a. is the out-patients' department OLD AGE, 11
old a.…the fear that it may go on too long OLD AGE, 45
Our parents' a.…has produced us AGE, 33
Thou has nor youth nor a. AGE, 53
treat…her a. with ambiguity AGE, 49
what a. takes away OLD AGE, 52
When men grow virtuous in their old a. VIRTUE, 15
when Mozart was my a. AGE, 35
who tells one her real a. AGE, 67
Years hence, perhaps, may dawn an a. FUTURE, 1
aged a. diplomats…bored than for young men to die DIPLOMACY, 1
a man of about a hundred and ten who had been a. OLD AGE, 51
the beauty /Of an a. face OLD AGE, 9
ageing Age only matters when one is a. OLD AGE, 32
Like so many a. college people ACADEMICS, 4
agenda Our a. is now exhausted AGREEMENT, 6
the a. winks at me BUREAUCRACY, 9
agent prime a. of all human perception IMAGINATION, 1
ages His acts being seven a. HUMAN CONDITION, 17
Our God, our help in a. past RELIGION, 64
Rock of a., cleft for me RELIGION, 59
aggregate the a. of the recipes SCIENCE, 44
aggression culture that worships a. VIOLENCE, 9
aging A.…the only…way to live a long time LONGEVITY, 1
agitate to a. a bag of wind FOOTBALL, 10
Agnes St A. Eve – Ah, bitter chill it was SEASONS, 9
agnostic rather a compliment to be called an a. HUMILITY, 3
agongy a lonely spasm of helpless a. DEATH, 63
agree colours will a. in the dark DIFFERENCE, 7
don't say you a. with me AGREEMENT, 7

If two men on the same job a. AGREEMENT, 8
those who a. with us AGREEMENT, 4
Two of a trade can ne'er a. ARGUMENTS, 6
agreeable I do not want people to be very a. NASTINESS, 2
My idea of an a. person AGREEMENT, 3
agreement My people and I have come to an a. FREEDOM, 11
Whenever you accept our views we shall be in full a. FLEXIBILITY, 1
agrees a person who a. with me AGREEMENT, 3
agricultural the a. labourers...commute COUNTRYSIDE, 7
agriculture when the nation depended on a. ECONOMICS, 18
Aids A. pandemic is a classic own-goal AIDS, 2
stop them catching A....the wife AIDS, 4; ILLNESS, 3
ail what can a. thee, knight at arms ILLNESS, 10
ain't bet you a hundred bucks he a. in here ESCAPE, 1; FUNERALS, 5
air cat is a diagram and pattern of subtle a. CATS, 5
Get your room full of good a. LONGEVITY, 2
my spirit found outlet in the a. FLYING, 1
the castles I have, are built with a. DREAMS, 10
to the Germans that of the a. EUROPE, 15
waste its sweetness on the desert a. WASTE, 2
airplane The a. stays up SCIENCE, 47
airplanes a....are wonderful things FLYING, 2
I feel about a. the way I feel about diets FLYING, 2
airth Let them bestow on every a. a limb EXECUTION, 9
aisle A.. Altar. Hymn MARRIAGE, 85; PUNS, 14
aitches We have nothing to lose but our a. CLASS, 25
Alamein Before A. we never had a victory WORLD WAR II, 15
alarms confused a. of struggle and flight WAR, 2
albatross I shot the a. BIRDS, 2
Albert A. was merely a young foreigner ROYALTY, 35
that A. married beneath him CRITICISM, 10
alcohol A....enables Parliament ALCOHOL, 55
A. is like love ALCOHOL, 19
discovered that a. was a food ALCOHOL, 66
alcoholic a. liquors have been used by the...best races ALCOHOL, 50
ale a. from the Country of the Young KNOWLEDGE, 36
no more cakes and a. MERRYMAKING, 3
the spicy nut-brown a. ALCOHOL, 45
Alexander Some talk of A., and some of Hercules HEROISM, 1
algebra What is a. exactly MATHEMATICS, 1
Algerian And drink of my A. wine INSULTS, 7
Alice A. – Mutton; Mutton – A. INTRODUCTIONS, 1
Oh! don't you remember sweet A., Ben Bolt MEMORY, 7
alien amid the a. corn BIRDS, 5
State socialism is totally a. SOCIALISM, 14
alike so many million of faces...none a. INDIVIDUALITY, 4
alimony Judges...in the matter of arranging a. MARRIAGE, 135
alive Bliss was it in that dawn to be a. FRENCH REVOLUTION, 3
he is no longer a. DEATH, 26
if I am a. DEATH, 54
needst not strive /...to keep a. KILLING, 2
not one will still be a. in a hundred years' time MORTALITY, 22
We intend to remain a. SELF-PRESERVATION, 7
all A. for one, and one for all UNITY, 8
A. good things ENDING, 1
a. our yesterdays LIFE, 45
A.'s well ENDING, 2
a man, take him for a. in a. ADMIRATION, 15; ADMIRATION, 15
are you sure they are a. horrid NASTINESS, 1
Christ is a., and in a. CHRISTIANITY, 5
Damn you, Jack – I'm a. right SELFISHNESS, 3
Ripeness is a. ENDURANCE, 17
'Tis a. thou art EQUALITY, 29
allegiance Not bound to swear a. to any master FREEDOM, 19
allegory headstrong as an a. MALAPROPISMS, 6
alley she lives in our a. LOVE, 36
allies former a. had blundered NAZISM, 4
all-round a wonderful a. man INSULTS, 6
ally An a. has to be watched MISTRUST, 10
Almighty If the A. himself played the violin EGOTISM, 6
almonds Don't eat too many a. FOOD, 15
alms a. for oblivion TIME, 35
alone A., alone, all, all alone SOLITUDE, 2
A. and palely loitering ILLNESS, 10
And we are left, or shall be left, a. DEFEAT, 9
better to be a. than in bad company FRIENDS, 15
I am here at the gate a. INVITATIONS, 2
I hate to be a. OBSESSIONS, 1
I want to be a. MISQUOTATIONS, 17; PRIVACY, 2; SOLITUDE, 6
No poet...has...meaning a. ARTS, 3
powerful but a. SOLITUDE, 14
She sleeps a. at last EPITAPHS, 1
To be a. is the fate of all great minds LONELINESS, 6; GREATNESS, 11
We perish'd, each a. DEATH, 40
woe to him that is a. when he falleth FRIENDSHIP, 8
You come into the world a. HUMAN CONDITION, 13
Alph Where A., the sacred river, ran PLEASURE, 8
alphabet the remaining twenty-two letters of the a. LEARNING, 7
altar Aisle. A.. Hymn MARRIAGE, 85; PUNS, 14
altars struggled in poverty to build these a. RELIGION, 53
alter I dare not a. these things INSPIRATION, 3
alternative a need to create an a. world FICTION, 3
I prefer old age to the a. OLD AGE, 12
always Minorities...are almost a. in the right MINORITY, 3
am in the infinite I A. IMAGINATION, 1
I think therefore I a. THINKING, 3
Amaryllis sport with A. in the shade PLEASURE, 22
amateur a. is an artist who supports himself with outside jobs ARTISTS, 5
America...is the prize a. nation AMERICA, 40; GERMANY, 9
In love...the a. status LOVE, 63
the last time that I will take part as an a. FUNERALS, 2
amateurs a disease that afflicts a. ARTS, 2
nation of a. BRITISH, 9
amaze How vainly men themselves a. VICTORY, 10
ambiguity treat...her age with a. AGE, 49
ambition A., Distraction, Uglification, and Derision EDUCATION, 9
A. should be made of sterner stuff AMBITION, 15
A writer's a. should be POSTERITY, 6
Every man has...an a. to be a wag HUMOUR, 16
Let not A. mock POVERTY, 13
Vaulting a., which o'er-leaps itself AMBITION, 16
What argufies pride and a. MORTALITY, 4
ambitious an a. man has as many masters AMBITION, 11
amblongus A. Pie NONSENSE, 21
ambulance Knocked down a doctor? With an a. ACCIDENTS, 7
Amen sound of a great A. MUSIC, 39
America A....based on the dreams of spinsters AMERICA, 31
A. became top nation HISTORY, 31
A.!.../God shed His grace on thee AMERICA, 4
A. has brought us McDonald's RUSSIA, 12
A....has gone directly from barbarism AMERICA, 8
A. is a country of young men AMERICA, 13
A. is a large, friendly dog AMERICA, 35
A. is just ourselves AMERICA, 1
A. is...the great Melting-Pot AMERICA, 42
A. is the only idealistic nation AMERICA, 39
A....is the prize amateur nation AMERICA, 40; GERMANY, 9
ask not what A. will do for you PATRIOTISM, 18
A.'s really only a kind of Russia FUTURE, 5
behind the discovery of A. JEWS, 11
first come to pass in the heart of A. AMERICA, 12
His foreparents came to A. EQUALITY, 12
my A.! my new-found-land LOVE, 49
The business of A. is business AMERICA, 10
the greatest that we owe to the discovery of A. SMOKING, 6
the more absolute silence of A. ENGLAND, 24
The national dish of A. AMERICA, 29
Vietnam was lost in the living rooms of A. TELEVISION AND RADIO, 4; WAR, 65
what makes A. what it is AMERICA, 32
when we think of thee, O A. AMERICA, 36
Why will A. not reach out...to Russia DIPLOMACY, 8
woman governs A. AMERICA, 25
American A. heiress wants to buy a man MATERIALISM, 14
A. system of rugged individualism AMERICA, 18
An A. is either a Jew, or an anti-Semite AMERICANS, 9
I am willing to love all mankind, *except an A.* AMERICANS, 5
If I were an A., as I am an Englishman PATRIOTISM, 24
It hasn't taken Winston long to get used to A. ways CHURCHILL, 1
I was born an A. PATRIOTISM, 31
Let's talk sense to the A. people ENDURANCE, 19
Scratch an A. AMERICANS, 4
spiteful to me in the A. press NEWSPAPERS, 14
the A. abroad AMERICANS, 10
the greatest A. friend we have ever known POLITICIANS, 48
We are all A. at puberty NATIONALITY, 10

whereby A. girls turn into A. women CAPITALISM, 3
Americanism hyphenated A. PATRIOTISM, 25
McCarthyism is A. POLITICS, 54
There can be no fifty-fifty A. PATRIOTISM, 26
Americans A. have been conditioned to respect newness AMERICANS, 11
because A. won't listen to sense AMERICANS, 6
Good A., when they die, go to Paris AMERICANS, 1
the matter with A. AMERICANS, 3
when good A. die they go to Paris AMERICANS, 13
amiable It destroys one's nerves to be a. MARRIAGE, 49
amis *Changez vos a.* FRIENDS, 8
ammunition Praise the Lord and pass the a. WAR, 37
amo *Odi et a.* LOVE AND HATE, 2
Amor *A. vincit insomnia* LOVE, 58; SLEEP, 9
amorous the silk stockings and white bosoms…excite my a. propensities LUST, 3
amplified I'm being a. by the mike OBESITY, 4
amputate Thank God they had to a. WAR, 99
am'rous dire offence from a. causes springs RESULTS, 5
amused how to be a. rather than shocked AGE, 16
I was *very* much a. ROYALTY, 38
one has to be very old before one learns how to be a. AGE, 16
We are not a. ROYALTY, 37
amusing Any a. deaths DEATH, 34
analogy Though a. is often misleading ANALOGY, 1
analysis historian fits a man for psychological a. PSYCHOLOGY, 2
anarchy a well-bred sort of emotional a. CLASSIFICATION, 2
grieved under a *democracy*, call it *a.* GOVERNMENT, 12
anatomy he has studied a. and dissected at least one woman MARRIAGE, 18
ancestor I am my own a. ANCESTRY, 1
ancestors a. on either side of the Battle of Hastings ANCESTRY, 4
when his half-civilized a. were hunting the wild boar JEWS, 2
ancestry I can trace my a. back to a…globule ANCESTRY, 2
ancient with the a. is wisdom OLD AGE, 6; WISDOM, 5
anecdotage man fell into his a. OLD AGE, 16
angel An a. writing in a book of gold DREAMS, 12
A. of Death has been abroad WAR, 17
A. of the Lord came down CHRISTMAS, 18
in action, how like an a. MANKIND, 27
in comparison with which…I am a A. EVIL, 8
In heaven an a. is nobody in particular IMPORTANCE, 2
Is man an ape or an a. EVOLUTION, 8
This was the A. of History WORLD WAR II, 18
woman yet think him an a. LOVE, 137
You may not be an a. LOVE, 52
angels A. can fly SERIOUSNESS, 1
fools rush in where a. fear to tread HASTE, 8
I…am on the side of the a. EVOLUTION, 8
Its visits, /Like those of a. DEATH, 32
Not Angles, but a. ENGLISH, 14
One more devils'-triumph and sorrow for a. DAMNATION, 1
People are not fallen a. CRITICISM, 27
Tears such as a. weep SORROW, 12
the tongues of men and of a. CHARITY, 6
anger A. is one of the sinews of the soul ANGER, 4
a. makes us all stupid ANGER, 6
A. supplies the arms ANGER, 7
Grief and disappointment give rise to a. EMOTION, 3
he that is slow to a. is better than the mighty SELF-CONTROL, 1
Juno's never-forgetting a. ENDURANCE, 23
Angles Not A., but angels ENGLISH, 14
angling A. is somewhat like poetry FISHING, 2
A. may be said to be…like the mathematics FISHING, 4
lovers of virtue…and go a-A. FISHING, 3
We may say of a. as Dr Boteler said of strawberries FISHING, 5
Anglo-Catholic Becoming an A. must…be a sad business CATHOLICISM, 11
Anglo-Saxon Come in, you A. swine INSULTS, 7
those are A. attitudes ENGLISH, 10
angry A. Young Man REBELLION, 7
The man who gets a.…in the right way ANGER, 1
anguish drinking deep of that divinest a. SUFFERING, 5
Making love is the sovereign remedy for a. SEX, 31
angular an oblong a. figure HUMOUR, 42
animal information vegetable, a. and mineral KNOWLEDGE, 16
Man is a gaming a. SPORT AND GAMES, 14
man is and will always be a wild a. MANKIND, 13
Man is an intellectual a. INTELLECT, 3
Man is a noble a. MANKIND, 9
man is…a religious a. RELIGION, 9
Man is a social a. SOCIETY, 9
Man is by nature a political a. POLITICS, 3
Man is the only a.…on friendly terms with the victims HYPOCRISY, 6
This a. is very bad SELF-PRESERVATION, 3
true to your a. instincts ANIMALISM, 3
Whenever you observe an a. closely ANIMALS, 8
animality its own a. either objectionable or funny HUMOUR, 18
animals All a. are equal EQUALITY, 18
all a. were created…for the use of man ANIMALS, 17
all there is to distinguish us from other a. MANKIND, 4
A. are such agreeable friends ANIMALS, 10
a.…know nothing…of what people say ANIMALS, 19
But if we stop loving a. LOVE, 129
differs in no respect from the ovules of other a. EVOLUTION, 3
give my wisdom and experience to a. CONSERVATION, 1
I could…live with a. ANIMALS, 22
My music…understood by children and a. MUSIC, 50
paragon of a. MANKIND, 27
some a. are more equal than others EQUALITY, 18
There are two things for which a. are…envied ANIMALS, 19
Wild a. never kill for sport HUNTING, 3
Anna great A.! whom three realms obey DRINKS, 7
annals short and simple a. of the poor POVERTY, 13
Anne Move Queen A.? Most certainly not MEMORIALS, 12
Annie for bonnie A. Laurie LOVE AND DEATH, 1
annihilating A. all that's made OBLIVION, 3
annihilation No a. REPRESENTATION, 2
Anno A. domini…the most fatal complaint DEATH, 61
annual A. income twenty pounds ECONOMICS, 7
annuity Buy an a. cheap MONEY, 20
annus it has turned out to be an 'a. horribilis' ROYALTY, 19
anomaly Poverty is an a. to rich people HUNGER, 2
Anon guess that A.…was often a woman WOMEN, 91
another A. year! – another deadly blow DEFEAT, 9
He who would do good to a. GOOD, 2
I would have given you a. CHIVALRY, 5
Life is just one damned thing after a. LIFE, 29
No man can…condemn a. JUDGMENT, 5
answer a. a fool according to his folly FOOLISHNESS, 10
A timid question will…receive a confident a. SHYNESS, 2
But a. came there none GREED, 5
give a. as need requireth LEARNING, 2
I do not a. questions like this MASCULINITY, 1
more than the wisest man can a. EXAMINATIONS, 1
The a.…is blowin' in the wind FREEDOM, 10
the inquisitive mind can…receive no a. PHILOSOPHY, 6
where no one asks, no one needs to a. PURPOSE, 4
would not stay for an a. TRUTH, 10
antagonistic the most a. to the Victorian age WRITERS, 93
antan *les neiges d'a.* NOSTALGIA, 22
anthology a. is like all the plums and orange peel BOOKS, 31
antic dance an a. hay DANCING, 6
anticipation the intelligent a. of facts JOURNALISM, 15
anti-clerical it makes me understand a. things CLERGY, 1
anti-climax everything afterward savours of a. PRECOCITY, 1
antidote the a. to desire DESIRE, 6
antipathy dislike the French from…vulgar a. FRANCE, 15
strong a. of good to bad PROVOCATION, 2
antiquity Damn the age. I'll write for a. POSTERITY, 7
anti-Semite An American is either a Jew, or an a. AMERICANS, 9
hated /by every a. /as if I were a Jew PREJUDICE, 7
anxious a. to do the wrong thing correctly ETIQUETTE, 7
anybody who you are, you aren't a. FAME, 17
anyone a. here whom I have not insulted INSULTS, 10
anywhere go a. I damn well please FREEDOM, 2
apartheid closed the book on a. SOUTH AFRICA, 5
We don't want a. liberalized RACISM, 29
apathy going about the country stirring up a. POLITICS, 89
sheer a. and boredom DISCOVERY, 4
ape having an a. for his grandfather EVOLUTION, 10
Is man an a. or an angel EVOLUTION, 8
It is not the a., nor the tiger HUMAN NATURE, 23
the a. from which he is descended EVOLUTION, 11
The exception is a naked a. MANKIND, 19

ape-like The a. virtues without which EDUCATION, 13
aphorisms The great writers of a. SAYINGS, 3
The hunter for a.…has to fish in muddy water SAYINGS, 2
aphrodisiac Fame is a powerful a. FAME, 11
Power is the ultimate a. POWER, 14
apologize a good rule in life never to a. APOLOGIES, 5
It's too late to a. INSULTS, 39
apology Never make a defence or a. ACCUSATION, 2
apostates malignity…characteristic of a. BETRAYAL, 5
apostle great a. of the Philistines PHILISTINISM, 2
Apostles The Septuagint minus the A. NUMBERS, 4
apparatus *Brain,* n. An a. with which we think MIND, 1
apparel a. oft proclaims the man CLOTHES, 16
appeal The whole of art is an a. to a reality ARTS, 6
appear Things are…what they a. to be APPEARANCES, 19
appearance secret of a successful a. APPEARANCE, 34
appearances A. are deceptive APPEARANCES, 2
A. are not…a clue to the truth APPEARANCES, 13
Keep up a. APPEARANCES, 11
shallow people…do not judge by a. APPEARANCES, 23
appeaser An a. is one who feeds a crocodile DIPLOMACY, 6
appetite A. comes with eating DESIRE, 13
a. may sicken and so die MUSIC, 46
the desire of satisfying a voracious a. LUST, 2
apple An a. a day HEALTH AND HEALTHY LIVING, 1
as the a. of his eye SUPPORT, 1
My a. trees will never get across NEIGHBOURS, 3
want the a. for the a.'s sake PERVERSITY, 6
When Eve ate this particular a. SEX, 30
apple-pie An a. without some cheese FOOD, 2
apples The silver a. of the moon DESIRE, 18
applications only a. of science SCIENCE, 32
applied no such things as a. sciences SCIENCE, 32
appreciate I never 'a.' BEAUTY, 29
appreciation total dependence on the a. of others CHARM, 2
apprehend Intelligence is quickness to a. ABILITY, 4
apprehensions elations and a. of growth AGE, 37
approve They that a.…call it opinion OPINIONS, 2
April And after A., when May follows MONTHS, 6
A. is the cruellest month MONTHS, 8
months…gloomy in England are March and A. SEASONS, 27
My regret /Becomes an A. violet SORROW, 25
Now that A.'s there ENGLAND, 8
Sweet A. showers MONTHS, 12
Aprille Whan that A. with his shoures sote MONTHS, 7
Arab I shook hands with a friendly A. PLACES, 13
Arabia All the perfumes of A. GUILT, 9
Arabs The Jews and A. should…settle their differences MIDDLE EAST, 3
arch All experience is an a. EXPERIENCE, 20
archaeologist An a. is the best husband MARRIAGE, 36
Archangel an A. a little damaged POETS, 48
archbishop the sign of an a. is a double-cross CLERGY, 6
arch-enemy love…has one a. – and that is life LOVE, 16
arches Underneath the a. DREAMS, 7
Archimedes familiar with truths for which A. SCIENCE, 37
architect Each man the a. of his own fate RESPONSIBILITY, 3
not a great sculptor or painter can be an a. ARCHITECTURE, 9
the a. can only advise MISTAKES, 20
architects a. were artists ARTISTS, 12
architecture A. in general is frozen music ARCHITECTURE, 11
Fashion is a. FASHION, 1
What has happened to a. ARCHITECTURE, 6
ardua *Per a. ad astra* AMBITION, 2
'arf An' rather less than 'a. CLOTHES, 10
arguing I am not a. with you ARGUMENTS, 18
In a. too, the parson own'd his skill KNOWLEDGE, 17
argument All a. is against it SUPERNATURAL, 9
I have found you an a. ARGUMENTS, 10
I love a., I love debate ARGUMENTS, 15
to get the best of an a. ARGUMENTS, 4
work of art must start an a. ART, 30
arguments beware of long a. and long beards BREVITY, 6
the world can be expressed in…a. THEORY, 3
Arian In three sips the A. frustrate DRINKS, 2
aristocracy an absentee a. IRELAND, 6
An a. in a republic is like a chicken ARISTOCRACY, 10
a.…government by the badly educated ARISTOCRACY, 5; DEMOCRACY, 3
a. to what is decent CLASS, 16
displeased with *a.*, call it *oligarchy* GOVERNMENT, 12
If human beings could be propagated…a. would be…sound ARISTOCRACY, 7
Unlike the male codfish…the British a. is ARISTOCRACY, 16
aristocrat gentleman from both the artist and the a. CLASS, 35
aristocratic To be a. in Art ART, 19
to distinguish…the a. class from the Philistines CLASS, 3
arithmetic different branches of A. EDUCATION, 9
Music is the a. of sounds MUSIC, 17
arm An a. /Rose up from…the lake ARTHURIAN LEGEND, 3
Don't carry away that a. till I have…my ring PRACTICALITY, 6
Human on my faithless a. SLEEP, 3
armchair She fitted into my biggest a. OBESITY, 12
arm'd a. with more than complete steel JUSTICE, 16
Armenteers A mademoiselle from A. FRANCE, 13
armies ignorant a. clash by night WAR, 2
not a.…but flocks of sheep DELUSION, 3
armistice an a. for twenty years WORLD WAR I, 10
a short a. with truth TRUTH, 17
armour Conceit is the finest a. CONCEIT, 12
Prayer makes the Christian's a. bright PRAYER, 10
arms Anger supplies the a. ANGER, 7
A. control so easily becomes an incantation WEAPONS, 4
For the theatre one needs long a. ACTING, 4
I never would lay down my a. PATRIOTISM, 24
I sing of a. and the man ENDURANCE, 23
opening time in the Sailors A. PUBLIC HOUSES, 4
So he laid down his a. PUNS, 8
army An a. is a nation within a nation ARMY, 4
An a. marches on its stomach FOOD, 43
Chief of the A. LAST WORDS, 45
contemptible little A. WAR, 132
If you don't want to use the a., I should like to borrow it SARCASM, 2
little ships of England brought the A. home BOATS, 8; WORLD WAR II, 20
The a. ages men sooner than the law ARMY, 6
The conventional a. loses if it does not win WAR, 57
arrest My father didn't create you to a. me POLICE, 6
One does not a. Voltaire RESPECT, 2
arrested Christ…would quite likely have been a. OPPRESSION, 3
arrive To travel hopefully is…better…than to a. ANTICIPATION, 7
arrow Every a.…feels the attraction of earth AMBITION, 13
I, said the Sparrow, /With my bow and a. NURSERY RHYMES, 68
I shot an a. into the air CHANCE, 3
arse a politician is an a. POLITICIANS, 3
Sit on your a. for fifty years INDIFFERENCE, 4
arsenal a. of democracy DEMOCRACY, 17
arson A., after all, is an artificial crime FIRE, 5
art All a. deals with the absurd ART, 20
All A. is quite useless ART, 33
An a. can only be learned LEARNING, 4
A. and religion first; then philosophy IMPORTANCE, 3
an A.-loving nation PHILISTINISM, 8
A.…can go on mattering ART, 5
a. constantly aspires towards…music ART, 21
A. for art's sake ART, 6, 8
A. has to move you ART, 11
A. is a jealous mistress ART, 7
A. is long, and Time is fleeting MORTALITY, 14
A. is not a mirror…but a hammer ART, 17
A. is not a special sauce ART, 14
a. is not a weapon ART, 12
A. is ruled…by the imagination IMAGINATION, 3
A. is the imposing of a pattern ART, 31
A. is the most intense mode ART, 34
A. is…the transmission of feeling ART, 28
a. is to give life a shape ART, 2
A. never expresses anything ART, 32
a. of pleasing consists PLEASURE, 12
A. will make our streets as beautiful as the woods DESIGN, 5
aspires…to the condition of a. LITERATURE, 2
Bullfighting is the only a. SPORT AND GAMES, 8
Desiring this man's a. DISCONTENT, 8
excellence of every a. is its intensity ARTS, 5
Fine a. is that in which the hand ART, 25
great parables…but false a. CRITICISM, 27
half a trade and half an a. LITERATURE, 7
I have discovered the a. DANCING, 4
industry without a. is brutality ART, 24

Insurrection is an a. REVOLUTION, 6
It's clever but is it a. ART, 13
Mr Goldwyn...you are only interested in a. ART, 26; MONEY, 45
nature is the a. of God NATURE, 1
Nature's handmaid, a. NATURE, 8
Politics is not a science...but an a. POLITICS, 9
princes learn no a. truly, but...horsemanship HORSES, 7
Rules and models destroy genius and a. RULES, 2
sombre enemy of good a. BABIES, 1
the a. of the possible POLITICS, 13
The whole of a. is an appeal to a reality ARTS, 6
To be aristocratic in A. ART, 19
True ease in writing comes from a. WRITING, 26
wonderful case of nature imitating a. ACTORS, 22
work of a. must start an argument ART, 30
artful The a. Dodger NAMES, 2
article It all depends upon that a. there SOLDIERS, 10
articles to pay for a....they do not want BORROWING, 4
artificial All things are a. NATURE, 1
nothing so a. as sinning nowadays SIN, 15
artist amateur is an a. who supports himself with outside jobs ARTISTS, 5
a. is someone who produces things ARTISTS, 8
As an a., a man has no home PARIS, 4
Beware of the a. who's an intellectual ARTISTS, 3
God is really only another a. GOD, 42
only one position for an a. anywhere WALES, 3
Remember I'm an a. ARTISTS, 2
the gentleman from both the a. and the aristocrat CLASS, 35
What is an a. ARTISTS, 6
artistic a. temperament...afflicts amateurs ARTS, 2
There never was an a. period PHILISTINISM, 8
artists architects were a. ARTISTS, 12
A. are not engineers of the soul ART, 12
Great a. have no country NATIONALITY, 7
You a. produce something that nobody needs ARTISTS, 9
arts If all the a. aspire to the condition of music SCIENCE, 38
Murder...one of the Fine A. MURDER, 6
secret of the a. is to correct nature ARTS, 8
ashamed I am a. of confessing INNOCENCE, 1
not a. of having been in love LOVE, 107
some habit of which he is deeply a. TELEVISION AND RADIO, 2
to see them not a. REGRET, 21
We are not a. of what we have done PRIDE, 6
ashes a. of Napoleon INDIFFERENCE, 6
Asia There is too much A. PLACES, 8
ask A. no questions CURIOSITY, 1
To labour and not a. for any reward SELFLESSNESS, 2
asks where no one a., no one needs to answer PURPOSE, 4
asleep The devil is a. LUCK, 10
you fall a. halfway through her name INSULTS, 8
aspect Meet in her a. BEAUTY, 14
aspens Willows whiten, a. quiver WEATHER, 27
aspicious two a. persons MALAPROPISMS, 1
aspirations The young have a. AGE, 50
aspires art constantly a. towards...music ART, 21
a....to the condition of art LITERATURE, 2
aspirin if tranquillizers could be bought as easily and cheaply as a. DRUGS, 8
aspirings The soul hath not her generous a. SMOKING, 10
ass every a. thinks he may kick at him WRITERS, 75
the law is a a. LAW, 9
assassination Absolutism tempered by a. RUSSIA, 7
A. has never changed ASSASSINATION, 1
A....the extreme form of censorship ASSASSINATION, 5
assemblance Care I for the...a. of a man APPEARANCES, 20
assemblies Kings govern by...a. only when MONARCHY, 12
assertions Pure mathematics consists entirely of a. MATHEMATICS, 13
asset the greatest a. a head of state can have SLEEP, 20
assigned purpose of God and the doom a. DESTINY, 23
associate good must a. UNITY, 7
I...like to a. with...priests CLERGY, 1
assure a. him that he'd live tomorrow DESTINY, 17
astonished a. at my own moderation MODERATION, 3
you are merely a. WORDS, 22
astonishment a little more reverence...and not so much a. SINGING, 3
Dear Sir, Your a.'s odd EXISTENCE, 1
astound Austria will a. the world DIPLOMACY, 18
astronauts The a.!...Rotarians in outer space SPACE, 8
astronomer Bach is like an a. MUSICIANS, 11
astronomy A. teaches the correct use ASTRONOMY, 4
asunder afar and a. PARTING, 4
let not man put a. MARRIAGE, 27
asylum world is...like a lunatic a. MADNESS, 9
asylums lunatic a....the stately homes STATELY HOMES, 5
atheism a., breast-feeding, circumcision INDULGENCE, 2
miracle to convince a. ATHEISM, 2
atheist an a. half believes a God FEAR, 15
An a....has no invisible means of support ATHEISM, 5
an a. if the king were SERVILITY, 4
An a. is one point ATHEISM, 1
an a. who trembles in the haunted corridor WRITERS, 95
He was an embittered a. ATHEISM, 8
I am an a....thank God ATHEISM, 4
scepticism kept her from being an a. SCEPTICISM, 5
very *chic* for an a. MEMORIALS, 9
Athens A. arose EUROPE, 19
A. holds sway over all Greece INFLUENCE, 9
athletic The only a. sport I ever mastered SPORT AND GAMES, 10
athletics a. as inferior forms of fox-hunting WOMEN, 87
Atlantic The Admiral of the A. ARROGANCE, 10
to have the East come to the A. WORLD WAR II, 19
atmosphere a. has been poisoned SPORT AND GAMES, 16
atom carbon a. possesses certain exceptional properties SCIENCE, 23
how the a. is split SCIENCE, 4
nearer to the a. than the stars SCIENCE, 11
The a. bomb is a paper tiger NUCLEAR WEAPONS, 12
There is no evil in the a. NUCLEAR WEAPONS, 18
They split the a. by firing particles at SCIENCE, 18
atomic The way to win an a. war NUCLEAR WEAPONS, 3
atoms fortuitous concurrence of a. CHANCE, 4
atone a. for the sins of your fathers INJUSTICE, 7
atrophy Music begins to a. ARTS, 7
attached men become a. even to Widnes ENGLAND, 39
attack A. is the best form CONFLICT, 1
love until after the first a. SCEPTICISM, 1
situation excellent. I shall a. WAR, 36
attainments rare a....but...can she spin WOMAN'S ROLE, 3
attention a. to the inside...contempt for the outside BOOKS, 14
take his a. away from the universe PRAYER, 11
attic A. wit HUMOUR, 22
brain a. stocked with all the furniture KNOWLEDGE, 13
glory of the A. stage LIFE, 6
attitudes Anglo-Saxon a. ENGLISH, 10
attorney the gentleman is an *a.* LAWYERS, 7
attraction Every arrow...feels the a. of earth AMBITION, 13
The chief a. of military service ARMY, 3
attractive if they are in the least a. TRANSLATION, 2
The most a. sentences are not perhaps the wisest LANGUAGE, 25
audacity a. of elected persons REVOLUTION, 12
Auden A. was someone you could laugh-at-with POETS, 54
W. H. A., a sort of gutless Kipling SOCIALISM, 13
audience I know two kinds of a. AUDIENCES, 5
the a. want to be surprised PLAYS, 3
the a. was a disaster PLAYS, 14
whether the a. thinks you are crying ACTING, 2
auld a. acquaintance be forgot FRIENDSHIP, 12
for a. lang syne FRIENDSHIP, 13
aunt Charley's a. from Brazil PLACES, 16
aunts bad a. and good a. FAMILY, 38
Aussie a dinkum hard-swearing A. PATRIOTISM, 14
Austen Jane A. WRITERS, 81
Jane A.'s books, too, are absent from this library WRITERS, 89
Miss A....husband-hunting butterfly WRITERS, 69
Miss A.'s novels...sterile in artistic invention WRITERS, 45
More can be learnt from Miss A. about...the novel WRITERS, 29
Austerlitz There rises the sun of A. WAR, 74
Australia guess...he was born in A. PLACES, 14
So you're going to A. PLACES, 11
Australian I'm going to write the Great A. Novel AMBITION, 19
Austria A. is Switzerland...with history added EUROPE, 14
A. will astound the world DIPLOMACY, 18
author An a. who speaks about his own books EGOTISM, 5; MOTHERHOOD, 7
bad novel tells us...about its a. NOVELS, 2
He is the richest a. that ever grazed WRITERS, 61
authority a. be a stubborn bear BRIBERY, 4

A. forgets a dying king ROYALTY, 36
man /Dress'd in a little brief a. MANKIND, 26
No morality can be founded on a. MORALITY, 2
Nothing destroyeth a. so much POWER, 5
place him in a. CHARACTER, 2
The defiance of established a. REBELLION, 1
the highest a. for believing that the meek shall inherit the Earth HUMILITY, 11
authors A. are easy to get on with WRITERS, 12
much exposed to a. WRITERS, 25
The faults of great a. WRITERS, 6
their a. could not endure being wrong CRIME, 2
The reciprocal civility of a. WRITERS, 11
The trouble with our younger a. is WRITERS, 15
automobile Money differs from an a. MONEY, 24
avarice rich beyond the dreams of a. WEALTH, 21
ave *a. atque vale* GREETINGS, 1
avenged satisfaction of knowing that we are a. REVENGE, 14
average Take the life-lie away from the a. man DELUSION, 4
aves Beadsman, after thousand a. told PRAYER, 14
Avilion To the island-valley of A. AFTERLIFE, 10
avocado fat content of an a. FOOD, 21
avoidance The a. of taxes…still carries…reward TAXATION, 8
avoiding ingenious device for a. thought READING, 6
Avon Sweet Swan of A. SHAKESPEARE, 11
a-waggle You must always be a. LOVE, 80
awake At last a. LIFE, 14
A.! for Morning in the Bowl of Night DAY, 5
I dream when I am a. REALITY, 2
The lilies and roses were all a. LOVE, 134
We're very wide a., /The moon and I APPEARANCES, 15
away Over the hills and far a. LOVE, 59
Take the soup a. FOOD, 27
the big one that got a. MARRIAGE, 46
aweary I gin to be a. of the sun WORLD-WEARINESS, 8
awful And felt how a. goodness is GOOD, 12
awfulness by its very a. MARRIAGE, 113
awoke I a. one morning FAME, 6
axe his keener eye /The a.'s edge did try EXECUTION, 16
Lizzie Borden took an a. MURDER, 1
axioms A. in philosophy are not axioms PHILOSOPHY, 8
expressed in…arguments…a. and theorems THEORY, 3
aye A., and what then PROOF, 3

B

baa B., b., black sheep NURSERY RHYMES, 4
God ha' mercy on such as we, /B.! Yah! Bah DEBAUCHERY, 7
Babbitt one thing wrong with the B. house HOME, 5
babbl'd b. of green fields DEATH, 112
Babel B.; because the Lord did there confound the language LANGUAGE, 2
the tower of B. should have got language all mixed up LANGUAGE, 26
babies bit the b. in the cradles ANIMALS, 5
If men had to have b. BIRTH, 6
Other people's b. BABIES, 4
putting milk into b. CHILDREN, 18
War will never cease until b. WAR, 66
wretched b. don't come until BABIES, 3
You breed b. and you eat chips FOOD, 53
baby Anybody can shock a b. SIMPLICITY, 7
Don't throw the b. out HASTE, 1
Every b. born into the world BABIES, 2
hanging the b. on the clothes line to dry INNOVATION, 2
Hush-a-bye, b., on the tree top NURSERY RHYMES, 19
my b. at my breast SUICIDE, 11
no new b. in the womb of our society RUSSIA, 5
Rock-a-bye b. on the tree top SLEEP, 4
The b. bounced gently off the wall of her uterus PREGNANCY, 1
Walking My B. Back Home LOVE, 142
Babylon By the waters of B. AMERICA, 36
How many miles to B. NURSERY RHYMES, 17
Bach B. is like an astronomer MUSICIANS, 11
J. S. B. CRITICISM, 3
Music owes as much to B. MUSICIANS, 15
bachelor B.'s fare MARRIAGE, 116
Never trust…a b. too near TRUST, 4
bachelors reasons for b. to go out WOMEN, 30
back any of you at the b. who do not hear me DISABILITY, 1
But at my b. I always hear AGE, 38
Either b. us or sack us SUPPORT, 3
I sit on a man's b. HYPOCRISY, 17
turn your b. upon the world PERFECTION, 4
Will ye no come b. again RETURN, 3
backs With our b. to the wall…fight on to the end WAR, 44; WORLD WAR I, 12
back-stairs Drama is the b. of the intellect THEATRE, 4
Bacon B. discovered the art of making reading-glasses SCIENTISTS, 12
When their lordships asked B. BRIBERY, 1
bad a b. novel tells us the truth about its author NOVELS, 2
A b. penny LUCK, 1
A truth that's told with b. intent TRUTH, 14
b. die late GOOD AND EVIL, 3
B. girls don't have the time DIARIES, 2
b. taste is better than no taste TASTE, 1
Defend the b. against the worse DECLINE, 3
It is as b. as b. can be FOOD, 30
never was a b. peace WAR AND PEACE, 6
nothing either good or b. THINKING, 10
Nothing so b. but it might have been worse OPTIMISM, 7
put up with b. things TOLERANCE, 8
resolved to do something b. DECISION, 3
she was a very b. cook SNOBBERY, 9
so much b. in the best of us GOOD AND EVIL, 1
strong antipathy of good to b. PROVOCATION, 2
the name of…obstinacy in a b. one STUBBORNNESS, 3
There's no such thing as a b. Picasso INFERIORITY, 4
what I feel really b. about LIBERALISM, 1
When b. men combine UNITY, 7
when I'm b. I'm better SEX, 65
badge Red B. of Courage COURAGE, 7
badly If you want to do a thing b. EFFORT, 6
Bailey When will you pay me? /Say the bells of Old B. LONDON, 2
baker The butcher, the b. NURSERY RHYMES, 45
balance The b. of power POWER, 27
balanced Food is an important part of a b. diet FOOD, 35
balances thou art weighed in the b. JUDGMENT, 1
bald being b. – one can hear snowflakes APPEARANCE, 11
Balfour Mr B.'s Poodle HOUSES OF PARLIAMENT, 12
Balham She has a Rolls body and a B. mind STUPIDITY, 11
Balkans some damned silly thing in the B. BOSNIA AND HERCEGOVINA, 2
ball B.…how very singular NAMES, 1
ballet it takes more than one to make a b. SUPPORT, 6
To enter the…B. is to enter a convent DANCING, 8
balloon the moon's /a b. MOON, 3
The Moon's a B. BOOK, SONG, AND PLAY TITLES, 20
ballot The b. is stronger than the bullet DEMOCRACY, 10
ballots employers…only like b. so long as you lose them STRIKES, 3
balm wash the b. from an anointed king MONARCHY, 21
bananas b. or oranges, the Americans would not go MIDDLE EAST, 11
hanging around like clumps of b. INSULTS, 23
Banbury Ride a cock-horse to B. Cross NURSERY RHYMES, 42
bandage Religion…the wound, not the b. RELIGION, 50
bandages to walk around…with only a few light b. on BEAUTY, 32
bands Brass b. are all very well in their place MUSIC, 4
ladies who pursue Culture in b. CULTURE, 4
bang Not with a b. but a whimper ENDING, 3
banish to b.…the dark divisive clouds of Marxist socialism MARXISM, 6
bank a b. that would lend money to such a poor risk ROWING, 2
b. and shoal of time ENDING, 5
better that a man should tyrannize over his b. balance TYRANNY, 4
I cried all the way to the b. CRITICISM, 29
the b. was mightier than the sword LIBERALISM, 3
the man who broke the B. at Monte Carlo WEALTH, 16
bankrupt B. of Life WORLD-WEARINESS, 1
banks cashiers of the Musical B. MONEY, 13
Ye b. and braes NATURE, 2
banned any book should be b. CENSORSHIP, 4
banner A b. with the strange device, /Excelsior AMBITION, 12
Baptist For good all round business work, I should have preferred a B. PROTESTANTISM, 2
bar an olfactory b. FAMILIARITY, 6
no moaning of the b. DUTY, 5

though hell should b. the way DETERMINATION, 13
When I went to the B. as a very young man LAW, 11
Barabbas B. was a publisher PUBLISHING, 4
Barbara Her name was B. Allen LOVE, 13
barbarians society distributes itself into B., Philistines, and Populace AMERICA, 1
barbarity the...b. of war WAR, 55
the English seem...to act with the b. of tyrants IRELAND, 19
barbarous the invention of a b. age POETRY, 31
bard This goat-footed b. POLITICIANS, 58
bards Portraits of famous b. and preachers PAINTING, 16
bare Our ingress.../Was naked and b. LIFE, 34
Pylons, those pillars /B. TECHNOLOGY, 13
bargains rule for b. BUSINESS, 5
barge The b. she sat in, like a burnish'd throne ADMIRATION, 13
baritones b. are born villains in opera OPERA, 8
bark to hear the watch-dog's honest b. DOGS, 5
barking B. dogs ACTION, 1
b. mad about crime CRIME, 7
Barnum the celebrated B.'s circus POLITICIANS, 46
barrage chemical b. has been hurled against the fabric of life ECOLOGY, 2
barrel out of the b. of a gun POWER POLITICS, 5
someone who has...drunk...a...b. EXPERIENCE, 10
barrenness quarrels which vivify its b. LOVE, 64
barricade At some disputed b. DEATH, 103
barring a schoolboy's b. out POLITICS, 78
bar-rooms It brings men together in crowds and mobs in b. SOCIETY, 10
bars Nor iron b. a cage IMPRISONMENT, 4
barter All government...is founded on compromise and b. COMPROMISE, 4
base doing good to b. fellows CHARITY, 11
It takes a certain courage...to be truly b. EVIL, 2
baseball as sensible as b. in Italian OPERA, 5
b. cap is just as valid as a felt hat FASHION, 6
based All progress is b. PROGRESS, 2; EXTRAVAGANCE, 2
basics time to get back to b. POLITICS, 51
basing b. morals on myth MORALITY, 15
basket Have you ever taken anything out of the clothes b. CLEANNESS, 3
bastard Because I am a b. NASTINESS, 4
I hope you will not publicly call me a b. INSULTS, 43
putting all my eggs in one b. ABORTION, 2
bastards It is a pity...that more politicians are not b. POLITICIANS, 31
that'll hold the little b. MISTAKES, 5
bat black b., night, has flown INVITATIONS, 2
They came to see me b. not to see you bowl CRICKET, 3
Twinkle, twinkle, little b. NONSENSE, 5
bath B....once a week CLEANNESS, 1
Oh! who can ever be tired of B. ENGLAND, 1
the nuns who never take a b. MODESTY, 6
bathing caught the Whigs b. POLITICS, 22
something between a large b. machine BOATS, 6
bathroom fierce and revolutionary in a b. AMERICANS, 7
he goes to church as he goes to the b. CLERGY, 3
bats b. in the belfry MADNESS, 10
battalions God is always on the side of the big b. POWER POLITICS, 7
God is on the side not of the heavy b. POWER POLITICS, 8
battering B. the gates of heaven EXCESS, 14
battle A b. of giants WAR, 127
greatest misery is a b. gained VICTORY, 19
next greatest misfortune to losing a b. VICTORY, 18
preferred to go into b. sitting down SOLDIERS, 9
The b. of Britain WORLD WAR II, 6
battlefield b. is fearful WORLD WAR I, 4
the most beautiful b. WAR, 73
we survive amongst the dead and the dying as on a b. OLD AGE, 43
battlements Fate sits on these dark b. DESTINY, 18
battles Dead b., like dead generals WAR, 120
mother of b. MIDDLE EAST, 9
bauble that fool's b., the mace DISMISSAL, 4
baying b. for broken glass ARISTOCRACY, 15
bayonet bullet and the b. are brother and sister WORLD WAR I, 20
bayonets A man may build...a throne of b. POWER POLITICS, 4
bays To win the palm, the oak, or b. VICTORY, 10
be If you want to b. happy, b. HAPPINESS, 29
To b., or not to b. SUICIDE, 12; LANGUAGE, 6
What must b., must b. DESTINY, 1
beaches we shall fight on the b. WORLD WAR II, 4
beacons Logical consequences are the scarecrows of fools and the b. of wise men LOGIC, 3
beadle a b. on boxin' day POETRY, 12
beads what glass b. are to African traders SORROW, 5
Beadsman The B., after thousand aves told PRAYER, 14
beak Take thy b. from out my heart EVIL, 13
beaker a b. full of the warm South ALCOHOL, 37
Beale Miss Buss and Miss B. /Cupid's darts do not feel SENSITIVITY, 1
be-all b. and the end-all here ENDING, 5
bean The home of the b. and the cod SNOBBERY, 2
bear a B. of Very Little Brain WORDS, 16
any man...who could not b. another's misfortunes...like a Christian MISFORTUNE, 13
authority be a stubborn b. BRIBERY, 4
Exit, pursued by a b. ANIMALS, 18
Human kind cannot b. REALITY, 3
never...sell the b.'s skin ANTICIPATION, 6
Round and round the garden /Like a teddy b. NURSERY RHYMES, 44
they think I shall be able to b. it best RESPONSIBILITY, 4
bear-baiting Puritan hated b. PURITANISM, 3
beard singed the Spanish king's b. WAR, 35
There was an Old Man with a b. APPEARANCE, 19
bearded hard to hear what a b. man is saying PUNS, 12
He reaps the b. grain at a breath DEATH, 79
beards beware of long arguments and long b. BREVITY, 6
men wore their b., like they wear their neckties APPEARANCE, 18
bears And dancing dogs and b. ANIMALS, 12
And some of the bigger b. try to pretend SUPERSTITION, 9
b. and lions growl and fight ANIMALS, 20
beast b. of the earth ANIMALS, 3; CREATION, 5
b....will be a monster computer COMPUTERS, 3
Dialect words – those terrible marks of the b. CLASS, 15
Either a b. or a god MANKIND, 2
for man or b. WEATHER, 10
hardly be a b. or a fool alone on a great mountain SOLITUDE, 9
Man's life is cheap as b.'s NECESSITY, 5
The B. stands for strong mutually antagonistic governments NEWSPAPERS, 14
the mark...of the b. DEVIL, 5
beastie Wee, sleekit, cow'rin', tim'rous b. ANIMALS, 7
beastliness It is called in our schools 'b.' SEX, 5
beastly Don't let's be b. to the Germans GERMANY, 12
beat make the b. keep time with short steps FUNERALS, 1
Two hearts that b. as one LOVE, 85
beaten I was b. up by Quakers SHYNESS, 1
learning was painfully b. into him EDUCATION, 43
beats It b. as it sweeps as it cleans ADVERTISING, 14
beautiful Against the b....one can wage a pitiless war BEAUTY, 19
b....for someone who could not read AMERICA, 7
food is, actually, very b. FOOD, 50
Give me my golf clubs...and a b. partner DESIRE, 1
light, shade, and perspective...make it b. BEAUTY, 16
many men, so b. GUILT, 4
most b. things...are the most useless BEAUTY, 33
Our love of what is b. RESULTS, 4
Rich men's houses are seldom b. WEALTH, 3
summer afternoon...two most b. words SEASONS, 8
The good is the b. GOOD, 13
the most b. battlefield WAR, 73
the most b. woman I've ever seen BEAUTY, 27
the name of which was B. ARCHITECTURE, 2
the work comes out more b. ARTS, 4
when a woman isn't b. BEAUTY, 15
beautifully B. done LAST WORDS, 66
beauty A thing of b. is a joy for ever BEAUTY, 23
B. and the lust for learning BEAUTY, 8
b. being the best of all we know BEAUTY, 10
B. in distress BEAUTY, 13
B. in things exists in the mind BEAUTY, 21
B. is altogether in the eye of the beholder BEAUTY, 22
b. is only sin deep BEAUTY, 34
B. is only skin-deep BEAUTY, 2
B. is potent BEAUTY, 3
B. is truth, truth beauty BEAUTY, 24; TRUTH, 33

B. itself doth of itself persuade /The eyes of men BEAUTY, 35
B. sat with me all the summer day BEAUTY, 11
B. stands /In the admiration…of weak minds BEAUTY, 28
better to be first with an ugly woman than the hundredth with a b. BEAUTY, 12
But b.'s self she is, /When all her robes are gone BEAUTY, 5
Clad in the b. of a thousand stars BEAUTY, 26
Exuberance is B. BEAUTY, 9
Fostered alike by b. and by fear SOUL, 12
her b. made /The bright world dim BEAUTY, 37
Love built on b. BEAUTY, 17
love permanence more than…b. BRITISH, 3
Mathematics possesses…b. MATHEMATICS, 14
perceive real b. in a person…older BEAUTY, 6
She walks in b. BEAUTY, 14
Teaches such b. as a woman's eye LEARNING, 8
the b. /Of an aged face OLD AGE, 9
the laws of poetic truth and poetic b. POETRY, 2
The pain passes, but the b. remains ENDURANCE, 14
There is no excellent b. BEAUTY, 7
this generation…found England a land of b. ECOLOGY, 4
What *is* b., anyway? There's no such thing BEAUTY, 29

because B. it is there MOTIVE, 3

Becket Thomas B. ASSASSINATION, 4

become What's b. of Waring ABSENCE, 5

becoming I believe I am b. a god LAST WORDS, 72
Sunburn is very b. APPEARANCE, 9

bed and die – in b. WAR, 101
And so to b. BED, 7
B.…is the poor man's opera SEX, 28
Each within our narrow b. DEATH, 37
Go to b. with the lamb BED, 2
Here comes a candle to light you to b. LONDON, 2
Lady Capricorn…was…keeping open b. PROMISCUITY, 2
Never go to b. mad ANGER, 3
nicer to stay in b. BED, 5
So I took her into b. and covered up her head SEX, 4
The b. be blest BLESSING, 1
the night the b. fell on my father MEMORY, 19
Wedlock…double b. after the…chaise-longue MARRIAGE, 34
Who goes to b. with whom OLD AGE, 37
woman who goes to b. with a man SEX, 40

bedfellows Misery acquaints…strange b. MISFORTUNE, 16

bedroom meeting in a darkened b. in a Brussels hotel EUROPE, 20

beds Minds like b. always made up INFLEXIBILITY, 4
Will there be b. for me and all who seek REST, 1

bedspring the triumphant twang of a b. SEX, 47

bee How doth the little busy b. WORK, 25
Sting like a b. SPORT AND GAMES, 1

Beecham B.'s pills are just the thing DRUGS, 2

beechen spare the b. tree TREES, 2

beef The roast b. of England FOOD, 23

beefsteak Dr Johnson's morality was as English…as a b. ENGLAND, 20

beer chronicle small b. TRIVIALITY, 12
Did you ever taste b. ALCOHOL, 24
Life isn't all b. and skittles LIFE, 30
that bitter b. that tastes sweet IMMORTALITY, 5

Beerbohm Max B. OLD AGE, 49

bees murmuring of innumerable b. SEASONS, 23
No b., no honey WORK, 2
No shade, no shine, no butterflies, no b. MONTHS, 10

bees-winged Or was it his b. eyes WRITERS, 33

Beethoven B.'s Fifth Symphony is the most sublime noise MUSIC, 21
Roll Over B. POP MUSIC, 4

before I have been here b. FAMILIARITY, 4

beg only the poor…are forbidden to b. POVERTY, 10

beggar'd b. all description ADMIRATION, 13

beggars B. can't be choosers NECESSITY, 1

beggary b. in the love that can be reckon'd LOVE, 116
no vice but b. HYPOCRISY, 15

begin Are you sitting comfortably? Then I'll b. BEGINNING, 13
B. at the beginning ORDER, 2

beginning a b., a muddle, and an end NOVELS, 8
As it was in the b. ETERNITY, 2
a whole is that which has a b., a middle, and an end PLAYS, 1
Begin at the b. ORDER, 2
b. of fairies FAIRIES, 2
b. of time according to our Chronologie CREATION, 14
end of the b. WORLD WAR II, 13
every man at the b. doth set forth good wine ALCOHOL, 14
I like a film to have a b., a middle and an end CINEMA, 4
in the b. God CREATION, 2
in the b. was the word WORDS, 1
Nothing so difficult as a b. POETRY, 8
the b. of the end DEFEAT, 8

beginnings end to the b. of all wars WAR, 94
mighty things from small b. NATURE, 8

begins my family b. with me ANCESTRY, 3

begot what they were about when they b. me FAMILY, 32

begotten Whatever is b., born, and dies MORTALITY, 23

beguine She refused to begin the 'B.' PETULANCE, 1
When they begin the b. HAPPINESS, 16

begun There is an old saying 'well b. is half done' BEGINNING, 11

behaving men are more interested in…justifying themselves than in…b. MOTIVE, 6

behaviour The quality of moral b. varies MORALITY, 7

behind In the dusk, with a light b. her AGE, 30
led his regiment from b. COWARDICE, 3
part my hair b. OLD AGE, 18

behold all which we b. /Is full of blessings OPTIMISM, 29
B. her, single in the field SOLITUDE, 16
b. it was a dream DREAMS, 3

beholder Beauty is…in the eye of the b. BEAUTY, 22

beige It's b.! My color ARCHITECTURE, 14

being in him we live, and move, and have our b. GOD, 5
Knowledge is proportionate to b. KNOWLEDGE, 20
To kill a human b. KILLING, 4

Belfast British troops were patrolling the streets of B. IRELAND, 5

belfry bats in the b. MADNESS, 10

belief *Action will furnish b.* BELIEF, 5

believe a verb meaning 'to b. falsely' BELIEF, 8
b. in the life to come AFTERLIFE, 1
B. it or not BELIEF, 6
B. nothing of what you hear BELIEF, 1
don't b. in…true love SCEPTICISM, 1
I b. because it is impossible BELIEF, 7
I b. I am becoming a god LAST WORDS, 72
I b. in the Church RELIGION, 55
I don't b. in fairies FAIRIES, 1
inclined to b. those whom we do not know TRUST, 3
Infidelity…consists in professing to b. INTEGRITY, 5
it brings you luck whether you b.…or not SUPERSTITION, 6
They didn't b. me BEAUTY, 30
undesirable to b. a proposition SCEPTICISM, 4
We can b. what we choose RESPONSIBILITY, 11
what we b. is not necessarily true OBJECTIVITY, 3
you must b. in God FAITH, 12

believes He b.…that there *is* such a thing as truth POLITICIANS, 35
politician never b. what he says POLITICIANS, 7

bell B., book, and candle MATERIALISM, 18
for whom the b. tolls DEATH, 45
I'll b. the cat COURAGE, 10
The b. strikes one TIME, 43
The sexton toll'd the b. PUNS, 5
Unto the B. at Edmonton MARRIAGE, 43

Bellamy I could eat one of B.'s veal pies LAST WORDS, 52; FOOD, 44

belle La b. Dame sans Merci SUPERNATURAL, 10

bellies their b. were full HUNGER, 3

bells Ring out, wild b., and let him die ENDING, 7
Rings on her fingers and b. on her toes NURSERY RHYMES, 42
The b. of hell go ting-a-ling-a-ling DEATH, 16
'Twould ring the b. of Heaven ANIMALS, 12
With silver b. and cockle shells GARDENS, 1

belly Every man with a b. full of the classics CLASSICS, 7
to banish hunger by rubbing the b. HUNGER, 5
upon thy b. shalt thou go SEXES, 2
victory under the b. of a Cossack's horse RUSSIAN REVOLUTION, 3

bellyful Rumble thy b. WEATHER, 20

below Capten, art tha sleepin' there b. WAR, 77
Down and away b. DEPARTURE, 1
What thy errand here b. PURPOSE, 6

Ben Adhem And lo! B.'s name led all the rest SUPERIORITY, 5

Ben Battle B. was a soldier bold PUNS, 8

bench What do you suppose I am on the B. for REPARTEE, 4

benefactors gratitude to most b. INGRATITUDE, 3

benefits B. make a man a slave MATERIALISM, 1

It is the nature of men to be bound by the b. they confer OBLIGATION, 2
benevolence husband render unto the wife due b. MARRIAGE, 24
bereav'd I am black, as if b. of light RACISM, 5
Berkeley A Nightingale Sang in B. Square BIRDS, 7
Berliner *Ich bin ein B.* GERMANY, 6
Bernhardt Sarah B.'s funeral ACTORS, 12
berries I come to pluck your b. TREES, 10
berth His death, which happen'd in his b. PUNS, 5
Things hitherto undone should be given...a wide b. ORIGINALITY, 1
Bertie I'm Burlington B. BED, 3
best all that's b. of dark and bright BEAUTY, 14
as in the b. it is MURDER, 11
beauty being the b. of all we know BEAUTY, 10
b. of life is but intoxication DRUNKENNESS, 10
b. that is known and thought in the world CRITICISM, 1
b. words in the b. order POETRY AND PROSE, 2
Culture, the acquainting ourselves with the b. CULTURE, 1
For home is b. HOME, 9
His worst is better than any other person's b. WRITERS, 55
It was the b. of times FRENCH REVOLUTION, 1
look at the b. book...price of a turbot BOOKS, 37
Men of few words are the b. BREVITY, 8
Stolen sweets are b. THEFT, 5
The b. is the enemy of the good EXCELLENCE, 4
The b. of friends FRIENDSHIP, 6
the b. of possible worlds OPTIMISM, 27
The b. things in life WEALTH, 1
the shortest works are always the b. BREVITY, 4
we live in the b. of all possible worlds OPTIMISM, 19; PESSIMISM, 3
we will do our b. WORLD WAR II, 10
bestial what remains is b. REPUTATION, 7
bestow Let them b. on every airth a limb EXECUTION, 9
best-seller A b....because it was selling well FAME, 5
A b. is the gilded tomb of a mediocre talent BOOKS, 40
bet I b. my money on the bob-tail nag HORSES, 6
Bethlehem O come ye to B. CHRISTMAS, 16
O little town of B. CHRISTMAS, 11
betimes to be up b. BED, 8
betray Nature never did b. NATURE, 18
betraying if I had to choose between b. my country and b. my friend BETRAYAL, 3
betrothed a bride's attitude towards her b. MARRIAGE, 85; PUNS, 14
better a far, far, b. thing EXECUTION, 6
always...trying to get the b. SPORT AND GAMES, 14
b. is he...who hath not seen the evil work EVIL, 3
b. strangers SEPARATION, 6
B. than a play HOUSES OF PARLIAMENT, 6
b. to have loved and lost LOVE, 132
b. to have no opinion of God GOD, 3
b. to marry than to burn MARRIAGE, 25
for b. for worse MARRIAGE, 30
He is no b. ILLNESS, 1
I am getting b. and b. REMEDIES, 8
if you knows of a b. 'ole WAR, 4
I've got to admit it's getting b. IMPROVEMENT, 2
something b. than our brains to depend upon ARISTOCRACY, 4
the old is b. AGE, 12; ALCOHOL, 15
when I'm bad I'm b. SEX, 65
When you meet someone b....turn your thoughts to becoming his equal SUPERIORITY, 4
You're a b. man than I am, Gunga Din SUPERIORITY, 6
bettering Black people are...b. themselves RACISM, 7
Beulah B., peel me a grape LUXURY, 6
bewailing the sum of life's b. REGRET, 7
beware all should cry, B. CAUTION, 9
B. of the dog DOGS, 1
B. of the man who does not return your blow FORGIVENESS, 15
bewildered Bewitched, Bothered and B. CONFUSION, 6
I was b. once CONFUSION, 2
bewitched B., Bothered and Bewildered CONFUSION, 6
beyond people live b. their incomes EXTRAVAGANCE, 4
Bible have used the B. as if it was a constable's handbook BIBLE, 6
searching through the B. for loopholes BIBLE, 5
that book is the B. BIBLE, 1
The B. is literature BIBLE, 10
the B. tells me so RELIGION, 62
The English B. BIBLE, 7
There's a B. on that shelf there BIBLE, 9
Bibles they have the land and we have the B. RACISM, 12
bicycle a b. made for two MARRIAGE, 44
Socialism can only arrive by b. SOCIALISM, 4
big A b. man has no time FAME, 9
A government...b. enough to give you all you want GOVERNMENT, 11
B. Brother is watching you AUTHORITARIANISM, 5
b. emotions come from b. words STYLE, 5
he was too b. for them CONCEIT, 5
the b. one that got away MARRIAGE, 46
The b. print giveth and the fine print taketh away BUSINESS, 20
bigger it's a great deal b. UNIVERSE, 3
bike he got on his b. UNEMPLOYMENT, 2
bill put 'Emily, I love you' on the back of the b. LOVE, 89
billboard A b. lovely as a tree TREES, 12
billboards the churches...bore for me the same relation to God that b. did to Coca-Cola RELIGION, 61
billiard The b. sharp whom any one catches PUNISHMENT, 11
billiards to play b. well SPORT AND GAMES, 22
Billy B..../Fell in the fire FIRE, 2
billy-bong Once a jolly swagman camped by a b. PLACES, 12
biographies History is the essence of...b. BIOGRAPHY, 3; HISTORY, 7
biography a man is nobody unless his b. OBITUARIES, 3
history...the b. of great men GREATNESS, 6; HISTORY, 8
how difficult it is to write b. BIOGRAPHY, 6
no history; only b. BIOGRAPHY, 5; HISTORY, 12
birch I'm all for bringing back the b. PUNISHMENT, 16
bird A b. in the hand PRUDENCE, 1
a b. of the air shall carry the voice SECRECY, 3
Lo! the B. is on the Wing TIME, 17
She's only a b. in a gilded cage IMPRISONMENT, 3
The B. of Time TIME, 17
bird-cage a b. played with toasting-forks MUSIC, 6
Robert Houdin who...invented the vanishing b. trick THEATRE, 15
birds All the b. of the air NURSERY RHYMES, 2
b....caught in the snare CHANCE, 2
B. of a feather SIMILARITY, 1
no b. sing ILLNESS, 10
No fruits, no flowers, no leaves, no b. MONTHS, 10
spring now comes unheralded by the return of the b. ECOLOGY, 1
that make fine b. CLOTHES, 1
Two little dicky b., /Sitting on a wall NURSERY RHYMES, 63
where late the sweet b. sang OLD AGE, 40
Birmingham Am in B. MEMORY, 4
One has no great hopes from B. ENGLAND, 2
birth B., and copulation, and death LIFE AND DEATH, 5
B. may be a matter of a moment BIRTH, 7
b. of the Universe UNIVERSE, 12
From b. to age eighteen, a girl needs good parents AGE, 63
no credentials...not even...a certificate of b. ARISTOCRACY, 8
no cure for b. and death LIFE AND DEATH, 12
The history of man for the nine months preceding his b. BIRTH, 5
what you were before your b. AFTERLIFE, 8
birthday A diplomat...always remembers a woman's b. AGE, 28
If one doesn't get b. presents GIFTS, 5
is it my b. or am I dying LAST WORDS, 5
birthplace accent of one's b. lingers HOMESICKNESS, 5
biscuit Can't a fellow even enjoy a b. THRIFT, 9
bishop a b....must be blameless CLERGY, 2
another B. dead CLERGY, 12
blonde to make a b. kick a hole APPEARANCE, 8
How can a b. marry CLERGY, 13
Make him a b., and you will silence him CLERGY, 5
May you be the mother of a b. BLESSING, 3; LAST WORDS, 8
the symbol of a b. is a crook CLERGY, 6
bisier he semed b. than he was APPEARANCES, 10
bit He b. his lip in a manner HUMOUR, 51
The dog.../Went mad and b. the man DOGS, 7
bitches burn the bloody b. CLERGY, 11
Now we are all sons of b. NUCLEAR WEAPONS, 1
bite b. the hand that fed them INGRATITUDE, 2
would b. some other of my generals REPARTEE, 3
bites when a man b. a dog that is news JOURNALISM, 11

biting if you don't stop b. your fingernails ARTISTS, 19
bitter never tasted what is b. SUFFERING, 2
black A lady asked me why...I wore b. MOURNING, 15
Any colour, so long as it's b. CHOICE, 1
B. people are...bettering themselves RACISM, 7
British Government sees b. people as expendable RACISM, 30
coffee that's too b.... You integrate it with cream RACISM, 20
I am b., as if bereav'd of light RACISM, 5
I don't believe in b. majority rule RACISM, 28
looking for a b. hat METAPHYSICS, 1
One b., and one white, and two khaki RACISM, 1
People think we do not understand our b.... countrymen RACISM, 6
Take that b. box away CINEMA, 11
That old b. magic SUPERNATURAL, 11
The Ethiopians say that their gods are...b. RELIGION, 72
The future is...b. RACISM, 3
There's a b. sheep FAMILY, 4
To like an individual because he's b. RACISM, 8
Two lovely b. eyes VIOLENCE, 4
blackbird When down came a b. NURSERY RHYMES, 48
Blackpool With my little stick of B. rock FOOD, 24
Blackshirt Before the organization of the B. movement FREEDOM, 37
Blake B. is damned good to steal from POETS, 35
B. is to the average poet...man in the street POETS, 55
B.... presents only the essential POETS, 34
That William B. /Who beat upon the wall POETS, 62
blame Everyone threw the b. on me RESPONSIBILITY, 4
blank Pain – has an Element of B. SUFFERING, 7
Where were you fellows when the paper was b. EDITORS, 1
blanks historians left b. in their writings HISTORIANS, 5
blasphemies All great truths begin as b. NOVELTY, 9
bleak In the b. mid-winter SEASONS, 18
bleed If you prick us, do we not b. EQUALITY, 22
blemish Christianity...the one immortal b. CHRISTIANITY, 35
Blenheim I dine at B. once a week SUPERIORITY, 1
bless God b. us, every one BLESSING, 6
blessed B. are the meek HUMILITY, 1
b. is the man that endureth temptation TEMPTATION, 4
B. is the man who expects nothing EXPECTATION, 4
blessing a b. that money cannot buy HEALTH AND HEALTHY LIVING, 12
Let the b.... be...upon all that are lovers of virtue FISHING, 3
blessings all which we behold /Is full of b. OPTIMISM, 29
nurse has become one of the great b. OCCUPATIONS, 15
blest It is twice b. MERCY, 2
The bed be b. BLESSING, 1
they b. him in their pain MARTYRDOM, 4
this b. man, let his just praise be given COMPLIMENTS, 8
blind A b. man in a dark room METAPHYSICS, 1
all the discomforts that will accompany my being b. BLINDNESS, 7
Booth died b. FAITH, 13
Country of the B. SUPERIORITY, 12
love is b. LOVE, 118
Painting is a b. man's profession PAINTING, 11
union of a deaf man to a b. woman MARRIAGE, 37
wing'd Cupid painted b. LOVE, 120
blinded with b. eyesight LEARNING, 9
blindness world was stumbling...in social b. BLINDNESS, 2
bliss B. was it in that dawn to be alive FRENCH REVOLUTION, 3
where ignorance is b., /'Tis folly to be wise IGNORANCE, 6
blithe Hail to thee, b. Spirit BIRDS, 10
No lark more b. than he HAPPINESS, 4
blitz A b. of a boy is Timothy Winters APPEARANCE, 7
block a chip off the old b. POLITICIANS, 40
there's a statue inside every b. of stone OBESITY, 8
blockhead No man but a b. ever wrote WRITING, 16
blocks philosophy ought to...unravel people's mental b. PHILOSOPHY, 10
blonde A b. to make a bishop kick a hole APPEARANCE, 8
blondes Gentlemen always seem to remember b. APPEARANCE, 23
blood b. and iron POWER POLITICS, 2
B. is thicker FAMILY, 1
B. sport is brought to its ultimate refinement JOURNALISM, 18
b., toil, tears and sweat EFFORT, 3
critics...desire our b., not our pain CRITICS, 13
drown in their own b. MIDDLE EAST, 8
He is all b., dirt and sucked sugar stick CRITICISM, 57
his b. be on us GUILT, 3
humble and meek are thirsting for b. HUMILITY, 7
I am in b. /Stepp'd in so far GUILT, 7
If I die today every drop of my b. LAST WORDS, 29
I have lived off the b. of Chopin MUSICIANS, 7
leeches have red b. LAST WORDS, 17
rather have b. on my hands COMMITMENT, 4
Seas of B. CHRISTIANITY, 39
shed his b. for the country JUSTICE, 21
The b. of the martyrs CHRISTIANITY, 44
the b. that she has spilt REVENGE, 9
the old savage England, whose last b. flows still ENGLAND, 23
There are two kinds of b. RACISM, 31
the River Tiber foaming with much b. PROPHECY, 11; RACISM, 26
thy brother's b. crieth unto me MURDER, 2
trading on the b. of my men EXPLOITATION, 3
without shedding of b. is no remission EXECUTION, 2
You can't get b. FUTILITY, 3
your b. of your lives will I require CRIME, 1; PUNISHMENT, 4
bloodiness symbol of the b. of family life FAMILY, 24
bloody All the faces...seem to be b. Poms ENGLISH, 11
My head is b., but unbowed ENDURANCE, 6
bloom It's a sort of b. on a woman CHARM, 1
lilac is in b. FLOWERS, 2
blossom Love's perfect b. LOVE, 98
blow A b. in cold blood VIOLENCE, 7
Another year! – another deadly b. DEFEAT, 9
Beware of the man who does not return your b. FORGIVENESS, 15
B., blow, thou winter wind INGRATITUDE, 4
B.... till you burst CONTEMPT, 2
B., winds, and crack your cheeks WEATHER, 19
but a word and a b. VIOLENCE, 3
themselves must strike the b. FREEDOM, 6
this b. /Might be the be-all and the end-all here ENDING, 5
bludgeoning the b. of the people DEMOCRACY, 23
blue Little Boy B., /Come blow your horn NURSERY RHYMES, 28
that little tent of b. IMPRISONMENT, 7
The b. ribbon of the turf HORSES, 5
The essence of any b. material HUMOUR, 17
What are those b. remembered hills NOSTALGIA, 10
blues Twentieth-Century B. MELANCHOLY, 4
blue-vested short, b. people FRANCE, 3
blunder poverty...is a b. POVERTY, 19
worse than a crime, it is a b. MISTAKES, 4
Youth is a b. AGE, 19
blunders b. usually do more to shape history MISTAKES, 17
blush a b. to the cheek of a young person EMBARRASSMENT, 1
b. to find it fame GOOD, 14
flower is born to b. unseen WASTE, 2
blushes Man is the only animal that b. EMBARRASSMENT, 2
take away the candle and spare my b. MODESTY, 1
Boadicea some bargain-basement B. POLITICIANS, 53
boar ancestors were hunting the wild b. JEWS, 2
boarding-house Any two meals at a b. FOOD, 33
boat a beautiful pea-green b. NONSENSE, 20
Do they allow tipping on the b. MONEY, 34
It was involuntary. They sank my b. MODESTY, 2
On a slow b. to China BOATS, 10
boating Jolly b. weather BOATS, 4
boats messing about in b. BOATS, 7
we look for happiness in b. and carriage rides TRAVEL, 12
Bobby B. Shafto's gone to sea NURSERY RHYMES, 5
bob-tail I bet my money on the b. nag HORSES, 6
Boche drove the B. across the Rhine WORLD WAR I, 23
bodies many b. of the saints which slept arose LAST WORDS, 11
our dead b. must tell the tale ENDURANCE, 16
well-developed b., fairly developed minds EDUCATION, 18
body A b. seriously out of equilibrium MADNESS, 11
a sound mind in a sound b. HEALTH AND HEALTHY LIVING, 11
b. of a man half my age HEALTH AND HEALTHY LIVING, 8
b. of a weak and feeble woman ROYALTY, 13
company...have neither a soul to lose nor a b. to kick BUSINESS, 22
fear made manifest on the b. DISEASE, 16
Happiness is beneficial for the b. SORROW, 18
Man has no B. distinct from his Soul SOUL, 4
mind that makes the b. rich APPEARANCES, 22
more familiar with Africa than my own b. INNOCENCE, 8
not being allowed to have control over her b. PREGNANCY, 3
Our b. is a machine for living REMEDIES, 13

the gigantic b., the huge massy face WRITERS, 67
the human b. is sacred MANKIND, 36
the soul is not more than the b. SELF, 20
Why be given a b. if you...keep it shut up NAKEDNESS, 5
Bognor Bugger B. LAST WORDS, 30
boil b. at different degrees INDIVIDUALITY, 5
boiler The United States is like a gigantic b. AMERICA, 16
boldness B., and again boldness COURAGE, 8
bomb god of science...has given us the atomic b. SCIENCE, 25
bombed no power on earth that can protect him from being b. WAR, 6
bombs b. *are* unbelievable until they...fall WEAPONS, 10
Come, friendly b., and fall on Slough ENGLAND, 4
drop b....hit civilians WAR, 42
Ears like b. APPEARANCE, 7
test the Russians, not the b. NUCLEAR WEAPONS, 6
bon to produce an occasional *b. mot* MARRIAGE, 16
Bonaparte The three-o'-clock in the morning courage, which B. thought was the rarest COURAGE, 24
Bonar Poor B. can't bear being called a liar POLITICIANS, 61
bondage Of Human B. BOOK, SONG, AND PLAY TITLES, 16
bone The nearer the b. FOOD, 5
boneless the b. wonder POLITICIANS, 46
bones Bleach the b. of comrades slain WAR, 50
Heat, madam!...to take off my flesh and sit in my b. WEATHER, 26
Of his b. are coral made DEATH, 108
The healthy b. of a single Pomeranian grenadier DIPLOMACY, 4
bonhomie Overcame his natural b. ECONOMICS, 3
bonjour *B. tristesse* SORROW, 7
bonkers If the British public falls for this...it will be...b. POLITICS, 32
bonnie *By the b. milldams o' Binnorie* LOVE, 15
My B. lies over the ocean SEPARATION, 1
Oh, bring back my B. to me SEPARATION, 1
bonny the child that is born on the Sabbath day / Is b. and blithe, and good and gay NURSERY RHYMES, 34
bonum *Summum b.* GOOD, 3
boojum Snark *was* a B. NONSENSE, 6
book A b. may be amusing BOOKS, 20
A b.'s a b., although there's nothing in't BOOKS, 10
A b. that furnishes no quotations QUOTATIONS, 9
a b. that is a b. flowers once BOOKS, 23
a b. to kill time CRITICISM, 32
A good b. is the best of friends BOOKS, 44
A good b. is the precious life-blood BOOKS, 28
An angel writing in a b. of gold DREAMS, 12
Another damned, thick, square b. WRITING, 9
any b. should be banned CENSORSHIP, 4
Bell, b., and candle MATERIALISM, 18
b. is not harmless...consciously offended BOOKS, 17
dainties that are bred in a b. IGNORANCE, 13
do not throw this b. about BOOKS, 7
Everybody writes a b. too many WRITERS, 20
Every b. must be chewed WRITING, 1
go away and write a b. about it SPEECHES, 1
Go, litel b. BOOKS, 13
half a library to make one b. WRITING, 13
he who destroys a good b., kills reason BOOKS, 27
If a b. is worth reading BOOKS, 35
I have only read one b. READING, 12
I'll drown my b. RENUNCIATION, 4
moral or an immoral b. BOOKS, 46
never got around to reading the b. CRITICISM, 33
Never judge a cover by its b. BOOKS, 24
that everyone has it in him to write one b. WRITING, 22
The number one b....was written by a committee BIBLE, 8
The possession of a b. OSTENTATION, 2
There are two motives for reading a b. READING, 13
There is not any b. / Or face DEATH, 127
There must be a man behind the b. WRITERS, 9
unprintable b. that is readable BOOKS, 30
What is the use of a b. BOOKS, 12
What you don't know would make a great b. IGNORANCE, 15
When a b. is boring, they yawn openly BOOKS, 39
without mentioning a single b. BOOKS, 32
Would you allow your wife...to read this b. PRUDERY, 1
You can't tell a b. APPEARANCES, 7
books against b. the Home Secretary is PHILISTINISM, 7
All b. are divisible into two classes BOOKS, 36
An author who speaks about his own b. EGOTISM, 5
be not swallowed up in b. LOVE, 146; KNOWLEDGE, 34
between a man of sense and his b. BOOKS, 14
B. and friends BOOKS, 1; FRIENDS, 1
B. are a load of crap BOOKS, 22
B. are...a mighty bloodless substitute for life BOOKS, 42
B. are made...like pyramids BOOKS, 18
B. are well written, or badly written BOOKS, 46
b. by which the printers have lost BOOKS, 19
B. cannot always please BOOKS, 15
b. cannot be killed by fire BOOKS, 34
B., I don't know what you see in them BOOKS, 45
B. must follow sciences BOOKS, 4
B....propose to *instruct* or to *amuse* BOOKS, 16
B. think for me READING, 9
b....written by people who don't understand them BOOKS, 25
Borrowers of b. BORROWING, 6
but b. never die BOOKS, 34
come not, Lucifer! / I'll burn my b. DAMNATION, 4
Few b. today are forgivable BOOKS, 21
Give me b., fruit, French wine and fine weather PLEASURE, 17
God has written all the b. SUBJECTIVITY, 2
His b. were read BOOKS, 6; PUNS, 1
If my b. had been any worse CINEMA, 1
I keep my b. at the British Museum BOOKS, 9
Morality's a gesture....learnt from b. MORALITY, 3
Motherhood meant I have written four fewer b. MOTHERHOOD, 5
No furniture so charming as b. BOOKS, 41
of making many b. there is no end BOOKS, 8
poring over miserable b. LEARNING, 9
Prolonged...reviewing of b. involves constantly *inventing* reactions CRITICISM, 36
proper study of mankind is b. LITERATURE, 6
replacing some of the timber used up by my b. TREES, 6
Some b. are to be tasted BOOKS, 3
Some b. are undeservedly forgotten BOOKS, 2
the b. of the hour BOOKS, 36
The b. one reads in childhood BOOKS, 29
the disease of writing b. WRITING, 23
The reading of all good b. LITERATURE, 3
To read too many b. READING, 11
We all know that b. burn BOOKS, 34
Whenever b. are burned CENSORSHIP, 1
When I think of all the b. I have read LIFE, 55
women dislike his b. WRITERS, 71
bookseller he once shot a b. PUBLISHING, 5
booksellers b. are generous liberal-minded men PUBLISHING, 9
nor even b. have put up with poets' being second-rate POETS, 8
boon Is life a b. MORTALITY, 7
boorish the opinionated, the ignorant, and the b. STUBBORNNESS, 2
boot imagine a b. stamping on a human face OPPRESSION, 6
Booth B. died blind FAITH, 13
boots before the truth has got its b. on LYING, 6
If ever he went to school without any b. CONCEIT, 5
Very well, then I shall not take off my b. PRACTICALITY, 7
Bo-peep Little B. has lost her sheep NURSERY RHYMES, 27
bordello return to earth as a gatekeeper of a b. THREATS, 3
border Through all the wide B. CHIVALRY, 9
bore A b. is a man who BORES, 5
A healthy male adult b. BORES, 8
B., n. A person who talks BORES, 1
Every hero becomes a b. HEROISM, 5
He is an old b. BORES, 7
Is not life...too short...to b. ourselves BOREDOM, 6
no greater b. than the travel b. TRAVEL, 19
proof that God is a b. PROTESTANTISM, 1
War is an organized b. WAR, 48
you are...the club B.: I am the club Liar SUPERIORITY, 11
bored aged diplomats to be b. DIPLOMACY, 1
Bores and *B.* BORES, 2
Dear World, I am leaving you because I am b. LAST WORDS, 60
I wanted to be b. to death BOREDOM, 2
Punctuality is the virtue of the b. PROMPTNESS, 5
We were as nearly b. as enthusiasm would permit CRITICISM, 17
When you're b. with yourself BOREDOM, 7
boredom sheer apathy and b. DISCOVERY, 4
The effect of b. on a large scale BOREDOM, 5

three great evils, b., vice, and poverty WORK, 24
bores he b. for England BORES, 4
the *B.* and *Bored* BORES, 2
boring curiously b. about...happiness SYMPATHY, 4
Men are b. to women SEXES, 16
Somebody's b. me, I think it's me BORES, 6
you ought to be ashamed of...being b. BOREDOM, 3
born a silly little mouse will be b. DISAPPOINTMENT, 3
As soon as man is b. DEATH, 3
a time to be b., and a time to die TIME, 12
best...never to have been b. at all PESSIMISM, 6
better if neither of us had been b. REGRET, 10
b. again, not of corruptible seed DEATH, 29
b. to obey OBEDIENCE, 2
B. under one law HUMAN CONDITION, 9
Every moment one is b. LIFE AND DEATH, 14
he is not conscious of being b. LIFE AND DEATH, 8
He was b. an Englishman NATIONALITY, 1
I was b. at the age of twelve CINEMA, 3
I was b. old AGE, 61
joy that a man is b. into the world BIRTH, 1
Man was b. free FREEDOM, 46
natural to die as to be b. DEATH, 23
No, thank you, I was b. intoxicated DRUNKENNESS, 18
One is not b. a woman WOMEN, 13
one of woman b. BIRTH, 9
Some are b. great GREATNESS, 12
Some men are b. mediocre MEDIOCRITY, 5
sucker b. every minute GULLIBILITY, 1
The house where I was b. NOSTALGIA, 9
to have been b. BIRTH, 4
to the manner b. CUSTOM, 3
We are all b. mad MADNESS, 1
Whatever is begotten, b., and dies MORTALITY, 23
born-again b. people...make you wish RELIGION, 69
boroughs The bright b., the circle-citadels there STARS, 3
borrow If you don't want to use the army, I should like to b. it SARCASM, 2
men who b. BORROWING, 5
borrowed B. garments BORROWING, 1
Britain has lived...on b. time BRITAIN, 5
borrower Neither a b. nor a lender be BORROWING, 8; INTEGRITY, 6
borrowers B. of books BORROWING, 6
borrowing banqueting upon b. BORROWING, 3
b. dulls the edge of husbandry BORROWING, 8; INTEGRITY, 6
Bosnia thread holding B. together BOSNIA AND HERCEGOVINA, 5
bosom Abraham's b. POVERTY AND WEALTH, 2
a capital b. to hang jewels upon APPEARANCE, 13
not a b. to repose upon APPEARANCE, 13
boss working...eight hours a day...get to be a b. WORK, 8
Boston A B. man AMERICANS, 2
this is good old B. SNOBBERY, 2
both Dreaming on b. AGE, 53
said on b. sides OBJECTIVITY, 1
bother long words B. me WORDS, 16
bothered Bewitched, B. and Bewildered CONFUSION, 6
Botticelli If B. were alive today ARTISTS, 21
bottinney b. means a knowledge of plants EDUCATION, 14
bottle Yo-ho-ho, and a b. of rum ALCOHOL, 60
bottles It is with...people as with...b. CHARACTER, 18
the English have hot-water b. ENGLISH, 24
bottom b. of the economic pyramid POVERTY, 27
the best reasons...for remaining at the b. AMBITION, 6
bough Loaf of Bread beneath the B. CONTENTMENT, 3
bought b. things because she wanted 'em WOMEN, 84
bouillabaisse B. is only good because cooked by the French FOOD, 19; FRANCE, 5
boulder When the torrent sweeps a man against a b. THEORY, 7
Boulogne There was an old man of B. INNUENDO, 1
bound grandmother's feet had been b. CHINA, 3
Tomorrow my hands will be b. EXECUTION, 1
bouquet the b. is better than the taste ALCOHOL, 49
bourgeois *B.*...is an epithet CLASS, 16
How beastly the b. is MEN, 8
bourgeoisie the British b. have spoken of themselves as gentlemen CLASS, 35
bourn from whose b. /No traveller returns AFTERLIFE, 9
bovine The cow is of the b. ilk ANIMALS, 16
bow B., b., ye lower middle classes CLASS, 13
I, said the Sparrow, /With my b. and arrow NURSERY RHYMES, 68
Says the great bell at B. LONDON, 2
bowels in the b. of Christ MISTAKES, 6
bower-bird I'm a bit of a b. WRITING, 36
bowl inverted B. we call The Sky DESTINY, 9
love in a golden b. WISDOM, 10
They came to see me bat not to see you b. CRICKET, 3
bow-wow Daddy wouldn't buy me a b. DOGS, 14
box B. about: 'twill come to my father anon FATHERS, 2
Take that black b. away CINEMA, 11
boxing loves b. is either a liar or a fool SPORT AND GAMES, 8
boy And said, What a good b. am I NURSERY RHYMES, 29
a secret way...of getting at a b. EVIL, 8
A thing of duty is a b. for ever POLICE, 4; PUNS, 15
every b. and every gal /That's born into the world alive POLITICS, 31
If...I were the only b. LOVE, 65
I'm farther off from heav'n /Than when...a b. INNOCENCE, 6
Let the b. win his spurs SELF-RELIANCE, 5
Love is a b. PUNISHMENT, 6; INDULGENCE, 1
Mad about the b. LOVE, 44
rarely...one can see in a little b. the promise of a man CHILDREN, 20
Shades of the prison-house begin to close /Upon the growing b. METAPHYSICS, 5
The b. I love is up in the gallery LOVE, 144
The b. stood on the burning deck COURAGE, 14
the little b. /Who lives down the lane NURSERY RHYMES, 4
When I was a little b. they called me a liar WRITERS, 22
boyhood The smiles, the tears, /Of b.'s years NOSTALGIA, 14
boys As flies to wanton b. DESTINY, 20
B. and girls come out to play NURSERY RHYMES, 6
B. are capital fellows in their own way CHILDREN, 32
B. do not grow up gradually CHILDREN, 19
b. plan for what...girls plan for whom SEXES, 10
B. will be boys SEXES, 12
Claret is the liquor for b. ALCOHOL, 32
Girls and b. grow up more normally together EDUCATION, 45
Where are the b. of the Old Brigade NOSTALGIA, 23
Written by office b. for office b. NEWSPAPERS, 11
bracelet diamond and safire b. lasts forever MATERIALISM, 13
braces I had b. on my teeth and got high marks APPEARANCE, 24
braes Ye banks and b. NATURE, 2
Brahms B....an extraordinary musician MUSICIANS, 16
brain a Bear of Very Little B. WORDS, 16
b. attic stocked with all the furniture KNOWLEDGE, 13
B., n. An apparatus with which we think MIND, 1
If it is for mind that we are seaching the b. MIND, 7
Let schoolmasters puzzle their b. ALCOHOL, 29
the human b. is a device to keep the ears from grating MIND, 2
Tobacco drieth the b. SMOKING, 22
we are supposing the b....more than a telephone-exchange MIND, 7
with no deep researches vex the b. CLARITY, 1
You've got the b. of a four-year-old boy STUPIDITY, 8
brains a girl with b. ought to do something else WOMEN, 47
b. enough to make a fool of himself WISDOM AND FOOLISHNESS, 7
I mix them with my b. PAINTING, 7
something better than our b. to depend upon ARISTOCRACY, 4
What good are b. to a man INTELLIGENCE, 8
braking British civil service...effective b. mechanism BUREAUCRACY, 10
branch Cut is the b. that might have grown DEATH, 81
brandy I am not well; pray get me...b. FIRST IMPRESSIONS, 3
brass B. bands are all very well in their place MUSIC, 4
Men's evil manners live in b. MEMORIALS, 10
sounding b. CHARITY, 6
brave Any fool can be b. on a battle field WAR, 68
b. new world...such people in't MANKIND, 28
Fortune favours the b. COURAGE, 23
land of the free, and the home of the b. AMERICA, 21
Many b. men...before Agamemnon's time OBLIVION, 1
the B. deserves the Fair COURAGE, 11
we could never learn to be b....if there were only joy ENDURANCE, 7
Brazil B., where the nuts come from PLACES, 16
breach a custom more honour'd in the b. CUSTOM, 3
Once more unto the b. COURAGE, 19

bread b. and cheese, and kisses MARRIAGE, 116
b. and circuses PUBLIC, 15
b. eaten in secret is pleasant SECRECY, 5
B. is the staff of life FOOD, 3
cast thy b. upon the waters OPPORTUNITY, 10
I am the b. of life FAITH, 8
Loaf of B. beneath the Bough CONTENTMENT, 3
One swears by wholemeal b. HEALTH AND HEALTHY LIVING, 9
that b. should be so dear POVERTY, 17
Their learning is like b. in a besieged town SCOTS, 6
This b. I break was once the oat AGRICULTURE, 6
breakdown symptoms of approaching nervous b. WORK, 21
breakfast b.. I told Jeeves to drink it himself ALCOHOL, 65
she must not reheat his sins for b. FORGIVENESS, 11
breakfast-table ready for the national b. OBITUARIES, 3
breakfast-time critical period in matrimony is b. MARRIAGE, 70
breast charms to soothe a savage b. MUSIC, 15
my baby at my b. SUICIDE, 11
breast-feeding atheism, b., circumcision INDULGENCE, 2
breasts they add weight to the b. FOOD, 15
breath blow hot and cold with the same b. INDECISION, 1
Can storied urn.../Back to its mansion call the fleeting b. DEATH, 57
He reaps the bearded grain at a b. DEATH, 79
in this harsh world draw thy b. in pain MOURNING, 13
The years to come seemed waste of b. FLYING, 4
wish the night /Had borne my b. away NOSTALGIA, 9
world will hold its b. WORLD WAR II, 21
breathed God...b. into his nostrils GARDENS, 3
breather I happen to be a chain b. SMOKING, 17
breed happy b. of men ENGLAND, 36
more careful of the b. of their horses and dogs than of their children FATHERS, 5
breeding formed by a different b. POVERTY AND WEALTH, 4
Good b. consists in concealing how...we think of ourselves MANNERS, 5
breeks taking the b. aff a wild Highlandman SCOTS, 10
breeze The fair b. blew EXPLORATION, 1
breezes spicy b. /Blow soft o'er Ceylon's isle MISANTHROPY, 1
brevity B. is the soul of lingerie BREVITY, 5; CLOTHES, 12
B. is the soul of wit BREVITY, 7
brewery O take me to a b. ALCOHOL, 9
bribe doing nothing for a b. CONTENTMENT, 7
The man who offers a b. BRIBERY, 3
You cannot hope to b. or twist JOURNALISM, 33
bribes How many b. he had taken BRIBERY, 1
bribing Money is good for b. yourself MONEY, 39
brick carried a...b. in his pocket BUSINESS, 23
he found it b. IMPROVEMENT, 1
He is a man of b. CHARACTER, 25
bricklayers B. kick their wives to death CLASS, 37
bride a b.'s attitude towards her betrothed MARRIAGE, 85; PUNS, 14
It helps...to remind your b. that you gave up a throne for her MARRIAGE, 134
unravish'd b. of quietness SILENCE, 9
bridge A B. Too Far BOOK, SONG, AND PLAY TITLES, 22
Beautiful Railway B. of the Silv'ry Tay DISASTER, 4
I am not going to speak to the man on the b. DEPARTURE, 3
I stood on the b. at midnight TIME, 25
Like a b. over troubled water COMFORT, 4
London B. is falling down NURSERY RHYMES, 32
over the B. of Sighs into eternity DEATH, 74
brief I strive to be b., and I become obscure BREVITY, 2
Out, out, b. candle LIFE, 45
brigade Forward the Light B. OBEDIENCE, 4
Where are the boys of the Old B. NOSTALGIA, 23
brigands B. demand your money WOMEN, 19
bright her beauty made /The b. world dim BEAUTY, 37
Look on the b. side OPTIMISM, 5
the creature hath a purpose and its eyes are b. with it PURPOSE, 5
Tiger! burning b. ANIMALS, 4
young lady named B. SCIENCE, 3
brightness To pass away ere life hath lost its b. DEATH, 59
Brighton Like B. pier...inadequate for getting to France TRAVEL, 15
bright-star Johnny-the-b. REALISM, 4
brilliance No b. is needed in the law LAW, 20
brilliant a far less b. pen than mine CONCEIT, 4
b. men...will come to a bad end GREATNESS, 2
The dullard's envy of b. men GREATNESS, 2
brillig Twas b., and the slithy toves NONSENSE, 7
brimstone b. and fire PUNISHMENT, 3
bring thou knowest not what a day may b. forth FUTURE, 3
Britain a time when B. had a savage culture CIVILIZATION, 2
battle of B. is about to begin WORLD WAR II, 6
B....Fabian Society writ large BRITAIN, 8
B. fit country for heroes to live in GOVERNMENT, 16
B. is no longer in the politics of the pendulum POLITICS, 81
B. is not...easily rocked by revolution BRITAIN, 8
Today in B., a fascist has won an election FASCISM, 5
to help B. to become a Third Programme BRITAIN, 14
When B. first, at heaven's command BRITAIN, 13
Britannia Rule, B., rule the waves BRITAIN, 13
British but we are B. – thank God HOMOSEXUALITY, 9
less known by the B. than these selfsame B. Islands BRITISH, 2;
socialism...alien to the B. character SOCIALISM, 14
The B., being brought up on team games HOUSES OF PARLIAMENT, 14
The B. love permanence BRITISH, 3
the magnificent fair play of the B. criminal law JUSTICE, 6
the most vulgar...is the B. tourist BRITISH, 7
when a B. Prime Minister sneezed BRITAIN, 12
you broke a B. square RACISM, 16
British Empire 'Can't' will be the epitaph of the B. BRITISH EMPIRE, 5
liquidation of the B. BRITISH EMPIRE, 2
British Museum a little room somewhere in the B. that MUSEUMS, 2
a reflection of the B. Reading Room INTELLECTUALS, 8
I keep my books at the B. BOOKS, 9
There is in the B. an enormous mind MUSEUMS, 3
British Rail it isn't easy to work with B. TRAINS, 3
Briton as only a free-born B. can do SERVILITY, 7
Britons B. never will be slaves BRITAIN, 13
B. were only natives HISTORY, 29
broad She is a smart old b. EVIL, 15
She's the B. and I'm the High ACADEMICS, 5
broken A b. head in Cold Bath Fields PAROCHIALISM, 2
baying for b. glass ARISTOCRACY, 15
He liked the sound of b. glass ARISTOCRACY, 2
Laws were made to be b. LAW, 21
peace has b. out PEACE, 5
broker An honest b. DIPLOMACY, 3
bronchitis nobody goes to the theatre unless he...has b. AUDIENCES, 1
Brontë Charlotte B....unlike them in being fortunate WRITERS, 63
bronze executed a memorial longer lasting than b. MEMORIALS, 5
brook b. no contradiction DOCTORS, 10
brothel a sort of metaphysical b. SENTIMENTALITY, 3
brothels b. with bricks of Religion HYPOCRISY, 4
brother Big B. is watching you AUTHORITARIANISM, 5
I want to be the white man's b. RACISM, 14
love God, and hateth his b. LOVE, 23
Pardon me...*I* am my b. MISTAKES, 9
brotherhood Freedom! Equality! B. HUMAN RIGHTS, 2
brother-in-law not his b. RACISM, 14
brotherly let b. love continue HOSPITALITY, 6
brothers All men are b. FAMILY, 28
am I my b. keeper MURDER, 2
B. all /In honour HONOUR, 7
the poor are our b. and sisters POVERTY, 31
brought never b. to min' FRIENDSHIP, 12
Brown's John B. body MEMORIALS, 4
bruise it shall b. thy head SEXES, 2
sweetest fragrance from the herb...tread on it and b. it WOMEN, 81
bruised it is often a comfort to...be b. in a new place CHANGE, 12
Brunswick Hamelin Town's in B. GERMANY, 11
Brussels B. is a madness EUROPE, 10
meeting in a darkened bedroom in a B. hotel EUROPE, 20
brutality industry without art is b. ART, 24
Sentimentality is a superstructure covering b. SENTIMENTALITY, 2
brute I never saw a b. I hated so EVIL, 6
brutes Exterminate all b. RUTHLESSNESS, 3
rise above the b. WORDS, 11
Brutus B. is an honourable man HONOUR, 5
Caesar had his B. TREASON, 4

BSE give my cows B. AGRICULTURE, 3
bubble Life is mostly froth and b. MISFORTUNE, 10
bubbles With beaded b. winking at the brim ALCOHOL, 37
buck The b. stops here RESPONSIBILITY, 16
Buckingham changing guard at B. Palace SOLDIERS, 3
buckle One, two, /B. my shoe NURSERY RHYMES, 37
bucks bet you a hundred b. he ain't in here ESCAPE, 1; FUNERALS, 5
bud And now in age I b. again OLD AGE, 22
Buddha plastic B. jars out a Karate screech TECHNOLOGY, 6
budding That which sets...The b. rose above the rose full blown FRENCH REVOLUTION, 4
budget b. is a method of worrying ECONOMICS, 2
buds Gather the flowers, but spare the b. FLOWERS, 8
the darling b. of May COMPLIMENTS, 4
buffalo give me a home where the b. roam HOMESICKNESS, 4
bugger B. Bognor LAST WORDS, 30
build let us think that we b. for ever ARCHITECTURE, 10
The *end* is to b. well ARCHITECTURE, 15
builder he can only be a *b.* ARCHITECTURE, 9
building twenty years of marriage make her...like a public b. MARRIAGE, 132
Well b. hath three Conditions ARCHITECTURE, 15
buildings b....condemned now in advance ARCHITECTURE, 12
I go amongst the b. of a city PURPOSE, 5
Luftwaffe –...knocked down our b. ARCHITECTURE, 3
built till we have b. Jerusalem ENGLAND, 5
bull Better send them a Papal B. MISTAKES, 7
Down at the old 'B. and Bush' PUBLIC HOUSES, 5
take the b. between the teeth MIXED METAPHORS, 3
When you take the b. by the horns... CHANCE, 5
bullet ballot is stronger than the b. DEMOCRACY, 10
b. and the bayonet are brother and sister WORLD WAR I, 20
Each b. has got its commission MORTALITY, 4
Every b. has its billet DESTINY, 25
The b. that is to kill me ARROGANCE, 6
bullets I heard the b. whistle WAR, 122
bullfighting B. is the only art SPORT AND GAMES, 8
bulrushes dam...the Nile with b. FREEDOM, 7
bump And things that go b. in the night PRAYER, 2; SUPERNATURAL, 1
bums art and literature are left to a lot of shabby b. AMERICA, 23
Bunbury an invaluable permanent invalid called B. DECEPTION, 7
bungalow proud of the position of the b. SUBURBIA, 2
bunk Exercise is b. HEALTH AND HEALTHY LIVING, 6
History is more or less b. HISTORY, 13
buns Hot cross b.! NURSERY RHYMES, 16
Bunsen and I'd left my B. burner home OPPORTUNITY, 18
Bunyan B., you're a lucky fellow HOSTAGES, 4
burden Take up the White Man's b. RACISM, 15
The dreadful b. IDLENESS, 2
burgling managed to do any b. CRIME, 4
Burgundy a Naive Domestic B. ALCOHOL, 62
Burlington I'm B. Bertie BED, 3
burn better to marry than to b. MARRIAGE, 25
b. the bloody bitches CLERGY, 11
come not, Lucifer! /I'll b. my books DAMNATION, 4
He would b. your house down EGOTISM, 4
I will b., but...continue our discussion in eternity MARTYRDOM, 3
burned every government...should have its old speeches b. GOVERNMENT, 28
Whenever books are b. CENSORSHIP, 1
burning The boy stood on the b. deck COURAGE, 14
The spirit b. but unbent DETERMINATION, 7
To keep a lamp b. CHARITY, 21
Burnings B. of people ART, 23
burnish'd Furnish'd and b. by Aldershot sun ADMIRATION, 1
burnt she is b. flesh SUPERNATURAL, 7
burr kind of b.; I shall stick PERSISTENCE, 12
burst Blow your pipe there till you b. CONTEMPT, 2
burthen the b. of the mystery.../Is lightened CONFUSION, 10
bury I come to b. Caesar, not to praise him EVIL, 16
the sort of woman...one would almost feel disposed to b. for nothing WOMEN, 27
bus Hitler has missed the b. WORLD WAR II, 2
business A b. that makes nothing but money BUSINESS, 8
All b. sagacity reduces itself...to...sabotage BUSINESS, 25
a successful b. BUSINESS, 6
a woman's b. to get married MARRIAGE, 107
B. as usual BRITISH, 5
B....may bring money...friendship hardly ever does MONEY, 6
B. underlies everything in our national life BUSINESS, 29
dinner lubricates b. BUSINESS, 17
don't advise any one to take it up as a b. proposition ARTISTS, 4
everybody's b. is nobody's b. GOSSIP, 10
For good all round b. work, I should have preferred a Baptist PROTESTANTISM, 2
friendship founded on b. BUSINESS, 16
If everybody minded their own b. CURIOSITY, 4
I have led a life of b. so long that I have lost my taste for reading READING, 17
I hope it will not interfere with the public b. FIRE, 3
it is...our b. to lose innocence INNOCENCE, 4
That's the true b. precept BUSINESS, 5
The b. of America is b. AMERICA, 10
The Swiss...are not a people so much as a...b. SWITZERLAND, 2
To b. that we love we rise betime ENTHUSIASM, 8
Your b. is to put me out of b. ADVICE, 7
businessmen My message to the b. of this country ILLNESS, 3
Buss Miss B. and Miss Beale /Cupid's darts do not feel INSENSITIVITY, 1
bust It's a funny thing about that b. AGE, 57
bustle the b. of man's worktime OPTIMISM, 17
busy How doth the little b. bee WORK, 25
It is a stupidity...to b. oneself with the correction of the world IMPROVEMENT, 3
The English are b. ENGLISH, 26
thou knowest how b. I must be this day PRAYER, 3
busyness Extreme *b.* EXCESS, 13
butcher The b., the baker NURSERY RHYMES, 45
butchers Governments needs to have both shepherds and b. GOVERNMENT, 31
Buthelezi bad case of the B. Blues SOUTH AFRICA, 7
butter b. will only make us fat POWER POLITICS, 3
b. wouldn't melt in her mouth ACTORS, 17
fine words b. no parsnips WORDS, 18
buttercup I'm called Little B. NAMES, 3
buttered a piece of toast...fell...always/ on the b. side PERVERSITY, 5
butterflies Literature and b. are the two sweetest passions LITERATURE, 14
No shade, no shine, no b., no bees MONTHS, 10
butterfly a man dreaming I was a b. DREAMS, 4
Float like a b. SPORT AND GAMES, 1
Happiness is like a b. HAPPINESS, 15
Miss Austen...husband-hunting b. WRITERS, 69
buttocks Two b. of one bum FRIENDSHIP, 24
button facility to do such things at the touch of a b. TECHNOLOGY, 8
buttress a b. of the church SUPPORT, 5
buy American heiress wants to b. a man MATERIALISM, 14
I could b. back my introduction INTRODUCTIONS, 2
would never b. my pictures PAINTING, 6
bygones Let b. be b. FORGIVENESS, 2
Byron A gifted B. rises in his wrath POETS, 26
a more worthless set than B. POETS, 12
B. is dead POETS, 23
B. tried to write Poetry with a capital P POETS, 19
B. was really a comedian, not a satirist POETS, 19
The world is rid of Lord B. POETS, 30
When B.'s eyes were shut in death POETS, 15

C

cabbages c. and kings NONSENSE, 9
The c. are coming now ENGLAND, 4
cabin'd c., cribb'd, confin'd, bound in FEAR, 11
cabs busy driving c. and cutting hair GOVERNMENT, 7
Caesar *Ave C., morituri te salutant* LAST WORDS, 4
C.! dost thou lie so low DEATH, 106
C. had his Brutus TREASON, 4
C.'s wife PURITY, 1
I always remember that I am C.'s daughter EXTRAVAGANCE, 3
I come to bury C. EVIL, 16
Not that I lov'd C. less PATRIOTISM, 28
Regions C. never knew ENGLAND, 13
Rose...where some buried C. bled FLOWERS, 4
that C. might be great RUTHLESSNESS, 2

Caesar's C. laurel crown POWER, 7
C. wife must be above suspicion INTEGRITY, 2
cage Marriage is like a c. MARRIAGE, 84
Nor iron bars a c. IMPRISONMENT, 4
robin redbreast in a c. IMPRISONMENT, 1
She's only a bird in a gilded c. IMPRISONMENT, 3
caged We think c. birds sing IMPRISONMENT, 6
Cain the Lord set a mark upon C. REVENGE, 7
caitiff If the rude c. smite the other too REVENGE, 10
cake Bake me a c. as fast as you can NURSERY RHYMES, 38
Let them eat c. HUNGER, 10
cakes no more c. and ale MERRYMAKING, 3
Calais 'C.' lying in my heart DEFEAT, 5
Calamities C. are of two kinds MISFORTUNE, 4
the c. of life CLASS, 8
calamity Whatsoever…the private c., I hope it will not interfere with the public business of the country FIRE, 3
calculating A dessicated c. machine POLITICIANS, 37
Caledonia C.! stern and wild SCOTLAND, 7
calf but the c. won't get much sleep MISTRUST, 3
he killed a c.…in a high style SHAKESPEARE, 2
the fatted c. PARTIES, 2
call one clear c. for me DUTY, 5
called c. a cold a cold ILLNESS, 2
calm sea is c. to-night SEA, 1
Wisdom has taught us to be c. and meek REVENGE, 10
calories the only thing that matters is c. HEALTH AND HEALTHY LIVING, 9
calumnies C. are answered best INSULTS, 22
Calvary the place, which is called C. EXECUTION, 3
Calvin land of C., oat-cakes, and sulphur SCOTLAND, 8
Cambridge C. people rarely smile CAMBRIDGE, 2
Oxford is on the whole more attractive than C. CAMBRIDGE, 1; OXFORD, 3
Spring and summer did happen in C. CAMBRIDGE, 4
The young C. group CLASSIFICATION, 2
To C. books CAMBRIDGE, 6; OXFORD, 6
With equal skill to C. books he sent CAMBRIDGE, 3; OXFORD, 4
came I c.; I saw; God conquered VICTORY, 16
I c., I saw, I conquered VICTORY, 1
I c. like Water LIFE AND DEATH, 6
camel easier for a c. to go through the eye of a needle WEALTH, 8
Camelot many-tower'd C. ARTHURIAN LEGEND, 2
To look down to C. CURSES, 4
camels the c. and the sand CINEMA, 10
camera I am a c. OBJECTIVITY, 4
The c. cannot lie. But… PHOTOGRAPHY, 4
Campland This is C., an invisible country IMPRISONMENT, 5
campus administrative problems on a c. EDUCATION, 28
can Talent does what it c. TALENT AND GENIUS, 3
cancel to c. half a Line DESTINY, 8
cancels debt which c. all others OBLIGATION, 1
cancer C.'s a Funny Thing DISEASE, 20
chronic diseases more destructive to life than c. DISEASE, 26
candid save me, from the c. friend FRANKNESS, 1
candidates C. should not attempt more than six BIBLE, 2
candle a c. of understanding UNDERSTANDING, 2
Bell, book, and c. MATERIALISM, 18
blow out your c.…to find your way GUIDANCE, 2
It is burning a farthing c. at Dover CRITICISM, 19
light a c. to the sun FUTILITY, 9
Like a c. burnt out TIME, 42
little c. throws his beams GOOD, 15
My c. burns at both ends PLEASURE, 21
Out, out, brief c. LIFE, 45
take away the c. and spare my blushes MODESTY, 1
we shall this day light such a c. EXECUTION, 15
candle-light Can I get there by c. NURSERY RHYMES, 17
candles She would rather light c. than curse the darkness COMPLIMENTS, 6
candlestick The butcher, the baker, /The c.-maker NURSERY RHYMES, 45
canem *Cave c.* DOGS, 1
canker killing as the c. to the rose CORRUPTION, 4
canned C. music is like audible wallpaper POP MUSIC, 7
cannibal Better sleep with a sober c. than a drunken Christian DRUNKENNESS, 16
cannon-ball c. took off his legs PUNS, 8
canoe every man paddle his own c. INDEPENDENCE, 3
Canossa We will not go to C. DETERMINATION, 6
cant clear your *mind* of c. REASON, 3
love – all the wretched c. of it LOVE, 64
where the Greeks had modesty, we have c. HYPOCRISY, 13
can't 'C.' will be the epitaph of the British Empire BRITISH EMPIRE, 5
capability Negative C. DOUBT, 6
capable c. of being well set to music MUSIC, 2
capital Boys are c. fellows in their own way CHILDREN, 32
capitalism C. re-creates POLITICS, 61
c.…process whereby American girls turn into American women CAPITALISM, 3
I am going to fight c. CAPITALISM, 11
imperialism is the monopoly stage of c. POLITICS, 45
Lenin was the first to discover that c. 'inevitably' caused war CAPITALISM, 14
militarism…is one of the chief bulwarks of c. CAPITALISM, 5
unacceptable face of c. CAPITALISM, 4
We cannot remove the evils of c. CAPITALISM, 6
capitalist C. production begets…its own negation CAPITALISM, 9
problem someone has with his girlfriend…due to…c.… production CAPITALISM, 8
capitulate I will be conquered; I will not c. DETERMINATION, 9
Capricorn Lady C.…was…keeping open bed PROMISCUITY, 2
captain C. of the *Pinafore* CONCEIT, 9
I am the c. of my soul RESPONSIBILITY, 8
captains C. of industry LEADERSHIP, 4
capten C., art tha sleepin' there below WAR, 77
captive Beauty stands…Led c. BEAUTY, 28
car always using a small c. to drive to the dockyard instead of my Rolls Royce ROYALTY, 25
The c. has become the carapace CARS, 4
carapace The car has become the c. CARS, 4
carbon c. atom possesses certain exceptional properties SCIENCE, 23
carbuncle Like a c. on the face ARCHITECTURE, 4
card wrestled with a self-adjusting c. table TECHNOLOGY, 14
cardinal unbecoming for a c. to ski badly SPORT AND GAMES, 11
cards an old age of c. OLD AGE, 33
I have not learned to play at c. SPORT AND GAMES, 12
care age is full of c. AGE, 55
Begone, dull c. WORRY, 5
C. /Sat on his faded cheek WORRY, 11
I c. for nobody SELFISHNESS, 2
I don't c. for war WAR, 75
Our progress…/Is trouble and c. LIFE, 34
People who are always taking c. of their health are like misers HYPOCHONDRIA, 2
pleasures are their only c. EXPLOITATION, 2
Sleep that knits up the ravell'd sleave of c. SLEEP, 15
so vain…c. for the opinion of those we don't c. for CONCEIT, 8
take c. of the minutes TIME, 15
Take c. of the pence THRIFT, 4
what is past my help is past my c. INDIFFERENCE, 1
career a lover with any other c. in view COMMITMENT, 6
having a c. of my own MARRIAGE, 15
Miss Madeleine Philips…was a c. COMMITMENT, 6
nothing which might damage his c. SCOTS, 1
science was the only c. worth following WORK, 10
careers The best c. advice OCCUPATIONS, 18
careful be very c. o' vidders CAUTION, 11
careless first fine c. rapture BIRDS, 1
carelessness To lose one parent…a misfortune; to lose both looks like c. LOSS, 8
with a slow deliberate c. READING, 10
cares Nobody c. much at heart about Titian ARTISTS, 20
the earth where c. abound BIRDS, 11
careth he that is married c.…how he may please his wife MARRIAGE, 26
cargo With a c. of ivory BOATS, 12
With a c. of Tyne coal BOATS, 13
caring take millions off the c. services PATRIOTISM, 19
Carling I'll bet he drinks C. Black Label ADVERTISING, 13
carpe *C. diem* PRESENT, 7
carpenter Walrus and the C. SEASIDE, 1
carpet a Turkey c. bears to a picture CRITICISM, 31
only men in rags…/Mistake themselves for c. bags ETIQUETTE, 5
carriage Go together like a horse and c. LOVE AND MARRIAGE, 1
very small second-class c. BOATS, 6
we look for happiness in boats and c. rides TRAVEL, 12

carriages when they think they are alone in railway c. HABIT, 6
cars c....equivalent of...cathedrals CARS, 1
Carthage C. must be destroyed WAR, 24
Cary Grant Old C. fine TELEGRAMS, 7
Casanova C. had lots of fun AIDS, 3
case If ever there was a c. of clearer evidence NONSENSE, 2
in our c. we have not got WEAPONS, 7
the c. is still before the courts ARGUMENTS, 7
the reason of the c. LAW, 22
there had been a lady in the c. WOMEN, 20
The world is everything that is the c. LOGIC, 4
casements Charm'd magic c. BIRDS, 5
cash Nothing links man to man like...c. MONEY, 46
One cannot assess in terms of c....a church tower ENVIRONMENT, 1
only the poor who pay c. MONEY, 23
take the C. in hand MONEY, 22
cashiers c. of the Musical Banks MONEY, 13
casino I have come to regard...courts...as a c. JUSTICE, 11
cask A c. of wine ALCOHOL, 1
casket seal the hushed c. of my soul SLEEP, 13
Cassius C. has a lean and hungry look MISTRUST, 9
cassock C., band, and hymn-book too CLERGY, 17
cassowary If I were a c. CLERGY, 17
cast c. thy bread upon the waters OPPORTUNITY, 10
he that is without sin...let him first c. a stone SIN, 4
pale c. of thought CONSCIENCE, 5
The die is c. IRREVOCABILITY, 1
caste measure the social c. of a person CLASS, 2
casteth perfect love c. out fear LOVE, 24; FEAR, 3
casting It is no good c. out devils DEVIL, 9
castle A c. called Doubting Castle DESPAIR, 3
A neurotic is the man who builds a c. in the air PSYCHIATRY, 11
The house of every one is to him as his c. PRIVACY, 1
Castlereagh Murder...had a mask like C. . MURDER, 12
castles C. in the air DREAMS, 9
Death kicks his way...into...c. of kings EQUALITY, 28
the c. I have, are built with air DREAMS, 10
casualty except the c. list of the World War MURDER, 3
The first c. when war comes WAR, 53
cat A c. has nine lives LUCK, 2
A c. may look EQUALITY, 1
a C. of such deceitfulness CATS, 2
c. is a diagram and pattern of subtle air CATS, 5
God...a cosmic Cheshire c. GOD, 27
Had Tiberius been a c. CATS, 1
He bought a crooked c. NURSERY RHYMES, 52
he is a very fine c. CATS, 4
Hey diddle diddle, /The c. and the fiddle NURSERY RHYMES, 14
I'll bell the c. COURAGE, 10
More ways of killing a c. CHOICE, 3
That tossed the dog, /That worried the c. NURSERY RHYMES, 57
The C., the Rat, and Lovell our dog INSULTS, 14
What c.'s averse to fish MATERIALISM, 8
When I play with my c. CATS, 6
When the c.'s away ABSENCE, 3
cataclysm Out of their c. but one poor Noah /Dare hope to survive SEX, 27
catastrophe to lose one's teeth is a c. TEETH, 5
When a man confronts c....a woman looks in her mirror SEXES, 27
catch Go, and c. a falling star NONSENSE, 11
only one c. and that was Catch-22 OBSTRUCTION, 3; SELF-PRESERVATION, 5
Catch-22 only one catch and that was C. OBSTRUCTION, 3; SELF-PRESERVATION, 5
catchwords Man is a creature who lives...by c. SEXES, 22
categorical This imperative is C. MORALITY, 8
cathedrals cars...equivalent of...c. CARS, 1
the ancient c. – grand, wonderful RELIGION, 53
Catherine I'm glad you like my C. PROMISCUITY, 6
Catholic I am a C.....I go to Mass every day PREJUDICE, 1
I have a C. soul, but a Lutheran stomach CATHOLICISM, 4
I'm still a C. CATHOLICISM, 12
quite lawful for a C. woman to avoid pregnancy by...mathematics CONTRACEPTION, 5
who, like you, your Holiness, is a Roman C. CATHOLICISM, 3
Catholics C. and Communists have committed great crimes COMMITMENT, 4
they may be C. but they are not Christians INSULTS, 31
We know these new English C. CATHOLICISM, 7
cats All c. are grey EQUALITY, 2
A lotta c. copy the Mona Lisa IMITATION, 1
what c. most appreciate...is...entertainment value CATS, 3
cattle Actors should be treated like c. ACTORS, 5
O Mary, go and call the c. home AGRICULTURE, 5
these who die as c. WORLD WAR I, 18
cause for what high c. /This darling of the Gods DESTINY, 14
the name of perseverance in a good c. STUBBORNNESS, 3
causes Home of lost c. OXFORD, 1
they should declare the c. which impel them to...separation INDEPENDENCE, 2
cavaliero a perfect c. HEROISM, 4
cavaliers C. (Wrong but Wromantic) HISTORY, 27
cave *C. canem* DOGS, 1
I should be like a lion in a c. of savage Daniels ENEMIES, 9
caverns Gluts twice ten thousand C. SEA, 8
Through c. measureless to man PLEASURE, 8
caves be c....in which his shadow will be shown GOD, 39
sunny pleasure-dome with c. of ice PLEASURE, 9
caviare c. to the general TASTE, 7
cease have their day and c. to be TRANSIENCE, 18
I will not c. from mental fight ENGLAND, 5
restless Cromwell could not c. POLITICIANS, 63
ceases forbearance c. to be a virtue TOLERANCE, 1
celebrate I c. myself SELF, 18
celebrity A c....works hard...to become known FAME, 1
The c....known for his well-knownness FAME, 4
celerity C. is never more admir'd IMPETUOSITY, 3
celery Genuineness...Like c. SINCERITY, 4
two thousand people crunching c. at the same time FOOD, 49
Celia Come, my C., let us prove LOVE, 76
celibacy c. is...a muddy horse-pond MARRIAGE, 91
cello The c. is not one of my favourite instruments MUSIC, 53
cemetery old c. in which nine of his daughters were lying SEX, 58
censor Deleted by French c. NEWSPAPERS, 2
censorship Assassination...the extreme form of c. ASSASSINATION, 5
C....depraving and corrupting CENSORSHIP, 3
censure All c. of a man's self SELF, 10
centre I love being at the c. of things COMMITMENT, 5
My c. is giving way WORLD WAR I, 9
century The c. on which we are entering...must be the c. of the common man PUBLIC, 19
The great man...walks across his c. INFLUENCE, 7
the twentieth c. will be...the c. of Fascism FASCISM, 2
cereal Do you *know* what breakfast c. is made of FOOD, 17
cerebrums larger c. and smaller adrenal glands WAR, 66
certain I am c. that we will win SELF-CONFIDENCE, 6
nothing is c. but death and taxes TAXATION, 5
Nothing is c. but death DEATH, 9
One thing is c. LIFE, 25
certainties begin with c. CERTAINTY, 1; DOUBT, 1
His doubts are better than...c. DOUBT, 5
cesspit people swirling about in a human c. AIDS, 1
cesspool London, that great c. LONDON, 6
Ceylon spicy breezes /Blow soft o'er C.'s isle MISANTHROPY, 1
chaff An editor...separates the wheat from the c. EDITORS, 3
not racially pure are mere c. RACISM, 13
chain A c. is no stronger UNITY, 1
the flesh to feel the c. IMPRISONMENT, 2
chains c. that tie /The hidden soul of harmony MUSIC, 33
It's often safer to be in c. FREEDOM, 24
Man...everywhere he is in c. FREEDOM, 46
nothing to lose but their c. MARXISM, 3
chair Give Dayrolles a c. LAST WORDS, 16
the age of the editorial c. PSYCHIATRY, 8
chaise All in a c. and pair MARRIAGE, 43
chaise-longue Wedlock – the...deep peace of the double bed after the...c. MARRIAGE, 34
chalices treen c. and golden priests CLERGY, 9
cham That great C. of literature, Samuel Johnson WRITERS, 84
chamber rapping at my c. door SUPERNATURAL, 12
Upstairs and downstairs /And in my lady's c. NURSERY RHYMES, 13
chambermaid as happy in the arms of a c. IMAGINATION, 6
chamois springing from blonde to blonde like the c. of the Alps AMERICANS, 14
champagne Fighting is like c. WAR, 68

like a glass of c. that has stood HOUSES OF PARLIAMENT, 2
water flowed like c. ABSTINENCE, 4
chance every c. brought out a noble knight NOSTALGIA, 19
Grab a c. OPPORTUNITY, 15
time and c. happeneth to them all CHANCE, 2
chancellor C. of the Exchequer TAXATION, 9
change C. is not made without inconvenience CHANGE, 11
c. is the very essence of life CHANGE, 8
I c., but I cannot die WEATHER, 23
If you leave a thing alone you leave it to a torrent of c. CONSERVATISM, 1
Most of the c. we think we see NOVELTY, 2
Most women set out to try to c. a man CHANGE, 5
Plus ça c. CONSTANCY, 3
Popularity?...glory's small c. POPULARITY, 4
The more things c. CONSTANCY, 3
There is a certain relief in c. CHANGE, 12
The wind of c. CHANGE, 15
changed All c., c. utterly BEAUTY, 41
changeth The old order c. CHANGE, 19
changez *C. vos amis* FRIENDS, 8
changing c. scenes of life CHANGE, 18
Woman is always fickle and c. WOMEN, 86
Channel dream you are crossing the C. BOATS, 6
let the last man...brush the C. with his sleeve WAR, 105; WORLD WAR I, 22
chaos a perfectly possible means of overcoming c. POETRY, 37
c. of a Labour council – a *Labour* council INCOMPETENCE, 2
chapel Devil always builds a c. there DEVIL, 7
chapels c. had been churches ACTION, 11
chaplain twice a day the C. called IMPRISONMENT, 8
Chaplin C. is no business man ACTORS, 15
chaps Biography is about C. BIOGRAPHY, 1
chapter c. of accidents MISFORTUNE, 8; ACCIDENTS, 8
character c. is something for which people are responsible CHARACTER, 11
I had become a woman of...c. CHARACTER, 6
I leave my c. behind REPUTATION, 10
What is c. but the determination of incident CHARACTER, 14
characteristic c. of Thatcherism SOCIETY, 1
typically English c. ENGLISH, 3; UNITY, 4
characters c. in one of my novels FICTION, 2
her c. are round, or capable of rotundity WRITERS, 48
involvements and feelings and c. of ordinary life WRITERS, 82
Most women have no c. WOMEN, 63
charge Electrical force...causes motion of electrical c. SCIENCE, 10
charged it was c. against me INDIFFERENCE, 7
Charing Cross between Heaven and C. HEAVEN, 13
I went out to C., to see Major-general Harrison hanged EXECUTION, 22
the full tide of human existence is at C. LONDON, 9
chariot Swing low sweet c. DEATH, 17
the dust beneath thy c. wheel HUMILITY, 5
Time's winged c. AGE, 38
charity c. at election time OPPRESSION, 5
C. begins at home CHARITY, 1, 10
C. is the power of defending that which we know to be indefensible CHARITY, 12; HOPE, 5
c. never faileth CHARITY, 6
c. suffereth long, and is kind CHARITY, 6
In c. there is no excess CHARITY, 3
knowledge puffeth up, but c. edifieth CHARITY, 7; KNOWLEDGE, 8
lectures or a little c. SELF, 19
now abideth faith, hope, c. CHARITY, 6
the greatest of these is c. CHARITY, 6
The living need c. CHARITY, 2
The man who leaves money to c. in his will BEQUESTS, 3
without c. are nothing worth CHARITY, 9
Charles Caesar had his Brutus – C. the First, his Cromwell TREASON, 4
gentlemen...in the navy of C. the Second NAVY, 3
Charley I'm C.'s aunt from Brazil PLACES, 16
Charlie C. is my darling ADMIRATION, 9
charm Conversation has a kind of c. CONVERSATION, 8
Oozing c....He oiled his way CHARM, 3
The c. is purely romantic IDEALISM, 7
charming c. people have something to conceal CHARM, 2
I heard the bullets whistle...c. in the sound WAR, 122
It is c. to totter into vogue AGE, 65
People are either c. or tedious CHARM, 4
charms Whose c. all other maids surpass ADMIRATION, 7
Charon C., seeing, may forget LUST, 5
Chartreuse religious system that produced green C. ALCOHOL, 51
chaste godly poet must be c. himself POETRY, 10
chastity Give me c. and continence PROCRASTINATION, 4
Chatterley Put thy shimmy on, Lady C. PARTING, 7
Chaucer C., I confess, is a rough diamond CHAUCER, 2
C....I think obscene and contemptible CHAUCER, 1
read C. still with as much pleasure CHAUCER, 3
Chawcer pity that C....was so unedicated CHAUCER, 4
cheap flesh and blood so c. POVERTY, 17
cheating *Peace...a period of c.* PEACE, 3
Chechens C. are especially disappointed RUSSIA, 2
check C. enclosed MONEY, 38
dreadful is the c. IMPRISONMENT, 2
cheek Care /Sat on his faded c. WORRY, 11
the c. that doth not fade APPEARANCE, 17
turn the other c. REVENGE, 10
whosoever shall smite thee on thy right c. ENEMIES, 2
cheeks Blow, winds, and crack your c. WEATHER, 19
cheer cups, /That c. but not inebriate DRINKS, 4
Don't c., boys; the poor devils are dying WAR, 86
cheerful God loveth a c. giver GENEROSITY, 2
cheerfulness No warmth, no c., no healthful ease MONTHS, 10
cheese 265 kinds of c. FRANCE, 6
bread and c., and kisses MARRIAGE, 116
c. – toasted, mostly DREAMS, 13
when the c. is gone NONSENSE, 4
chemical c. barrage has been hurled against the fabric of life ECOLOGY, 2
Shelley and Keats were...up to date in...c. knowledge POETS, 7; SCIENCE, 17
cheque Any general statement is like a c. GENERALIZATIONS, 3
Mrs Claypool's c. will come back to you HUMOUR, 47
Chequer-board a C. of Nights and Days DESTINY, 7
cherish to love and to c. MARRIAGE, 30
cherry Before the c. orchard was sold WORRY, 9
C. ripe, ripe, ripe BUSINESS, 13
Loveliest of trees, the c. TREES, 5
Till 'C. ripe' themselves do cry ADMIRATION, 4
chess Life's too short for c. SPORT AND GAMES, 3
the devil played at c. with me EXPLOITATION, 1
chess-board c. is the world GOD, 28
chest Fifteen men on the dead man's c. ALCOHOL, 60
chestnut O c. tree NATURE, 22
Under the spreading c. tree OCCUPATIONS, 10
chestnuts warmongers who...have others pull the c. out of the fire POLITICS, 71
chew he can't fart and c. gum at the same time STUPIDITY, 5
chewing c. little bits of String FOOD, 8
chic very *c.* for an atheist MEMORIALS, 9
chicken a c. in his pot every Sunday POVERTY, 15
England will have her neck wrung like a c. WORLD WAR II, 30
Some c. WORLD WAR II, 12
chickens children are more troublesome and costly than c. MANKIND, 29
count their c. ere they're hatched ANTICIPATION, 5
Don't count your c. ANTICIPATION, 4
If I didn't start painting, I would have raised c. OCCUPATIONS, 13
You don't set a fox to watching the c. EXPERIENCE, 21
chief C. Defect of Henry King FOOD, 8
C. of the Army LAST WORDS, 45
child A c. becomes an adult when RIGHT, 2
A c. deserves the maximum respect CHILDREN, 29
A c.'s a plaything for an hour CHILDREN, 33
all any reasonable c. can expect SEX, 44
better...a poor and a wise c. than an old and foolish king OLD AGE, 5; YOUTH, 1
C.! do not throw this book about BOOKS, 7
c. of five would understand this SIMPLICITY, 5
desire to have a c. CHILDREN, 28
flourish in a c. of six CHILDREN, 9
getting wenches with c. YOUTH, 16
He who shall teach the c. to doubt DOUBT, 3
If you strike a c. VIOLENCE, 7
nobody's c. LONELINESS, 1
Now at last our c. is just like all children EQUALITY, 27
One stops being a c. when...telling one's trouble does not make it better DISILLUSION, 5
receive one such little c. in my name CHILDREN, 14

right to have a c. MOTHERHOOD, 3
spoil the c. PUNISHMENT, 6; INDULGENCE, 1
sweetest Shakespeare, Fancy's c. SHAKESPEARE, 13
The business of being a c. CHILDREN, 26
The C. is Father of the Man AGE, 69
The mother-c. relationship is paradoxical MOTHERHOOD, 9
There are only two things a c. will share willingly CHILDREN, 39
unless the play is stopped, the c. cannot…go on AUDIENCES, 2
unto us a c. is born CHRISTMAS, 6
What is the use of a new-born c. PURPOSE, 2
when I was a c., I spake as a c. CHARITY, 6
wise father that knows his own c. FATHERS, 6
childbirth Death and taxes and c. EXPEDIENCY, 5
Mountains will heave in c. DISAPPOINTMENT, 3
the male equivalent of c. PUBLISHING, 1
Childe C. Roland to the Dark Tower SUMMONS, 4
childhood The books one reads in c. BOOKS, 29
childish I put away c. things CHARITY, 6
Sweet c. days NOSTALGIA, 24
childishness second c. OLD AGE, 38
children a Friend for little c. /Above the bright blue sky GOD, 36
Anybody who hates c. and dogs CHILDREN, 21; DOGS, 6
Are the c. all in their beds? NURSERY RHYMES, 64
as c. fear to go in the dark DEATH, 22
a wicked man that comes after c. SLEEP, 10
c. are more troublesome and costly than chickens MANKIND, 29
C. aren't happy with nothing to ignore FAMILY, 26
c. are true judges of character CHILDREN, 4; DISEASE, 7
C. have never been very good at listening CHILDREN, 6
C.…have no use for psychology. BOOKS, 39
c., obey your parents OBEDIENCE, 1
C. should acquire…heroes and villains from fiction HISTORY, 3
C. sweeten labours CHILDREN, 5
C. with Hyacinth's temperament…merely know more CHARACTER, 19
Come dear c. DEPARTURE, 1
desire not a multitude of unprofitable c. CHILDREN, 11
Do you hear the c. weeping SORROW, 2
English are growing demented about c. CHILDREN, 42
except ye…become as little c. CHILDREN, 13
Familiarity breeds…c. SEX, 60
Far too good to waste on c. YOUTH, 17
He that has no c. ADVICE, 3
He that loves not his wife and c. MARRIAGE, 118
his wife is beautiful and his c. smart TOLERANCE, 5
I love all my c. MOTHERHOOD, 6
in sorrow thou shalt bring forth c. SEXES, 2
I've lost one of my c. this week LOSS, 7
Let our c. grow tall TALENT, 7
like a c.'s party taken over by the elders AGE, 26
make your c. *capable of honesty* HONESTY, 7
Many c. are suffering from muesli-belt malnutrition FOOD, 38
Men are but c. of a larger growth AGE, 21
more careful of the breed of their horses and dogs than of their c. FATHERS, 5
Most of the people…will be c. FUNERALS, 1
My music…understood by c. and animals MUSIC, 50
Never have c. CHILDREN, 41
Now at last our child is just like all c. EQUALITY, 27
Parents learn a lot from their c. CHILDREN, 38
Problem c. tend to grow up into problem adults FAMILY, 11
provoke not your c. FATHERS, 3
She had so many c. she didn't know what to do NURSERY RHYMES, 54
the c. I might have had CHILDREN, 35
the early marriages of silly c. MARRIAGE, 81
To bear many c. is considered…an investment CHILDREN, 22
We have no c., except me CHILDREN, 7
Were we closer to the ground as c. NOSTALGIA, 1
when they started life as c. CHILDREN, 3
write for c.…as you do for adults WRITING, 10
You can do anything with c. if you only play with them CHILDREN, 16
chill St Agnes Eve – Ah, bitter c. it was SEASONS, 9
chime to set a c. of words tinkling PURPOSE, 7
chimes c. at midnight MERRYMAKING, 4
chimney sixty horses wedged in a c. JOURNALISM, 24
chimney-sweepers As c., come to dust MORTALITY, 16
China Hooligan was probably invented in C. CHINA, 9
On a slow boat to C. BOATS, 10
The infusion of a C. plant DRINKS, 1
Chinese Nothing…can destroy the C. people CHINA, 1
chip c. off the old block POLITICIANS, 40
chips You breed babies and you eat c. FOOD, 53
chirche-dore Housbondes at c. MARRIAGE, 35
chivalry age of c. is gone EUROPE, 2
The age of c. is never past CHIVALRY, 6
Chi Wen Tzu C. always CAUTION, 10
Chloë In the spring…your lovely C. APPEARANCE, 32
chocolate a c. cream soldier SOLDIERS, 6
both its national products, snow and c., melt SWITZERLAND, 1
Venice is like eating…c. liqueurs VENICE, 2
choice Hebrew word…*timshel*…gives a c. CHOICE, 5
choir Sweet singing in the c. CHRISTMAS, 5
choirs Bare ruin'd c. OLD AGE, 40
choose *We can believe what we c.* RESPONSIBILITY, 11
Chopin I have lived off the blood of C. MUSICIANS, 7
to bridge the awful gap between Dorothy and C. MUSIC, 3
chord c. of music MUSIC, 39
chorus a dozen are only a c. BEAUTY, 18
chose *plus c'est la même c.* CONSTANCY, 3
Christ C. is all, and in all CHRISTIANITY, 5
C.…would quite likely have been arrested OPPRESSION, 3
churches have kill'd their C. CLERGY, 16
I beseech you, in the bowels of C. MISTAKES, 6
only a male can represent C. CLERGY, 4
The Jews have produced…C., Spinoza, and myself CONCEIT, 16
We're more popular than Jesus C. POPULARITY, 6
Who dreamed that C. has died in vain CHRISTIANITY, 39
Christendom wisest fool in C. FOOLISHNESS, 13
Christian A C.…feels /Repentance on a Sunday HYPOCRISY, 19
any man…who could not bear another's misfortunes…like a C. MISFORTUNE, 13
Better sleep with a sober cannibal than a drunken C. DRUNKENNESS, 16
centres of strong C. presence…kind of Walt Disney Theme Park COMMERCIALISM, 1
C. Science explains all cause and effect as mental RELIGION, 20
How very hard…/To be a C. CHRISTIANITY, 20
I die a C. EXECUTION, 4
in what peace a C. can die LAST WORDS, 3
I was born of C. race RELIGION, 63
No Jew was ever fool enough to turn C. RELIGION, 73
object…to form C. men EDUCATION, 3
Onward, C. soldiers CHRISTIANITY, 3
several young women…would render the C. life intensely difficult CHRISTIANITY, 31
The C. religion not only was at first attended with miracles CHRISTIANITY, 29
The C. religion…cannot be believed by any reasonable person without one CHRISTIANITY, 29
Christianity C. accepted as given a metaphysical system CHRISTIANITY, 30
C.…but why journalism CHRISTIANITY, 2; JOURNALISM, 3
C. has done a great deal for love CHRISTIANITY, 24
C. has made of death a terror CHRISTIANITY, 36
C. is part of the Common Law of England CHRISTIANITY, 26
C. is the most materialistic of all great religions CHRISTIANITY, 42
C.…says that they are all fools MANKIND, 11
C. the one great curse CHRISTIANITY, 35
C.…the one immortal blemish of mankind CHRISTIANITY, 35
decay of C. ALCOHOL, 51
His C. was muscular CHRISTIANITY, 23
local cult called C. CHRISTIANITY, 28
loving C. better than Truth CHRISTIANITY, 22
Rock and roll or C. POPULARITY, 6
Christians C. awake, salute the happy morn CHRISTMAS, 12
Onward, C., onward go ENDURANCE, 24
settle their differences like good C. MIDDLE EAST, 3
these C. love one another CHRISTIANITY, 45
they may be Catholics but they are not C. INSULTS, 31
Christ-like C. heroes and woman-worshipping Don Juans MEN, 9
Christmas At C. I no more desire a rose SUITABILITY, 4
C. should fall out in the Middle of Winter CHRISTMAS, 1

Eating a C. pie NURSERY RHYMES, 29
For C. comes but once a year CHRISTMAS, 19
I'm walking backwards till C. NONSENSE, 23
Let them know it's C. CHARITY, 4
perceive C. through its wrapping CHRISTMAS, 20
'Twas the night before C. CHRISTMAS, 14
Christopher C. Robin went down with Alice SOLDIERS, 3
chronicle c. small beer TRIVIALITY, 12
the c. of wasted time HISTORY, 32
Chronologie beginning of time according to our C. CREATION, 14
church an alien C. IRELAND, 6
Beware when you take on the C. of God RELIGION, 60
But get me to the c. on time MARRIAGE, 79
C. produced no geometers CHURCH, 6
he'd go to c., start a revolution – *something* MATERIALISM, 15
he goes to c. as he goes to the bathroom CLERGY, 3
I believe in the C. RELIGION, 55
If I really believed that the C. of England RELIGION, 6
straying away from the c. RELIGION, 7
The blood of the martyrs is the seed of the C. CHRISTIANITY, 44
The C. exists CHURCH, 8
The C.'s one foundation CHRISTIANITY, 40
The farther you go from the c. of Rome PROTESTANTISM, 3
There are many who stay away from c. RELIGION, 44
There is no salvation outside the c. RELIGION, 3
There was I, waiting at the c. MARRIAGE, 78
where MCC ends and the C. of England begins CHURCH, 7
churches chapels had been c. ACTION, 11
c. have kill'd their Christ CLERGY, 16
the c.…bore for me the same relation to God that billboards did to Coca-Cola RELIGION, 61
The itch of disputing…the scab of c. RELIGION, 71
church-goers Hunting people tend to be c. HUNTING, 6
churchman a species of person called a 'Modern C.' RELIGION, 66
churchyard A piece of c. fits everybody DEATH, 2
Cicero C. /And…Homer were /*Mad as the mist and snow* MADNESS, 18
cider c. and tinned salmon FOOD, 51
cigar a good c. is a smoke WOMEN, 44
It is like a c.….it never tastes quite the same LOVE, 145
cigarette A c. is…a perfect pleasure SMOKING, 23
I kissed my first woman, and smoked my first c. SMOKING, 19
Cinderella poetry, 'The C. of the Arts.' POETRY, 33
cinema c. is truth twenty-four times a second CINEMA, 5
circle All things from eternity…come round in a c. HISTORY, 5
circumcised our fingers are c. MUSICIANS, 6
When they c. Herbert Samuel INSULTS, 27
circumcision atheism, breast-feeding, c. INDULGENCE, 2
circumlocution C. Office BUREAUCRACY, 5
circumstance Pride, pomp, and c. WAR, 108
To a philosopher no c.…is too minute PHILOSOPHERS, 3
circumstances to face straitened c. at home POVERTY, 22
circumstantial Some c. evidence is very strong PROOF, 6
circus run away from the c. POLITICIANS, 32
circuses bread and c. PUBLIC, 15
cities I have sung women in three c. WOMEN, 66
many c. had rubbed him smooth TRAVEL, 10
The government burns down whole c. INJUSTICE, 10
citizen a c. of the world NATIONALITY, 8; COURTESY, 2
citizens All free men…are c. of Berlin GERMANY, 6
city every man in the c. wants a farm ENVY, 5
first c. Cain GARDENS, 6
great c.…has the greatest men and women GREATNESS, 15
hiring taxis to scuttle around a c. INCOMPETENCE, 2
I go amongst the buildings of a c. PURPOSE, 5
It is a c. where you can see a sparrow fall IRELAND, 14
the c. is not a concrete jungle, it is a human zoo MANKIND, 18
the c. of perspiring dreams CAMBRIDGE, 5
civilian forget about this c. WAR, 42
civilians drop bombs…hit c. WAR, 42
civilisation Disinterested intellectual curiosity…life blood of…c. CURIOSITY, 9
civility C. costs nothing COURTESY, 1
The reciprocal c. of authors WRITERS, 11
civilization As c. advances, poetry…declines CIVILIZATION, 8
C. is a method of living CIVILIZATION, 1
C. is…equal respect for all men CIVILIZATION, 1
How idiotic c. is NAKEDNESS, 5
If people dug up the remains of this c. ARTISTS, 16
It is so stupid of modern c. DEVIL, 8
little in c. to appeal to a Yeti CIVILIZATION, 7
Madam, I am the c. they are fighting to defend WAR, 40
Our c. is founded on the shambles DEATH, 63
The degree of a nation's c. CIVILIZATION, 9
the Renaissance was…the green end of one of c.'s hardest winters CIVILIZATION, 5
without the usual interval of c. AMERICA, 8
You can't say c. don't advance PROGRESS, 10
civilized it proved that I was in a c. society EXECUTION, 21
Woman will be the last thing c. by Man WOMEN, 52
civil service British c.…effective braking mechanism BUREAUCRACY, 10
civil war In a c., a general must know WAR, 89
civil wars Foreigners fooling about in others' c. WAR AND PEACE, 15
clap Don't c. too hard ENTHUSIASM, 6
clapped c. the glass to his sightless eye BLINDNESS, 6
claret C. is the liquor for boys ALCOHOL, 32
drink a dozen of C. on my Tomb ALCOHOL, 35
look for the second cheapest c.…and say, 'Number 22' ALCOHOL, 48
said of c. ALCOHOL, 11
class an…young Englishman of our upper c. ARISTOCRACY, 1
a special machine for the suppression of one c. by another CAPITALISM, 7
Because there's no fourth c. HUMILITY, 8
Discussion in c., which means EDUCATION, 39
Every c. is unfit to govern GOVERNMENT, 2
for one c. to appreciate the wrongs of another CLASS, 32
For this c. we have…the designation of Philistines PHILISTINISM, 1
Like many of the upper c. ARISTOCRACY, 2
Poets and painters are outside the c. system ARTISTS, 1
Poets and painters…constitute a special c. POETS, 1
The constitution…first and second c. citizens CLASS, 40
The history of all…society is the history of c. struggles CLASS, 22
The one c. you do *not* belong to CLASS, 23
the proletariat will…wage a c. struggle for Socialism CLASS, 18
The state is an instrument…of the ruling c. STATE, 5
Without c. differences…living theatre ENGLAND, 9
classes back the masses against the c. CLASS, 14
Hats divide generally into three c. CLOTHES, 19
I'm not interested in c. CLASS, 20
responsible and the irresponsible c. CLASS, 17
classical c. Canon and the multicultural cause POLITICAL CORRECTNESS, 3
C. quotation is the *parole* of literary men QUOTATIONS, 4
That's the c. mind at work MIND, 5
The basic difference between c. music and jazz MUSIC, 38
Classicism C.…the literature that gave…pleasure to their great-grandfathers LITERATURE, 17
classics Every man with a belly full of the c. CLASSICS, 7
The c. are only primitive literature CLASSICS, 6
clay absorbs a c. /After his labours SMOKING, 3
clean Bath…once a day to be passably c. CLEANNESS, 1
c. your plate POLITICS, 64
hard to be funny when you have to be c. HUMOUR, 30
clear His right was c., his will was strong RIGHT, 1
if he could make *me* understand…it would be c. to all UNDERSTANDING, 10
clearing-house the C. of the World ECONOMICS, 5
cleft Rock of ages, c. for me RELIGION, 59
Clementine Dwelt a miner, Forty-niner, /And his daughter, C. MOURNING, 7
clenched You cannot shake hands with a c. fist INFLEXIBILITY, 2
Cleopatra Had C.'s nose been shorter APPEARANCE, 29
clergy c. are men CLERGY, 7
I never saw…the c. were beloved in any nation CLERGY, 14
clergyman c. whose mendicity is only equalled by their mendacity CLERGY, 15
good enough to be a c. CLERGY, 10
clerk diplomatic history is…what one c. said to another c. HISTORY, 37
the smartness of an attorney's c. INSULTS, 15
clever Be good, sweet maid, and let who can be c. VIRTUE, 12
c. man…came of…stupid people INTELLIGENCE, 2
It's c., but is it art ART, 13

never wise to try to appear...more c. WISDOM, 24
no use trying to be *c.* ACADEMICS, 3
To be c. enough to get...money, one must be stupid MATERIALISM, 6
cleverest You're the c. member of...the c. nation in the world SELF-CONFIDENCE, 7
cleverness height of c. is...to conceal it INTELLIGENCE, 7
cliché The c. is dead poetry LANGUAGE, 3
climate common where the c.'s sultry ADULTERY, 1
If it's heaven for c. PERVERSITY, 1
climb Fain would I c., yet fear I to fall AMBITION, 14
clime change their c., not their frame of mind, who rush across the sea TRAVEL, 12
Clive What I like about C. DEATH, 26
clock c. in the steeple strikes one ALCOHOL, 68
grandfather's c. CLOCKS, 2
Rock Around the C. POP MUSIC, 13
Stands the Church c. at ten to three NOSTALGIA, 3
The c. struck one, /The mouse ran down NURSERY RHYMES, 15
The mouse ran up the c. NURSERY RHYMES, 15
clocks hands of c. in railway stations CHILDREN, 19
pass my declining years saluting...grandfather c. OLD AGE, 31
the c. were striking the hour TIME, 25
clogs From c. to c. POVERTY, 1
cloke knyf under the c. HYPOCRISY, 7
Clootie Satan, Nick, or C. DEVIL, 6
close a breathless hush in the C. tonight CRICKET, 5
regretted living so c. to Marie LOVE, 103
closed Mankind is a c. society MANKIND, 25
the transition from the...'c. society' SOCIETY, 6
closet sleep in your c. rather than ENGLISH, 8
close-up Life is a tragedy...in c. LIFE, 18
closing c. time in the gardens of the West CAPITALISM, 1
clothe feed and c. 1.2 billion Chinese CHINA, 7
clothes After that you just take the girl's c. off ALCOHOL, 19
as if she were taking off all her c. SEX, 16
bought her wedding c. WOMEN, 7
enterprises that require new c. THRIFT, 11
Fine c. are good CLOTHES, 9
hanging the baby on the c. line to dry INNOVATION, 2
Have you ever taken anything out of the c. basket CLEANNESS, 3
if it be our c. alone which fit us for society CLOTHES, 4
most fun you can have with your c. on ADVERTISING, 3
Nothing to wear but c. PESSIMISM, 7
No woman so naked as...underneath her c. NAKEDNESS, 4
walked away with their c. POLITICS, 22
wrapped him in swaddling c. CHRISTMAS, 7
cloud Every c. has a silver lining OPTIMISM, 2
fiend hid in a c. BIRTH, 3
I wandered lonely as a c. FLOWERS, 14
clouds But trailing c. of glory METAPHYSICS, 5
c. that gather round the setting sun MORTALITY, 21
clout Ne'er cast a c. MONTHS, 2
clown I remain just one thing...and that is a c. HUMOUR, 6
club I don't want to belong to any c. HUMOUR, 48
Mankind is a c. MANKIND, 12
takes you so far from the c. house GOLF, 3
the best c. in London HOUSES OF PARLIAMENT, 7
the most exclusive c. there is ENGLISH, 29
cluster The human face is...a whole c. of faces MANKIND, 21
Clyde the bonny banks of C. SCOTLAND, 6
CMG Members rise from C. TITLES, 9
coach c. and six horses through the Act of Settlement IRELAND, 16
indifference and a c. and six LOVE, 40
coal though the whole world turn to c. VIRTUE, 11
coals heap c. of fire upon his head RETRIBUTION, 8
coaster Dirty British c. BOATS, 13
cobwebs Laws are like c. LAW, 28
laws were like c. LAW, 6
Coca-Cola the churches...bore for me the same relation to God that billboards did to C. RELIGION, 61
Coca Colas Instead of drinking C. WATER, 3
cocaine C. is God's way of saying DRUGS, 15
C. isn't habit-forming ADDICTION, 1
cock He was like a c. ARROGANCE, 3
That kept the c. that crowed in the morn NURSERY RHYMES, 57
waiting for the c. to crow BETRAYAL, 4
we owe a c. to Aesculapius LAST WORDS, 65
cockles Crying, C. and mussels! alive, alive, O BUSINESS, 1
cockroach to choose between him and a c. INSULTS, 46
cocksure as c. of anything SELF-CONFIDENCE, 3
cod piece of c. passes all understanding FOOD, 36
serve both c. and salmon PUNS, 11
the c.'s wallop is always fresh made COMMUNISM, 5
The home of the bean and the c. SNOBBERY, 2
codfish Unlike the male c....the British aristocracy is ARISTOCRACY, 16
coffee c. that's too black RACISM, 20
C. which makes the politician wise DRINKS, 6
measured out my life with c. spoons LIFE, 24
coffee-house It is folly...to mistake the echo of a...c. for the...kingdom OPINIONS, 6
coffin the silver plate on a c. INSULTS, 32
cogito *C., ergo sum* THINKING, 3
cognitive I have created a lot of c. dissonance CONFUSION, 5
coil shuffled off this mortal c. SUICIDE, 12
coke Happiness is like c. HAPPINESS, 11
cold a period of c. peace COLD WAR, 5
blow hot and c. with the same breath INDECISION, 1
C. Pastoral ETERNITY, 3
C. War and is in danger of...C. Peace COLD WAR, 6
I beg c. comfort COMFORT, 3
she should catch a c. on overexposure TRUTH, 16
The Irish...are needed in this c. age IRISH, 4
we are...in the midst of a c. war COLD WAR, 2
We called a c. a c. ILLNESS, 2
coldly c. she turns from their gaze, and weeps MOURNING, 8
Coliseum While stands the C., Rome shall stand EUROPE, 5
collapse Russia is a c., not a revolution RUSSIA, 5
collapses Force...c. through its own mass JUDGMENT, 9
collar no shirt or c. ever comes back twice NEGLECT, 2
collections those mutilators of c. BORROWING, 6
collective the greatest c. work of science SCIENCE, 2
college I am Master of this c. ACADEMICS, 2
Like so many ageing c. people ACADEMICS, 4
colleges a liberal education at the C. of Unreason REASON, 1
colonel The gatling's jammed and the c. dead WAR, 76
colonnade whispering sound of the cool c. TREES, 3
colour an incurable disease – c. blindness RACISM, 9
Any c., so long as it's black CHOICE, 1
water, is unsuitable in c. WATER, 5
coloured I'm a c., one-eyed Jew DISABILITY, 2; RACISM, 10
colourless C. green ideas NONSENSE, 10
colours All c. will agree in the dark DIFFERENCE, 7
clashed his c. together like cymbals ARTISTS, 10
combine When bad men c. UNITY, 7
combustion the Immaculate Conception was spontaneous c. CATHOLICISM, 9
come C. what come may TIME, 32
Mr Watson, c. here; I want you SUMMONS, 3
O c. all ye faithful CHRISTMAS, 16
Thou'lt c. no more MOURNING, 9
Whistle and she'll c. to you SUMMONS, 2
Why don't you c. up sometime MISQUOTATIONS, 23; INVITATIONS, 3
Will ye no c. back again RETURN, 3
comedian A c. can only last HUMOUR, 25
comedies c. are ended by a marriage THEATRE, 6
comedy All I need to make a c. HUMOUR, 5
at a c. we only look THEATRE, 10
c. at the moment of deepest hysteria HUMOUR, 21
C. is if I walk into an open sewer and die THEATRE, 5
C., like sodomy, is an unnatural act HUMOUR, 12
C., we may say, is society HUMOUR, 24
Farce refined becomes high c. THEATRE, 9
Life is...a c. in long-shot LIFE, 18
What a fine c. this world would be LIFE, 21
world is a c. to those who think LIFE, 53
comes Everything c. to him who waits PATIENCE, 2
comfort carrion c., Despair, not feast on thee DESPAIR, 4
From ignorance our c. flows IGNORANCE, 12
I beg cold c. COMFORT, 3
thought of suicide is a great...c. SUICIDE, 6
Two loves I have, of c. and despair CONFLICT, 7
until his friends came to c. him ENDURANCE, 8
comfortable to be baith grand and c. LUXURY, 1
comfortably Are you sitting c.? Then I'll begin BEGINNING, 13
comic It is so c. to hear oneself called old OLD AGE, 23
coming C. through the rye LOVE, 34
he...c. after me is preferred before me CHRISTIANITY, 11

command mortals to c. success SUCCESS, 3
one of those born neither to obey nor to c. NASTINESS, 5
people c. rather badly OBEDIENCE, 2
commandments fear God, and keep his c. GOD, 9
gods handing down new c. SCIENTISTS, 4
Where there aren't no Ten C. DESIRE, 9
commas absence of inverted c. guarantees…originality QUOTATIONS, 2
commend forced to c. her highly INSINCERITY, 3
into thy hands I c. my spirit LAST WORDS, 10
commended The man who gets angry…in the right way…is c. ANGER, 1
commendeth obliquely c. himself CRITICISM, 7
comment C. is free but facts are sacred JOURNALISM, 27
commentators rather give me c. plain CLARITY, 1
commerce Friendship is a disinterested c. between equals LOVE AND FRIENDSHIP, 2
honour sinks where c. long prevails BUSINESS, 12
commercing looks c. with the skies SOUL, 10
commission A Royal C. is a broody hen BUREAUCRACY, 6
Each bullet has got its c. MORTALITY, 4
commit woman alone, can…c. them SEXES, 25
committee A c. is a cul-de-sac BUREAUCRACY, 4
A c. should consist of three men DEMOCRACY, 21
The number one book…was written by a c. BIBLE, 8
commodity *C., Firmness,* and *Delight* ARCHITECTURE, 15
common C. Law of England LAW, 16
C. sense is the collection of prejudices PREJUDICE, 3
good thing, to make it too c. ENGLAND, 37
He nothing c. did or mean EXECUTION, 16
lose the c. touch IDEALISM, 2
seldom attribute c. sense AGREEMENT, 4
the happiness of the c. man GOVERNMENT, 6
The trivial round, the c. task SIMPLICITY, 4
'Tis education forms the c. mind EDUCATION, 44
trained and organized c. sense SCIENCE, 20
common-looking The Lord prefers c. people APPEARANCE, 21
common man I have no concern for the c. PUBLIC, 21
commonplace nothing so unnatural as the c. TRIVIALITY, 7
renders…c. things and characters interesting WRITERS, 81
unassuming c. /Of Nature FLOWERS, 13
commonplaces c. are the great poetic truths TRIVIALITY, 13
Commons The C., faithful to their system GOVERNMENT, 17
Commonwealth a C. of Nations BRITISH EMPIRE, 7
turn to the wider vision of the C. POLITICS, 47
Communism arrested under the Suppression of C. Act OPPRESSION, 3
C. continued to haunt Europe as a spectre COMMUNISM, 10
C. is like prohibition COMMUNISM, 6
C. is Soviet power plus the electrification COMMUNISM, 4
For us in Russia c. is a dead dog COMMUNISM, 7
communist Every c. has a fascist frown COMMUNISM, 8; FASCISM, 5
your grandson will…be a C. COMMUNISM, 3
Communists Catholics and C. have committed great crimes COMMITMENT, 4
In Germany, the Nazis came for the C. NAZISM, 5
community journalism….keeps us in touch with the ignorance of the c. JOURNALISM, 32
Marriage…a c.…making in all two MARRIAGE, 29
party of the c. INDIVIDUALITY, 4
the c. of Europe EUROPE, 17
commute the agricultural labourers…c. from London COUNTRYSIDE, 7
commuter C.…riding to and from his wife TRAINS, 6; TRAVEL, 25
compact the damned, c., liberal majority MAJORITY, 4
companion to choose between him and a cockroach as a c. INSULTS, 46
companionable so c. as solitude SOLITUDE, 13
companions Boys…are unwholesome c. for grown people CHILDREN, 32
c. for middle age MARRIAGE, 13
company better to be alone than in bad c. FRIENDS, 15
c.…have neither a soul to lose nor a body to kick BUSINESS, 22
Crowds without c. LONDON, 7
find myself in the c. of scientists SCIENTISTS, 1
I've been offered titles…get one into disreputable c. TITLES, 11
pleasure of your c. MOUNTAINS, 2
Take the tone of the c. CONFORMITY, 3
Tell me what c. thou keepest FRIENDS, 4
You have your own c. CARS, 6
You never expected justice from a c. BUSINESS, 22
comparative progress is simply a c. PROGRESS, 3
compare any she belied with false c. ANALOGY, 4
c. thee to a summer's day COMPLIMENTS, 4
Learn, c., collect the facts EDUCATION, 42
compared The war we have just been through…is not to be c. WAR, 134
comparisons c. are odious ANALOGY, 2
C. are odorous MALAPROPISMS, 2
compass my heart shall be /The faithful c. FAITHFULNESS, 4
compassion a certain Samaritan…had c. CHARITY, 8
competition happiest conversation where there is no c. CONVERSATION, 5
complacency c. and satisfaction…in…a new-married couple MARRIAGE, 75
complain one hardly knows to whom to c. COMPLAINTS, 2
complaint Anno domini…the most fatal c. DEATH, 61
how is the old c. MEMORY, 5
I want to register a c. COMPLAINTS, 5
complaints The imaginary c. of indestructible old ladies HYPOCHONDRIA, 3
complete now I feel like a c. idiot INFERIORITY, 1
complex Wherever an inferiority c. exists INFERIORITY, 2
complexities c. of poetry are destroyed by the media THEATRE, 5
compliance by a timely c. SEX, 19
compliment returned the c. GOD, 50
compose Never c.…unless…not composing…becomes a positive nuisance MUSIC, 24
composed When I c. that, I was…inspired by God MUSIC, 9
composer A good c. does not imitate MUSICIANS, 9
composition difference between…prose and metrical c. POETRY AND PROSE, 7
comprehended c. two aspicious persons MALAPROPISMS, 1
compromise All government…is founded on c. and barter COMPROMISE, 4
C. used to mean that half a loaf COMPROMISE, 5
not a question that leaves much room for c. SELF-PRESERVATION, 7
compulsion seized by the stern hand of C. WOMEN, 79
compulsory c. and irreproachable idleness ARMY, 3
computer put your disk into someone's c. COMPUTERS, 2
computers so many c.…use them in the search for love COMPUTERS, 6
wipe all the information off everybody's c. COMPUTERS, 1
comrade stepping where his c. stood COURAGE, 18
comrades Bleach the bones of c. slain WAR, 50
conceal Addresses…c. our whereabouts ADDRESSES, 1
height of cleverness is…to c. it INTELLIGENCE, 7
speech only to c. their thoughts HUMAN NATURE, 24
concealed Much truth is spoken…more…c. TRUTH, 21
concealing Good breeding consists in c. how…we think of ourselves MANNERS, 5
concealment c., like a worm i' th' bud LOVE, 126
conceit C. is the finest armour CONCEIT, 12
conceited I would grow intolerably c. CONCEIT, 21
what man will do any good who is not c. SELF-RESPECT, 2
If the c. of God has RELIGION, 5
concept Political correctness is a really inane c. POLITICAL CORRECTNESS, 4
conception if the dad is present at the c. SEX, 44
the Immaculate C. was spontaneous combustion CATHOLICISM, 9
concepts walks up the stairs of his c. MANKIND, 30
concessions The c. of the weak are the c. of fear YIELDING, 1
conclusions Life is the art of drawing…c. LIFE, 17
concord toleration produced…religious c. RELIGION, 27
Yes – around C. TRAVEL, 24
concurrence fortuitous c. of atoms CHANCE, 4
condemn No man can justly censure or c. another JUDGMENT, 5
condemned If God were suddenly c. to live the life HUMAN CONDITION, 6
Man is c. to be free FREEDOM, 48
condemning examine oneself…before…c. others SELF, 11
condition fools decoyed into our c. MARRIAGE, 93
hopes for the human c. PESSIMISM, 4
The c. of man…is a c. of war HUMAN CONDITION, 10
the Jews have made a contribution to the human c. JEWS, 14
To be a poet is a c. POETS, 6

wearisome c. of humanity HUMAN CONDITION, 9
conditioned Americans have been c. to respect newness AMERICANS, 11
conditions my people live in such awful c. POVERTY, 12
condoms hope people will learn to love c. AIDS, 3
conduct C....to the prejudice of good order and military discipline ARMY, 2
conductor c. has the advantage MUSICIANS, 5
conference naked into the c. chamber WEAPONS, 1
confess It's easy to make a man c....lies TRUTH, 30
Men will c. HUMOUR, 8
only c. our little faults IMPERFECTION, 11
We c. our bad qualities...out of fear SELF-KNOWLEDGE, 2
confessing I am ashamed of c. INNOCENCE, 1
women...ill-using them and then c. it WOMEN, 81
confidence something you have complete c. in FANATICISM, 3
Three addresses always inspire c. ADDRESSES, 2
confident There are two things which I am c. I can do very well CRITICISM, 18
confin'd cabin'd, cribb'd, c., bound in FEAR, 11
confined their elegant but c. houses WRITERS, 36
conflict We are in an armed c. MIDDLE EAST, 7
conform how to rebel and c. at the same time YOUTH, 5
conformable Nature is very consonant and c. NATURE, 12
confound the weak things of the world to c. the...mighty WISDOM AND FOOLISHNESS, 3
Congreve C. is the only sophisticated playwright WRITERS, 88
Congs Kinquering C. their titles take SPOONERISMS, 3
connect Only c. COMMUNICATION, 1
conquer in the end the truth will c. TRUTH, 48
They will c., but...not convince PERSUASION, 1
We'll fight and we'll c. COURAGE, 13
when we c. without danger VICTORY, 3
conquered I came; I saw; God c. VICTORY, 16
I came, I saw, I c. VICTORY, 1
I will be c.; I will not capitulate DETERMINATION, 9
the English seem...to have c. and peopled half the world BRITISH EMPIRE, 8
conquering C. kings ROYALTY, 9
not c. but fighting well VICTORY, 4
See, the c. hero comes VICTORY, 12
conquest The Roman C. was, however, a *Good Thing* HISTORY, 29
conscience a Nonconformist c. WOMEN, 89
As guardian of His Majesty's c. MONARCHY, 24
c. does make cowards of us all CONSCIENCE, 5
C. is a coward CONSCIENCE, 3
C. is the inner voice CONSCIENCE, 4
C. is the internal perception of the rejection of a particular wish CONSCIENCE, 2
dilemmas of c. and egotism POWER, 22
freedom of speech, freedom of c., and the prudence never to practise...them FREEDOM, 51
go to the polling booth without a bad c. SOUTH AFRICA, 3
I cannot...cut my c. to fit this year's fashions INTEGRITY, 3
I'll catch the c. of the King PLAYS, 11
Now war has a bad c. WAR, 54
Science without c. SCIENCE, 36
why is my liberty judged of another man's c. CONSCIENCE, 1; FREEDOM, 3
consent No one can make you feel inferior without your c. INFERIORITY, 5
consequence physicians...mistake subsequence for c. DOCTORS, 5
consequences men never violate the laws of God without suffering the c. RETRIBUTION, 9
conservatism c....adherence to the old and tried CONSERVATISM, 5
c. is based upon the idea CONSERVATISM, 1
conservative C. government is an organized hypocrisy POLITICS, 21
Or else a little C. POLITICS, 31
The radical invents the views....the c. adopts them CONSERVATISM, 7
to what is called the Tory...called the C., party POLITICS, 20
which makes a man more c. CONSERVATISM, 4
consider When I c. how my light is spent BLINDNESS, 5
considerable to appear c. in his native place FAME, 12
consistency C. is contrary to nature CONSTANCY, 2
consonant Nature is very c. and conformable NATURE, 12
conspiracy not a Party, it is a c. COMMUNISM, 1
People of the same trade...conversation ends in a c. BUSINESS, 21
conspirators All the c. NOBILITY, 4
constabulary When c. duty's to be done POLICE, 1
constant A c. guest HOSPITALITY, 1
Friendship is c. in all other things LOVE AND FRIENDSHIP, 3
constitution The c....first and second class citizens CLASS, 40
The principles of a free c. GOVERNMENT, 10
constitutional A c. king must learn to stoop MONARCHY, 14
c. right DEMOCRACY, 11
definition of a c. statesman POLITICIANS, 1
construction Our object in the c. of the state REPUBLIC, 1
consultations dictator...always take some c. AUTHORITARIANISM, 6
consulted the right to be c....to encourage MONARCHY, 2
consume more history than they can c. EUROPE, 16
statistics, born to c. resources STATISTICS, 3
consumer In a c. society there are...two kinds of slaves MATERIALISM, 10
consumes Man...c. without producing CAPITALISM, 10
consummation a c. /Devoutly to be wish'd SUICIDE, 12
consumption Conspicuous c....is a means of reputability MATERIALISM, 20
this c. of the purse MONEY, 42
contemplates Beauty in things exists in the mind which c. them BEAUTY, 21
contemplation right mindfulness, right c. RELIGION, 8
contemporary I am no one's c. – ever DENIAL, 2
to trade a hundred c. readers for POSTERITY, 6
contempt attention to the inside...c. for the outside BOOKS, 14
she was only an Object of C. CONTEMPT, 1
To show pity is felt as a sign of c. SYMPATHY, 5
contemptible c. little Army WAR, 132; WORLD WAR I, 25
content desire is got without c. CONTENTMENT, 6
contented How is it...that no one lives c. DISCONTENT, 4
If you are foolish enough to be c., don't show it COMPLAINTS, 3
With what I most enjoy c. least DISCONTENT, 8
contentment C. and fulfilment don't make for very good fiction FICTION, 5
Where wealth and freedom reign, c. fails BUSINESS, 12
contests mighty c. rise from trivial things RESULTS, 5
continence Give me chastity and c. PROCRASTINATION, 4
that melancholy sexual perversion known as c. ABSTINENCE, 6
continent On the C. people have good food MANNERS, 4
continental C. people have sex life ENGLISH, 24
continual c. state of inelegance WEATHER, 7
continuation All diplomacy is a c. of war DIPLOMACY, 14
War is the c. of politics WAR, 30
contraception a terrific story about oral c. CONTRACEPTION, 2
contraceptive It's like having a totally efficient c. FUTURE, 5
contraceptives C. should be used CONTRACEPTION, 6
Skullion had little use for c. CONTRACEPTION, 7
contract Every law is a c. LAW, 23
Marriage is...but a civil c. MARRIAGE, 103
contradict Do I c. myself SELF, 21
contradiction brook no c. DOCTORS, 10
Man is...an everlasting c. to himself INTELLECT, 3
Woman's at best a c. WOMEN, 65
contrairy everythink goes c. with me MISFORTUNE, 9
contraries Without C. is no progression CONFLICT, 4
contrariwise 'C.,' continued Tweedledee LOGIC, 1
contrary Mary, Mary, quite c. GARDENS, 1; NURSERY RHYMES, 33
On the c. LAST WORDS, 40
control we ought to c. our thoughts SELF-CONTROL, 3
controversies savage c....no good evidence either way ARGUMENTS, 14
controversy that c. is either superfluous ARGUMENTS, 12
convenient always to seek what is more c. DISEASE, 37
Nobody is forgotten when it is c. to remember him EXPEDIENCY, 3
convent To enter the...Ballet is to enter a c. DANCING, 8
convention a c. which says you must not make species extinct CONSERVATION, 7
conventional The c. army loses if it does not win WAR, 57
conventionally to fail c. ORTHODOXY, 3
conversation a c. with the finest men LITERATURE, 3
And third-rate c. MEDIOCRITY, 7
a proper subject of c. RELIGION, 13
C....elicits secrets from us CONVERSATION, 8

C. has a kind of charm CONVERSATION, 8
c. must be an exchange of thought CONVERSATION, 7
happiest c. where there is no competition CONVERSATION, 5
make his c. perfectly delightful INSULTS, 35
never-ending worldwide c. COMPUTERS, 5
Questioning is not the mode of c. CONVERSATION, 4
There is no such thing as c. CONVERSATION, 10
Writing...is but a different name for c. WRITING, 31
Your ignorance cramps my c. IGNORANCE, 8
conversationalist the c. who adds 'in other words' CONVERSATION, 6
conversing Even when c. he could not keep still WRITERS, 76
converted difficult for a Jew to be c. JEWS, 6
convince They will conquer, but...not c. PERSUASION, 1
cook a good c., as cooks go HUMOUR, 54
Any c. should be able to GOVERNMENT, 15
C. is a little unnerved ETIQUETTE, 1
ill c. that cannot lick his own fingers SELF-CONFIDENCE, 4
she was a very bad c. SNOBBERY, 9
cookery c. do FOOD, 40
cooking woman accepted c. FOOD, 46
cooks Too many c. HELP, 5
Coolidge C. is a better example of evolution POLITICIANS, 69
copier c. of nature can never produce anything IMITATION, 4
copies more c. of my works are left behind WRITERS, 32
copulation Birth, and c., and death LIFE AND DEATH, 5
copy A lotta cats c. the Mona Lisa IMITATION, 1
copying by defying their parents and c. one another YOUTH, 5
copyright no c. on your own life PRIVACY, 3
coral C. is far more red ANALOGY, 3
Of his bones are c. made DEATH, 108
cord a threefold c. is not quickly broken UNITY, 5
cordial gold in phisik is a c. MATERIALISM, 5
cordiale *La c. entente* DIPLOMACY, 15
corn amid the alien c. BIRDS, 5
make two ears of c....grow POLITICIANS, 27
That ate the c. NURSERY RHYMES, 57
the meadows rich with c. AMERICA, 37
corner a c. in the thing I love JEALOUSY, 6
some c. of a foreign field WAR, 18
corners people standing in the c. of our rooms TELEVISION AND RADIO, 1
Cornish twenty thousand C. men EXECUTION, 10
Coromandel On the Coast of C. NONSENSE, 16
coronets Kind hearts are more than c. ARISTOCRACY, 12
corps English characteristic...*esprit de c.* ENGLISH, 3
corpse He'd make a lovely c. DEATH, 41
he makes a very handsome c. DEATH, 56
corpses They are for prima donnas or c. FLOWERS, 11
corpuscles make the c. of the blood glow JEWS, 8
correct Astronomy teaches the c. use ASTRONOMY, 4
correction the c. of the world IMPROVEMENT, 3
correctly anxious to do the wrong thing c. ETIQUETTE, 7
corridors c. of power POWER, 22
corroboration c....in the records of Somerset House HUMILITY, 11
corrupt Among a people generally c. CORRUPTION, 1
power is apt to c. POWER, 19
Power tends to c. POWER, 3
corrupted They had been c. by money SENTIMENTALITY, 1
corruptible born again, not of c. seed DEATH, 29
corruption C., the most infallible symptom of constitutional liberty CORRUPTION, 2
corrupts lack of power c. absolutely POWER, 24
corse As his c. to the rampart FUNERALS, 10
cosmetic sunlight as a kind of c. effulgence SUN, 4
cosmetics In the factory we make c. COSMETICS, 3
cosmopolitan I was told I am a true c. MELANCHOLY, 11
cosmos c. is about the smallest hole UNIVERSE, 5
obligation to survive is owed...to that c. SURVIVAL, 6
cost To give and not to count the c. SELFLESSNESS, 2
cottage Love and a c. LOVE, 40
poorest man may in his c. bid defiance PRIVACY, 4
your friend's country establishment as a 'c.' WORDS, 17
cottages Pale Death kicks his way equally into the c. of the poor EQUALITY, 28
couch the century of the psychiatrist's c. PSYCHIATRY, 8
time as a tool not as a c. TIME, 22
when on my c. I lie SOLITUDE, 15
cough Jeeves coughed one soft, low, gentle c. ANALOGY, 5
coughing keeping people from c. ACTING, 9
council The grotesque chaos of a Labour c. INCOMPETENCE, 2
counsel C. of her country's gods BRITAIN, 7
sometimes c. take – and sometimes Tea DRINKS, 7
count Don't c. your chickens ANTICIPATION, 4
If you can...c. your money WEALTH, 15
To give and not to c. the cost SELFLESSNESS, 2
countenance the Lord lift up his c. upon thee BLESSING, 4
counter-democratic Proportional Representation...is fundamentally c. POLITICS, 43
counterpoint Too much c.; what is worse, Protestant c. CRITICISM, 3
counties see the coloured c. COUNTRYSIDE, 6
countries preferreth all c. before his own DISCONTENT, 7
country absolved from all duty to his c. MARRIAGE, 92
a c. diversion COUNTRYSIDE, 1
A c. governed by a despot TYRANNY, 3
a c. of young men AMERICA, 13
affections must be confined...to a single c. PATRIOTISM, 10
A man should know something of his own c. TRAVEL, 20
an honest man sent to lie abroad for...his c. DIPLOMACY, 21
Anybody can be good in the c. COUNTRYSIDE, 10
Anyone who loves his c., follow me PATRIOTISM, 11
Counsel of her c.'s gods BRITAIN, 7
c. from whose bourn no traveller returns AFTERLIFE, 9
God made the c. COUNTRYSIDE, 2
go down into the c. DECEPTION, 7
Great artists have no c. NATIONALITY, 7
How I leave my c. LAST WORDS, 51
I have but one life to lose for my c. PATRIOTISM, 13
I love thee still, My c. PATRIOTISM, 7
I would die for my c. PATRIOTISM, 20
loathe the c. COUNTRYSIDE, 1
My c., right or wrong PATRIOTISM, 5
nothing good...in the c. COUNTRYSIDE, 4
Our c. is the world AMERICA, 14
our c., right or wrong PATRIOTISM, 8
proud of the position of the bungalow...in the c. SUBURBIA, 2
she is my c. still PATRIOTISM, 6
That is no c. for old men MORTALITY, 23
The history of every c. begins in the heart HISTORY, 9
The idiot who praises...every c. but his own DISCONTENT, 2
The past is a foreign c. PAST, 5
The soil of our c. RACISM, 21
The undiscover'd c. AFTERLIFE, 9
This c....belongs to the people who inhabit it DEMOCRACY, 11
to leave his c. as good as he had found it DUTY, 1
understanding the problems of running a c. POLITICS, 79
we can die but once to serve our c. PATRIOTISM, 1
what was good for our c. BUSINESS, 28
When I am in the c. I wish to vegetate COUNTRYSIDE, 5
countryside a more dreadful record of sin than...c. SIN, 12
c. is one of the most heavily man-made habitats CONSERVATION, 8
county The sound of the English c. families ARISTOCRACY, 15
couple A married c. are well suited MARRIAGE, 98
the perfect c....a mother and child MOTHERHOOD, 8
couples so many c....not getting the right proteins SEX, 12
courage be strong and of a good c. GOD, 8
C. is the price...for granting peace COURAGE, 12
c. to love...courage to suffer LOVE, 140
good deal of physical c. to ride a horse ALCOHOL, 40; HORSES, 8
tale...of...c. of my companions ENDURANCE, 16
The Red Badge of C. COURAGE, 7
three o'clock in the morning c. COURAGE, 24
Whistling aloud to bear his c. up WHISTLING, 1
course c. of true love never did run smooth LOVE, 119
courteous If a man be...c. to strangers COURTESY, 2
courtesy C. is not dead COURTESY, 4
courting When you are c. a nice girl SCIENCE, 12
courts I have come to regard...c....as a casino JUSTICE, 11
the case is still before the c. ARGUMENTS, 7
courtship C. to marriage MARRIAGE, 39
covenant a c. between me and the earth PROMISES, 2
a c. with death SLAVERY, 4
cover Never judge a c. by its book BOOKS, 24
covet thou shalt not c. GOD, 10
cow A c. is a very good animal in the field SUITABILITY, 2
That milked the c. with the crumpled horn NURSERY RHYMES, 57
The c. is of the bovine ilk ANIMALS, 16
The c. jumped over the moon NURSERY RHYMES, 14
till the c. comes home ETERNITY, 1
Truth, Sir, is a c. SCEPTICISM, 3

Why buy a c. FUTILITY, 1
coward better to be the widow of a hero than the wife of a c. COURAGE, 15
Conscience is a c. CONSCIENCE, 3
No c. soul is mine COURAGE, 3
None but a c....has never known fear COWARDICE, 2
The c. does it with a kiss KILLING, 8
cowardice guilty of Noël C. COWARDICE, 1
cowardly Marriage is the only adventure open to the c. MARRIAGE, 127
cowards C. die many times COWARDICE, 9
the future...makes c. of us PRESENT, 3
Thus conscience does make c. of us all CONSCIENCE, 5
cowboy easier to get an actor to be a c. ACTING, 6
cows explain...that c. can be eaten RELIGION, 26
'Horses' should have read 'C.' MISTAKES, 10
The c. in the corn NURSERY RHYMES, 28
coxcomb to hear a c. ask two hundred guineas CRITICISM, 45
coyness This c., lady, were no crime SHYNESS, 5
compassion C. is not a sloppy, sentimental feeling SOCIALISM, 8
cracked The c. looking glass of a servant IRELAND, 10
cradle Between the c. and the grave TRANSIENCE, 12
Rocked in the c. of the deep SEA, 11
The hand that rocks the c. INFLUENCE, 10
cradles bit the babies in the c. ANIMALS, 5
craft the c. so long to lerne MORTALITY, 3
The life so short, the c. so long to learn MORTALITY, 12
craftsmanship Skill without imagination is c. ART, 27
crafty too c. a woman to invent a new lie LYING, 9
crankshaft spheres geared to God's c. UNIVERSE, 13
cranny We seek...In every c. but the right PERVERSITY, 3
crap Books are a load of c. BOOKS, 22
Craven mistress of the Earl of C. SEX, 66
crazy going to go c., living this epidemic DISEASE, 24
grow a little c....like all men at sea MADNESS, 5
cream coffee that's too black...You integrate it with c. RACISM, 20
create My father didn't c. you to arrest me POLICE, 6
created God c....the earth CREATION, 2
man alone leaves traces of what he c. MANKIND, 8
Man...had been c. to jab the life out of Germans WAR, 98
Thou hast c. us for Thyself HUMAN CONDITION, 2
we cannot be c. for this sort of suffering AFTERLIFE, 6
creates he c. Gods by the dozen RELIGION, 46
creation greatest week...since the c. SPACE, 6
Had I been present at the C. UNIVERSE, 1
The art of c. /is older CREATION, 16
creator All right, my lord c., Don Miguel DEATH, 69
c. had a purpose in equipping us with a neck COURAGE, 16
Man...hasn't been a c., only a destroyer ECOLOGY, 3
virtue in the c. is not the same CREATION, 12
creature No c. smarts...as a fool FOOLISHNESS, 17
the c. hath a purpose PURPOSE, 5
Who kills a man kills a reasonable c. BOOKS, 27
creatures call these delicate c. ours JEALOUSY, 6
From fairest c. we desire increase BEAUTY, 36
creche c....happens between two Range Rovers POLITICS, 67
credentials no c....not even...a certificate of birth ARISTOCRACY, 8
credit not to mind who gets the c. SELFLESSNESS, 1
creditors my oldest c. would hardly know me APPEARANCE, 14
not everyone who wishes makes c. BORROWING, 7
credits c. would still read 'Rubinstein, God, and Piatigorsky' EGOTISM, 6
credulity C. is...the child's strength INNOCENCE, 7
creed got the better of his c. RELIGION, 54
the c. of a second-rate man POLITICIANS, 1
wrought /...the c. of creeds CHRISTIANITY, 43
creeds So many gods, so many c. RELIGION, 70; KINDNESS, 6
Vain are the thousand c. BELIEF, 3
creep I wants to make your flesh c. FEAR, 8
Wit that can c. SERVILITY, 5
creepers Jeepers C. EYES, 2
creetur lone lorn c. MISFORTUNE, 9
crème you would have been the c. de la c. EXCELLENCE, 3
Crete The people of C....make more history EUROPE, 16
cricket c. as organised loafing CRICKET, 7
c. is the greatest thing that God ever created CRICKET, 6
I do love c. – it's so very English CRICKET, 2; FOOTBALL, 2
It's not in support of c. CRICKET, 1; GOLF, 1
playing c. with their peasants ARISTOCRACY, 13; CRICKET, 8
the c. on the hearth MELANCHOLY, 9
where the c. sings PEACE, 17
Cricklewood Midland, bound for C. TRAINS, 1
cried I c. all the way to the bank CRITICISM, 29
crieth thy brother's blood c. unto me MURDER, 2
crime all c. is due to the repressed desire CRIME, 9
Arson, after all, is an artificial c. FIRE, 5
C., like virtue, has its degrees CRIME, 6
Do you call poverty a c. POVERTY, 30
If poverty is the mother of c., stupidity is its father CRIME, 5
man's greatest c. BIRTH, 4
no...c. so shameful as poverty POVERTY, 8
terrorism inflicted on society by c. figures CRIME, 8
The atrocious c. of being a young man YOUTH, 14
the Napoleon of c. CRIME, 3
The punishment fit the c. PUNISHMENT, 10
This coyness, lady, were no c. SHYNESS, 5
Treason was no C. TREASON, 2
worse than a c., it is a blunder MISTAKES, 4
worst c. is faking it HONESTY, 4
crimes Catholics and Communists have committed great c. COMMITMENT, 4
history...a tableau of c. and misfortunes HISTORY, 35
how many c. committed CRIME, 2
Oh liberty!...What c. EXECUTION, 27; FREEDOM, 45
Crippen strong suspicions that C. London cellar murderer TECHNOLOGY, 7; TELEGRAMS, 9
crisis c. is not a c. of information ACTION, 14
Kuwaitis enjoy a c. MIDDLE EAST, 15
crisp Deep and c. and even CHRISTMAS, 15
critic A c. is a man who CRITICS, 20
A good c....narrates the adventures of his mind CRITICS, 5
A good drama c. is CRITICS, 21
c. spits on what is done CRITICS, 8
Nor in the c. let the man be lost CRITICS, 14
the function of the c. CRITICS, 1
critical c. judgement is so exquisite CRITICS, 6
nothing if not c. CRITICISM, 46
criticism A great deal of contemporary c. CRITICISM, 8
As far as c. is concerned CRITICISM, 52
c. is a letter to the public CRITICISM, 41
my own definition of c. CRITICISM, 1
People ask you for c. CRITICISM, 34
The Stealthy School of C. CRITICISM, 43
criticize don't c. /What you can't understand CHANGE, 6
criticizing The pleasure of c. CRITICISM, 26
critics Asking a working writer...about c. CRITICS, 7
c. all are ready made CRITICS, 2
C. are more malicious about poetry CRITICS, 9
c....desire our blood, not our pain CRITICS, 13
music c.....small and rodent-like CRITICS, 18
The greater part of c. are parasites CRITICS, 16
crocodile An appeaser is one who feeds a c. DIPLOMACY, 6
crocodiles wisdom of the c. HYPOCRISY, 2
Cromwell Charles the First, his C. TREASON, 4
restless C. could not cease POLITICIANS, 63
ruins that C. knocked about a bit INNUENDO, 2
crony government by c. NEPOTISM, 1
crook A writer of c. stories POLITICS, 86
I am not a c. DENIAL, 3
the symbol of a bishop is a c. CLERGY, 6
crooked the c. timber of humanity HUMAN NATURE, 15
There was a c. man, and he walked a c. mile NURSERY RHYMES, 52
crop watering the last year's c. FUTILITY, 6
crops Man.../Laid the c. low AGRICULTURE, 6
cross Don't c. the bridge ANTICIPATION, 2
Hot c. buns! NURSERY RHYMES, 16
no c., no crown ENDURANCE, 12
The orgasm has replaced the C. SEX, 42
When I survey the wondrous C. HUMILITY, 13
cross-bow With my c. /I shot BIRDS, 2
crossed a girl likes to be c. in love WOMEN, 9
crosses wooden c. on the roadside WORLD WAR I, 16
crossword fills up his c. puzzle in ink OPTIMISM, 25
crow sun had risen to hear him c. ARROGANCE, 3
waiting for the cock to c. BETRAYAL, 4
crowd a c. like that...brings a lump to my wallet MATERIALISM, 22
And hid his face amid a c. of stars LOVE, 150
Far from the madding c. SOLITUDE, 7
crowds C. without company LONDON, 7

If you can talk with c. and keep your virtue IDEALISM, 2
It brings men together in c. and mobs in bar-rooms SOCIETY, 10
crown no cross, no c. ENDURANCE, 12
poorest man… bid defiance to…the C. PRIVACY, 4
the c. of life TEMPTATION, 4
The influence of the C. has increased MONARCHY, 10
Uneasy lies the head that wears a c. MONARCHY, 22
within the hollow c. ROYALTY, 32
crucible America is God's C. AMERICA, 42
crucified Where the dear Lord was c. CHRISTIANITY, 1
you might try getting c. CHRISTIANITY, 41
crucify Diseases c. the soul of man DISEASE, 11
Do you want to c. the boy CHRISTIANITY, 25
cruel A c. story runs on wheels CRUELTY, 4
C., but composed and bland CATS, 1
cruellest April is the c. month MONTHS, 8
cruelty Man's inhumanity to man
we are all on our last c. MORTALITY, 18
crumbs c. which fell from the rich man's table POVERTY AND WEALTH, 2
cry I often want to c. SEXES, 20
make 'em c. WRITING, 27
mother, do not c. LAST WORDS, 23
She likes stories that make her c. SENTIMENTALITY, 5
the c. of him that ruleth among fools WISDOM, 3
the only advantage women have over men…they can c. SEXES, 20
We think caged birds sing, when indeed they c. IMPRISONMENT, 6
when we c. to Thee SEA, 14
crying An infant c. in the night HUMAN CONDITION, 20
It is no use c. REGRET, 1
cubic One c. foot less SMALLNESS, 3
cuckoo the c. clock was invented SWITZERLAND, 1
The c. comes in April MONTHS, 3
This is the weather the c. likes WEATHER, 13
cucumber A c. should be well sliced FOOD, 31
cucumbers they are but c. after all CRITICISM, 25
cul-de-sac A committee is a c. BUREAUCRACY, 4
cult local c. called Christianity CHRISTIANITY, 28
What's a c. MINORITY, 1
cultivate c. our garden PAROCHIALISM, 3
cultivated I do not want to die…until I have…c. the seed ACHIEVEMENT, 6
culture C. is an instrument wielded by professors CULTURE, 3
C. is the passion for sweetness and light CULTURE, 2
C., the acquainting ourselves with the best CULTURE, 1
c., you'll find more on…yoghurt ROYALTY, 24
ladies who pursue C. in bands CULTURE, 4
terrible revenge by the c. of the Negroes POP MUSIC, 15
two half-cultures do not make a c. HALF MEASURES, 1
When I hear anyone talk of C. PHILISTINISM, 4
You can lead a whore to c. PUNS, 16
cultures apt to leave his c. exposed SCIENTISTS, 13
cumulative they underestimate the c. effect POLITICAL CORRECTNESS, 5
cup Ah, fill the C. TIME, 18
Come, fill the C., and in the Fire of Spring TIME, 17
tak a c. o' kindness yet FRIENDSHIP, 13
cupboard The c. was bare NURSERY RHYMES, 36
Cupid wing'd C. painted blind LOVE, 120
cups c., That cheer but not inebriate DRINKS, 4
curators more philosophical than…c. of the museums MUSEUMS, 1; PRACTICALITY, 3
cur'd C.…of my disease DOCTORS, 8
curds Eating her c. and whey NURSERY RHYMES, 30
cure a c. for which there was no disease REMEDIES, 5
C. the disease DISEASE, 8; REMEDIES, 1
no c. for birth and death LIFE AND DEATH, 12
Show me a sane man and I will c. him for you MADNESS, 6
the c. for admiring the House of Lords HOUSES OF PARLIAMENT, 3
There are maladies we must not seek to c. REMEDIES, 11
Work is the grand c. WORK, 6
cured disease you don't look forward to being c. of DEATH, 80
What can't be c. ENDURANCE, 3
curfew C. shall not ring tonight! MERCY, 3
The C. tolls the knell of parting day DAY, 6
curiosities How these c. would be quite forgot GOSSIP, 7
curiosity C. killed the cat CURIOSITY, 2
C. will conquer fear CURIOSITY, 8
Disinterested intellectual c. CURIOSITY, 9
I would rather be a brilliant memory than a c. RENUNCIATION, 2
curious Be not c. in unnecessary matters CURIOSITY, 3
I am c. to see what happens…to one who dies unshriven LAST WORDS, 50
'That was the c. incident,' remarked…Holmes TRIVIALITY, 8
curiouser C. and curiouser CONFUSION, 3
curl There was a little girl /Who had a little c. SEX, 39
curly Curly locks, C. locks, /Wilt thou be mine NURSERY RHYMES, 8
currency I will not be a party to debasing the c. ECONOMICS, 11
curse A c. is on her if she stay CURSES, 4
Christianity the one great c. CHRISTIANITY, 35
c. not the king, no not in thy thought SECRECY, 3
Don't c. the darkness FUTILITY, 4
rather light candles than c. the darkness COMPLIMENTS, 6
The c. is come upon me CURSES, 3
Work is the c. of the drinking classes WORK, 26
cursed thou art c. above all cattle SEXES, 2
curses C.…always come home to roost CURSES, 2
curst C. be the verse POETRY, 35
curtain An iron c. COLD WAR, 3
I saw it at a disadvantage – the c. was up CRITICISM, 54
Ring down the c. LAST WORDS, 55
cushion Like a c., he always bore IMPRESSIONABILITY, 2
custodiet *Quis c. ipsos /custodes* MISTRUST, 7
custom A c. loathsome to the eye SMOKING, 7
Age…nor c. stale her infinite virginity PURITY, 5
C. calls me to't CUSTOM, 4
c. /More honour'd in the breach than the observance CUSTOM, 3
c. stale /Her infinite variety ADMIRATION, 14
C., then, is the great guide of human life CUSTOM, 2
customer The c. is always right BUSINESS, 18
customers When you are skinning your c. BUSINESS, 14
cut c. to the heart ANGER, 2
Don't c. off your nose REVENGE, 1
the human pack is shuffled and c. EDUCATION, 31
cuts he that c. off twenty years of life DEATH, 105
cutting busy driving cabs and c. hair GOVERNMENT, 7
cycles opinions have arisen among men in c. OPINIONS, 1
cymbal a tinkling c. CHARITY, 6
cymbals clashed his colours together like c. ARTISTS, 10
Cynara faithful to thee, C. FAITHFULNESS, 3
cynic c. is a man who CYNICISM, 3
cynicism C. is an unpleasant way of saying the truth CYNICISM, 2
C. is humour in ill-health CYNICISM, 4
no literature can outdo the c. of real life EXPERIENCE, 10

D

dad if the d. is present at the conception SEX, 44
They fuck you up, your mum and d. FAMILY, 19
Daddy D. wouldn't buy me a bow-wow DOGS, 14
daffodils Fair d., we weep to see TRANSIENCE, 14
host, of golden d. FLOWERS, 14
I never saw d. so beautiful FLOWERS, 12
dagger never be left holding the d. POLITICS, 91
Daily Telegraph Wilde…persecutors…letters page of the *D.* HOMOSEXUALITY, 10
dainties d. that are bred in a book IGNORANCE, 13
dainty Nothing's so d. sweet MELANCHOLY, 1
Daisy D., give me your answer, do MARRIAGE, 44
Dalhousie Alas! Lord and Lady D. are dead DEATH, 86
dalliance primrose path of d. EXAMPLE, 8
damage nothing which might d. his career SCOTS, 1
dame La belle D. sans Merci SUPERNATURAL, 10
one for the d. NURSERY RHYMES, 4
dammed Holland…lies so low they're only saved by being d. EUROPE, 8
damn D. the age. I'll write for antiquity POSTERITY, 7
D. with faint praise CRITICISM, 40
D. you, England. You're rotting ENGLAND, 32
I don't care a twopenny d. INDIFFERENCE, 6
not worth a d. OFFICERS, 15
The public doesn't give a d. MUSIC, 7
damnation there would be no d. SIN, 20
the terminal point of addiction is…d. SIN, 2
damnations Twenty-nine distinct d. BIBLE, 3

damn'd thou must be d. perpetually DAMNATION, 3
damned a d. serious business WAR, 125
d. good-natured friend FRIENDS, 14
d. if you do – And…damned if you don't DAMNATION, 2
Life is just one d. thing after another LIFE, 29
Publish and be d. PUBLISHING, 11
The public be d. CAPITALISM, 15
Danaos *timeo D. et dona ferentis* MISTRUST, 11
dance A D. to the Music of Time BOOK, SONG, AND PLAY TITLES, 21
d. an antic hay DANCING, 6
D., dance, dance little lady DANCING, 3
I could d. with you till the cows come home HUMOUR, 44
I have discovered the d. DANCING, 4
On with the d. DANCING, 1
will you join the d. DANCING, 2
danced I've d. with a man SNOBBERY, 4
dancers ghastly season…for you Spanish d. CHARITY, 5
dancing And d. dogs and bears ANIMALS, 12
d. on a volcano REVOLUTION, 5
the manners of a d. master CRITICISM, 22
danger A nation is not in d. ECONOMICS, 17
d.…lies in acting well EXCELLENCE, 2
industry has created many new sources of d. DISEASE, 36
I realized there was a measure of d. DANGER, 5
Oft in d., oft in woe ENDURANCE, 24
the only real d. that exists is man himself HUMAN NATURE, 14
when we conquer without d. VICTORY, 3
dangerous A d. person to disagree with WRITERS, 44
A little learning is a d. thing KNOWLEDGE, 30
He thinks too much. Such men are d. MISTRUST, 9
If a little knowledge is d. KNOWLEDGE, 21
if a little knowledge was a d. thing KNOWLEDGE, 32
more d. the abuse POWER, 8
What is d. about the tranquillizer DRUGS, 9
dangerously *live d.* DANGER, 6
dangers D. by being despised DANGER, 4
Daniels like a lion in a cave of savage D. ENEMIES, 9
Danny Deever they're hangin' D. in the mornin' EXECUTION, 14
Dante D. makes me sick LAST WORDS, 13
dappled Glory be to God for d. things BEAUTY, 20
dare d. to eat a peach OLD AGE, 18
Darien Silent, upon a peak in D. DISCOVERY, 5
daring d. to excel EXCELLENCE, 2
Darjeeling There was an old man from D. HUMOUR, 33
dark A blind man in a d. room METAPHYSICS, 1
children fear…the d. DEATH, 22
colours will agree in the d. DIFFERENCE, 7
d. sayings WISDOM, 7
Genuineness only thrives in the d. SINCERITY, 4
great leap in the d. LAST WORDS, 38
never to refuse a drink after d. ALCOHOL, 43
O d., d., d., amid the blaze of noon BLINDNESS, 4
slow, sure doom falls pitiless and d. HUMAN CONDITION, 15
The d. night of the soul SOUL, 8
Turn up the lights, I don't want to go home in the d. LAST WORDS, 37
we are for the d. ENDING, 6
What in me is d. /Illumine GOD, 38
darken never d. my towels again DISMISSAL, 5
darkest The d. hour OPTIMISM, 8
darkling as on a d. plain WAR, 2
D. I listen DEATH, 70
darkly through a glass, d. CHARITY, 6
darkness Before us pass'd the door of D. DEATH, 50
d. was upon the face of the deep CREATION, 2
men loved d.…because their deeds were evil EVIL, 5
rather light candles than curse the d. COMPLIMENTS, 6
The d. falls at Thy behest DAY, 4
the d. inside houses FEAR, 7
darlin he's a d.' man FRIENDS, 11
darling Charlie is my d. ADMIRATION, 9
d. of the Gods was born DESTINY, 14
Thrice welcome, d. of the spring BIRDS, 14
darn a d. is…poverty THRIFT, 10
dates Its history d. from today ROYALTY, 39
daughter as is the mother, so is her d. FAMILY, 7
d. of Earth and Water WEATHER, 23
Don't put your d. on the stage THEATRE, 8
Dwelt a miner, Forty-niner, /And his d., Clementine MOURNING, 7
I always remember that I am Caesar's d. EXTRAVAGANCE, 3
skipper had taken his little d. BOATS, 11
daughters cemetery in which nine of his d. were lying SEX, 58
Words are men's d. WORDS, 14
dauntless faithful in love…d. in war CHIVALRY, 10
David's Once in royal D. city CHRISTMAS, 2
Davy Sir Humphry D. SCIENTISTS, 7
dawn a grey d. breaking SEA, 10
Bliss was it in that d. to be alive FRENCH REVOLUTION, 3
the dappled d. doth rise BIRDS, 8
They sighed for the d. and thee LOVE, 134
dawned each day that has d. is your last PRESENT, 10
day As I was saying the other d. INTERRUPTIONS, 2
compare thee to a summer's d. COMPLIMENTS, 4
count as profit every d. that Fate allows you PRESENT, 8
each d. is like a year IMPRISONMENT, 10
each d. that has dawned is your last PRESENT, 10
every dog has his d. SATISFACTION, 1
from this d. forward MARRIAGE, 30
God called the light D. CREATION, 2
Good morning to the d.: and, next, my gold MATERIALISM, 12
If every d. in the life of a school EDUCATION, 30
I look upon every d. to be lost FRIENDSHIP, 20
in the d. of judgement DEATH, 33
It takes place every d. DOOMSDAY, 4
It was such a lovely d. BED, 6
Live this d., as…thy last PRESENT, 12
long d.'s task is done REST, 2
Night and d. LOVE, 101
Now the d. is over DAY, 1
Our little systems have their d. TRANSIENCE, 18
Seize the d. PRESENT, 7
So foul and fair a d. WEATHER, 22
spend a single d. really well GOOD, 6
Stay, stay, /Until the hasting d. /Has run TRANSIENCE, 14
Sweet d., so cool, so calm DAY, 8
That fellow would vulgarize the d. of judgment VULGARITY, 3
The bright d. is done ENDING, 6
The d. begins to droop DAY, 2
the twenty-four hour d. TIME, 10
thou knowest not what a d. may bring forth FUTURE, 3
Without all hope of d. BLINDNESS, 4
daylight a rule never to drink by d. ALCOHOL, 43
Dayrolles Give D. a chair LAST WORDS, 16
days D. and moments quickly flying DEATH, 37
D. off LEISURE, 5
d. of wine and roses TRANSIENCE, 11
Do not let us speak of darker d. WORLD WAR II, 11
Shuts up the story of our d. FAITH, 17
Sweet childish d. NOSTALGIA, 24
Thirty d. hath November MONTHS, 9
dead Add: 'provided he is really d.' ADMIRATION, 6
And what was d. was Hope IMPRISONMENT, 9
A statesman is a politician who's been d. POLITICIANS, 29
But he's just as d. as if he'd been wrong RIGHT, 1
Come not, when I am d. HYPOCRISY, 16
D.! and…never called me mother DEATH, 132
d., but in the Elysian fields HOUSES OF PARLIAMENT, 8
D. men tell no tales DEATH, 4
Either he's d. or my watch has stopped DEATH, 83
England mourns for her d. across the sea MOURNING, 3
Fifteen men on the d. man's chest ALCOHOL, 60
for those who like it better d. CRITICISM, 32
God is d. GOD, 39
great deal to be said for being d. DEATH, 26
Here lies Fred, /Who was alive and is d. ROYALTY, 3
He was a great patriot…provided…that he really is d. ADMIRATION, 17
if I am d. he would like to see me DEATH, 54
If the d. talk to you, you are a spiritualist MADNESS, 15
I have been drinking it for sixty-five years and I am not d. DRINKS, 9
It does not then concern either the living or the d. DEATH, 47
I've just read that I am d. OBITUARIES, 2
more to say when I am d. DEATH, 98
most of 'em d. WAR, 102
Mother is the d. heart of the family WOMAN'S ROLE, 2
move in a world of the d. HISTORIANS, 2
My husband is d. DEATH, 84
Nobody heard him, the d. man DROWNING, 3
Now he is d. DEATH, 19

Now I'm d. in the grave with my lips moving POSTERITY, 8
O pity the d. that are d. DEATH, 75
she was d.; but my father he kept ladling gin REMEDIES, 12
The d. don't die DEATH, 76
The d....look on and help DEATH, 76
the d. shall be raised incorruptible DEATH, 28
The noble living and the noble d. NOBILITY, 6
The novel being d. NOVELS, 17
The only completely consistent people are the d. CONSTANCY, 2
The only good Indians I ever saw were d. ENEMIES, 7
The past is the only d. thing PAST, 7
the people we should have been seen d. with SNOBBERY, 10
To one d. deathless hour POETRY, 38
to resuscitate the d. art /Of poetry POETRY, 36
to the d. we owe only truth RESPECT, 4
we are all d. DEATH, 73
we survive amongst the d. and the dying OLD AGE, 43
When I am d., and laid in grave MEMORIALS, 1
When I am d., my dearest DEATH, 99
who quoted d. languages CRITICS, 19
deadener Habit is a great d. HABIT, 2
deadly Soap and education...are more d. EDUCATION, 56
the female of the species is more d. than the male WOMEN, 43
deaf Historians are like d. people HISTORIANS, 7
union of a d. man to a blind woman MARRIAGE, 37
deal a new d. for the American people AMERICA, 30
Shed his blood...given a square d. JUSTICE, 21
dean no dogma, no D. RELIGION, 17
the queer old D. SPOONERISMS, 4
dear D. 338171 HUMOUR, 36
that bread should be so d. POVERTY, 17
dearer d. still is truth TRUTH, 8
death a covenant with d. SLAVERY, 4
added another terror to d. BIOGRAPHY, 4
After the first d., there is no other DEATH, 125
After your d. you will be AFTERLIFE, 8
Angel of D. has been abroad WAR, 17
an intelligent man at the point of d. DEATH, 15
Any man's d. diminishes me DEATH, 45
A physician can sometimes parry the scythe of d. TIME, 28
a Reaper whose name is D. DEATH, 79
a remedy for everything except d. REMEDIES, 6
artist is in danger of d. SPORT AND GAMES, 8
A single d. is a tragedy STATISTICS, 9
a tie that only d. can sever MARRIAGE, 83
A useless life is an early d. PURPOSE, 3
author of the Satanic Verses...sentenced to d. RELIGION, 37
Because I could not stop for D. DEATH, 42
Birth, and copulation, and d. LIFE AND DEATH, 5
Christianity has made of d. a terror CHRISTIANITY, 36
d. after life does greatly please DEATH, 119
D. and taxes and childbirth EXPEDIENCY, 5
D. be not proud DEATH, 44
D. cometh soon or late COURAGE, 17
D. defies the doctor DEATH, 5
D. destroys a man DEATH, 52
D. is a delightful hiding-place WORLD-WEARINESS, 3
D. is my neighbour now DEATH, 48
D. is nothing AFTERLIFE, 5
D. is not the greatest of ills WORLD-WEARINESS, 9
D. is still working like a mole DEATH, 60
D. is the great leveller DEATH, 6
D. is the veil DEATH, 114
d. itself must be...a mockery DEATH, 115
d.'s own hand is warmer than my own WORLD-WEARINESS, 4
d....the least of all evils DEATH, 20
d., the most terrifying of ills DEATH, 47
D. took him by the heart DEATH, 90
D. was but /A scientific fact IMPRISONMENT, 8
D....we haven't succeeded in...vulgarizing DEATH, 62
D. will disprove you DEATH, 128
dread disease which so prepares its victim...for d. DISEASE, 14
dread of something after d. AFTERLIFE, 9
easy d. only to the just DEATH, 14
enormously improved by d. WRITERS, 79
Football isn't a matter of life and d. FOOTBALL, 8
give me liberty or give me d. FREEDOM, 16
Go and try to disprove d. DEATH, 128
Graveyards...people associate them with d. DEATH, 25
Growth is a greater mystery than d. AGE, 37
half in love with easeful D. DEATH, 70
He who pretends to look on d. without fear lies DEATH, 100
His d., which happen'd in his berth PUNS, 5
I am able to follow my own d. step by step DEATH, 67
I am signing my d. warrant PROPHECY, 3
Ideal mankind would abolish d. IDEALISM, 3
I do really think that d. will be marvellous DEATH, 117
I know I shall love d. as well DEATH, 121
in their d. they were not divided FRIENDSHIP, 9
Into the jaws of D. COURAGE, 22
Into the valley of D. OBEDIENCE, 4
I prepare for a journey...as though for d. TRAVEL, 17
I shall but love thee better after d. LOVE, 30
it is not d., but dying, which is terrible DEATH, 49
it may be so the moment after d. AFTERLIFE, 4
I've been accused of every d. MURDER, 3
I wanted to be bored to d. BOREDOM, 2
man fears...only the stroke of d. DEATH, 21
Many men would take the d.-sentence LIFE AND DEATH, 10
Men fear d. DEATH, 22
message of d. for our young men WORLD WAR I, 27
no cure for birth and d. LIFE AND DEATH, 12
no drinking after d. ALCOHOL, 26
nothing is certain but d. and taxes TAXATION, 5
O d., where is thy sting DEATH, 28, 94
O D., where is thy sting-a-ling-a-ling DEATH, 16
one of those unfortunates to whom d. is EXPLANATIONS, 1
one that had been studied in his d. DEATH, 110
Pale D. kicks his way equally into the cottages of the poor and the castles of kings EQUALITY, 28
Railing at life, and yet afraid of d. OLD AGE, 13
read the d. of Little Nell without laughing DICKENS, 4
Reports of my d. are greatly exaggerated OBITUARIES, 4; TELEGRAMS, 11
sad stories of the d. of kings ROYALTY, 32
sentenced to d. in my absence JUSTICE, 2
Sickness, sin and d....do not originate in God RELIGION, 21
Sin brought d. DEATH, 46; SIN, 14
Sleeping as quiet as d. OLD AGE, 46
Sleep is good, d. is better PESSIMISM, 6
Sleep...knows not D. SLEEP, 16
Soldiers are citizens of d.'s grey land SOLDIERS, 5
Swarm over, D. ENGLAND, 4
that...turneth the shadow of d. into the morning GOD, 6
the d. of Little Nell without laughing INSENSITIVITY, 4
the idea of d. as an individual NUCLEAR WEAPONS, 9
the last enemy...is d. AUTHORITARIANISM, 2
there's always d. DEATH, 89
the struggle against d. LIFE AND DEATH, 7
this is d., and the sole d. DEATH, 35
this may be play to you, 'tis d. to us SERIOUSNESS, 2
Thou wast not born for d. BIRDS, 5
till d. us do part MARRIAGE, 30
Time flies, d. urges TIME, 44
to abolish the d. penalty EXECUTION, 13
tragedies are finished by a d. THEATRE, 6
valiant never taste of d. but once COWARDICE, 9
way to dusty d. LIFE, 45
we all contain failure and d. within us AGE, 37
we owe God a d. DEATH, 113
what a man still plans...injustice in his d. DEATH, 36
who fears dishonour more than d. HAPPINESS, 9
worse than d. SEPARATION, 3
you impart knowledge of it through another's d. RESEARCH, 1
deaths Any amusing d. DEATH, 34
it is chiefly our own d. that we mourn for FUNERALS, 3
debasing I will not be a party to d. the currency ECONOMICS, 11
debate I love argument, I love d. ARGUMENTS, 15
debauchee *D.*, n. One who has...pursued pleasure DEBAUCHERY, 3
debt A promise made is a d. unpaid PROMISES, 5
d. which cancels all others OBLIGATION, 1
Out of d. MONEY, 2
The nations which have put mankind...most in their d. NATIONS, 2
debtor Not everyone is a d. BORROWING, 7
debts He that dies pays all d. DEATH, 109
decade fun to be in the same d. AGE, 48
decadence The difference between our d. and the Russians' DECLINE, 12

decades D. have a delusive edge CLASSIFICATION, 3
decay As quick a growth to meet d. TRANSIENCE, 14
D. and disease are often beautiful DISEASE, 39
Macmillan seemed...to embody the national d. DECLINE, 5
Time drops in d. TIME, 42
woods d. and fall MORTALITY, 19
deceit love we swore...seems d. TRANSIENCE, 10
philosophy and vain d. CHRISTIANITY, 4
temper discretion with d. EDUCATION, 60
Where rumour of oppression and d. SOLITUDE, 3
deceitfulness a Cat of such d. CATS, 2
deceive if we say that we have no sin, we d. SIN, 5
To d. oneself DECEPTION, 1
deceived take heed...that your heart be not d. CHRISTIANITY, 6
deceiving without quite d. your enemies PROPAGANDA, 1
decent aristocracy to what is d. CLASS, 16
d. means poor RESPECTABILITY, 3
the only d. thing...is to die at once BEQUESTS, 1
decision he is going to make 'a realistic d.' DECISION, 3
if usage so choose, with whom resides the d. WORDS, 10
decisive Marriage is a step so grave and d. MARRIAGE, 113
deck I am not going to spit on the d. DEPARTURE, 3
declaim when you are declaiming, d. COMPLAINTS, 4
declare they should d. the causes INDEPENDENCE, 2
declining pass my d. years saluting...grandfather clocks OLD AGE, 31
decompose d. in a barrel of porter FUNERALS, 6
decomposing d. in the eternity of print CRITICISM, 55
decorated proverb...much matter d. SAYINGS, 4
decorum *Dulce et d. est* PATRIOTISM, 15
Let them cant about d. RESPECTABILITY, 2
decrepit you are not yet d. enough AGE, 22
decussated Anything reticulated or d. WORDS, 12
dedicated never d. to something you have complete confidence in FANATICISM, 3
Dee Across the sands of D. AGRICULTURE, 5
deed a good d. to forget a poor joke HUMOUR, 4
good d. in a naughty world GOOD, 15
right d. for the wrong reason MOTIVE, 2
The better day, the worse d. SUNDAY, 4
deeds better d. shall be in water writ MEMORIALS, 2
The bitterest tears...are for words...unsaid and d....undone REGRET, 20
deep beauty is only sin d. BEAUTY, 34
D. and crisp and even CHRISTMAS, 15
Rocked in the cradle of the d. SEA, 11
what a very singularly d. young man ARROGANCE, 4
deeper d. than did ever plummet sound RENUNCIATION, 4
whelm'd in d. gulphs DEATH, 40
deeth D. is an ende of every worldly sore LIFE AND DEATH, 4
defeat a d. without a war WORLD WAR II, 3
d. is an orphan SUCCESS, 10
D. of Germany means WORLD WAR II, 27
every victory turns into a d. DISILLUSION, 2
In d. unbeatable OFFICERS, 3
defeated man can be destroyed...not d. DEFEAT, 3
defect Chief D. of Henry King FOOD, 8
defence Never make a d. or apology ACCUSATION, 2
Preparing for suicide...means of d. NUCLEAR WEAPONS, 8
The best immediate d. of the United States WORLD WAR II, 26
The only d. is in offence WAR, 5
Truth telling is not compatible with the d. of the realm TRUTH, 40
When you think about the d. of England ENGLAND, 3
defend D. us BOSNIA AND HERCEGOVINA, 3
I disapprove of what you say, but I will d....your right to say it FREEDOM, 52
defiance in defeat, d. WAR AND PEACE, 3
poorest man may in his cottage bid d. to...the Crown PRIVACY, 4
The d. of established authority REBELLION, 1
defied Age will not be d. AGE, 7
defiles What a man does d. him RESPONSIBILITY, 7
defining Language is...a d. framework LANGUAGE, 28
definition Science fiction is the search for a d. of mankind SCIENCE FICTION, 2
deflowering this d. of Europe WORLD WAR I, 17
defying by d. their parents and copying one another YOUTH, 5
degenerates everything d. in the hands of man MANKIND, 23
world d. and grows worse every day WORLD, 3
degeneration fatty d. of his moral being MARRIAGE, 115
degradation a...sense of intellectual d. after an interview with a doctor DOCTORS, 4
degrading by labour d. to the makers DESIGN, 4
degree d. of delight SUFFERING, 6
when d. is shak'd ORDER, 4
degrees Crime, like virtue, has its d. CRIME, 6
We boil at different d. INDIVIDUALITY, 5
deid Gey few, and they're a' d. INDIVIDUALITY, 1
deities the d. so kindly DESTINY, 17
Deity doubted the existence of the D. SCIENTISTS, 6
to distinguish between the D. and the Drains GOD, 47
deleted D. by French censor NEWSPAPERS, 2
deliberate with a slow d. carelessness READING, 10
deliberates woman that d. is lost WOMEN, 6
deliberation D. is the work of many men ACTION, 9
delicacy the talent of flattering with d. FLATTERY, 2
delight a degree of d. SUFFERING, 6
Commodity, Firmness, and D. ARCHITECTURE, 15
Energy is Eternal D. EFFORT, 2
go to't with d. ENTHUSIASM, 8
Studies serve for d. EDUCATION, 5
Teach us d. in simple things GOOD, 7
The leaping light for your d. discovers DISCOVERY, 2
very temple of d. MELANCHOLY, 8
wept with d. when you gave her a smile MEMORY, 7
delighted Whosoever is d. in solitude SOLITUDE, 1
You have d. us long enough DISMISSAL, 2
delightful make his conversation perfectly d. INSULTS, 35
What a d. thing this perspective is ART, 29
delights Man d. not me MANKIND, 27
deliver d. me from myself SELF, 5
deluge After us the d. PROPHECY, 10
Après nous le d. PROPHECY, 10
delusion he who can analyze his d. PHILOSOPHERS, 1
delusions Many people have d. of grandeur DELUSION, 5
delusive Decades have a d. edge CLASSIFICATION, 3
delved When Adam d. CLASS, 4
demagogues the vilest specimens...found among d. POLITICS, 46
demand D. bare walls in your bedroom DESIGN, 1
demands the populace cannot exact their d. HOUSES OF PARLIAMENT, 19
democracy arsenal of d. DEMOCRACY, 17
D. can't work DEMOCRACY, 6
D....government by the uneducated ARISTOCRACY, 5; DEMOCRACY, 3
D. is only an experiment in government DEMOCRACY, 7
D. means government by discussion DEMOCRACY, 1
D. passes into despotism DEMOCRACY, 15
D. resumed her reign POLITICS, 4
Development requires d. DEMOCRACY, 20
extreme d. or absolute oligarchy...will come GOVERNMENT, 4
grieved under a *d.*, call it *anarchy* GOVERNMENT, 12
In Switzerland they had...five hundred years of d. and peace SWITZERLAND, 5
Man's capacity for evil makes d. necessary DEMOCRACY, 14
no d. in Russia RUSSIA, 9
not the voting that's d. DEMOCRACY, 19
war wasn't fought about d. MIDDLE EAST, 5
world...made safe for d. DEMOCRACY, 24
you often need less, not more, d. DEMOCRACY, 13
democratic the ideal of a d. and free society RACISM, 22
thoroughly d. and patronise everybody DEMOCRACY, 18
demon woman wailing for her d.-lover SUPERNATURAL, 6
demonstrations d. from Chengdu to Tiananmen Square CHINA, 4
denial the highest praise of God consists in the d. of Him ATHEISM, 9
denies spirit that always d. DENIAL, 1
Denmark rotten in the state of D. CORRUPTION, 7
denounce We thus d....the arms race NUCLEAR WEAPONS, 7
dentist fuss about sleeping together...sooner go to my d. SEX, 62
dentists gratitude to most benefactors is the same as...for d. INGRATITUDE, 3
I have let d. ride roughshod over my teeth TEETH, 1
The thought of d. gave him just the same sick horror FEAR, 14
deny let him d. himself CHRISTIANITY, 19
Those who d. freedom FREEDOM, 29
depart D....and let us have done with you DISMISSAL, 1
lettest thou thy servant d. in peace DEATH, 30

when the great and good d. MORTALITY, 20
departure the time of my d. is at hand FAITH, 6
depends It all d. upon that article there SOLDIERS, 10
depraved No one...suddenly became d. DEBAUCHERY, 6
depression Recession...a neighbour loses...d....you lose ECONOMICS, 19
depth out of your d. SELF-CONFIDENCE, 5
derangement a nice d. of epitaphs MALAPROPISMS, 8
derision Ambition, Distraction, Uglification, and D. EDUCATION, 9
descend Never d. to the ways of those above you EQUALITY, 16
descended D. from the apes EVOLUTION, 1
description beggar'd all d. ADMIRATION, 13
descriptions d. of the fairest wights HISTORY, 32
desert The sand of the d. is sodden red WAR, 76
Use every man after his d. MERIT, 6
deserts D. of vast eternity AGE, 38
deserve I have arthritis, and I don't d. that either MERIT, 2
deserved I wasn't lucky. I d. it MERIT, 7
deserves At 50, everyone has the face he d. AGE, 43
the government it d. GOVERNMENT, 18
designing I am d. St Paul's ARCHITECTURE, 1
desire antidote to d. DESIRE, 6
a universal innate d. PROGRESS, 2; EXTRAVAGANCE, 2
d. is got without content CONTENTMENT, 6
D. is the very essence of man DESIRE, 16
d. should so many years outlive performance SEX, 52
d. to be praised twice over PRAISE, 6
It provokes the d. ALCOHOL, 53
nothing like d. for preventing the thing one says DESIRE, 12
The D. of Man being Infinite INFINITY, 1
Those who restrain D. DESIRE, 2
to have few things to d. FEAR, 1
to lose your heart's d. DESIRE, 15
desired war which...left nothing to be d. WAR, 15
desires He who d. but acts not ACTION, 7
Man's D. are limited by his Perceptions PERCEPTION, 2; DESIRE, 4
Strong enough to answer back to d. CHARACTER, 12
than nurse unacted d. DESIRE, 3
desiring pessimists end up by d. the things they fear PESSIMISM, 9
desist to d. from the experiment in despair SCOTS, 7
desk what risks you take...to find money in a d. THEFT, 4
desks Stick...to your d. and never go to sea OFFICERS, 7
desolate d. and sick of an old passion LOVE, 51
despair carrion comfort, D., not feast on thee DESPAIR, 4
Don't d., not even over...despair DESPAIR, 5
Patience, n. A minor form of d. PATIENCE, 8
some divine d. SORROW, 26
to desist from the experiment in d. SCOTS, 7
without understanding d. PSYCHIATRY, 6
despairs He who d. over an event is a coward PESSIMISM, 4
desperate D. cuts RESULTS, 1
desperation lives of quiet d. DESPAIR, 6
despise I d. Shakespeare SHAKESPEARE, 16
some other Englishman d. him ENGLISH, 32
despised A poor man is d. the whole world over POVERTY, 19
I doubt if the philosopher lives...who could know himself...d. by a street boy PHILOSOPHERS, 5
despises A woman d. a man for loving her LOVE, 130
despond name of the slough was D. DESPAIR, 2
despot A country governed by a d. TYRANNY, 3
despotism Democracy passes into d. DEMOCRACY, 15
extreme democracy or absolute oligarchy or d. will come GOVERNMENT, 4
France was a long d. FRANCE, 2
dessicated A d. calculating machine POLITICIANS, 37
destination I do not think this poem will reach its d. CRITICISM, 51
destiny I were walking with d. DESTINY, 4
man of d. SOUTH AFRICA, 6
Riddle of d. PURPOSE, 6
destroy Doth the wingèd life d. PLEASURE, 5
He would like to d. his old diaries CONCEIT, 20
Man...builds machines to d. WORLD WAR I, 16
sought to d. institutions INDIFFERENCE, 7
they shall not hurt nor d. in all my holy mountain PEACE, 1
whom God wishes to d. MADNESS, 4
Whom the gods wish to d. TALENT, 1
destroy'd a bold peasantry.../When once d. PUBLIC, 12
destroyed man can be d....not defeated DEFEAT, 3
destroyer Man...hasn't been a creator, only a d. ECOLOGY, 3
destroying simplifying something by d. CIVILIZATION, 4
destroys he who d. a good book, kills reason BOOKS, 27
destruction one purpose...d. of Hitler HITLER, 3
Pride goeth before d. MISQUOTATIONS, 10
detail life is frittered away by d. SIMPLICITY, 8
details a mind that reveres d. UNDERSTANDING, 9
detective The d. novel is NOVELS, 13
detente D. is like the race POLITICS, 16
deterrent the d. is a phallic symbol NUCLEAR WEAPONS, 19
detest they d. at leisure LOVE AND HATE, 1
detestable D. person but needs watching WRITERS, 78
detested D. sport HUNTING, 2
Deutschland *D., D. über alles* GERMANY, 13
device A banner with the strange d., /Excelsior AMBITION, 12
devil Abashed the d....felt how awful goodness is GOOD, 12
between any sort of d. and the deep blue sea SUICIDE, 8
cleft the D.'s foot NONSENSE, 11
D. always builds a chapel there DEVIL, 7
d. can cite Scripture QUOTATIONS, 12
given up believing in the d. DEVIL, 8
I do not see...why the d. should have all the good tunes MUSIC, 23
Milton's D. as a moral being is far superior MILTON, 3
nickname is the heaviest stone that the d. can throw NAMES, 4
Renounce the d. RENUNCIATION, 1
sacrifice...of the d.'s leavings VIRTUE, 15
Sarcasm...the language of the d. SARCASM, 1
The d. finds work IDLENESS, 1
The D. is a gentleman DEVIL, 11
The d. is not so black DEVIL, 1
the D. knows Latin LANGUAGE, 17
The d. looks after his own LUCK, 5
the d. played at chess with me EXPLOITATION, 1
the world, the flesh, and the d. JOURNALISM, 25; TEMPTATION, 5
devilish eyes flamed red with d. passion SUPERNATURAL, 16
devil's d. walking parody ANIMALS, 9
It is no good casting out d. DEVIL, 9
One more d.'-triumph and sorrow for angels DAMNATION, 1
devotion dollar...object of universal d. MATERIALISM, 11
devour shed tears when they would d. HYPOCRISY, 2
dew Just to save her from the foggy, foggy d. SEX, 4
dexterity Your d. seems a happy compound INSULTS, 15
diabetic Many a d. has stayed alive DISEASE, 19
diagram cat is a d. and pattern of subtle air CATS, 5
dialect a d. I understand very little LANGUAGE, 19
D. words – those terrible marks of the beast CLASS, 15
diamond A d. is forever ADVERTISING, 6
Chaucer, I confess, is a rough d. CHAUCER, 2
D.! D. ACCIDENTS, 5
more of rough than polished d. BRITISH, 4
diamonds D. Are MATERIALISM, 17
D. Are Forever BOOK, SONG, AND PLAY TITLES, 8
My goodness those d. are lovely GOOD, 17
to give him d. back MATERIALISM, 7
diaries He would like to destroy his old d. CONCEIT, 20
Let d., therefore DIARIES, 1
Only good girls keep d. DIARIES, 2
diary I never travel without my d. DIARIES, 6
To write a d....returning to one's own vomit DIARIES, 4
What is a d. as a rule DIARIES, 5
Dickens D....never quite took DICKENS, 1
D.'s style it is impossible to speak in praise DICKENS, 3
D.' world is not life-like DICKENS, 2
dictation God wrote it. I merely did his d. INSPIRATION, 6
dictator and finally a single d. substitutes himself COMMUNISM, 11
I am painted as the greatest little d. AUTHORITARIANISM, 6
I believe in benevolent dictatorship provided I am the d. LEADERSHIP, 3
dictators D. ride to and fro upon tigers AUTHORITARIANISM, 3
dictatorship The d. of the proletariat MARXISM, 5
dictionaries To make d. is dull work LEXICOGRAPHY, 5
dictionary send the reader to the d. STYLE, 4
The responsibility of a d. LEXICOGRAPHY, 3
this is the first time I ever made the d. LEXICOGRAPHY, 7
words never seen...before outside of a d. POETS, 50
diddle Hey d. d., /The cat and the fiddle NURSERY RHYMES, 14
die A man can d. DEATH, 1
argue that I shall some day d. DEATH, 77

better to d. on your feet SELF-RESPECT, 1
but to do and d. OBEDIENCE, 4
D....the last thing I shall do LAST WORDS, 49
D. when I may REPUTATION, 4
either do, or d. ACTION, 6
Everybody has got to d..... Now what LAST WORDS, 61
for me to d., for you to go on living GOD, 45
have to d. beyond my means LAST WORDS, 74
How often are we to d. DEATH, 96
I am ready to d. for my Lord LAST WORDS, 7
I d. a Christian EXECUTION, 4
I d. because I do not d. DEATH, 65
I d. happy LAST WORDS, 27
I do not want to d. ACHIEVEMENT, 6
If a man hasn't discovered something that he would d. for IDEALISM, 1
If I d. today every drop of my blood LAST WORDS, 29
If I should d. WAR, 18
I have been learning how to d. DEATH, 129
in what peace a Christian can d. LAST WORDS, 3
I shall be like that tree; I shall d. from the top DECLINE, 10
It is natural to d. DEATH, 23
it is worse to want to d. WORLD-WEARINESS, 9
it is youth that must fight and d. WAR, 49
I will d. in peace LAST WORDS, 75
I will d. in the last ditch PATRIOTISM, 33
I would d. for my country PATRIOTISM, 20
let me d. drinking in an inn ALCOHOL, 41
Let us determine to d. here DETERMINATION, 5
Let us do or d. ACTION, 8
live for ever or d. in the attempt IMMORTALITY, 3
man can d. but once DEATH, 113
Many people would sooner d. than think THINKING, 8
Never say d. PERSISTENCE, 2
No young man believes he shall ever d. IMMORTALITY, 2
one may d. without ever laughing LAUGHTER, 8
place...to d. in WORLD, 1
Rather suffer than d. SUFFERING, 10
Ring out, wild bells, and let him d. ENDING, 7
save your world you asked this man to d. WAR, 3
The dead don't d. DEATH, 76
The d. is cast IRREVOCABILITY, 1
the only decent thing...is to d. at once BEQUESTS, 1
those who are about to d. salute you LAST WORDS, 4
to d., and go we know not where DEATH, 107
To d. will be an awfully big adventure DEATH, 24
trains all night groan on the rail /To men that d. at morn EXECUTION, 11
we can d. but once to serve our country PATRIOTISM, 1
We d. – does it matter when DEATH, 123
we must live as though...never going to d. ACHIEVEMENT, 9
when good Americans d. they go to Paris AMERICANS, 13
died dog it was that d. DOGS, 8
I d....of my physician DOCTORS, 8
Men have d. from time to time LOVE AND DEATH, 6
there were people who d. of dropsies ALCOHOL, 33
'Tis said that some have d. for love LOVE AND DEATH, 7
diem *Carpe d.* PRESENT, 7
dies a young person, who...marries or d. HUMAN NATURE, 1
because a man d. for it MARTYRDOM, 5
Every moment d. a man LIFE AND DEATH, 1
he d. in pain LIFE AND DEATH, 8
He that d. pays all debts DEATH, 109
It matters not how a man d. DEATH, 66
king never d. MONARCHY, 5
One d. only once DEATH, 88
Whatever is begotten, born, and d. MORTALITY, 23
diet As the low-fat d. unfolded FOOD, 16
Food is an important part of a balanced d. FOOD, 35
The right d. directs sexual energy FOOD, 14
diets I feel about airplanes the way I feel about d. FLYING, 2
difference Because there is no d. LIFE AND DEATH, 15
d. between...prose and metrical composition POETRY AND PROSE, 7
made the d. of forty thousand men OFFICERS, 16
more d. within the sexes than between them SEXES, 5
differences If we cannot now end our d. DIFFERENCE, 8
The Jews and Arabs should...settle their d. MIDDLE EAST, 3
different populism that rejects anything d. DEMOCRACY, 4
rich are d. WEALTH, 12
differently I would have done it d. ARROGANCE, 9
differeth one star d. from another...in glory ASTRONOMY, 1
difficult D. do you call it, Sir CRITICISM, 24
It is d. to be humble HUMILITY, 4
It is very d. to get up resentment BITTERNESS, 2
persuade you that things are too d. DETERMINATION, 3
When a piece gets d. MUSICIANS, 14
difficulties settle up these little local d. POLITICS, 47
difficulty A d. for every solution BUREAUCRACY, 7
I feel...a certain d. in continuing to exist LAST WORDS, 26
digest mark, learn and inwardly d. LEARNING, 3
my stomach must just d. in its waistcoat ALCOHOL, 57
digestion Things sweet to taste prove in d. sour REGRET, 14
digestions Few radicals have good d. POLITICS, 14
digital d. watches are a pretty neat idea SCIENCE FICTION, 1
digitalis I use d. in doses the text books say are dangerous DRUGS, 14
dignity human beings are born free...d. and rights HUMAN RIGHTS, 1
man added to his d. by standing on it PRIDE, 3
Official d....in inverse ratio to...importance DIPLOMACY, 12
dilemmas d. of conscience and egotism POWER, 22
diligently Had I...served God as d. LOYALTY, 11
dim my lamp burns low and d. ENVY, 3
dime Brother, can you spare a d. MISQUOTATIONS, 19
dimensions sickness enlarges the d. ILLNESS, 11
diminished ought to be d. MONARCHY, 10
dimmed The eyes that shone, /Now d. and gone NOSTALGIA, 14
dimple A d. in the chin, a devil within SUPERSTITION, 1
din made such a frightful d. on the piano MUSICIANS, 18
dine wretches hang that jury-men may d. JUSTICE, 19
dined More d. against than dining FOOD, 10
when Thomas Jefferson d. alone TALENT, 5
you have d. in every house in London – *once* BORES, 9
diners Observe d. arriving at any restaurant HUMAN NATURE, 19
diners-out d. from whom we guard our spoons MISTRUST, 8
ding D. dong, bell, /Pussy's in the well NURSERY RHYMES, 9
dinkum a 'd. hard-swearing Aussie' PATRIOTISM, 14
dinky Hinky, d., par-lee-voo FRANCE, 13
dinner A d. lubricates business BUSINESS, 17
A man is...better pleased when he has a good d. upon his table WOMAN'S ROLE, 4
Breakfast, D., Lunch and Tea FOOD, 7
people...would ask him to d. BELIEF, 4
refuse a good d. UNDERSTANDING, 5
This was a good d. enough FOOD, 29
dinner-table dominate a London d. INFLUENCE, 11
diplomacy All d. is a continuation of war DIPLOMACY, 14
diplomat A d....remembers a woman's birthday AGE, 28
d. these days is nothing but a head-waiter DIPLOMACY, 19
diplomatic d.history...what one clerk said HISTORY, 37
diplomats aged d. to be bored DIPLOMACY, 1
Dirce With D. in one boat conveyed LUST, 5
direct can't d. a Laughton picture ACTORS, 16
direction 'God knows how you Protestants...have any sense of d. CATHOLICISM, 12
directions rode madly off in all d. NONSENSE, 15
director Every d. bites the hand MIXED METAPHORS, 2
Theatre d.: a person ACTING, 1
dirt d. doesn't get any worse HOUSEWORK, 3
I know d. when I smell it and here it is WRITERS, 77
Throw d. enough GOSSIP, 5
dirty Is sex d. SEX, 1
disadvantage d. of merely counting votes DEMOCRACY, 7
disagree Who shall decide when doctors d. DOCTORS, 7
disappointment Grief and d. give rise to anger EMOTION, 3
disapprove I d. of what you say, but I will defend...your right to say it FREEDOM, 52
disarmament precede the d. of the victors WAR, 27
disaster the audience was a d. PLAYS, 14
disasters the middle station had the fewest d. CLASS, 8
trace...the d. of English history to...Wales WALES, 5
disbelief willing suspension of d. POETRY, 11
disciples d....mark its ways and note...its mysteries LUCK, 7
discomforts all the d. that will accompany my being blind BLINDNESS, 7
discommendeth He who d. others CRITICISM, 7
discontent lent /To youth and age...d. DISCONTENT, 1
To be discontented with the divine d. VIRTUE, 13
winter of our d. OPTIMISM, 23
discontents the family...source of all our d. FAMILY, 20
discourse their d. was about hunting LANGUAGE, 19

discovered We have d. the secret of life SCIENCE, 7
discoverers ill d. that think there is no land DISCOVERY, 3
discovery behind the d. of America JEWS, 11
D. consists of seeing what everybody has seen DISCOVERY, 8
he who never made a mistake never made a d. MISTAKES, 16
Scientific d. is a private event SCIENCE, 29
discretion better part of valour is d. SELF-PRESERVATION, 8
temper d. with deceit EDUCATION, 60
the years of d. AGE, 14
discrimination sympathetic without d. SYMPATHY, 2
discussion D. in class, which means EDUCATION, 39
more time for d.…more mistakes MISTAKES, 19
disdains He d. all things above his reach DISCONTENT, 7
disease a cure for which there was no d. REMEDIES, 5
amusing the patient while Nature cures the d. MEDICINE, 12
an incurable d. – colour blindness RACISM, 9
Cur'd…of my d. DOCTORS, 8
Cure the d. REMEDIES, 1
Decay and d. are often beautiful DISEASE, 39
D. is…of the place DISEASE, 34
d. known is half cured DISEASE, 1
dread d. which so prepares its victim…for death DISEASE, 14
Evil comes…like the d. GOOD AND EVIL, 2
I am suffering from the particular d. HYPOCHONDRIA, 1
if the physician had the same d. EXAMPLE, 7
I have Bright's d. HUMOUR, 52
Life is an incurable d. DISEASE, 13; LIFE, 20
only d. you don't look forward to being cured of DISEASE, 25
Only those in the last stage of d. CHILDREN, 4
remedies…suggested for a d. REMEDIES, 7
remedy is worse than the d. REMEDIES, 2
strange d. of modern life DISEASE, 6; LIFE, 5
the d. of writing books WRITING, 23
the incurable d. of writing WRITING, 17
the only d. you don't look forward to being cured of DEATH, 80
this long d., my life ENDURANCE, 13
diseases D. are the tax DISEASE, 31
d.…no less natural than the instincts DISEASE, 32
Extreme remedies…for extreme d. REMEDIES, 10
Hungry Joe collected lists of fatal d. ILLNESS, 6
disgrace a d. to our family name of Wagstaff FAMILY, 23
disgracefully The world is d. managed COMPLAINTS, 2
disguise virtues are…vices in d. VIRTUE AND VICE, 2
dish And the d. ran away with the spoon NURSERY RHYMES, 14
a side d. he hadn't ordered CONTEMPT, 3
The national d. of America AMERICA, 29
dishes Thou shalt not wash d. NURSERY RHYMES, 8
dishonour honour rooted in d. UNFAITHFULNESS, 6
who fears d. more than death HAPPINESS, 9
disillusionments d. in the lives of the medieval saints DECLINE, 9
disinclination d. to inflict pain upon oneself GOOD, 11
disinterested D. intellectual curiosity CURIOSITY, 9
disk put your d. into someone's computer COMPUTERS, 2
dislike I d. what I fancy I feel SUFFERING, 3
that *my* statue should be moved, which I should much d. MEMORIALS, 12
The law of d. for the unlike JEWS, 15
disliked I have always d. myself SELF, 6
dismal the D. Science ECONOMICS, 4
Disney D. the most significant figure ART, 15
Walt D. Theme Park COMMERCIALISM, 1
disobedience Of Man's first d. SIN, 16
disorder A sweet d. in the dress CLOTHES, 7
disposes God d. GOD, 30
dispute Many a long d. among divines ARGUMENTS, 5
disputing The itch of d.…the scab of churches RELIGION, 71
disreputable titles…get one into d. company TITLES, 11
disrespectfully Never speak d. of Society SNOBBERY, 12
dissipated still keep looking so d. DEBAUCHERY, 2
dissipation d. of energy begin SPORT AND GAMES, 13
d. without pleasure LONDON, 7
other things than d.…thicken the features APPEARANCE, 40
dissolve Fade far away, d. HUMAN CONDITION, 12
dissonance I have created a lot of cognitive d. CONFUSION, 5
distance The d. doesn't matter BEGINNING, 8
disthressful She's the most d. country IRELAND, 2
distinguish all there is to d. us from other animals MANKIND, 4
distinguished a sparrow alight upon my shoulder…I was more d. by that HONOUR, 6
So it has come at last, the d. thing LAST WORDS, 41
When a d. but elderly scientist states SCIENCE, 6
distraction Ambition, D., Uglification, and Derision EDUCATION, 9
distress All pray in their d. PRAYER, 5
the mean man is always full of d. SUPERIORITY, 2
distrust shameful to d. one's friends FRIENDS, 12
stay together, but we d. one another MARRIAGE, 31
distrusts him who d. himself SILENCE, 10
disturb What isn't part of ourselves doesn't d. us HATE, 5
disturbances think of diseases as isolated d. DISEASE, 3
ditch if he wasn't as dull as d. water STUPIDITY, 2
ditchwater Is d. dull NATURE, 5
diversion d.…imitation of fighting WAR, 116
'tis a country d. COUNTRYSIDE, 1
diversity make the world safe for d. DIFFERENCE, 8
divide D. and rule POWER, 1
divided in their death they were not d. FRIENDSHIP, 9
Obstinate people can be d. into STUBBORNNESS, 2
Thought must be d. against itself UNDERSTANDING, 8
divine attain to the d. perfection PERFECTION, 4
The Hand that made us is d. CREATION, 1
The right d. of kings to govern wrong MONARCHY, 17
To be discontented with the d. discontent VIRTUE, 13
To err is human, to forgive, d. MISTAKES, 13; FORGIVENESS, 14
divines Many a long dispute among d. ARGUMENTS, 5
divinity a d. that shapes our ends DESTINY, 19
a piece of d. in us NOBILITY, 1
d. in odd numbers SUPERSTITION, 10
There's such d. doth hedge a king MONARCHY, 20
divisions How many d. has *he* got CATHOLICISM, 10
divorce D.? Never. But murder often MARRIAGE, 124
not wanting to consent to the d. PROPHECY, 7
do D. as I say, not as I do DISEASE, 33
D. as you would be done by EXAMPLE, 3
D. other men BUSINESS, 5
d. what the mob d. MAJORITY, 1
either d., or die ACTION, 6
for they know not what they d. FORGIVENESS, 5
I am to d. what I please FREEDOM, 11
Let us d. or die ACTION, 8
Nature…hath done her part; D. thou but thine RESPONSIBILITY, 10
Now what d. I d. with *this* ROYALTY, 40
Preachers say, D. as I say, not as I do EXAMPLE, 7
so much to d., /So little done ACTION, 12
they would d. you BUSINESS, 5
to d. something is to create existence EXISTENCE, 5
Dobest Dowel, Dobet and D. GOOD, 10
Dobet Dowel, D. and Dobest GOOD, 10
doctor A d.…is a patient half-cured OCCUPATIONS, 16
a…sense of intellectual degradation after an interview with a d. DOCTORS, 4
D. Foster went to Gloucester NURSERY RHYMES, 10
Evil comes…like the disease; good…like the d. GOOD AND EVIL, 2
I do not love thee, D. Fell HATE, 1
Imperative drugging…no longer…the chief function of the d. DRUGS, 12
Knocked down a d.? With an ambulance ACCIDENTS, 7
Passion…can be destroyed by a d. PASSION, 7
The d. found…/Her last disorder mortal DOCTORS, 3
doctors Who shall decide when d. disagree DOCTORS, 7
doctrine a d. so illogical and so dull MARXISM, 2
doctrines What makes all d. plain MONEY, 15
documents sign d. which they do not read BORROWING, 4
Dodger artful D. NAMES, 2
does It's dogged as d. it ACTION, 13
dog A door is what a d. is…on the wrong side of DOGS, 10
A good d. MERIT, 1
America is a large, friendly d. AMERICA, 35
And every d. his day YOUTH, 12
A woman's preaching is like a d.'s walking on his hinder legs WOMEN, 41
Beware of the d. DOGS, 1
D. does not eat dog LOYALTY, 1
d. that praised his fleas PARASITES, 4
end up eating our d. ECOLOGY, 7
Every d. has his day OPPORTUNITY, 2; SATISFACTION, 1
Every d. is allowed LAW, 2
Give a d. a bad name INJUSTICE, 1
I am His Highness' d. at Kew DOGS, 11

If a d. jumps...but if a cat CATS, 7
I ope my lips let no d. bark EGOTISM, 8
That tossed the d., /That worried the cat NURSERY RHYMES, 57
The d. it was that died DOGS, 8
The d..../Went mad and bit the man DOGS, 7
The great pleasure of a d. DOGS, 4
The little d. laughed /To see such sport NURSERY RHYMES, 14
The world regards such a person as...an unmuzzled d. CLASSIFICATION, 1
whose d. are you DOGS, 11
Why keep a d. FUTILITY, 2
dogged It's d. as does it ACTION, 13
dogging A case of the tail d. the wag HUMOUR, 53
dogma Any stigma...to beat a d. PUNS, 4
no d., no Dean RELIGION, 17
You can't teach an old d. CONSERVATISM, 6; PUNS, 17
dogmas these d. or goals are in doubt FANATICISM, 3
dogs And dancing d. and bears ANIMALS, 12
Anybody who hates children and d. CHILDREN, 21; DOGS, 6
d. delight to bark and bite ANIMALS, 20
D., like horses, are quadrupeds ANIMALS, 15
how much more d. are animated when they hunt in a pack UNITY, 11
I loathe people who keep d. DOGS, 13
let slip the d. of war WAR, 107
like asking a lamp-post...about d. CRITICS, 7
more careful of the breed of their horses and d. than of their children FATHERS, 5
Rats...fought the d. ANIMALS, 5
Stop...those d....peeing on my cheapest rug DOGS, 9
The woman who is really kind to d. DOGS, 2; WOMEN, 14
doing Anything that is worth d. ORIGINALITY, 1
D. is better than saying ACTION, 2
Find out what you like d. best and get someone to pay you for d. it OCCUPATIONS, 18
let us not be weary in well d. RETRIBUTION, 4
we learn by d. LEARNING, 1
Whatever is worth d. EXCELLENCE, 1
doings All our d. without charity CHARITY, 9
do-it-yourself Edison...a supreme 'd.' man SCIENTISTS, 8
dollar The almighty d....object of universal devotion MATERIALISM, 11
dollars What's a thousand d. MONEY, 33; PUNS, 13
dominate d. the world INFLUENCE, 11
dominions The sun does not set in my d. ROYALTY, 30
dona *timeo Danaos et d. ferentis* MISTRUST, 11
done bright day is d. ENDING, 6
Do as you would be d. by EXAMPLE, 3
d. those things we ought not SIN, 9
If it were d. when 'tis d. HASTE, 10
Justice should...be seen to be d. JUSTICE, 10
Let justice be d. JUSTICE, 7
long day's task is d. REST, 2
Oh, he's d. for AGE, 29
One never notices what has been d. ACHIEVEMENT, 4
so little d. ACTION, 12
the dread of doing what has been d. before ORIGINALITY, 7
The way to get things d. is not to mind who gets the credit SELFLESSNESS, 1
thy worldly task hast d. MORTALITY, 16
What's d. cannot be undone REGRET, 3
What you do not want d. to yourself EXAMPLE, 4
Dong The D. with a luminous Nose NONSENSE, 17
Don Juan *D.* when anger is subsiding LITERATURE, 13
Don Juans woman-worshipping D. MEN, 9
donkeys lions led by d. OFFICERS, 8
Don Miguel All right, my lord creator, D. DEATH, 69
Donne D.'s Body only, lyes below POETS, 13
D....sublimation of subtlety POETS, 31
D.'s verses...pass all understanding POETS, 42
Don Quixote the only absolutely original creation...is D. FICTION, 4
dons If the D. sight Devon PATRIOTISM, 21
It is the little d. I complain about CRITICS, 15
donsmanship D....the art of criticizing INATTENTION, 3
don't-knows One day the d. will get in GOVERNMENT, 20
Doodle Yankee D. came to town AMERICA, 3; NURSERY RHYMES, 69
doom bears it out even to the edge of d. LOVE, 124
purpose of God and the d. assigned DESTINY, 23
regardless of their d. IGNORANCE, 7
slow, sure d. falls pitiless and dark HUMAN CONDITION, 15
door A d. is what a dog is...on the wrong side of DOGS, 10
sweetest thing that ever grew /Beside a human d. ADMIRATION, 18
When one d. shuts OPTIMISM, 10
world will make a beaten path to his d. FAME, 8
Youth will come...beat on my d. YOUTH, 10
doors the d. of perception were cleansed PERCEPTION, 1
doping struggle against d. SPORT AND GAMES, 16
Dorchester All terrorists...end up with drinks at the D. POLITICS, 24
dosed d. her children with every specific DRUGS, 5
dots those damned d. MATHEMATICS, 2
double down the grassgreen gooseberried d. bed SEX, 57
make that a d. LAST WORDS, 35
double-crossing You dirty d. rat MISQUOTATIONS, 12
double-entendre But the horrible d. INNUENDO, 1
doublethink D. means OPPOSITES, 6
doubt a life of d. diversified by faith DOUBT, 4
all my mind is clouded with a d. AFTERLIFE, 10
Humility is only d. HUMILITY, 2
new Philosophy calls all in d. SCIENCE, 9
No...shadow of d. CERTAINTY, 2
O thou of little faith, wherefore didst thou d. DOUBT, 2
these dogmas or goals are in d. FANATICISM, 3
Through the night of d. and sorrow ENDURANCE, 5
When a man is in d. about...his writing POSTERITY, 4
When in d., win the trick SPORT AND GAMES, 9
Doubting castle called D. Castle DESPAIR, 3
doubts end in d. CERTAINTY, 1; DOUBT, 1
His d. are better than...certainties DOUBT, 5
douche the rattling of a thousand d. bags CHILDREN, 35
dove No visit to D. Cottage, Grasmere HUMOUR, 35
the wings of a d. SOLITUDE, 4
Dover It is burning a farthing candle at D. CRITICISM, 19
Dowel D., Dobet and Dobest GOOD, 10
dower forfeited their ancient English d. DECLINE, 15
down for coming d. let me shift for myself EXECUTION, 18
He that is d. PRIDE, 2
I started at the top and worked my way d. DECLINE, 13
put it d. a we SPELLING, 1
Yes, and they went d. very well too WAR, 126
downcast causes many people to feel a little d. DEATH, 86
downhearted Are we d.? No OPTIMISM, 12
dozen a d. are only a chorus BEAUTY, 18
drain you will leave Oxford by the town d. SPOONERISMS, 5
drainpipe wrong end of a municipal d. POLITICIANS, 62
drains to distinguish between the Deity and the D. GOD, 47
Drake D. he's in his hammock WAR, 77
drama A good d. critic is CRITICS, 21
D. is the back-stairs THEATRE, 4
D. never changed anybody's mind THEATRE, 11
dramatist Sherard Blaw, the d. who had discovered himself WRITERS, 80
draught O, for a d. of vintage ALCOHOL, 36
draw I d. what I feel in my body ART, 9
drawbacks everything has its d. FAMILY, 17
One of the d. of Fame FAME, 13
drawing the Suez Canal was flowing through my d. room POLITICS, 23
dread The d. of beatings EDUCATION, 7
the d. of doing what has been done before ORIGINALITY, 7
dreadful d. is the check IMPRISONMENT, 2
Other people are quite d. MISANTHROPY, 4
Portions and parcels of the d. Past TIME, 37
some have called thee /Mighty and d. DEATH, 44
dreadnoughts Duke costs as much...as two D. ARISTOCRACY, 9
dream All men d.: but not equally DREAMS, 11
A sight to d. of DESIRE, 5
awakened from the d. of life LIFE AND DEATH, 13
Awoke one night from a deep d. of peace DREAMS, 12
behold it was a d. DREAMS, 3
d. of perfect bliss DREAMS, 2
For life is but a d. LIFE, 52
God pity a one-d. man DREAMS, 8
God will cease to d. you DEATH, 69
Happiness is no vague d. HAPPINESS, 21
hope is...the d. of those that wake HOPE, 9
I d. when I am awake REALITY, 2
I have a d. EQUALITY, 15
The young men's vision, and the old men's d. DREAMS, 5
To sleep, perchance to d. SUICIDE, 12
warned of God in a d. CHRISTMAS, 10

Where is it now, the glory and the d. METAPHYSICS, 5
you d. you are crossing the Channel BOATS, 6
dreamer The poet and the d. are distinct OPPOSITES, 3
dreamers the d. of the day are dangerous men DREAMS, 11
dreamin' d.…o' Plymouth Hoe WAR, 77
dreaming after-dinner's sleep, d. on both AGE, 53
a man d. I was a butterfly DREAMS, 4
City with her d. spires OXFORD, 2
dreams doubtful d. of d. PEACE, 15
do we not live in d. DREAMS, 14
dream our d. away DREAMS, 7
D. and predictions DREAMS, 1
Fanatics have their d. FANATICISM, 2
For one person who d. of making fifty thousand pounds LAZINESS, 3
I, being poor, have only my d. POVERTY, 34
In d. begins responsibility RESPONSIBILITY, 17
show life…as we see it in our d. WRITING, 5
spread my d. under your feet DREAMS, 15
Than this world d. of PRAYER, 17
the city of perspiring d. CAMBRIDGE, 5
We are such stuff /As d. are made on MORTALITY, 17
what d. may come SUICIDE, 12
dreamt d. of in your philosophy SUPERNATURAL, 13
I d. that I was making a speech SPEECHES, 4
dreary d. intercourse of daily life OPTIMISM, 29
Dying is a very dull, d. affair DEATH, 85
If your morals make you d. MORALITY, 21
Once upon a midnight d. SUPERNATURAL, 12
dress I have no d. except the one I wear PRACTICALITY, 1
put on a d. of guilt GUILT, 6
sweet disorder in the d. CLOTHES, 7
Those who make their d.…themselves CLOTHES, 6
dress'd D. in a little brief authority MANKIND, 26
dressed All d. up, with nowhere to go FUTILITY, 11
Some fruit for Him that d. me SERVICE, 2
Today I d. to meet my father's eyes SUITABILITY, 3
dresses long d.…cover a multitude of shins CLOTHES, 18
drink A good d. ALCOHOL, 3
A little in d. MARRIAGE, 111
Another little d. ALCOHOL, 58
a rule never to d. by daylight ALCOHOL, 43
A taste for d., combined with gout ALCOHOL, 28
D. and the devil ALCOHOL, 60
D. deep, or taste not the Pierian spring KNOWLEDGE, 30
D.! for you know not whence you came DESTINY, 10
d. may be said to be an equivocator with lechery ALCOHOL, 53
D. to me only with thine eyes LOVE, 75
First you take a d.…then the d. takes you ALCOHOL, 25
I commended mirth…to eat…to d., and to be merry PLEASURE, 4
let us eat and d. MISQUOTATIONS, 7; TRANSIENCE, 7
never to refuse a d. after dark ALCOHOL, 43
no one has yet found a way to d. for a living ALCOHOL, 38
Nor any drop to d. WATER, 2
One reason I don't d. DRUNKENNESS, 6
she would never take a d. ABSTINENCE, 11
soft d. at a party ABSTINENCE, 2
that he has taken to d. ALCOHOL, 61
There are five reasons we should d. ALCOHOL, 8
we d. too much tea DRINKS, 8
willing to taste any d. once DRINKS, 3
woe unto them that…follow strong d. ALCOHOL, 12
you shall d. twice while I d. once DRUNKENNESS, 20
drinka D. a pinta milka day ADVERTISING, 8
drinkers no verse can give pleasure…that is written by d. of water WATER, 6
drinking D.…and making love MANKIND, 4
d. deep of that divinest anguish SUFFERING, 5
I have been d. it for sixty-five years DRINKS, 9
let me die d. in an inn ALCOHOL, 41
no d. after death ALCOHOL, 26
resolve to give up smoking, d. and loving ABSTINENCE, 5
smoking cigars and…d. of alcohol ALCOHOL, 21; SMOKING, 4
there's nothing like d. ALCOHOL, 23
'Tis not the d.…but the excess EXCESS, 7
two reasons for d. THIRST, 1
Work is the curse of the d. classes WORK, 26
drinks He who d. a little too much ALCOHOL, 4
dripping Constant d. hollows out a stone PERSISTENCE, 10
electricity was d. invisibly SCIENCE, 41
driver in the d.'s seat POWER, 6
driving busy d. cabs and cutting hair GOVERNMENT, 7
I would spend my life in d. briskly PLEASURE, 16
drizzle the blasted English d. DISCONTENT, 6
droghte d. of Marche MONTHS, 7
dromedary Donne, whose muse on d. trots POETS, 28
droop The day begins to d. DAY, 2
drop Nor any d. to drink WATER, 2
there are people whom one should like very well to d. HURT, 2
dropping peace comes d. slow PEACE, 17
dropsies there were people who died of d. ALCOHOL, 33
dropt Mrs Montagu has d. me HURT, 2
drown d. in their own blood MIDDLE EAST, 8
I'll d. my book RENUNCIATION, 4
what pain it was to d. DROWNING, 2
drowning A d. man HOPE, 1
Being an old maid is like death by d. MARRIAGE, 55
If I rescued a child from d. POLITICIANS, 36; JOURNALISM, 7
not waving but d. DROWNING, 3
drudge a harmless d. LEXICOGRAPHY, 6
drudgery Learn to innure yourself to d. in science EDUCATION, 42
drug A miracle d. is MEDICINE, 3
d. is that substance which DRUGS, 1
Television – the d. of the nation TELEVISION AND RADIO, 7
Words are…the most powerful d. WORDS, 13
drugging Imperative d.…no longer…the chief function of the doctor DRUGS, 12
drugs Half the modern d. could well be thrown out the window DRUGS, 7
if you're on d. then you're in trouble DRUGS, 3
drum brave Music of a *distant* D. MONEY, 22
Not a d. was heard FUNERALS, 10
Take my d. to England PATRIOTISM, 21
drums the beating of war d. WAR, 58
drunk If, d. with sight of power, we loose BOASTS, 4
man…must get d. DRUNKENNESS, 10
My mother, d. or sober PATRIOTISM, 5
not so think as you d. DRUNKENNESS, 19
someone who has…d.…a…barrel EXPERIENCE, 10
this meeting is d. DRUNKENNESS, 11
drunkards There are more old d. DRUNKENNESS, 1
drunken Better sleep with a sober cannibal than a d. Christian DRUNKENNESS, 16
He uses statistics as a d. man uses lamp-posts STATISTICS, 4
What shall we do with the d. sailor DRUNKENNESS, 4
drunkenness A branch of the sin of d. DRUNKENNESS, 14
If…'feeling good' could decide, d. would be…supremely valid DRUNKENNESS, 13
dry old man in a d. month AGE, 23
out of these wet clothes and into a d. Martini ALCOHOL, 67
Dublin D., though…much worse than London PLACES, 7
In D.'s fair city, where the girls are so pretty BUSINESS, 1
duckling The Ugly D. BOOK, SONG, AND PLAY TITLES, 3
ducks you go about the country stealing d. THEFT, 3
your precious 'lame d.' WEAKNESS, 3
dug If people d. up the remains of this civilization ARTISTS, 16
duke D. costs as much…as two Dreadnoughts ARISTOCRACY, 9
naked D. of Windlestraw NAKEDNESS, 2
dulce *D. et decorum est* PATRIOTISM, 15
dull a doctrine so illogical and so d. MARXISM, 2
a very d. Play MARRIAGE, 39
Heaven…is a place so inane, so d. HEAVEN, 12
He was d. in a new way POETS, 43
if he wasn't as d. as ditch water STUPIDITY, 2
Music-hall songs provide the d. with wit STUPIDITY, 9
not only d. in himself STUPIDITY, 3
The prospect of a lot /Of d. MPs POLITICIANS, 11
To make dictionaries is d. work LEXICOGRAPHY, 5
dullard The d.'s envy of brilliant men GREATNESS, 2
dumplings I am the emperor, and I want d. PETULANCE, 3
Dunblane D. Primary School EVIL, 17; WEAPONS, 8
dunces the d. are all in confederacy against him GENIUS, 9
dupe The d. of friendship, and the fool of love BITTERNESS, 1
dusk In the d., with a light behind her AGE, 30
slow d. a drawing-down of blinds WAR, 81
dusky Midnight brought on the d. hour DAY, 12
dust A heap of d. alone remains EQUALITY, 29
As chimney-sweepers, come to d. MORTALITY, 16
d. shalt thou eat SEXES, 2

fear in a handful of d. FEAR, 9
fly...said, what a d. do I raise CONCEIT, 3
pride that licks the d. SERVILITY, 5
raised a d. COMPLAINTS, 1
The d. and silence of the upper shelf NEGLECT, 3
the d. beneath thy chariot wheel HUMILITY, 5
The d. of great persons' graves EQUALITY, 26
this quintessence of d. MANKIND, 27
Dutch my dear old D. LOVE, 37
duties he devotes to the neglect of his d. NEGLECT, 4
Property has its d. CAPITALISM, 2
duty absolved from all d. to his country MARRIAGE, 92
a stupid man...always declares that it is his d. DUTY, 4
A thing of d. is a boy for ever POLICE, 4; PUNS, 15
Do your d. and leave the rest to the Gods DUTY, 2
d. of an opposition OPPOSITION, 2
England expects every man will do his d. DUTY, 3
It is my d. to warn you that it will be used against you JUSTICE, 6
more than a moral d. to speak one's mind FRANKNESS, 4
Nor law, nor d. bade me fight FLYING, 4
Patriotism...is a revolutionary d. PATRIOTISM, 30
right of all...d. of some SEPARATION, 4
the d. of being happy HAPPINESS, 27
this is the whole d. of man GOD, 9
What's a man's first d. SINCERITY, 5
when constabulary d.'s to be done POLICE, 1
dwarfs A number of anxious d. POLITICIANS, 22
dwell Let other pens d. on guilt and misery OPTIMISM, 14
dwelt She d. among the untrodden ways LONELINESS, 9
dyin' Young man, I think you're d.! LOVE, 13
dying alike are the groans of love to...d. LOVE AND DEATH, 4
All men are afraid of d. DEATH, 100
Don't cheer, boys; the poor devils are d. WAR, 86
D. for an idea MARTYRDOM, 2
D. is a very dull, dreary affair DEATH, 85
folly to shrink in fear, if this is d. DEATH, 92
For a priest to turn a man when he lies a-d. PERSUASION, 3
good for a writer to think he's d. WRITERS, 26
He had been, he said, a most unconscionable time d. DEATH, 38
Here am I, d. DEATH, 95
I cannot forgive my friends for d. DEATH, 116
If this is d. LAST WORDS, 67
is it my birthday or am I d. LAST WORDS, 5
it is not death, but d., which is terrible DEATH, 49
'Tis not the d. for a faith FAITH, 18
Truth sits upon the lips of d. men TRUTH, 9
victim of the whole d. industry DEATH, 78
we survive amongst the dead and the d. OLD AGE, 43
dyke February, fill the d. MONTHS, 11
dykes our d....are ten feet deep BOASTS, 6
dynamic class people as static and d. SEXES, 29
play is a d. thing NOVELS, 16; PLAYS, 13
dyspepsia when they are troubled with d. RELIGION, 35

E

ear a pistol let off at the e. PUNS, 10
jest's prosperity lies in the e. HUMOUR, 28
more is meant than meets the e. INNUENDO, 3
the e. begins to hear IMPRISONMENT, 2
Earl As far as the 14th E. is concerned TITLES, 1
ground to a halt with a 14th E. TITLES, 12
early A useless life is an e. death PURPOSE, 3
E. to bed BED, 1
E. to rise and early to bed BED, 9
good die e. GOOD AND EVIL, 3
nobody who does not rise e. BED, 4
The e. bird ANTICIPATION, 3
earn this is the week I e. my salary MERIT, 5
earned Old age...gives us what we have e. OLD AGE, 8
earning learning, e. and yearning LIFE, 38
ears A hungry stomach has no e. HUNGER, 8
can you waggle your e. BOOKS, 5
device to keep the e. from grating MIND, 2
Romans, countrymen, lend me your e. EVIL, 16
earth a covenant between me and the e. PROMISES, 2
But did thee feel the e. move SEX, 24
Cool'd...in the deep-delved e. ALCOHOL, 36
E. fills her lap with pleasures NATURE, 19
E. has not anything to show more fair LONDON, 14
E. is just too small and fragile a basket SPACE, 4
from whose face the e. and the heaven fled JUDGMENT, 4
God called the dry land E. CREATION, 3
God created...the e. CREATION, 2
heaven and e. shall pass away TRANSIENCE, 8
heav'n on e. HEAVEN, 6
hell upon e....in a melancholy man's heart MELANCHOLY, 3
I will move the e. TECHNOLOGY, 1
lards the lean e. as he walks OBESITY, 10
mine were princes of the e. JEWS, 2
more things in heaven and e. SUPERNATURAL, 13
on this e. to read *Ulysses* LEISURE, 2
passenger on the spaceship, E. SPACE, 3
so much of e....of heaven IMPETUOSITY, 4
the cool flowery lap of e. POETS, 16
The e. does not argue HUMAN NATURE, 25
the e. of England is in my two hands VICTORY, 20
the e. where cares abound BIRDS, 11
The meek do not inherit the e. HUMILITY, 6
This e. of majesty ENGLAND, 36
When e. was nigher heaven PAST, 3
ease done with so much e. CHARACTER, 7
Joys in another's loss of e. LOVE, 28
No warmth, no cheerfulness, no healthful e. MONTHS, 10
Prodigal of E. WORLD-WEARINESS, 1
True e. in writing comes from art WRITING, 26
easeful half in love with e. Death DEATH, 70
easier E. said than done ACTION, 3
it is much e. to say what it is not POETRY, 21
east E. is E., and West is West OPPOSITES, 4
E., west HOME, 1
hold the gorgeous e. in fee VENICE, 4
Now we can look the E. End in the face WORLD WAR II, 17
the e. wind made flesh AMERICANS, 2
to have the E. come to the Atlantic WORLD WAR II, 19
to prevent us from going into the E. WORLD WAR II, 19
wise men from the e. CHRISTMAS, 9
easy E. come MONEY, 1
It is e. to bear MISFORTUNE, 1
It is e. to be wise WISDOM, 1
It's either e. or impossible PAINTING, 4
eat Don't e. too many almonds FOOD, 15
E. as much as you like OBESITY, 9
e. moderately, having an ordinary mixed diet HEALTH AND HEALTHY LIVING, 9
E. to live FOOD, 4
e. to live, not live to e. FOOD, 41
great ones e. up the little ones RUTHLESSNESS, 5
I commended mirth...to e....to drink, and to be merry PLEASURE, 4
I could e. one of Bellamy's veal pies LAST WORDS, 52; FOOD, 44
if any would not work, neither should he e. WORK, 4
Let them e. the lie NONCOMMITMENT, 2
let us e. and drink MISQUOTATIONS, 7; TRANSIENCE, 7
So I did sit and e. LOVE, 68
Some hae meat, and canna e. FOOD, 11
To e. well in England FOOD, 39
eaten daring...to explain...that cows can be e. RELIGION, 26
e. me out of house and home GREED, 11
eating Appetite comes with e. DESIRE, 13
E. people is wrong CANNIBALISM, 1; BOOK, SONG, AND PLAY TITLES, 4
sign something is e. us GREED, 6
someone e. out of your hand POWER, 9
eats e., sleeps and watches the television WOMAN'S ROLE, 2
on friendly terms with the victims...he e. HYPOCRISY, 6
ecclesiastic E. tyranny's the worst CHURCH, 5
ecclesiastical lay interest in e. matters...often a prelude to insanity RELIGION, 65
echo The sound must seem an e. to the sense WRITING, 26
economic bottom of the e. pyramid POVERTY, 27
economics E. is a subject that ECONOMICS, 12
prepared to accept the e. of a housewife ECONOMICS, 6
economist Give me a one-handed e. ECONOMICS, 21
Jesus was...a first-rate political e. CHRISTIANITY, 38
Practical men...slaves of some defunct e. INFLUENCE, 6
economists All races have...e., with the exception of the Irish IRISH, 5
If all e. were laid end to end ECONOMICS, 20

economy E. is going without something you do want THRIFT, 8
Everybody is always in favour of general e. THRIFT, 7
eczema style...often hides e. STYLE, 2
Eden a garden eastward in E. GARDENS, 3
futile to attempt a picnic in E. INNOCENCE, 4
Sir Anthony E. BORES, 4
the garden of E. TREES, 1; KNOWLEDGE, 7
This other E., demi-paradise ENGLAND, 36
edge his keener eye /The axe's e. did try EXECUTION, 16
We stand today on the e. of a new frontier BEGINNING, 12
Edison E....a supreme 'do-it-yourself' man SCIENTISTS, 8
editor An e....separates the wheat from the chaff EDITORS, 3
editorial the age of the e. chair PSYCHIATRY, 8
Edmonton If wife should dine at E. MARRIAGE, 42
Unto the Bell at E. MARRIAGE, 43
Edna Aunt E. is universal AUDIENCES, 4
educate e. a woman you e. a family EDUCATION, 33
e. with the head instead of with the hand EDUCATION, 29
got to e. him first EDUCATION, 47
'tis the schoolboys that e. my son EDUCATION, 15
education a liberal e. at the Colleges of Unreason REASON, 1
E....has produced a vast population able to read READING, 16
e. is a leading out of what is...in the pupil's soul EDUCATION, 55
E. is...the soul of a society EDUCATION, 11
E. is what survives EDUCATION, 54
E. made us what we are EDUCATION, 21
fortunate in escaping regular e. WRITERS, 14
His English e....preserved his intellect...at the stage of boyhood EDUCATION, 10
if e. is...a mere transmission of knowledge EDUCATION, 37
make your children *capable of honesty* is the beginning of e. HONESTY, 7
one of the ultimate advantages of an e. EDUCATION, 53
part of English middle-class e. is devoted to the training of servants EDUCATION, 65
Soap and e. are not as sudden as a massacre, but they are more deadly EDUCATION, 56
'Tis e. forms the common mind EDUCATION, 44
Travel...is a part of e. TRAVEL, 2
with e. and whisky the price it is CHARACTER, 26
woman of e. WOMEN, 84
educations feeble minds with classical e. EDUCATION, 23
Edwardian plants left over from the E. Wilderness CHANGE, 17
Edwardians E....were nomadic TRAVEL, 26
eena E., meena, mina, mo NURSERY RHYMES, 11
effect little e. after much labour RESULTS, 2
efficient be e. if you're going to be lazy LAZINESS, 1
effort What is written without e. WRITING, 14
efforts One is happy as a result of one's own e. HAPPINESS, 21
egalitarianism The majestic e. of the law EQUALITY, 8
égalité *Liberté! É! Fraternité* HUMAN RIGHTS, 2
egg a broody hen sitting on a china e. BUREAUCRACY, 6
Go to work on an e. ADVERTISING, 9
hand that lays the golden e. MIXED METAPHORS, 2
the learned roast an e. FOOD, 45
The vulgar boil...an e. FOOD, 45
throw an e. into an electric fan AMBITION, 9
eggs Don't put all your e. in one basket CAUTION, 2
I've met a lot of hardboiled e. CHARACTER, 27
putting all my e. in one bastard ABORTION, 2
to cook himself a couple of e. EGOTISM, 4
ways to dress e. FRANCE, 11
eggyellow his nicotine e. weeping walrus Victorian moustache APPEARANCE, 37
egotism dilemmas of conscience and e. POWER, 22
egotist *E.*, n. ...more interested in himself EGOTISM, 3
Egypt Remember you're in E. PRONUNCIATION, 2
We are not at war with E. MIDDLE EAST, 7
Egyptians the E. worshipped an insect POLITICIANS, 51
eight E. maids a-milking NURSERY RHYMES, 55
Pieces of e. MONEY, 47
eighteen From birth to age e., a girl needs good parents AGE, 63
I knew almost as much at e. as I do now KNOWLEDGE, 25
speaks e. languages. And she can't say 'No' PROMISCUITY, 5
Ein And no one can understand E. HUMOUR, 31
There's Gert and there's Epp and there's E. HUMOUR, 31
Einstein E. – the greatest Jew since Jesus SCIENTISTS, 11
Let E. be SCIENTISTS, 15
elations e. and apprehensions of growth AGE, 37
elderly see it as an e. lady CHURCH, 4
When a distinguished but e. scientist states SCIENCE, 6
elders miss not the discourse of the e. LEARNING, 2
elected audacity of e. persons REVOLUTION, 12
election charity at e. time OPPRESSION, 5
I am certain that we will win the e. SELF-CONFIDENCE, 6
Today in Britain, a fascist has won an e. FASCISM, 4
electric e. light will close with it PROPHECY, 15
the e. display of God the Father LIFE, 39
electrical E. force...causes motion SCIENCE, 10
electricity e. was dripping invisibly SCIENCE, 41
electrification Communism is Soviet power plus the e. COMMUNISM, 4
electronic They are e. lice POP MUSIC, 6
elegant English women are e. ENGLISH, 25
element One God, one law, one e. DESTINY, 22
elementary 'E.,' said he MISQUOTATIONS, 15; SIMPLICITY, 1
elements I tax not you, you e., with unkindness WEATHER, 20
something that was before the e. NOBILITY, 1
elephant I shot an e. in my pajamas HUMOUR, 43
they couldn't hit an e. LAST WORDS, 63
elevate E. them guns a little lower WAR, 51
eleven E. ladies dancing NURSERY RHYMES, 55
eliminate I e. my individualism CHINA, 5
eloquence Talking and e. are not the same SPEECH, 11
else Lord High Everything E. TITLES, 4
Suppose it had been someone e. who found you like this ADULTERY, 8
elusive One's prime is e. AGE, 58
Elysian dead, but in the E. fields HOUSES OF PARLIAMENT, 8
emancipated e. from...time and space IMAGINATION, 2
embalmer A triumph of the e.'s art INSULTS, 40
soft e. of the still midnight SLEEP, 12
embarras *l'e. des richesses* EXCESS, 1
embarrassment God could cause us considerable e. DISCOVERY, 4
embittered He was an e. atheist ATHEISM, 8
embody I, my lords, e. the Law LAW, 12
embrace I e. the purpose of God DESTINY, 23
none, I think, do there e. DEATH, 82
whether I e. your lordship's principles or your mistress REPARTEE, 5
emotion Poetry is not a turning loose of e. POETRY, 14
Sorrow is tranquillity remembered in e. SORROW, 14
the degree of my aesthetic e. CRITICS, 1
emotional a well-bred sort of e. anarchy CLASSIFICATION, 2
emotions a sort of metaphysical brothel for e. SENTIMENTALITY, 3
big e. come from big words STYLE, 5
noble grounds for the noble e. POETRY, 39
She ran...e. from A to B CRITICISM, 37
emperor An e. ought at least to die on his feet LAST WORDS, 72
I am the e., and I want dumplings PETULANCE, 3
the E. has nothing on INNOCENCE, 3
emperors e. can't do it all by themselves SUPPORT, 2
empire An e. founded by war WAR, 70
Great Britain has lost an E. BRITAIN, 1
How is the E. LAST WORDS, 31; BRITISH EMPIRE, 4
the downfall of the British E. BRITISH EMPIRE, 1
the Holy Roman Empire was neither holy, nor Roman, nor an e. NATIONS, 3
to the French the e. of the land EUROPE, 15
empires The day of E. has come NATIONS, 1
employed innocently e. than in getting money MONEY, 28
The rise in the...e. is governed by Parkinson's Law WORK, 14
employee capitalist society has converted Eros into an e. COMMERCIALISM, 3
employees e. who have not yet reached...incompetence INCOMPETENCE, 4
employer ideal of the e....production without employees INDUSTRIAL RELATIONS, 3
employers e....only like ballots so long as you lose them STRIKES, 3
employment to seek...gainful e. GOVERNMENT, 1
empty Bring on the e. horses LANGUAGE, 11
E. vessels FOOLISHNESS, 5
You can't think rationally on an e. stomach THINKING, 6
enchantment distance lends e. to the view PERSPECTIVE, 1
enclose A vacuum can only exist...by the things which e. it SCIENCE, 16
enclosed Check e. MONEY, 38

encourage the right to be consulted...to e. MONARCHY, 2
to e. the others EXAMPLE, 9
encourager *pour e. les autres* EXAMPLE, 9
encyclopaedia a whole E. behind SCIENCE, 26
end a beginning, a muddle, and an e. NOVELS, 8
an e. to the beginnings of all wars WAR, 94
a whole is that which has a beginning, a middle, and an e. PLAYS, 1
beginning of the e. DEFEAT, 8
God be at my e., /And at my departing GOD, 1
I like a film to have a beginning, a middle and an e. CINEMA, 4
I move softly towards the e. DEATH, 67
Keep right on to the e. of the road PERSISTENCE, 8
looks like the e. of the world ENVIRONMENT, 4
of making many books there is no e. BOOKS, 8
our minutes hasten to their e. TIME, 34
the e. is not yet WAR, 9
The *e.* is to build well ARCHITECTURE, 15
the e. of the beginning WORLD WAR II, 13
Walt Whitman who laid e. to e. POETS, 50
we're forbidden to know – what e. the gods have in store DESTINY, 13
world without e. ETERNITY, 2
Yes, to the very e. ENDURANCE, 15
endeavour To e. to forget anyone MEMORY, 8
ended My life with girls has e. SEX, 25
The day Thou gavest, Lord, is e. DAY, 4
ending The quickest way of e. a war WAR, 80
endless History is an e. repetition HISTORY, 11
ends divinity that shapes our e. DESTINY, 19
my family begins...yours e. with you ANCESTRY, 3
endurance patient e. is godlike ENDURANCE, 9
endure For his mercies ay e. GOD, 37
It is flattering some men to e. them TOLERANCE, 3
Jazz will e. POP MUSIC, 18
Youth's a stuff will not e. PRESENT, 13
endured Job e. everything – until his friends came ENDURANCE, 8
endures When a man is in love he e. more LOVE, 92
endureth blessed is the man that e. temptation TEMPTATION, 4
enemies Better a thousand e. ENEMIES, 1
designing mausoleums for his e. HATE, 6
do not have to forgive my e. LAST WORDS, 46; RUTHLESSNESS, 4
Even a paranoid can have e. ENEMIES, 4
love your e. ENEMIES, 3
Mountains interposed /Make e. of nations MOUNTAINS, 1
Peace is made with yesterday's e. MIDDLE EAST, 12
The e. of Freedom OPPRESSION, 4
we have been mortal e. ever since ENEMIES, 5
enemy Every man is his own worst e. SELF, 1
hasn't an e. in the world POPULARITY, 9
I cannot get any sense of an e. WORLD WAR I, 14
It takes your e. and your friend..., to hurt you HURT, 3
no more sombre e. of good art BABIES, 1
Poverty is a great e. to human happiness POVERTY, 20
We have met the e., and they are ours VICTORY, 13
we must be just to our e. PUBLISHING, 5
enemy-friends what we call the 'e.' MIDDLE EAST, 1
energies quarrel...e. displayed in it are fine ARGUMENTS, 11
energy dissipation of e. begin SPORT AND GAMES, 13
E. is Eternal Delight EFFORT, 2
enfants *Allons, e., de la patrie* FRANCE, 10
Les e. terribles YOUTH, 8
engaged one of the nicest girls I was ever e. to MARRIAGE, 136
engine indefatigable and unsavoury e. of pollution DOGS, 12
England A grain, which in E. is generally given to horses SCOTLAND, 3
Be E. what she will PATRIOTISM, 6
but the King of E. cannot enter PRIVACY, 4
Christianity is part of the Common Law of E. CHRISTIANITY, 26
Common Law of E. LAW, 16
Damn you, E.. You're rotting ENGLAND, 32
E. elects a Labour Government POLITICS, 63
E. expects every man will do his duty DUTY, 3
E. is a nation of shopkeepers ENGLISH, 28
E. is a paradise for women NATIONALITY, 3
E. is the mother of parliaments ENGLAND, 6
E. is the paradise of women ENGLAND, 17
E. is the paradise of individuality ENGLAND, 35
E. mourns for her dead across the sea MOURNING, 3
E.'s green and pleasant land ENGLAND, 5
E.'s pleasant pastures ENGLAND, 5
E....the envy of less happy lands ENGLAND, 14
E....the workshop of the world ENGLAND, 16
E.!.../What love I bore to thee HOMESICKNESS, 9
E. will have her neck wrung like a chicken WORLD WAR II, 30
E., with all thy faults PATRIOTISM, 7
For E. the one land ENGLAND, 7
For God's sake, madam, don't say that in E. for...they will surely tax it TAXATION, 12
go back to thy stately homes of E. PARTING, 7
hardly be a town in the South of E. ENGLAND, 31
he bores for E. BORES, 4
in E. people have good table manners MANNERS, 4
In E., pop art and fine art ART, 16
In E. there is only silence or scandal ENGLAND, 27
It was twenty-one years ago that E. and I ENGLAND, 29
little ships of E. brought the Army home BOATS, 8; WORLD WAR II, 20
Living in E....must be like being married to a stupid...wife ENGLAND, 18
no man in E. will take away my life ARROGANCE, 2
occurred nowhere but in E. ENGLAND, 11
Oh, to be in E. ENGLAND, 8
Old E. is lost BRITAIN, 10
rather hew wood than be...King of E. MONARCHY, 6
should they know of E. who only E. know ENGLAND, 22
Speak for E. PATRIOTISM, 2
Stately Homes of E. ARISTOCRACY, 6; STATELY HOMES, 2
that is forever E. WAR, 18
The best thing I know between France and E. FRANCE, 8
the earth of E. is in my two hands VICTORY, 20
the Kings of E., Diamonds, Hearts, Spades and Clubs MONARCHY, 11
The Law of E. is a very strange one LAW, 8
The national sport of E. ENGLISH, 35
the old savage E., whose last blood flows still ENGLAND, 23
There'll always be an E. ENGLAND, 33
The roast beef of E. FOOD, 23
The stately homes of E. STATELY HOMES, 4
this generation...found E. a land of beauty ECOLOGY, 4
this realm, this E. ENGLAND, 36
we are the people of E. ENGLISH, 12
When people say E. ENGLAND, 28
When you think about the defence of E. ENGLAND, 3
English Dr Johnson's morality was as E....as a beefsteak ENGLAND, 20
E. people...are surely the *nicest* ENGLISH, 21
E. soldiers fight like lions OFFICERS, 8
E....the language of an imaginative race LANGUAGE, 3
E. women are elegant ENGLISH, 25
especially if he went among the E. BRITISH, 1
exterminate...the treacherous E. WAR, 132
forfeited their ancient E. dower DECLINE, 15
I do love cricket – it's so very E. CRICKET, 2; FOOTBALL, 2
If the E. language had been properly organized LANGUAGE, 18
If you get the E. people into the way of making kings ROYALTY, 24
one of the few E. novels for grown up people CRITICISM, 56
Opera in E. OPERA, 5
our E. nation, if they have a good thing, to make it too common ENGLAND, 37
part of E. middle-class education is devoted to the training of servants EDUCATION, 65
stones kissed by the E. dead WAR, 82
The attitude of the E....toward E. history ENGLISH, 16
The baby doesn't understand E. LANGUAGE, 17
The E....are rather a foul-mouthed nation ENGLISH, 18
the E. are...the least a nation of pure philosophers ENGLISH, 5
the E. have hot-water bottles ENGLISH, 24
The E. have no respect for their language ENGLISH, 32
The E. instinctively admire ENGLISH, 4
The E. may not like music MUSIC, 5
the E. seem...to have conquered and peopled half the world BRITISH EMPIRE, 8
The E. take their pleasures ENGLAND, 38
The E. want *inferiors* PRIDE, 11
This is the sort of E. GRAMMAR, 4
To Americans E. manners are...frightening MANNERS, 3
to the E. that of the sea EUROPE, 15

typically E. characteristic ENGLISH, 3; UNITY, 4
Englishman Am I not punished enough in not being born an E. NATIONALITY, 9
An E.…forms an orderly queue of one ENGLISH, 23
an E.'s heaven-born privilege of doing as he likes PUBLIC, 2
An E.'s way of speaking CLASS, 19
An E.'s word ENGLISH, 2
an…young E. of our upper class ARISTOCRACY, 1
E.…is afraid to feel EDUCATION, 17
E. never enjoys himself except for a noble purpose ENGLISH, 19
He was born an E. NATIONALITY, 1
If I were an American, as I am an E. PATRIOTISM, 24
in spite of all temptations…He remains an E. NATIONALITY, 5
it takes a great deal to produce ennui in an E. ENGLISH, 15
never find an E. among the underdogs ENGLAND, 41
Remember that you are an E. ENGLISH, 31
some other E. despise him ENGLISH, 32
tale…which would have stirred…E. ENDURANCE, 16
To be an E. ENGLISH, 29
to behold the E. at his *best* ENGLISH, 13
You may be the most liberal Liberal E. CLASS, 17
Englishmen to create Frenchmen in the image of E. NATIONALITY, 4
to see the absurd nature of E. ENGLISH, 30
When two E. meet, their first talk is of the weather ENGLISH, 20; WEATHER, 15
Englishwoman This E. is so refined WOMEN, 72
enigma a riddle wrapped in a mystery inside an e. RUSSIA, 3
enjoy Certainly, there is nothing else here to e. PARTIES, 6
He knew everything about literature except how to e. it LITERATURE, 5
Since God has given us the papacy…e. it CATHOLICISM, 8
ennui it takes a great deal to produce e. in an Englishman ENGLISH, 15
enough It comes soon e. FUTURE, 6
patriotism is not e. LAST WORDS, 14
entente *La cordiale e.* DIPLOMACY, 15
enter but the King of England cannot e. PRIVACY, 4
enterprises e. that require new clothes THRIFT, 11
entertained Television…permits you to be e. in your living room TELEVISION AND RADIO, 3
entertainment what cats most appreciate…is…e. value CATS, 3
enthusiasm Nothing great was ever achieved without e. ENTHUSIASM, 4
Nothing is so contagious as e. ENTHUSIASM, 3
We were as nearly bored as e. would permit CRITICISM, 17
enthusiastic Latins are tenderly e. PLACES, 4
enthusiasts so few e. can be trusted ENTHUSIASM, 2
entities E. should not be multiplied SIMPLICITY, 6
entrance all men have one e. into life BIRTH, 2
envied Better be e. ENVY, 1
There are two things for which animals are…e. ANIMALS, 19
environment President Robbins was so well adjusted to his e. ADAPTABILITY, 3
environmental Population growth…e. damage CONSERVATION, 3
envy 2 percent moral, 48 percent indignation and 50 percent e. MORALITY, 20
e. is a kind of praise ENVY, 6
prisoners of addiction and…prisoners of e. MATERIALISM, 10
The dullard's e. of brilliant men GREATNESS, 2
the upbringing a nun would e. INNOCENCE, 8
Epicurus one of E.' herd of pigs PRESENT, 10
epidemic feel snubbed if an e. overlooks them DISEASE, 22
going to go crazy, living this e. every minute DISEASE, 24
living this e. every minute AIDS, 6
epidemics E. have often been more influential DISEASE, 15
epigrams long despotism tempered by e. FRANCE, 2
epilogue good play needs no e. PLAYS, 10
Epipsychidion You understand *E.* best when you are in love LITERATURE, 13
epitaph 'Can't' will be the e. of the British Empire BRITISH EMPIRE, 5
epitaphs a nice derangement of e. MALAPROPISMS, 8
epithet *Bourgeois*…is an e. CLASS, 16
epitome all Mankind's E. HUMAN NATURE, 9
epoch From today…there begins a new e. in the history of the world BEGINNING, 9
Epp E.'s statues are junk HUMOUR, 31
There's Gert and there's E. and there's Ein HUMOUR, 31
Epstein The E. makes me feel physically sick ARTISTS, 14
equal All animals are e. EQUALITY, 18
all men are created e. EQUALITY, 15; HUMAN RIGHTS, 3
All shall e. be CLASS, 11
Everybody should have an e. chance EQUALITY, 24
Inferiors revolt…that they may be e. REVOLUTION, 1
some animals are more e. than others EQUALITY, 18
That all men are e. is a proposition EQUALITY, 10
When you meet someone better…turn your thoughts to becoming his e. SUPERIORITY, 4
equality E.…is the thing EQUALITY, 19
E. may perhaps be a right, but no…fact EQUALITY, 3
e.…with our superiors EQUALITY, 5
Freedom! E.! Brotherhood HUMAN RIGHTS, 2
pushes for e.…declared "PC" POLITICAL CORRECTNESS, 1
The cry of e. pulls everyone down EQUALITY, 17
equally I hate everyone e. HATE, 3
It comes e. to us all EQUALITY, 26
Pale Death kicks his way e. into the cottages of the poor EQUALITY, 28
That all who are happy, are e. happy HAPPINESS, 12
equanimity an e. bordering on indifference INDIFFERENCE, 3
erect faced the firing squad; e. and motionless EXECUTION, 28
ergo *Cogito, e. sum* THINKING, 3
erogenous The mind can also be an e. zone MIND, 9
Eros capitalist society has converted E. into an employee COMMERCIALISM, 3
Unarm, E. REST, 2
err The Most may e. as grosly PUBLIC, 11
those /Who e. each other must respect LOVE, 98
To e. is human IMPERFECTION, 3
To e. is human, to forgive, divine MISTAKES, 13; FORGIVENESS, 14
errand What thy e. here below PURPOSE, 6
erred We have e., and strayed from thy ways SIN, 8
error A new maxim is often a brilliant e. SAYINGS, 5
show a man that he is in an e. TRUTH, 34
errors E., like Straws, upon the surface flow TRUTH, 24
few e. they have ever avoided PLACES, 3
the e. of those who think they are strong MISTAKES, 3
escape Gluttony is an emotional e. GREED, 6
Let no guilty man e. JUSTICE, 9
escaped e. from a mad and savage master SEX, 54
escaping fortunate in e. regular education WRITERS, 14
esprit English characteristic…*e. de corps* ENGLISH, 3; UNITY, 4
essay an over-ambitious e. by a second-year student CRITICS, 15
essence change is the very e. of life CHANGE, 8
Desire is the very e. of man DESIRE, 16
The poet gives us his e. POETRY AND PROSE, 6
establishment to refer to your friend's country e. as a 'cottage' WORDS, 17
estate a fourth e. of the realm JOURNALISM, 21
e. o' th' world were now undone WORLD-WEARINESS, 8
état *L'é. c'est moi* MONARCHY, 15
etchings I'll bring the e. down HUMOUR, 56
eternal Hope springs e. in the human breast HOPE, 8
The e. *not ourselves* that makes for righteousness RIGHTEOUSNESS, 1
We feel…we are e. IMMORTALITY, 6
eternity All things from e.…come round in a circle HISTORY, 5
Deserts of vast e. AGE, 38
E. by term DEATH, 43
E. in an hour WONDER, 2
E.'s a terrible thought ETERNITY, 4
from e. spinning the thread of your being DESTINY, 2
impress on e. INFLUENCE, 3
I will burn, but…continue our discussion in e. MARTYRDOM, 3
over the Bridge of Sighs into e. DEATH, 74
Tears of e. and sorrow SORROW, 10
without injuring e. TIME, 39
ethereal E. minstrel BIRDS, 11
Ethiopians The E. say that their gods are…black RELIGION, 72
ethnic cleansing undergoing e. BOSNIA AND HERCEGOVINA, 1
Eton the Battle of Waterloo *was* won on the playing-fields of E. WAR, 79
the playing fields of E. EDUCATION, 64
eunuch a kind of moral e. MORALITY, 19
prerogative of the e. RESPONSIBILITY, 14
Eureka *E.* DISCOVERY, 1
Euripides E. portrays them as they are THEATRE, 13
Europe another war in E. BOSNIA AND HERCEGOVINA, 2

Communism continued to haunt E. as a spectre COMMUNISM, 10
E. is a state of mind EUROPE, 9
E. is the unfinished negative AMERICA, 27
glory of E. is extinguished EUROPE, 2
In Western E. there are now only small countries EUROPE, 12
lamps are going out over all E. PROPHECY, 5
sick man of E. DECLINE, 7
That E.'s nothin' on earth EUROPE, 22
the community of E. EUROPE, 17
the race of men is almost extinct in E. MEN, 9
This going into E. EUROPE, 20
United States of E. EUROPE, 6
European taking very good E. films CINEMA, 3
to shoot down a E. OPPRESSION, 7
Europeanism Their E. is...imperialism with an inferiority complex POLITICS, 34
Europeans really materialistic people...E. MATERIALISM, 14
Eva If a woman like E. Peron with no ideals POLITICIANS, 75
evacuations Wars are not won by e. WORLD WAR II, 14
evah Well, did you e.! What a swell party PARTIES, 5
eve from noon to dewy e. DECLINE, 4
Eve When E. ate this particular apple SEX, 30
even Deep and crisp and e. CHRISTMAS, 15
evening e. is spread out against the sky DEPARTURE, 6
Now came still E. on DAY, 11
Soup of the e. FOOD, 13
the quiet-coloured end of e. DAY, 3
thou art fairer than the e. air BEAUTY, 26
event greatest e....that ever happened FRENCH REVOLUTION, 2
hurries to the main e. PLAYS, 5
one far-off divine e. DESTINY, 22
thinking too precisely on th' e. COWARDICE, 7
eventide Abide with me; fast falls the e. RELIGION, 41
events all great e. and personalities...reappear HISTORY, 20
E. which...never happened HISTORY, 17
There are only three e. in a man's life LIFE AND DEATH, 8
When in the course of human e., it becomes necessary INDEPENDENCE, 2
ever for e. hold his peace OPPORTUNITY, 11
Everest the summit of E. was hardly the place PHOTOGRAPHY, 5
treating the *mons Veneris* as...Mount E. SEX, 26
every E. day in e. way REMEDIES, 8
God bless us, e. one BLESSING, 6
everybody E. has got to die.... Now what LAST WORDS, 61
E. is always in favour of general economy THRIFT, 7
E. was up to something INTRIGUE, 2
Everyman E., I will go with thee GUIDANCE, 1
everyone e. against e. HUMAN CONDITION, 10
I hate e. equally HATE, 3
stop e. from doing it PERVERSITY, 4
everything A place for e. ORDER, 6
destroying nearly e. CIVILIZATION, 4
e. in its place ORDER, 6
E. is funny HUMOUR, 26
E. is only for a day TRANSIENCE, 1
E.'s got a moral PURPOSE, 1
e. that lives is holy LIFE, 13
God made e. out of nothing CREATION, 15
making e. the concern of all RESPONSIBILITY, 13
men we like are good for e. SUBJECTIVITY, 3
One fifth of the people are against e. OPPOSITION, 4
Was E. by starts HUMAN NATURE, 9
evidence If ever there was a case of clearer e. NONSENSE, 2
men...give e. against their own understanding SPEECH, 10
Some circumstantial e. is very strong PROOF, 6
evil about the dreadful wood /Of conscious e. GUILT, 2
a thing may look e. in theory THEORY, 1
belief in a supernatural source of e. EVIL, 7
better is he...who hath not seen the e. work EVIL, 3
deliver us from e. PRAYER, 4
E., be thou my Good EVIL, 12
E. be to him who evil thinks EVIL, 1
E. comes at leisure DISEASE, 12
E. comes...like the disease GOOD AND EVIL, 2
e. is wrought by want of thought EVIL, 10
e. men and seducers EVIL, 4
E. visited us EVIL, 17
first to Touch for the E. according to costome REMEDIES, 9
Government...is but a necessary e. GOVERNMENT, 22
He who passively accepts e. EVIL, 11
know all the e. he does EVIL, 14
love of money is the root of all e. MONEY, 11
Man's capacity for e. makes democracy necessary DEMOCRACY, 14
men loved darkness...because their deeds were e. EVIL, 5
Men's e. manners live in brass MEMORIALS, 10
No man is justified in doing e. EXPEDIENCY, 6
Only lies and e. come from letting people off FORGIVENESS, 13
Put off the e. hour PROCRASTINATION, 2
science is...neither a potential for good nor for e. SCIENCE, 39
The e. that men do lives after them EVIL, 16
the fear of one e. VICE, 3
the love of money is the root of all e. MONEY, 14
There is no e. in the atom NUCLEAR WEAPONS, 18
Vice itself lost half its e. VICE, 5
we are the origin of all coming e. HUMAN NATURE, 14
woe unto them that call e. good LYING, 4
evils death...the least of all e. DEATH, 20
He...must expect new e. INNOVATION, 1
There exist some e. so terrible...that we dare not think of them MISFORTUNE, 12
To great e. we submit TRIVIALITY, 9
We cannot remove the e. of capitalism CAPITALISM, 6
Whenever I'm caught between two e. VICE, 9
Work banishes those three great e. WORK, 24
evolution Coolidge is a better example of e. POLITICIANS, 69
e. of the human race MANKIND, 13
sex...must itself be subject...to e. SEXES, 3
exact Politics is not an e. science POLITICS, 8
exaggerated Reports of my death are greatly e. OBITUARIES, 4
examine One should e. oneself...before...condemning others SELF, 11
example E. is the school of mankind EXAMPLE, 2
George the Third...*may profit by their e.* TREASON, 4
exasperating that the afterlife will be any less e. AFTERLIFE, 3
excel daring to e. EXCELLENCE, 2
excellence acute limited e. at twenty-one PRECOCITY, 1
excellences e. carried to an excess WRITERS, 6
excellent everything that's e. LAW, 12
Excelsior A banner with the strange device, /E. AMBITION, 12
exception I never forget a face, but I'll make an e. MEMORY, 9
The e. proves the rule RULES, 1
excess excellences carried to an e. WRITERS, 6
e. is most exhilarating EXCESS, 2
Give me e. of it MUSIC, 46
In charity there is no e. CHARITY, 3
Nothing succeeds like e. MODERATION, 5; EXCESS, 15
The road of e. EXCESS, 3
'Tis not the drinking...but the e. EXCESS, 7
exchange conversation must be an e. of thought CONVERSATION, 7
I stopped...to e. ideas INFERIORITY, 1
Exchequer Chancellor of the E. TAXATION, 9
exciting He found it less e. COWARDICE, 3
Jam today, and men aren't at their most e. PROMISES, 6
exclude we cannot e. the intellect INTELLECT, 4
excluded when you have e. the impossible TRUTH, 23
exclusive the most e. club there is ENGLISH, 29
excuse bet he's just using that as an e. DEATH, 84
execution some are daily led to e. EXECUTION, 23
executioner I am mine own E. SELF, 7
executioners victims who respect their e. RESPECT, 3
executive the e. expression of human immaturity POLITICS, 11
exercise E. is bunk HEALTH AND HEALTHY LIVING, 6; SPORT AND GAMES, 7
Prostitution...provides fresh air and wholesome e. SEX, 23
exertion success depends...upon individual initiative and e. EFFORT, 5; SUCCESS, 13
the e. is too much for me LAUGHTER, 9
exhausted Our agenda is now e. AGREEMENT, 6
exile New York...where every one is an e. AMERICA, 15
exist Facts do not cease to e. FACTS, 2
I e. by what I think THINKING, 9
I feel...a certain difficulty in continuing to e. LAST WORDS, 26
If God did not e. GOD, 49
liberty cannot long e. CORRUPTION, 1
No more things should be presumed to e. SIMPLICITY, 6
existence A God who let us prove his e. GOD, 15
disregard for the necessities of e. CIVILIZATION, 9

Does it contain any experimental reasoning, concerning matter of fact and e. PHILOSOPHY, 3
doubted the e. of the Deity SCIENTISTS, 6
individual e. goes out in a lonely spasm of helpless agony DEATH, 63
Let us contemplate e. EXISTENCE, 2
mere e. is swollen to a horror IDEALISM, 3
the sole purpose of human e. is to kindle a light EXISTENCE, 3
the struggle for e. EVOLUTION, 5
to deny the e. of an unseen kingdom is bad SPECULATION, 1
to do something is to create e. EXISTENCE, 5
exit E., pursued by a bear ANIMALS, 18
exits They have their e. and their entrances HUMAN CONDITION, 17
expect all any reasonable child can e. SEX, 44
people e. me to neigh, grind my teeth HORSES, 1
the audience want to be surprised...by things that they e. PLAYS, 3
you e. other people to be...to your liking TOLERANCE, 4
expectation the distinction between hope and e. REALISM, 3
expectations the difference between our talents and our e. DISAPPOINTMENT, 1
expects Blessed is the man who e. nothing EXPECTATION, 4
England e. every man will do his duty DUTY, 3
expediency the most useful thing about a principle... sacrificed to e. EXPEDIENCY, 4
expendable British Government sees black people as e. RACISM, 30
expenditure annual e. nineteen nineteen six ECONOMICS, 7
in favour of...particular e. THRIFT, 7
expense flatterers live at the e. of those who listen FLATTERY, 6
who /Would be at the e. of two GOD, 17
experience All e. is an arch EXPERIENCE, 20
An e. of women EXPERIENCE, 12
E. is a good teacher EXPERIENCE, 6
E. is never limited EXPERIENCE, 16
E. isn't interesting EXPERIENCE, 9
E. is the best teacher EXPERIENCE, 2
E. is the mother EXPERIENCE, 3
I can't see that it's wrong to give him a little legal e. NEPOTISM, 2
Language is not simply a reporting device for e. LANGUAGE, 28
moment's insight...worth a life's e. EXPERIENCE, 15
my e. of life has been drawn from life itself EXPERIENCE, 8
Notwithstanding the poverty of my...e. CONTENTMENT, 4
Reason, Observation, and E. SCIENCE, 22
the light which e. gives EXPERIENCE, 11
The triumph of hope over e. MARRIAGE, 73
experiences the child should be allowed to meet the real e. of life CHILDREN, 31
experiment A theory can be proved by e. THEORY, 2
existence remains a...lamentable e. HAPPINESS, 22
no path leads from e. to...theory THEORY, 2
to desist from the e. in despair SCOTS, 7
experimental *Does it contain any e. reasoning, concerning matter of fact and existence* PHILOSOPHY, 3
experiments divers e. in Mr Boyle's Pneumatic Engine SCIENTISTS, 10
expert An e....has made all the mistakes...in a very narrow field EXPERTS, 2
An e....knows some of the worst mistakes EXPERTS, 3
Prince Philip....a world e. on leisure ROYALTY, 20
explanations less hideous than e. EXPLANATIONS, 1
export I integrate the current e. drive BUSINESS, 4
exposes A man who e. himself when he is intoxicated DRUNKENNESS, 15
ex-president No candidate...elected e. by such a large majority DEFEAT, 7
expression supreme e. of the mediocrity RUSSIA, 10
the executive e. of human immaturity POLITICS, 11
exquisite It is e., and it leaves one unsatisfied SMOKING, 23
the e. touch...is denied to me WRITERS, 81
ex-secretary attacking an e. of state CHURCHILL, 1
exterminate E. all brutes RUTHLESSNESS, 3
e....the treacherous English WAR, 132
extinct a convention which says you must not make species e. CONSERVATION, 7
the Tasmanians...are now e. ADULTERY, 7
extinguished glory of Europe is e. EUROPE, 2
extraordinary Little minds are interested in the e. TRIVIALITY, 10
the most e. collection of talent TALENT, 5
this is an e. man POLITICIANS, 56
extravagance e....thrift and adventure THRIFT, 5
Our love of what is beautiful does not lead to e. RESULTS, 4
extreme E. remedies...for extreme diseases REMEDIES, 10
extremism e. in the defence of liberty is no vice EXCESS, 4
exuberance E. is Beauty BEAUTY, 9
e. of his own verbosity VERBOSITY, 2
ex-wife no fury like an e. searching for a new lover WOMEN, 24
eye A custom loathsome to the e. SMOKING, 7
A person may be indebted for a nose or an e....to a great-aunt FAMILY, 15
a sober colouring from an e. MORTALITY, 21
as the apple of his e. SUPPORT, 1
clapped the glass to his sightless e. BLINDNESS, 6
Every tear from every e. SORROW, 1
e. for e. RETRIBUTION, 3
He had but one e. APPEARANCE, 12
his keener e. /The axe's edge did try EXECUTION, 16
less in this than meets the e. CRITICISM, 2
man who looks you...in the e....hiding something INSINCERITY, 1
neither e. to see, nor tongue to speak HOUSES OF PARLIAMENT, 11
such beauty as a woman's e. LEARNING, 8
The e. is bigger GREED, 3
There is a road from the e. to the heart EMOTION, 1
the sort of e. that can open an oyster at sixty paces APPEARANCE, 42
with an e. made quiet.../We see into the life of things DEATH, 134
with the jaundiced e. PASSION, 8
eyeless E. in Gaza BLINDNESS, 3
eye-lids the opening e. of the morn DAY, 10
tir'd e. upon tir'd eyes MUSIC, 51
When she raises her e. SEX, 16
eyes And on his grave, with shining e. DEATH, 19
and throws...sand in their e. SLEEP, 10
Drink to me only with thine e. LOVE, 75
fortune and men's e. DISCONTENT, 8
God be in my e., /And in my looking GOD, 1
I first set my e. on sweet Molly Malone BUSINESS, 1
Look at that man's e. POLITICIANS, 60
Look not in my e. LOVE, 71
Love looks not with the e. LOVE, 120
Mine e. have seen the glory of the coming of the Lord GOD, 26
pearls that were his e. DEATH, 108
the creature hath a purpose and its e. are bright PURPOSE, 5
the e. are the windows of the soul EYES, 1
The e. are the window SOUL, 1
The e. that shone, /Now dimmed and gone NOSTALGIA, 14
the whites of their e. WAR, 87
Thy rapt soul sitting in thine e. SOUL, 10
Two lovely black c. VIOLENCE, 4
you'll wear your e. out STARING, 2
Your e. shine like the pants COMPLIMENTS, 3
eyesight with blinded e. LEARNING, 9
Eyre I wish you had not sent me Jane E. WRITERS, 85

F

Fabian Britain...F. Society writ large BRITAIN, 8
Fabians A good man fallen among F. WRITERS, 64
fabric chemical barrage has been hurled against the f. of life ECOLOGY, 2
the baseless f. of this vision MORTALITY, 17
face Accustomed to her f. FAMILIARITY, 3
a garden in her f. ADMIRATION, 4
A good f. is a letter of recommendation BEAUTY, 1
And hid his f. amid a crowd of stars LOVE, 150
At 50, everyone has the f. he deserves AGE, 43
everybody's f. but their own SATIRE, 3
every man is responsible for his f. APPEARANCE, 6
False f. must hide DECEPTION, 5
from whose f. the earth and the heaven fled JUDGMENT, 4
I have looked upon the f. of Agamemnon HISTORY, 24
I never forget a f., but I'll make an exception MEMORY, 9

Look in my f.; my name is Might-have-been DISAPPOINTMENT, 6
Looks the whole world in the f. RIGHTEOUSNESS, 7
My f. is my fortune, sir, she said NURSERY RHYMES, 67
painting a f. and not washing APPEARANCE, 15
Socialism with a human f. COMMUNISM, 2
the f. that launch'd a thousand ships BEAUTY, 25
The human f. is…a whole cluster of faces MANKIND, 21
There is not any book /Or f. DEATH, 127
to order a new stamp…with my f. on it TRIVIALITY, 11
your whole life shows in your f. AGE, 6
faces All, all are gone, the old familiar f. NOSTALGIA, 12
among so many million of f. INDIVIDUALITY, 4
facetious not…foolish because I am f. SERIOUSNESS, 3
fact slaying of a beautiful hypothesis by an ugly f. SCIENCE, 21
faction To die for f. EXECUTION, 7
factory In the f. we make cosmetics COSMETICS, 3
facts Comment is free but f. are sacred JOURNALISM, 27
F. alone are wanted in life FACTS, 1
F. do not cease to exist FACTS, 2
F. speak louder than statistics FACTS, 3; STATISTICS, 11
Learn, compare, collect the f. EDUCATION, 42
Once a newspaper touches a story, the f. are lost JOURNALISM, 22
phantom beings loaded up with f. SCIENCE, 43
fade the cheek that doth not f. APPEARANCE, 17
fail If they succeed, they f. HOMOSEXUALITY, 3
Others must f. RUTHLESSNESS, 7
to f. conventionally ORTHODOXY, 3
failed Here lies Joseph, who f. in everything FAILURE, 4
faileth charity never f. CHARITY, 6
fails If thy heart f. thee AMBITION, 7
failure All political lives…end in f. POLITICIANS, 20
no success like f. FAILURE, 2
we all contain f. and death within us AGE, 37
faint Damn with f. praise CRITICISM, 40
fair All is f. LOVE, 1
all's f. in love and war JUSTICE, 8
F. stood the wind for France BOATS, 5
Grief has turned her f. APPEARANCE, 41
Monday's child is f. of face NURSERY RHYMES, 34
Serious sport has nothing to do with f. play SPORT AND GAMES, 18
So foul and f. a day WEATHER, 22
the Brave deserves the F. COURAGE, 11
There was a f. maid dwellin' LOVE, 13
Whitehall…our attempts to be f. to everybody BRITAIN, 3
faire *Laissez f.* FREEDOM, 43
fairer thou art f. than the evening air BEAUTY, 26
fairest the f. things have the worst fate TRANSIENCE, 17
fairies I don't believe in f. FAIRIES, 1
the beginning of f. FAIRIES, 2
There are f. at the bottom of our garden FAIRIES, 3
fairy A myth is, of course, not a f. story MYTHS, 2
the f. tales of science EXPERIENCE, 19
fairyland The Fleet's lit up. It is like f. NAVY, 4
faith a life of doubt diversified by f. DOUBT, 4
an absolute f. that all things are possible to God FAITH, 10
And f. shines equal COURAGE, 3
by f. the walls of Jericho fell down FAITH, 2
F.…an illogical belief in…the improbable FAITH, 14
F. consists in believing FAITH, 19
f., if it hath not works, is dead FAITH, 7
f. is the substance of things hoped for FAITH, 3
f. unfaithful kept him falsely true UNFAITHFULNESS, 6
F. will move mountains FAITH, 1
no need for any other f. than…in human beings FAITH, 9
now abideth f., hope, charity CHARITY, 6
O thou of little f., wherefore didst thou doubt DOUBT, 2
Reason is itself a matter of f. REASON, 2
the f. and morals hold /Which Milton held FREEDOM, 54
'Tis not the dying for a f. FAITH, 18
we walk by f., not by sight FAITH, 5
When your ladyship's f. has removed them RELIGION, 14
whoever is moved by f. to assent to it CHRISTIANITY, 29
faithful f. in love…dauntless in war CHIVALRY, 10
f. to thee, Cynara FAITHFULNESS, 3
happiness of man that he be mentally f. INTEGRITY, 5
If this man is not f. to his God LOYALTY, 9
if you had been f. LOVE, 105
my heart shall be /The f. compass FAITHFULNESS, 4
O come all ye f. CHRISTMAS, 16
thou good and f. servant SERVICE, 1
Translations (like wives) are seldom f. TRANSLATION, 2
fake If I like it…it's mine. If I don't…it's a f. PAINTING, 9
faking worst crime is f. it HONESTY, 4
fall and an haughty spirit before a f. PRIDE, 1
Fain would I climb, yet fear I to f. AMBITION, 14
The airplane stays up because it doesn't have the time to f. SCIENCE, 47
Whenever you f., pick up something OPPORTUNITY, 8
fallen A good man f. among Fabians WRITERS, 64
y-f. out of heigh degree. Into miserie MISFORTUNE, 6
falleth woe to him that is alone when he f. FRIENDSHIP, 8
fallow lie f. for a while REST, 3
false beware of f. prophets DECEPTION, 2
F. face must hide what the false heart DECEPTION, 5
f. to his friends…true to the public HONESTY, 3
natural f. teeth TEETH, 3
The religions we call f. were once true RELIGION, 23
Thou canst not then be f. BORROWING, 8; INTEGRITY, 6
thou shalt not bear f. witness GOD, 10
True and F. are attributes of speech, not of things TRUTH, 29
Vain wisdom all, and f. philosophy WISDOM, 19
falsehood Let her and F. grapple TRUTH, 36
falsely a verb meaning 'to believe f.' BELIEF, 8
Falstaff F. sweats to death OBESITY, 10
fame blush to find it f. GOOD, 14
F. is a powerful aphrodisiac FAME, 11
F. is like a river FAME, 2
F. is sometimes like unto a…mushroom FAME, 10
F. is the spur FAME, 14
Here rests…/A youth to fortune and to f. unknown DEATH, 58
Love of f. is the last thing…to be parted from FAME, 19
One of the drawbacks of F. FAME, 13
The book written against f.…has the author's name on the title-page HYPOCRISY, 9
familiar old f. faces NOSTALGIA, 12
familiarity F. breeds contempt FAMILIARITY, 1
F. breeds contempt – and children SEX, 60
I like f. FAMILIARITY, 5
families All happy f. resemble one another FAMILY, 34
Good f. are generally worse than any others FAMILY, 16
Murder, like talent, seems…to run in f. MURDER, 9
the best-regulated f. ACCIDENTS, 2
There are only two f. in the world POVERTY AND WEALTH, 3
family A f. with the wrong members in control ENGLAND, 30
a tense and peculiar f., the Oedipuses CLASSICS, 1
educate a woman you educate a f. EDUCATION, 33
Mother is the dead heart of the f. MOTHERHOOD, 10
my f. begins with me ANCESTRY, 3
symbol of the bloodiness of f. life FAMILY, 24
the f.…source of all our discontents FAMILY, 20
The f. that prays together FAMILY, 3
famine They that die by f. die by inches HUNGER, 6
you look as if there were f. in the land APPEARANCE, 33
famous everyone will be f. for 15 minutes FAME, 23
I awoke…found myself f. FAME, 6
I'm never going to be f. FAME, 16
let us now praise f. men PRAISE, 3
so f., that it would permit me…to break wind in society FAME, 3
What are you f. *for*?' FAME, 15
fan 'F. vaulting'…belongs to the 'Last-supper-carved-on-a-peach-stone' ARCHITECTURE, 5
throw an egg into an electric f. AMBITION, 9
fanatic f.…over-compensates a…doubt FANATICISM, 1
fanatics F. have their dreams FANATICISM, 2
when f. are on top there is no limit GOVERNMENT, 19
fancies All universal moral principles are idle f. MORALITY, 14
fancy Ever let the f. roam DISCONTENT, 5
F. is…a mode of memory IMAGINATION, 2
f. wit will come STUPIDITY, 13
hopeless f. feign'd NOSTALGIA, 20
In the Spring a young man's f. SEASONS, 24
little of what you f. does you good PLEASURE, 19
sweetest Shakespeare, F.'s child SHAKESPEARE, 13
Fanny F. by Gaslight BOOK, SONG, AND PLAY TITLES, 23
fantastic the light f. toe DANCING, 7
far a f., f., better thing EXECUTION, 6
how f. we may go too f. TACT, 5
The night is dark, and I am f. from home FAITH, 16
Thursday's child has f. to go NURSERY RHYMES, 34

Faraday remain plain Michael F. to the last TITLES, 3
farce But not as hard as f. ACTING, 7
F. is the essential theatre THEATRE, 9
Parliament is the longest running f. GOVERNMENT, 27
the f. is over LAST WORDS, 55
the wine was a f. and the food a tragedy FOOD, 47
farewell F., a long farewell, to all my greatness HUMAN CONDITION, 16
F., my poor hands MUSICIANS, 13
F.! thou art too dear for my possessing PARTING, 11
hail and f. GREETINGS, 1
long journey…must bid the company f. LAST WORDS, 57
farmer This is the f. sowing his corn NURSERY RHYMES, 57
To the average British f., organic farming is…as relevant as caviar ECOLOGY, 9
farm-yard distinguish human society from the f. MANKIND, 29
the f. world of sex ANIMALISM, 2
far-reaching Life's short span forbids us to enter on f. hopes MORTALITY, 13
fart can't f. and chew gum MISQUOTATIONS, 21; STUPIDITY, 5
farthing It is burning a f. candle at Dover CRITICISM, 19
steal one poor f. without excuse SIN, 18
fascinates I like work; it f. me IDLENESS, 6
fascination Philosophy…is a fight against…f. PHILOSOPHY, 17
war…will always have its f. WAR, 130
fascism F. is a religion FASCISM, 2
F. is not an article for export FASCISM, 3
F. means war FASCISM, 6
the twentieth century will be…the century of F. FASCISM, 2
fascist Every communist has a f. frown COMMUNISM, 8; FASCISM, 5
fascist Today in Britain, a f. has won an election FASCISM, 4
fashion after the f. of their country ENGLAND, 38
A love of f. makes the economy go round FASHION, 9
as…be…out of the f. FASHION, 2
Every man after his f. DIFFERENCE, 1
faithful to thee, Cynara! in my f. FAITHFULNESS, 3
F. is architecture FASHION, 1
Nothing else holds f. SEX, 53
the unreasoning laws of markets and f. ART, 1
true to you, darlin', in my f. FAITHFULNESS, 5
fashionable an idea…to be f. is ominous FASHION, 7
fashions F.…only induced epidemics FASHION, 8
I cannot…cut my conscience to fit this year's f. INTEGRITY, 3
fast none so f. as stroke BOATS, 2
they stumble that run f. HASTE, 11
US has to move very f. AMERICA, 20
faster Will you walk a little f. HASTE, 5
fastidious to set a chime of words tinkling in…a few f. people PURPOSE, 7
fat butter will only make us f. POWER POLITICS, 3
Enclosing every thin man, there's a f. man APPEARANCE, 39
f. content of an avocado FOOD, 21
in every f. man a thin one OBESITY, 5
Let me have men about me that are f. MISTRUST, 9
O f. white woman OBESITY, 6
Outside every f. man…an even fatter man OBESITY, 1
The opera isn't over till the f. lady sings OPERA, 3
there's a thin man inside every f. man OBESITY, 8
Who's your f. friend OBESITY, 2
you will come and find me f. and sleek PRESENT, 10
fatal Anno domini…the most f. complaint DEATH, 61
Nature has never put the f. question as to the meaning of their lives PURPOSE, 4
when he does it is nearly always f. LOVE AND DEATH, 5
fate count as profit every day that F. allows you PRESENT, 8
Each man the architect of his own f. RESPONSIBILITY, 3
F. sits on these dark battlements DESTINY, 18
hostages given to f. FAMILY, 21
How wayward the decrees of F. GREATNESS, 14; WISDOM, 23
jeers at F. ENVY, 2
Leave the flesh to the f. it was fit for SOUL, 5
master of his f. RESPONSIBILITY, 15
mortifying f. of most English universities NOVELTY, 6
the fairest things have the worst f. TRANSIENCE, 17
the life-sentence which f. carries LIFE AND DEATH, 10
the master of my f. RESPONSIBILITY, 8
the severity of f. DESTINY, 11
We may become the makers of our f. DESTINY, 16
when F. summons MORTALITY, 5
father a wise f. that knows his own child FATHERS, 6
Box about: 'twill come to my f. anon FATHERS, 2
brood of Folly without f. PLEASURE, 23
Dreading to find its F. GUILT, 2
except to shoot rabbits and hit his f. on the jaw NASTINESS, 5
F.…come home with me now ALCOHOL, 68
Full fathom five thy f. lies DEATH, 108
God is…an exalted f. GOD, 22
he had rather /Have a turnip than his f. NONSENSE, 13
If poverty is the mother of crime, stupidity is its f. CRIME, 5
in my F.'s house are many mansions HEAVEN, 3
left me by my F. EXECUTION, 4
Like f., like son FATHERS, 1
My f. didn't create you to arrest me POLICE, 6
No man is responsible for his f. FATHERS, 7
our F. PRAYER, 4
The Child is F. of the Man AGE, 69
the electric display of God the F. LIFE, 39
the F. of lights GIFTS, 1
the night the bed fell on my f. MEMORY, 19
Today I dressed to meet my f.'s eyes SUITABILITY, 3
You are old, F. William OLD AGE, 42
fatherhood Mirrors and f. are abominable UNIVERSE, 2
fatherland Germany is our f. GERMANY, 7
fathers atone for the sins of your f. INJUSTICE, 7
Come mothers and f. /Throughout the land CHANGE, 6
f., provoke not your children FATHERS, 3
land of my f. WALES, 2
Victory has a thousand f. SUCCESS, 10
fathom f. the inscrutable workings of Providence REPARTEE, 4
Full f. five thy father lies DEATH, 108
fatted the f. calf PARTIES, 2
fattening the things I really like…are either immoral, illegal, or f. PLEASURE, 31
fatter But the valley sheep are f. GREED, 7
fatty f. degeneration of his moral being MARRIAGE, 115
fatuity English…to act with…f. of idiots IRELAND, 19
fault only one f.. It was…lousy CRITICISM, 49
Shakespeare never had six lines together without a f. SHAKESPEARE, 9
the f. were on only one side ARGUMENTS, 13
The fundamental f. of the female character WOMEN, 68
faultless Whoever thinks a f. piece to see PERFECTION, 6
faults by pointing out to a man the f. of his mistress IMPERFECTION, 10
Don't tell your friends their social f. ADVICE, 13
England, with all thy f. PATRIOTISM, 7
f., do not fear to abandon them IMPERFECTION, 6
If we had no f. of our own IMPERFECTION, 12
only confess our little f. IMPERFECTION, 11
When you have f. IMPERFECTION, 6
favour accepts a smaller as a f. INJUSTICE, 3
Many terms…out of f., will be revived WORDS, 10
truths being in and out of f. NOVELTY, 2
favoured play-actors…they're a f. race ACTORS, 3
favours On whom their f. fall WOMEN, 76
Whether a pretty woman grants or withholds her f. WOMEN, 58
fav'rite A f. has no friend LONELINESS, 2
fear concessions of f. YIELDING, 1
Curiosity will conquer f. CURIOSITY, 8
do I f. thy nature KINDNESS, 4
f. God, and keep his commandments GOD, 9
F. has many eyes FEAR, 4
f. in a handful of dust FEAR, 9
F. lent wings to his feet FEAR, 13
f. made manifest on the body DISEASE, 16
F. no more the heat o' th' sun MORTALITY, 16
F. of death DEATH, 7
fools rush in where angels f. to tread HASTE, 8
Fostered alike by beauty and by f. SOUL, 12
freedom from f. HUMAN RIGHTS, 4
have…many things to f. FEAR, 1
He who pretends to look on death without f. lies DEATH, 100
Men f. death DEATH, 22
None but a coward…has never known f. COWARDICE, 2
one has…ceased to be an object of *f.* SYMPATHY, 5
only thing we have to f. is f. itself FEAR, 10
perfect love casteth out f. LOVE, 24; FEAR, 3
Perhaps your f. in passing judgement COURAGE, 4
pessimists end up by desiring the things they f. PESSIMISM, 9
the f. of one evil VICE, 3
fearful facing f. odds COURAGE, 17
thy f. symmetry ANIMALS, 4

fears A man who f. suffering SUFFERING, 11
enough for fifty hopes and f. WORRY, 8
man f....only the stroke of death DEATH, 21
The sum of their f. FEAR, 5
feast Life is not a...f. LIFE, 42
Paris is a moveable f. PARIS, 1
feather a f. to tickle the intellect PUNS, 10
feathers Fine f. APPEARANCE, 1
not only fine f. CLOTHES, 1
February Excepting F. alone NURSERY RHYMES, 56
F., fill the dyke MONTHS, 11
fecund to mistake for the first-rate, the f. rate WRITERS, 18
fed bite the hand that f. them INGRATITUDE, 2
fee hold the gorgeous east in f. VENICE, 4
feed f. and clothe 1.2 billion Chinese CHINA, 7
F. the World CHARITY, 4
he shall f. his flock CHRISTIANITY, 10
Why rob one to f. the other DEATH, 68
You cannot f. the hungry on statistics STATISTICS, 5
feeding Spoon f....teaches us nothing EDUCATION, 19
feel Englishman...is afraid to f. EDUCATION, 17
I draw what I f. in my body ART, 9
what I f. really bad about LIBERALISM, 1
feeling A man is as old as he's f. AGE, 18
Compassion is not a sloppy, sentimental f. SOCIALISM, 8
feelings First f. are always the most natural FIRST IMPRESSIONS, 5
feels A really intelligent man f. INTELLIGENCE, 5
feet Alan will always land on somebody's f. HUMOUR, 50
An emperor ought at least to die on his f. LAST WORDS, 72
better to die on your f. SELF-RESPECT, 1
both f. firmly planted in the air IDEALISM, 6
Fear lent wings to his f. FEAR, 13
those f. in ancient time ENGLAND, 5
feigning truest poetry is the most f. POETRY, 40
felicity likely to mar the general f. MARRIAGE, 33
fell by faith the walls of Jericho f. down FAITH, 2
crumbs which f. from the rich man's table POVERTY AND WEALTH, 2
Doctor F. HATE, 1
men f. out WAR, 21
felled The poplars are f. TREES, 3
fellow f. of infinite jest MOURNING, 10
fellows Boys are capital f. in their own way CHILDREN, 32
fellowship such a f. of good knights shall never be together LOSS, 3
female male and f. created he them MANKIND, 5; CREATION, 6
the f. character...has no sense of justice WOMEN, 68
the f. of the species is more deadly than the male WOMEN, 43
The fundamental fault of the f. character WOMEN, 68
The seldom f. SEXES, 18
What f. heart can gold despise MATERIALISM, 8
feminine Taste is the f. of genius TASTE, 3
fence gentleman has sat so long on the f. NONCOMMITMENT, 3
fences Good f. make good neighbours NEIGHBOURS, 3
fettered so f. fast we are FREEDOM, 4
fever F. the eternal reproach DISEASE, 27
hand that signed the treaty bred a f. SIGNATURES, 3
Février Generals Janvier and F. SEASONS, 15
few err as grosly as the F. PUBLIC, 11
How f. of his friends' houses ILLNESS, 9
owed by so many to so f. WORLD WAR II, 7
fickle Woman is always f. and changing WOMEN, 86
fiction ancient history...accepted f. HISTORY, 34
an improbable f. REALITY, 6
Children should acquire...heroes and villains from f. HISTORY, 3
one form of continuous f. JOURNALISM, 10
Poetry is a comforting piece of f. POETRY, 29
Science f. is no more written for scientists FICTION, 1
Stranger than f. TRUTH, 18
fiddle consider your puny little f. when He speaks to me MUSIC, 9
Hey diddle diddle, /The cat and the f. NURSERY RHYMES, 14
keep it shut up...like a rare, rare f. NAKEDNESS, 5
When I play on my f. in Dooney MUSIC, 56
field A cow is a very good animal in the f. SUITABILITY, 2
Behold her, single in the f. SOLITUDE, 16
Man for the f. and woman for the hearth SEXES, 24
shepherds abiding in the f. CHRISTMAS, 8
some corner of a foreign f. WAR, 18
What though the f. be lost DETERMINATION, 12
fields babbl'd of green f. DEATH, 112
East and west on f. forgotten WAR, 50
Now there are f. where Troy once was DECLINE, 8
We plough the f., and scatter AGRICULTURE, 1
fiend a f. hid in a cloud BIRTH, 3
a frightful f. /Doth close behind him tread FEAR, 6
fierce f. and bald and short of breath WAR, 100
fiery Nightingale.../A creature of a 'f. heart' BIRDS, 12
fifteen F. men on the dead man's chest ALCOHOL, 60
fifth Beethoven's F. Symphony is the most sublime MUSIC, 21
One f. of the people are against everything OPPOSITION, 4
fifty dreams of making f. thousand pounds LAZINESS, 3
Sit on your arse for f. years INDIFFERENCE, 4
'You'll see, when you're f. AGE, 52
fifty-fifty There can be no f. Americanism PATRIOTISM, 26
fifty-two refuse to admit that I am more than f. AGE, 5
fight a great cause to f. for PRIDE, 6
easier to f. for one's principles PRINCIPLES, 1
f., f., f., and f. again POLITICS, 25
F. fire CONFLICT, 2
F. the good f. with all thy might CHRISTIANITY, 33
I dare not f. COWARDICE, 8
I have not yet begun to f. DETERMINATION, 10
I purpose to f. it out on this line DETERMINATION, 8
I shall f. before Paris WORLD WAR I, 7
I will not cease from mental f. ENGLAND, 5
Nor law, nor duty bade me f. FLYING, 4
The only time...ever put up a f. INSULTS, 13
To f. and not to heed the wounds SELFLESSNESS, 2
too proud to f. WAR, 133
Ulster will f. IRELAND, 4
We don't want to f., but, by jingo if we do PATRIOTISM, 16
We'll f. and we'll conquer COURAGE, 13
we shall f. on the beaches WORLD WAR II, 4
when the f. begins within CONFLICT, 5
With our backs to the wall...each...must f. WAR, 44
You cannot f. against the future PROGRESS, 7
fighting F. is like champagne WAR, 68
Most sorts of diversion...are an imitation of f. WAR, 116
not conquering but f. well VICTORY, 4
What are we f. for WAR, 106
fights He that f. and runs away SELF-PRESERVATION, 2
I can't spare this man; he f. OFFICERS, 9
figure an oblong angular f. HUMOUR, 42
figures prove anything by f. STATISTICS, 1
film A wide screen...makes a bad f. twice as bad CINEMA, 7
I like a f. to have a beginning, a middle and an end CINEMA, 4
filmed written or thought, it can be f. CINEMA, 8
films Why...pay money to see bad f. CINEMA, 6
finality F. is death. Perfection is f. PERFECTION, 9
find terrible thing for a man to f. out HONESTY, 13
your sin will f. you out SIN, 7
finders F. keepers LUCK, 3
fine f. feathers that make f. birds CLOTHES, 1
In England, pop art and f. art ART, 16
The big print giveth and the f. print taketh away BUSINESS, 20
finer every baby...is a f. one BABIES, 2
finest their f. hour WORLD WAR II, 5
finger Moving F. writes DESTINY, 8
The least pain in our little f. SELF-INTEREST, 4
fingerlickin' It's f. good ADVERTISING, 15
fingernails if you don't stop biting your f. ARTISTS, 19
fingers F. were made before forks BEGINNING, 2
ill cook that cannot lick his own f. SELF-CONFIDENCE, 4
our f. are circumcised MUSICIANS, 6
finger-tips An accomplished man to his f. EXPERTS, 4
fings F. Ain't Wot They Used T'Be NOSTALGIA, 15
finished it is f. LAST WORDS, 9
We have f. the job TELEGRAMS, 10
finite Our knowledge can only be f. KNOWLEDGE, 31
fir The f. trees dark and high INNOCENCE, 6
fire All things, oh priests, are on f. FIRE, 1
Billy.../Fell in the f. FIRE, 2
bound /Upon a wheel of f. SUFFERING, 14
F. – without hatred WAR, 93
French Guard, f. first WAR, 45
heap coals of f. upon his head RETRIBUTION, 8
He had a f. in his eye, a fever in his blood POETS, 40
how great a matter a little f. kindleth SPEECH, 5
Ideas that enter the mind under f. INDOCTRINATION, 3

It is with our passions as it is with f. and water PASSION, 4
it is your business, when the wall next door catches f. NEIGHBOURS, 4
I warmed both hands before the f. of life LIFE AND DEATH, 9
London burnt by f. in three times twenty plus six PROPHECY, 9
The f. which in the heart resides SOUL, 2
two irons in the f. PRUDENCE, 5
what wind is to f. ABSENCE, 6
firearms Though loaded f. were strictly forbidden at St Trinian's WEAPONS, 9
fire-folk the f. sitting in the air STARS, 3
fireirons Saint Preux never kicked the f. IMPERFECTION, 5
fires Husbands are like f. MARRIAGE, 61
fireside allowed to take a glass of wine by his own f. FIRE, 4
firing he faced the f. squad; erect and motionless EXECUTION, 28
firm not a family; we're a f. ROYALTY, 19
firmness *Commodity, F.*, and *Delight* ARCHITECTURE, 15
first Because of my title, I was the f. COURAGE, 2
F. come HASTE, 2
F. impressions FIRST IMPRESSIONS, 1
F. things first PATIENCE, 3
If at f. you don't succeed PERSISTENCE, 5
many that are f. shall be last MERIT, 3
The constitution…f. and second class citizens CLASS, 40
The f. day a guest HOSPITALITY, 3
there is no last or f. EQUALITY, 6
which came f., the Greeks or the Romans IGNORANCE, 5
Who ever loved, that loved not at f. sight FIRST IMPRESSIONS, 6
first-aid His ideas of f. INCOMPETENCE, 6
first-rate the powers of a f. man and the creed of a second-rate man POLITICIANS, 1
to mistake for the f., the fecund rate WRITERS, 18
fish F. and guests HOSPITALITY, 2
F. die belly-upward OPPOSITES, 2
F. fuck in it WATER, 4
I have my own f. to fry NONCOMMITMENT, 2
No human being…was ever so free as a f. FREEDOM, 47
Phone for the f. knives Norman ETIQUETTE, 1
This man…is a poor f. MARRIAGE, 46
What cat's averse to f. MATERIALISM, 8
white wine came up with the f. ETIQUETTE, 4
fishbone The monument sticks like a f. MEMORIALS, 7
fishermen a bite every time for f. HUMOUR, 49
fishes f. live in the sea RUTHLESSNESS, 5
So are the f. WORLD WAR II, 8
fishing Time is but the stream I go a-f. in TIME, 38
fishmonger She was a f., but sure 'twas no wonder BUSINESS, 1
fishy something f. about the French FRANCE, 4
fist You cannot shake hands with a clenched f. INFLEXIBILITY, 2
fit a pleasing f. of melancholy MELANCHOLY, 10
It is not f. that you should sit here DISMISSAL, 3
let the punishment f. the crime PUNISHMENT, 10
news that's f. to print NEWSPAPERS, 9
only the F. survive SURVIVAL, 6
fits periodical f. of morality MORALITY, 10
Strange f. of passion PASSION, 9
fittest Survival of the F. EVOLUTION, 7
five child of f. would understand this SIMPLICITY, 5
F. gold rings NURSERY RHYMES, 55
If you don't find a God by f. o'clock this afternoon ATHEISM, 7
practise f. things VIRTUE, 7
The formula 'Two and two make f.' PHILOSOPHY, 2
five-pound get a f. note as…a light GENEROSITY, 4
five-year-old real menace in dealing with a f. CHILDREN, 30
fixed Nothing to be f. except TELEGRAMS, 5
flabbiness The moral f. born of…Success SUCCESS, 9
flag But spare your country's f. PATRIOTISM, 32
keep the red f. flying here SOCIALISM, 3
Tonight the American f. floats from yonder hill WAR, 113
flame like a moth, the simple maid /Still plays about the f. WOMEN, 34
flames Commit it then to the f. PHILOSOPHY, 3
Superstition sets the whole world in f. SUPERSTITION, 11
Flanders In F. fields MEMORIALS, 8
You have sent me a F. mare FIRST IMPRESSIONS, 4
flashing His f. eyes, his floating hair CAUTION, 9
flat Very f., Norfolk ENGLAND, 12
Vile snub-nose, f.-nosed ass APPEARANCE, 31
flatter not f. me REALISM, 1
We f. those we scarcely know HURT, 4
flatterer the brave beast is no f. HORSES, 7
flatterers f. live at the expense of those who listen FLATTERY, 6
Self-love…greatest of all f. CONCEIT, 14
flattering It is f. some men to endure them TOLERANCE, 3
the talent of f. with delicacy FLATTERY, 2
flattery consider whether…your f. is worth his having FLATTERY, 5
F. is all right FLATTERY, 8
f.'s the food of fools FLATTERY, 9
Imitation is the sincerest form of f. IMITATION, 2
ne'er /Was f. lost POETS, 10
woman…to be gained by…f. FLATTERY, 4
flaunt if you've got it, f. it OSTENTATION, 1
flautists f. are most obviously the ones who know something we don't know MUSICIANS, 4
flea English literature's performing f. WRITERS, 60
man's whole frame is obvious to a f. CLARITY, 3
The guerrilla fights the war of the f. WAR, 117
the point of precedency between a louse and a f. POETS, 9
fleas dog that praised his f. PARASITES, 4
F.…upon the body of a giant PERSPECTIVE, 3
the f. in my bed were as good COMPLIMENTS, 1
The f. that tease in the high Pyrenees NONSENSE, 3
these have smaller f. to bite 'em PARASITES, 3
fled I f. Him, down the nights RELIGION, 58
fleet The F.'s lit up. It is like fairyland NAVY, 4
flesh all f. is as grass DEATH, 29
doesn't seem to be any moral place for f. MORALITY, 5
f. and blood so cheap POVERTY, 17
f. to feel the chain IMPRISONMENT, 2
Heat, madam!…to take off my f. and sit in my bones WEATHER, 26
I, born of f. and ghost DEATH, 124
I have more f. than another man OBESITY, 11
Ishmaelites…will not publicly eat human f. CANNIBALISM, 2
I wants to make your f. creep FEAR, 8
Leave the f. to the fate it was fit for SOUL, 5
Rehearsing a play is making the word f. PLAYS, 9
she is burnt f. SUPERNATURAL, 7
the f. is weak IMPERFECTION, 4
the f. lusteth against the Spirit COMPROMISE, 3
the way of all f. DEATH, 39; HUMAN NATURE, 21
the way of all f.…towards the kitchen FOOD, 52
the world, the f., and the devil JOURNALISM, 25; TEMPTATION, 5
fleshly The F. School of Poetry POETS, 2
flies As f. to wanton boys DESTINY, 20
certain, that Life f. LIFE, 25
Time f., death urges TIME, 44
flight Above the vulgar f. of common souls SUPERIORITY, 8
fling I'll have a f. FREEDOM, 1
flirt f. with their own husbands LOVE AND MARRIAGE, 6
float rather be an opportunist and f. EXPEDIENCY, 2
flock he shall feed his f. CHRISTIANITY, 10
keeping watch over their f. by night CHRISTMAS, 8
flogging There is now less f. in our great schools EDUCATION, 27
flood Which, taken at the f. OPPORTUNITY, 16
floor stood ninety years on the f. CLOCKS, 2
flowed water f. like champagne ABSTINENCE, 4
flower A lovelier f. /…was never sown DEATH, 133
I have always plucked a thistle and planted a f. REPUTATION, 4
just miss the prizes at the f. show MEDIOCRITY, 3
many a f. is born to blush unseen WASTE, 2
The F. that once has blown LIFE, 25
the meanest f.…can give /Thoughts NATURE, 21
flowers a book that is a book f. once BOOKS, 23
Do spring May f. MONTHS, 12
Gather the f., but spare the buds FLOWERS, 8
Letting a hundred f. blossom CHINA, 8
No fruits, no f., no leaves, no birds MONTHS, 10
Say it with f. FLOWERS, 10
The f. that bloom in the spring APPEARANCE, 16
Their f. the tenderness of patient minds WAR, 81
Too late for fruit, too soon for f. ILLNESS, 13
Where have all the f. gone LOSS, 5
flowery A little thin, f. border GARDENS, 9
flows Everything f. and nothing stays CHANGE, 9

flung he f. himself from the room NONSENSE, 15
fly A f., Sir, may sting a stately horse CRITICS, 11
f.…said, what a dust do I raise CONCEIT, 3
said a spider to a f. INVITATIONS, 1
small gilded f. /Does lecher ANIMALISM, 7
Who saw him die? /I, said the F. NURSERY RHYMES, 68
flying Days and moments quickly f. DEATH, 37
foam the f. /Of perilous seas BIRDS, 5
the white f. flew EXPLORATION, 1
foe Heat not a furnace for your f. EXCESS, 11
he is the sworn f. of our nation PUBLISHING, 5
He…who never made a f. ENEMIES, 8
foeman When the f. bares his steel COWARDICE, 4
foes judge of a man by his f. JUDGMENT, 7
fog a London particular…A f. WEATHER, 9
Folies-Bergère A psychiatrist is a man who goes to the F. PSYCHIATRY, 9
folk-dancing except incest and f. EXPERIENCE, 7
folks for de old f. at home HOMESICKNESS, 3
follies f. as the special evidences of our wisdom PRIDE, 12
lovers cannot see the pretty f. LOVE, 118
the f. of the town crept slowly among us VICE, 7
The f. which a man regrets REGRET, 12
follow F. up!…/Till the field ring again SPORT AND GAMES, 2
He would rather f. public opinion POLITICIANS, 55
I have to f. them, I am their leader LEADERSHIP, 6
take up his cross, and f. me CHRISTIANITY, 19
folly brood of F. without father PLEASURE, 23
f. to shrink in fear, if this is dying DEATH, 92
His foe was f. and his weapon wit HUMOUR, 15
the slightest f. /That ever love did make thee run LOVE, 117
When lovely woman stoops to f. GULLIBILITY, 2
where ignorance is bliss, /'Tis f. to be wise IGNORANCE, 6
fond He is very f. of making things FUTILITY, 7
fonder Absence makes the heart grow f. ABSENCE, 4
food discovered that alcohol was a f. ALCOHOL, 66
distinction between f. and medicine CHINA, 6
flattery's the f. of fools FLATTERY, 9
f. in music MUSIC, 29
f. is, actually, very beautiful FOOD, 50
F. is an important part of a balanced diet FOOD, 35
f. is not necessarily essential CHILDREN, 43
f. to one man is bitter poison to others TASTE, 5
Nothing to eat but f. PESSIMISM, 7
On the Continent people have good f. MANNERS, 4
respond with f. FORGIVENESS, 4
Spleen can subsist on any kind of f. ANGER, 5
The perpetual struggle for room and f. SURVIVAL, 3
the wine was a farce and the f. a tragedy FOOD, 47
tinned f. is a deadlier weapon WEAPONS, 3
fool a f. among fools or a f. alone MANKIND, 37
A f. and his money FOOLISHNESS, 1
A f. at forty FOOLISHNESS, 2
A f. bolts pleasure, then complains DEBAUCHERY, 1
A f. sees not the same tree WISDOM AND FOOLISHNESS, 5
a greater f. to admire him ADMIRATION, 3
answer a f. according to his folly FOOLISHNESS, 10
a worm at one end and a f. at the other FISHING, 1
Better be a f. than a knave FOOLISHNESS, 4
brains enough to make a f. of himself WISDOM AND FOOLISHNESS, 7
Busy old f., unruly Sun SUN, 2
f. his whole life long PLEASURE, 20
He who holds hopes…is a f. PESSIMISM, 4
Love is the wisdom of the f. LOVE, 74
loves boxing is either a liar or a f. SPORT AND GAMES, 8
more of the f. than of the wise HUMAN NATURE, 3
No creature smarts…as a f. FOOLISHNESS, 17
One f.…in every married couple MARRIAGE, 59
The dupe of friendship, and the f. of love BITTERNESS, 1
the greatest f. may ask more EXAMINATIONS, 1
the old man who will not laugh is a f. AGE, 51; WISDOM, 20
There's no f. like an old f. FOOLISHNESS, 8
The wisest f. in Christendom FOOLISHNESS, 13
Wise Man or a F. WISDOM, 11
You can f. too many of the people DECEPTION, 6
foolish A f. consistency CONSTANCY, 1
anything very f. MOTIVE, 4
If you are f. enough to be contented COMPLAINTS, 3
the f. things of the world WISDOM AND FOOLISHNESS, 3
think me…f. because I am facetious SERIOUSNESS, 3
foolishness Mix a little f. with your serious plans FOOLISHNESS, 14
fools Christianity…says that they are all f. MANKIND, 11
flattery's the food of f. FLATTERY, 9
f. and passengers drink at sea BOATS, 15
F. are in a terrible, overwhelming majority FOOLISHNESS, 15
F. build houses FOOLISHNESS, 6
f. decoyed into our condition MARRIAGE, 93
F. live poor FOOLISHNESS, 7
f. rush in where angels fear to tread HASTE, 8
Fortune, that favours f. LUCK, 8
I am two f. LOVE, 48
Is Pride, the never-failing vice of f. PRIDE, 8
Many have been the wise speeches of f. WISDOM AND FOOLISHNESS, 6
suffer f. gladly WISDOM AND FOOLISHNESS, 4
the greater part of the law is learning to tolerate f. LAW, 19
Thirty millions, mostly f. ENGLISH, 9
this great stage of f. HUMAN CONDITION, 18
To suckle f. and chronicle TRIVIALITY, 12
what f. these mortals be FOOLISHNESS, 18
world is made up…of f. and knaves FOOLISHNESS, 11
foot noiseless f. of Time TIME, 33
football F.…is a species of fighting FOOTBALL, 5
F. isn't a matter of life and death FOOTBALL, 8
Professional f. is no longer a game FOOTBALL, 1
spontaneity is fundamental in art and f. FOOTBALL, 4
footballs streets were full of f. FOOTBALL, 6
footeball F.…causeth fighting FOOTBALL, 9
footprints F. on the sands of time ACTION, 4
those f. scare me, all directed your way MISTRUST, 5
you can have my f. HUMOUR, 46
footsteps home his f. he hath turn'd HOMESICKNESS, 6
foppery excellent f. of the world MISFORTUNE, 18
for neither f. nor against institutions INDIFFERENCE, 7
forbearance f. ceases to be a virtue TOLERANCE, 1
forbidden F. fruit TEMPTATION, 1
he wanted it only because it was f. PERVERSITY, 6
we're f. to know – what end the gods have in store DESTINY, 13
force f. alone is but *temporary* FORCE, 2
F., if unassisted by judgement, collapses JUDGMENT, 9
F. is not a remedy FORCE, 1
Hence no f. however great POETRY, 51
Other nations use 'f.'; we Britons…use 'Might' BRITISH, 10
Who overcomes /By f. VICTORY, 11
forced f. to commend her highly INSINCERITY, 3
force-feeding This universal, obligatory f. with lies INDOCTRINATION, 2
forces one of the f. of nature GREATNESS, 10
Ford Jerry F. is so dumb STUPIDITY, 5
forefathers Think of your f. POSTERITY, 1
forehead A burning f., and a parching tongue PASSION, 3
foreign pronounce f. names as he chooses PRONUNCIATION, 1
wandering on a f. strand HOMESICKNESS, 6
foreigner f. should…be wiser than ourselves PRIDE, 12
foreigners f. speak English when our backs are turned LANGUAGE, 10
f.…spell better than they pronounce PRONUNCIATION, 3; SPELLING, 2
Sympathy…for being f. SYMPATHY, 1
foreparents His f. came to America EQUALITY, 12
forest His f. fleece the Wrekin heaves TREES, 4
Wandering in a vast f. at night GUIDANCE, 2
forests the f. of the night ANIMALS, 4
foretaste Every parting gives a f. of death SEPARATION, 5
forever That is f. England WAR, 18
forewarned F. is forearmed PRUDENCE, 2
forget Better by far you should f. and smile MEMORY, 14
Fade far away, dissolve, and…f. HUMAN CONDITION, 12
I f. what I was taught KNOWLEDGE, 35
I'll not f. old Ireland HOMESICKNESS, 1
I never f. a face, but I'll make an exception MEMORY, 9
Oh Lord!…if I f. thee, do not thou f. me PRAYER, 3
Old men f. MEMORY, 16
To endeavour to f. anyone MEMORY, 8
Were it not better to f. REGRET, 6
When I f. my sovereign LOYALTY, 10
forgivable Few books today are f. BOOKS, 21
forgive do not have to f. my enemies LAST WORDS, 46; RUTHLESSNESS, 4
Father, f. them FORGIVENESS, 5

F. and forget FORGIVENESS, 1
how oft shall...I f. him FORGIVENESS, 7
Men will f. a man PROSE, 2
To err is human, to f., divine MISTAKES, 13; FORGIVENESS, 14
forgiven her sins, which are many, are f. FORGIVENESS, 6; SIN, 6
Once a woman has f. her man FORGIVENESS, 11
forgot auld acquaintance be f. FRIENDSHIP, 12
How these curiosities would be quite f. GOSSIP, 7
I have f. my part FAILURE, 6
forgotten God has f. me LIFE AND DEATH, 3
I have f. more law than you ever knew INSULTS, 30
Nobody is f. when it is convenient to remember him EXPEDIENCY, 3
The f. man POVERTY, 27
what has been learnt has been f. EDUCATION, 54
fork he had a f. INSULTS, 26
forks I had a knife and two f. left ETIQUETTE, 6
forlorn faery lands f. BIRDS, 5
postgraduate student is a lonely f. soul EDUCATION, 31
form significant f. ART, 4
formed not f. by nature to bear ENDURANCE, 4
formidable Examinations are f. EXAMINATIONS, 1
forms from outward f. to win APPEARANCES, 12
formula Matter...a convenient f. PHILOSOPHY, 11
fornicated f. and read the papers MANKIND, 10
fornication F.: but that was in another country SEX, 35
forsaken my God, why hast thou f. me DESPAIR, 1
fortress f. built by Nature ENGLAND, 36
fortuitous f. concurrence of atoms CHANCE, 4
fortune f. and men's eyes DISCONTENT, 8
F. favours the brave COURAGE, 23
F., that favours fools LUCK, 8
greater virtues to sustain good f. LUCK, 11
Here rests.../A youth to f. and to fame unknown DEATH, 58
hostages to f. FAMILY, 5
people of f....a few delinquencies POVERTY AND WEALTH, 5
slings and arrows of outrageous f. SUICIDE, 12
to make your f....let people see...it is in their interests to promote yours SUCCESS, 11
What is your f., my pretty maid NURSERY RHYMES, 67
fortunes f. sharp adversitee MISFORTUNE, 7
share in the good f. of the mighty INJUSTICE, 2
forty F. years on PARTING, 4
I am just turning f. AGE, 36
I have been talking prose for over f. years PROSE, 3
Life begins at f. AGE, 62
look young till f. AGE, 20
made the difference of f. thousand men OFFICERS, 16
When you are f. OLD AGE, 3
forty-five That should assure us of...f. minutes of undisturbed privacy INATTENTION, 2
forty-niner Dwelt a miner, F. MOURNING, 7
forty-three She may very well pass for f. AGE, 30
forward looking f. to the past NOSTALGIA, 17
foster-child f. of silence and slow time SILENCE, 9
fou I wasna f. SATISFACTION, 2
fought better to have f. and lost DEFEAT, 1
I have f. a good fight FAITH, 6
foul Murder most f. MURDER, 11
So f. and fair a day WEATHER, 22
foul-mouthed English...are rather a f. nation ENGLISH, 18
found he f. it brick IMPROVEMENT, 1
I have f. it DISCOVERY, 1
Pleasure is...seldom f. where it is sought PLEASURE, 14
Suppose it had been someone else who f. you ADULTERY, 8
foundation The Church's one f. CHRISTIANITY, 40
four age of f....we're all Generals AUTHORITARIANISM, 8
F. colly birds NURSERY RHYMES, 55
f. essential human freedoms HUMAN RIGHTS, 4
Great God grant that twice two be not f. PRAYER, 18
fourth a f. estate of the realm JOURNALISM, 21
Because there's no f. class HUMILITY, 8
on the f. day they will say 'To hell with you!' PROMISES, 4
four-year-old You've got the brain of a f. boy STUPIDITY, 8
fox a f. from his lair HUNTING, 4
Charles James F. MORTALITY, 20
The f. came home and he went to ground ANIMALS, 13
The f. knows many things ANIMALS, 2
the...f. said...those footprints scare me MISTRUST, 5
You don't set a f. to watching the chickens EXPERIENCE, 21
fox-hunting athletics as inferior forms of f. WOMEN, 87
fraction Only a residual f. is thought BUREAUCRACY, 8
fractions distinguish proper from improper f. MATHEMATICS, 7
fragrant a thousand f. posies FLOWERS, 7
frailty F., thy name is woman WEAKNESS, 4; WOMEN, 70
more flesh...more f. OBESITY, 11
frame all the Human F. requires FOOD, 7
change their clime, not their f. of mind, who rush across the sea TRAVEL, 12
man's whole f. is obvious to a flea CLARITY, 3
frames The finest collection of f. PHILISTINISM, 3
framework Language is...a defining f. LANGUAGE, 28
France all roads lead to F. WAR, 119
Fair stood the wind for F. BOATS, 5
F. is a country where the money falls apart FRANCE, 16
F. was a long despotism FRANCE, 2
Had we gone the way of F. ECOLOGY, 8
Like Brighton pier...inadequate for getting to F. TRAVEL, 15
The best thing I know between F. and England FRANCE, 8
Francis cousin F. and I are in perfect accord AGREEMENT, 1
frankincense gold, and f., and myrrh CHRISTMAS, 10
fraternité *Liberté! Égalité! F.* HUMAN RIGHTS, 2
frauds many of the great men of history are f. GREATNESS, 9
pious f. of friendship FRIENDSHIP, 18
free a f. society...where it is safe to be unpopular FREEDOM, 50
All f. men...are citizens of Berlin GERMANY, 6
All human beings are born f. HUMAN RIGHTS, 1
all men everywhere could be f. FREEDOM, 28
f. as the road FREEDOM, 17
F. Will and Predestination DESTINY, 5
Greece might still be f. EUROPE, 4
I'm with you on the f. press JOURNALISM, 29
In a f. society the state...administers justice STATE, 3
land of the f., and the home of the brave AMERICA, 21
Man is condemned to be f. FREEDOM, 48
Man was born f. FREEDOM, 46
No human being...was ever so f. as a fish FREEDOM, 47
none the less f. than you were ADAPTABILITY, 1
no such thing as a f. lunch FRIENDSHIP, 7
Only f. men can negotiate SOUTH AFRICA, 9
safer to be in chains than to be f. FREEDOM, 24
So f. we seem FREEDOM, 4
the truth shall make you f. TRUTH, 12
Thou art f. SHAKESPEARE, 1
truth that makes men f. TRUTH, 7
We have to believe in f. will CHOICE, 4
We must be f. or die FREEDOM, 54
Who would be f. FREEDOM, 6
freedom enemies of F. OPPRESSION, 3
fit to use their f. FREEDOM, 30
flame of f. in their souls KNOWLEDGE, 33
F.! Equality! Brotherhood HUMAN RIGHTS, 2
F. is an indivisible word HUMAN RIGHTS, 5
F. is the right to tell...do not want to hear FREEDOM, 39
f. of speech, f. of conscience, and the prudence never to practise...them FREEDOM, 51
F.'s just another word FREEDOM, 26
f. to print...proprietor's prejudices ADVERTISING, 5; JOURNALISM, 30
If f. were not so economically efficient ECONOMICS, 8
In solitude alone can he know true f. SOLITUDE, 12
Me this unchartered f. tires FREEDOM, 53
Necessity is the plea for every infringement of human f. NECESSITY, 4
None can love f. heartily, but good men FREEDOM, 35
only f. can make security secure FREEDOM, 41
So long as the state exists there is no f. STATE, 2
stand up for f. of the imagination RELIGION, 52
The worst enemy of truth and f. MAJORITY, 4
Those who deny f. to others FREEDOM, 29
Until you've lost your reputation, you never realize...what f. really is REPUTATION, 5
what is F. FREEDOM, 8
Your f. and mine cannot be separated FREEDOM, 32
You took my f. away a long time ago FREEDOM, 49
freedoms few remaining f. FREEDOM, 25
four essential human f. HUMAN RIGHTS, 4
free-loader A f. is a confirmed guest PARASITES, 2
freely nothing so f. as advice ADVICE, 12
freemasonry a kind of bitter f. LOVE, 20
free-will believe in f.. We've got no choice HUMAN CONDITION, 19

French Bouillabaisse is only good because cooked by the F. FOOD, 19; FRANCE, 5
dislike the F. from...vulgar antipathy FRANCE, 15
everyone would always have spoken F. LANGUAGE, 26
F. governments more selfish than most GOVERNMENT, 8
F. Guard, fire first WAR, 45
Give me books, fruit, F. wine and fine weather PLEASURE, 17
I hate the F. FRANCE, 7
Imagine the Lord talking F. LANGUAGE, 12
I speak...Italian to women, F. to men LANGUAGE, 7
My suit is pale yellow. My nationality is F. NORMALITY, 2
something fishy about the F. FRANCE, 4
The F. are wiser than they seem APPEARANCES, 9
The F. want no-one to be their *superior* PRIDE, 11
The F. will only be united under the threat of danger FRANCE, 6
the German text of F. operas OPERA, 10
There's something Vichy about the F. FRANCE, 12
to the F. the empire of the land EUROPE, 15
Frenchman F. must be always talking FRANCE, 9
You must hate a F. ENEMIES, 6
Frenchmen F. drink wine just like ALCOHOL, 39
to create F. in the image of Englishmen NATIONALITY, 4
frenzy poet's eye, in a fine f. rolling POETRY, 41
fresh f. as is the month of May CHARACTER, 4
the cod's wallop is always f. made COMMUNISM, 5
freshen a mighty storm...to f. us up CHANGE, 3
fret weariness, the fever, and the f. HUMAN CONDITION, 12
Freud The trouble with F. PSYCHIATRY, 2
Freudian the F., it is a very low, Central European sort of humour HUMOUR, 13
Friday F.'s child is loving and giving NURSERY RHYMES, 34
Worse on F. NURSERY RHYMES, 49
friend A fav'rite has no f. LONELINESS, 2
a F. for little children GOD, 36
A f. in need FRIENDSHIP, 1
A f. in power POWER, 4
A f. should bear his f.'s infirmities FRIENDS, 13
a good f., but bad acquaintance FRIENDS, 3
A good f. is my nearest relation FRIENDSHIP, 2
a new f. is as new wine FRIENDS, 2
A woman can become a man's f. FRIENDSHIP, 15
damned good-natured f. FRIENDS, 14
Every time I paint a portrait I lose a f. PAINTING, 15
forsake not an old f. FRIENDS, 2
F....masterpiece of Nature FRIENDS, 7
f., wherefore art thou come BETRAYAL, 1
He makes no f. ENEMIES, 8
I might give my life for my f. FRIENDSHIP, 27
In every f. we lose a part of ourselves DEATH, 96
It takes your enemy and your f...., to hurt you HURT, 3
no f. like a sister FAMILY, 29
save me, from the candid f. FRANKNESS, 1
that a man lay down his wife for a f. FRIENDSHIP, 21
trust ye not in a f. TRUST, 1
When a f. dies out on us FRIENDSHIP, 23
Whenever a f. succeeds ENVY, 8
friendly Man is the only animal...on f. terms with the victims...he eats HYPOCRISY, 6
so large, /So f., and so rich AMERICA, 2
friends Animals are such agreeable f. ANIMALS, 10
better to drop thy f. CLASS, 5
false to his f....true to the public HONESTY, 3
F., Romans, countrymen EVIL, 16
Good thoughts his only f. RIGHTEOUSNESS, 5
guessed you were f. FRIENDSHIP, 10
Have no f. not equal FRIENDS, 5
His best f. hear no more MARRIAGE, 108
How few of his f.' houses ILLNESS, 9
How to Win F. INFLUENCE, 2
I cannot forgive my f. for dying DEATH, 116
I don't trust him. We're f. FRIENDSHIP, 11
I let down my f. BETRAYAL, 6
In the misfortune of our best f. MISFORTUNE, 15
Job endured everything – until his f. came ENDURANCE, 8
lay down his f. for his life SELF-PRESERVATION, 10
Money can't buy f. MONEY, 36
none of his f. like him POPULARITY, 9
not so much our f.' help that helps us FRIENDSHIP, 17
Once more unto the breach, dear f. COURAGE, 19
our f. are true and our happiness OPTIMISM, 15
shameful to distrust one's f. FRIENDS, 12
that a man lay down his life for his f. LOVE, 25
the best of f. must part PARTING, 2
troops of unrecording f. LIFE, 50
with a little help from my f. FRIENDS, 10
without three good f. MONEY, 41
you choose your f. FAMILY, 9; FRIENDS, 6
friendship A man, Sir, should keep his f. in constant repair FRIENDS, 9
Business...may bring money...f. hardly ever does MONEY, 6
f. closes its eyes LOVE AND FRIENDSHIP, 1; FRIENDSHIP, 5
F. is a disinterested commerce between equals LOVE AND FRIENDSHIP, 2
F. is constant in all other things LOVE AND FRIENDSHIP, 3
F. is unnecessary FRIENDSHIP, 22
love...looks more like hatred than like f. LOVE AND HATE, 5
Most f. is feigning INSINCERITY, 4
Society, f., and love SOLITUDE, 4
The dupe of f., and the fool of love BITTERNESS, 1
To like...the same things, that is...true f. FRIENDSHIP, 26
true bond of f. FRIENDSHIP, 25
frighten by God, they f. me OFFICERS, 13
f. the horses SEX, 9
frightened My father was f. of his mother FAMILY, 13
frittered life is f. away by detail SIMPLICITY, 8
frivolity gay without f. FUTURE, 1
frocks f. are built in Paris FASHION, 6
frog A f. he would a-wooing go NURSERY RHYMES, 1
frogs F. and snails /And puppy-dogs' tails NURSERY RHYMES, 65
frontier We stand today on the edge of a new f. BEGINNING, 12
froth Life is mostly f. and bubble MISFORTUNE, 10
fruit every good tree bringeth forth good f. ACHIEVEMENT, 1; RESULTS, 3
Ignorance is like a delicate exotic f. IGNORANCE, 17
Some f. for Him that dressed me SERVICE, 2
the f. /Of that forbidden tree SIN, 16
the f. of the Spirit is love, joy, peace CHRISTIANITY, 8
Too late for f., too soon for flowers ILLNESS, 13
fruitful be f. and multiply MANKIND, 5; CREATION, 6
The command 'Be f. and multiply CONTRACEPTION, 4
fruitfulness reaping the greatest f....from life DANGER, 6
fruits by their f. ye shall know them ACHIEVEMENT, 1; RESULTS, 3
No f., no flowers, no leaves, no birds MONTHS, 10
frustrate In three sips...Arian f. DRINKS, 2
Fry Dear Roger F. whom I love as a man CRITICS, 12
fuck Fish f. in it WATER, 4
They f. you up, your mum and dad FAMILY, 19
fucking all this cold-hearted f. ANIMALISM, 4
fugitive a f. and a vagabond PUNISHMENT, 2
fulfilment Contentment and f. don't make for very good fiction FICTION, 5
full f. of new wine DRUNKENNESS, 8
Reading maketh a f. man READING, 1
fun Casanova had lots of f. AIDS, 3
f. to be in the same decade AGE, 48
Most people get a fair amount of f. out of their lives LIFE, 40
No woman has an abortion for *f.* ABORTION, 3
People must not do things for f. PLEASURE, 13
the most f. I ever had without laughing SEX, 2
the people have f. PLEASURE, 24
Work is much more f. than f. WORK, 7
you feel as if a human being sitting inside were making f. of you ANIMALS, 8
function f. of the critic CRITICS, 1
funeral F. marches to the grave MORTALITY, 14
funerals If you don't go to other men's f. FUNERALS, 4
weddings is sadder than f. MARRIAGE, 21
funny Everything is f. HUMOUR, 26
F. peculiar, or funny ha-ha HUMOUR, 14
F. without being vulgar CRITICISM, 15
hard to be f. when you have to be clean HUMOUR, 30
its own animality either objectionable or f. HUMOUR, 18
Kings...are just as f. ROYALTY, 29
to accuse someone of trying to be f. is highly abusive HUMOUR, 20
furiously sleep f. NONSENSE, 10
furnace a burning fiery f. DOOMSDAY, 1
Heat not a f. for your foe EXCESS, 11
furniture brain attic stocked with all the f. KNOWLEDGE, 13
fury full of sound and f. LIFE, 45
hell a f. like a woman scorned LOVE AND HATE, 3
no f. like an ex-wife searching for a new lover WOMEN, 24
strength and f. PATIENCE, 11

the F. of a Patient Man PATIENCE, 10
fustest f. with the mostest MISQUOTATIONS, 16
I got there f. with the mostest WAR, 38
future *F.*, n. That period of time in which OPTIMISM, 15
how pleasant...not to have any f. FUTURE, 5
If you want a picture of the f. OPPRESSION, 6
if you would divine the f. PAST, 4
I have a vision of the f. FUTURE, 2
I have seen the f. FUTURE, 7
I mean a F. Life AFTERLIFE, 2
I never think of the f. FUTURE, 6
people who live in the f. PROGRESS, 1
pick today's fruits, not relying on the f. PRESENT, 9
The f. is...black RACISM, 3
The f. is made of the same stuff FUTURE, 8
The f. is the only kind of property SLAVERY, 1
the f....makes cowards of us PRESENT, 3
The past was nothing...The f. was a mystery PRESENT, 2
Who controls the past controls the f. POWER, 18
You cannot fight against the f. PROGRESS, 7
Fuzzy-Wuzzy to you, F., at your 'ome in the Soudan RACISM, 16

G

gaiety the only concession to g. WELSH, 2
gain never broke the Sabbath, but for G. SIN, 13
richest g. I count but loss HUMILITY, 13
gained learning hath g. most BOOKS, 19
gainful to seek...g. employment GOVERNMENT, 1
gains no g. without pains ENDURANCE, 19; SUCCESS, 16
Galatians a great text in G. BIBLE, 3
Galileo If G. had said in verse that the world moved POETRY, 19
gall in a hospital...the assumption...that because you have lost your g. bladder HOSPITALITY, 7
gallant a loyal, a g., a generous, an ingenious, and good-temper'd people FRANCE, 14
gallantry What men call g. ADULTERY, 1
gallery The boy I love is up in the g. LOVE, 144
galloped I g., Dirck g. HORSES, 3
gallows You will die either on the g., or of the pox REPARTEE, 5
gamble Life is a g. LIFE, 48
gambling primary notion back of most g. is the excitement SPECULATION, 3
game He no play-a da g. CONTRACEPTION, 3
how you played the g. SPORT AND GAMES, 20; VICTORY, 15
I don't like this g. SPORT AND GAMES, 17
It's more than a g.. It's an institution CRICKET, 4
Play up! play up! and play the g. WAR, 76
win this g. and thrash the Spaniards SPORT AND GAMES, 5; WAR, 34
woman is his g. SEXES, 23
gameboy g. down a well POP MUSIC, 8
gamekeeping the book cannot take the place of...*Practical G.* WRITERS, 46
games The most important thing in the Olympic G. VICTORY, 4
gamesmanship G. or The Art of Winning Games SPORT AND GAMES, 19
gaming Man is a g. animal SPORT AND GAMES, 14
gangsters great nations have always acted like g. DIPLOMACY, 13
Garbo one sees in G. sober COMPLIMENTS, 7
garden a g. in her face ADMIRATION, 4
A g. is a lovesome thing GARDENS, 4
Come into the g., Maud INVITATIONS, 2
cultivate our g. PAROCHIALISM, 3
Don't go into Mr McGregor's g. CAUTION, 12
God Almighty first planted a g. GARDENS, 2
God the first g. made GARDENS, 6
I have a g. of my own GARDENS, 10
My heart shall be thy g. LOVE, 91
nearer God's Heart in a g. GARDENS, 7
the g. of Eden TREES, 1; KNOWLEDGE, 7
There are fairies at the bottom of our g. FAIRIES, 3
gardener Every time I talk to...my g., I'm convinced of the opposite HAPPINESS, 19
Nor does a...g. scent his roses POETS, 4
Oh, Adam was a g. GARDENS, 8
gardens closing time in the g. of the West CAPITALISM, 1
garland wither'd is the g. of the war MOURNING, 11
garlands gather g. there COUNTRYSIDE, 8
Garrick G. was pure gold ACTORS, 11
garrulous That g. monk HITLER, 5
Garter I like the G. TITLES, 5
gas effects of the successful g. attack were horrible WORLD WAR I, 5
If silicon had been a g. I should have been a major-general EXAMINATIONS, 3
gaslight Fanny by G. BOOK, SONG, AND PLAY TITLES, 23
gas-masks digging trenches and trying on g. WORLD WAR II, 1
gate I am here at the g. alone INVITATIONS, 2
I said to the man who stood at the g. of the year FAITH, 11
matters not how strait the g. RESPONSIBILITY, 8
the g. of heaven HEAVEN, 2
gatekeeper After I die, I shall return to earth as a g. of a bordello THREATS, 3
gates Battering the g. of heaven EXCESS, 14
the g. of the day LONELINESS, 10
the iron g. of life LOVE, 88
gateway 'Sex,'...'is the g. to life.' SEX, 6
gather G. the flowers... FLOWERS, 8
G. ye rosebuds while ye may PRESENT, 6
gathered where two or three are g. together CHURCH, 2; PRAYER, 6
gatling The g.'s jammed and the colonel dead WAR, 76
gaudy round, neat, not g. GARDENS, 9
Gaul G. is divided into three FRANCE, 1
Gaullist I...have become a G....little by little POLITICS, 30
gave God...g. his only begotten Son CHRISTIANITY, 13
gay g. without frivolity FUTURE, 1
when its g. priests NEWSPAPERS, 8
gays wouldn't be discriminating against g. HOMOSEXUALITY, 9
Gaza Eyeless in G. BLINDNESS, 3
gazelle never nurs'd a dear g. ANIMALS, 14
G.B.S G. looked aged and feeble WRITERS, 38
general caviare to the g. TASTE, 7
In a civil war, a g. must know WAR, 89
was good for G. Motors BUSINESS, 28
generalizations All g. are dangerous GENERALIZATIONS, 2
generalize To g. is to be an idiot GENERALIZATIONS, 1
generals at the age of four with paper hats and wooden swords we're all G. AUTHORITARIANISM, 8
Dead battles, like dead g. WAR, 120
It is not the business of g. to shoot one another OFFICERS, 14
that's not against the law for g. OFFICERS, 12
to be left to the g. OFFICERS, 5
wish he would *bite*...my g. REPARTEE, 3
generation Each g. imagines itself...more intelligent AGE, 44
You are a lost g. WAR, 114
generations g....have struggled in poverty to build these altars RELIGION, 53
g....pass in a short time MORTALITY, 15
No hungry g. tread thee down BIRDS, 5
generosity The poor...their function...is to exercise our g. POVERTY, 28
generous a loyal, a gallant, a g., an ingenious, and good-temper'd people FRANCE, 14
genes preserve the selfish molecules known as g. SURVIVAL, 3
genitalia D.H.L.'s interest in the human g. WRITERS, 66
genius a country full of g., but with absolutely no talent IRELAND, 11
A g.! For thirty-seven years I've practiced...and now they call me a g. GENIUS, 8
a German and a g. LAST WORDS, 68
Ah, a German and a g. MUSICIANS, 21
G....capacity of taking trouble GENIUS, 2
G. does what it must TALENT AND GENIUS, 3
G. is an infinite capacity GENIUS, 1
G. is one per cent inspiration GENIUS, 5
He identified g. with immunity from...cravings WRITERS, 58
His thoughts...borne on the gusts of g. POETS, 39
Milton, Madam, was a g. MILTON, 2; POETS, 44
Nothing, except my g. CONCEIT, 25
Only an organizing g. INCOMPETENCE, 1
Rules and models destroy g. and art RULES, 2
Since when was g....respectable RESPECTABILITY, 1
talent instantly recognizes g. MEDIOCRITY, 3; TALENT AND GENIUS, 2
Taste is the feminine of g. TASTE, 3
the difference between talent and g. TALENT AND GENIUS, 1
the most *vulgar-minded* g. POETS, 33
The poor little woman of g. WRITERS, 86

true g. is a mind of large general powers GENIUS, 7
True g. walks along a line GENIUS, 6
Unless one is a g. COMMUNICATION, 2
What a commonplace g. he has WRITERS, 62
When a true g. appears GENIUS, 9
geniuses G. don't die GENIUS, 3
genocide turning away from…g. BOSNIA AND HERCEGOVINA, 5
gent what a man is to a g. INTELLIGENCE, 1
gentil verray parfit g. knight CHIVALRY, 4
Gentiles a light to lighten the G. DEATH, 30
gentleman A g. need not know Latin EDUCATION, 34
a g.…never inflicts pain CHIVALRY, 8
A g.…wouldn't hit a woman with his hat on CHIVALRY, 1
g. of leisure MATERIALISM, 20
g.….robbing the poor CLASS, 30
God is a g. GOD, 40
last g. in Europe WRITERS, 65
Not a g.; dresses too well CLOTHES, 14
The Devil is a g. DEVIL, 11
the g. is an *attorney* LAWYERS, 7
Who was then the g. CLASS, 4
gentlemanly secondly, g. conduct EDUCATION, 2
gentlemen by g. for g. NEWSPAPERS, 13
extremely difficult to behave like g. WOMEN, 48
g., let us do something today WAR, 31
G.…remember blondes APPEARANCE, 23
God rest you merry, g. CHRISTMAS, 4
Good-morning, g. both INSULTS, 16
one of Nature's G. CHIVALRY, 7
religion for g. RELIGION, 12
Scholars and g. HONOUR, 7
the British bourgeoisie have spoken of themselves as g. CLASS, 35
There were g. and…seamen in the navy NAVY, 3
the seamen were not g. NAVY, 3
gentlewoman gravest sins it was possible for a g. to commit READING, 18
genuineness G. only thrives in the dark SINCERITY, 4
geographical India is a g. term PLACES, 2
geography G. is about Maps BIOGRAPHY, 1
geometers Church produced no g. CHURCH, 6
geometrical Population…increases in a g. ratio ECONOMICS, 16
geometricians we are g. only by chance PHILOSOPHY, 4
geometry G. is not true MATHEMATICS, 8
Poetry is as exact a science as g. POETRY, 15
There is no 'royal road' to g. MATHEMATICS, 4
George *Death of King G. V* HUNTING, 1
G. the Third…*may profit by their example* TREASON, 4
King G. will be able to read that SIGNATURES, 2
Georgia marching through G. GLORY, 5
Georgie G. Porgie, pudding and pie NURSERY RHYMES, 12
German a G. and a genius LAST WORDS, 68
Ah, a G. and a genius MUSICIANS, 21
I speak…G. to my horse LANGUAGE, 7
Life is too short to learn G. LANGUAGE, 21
the G. text of French operas OPERA, 10
Germans created to jab the life out of G. WAR, 98; WORLD WAR I, 19
Don't let's be beastly to the G. GERMANY, 12
How…thorough these G. always managed to be GERMANY, 15
The G.…are going to be squeezed RETRIBUTION, 10
to the G. that of the air EUROPE, 15
Germany Defeat of G. means WORLD WAR II, 27
G., G. before all else GERMANY, 13
G. was the cause of Hitler HITLER, 8
G. will be…a world power GERMANY, 14
If we see that G. is winning WORLD WAR II, 29
In G., the Nazis came for the Communists NAZISM, 5
Nazi G. had become a menace to all mankind NAZISM, 4
Gert There's G. and there's Epp and there's Ein HUMOUR, 31
gesture g. by the individual to himself BUSINESS, 11
get I thought it was a pity to g. up BED, 6
getting a secret way…of g. at a boy EVIL, 8
G. and spending WASTE, 3
ghost I, born of flesh and g. DEATH, 124
the G. in the Machine MIND, 6
The Papacy is not other than the G. of the deceased Roman Empire CATHOLICISM, 5
There is a g. /That eats handkerchiefs LOSS, 4
yielded up the g. LAST WORDS, 11
ghoulies From g. and ghosties and long-leggety beasties PRAYER, 2; SUPERNATURAL, 1
giant Fleas…upon the body of a g. PERSPECTIVE, 3
owner whereof was G. Despair DESPAIR, 3
we have only awakened a sleeping g. WORLD WAR II, 31
giants A battle of g. WAR, 127
it is by standing on the shoulders of g. PROGRESS, 9
not g. but windmills DELUSION, 2
war of the g. is over WORLD WAR II, 16
Gideon Why do they put the G. Bibles SEX, 41
gift Never look a g. horse INGRATITUDE, 1
the timeliness of the g. PROMPTNESS, 1
True love's the g. which God has given LOVE, 113
worth more than the g. GIFTS, 4
gifts deserves the name of happy who knows how to use the gods' g. wisely HAPPINESS, 9
God's g. put man's best g. GOD, 16
I fear the Greeks even when they bring g. MISTRUST, 11
The Gods themselves cannot recall their g. IRREVOCABILITY, 2
gild To g. refined gold EXCESS, 10
gilded g. tomb of a mediocre talent BOOKS, 40
She's only a bird in a g. cage IMPRISONMENT, 3
gin G. was mother's milk ALCOHOL, 56
No man is genuinely happy, married, who has to drink worse g. ALCOHOL, 44
she was dead; but my father he kept ladling g. REMEDIES, 12
The shortest way out of Manchester is…g. PLACES, 1
girded Pavilioned in splendour, and g. with praise GOD, 23
girl Every little g. knows about love LOVE, 111
From birth to age eighteen, a g. needs good parents AGE, 63
g. with brains WOMEN, 47
Give me a g. at an impressionable age IMPRESSIONABILITY, 3
If you were the only g. in the world LOVE, 65
one can…see in a little g. the threat of a woman CHILDREN, 20
One g. can be pretty BEAUTY, 18
park, a policeman and a pretty g. HUMOUR, 5
There was a little g. /Who had a little curl SEX, 39
girlfriend Not every problem someone has with his g. is…due to…capitalist…production CAPITALISM, 8
girls Boys and g. come out to play NURSERY RHYMES, 6
G. and boys grow up more normally together EDUCATION, 45
g. are so queer WOMEN, 8
g. from being g. SEXES, 12
g.…say No when they mean Yes WOMEN, 8
g. who wear glasses APPEARANCE, 27
if ever I was to have a dozen g., I'd call 'em all Jane NAMES, 8
little g.…slamming doors CHILDREN, 10
My life with g. has ended SEX, 25
one of the nicest g. I was ever engaged to MARRIAGE, 136
the…rift between the sexes is…widened by…teaching…to the g. SEXES, 22
Treaties are like roses and young g. DIPLOMACY, 10
When you see what some g. marry MARRIAGE, 100
Where…boys plan for what…g. plan for whom SEXES, 10
give freely ye have received, freely g. GENEROSITY, 3; GIFTS, 2
g. me liberty or g. me death FREEDOM, 16
G. me your tired…/Your huddled masses AMERICA, 22
my peace I g. unto you PEACE, 2
such as I have g. I thee REMEDIES, 3
To g. and not to count the cost SELFLESSNESS, 2
When I g. I g. myself SELF, 19
given I wish that God had not g. me what I prayed for DISAPPOINTMENT, 7
I would have g. you another CHIVALRY, 5
gives He g. twice who g. promptly PROMPTNESS, 4
giving The manner of g. GIFTS, 4
gizzard My wife hath something in her g. PROVOCATION, 1
glad A heart…too soon made g. IMPRESSIONABILITY, 1
with a love like that you know you should be g. LOVE, 83
you would have been very g. if I had written it PLAYS, 6
gladsome Let us with a g. mind /Praise the Lord GOD, 37
Gladstone G. POLITICIANS, 35
Mr G. read Homer for fun CLASSICS, 2
glamorous g. only in retrospect TRAVEL, 23
Glasgow never played the G. Empire PSYCHIATRY, 2
glass baying for broken g. ARISTOCRACY, 15
He liked the sound of broken g. ARISTOCRACY, 2
on the other side of the g. LIFE, 11
Satire is a sort of g. SATIRE, 3
through a g., darkly CHARITY, 6

you won't intoxicate with one g. EXPERIENCE, 10
glasses girls who wear g. APPEARANCE, 27
glimpse I...catch a g. of a stoat PURPOSE, 5
Same old g. of /Paradise MARRIAGE, 76
glisters Nor all that g. gold TEMPTATION, 6
glittering world continues to offer g. prizes RUTHLESSNESS, 6
glitters All that g. is not gold APPEARANCES, 1
gloamin Roamin' in the g.' SCOTLAND, 6
global my wars /Were g. WAR, 90
the world in the image of a g. village TECHNOLOGY, 9
globe the great g. itself MORTALITY, 17
globule I can trace my ancestry back to a...g. ANCESTRY, 2
gloire *Le jour de g. est arrivé* FRANCE, 10
gloria *Sic transit g. mundi* GLORY, 3
glorious G. things of thee are spoken HEAVEN, 7
Happy and g. BRITAIN, 6
glory Another g. awaits us in heaven HEAVEN, 8
But trailing clouds of g. METAPHYSICS, 5
G. be to God for dappled things BEAUTY, 20
g., jest, and riddle of the world HUMAN CONDITION, 14
greatest g. is not in never falling ACHIEVEMENT, 3
I go on to g. LAST WORDS, 20
It is a great g. in a woman WOMEN, 78
Land of Hope and G. BRITAIN, 4
Mine eyes have seen the g. of the coming of the Lord GOD, 26
paths of g. lead but to the grave MORTALITY, 10
Popularity?...g.'s small change POPULARITY, 4
the g. of Europe is extinguished for ever EUROPE, 2
the Son of man coming...with power and great g. DOOMSDAY, 2
To the greater g. of God CATHOLICISM, 2
we left him alone with his g. FUNERALS, 11
Where is it now, the g. and the dream METAPHYSICS, 5
Gloucester Doctor Foster went to G. NURSERY RHYMES, 10
glow make the corpuscles of the blood g. JEWS, 8
Glum I've examined your son's head, Mr G. STUPIDITY, 12
speed g. heroes...to death WAR, 100
gluttony G. is an emotional escape GREED, 6
gnomes the little g. of Zürich MONEY, 52
go a good cook, as cooks g. HUMOUR, 54
In the name of God, *g.!* DISMISSAL, 1
I shall be the last to g. out COURAGE, 2
Let us g. then, you and I DEPARTURE, 6
not to g. anywhere, but to g. TRAVEL, 22
stopped short – never to g. again CLOCKS, 3
whither thou goest, I will g. LOYALTY, 5
goal The g. stands up FOOTBALL, 4
goat-footed This g. bard POLITICIANS, 58
God Act of G....*something which no reasonable man could have expected* DISASTER, 3
A G. who let us prove his existence GOD, 15
a kind of Providence will...end...the acts of G. DISASTER, 2
A man with G. GOD, 31
America is G.'s Crucible AMERICA, 42
an absolute faith that all things are possible to G. FAITH, 10
an atheist half believes a G. FEAR, 15
An honest G. GOD, 29
Are G. and Nature then at strife NATURE, 15
better to have no opinion of G. GOD, 3
but for the grace of G. goes LUCK, 6
charged with the grandeur of G. GOD, 25
concept of G. has any validity RELIGION, 5
cricket is the greatest thing that G. ever created CRICKET, 6
diet unfolded...that G. was showing me FOOD, 16
effect Whose cause is G. NATURE, 6
Either a beast or a g. MANKIND, 2
either a wild beast or a g. SOLITUDE, 1
Even G. cannot change the past PAST, 1
even G. was born /too late RELIGION, 39
Every man thinks G. is on his side GOD, 2
final proof of G.'s omnipotence GOD, 19
for which...the good G. prepare me BLINDNESS, 7
G. alone deserves to be loved LOVE, 112
G. as a working hypothesis GOD, 14
G. bless ... G. damn LAST WORDS, 69
'G. bless us every one!' BLESSING, 6
G. can stand being told GOD, 43
G. could cause us considerable embarrassment DISCOVERY, 4
G. defend me from my friends FRIENDSHIP, 4
G. disposes GOD, 30
G. does not play dice SCIENCE, 15
G. erects a house of prayer DEVIL, 7
G....first planted a garden GARDENS, 2
G. has written all the books SUBJECTIVITY, 2
G. helps them SELF, 2
G. is a gentleman GOD, 40
G. is always on the side of the big battalions POWER POLITICS, 7
G. is beginning to resemble...the last fading smile of a cosmic Cheshire cat GOD, 27
G. is dead GOD, 39
G. is nothing more than an exalted father GOD, 22
G. is on the side...of the best shots POWER POLITICS, 8
G. is really only another artist GOD, 42
G. is subtle but he is not malicious GOD, 21
G. is the immemorial refuge of the incompetent GOD, 35
G.....just had the power to kill her RELIGION, 1
G. made everything out of nothing CREATION, 15
G. made the country COUNTRYSIDE, 2
G. save our gracious King BRITAIN, 6
G.'s gifts put man's best gifts GOD, 16
G. should go before such villains GOD, 44
G.'s in His heaven PERFECTION, 2
G. the first garden made GARDENS, 6
G. will cease to dream you DEATH, 69
G. will grant an end to these too ENDURANCE, 21
G. will pardon me. It is His trade LAST WORDS, 36
going back to G. RELIGION, 7
Great G. grant that twice two be not four PRAYER, 18
Had I but serv'd my G. with half the zeal /I serv'd my King REGRET, 19
Had I...served G. as diligently as I have served the king LOYALTY, 11
have one G. only GOD, 17
her conception of G. was certainly not orthodox GOD, 47
Holy, holy, holy, Lord G. Almighty GOD, 24
How could G. do this to me INJUSTICE, 9
I am glad...he thanks G. for anything GRATITUDE, 2
I believe I am becoming a g. LAST WORDS, 72
I did not write it. G. wrote it INSPIRATION, 6
If G. did not exist GOD, 49
If G. made us in His image GOD, 50
If G. were suddenly condemned to live the life HUMAN CONDITION, 6
If this man is not faithful to his G. LOYALTY, 9
if triangles invented a g. RELIGION, 47
If you don't find a G. by five o'clock this afternoon ATHEISM, 7
If you talk to G., you are praying MADNESS, 15
It takes a long while for a...trustful person to reconcile himself to...G. FAITH, 15
I wouldn't give up writing about G. WRITERS, 90
I wretch lay wrestling with...my G. SOUL, 7
justify the ways of G. to men GOD, 38
Just what G. would have done if he had the money WEALTH, 30
Kill everyone, and you are a g. KILLING, 7
Know then thyself, presume not G. to scan SELF-KNOWLEDGE, 5
Live among men as if G. beheld you RIGHTEOUSNESS, 8
Many people believe that they are attracted by G. RELIGION, 34
May G. deny you peace GLORY, 2
nature is the art of G. NATURE, 1
Nearer, my G., to thee RELIGION, 2
none deny there is a G. ATHEISM, 3
One G., one law, one element DESTINY, 22
One on G.'s side is a majority GOD, 41
only G. can make a tree TREES, 9
Our G., our help in ages past RELIGION, 64
poems...for the love of Man and in praise of G. POETRY, 48
proof that G. is a bore PROTESTANTISM, 1
prose for G. LANGUAGE, 13
put your hand into the hand of G. FAITH, 11
Sickness, sin and death...do not originate in G. RELIGION, 21
Since G. has given us the papacy...enjoy it CATHOLICISM, 8
speak to G. as if men were listening RIGHTEOUSNESS, 8
that G. is interested only...in religion GOD, 48
that great Leviathan, or rather...that *Mortal G.* STATE, 1
The Act of G. designation ACCIDENTS, 1
the dear G. who loveth us PRAYER, 9
the electric display of G. the Father LIFE, 39

the highest praise of G. consists in the denial of Him ATHEISM, 9
the nearer you are to G. PROTESTANTISM, 3
the one G. whose worshippers…still trust in Him LUCK, 7
There, but for the Grace of G., goes G. ARROGANCE, 5
There once was a man who said G. EXISTENCE, 4
The true G.…G. of ideas INSPIRATION, 7
Those who marry G.…can become domesticated RELIGION, 29
To understand G.'s thoughts STATISTICS, 7
we come /From G., who is our home METAPHYSICS, 5
we owe G. a death DEATH, 113
What G. does, He does well GOD, 32
What sort of G. are we portraying GOD, 20
When I composed that, I was…inspired by G. MUSIC, 9
when one has loved a man it is very different to love G. LOVE, 112
whom G. wishes to destroy MADNESS, 4
yearning like a G. in pain SUFFERING, 9
you hardly ever mention G. any more RELIGION, 44
you must believe in G. FAITH, 12

godlike patient endurance is g. ENDURANCE, 9

gods Against stupidity the g.…struggle in vain STUPIDITY, 14
by force of the g. ENDURANCE, 23
deserves the name of happy who knows how to use the g.' gifts wisely HAPPINESS, 9
for what high cause /This darling of the G. DESTINY, 14
g. handing down new commandments SCIENTISTS, 4
G. help them SELF-RELIANCE, 2
Kings are earth's g. ROYALTY, 31
leave the rest to the G. DUTY, 2
Live with the g. CONTENTMENT, 1
man's ignorance of the g. SPONTANEITY, 1
no other g. before me GOD, 10
So many g., so many creeds RELIGION, 70; KINDNESS, 6
The Ethiopians say that their g. are…black RELIGION, 72
The G. themselves cannot recall their gifts IRREVOCABILITY, 2
what end the g. have in store DESTINY, 13
Whom the g. love DEATH, 87
Whom the g. wish to destroy TALENT, 1

goe to morowe longe I to g. to God FAMILY, 25

going I am just g. outside LAST WORDS, 48
Men must endure /Their g. hence ENDURANCE, 17
Stand not upon the order of your g. DISMISSAL, 8

gold A g. rush is what happens when MATERIALISM, 23
all the g. that the goose could give MATERIALISM, 2
An angel writing in a book of g. DREAMS, 12
cursed /craving for g. MATERIALISM, 21
For g. in phisik is a cordial MATERIALISM, 5
Garrick was pure g. ACTORS, 11
gild refined g. EXCESS, 10
Good morning to the day: and next my g. MATERIALISM, 12
Nor all that glisters g. TEMPTATION, 6
silver and g. have I none REMEDIES, 3
Silver threads among the g. OLD AGE, 35
The ring so worn…is yet of g. APPEARANCE, 10
To a shower of g. BRIBERY, 2
travell'd in the realms of g. TRAVEL, 14
Were't not for g. and women SIN, 20
What female heart can g. despise MATERIALISM, 8
When every…thing you hold /Is made of silver, or of g. ECONOMICS, 9

golden G. slumbers kiss your eyes SLEEP, 7
In good King Charles's g. days SELF-PRESERVATION, 4
In old time we had treen chalices and g. priests CLERGY, 9
Jerusalem the g. MIDDLE EAST, 10
perhaps, the g. rule ABSTINENCE, 10
The g. apples of the sun DESIRE, 18
the G. Road to Samarkand KNOWLEDGE, 14
there are no g. rules RULES, 3

Goldwyn Mr G.…you are only interested in art ART, 26; MONEY, 45

golf an earnest protest against g. CRICKET, 1; GOLF, 1
G.…a form of moral effort GOLF, 2

golf clubs Give me my g.…and a beautiful partner DESIRE, 1

Gomorrah Sodom and…G. PUNISHMENT, 3

gone g. with the wind MEMORY, 6
G. With the Wind BOOK, SONG, AND PLAY TITLES, 19

gongs women should be struck…like g. WOMEN, 25

good a gigantic reservoir of g. will AMERICA, 38
A g. man fallen among Fabians WRITERS, 64
A g. novel tells us the truth NOVELS, 2
A G. Time Was Had by All PLEASURE, 28
All g. writing WRITING, 7
Anybody can be g. in the country COUNTRYSIDE, 10
Be g., sweet maid, and let who can be clever VIRTUE, 12
being really g. all the time HYPOCRISY, 18
dedicate this nation to the policy of the g. neighbor CHARITY, 16
Do g. by stealth GOOD, 14
doing g.…professions which are full CHARITY, 22
doing g. to base fellows CHARITY, 11
dull prospect of a distant g. PLEASURE, 11
every man at the beginning doth set forth g. wine ALCOHOL, 14
Every man loves what he is g. at ENTHUSIASM, 7
Evil, be thou my G. EVIL, 12
Evil comes…like the disease; g.…like the doctor GOOD AND EVIL, 2
Far too g. to waste on children YOUTH, 17
For the g. are always the merry HAPPINESS, 32
General G. is the plea of the scoundrel GOOD, 2
God saw that it was g. CREATION, 3
G., but not religious-g. VIRTUE, 9
G. isn't the word CRITICISM, 16
g. shepherd giveth his life for the sheep CHRISTIANITY, 15
G. things, when short, are twice as good BREVITY, 1
g. tidings of great joy CHRISTMAS, 8
greatest g. GOOD, 3
happiness makes them g. GOOD, 9
He who would do g. to another GOOD, 2
how *can* they become g. people PREJUDICE, 5
How g. is man's life, the mere living LIFE, 15
If…'feeling g.' could decide, drunkenness would be DRUNKENNESS, 13
If to do were as easy as to know what were g. ACTION, 11
If you can't be g. TEMPTATION, 2
I have fought a g. fight FAITH, 6
it cannot come to g. PESSIMISM, 11
It is g. to know what a man is UNDERSTANDING, 3
It is seldom…one parts on g. terms PARTING, 9
little of what you fancy does you g. PLEASURE, 19
Men have never been g. GOOD, 1
never was a g. war WAR AND PEACE, 6
no hint throughout the universe /Of g. or ill NECESSITY, 8
Nothing can harm a g. man GOOD, 16
nothing either g. or bad THINKING, 10
nothing g. to be had in the country COUNTRYSIDE, 4
One man is as g. as another WRITERS, 13
Only g. girls keep diaries DIARIES, 2
our people have never had it so g. WEALTH, 18
Roman Conquest…a G. Thing HISTORY, 29
science is…neither a potential for g. nor for evil SCIENCE, 39
strong antipathy of g. to bad PROVOCATION, 2
suppose the people g. CORRUPTION, 6
The g. die early GOOD AND EVIL, 3
The g. die first GOOD AND EVIL, 5
The g. die young DEATH, 10
The g. is oft interred with their bones EVIL, 16
The g. is the beautiful GOOD, 13
the g. must associate UNITY, 7
The g. of the people LAW, 7
The g. old times NOSTALGIA, 5
The king has been very g. to me MARTYRDOM, 1
the name of perseverance in a g. cause STUBBORNNESS, 3
The only g. Indians I ever saw were dead ENEMIES, 7
There is so much g. in the worst of us GOOD AND EVIL, 1
the thing which is g. PUNISHMENT, 1; SIN, 3
those who go about doing g. CHARITY, 13
thou g. and faithful servant SERVICE, 1
three ingredients in the g. life LIFE, 38
to write g. prose is an affair of g. manners POETRY AND PROSE, 4
what g. came of it at last VICTORY, 17
What's the g. of a home ABSENCE, 7
Whenever two g. people argue over principles PRINCIPLES, 3
When I'm g. I'm very g. SEX, 65
when the great and g. depart MORTALITY, 20
Why care for grammar as long as we are g. GRAMMAR, 8
You shouldn't say it is not g. GOOD, 18

goodbye G. to All That BOOK, SONG, AND PLAY TITLES, 10
Without a single kiss or a g. PARTING, 8

Good-bye-ee G.! – g. PARTING, 12

goodness And felt how awful g. is GOOD, 12

G. does not...make men happy GOOD, 9
My g. those diamonds are lovely GOOD, 17
Not to be wronged is to forgo...g. INJUSTICE, 13
goods isn't a bad bit of g., the Queen COMPLIMENTS, 1
good-temper'd an ingenious, and g. people FRANCE, 14
goodwill in peace, g. WAR AND PEACE, 3
goose all the gold that the g. could give MATERIALISM, 2
Goosey G., g. gander NURSERY RHYMES, 13
gored you tossed and g. several persons CONVERSATION, 3
gorgeous hold the g. east in fee VENICE, 4
Gospels We had no use for the policy of the G. REVENGE, 12
gossips No one g. about...secret virtues GOSSIP, 8
got Which in our case we have not g. WEAPONS, 7
gout A taste for drink, combined with g. ALCOHOL, 28
drink wine you have the g. DISEASE, 38
G....physician's name for DISEASE, 10
If gentlemen love the pleasant titillation of the g. DISEASE, 21
that old enemy the g. /Had taken him in toe PUNS, 6; ILLNESS, 7
what is a cure for g. DISEASE, 2
govern Every class is unfit to g. GOVERNMENT, 2
Grammar, which can g. even kings GRAMMAR, 6
He that would g. others SELF-CONTROL, 6
I will g. according to the common weal MONARCHY, 13
king reigns, but does not g. MONARCHY, 26
Kings g. by...assemblies only when MONARCHY, 12
Labour is not fit to g. POLITICS, 18
No man is good enough to g. another man DEMOCRACY, 9
Under socialism *all* will g. SOCIALISM, 10
governed not willing to be g. GOVERNMENT, 30
with how little wisdom the world is g. GOVERNMENT, 21
governing become accustomed to no one g. SOCIALISM, 10
the right of g. was not property but a trust GOVERNMENT, 9
government A g....big enough to give you all you want GOVERNMENT, 11
a g. organization could do it that quickly BUREAUCRACY, 3
All g....is founded on compromise and barter COMPROMISE, 4
As to religion...duty of g. to protect all...professors thereof GOVERNMENT, 23
Democracy is only an experiment in g. DEMOCRACY, 7
every g....should have its old speeches burned GOVERNMENT, 28
g. by crony NEPOTISM, 1
g. gives us is charity at election time OPPRESSION, 5
G....is but a necessary evil GOVERNMENT, 22
g. of the people, by the people, and for the people MEMORIALS, 6; DEMOCRACY, 12
I would not give half a guinea to live under one form of g. GOVERNMENT, 13
Monarchy is a strong g. MONARCHY, 1
no man believes, that want of g., is any new kind of g. GOVERNMENT, 12
people's g. GOVERNMENT, 33
prepare for g. POLITICS, 73
The g. burns down whole cities INJUSTICE, 10
the g. it deserves GOVERNMENT, 18
the President is dead, but the G. lives ASSASSINATION, 2
there was no form of g. common to the peoples REPUBLIC, 2
the things which g. does...social progress GOVERNMENT, 32
The worst g. is the most moral GOVERNMENT, 19
We live under a g. of men and...newspapers GOVERNMENT, 24; JOURNALISM, 26
governments all G. are selfish GOVERNMENT, 8
G. needs to have both shepherds and butchers GOVERNMENT, 31
The Beast stands for strong mutually antagonistic g. NEWSPAPERS, 14
governors Our supreme g., the mob PUBLIC, 20
Gower moral G. BOOKS, 13
grace but for the g. of God, goes LUCK, 6
God in his mercy lend her g. BEAUTY, 39
g. a summer queen COUNTRYSIDE, 8
He had at least the g. BRIBERY, 1
Lord, I ascribe it to Thy g. RELIGION, 63
Such g. had kings ROYALTY, 6
Tuesday's child is full of g. NURSERY RHYMES, 34
graces the G. do not seem...natives of Great Britain BRITISH, 4
gracious A life that moves to g. ends LIFE, 50
gradually Boys do not grow up g. CHILDREN, 19
Grail What were they going to do with the G. ARTHURIAN LEGEND, 1
grain A g., which in England is generally given to horses SCOTLAND, 3
He reaps the bearded g. at a breath DEATH, 79
grammar down to posterity talking bad g. GRAMMAR, 5
G., which can govern even kings GRAMMAR, 6
I am...above g. GRAMMAR, 7
Shakespeare...g. school kids LITERATURE, 4
Why care for g. as long as we are good GRAMMAR, 8
grammatical to refine our language to g. purity LANGUAGE, 14
gramophones waxworks inhabited by g. WORDS, 15
grand A 'G. Old Man' OLD AGE, 26
that g. old man POLITICIANS, 67
The g. Perhaps POSSIBILITY, 1
the g. style arises in poetry POETRY, 3
to be baith g. and comfortable LUXURY, 1
Grand Canyon coming across him at the G. INSULTS, 33
grandeur g. is a dream WEALTH, 11
g. of God GOD, 25
Many people have delusions of g. DELUSION, 5
grandfather g.'s clock CLOCKS, 2
having an ape for his g. EVOLUTION, 10
I don't know who my g. was ANCESTRY, 5
pass my declining years saluting...g. clocks OLD AGE, 31
grandmother I murdered my g. this morning INATTENTION, 4
We have become a g. AFFECTATION, 1
grandmothers selected...not on the basis of their g. NAZISM, 2
grandson concerned to know what his g. will be ANCESTRY, 5
your g. will...be a Communist COMMUNISM, 3
granny G. caught her tit in the mangle PLEASURE, 29
Grant Old Cary G. fine AGE, 31
granted infinite capacity for taking things for g. HUMAN NATURE, 13
grape Beulah, peel me a g. LUXURY, 6
grapes I am sure the g. are sour ENVY, 4
trampling out the vintage where the g. of wrath GOD, 26
grasp man's reach should exceed his g. AMBITION, 3
grass all flesh is as g. DEATH, 29
There's a snake hidden in the g. DANGER, 7
grassgreen down the g. gooseberried double bed SEX, 57
gratification I have had no real g....more than my neighbor...who is worth only half a million LAST WORDS, 71; WEALTH, 28
gratifying It is quite g. to feel guilty GUILT, 1
gratuite *L'acte g.* SPONTANEITY, 2
grave a-mouldering in the g. MEMORIALS, 4
And digs my g. at each remove DEATH, 60
And on his g., with shining eyes DEATH, 19
Between the cradle and the g. TRANSIENCE, 12
Dig the g. and let me lie DEATH, 120
Funeral marches to the g. MORTALITY, 14
her heart in his g. is lying MOURNING, 8
I may dread /The g. as little DEATH, 72
I shall soon be laid in the quiet g. DEATH, 71
Marriage is a step so g. and decisive MARRIAGE, 113
no work, nor device, nor knowledge...in the g. TRANSIENCE, 6, WORK, 3
O g., where is thy victory DEATH, 28, 94
paths of glory lead but to the g. MORTALITY, 10
The g.'s a fine and private place DEATH, 82
the g. yawns for him BORES, 7
To that dark inn, the g. DEATH, 101
grave-digger if I were a g., or...a hangman OCCUPATIONS, 8
graven any g. image GOD, 10
graves Six million young men lie in premature g. WORLD WAR I, 2
The bitterest tears shed over g. REGRET, 20
The dust of great persons' g. EQUALITY, 26
graveyards G....people associate them with death DEATH, 25
gravity He rose by g.; I sank by levity SERIOUSNESS, 4
gray When you are old and g. OLD AGE, 54
Gray Robin G., he was gudeman to me MARRIAGE, 19
grazed He is the richest author that ever g. WRITERS, 61
great All my shows are g. CONCEIT, 11
All things both g. and small PRAYER, 9
Everything g. in the world is done by neurotics NEUROSIS, 2
everything that is g....done by youth YOUTH, 6
fate of the g. wen LONDON, 5
G. men are but life-sized GREATNESS, 3
g. men have not commonly been g. scholars GREATNESS, 8
G. oaks BEGINNING, 4

History is full of ignominious getaways by the g. COWARDICE, 5
how g. a matter a little fire kindleth SPEECH, 5
How very small the very g. GREATNESS, 14; WISDOM, 23
If I am a g. man GREATNESS, 9
many of the g. men of history are frauds GREATNESS, 9
No g. man lives in vain GREATNESS, 6; HISTORY, 8
On earth there is nothing g. but man MANKIND, 14
Some are born g. GREATNESS, 12
the g. break through LAW, 26
The g. man...walks across his century INFLUENCE, 7
the g. ones eat up the little ones RUTHLESSNESS, 5
the shade /Of that which once was g. REGRET, 23
To be g. is to be misunderstood GREATNESS, 7
when the g. and good depart MORTALITY, 20
you...who have made me too g. for my house ROYALTY, 4
great-aunt indebted for a nose or an eye...to a g. FAMILY, 15
Great Britain G. could say that she supported both sides DIPLOMACY, 17
G. has lost an Empire BRITAIN, 1
G. is going to make war on a kindred nation WORLD WAR I, 3
To make a union with G. WORLD WAR II, 24
greater g. love hath no man LOVE, 25
The g. the power POWER, 8
Thy need is yet g. than mine SELF-DENIAL, 2
greatest great city...has the g. men and women GREATNESS, 15
I'm the g. CONCEIT, 1
the g. deeds require a certain insensitiveness INSENSITIVITY, 3
The g. happiness of the g. number HAPPINESS, 3
the g. of these is charity CHARITY, 6
great-grandfathers Classicism...the literature that gave... pleasure to their g. LITERATURE, 17
greatness long farewell to all my g. HUMAN CONDITION, 16
Men who have g....don't go in for politics POLITICIANS, 2
some have g. thrust upon 'em GREATNESS, 12
Greece Athens holds sway over all G. INFLUENCE, 9
G. might still be free EUROPE, 4
The isles of G. EUROPE, 3
Greek I...impress upon you the study of G. literature CLASSICS, 3
it was G. to me CONFUSION, 9
neither Jew nor G. CHRISTIANITY, 7
Nobody can say a word against G. CLASSICS, 8
small Latin and less G. CLASSICS, 5
the intrigue of a G. of the lower empire INSULTS, 15
The word is half G. and half Latin TELEVISION AND RADIO, 5
We were taught...Latin and G. CLASSICS, 9
Greeks G. Had a Word LANGUAGE, 1
I fear the G. even when they bring gifts MISTRUST, 11
To the G. the Muse gave native wit CLASSICS, 4
uncertainty: a state unknown to the G. UNCERTAINTY, 2
which came first, the G. or the Romans IGNORANCE, 5
green a g. thought in a g. shade OBLIVION, 3
for the wearin' o' the G. IRELAND, 2
G. grow the rashes O LOVE, 32
G. politics is not about being far left CONSERVATION, 5
I was g. in judgment YOUTH, 15
religious system that produced g. Chartreuse ALCOHOL, 51
There is a g. hill far away CHRISTIANITY, 1
tree of life is g. REALITY, 4; THEORY, 4
When the g. woods laugh HAPPINESS, 5
green-ey'd jealousy...g. monster JEALOUSY, 5
Greenland From G.'s icy mountains PLACES, 6
green-rob'd g. senators of mighty woods TREES, 7
green shoots g. of economic spring ECONOMICS, 13
Greensleeves G. was all my joy LOVE, 14
greenwood Under the g. tree COUNTRYSIDE, 9
greetings g. where no kindness is OPTIMISM, 29
perhaps the g. are intended for me POPULARITY, 1
grenadier bones of a single Pomeranian g. DIPLOMACY, 4
With a tow...row for the British G. HEROISM, 1
grew Three years she g. DEATH, 133
grey G. hairs are death's blossoms OLD AGE, 1
theory is all g. REALITY, 4; THEORY, 4
There is only one cure for g. hair....the guillotine REMEDIES, 15
well-belovèd's hair has threads of g. AGE, 70
grief A g. too much to be told SORROW, 27
calms one's g. by recounting it SORROW, 4
G. and disappointment give rise to anger EMOTION, 3
G. has turned her fair APPEARANCE, 41
in much wisdom is much g. KNOWLEDGE, 6; WISDOM, 2
Should be past g. REGRET, 15
The heart which g. hath cankered ALCOHOL, 18
grievances redress of the g. of the vanquished WAR, 27
grieve G. not that I die young DEATH, 59
Men are we, and must g. REGRET, 23
grill be careful not to look like a mixed g. APPEARANCE, 9
grimace only pianist I have ever seen who did not g. MUSICIANS, 19
grin All Nature wears one universal g. NATURE, 9
ending with the g., which remained some time SUPERNATURAL, 5
grind mills of God g. slowly GOD, 34
yet they g. exceeding small GOD, 34
grinders Writers, like teeth, are divided into incisors and g. WRITERS, 2
grist All's g. that comes to the mill OPPORTUNITY, 1
groan men sit and hear each other g. HUMAN CONDITION, 12
groans How alike are the g. of love to those of the dying LOVE AND DEATH, 4
Gromyko the G. of the Labour party POLITICIANS, 54
grooves specialists...tend to think in g. EXPERTS, 6
Groucho had Marx been G. instead of Karl HUMOUR, 3
No, G. is not my real name NAMES, 5
group A g. of closely related persons FAMILY, 22
groupies We don't get g. POP MUSIC, 19
grovelled Whenever he met a great man he g. SERVILITY, 7
groves And seek for truth in the g. of Academe EDUCATION, 22
grow Green g. the rashes O LOVE, 32
make two ears of corn...g. POLITICIANS, 27
make two questions g. where only one RESEARCH, 6
some of us never g. out AUTHORITARIANISM, 8
They shall g. not old MEMORIALS, 3
grow'd 'I 'spect I g..' CREATION, 13
growing Be not afraid of g. slowly ACHIEVEMENT, 2
G. old is like being increasingly penalized OLD AGE, 34
growl I hate a fellow...who does nothing...but sit and g. PETULANCE, 4
grown Boys...are unwholesome companions for g. people CHILDREN, 32
one of the few English novels for g. up people CRITICISM, 56
grown-ups g....have forgotten what it is like to be a child CHILDREN, 27
grows Nothing g. well in the shade GREATNESS, 5
growth as short a Spring; /As quick a g. to meet decay TRANSIENCE, 14
elations and apprehensions of g. AGE, 37
G. is a greater mystery than death AGE, 37
grub it is poor g., poor pay, and easy work AMERICA, 24; ENGLAND, 25
grumbling the muttering grew to a g. ANIMALS, 6
gruntled far from feeling g. DISCONTENT, 9
he was far from being g. HUMOUR, 58
guarantee No one can g. success in war WAR, 29
guard That g. our native seas NAVY, 1
guardian As g. of His Majesty's conscience MONARCHY, 24
guards Up, G., and at 'em WAR, 128
Who is to guard the g. themselves MISTRUST, 7
gudeman Robin Gray, he was g. to me MARRIAGE, 19
guerre *ce n'est pas la g.* WAR, 12
guerrilla The g. fights the war of the flea WAR, 117
The g. wins if he does not lose WAR, 57
guest A free-loader is a confirmed g. PARASITES, 2
Earth, receive an honoured g. POETS, 18
The g. who outstays HOSPITALITY, 4
guests the g. must be chosen as carefully as the wine ALCOHOL, 52
guide Custom, then, is the great g. of human life CUSTOM, 2
Everyman, I will go with thee, and be thy g. GUIDANCE, 1
I have only a faint light to g. me GUIDANCE, 2
guiding little onward lend thy g. hand GUIDANCE, 3
guillotine one cure for grey hair....the g. REMEDIES, 15
guilt Let other pens dwell on g. and misery OPTIMISM, 14
Life without industry is g. ART, 24
put on a dress of g. GUILT, 6
guiltless Whose g. heart is free RIGHTEOUSNESS, 4
guilty g. of Noël Cowardice COWARDICE, 1
It is quite gratifying to feel g. GUILT, 1
Let no g. man escape JUSTICE, 9
ten g. persons escape than one innocent suffer JUSTICE, 3
tremble like a g. thing surprised DOUBT, 8

guinea a round disc of fire somewhat like a g. PERCEPTION, 3
I would not give half a g. to live under one form of government GOVERNMENT, 13
there go two-and-forty sixpences…to one g. MERIT, 4
guineas I have only five g. in my pocket GENEROSITY, 5
Guinness G. is good for you ADVERTISING, 10
gulphs whelm'd in deeper g. than he DEATH, 40
gum can't fart and chew g. MISQUOTATIONS, 21
gun g. is the ideal weapon WEAPONS, 5
it is necessary to take up the g. WAR, 64
The difference between a g. and a tree TREES, 13
we have got /The Maxim G. POWER POLITICS, 1
gunfire Thanks to the movies, g. has always sounded unreal CINEMA, 12
Gunga Din You're a better man than I am, G. SUPERIORITY, 6
gunpowder G., Printing, and the Protestant Religion CIVILIZATION, 3
ingredients of g.…were known to him SCIENTISTS, 12
guns But it's 'Saviour of 'is country' when the g. SOLDIERS, 1
Elevate them g. a little lower WAR, 51
G. will make us powerful POWER POLITICS, 3
gutless W. H. Auden, a sort of g. Kipling SOCIALISM, 13
gutter We are all in the g. OPTIMISM, 28
gypsies Play with the g. in the wood NURSERY RHYMES, 35

H

habit a h. the pleasure of which increases LETTER-WRITING, 1
H. is a great deadener HABIT, 2
honour peereth in the meanest h. APPEARANCES, 22
some h. of which he is deeply ashamed TELEVISION AND RADIO, 2
habitation to airy nothing /A local h. POETRY, 41
habits Cultivate only the h. HABIT, 5
Curious things, h. HABIT, 3
h. that carry them far apart HABIT, 4
Old h. die hard HABIT, 1
hack Do not h. me EXECUTION, 17
had you h. it in you EXPECTATION, 3
hae Scots, wha h. WAR, 20
ha-ha Funny peculiar, or funny h. HUMOUR, 14
hail All h., the power of Jesus' name CHRISTIANITY, 37
h. and farewell GREETINGS, 1
H., h. rock'n'roll' POP MUSIC, 5
the flail of the lashing h. WEATHER, 24
hair busy driving cabs and cutting h. GOVERNMENT, 7
if a woman have long h. APPEARANCE, 5
part my h. behind OLD AGE, 18
Take a h. of the dog ALCOHOL, 5
To Crystal, h. was the most important APPEARANCE, 26
you have lovely h. BEAUTY, 15
half And when they were only h. way up ARMY, 1
h. a loaf is better than a whole COMPROMISE, 5
I am only h. there when I am ill ILLNESS, 12
I have not told h. of what I saw LAST WORDS, 53
longest h. of your life YOUTH, 18
One h.…cannot understand…the other PLEASURE, 3
There is an old saying 'well begun is h. done' BEGINNING, 11
half-a-dozen six of one and h. of the other SIMILARITY, 5
half-developed the working-class which, raw and h. PUBLIC, 2
half-wits a wit out of two h. FOOLISHNESS, 16
halitosis h. of the intellect STUPIDITY, 4
hall one of the sparrows…flew…through the h. LIFE, 9
We met…Dr H. in such very deep mourning MOURNING, 1
hallowed The place of justice is a h. place JUSTICE, 1
halt has ground to a h. with a 14th Earl TITLES, 12
halters talk of h. in the hanged man's house TACT, 4
halves Never do things by h. COMMITMENT, 2
hamburger British h. thus symbolised…failure to provide its ordinary people with food FOOD, 28
Why have h. out MARRIAGE, 89
Hamelin H. Town's in Brunswick GERMANY, 11
hammer Art is not a mirror…but a h. ART, 17
hand bite the h. that fed them INGRATITUDE, 2
educate with the head instead of with the h. EDUCATION, 29
h. that signed the treaty bred a fever SIGNATURES, 3
little onward lend thy guiding h. GUIDANCE, 3
No, this right h. shall work it all off WRITING, 30
one of those parties which got out of h. CHRISTIANITY, 21
Our h. will not tremble RUSSIAN REVOLUTION, 1
put your h. into the h. of God FAITH, 11
sweeten this little h. GUILT, 9
The H. that made us is divine CREATION, 1
The h. that rocks the cradle WOMEN, 4
This h. hath offended REGRET, 5
touch his weaknesses with a delicate h. IMPERFECTION, 8
handbook used the Bible as if it was a constable's h. BIBLE, 6
handful for a h. of silver he left us BETRAYAL, 2
handicraft Art is not a h. ART, 28
handkerchiefs There is a ghost /That eats h. LOSS, 4
handle polished up the h. of the big front door OFFICERS, 6
hands don't raise your h. because I am also nearsighted DISABILITY, 1
Farewell, my poor h. MUSICIANS, 13
He hath shook h. with time DEATH, 51
he shakes h. with people's hearts JOURNALISM, 5
into thy h. I commend my spirit LAST WORDS, 10
I think with my h. PRACTICALITY, 4
Licence my roving h. LUST, 1
Many h. make light work HELP, 2
Pale h. I loved beside the Shalimar LOVE, 70
Pilate…washed his h. GUILT, 3
the earth of England is in my two h. VICTORY, 20
To be played with both h. in the pocket MUSIC, 42
Tomorrow my h. will be bound EXECUTION, 1
You cannot shake h. with a clenched fist INFLEXIBILITY, 2
handsome H. is as handsome does APPEARANCE, 2
hang all you have to do is to h. it beautifully PAINTING, 12
I will find something…to h. him EXECUTION, 26
I will not h. myself today SUICIDE, 2
They h. us now in Shrewsbury jail EXECUTION, 11
We must indeed all h. together UNITY, 9
wretches h. that jury-men may dine JUSTICE, 19
hanged if they were going to see me h. PUBLIC, 9
I went out to Charing Cross, to see Major-general Harrison h. EXECUTION, 22
Men are not h. for stealing EXAMPLE, 5
talk of halters in the h. man's house TACT, 4
to be h. for nonsense EXECUTION, 7
when a man knows he is to be h. in a fortnight EXECUTION, 12
hangin' they're h. Danny Deever in the mornin' EXECUTION, 14
hanging H. and wiving goes by destiny DESTINY, 21
h. prevents a bad marriage MARRIAGE, 105
hangman if I were a grave-digger, or…a h. OCCUPATIONS, 8
Hansard H. is history's ear GOVERNMENT, 26
happen poetry makes nothing h. POETRY, 5
happened most of which had never h. WORRY, 10
happening h. to somebody else HUMOUR, 26
happens Everything that h. h. as it should DESTINY, 3
I just don't want to be there when it h. DEATH, 13
life…seems to me preparation for something that never h. LIFE, 55
Nothing h. BOREDOM, 1
happiest h. time of all the glad New-year MERRYMAKING, 5
Poetry is the record of the best and h. moments POETRY, 44
happiness A lifetime of h.…hell on earth HAPPINESS, 24
a man is always seeking for h. MARRIAGE, 50
curiously boring about…h. SYMPATHY, 4
greatest h. of the greatest number HAPPINESS, 3
h. fails, existence remains…experiment HAPPINESS, 22
H. in marriage MARRIAGE, 11
H. is a mystery like religion HAPPINESS, 7
H. is an imaginary condition HAPPINESS, 28
H. is beneficial for the body SORROW, 18
H. is like a butterfly HAPPINESS, 15
H. is like coke HAPPINESS, 11
H. is no laughing matter HAPPINESS, 30
h. is not an ideal of reason HAPPINESS, 13
H. is not best achieved HAPPINESS, 18
H. is no vague dream HAPPINESS, 21
H. is the only sanction of life HAPPINESS, 22
h. makes them good GOOD, 9
h. of man that he be mentally faithful INTEGRITY, 5
H.? That's nothing more than health HAPPINESS, 23
In Hollywood, if you don't have h. CINEMA, 9
In solitude /What h. SOLITUDE, 10
I thought that success spelled h. HAPPINESS, 15
It is of no moment to the h. of an individual GOVERNMENT, 13
life, liberty, and the pursuit of h. HUMAN RIGHTS, 3

nothing...by which so much h. is produced as by a good tavern PUBLIC HOUSES, 2
one may fail to find h. in theatrical life DANCING, 8
our friends are true and our h. OPTIMISM, 15
Poverty is a great enemy to human h. POVERTY, 20
recall a time of h. when in misery SORROW, 6
result h. ECONOMICS, 7
the greatest h. of the whole REPUBLIC, 1
the greatest h. for the greatest numbers HAPPINESS, 10
the h. of the common man GOVERNMENT, 6
where...We find our h. FRENCH REVOLUTION, 5
Who never knew the price of h. HAPPINESS, 33
you'll give h. and joy MUSICIANS, 2
you take away his h. DELUSION, 4
happy Ask...whether you are h. HAPPINESS, 14
be h. later on, but it's much harder HAPPINESS, 2
Few people can be h. unless they hate HATE, 7
Goodness does not...make men h. GOOD, 9
H. Days HAPPINESS, 31
h. families resemble each other FAMILY, 34
H. the hare at morning IGNORANCE, 4
H. the Man PRESENT, 4
If you want to be h., be HAPPINESS, 29
I have wanted only one thing to make me h. DISCONTENT, 3
I've had a h. life LAST WORDS, 34
I were but little h. SILENCE, 12
laugh before one is h. LAUGHTER, 8
Let us all be h., and live within our means BORROWING, 12
man is h. so long as he choose to be h. HAPPINESS, 26
Mankind are always h. for having been h. HAPPINESS, 25
Not the owner of many possessions will you be right to call h. HAPPINESS, 9
One is h. as a result of one's own efforts HAPPINESS, 21
People are never h. who want change CONFORMITY, 5
policeman's lot is not a h. one POLICE, 1
Puritanism – The haunting fear that someone...may be h. PURITANISM, 4
That all who are h., are equally h. HAPPINESS, 12
the duty of being h. HAPPINESS, 27
the one and only thing...that can make a man h. HAPPINESS, 8
There is a h. land HEAVEN, 15
To make men h. ADMIRATION, 10
We are never so h. nor so unhappy as we imagine HAPPINESS, 17
what it is that makes a Scotchman h. ALCOHOL, 34
hard Don't clap too h. ENTHUSIASM, 6
H. and high to the stars AMBITION, 2
I'm not h. – I'm frightfully soft CHARACTER, 24
It's been a h. day's night WORK, 12
Saturday's child works h. for his living NURSERY RHYMES, 34
hard-faced A lot of h. men HOUSES OF PARLIAMENT, 4
hardly summit of Everest was h. the place PHOTOGRAPHY, 5
hardness without h. will be sage FUTURE, 1
hardships we shall be glad to remember even these h. ENDURANCE, 22
Hardy But Mr H.'s women are moulded of...flesh WRITERS, 52
Kiss me, H. LAST WORDS, 47
No one has written worse English than Mr H. WRITERS, 94
hare First catch your h. MISQUOTATIONS, 18
Happy the h. at morning IGNORANCE, 4
Take your h. when it is cased FOOD, 25
hares And little hunted h. ANIMALS, 12
harlot society...pays a h. 25 times as much as it pays its Prime Minister INJUSTICE, 14
the prerogative of the h. through the ages RESPONSIBILITY, 2; JOURNALISM, 2
harm No people do so much h. CHARITY, 13
harmony chains that tie /The hidden soul of h. MUSIC, 33
h. imposes compatibility upon the incongruous MUSIC, 32
harp his wild h. slung behind him WAR, 72
The h. that once IRELAND, 13
harps To touch their h. of gold CHRISTMAS, 17
harpsichon play on the h. INSINCERITY, 3
harpsichord The sound of the h. MUSIC, 6
harsh in this h. world MOURNING, 13
hart As pants the h. for cooling streams THIRST, 3
harvest His Royal Highness...prides himself upon...the excellent h. ARROGANCE, 7
In seed time learn, in h. teach SUITABILITY, 1
haste H. makes waste HASTE, 3
Men love in h. LOVE AND HATE, 1
More h., less speed HASTE, 4
You h. away TRANSIENCE, 14
Hastings ancestors on either side of the Battle of H. ANCESTRY, 4
hat A gentleman...wouldn't hit a woman with his h. on CHIVALRY, 1
baseball cap...valid as...hat FASHION, 5
call that thing under your h. a head INSULTS, 19
He forbade me to put off my h. PRIDE, 4
little man wears a shocking bad h. CLOTHES, 20
looking for a black h. METAPHYSICS, 1
Where did you get that h. CLOTHES, 13
hatched chickens before they are h. ANTICIPATION, 4
count their chickens ere they're h. ANTICIPATION, 5
hatchet I did it with my little h. HONESTY, 11
hate feel no h. for him LOVE AND HATE, 4
Few...can be happy unless they h. HATE, 7
If you h. a person, you h....yourself HATE, 5
I h. a fellow...who does nothing...but sit and *growl* PETULANCE, 4
I h. and love LOVE AND HATE, 2
I h. everyone equally HATE, 3
I h. the whole race...your professional poets POETS, 12
I love or I h. BEAUTY, 29
Let them h. RESPECT, 1
never h. a song that has sold half a million copies POP MUSIC, 3
not to weep at them, nor to h. them UNDERSTANDING, 11
scarcely h. any one that we know HATE, 4
to h. the man you have hurt HUMAN NATURE, 22
You must h. a Frenchman ENEMIES, 6
hated h. /by every anti-semite /as if I were a Jew PREJUDICE, 7
h. of all men for my name's sake PERSISTENCE, 4
I never h. a man enough MATERIALISM, 7
I never saw a brute I h. so EVIL, 6
hates Anybody who h. children and dogs CHILDREN, 21; DOGS, 6
Everybody h. house-agents OCCUPATIONS, 17
Everybody h. me POPULARITY, 2
hateth love God, and h. his brother LOVE, 23
Hathaway reproductions of Anne H.'s cottage HOUSES, 3
hating patriotism which consists in h. all other nations PATRIOTISM, 12
hatred a deep burning h. for the Tory Party POLITICS, 7
An intellectual h. HATE, 8
Fire – without h. WAR, 93
h. is...the longest pleasure LOVE AND HATE, 1
love...looks more like h. than like friendship LOVE AND HATE, 5
hats H. divide generally into three classes CLOTHES, 19
Hatter 'Not the same thing a bit!' said the H. MEANING, 1
haunted e'er beneath a waning moon was h. SUPERNATURAL, 6
have To h. and to hold MARRIAGE, 30
Haves *H.* and the *Have-nots* POVERTY AND WEALTH, 3
havoc h. of the German bombs ARCHITECTURE, 13
hay Make h. while the sun shines OPPORTUNITY, 4
he For every h. has got him a she MERRYMAKING, 1
head anyone who slapped us...would get his h. kicked off REVENGE, 12
call that thing under your hat a h. INSULTS, 19
educate with the h. instead of with the hand EDUCATION, 29
God be in my h., /And in my understanding GOD, 1
Here comes a chopper to chop off your h. LONDON, 2
If you can keep your h. SELF-CONTROL, 5
I'll hold my h. so high it'll strike the stars PRIDE, 5
in politics there is no heart, only h. POLITICS, 57
it shall bruise thy h. SEXES, 2
Lay your sleeping h. SLEEP, 3
no matter which way the h. lies EXECUTION, 24
ought to have his h. examined PSYCHIATRY, 4
Scheherazade...a woman saving her h. SELF-PRESERVATION, 11
shorter by a h. ROYALTY, 15
show my h. to the people EXECUTION, 5
the greatest asset a h. of state can have SLEEP, 20
Uneasy lies the h. that wears a crown MONARCHY, 22
you are like a pin, but without...h. or...point BORES, 3
you incessantly stand on your h. OLD AGE, 10
head-in-air Johnny h. IDEALISM, 5
Little Johnny H. CHILDREN, 24
headmasters H. have powers EDUCATION, 12
heads H. I win VICTORY, 5
Two h. are better than one HELP, 6

head-waiter A pompous woman...complaining that the h. EGOTISM, 9
diplomat...is nothing but a h. DIPLOMACY, 19
heal I will h. me of my grievous wound AFTERLIFE, 10
physician, h. thyself DOCTORS, 2
health for h. is the second blessing HEALTH AND HEALTHY LIVING, 12
h. is all they get for it SMOKING, 20
H. is better than wealth HEALTH AND HEALTHY LIVING, 2
h. is his most valuable possession HEALTH AND HEALTHY LIVING, 8
Here's a h. unto his Majesty LOYALTY, 4
in sickness and in h. MARRIAGE, 30
Look to your h. HEALTH AND HEALTHY LIVING, 12
Only do always in h. what you have often promised to do when you are sick ILLNESS, 14
selling them in h. food shops FOOD, 42
They pay this price for h. SMOKING, 20
healthy h. and wealthy and dead BED, 9
He that goes to bed thirsty rises h. ALCOHOL, 30
Nobody is h. in London LONDON, 3
the h. type that was essentially middle-class CLASS, 10
think of diseases as isolated disturbances in a h. body DISEASE, 3
hear any of you at the back who do not h. me DISABILITY, 1
ear begins to h. IMPRISONMENT, 2
make any man sick to h. her INSINCERITY, 3
one is always sure to h. of it FRIENDS, 14
truth which men prefer not to h. TRUTH, 7
heard first been vividly h. by an inner ear MUSICIANS, 17
I have already h. it MUSIC, 40
hearsay to replace X-ray by h. GOSSIP, 9
heart Absence makes the h. grow fonder ABSENCE, 4
Because my h. is pure INTEGRITY, 7
by want of thought, as well as want of h. EVIL, 10
cold untroubled h. of stone SELFISHNESS, 4
cut to the h. ANGER, 2
Death took him by the h. DEATH, 90
first come to pass in the h. of America AMERICA, 12
God be in my h., /And in my thinking GOD, 1
Great thoughts come from the h. THINKING, 12
h. and stomach of a King ROYALTY, 13
holiness of the h.'s affections IMAGINATION, 7; TRUTH, 31
I am sick at h. COMFORT, 2
If thou didst ever hold me in thy h. MOURNING, 13
I love thee for a h. that's kind KINDNESS, 2
in politics there is no h., only head POLITICS, 57
let not your h. be troubled PEACE, 2
lonely of h. is withered away LONELINESS, 10
look in thy h. and write INSPIRATION, 5
Mother is the dead h. of the family WOMAN'S ROLE, 2
My h. aches MELANCHOLY, 7
My h. is a lonely hunter LONELINESS, 5
my h.'s abhorrence HATE, 2
my h. shall be /The faithful compass FAITHFULNESS, 4
My h. shall be thy garden LOVE, 91
My h.'s in the Highlands SCOTLAND, 2
Once a woman has given you her h. WOMEN, 85
our h. is not quiet until it rests in Thee HUMAN CONDITION, 2
She had /A h....too soon made glad IMPRESSIONABILITY, 1
So the h. be right EXECUTION, 24
strings...in the human h. EMOTION, 2
take heed...that your h. be not deceived CHRISTIANITY, 6
Take thy beak from out my h. EVIL, 13
that mighty h. is lying still SLEEP, 21
The fire which in the h. resides SOUL, 2
The h. has its reasons MOTIVE, 5
The H. Is a Lonely Hunter BOOK, SONG, AND PLAY TITLES, 18
The h. that loved her NATURE, 18
The history of every country begins in the h. HISTORY, 9
The intellect is always fooled by the h. EMOTION, 4
Their h.'s in the right place MANKIND, 17
There is a road from the eye to the h. EMOTION, 1
the waters of the h. /Push in their tides EMOTION, 5
The way to a man's h. is through his stomach FOOD, 22
to lose your h.'s desire DESIRE, 15
What comes from the h. SINCERITY, 2
With rue my h. is laden NOSTALGIA, 11
with the palsied h. PASSION, 8
hearth Man for the field and woman for the h. SEXES, 24
the cricket on the h. MELANCHOLY, 9
hearts he shakes hands with people's h. JOURNALISM, 5
Kind h. are more than coronets ARISTOCRACY, 12
One equal temper of heroic h. DETERMINATION, 15
The Queen of H. /She made some tarts FOOD, 12; NURSERY RHYMES, 51
the song that is sung in our h. MUSIC, 34
The Worldly Hope men set their H. upon TRANSIENCE, 13
those who have stout h. and sharp swords RUTHLESSNESS, 6
Two h. that beat as one LOVE, 85
well-developed bodies, fairly developed minds, and undeveloped h. EDUCATION, 18
heat Britain...is going to be forged in the white h. of this revolution SOCIALISM, 15
can't stand the h., get out of the kitchen ENDURANCE, 20
H., madam!...to take off my flesh and sit in my bones WEATHER, 26
heathen I was born of Christian race, /And not a H., or a Jew RELIGION, 63
heaven a H. in Hell's despair LOVE, 27
all H. in a rage IMPRISONMENT, 1
All place shall be hell that is not h. DOOMSDAY, 5
Another glory awaits us in h. HEAVEN, 8
ascend to h. EXECUTION, 8
between H. and Charing Cross HEAVEN, 13
from whose face the earth and the h. fled JUDGMENT, 4
God created the h. CREATION, 2
h. and earth shall pass away TRANSIENCE, 8
H. has granted me no offspring CONCEIT, 24
H. in a wild flower WONDER, 2
H....is a place so inane, so dull HEAVEN, 12
H. was in him, before he was in heaven COMPLIMENTS, 8
H. without being naturally qualified HEAVEN, 11
Home is h. DEBAUCHERY, 8
If it's h. for climate PERVERSITY, 1
If Max gets to H. BUSINESS, 26
If this belief from h. be sent MANKIND, 39
In h. an angel is nobody in particular IMPORTANCE, 2
it were better for sun and moon to drop from h. SIN, 18
make a H. of Hell, a Hell of H. MIND, 4
man is as H. made him CHARACTER, 3
Marriage is...excluded from h. MARRIAGE, 33
more things in h. and earth SUPERNATURAL, 13
no invention came more easily to man than H. HEAVEN, 5
Now: h. knows FREEDOM, 42
Order is h.'s first law ORDER, 3
Parting is all we know of h. PARTING, 5
Pennies do not come from h. WORK, 23
Pennies from H. OPTIMISM, 18
so much of earth...of h. IMPETUOSITY, 4
steep and thorny way to h. EXAMPLE, 8
the Hell I suffer seems a H. HELL, 5
The mind...Can make a H. of Hell MIND, 4
there was war in h. DEVIL, 4
the starry h. above me WONDER, 3
to be young was very h. FRENCH REVOLUTION, 3
'Twould ring the bells of H. ANIMALS, 12
We are all going to H. LAST WORDS, 28
We are as near to h. by sea as by land LAST WORDS, 32; SEA, 5
what's a h. for AMBITION, 3
What they do in h. MARRIAGE, 117
When earth was nigher h. PAST, 3
heavenward A homely face...aided many women h. APPEARANCE, 3
heavier O you who have borne even h. things ENDURANCE, 21
heaviest nickname is the h. stone that the devil can throw NAMES, 4
heav'n h. on earth HEAVEN, 6
I'm farther off from h. /Than when...a boy INNOCENCE, 6
hedge A leap over the h. PRAYER, 7
hedgehogs If you start throwing h. under me THREATS, 2
heed To fight and not to h. the wounds SELFLESSNESS, 2
heels Time wounds all h. TIME, 27
heesh If John or Mary comes h. will want to play LANGUAGE, 18
heights If suffer we must, let's suffer on the h. SUFFERING, 8
Heineken H. refreshes the parts ADVERTISING, 11
heiress American h. wants to buy a man MATERIALISM, 14
hell a H. in Heaven's despite LOVE, 28
A lifetime of happiness...h. on earth HAPPINESS, 24
All place shall be h. that is not heaven DOOMSDAY, 5
all we need of h. PARTING, 5
Better to reign in H. POWER, 17
h. a fury like a woman scorned LOVE AND HATE, 3

H. is a city much like London LONDON, 12
H. is other people HELL, 6
h. upon earth…in a melancholy man's heart MELANCHOLY, 3
Italy…h. for women NATIONALITY, 3
make a Heaven of H., a H. of Heaven MIND, 4
Old age is woman's h. OLD AGE, 27
on the fourth day they will say 'To h. with you!' PROMISES, 4
out of h. leads up to light HELL, 4
Raises from H. a human soul HELL, 1
the H. I suffer seems a Heaven HELL, 5
the h. of horses ENGLAND, 17
the little holiday steamers made an excursion to h. WORLD WAR II, 25
The mind…Can make a Heaven of H. MIND, 4
The road to h. is paved PROCRASTINATION, 3
though h. should bar the way DETERMINATION, 13
To h. with you TELEGRAMS, 1
Ugly h., gape not DAMNATION, 4
War is h. WAR, 110
way down to H. is easy HELL, 7
Which way I fly is H.; myself am H. HELL, 5

help gods h. them that h. themselves SELF-RELIANCE, 2
going in without the h. of Russia WORLD WAR II, 22
not so much our friends' h. that helps us FRIENDSHIP, 17
People must h. one another HELP, 7
Since there's no h. PARTING, 6
The dead…look on and h. DEATH, 76
the h. of too many physicians DOCTORS, 1
what is past my h. is past my care INDIFFERENCE, 1
with a little h. from my friends FRIENDS, 10

helpless Help of the h. RELIGION, 41

helps He h. little SELF, 3
not so much our friends' help that h. us FRIENDSHIP, 17

hem only touch the h. of his garment REMEDIES, 4

hen a broody h. sitting on a china egg BUREAUCRACY, 6
Two Owls and a H. APPEARANCE, 19

Henry He is without strict doubt a Hoorah H. ARISTOCRACY, 11
How H. would have loved it FUNERALS, 9

Herald Price of H. three cents daily NEWSPAPERS, 3; TELEGRAMS, 4

herb sweetest fragrance from the h.…tread on it WOMEN, 81

herbs nature runs either to h., or to weeds HUMAN NATURE, 2

Hercules Some talk of Alexander, and some of H. HEROISM, 1

herd the H. of such, /Who think too little VERBOSITY, 3

herd-morality Morality…is h. MORALITY, 12

here bet you a hundred bucks he ain't in h. ESCAPE, 1; FUNERALS, 5
h. today and gone tomorrow TRANSIENCE, 3
What you are looking for is h., is at Ulubrae TRAVEL, 12

heresies new truths…begin as h. NOVELTY, 4

heresy h. signifies no more than private opinion OPINIONS, 2

heritage I summon age /To grant youth's h. AGE, 15

hero Being a h. HEROISM, 6
better to be the widow of a h. COURAGE, 15
Every h. becomes a bore HEROISM, 5
No man is a h. to his valet FAMILIARITY, 2
The h. is strangely akin DEATH, 97
to his very valet seem'd a h. HEROISM, 4

herod It out-h.s Herod EXCESS, 12

heroes Children should acquire…h. and villains from fiction HISTORY, 3
fit country for h. to live in GOVERNMENT, 16
speed glum h.…to death WAR, 100
Unhappy the land that has no h. HEROISM, 3

heroic human beings are h. NOBILITY, 3

hesitate A leader who doesn't h.…is not fit LEADERSHIP, 7

hesitates A science which h. to forget SCIENCE, 46
He who h. is lost DETERMINATION, 1

Hesperus the schooner H. BOATS, 11

heterodoxy H. or Thy-doxy ORTHODOXY, 1

heterosexuality failed to convert me to h. HOMOSEXUALITY, 11

hickory H., dickory, dock NURSERY RHYMES, 15

hidden Nature is often h. HUMAN NATURE, 4

hide He can run, but he can't h. ESCAPE, 2
I have a big house – and I h. a lot CHILDREN, 40
Robes and furr'd gowns h. all APPEARANCES, 21

hideous less h. than explanations EXPLANATIONS, 1

hiding man who looks you…in the eye…h. something INSINCERITY, 1

high civil fury first grew h. WAR, 21
he killed a calf…in a h. style SHAKESPEARE, 2
She's the Broad and I'm the H. ACADEMICS, 5
to put off my hat to…h. or low PRIDE, 4
up in the h. numbers NUMBERS, 2
ye'll tak' the h. road SCOTLAND, 1

highbrow What is a h. INTELLECTUALS, 9

highest h. type of human nature POLITICS, 70

Highland Yon solitary H. lass SOLITUDE, 16

Highlandman taking the breeks aff a wild H. SCOTS, 10

Highlands My heart's in the H. SCOTLAND, 2

Highness His Royal H.…prides himself upon…the excellent harvest ARROGANCE, 7

high-water h. mark of my youth MEMORY, 19

hill If the h. will not come to Mahomet ADAPTABILITY, 2
There is a green h. far away CHRISTIANITY, 1
they call you…from the h. SUMMONS, 1
Tonight the American flag floats from yonder h. WAR, 113

hills a fine thing to be out on the h. alone SOLITUDE, 9
Over the h. and far away LOVE, 59
What are those blue remembered h. NOSTALGIA, 10

him he could not avoid making H. set the world in motion CREATION, 11

himself ever written out of reputation but by h. REPUTATION, 2
Every man for h., and the devil SELF-INTEREST, 1
gesture by the individual to h. BUSINESS, 11
He would kill H. HUMAN CONDITION, 6

hinder men that…h. the reception of every work CRITICS, 10

hindsight H. is always twenty-twenty HISTORY, 26

hinky H., dinky, par-lee-voo FRANCE, 13

Hippocrene the blushful H. ALCOHOL, 37

historian A good h. is timeless HISTORIANS, 1
A h. is a prophet in reverse HISTORIANS, 6
Great abilities are not requisite for an H. HISTORIANS, 3
h. fits a man for psychological analysis PSYCHOLOGY, 2
The h. must have…some conception of how men…behave HISTORIANS, 2

historians H. are like deaf people HISTORIANS, 7
h. left blanks in their writings HISTORIANS, 5
H. tell the story of the past NOVELS, 6

history ancient h.…is no more than accepted fiction HISTORY, 34
Austria is Switzerland…with h. added EUROPE, 14
blunders usually do more to shape h. than…wickedness MISTAKES, 17
deal of h. to produce…literature LITERATURE, 8; HISTORY, 18
diplomatic h. is…what one clerk said HISTORY, 37
From today…there begins a new epoch in the h. of the world BEGINNING, 9
He was…a student of h. EXPERIENCE, 18
h.…a tableau of crimes and misfortunes HISTORY, 35
H. does not repeat itself HISTORY, 6
H. gets thicker HISTORY, 33
H. is more or less bunk HISTORY, 13
H. is past politics POLITICS, 66; HISTORY, 25
H. is philosophy teaching by examples HISTORY, 10
H. is the essence of…biographies BIOGRAPHY, 3; HISTORY, 7
H. is the sum total HISTORY, 2
H. is…the wrong way of living HISTORY, 11
H. is too serious HISTORIANS, 4
h. must be false HISTORY, 36
h. of the human spirit CULTURE, 1
H. repeats itself HISTORY, 1
'H.', Stephen said, 'is a nightmare' HISTORY, 19
h.…the biography of great men GREATNESS, 6; HISTORY, 8
h.…register of…misfortunes of mankind HISTORY, 16
If men could learn from h. EXPERIENCE, 11
It is impossible to write ancient h. HISTORY, 21
Its h. dates from today ROYALTY, 39
more h. than they can consume locally EUROPE, 16
never looks like h. HISTORY, 15
no h.; only biography BIOGRAPHY, 5; HISTORY, 12
one of these is the h. of political power HISTORY, 22
people…never have learned anything from h. EXPERIENCE, 14
poetry is…more philosophical…than h. POETRY, 1
Political h. is far too criminal HISTORY, 3
Stratford…suggests powdered h. ENGLAND, 19
The attitude of the English…toward English h. ENGLISH, 16
the greatest week in the h. of the world SPACE, 6
The h. of all…society is the h. of class struggles CLASS, 22
The h. of every country begins in the heart HISTORY, 9
The most persistent sound…through men's h. WAR, 58
the Thames is liquid h. RIVERS, 1
This was the Angel of H. WORLD WAR II, 18
trace…the disasters of English h. to…Wales WALES, 5

War makes...good h. WAR AND PEACE, 7
history-making Man is a h. creature HISTORY, 4
hit a medley of your h. INSULTS, 25
if a man h. you VIOLENCE, 2
If you would h. the mark AMBITION, 13
hither Come h. COUNTRYSIDE, 9
Hitler every time H. occupies a country HITLER, 4
Germany was the cause of H. HITLER, 8
H. has carried out a revolution on our lines FASCISM, 1
H. has missed the bus WORLD WAR II, 2
H. showed surprising loyalty to Mussolini HITLER, 2
H. was a nuisance. Mussolini was bloody POLITICS, 50
I wouldn't believe H. was dead HITLER, 6
one purpose, the destruction of H. HITLER, 3
The people H. never understood HITLER, 1
tipster who...reached H.'s level of accuracy HITLER, 7
hobby-horse So long as a man rides his h. TOLERANCE, 7
hobgoblin the h. of little minds CONSTANCY, 1
hock He sipped at a weak h. and seltzer WRITERS, 33
hog Rule all England under a h. INSULTS, 14
hoi polloi the multitude, the *h.* PUBLIC, 10
hoist H. your sail OPPORTUNITY, 3
hold h. your tongue and let me love SILENCE, 5
To have and to h. MARRIAGE, 30
When every...thing you h. /Is made of silver, or of gold ECONOMICS, 9
holder office sanctifies the h. POWER, 3
hole A h. is the accident THRIFT, 10
if you knows of a better h. WAR, 4
out of a black h. HOSTAGES, 3
smallest h....man can hide his head in UNIVERSE, 5
What happens to the h. when the cheese is gone NONSENSE, 4
holes the first law of h....stop digging ADVICE, 9
holiday the little h. steamers made an excursion to hell WORLD WAR II, 25
holiness put off H. WISDOM, 11
the h. of the heart's affections IMAGINATION, 7; TRUTH, 31
who, like you, your H., is a Roman Catholic CATHOLICISM, 3
Holland H....lies so low they're only saved EUROPE, 8
hollers whatever you try to do, somebody jumps up and h. HUMAN NATURE, 11
hollow within the h. crown ROYALTY, 32
holly The h. and the ivy CHRISTMAS, 5
The h. bears the crown CHRISTMAS, 5
Hollywood In H., if you don't have happiness CINEMA, 9
I should not have been invited to H. CINEMA, 1
the attitude of a H. director toward love ENGLISH, 16
trend in H. of taking very good European films CINEMA, 3
holy dropped the word 'H.' BIBLE, 4
everything that lives is h. LIFE, 13
H., h., h., Lord God Almighty GOD, 24
the H. Roman Empire was neither h., nor Roman, nor an empire NATIONS, 3
'Twas on a H. Thursday CHILDREN, 17
home against books the H. Secretary is PHILISTINISM, 7
Charity begins at h. CHARITY, 10
Comin' for to carry me h. DEATH, 17
eaten me out of house and h. GREED, 11
English should give Ireland h. rule IRELAND, 17
Father...come h. with me now ALCOHOL, 68
for de old folks at h. HOMESICKNESS, 3
For h. is best HOME, 9
For the old Kentucky H. far away HOMESICKNESS, 2
give me a h. where the buffalo roam HOMESICKNESS, 4
h. his footsteps he hath turn'd HOMESICKNESS, 6
H. is heaven DEBAUCHERY, 8
H. is h. HOME, 3
H. is the sailor, h. from sea DEATH, 120
H. is where HOME, 2
H. of lost causes OXFORD, 1
H....where...they have to take you in HOME, 4
I can get all that at h. THEATRE, 7
Irish H. Rule is conceded IRELAND, 18
Many a man who thinks to found a h. PARASITES, 1
no h....save in Paris PARIS, 4
people you wouldn't have in your h. TELEVISION AND RADIO, 3
Pleasure never is at h. DISCONTENT, 5
She's leaving h. DEPARTURE, 8
stress...worse at h. VIOLENCE, 8
The Life and Soul, the man who will never go h. PARTIES, 9
there's no place like h. HOME, 7
till the cow comes h. ETERNITY, 1
we come /From God, who is our h. METAPHYSICS, 5
What's the good of a h. ABSENCE, 7
home-keeping h. youth HOME, 8
homely A h. face...aided many women heavenward APPEARANCE, 3
be never so h. HOME, 3
h. wits HOME, 8
Homer Cicero /And...H. were */Mad as the mist and snow* MADNESS, 18
even excellent H. nods IMPERFECTION, 9
Mr Gladstone read H. for fun CLASSICS, 2
Seven cities warr'd for H., being dead POVERTY, 16
The author of that poem is either H. ARGUMENTS, 8
homes go back to thy stately h. of England PARTING, 7
the Stately H. of England DECLINE, 1; STATELY HOMES, 3
home-sickness In h. you must keep moving HOMESICKNESS, 7
homo The 'h.' is the legitimate child HOMOSEXUALITY, 5
homos one of the stately h. of England HOMOSEXUALITY, 2
homosexuals h....set out to win the love of a 'real' man HOMOSEXUALITY, 3
honest An h. broker DIPLOMACY, 3
An h. God GOD, 29
an h. man sent to lie abroad for...his country DIPLOMACY, 21
An h. man's word HONESTY, 1
give me six lines...by the most h. man EXECUTION, 26
I am as h. as any man living HONESTY, 9
It's better to be quotable than...h. QUOTATIONS, 13
not an h. man HONESTY, 12
She was poor but she was h. POVERTY AND WEALTH, 1
then they get *h.* DOCTORS, 9
Though I am not naturally h. HONESTY, 10
Though I be poor, I'm h. HONESTY, 6
honestly If possible h., if not, somehow, make money MONEY, 25
honesty H. is the best policy HONESTY, 2, 12
make your children *capable of h.* HONESTY, 7
Philosophers never balance between profit and h. PHILOSOPHERS, 4
honey a land of oil olive, and h. WEALTH, 5
gather h. all the day WORK, 25
h. still for tea NOSTALGIA, 3
They took some h., and plenty of money NONSENSE, 20
honey'd the h. middle of the night LOVE, 78
honey-dew on h. hath fed CAUTION, 9
honi *H. soit qui mal y pense* EVIL, 1
honour All is lost save h. DEFEAT, 2
a prophet is not without h. HONOUR, 1
Brothers all /In h. HONOUR, 7
His h. rooted in dishonour UNFAITHFULNESS, 6
h. is for the poor HUMILITY, 12
H. pricks me on HONOUR, 4
h. sinks where commerce long prevails BUSINESS, 12
h. thy father and thy mother GOD, 10
if I accepted the h....I would not answer for the integrity of my intellect TITLES, 3
Let us h. if we can POSTERITY, 3
only h. and life have been spared DEFEAT, 2
peace I hope with h. PEACE, 8
So h. peereth in the meanest habit APPEARANCES, 22
That chastity of h. HONOUR, 2
then they get *h.* DOCTORS, 9
There is h. among thieves LOYALTY, 2
To h. we call you COURAGE, 13
Wealth has never been a sufficient source of h. OSTENTATION, 3
we're fighting for this woman's h. HONOUR, 3
honourable His designs were strictly h. MARRIAGE, 56
hoof I see many h.-marks going in MISTRUST, 2
hooligan H. was probably invented in China CHINA, 9
hoorah He is without strict doubt a H. Henry ARISTOCRACY, 11
hooray Dear Mrs A., h. h. TELEGRAMS, 6
H. and up she rises DRUNKENNESS, 4
hope Abandon h., all ye who enter here HELL, 2
a faint h. that he will die HUMAN NATURE, 10
And what was dead was H. IMPRISONMENT, 9
beacon of h. for the world SOUTH AFRICA, 14
H. for the best HOPE, 2
h. is...the dream of those that wake HOPE, 9
H. is the power of being cheerful CHARITY, 12; HOPE, 5
H. may vanish, but can die not OPTIMISM, 24
H. springs eternal in the human breast HOPE, 8

Land of H. and Glory BRITAIN, 4
no other medicine but only h. HOPE, 10
Not to h. for things to last for ever TRANSIENCE, 15
now abideth faith, h., charity CHARITY, 6
Our h. for years to come RELIGION, 64
the distinction between h. and expectation REALISM, 3
The triumph of h. over experience MARRIAGE, 73
The Worldly H. men set their Hearts upon TRANSIENCE, 13
unconquerable h. HOPE, 4
What a strange thing is memory, and h. MEMORY, 10
what difficulty a mind…admits h. SUFFERING, 15
While there is life, there's h. HOPE, 6
Without all h. of day BLINDNESS, 4
hopeless controversy is either superfluous or h. ARGUMENTS, 12
hopes enough for fifty h. and fears WORRY, 8
Life's short span forbids us to enter on far-reaching h. MORTALITY, 13
My h. no more must change their name FREEDOM, 53
Horatius brave H. COURAGE, 17
horde Society is now one polish'd h. BORES, 2
horizontal we value none /But the h. one POSTERITY, 3
Horner Little Jack H. /Sat in the corner NURSERY RHYMES, 29
Hornie Auld H., Satan, Nick DEVIL, 6
horns Memories are hunting h. MEMORY, 1
When you take the bull by the h. CHANCE, 5
horny-handed H. sons of toil WORK, 11
horribilis it has turned out to be an 'annus h.' ROYALTY, 19
horrible A strange, h. business…good enough for Shakespeare's day CRITICISM, 50
horrid are they all h. NASTINESS, 1
horror I have a h. of sunsets SUN, 3
mere existence is swollen to a h. IDEALISM, 3
The thought of dentists gave him just the same sick h. FEAR, 14
horror movies America has brought us McDonald's and h. RUSSIA, 12
horrors I have supp'd full with h. WORLD-WEARINESS, 7
horse A fly, Sir, may sting a stately h. CRITICS, 11
a pale h. DEATH, 31
A Protestant with a h. NATIONALITY, 2
Do not trust the h., Trojans MISTRUST, 11
good deal of physical courage to ride a h. ALCOHOL, 40; HORSES, 8
Go together like a h. and carriage LOVE AND MARRIAGE, 1
I feel as a h. must feel INJUSTICE, 5
I know two things about the h. HORSES, 2
like to be a h. ROYALTY, 16
my kingdom for a h. HORSES, 10
nobody has any business to go around looking like a h. APPEARANCE, 28
Ride a cock-h. to Banbury Cross NURSERY RHYMES, 42
the h., as a means of locomotion, is obsolete HORSES, 11
To confess that you are totally Ignorant about the H. HORSES, 9
victory under the belly of a Cossack's h. RUSSIAN REVOLUTION, 3
You can be in the H. Guards CLASS, 27
You can lead a h. to the water STUBBORNNESS, 1
You may have my husband, but not my h. MASCULINITY, 2
horsemanship princes learn no art truly, but…h. HORSES, 7
horse-pond celibacy is…a muddy h. MARRIAGE, 91
horses A grain, which in England is generally given to h. SCOTLAND, 3
Bring on the empty h. LANGUAGE, 11
Dogs, like h., are quadrupeds ANIMALS, 15
England…hell for h. NATIONALITY, 3
England…hell of h. ENGLAND, 17
frighten the h. SEX, 9
'H.' should have read 'Cows' MISTAKES, 10
Men are… more careful of the breed of their h. and dogs FAMILY, 33
sixty h. wedged in a chimney JOURNALISM, 24
swap h. in mid-stream CHANGE, 13
hospital h. is the assumption on the part of the staff MEDICINE, 4
in a h.…the assumption…that because you have lost your gall bladder HOSPITALITY, 7
the h. desirable for patients with serious ailments OCCUPATIONS, 11
the world, I count it not an inn, but an h. WORLD, 1
host a happy h. makes a sad guest HOSPITALITY, 5
an innumerable company of the heavenly h. PERCEPTION, 3
of all this h. of men not one will still be alive in a hundred years' time MORTALITY, 22
hostages h. given to fate FAMILY, 21
h. to fortune FAMILY, 5
holding h. HOSTAGES, 1
hostile The universe is not h. UNIVERSE, 9
hostility your h. towards him FRIENDSHIP, 10
hot blow h. and cold with the same breath INDECISION, 1
H. cross buns! NURSERY RHYMES, 16
hotel-keepers h. continue to give them TOLERANCE, 8
hotels I prefer temperance h. ALCOHOL, 64
hot-water the English have h. bottles ENGLISH, 24
Houdin Robert H. who…invented the vanishing bird-cage trick THEATRE, 15
Houdini Harry H. ESCAPE, 1; FUNERALS, 5
hounded I will not be h. CHARACTER, 24
hounds And the cry of his h. HUNTING, 4
hour A child's a plaything for an h. CHILDREN, 33
An h. in the morning TIME, 1
at the rate of sixty minutes an h. TIME, 24
I also had my h. GLORY, 1
In the h. of death DEATH, 33
Milton! thou shouldst be living at this h. DECLINE, 15
nothing can bring back the h. REGRET, 22
one bare h. to live DAMNATION, 3
One h.'s sleep SLEEP, 1
Some h. to which you have not been looking forward will prove lovely PRESENT, 10
the clocks were striking the h. TIME, 25
their finest h. WORLD WAR II, 5
Time and the h. runs through TIME, 32
To one dead deathless h. POETRY, 38
hourglass the sand in the h. TIME, 28
hours h. will take care of themselves TIME, 15
Three h. a day WRITING, 34
housbondes H. at chirche-dore MARRIAGE, 35
house A h. is a machine for living in HOUSES, 2
A man in the h. is worth two MEN, 14
Cleaning your h. while your kids are still growing HOUSEWORK, 4
get thee out…from thy father's h. JEWS, 3
in my Father's h. are many mansions HEAVEN, 3
The h. of every one is to him as his castle PRIVACY, 1
The H. of Lords, an illusion RESPONSIBILITY, 14
The H. of Lords…how to care for the elderly HOUSES OF PARLIAMENT, 9
The h. where I was born NOSTALGIA, 9
they all lived together in a little crooked h. NURSERY RHYMES, 52
you…who have made me too great for my h. ROYALTY, 4
house-agents Everybody hates h. OCCUPATIONS, 17
housekeeping H. ain't no joke HOUSEWORK, 1
housemaids damp souls of the h. MELANCHOLY, 5
House of Commons leader of the H. POLITICIANS, 51
House of Lords Every man has a H. in his own head HOUSES OF PARLIAMENT, 13
The H., an illusion HOUSES OF PARLIAMENT, 18
The H. is a perfect eventide home HOUSES OF PARLIAMENT, 17
The H. is the British Outer Mongolia HOUSES OF PARLIAMENT, 5
The H.…kept efficient by…persistent absenteeism HOUSES OF PARLIAMENT, 15
House of Peers The H.…Did nothing HOUSES OF PARLIAMENT, 10
houses H. are built to live in HOUSES, 1
plague o' both your h. CURSES, 1
Rich men's h. are seldom beautiful WEALTH, 3
the darkness inside h. FEAR, 7
housewife don't pretend to be an ordinary h. ACTORS, 19
h's drop thy 'H.' CLASS, 5
Hubbard Old Mother H. /Went to the cupboard NURSERY RHYMES, 36
hue native h. of resolution CONSCIENCE, 5
Hugo *H. – hélas!* POETS, 36
human Adam was but h. PERVERSITY, 6
All that is h. must retrograde PROGRESS, 6
evolution of the h. race MANKIND, 13
h. beings are heroic NOBILITY, 3
h. beings…capacity for taking things for granted HUMAN NATURE, 13
H. beings were invented by water WATER, 8

H. beings, yes, but not surgeons MEDICINE, 11
H. kind cannot bear REALITY, 3
h. nature...more of the fool HUMAN NATURE, 3
H. on my faithless arm SLEEP, 3
If h. beings could be propagated...aristocracy would be... sound ARISTOCRACY, 7
I got disappointed in h. nature HUMAN NATURE, 8
I have got lots of h. weaknesses IMPERFECTION, 13
imagine a boot stamping on a h. face OPPRESSION, 6
Ishmaelites...will not publicly eat h. flesh CANNIBALISM, 2
I wish I loved the H. Race MANKIND, 22
Mercy has a h. heart MANKIND, 6
my opinion of the h. race MANKIND, 17
No h. being...was ever so free as a fish FREEDOM, 47
no need for any other faith than...faith in h. beings FAITH, 9
nothing h. foreign to me MANKIND, 32
nothing to distinguish h. society from the farm-yard MANKIND, 29
not linen you're wearing out, /But h. creatures' lives WOMEN, 40
the full tide of h. existence is at Charing-Cross LONDON, 9
The h. face is...a whole cluster of faces MANKIND, 21
The h. race...many of my readers HUMAN CONDITION, 5
the importance of the h. factor INDUSTRIAL RELATIONS, 1
the vilest specimens of h. nature are...found among demagogues POLITICS, 46
To err is h., to forgive, divine MISTAKES, 13; FORGIVENESS, 14
To kill a h. being KILLING, 4
When in the course of h. events, it becomes necessary INDEPENDENCE, 2
you feel as if a h. being sitting inside were making fun of you ANIMALS, 8

humanity Every year h. takes a step towards Communism COMMUNISM, 3
H. is just a work in progress MANKIND, 38
Oh wearisome condition of h. HUMAN CONDITION, 9
That unremitting h. DICKENS, 1
the crooked timber of h. HUMAN NATURE, 15
The still, sad music of h. EXPERIENCE, 22

human life being alone is a fundamental quality of h. HUMAN CONDITION, 13

humble for the last time in my life, Your H. Servant ARGUMENTS, 17
He'll h. her MEN, 7
h. and meek are thirsting for blood HUMILITY, 7
It is difficult to be h. HUMILITY, 4

humiliating Corporal punishment is...h. PUNISHMENT, 13

humiliation the last h. of an aged scholar OLD AGE, 15
the moment of greatest h. is...when the spirit is proudest PRIDE, 6

humility H. is only doubt HUMILITY, 2

humour Cynicism is h. in ill-health CYNICISM, 4
deficient in a sense of h. HUMOUR, 9
Freudian...low...sort of h. HUMOUR, 13
God withheld the sense of h. from women WOMEN, 21
H....the first of the gifts to perish TRANSLATION, 5
own up to a lack of h. HUMOUR, 8
Total absence of h. HUMOUR, 10

hump A woman...without a positive h., may marry whom she likes MARRIAGE, 121

Humpty H. Dumpty sat on a wall NURSERY RHYMES, 18

hunchback The h. in the park LONELINESS, 8

hundred a h. schools of thought contend CHINA, 8
bet you a h. bucks he ain't in here ESCAPE, 1; FUNERALS, 5
it would be all the same a h. years hence TRIVIALITY, 3
I've done it a h. times SMOKING, 21
Letting a h. flowers blossom CHINA, 8
of all this host of men not one will still be alive in a h. years' time MORTALITY, 22
to trade a h. contemporary readers for POSTERITY, 6

Hungarian It's not enough to be H. EUROPE, 11; TALENT, 6

hunger best sauce...is h. HUNGER, 4
H. is the best sauce HUNGER, 1
The war against h. HUNGER, 7
to banish h. by rubbing the belly HUNGER, 5

hungry A h. stomach has no ears HUNGER, 8
h. as a hunter HUNGER, 9
h. hare has no frontiers POLITICS, 85
H. Joe collected lists of fatal diseases ILLNESS, 6
h. sheep look up, and are not fed CORRUPTION, 3
she makes h. /Where most she satisfies ADMIRATION, 14
You cannot feed the h. on statistics STATISTICS, 5

hunt how much more dogs are animated when they h. in a pack UNITY, 11
people who h. are the right people HUNTING, 7

hunted tell the others by their h. expression CHARITY, 15

hunter hungry as a h. HUNGER, 9
Man is the h. SEXES, 23
My heart is a lonely h. LONELINESS, 5
The Heart Is a Lonely H. BOOK, SONG, AND PLAY TITLES, 18

Hunter Dunn Miss J. H., Miss J. H. ADMIRATION, 1

hunting ancestors were h. the wild boar JEWS, 2
H. people tend to be church-goers HUNTING, 6
Memories are h. horns MEMORY, 1
their discourse was about h. LANGUAGE, 19

hurrah h.! we bring the Jubilee GLORY, 5

hurricane h. on the way WEATHER, 11

hurricanoes You cataracts and h. WEATHER, 19

hurries h. to the main event PLAYS, 5

hurry An old man in a h. POLITICIANS, 45
H.! I never hurry. I have no time to hurry HASTE, 12
So who's in a h. ALCOHOL, 10

hurrying I see a man h. along – to what PURPOSE, 5

hurt It doesn't h. to lose my crown FAILURE, 3
it h. too much to laugh DISAPPOINTMENT, 8
It takes your enemy and your friend..., to h. you HURT, 3
Those have most power to h. HURT, 1
wish to h. CRUELTY, 1

hurting Art...can go on mattering once it has stopped h. ART, 5

husband An archaeologist is the best h. MARRIAGE, 36
at all times yr faithful h. MARRIAGE, 111
Being a h. is a whole-time job MARRIAGE, 22
easier to be a lover than a h. MARRIAGE, 16
happened unawares to look at her h. MARRIAGE, 12
h. render unto the wife due benevolence MARRIAGE, 24
in love with...Her own h. LOVE AND MARRIAGE, 2
light wife doth make a heavy h. MARRIAGE, 104
My h. and I ROYALTY, 17
My h. is dead DEATH, 84
Never trust a h. too far TRUST, 4
that monstrous animal a h. and wife MARRIAGE, 57
The h. frae the wife despises MARRIAGE, 32
trust my h. not to fall asleep POLITICS, 80
You may have my h., but not my horse MASCULINITY, 2

husbandry borrowing dulls the edge of h. BORROWING, 8; INTEGRITY, 6

husbands flirt with their own h. LOVE AND MARRIAGE, 6
h. and wives...belong to different sexes SEXES, 8
h. and wives make shipwreck of their lives MARRIAGE, 50
H. are like fires MARRIAGE, 61
h., love your wives MARRIAGE, 23
h. remind me of an orangutang MARRIAGE, 17
h. to stay at home WOMEN, 30

hush a breathless h. in the Close tonight CRICKET, 5

hut Love in a h. LOVE, 77
The Arab who builds...a h. out of...a temple...is more philosophical than...curators of the museums MUSEUMS, 1; PRACTICALITY, 3

hyacinth Children with H.'s temperament...merely know more CHARACTER, 19
every H. the Garden wears FLOWERS, 4

hydrostatics It gives me the h. MALAPROPISMS, 5

hymn Aisle. Altar. H. MARRIAGE, 85; PUNS, 14

hymn-book Cassock, band, and h. too CLERGY, 17

hymns My poems are h. of praise POETRY, 46

hyper-thyroid Shelley had a h. face APPEARANCE, 36

hyphenated h. Americanism PATRIOTISM, 25

hypocrisy an organized h. POLITICS, 21
H....is a whole-time job HYPOCRISY, 11
H. is the homage paid by vice to virtue HYPOCRISY, 14
H. is the most...nerve-racking vice HYPOCRISY, 11
neither man nor angel can discern /H. HYPOCRISY, 12
That would be h. HYPOCRISY, 18

hypocrite No man is a h. in his pleasures PLEASURE, 15
see...into a h. HYPOCRISY, 8

hypocritical Man...learns by being h. HYPOCRISY, 10

hypodermic man who cannot work without his h. needle DRUGS, 6

hypothesis I have no need of that h. GOD, 33
the slaying of a beautiful h. by an ugly fact SCIENCE, 21
to discard a pet h. every day THEORY, 6

hysteria comedy at the moment of deepest h. HUMOUR, 21

I

I I also had my hour GLORY, 1
in the infinite I AM IMAGINATION, 1
I would have done it differently ARROGANCE, 9
ice skating over thin i. HASTE, 6
The i. was all around SEA, 4
ice-cream just enjoy your i. while it's on your plate PHILOSOPHY, 16
iced three parts i. over AGE, 4
icicles When i. hang by the wall SEASONS, 20
icumen Sumer is i. in SEASONS, 1
id put the i. back in yid JEWS, 12
idea An i. does not pass from one language TRANSLATION, 4
An i. isn't responsible for the people IDEAS, 5
best way to kill an i. BUREAUCRACY, 2
constant repetition…in imprinting an i. PUBLIC, 14
Dying for an i. MARTYRDOM, 2
i.'s worth having once IDEAS, 7
I think it would be a good i. CIVILIZATION, 6
no stand can be made against invasion by an i. IDEAS, 2
That fellow seems to me to possess but one i. STUPIDITY, 6
the i. of death as an individual NUCLEAR WEAPONS, 9
they will end by ruining our i. FASCISM, 1
ideal an i. for which I am prepared to die SOUTH AFRICA, 8
at fourteen every boy should be in love with some i. woman…on a pedestal SEXES, 17
the i. American AMERICANS, 3
idealist An i.…on noticing that a rose smells better than a cabbage IDEALISM, 4
people call me an i. AMERICA, 39
ideals Away with all i. SPONTANEITY, 3
think how far I can go with all the i. that I have POLITICIANS, 75
ideas down which i. are lured and…strangled BUREAUCRACY, 4
Human Stupidity consists in having lots of i. STUPIDITY, 10
i. are of more importance than values INTELLECTUALS, 4
i. simply pass through him STUPIDITY, 1
I. that enter the mind under fire INDOCTRINATION, 3
I stopped…to exchange i. INFERIORITY, 1
Learn our i., or otherwise get out RACISM, 17
Many i. grow better when transplanted IDEAS, 3
Morality which is based on i. MORALITY, 9
she's only got two i. in her head STUPIDITY, 7
the addiction of political groups to the i. POLITICS, 27
The true God…God of i. INSPIRATION, 7
ides Beware the i. of March PROPHECY, 12
idiot now I feel like a complete i. INFERIORITY, 1
tale told by an i. LIFE, 45
The i. who praises…every country but his own DISCONTENT, 2
To generalize is to be an i. GENERALIZATIONS, 1
idiots English…act with…the fatuity of i. IRELAND, 19
idle As i. as a painted ship BOATS, 3
I am happiest when I am i. IDLENESS, 9
Satan finds…mischief…/For i. hands IDLENESS, 10
We would all be i. IDLENESS, 7
idleness compulsory and irreproachable i. ARMY, 3
i. and indifference CHANGE, 3
I.…the refuge of weak minds IDLENESS, 3
Research! A mere excuse for i. RESEARCH, 2
idling It is impossible to enjoy i. IDLENESS, 5
idol one-eyed yellow i. to the north of Khatmandu MOURNING, 5
idolatry There is no i. in the Mass CATHOLICISM, 6
if I. you can keep your head SELF-CONTROL, 5
much virtue in I. POSSIBILITY, 3
ifs If i. and ans UNCERTAINTY, 1
ignominious History is full of i. getaways by the great COWARDICE, 5
ignorance From i. our comfort flows IGNORANCE, 12
I. is like a delicate exotic fruit IGNORANCE, 17
i. is never better than knowledge DESTINY, 6
I., madam, pure i. IGNORANCE, 9
I. of the law excuses LAW, 24
journalism.…keeps us in touch with the i. of the community JOURNALISM, 32
Lawyers are the only persons in whom i.…is not punished LAWYERS, 4
man's i. of the gods SPONTANEITY, 1
no sin but i. IGNORANCE, 11
Somebody else's i. is bliss IGNORANCE, 16
where i. is bliss, /'Tis folly to be wise IGNORANCE, 6
Your i. cramps my conversation IGNORANCE, 8
ignorant Let no one i. of mathematics enter MATHEMATICS, 9
The i. man always adores IGNORANCE, 10
the opinionated, the i., and the boorish STUBBORNNESS, 2
To confess that you are totally I. about the Horse HORSES, 9
what may follow it, or what preceded it, we are absolutely i. LIFE, 9
ill Cannot be i.; cannot be good SUPERNATURAL, 14
human i. does not dawn seem…an alternative HUMAN CONDITION, 22
I am only half there when I am i. ILLNESS, 12
If…someone is speaking i. of you CRITICISM, 12
no hint throughout the universe /Of good or i. NECESSITY, 8
very fine country to be acutely i. BRITAIN, 11
woman colour'd i. CONFLICT, 7
illegal collect legal taxes from i. money TAXATION, 2
the things I really like…are either immoral, i., or fattening PLEASURE, 31
illegitimate There are no i. children ILLEGITIMACY, 2
ill-health Cynicism is humour in i. CYNICISM, 4
illiteracy The ratio of literacy to i. LITERACY, 1
illiterate I. him…from your memory MALAPROPISMS, 4
illness I. is the night-side of life ILLNESS, 15
illogical Faith…an i. belief in…the improbable FAITH, 14
ills sharp remedy…for all i. EXECUTION, 25
ill-spent sign of an i. youth SPORT AND GAMES, 22
illumine What in me is dark /I. GOD, 38
illusion contain nothing but sophistry and i. PHILOSOPHY, 3
Religion is an i. RELIGION, 24
The House of Lords, an i. RESPONSIBILITY, 14; HOUSES OF PARLIAMENT, 18
visible universe was an i. UNIVERSE, 2
illusions It's life's i. I recall LIFE, 37
time…for innocence and i. GERMANY, 10
illustrious This i. man, the largest and most spacious intellect POETS, 32
ill-will I bear no i. against those responsible FORGIVENESS, 17
image any graven i. GOD, 10
A photograph is not only an i. PHOTOGRAPHY, 8
fall down and worship the golden i. DOOMSDAY, 1
If God made us in His i. GOD, 50
make man in our own i. MANKIND, 5; CREATION, 6
Why should I consent to the perpetuation of the i. of this i. PAINTING, 13
imaginary Happiness is an i. condition HAPPINESS, 28
imagination A lady's i. is very rapid WOMEN, 11
Art is ruled…by the i. IMAGINATION, 3
I. and fiction…three quarters of our real life IMAGINATION, 10
I.!…I put it first years ago ACTING, 11
I. is more important IMAGINATION, 4
I. without skill gives us modern art ART, 27
no i. and…no compassion IMAGINATION, 5
not an ideal of reason but of i. HAPPINESS, 13
of i. all compact LOVE, 121; POETRY, 43
stand up for freedom of the i. RELIGION, 52
The primary i. IMAGINATION, 1
treat your facts with i. is one thing TRUTH, 15
truth of i. IMAGINATION, 7; TRUTH, 31
imagine never so happy…as we i. HAPPINESS, 17
imagined What is now proved was…i. PROOF, 2
imagining reconcile this world…with…my i. BLINDNESS, 2
imitate A good composer does not i. MUSICIANS, 9
An original writer is…one whom nobody can i. ORIGINALITY, 2
never failed to i. CHILDREN, 6
obliged to i. himself, and to repeat IMITATION, 5
people…usually i. each other IMITATION, 3
imitates Photography can never grow up if it i. PHOTOGRAPHY, 1
imitation I. is the sincerest form of flattery FLATTERY, 1; IMITATION, 2
Man…is an i. MANKIND, 20
immaculate the I. Conception was spontaneous combustion CATHOLICISM, 9
Immanuel call his name I. CHRISTIANITY, 9
immature the i. man…wants to die nobly for a cause AGE, 59
immaturity common symptom of i. ORIGINALITY, 7
the executive expression of human i. POLITICS, 11
immoral moral or an i. book BOOKS, 46
the things I really like…are either i., illegal, or fattening PLEASURE, 31

worse than i. MISTAKES, 2
immorality the most rigid code of i. ENGLISH, 6
immortal I have lost the i. part REPUTATION, 7
make me i. with a kiss BEAUTY, 25
Our souls have sight of that i. sea METAPHYSICS, 6
Why are you weeping? Did you imagine that I was i. LAST WORDS, 44
immortality I...want to achieve i....through not dying IMMORTALITY, 1
just ourselves /And I. DEATH, 42
immutable Few things are as i. POLITICS, 27
impediment cause, or just i. OBSTRUCTION, 2
imperative This i. is Categorical MORALITY, 8
imperfection i. itself may have its...perfect state IMPERFECTION, 7
imperial be yourself, i., plain and true SINCERITY, 1
imperialism i. is the monopoly stage of capitalism POLITICS, 45
Their Europeanism is...i. with an inferiority complex POLITICS, 34
impersonal In the philosopher there is nothing whatever i. PHILOSOPHERS, 6
impertinent ask an i. question SCIENCE, 1
impetuous such i. blood IMPETUOSITY, 4
importance Official dignity...in inverse ratio to...i. DIPLOMACY, 12
important One doesn't recognize...the really i. moments... until it's too late REGRET, 4
that basic weekendmanship should contain...I. Person Play ONE-UPMANSHIP, 2
the little things are infinitely the most i. TRIVIALITY, 6
imposed wish to be i. on, and then are EXPLOITATION, 2
impossibility a physical and metaphysical i. POETS, 3
impossible complete sorrow is as i. EMOTION, 6
I believe because it is i. BELIEF, 7
It's either easy or i. PAINTING, 4
something is i., he is...wrong SCIENCE, 6
when you have excluded the i. TRUTH, 23
impotent an i. people, /Sick with inbreeding WELSH, 3
impregnator the writer...is the i. READING, 19
impression knowledge and wonder...is an i. of pleasure KNOWLEDGE, 5; WONDER, 1
impressionable Give me a girl at an i. age IMPRESSIONABILITY, 3
impressions i....lasting as...an oar upon the water INSIGNIFICANCE, 1
improbable an i. fiction REALITY, 6
Faith...an illogical belief in...the i. FAITH, 14
whatever remains, however i., must be the truth TRUTH, 23
improper I only hope it is not i. ETIQUETTE, 3
impropriety I. is the soul of wit HUMOUR, 19
improved enormously i. by death WRITERS, 79
improvement most schemes of political i. are very laughable POLITICS, 40
impulse the i. of the moment FLATTERY, 2
the need to talk is a primary i. IMPETUOSITY, 1
impulses Mistrust first i. FIRST IMPRESSIONS, 7
impure To the Puritan all things are i. PURITANISM, 2
in you had it i. you EXPECTATION, 3
inactivity wise and masterly i. GOVERNMENT, 17
inadequate Like Brighton pier...i. for getting to France TRAVEL, 15
inarticulate speak for the i. and the submerged JOURNALISM, 4
inartistic He was unperfect, unfinished, i. WRITERS, 60
inbreeding an impotent people, /Sick with i. WELSH, 3
incest except i. and folk-dancing EXPERIENCE, 7
inch every i. a king ROYALTY, 33
Give him an i. GREED, 1
inches They that die by famine die by i. HUNGER, 6
incident What is i. but the illustration of character CHARACTER, 14
incisors Writers, like teeth, are divided into i. and grinders WRITERS, 2
inclination A man ought to read just as i. leads READING, 8
incoherent I'm not i. CONFUSION, 8
income Annual i. twenty pounds ECONOMICS, 7
difficult to love mankind...private i. SELF-INTEREST, 5
hardest thing...to understand is i. tax TAXATION, 3
her Majesty...must not...look upon me as a source of i. TAXATION, 7
live beyond its i. PROGRESS, 2; EXTRAVAGANCE, 2
incomes people live beyond their i. EXTRAVAGANCE, 4
incompetence Work...by those employees who have not yet reached...i. INCOMPETENCE, 4
incompetent a tax on pianos for the i. MUSIC, 47
God is the immemorial refuge of the i. GOD, 35
i. swine WAR, 102
incomplete A man in love is i. until...married MARRIAGE, 62
incomprehensible an old, wild, and i. man POLITICIANS, 77
inconvenience Change is not made without i. CHANGE, 11
inconveniences A good many i. attend play-going PLAYS, 12
inconvenient i. to be poor POVERTY, 5
incorruptible seagreen I. POLITICIANS, 43
the dead shall be raised i. DEATH, 28
increase from fairest creatures we desire i. BEAUTY, 36
increased influence of the Crown has i. MONARCHY, 10
incredible i. feeling, like falling in love SOUTH AFRICA, 13
incurable Not even medicine can master i. diseases MEDICINE, 7
the i. disease of writing WRITING, 17
Ind Outshone the wealth of Ormus and of I. DEVIL, 10
indecency prejudicial...as a public i. SIN, 10
The older one grows the more one likes i. AGE, 68
indecent assume such i. postures CRICKET, 9
much more i....than a good smack PUNISHMENT, 14
sent down for i. behaviour EDUCATION, 58
indecision Nothing is so exhausting as i. INDECISION, 2
indefatigable i. and unsavoury engine of pollution DOGS, 12
indefensible political speech and writing are largely the defence of the i. POLITICS, 58
independent an I. Labour Party PARTIES, 8
An i....wants to take the politics out of politics POLITICS, 75
to become fully i. MOTHERHOOD, 9
To be poor and i. POVERTY, 4
India From I.'s coral strand PLACES, 6
I. is a geographical term PLACES, 2
I....the strength and the greatness of England BRITISH EMPIRE, 3
What have we to say to I. COMMUNICATION, 4
Indian base I., threw a pearl away LOVE, 128
in a world of Gary Coopers you are the I. RACISM, 2
lay out ten to see a dead I. CHARITY, 17
Indians The only good I. I ever saw were dead ENEMIES, 7
indictment an i. against an whole people ACCUSATION, 1
indifference and cold i. came INDIFFERENCE, 5
equanimity bordering on i. INDIFFERENCE, 3
idleness and i. CHANGE, 3
i. and a coach and six LOVE, 40
Nothing is so fatal to religion as i. INDIFFERENCE, 2
veil of i. COLD WAR, 4
indigestion I., n. A disease which the patient and his friends frequently mistake for deep religious conviction RELIGION, 4
I. is charged by God ILLNESS, 8
indignation Moral i. is in most cases 2 percent moral MORALITY, 20
puritan pours righteous i. PURITANISM, 1
the mists of righteous i. PRUDERY, 3
Wrongdoing can only be avoided if those who are not wronged feel the same i. VICE, 8
indignity ultimate i. is to be given a bedpan MEDICINE, 5
indiscretion lover without i. LOVE, 67
indispensables She was one of those i. INSIGNIFICANCE, 2
indistinguishable i. from any other decent business man AMERICA, 23
individual gesture by the i. to himself BUSINESS, 11
It is of no moment to the happiness of an i. GOVERNMENT, 13
party of the i. INDIVIDUALITY, 4
the idea of death as an i. NUCLEAR WEAPONS, 9
The liberty of the i. must be thus far limited FREEDOM, 34
The psychic development of the i. PSYCHIATRY, 3
individualism American system of rugged i. AMERICA, 18
Art is the most intense mode of i. ART, 34
I eliminate my i. CHINA, 5
individuality England is the paradise of i. ENGLAND, 35
indulgence An only son, sir, might expect more i. FATHERS, 4
industrial I. relations are like sexual relations INDUSTRIAL RELATIONS, 2
industry Captains of i. LEADERSHIP, 4
i. has created many new sources of danger DISEASE, 36
i. will supply their deficiency WORK, 19
Life without i. is guilt ART, 24
national i. of Prussia WAR, 67

inebriated i. with…his own verbosity VERBOSITY, 2
inelegance a continual state of i. WEATHER, 7
inexactitude terminological i. LYING, 7
infallible an i. sign of the second-rate INFERIORITY, 3
No man is i. IMPERFECTION, 2
The only i. criterion of wisdom SUCCESS, 7
We are none of us i. IMPERFECTION, 14
infancy Heaven lies about us in our i. METAPHYSICS, 5
infant a mixed i. CHILDREN, 8
An i. crying in the night HUMAN CONDITION, 20
Sooner murder an i. in its cradle DESIRE, 3
infanticide as indefensible as i. CENSORSHIP, 4
inferior No one can make you feel i. INFERIORITY, 5
Switzerland…an i. sort of Scotland SWITZERLAND, 3
inferiority minds so impatient of i. GRATITUDE, 1
Their Europeanism is…imperialism with an i. complex POLITICS, 34
Wherever an i. complex exists, there is…reason INFERIORITY, 2
inferiors I. revolt in order that they may be equal REVOLUTION, 1
The English want *i.* PRIDE, 11
inferno A man who has not passed through the i. of his passions PASSION, 2
infidelity I.…consists in professing to believe INTEGRITY, 5
infinite The Desire of Man being I. INFINITY, 1
The sight…gave me i. pleasure EXECUTION, 21
infinitive When I split an i. GRAMMAR, 2
infinity I cannot help it;…i. torments me INFINITY, 2
I. in the palm of your hand WONDER, 2
infirmities friend should bear his friend's i. FRIENDS, 13
infirmity last i. of noble mind FAME, 14
inflation a little i. is like being a little pregnant ECONOMICS, 10
I. in the Sixties was a nuisance ECONOMICS, 14
unemployment…the price…to get i. down UNEMPLOYMENT, 1
influence How to…I. People INFLUENCE, 2
i. of the Crown has increased MONARCHY, 10
influenza call it i. if ye like ILLNESS, 2
inform not to i. the reader BUREAUCRACY, 1
information wipe all the i. off everybody's computers COMPUTERS, 1
infortune The worst kinde of i. is this MISFORTUNE, 7
infringement Necessity is the plea for every i. of human freedom NECESSITY, 4
infusion The i. of a China plant DRINKS, 1
ingenious a loyal, a gallant, a generous, an i., and good-temper'd people FRANCE, 14
inglorious the i. arts of peace POLITICIANS, 63
ingratitude I hate i. more in a man INGRATITUDE, 6
I., thou marble-hearted fiend INGRATITUDE, 5
man's i. INGRATITUDE, 4
ingress Our i.…/Was naked and bare LIFE, 34
inherit Russia will certainly i. the future RUSSIA, 4
inhumanity Man's i. to man CRUELTY, 2
initiative success depends…upon individual i. and exertion EFFORT, 5; SUCCESS, 13
injured Never trust the man who…hath i. you TRUST, 2
injury An i. is much sooner forgotten INSULTS, 12
Recompense i. with justice KINDNESS, 1
injustice A lawyer has no business with…justice or i. JUSTICE, 13
fear of suffering i. JUSTICE, 20
threatened with a great i. INJUSTICE, 3
what a man still plans…shows the…i. in his death DEATH, 36
injustices thought only to justify their i. HUMAN NATURE, 24
ink an optimist…fills up his crossword puzzle in i. OPTIMISM, 25
inn no room for them in the i. CHRISTMAS, 7
To that dark i., the grave DEATH, 101
inner Conscience is the i. voice CONSCIENCE, 4
first been vividly heard by an i. ear MUSICIANS, 17
Innisfree I will arise and…go to I. SOLITUDE, 17
innocence it is…our business to lose i. INNOCENCE, 4
my i. begins to weigh me down INNOCENCE, 2
Ralph wept for the end of i. INNOCENCE, 5
time…for i. and illusions GERMANY, 10
innocent Every one is i. LAW, 3
ten guilty persons escape than one i. suffer JUSTICE, 3
innocently i. employed than in getting money MONEY, 28
innovator time is the greatest i. INNOVATION, 1
inquiry The world is but a school of i. CURIOSITY, 6
inquisitive the i. mind can…receive no answer PHILOSOPHY, 6
insane Man is quite i. RELIGION, 46
insanity lay interest in ecclesiastical matters…often a prelude to i. RELIGION, 65
inscrutable Dumb, i. and grand CATS, 1
fathom the i. workings of Providence REPARTEE, 4
insect the Egyptians worshipped an i. POLITICIANS, 51
insemination Surely you don't mean by unartificial i. SEX, 59
insensitiveness the greatest deeds require a certain i. SENSITIVITY, 3
inside attention to the i.…contempt for the outside BOOKS, 14
insight moment's i.…worth a life's experience EXPERIENCE, 15
insignificance A man of…the utmost i. POLITICIANS, 50
insignificant as i. men as any in England ARISTOCRACY, 14
utterly i. little blue green planet SCIENCE FICTION, 1
insolence a wretch who supports with i. PATRONAGE, 1
i. is not invective PETULANCE, 2; IMPERTINENCE, 1
the i. of wealth WEALTH, 17
insolent their i. and unfounded airs of superiority FRANCE, 15
insomnia *Amor vincit i.* LOVE, 58; SLEEP, 9
every man's i. is as different from his neighbor's SLEEP, 8
inspiration Genius is one per cent i. GENIUS, 5
Ninety per cent of i. INSPIRATION, 2
instinct the i. for being unhappy SORROW, 20
instincts diseases…no less natural than the i. which preserve him DISEASE, 32
institution Any i. which does not suppose the people good CORRUPTION, 6
more than a game. It's an i. CRICKET, 4
institutions working of great i. BUREAUCRACY, 8
instrument An i. to tickle human ears MUSIC, 10
there you sit with that magnificent i. between your legs INCOMPETENCE, 5
The state is an i.…of the ruling class STATE, 5
insufferable It is Oxford that has made me i. EDUCATION, 14
insult adding i. to injuries AGGRAVATION, 1
A man should not i. his wife publicly MARRIAGE, 125
Marriage is an i. MARRIAGE, 88
sooner forgotten than an i. INSULTS, 12
insulted anyone here whom I have not i. INSULTS, 10
insured you cannot be i. for the accidents…most likely to happen ACCIDENTS, 1
insurrection I. is an art REVOLUTION, 6
integrate I i. the current export drive BUSINESS, 4
integrity if I accepted the honour…I would not answer for the i. of my intellect TITLES, 3
I. without knowledge is weak INTEGRITY, 4; KNOWLEDGE, 24
intellect a feather to tickle the i. PUNS, 10
a road…that does not go through the i. EMOTION, 1
halitosis of the i. STUPIDITY, 4
his i. is not replenished IGNORANCE, 13
i. is…fooled by the heart EMOTION, 4
I. is invisible INTELLECT, 7
put on I. WISDOM, 11
take care not to make the i. our god INTELLECT, 1
the soul of a martyr with the i. of an advocate POLITICIANS, 35
The voice of the i. is a soft one INTELLECT, 2
we cannot exclude the i. INTELLECT, 4
intellects highest i., like the tops of mountains INTELLECT, 5
There is a wicked inclination…to suppose an old man decayed in his i. OLD AGE, 24
intellectual an i.…mind watches itself INTELLECTUALS, 5
Beware of the artist who's an i. ARTISTS, 3
Every i. attitude is latently political POLITICS, 52
i., but I found it too difficult HUMILITY, 9
i.…doesn't know how to park a bike INTELLECTUALS, 1
I've been called many things, but never an i. INTELLECTUALS, 3
Man is an i. animal INTELLECT, 3
The word I. suggests INTELLECTUALS, 2
thirdly, i. ability EDUCATION, 2
intellectuals vanishing race.…the i. INTELLECTUALS, 7
intelligence I. is almost useless INTELLIGENCE, 3
I. is quickness to apprehend ABILITY, 4
i. is the great polluter ENVIRONMENT, 5
The more i.…the more…one finds original INTELLIGENCE, 6
intelligent A really i. man feels what other men…know INTELLIGENCE, 5
Each generation imagines itself…more i. AGE, 44
i. people…are socialists SOCIALISM, 1
stupid are cocksure…i. full of doubt DOUBT, 7
The i. are to the intelligentsia INTELLIGENCE, 1
intelligentsia intelligent are to the i. INTELLIGENCE, 1

intelligible to aim at being i. COMMUNICATION, 2
intended i. to give you some advice ADVICE, 8
intensity excellence of every art is its i. ARTS, 5
intent A truth that's told with bad i. TRUTH, 14
prick the sides of my i. AMBITION, 16
intercourse dreary i. of daily life OPTIMISM, 29
Sexual i. began /In nineteen sixty-three SEX, 29
interest How can I take an i. in my work ENTHUSIASM, 1
It is not my i. to pay the principal, nor my principle to pay the i. BORROWING, 10
interested always been i. in people MISANTHROPY, 2
The average man is…i. in a woman who is i. in him SEXES, 7
interests all these great i. entrusted to the shaking hand POLITICIANS, 77
intérieur 'Vive l'i. HISTORY, 30; HUMOUR, 55
intermission Pleasure is…i. of pain PLEASURE, 27
international I. Woman's Day RUSSIAN REVOLUTION, 2
science is essentially i. SCIENCE, 8
interrupt excuse me while I i. myself INTERRUPTIONS, 3
interrupted Mr Wordsworth is never i. INTERRUPTIONS, 4
interval an opera without an i., or an i. without an opera OPERA, 6
intolerably I would grow i. conceited CONCEIT, 21
intoxicate you won't i. with one glass EXPERIENCE, 10
intoxicated exposes himself when he is i. DRUNKENNESS, 15
No, thank you, I was born i. DRUNKENNESS, 18
intoxication best of life is…i. DRUNKENNESS, 10
intrigue the i. of a Greek of the lower empire INSULTS, 15
introduce let me i. you to that leg of mutton INTRODUCTIONS, 1
introduction I could buy back my i. INTRODUCTIONS, 2
introspection I.…he never achieved WRITERS, 40
intrudes society, where none i. NATURE, 3
invade when religion is allowed to i.…private life RELIGION, 43
invalid an invaluable permanent i. called Bunbury DECEPTION, 7
invasion no stand can be made against i. by an idea IDEAS, 2
the long-promised i. WORLD WAR II, 8
invective insolence is not i. PETULANCE, 2; IMPERTINENCE, 1
invent it would be necessary to i. Him GOD, 49
inventing Prolonged…reviewing of books involves constantly *i.* reactions CRITICISM, 36
invention A long poem is a test of i. POETRY, 23
Woman's virtue is man's greatest i. SEXES, 21
inventions All one's i. are true POETRY, 15
investment There is no finer i. CHILDREN, 18
To bear many children is considered…an i. CHILDREN, 22
inviolable the i. shade HOPE, 4
invisible the only evil that walks /I. HYPOCRISY, 12
invisibly electricity was dripping i. SCIENCE, 41
invited People were not i. – they went there PARTIES, 4
involuntary It was i.. They sank my boat MODESTY, 2
inward They flash upon that i. eye SOLITUDE, 15
inwards he looked i., and found her SHAKESPEARE, 6
Ireland a picture of a relief map of I. APPEARANCE, 4
English should give I. home rule IRELAND, 17
How's poor ould I., and how does she stand IRELAND, 2
I'll not forget old I. HOMESICKNESS, 1
I never met anyone in I. who understood the Irish question IRELAND, 7
I. is the old sow IRELAND, 9
I would have liked to go to I. IRELAND, 20
Now I. has her madness POETRY, 5
The moment…I. is mentioned IRELAND, 19
The problem with I. IRELAND, 11
Irish All races have…economists, with the exception of the I. IRISH, 5
as I. as Black Americans IRISH, 6
I.…devotion to higher arts IRISH, 5
That is the I. Question IRELAND, 6
The English and Americans dislike only *some* I. IRISH, 3
The I. and the Jews have a psychosis IRISH, 2; JEWS, 1
The I. are a fair people IRISH, 7
The I.…are needed in this cold age IRISH, 4
The I. don't know what they want IRISH, 8
Irishman Put an I. on the spit IRISH, 1
iron An i. curtain COLD WAR, 3
blood and i. POWER POLITICS, 2
I do, and I also wash and i. them HOUSEWORK, 5
muscles…/Are strong as i. bands OCCUPATIONS, 10
rule them with a rod of i. LEADERSHIP, 2
the I. Curtain has been demolished COLD WAR, 1
the i. enter into his soul BITTERNESS, 3
the i. has entered his soul NONCOMMITMENT, 3
will wink and hold out mine i. COWARDICE, 8
ironies Life's Little I. LIFE, 27
irons two i. in the fire PRUDENCE, 5
irony everyone gets i. nowadays HUMOUR, 29
irrelevant the most i. thing in nature FAMILY, 18
irreproachable compulsory and i. idleness ARMY, 3
irresponsible better to be i. and right RESPONSIBILITY, 5; RIGHTEOUSNESS, 6
Irving I. reminded me of a pig ACTORS, 20
Ishmaelites I.…will not publicly eat human flesh uncooked in Lent CANNIBALISM, 2
Islam In some remote regions of I. MODESTY, 3
I. unashamedly came with a sword RELIGION, 51
island No man is an I. SOCIETY, 4
islands less known by the British than these selfsame British I. BRITISH, 2
isle Kelly from the I. of Man ABSENCE, 8
this sceptred i. ENGLAND, 36
isles The i. of Greece EUROPE, 3
Israel When I. was in Egypt land OPPRESSION, 1
Israelis I. are…'enemy-friends' MIDDLE EAST, 1
Italian as sensible as baseball in I. OPERA, 5
I speak…I. to women, French to men LANGUAGE, 7
Italians The I. will laugh at me HITLER, 4
Italy A man who has not been in I. TRAVEL, 13
I. a paradise for horses NATIONALITY, 3
itch The i. of disputing…the scab of churches RELIGION, 71
the i. of literature WRITING, 20
iteration i. of nuptials MARRIAGE, 40
itself Love seeketh not i. to please LOVE, 27
ivy The holly and the i. CHRISTMAS, 5

J

jab created to j. the life out of Germans WAR, 98
J'accuse *J.* ACCUSATION, 3
Jack Damn you, J. – I'm all right SELFISHNESS, 3
J. and Jill went up the hill /To fetch a pail of water NURSERY RHYMES, 24
J. of all trades OCCUPATIONS, 3
J. Sprat could eat no fat NURSERY RHYMES, 25
Little J. Horner /Sat in the corner NURSERY RHYMES, 29
the house that J. built NURSERY RHYMES, 57
jackals J. piss at their foot BOOKS, 18
Jackson J. standing like a stone wall DETERMINATION, 5
Jacob Talk to him of J.'s ladder PRACTICALITY, 5
the traffic of J.'s ladder HEAVEN, 13
jail being in a ship is being in a j. BOATS, 9
jam J. today, and men aren't at their most exciting PROMISES, 6
The rule is, j. tomorrow and j. yesterday PROMISES, 3
James The work of Henry J. WRITERS, 54
Jane if ever I was to have a dozen girls, I'd call 'em all J. NAMES, 8
Time's up for Sir John, an' for little Lady J. PARTING, 7
Janvier Generals J. and Février SEASONS, 15
Japan There was a young man of J. VERBOSITY, 1
Japanese The J. have perfected good manners PLACES, 15
jaundiced with the j. eye PASSION, 8
jaw-jaw To j. is better than to war-war DIPLOMACY, 5
jazz J.…people hear it through their feet MUSIC, 48
J. will endure POP MUSIC, 18
The basic difference between classical music and j. MUSIC, 38
the J. Age…became less and less an affair of youth AGE, 26
jealous a j. God GOD, 10
Art is a j. mistress ART, 7
jealousy J.…feeling alone among smiling enemies JEALOUSY, 2
of j.; /It is the green-ey'd monster JEALOUSY, 5
the ear of j. heareth all things JEALOUSY, 1
Jeepers J. Creepers EYES, 2
jeering laughing and j. at everything…strange ENGLISH, 30
jeers j. at Fate ENVY, 2
Jeeves J. coughed one soft, low, gentle cough ANALOGY, 5
like P. G. Wodehouse dropping J. WRITERS, 90
Jefferson when Thomas J. dined alone TALENT, 5
jelly Out vile j. EYES, 3
Jemmy Young J. Grove on his death-bed lay LOVE, 13
Jenny J. kissed me when we met KISSING, 2
Jericho by faith the walls of J. fell down FAITH, 2

Jerusalem J. ENGLAND, 5
J. the golden MIDDLE EAST, 10
Till we have built J. ENGLAND, 5
J. the golden MIDDLE EAST, 10
jest a fellow of infinite j. MOURNING, 10
A j.'s prosperity lies in the ear HUMOUR, 28
glory, j., and riddle of the world HUMAN CONDITION, 14
Life is a j. LIFE, 26
jesting j. Pilate TRUTH, 10
Jesus All hail, the power of J.' name CHRISTIANITY, 37
Gentle J. HUMILITY, 14
If J. Christ were to come to-day BELIEF, 4
J. loves me – this I know RELIGION, 62
J. was…a first-rate political economist CHRISTIANITY, 38
We're more popular than J. Christ now POP MUSIC, 14
when J. was born in Bethlehem of Judaea CHRISTMAS, 9
jeunesse *Si j. savait* AGE, 24
Jew American is either a J., or an anti-Semite AMERICANS, 9
difficult for a J. to be converted JEWS, 6
hated /by every anti-semite /as if I were a J. PREJUDICE, 7
Hath not a J. eyes EQUALITY, 22
I'm a coloured, one-eyed J. DISABILITY, 2; RACISM, 10
I'm not really a J.; just J.-ish HALF MEASURES, 2
I was born of Christian race, /And not a Heathen, or a J. RELIGION, 63
neither J. nor Greek CHRISTIANITY, 7
no intellectual society can flourish where a J. feels…uneasy JEWS, 7
No J. was ever fool enough to turn Christian RELIGION, 73
Pessimism is a luxury that a J. never can allow himself JEWS, 9
jewelry she did not remember…her j. PRUDENCE, 9
jewels a capital bosom to hang j. upon APPEARANCE, 13
Jewish A J. man with parents alive JEWS, 13
a *total solution* of the J. question NAZISM, 1
best that is in the J. blood JEWS, 8
I'm not really a Jew; just J. HALF MEASURES, 2
Jewry Modern Physics is an instrument of J. SCIENCE, 42
Jews But spurn the J. JEWS, 5
King of the J. CHRISTMAS, 9
not enough prisons…in Palestine to hold all the J. JEWS, 10
The Irish and the J. have a psychosis IRISH, 2; JEWS, 1
The J. and Arabs…settle their differences MIDDLE EAST, 3
the J. bring the unlike into the heart of *every milieu* JEWS, 15
the J. have made a contribution to the human condition JEWS, 14
The J. have produced…Christ, Spinoza, and myself CONCEIT, 16
To choose /The J. JEWS, 4
Jill Jack and J. went up the hill NURSERY RHYMES, 24
jingo We don't want to fight, but, by j. if we do PATRIOTISM, 16
jo John Anderson my j. NOSTALGIA, 4
job Being a husband is a whole-time j. MARRIAGE, 22
If two men on the same j. agree AGREEMENT, 8
We have finished the j. TELEGRAMS, 10; WORLD WAR II, 28
we will finish the j. WORLD WAR II, 9
woman's ability to stick to a j. WOMEN, 77
Job J. endured everything – until his friends came ENDURANCE, 8
jockey the…cup is given to the j. INJUSTICE, 5
Joe Hungry J. collected lists of fatal diseases ILLNESS, 6
John D'ye ken J. Peel HUNTING, 4
J. Anderson my jo NOSTALGIA, 4
J. Brown's body MEMORIALS, 4
Matthew, Mark, Luke and J. BLESSING, 1
Time's up for Sir J., an' for little Lady Jane PARTING, 7
Johnny J. head-in-air IDEALISM, 5
J.-the-bright-star REALISM, 4
J. underground IDEALISM, 5
Little J. Head-in-Air CHILDREN, 24
Johnson Dr J.'s morality was as English…as a beefsteak ENGLAND, 20
Dr J.'s sayings WRITERS, 57
Old dread-death and dread-evil J. WRITERS, 41
That great Cham of literature, Samuel J. WRITERS, 84
There is no arguing with J. WRITERS, 51
John Wayne J. is dead ACTORS, 9
join He's gone to j. the majority DEATH, 18
will you j. the dance DANCING, 2
joined what…God hath j. together MARRIAGE, 27
Why haven't you j. WORLD WAR I, 21
joke A j.'s a very serious thing HUMOUR, 7
a j. with a double meaning HUMOUR, 2
A rich man's j. is always funny FLATTERY, 3
good deed to forget a poor j. HUMOUR, 4
Housekeeping ain't no j. HOUSEWORK, 1
The coarse j. proclaims HUMOUR, 18
different taste in j. is a…strain on the affections HUMOUR, 11
Forgive…my little j. on Thee PRAYER, 12
He cannot bear old men's j. OLD AGE, 20
I don't make j. GOVERNMENT, 25
joking My way of j. is to tell the truth TRUTH, 41
jolly There was a j. miller HAPPINESS, 4
Joneses drag the J. down to my level ONE-UPMANSHIP, 1
Joseph Here lies J., who failed in everything FAILURE, 4
journalism Christianity…but why j. CHRISTIANITY, 2; JOURNALISM, 3
J. is the only job that requires no degrees JOURNALISM, 12
j.….keeps us in touch with the ignorance of the community JOURNALISM, 32
J. largely consists of saying 'Lord Jones is dead' JOURNALISM, 13
J.…the challenge of filling…space JOURNALISM, 31
j. what will be grasped at once LITERATURE, 1; JOURNALISM, 14
journalist the functions of the modern j. JOURNALISM, 15
to bribe or twist…the British j. JOURNALISM, 33
journalists j. put theirs on the front page OCCUPATIONS, 7
J. say a thing that they know isn't true JOURNALISM, 8
journey I prepare for a j.…as though for death TRAVEL, 17
long j.…must bid the company farewell LAST WORDS, 57
One of the pleasantest things in the world is going on a j. SOLITUDE, 8; TRAVEL, 11
Our j. had advanced DEATH, 43
journeying how strange it seemed to be j. TRAINS, 4
Jowett First come I; my name is J. ACADEMICS, 2
joy a father's j. EXPECTATION, 5
A thing of beauty is a j. for ever BEAUTY, 23
let j. be unconfined DANCING, 1
One j. scatters a hundred griefs HAPPINESS, 1
Silence is the perfectest herald of j. SILENCE, 12
Strength through j. NAZISM, 3
'tis little j./ To know I'm father off from heav'n INNOCENCE, 6
we could never learn to be brave…if there were only j. ENDURANCE, 7
joys For present j. PLEASURE, 11
Hence, vain deluding J. PLEASURE, 23
j. of parents are secret FAMILY, 6
jubilation day of j., a day of remembrance GERMANY, 8
Jubilee hurrah! we bring the J. GLORY, 5
judge A j. is not supposed to know JUSTICE, 18
A j. knows nothing LAW, 1
j. not, that ye be not judged JUDGMENT, 2
J. not the play JUDGMENT, 8
j. of a man by his foes JUDGMENT, 7
Never j. from appearances APPEARANCES, 3
salutary check for a j. LAWYERS, 8
shallow people…do not j. by appearances APPEARANCES, 23
judged they were j. every man according to their works JUDGMENT, 4
why is my liberty j. of another man's conscience SCIENCE, 1; FREEDOM, 3
judgement day of j. DEATH, 33
Don't wait for the Last J. DOOMSDAY, 4
Force, if unassisted by j., collapses JUDGMENT, 9
let my will replace reasoned j. AUTHORITARIANISM, 4
no one complains of his j. JUDGMENT, 12
Perhaps your fear in passing j. COURAGE, 4
your j. will probably be right JUDGMENT, 11
Your representative owes you…his j. JUDGMENT, 6
judgment That fellow would vulgarize the day of j. VULGARITY, 3
'Tis the Last J.'s fire DOOMSDAY, 3
judgments 'Tis with our j. as our watches OPINIONS, 4
jug Little brown j., don't I love thee DRUNKENNESS, 5
Julia Whenas in silks my J. goes CLOTHES, 8
Jumblies the lands where the J. live NONSENSE, 18
jump We'd j. the life to come ENDING, 5
Juno J.'s never-forgetting anger ENDURANCE, 23
jury how should you like…to be tried before a j. JUSTICE, 12
Trial by j. itself…will be a delusion JUSTICE, 5
jury-men wretches hang that j. may dine JUSTICE, 19
just it raineth on the j. JUSTICE, 4
rain on the j. and on the unjust ENEMIES, 3
justice A lawyer has no business with…j. JUSTICE, 13

In a free society the state...administers j. among men STATE, 3
J. is open to all JUSTICE, 17
J. is such a fine thing JUSTICE, 15
J. is the means by which established injustices are sanctioned INJUSTICE, 6
J. is the...perpetual wish JUSTICE, 14
j. must be seen to be more or less done JUSTICE, 23
J. should not only be done JUSTICE, 10
Let j. be done JUSTICE, 7
moderation in the pursuit of j. is no virtue EXCESS, 4
Recompense injury with j. KINDNESS, 1
Revenge is a kind of wild j. REVENGE, 4
She's like the old line about j. OSTENTATION, 5
the female character...has no sense of j. WOMEN, 68
The j. of my quarrel JUSTICE, 16
The love of j. in most men JUSTICE, 20
The place of j. is a hallowed place JUSTICE, 1
You never expected j. from a company BUSINESS, 22
justification carry its j. in every line LITERATURE, 2
justified No man is j. in doing evil EXPEDIENCY, 6
justify thought only to j. their injustices HUMAN NATURE, 24
justifying more interested in...j. themselves MOTIVE, 6

K

Kaiser Belgium put the kibosh on the K. WORLD WAR I, 1
she took down the signed photograph of the K. WAR, 123
kaleidoscope a girl with k. eyes IMAGINATION, 8
Karl had Marx been Groucho instead of K. HUMOUR, 3
Keats Here is Johnny K.' piss-a-bed poetry POETS, 22
K.'s vulgarity with a Public School accent CRITICISM, 28
Mister John K. five feet high ADMIRATION, 5
Shelley and K. were...up to date in...chemical knowledge POETS, 7; SCIENCE, 17
we think of the verse, not of John K. POETS, 49
keen out of a k. city /in the sky MOON, 3
Satire should, like a polished razor k. SATIRE, 2
keep if they k. on saying it...it will be true JOURNALISM, 8
K. up appearances APPEARANCES, 11
they should k. who can POWER, 28
keeper am I my brother's k. MURDER, 2
a poacher a k. turned inside out OCCUPATIONS, 9
k. stands up FOOTBALL, 4
Kelly Has anybody here seen K. ABSENCE, 8
ken When a new planet swims into his k. DISCOVERY, 5
Kennedy the kind of nation...President K. died for AMBITION, 10
Kennedys I don't feel the attraction of the K. at all INSULTS, 31
Kent K., sir – everybody knows K. ENGLAND, 15
Kentucky For the old K. Home far away HOMESICKNESS, 2
kept Married women are k. women MARRIAGE, 109
kettle Polly put the k. on NURSERY RHYMES, 40
Kew I am His Highness' dog at K. DOGS, 11
key lawyers...have taken away the k. of knowledge LAWYERS, 5
turn the k. deftly SLEEP, 13
keys don't go around hitting too many white k. MUSIC, 11; RACISM, 4
the k. of the kingdom of heaven CHURCH, 1
khaki One black, and one white, and two k. RACISM, 1
Khatmandu one-eyed yellow idol to the north of K. MOURNING, 5
kibosh Belgium put the k. on the Kaiser WORLD WAR I, 1
kick every ass thinks he may k. at him WRITERS, 75
if I were under water I would scarcely k. MELANCHOLY, 6
k. you out, but...never let you down EDUCATION, 61
kicked anyone who slapped us...would get his head k. off REVENGE, 12
he had known many k. down stairs PROMOTION, 2
Saint Preux never k. the fireirons IMPERFECTION, 5
kid Here's looking at you, k. ADMIRATION, 2
kiddies k. have crumpled the serviettes ETIQUETTE, 1
kidnapped my parents finally realize that I'm k. EXPEDIENCY, 1
kids Cleaning your house while your k. are still growing HOUSEWORK, 4
K. haven't changed much CHILDREN, 34
nice thing about having relatives' k. CHILDREN, 37
kill a man can't step up and k. a woman CHIVALRY, 2
churchmen fain would k. their church CLERGY, 16
God....just had the power to k. her RELIGION, 1
good to k. an admiral EXAMPLE, 9
He would k. Himself HUMAN CONDITION, 6
K. a man, and you are a murderer KILLING, 7
k. a wife with kindness KINDNESS, 5
K. everyone, and you are a god KILLING, 7
K. not the goose GREED, 2
k. the patient REMEDIES, 1
k. us for their sport DESTINY, 20
likely to k. you is yourself MURDER, 14
Next week...I'll k. myself SUICIDE, 9
only k. you once COMFORT, 1
The bullet that is to k. me ARROGANCE, 6
The word 'revolution' is a word for which you k. REVOLUTION, 10
they k. you a new way PROGRESS, 10
thou shalt not k. GOD, 10
To k. a human being KILLING, 4
When you have to k. a man DIPLOMACY, 7
killed A Woman K. with Kindness BOOK, SONG, AND PLAY TITLES, 11
He must have k. a lot of men WEALTH, 20
I don't mind your being k. ROYALTY, 21
killer the first trained k. to be a party leader POLITICIANS, 36
killing K. /Is the ultimate KILLING, 5
k. time /Is only...another of the multifarious ways /By which Time kills us TIME, 36
More ways of k. a cat CHOICE, 3
no difference between...k. and making decisions that...kill KILLING, 6
The man is k. time TIME, 26
To save a man's life against his will is...k. him KILLING, 3
kills Time is a great teacher, but...k. all its pupils TIME, 11
time quietly k. them TIME, 13
Who k. a man k. a reasonable creature BOOKS, 27; BOOKS, 27
Yet each man k. the thing he loves KILLING, 8
kilt The k. is an unrivalled garment for fornication SCOTS, 9
kind a k. parent...or a merciless step-mother NATURE, 13
being k. /Is all the sad world needs RELIGION, 70; KINDNESS, 6
charity suffereth long, and is k. CHARITY, 6
He was a vicious man, but very k. CHARACTER, 15
I love thee for a heart that's k. KINDNESS, 2
One k. word KINDNESS, 3
try to be *k.* ACADEMICS, 3
kindle the sole purpose of human existence is to k. a light EXISTENCE, 3
kindly a young person, who...marries or dies, is sure to be k. spoken of HUMAN NATURE, 1
the deities so k. DESTINY, 17
kindness a cup o' k. yet FRIENDSHIP, 13
A Woman Killed with K. BOOK, SONG, AND PLAY TITLES, 11
full o' th' milk of human k. KINDNESS, 4
greetings where no k. is OPTIMISM, 29
kill a wife with k. KINDNESS, 5
recompense k. with k. KINDNESS, 1
set a high value on spontaneous k. FRIENDSHIP, 19
the k. of strangers CHARITY, 23
unremembered acts /Of k. and of love KINDNESS, 7
kindred Like k. drops, been mingled MOUNTAINS, 1
king A constitutional k. must learn to stoop MONARCHY, 14
A k. is a thing MONARCHY, 18
a k. may make a nobleman CHIVALRY, 3
A k. of shreds and patches INFERIORITY, 6
All the k.'s horses, /And all the k.'s men NURSERY RHYMES, 18
an atheist if the k. were SERVILITY, 4
Authority forgets a dying k. ROYALTY, 36
A worse k. never left a realm undone ROYALTY, 8
better...a poor and a wise child than an old and foolish k. OLD AGE, 5; YOUTH, 1
but the K. of England cannot enter PRIVACY, 4
curse not the k., no not in thy thought SECRECY, 3
every inch a k. ROYALTY, 33
Every subject's duty is the K.'s MONARCHY, 19
God save our Gracious K. BRITAIN, 6
half the zeal I serv'd my K. REGRET, 19
harm that cometh of a k.'s poverty TAXATION, 4
heart and stomach of a K. ROYALTY, 13
He played the K. as though CRITICISM, 13
if I were not k., I should lose my temper ROYALTY, 23
I'm the k. of the castle NURSERY RHYMES, 23
I think the K. is but a man EQUALITY, 21
k. reigns, but does not govern MONARCHY, 26
rather hew wood than be...K. of England MONARCHY, 6
such divinity doth hedge a k. MONARCHY, 20

That whatsoever K. shall reign, /I'll be the Vicar of Bray, Sir SELF-PRESERVATION, 4
the k. can do no wrong MONARCHY, 4
The k. has been very good to me MARTYRDOM, 1
The k. never dies MONARCHY, 5
The K. of Spain's daughter /Came to visit me NURSERY RHYMES, 20
The K. over the Water ROYALTY, 1
The k. reigns, and the people govern themselves MONARCHY, 23
The k. was in his counting-house, /Counting out his money NURSERY RHYMES, 48
The present life of men on earth, O k. LIFE, 9
this house will in no circumstances fight for its K. and country PATRIOTISM, 3
wash the balm from an anointed k. MONARCHY, 21

kingdom It is folly...to mistake the echo of a...coffee-house for the...k. OPINIONS, 6
my k. for a horse HORSES, 10
No k. has...had as many...wars as the k. of Christ CHRISTIANITY, 34
the k. of God is not in word, but in power GOD, 12

kings Conquering k. their titles take ROYALTY, 9
Grammar, which can govern even k. GRAMMAR, 6
If you get the English people into the way of making k. ROYALTY, 24
K. are earth's gods ROYALTY, 31
K....are just as funny ROYALTY, 29
K. are naturally lovers of low company ROYALTY, 7
K. govern by...assemblies only when MONARCHY, 12
Or walk with K. IDEALISM, 2
Pale Death kicks his way...into...the castles of k. EQUALITY, 28
sad stories of the death of k. ROYALTY, 32
Such grace had k. ROYALTY, 6
teeming womb of royal k. ENGLAND, 36
the K. of England, Diamonds, Hearts, Spades and Clubs MONARCHY, 11
This royal throne of k. ENGLAND, 36
till philosophers become k. PHILOSOPHY, 9
'Twixt k. and tyrants there's this difference TYRANNY, 2

kingship k. approaches tyranny it is near its end TYRANNY, 5

kinquering K. Congs their titles take SPOONERISMS, 3

Kipling W. H. Auden, a sort of gutless K. SOCIALISM, 13

kippers like two old k. in a box OLD AGE, 46

kiss A k. without a moustache KISSING, 4
come let us k. and part PARTING, 6
K. me, Hardy LAST WORDS, 47
make me immortal with a k. BEAUTY, 25
The coward does it with a k. KILLING, 8
The k. of sun for pardon GARDENS, 7
Then come k. me, sweet and twenty PRESENT, 13
Without a single k. or a good-bye PARTING, 8
you must not k. and tell SECRECY, 7
You must remember this; /A k. is just a k. TIME, 20

kissed Being k. by a man who didn't wax his moustache KISSING, 3
hail, master; and k. him BETRAYAL, 1
I k. her little sister UNFAITHFULNESS, 4
Jenny k. me when we met KISSING, 2
k. her once by the pig-sty EXPECTATION, 6
K. the girls and made them cry NURSERY RHYMES, 12
Wherever one wants to be k. COSMETICS, 2

kisses bread and cheese, and k. MARRIAGE, 116
remembered k. after death NOSTALGIA, 20
Stolen sweets are always sweeter, /Stolen k. much completer THEFT, 7

kissing K. don't last FOOD, 40
K. Had to Stop BOOK, SONG, AND PLAY TITLES, 7
The President spends most of his time k. PERSUASION, 4
when the k. had to stop KISSING, 1

kit-bag pack up your troubles in your old k. OPTIMISM, 13

kitchen can't stand the heat, get out of the k. ENDURANCE, 20
the way of all flesh...towards the k. FOOD, 52

Kitchener If K. was not a great man, he was...a great poster OFFICERS, 2

K-K-Katy K., beautiful Katy LOVE, 94

knave The K. of Hearts /He stole the tarts NURSERY RHYMES, 51

knaves world is made up...of fools and k. FOOLISHNESS, 11

knee-cap The soul started at the k. ANIMALISM, 5

knew I k. him, Horatio MOURNING, 10
much righter than one k. at say 17 or 23 AGE, 46
We all k. you had it in you PREGNANCY, 4

knife I had a k. and two forks left ETIQUETTE, 6
it keeps them on the k. FOOD, 6
last twist of the k. LIFE, 23
War even to the k. WAR, 22

knight a verray parfit gentil k. CHIVALRY, 4
every chance brought out a noble k. NOSTALGIA, 19
I never realized that I'd end up being the shortest k. of the year PUNS, 19; TITLES, 8
Poor K.! he really had two periods WRITING, 25
There came a k. to be their wooer LOVE, 15
what can ail thee, k. at arms ILLNESS, 10

knights sorrier for my good k.' loss than for...my fair queen LOSS, 3

knitter a beautiful little k. WRITERS, 83

knives Phone for the fish k. Norman ETIQUETTE, 1

knock Don't k. it SEX, 3
K. as you please STUPIDITY, 13
k. him down first, and pity him afterwards SELF-PRESERVATION, 6
Three, four, /K. at the door NURSERY RHYMES, 37

know all /Ye k. on earth BEAUTY, 24; TRUTH, 33
A really intelligent man feels what other men...k. INTELLIGENCE, 5
Children with Hyacinth's temperament...merely k. more CHARACTER, 19
flautists are most obviously the ones who k. something we don't k. MUSICIANS, 4
for they k. not what they do FORGIVENESS, 5
I do not k. myself SELF-KNOWLEDGE, 4
I k. myself SELF-KNOWLEDGE, 3
I k. what I like SUBJECTIVITY, 1
K. then thyself, presume not God to scan SELF-KNOWLEDGE, 5
scarcely hate any one that we k. HATE, 4
the only person...I should like to k. EGOTISM, 11
To k. how to say what others only...think SPEECH, 7
What we k. of the past HISTORY, 17
What you don't k. IGNORANCE, 3
What you don't k. would make a great book IGNORANCE, 15
You k....what you are KNOWLEDGE, 20

knowed The clever men at Oxford /Know all that there is to be k. KNOWLEDGE, 18

knowing A woman, especially if she have the misfortune of k. anything WOMEN, 10

knowledge a k. of nothing KNOWLEDGE, 12
All k. is of itself of some value KNOWLEDGE, 23
all k. to be my province KNOWLEDGE, 4
all our k. is, ourselves to know SELF-KNOWLEDGE, 6
an age in which useless k. KNOWLEDGE, 22
an intimate k. of its ugly side DISILLUSION, 1
ask it for the k. of a lifetime ARTISTS, 22
civilizations...abandon the quest for k. KNOWLEDGE, 27
he giveth...k. to them that know understanding GOD, 7
If a little k. is dangerous, where is the man...out of danger KNOWLEDGE, 21
if a little k. was a dangerous thing KNOWLEDGE, 32
if education is...a mere transmission of k. EDUCATION, 37
Integrity without k. is weak INTEGRITY, 4; KNOWLEDGE, 24
K. advances by steps KNOWLEDGE, 28
k. and wonder...is an impression of pleasure KNOWLEDGE, 5; WONDER, 1
K. can be communicated but not wisdom WISDOM, 17
K. dwells /In heads replete KNOWLEDGE, 11; WISDOM, 15
K. is Life with wings KNOWLEDGE, 15
K. is of two kinds KNOWLEDGE, 26
K. is proportionate to being KNOWLEDGE, 20
K. is the mother KNOWLEDGE, 1
K. itself is power KNOWLEDGE, 3
k. puffeth up CHARITY, 7; KNOWLEDGE, 8
lawyers...have taken away the key of k. LAWYERS, 5
let him receive the new k. HEAVEN, 4
light of k. in their eyes KNOWLEDGE, 33
never has a man turned so little k. to such great account SHAKESPEARE, 7
Our k. can only be finite KNOWLEDGE, 31
Out-topping k. SHAKESPEARE, 1
province of k. to speak KNOWLEDGE, 19; WISDOM, 18
the river of k. has too often turned back on itself SCIENCE, 24
the search for k. PHILOSOPHERS, 8
the tree of the k. of good and evil GARDENS, 3
What I don't know isn't k. ACADEMICS, 2

worth a pound of k. LOVE, 146; KNOWLEDGE, 34
you impart k. of it through another's death RESEARCH, 1
known apart from the k. and the unknown METAPHYSICS, 4
knows a woman who k. all...that can be taught KNOWLEDGE, 9
He that k. little IGNORANCE, 1
He that k. nothing IGNORANCE, 2
he thinks he k. everything POLITICIANS, 24
He who k. only his own side...knows little SUBJECTIVITY, 4
Only the nose k.... SECRECY, 1
knuckle-end k. of England SCOTLAND, 8
knyf The smyler with the k. HYPOCRISY, 7
Kodak painted...by the great artist K. PHOTOGRAPHY, 7
Kubla In Xanadu did K. Khan PLEASURE, 8
Kuwait K. is an oil monarchy MIDDLE EAST, 11
Kuwaitis K. enjoy a crisis MIDDLE EAST, 15

L

laboratorium *L. est oratorium* SCIENCE, 30
laboratory apt to leave his cultures exposed on the l. table SCIENTISTS, 13
We're all of us guinea pigs in the l. of God MANKIND, 38
labour all ye that l. and are heavy laden CHRISTIANITY, 18
A mountain in l. shouted so loud DISAPPOINTMENT, 4
an Independent L. Party PARTIES, 8
disastrous element in the L. party POLITICS, 19
England elects a L. Government POLITICS, 63
genius the L. Party has for cutting itself in half POLITICS, 17
L. is not fit to govern POLITICS, 18
little effect after much l. RESULTS, 2
Man...can only find relaxation from one...l. by taking up another CHANGE, 7
model L. voter POLITICS, 42
the Gromyko of the L. party POLITICIANS, 54
The grotesque chaos of a L. council – a *L.* council INCOMPETENCE, 2
The L. party is like a stage-coach POLITICS, 90
To l. and not ask for any reward SELFLESSNESS, 2
labours absorbs a clay /After his l. SMOKING, 3
Children sweeten l. CHILDREN, 5
labyrinthine I fled Him, down the l. ways RELIGION, 58
lack l. of power corrupts absolutely POWER, 24
own up to a l. of humour HUMOUR, 8
lad many a lightfoot l. NOSTALGIA, 11
ladder behold a l. set up on earth HEAVEN, 1
Talk to him of Jacob's l. PRACTICALITY, 5
the traffic of Jacob's l. HEAVEN, 13
We make ourselves a l. out of our vices VICE, 2
ladies How sweet are looks that l. bend WOMEN, 76
lion among l. FEAR, 12
lady Dance, dance, dance little l. DANCING, 3
l. doth protest too much EXCESS, 8
l. of a certain age AGE, 17
My fair l. NURSERY RHYMES, 32
Put thy shimmy on, L. Chatterley PARTING, 7
the L. Is a Tramp DECLINE, 2
The l.'s not for turning INFLEXIBILITY, 3
there had been a l. in the case WOMEN, 20
There is a l. sweet and kind FIRST IMPRESSIONS, 2
young l. named Bright SCIENCE, 3
ladybird L., l., /Fly away home NURSERY RHYMES, 26
Lady Chatterley *L.'s Lover*...all Christians might read with profit PORNOGRAPHY, 5
ladyship When your l.'s faith has removed them RELIGION, 14
Lafayette L., we are here GREETINGS, 4
laid all the young ladies who attended the Yale promenade dance were l. end to end SEX, 45
l. on with a trowel EXCESS, 9
laissez *L. faire* FREEDOM, 43
L. faire, l. passer FREEDOM, 13
lake An arm /Rose up from...the l. ARTHURIAN LEGEND, 3
Marriage may often be a stormy l. MARRIAGE, 91
sedge is wither'd from the l. ILLNESS, 10
lamb Did he who made the L. make thee CREATION, 7
Little L., who made thee CREATION, 8
Mary had a little l. ANIMALS, 11
Pipe a song about a L. MUSIC, 13
the L. of God CHRISTIANITY, 12
to make the lion lie down with the l. HUMAN NATURE, 18
Lambeth doin' the L. walk DANCING, 5
lambs We're poor little l. DEBAUCHERY, 7
lame your precious 'l. ducks' WEAKNESS, 2
lament reason to l. /What man has made of man MANKIND, 39
lamp my l. burns low and dim ENVY, 3
To keep a l. burning CHARITY, 21
lampada *vitai l.* MORTALITY, 15
lamp-post I'm leaning on a l. LOVE, 57
like asking a l....about dogs CRITICS, 7
share a quick pee over a common l. WRITERS, 8
lamp-posts He uses statistics as a drunken man uses l. STATISTICS, 4
lamps l. are going out all over Europe PROPHECY, 5
new l. for old ones BUSINESS, 3
the people are forbidden to light l. INJUSTICE, 10
Ye living l. BIRDS, 6
Lancelot bold Sir L. CHIVALRY, 11
land England's green and pleasant l. ENGLAND, 5
For England's the one l. ENGLAND, 7
L. of Hope and Glory BRITAIN, 4
My native L. DEPARTURE, 5
the l. grows poorer and uglier every day ECOLOGY, 3
The l. of my fathers WALES, 2
There is a happy l. HEAVEN, 15
They are ill discoverers that think there is no l. DISCOVERY, 3
they have the l. and we have the Bibles RACISM, 12
to the French the empire of the l. EUROPE, 15
Unhappy the l. that has no heroes HEROISM, 3
We are as near to heaven by sea as by l. LAST WORDS, 32; SEA, 5
why Absurdist plays take place in No Man's L. THEATRE, 1
landlady The l....is a parallelogram HUMOUR, 42
landlord Come l., fill the flowing bowl DRUNKENNESS, 3
the l. does not intend to repair LAST WORDS, 2
lands in faery l. forlorn BIRDS, 5
l. where the Jumblies live NONSENSE, 18
landscape half the l. is...covered by useless water SEASIDE, 2
When will the l. tire the view COUNTRYSIDE, 3
lane the little boy /Who lives down the l. NURSERY RHYMES, 4
language Babel; because the Lord did there confound the l. LANGUAGE, 2
characteristics of parliamentary l. POLITICS, 10
governed by those who do not speak their l. GOVERNMENT, 30
I have laboured to refine our l. to grammatical purity LANGUAGE, 14
L. grows out of life LANGUAGE, 23
L. is not simply a reporting device for experience LANGUAGE, 28
L. is only the instrument of science LANGUAGE, 16
L., man!...it's LITERATURE LITERATURE, 19
Literature is simply l. charged with meaning LITERATURE, 16
she knows her l. better than most ladies do WRITERS, 85
The English have no respect for their l. ENGLISH, 32
the tower of Babel should have got l. all mixed up LANGUAGE, 26
the whole earth was of one l. UNITY, 6
what l. an opera is sung in OPERA, 1
when his l. performs what is required of it without shyness STYLE, 3
with l. profane and obscene PETULANCE, 1
with no l. but a cry HUMAN CONDITION, 20
languages l. are the pedigree of nations LANGUAGE, 15
she speaks eighteen l.. And she can't say 'No' in any of them PROMISCUITY, 5
the man who can be silent in several l. DIPLOMACY, 11
who quoted dead l. CRITICS, 19
lap the cool flowery l. of earth POETS, 16
lap-dogs when l. breathe their last SORROW, 16
lards And l. the lean earth as he walks OBESITY, 10
lark No l. more blithe than he HAPPINESS, 4
To hear the l. begin his flight BIRDS, 8
larks Four L. and a Wren APPEARANCE, 19
lascivious Poetry...set to more or less l. music POETRY, 29
lash rum, sodomy, and the l. NAVY, 2
lass On Richmond Hill there lives a l. ADMIRATION, 7
lasses Come l. and lads, get leave of your dads MERRYMAKING, 1
lassie I love a l. LOVE, 79
last as if it were the l. LIFE, 35
Die...the l. thing I shall do LAST WORDS, 49
Don't wait for the L. Judgement DOOMSDAY, 4
each day that has dawned is your l. PRESENT, 10
'Fan vaulting'...belongs to the 'L.-supper-carved-on-a-peach-stone' ARCHITECTURE, 5

for the l. time in my life, Your Humble Servant ARGUMENTS, 17
hoping that it will eat him l. DIPLOMACY, 6
I shall be the l. to go out COURAGE, 2
l. act crowns the play PLAYS, 8
l. day but one EDUCATION, 30
Nice guys finish l. GOOD, 4
the feeling that I could l. for ever YOUTH, 4
the l. shall be first MERIT, 3
The l. straw ENDURANCE, 2
the l. time that I will take part as an amateur FUNERALS, 2
there is no l. or first EQUALITY, 6
'Tis the L. Judgment's fire DOOMSDAY, 3
we are all on our l. cruise MORTALITY, 18
What is it that will l. TIME, 37
late Better never than l. PROMPTNESS, 3
Never too l. to learn AGE, 1
One doesn't recognize…the really important moments… until it's too l. REGRET, 4
So l. into the night DEBAUCHERY, 4
We have met too l. INFLUENCE, 5
later It is l. than you think TIME, 31
Latin A gentleman need not know L. EDUCATION, 34
A silly remark can be made in L. LANGUAGE, 5
Don't quote L. SPEECHES, 6
small L., and less Greek CLASSICS, 5
the Devil knows L. LANGUAGE, 17
The word is half Greek and half L. TELEVISION AND RADIO, 5
We were taught…L. and Greek CLASSICS, 9
Latins L. are tenderly enthusiastic PLACES, 4
latrine used as a l. by some small animal DRUNKENNESS, 2
laudanum Whipping and abuse are like l. CRUELTY, 5
laugh I make myself l. at everything LAUGHTER, 4
L. and grow fat LAUGHTER, 1
L., and the world laughs with you LAUGHTER, 10
L. before breakfast LAUGHTER, 2
l. before one is happy LAUGHTER, 8
Make 'em l. WRITING, 27
not to l. at human actions UNDERSTANDING, 11
old man who will not l. AGE, 51; WISDOM, 20
The Italians will l. at me HITLER, 4
laughable most schemes of political improvement are very l. POLITICS, 40
laugh-at-with Auden was someone you could l. POETS, 54
laughed Few women care to be l. at RIDICULE, 2
on which one has not l. LAUGHTER, 6
When the first baby l. FAIRIES, 2
laughing Happiness is no l. matter HAPPINESS, 30
l. and jeering at everything…strange ENGLISH, 30
One cannot be always l. at a man MEN, 1
one may die without ever l. LAUGHTER, 8
read the death of Little Nell without l. DICKENS, 4; INSENSITIVITY, 4
the most fun I ever had without l. SEX, 2
laughter I said of l., it is mad LAUGHTER, 5
I was convulsed with l. INSULTS, 29
L. is pleasant LAUGHTER, 9
L. is the best medicine LAUGHTER, 3
l. is weakness LAUGHTER, 7
present l. PRESENT, 13
you can draw l. from an audience MARRIAGE, 74
Laughton can't direct a L. picture ACTORS, 16
Launcelot Sir L. saw her visage, but he wept not greatly SORROW, 11
laundries Land of L. TRAINS, 1
laundry Give me a l.-list MUSIC, 41
The general idea…in any first-class l. NEGLECT, 2
laurel Caesar's l. crown POWER, 7
laurel-bough burned is Apollo's l. DEATH, 81
laurels Nothing is harder on your l. SUCCESS, 2
once more, O ye l. TREES, 10
The l. all are cut ENDING, 4
Laurie for bonnie Annie L. LOVE AND DEATH, 1
law Born under one l. HUMAN CONDITION, 9
Common L. of England LAW, 16
each man must struggle, lest the moral l. become…separated MORALITY, 1
Every l. is a contract LAW, 23
Ignorance of the l. LAW, 24
I have forgotten more l. than you ever knew INSULTS, 30
No brilliance is needed in the l. LAW, 20
Nor l., nor duty bade me fight FLYING, 4
nothing is l. that is not reason LAW, 22
Order is heaven's first l. ORDER, 3
Or lesser breeds without the L. BOASTS, 4
Prisons are built with stones of L. HYPOCRISY, 4
rich men rule the l. LAW, 14
The army ages men sooner than the l. ARMY, 6
the first l. of holes…stop digging ADVICE, 9
the greater part of the l. is learning to tolerate fools LAW, 19
The l. does not concern itself LAW, 5
the l. is a ass LAW, 9
The L. is the true embodiment LAW, 12
The l. of dislike for the unlike JEWS, 15
The L. of England is a very strange one LAW, 8
the L. of the Yukon SURVIVAL, 6
the magnificent fair play of the British criminal l. JUSTICE, 6
The majestic egalitarianism of the l. EQUALITY, 8
the moral l. WONDER, 3
There is no universal l. SPONTANEITY, 3
There's one l. for the rich CLASS, 1
The rise in the…employed is governed by Parkinson's L. WORK, 14
th' windy side of the l. LAW, 25
whole lives and not know the l. LAW, 11
Lawrence For L., existence was one continuous convalescence WRITERS, 59
L., that provincial genius WRITERS, 50
L.…the only prophetic novelist writing today WRITERS, 47
Mr L. has penned another novel WRITERS, 77
laws I know not whether L. be right IMPRISONMENT, 10
L. are generally found to be nets LAW, 26
L. are like cobwebs LAW, 28
L. are like spider's webs LAW, 27
L. grind the poor LAW, 14
l. were like cobwebs LAW, 6
L. were made to be broken LAW, 21
not governed by the same l. POVERTY AND WEALTH, 4
rules of the game are what we call the l. of Nature GOD, 28
the individual subject…'has nothing to do with the l. but to obey them.' LAW, 17
the l. of poetic truth and poetic beauty POETRY, 2
the repeal of bad or obnoxious l. LAW, 15
Where l. end, tyranny begins TYRANNY, 6
you do not make the l. but…are the wives…of those who do WOMEN, 37
lawyer A client is fain to hire a l. to keep from…other lawyers LAWYERS, 6
A l. has no business with…justice or injustice JUSTICE, 13
A l. never goes LAWYERS, 2
A l.'s opinion LAWYERS, 3
He that is his own l. LAWYERS, 1
No poet ever interpreted nature…as a l. interprets truth LAW, 13
lawyers L. are the only persons in whom ignorance…is not punished LAWYERS, 4
woe unto you, l. LAWYERS, 5
laxative Now Spring, sweet l. of Georgian strains SEASONS, 6; STATELY HOMES, 1
lay I never would l. down my arms PATRIOTISM, 24
L. your sleeping head SLEEP, 3
Lazarus L.…laid at his gate, full of sores POVERTY AND WEALTH, 2
L. was not /Questioned about after-lives DEATH, 64
lazy be efficient if you're going to be l. LAZINESS, 1
There are no ugly women, only l. ones BEAUTY, 31
lead L., kindly Light FAITH, 16
leader A l. who doesn't hesitate…is not fit to be a l. LEADERSHIP, 7
I have to follow them, I am their l. LEADERSHIP, 6
leadership men do not approach to l. LEADERSHIP, 1
leap a great l. in the dark LAST WORDS, 38
A l. over the hedge PRAYER, 7
And twenty-nine in each l. year NURSERY RHYMES, 56
one giant l. for mankind SPACE, 1
leapt Into the dangerous world I l. BIRTH, 3
learn L., compare, collect the facts EDUCATION, 42
The life so short, the craft so long to l. MORTALITY, 12
we could never l. to be brave…if there were only joy ENDURANCE, 7
What we have to l. to do LEARNING, 1
learned A l. man is an idler EDUCATION, 50
He was naturally l. SHAKESPEARE, 6
I am…of the opinion with the l. AGREEMENT, 2

Misquotation is the pride and privilege of the l. MISQUOTATIONS, 2
people...never have l. anything from history EXPERIENCE, 14
the l. roast an egg FOOD, 45
learning A little l. is a dangerous thing KNOWLEDGE, 30
A progeny of l. MALAPROPISMS, 3
beauty and the lust for l. BEAUTY, 8
I have been l. how to die DEATH, 129
I thought that I was l. how to live DEATH, 129
l., earning and yearning LIFE, 38
L. hath gained most BOOKS, 19
L. is a treasure KNOWLEDGE, 2
L. is but an adjunct LEARNING, 8
L. without thought is labour lost KNOWLEDGE, 10
public school, where...l. was painfully beaten into him EDUCATION, 43
Their l. is like bread in a besieged town SCOTS, 6
learnt I only remember what I've l. KNOWLEDGE, 35
Soon l. EDUCATION, 1
what has been l. has been forgotten EDUCATION, 54
least death...the l. of all evils DEATH, 20
L. said soonest mended ARGUMENTS, 2
Strongest minds /...the noisy world /Hears l. MIND, 11
leave Fare thee well, for I must l. thee PARTING, 2
How I l. my country LAST WORDS, 51
If you l. a thing alone you l. it to a torrent of change CONSERVATISM, 1
L. well alone TACT, 1
to l. his country as good as he had found it DUTY, 1
leaves before the l. have fallen WAR, 131
before the l. have fallen from the trees WORLD WAR I, 24
If poetry comes not...as l. to a tree POETRY, 25
No fruits, no flowers, no l., no birds MONTHS, 10
Though l. are many, the root is one AGE, 72
With vine l. in his hair RETURN, 2
Words are like l. VERBOSITY, 6
leaving became him like the l. it DEATH, 110
She's l. home DEPARTURE, 8
leavings sacrifice...of the devil's l. VIRTUE, 15
lecher small gilded fly does l. ANIMALISM, 7
lechery drink...an equivocator with l. ALCOHOL, 53
Still wars and l. SEX, 53
lectures l. or a little charity SELF, 19
led l. by the nose with gold BRIBERY, 4
leeches l. have red blood LAST WORDS, 17
left a handful of silver he l. us BETRAYAL, 2
And we are l., or shall be l., alone DEFEAT, 9
better to be l. than never to have been loved LOVE, 43
not l. to Spain MARTYRDOM, 4
You just press the accelerator to the floor and steer l. SPORT AND GAMES, 24
leg here I leave my second l. PUNS, 9
legal collect l. taxes from illegal money TAXATION, 2
l. system will not support...professional slavery EXPLOITATION, 4
legality do not let so great an achievement suffer from...l. LAW, 18
legs apart from having two good l. INTELLIGENCE, 4
cannon-ball took off his l. PUNS, 8
there you sit with that magnificent instrument between your l. INCOMPETENCE, 5
You were born with your l. apart PROMISCUITY, 4
Leicester Square Good-bye Piccadilly, Farewell L. HOMESICKNESS, 8
leisure Evil comes at l. DISEASE, 12
gentleman of l. MATERIALISM, 20
Men...detest at l. LOVE AND HATE, 1
Prince Philip....a world expert on l. ROYALTY, 20
The secret of being miserable is to have l. SORROW, 23
wisdom...cometh by opportunity of l. LEISURE, 1; WISDOM, 4
lemon The Germans...squeezed, as a l. RETRIBUTION, 10
lend I would not l. my pony now NURSERY RHYMES, 21
lender Neither a borrower nor a l. be BORROWING, 8; INTEGRITY, 6
lene As l. was his hors as is a rake HORSES, 4
Lenin L.'s method leads to this COMMUNISM, 11
L. was the first to discover that capitalism 'inevitably' caused war CAPITALISM, 14
Lent Ishmaelites...will not publicly eat human flesh uncooked in L. CANNIBALISM, 2
Leonardo Disney the most significant figure...since L. ART, 15
leopard or the l. his spots CHANGE, 1
leprosy It is full of l. PRACTICALITY, 2
lerne gladly wolde he l. CHARACTER, 5
lesbian not making me a l. SEX, 22
lesbians wouldn't be discriminating against gays and l. HOMOSEXUALITY, 9
less found it l. exciting COWARDICE, 3
I love not Man the l. NATURE, 3
l. in this than meets the eye CRITICISM, 2
more and more about l. and l. EXPERTS, 5
the l. they have...the more noise they make CHARACTER, 18
let I l. down my friends BETRAYAL, 6
kick you out, but...never l. you down EDUCATION, 61
L. it be, l. it pass FREEDOM, 43
Lethe go not to L. OBLIVION, 2
letter I have made this l. longer VERBOSITY, 5
thou unnecessary l. INSULTS, 34
writing a l. and forgetting to sign his name INSULTS, 5
letters His sayings are generally like women's l. LETTER-WRITING, 3
The profession of l....in which one can make no money without being ridiculous WRITING, 28
the republic of l. MANKIND, 1
When I pass my name in such large l. FAME, 22
level-headed When things are steep, remember to stay l. SELF-CONTROL, 4
levellers Your l. wish to level *down* as far as themselves EQUALITY, 13
Leviathan that great L., or rather...that *Mortal God* STATE, 1
levity He rose by gravity; I sank by l. SERIOUSNESS, 4
lexicographer L....harmless drudge LEXICOGRAPHY, 6
to wake a l. LEXICOGRAPHY, 4
liaison partly a l. man and partly P.R.O BUSINESS, 4
liar A l. is worse LYING, 1
He did not feel a l. LYING, 12
loves boxing is either a l. or a fool SPORT AND GAMES, 8
Mr. Speaker, I said the honorable member was a l. APOLOGIES, 4
Poor Bonar can't bear being called a l. POLITICIANS, 61
When I was a little boy they called me a l. WRITERS, 22
you are...the club Bore: I am the club L. SUPERIORITY, 11
liars It has made more l. LYING, 14
liberal a l. education at the Colleges of Unreason REASON, 1
either a little L. POLITICS, 31
ineffectual l.'s problem LIBERALISM, 1
Just like an old l. /Between the wars LIBERALISM, 3
the damned, compact, l. majority MAJORITY, 4
When a l. is abused, he says LIBERALISM, 2
liberality L. lies less in giving liberally PROMPTNESS, 1
liberal-minded booksellers are generous l. men PUBLISHING, 9
Liberal party task of the L. is to strangle it at birth POLITICS, 68
liberation truly mankind's war of l. HUNGER, 7
liberté *L.! Égalité! Fraternité* HUMAN RIGHTS, 2
liberties government will protect all l. but one FREEDOM, 38
liberty condition upon which God hath given l. FREEDOM, 9
Corruption...symptom of constitutional l. CORRUPTION, 2
extremism in the defence of l. is no vice EXCESS, 4
give me l. or give me death FREEDOM, 16
If men are to wait for l. FREEDOM, 30
It is true that l. is precious FREEDOM, 27
l. cannot long exist CORRUPTION, 1
l. for one person is constrained only EQUALITY, 11
L. is the right to do everything FREEDOM, 36
L. means responsibility LIBERTY, 2
L. of action FREEDOM, 13
L., too, must be limited FREEDOM, 5
life, l., and the pursuit of happiness HUMAN RIGHTS, 3
love of l. is the love of others FREEDOM, 15
Oh l.!...What crimes are committed in thy name EXECUTION, 27; FREEDOM, 45
Power...and L....are seldom upon good Terms POWER, 12; FREEDOM, 14
The l. of the individual must be thus far limited FREEDOM, 34
The L. of the press FREEDOM, 23
the price of l. FREEDOM, 40
The tree of l. must be refreshed FREEDOM, 21
thy chosen music, L. FREEDOM, 55
Venice, the eldest Child of L. VENICE, 3
When the People contend for their L. REBELLION, 4
why is my l. judged of another man's conscience CONSCIENCE, 1; FREEDOM, 3

Liberty-Hall This is L. FREEDOM, 12
library A l. is thought in cold storage BOOKS, 38
half a l. to make one book WRITING, 13
put away in the lumber room of his l. KNOWLEDGE, 13
lice They are electronic l. POP MUSIC, 6
licence a l. to print your own money BUSINESS, 24
A universal l. to be good FREEDOM, 8
L. my roving hands LUST, 1
Painters and poets…l. to dare anything FREEDOM, 18
the rest love…l. FREEDOM, 35
licks pride that l. the dust SERVILITY, 5
lie A l. can be half-way round the world LYING, 6
A l. is…help in trouble LYING, 16
a l. which is part a truth LYING, 17
A lot of people…tell a l. with their last gasp LAST WORDS, 1
a man…should never venture to l. LYING, 11
an honest man sent to l. abroad for…his country DIPLOMACY, 21
Better a l. that heals TRUTH, 1
Father, I cannot tell a l. HONESTY, 11
He who does not need to l. is proud LYING, 13
L. follows by post APOLOGIES, 1
more easily fall victim to a big l. LYING, 8
My love and I would l. COUNTRYSIDE, 6
Nature admits no l. NATURE, 4
The camera cannot l.. But… PHOTOGRAPHY, 4
The greater the l. PROPAGANDA, 2
the l. has become…a pillar of the State LYING, 15
The old L. PATRIOTISM, 23
Those who live by…a l., and those who live by…the truth HONESTY, 5
too crafty a woman to invent a new l. LYING, 9
you would l. if you were in his place TRUTH, 35
lied because our fathers l. WORLD WAR I, 13
lies believing their own l. POLITICS, 2
It's easy to make a man confess…l. TRUTH, 30
l., damned l. and statistics STATISTICS, 2
Only l. and evil come from letting people off FORGIVENESS, 13
Optimistic l. MEDICINE, 8
polite by telling l. COURTESY, 3
The cruellest l. are…told in silence SILENCE, 14
This universal, obligatory force-feeding with l. INDOCTRINATION, 2
which way the head l. EXECUTION, 24
life a keen observer of l. INTELLECTUALS, 2
A l. that moves to gracious ends LIFE, 50
Anythin' for a quiet l. PEACE, 7
As our l. is very short LIFE, 49
A well-written L. BIOGRAPHY, 2
Bankrupt of L. WORLD-WEARINESS, 1
because I love this l. DEATH, 121
believe in the l. to come AFTERLIFE, 1
Books are…a mighty bloodless substitute for l. BOOKS, 42
brief is l. but love is long LOVE, 135
chemical barrage has been hurled against the fabric of l. ECOLOGY, 2
death after l. does greatly please DEATH, 119
doctrine of the strenuous l. WORK, 20
dreary intercourse of daily l. OPTIMISM, 29
Football isn't a matter of l. and death FOOTBALL, 8
For l. is but a dream LIFE, 52
good shepherd giveth his l. for the sheep CHRISTIANITY, 15
half of them prefer hiring their servants for l. SLAVERY, 2
help me through this long disease, my l. DISEASE, 29
hymns of praise to the glory of l. POETRY, 46
I am the bread of l. FAITH, 8
I am the resurrection, and the l. CHRISTIANITY, 16
I am the way, the truth, and the l. CHRISTIANITY, 17
I have but one l. to lose for my country PATRIOTISM, 13
I have measured out my l. LIFE, 24
Illness is the night-side of l. ILLNESS, 15
I might give my l. for my friend FRIENDSHIP, 27
Is l. a boon MORTALITY, 7
Is not l.…too short…to bore ourselves BOREDOM, 6
isn't l. a terrible thing LIFE, 51
Is there another l. AFTERLIFE, 6
It doesn't…matter what you do…so long as you have your l. LIFE, 31
It is only in the microscope that our l. looks so big LIFE, 43
Its private l. is a disgrace RABBITS, 1
I've had a happy l. LAST WORDS, 34
I've looked at l. from both sides now LIFE, 37
I warmed both hands before the fire of l. LIFE AND DEATH, 9
lay down his friends for his l. SELF-PRESERVATION, 10
L. begins at forty LIFE, 1; AGE, 62
l.…effort to prevent…thinking THINKING, 5
L. exists in the universe SCIENCE, 23
L. flies LIFE, 25
l.…happens almost exclusively in newspapers JOURNALISM, 1
L.…happens…while you're busy making other plans LIFE, 33
L. is a gamble LIFE, 48
L. is a great surprise LIFE AND DEATH, 11
L. is a jest LIFE, 26
L. is a maze in which we take the wrong turning LIFE, 19
L. is an incurable disease DISEASE, 13; LIFE, 20
L.…is a predicament LIFE, 42
L. is as tedious as a twice-told tale LIFE, 44
L. is a tragedy…in close-up LIFE, 18
L. is just a bowl LIFE, 2
L. is just one damned thing after another LIFE, 29
L. is like a sewer LIFE, 32
L. is mostly froth and bubble MISFORTUNE, 10
L. is not a spectacle or a feast LIFE, 42
L. isn't all beer and skittles LIFE, 30
L. is one long process LIFE, 16
L. is sweet LIFE, 3
L. is the art of drawing sufficient conclusions LIFE, 17
L. is the ensemble of functions LIFE, 12
l. is the thing READING, 14
L. is too short to do anything for oneself WORK, 13
L. is too short to learn German LANGUAGE, 21
l., liberty, and the pursuit of happiness HUMAN RIGHTS, 3
L.'s but a walking shadow LIFE, 45
l.…seems to me preparation for something that never happens LIFE, 55
L.'s Little Ironies LIFE, 27
L.'s short span forbids us to enter on far-reaching hopes MORTALITY, 13
l. stands explained MADNESS, 16
L.'s too short for chess SPORT AND GAMES, 3
L. to me is like boarding-house wallpaper LIFE, 36
L. without industry is guilt ART, 24
L. would be tolerable PLEASURE, 18
like runners hand on the torch of l. MORTALITY, 15
longest half of your l. YOUTH, 18
lot of trouble in his l. WORRY, 10
love…has one arch-enemy – and that is l. LOVE, 16
meddling with any practical part of l. OBJECTIVITY, 2
moment's insight…worth a l.'s experience EXPERIENCE, 15
money has something to do with l. MONEY, 30
my experience of l. has been drawn EXPERIENCE, 8
My wife…is troubled with her lonely l. WOMEN, 60
no copyright on your own l. PRIVACY, 3
no man loses any other l. than…he now lives LIFE, 7
Nothing in his l. /Became him like the leaving DEATH, 110
only honour and l. have been spared DEFEAT, 2
our l. is what our thoughts make it LIFE, 8
passion and the l.…within APPEARANCES, 12
secret of reaping the greatest fruitfulness…from l. DANGER, 6
Sex…is the gateway to l. SEX, 6
she is mine for l. IMPRESSIONABILITY, 3
show l. neither as it is nor as it ought to be WRITING, 5
strange disease of modern l. LIFE, 5
Superstition is the poetry of l. SUPERSTITION, 8
take my l. WORLD-WEARINESS, 2
Than to ever let a woman in my l. MISOGYNY, 3
that a man lay down his l. for his friends LOVE, 25
The best part of married l. is the fights MARRIAGE, 133
The Book of L. begins BIBLE, 11
the child should be allowed to meet the real experiences of l. CHILDREN, 31
the crown of l. TEMPTATION, 4
The essential thing in l. VICTORY, 4
The first rule in opera is the first rule in l. SELF-RELIANCE, 6
The Leaves of L. keep falling MORTALITY, 6
The L. and Soul, the man who will never go home PARTIES, 9
the l. of man, solitary, poor, nasty, brutish, and short HUMAN CONDITION, 11
the l.-sentence which fate carries LIFE AND DEATH, 10
The l. so short, the craft so long to learn MORTALITY, 12
The love of l. is necessary to…any undertaking ENTHUSIASM, 5

The present l. of men on earth, O king LIFE, 9
There are only three events in a man's l. LIFE AND DEATH, 8
therefore choose l. LIFE AND DEATH, 2
the stuff l. is made of TIME, 19
the tree of l. GARDENS, 3
The vanity of human l. is like a river LIFE, 41
the veil which those who live call l. DEATH, 114
The Wine of L. keeps oozing MORTALITY, 6
they get about ten percent out of l. LIFE, 22
this l. /Is nobler CONTENTMENT, 7
this long disease, my l. ENDURANCE, 13
three ingredients in the good l. LIFE, 38
Three passions…have governed my l. PHILOSOPHERS, 8
to prolong l. MEDICINE, 1
To save a man's l. against his will is…killing him KILLING, 3
total of such moments is my l. SELF, 6
value l. less than sport WEAPONS, 8
veil which those who live /Call l. LIFE, 47
We'd jump the l. to come ENDING, 5
We have discovered the secret of l. SCIENCE, 7
We see into the l. of things DEATH, 134
what a queer thing L. is LIFE, 54
when religion is allowed to invade…private l. RELIGION, 43
While there is l. HOPE, 6
While there's l. OPTIMISM, 11
Who saw l. steadily LIFE, 6
your whole l. shows in your face AGE, 6
life-blood A good book is the precious l. BOOKS, 28
lifeboat This is a movie, not a l. EQUALITY, 23
life-insurance I detest l. agents IMMORTALITY, 4
life-lie Take the l. away from the average man DELUSION, 4
life-sized Great men are but l. GREATNESS, 3
lifetime ask it for the knowledge of a l. ARTISTS, 22
light a l. to lighten the Gentiles DEATH, 30
Culture is the passion for sweetness and l. CULTURE, 2
Fond Memory brings the l. /Of other days NOSTALGIA, 14
Forward the L. Brigade OBEDIENCE, 4
Give me a l. that I may tread safely into the unknown FAITH, 11
I am the l. of the world CHRISTIANITY, 14
I can't stand a naked l. bulb VULGARITY, 6
I have only a faint l. to guide me GUIDANCE, 2
Lead, kindly L. FAITH, 16
let there be l. CREATION, 2
l. a candle of understanding UNDERSTANDING, 2
L. breaks where no sun shines EMOTION, 5
l. dwelleth with him GOD, 7
Lolita, l. of my life LUST, 6
one might get a five-pound note as one got a l. for a cigarette GENEROSITY, 4
Put out the l. MURDER, 10
speed was far faster than l. SCIENCE, 3
The leaping l. for your delight discovers DISCOVERY, 2
the l. fantastic toe DANCING, 7
The L. that Failed BOOK, SONG, AND PLAY TITLES, 12
the l. that led astray DELUSION, 1
Truth is so seldom the sudden l. TRUTH, 20
we shall this day l. such a candle EXECUTION, 15
When I consider how my l. is spent BLINDNESS, 5
wisdom excelleth folly, as…l. excelleth darkness WISDOM AND FOOLISHNESS, 2
light bulb like a l. COMPUTERS, 4
lightened brooding tragedy and its dark shadows can be l. HISTORY, 14
lightfoot many a l. lad NOSTALGIA, 11
light-headed l., variable men MARRIAGE, 113
lighthouse sitivation at the l. PEACE, 7
lightly Angels…take themselves l. SERIOUSNESS, 1
lightning beheld Satan as l. fall from heaven DEVIL, 2
reading Shakespeare by flashes of l. CRITICISM, 9
snatched the l. shaft from heaven SCIENTISTS, 16
lights God made two great l. CREATION, 4; STARS, 2
the Father of l. GIFTS, 1
Turn up the l., I don't want to go home in the dark LAST WORDS, 37
like I don't l. your Christian name MARRIAGE, 20
If I l. it…it's mine. If I don't…it's a fake PAINTING, 9
I know what I l. SUBJECTIVITY, 1
I shall not look upon his l. ADMIRATION, 15
L. breeds like SIMILARITY, 3
L. doth quit like JUSTICE, 22
men we l. are good for everything SUBJECTIVITY, 3
People who l. this sort of thing CRITICISM, 30
To l.…the same things, that is…true friendship FRIENDSHIP, 26
Where wilt thou find their l. agen ADMIRATION, 12
liked He's l., but he's not well l. POPULARITY, 7
I'm so universally l. POPULARITY, 2
likes I know she l. me LOVE, 131
liking it saves me the trouble of l. them NASTINESS, 2
this l. for war WAR, 8
you expect other people to be…to your l. TOLERANCE, 4
lilac the l. is in bloom FLOWERS, 2
lilacs l. out of the dead land MONTHS, 8
lilies consider the l. of the field WORRY, 6
L. that fester CORRUPTION, 8
The l. and roses were all awake LOVE, 134
lily paint the l. EXCESS, 10
limb Let them bestow on every airth a l. EXECUTION, 9
perils…of wind and l. FAITHFULNESS, 2
limericks Whose l. never would scan VERBOSITY, 1
limit In order to draw a l. to thinking THINKING, 13
No one who cannot l. himself SELF-CONTROL, 2
limited Liberty too must be l. FREEDOM, 5
limousine One perfect l. MATERIALISM, 16
line cancel half a L. DESTINY, 8
carved not a l. FUNERALS, 11
draw a l. in the sand MIDDLE EAST, 4
I purpose to fight it out on this l. DETERMINATION, 8
l. that fits the music POP MUSIC, 16
thin red l. tipped with steel WAR, 95
True genius walks along a l. GENIUS, 6
linen It is not l. you're wearing out WOMEN, 40
washing one's clean l. in public LOVE AND MARRIAGE, 6
lines give me six l.…by the most honest man EXECUTION, 26
Pray to God and say the l. ACTING, 5
lingerie Brevity is the soul of l. BREVITY, 5; CLOTHES, 12
lingering Something l.…I fancy DEATH, 55
linguistics Essay in Sociological L. CLASS, 28
links Nothing l. man to man like…cash MONEY, 46
lion A l. among ladies FEAR, 12
I hear the l. roar MERCY, 1
I should be like a l. in a cave of savage Daniels ENEMIES, 9
Now that the old l. is dead WRITERS, 75
the…fox said…to the sick l.: 'Because those footprints scare me MISTRUST, 5
The l. and the unicorn NURSERY RHYMES, 50
The nation had the l.'s heart CHURCHILL, 5
the wary fox said…to the sick l. MISTRUST, 5
to make the l. lie down with the lamb HUMAN NATURE, 18
lioness feeds a l. at home MARRIAGE, 118
lionized wasn't spoilt by being l. FAME, 21
lions bears and l. growl and fight ANIMALS, 20
English soldiers fight like l. OFFICERS, 8
l. led by donkeys OFFICERS, 8
lip He bit his l. in a manner HUMOUR, 51
stiff upper l. COURAGE, 5
lips l. that touch liquor must never touch mine ABSTINENCE, 12
My l. are sealed SECRECY, 2
read my l., no new taxes TAXATION, 1
Red l. are not so red WAR, 82
liquefaction That l. of her clothes CLOTHES, 8
liquidation the l. of the British Empire BRITISH EMPIRE, 2
liquor If…Orientals…drank a l. ALCOHOL, 17
lips that touch l. must never touch mine ABSTINENCE, 12
liquors alcoholic l. have been used by the…best races ALCOHOL, 50
Lisa A lotta cats copy the Mona L. IMITATION, 1
list victim must be found /I've got a little l. PUNISHMENT, 9
listen privilege of wisdom to l. KNOWLEDGE, 19; WISDOM, 18
they will l. today, they will l. tomorrow PROMISES, 4
listener A good l. is a good talker with a sore throat CONVERSATION, 11
literacy The ratio of l. to illiteracy LITERACY, 1
literary Classical quotation is the *parole* of l. men QUOTATIONS, 4
'Joe,'…the first great nonstop l. drinker ALCOHOL, 63
L. men are…a perpetual priesthood WRITERS, 4
literature All that is l. seeks to communicate power BOOKS, 16
All the rest is l. SCIENCE, 44
American professors like their l.…dead LITERATURE, 11
great deal of history to produce a little l. LITERATURE, 8; HISTORY, 18

He knew everything about l. except how to enjoy it LITERATURE, 5
If we can't stamp out l. PHILISTINISM, 7
I...impress upon you the study of Greek l. CLASSICS, 3
itch of l. WRITING, 20
Language, man!...it's L. LITERATURE, 19
L. and butterflies are the two sweetest passions LITERATURE, 14
L. flourishes best LITERATURE, 7
L. is mostly about having sex LITERATURE, 12
L. is news LITERATURE, 15
L. is simply language charged with meaning LITERATURE, 16
L. is strewn with the wreckage of men WRITERS, 27
L. is the orchestration of platitudes LITERATURE, 20
l....poisoned by its own secretions LANGUAGE, 3
L....something that will be read twice LITERATURE, 1; JOURNALISM, 14
no l. can outdo the cynicism of real life EXPERIENCE, 10
That great Cham of l., Samuel Johnson WRITERS, 84
The Bible is l. BIBLE, 10
litter social virtues...but the virtue of pigs in a l. SOCIETY, 10
little Every l. helps HELP, 1
He who knows only his own side...knows l. SUBJECTIVITY, 4
it was a very l. one ILLEGITIMACY, 1
L. things affect little minds TRIVIALITY, 4
Man wants but l. MORTALITY, 9, 24
read the death of L. Nell without laughing DICKENS, 4; INSENSITIVITY, 4
So l. done, so much to do LAST WORDS, 58
the l. things are infinitely the most important TRIVIALITY, 6
littleness the l. of those that should carry them out SUPPORT, 2
live anything but l. for it RELIGION, 16
better to die on your feet than to l. on your knees SELF-RESPECT, 1
Come l. with me, and be my love LOVE, 47, 87
Do you want to l. for ever WAR, 32
eat to l., not l. to eat FOOD, 41
he forgets to l. LIFE AND DEATH, 8
Houses are built to l. in HOUSES, 1
If God were suddenly condemned to l. the life HUMAN CONDITION, 6
If you l. long enough, the venerability factor creeps in LONGEVITY, 3
I have learned to l. each day as it comes PRESENT, 3
in him we l., and move, and have our being GOD, 5
in Rome, l. as the Romans CONFORMITY, 2
I thought that I was learning how to l. DEATH, 129
I want to love first, and l. incidentally LOVE, 55
Like a rose, she has lived as long as roses l. TRANSIENCE, 17
L. all you can; it's a mistake not to LIFE, 31
L. among men as if God beheld you RIGHTEOUSNESS, 8
L. and learn EXPERIENCE, 4
l. beyond its income PROGRESS, 2; EXTRAVAGANCE, 2
l. dangerously DANGER, 6
l. for ever or die in the attempt IMMORTALITY, 3
L. that thou mayest desire to live again AFTERLIFE, 7
Live that thou mayest desire to l. again AFTERLIFE, 7
L. this day, as...thy last PRESENT, 12
l. to fight another day SELF-PRESERVATION, 2
L. with the gods CONTENTMENT, 1
One can't l. on love alone LOVE, 139
People do not l. nowadays LIFE, 22
people l. beyond their incomes EXTRAVAGANCE, 4
Rascals, would you l. for ever WAR, 39
self-willed determination to l. LIFE AND DEATH, 7
Teach me to l. DEATH, 72
than to l. up to them PRINCIPLES, 1
there shall no man see me, and l. GOD, 11
those who l....believe...to be the truth HONESTY, 5
Those who l. by...a lie, and those who l. by...the truth HONESTY, 5
To l. with thee, and be thy love LOVE, 106
we l. but to make sport RIDICULE, 1
We l. in stirring times PRESENT, 11
we must l. as though...never going to die ACHIEVEMENT, 9
You might as well l. SUICIDE, 7
lived Never to have l. is best LIFE, 56
no man...hath l. better than I ACHIEVEMENT, 7
She...has never l. LOVE, 60
slimy things L. on GUILT, 4
livelihood slave for l. ENVY, 3
lives He that l. long SUFFERING, 1
He who l. by the sword CONFLICT, 3
he who l. more l. than one DEATH, 131
live their whole l. and not know the law LAW, 11
l. of quiet desperation DESPAIR, 6
men devote the greater part of their l. MANKIND, 15
no man loses any other life than...he now l. LIFE, 7
living A house is a machine for l. in HOUSES, 2
Civilization is a method of l. CIVILIZATION, 1
History is...the wrong way of l. HISTORY, 11
How good is man's life, the mere l. LIFE, 15
I make war on the l. REVENGE, 8
It does not then concern either the l. or the dead DEATH, 47
let the earth bring forth the l. creature ANIMALS, 3; CREATION, 5
life had prepared Podduyev for l. DEATH, 118
L. frugally...he died early ABSTINENCE, 1
l. need charity CHARITY, 2
no one has yet found a way to drink for a l. ALCOHOL, 38
search the land of l. men ADMIRATION, 12
Television...permits you to be entertained in your l. room TELEVISION AND RADIO, 3
The noble l. and the noble dead NOBILITY, 6
two people l. together for 25 years without having a cross word MARRIAGE, 69
Vietnam was lost in the l. rooms of America TELEVISION AND RADIO, 4; WAR, 65
We owe respect to the l. RESPECT, 4
Livingstone Dr L., I presume GREETINGS, 3
Lloyd George L. POWER, 6
L. could not see a belt...hitting below it INSULTS, 3
loaf half a l. is better than a whole l. COMPROMISE, 5
loafed It is better to have l. and lost LAZINESS, 4
loathe I l. the country COUNTRYSIDE, 1
lobby not a man would go into the L. against us SECRECY, 2
local settle up these little l. difficulties POLITICS, 47
Lochinvar young L. CHIVALRY, 9
lodge a l. in some vast wilderness SOLITUDE, 3
log-cabin L. to White House ACHIEVEMENT, 8
logic L. must take care of itself LOGIC, 5
people...not dealing with creatures of l. HUMAN NATURE, 7
That's l. LOGIC, 1
the l. of our times DECLINE, 3
The principles of l. and metaphysics are true PHILOSOPHY, 1
You can only find truth with l. LOGIC, 2; TRUTH, 19
logical L. consequences are the scarecrows of fools LOGIC, 3
loitered I l. my life away, reading books DISCONTENT, 3
loitering Alone and palely l. ILLNESS, 10
Lolita L., light of my life LUST, 6
Lomon' On the bonnie...banks o' Loch L. SCOTLAND, 1
London dominate a L. dinner-table INFLUENCE, 11
Dublin, though...much worse than L. PLACES, 7
Hell is a city much like L. LONDON, 12
I've been to L. to look at the queen NURSERY RHYMES, 41
L....Clearing-house of the World ECONOMICS, 5
L., that great cesspool LONDON, 6
L., that great sea LONDON, 11
Nobody is healthy in L. LONDON, 3
the agricultural labourers...commute from L. COUNTRYSIDE, 7
the best club in L. HOUSES OF PARLIAMENT, 7
the lowest and vilest alleys of L. SIN, 12
When a man is tired of L. LONDON, 10
you have dined in every house in L. – *once* BORES, 9
You will hear more good things on...a stagecoach from L. to Oxford INTELLECTUALS, 6
loneliness L....is the most terrible poverty LONELINESS, 7
l. may spur you into finding something LONELINESS, 3
lonely All the l. people LONELINESS, 4
l. of heart is withered away LONELINESS, 10
None But the L. Heart BOOK, SONG, AND PLAY TITLES, 15
She left l. for ever DEPARTURE, 2
the l. sea and the sky SEA, 10
Lonelyhearts Write to Miss L. ADVICE, 17
lonesome A l. man...who does not know how to read READING, 4
one, that on a l. road FEAR, 6
long a l., l. way to Tipperary HOMESICKNESS, 8
It is a l. lane HOPE, 3
Like German opera, too l. and too loud OPERA, 9; WAR, 124
L. is the way /And hard HELL, 4
Not that the story need be l. WRITING, 33
longer I have made this letter l. VERBOSITY, 5

Was there ever yet anything written...that was wished l. by its readers LITERATURE, 9
longest chapter of accidents is the l....in the book ACCIDENTS, 8
l. half of your life YOUTH, 18
The weariest nights, the l. days ENDURANCE, 11
longing the l. for love PHILOSOPHERS, 8
longitude A l. with no platitude MEANING, 4
longueurs Very good, but it has its *l.* CRITICISM, 42
look Cassius has a lean and hungry l. MISTRUST, 9
L. before you leap CAUTION, 8
L., stranger, at this island now DISCOVERY, 2
sit and l. at it for hours IDLENESS, 6
To l. down to Camelot CURSES, 4
looked better to be l. over than overlooked STARING, 1
looker-on sit thou a patient l. PLAYS, 8
looking Don't go on l. at me STARING, 2
Here's l. at you, kid ADMIRATION, 2
somebody may be l. CONSCIENCE, 4
looking-glasses Women have served...as l. WOMEN, 92
looks A woman as old as she l. AGE, 18
l. commercing with the skies SOUL, 10
man who l. you...in the eye...hiding something INSINCERITY, 1
Well, he l. like a man HOMOSEXUALITY, 6
loose let l. upon the world with £300 BRITISH, 1
lord And I replied, 'My L..' RELIGION, 31
drunk as a l. DRUNKENNESS, 17
Let us with a gladsome mind /Praise the L. GOD, 37
L. High Everything Else TITLES, 4
l. of all things, yet a prey to all HUMAN CONDITION, 14
Mine eyes have seen the glory of the coming of the L. GOD, 26
Praise the L. and pass the ammunition WAR, 37
This man I thought had been a L. among wits CRITICISM, 21
lords a naked Duke of Windlestraw addressing a naked House of L. NAKEDNESS, 2
Great l. have their pleasures PLEASURE, 24
the cure for admiring the House of L. HOUSES OF PARLIAMENT, 3
The House of L., an illusion RESPONSIBILITY, 14
The House of L....how to care for the elderly HOUSES OF PARLIAMENT, 9
lordships good enough for their l. on a hot summer afternoon HOUSES OF PARLIAMENT, 1
lorn a lone l. creetur MISFORTUNE, 9
lose A man who does not l. his reason REASON, 4
In every friend we l. a part of ourselves DEATH, 96
I shall l. no time in reading it INATTENTION, 1
It doesn't hurt to l. my crown FAILURE, 3
l. the substance GREED, 4
nothing to l. but their chains MARXISM, 3
tails you l. VICTORY, 5
We Don't Want To L. You DISMISSAL, 7
loser good and gracious l. FAILURE, 5
losers In war...all are l. WAR, 25
no place...for good l. VICTORY, 7
loses no man l. any other life than...he now lives LIFE, 7
The conventional army l. if it does not win WAR, 57
loss richest gain I count but l. HUMILITY, 13
lost All is l. save honour DEFEAT, 2
All is not l. DETERMINATION, 12
better to have fought and l. DEFEAT, 1
better to have loved and l. LOVE, 132
he was l., and is found PARTIES, 2
Home of l. causes OXFORD, 1
I can't say I was ever l. CONFUSION, 2
I have discovered the art...l. for two thousand years DANCING, 4
I look upon every day to be l. FRIENDSHIP, 20
It is better to have loafed and l. LAZINESS, 4
I've l. one of my children this week LOSS, 7
l. and gone for ever MOURNING, 7
never to have l. at all LOSS, 1
What though the field be l. DETERMINATION, 12
woman that deliberates is l. WOMEN, 6
You are a l. generation WAR, 114
lot policeman's l. is not a happy one POLICE, 1
lots they parted his raiment, and cast l. FORGIVENESS, 5
loud A l. noise at one end BABIES, 5
Like German opera, too long and too l. OPERA, 9; WAR, 124
Louis Son of Saint L. EXECUTION, 8
louse the point of precedency between a l. and a flea POETS, 9
lousy It was kind of l. CRITICISM, 49
lov'd I never writ, nor no man ever l. LOVE, 124
Of one that l. not wisely, but too well LOVE, 128
love Absence is to l. ABSENCE, 6
a comfort in the strength of l. LOVE, 149
a girl likes to be crossed in l. a little now and then WOMEN, 9
Alcohol is like l. ALCOHOL, 19
alike are the groans of l. to...dying LOVE AND DEATH, 4
All mankind l. a lover LOVE, 53
all's fair in l. and war JUSTICE, 8
all the world and l. were young LOVE, 106
And l. to all men GOOD, 7
An ounce of l. LOVE, 146; KNOWLEDGE, 34
ashamed of having been in l. LOVE, 107
Because women can do nothing except l. WOMEN, 51
brief is life but l. is long LOVE, 135
But L. has pitched his mansion LOVE, 151
Christianity has done a great deal for l. CHRISTIANITY, 24
Come live with me, and be my l. LOVE, 87
corner in the thing I l. JEALOUSY, 6
courage to l....courage to suffer LOVE, 140
Dear Roger Fry whom I l. as a man CRITICS, 12
Deep as first l. NOSTALGIA, 20
Do not l. your neighbour as yourself SELF, 13
Drinking...and making l. MANKIND, 4
England!.../What l. I bore to thee HOMESICKNESS, 9
Every little girl knows about l. LOVE, 111
Every l. is the l. before LOVE, 96
folly...l. did make thee run into LOVE, 117
God is l. LOVE, 22
greater l. hath no man LOVE, 25
He fell in l. with himself CONCEIT, 13
help...of the woman I l. LOVE, 147
he told men to l. their neighbour HUNGER, 3
how difficult it is to write biography...many people know the...truth about his or her l. affairs BIOGRAPHY, 6
husbands, l. your wives MARRIAGE, 23
I do not l. thee LOVE, 93
I do not l. thee, Doctor Fell HATE, 1
if men and women marry those whom they do not l. LOVE AND MARRIAGE, 4
If music be the food of l. MUSIC, 46
I hate and l. LOVE AND HATE, 2
I l. or I hate BEAUTY, 29
I'm tired of L. MONEY, 9
In l....the amateur status LOVE, 63
In Switzerland they had brotherly l. SWITZERLAND, 5
I rather suspect her of being in l. LOVE AND MARRIAGE, 2
I shall but l. thee better after death LOVE, 30
Is thy l. a plant /Of such weak fibre ABSENCE, 10
I think my l. as rare ANALOGY, 4
it jumps from admiration to l. WOMEN, 11
I understand only because I l. LOVE, 138; UNDERSTANDING, 12
I want to l. first, and live incidentally LOVE, 55
law of nature which l. alone can alter SEX, 14
let brotherly l. continue HOSPITALITY, 6
Let's Fall in L. LOVE, 102
let us prove...the sports of l. LOVE, 76
let us too give in to L. LOVE, 143
live with me, and be my l. LOVE, 47
longing for l. PHILOSOPHERS, 8
l. – all the wretched cant of it LOVE, 64
L. and all his pleasures SEX, 10
l. and marriage LOVE AND MARRIAGE, 1
l. and murder will out LOVE, 41; MURDER, 5
l., an...intercourse between tyrants and slaves LOVE AND FRIENDSHIP, 2
l. a place the less for having suffered SUFFERING, 4
L. bade me welcome GUILT, 5
L. built on beauty BEAUTY, 17
L. ceases to be a pleasure LOVE, 21
L. conquers all things LOVE, 143
l. dwells in gorgeous palaces LOVE, 29
L. fled LOVE, 150
l. God, and hateth his brother LOVE, 23
l....has one arch-enemy – and that is life LOVE, 16
L.? I make it constantly but I never talk about it SEX, 49
l. in a golden bowl WISDOM, 10
L. in a hut LOVE, 77
L. is a boy PUNISHMENT, 6; INDULGENCE, 1
L. is a sickness LOVE, 45

L. is based on a view of women LOVE, 90
l. is blind LOVE, 118
L. is blind LOVE AND FRIENDSHIP, 1
L. is like quicksilver LOVE, 97
L. is like the measles LOVE, 72
L. is moral even without...marriage LOVE AND MARRIAGE, 3
L. is my religion LOVE AND DEATH, 3
L. is not love /Which alters LOVE, 123
L. is the wisdom of the fool LOVE, 74
L. itself shall slumber on MEMORY, 17
L. laughs at locksmiths LOVE, 3
l., like a running brook, is disregarded LOVE, 61
l....looks more like hatred than like friendship LOVE AND HATE, 5
L. looks not with the eyes LOVE, 120
L. makes the world LOVE, 4
L. means never having to say APOLOGIES, 3
L. means the pre-cognitive flow LOVE, 81
L. me, love my dog LOVE, 5
l. of justice in most men JUSTICE, 20
l. of liberty is the l. of others FREEDOM, 15
l. of money is the root of all evil MONEY, 11
l. robs those who have it of their wit LOVE, 46
L. seeketh not itself to please LOVE, 27
L. seeketh only Self to please LOVE, 28
L.'s like the measles LOVE, 73
L. sought is good LOVE, 127
L.'s pleasure lasts but a moment LOVE, 56
l. that loves a scarlet coat PUNS, 7
L....the gift of oneself LOVE, 17
L., the human form divine MANKIND, 6
l. the Lord thy God with all thy heart LOVE, 26
l. thy neighbour as thyself LOVE, 26
l. until after the first attack SCEPTICISM, 1
l....was not as l. is nowadays NOSTALGIA, 13
l. we swore...seems deceit TRANSIENCE, 10
L. will find a way LOVE, 6
l. your enemies ENEMIES, 3
L. your neighbour NEIGHBOURS, 1
Making l. is the sovereign remedy for anguish SEX, 31
Many a man has fallen in l. with a girl LOVE, 38
Men l. in haste LOVE AND HATE, 1
My l. and I would lie COUNTRYSIDE, 6
My L. in her attire doth show her wit BEAUTY, 5
My l. is like a red red rose LOVE, 33
My l. she's but a lassie yet LOVE, 69
No l. like the first l. LOVE, 8
no man dies for l., but on the stage LOVE AND DEATH, 2
Nuptial l. maketh mankind LOVE, 19
office and affairs of l. LOVE AND FRIENDSHIP, 3
O Lord, to what a state...those who l. Thee RELIGION, 56
One can l....vulgarity VULGARITY, 2
One can't live on l. alone LOVE, 139
O tell me the truth about l. LOVE, 18
Our l. of what is beautiful does not lead to extravagance RESULTS, 4
perfect l. casteth out fear LOVE, 24; FEAR, 3
poet without l. POETS, 3
Religion is l. RELIGION, 67
Saying 'Farewell, blighted l.' POVERTY AND WEALTH, 1
scientist who has ever been in l. LOVE, 84
She makes l. just like a woman WOMEN, 29
She never told her l. LOVE, 126
Society, friendship, and l. SOLITUDE, 4
so many computers...use them in the search for l. COMPUTERS, 6
Such ever was l.'s way LOVE, 31
The boy I l. is up in the gallery LOVE, 144
The dupe of friendship, and the fool of l. BITTERNESS, 1
The l. of life is necessary to...any undertaking ENTHUSIASM, 5
the L. that dare not speak its name HOMOSEXUALITY, 4
the most intense l. on the mother's side MOTHERHOOD, 9
There can be no peace of mind in l. LOVE, 104
these Christians l. one another CHRISTIANITY, 45
Those have most power to hurt us that we l. HURT, 1
'Tis said that some have died for l. LOVE AND DEATH, 7
To be wise and l. LOVE, 125
To business that we l. we rise betime ENTHUSIASM, 8
To fear l. is to fear life LOVE, 109
To live with thee, and be thy l. LOVE, 106
to l. and to cherish MARRIAGE, 30
To l. oneself is the beginning of a lifelong romance CONCEIT, 26
True l.'s the gift which God has given /To man alone LOVE, 113
Try thinking of l. LOVE, 58; SLEEP, 9
vanity and l....universal characteristics WOMEN, 22
violence masquerading as l. VIOLENCE, 6
War is like l. WAR, 16
Were you ever in l., Beach LOVE, 148
we two had made such wise provision in all our l. MARRIAGE, 95
what a mischievous devil L. is LOVE, 35
What are your views on l. SEX, 49
What is commonly called l. LUST, 2
What is l.? 'Tis not hereafter PRESENT, 13
When a man is in l. he endures more LOVE, 92
when l. is grown /To ripeness LOVE, 136
when one has loved a man it is very different to l. God LOVE, 112
where the course of true l. may be expected to run smooth AMERICA, 26
whom to look at was to l. LOVE, 133
with a l. like that you know you should be glad LOVE, 83
with l. from me to you LOVE, 82
worms have eaten them, but not for l. LOVE AND DEATH, 6
yet I l. her till I die FIRST IMPRESSIONS, 2
you should l. your enemies MIDDLE EAST, 14
loved And the l. one all together PERVERSITY, 2
better to be left than never to have been l. LOVE, 43
better to have l. and lost LOSS, 1
God alone deserves to be l. LOVE, 112
I have l. him too much LOVE AND HATE, 4
It seems to me that he has never l. LOVE, 50
l., to have thought, to have done LIFE, 4
never to have l. at all LOVE, 132
She who has never l. has never lived LOVE, 60
'Tis better to have l. and lost LOVE, 132
Who ever l., that l. not at first sight FIRST IMPRESSIONS, 6
lovelier A l. flower /...was never sown DEATH, 133
lovelies Fifty l. in the rude OPPORTUNITY, 18
loveliest L. of trees, the cherry TREES, 5
loveliness A woman of so shining l. BEAUTY, 40
lovely It's all been rather l. LAST WORDS, 43
It was such a l. day BED, 6
l. and pleasant in their lives FRIENDSHIP, 9
Some hour to which you have not been looking forward will prove l. PRESENT, 10
lover All mankind love a l. LOVE, 53
a l. with any other career in view COMMITMENT, 6
A l. without indiscretion is no l. LOVE, 67
an ex-wife searching for a new l. WOMEN, 24
easier to be a l. than a husband MARRIAGE, 16
lunatic, the l., and the poet LOVE, 121; POETRY, 43
satisfied with her l.'s mind LOVE, 141
loverly Oh, wouldn't it be l. DESIRE, 10
lovers Hello, Young L., Wherever You Are LOVE, 66
l. cannot see /The pretty follies LOVE, 118
l. fled away into the storm DEPARTURE, 7
make two l. happy LOVE, 99
one makes l. as fast as one pleases LOVE, 42
those of us meant to be l. LOVE, 39
two young l. lately wed MARRIAGE, 119
loves Anyone who l. his country, follow me PATRIOTISM, 11
Every man l. what he is good at ENTHUSIASM, 7
He that l. not his wife and children MARRIAGE, 118
I have reigned with your l. ROYALTY, 14
Two l. I have, of comfort and despair CONFLICT, 7
lovesome garden is a l. thing GARDENS, 4
loveth God l. a cheerful giver GENEROSITY, 2
He prayeth best who l. best PRAYER, 9
loving A woman despises a man for l. her LOVE, 130
But if we stop l. animals LOVE, 129
Friday's child is l. and giving NURSERY RHYMES, 34
l. himself better than all CHRISTIANITY, 22
most l. mere folly INSINCERITY, 4
low Caesar! dost thou lie so l. DEATH, 106
He that is l. PRIDE, 2
Holland...lies so l. they're only saved EUROPE, 8
I'll tak' the l. road SCOTLAND, 1
Kings are naturally lovers of l. company ROYALTY, 7
my lamp burns l. and dim ENVY, 3
to put off my hat to...high or l. PRIDE, 4

when your powder's runnin' l. PATRIOTISM, 21
lower if the l. orders don't set us a good example CLASS, 39
The l. one's vitality ART, 3
lower-middle No one ever describes himself as belonging to the l. class CLASS, 23
lowly In l. pomp ride on to die CHRISTIANITY, 32
meek and l. in heart CHRISTIANITY, 18
Lowry Malcolm L. /Late of the Bowery EPITAPHS, 19
loyal a l....and good-temper'd people FRANCE, 14
loyalty Hitler showed surprising l. to Mussolini HITLER, 2
Party l. lowers the greatest of men POLITICS, 12
When l. no harm meant SELF-PRESERVATION, 4
Lucifer come not, L.! /I'll burn my books DAMNATION, 4
that same star, /That fitful, fiery L. STARS, 6
luck A self-made man...believes in l. SELF-MADE MEN, 3
it brings you l. whether you believe...or not SUPERSTITION, 6
l....the harder I work the more I have LUCK, 9
l. to give the roar CHURCHILL, 5
luckiest People who need people are the l. SOCIETY, 5
lucky Bunyan, you're a l. fellow HOSTAGES, 4
It is better to be born l. LUCK, 4
I wasn't l.. I deserved it MERIT, 7
L. at cards LOVE, 7
L. Jim BOOK, SONG, AND PLAY TITLES, 2
ludicrous He has no sense of the l. POETS, 37
lumber put away in the l. room of his library KNOWLEDGE, 13
luminous Dong with a l. Nose NONSENSE, 17
lump a crowd like that...brings a l. to my wallet MATERIALISM, 22
lunatic l. asylums...the stately homes STATELY HOMES, 5
l., the lover, and the poet LOVE, 121; POETRY, 43
lunatics All are l. PHILOSOPHERS, 1
luncheon to read a novel before l. was one of the gravest sins READING, 18
lungs don't keep using your l. LONGEVITY, 2
lured down which ideas are l. and...strangled BUREAUCRACY, 4
lust l. in action LUST, 7
Nonconformity and l. stalking hand in hand LUST, 8
lusteth the flesh l. against the Spirit COMPROMISE, 3
Lutheran I have a Catholic soul, but a L. stomach CATHOLICISM, 4
luxuries Give us the l. of life LUXURY, 4
luxury Blesses his stars, and thinks it l. PLEASURE, 2
Every l....atheism, breast-feeding, circumcision INDULGENCE, 2
The saddest thing...to get used to l. LUXURY, 2
lyf That l. so short MORTALITY, 3
lying One of you is l. LOVE, 95
the air of someone who is l....to a policeman POLICE, 7
lynching he could have attended a l. every day TOLERANCE, 6
lyre on this wall hang my weapons and my l. SEX, 25
lyric if you include me among the l. poets PRIDE, 5

M

macaroni He stuck a feather in his cap /And called it m. AMERICA, 3; NURSERY RHYMES, 69
Macaulay apostle of the Philistines, Lord M. PHILISTINISM, 2
Lord M. INSULTS, 35
Macavity there's no one like M. CATS, 2
McCarthyism M. is Americanism POLITICS, 54
MacDonald Ramsay M. POLITICIANS, 64
McDonald's America has brought us M. RUSSIA, 12
mace that fool's bauble, the m. DISMISSAL, 4
McGregor Don't go into Mr M.'s garden CAUTION, 12
machine A m. for living in DESIGN, 2
a taxing m. TAXATION, 9
One m. can do the work of fifty ordinary men TECHNOLOGY, 5
Our body is a m. for living REMEDIES, 13
that magical m., with its flying white breath TRAINS, 4
the Ghost in the M. MIND, 6
the great intangible m. of commercial tyranny DESIGN, 3
The m. threatens TECHNOLOGY, 12
The tall modern office building is the m. DESIGN, 8
machine-gun a m. riddling her hostess SYMPATHY, 3
machines no reason...these m. will ever force themselves into general use TRAINS, 7
machine tools I would like to suggest we...make him sit on a crate of m. ECONOMICS, 18
mackerel M. sky and mares' tails WEATHER, 1
Macmillan M. is the best prime minister POLITICIANS, 41
M. seemed...to embody the national decay DECLINE, 5
mad barking m. about crime CRIME, 7
escaped from a m. and savage master SEX, 54
Every one is more or less m. on one point MADNESS, 7
half of the nation is m. ENGLISH, 33
he ceased to be m. he became merely stupid REMEDIES, 11
he first makes m. MADNESS, 4
I said of laughter, it is m. LAUGHTER, 5
let me not be m. MADNESS, 14
M. about the boy LOVE, 44
M. as the Mist and Snow MADNESS, 18
M., bad, and dangerous to know POETS, 46
Men will always be m. MADNESS, 17
Never go to bed m. ANGER, 3
The dog.../Went m. and bit the man DOGS, 7
There is no doubt that this poor man was m. POETS, 60
We all are born m. MADNESS, 1
When we remember that we are all m. MADNESS, 16
who turns m. for a reason MADNESS, 2
madam M. I may not call you TITLES, 2
madame Call me m. TITLES, 7
Madame Bovary All I could think of...was: *M.* NOVELS, 11
maddest those who think they can cure them are the m. MADNESS, 17
made Annihilating all that's m. OBLIVION, 3
Don't you think I was m. for you LOVE, 54
Do you know who m. you CREATION, 13
Little Lamb, who m. thee CREATION, 8
we're all m. the same SIMILARITY, 4
Madeira We're from M. EUROPE, 18
madeleine The taste was that of the little crumb of m. MEMORY, 11
mademoiselle A m. from Armenteers FRANCE, 13
Madison How were the receipts today in M. Square Garden LAST WORDS, 6
madman If a m. were to come into this room SELF-PRESERVATION, 6
The m....has lost everything except his reason MADNESS, 3
The m. is not the man who has lost his reason MADNESS, 3
Thou call'st me m. INSULTS, 9
madness Brussels is a m. EUROPE, 10
devil's m. – War WAR, 106
Great Wits...to M. near alli'd GENIUS, 4
M. and suffering can set themselves no limit MADNESS, 11
M. in great ones MADNESS, 13
M. need not be all breakdown MADNESS, 8
Now Ireland has her m. POETRY, 5
maestro Music, M., Please MUSIC, 30
maggot how to create a m. RELIGION, 46
magic men mistook m. for medicine MEDICINE, 10
That old black m. SUPERNATURAL, 11
magicians if the way had not been prepared by m. SCIENCE, 31
magistrate Obscenity...happens to shock some elderly...m. PRUDERY, 4
suppose...the m. corruptible CORRUPTION, 6
Magna Charta M. is such a fellow MONARCHY, 9
magnanimity in victory, m. WAR AND PEACE, 3
magnificent some m. myth PROPAGANDA, 3
there you sit with that m. instrument between your legs INCOMPETENCE, 5
magnifique *c'est m., mais* WAR, 13
Mahomet If the hill will not come to M. ADAPTABILITY, 2
maid Being an old m. is like death by drowning MARRIAGE, 55
like a moth, the simple m. WOMEN, 34
The m. was in the garden, /Hanging out the clothes NURSERY RHYMES, 48
Where are you going to, my pretty m. NURSERY RHYMES, 66
maiden A simple m. in her flower PURITY, 3
I've a neater, sweeter m. DISCONTENT, 6
many a rose-lipt m. NOSTALGIA, 11
That kissed the m. all forlorn NURSERY RHYMES, 57
maids And pretty m. all in a row GARDENS, 1
Three little m. from school CHILDREN, 23
majesty A sight so touching in its m. LONDON, 14
Her M. is not a subject ROYALTY, 12
her M....must not...look upon me as a source of income TAXATION, 7

Her M.'s Opposition OPPOSITION, 1
How can I…dislike a sex to which Your M. belongs MISOGYNY, 5
If Her M. stood for Parliament POLITICS, 69
Ride on! ride on in m. CHRISTIANITY, 32
This earth of m. ENGLAND, 36
When I invented the phrase 'His M.'s Opposition' OPPOSITION, 3
major-general very model of a modern M. KNOWLEDGE, 16
majority A m. is always the best repartee MAJORITY, 2
Fools are in a terrible…m. FOOLISHNESS, 15
He's gone to join the m. DEATH, 18
I am certain that we will win the election with a good m. SELF-CONFIDENCE, 6
No candidate…elected ex-president by such a large m. DEFEAT, 7
One on God's side is a m. GOD, 41
the damned, compact, liberal m. MAJORITY, 4
the great silent m. MAJORITY, 5
The m. has the might MAJORITY, 3; MINORITY, 2
majors scarlet M. WAR, 100
make a Scotsman on the m. SCOTS, 2
Love? I m. it constantly SEX, 49
The white man knows how to m. everything CHARITY, 19
maker he adores his m. CONCEIT, 7; SELF-MADE MEN, 1
making He is very fond of m. things FUTILITY, 7
If you get the English people into the way of m. kings ROYALTY, 24
maladies all the m. and miseries WORK, 6
Medical men…call all sorts of m.…by one name MEDICINE, 2
There are m. we must not seek to cure REMEDIES, 11
malady It is the m. of our age YOUTH, 9
malaise Wembley, adj. Suffering from a vague *m.* HUMOUR, 39
male especially the m. of the species MEN, 8
In the sex-war thoughtlessness is the weapon of the m. SEXES, 6
m. and female created he them MANKIND, 5; CREATION, 6
more deadly than the m. WOMEN, 43
only a m. can represent Christ CLERGY, 4
preserve one last m. thing MASCULINITY, 2
malice M. is like a game of poker NASTINESS, 9
malicious Critics are more m. about poetry CRITICS, 9
God is subtle but he is not m. GOD, 21
malign rather m. oneself EGOTISM, 7
malignant the only part of Randolph that was not m. INSULTS, 41
malignity that peculiar m.…characteristic of apostates BETRAYAL, 5
malingering Neurosis has an absolute genius for m. NEUROSIS, 1
malt M. does more than Milton can ALCOHOL, 31; MILTON, 1
mamas The Last of the Red-Hot M. SINGERS, 3
mammon M. wins his way where Seraphs might despair MATERIALISM, 4
man A 'Grand Old M.' OLD AGE, 26
all animals were created…for the use of m. ANIMALS, 17
a m. can die but once DEATH, 113
a m. has no reason to be ashamed of having an ape for his grandfather EVOLUTION, 10
A m. in the house is worth two MEN, 14
a m. is always seeking for happiness MARRIAGE, 50
A m. is only as old as the woman AGE, 39
A m.…is *so* in the way MEN, 5
A m. must serve his time to every trade CRITICS, 2
A m. of straw WOMEN, 1
A m.'s a m. for a' that MEN, 2
A m. should never put on his best trousers FREEDOM, 20
A m. should…own he has been in the wrong MISTAKES, 12
A m. with God GOD, 31
an old m. in a dry month AGE, 23
apparel oft proclaims the m. CLOTHES, 16
'A was a m., take him for all in all ADMIRATION, 15
big m. has no time FAME, 9
Brutus is an honourable m. HONOUR, 5
condition of m. is a condition of war HUMAN CONDITION, 10
England expects every m. will do his duty DUTY, 3
Every m. is as Heaven made him CHARACTER, 3
Every m. is wanted HUMAN CONDITION, 7
Every m. meets his Waterloo DEFEAT, 6
figure of 'The Reasonable M.' LAW, 16
follies which a m. regrets the most MISTAKES, 14
for m. or beast WEATHER, 10
Glory to M. in the highest MANKIND, 31
God made the woman for the m. WOMEN, 75
Go West, young m. EXPLORATION, 2
hate ingratitude more in a m. INGRATITUDE, 6
He is a m. of brick CHARACTER, 25
he owes not any m. RIGHTEOUSNESS, 7
He was her m., but he done her wrong UNFAITHFULNESS, 2
I care not whether a m. is Good WISDOM, 11
If a m. be gracious and courteous COURTESY, 2
If a m. stays away from his wife MARRIAGE, 45
I love not M. the less NATURE, 3
I said to the m. who stood at the gate of the year FAITH, 11
I see a m. hurrying along – to what PURPOSE, 5
I sing of arms and the m. ENDURANCE, 23
It is good to know what a m. is UNDERSTANDING, 3
It takes…twenty years to make a m. LOVE, 108
Kelly from the Isle of M. ABSENCE, 8
King is but a m. EQUALITY, 21
little m. wears a shocking bad hat CLOTHES, 20
make m. in our own image MANKIND, 5; CREATION, 6
m. alone leaves traces of what he created MANKIND, 8
M., being reasonable, must get drunk DRUNKENNESS, 10
M.…can neither repeat his past nor leave it behind HISTORY, 4
M.…can only find relaxation from one…labour by taking up another CHANGE, 7
M.…consumes without producing CAPITALISM, 10
M. delights not me MANKIND, 27
m. fell into his anecdotage OLD AGE, 16
M. for the field and woman for the hearth SEXES, 24
M.…grows beyond his work MANKIND, 30
M. has his will SEXES, 11
m. has stopped moving EVOLUTION, 2
m. hath penance done PUNISHMENT, 7
M. is a history-making creature HISTORY, 4
M. is…an everlasting contradiction to himself INTELLECT, 3
M. is an intellectual animal INTELLECT, 3
M. is a noble animal MANKIND, 9
M. is…a political animal POLITICS, 3
m. is…a religious animal RELIGION, 9
M. is a social animal SOCIETY, 9
m. is as old as he's feeling AGE, 18
M. is a tool-making animal TECHNOLOGY, 4
m. is…a wild animal MANKIND, 13
M. is not a solitary animal SOCIETY, 7
M. is something that is to be surpassed SUPERIORITY, 9
M. is the hunter SEXES, 23
M. is the master of things MANKIND, 31
M. is the only animal that can remain on friendly terms HYPOCRISY, 6
M.…/Laid the crops low AGRICULTURE, 6
m. made the town COUNTRYSIDE, 2
M. proposes GOD, 30
m. right fair CONFLICT, 7
m.'s greatest crime BIRTH, 4
M.'s inhumanity to m.
M.'s life is cheap as beast's NECESSITY, 5
M.'s love is of man's life a thing apart SEXES, 4
m. so various HUMAN NATURE, 9
m.'s worth something CONFLICT, 5
m. that hath no music in himself MUSIC, 45
m. that is born of a woman HUMAN CONDITION, 3
m. that is young in years AGE, 8
M. to command and woman to obey SEXES, 24
M. wants but little MORTALITY, 9
M. was born free FREEDOM, 46
m. who…had the largest…soul SHAKESPEARE, 5
m. who's untrue to his wife INTELLECTUALS, 2
m. with all his noble qualities EVOLUTION, 4
M. with the head and woman with the heart SEXES, 24
mean m. is always full of distress SUPERIORITY, 2
My mother said it was simple to keep a m. WOMEN, 38
no m.…hath lived better than I ACHIEVEMENT, 7
No m. is an Island SOCIETY, 4
No m. is good enough to govern another DEMOCRACY, 9
Nor in the critic let the m. be lost CRITICS, 14
Nothing happens to any m. ENDURANCE, 4
Nothing links m. to m. like…cash MONEY, 46
No young m. believes he shall ever die IMMORTALITY, 2
Of M.'s first disobedience SIN, 16

On earth there is nothing great but m. MANKIND, 14
One cannot be always laughing at a m. MEN, 1
one m. pick'd out of ten thousand HONESTY, 8
One m. shall have one vote DEMOCRACY, 2
one small step for m. SPACE, 1
only m. is vile MISANTHROPY, 1
only place where a m. can feel…secure MEN, 6
rarely…one can see in a little boy the promise of a m. CHILDREN, 20
reason to lament /What m. has made of m. MANKIND, 39
She is clearly the best m. among them POLITICIANS, 44
single sentence…for modern m. MANKIND, 10
some meannesses…too mean even for m. SEXES, 25
Style is the m. himself STYLE, 1
superior m. is distressed by his want of ability ABILITY, 1; SUPERIORITY, 3
superior m. is satisfied SUPERIORITY, 2
Tears of eternity, and sorrow, /Not mine, but m.'s SORROW, 10
that grand old m. POLITICIANS, 67
That married the m. all tattered and torn NURSERY RHYMES, 57
That's one small step for m. MISQUOTATIONS, 5
The atrocious crime of being a young m. YOUTH, 14
the century of the common m. PUBLIC, 19
The Child is Father of the M. AGE, 69
The history of m. for the nine months preceding his birth BIRTH, 5
the honest m. who married MARRIAGE, 65
The m. who makes no mistakes MISTAKES, 11
the m. whose second thoughts are good THINKING, 1
the only real danger that exists is m. himself HUMAN NATURE, 14
The proper study of Mankind is M. SELF-KNOWLEDGE, 5
The really original woman…imitates a m. WOMEN, 74
There must be a m. behind the book WRITERS, 9
There once was a m. who said 'God EXISTENCE, 4
the state…M. is in GOD, 39
This is the state of m. HUMAN CONDITION, 16
this is the whole duty of m. GOD, 9
'This was a m.!' NOBILITY, 5
'Tis strange what a m. may do LOVE, 137
To the m.-in-the-street, who INTELLECTUALS, 2
True love's the gift which God has given /To m. alone LOVE, 113
uneducated m. to read books of quotations QUOTATIONS, 1
We have on our hands a sick m. DECLINE, 7
We know nothing of m., far too little HUMAN NATURE, 14
Well, he looks like a m. HOMOSEXUALITY, 6
what a m. is to a gent INTELLIGENCE, 1
What a piece of work is a m. MANKIND, 27
what a very singularly deep young m. ARROGANCE, 4
What is m.…a…machine for turning…the red wine of Shiraz into urine MANKIND, 7
What's a m.'s first duty SINCERITY, 5
When a m. is in love he endures more LOVE, 92
When a woman behaves like a m. WOMEN, 32
whether he is a Wise M. or a Fool WISDOM, 11
Whoso would be a m. CONFORMITY, 4
Why can't a woman be more like a m. MEN, 10
Women who love the same m. LOVE, 20
you asked this m. to die WAR, 3
You cannot make a m. by standing a sheep PUBLIC, 4
you'll be a M. my son IDEALISM, 2
young m. not yet MARRIAGE, 14
Manchester In M., you…become a musician POP MUSIC, 12
The shortest way out of M. is…gin PLACES, 1
Mandalay On the road to M. PLACES, 9
Mandela Mr M. has walked a long road SOUTH AFRICA, 6
Manderley I dreamt I went to M. again DREAMS, 6
mandrake Get with child a m. root NONSENSE, 11
manger In a m. for His bed CHRISTMAS, 2
laid him in a m. CHRISTMAS, 7
mangle Granny caught her tit in the m. PLEASURE, 29
Manhattan I like to walk around M. AMERICA, 33
manhood m. a struggle AGE, 19
mankind about the dreadful wood…runs a lost m. GUILT, 2
a decent respect to the opinions of m. INDEPENDENCE, 2
all M.'s epitome HUMAN NATURE, 9
As I know more of m. EXPECTATION, 2
difficult to love m.…private income SELF-INTEREST, 5
giant leap for m. SPACE, 1
Human reason won. M. won VICTORY, 8
I am willing to love all m., *except an American* AMERICANS, 5
Ideal m. would abolish death IDEALISM, 3
I love m. MANKIND, 24; MISANTHROPY, 3
M. is a closed society MANKIND, 25
M. is a club MANKIND, 12
M. is not a tribe of animals MANKIND, 12
Nazi Germany had become a menace to all m. NAZISM, 4
proper study of m. is books LITERATURE, 6
Spectator of m. OBJECTIVITY, 2
The nations which have put m.…most in their debt NATIONS, 2
The proper study of M. is Man SELF-KNOWLEDGE, 5
truly m.'s war of liberation HUNGER, 7
man-made countryside is one of the most heavily m. habitats CONSERVATION, 8
manners in England people have good table m. MANNERS, 4
leave off first for m.' sake MANNERS, 1
M. are…the need of the plain MANNERS, 7
M. maketh man MANNERS, 8
The Japanese have perfected good m. PLACES, 15
the m. of a dancing master CRITICISM, 22
the m. of a Marquis CLASS, 12
To Americans English m. are…frightening MANNERS, 3
Tom Jones…picture of human m. NOVELS, 5
to write good prose is an affair of good m. POETRY AND PROSE, 4
who are…ordered by different m. POVERTY AND WEALTH, 4
mansion Back to its m. call the fleeting breath DEATH, 57
mansions in my Father's house are many m. HEAVEN, 3
manure The tree of liberty must be refreshed… It is its natural m. FREEDOM, 21
many m. men, m. women, and m. children CRITICISM, 23
so much owed by so m. WORLD WAR II, 7
what can two do against so m. AUDIENCES, 6
map a picture of a relief m. of Ireland APPEARANCE, 4
Roll up that m. PEACE, 13
The books one reads in childhood…create in one's mind a…false m. BOOKS, 29
maps Geography is about M. BIOGRAPHY, 1
mar likely to m. the general felicity MARRIAGE, 33
Marathon mountains look on M. EUROPE, 4
marble he…left it m. IMPROVEMENT, 1
Not m., nor the gilded monuments POETRY, 42
March Beware the ides of M. PROPHECY, 12
M. comes in like a lion MONTHS, 1
M., whan God first maked man CREATION, 9
months…gloomy in England are M. and April SEASONS, 27
Napoleon's armies used to m. on their stomachs TORY, 30; HUMOUR, 55
Truth is on the m. TRUTH, 49
Marche The droghte of M. MONTHS, 7
marched He m. them up to the top of the hill ARMY, 1
March Hare 'you should say what you mean', the M. went on MEANING, 1
marching m. through Georgia GLORY, 5
mare Though patience be a tired m. PATIENCE, 12
You have sent me a Flanders m. FIRST IMPRESSIONS, 4
Margery See-saw, M. Daw NURSERY RHYMES, 46
Marie regretted living so close to M. LOVE, 103
Mariners Ye M. of England NAVY, 1
mark an ever-fixed m. LOVE, 123
If you would hit the m. AMBITION, 13
the Lord set a m. upon Cain REVENGE, 7
the m.…of the beast DEVIL, 5
markets the unreasoning laws of m. and fashion ART, 1
marmalade tangerine trees and m. skies IMAGINATION, 8
Marquis the manners of a M. CLASS, 12
marriage comedies are ended by a m. THEATRE, 6
hanging prevents a bad m. MARRIAGE, 105
Happiness in m. MARRIAGE, 11
In no country…are the m. laws so iniquitous as in England ENGLAND, 26; MARRIAGE, 82
It should be a very happy m. MARRIAGE, 123
It takes two to make a m. MARRIAGE, 102
love and m. LOVE AND MARRIAGE, 1
Love is moral even without…m. LOVE AND MARRIAGE, 3
M.…a community…making in all two MARRIAGE, 29
M.…a woman's best investment MARRIAGE, 129
M. has many pains MARRIAGE, 72
m. in a registry office MARRIAGE, 7
M. is a great institution MARRIAGE, 128
M. is an insult MARRIAGE, 88

M. is a step so grave and decisive MARRIAGE, 113
M. is a wonderful invention MARRIAGE, 41
M. is...but a civil contract MARRIAGE, 103
M. is...excluded from heaven MARRIAGE, 33
M. is like a cage MARRIAGE, 84
M. is like life in this MARRIAGE, 114
M. is popular MARRIAGE, 106
M. is the only adventure open to the cowardly MARRIAGE, 127
M. may often be a stormy lake MARRIAGE, 91
m....not a public conveyance MARRIAGE, 86
m. of true minds LOVE, 123
m....resembles a pair of shears MARRIAGE, 110
rob a lady of her fortune by way of m. MARRIAGE, 56
they neither marry, nor are given in m. MARRIAGE, 117
twenty years of m. make her...like a public building MARRIAGE, 132
Why should m. bring only tears UNFAITHFULNESS, 8
Women...care fifty times more for a m. than a ministry WOMEN, 12

marriages M. are made in heaven MARRIAGE, 2
m. don't add two people together MARRIAGE, 60
Nearly all m....are mistakes MARRIAGE, 126
the early m. of silly children MARRIAGE, 81
When widows exclaim loudly against second m. MARRIAGE, 58

married A man in love is incomplete until...m. MARRIAGE, 62
A m. couple are well suited MARRIAGE, 98
a woman's business to get m. MARRIAGE, 107
complacency and satisfaction...in...a new-m. couple MARRIAGE, 75
cross between a very severe virus and getting m. ACTORS, 22
don't sleep with m. men ADULTERY, 6
he that is m. careth...how he may please his wife MARRIAGE, 26
I am...thankful for not having m. MARRIAGE, 80
if ever we had been m. MARRIAGE, 63
I m. beneath me MARRIAGE, 9
I'm getting m. in the morning MARRIAGE, 79
In m. life three is company MARRIAGE, 131
Living in England...like being m. to a stupid wife ENGLAND, 18
m....like jumping into a hole in the ice MARRIAGE, 68
m. past redemption MARRIAGE, 53
m. to the only man north of the Tiber...untidier than I am MARRIAGE, 130
M. women are kept women MARRIAGE, 109
No man is genuinely happy, m., who has to drink worse gin ALCOHOL, 44
no taste when you m. me TASTE, 8
that Albert m. beneath him CRITICISM, 10
the honest man who m. MARRIAGE, 65
what delight we m. people have to see MARRIAGE, 93
When m. people don't get on MARRIAGE, 83
Writing is like getting m. MARRIAGE, 87; WRITING, 24
You are playing it like m. men LOVE AND MARRIAGE, 5

marries a young person, who...m. or dies, is sure to be kindly spoken of HUMAN NATURE, 1
doesn't much signify whom one m. MARRIAGE, 97
When a man m., dies MARRIAGE, 108

marry as easy to m. a rich woman as a poor woman MARRIAGE, 120
A woman...may m. whom she likes MARRIAGE, 121
better to m. than to burn MARRIAGE, 25
Every woman should m. MARRIAGE, 48
friends chose to m. the people they did MARRIAGE, 137
if men and women m. those whom they do not love LOVE AND MARRIAGE, 4
if only you could persuade him to m. CHRISTIANITY, 31
M. in haste MARRIAGE, 3
M. in Lent MARRIAGE, 4
M. in May MARRIAGE, 5
No man should m. MARRIAGE, 18
no woman should m. a teetotaller ABSTINENCE, 10
Then I can't m. you, my pretty maid NURSERY RHYMES, 67
Those who m. God...can become domesticated too RELIGION, 29
To m. a man out of pity is folly MARRIAGE, 8
when a man should m. MARRIAGE, 14
When you see what some girls m. MARRIAGE, 100
while ye may, go m. MARRIAGE, 71

marry'd M. in haste MARRIAGE, 38

Mars A M. a day helps you work rest and play ADVERTISING, 7
seat of M. ENGLAND, 36

marshal We may pick up a m. or two OFFICERS, 15

Martini out of these wet clothes and into a dry M. ALCOHOL, 67

martyr a m. to music MUSIC, 52
Now he will raise me to be a m. MARTYRDOM, 1
the soul of a m. with the intellect of an advocate POLITICIANS, 35

martyrdom M. is the test FREEDOM, 22

martyrs The blood of the m. is the seed of the Church CHRISTIANITY, 44

marvel To m. at nothing is just about the one and only thing HAPPINESS, 8

Marx had M. been Groucho instead of Karl HUMOUR, 3
M. is a case in point ILLNESS, 4
not even M. is more precious...than the truth TRUTH, 46

Marxian M. Socialism must always remain a portent MARXISM, 2

Marxist to banish...M. socialism MARXISM, 6
wasn't a M. all the time MARXISM, 1

Mary Hail M., full of grace PRAYER, 1
I'm sitting on the stile, M. NOSTALGIA, 8
M. had a little lamb ANIMALS, 11
M., M., quite contrary GARDENS, 1; NURSERY RHYMES, 33
O M., go and call the cattle home AGRICULTURE, 5

Maryland the hills of M. AMERICA, 37

masculine Fighting is essentially a m. idea WOMEN, 36
It makes me feel m. to tell you MASCULINITY, 1
partly from m. clannishness MEN, 12

mass I am a Catholic...I go to M. every day PREJUDICE, 1
Paris is worth a m. PARIS, 2
There is no idolatry in the M. CATHOLICISM, 6

masses Give me your tired.../Your huddled m. AMERICA, 22
I will back the m. against the classes CLASS, 14
The uprising of the m. REVOLUTION, 3

master A m. is dead MUSICIANS, 10
commerce between m. and slave is...exercise of... boisterous passions SLAVERY, 5
Man is the m. of things MANKIND, 31
m. of himself SELF-CONTROL, 6
Not bound to swear allegiance to any m. FREEDOM, 19
One for the m. NURSERY RHYMES, 4
the M. Mistress of my passion LOVE, 122
the m. of my fate RESPONSIBILITY, 8
the morals of a whore, and the manners of a dancing m. CRITICISM, 22

masterpiece the m. of Nature FRIENDS, 7
Who am I to tamper with a m. CONCEIT, 27

masters an ambitious man has as many m. AMBITION, 11
Assistant m....liked little boys EDUCATION, 63
Buy old m. PAINTING, 1
By studying the m. EXPERTS, 1
good servants, but bad m. PASSION, 4
people are the m. PUBLIC, 6
that the m. willingly concede to slaves SLAVERY, 1
We are the m. at the moment POWER, 21

masturbation m. of war WAR, 88
M.: the primary sexual activity SEX, 55

match man who had missed the last home m. FOOTBALL, 7

material that which was most m. in the postscript LETTER-WRITING, 2

materialistic Christianity is the most m. CHRISTIANITY, 42
only really m. people...Europeans MATERIALISM, 14

materialists all the books with which m. have pestered the world SOUL, 11

maternity M. is...an unsocial experience MOTHERHOOD, 14

mates moves, and m., and slays DESTINY, 7

mathematics Angling may be said to be...like the m. FISHING, 4
As far as the laws of m. refer to reality MATHEMATICS, 3
How are you at M. MATHEMATICS, 6
Let no one ignorant of m. enter here MATHEMATICS, 9
M. may be defined as the subject MATHEMATICS, 12
M. possesses not only truth, but supreme beauty MATHEMATICS, 14
Pure m. consists entirely of assertions MATHEMATICS, 13
quite lawful for a Catholic woman to avoid pregnancy by... m. CONTRACEPTION, 5
spirit of delight...in m. MATHEMATICS, 10

Matilda You'll come a-waltzing, M. PLACES, 12

matinée Robert Houdin who...invented the...theater m. THEATRE, 15

mating Only in the m. season ANIMALISM, 6
matrimony critical period in m. is breakfast-time MARRIAGE, 70
it jumps from…love to m. WOMEN, 11
m., which I always thought a highly overrated performance MARRIAGE, 54
matter It is not much m. which we say UNITY, 12
M.…a convenient formula PHILOSOPHY, 11
proverb is much m. decorated SAYINGS, 4
We die – does it m. when DEATH, 123
Women represent…m. over mind SEXES, 31
mattering Art…can go on m. once it has stopped hurting ART, 5
matters Nothing m. very much TRIVIALITY, 1
Matthew M., Mark, Luke and John BLESSING, 1
maturing Do you think my mind is m. late AGE, 42
maturity m. is only a short break in adolescence AGE, 25
Maud Come into the garden, M. INVITATIONS, 2
maunder m. and mumble PUBLIC, 8
mausoleums designing m. for his enemies HATE, 6
Max If M. gets to Heaven BUSINESS, 26
maxim A new m. is often a brilliant error SAYINGS, 5
we have got /The M. Gun POWER POLITICS, 1
May And after April, when M. follows MONTHS, 6
as fresh as is the month of M. CHARACTER, 4
darling buds of M. COMPLIMENTS, 4
Do spring M. flowers MONTHS, 12
I'm to be Queen o' the M. MERRYMAKING, 5
the merry month of M. MONTHS, 5
wish a snow in M. SUITABILITY, 4
maze Life is a m. LIFE, 19
mazes The melting voice through m. running MUSIC, 33
MCC where M. ends and the Church of England begins CHURCH, 7
me Besides Shakespeare and m., who do you think there is CONCEIT, 15
between m. and the sun REPARTEE, 2
My thought is m. THINKING, 9
we never talk about anything except m. CONCEIT, 23; TELEGRAMS, 13
meal A m. without flesh FOOD, 1
meals Any two m. at a boarding-house FOOD, 33
mean Down these m. streets COURAGE, 6
He nothing common did or m. EXECUTION, 16
He who meanly admires m. things is a Snob SNOBBERY, 7
it means just what I choose it to m. MEANING, 3
She was a woman of m. understanding INSULTS, 4
'you should say what you m.', the March Hare went on MEANING, 1
meaner A patronizing disposition…has its m. side CHARACTER, 8
motives m. than your own MOTIVE, 1
meanest the m.…deeds require spirit and talent INSENSITIVITY, 3
the m. of his creatures /Boasts two soul-sides HYPOCRISY, 5
meaning Even when poetry has a m. POETRY, 20; UNDERSTANDING, 7
Literature is simply language charged with m. LITERATURE, 16
Nature has never put the fatal question as to the m. of their lives PURPOSE, 4
The least of things with a m. is worth more…than the greatest MEANING, 5
meannesses some m.…too mean even for man SEXES, 25
means Errors look so very ugly in persons of small m. POVERTY AND WEALTH, 5
I shall have to die beyond my m. EXTRAVAGANCE, 5
Let us all be happy, and live within our m. BORROWING, 12
m. just what I choose it to mean MEANING, 3
Private M. is dead PUNS, 20
We are living beyond our m. ECOLOGY, 5
measles Love is like the m. LOVE, 72, 73
measure M. still for M. JUSTICE, 22
Shrunk to this little m. DEATH, 106
measureless caverns m. to man PLEASURE, 8
meat man loves the m. in his youth AGE, 54
one man is appointed to buy the m. MONARCHY, 18
One man's m. DIFFERENCE, 3
Some hae m., and canna eat FOOD, 11
The public buys its opinions as it buys its m. PUBLIC, 7
meddling He was m. too much in my private life PSYCHIATRY, 12
media complexities of poetry are destroyed by the m. THEATRE, 5
reputation doesn't really matter to…m. REPUTATION, 6
medical m. attention – a dog licked me MEDICINE, 9
We shall not refuse tobacco the credit of being…m. SMOKING, 18
medicine art of m. consists of DISEASE, 40
distinction between food and m. CHINA, 6
I never read a patent m. advertisement HYPOCHONDRIA, 1
men mistook magic for m. MEDICINE, 10
miserable have no other m. HOPE, 10
The art of m. is generally a question of time MEDICINE, 6
medieval disillusionments in the lives of the m. saints DECLINE, 9
mediocre A best-seller is the gilded tomb of a m. talent BOOKS, 40
Some men are born m. MEDIOCRITY, 5
Titles distinguish the m. TITLES, 10
Women want m. men MEDIOCRITY, 6
mediocrity It isn't evil…but m. MEDIOCRITY, 8
m.…always at its best MEDIOCRITY, 2
M. knows nothing higher MEDIOCRITY, 4; TALENT AND GENIUS, 2
supreme expression of the m. RUSSIA, 10
Mediterranean All my wife has ever taken from the M. PHILISTINISM, 6
medium The m. is the message COMMUNICATION, 3
medley a m. of your hit INSULTS, 25
meek Blessed are the m. HUMILITY, 1
humble and m. are thirsting for blood HUMILITY, 7
m. and lowly in heart CHRISTIANITY, 18
m. and mild HUMILITY, 14
the highest authority for believing that the m. shall inherit the Earth HUMILITY, 11
The m. do not inherit the earth HUMILITY, 6
The m.…not the mineral rights WEALTH, 14
Wisdom has taught us to be calm and m. REVENGE, 10
meet M. on the stairs SUPERSTITION, 2
never the twain shall m. OPPOSITES, 4
The only way for writers to m. WRITERS, 8
Two may talk…yet never really m. FRIENDSHIP, 14
We only part to m. again FAITHFULNESS, 4
meeting as if I was a public m. POLITICIANS, 78
My life's been a m., Dad BUREAUCRACY, 9
this m. is drunk DRUNKENNESS, 11
megalomaniac m.…seeks to be feared POWER, 20
melancholy a pleasing fit of m. MELANCHOLY, 10
hell upon earth…in a m. man's heart MELANCHOLY, 3
M. has her sovran shrine MELANCHOLY, 8
Most musical, most m. BIRDS, 9
so sweet as M. MELANCHOLY, 2
Melba Dame Nellie M. PATRIOTISM, 14
mellows A tart temper never m. with age CHARACTER, 13
melodies Heard m. are sweet MUSIC, 27
melody m. imposes continuity upon the disjointed MUSIC, 32
melting the races of Europe are m. AMERICA, 42
melting-pot America is…the great M. AMERICA, 42
member the tongue is a little m. SPEECH, 5
même *plus c'est la m. chose* CONSTANCY, 3
memorandum A m. is written BUREAUCRACY, 1
memorial executed a m. longer lasting than bronze MEMORIALS, 5
memories M. are hunting horns MEMORY, 1
memory Everyone complains of his m. JUDGMENT, 12
Fond M. brings the light /Of other days NOSTALGIA, 14
For my name and m., I leave it to…the next ages REPUTATION, 1
His m. is going OLD AGE, 24
How sweet their m. still NOSTALGIA, 7
Illiterate him…from your m. MALAPROPISMS, 4
I would rather be a brilliant m. than a curiosity RENUNCIATION, 2
m. is a painter MEMORY, 10
O m., hope, love of finished years NOSTALGIA, 18
Time whereof the m. of man MEMORY, 3
Unless a man feels he has a good enough m. LYING, 11
What a strange thing is m., and hope MEMORY, 10
men all m. are created equal HUMAN RIGHTS, 3
all m. have one entrance into life BIRTH, 2
all m. would be tyrants TYRANNY, 1
Christ called as his Apostles only m. SEXES, 13
depict m. as they ought to be THEATRE, 13
don't sleep with married m. ADULTERY, 6

England…purgatory of m. ENGLAND, 17
give place to better m. DISMISSAL, 3
great city…has the greatest m. and women GREATNESS, 15
Great m. are almost always bad m. POWER, 3
great m. have not commonly been great scholars GREATNESS, 8
happy breed of m. ENGLAND, 36
I don't think m. and women were meant to live together SEXES, 9
It brings m. together in crowds and mobs in bar-rooms SOCIETY, 10
It is m. who face the biggest problems MEN, 3
It's not the m. in my life that count SEX, 64
Many m. would take the death-sentence LIFE AND DEATH, 10
m. about me that are fat MISTRUST, 9
m. and sea interpenetrate ENGLAND, 11
M. are boring to women SEXES, 16
M. are but children of a larger growth AGE, 21
M. are…more careful of the breed of their horses and dogs FATHERS, 5
M. are not hanged for stealing horses EXAMPLE, 5
M. are we, and must grieve REGRET, 23
m.…capable of every wickedness EVIL, 7
M. come of age at sixty AGE, 60
m. devote the greater part of their lives MANKIND, 15
m. everywhere could be free FREEDOM, 28
M. fear death DEATH, 22
M. have never been good GOOD, 1
M. of few words are the best m. BREVITY, 8
m. represent…mind over morals SEXES, 31
M.'s natures are alike HABIT, 4
m. think all m. mortal ARROGANCE, 11
M. will always be mad MADNESS, 17
M. will confess HUMOUR, 8
Most m. admire /Virtue VIRTUE, 14
O! m. with sisters dear WOMEN, 40
Our Lord chose m. SEXES, 32
rich m. rule the law LAW, 14
schemes o' mice an' m. DISAPPOINTMENT, 2
So many m., so many opinions OPINIONS, 7
Such m. are dangerous MISTRUST, 9
That all m. are equal EQUALITY, 10
The many m., so beautiful GUILT, 4
The mass of m. lead lives DESPAIR, 6
the m. who borrow, and the m. who lend BORROWING, 5
the only advantage women have over m.…they can cry SEXES, 20
the race of m. is almost extinct in Europe MEN, 9
the tongues of m. and of angels CHARITY, 6
The War between M. and Women SEXES, 26
those m. have their price CORRUPTION, 10
tide in the affairs of m. OPPORTUNITY, 16
To famous m. all the earth is a sepulchre FAME, 20
to form Christian m. EDUCATION, 3
We live under a government of m. and…newspapers GOVERNMENT, 24; JOURNALISM, 26
when m. and mountains meet GREATNESS, 4
Why are women…so much more interesting to m. SEXES, 33
Women…are either better or worse than m. WOMEN, 46
Women have smaller brains than m. SEXES, 19
menace Foreigners fooling about in others' civil wars are a m. WAR AND PEACE, 15
Nazi Germany had become a m. to all mankind NAZISM, 4
mend God won't, and we can't m. it CONFUSION, 5
mendacity clergyman whose mendicity is only equalled by their m. CLERGY, 15
mental Christian Science explains all cause and effect as m. RELIGION, 20
philosophy ought to…unravel people's m. blocks PHILOSOPHY, 10
mentally happiness of man that he be m. faithful INTEGRITY, 5
merci La belle Dame sans M. SUPERNATURAL, 10
mercies For his m. ay endure GOD, 37
merciless a kind parent…or a m. step-mother NATURE, 13
mercury 'Twas a chilly day for Willie /When the m. went down HUMOUR, 32
mercy And that is M.'s door MERCY, 1
For M. has a human heart MANKIND, 6
quality of m. is not strain'd MERCY, 2
To M., Pity, Peace, and Love PRAYER, 5
merit no damned m. in it TITLES, 5
Satan exalted sat, by m. raised DEVIL, 10
meritocracy The Rise of the M. MERIT, 8
Mermaid Choicer than the M. Tavern PUBLIC HOUSES, 3
mermaids I have heard the m. singing OLD AGE, 18
merry For the good are always the m. HAPPINESS, 32
For tonight we'll m., m. be DRUNKENNESS, 3
I am never m. when I hear sweet music MUSIC, 44
I commended mirth…to eat…to drink, and to be m. PLEASURE, 4
merryman It's a song of a m. LOVE, 62
message the electric m. came ILLNESS, 1
The medium is the m. COMMUNICATION, 3
Messiah He was the M. of the new age POLITICIANS, 72
messing m. about in boats BOATS, 7
met I m. a man who wasn't there NONSENSE, 22
We have m. too late INFLUENCE, 5
metaphor all m. is poetry LANGUAGE, 9
metaphysical a physical and m. impossibility POETS, 3
a sort of m. brothel for emotions SENTIMENTALITY, 3
metaphysics M. is the finding of bad reasons METAPHYSICS, 2
metaquizzical The great M. poet POETS, 21
method madness, yet there is m. in't MADNESS, 12
Traditional scientific m. has always been SCIENCE, 33
You know my m. TRIVIALITY, 5
metre Poetry is opposed to science…prose to m. POETRY AND PROSE, 1
without…understanding what m. POETS, 29
metrical difference between…prose and m. composition POETRY AND PROSE, 7
Mexico Poor M. AMERICA, 11
mice schemes o' m. an' men DISAPPOINTMENT, 2
Three blind m., see how they run NURSERY RHYMES, 59
Michelangelo If M. had been straight HOMOSEXUALITY, 11
Talking of M. WOMEN, 31
microbe The M. is so very small SMALLNESS, 2
microscope It is only in the m. that our life looks so big LIFE, 43
middle a whole is that which has a beginning, a m., and an end PLAYS, 1
Bow, bow, ye lower m. classes CLASS, 13
I like a film to have a beginning, a m. and an end CINEMA, 4
no m. course between the throne and the scaffold MONARCHY, 7
One of the pleasures of m. age is to *find out* that one WAS right AGE, 46
people who stay in the m. of the road COMPROMISE, 2; NONCOMMITMENT, 1
the ease…move into the m. class CLASS, 33
middle-class part of English m. education is devoted to the training of servants EDUCATION, 65
respectable, m. …lady AUDIENCES, 4
the healthy type that was essentially m. CLASS, 10
Midland M., bound for Cricklewood TRAINS, 1
midnight chimes at m. MERRYMAKING, 4
I stood on the bridge at m. TIME, 25
It came upon the m. clear CHRISTMAS, 17
M. brought on the dusky hour DAY, 12
m. never come DAMNATION, 3
Not to be abed after m. BED, 8
Once upon a m. dreary SUPERNATURAL, 12
See her on the bridge at m. POVERTY AND WEALTH, 1
soft embalmer of the still m. SLEEP, 12
To cease upon the m. with no pain DEATH, 70
mid-stream best to swap horses in m. CHANGE, 13
mid-winter In the bleak m. SEASONS, 18
might Fight the good fight with all thy m. CHRISTIANITY, 33
The majority has the m. MAJORITY, 3; MINORITY, 2
We m. have been REGRET, 7
Might-have-been Look in my face; my name is M. DISAPPOINTMENT, 6
mightier pen is m. than the sword WRITING, 3
mighty Another m. empire overthrown DEFEAT, 9
How are the m. fallen MOURNING, 2
share in the good fortunes of the m. INJUSTICE, 2
the weak things of the world to confound the…m. WISDOM AND FOOLISHNESS, 3
mike I'm being amplified by the m. OBESITY, 4
Milan he wants M., and so do I AGREEMENT, 1
miles m. to go before I sleep TRAVEL, 9
militant I am an optimist, unrepentant and m. OPTIMISM, 26
militarism m.…is one of the chief bulwarks of capitalism CAPITALISM, 5
military The chief attraction of m. service ARMY, 3

milk as when you find a trout in the m. PROOF, 6
drunk the m. of Paradise CAUTION, 9
Gin was mother's m. ALCOHOL, 56
putting m. into babies CHILDREN, 18
reform for me will be when the m. isn't sour RUSSIA, 3
too full o' th' m. of human kindness KINDNESS, 4
Mill John Stuart M. /By a mighty effort of will ECONOMICS, 3
miller There was a jolly m. HAPPINESS, 4
million I have had no real gratification…more than my neighbor…who is worth only half a m. LAST WORDS, 71; WEALTH, 28
man who has a m. dollars WEALTH, 4
million m. spermatozoa, /All of them alive SEX, 27
'Son, here's a m. dollars ADVICE, 11
millionaire He must be a m. WEALTH, 16
I am a m.. That is my religion WEALTH, 24
Who Wants to Be a M. WEALTH, 23
millions take m. off the caring services PATRIOTISM, 19
unrewarded m. without whom Statistics would be a bankrupt science STATISTICS, 8
mills m. of God grind slowly GOD, 34
millstone a m.…hanged about his neck CHILDREN, 14
Milton Malt does more than M. can ALCOHOL, 31; MILTON, 1
M., Madam, was a genius MILTON, 2; POETS, 44
M.'s Devil as a moral being is far superior MILTON, 3
M.! thou shouldst be living at this hour DECLINE, 15
The divine M. MILTON, 4
the faith and morals hold /Which M. held FREEDOM, 54
the making up of a Shakespeare or a M. WRITERS, 5
mimsy All m. were the borogoves NONSENSE, 7
min never brought to m.' FRIENDSHIP, 12
mince dined on m., and slices of quince FOOD, 34
mind A good critic…narrates the adventures of his m. CRITICS, 5
an exaggerated stress on not changing one's m. DECISION, 2
an unseemly exposure of the m. NASTINESS, 3
A short neck denotes a good m. APPEARANCE, 35
a sound m. in a sound body HEALTH AND HEALTHY LIVING, 11
Beauty in things exists in the m. which contemplates them BEAUTY, 21
change their clime, not their frame of m., who rush across the sea TRAVEL, 12
clear your *m.* of cant REASON, 3
Do you think my m. is maturing late AGE, 42
Drama never changed anybody's m. THEATRE, 11
Europe is a state of m. EUROPE, 9
If it is for m. that we are seaching the brain MIND, 7
it's all in the m. ILLNESS, 16
making things plain to uninstructed people was…best means of clearing…one's own m. EDUCATION, 24
Many ideas grow better when transplanted into another m. IDEAS, 3
men represent…m. over morals SEXES, 31
m., once expanded MIND, 10
m. that makes the body rich APPEARANCES, 22
never to ransack any m. but his own IMITATION, 5
No m. is thoroughly well organized HUMOUR, 9
our love…of the m. does not make us soft RESULTS, 4
prodigious quantity of m. INDECISION, 3
Reading is to the m. READING, 15
someone whose m. watches itself INTELLECTUALS, 5
spirit… of a sound m. FEAR, 2
That's the classical m. at work MIND, 5
the inquisitive m. can…receive no answer PHILOSOPHY, 6
The m. can also be an erogenous zone MIND, 9
The m.…Can make a Heaven of Hell MIND, 4
The m. is its own place MIND, 4
The pendulum of the m. oscillates between sense and nonsense MIND, 3
There is in the British Museum an enormous m. MUSEUMS, 3
'Tis education forms the common m. EDUCATION, 44
to change your m. ADAPTABILITY, 1
To know the *m.* of a woman LOVE, 81
true genius is a m. of large general powers GENIUS, 7
what difficulty a m.…admits hope SUFFERING, 15
Women represent…matter over m. SEXES, 31
minded If everybody m. their own business CURIOSITY, 4
minds All things can corrupt perverted m. CORRUPTION, 5
Great m. think alike SIMILARITY, 2
Little m. are interested in the extraordinary TRIVIALITY, 10
marriage of true m. LOVE, 123
M. are not ever craving BOOKS, 15
M. like beds always made up INFLEXIBILITY, 4
m. so impatient of inferiority GRATITUDE, 1
Strongest m. /…the noisy world /Hears least MIND, 11
Superstition is the religion of feeble m. SUPERSTITION, 7
the hobgoblin of little m. CONSTANCY, 1
To be alone is the fate of all great m. LONELINESS, 6; GREATNESS, 11
well-developed bodies, fairly developed m. EDUCATION, 18
When people will not weed their own m. MIND, 8
miner Dwelt a m., Forty-niner, /And his daughter, Clementine MOURNING, 7
miners it is only because m. sweat their guts out SUPERIORITY, 10
the Vatican, the Treasury and the m. DIPLOMACY, 2
mingled Like kindred drops, been m. MOUNTAINS, 1
ministers I don't mind how much my m. talk AUTHORITARIANISM, 7
my actions are my m.' REPARTEE, 1
ministries *The Times* has made many m. NEWSPAPERS, 1
ministry Women…more for a marriage than a m. WOMEN, 12
minorities M.…are almost always in the right MINORITY, 3
minority not enough people to make a m. MINORITY, 1
The m. is always right MAJORITY, 3; MINORITY, 2
minstrel A wandering m. I SINGERS, 2
Ethereal m. BIRDS, 11
The M. Boy WAR, 72
minute M. Particulars GOOD, 2
not a m. on the day STRIKES, 1
sucker born every m. GULLIBILITY, 1
To a philosopher no circumstance…is too m. PHILOSOPHERS, 3
minutes at the rate of sixty m. an hour TIME, 24
take care of the m. TIME, 15
Yes, about ten m. SERMONS, 3
miracle a m. of rare device PLEASURE, 9
man prays…for a m. PRAYER, 18
quiet m. of a normal life MIDDLE EAST, 6
miracles before we *know* he is a saint, there will have to be m. PROOF, 4
The Christian religion not only was at first attended with m. CHRISTIANITY, 29
mirror A novel is a m. NOVELS, 15
Art is not a m.…but a hammer ART, 17
Look not in my eyes, for fear /They m. true the sight I see LOVE, 71
When a man confronts catastrophe…a woman looks in her m. SEXES, 27
mirrors M. and fatherhood are abominable UNIVERSE, 2
M. should think longer THINKING, 2
mirth I commended m.…to eat…to drink, and to be merry PLEASURE, 4
I love such m. as does not make friends ashamed MERRYMAKING, 6
miscarriage success and m. are empty sounds DISILLUSION, 4
miscast George Bernard Shaw is sadly m. CRITICISM, 48
mischief If you want to make m.…papers JOURNALISM, 6
Satan finds…m.…/For idle hands IDLENESS, 10
thou little knowest the m. done ACCIDENTS, 5
To mourn a m. that is past REGRET, 17
mischievous what a m. devil Love is LOVE, 35
miserable m. have no other medicine HOPE, 10
poring over m. books LEARNING, 9
The secret of being m. is to have leisure SORROW, 23
miserie y-fallen out of heigh degree. Into m. MISFORTUNE, 6
miseries all the maladies and m. WORK, 6
misery certain amount of m.…to distribute as fairly as he can TAXATION, 9
greatest m. is a battle gained VICTORY, 19
he /Who finds himself, loses his m. SELF-KNOWLEDGE, 1
Let other pens dwell on guilt and m. OPTIMISM, 14
M. acquaints a man with strange bedfellows MISFORTUNE, 16
Thou art so full of m. SUICIDE, 13
misfortune In the m. of our best friends MISFORTUNE, 15; HUMAN NATURE, 20
next greatest m. to losing a battle VICTORY, 18
the most unhappy kind of m. HAPPINESS, 6
misfortunes any man…who could not bear another's m. MISFORTUNE, 13
history…a tableau of crimes and m. HISTORY, 35
history…the register of the…m. of mankind HISTORY, 16
if a man talks of his m. MISFORTUNE, 11

strong enough to bear the m. of others MISFORTUNE, 14
The m. of poverty POVERTY, 21
the real m. and pains of others SUFFERING, 6
misguided We have guided missiles and m. men WAR, 56
mislead One to m. the public, another to m. the Cabinet GOVERNMENT, 5
misleading Though analogy is often m. ANALOGY, 1
misquotation M. is the pride and privilege of the learned MISQUOTATIONS, 2
misquotations M. are…never misquoted MISQUOTATIONS, 1
miss A m. is as good FAILURE, 1
to m. the one before it TRAINS, 2
missed who never would be m. PUNISHMENT, 9
missiles We have guided m. and misguided men WAR, 56
missionary I would eat a m. CLERGY, 17
mist Mad as the M. and Snow MADNESS, 18
The rolling m. came down DROWNING, 1
mistake he who never made a m. never made a discovery MISTAKES, 16
Live all you can; it's a m. not to LIFE, 31
Woman was God's *second* m. WOMEN, 55
mistaken think it possible you may be m. MISTAKES, 6
mistakes An expert…knows some of the worst m. that can be made EXPERTS, 3
Nearly all marriages…are m. MARRIAGE, 126
The man who makes no m. MISTAKES, 11
Young men make great m. in life YOUTH, 11
mistress a m., and only then a friend FRIENDSHIP, 15
A m. should be like a…retreat SEX, 67
Art is a jealous m. ART, 7
by pointing out to a man the faults of his m. IMPERFECTION, 10
Master M. of my passion LOVE, 122
m. I am ashamed to call you TITLES, 2
first Prince of Wales…not to have a m. ADULTERY, 6
whether I embrace your lordship's principles or your m. REPARTEE, 5
why and how I became…m. of the Earl of Craven SEX, 66
mistresses a better price than old m. PAINTING, 1
No, I shall have m. MARRIAGE, 64
one wife and hardly any m. MARRIAGE, 101
Wives are young men's m. MARRIAGE, 13
mistrust M. first impulses FIRST IMPRESSIONS, 7
mists Season of m. and mellow fruitfulness SEASONS, 12
misunderstood To be great is to be m. GREATNESS, 7
Mitty Walter M., the undefeated EXECUTION, 28
mix I m. them with my brains PAINTING, 7
mixed a m. infant CHILDREN, 8
not to look like a m. grill APPEARANCE, 9
mob do what the m. do MAJORITY, 1
Our supreme governors, the m. PUBLIC, 20
mobs It brings men together in crowds and m. in bar-rooms SOCIETY, 10
mock Let not Ambition m. POVERTY, 13
Mock on, m. on, Voltaire, Rousseau FUTILITY, 5
mockery death itself must be…a m. DEATH, 115
mockingbird to kill a m. BOOK, SONG, AND PLAY TITLES, 13
mode Fancy is…a m. of memory IMAGINATION, 2
model m. Labour voter…is patronizing POLITICS, 42
very m. of a modern Major-General KNOWLEDGE, 16
models Rules and m. destroy genius and art RULES, 2
moderation astonished at my own m. MODERATION, 3
M. in all things MODERATION, 1
m. in the pursuit of justice is no virtue EXCESS, 4
modern Imagination without skill gives us m. art ART, 27
It is so stupid of m. civilization DEVIL, 8
The m. pantheist not only PHOTOGRAPHY, 6
modest and is m. about it ENGLISH, 4
modester People ought to be m. UNIVERSE, 3
modesty a woman…ought to lay aside…m. with her skirt SEX, 40
Enough for m. CLOTHES, 2
I don't think that m. POLITICS, 35
I have often wished I had time to cultivate m. MODESTY, 7
There is false m., but there is no false pride PRIDE, 9
where the Greeks had m., we have cant HYPOCRISY, 13
Mohamed M. wanted equality for women EQUALITY, 3
Mohammed If the mountain will not come to M. ADAPTABILITY, 2
moi *L'État c'est m.* MONARCHY, 15
mole Death is still working like a m. DEATH, 60
Molly M. Stark sleeps a widow WAR, 113
moment a m. of time LAST WORDS, 22
A m. of time may make us unhappy for ever SORROW, 8
Every m. one is born LIFE AND DEATH, 14
Mona A lotta cats copy the M. Lisa IMITATION, 1
I have…several original M. Lisas PHOTOGRAPHY, 7
monarch m. of all I survey SOLITUDE, 5
monarchy M. is a strong government MONARCHY, 1
The m. is a labour-intensive industry MONARCHY, 25
The m.…oldest profession in the world ROYALTY, 11
The Sovereign has, under a constitutional m.…three rights MONARCHY, 2
They that are discontented under *m.*, call it *tyranny* GOVERNMENT, 12
tourists…take in the M.…with…the pigeons LONDON, 8
Monday is going to do on M. HYPOCRISY, 19
M.'s child CHARACTER, 1; NURSERY RHYMES, 34
Solomon Grundy, /Born on a M. NURSERY RHYMES, 49
monetarist 'Starve a cold'; she was a m. ECONOMICS, 15
money a bank that would lend m. to such a poor risk BORROWING, 2
a blessing that m. cannot buy HEALTH AND HEALTHY LIVING, 13
a licence to print your own m. BUSINESS, 24
always try to rub up against m. MONEY, 40
art…of draining m. TAXATION, 11
Brigands demand your m. or your life WOMEN, 19
Business…may bring m.…friendship hardly ever does MONEY, 6
collect legal taxes from illegal m. TAXATION, 2
descriptions of m. changing hands MONEY, 19
easiest way for your children to learn about m. MONEY, 50
except for large sums of m. RIDICULE, 2
France is a country where the m. falls apart FRANCE, 16
Good Samaritan…had m. as well MONEY, 49
He that wants m., means, and content MONEY, 41
If possible honestly, if not, somehow, make m. MONEY, 25
If women didn't exist…m.…no meaning WOMEN, 57
If you can…count your m. you are not…rich man WEALTH, 15
innocently employed than in getting m. MONEY, 28
Just what God would have done if he had the m. WEALTH, 30
killed a lot of men to have made so much m. WEALTH, 20
Lack of m. MONEY, 44
love of m. is the root of all evil MONEY, 11
m. answereth all things MONEY, 10
M. can't buy friends MONEY, 36
m. can't buy me love MONEY, 31
M. gives me pleasure MONEY, 9
m. has something to do with life MONEY, 30
M. is good for bribing yourself MONEY, 39
M. is like a sixth sense MONEY, 35
M. is like manure MONEY, 27
M. is like muck MONEY, 7
M., it turned out, was exactly like sex MONEY, 8; SEX, 7
pleasant it is to have m. MONEY, 18
Put m. in thy purse MONEY, 43
Some people's m. is merited MONEY, 37
spiritual snobbery…happy without m. MONEY, 16
the love of m. is the root of all evil MONEY, 14
The man who leaves m. to charity in his will BEQUESTS, 3
the poor person…thinks m. would help MONEY, 29
The profession…in which one can make no m. WRITING, 28
The working classes are never embarrassed by m. MONEY, 32
They had been corrupted by m. SENTIMENTALITY, 1
they have more m. WEALTH, 12
time is m. BUSINESS, 10
To be clever enough to get…m., one must be stupid MATERIALISM, 6
to waste my time making m. MONEY, 4
We all know how the size of sums of m. appears to vary MONEY, 26
We haven't the m., so we've got to think RESEARCH, 5
we've got the men, we've got the m. too PATRIOTISM, 16
what risks you take…to find m. in a desk THEFT, 4
Where large sums of m. are concerned MONEY, 17
with m.…they have not got BORROWING, 4
You can be young without m. MONEY, 51
monkey no reason to attack the m. POLITICIANS, 38
the biggest asset the m. possesses POLITICIANS, 69
monopoly imperialism is the m. stage of capitalism POLITICS, 45
No party has a m. over what is right TOLERANCE, 2

Monroe Marilyn M.'s FUNERALS, 7
mons treating the *m. Veneris* as...Mount Everest SEX, 26
monster jealousy...green-ey'd m. JEALOUSY, 5
monstrous US is a truly m. force AMERICA, 28
Montagu Mrs M. has dropt me HURT, 2
Monte Carlo M. LUCK, 7
the man who broke the Bank at M. WEALTH, 16
month April is the cruellest m. MONTHS, 8
months two m. of every year WEATHER, 8
monument like Patience on a m. LOVE, 126
sonnet is a moment's m. POETRY, 38
The m. sticks like a fishbone MEMORIALS, 7
monuments Not marble, nor the gilded m. POETRY, 42
moo You silly m. INSULTS, 36
moon For years politicians have promised the m. MOON, 5
I saw the new m. late yestreen MOON, 1; PROPHECY, 1
I see the m., /And the m. sees me BLESSING, 2
moving M. went up the sky MOON, 2
nothing left remarkable beneath the...m. MOURNING, 11
shine on, shine on, harvest m. MOON, 6
The M. and Sixpence BOOK, SONG, AND PLAY TITLES, 17
The m. doth shine as bright as day NURSERY RHYMES, 6
the m.'s /a balloon MOON, 3
They danced by the light of the m. FOOD, 34
th' inconstant m. UNFAITHFULNESS, 5
We're very wide awake, /The m. and I APPEARANCES, 15
moonlight Look for me by m. DETERMINATION, 13
moons So sicken waning m. too near the sun MOON, 4
moral All universal m. principles are idle fancies MORALITY, 14
doesn't seem to be any m. place for flesh MORALITY, 5
each man must struggle, lest the m. law become... separated MORALITY, 1
Everything's got a m. PURPOSE, 1
it should preach a high m. lesson PURPOSE, 8
Let us be m. EXISTENCE, 2
Love is m. even without...marriage LOVE AND MARRIAGE, 3
m. attribute of a Scotsman SCOTS, 1
M. indignation is in most cases 2 percent moral MORALITY, 20
m. is what you feel good after MORALITY, 6
m. or an immoral book BOOKS, 46
more than a m. duty to speak one's mind FRANKNESS, 4
one is unhappy one becomes m. SORROW, 17
The highest possible stage in m. culture SELF-CONTROL, 3
the m. law WONDER, 3
The worst government is the most m. GOVERNMENT, 19
moralist A Scotchman must be a very sturdy m. SCOTS, 3
no sterner m. than Pleasure PLEASURE, 7
morality Dr Johnson's m. was as English...as a beefsteak ENGLAND, 20
live for others...middle class m. CLASS, 31
M. consists in suspecting MORALITY, 16
M....is herd-morality MORALITY, 12
M.'s a gesture....learnt from books MORALITY, 3
M.'s not practical MORALITY, 3
M. which is based on ideas MORALITY, 9
new m....the old immorality condoned MORALITY, 18
No m. can be founded on authority MORALITY, 2
periodical fits of m. MORALITY, 10
This imperative may be called that of M. MORALITY, 8
two kinds of m. MORALITY, 13
morals basing m. on myth MORALITY, 15
If your m. make you dreary MORALITY, 21
men represent...mind over m. SEXES, 31
M. are an acquirement MORALITY, 23
the faith and m. hold /Which Milton held FREEDOM, 54
the m. of a whore, and the manners of a dancing master CRITICISM, 22
mordre M. wol out MURDER, 4
more As I know m. of mankind EXPECTATION, 2
Oliver Twist has asked for m. COURAGE, 9
Specialist – A man who knows m. and m. about less and less EXPERTS, 5
take *m.* than nothing LANGUAGE, 4
the m. you get the m. you spend MONEY, 5
mores *O tempora! O m.!* CUSTOM, 1
morn From m. to night, my friend ENDURANCE, 15
From m. /To noon he fell DECLINE, 4
He rose the morrow m. WISDOM, 13
the opening eye-lids of the m. DAY, 10
mornin' nice to get up in the m. BED, 5
morning Early one m., just as the sun was rising UNFAITHFULNESS, 1
I awoke one m. FAME, 6
I'm getting married in the m. MARRIAGE, 79
M. in the Bowl of Night DAY, 5
Oh, what a beautiful m. DAY, 7
she has lived...the space of one m. TRANSIENCE, 17
that...turneth the shadow of death into the m. GOD, 6
'Tis always m. somewhere BEGINNING, 10
Morocco We're M. bound LEXICOGRAPHY, 2
morrow take...no thought for the m. WORRY, 7
mortal All men are m. MORTALITY, 1
I was not unaware that I had begotten a m. MORTALITY, 8
men think all men m. ARROGANCE, 11
that M. God STATE, 1
The doctor found.../Her last disorder m. DOCTORS, 3
we have been m. enemies ever since ENEMIES, 5
mortality kept watch o'er man's m. MORTALITY, 21
M., behold and fear MORTALITY, 2
mortals A novelist is, like all m. WRITERS, 16
We m. cross the ocean HUMAN CONDITION, 4
what fools these m. be FOOLISHNESS, 18
Moscow don't march on M. WAR, 71
Moses he saw his role as being that of M. LEADERSHIP, 5
there arose not a prophet...like unto M. PROPHECY, 2
most The M. may err as grosly PUBLIC, 11
mostest I got there fustest with the m. MISQUOTATIONS, 16; WAR, 38
mote the m. that is in thy brother's eye CRITICISM, 6; JUDGMENT, 3
moth like a m., the simple maid WOMEN, 34
The desire of the m. for the star HUMOUR, 40
mother A m.! What are we worth really MOTHERHOOD, 17
And Her M. Came Too MOTHERHOOD, 12
as is the m., so is her daughter FAMILY, 7
Dead! and...never called me m. DEATH, 132
I am old enough to be – in fact am – your m. AGE, 40
If poverty is the m. of crime, stupidity is its father CRIME, 5
I was born...at an extremely tender age because my m. needed a fourth at meals BIRTH, 8
I wished to be near my m. BIRTH, 10
May you be the m. of a bishop BLESSING, 3; LAST WORDS, 8
most automated appliance in a household is the m. MOTHERHOOD, 11
M. is far too clever to understand PREJUDICE, 2
M. is the dead heart of the family MOTHERHOOD, 10; WOMAN'S ROLE, 2
m. of battles MIDDLE EAST, 9
M. of the Free BRITAIN, 4
My m., drunk or sober PATRIOTISM, 5
My m. said it was simple to keep a man WOMEN, 38
No matter how old a m. is MOTHERHOOD, 15
the most intense love on the m.'s side MOTHERHOOD, 9
The m.-child relationship is paradoxical MOTHERHOOD, 9
the m. of parliaments ENGLAND, 6
the perfect couple...a m. and child MOTHERHOOD, 8
this war...which did not justify the sacrifice of a single m.'s son WAR, 83
watched a m. stroke her child's cheek MOTHERHOOD, 13
motherhood m. is the most important of all the professions MOTHERHOOD, 16
M. meant I have written four fewer books MOTHERHOOD, 5
The best thing that could happen to m. MOTHERHOOD, 1
wifehood and m. are but incidental relations WOMEN, 73
Womanliness means only m. MOTHERHOOD, 4
mother-in-law as the man said when his m. died FAMILY, 17
What a marvellous place to drop one's m. FAMILY, 12
mothers Come m. and fathers /Throughout the land CHANGE, 6
O! men with m. and wives WOMEN, 40
women become like their m. SEXES, 30
Women...the m. of all mischief MOTHERHOOD, 2
mothers-in-law Two m. FAMILY, 30
motives m. meaner than your own MOTIVE, 1
motorists M....were utterly irresponsible in their dealings with each other CARS, 3
motors was good for General M. BUSINESS, 28
mould If you cannot m. yourself TOLERANCE, 4
Nature made him, and then broke the m. INDIVIDUALITY, 2
There is...an instrument to m. the minds of the young CENSORSHIP, 2
mountain A m. in labour shouted so loud DISAPPOINTMENT, 4

hardly be a beast or a fool alone on a great m. SOLITUDE, 9
I don't...care if I never see another m. MOUNTAINS, 2; POETS, 47
If the m. will not come to Mohammed ADAPTABILITY, 2
Land of the m. and the flood SCOTLAND, 7
mountains all faith, so that I could remove m. CHARITY, 6
England's m. green ENGLAND, 5
highest intellects, like the tops of m. INTELLECT, 5
if the Swiss had designed these m. MOUNTAINS, 4; SWITZERLAND, 4
M. interposed /Make enemies of nations MOUNTAINS, 1
m. look on Marathon EUROPE, 4
M....the beginning and the end of all natural scenery MOUNTAINS, 3
M. will heave in childbirth DISAPPOINTMENT, 3
Two voices...one is of the sea, /One of the m. FREEDOM, 55
when men and m. meet GREATNESS, 4
mourn countless thousands m. CRUELTY, 2
it is chiefly our own deaths that we m. for FUNERALS, 3
To m. a mischief that is past REGRET, 17
mourning I'm in m. for my life MOURNING, 4
in m....for the world MOURNING, 15
tedium is the very basis of m. BOREDOM, 4
We met...Dr Hall in such very deep m. MOURNING, 1
What we call m. for our dead MOURNING, 6
with my m....and new periwig APPEARANCE, 30
mouse a silly little m. will be born DISAPPOINTMENT, 3
He bought a crooked cat, which caught a crooked m. NURSERY RHYMES, 52
leave room for the m. EXCESS, 6
she brought forth a m. DISAPPOINTMENT, 4
The m. ran up the clock NURSERY RHYMES, 15
mouse-trap If a man make a better m. FAME, 8
moustache A kiss without a m. KISSING, 4
a man outside with a big black m. APPEARANCE, 25
Being kissed by a man who didn't wax his m. KISSING, 3
his nicotine eggyellow weeping walrus Victorian m. APPEARANCE, 37
mouth A politician is a statesman...with an open m. POLITICIANS, 26
butter wouldn't melt in her m. ACTORS, 17
God be in my m., /And in my speaking GOD, 1
Keep your m. shut and your eyes open CAUTION, 6
mouth-brothels Great restaurants are...nothing but m. FOOD, 48
move But did thee feel the earth m. SEX, 24
in him we live, and m., and have our being GOD, 5
I will m. the earth TECHNOLOGY, 1
The great affair is to m. TRAVEL, 22
movement I want to be a m. SOLITUDE, 11
We are the true peace m. PEACE, 16
moves m., and mates, and slays DESTINY, 7
Yet it m. ASTRONOMY, 3
movie This is a m., not a lifeboat EQUALITY, 23
movies Thanks to the m., gunfire has always sounded unreal CINEMA, 12
violence in the m. can be cool VIOLENCE, 10
moving In home-sickness you must keep m. HOMESICKNESS, 7
m. Moon went up the sky MOON, 2
people under suspicion are better m. JUDGMENT, 10
The M. Finger writes DESTINY, 8
Mozart The sonatas of M. are unique MUSIC, 43
when M. was my age AGE, 35
MP rent an M. just like...a London taxi POLITICIANS, 12
MPs The prospect of a lot /Of dull M. POLITICIANS, 11
much m....said on both sides OBJECTIVITY, 1
So little done, so m. to do LAST WORDS, 58
so m. owed by so many to so few WORLD WAR II, 7
muchness Much of a m. MEDIOCRITY, 9
muck Money is like m. MONEY, 7
sing 'em m. PLACES, 11
mud One sees the m., and one the stars OPTIMISM, 21
muddle a beginning, a m., and an end NOVELS, 8
muddle-headed He's a m. fool FOOLISHNESS, 12
muddy The hunter for aphorisms...has to fish in m. water SAYINGS, 2
muesli Many children are suffering from m.-belt malnutrition FOOD, 38
Muffet Little Miss M. /Sat on a tuffet NURSERY RHYMES, 30
multicultural classical Canon and the m. cause POLITICAL CORRECTNESS, 3
multiplied Entities should not be m. SIMPLICITY, 6
multiply be fruitful and m. MANKIND, 5; CREATION, 6
multitude long dresses...cover a m. of shins CLOTHES, 18
The m. is always in the wrong PUBLIC, 17
this massed m. of silent witnesses to...war WAR, 41
multitudes I contain m. SELF, 21
mum M.'s the word SECRECY, 6
They fuck you up, your m. and dad FAMILY, 19
mumble maunder and m. PUBLIC, 8
mundi *Sic transit gloria m.* GLORY, 3
murder Divorce? Never. But m. often MARRIAGE, 124
love and m. will out LOVE, 41; MURDER, 5
m. back into its rightful setting – in the home MURDER, 7
M. considered as one of the Fine Arts MURDER, 6
M....had a mask like Castlereagh MURDER, 12
M., like talent, seems...to run in families MURDER, 9
M. most foul MURDER, 11
m. shrieks out MURDER, 13
Never m. a man who is committing suicide SUICIDE, 14
Olivier had m. in his heart ACTORS, 14
put m. on a mass-production basis DESIGN, 6
So it was m. DEATH, 84
Sooner m. an infant in its cradle DESIRE, 3
murdered I m. my grandmother this morning INATTENTION, 4
murderer Kill a man, and you are a m. KILLING, 7
strong suspicions that Crippen London cellar m. TECHNOLOGY, 7
murderous at Yuletide men / are the more m. CHRISTMAS, 13
murmuring m. of innumerable bees SEASONS, 23
muscular His Christianity was m. CHRISTIANITY, 23
Muse To the Greeks the M. gave native wit CLASSICS, 4
mused Lancelot m. a little space BEAUTY, 39
museum the m. of this world MASCULINITY, 2
museums more philosophical than...curators of the m. PRACTICALITY, 3
The Arab...is more philosophical than...curators of the m. MUSEUMS, 1
mushroom a supramundane m. NUCLEAR WEAPONS, 11
Fame is sometimes like unto a...m. FAME, 10
to stuff a m. HOUSEWORK, 2
music a martyr to m. MUSIC, 52
Architecture...is frozen m. ARCHITECTURE, 11
art constantly aspires towards...m. ART, 21
a young man who would...play his m. and be whistled at for it MUSIC, 19
Canned m. is like audible wallpaper POP MUSIC, 7
capable of being well set to m. MUSIC, 2
century of aeroplanes deserves its own m. MUSIC, 18
chord of m. MUSIC, 39
food in m. MUSIC, 29
God tells me how he wants this m. played MUSIC, 54
Having verse set to m. POETRY, 50
how potent cheap m. is MUSIC, 16
How sour sweet m. is ORDER, 5
I don't write modern m. MUSIC, 49
If all the arts aspire to the condition of m. SCIENCE, 38
If m. be the food of love MUSIC, 46
I'll set it to m. MUSIC, 41
In m., the punctuation is absolutely strict ACTING, 10
line that fits the m. POP MUSIC, 16
making m. throatily and palpitatingly sexual MUSIC, 25
man that hath no m. in himself MUSIC, 45
m....affects your nerves MUSIC, 28
M. and women I cannot but give way to MUSIC, 37
M. begins to atrophy ARTS, 7
M....confirm human loneliness MUSIC, 20
M. creates order out of chaos MUSIC, 32
m. critics....small and rodent-like with padlocked ears CRITICS, 18
M. has charms to soothe MUSIC, 15
M. helps not MUSIC, 1
M. is not written in red, white and blue MUSIC, 31
M. is the arithmetic of sounds MUSIC, 17
M. is your own experience MUSIC, 36
M., Maestro, Please MUSIC, 30
M. owes as much to Bach MUSICIANS, 15
M. that gentlier on the spirit lies MUSIC, 51
M., when soft voices die MEMORY, 17
never merry when I hear sweet m. MUSIC, 44
Poetry...set to more or less lascivious m. POETRY, 29
popular m....made giant strides in reverse POP MUSIC, 10
potent cheap m. is POP MUSIC, 9
public doesn't want a new m. MUSICIANS, 3

silence sank like m. SILENCE, 3
sometimes I don't even like m. MUSIC, 55
The English may not like m. MUSIC, 5
The hills are alive with the sound of m. MUSIC, 22
The m. teacher came twice each week MUSIC, 3
thy chosen m., Liberty FREEDOM, 55
Van Gogh's ear for m. INSULTS, 44
Wagner is the Puccini of m. MUSICIANS, 12
musical cashiers of the M. Banks MONEY, 13
Most m., most melancholy BIRDS, 9
music-hall M. songs provide the dull with wit STUPIDITY, 9
musician Brahms…an extraordinary m. MUSICIANS, 16
musicians M. don't retire MUSICIANS, 1
musicologist A m.…can read music but can't hear it MUSIC, 8
Mussolini Hitler was a nuisance. M. was bloody POLITICS, 50
must Genius does what it m. TALENT AND GENIUS, 3
Is *m.* a word to be addressed to princes IMPERTINENCE, 2
muttering the m. grew to a grumbling ANIMALS, 6
mutton Alice – M.; M. – Alice INTRODUCTIONS, 1
I could no longer stand their eternal cold m. ENGLAND, 34
myriad-minded m. Shakespeare SHAKESPEARE, 3
myself deliver me from m. SELF, 5
I am always with m. SELF, 15
I have always disliked m. SELF, 6
I know m. SELF-KNOWLEDGE, 3
I like to go by m. SOLITUDE, 8; TRAVEL, 11
I've over-educated m. DEBAUCHERY, 5
not only witty in m. HUMOUR, 27
The Jews have produced…Christ, Spinoza, and m. CONCEIT, 16
mysteries disciples…mark its ways and note…its m. LUCK, 7
mysterious God moves in a m. way GOD, 18
the ancient cathedrals – grand, wonderful, m. RELIGION, 53
mystery a riddle wrapped in a m. inside an enigma RUSSIA, 3
Growth is a greater m. than death AGE, 37
Happiness is a m. like religion HAPPINESS, 7
In m. our soul abides SOUL, 2
mystic The m. sees the ineffable PSYCHIATRY, 7
myth A m. is, of course, not a fairy story MYTHS, 2
basing morals on m. MORALITY, 15
some magnificent m. PROPAGANDA, 3
myths Science must begin with m. MYTHS, 1; SCIENCE, 34

N

nails I used to bite my n. FAME, 16
naive the n. forgive FORGIVENESS, 16
naked a n. Duke of Windlestraw addressing a n. House of Lords NAKEDNESS, 2
a pretty girl who n. is NAKEDNESS, 3
I can't stand a n. light bulb VULGARITY, 6
n. into the conference chamber NUCLEAR WEAPONS, 2; WEAPONS, 1
No woman so n. as…underneath her clothes NAKEDNESS, 4
Our ingress…/Was n. and bare LIFE, 34
Poor n. wretches WEATHER, 21
The exception is a n. ape MANKIND, 19
they were both n. WOMEN, 15
nakedness N. is uncomely NAKEDNESS, 1
name a good n. is better than precious ointment VIRTUE, 3
And lo! Ben Adhem's n. led all the rest SUPERIORITY, 5
Good n. in man and woman REPUTATION, 8
his n. shall be called, Wonderful, Counsellor CHRISTMAS, 6
How I loathe that other with my n. DENIAL, 2
I don't like your Christian n. MARRIAGE, 20
I remember your n. perfectly SPOONERISMS, 2
local habitation and a n. POETRY, 41
No, Groucho is not my real n. NAMES, 5
Oh liberty!…What crimes are committed in thy n. EXECUTION, 27; FREEDOM, 45
People you know, yet can't quite n. OLD AGE, 25
rose by any other n. NAMES, 7
signing his n. and forgetting to write the letter INSULTS, 5
the n. of which was Beautiful ARCHITECTURE, 2
thou shalt not take the n. of…God in vain GOD, 10
two or three…gathered together in my n. CHURCH, 2
What's in a n. NAMES, 7
When I pass my n. in such large letters FAME, 22
you fall asleep halfway through her n. INSULTS, 8
name-dropper One must not be a n. SNOBBERY, 6
names No n., no pack-drill GOSSIP, 3
naming Today we have n. of parts WEAPONS, 6
Napoleon ashes of N. INDIFFERENCE, 6
N. OFFICERS, 16
the N. of crime CRIME, 3
narcissist megalomaniac differs from the n. POWER, 20
narcotics Two great European n. DRUGS, 11
nastier she could have found anything n. to say NASTINESS, 7
nasty how n. the nice people can be NASTINESS, 6
Something n. in the woodshed EVIL, 9
nation America became top n. HISTORY, 31
An army is a n. within a n. ARMY, 4
A n. is not in danger ECONOMICS, 17
a n. of amateurs BRITISH, 9
dedicate this n. to the policy of the good neighbor CHARITY, 16
England is a n. of shopkeepers ENGLISH, 28
he is the sworn foe of our n. PUBLISHING, 5
I will make of thee a great n. JEWS, 3
n.…fall victim to a big lie LYING, 8
n. had the lion's heart CHURCHILL, 5
n. shall not lift up sword against n. WAR AND PEACE, 2
n. shall rise against n. WAR, 9
N. shall speak peace PEACE, 14
No n. is fit to sit in judgement DIPLOMACY, 20
No n. was ever ruined by trade BUSINESS, 9
Television – the drug of the n. TELEVISION AND RADIO, 7
the English are…the least a n. of pure philosophers ENGLISH, 5
the kind of n.…President Kennedy died for AMBITION, 10
the kind of n. that President Roosevelt hoped for AMBITION, 10
nationalism N. is…the measles of mankind PATRIOTISM, 9
nationality My n. is French NORMALITY, 2
Other people have a n. IRISH, 2; JEWS, 1
nations Commonwealth of N. BRITISH EMPIRE, 7
extends over many n. and three continents EXPERIENCE, 12
If people behaved in the way n. do GOVERNMENT, 34
languages are the pedigree of n. LANGUAGE, 15
The day of small n. has long passed away NATIONS, 1
The great n. have always acted like gangsters DIPLOMACY, 13
The n. which have put mankind and posterity most in their debt NATIONS, 2
'Two n. POVERTY AND WEALTH, 4
native My n. Land – Good Night DEPARTURE, 5
my own, my n. land HOMESICKNESS, 6
to appear considerable in his n. place FAME, 12
white man…looks into the eyes of a n. RACISM, 18
natives Britons were only n. HISTORY, 29
natural First feelings are always the most n. FIRST IMPRESSIONS, 5
It is n. to die DEATH, 23
n. false teeth TEETH, 3
N. Selection EVOLUTION, 6
Nothing prevents us from being n. SPONTANEITY, 4
'twas N. to please CHARACTER, 7
naturally Though I am not n. honest HONESTY, 10
nature Accuse not N., she hath done her part RESPONSIBILITY, 10
All N. wears one universal grin NATURE, 9
Allow not n. more than n. needs NECESSITY, 5
a noble n.…treats…a serious subject POETRY, 3
but N. more NATURE, 3
Consistency is contrary to n. CONSTANCY, 2
drive out n. with a pitchfork HUMAN NATURE, 12
fortress built by N. ENGLAND, 36
Friend…masterpiece of N. FRIENDS, 7
God and N. then at strife NATURE, 15
Human n. is so well disposed HUMAN NATURE, 1
I got disappointed in human n. HUMAN NATURE, 8
I have learned /To look on n. EXPERIENCE, 22
In n. there are neither rewards nor punishments NATURE, 11
law of n. which love alone can alter SEX, 14
Let N. be your Teacher NATURE, 20
Little we see in N. that is ours WASTE, 3
N. abhors a vacuum NATURE, 14
N. admits no lie NATURE, 4
N. has left this tincture TYRANNY, 1
N. has never put the fatal question as to the meaning of their lives PURPOSE, 4
N. is but a name for an effect NATURE, 6
N. is creeping up ARROGANCE, 8
N. is often hidden HUMAN NATURE, 4
n. is the art of God NATURE, 1

N. is usually wrong NATURE, 16
N. is very consonant and conformable NATURE, 12
N. made him, and then broke the mould INDIVIDUALITY, 2
N.…must be obeyed HUMAN NATURE, 5
N. never did betray NATURE, 18
N. remains NATURE, 17
N.'s handmaid, art NATURE, 8
n.'s law HELP, 7
new sights of N. made me rejoice NATURE, 7
not formed by n. to bear ENDURANCE, 4
o'erstep not the modesty of n. ACTION, 10
one of N.'s Gentlemen CHIVALRY, 7
one of the forces of n. GREATNESS, 10
rules of the game are what we call the laws of N. GOD, 28
science…is…the interplay between n. and ourselves NATURE, 10
secret of the arts is to correct n. ARTS, 8
the most irrelevant thing in n. FAMILY, 18
the spectacles of books to read n. SHAKESPEARE, 6
to see the absurd n. of Englishmen ENGLISH, 30
True wit is n. to advantage dress'd HUMOUR, 23
unassuming common-place /Of N. FLOWERS, 13
We need more understanding of human n. HUMAN NATURE, 14
wonderful case of n. imitating art ACTORS, 22
you can't call yourself a great work of n. INSULTS, 42

natures Men's n. are alike HABIT, 4
N. ancient power was lost DECLINE, 11

naught N. so sweet as Melancholy MELANCHOLY, 2

nauseate I n. walking COUNTRYSIDE, 1

Navee Ruler of the Queen's N. OFFICERS, 6
Rulers of the Queen's N. OFFICERS, 7

navy There were gentlemen and…seamen in the n. of Charles the Second NAVY, 3

Nazi N. Germany had become a menace to all mankind NAZISM, 4

Nazis In Germany, the N. came for the Communists NAZISM, 5

near I wished to be n. my mother BIRTH, 10

nearer N., my God, to thee RELIGION, 2
the n. you are to God PROTESTANTISM, 3

nearest the n. run thing you ever saw WAR, 125

nearsighted don't raise your hands because I am also n. DISABILITY, 1

neat round, n., not gaudy GARDENS, 9

necessary Government…is but a n. evil GOVERNMENT, 22

necessities disregard for the n. of existence CIVILIZATION, 9
we will dispense with its n. LUXURY, 4

necessity I find alone N. Supreme NECESSITY, 8
N. is the mother NECESSITY, 2
N. is the plea for every infringement of human freedom NECESSITY, 4
N. knows no law NECESSITY, 7
no virtue like n. NECESSITY, 6

neck A short n. denotes a good mind APPEARANCE, 35
creator had a purpose in equipping us with a n. COURAGE, 16
England will have her n. wrung like a chicken WORLD WAR II, 30
go to the bottom with my principles round my n. EXPEDIENCY, 2
my n. is very short EXECUTION, 19
Some n. WORLD WAR II, 12
the Roman people had but one n. RUTHLESSNESS, 1

necking Whoever named it n. SEX, 36

neckties men wore their beards, like they wear their n. APPEARANCE, 18

Ned no more work for poor old N. DEATH, 53

need artist is someone who produces things that people don't n. ARTISTS, 8
reason not the n. NECESSITY, 5
Thy n. is yet greater than mine SELF-DENIAL, 2

needle easier for a camel to go through the eye of a n. WEALTH, 8

needs N. must NECESSITY, 3
to each according to his n. MARXISM, 4
You artists produce something that nobody n. ARTISTS, 9

negation Capitalist production begets…its own n. CAPITALISM, 9

negative Europe is the unfinished n. AMERICA, 27
N. Capability DOUBT, 6

neglect A little n. may breed mischief NEGLECT, 1
he devotes to the n. of his duties NEGLECT, 4

negligent Celerity…admired…by the n. IMPETUOSITY, 3

Negro makes a N. unpleasant to white folk RACISM, 23

Negroes revenge by the culture of the N. MUSIC, 35

neiges *les n. d'antan* NOSTALGIA, 22

neighbor I have had no real gratification…more than my n. LAST WORDS, 71; WEALTH, 28

neighbour better mouse-trap than his n. FAME, 8
death…had been his next-door n. DEATH, 102
Death is my n. now DEATH, 48
Do not love your n. as yourself SELF, 13
It's a recession when your n. UNEMPLOYMENT, 3
love thy n. as thyself LOVE, 26
told men to love their n. HUNGER, 3

neighbours fear of what the n. might say SUICIDE, 5
improper thoughts about n. MORALITY, 4
make sport for our n. RIDICULE, 1

neither better if n. of us had been born REGRET, 10

Nell read the death of Little N. without laughing DICKENS, 4; INSENSITIVITY, 4

Nelly let not poor N. starve LAST WORDS, 15

Nelson keep the N. touch OFFICERS, 10; PATRIOTISM, 22
N., born in a fortunate hour OFFICERS, 11

nerve called a n. specialist because it sounds better PSYCHIATRY, 13

nerves It destroys one's n. to be amiable every day MARRIAGE, 49

nervous One of the symptoms of approaching n. breakdown WORK, 21

nest broods a n. of sorrows MARRIAGE, 118

nets Laws are generally found to be n. LAW, 26

nettle stroke a n., /And it stings you for your pains DECISION, 1

nettles apt to be overrun with n. MIND, 8

neurosis N. has an absolute genius for malingering NEUROSIS, 1
N. is the way of avoiding non-being NEUROSIS, 3

neurotic Acting is the expression of a n. impulse ACTING, 3
A n. is the man who builds a castle in the air PSYCHIATRY, 11
Psychiatrists classify a person as n. PSYCHIATRY, 10

neurotics Everything great in the world is done by n. NEUROSIS, 2

neutrality 'positive n.' is a contradiction in terms POLITICS, 55

never Better n. than late PROMPTNESS, 3
I n. would lay down my arms PATRIOTISM, 24
Love? I make it constantly but I n. talk about it SEX, 49
N., n., n., n. MOURNING, 9
our people have n. had it so good WEALTH, 18
Than n. to have loved at all LOVE, 132

nevermore Quoth the Raven, 'N.' EVIL, 13

Nevershit like you was Lady N. AFFECTATION, 2

new He that will not apply n. remedies INNOVATION, 1
He was dull in a n. way POETS, 43
He was the Messiah of the n. age POLITICIANS, 72
n. book is published, read an old one BOOKS, 33
n. deal for the American people AMERICA, 30
N. roads: new ruts PROGRESS, 4
Revolution is…the setting-up of a n. order REVOLUTION, 4
something impossibly n. ORIGINALITY, 6
something n. out of Africa NOVELTY, 8
There are no n. truths NOVELTY, 7
there is no n. thing under the sun NOVELTY, 1
we shall find something n. NOVELTY, 10
We stand today on the edge of a n. frontier BEGINNING, 12
You suddenly understand something…in a n. way LEARNING, 6
Youth is something very n. YOUTH, 3

new-found-land my n. LOVE, 49

newness conditioned to respect n. AMERICANS, 11

news Bad n. travels fast DISASTER, 1
Literature is n. LITERATURE, 15
n. that's fit to print NEWSPAPERS, 9
No n. is good n. OPTIMISM, 6; JOURNALISM, 9
Nothing is n. until it has appeared in *The Times*. NEWSPAPERS, 7
only n. until he's read it. After that it's dead NEWSPAPERS, 15
when a man bites a dog that is n. JOURNALISM, 11

newspaper good n.…is a nation talking to itself JOURNALISM, 23
I read the n. avidly JOURNALISM, 10
Once a n. touches a story, the facts are lost JOURNALISM, 22
Reading someone else's n. NEWSPAPERS, 4
With the n. strike on OBITUARIES, 1

newspapers I'm with you on the free press. It's the n. JOURNALISM, 29
life...happens almost exclusively in n. JOURNALISM, 1
N. always excite curiosity JOURNALISM, 19
We live under a government of men and...n. GOVERNMENT, 24; JOURNALISM, 26
Newton Let *N. be!* SCIENTISTS, 14
Newtons souls of five hundred Sir Isaac N. SCIENTISTS, 9; WRITERS, 5
New York N. is a small place AMERICA, 41
N....that unnatural city AMERICA, 15
Niagara one wouldn't *live* under N. INSULTS, 11
nice Be n. to people on your way up PRUDENCE, 10
how nasty the n. people can be NASTINESS, 6
N. guys finish last GOOD, 4
Sugar and spice /And all that's n. NURSERY RHYMES, 65
Nicely-Nicely what N. dies of will be over-feeding GREED, 8
nicest English people...are surely the *n.* ENGLISH, 21
Nicholas St N. soon would be there CHRISTMAS, 14
Nick Satan, N., or Clootie DEVIL, 6
nickname n. is the heaviest stone that the devil can throw NAMES, 4
nicotine his n. eggyellow weeping walrus Victorian moustache APPEARANCE, 37
nigger Catch a n. by his toe NURSERY RHYMES, 11
niggers He's gone whar de good n. go DEATH, 53
night An infant crying in the n. HUMAN CONDITION, 20
calm passage...across many a bad n. SUICIDE, 6
Come to me in the silence of the n. NOSTALGIA, 18
Do not go gentle into that good n. DEATH, 126
From morn to n., my friend ENDURANCE, 15
Gwine to run all n. HORSES, 6
ignorant armies clash by n. WAR, 2
It ain't a fit n. out WEATHER, 10
money in a desk by n. THEFT, 4
moonless n. in the small town RELIGION, 57
Morning in the Bowl of N. DAY, 5
N. and day LOVE, 101
Oft in the stilly n., /Ere Slumber's chain NOSTALGIA, 14
only one man...can count on steady work – the n. watchman THEATRE, 2
perils...of this n. DANGER, 3
real dark n. of the soul SOUL, 6
returned home the previous n. SCIENCE, 3
Ships that pass in the n. TRANSIENCE, 16
So late into the n. DEBAUCHERY, 4
sound of revelry by n. MERRYMAKING, 2
the black bat, n., has flown INVITATIONS, 2
the darkness he called N. CREATION, 2
The dark n. of the soul SOUL, 8
the honey'd middle of the n. LOVE, 78
The n. is dark, and I am far from home FAITH, 16
wish the n. /Had borne my breath away NOSTALGIA, 9
nightingale A N. Sang in Berkeley Square BIRDS, 7
N..../A creature of a 'fiery heart' BIRDS, 12
The n. does sit so late BIRDS, 6
nightingales From Wales /Whose n. WALES, 4
nightmare 'History', Stephen said, 'is a n.' HISTORY, 19
nights a Chequer-board of N. and Days DESTINY, 7
The weariest n....must...end ENDURANCE, 11
They shorten tedious n. SEX, 10
nihilist a part-time n. COMMITMENT, 3
Nile dam...the N. with bulrushes FREEDOM, 7
nine N. drummers drumming NURSERY RHYMES, 55
ninepence I have but n. in ready money CONVERSATION, 2
ninety stood n. years on the floor CLOCKS, 2
Nineveh Quinquireme of N. BOATS, 12
nip I'll n. him in the bud MIXED METAPHORS, 4
Nixon N....would cut down a redwood tree POLITICIANS, 73
standing between N. and the White House POLITICIANS, 57
You won't have N. to kick around RENUNCIATION, 3
no become accustomed to n. one governing SOCIALISM, 10
girls...say N. when they mean Yes WOMEN, 8
It's n. go the picture palace INDIFFERENCE, 4
rebel...man who says n. REBELLION, 2
she speaks eighteen languages. And she can't say 'N.' in any of them PROMISCUITY, 5
why Absurdist plays take place in N. Man's Land THEATRE, 1
Noah Out of their cataclysm but one poor N. SEX, 27
nobility N. has its own obligations NOBILITY, 2
The n....snored through the Sermon ARISTOCRACY, 3
noble a n. nature...treats...a serious subject POETRY, 3
Englishman never enjoys himself except for a n. purpose ENGLISH, 19
n. grounds for the n. emotions POETRY, 39
Ridicule...smothers that which is n. RIDICULE, 4
The n. living and the n. dead NOBILITY, 6
nobleman a king may make a n. CHIVALRY, 3
nobleness perfect plainness of speech...perfect n. BIBLE, 1
noblesse If the French n. had been capable of playing cricket with their peasants ARISTOCRACY, 13; CRICKET, 8
noblest n. man /That ever lived in the tide of times REGRET, 16
n. Roman of them all NOBILITY, 4
nobly the immature man...wants to die n. for a cause AGE, 59
nobody a man is n. unless his biography OBITUARIES, 3
I care for n. SELFISHNESS, 2
N. asked you, sir, she said NURSERY RHYMES, 67
whom n. loves OBESITY, 6
nod A n. is as good as a wink BLINDNESS, 1
the land of N. REVENGE, 7
nods even excellent Homer n. IMPERFECTION, 9
noise A loud n. at one end BABIES, 5
dreadful n. of waters in my ears DROWNING, 2
the less they have...the more n. they make CHARACTER, 18
they...love the n. it makes MUSIC, 5
Those people...are making such a n. AUDIENCES, 3
noises Like n. in a swound SEA, 4
noisy Strongest minds /...the n. world /Hears least MIND, 11
The people would be just as n. PUBLIC, 9
nominated I will not accept if n. POLITICIANS, 71
No-more I am also called N. DISAPPOINTMENT, 6
non-being Neurosis is the way of avoiding n. NEUROSIS, 3
non-combatant War hath no fury like a n. WAR, 69
nonconformist a N. conscience WOMEN, 89
man must be a n. CONFORMITY, 4
Why do you have to be a n. CONFORMITY, 6
nonconformity N. and lust stalking hand in hand LUST, 8
none N. but the Brave COURAGE, 11
nonsense you intend to talk n. AMERICANS, 6
non-U U and N. CLASS, 28
non-violence to disagree...about...n. without wanting to kick VIOLENCE, 5
noon From morn /To n. he fell DECLINE, 4
from n. to dewy eve DECLINE, 4
O dark, dark, dark, amid the blaze of n. BLINDNESS, 4
Norfolk bear him up the N. sky HUNTING, 1
Very flat, N. ENGLAND, 12
Norgay Tenzing N. PHOTOGRAPHY, 5
Norma Jean Goodbye N. ACTORS, 18
normal quiet miracle of a n. life MIDDLE EAST, 6
the n. is so...interesting NORMALITY, 1
Normans The Saxon is not like us N. NATIONALITY, 6
north The n. wind does blow WEATHER, 6
nose A custom loathsome to the eye, hateful to the n. SMOKING, 7
A person may be indebted for a n....to a great-aunt FAMILY, 15
Dong with a luminous N. NONSENSE, 17
Had Cleopatra's n. been shorter APPEARANCE, 29
led by the n. with gold BRIBERY, 4
My n. is huge APPEARANCE, 31
Only the n. knows SECRECY, 1
This fellow did not see further than his...n. PAROCHIALISM, 1
will it come without warning /Just as I'm picking my n. LOVE, 18
nostrils God...breathed into his n. GARDENS, 3
not Believe it or n. BELIEF, 6
HOW N. TO DO IT BUREAUCRACY, 5
note The world will little n., nor long remember MEMORIALS, 6
notes the pauses between the n. MUSICIANS, 8
nothin You ain't heard n.' yet PROPHECY, 6
nothing Blessed is the man who expects n. EXPECTATION, 4
Certainly, there is n. else here to enjoy PARTIES, 6
Children aren't happy with n. to ignore FAMILY, 26
Death is n. AFTERLIFE, 5
doing n. for each other FRIENDSHIP, 16
from n. to a state of extreme poverty POVERTY, 26
God made everything out of n. CREATION, 15
have n. whatever to do with it DEATH, 85
N. can be created out of nothing NOTHING, 1
n. can bring back the hour REGRET, 22
n. either good or bad THINKING, 10
N., except my genius CONCEIT, 25

N. happens BOREDOM, 1
n. if not critical CRITICISM, 46
n. is certain but death and taxes TAXATION, 5
n....is greater...than one's self SELF, 20
n. is had for n. EFFORT, 4
n. is law that is not reason LAW, 22
N. long HUMAN NATURE, 9
N. matters very much TRIVIALITY, 1
N. to do but work PESSIMISM, 7
n. to do with the case APPEARANCE, 16
N. will come of n. NOTHING, 2
opened it only to find – n. MATERIALISM, 2
Signifying n. LIFE, 45
sooner read a time-table...than n. NOVELS, 10
take *more* than n. LANGUAGE, 4
The House of Peers...Did n. HOUSES OF PARLIAMENT, 10
the sort of woman...one would almost feel disposed to bury for n. WOMEN, 27
The temerity to believe in n. SCEPTICISM, 6
those who were up to n. INTRIGUE, 2
To marvel at n. is just about the one and only thing HAPPINESS, 8
When you have n. to say, say n. SILENCE, 4
Where some people are very wealthy and others have n. GOVERNMENT, 4

nothingness the n. shows through CREATION, 15
notice The State...takes no n. of their opinions LOYALTY, 6
notices One never n. what has been done ACHIEVEMENT, 4
nought N.'s had, all's spent CONTENTMENT, 6
nourisher Chief n. in life's feast SLEEP, 15
nourishment n. of the body into a painful attack FOOD, 18
novel A n. is a mirror NOVELS, 15
A n. is a static thing NOVELS, 16; PLAYS, 13
because a n.'s invented, it isn't true NOVELS, 12
choice of the moment...to begin his n. WRITERS, 21
good n. tells us the truth NOVELS, 2
I'm going to write the Great Australian N. AMBITION, 19
not a n. to be tossed aside lightly CRITICISM, 38
scrofulous French n. NOVELS, 1
The detective n. is NOVELS, 13
the last fashionable n. on the tables of young ladies WRITING, 21
The n. being dead NOVELS, 17
the n. tells a story NOVELS, 4
The only obligation to which...we may hold a n. NOVELS, 7
the sex n. is now normal NOVELS, 14
to read a n. before luncheon was one of the gravest sins READING, 18
When I want to read a n. NOVELS, 3
novelist A n. is, like all mortals WRITERS, 16
n. who writes nothing for 10 years WRITERS, 19
the most precious gift a n. can possess WRITERS, 68
novelists if a third of all the n....dropped dead WRITERS, 17
n. the story of the present NOVELS, 6
There are many reasons why n. write FICTION, 3
novels characters in one of my n. FICTION, 2
It is a sad feature...that only women...have time to write n. WRITERS, 24
one of the few English n. for grown up people CRITICISM, 56
novelty Novelty, n., n. NOVELTY, 3
November N. MONTHS, 10
Please to remember the Fifth of N. TREASON, 1
Thirty days hath N. MONTHS, 9
now We are all Socialists n. SOCIALISM, 7
nowhere All dressed up, with n. to go FUTILITY, 11
He's a real N. Man FUTILITY, 8
noxious the most n. is a tourist BRITISH, 7
nuclear adopt n. disarmament NUCLEAR WEAPONS, 16
Wars cannot be fought with n. weapons NUCLEAR WEAPONS, 13
nude To keep one from going n. PESSIMISM, 7
nudity you don't need the n. CINEMA, 15
nuisance exchange of one n. for another n. PROGRESS, 5
Inflation in the Sixties was a n. ECONOMICS, 14
Never compose...unless...not composing...becomes a positive n. MUSIC, 24
nuisances a change of n. is as good as a vacation CHANGE, 14
number *abstract reasoning concerning quantity or n.* PHILOSOPHY, 3
a very interesting n. NUMBERS, 3
Look after n. one SELF-PRESERVATION, 1
numbers divinity in odd n. SUPERSTITION, 10
N....only universal language MATHEMATICS, 15
Round n. NUMBERS, 1
the greatest happiness for the greatest n. HAPPINESS, 10
up in the high n. NUMBERS, 2
numble We live in a n. abode SERVILITY, 2
numbness drowsy n. pains /My sense MELANCHOLY, 7
nun the upbringing a n. would envy INNOCENCE, 8
nuns the n. who never take a bath MODESTY, 6
nuptials prone to any iteration of n. MARRIAGE, 40
nurse any other definition of what a n. should be OCCUPATIONS, 14
N. unupblown BREVITY, 9; TELEGRAMS, 12
The trained n. has become one of the great blessings of humanity OCCUPATIONS, 15
The trained n. has given nursing the human...touch OCCUPATIONS, 11
nurseries n. of all vice EDUCATION, 16
nurses old men's n. MARRIAGE, 13
nut I had a little n. tree, /Nothing would it bear NURSERY RHYMES, 20
nut-brown the spicy n. ale ALCOHOL, 45
nutmeg But a silver n. NURSERY RHYMES, 20

O

oak Heart of o. are our ships COURAGE, 13
To win the palm, the o., or bays VICTORY, 10
oar impressions...lasting as...an o. upon the water INSIGNIFICANCE, 1
oat This bread I break was once the o. AGRICULTURE, 6
oat-cakes land of Calvin, o., and sulphur SCOTLAND, 8
oaths O. are but words WORDS, 4
obedience The reluctant o. of distant provinces DIPLOMACY, 16
obey born to o. OBEDIENCE, 2
children, o. your parents OBEDIENCE, 1
one of those born neither to o. nor to command NASTINESS, 5
safer to o. than to rule OBEDIENCE, 3
obeyed Nature...must be o. HUMAN NATURE, 5
object o. will be, if possible to form Christian men EDUCATION, 3
objectionable its own animality either o. or funny HUMOUR, 18
obligation The only o. to which...we may hold a novel NOVELS, 7
To the University of Oxford I acknowledge no o. EDUCATION, 20
obligations hothouse of o. HOSTAGES, 2
oblige One should o. everyone ABILITY, 3; PRUDENCE, 8
oblivion alms for o. TIME, 35
o. which awaits the uncreative mind SCIENTISTS, 11
oblong an o. angular figure HUMOUR, 42
obscene Chaucer...I think o. and contemptible CHAUCER, 1
would not say that our Press is o. JOURNALISM, 20
obscenity O....happens to shock some elderly...magistrate PRUDERY, 4
obscure I strive to be brief, and I become o. BREVITY, 2
observance More honour'd in the breach than the o. CUSTOM, 3
the o. of trifles TRIVIALITY, 5
observation Reason, O., and Experience SCIENCE, 22
observations To o. which ourselves we make SUBJECTIVITY, 6
observe Whenever you o. an animal closely ANIMALS, 8
obsolete the horse, as a means of locomotion, is o. HORSES, 11
obstinacy the name of...o. in a bad one STUBBORNNESS, 3
obstinate O. people can be divided into STUBBORNNESS, 2
occupation for ever apologizing for his o. BUSINESS, 15
occur Accidents will o. ACCIDENTS, 2
ocean A life on the o. wave SEA, 13
on the o. of life we pass TRANSIENCE, 16
We mortals cross the o. HUMAN CONDITION, 4
whilst the great o. of truth lay all undiscovered before me DISCOVERY, 6
o'clock Three o. is always too late or too early DAY, 13
octopus dear o. from whose tentacles we never quite escape FAMILY, 31
odd How o. /Of God JEWS, 4
This world is very o. we see CONFUSION, 5
odds The o. is gone MOURNING, 11
odi *O. et amo* LOVE AND HATE, 2
odious comparisons are o. ANALOGY, 2
little o. vermin ENGLISH, 34

One is not superior...because one sees the world in an o. light CYNICISM, 1
odorous Comparisons are o. MALAPROPISMS, 2
Oedipuses a tense and peculiar family, the O. CLASSICS, 1
o'er Returning were as tedious as go o. GUILT, 7
o'er-leaps Vaulting ambition, which o. itself AMBITION, 16
off Days o. LEISURE, 5
offence dire o. from am'rous causes springs RESULTS, 5
greatest o. against virtue VIRTUE, 10
It is a public scandal that gives o. MORALITY, 11
The only defence is in o. WAR, 5
offend the kind of pride least likely to o. MODESTY, 5
Those who o. us are generally punished REVENGE, 14
offended This hand hath o. REGRET, 5
This hath not o. the king EXECUTION, 20
When people do not respect us we are sharply o. SELF-RESPECT, 4
offensive You are extremely o. IMPERTINENCE, 4
office in o. but not in power GOVERNMENT, 14
not describe holding public o. GOVERNMENT, 1
o. sanctifies the holder POWER, 3
Written by o. boys for o. boys NEWSPAPERS, 11
officer unbecoming the character of an o. OFFICERS, 1
official O. dignity...in inverse ratio DIPLOMACY, 12
offspring Heaven has granted me no o. CONCEIT, 24
often 'Do you come here o. ANIMALISM, 6
oil Kuwait is an o. monarchy MIDDLE EAST, 11
oiled Oozing charm...He o. his way CHARM, 3
ointment a good name is better than precious o. VIRTUE, 3
Okie O. use' to mean you was from Oklahoma INSULTS, 37
Oklahoma Okie use' to mean you was from O. INSULTS, 37
old All evil comes from the o. AGE, 3
an o., wild, and incomprehensible man POLITICIANS, 77
a sight to make an o. man young BEAUTY, 38
Before we grow o. and die AGE, 73
being o. is having lighted rooms OLD AGE, 25
Better be an o. man's darling MARRIAGE, 1
for de o. folks at home HOMESICKNESS, 3
Growing o. is like being increasingly penalized OLD AGE, 34
He cannot bear o. men's jokes OLD AGE, 20
I am o. enough to be – in fact am – your mother AGE, 40
J grow o....I grow o. OLD AGE, 17
I love everything that's o. CONSERVATISM, 2
inclination...to suppose an o. man decayed in his intellects OLD AGE, 24
It is so comic to hear oneself called o. OLD AGE, 23
I was born o. AGE, 61
I will never be an o. man OLD AGE, 4
man...as o. as the woman he feels AGE, 39
new book is published, read an o. one BOOKS, 33
no more work for poor o. Ned DEATH, 53
o., but I'm not cold SPORT AND GAMES, 4
O. men are dangerous OLD AGE, 41
O. men forget MEMORY, 16
O. sins SIN, 1
one has to be very o. before one learns how to be amused AGE, 16
redress the balance of the O. AMERICA, 5
Say I'm growing o., but add, /Jenny kissed me KISSING, 2
so few who can grow o. with a good grace OLD AGE, 44
Tell me the o., o. story CHRISTIANITY, 7
terrible thing for an o. woman to outlive her dogs OLD AGE, 50
that grand o. man POLITICIANS, 67
That is no country for o. men MORTALITY, 23
that o. serpent DEVIL, 4
the o. have reminiscences AGE, 50
the o. have rubbed it into the young that they are wiser OLD AGE, 28
the o. is better AGE, 12; ALCOHOL, 15
The o. man has his death DEATH, 11
There are no o. men any more AGE, 64
They shall grow not o. MEMORIALS, 3
they think he is growing o. AGE, 34
To be o. is to be part of a...multitude OLD AGE, 7
too much Asia and she is too o. PLACES, 8
too o. to go again to my travels ROYALTY, 10
When you are o. and gray OLD AGE, 54
Where are the boys of the O. Brigade NOSTALGIA, 23
'You are o., Father William OLD AGE, 10
old age first sign of o. AGE, 32
gift of perpetual o. OLD AGE, 49
I prefer o. to the alternative OLD AGE, 12
nothing funny or commendable about o. OLD AGE, 48
o. a regret AGE, 19
O. brings...the comfort that you will soon be out of it OLD AGE, 19
O. is...crossed off names in an address book AGE, 13
o. is...older than I am OLD AGE, 4
O. is the out-patients' department OLD AGE, 11
o....the fear that it may go on too long OLD AGE, 45
older make way for an o. man DISMISSAL, 6
O. men declare war WAR, 49
perceive real beauty in a person...o. BEAUTY, 6
The o. one grows the more one likes indecency AGE, 68
to go on getting o. SURVIVAL, 1
old-fashioned o. respect for the young RESPECT, 5
O. ways which no longer apply WOMEN, 5
olfactory an o. bar FAMILIARITY, 6
oligarchy displeased with *aristocracy*, call it *o.* GOVERNMENT, 12
extreme democracy or absolute o....will come GOVERNMENT, 4
olive a land of oil o., and honey WEALTH, 5
Olivier O. had murder in his heart ACTORS, 14
Olympic The most important thing in the O. Games VICTORY, 4
ominous an idea...to be fashionable is o. FASHION, 7
omnipotence final proof of God's o. GOD, 19
on O. with the dance DANCING, 1
they get *o.*, then they get ***honour*** DOCTORS, 9
once For Christmas comes but o. a year CHRISTMAS, 19
O. more unto the breach, dear friends COURAGE, 19
One dies only o. DEATH, 88
you have dined in every house in London – *o.* BORES, 9
you shall drink twice while I drink o. DRUNKENNESS, 20
one All for o., and o. for all UNITY, 8
How to be o. up ONE-UPMANSHIP, 3
if we knew o., we knew two METAPHYSICS, 3
o. and o. are two METAPHYSICS, 3
The number o. book...was written by a committee BIBLE, 8
one-eyed o. yellow idol to the north of Khatmandu MOURNING, 5
the O. Man is King SUPERIORITY, 12
one-handed Give me a o. economist ECONOMICS, 21
oneself It is a stupidity...to busy o. with the correction of the world IMPROVEMENT, 3
One should examine o....before...condemning others SELF, 11
only possible society is o. MISANTHROPY, 4
onions carry their own o. when cycling abroad FRANCE, 3
onward little o. lend thy guiding hand GUIDANCE, 3
O., Christian soldiers CHRISTIANITY, 3
O., Christians, onward go ENDURANCE, 24
open I declare this thing o. – whatever it is ARCHITECTURE, 8
O. Sesame SUPERNATURAL, 2
opening o. time in the Sailors Arms PUBLIC HOUSES, 4
opera an o. without an interval, or an interval without an o. OPERA, 6
baritones are born villains in o. OPERA, 8
Bed...is the poor man's o. SEX, 28
Like German o., too long and too loud OPERA, 9; WAR, 124
No good o. plot can be sensible OPERA, 2
O. in English OPERA, 5
o. isn't what it used to be OPERA, 4
The first rule in o. is the first rule in life SELF-RELIANCE, 6
The o. isn't over till the fat lady sings OPERA, 3
what language an o. is sung in OPERA, 1
operas the German text of French o. OPERA, 10
opinion A man...must have a very good o. of himself CONCEIT, 2
better to have no o. of God GOD, 3
fact that an o. has been widely held OPINIONS, 5
give him my o. MARRIAGE, 47
he is.../Now but a climate of o. PSYCHIATRY, 1
heresy signifies no more than private o. OPINIONS, 2
He would rather follow public o. POLITICIANS, 55
I agree with no man's o. OPINIONS, 8
I am...of the o. with the learned AGREEMENT, 2
Nobody holds a good o. of a man who has a low o. of himself SELF-RESPECT, 2
nothing to admire except his o. CRITICS, 6
of his own o. still YIELDING, 2

so vain...care for the o. of those we don't care for CONCEIT, 8
the English think of an o. as something...to hide ENGLISH, 17
The superiority of one man's o. over another's OPINIONS, 3
They that approve...call it o. OPINIONS, 2
opinionated the o., the ignorant, and the boorish STUBBORNNESS, 2
opinions a decent respect to the o. of mankind INDEPENDENCE, 2
New o. are always suspected NOVELTY, 5
not a writer's business to hold o. WRITERS, 28
So many men, so many o. OPINIONS, 7
the proper o. for the time of year PUBLIC, 3
The public buys its o. as it buys its meat PUBLIC, 7
There are only o., some of which are preferable TRUTH, 29
the same o. have arisen among men in cycles OPINIONS, 1
The State, in choosing men...takes no notice of their o. LOYALTY, 6
The wish to spread those o. that we hold ENGLISH, 7
opium Religion...is the o. of the people RELIGION, 42
opium-dose an o. for keeping beasts of burden BIBLE, 6
opponent Never ascribe to an o. motives meaner than your own MOTIVE, 1
opportunist rather be an o. and float EXPEDIENCY, 2
opportunities A wise man will make more o. OPPORTUNITY, 9
One can present people with o. OPPORTUNITY, 13
O. are usually disguised as hard work OPPORTUNITY, 12
opportunity Equality of o. OPPORTUNITY, 14
follies...he didn't commit when he had the o. REGRET, 12
O. seldom knocks twice OPPORTUNITY, 6
oppose duty...to o. OPPOSITION, 2
opposition Her Majesty's O. OPPOSITION, 1
I have spent many years...in o. OPPOSITION, 5
The duty of an o. OPPOSITION, 2
When I invented the phrase 'His Majesty's O.' OPPOSITION, 3
oppression when fanatics are on top there is no limit to o. GOVERNMENT, 19
Where rumour of o. and deceit SOLITUDE, 3
oppressive Vatican is an o. regime CHURCH, 3
optimism Pessimism...is just as agreeable as o. PESSIMISM, 1
The place where o. most flourishes OPTIMISM, 20
optimist an o....fills up his crossword puzzle in ink OPTIMISM, 25
I am an o., unrepentant and militant OPTIMISM, 26
The o. proclaims OPTIMISM, 19; PESSIMISM, 3
optimistic O. lies MEDICINE, 8
Oracle 'I am Sir O. EGOTISM, 8
oracular the use of my o. tongue MALAPROPISMS, 8
oral a terrific story about o. contraception CONTRACEPTION, 2
orange Oh that I were an o.-tree SERVICE, 2
oranges bananas or o. MIDDLE EAST, 11
O. and lemons, /Say the bells of St Clement's LONDON, 2
orangutang an o. trying to play the violin MARRIAGE, 17
oratorium *Laboratorium est o.* SCIENCE, 30
orchard Before the cherry o. was sold WORRY, 9
orchestra two golden rules for an o. MUSIC, 7
orchestration Literature is the o. of platitudes LITERATURE, 20
order O. is heaven's first law ORDER, 3
The old o. changeth CHANGE, 19
upon the o. of your going DISMISSAL, 8
wisdom...sweetly doth...o. all things WISDOM, 9
words in the best o. POETRY AND PROSE, 2
ordered a side dish he hadn't o. CONTEMPT, 3
ordering the better o. of the universe UNIVERSE, 1
orderly Being o....can be excessively tiresome ORDER, 1
ordinary One machine can do the work of fifty o. men TECHNOLOGY, 5
organ my second favourite o. ANIMALISM, 1
Seated...at the o. MUSIC, 39
organ-grinder no reason to attack the monkey when the o. is present POLITICIANS, 38
organic O. life...has developed...from the protozoon to the philosopher PROGRESS, 11
organization a government o. could do it that quickly BUREAUCRACY, 3
organized War is an o. bore WAR, 48
organs he'd have given us all more o. SEX, 8
orgasm The o. has replaced the Cross SEX, 42
orgies o. are vile DEBAUCHERY, 8
orgy An o. looks particularly alluring PRUDERY, 3
you need an o., once in a while DEBAUCHERY, 8
Orientals If...O....drank a liquor which...made them vomit ALCOHOL, 17
origin the indelible stamp of his lowly o. EVOLUTION, 4
original An o. writer is...one whom nobody can imitate ORIGINALITY, 2
Mona did researches in o. sin SEX, 48
o. is unfaithful to the translation TRANSLATION, 1
The more intelligence...the more...one finds o. INTELLIGENCE, 6
the only absolutely o. creation...is Don Quixote FICTION, 4
thought is often o. ORIGINALITY, 3
originality absence of inverted commas guarantees...o. QUOTATIONS, 2
All good things...are the fruits of o. ORIGINALITY, 4
without o. or moral courage CHARACTER, 23
originator quotes...give us a nodding acquaintance with the o. QUOTATIONS, 15
Ormus Outshone the wealth of O. and of Ind DEVIL, 10
ornamental not merely...useful and o. PURPOSE, 8
orphan defeat is an o. SUCCESS, 10
orthodoxy 'o.'...no longer means being right ORTHODOXY, 2
O. or My-doxy ORTHODOXY, 1
Oscar We all assume that O. said it QUOTATIONS, 7; WRITERS, 73
Oscar Wilde if...O. had lived into his nineties OLD AGE, 30
ostrich the wings of an o. IMAGINATION, 9
other O. people are quite dreadful MISANTHROPY, 4
you expect o. people to be...to your liking TOLERANCE, 4
others By persuading o. we convince ourselves PERSUASION, 2
delight in...misfortunes...of o. SUFFERING, 6
some more than o. SIMILARITY, 4
tell the o. by their hunted expression CHARITY, 15
to encourage the o. EXAMPLE, 9
otherwise Some folk...are o. WISDOM, 21
Otis Miss O. regrets APOLOGIES, 2
ounce An o. of a man's own wit WISDOM, 22
ours We have met the enemy, and they are o. VICTORY, 13
ourselves all our knowledge is, o. to know SELF-KNOWLEDGE, 6
By persuading others we convince o. PERSUASION, 2
In every friend we lose a part of o. DEATH, 96
remedies oft in o. do lie SELF-RELIANCE, 8
we but praise o. in other men PRAISE, 5
What isn't part of o. doesn't disturb us HATE, 5
'ousemaids I walks with fifty 'o. outer Chelsea to the Strand DISCONTENT, 6
'ouses It's 'aving 'o. built by men HOUSES, 5
out Mordre wol o. MURDER, 4
once o., what you've said can't be stopped PUBLISHING, 7
O., damned spot GUILT, 8
outlive o. this powerful rhyme POETRY, 42
outlook religious o. on life RELIGION, 36
outrun We may o. EXCESS, 11
outside I am just going o. LAST WORDS, 48
I support it from the o. SUPPORT, 5
outward I may not hope from o. forms APPEARANCES, 12
over Now the day is o. DAY, 1
we're coming o., /And we won't come back till it's o., o. there. WORLD WAR I, 8
overcomes Who o. /By force VICTORY, 11
over-confident Not that I am ever o. SELF-CONFIDENCE, 6
over-dressed He was o., pompous...and vain WRITERS, 91
over-educated I've o. myself in all the things DEBAUCHERY, 5
overexposure she should catch a cold on o. TRUTH, 16
overfed They're overpaid, o., oversexed and over here SOLDIERS, 8
over-feeding what Nicely-Nicely dies of will be o. GREED, 8
overlooked better to be looked over than o. STARING, 1
overpaid They're o., overfed, oversexed and over here SOLDIERS, 8
overrated matrimony, which I always thought a highly o. performance MARRIAGE, 54
overrun apt to be o. with nettles MIND, 8
over-running and lose by o. EXCESS, 11
oversexed They're overpaid, overfed, o. and over here SOLDIERS, 8
overtakers It is the o. who CARS, 7
overthrown Another mighty empire o. DEFEAT, 9
overtures I tried to resist his o. PUNS, 18
ovule Man is developed from an o. EVOLUTION, 3
ovules differs in no respect from the o. of other animals EVOLUTION, 3
owe I don't o. a penny to a single soul BORROWING, 13
owed so much o. by so many to so few WORLD WAR II, 7

owes A nation is not in danger...because it o. itself money ECONOMICS, 17
he o. not any man RIGHTEOUSNESS, 7
owl The O. and the Pussy-Cat went to sea NONSENSE, 20
owls Two O. and a Hen APPEARANCE, 19
own mine o. Executioner SELF, 7
ownership its source of power: o. CAPITALISM, 6
spread of personal o. is in harmony BRITISH, 8
transform this society without...extension of public o. SOCIALISM, 9
own-goal Aids pandemic is a classic o. AIDS, 2
ox When he stands like an o. in the furrow NATIONALITY, 6
Oxford a secret in the O. sense SECRECY, 10
It is O. that has made me insufferable EDUCATION, 6
nice sort of place, O. OXFORD, 5
O....full of a particular non-social snobbiness OXFORD, 7
O. is on the whole more attractive than Cambridge CAMBRIDGE, 1; OXFORD, 3
The clever men at O. /Know all that there is to be knowed KNOWLEDGE, 18
The King to O. sent a troop of horse CAMBRIDGE, 3; OXFORD, 4
To the University of O. I acknowledge no obligation EDUCATION, 20
You will hear more good things on...a stagecoach from London to O. INTELLECTUALS, 6
you will leave O. by the town drain SPOONERISMS, 5
oyster bold man that first eat an o. COURAGE, 20; FOOLISHNESS, 19
nothing...quite matches the sympathetic unselfishness of an o. PERFECTION, 7
the sort of eye that can open an o. at sixty paces APPEARANCE, 42
world's mine o. OPPORTUNITY, 17
oysters Poverty and o. POVERTY, 6

P

pace this petty p. from day to day LIFE, 45
Pacific salutes the Admiral of the P. ARROGANCE, 10
pacifism My p. is not based on...intellectual theory WAR AND PEACE, 5
pack how much more dogs are animated when they hunt in a p. UNITY, 11
the human p. is shuffled and cut EDUCATION, 31
paddle every man p. his own canoe INDEPENDENCE, 3
padlocked music critics....small and rodent-like with p. ears CRITICS, 18
pagan A P. suckled in a creed outworn DISCONTENT, 10
pageant insubstantial p. faded MORTALITY, 17
paid I do not answer questions like this without being p. MASCULINITY, 1
pain a gentleman...never inflicts p. CHIVALRY, 8
Although p. isn't real SUFFERING, 3
critics...desire our blood, not our p. CRITICS, 13
disinclination to inflict p. upon oneself GOOD, 11
I feel no p., dear mother, now ALCOHOL, 9
momentary intoxication with p. CRUELTY, 1
Neither shame nor physical p. have any...effect PUNISHMENT, 13
owes its pleasures to another's p. HUNTING, 2
P. – has an Element of Blank SUFFERING, 7
Pleasure is...intermission of p. PLEASURE, 27
Remember that p. has this most excellent quality SUFFERING, 13
The least p. in our little finger SELF-INTEREST, 4
The p. passes, but the beauty remains ENDURANCE, 14
they blest him in their p. MARTYRDOM, 4
what p. it was to drown DROWNING, 2
yearning like a God in p. SUFFERING, 9
painful nourishment of the body into a p. attack FOOD, 18
pains no gains without p. ENDURANCE, 19
paint flinging a pot of p. in the public's face CRITICISM, 45
I p. objects as I think them ARTISTS, 17; PAINTING, 10
My business is to p....what I see PAINTING, 17
not p. a portrait to look like the subject ARTISTS, 13
to p. the lily EXCESS, 10
painted As idle as a p. ship BOATS, 3
I am p. as the greatest little dictator AUTHORITARIANISM, 6
Most women are not so young as they are p. COSMETICS, 1
p....by the great artist Kodak PHOTOGRAPHY, 7
painter A p. should not paint what he sees ARTISTS, 7
I am married to Beatrice Salkeld, a p. CHILDREN, 7
I could have become a real p. LAST WORDS, 39
memory is a p. MEMORY, 10
not a great sculptor or p. can be an architect ARCHITECTURE, 9
painters Good p. imitate nature PAINTING, 3
P. and poets...licence to dare anything FREEDOM, 18
Poets and p. are outside the class system ARTISTS, 1; POETS, 1
painting a great difference between p. a face APPEARANCE, 15
If I didn't start p., I would have raised chickens OCCUPATIONS, 13
If people only knew...about p. PAINTING, 6
I just keep p. till I feel like pinching. Then I know it's right PAINTING, 14
P. is a blind man's profession PAINTING, 11
p. on a square of ivory WRITERS, 48
P....protecting flat surfaces from the weather PAINTING, 2
pajamas I shot an elephant in my p. HUMOUR, 43
palace Love in a p. LOVE, 77
palaces Mid pleasures and p. though we may roam HOME, 7
pale a p. horse DEATH, 31
Palestine not enough prisons...in P. to hold all the Jews JEWS, 10
pall The pallor of girls' brows shall be their p. WAR, 81
Palladium Liberty of the press is the *P.* of...rights FREEDOM, 23
pallor The p. of girls' brows shall be their pall WAR, 81
palm happy state of getting the victor's p. without the dust of racing VICTORY, 6
To win the p., the oak, or bays VICTORY, 10
palms p. before my feet GLORY, 1
palsied with the p. heart PASSION, 8
pan Put on the p.; /Says Greedy Nan NURSERY RHYMES, 7
Pandora open that P.'s Box...Trojan 'orses will jump out MIXED METAPHORS, 1
Panjandrum the grand P. NONSENSE, 12
pantheist The modern p. not only PHOTOGRAPHY, 6
pants There were times my p. were so thin POVERTY, 32
Your eyes shine like the p. COMPLIMENTS, 3
papacy Since God has given us the p....enjoy it CATHOLICISM, 8
The P. is not other than the Ghost of the deceased Roman Empire CATHOLICISM, 5
paper reactionaries are p. tigers POLITICS, 53
The atom bomb is a p. tiger NUCLEAR WEAPONS, 12
This p. will no doubt be found interesting CRITICISM, 11
Where were you fellows when the p. was blank EDITORS, 1
papers fornicated and read the p. MANKIND, 10
only two posh p. on a Sunday NEWSPAPERS, 10
papyromania *P.* – compulsive accumulation OBSESSIONS, 2
papyrophobia *P.* – abnormal desire OBSESSIONS, 2
parables great p....but false art CRITICISM, 27
parade the chief employment of riches consists in the p. of riches OSTENTATION, 6; WEALTH, 25
paradise A p. for a sect FANATICISM, 2
drunk the milk of P. CAUTION, 9
England is a p. for women NATIONALITY, 3
England is the p. of individuality ENGLAND, 35
Grant me p. in this world HEAVEN, 14
If a man could pass through P. PROOF, 3
Same old glimpse of /P. MARRIAGE, 76
to hope for P. is to live in P. HEAVEN, 9
Wilderness is P. enow CONTENTMENT, 3
paradox p. in South Africa SOUTH AFRICA, 15
paragon the p. of animals MANKIND, 27
parallel passion...which...we may not find a p. SELF, 8
parallelogram The landlady...is a p. HUMOUR, 42
paralyse p. it by encumbering it with remedies REMEDIES, 13
paranoid Even a p. can have enemies ENEMIES, 4
parasite The sick man is a p. of society PATIENTS, 2
parcels Portions and p. of the dreadful Past TIME, 37
pardon God may p. you, but I never can FORGIVENESS, 12
God will p. me. It is His trade LAST WORDS, 36
the government that should ask me for a p. FORGIVENESS, 10
pardoned The women p. all FORGIVENESS, 9
parent a kind p....or a merciless step-mother NATURE, 13
To lose one p....a misfortune; to lose both looks like carelessness LOSS, 8
parents A Jewish man with p. alive JEWS, 13
by defying their p. and copying one another YOUTH, 5
children, obey your p. OBEDIENCE, 1
Don't hold your p. up to contempt FAMILY, 36
From birth to age eighteen, a girl needs good p. AGE, 63
joys of p. are secret FAMILY, 6

necessary precautions to avoid having p. FAMILY, 8
P.…a disappointment to their children FAMILY, 27
P.…bones on which children sharpen their teeth FAMILY, 35
P. learn a lot from their children CHILDREN, 38
the way p. obey their children FAMILY, 37
what p. were created for FAMILY, 26
Paris delivered of a city bigger than P. DISAPPOINTMENT, 4
Good Americans, when they die, go to P. AMERICANS, 1
I love P. PARIS, 5
Is P. burning PARIS, 3
no home…save in P. PARIS, 4
P. is worth a mass PARIS, 2
when good Americans die they go to P. AMERICANS, 13
parish all the world as my p. RELIGION, 68
park The hunchback in the p. LONELINESS, 8
Parkinson The rise in the…employed is governed by P.'s Law WORK, 14
par-lee-voo Hinky, dinky, p. FRANCE, 13
Parliament build your House of P. upon the river HOUSES OF PARLIAMENT, 19
He stood twice for P. POLITICS, 87
If Her Majesty stood for P. POLITICS, 69
no reference to fun in any Act of P. PLEASURE, 13
P. is the longest running farce GOVERNMENT, 27
parliaments England…mother of p. ENGLAND, 6
parlour Will you walk into my p. INVITATIONS, 1
parochial worse than provincial – he was p. WRITERS, 60
parody devil's walking p. ANIMALS, 9
parole Classical quotation is the *p.* of literary men QUOTATIONS, 4
parrot to sell the family p. RESPECTABILITY, 4
parsnips fine words butter no p. WORDS, 18
parson If P. lost his senses ANIMALS, 12
In arguing too, the p. own'd his skill KNOWLEDGE, 17
Once a p. OCCUPATIONS, 5
parsons Our dourest p. PRAYER, 15
part I have forgot my p. FAILURE, 6
In every friend we lose a p. of ourselves DEATH, 96
it is a little flesh and breath, and the ruling p. MANKIND, 3
let us kiss and p. PARTING, 6
p. never calls for it NAKEDNESS, 6
till death us do p. MARRIAGE, 30
We only p. to meet again FAITHFULNESS, 4
particular a London p.…A fog WEATHER, 9
did nothing in p. HOUSES OF PARLIAMENT, 10
particulars Minute P. GOOD, 2
parties it is always like that at p. REGRET, 11
one of those p. which got out of hand CHRISTIANITY, 21
parting Every p. gives a foretaste of death SEPARATION, 5
P. is all we know of heaven PARTING, 5
P. is such sweet sorrow PARTING, 10
partisanship P. is our great curse SUBJECTIVITY, 7
partly Man p. is AMBITION, 4
partridge well-shot woodcock, p., snipe HUNTING, 1
parts It is seldom…one p. on good terms PARTING, 9
one man in his time plays many p. HUMAN CONDITION, 17
Today we have naming of p. WEAPONS, 6
part-time p. nihilist COMMITMENT, 3
party A great p. is not to be brought down POLITICS, 33
best number for a dinner p. is two FOOD, 26
Heard there was a p. ACCIDENTS, 4
I always voted at my p.'s call POLITICIANS, 10
No p. has a monopoly over what is right TOLERANCE, 2
p. of the individual…p. of the community INDIVIDUALITY, 4
soft drink at a p. ABSTINENCE, 2
The p. is the rallying-point for the…working class COMMUNISM, 9
The sooner every p. breaks up the better PARTIES, 1
Well, did you evah! What a swell p. PARTIES, 5
pass ideas simply p. through him STUPIDITY, 1
I shall not p. this way again MORTALITY, 11
p. for forty-three AGE, 30
Praise the Lord and p. the ammunition WAR, 37
They shall not p. DETERMINATION, 14
To p. away ere life hath lost its brightness DEATH, 59
passage calm p.…across many a bad night SUICIDE, 6
Patience and p. of time PATIENCE, 11
passageways smell of steaks in p. FOOD, 20
passed That p. the time TIME, 9
passengers fools and p. drink at sea BOATS, 15
passeront *Ils ne p. pas* DETERMINATION, 14
passes Men seldom make p. APPEARANCE, 27
passeth the peace of God, which p. all understanding BLESSING, 5
passion All breathing human p. far above PASSION, 3
cheated into p., but…reasoned into truth TRUTH, 25
Culture is the p. for sweetness and light CULTURE, 2
desolate and sick of an old p. LOVE, 51
Master Mistress of my p. LOVE, 122
one master-p.…/swallows up the rest PASSION, 5
p. and party blind our eyes EXPERIENCE, 11
P.…can be destroyed by a doctor PASSION, 7
p. in the human soul MUSIC, 29
So I triumphed ere my p. PASSION, 8
Strange fits of p. PASSION, 9
The p. and the life, whose fountains are within APPEARANCES, 12
The ruling p. conquers reason still PASSION, 6
We never remark any p.…in others SELF, 8
passions inferno of his p. PASSION, 2
It is with our p. as it is with fire and water PASSION, 4
Literature and butterflies are the two sweetest p. LITERATURE, 14
not his reason, but his p. RELIGION, 54
The man who is master of his p. PASSION, 1
Three p., simple but overwhelmingly strong, have governed my life PHILOSOPHERS, 8
past Even God cannot change the p. PAST, 1
half of you belongs to the p. OLD AGE, 3
Historians tell the story of the p. NOVELS, 6
I do not…prejudge the p. PREJUDICE, 6
Keep off your thoughts from things that are p. PAST, 8
looking forward to the p. NOSTALGIA, 17
Nothing recalls the p. so potently as a smell NOSTALGIA, 6
people who live in the p. PROGRESS, 1
Portions and parcels of the dreadful P. TIME, 37
remembrance of things p. REGRET, 18
something…absurd about the p. PAST, 2
Study the p. PAST, 4
The only thing I regret about my p. life AGE, 9
The p., at least, is secure PAST, 9
The p. is a foreign country PAST, 5
The p. is the only dead thing PAST, 7
The p. was a sleep BEGINNING, 7
The p. was nothing…The future was a mystery PRESENT, 2
Those who cannot remember the p. HISTORY, 23
to know nothing but the present, or nothing but the p. CONSERVATISM, 4
what is p. my help is p. my care INDIFFERENCE, 1
what's p. help /Should be p. grief REGRET, 15
What we know of the p. is HISTORY, 17
Who controls the p. controls the future POWER, 18
pastoral Cold P. ETERNITY, 3
pastures fresh woods, and p. new CHANGE, 16
pat P.-a-cake, pat-a-cake, baker's man NURSERY RHYMES, 38
P. it and prick it, and mark it with B NURSERY RHYMES, 38
patches king of shreds and p. INFERIORITY, 6
thing of shreds and p. SINGERS, 2
pate You beat your p. STUPIDITY, 13
patent The people – could you p. the sun DISCOVERY, 7
path the primrose p. of dalliance EXAMPLE, 8
world will make a…p. to his door FAME, 8
patience like P. on a monument LOVE, 126
P. and passage of time PATIENCE, 11
P. is a virtue PATIENCE, 4
P., n. A minor form of despair PATIENCE, 8
the years teach us p. PATIENCE, 13
Though p. be a tired mare PATIENCE, 12
patient A disease which the p. and his friends frequently mistake for deep religious conviction RELIGION, 4
A doctor…is a p. half-cured OCCUPATIONS, 16
amusing the p. while Nature cures the disease MEDICINE, 12
Fury of a P. Man PATIENCE, 10
kill the p. REMEDIES, 1
Like a p. etherized upon a table DEPARTURE, 6
p. endurance is godlike ENDURANCE, 9
patients the faults of the p. PATIENTS, 1
patrie *Allons, enfants, de la p.* FRANCE, 10
patriot A good historian…is a p. HISTORIANS, 1
He was a great p.…provided…that he really is dead ADMIRATION, 17
The summer soldier and the sunshine p. COWARDICE, 6
patriotism Blimpish p. in the mode of Margaret Thatcher PATRIOTISM, 19

P....is a revolutionary duty PATRIOTISM, 30
p. is not enough LAST WORDS, 14
P....looking out for yourself while AMERICA, 9
P....the last refuge PATRIOTISM, 4, 17
p. which consists in hating all other nations PATRIOTISM, 12
True p. is of no party PATRIOTISM, 29
patriots P. always talk of dying for their country PATRIOTISM, 27
patron Is not a P., my Lord, one who looks with unconcern PATRONAGE, 2
patronise He liked to p. coloured people RACISM, 27
patronizing A p. disposition...has its meaner side CHARACTER, 8
The idea that there is a model Labour voter...is p. POLITICS, 42
pattern p. of excelling nature MURDER, 10
paucity the p. of human pleasures HUNTING, 5
Paul One named Peter, /The other named P. NURSERY RHYMES, 63
Paul's I am designing St P. ARCHITECTURE, 1
pause Now I'll have *eine kleine P.* LAST WORDS, 24
pauses the p. between the notes MUSICIANS, 8
pavilion The p. of Heaven is bare WEATHER, 23
pavilioned P. in splendour, and girded with praise GOD, 23
pay better...not vow, than...vow and not p. PROMISES, 1
get someone to p. you for doing it OCCUPATIONS, 18
it is poor grub, poor p., and easy work AMERICA, 24; ENGLAND, 25
Life is too short to do anything...one can p. others to do WORK, 13
Not a penny off the p. STRIKES, 1
we cannot p. too dearly for it JUSTICE, 15
pays He who p. the piper POWER, 2
PC pushes for equality...is declared "P." POLITICAL CORRECTNESS, 1
peace And who will bring white p. PEACE, 11
a period of cold p. COLD WAR, 5
Arms alone are not enough to keep the p. PEACE, 10
Courage is the price...for granting p. COURAGE, 12
depart in p. DEATH, 30
hereafter for ever hold his p. OPPORTUNITY, 11
In Switzerland they had brotherly love...and p. SWITZERLAND, 5
in what p. a Christian can die LAST WORDS, 3
it is in the minds of men that the defences of p. must be constructed WAR AND PEACE, 1
I will die in p. LAST WORDS, 75
Let him who desires p., prepare for war WAR AND PEACE, 13
Let us have p. PEACE, 9
life is more interesting in war than in p. WAR AND PEACE, 10
make a wilderness and call it p. WAR, 118
makes a good war makes a good p. WAR AND PEACE, 8
May God deny you p. GLORY, 2
my p. I give unto you PEACE, 2
Nation shall speak p. PEACE, 14
never was a good war or a bad p. WAR AND PEACE, 6
no p....unto the wicked PEACE, 2; PUNISHMENT, 5
P....a period of cheating PEACE, 3
p. comes dropping slow PEACE, 17
p. for our time PEACE, 6
p. has broken out PEACE, 5
P. hath her victories WAR AND PEACE, 11
p. I hope with honour PEACE, 8
p. in our time PEACE, 4
P. is made with yesterday's enemies MIDDLE EAST, 12
P. is not only better than war WAR AND PEACE, 12
P. is poor reading WAR AND PEACE, 7
p. process will be irreversible IRELAND, 1
P., the human dress MANKIND, 6
P. took them all prisoner WAR AND PEACE, 9
p. with honour PEACE, 6
price which is too great to pay for p. WORLD WAR I, 28
The Bomb brought p. but man alone NUCLEAR WEAPONS, 4
the inglorious arts of p. POLITICIANS, 63
the p. of God, which passeth all understanding BLESSING, 5
the Prince of P. CHRISTMAS, 6
There can be no p. of mind in love LOVE, 104
They made p. between us ENEMIES, 5
those who could make a good p. WAR AND PEACE, 4
War is P. OPPOSITES, 5
We are the true p. movement PEACE, 16
We wanted p. on earth PEACE, 12
When there was p., he was for p. PUBLIC, 3
peach dare to eat a p. OLD AGE, 18
'Fan vaulting'...belongs to the 'Last-supper-carved-on-a-p.-stone' ARCHITECTURE, 5
peaches poetry in p. POETRY, 18
with p. and women, it's...the side next the sun that's tempting TEMPTATION, 8
peak One sees...only small things from the p. PERSPECTIVE, 2
Silent, upon a p. in Darien DISCOVERY, 5
pear And a golden p. NURSERY RHYMES, 20
pearl base Indian, threw a p. away LOVE, 128
pearls He who would search for P. TRUTH, 24
p. before swine FOOLISHNESS, 9
p. that were his eyes DEATH, 108
peas I always eat p. with honey FOOD, 6
peasantry a bold p..../When once destroy'd PUBLIC, 12
peasants If the French noblesse had been capable of playing cricket with their p. ARISTOCRACY, 13; CRICKET, 8
peck Peter Piper picked a p. of pickled pepper NURSERY RHYMES, 39
peculiar a tense and p. family, the Oedipuses CLASSICS, 1
Funny p., or funny ha-ha HUMOUR, 14
pedestal at fourteen every boy should be in love with some ideal woman...on a p. SEXES, 17
pedigree languages are the p. of nations LANGUAGE, 15
pee share a quick p. over a common lamp-post WRITERS, 8
Peel D'ye ken John P. HUNTING, 4
P.'s smile INSULTS, 32
Sir Robert P. POLITICIANS, 1
peer A life p. is like a mule HOUSES OF PARLIAMENT, 16
peerage When I want a p., I shall buy one TITLES, 6
peers Fears, prejudices, misconceptions – those are the p. HOUSES OF PARLIAMENT, 13
pen how much more cruel the p. WRITING, 4
less brilliant p. than mine CONCEIT, 4
nothing can cure it but the scratching of a p. WRITING, 20
p. is mightier than the sword WRITING, 3
penance The man hath p. done PUNISHMENT, 7
pence Take care of the p. MONEY, 3
Take care of the p. THRIFT, 4
pendulum politics of the p., but of the ratchet POLITICS, 81
The p. of the mind oscillates between sense and nonsense MIND, 3
penetrable most things are p. BRIBERY, 2
pennies P. do not come from heaven WORK, 23
P. from Heaven OPTIMISM, 18
penny A p. saved THRIFT, 1
One a p., two a p. NURSERY RHYMES, 16
I don't owe a p. to a single soul BORROWING, 13
In for a p. COMMITMENT, 1
Not a p. off the pay STRIKES, 1
P. wise THRIFT, 3
pens Let other p. dwell on guilt and misery OPTIMISM, 14
people a loyal, a gallant, a generous, an ingenious, and good-temper'd p. FRANCE, 14
always been interested in p. MISANTHROPY, 2
Be nice to p. on your way up PRUDENCE, 10
Boys...are unwholesome companions for grown p. CHILDREN, 32
good of the p. LAW, 7
government of the p., by the p., and for the p. DEMOCRACY, 12; MEMORIALS, 6
Hell is other p. HELL, 6
How do p. go to sleep SLEEP, 14
If p. behaved in the way nations do GOVERNMENT, 34
if the p....can be reached with the truth DEMOCRACY, 16
indictment against an whole p. ACCUSATION, 1
It is with...p. as with...bottles CHARACTER, 18
Most of the p....will be children FUNERALS, 1
my p. live in such awful conditions POVERTY, 12
Once the p. begin to reason PUBLIC, 18
p....are attracted by God RELIGION, 34
P. are either charming or tedious CHARM, 4
P. are not fallen angels CRITICISM, 27
p. are the masters PUBLIC, 6
p. may be made to follow a course of action UNDERSTANDING, 4
P. must help one another HELP, 7
p....not dealing with creatures of logic HUMAN NATURE, 7
p.'s government GOVERNMENT, 33
p. standing in the corners of our rooms TELEVISION AND RADIO, 1

p. under suspicion are better moving JUDGMENT, 10
p....usually imitate each other IMITATION, 3
P. who like this sort of thing CRITICISM, 30
P. who need people are the luckiest SOCIETY, 5
p. whose company is coveted OSTENTATION, 4
p. who stay in the middle of the road NONCOMMITMENT, 1
P. will cross the road...to say 'We saw you on the telly' TELEVISION AND RADIO, 2
Pleasant p. are just as real as horrible p. HUMAN NATURE, 6
Religion...is the opium of the p. RELIGION, 42
show my head to the p. EXECUTION, 5
the bludgeoning of the p. DEMOCRACY, 23
The Lord prefers common-looking p. APPEARANCE, 21
the p. are forbidden to light lamps INJUSTICE, 10
The p. – could you patent the sun DISCOVERY, 7
the p. we should have been seen dead with SNOBBERY, 10
The p. would be just as noisy PUBLIC, 9
The Swiss...are not a p. so much as a...business SWITZERLAND, 2
This country...belongs to the p. who inhabit it DEMOCRACY, 11
thy p. shall be my p. LOYALTY, 5
two p. with one pulse LOVE, 86
victory for all the p. of South Africa SOUTH AFRICA, 10
we are not a small p. BRITAIN, 9
When...it becomes necessary for one p. to dissolve...political bonds INDEPENDENCE, 2
When the P. contend for their Liberty REBELLION, 4
You can fool too many of the p. DECEPTION, 6
people's The p. flag is deepest red SOCIALISM, 3
pepper Peter Piper picked a peck of pickled p. NURSERY RHYMES, 39
Sergeant P.'s BOOK, SONG, AND PLAY TITLES, 14
perception any truth but from a clear p. TRUTH, 32
doors of p. were cleansed PERCEPTION, 1
prime agent of all human p. IMAGINATION, 1
perceptions Man's Desires are limited by his P. PERCEPTION, 2; DESIRE, 4
perfect A cigarette is...a p. pleasure SMOKING, 23
p. love casteth out fear LOVE, 24; FEAR, 3
perfection attain to the divine p. PERFECTION, 4
Finality is death. P. is finality PERFECTION, 9
P. has one grave defect PERFECTION, 5
The pursuit of p. PERFECTION, 1
performance desire should...outlive p. SEX, 52
it takes away the p. ALCOHOL, 53
verses...as a literary p. POETRY, 52
performing English literature's p. flea WRITERS, 60
perfume As a p. doth remain MEMORY, 18
perfumes All the p. of Arabia GUILT, 9
perhaps I am going in search of a great p. LAST WORDS, 56
The grand P. POSSIBILITY, 1
peril For those in p. on the sea SEA, 14
perils all p. and dangers of this night DANGER, 3
smile at p. past PAST, 6
periods Decades...are not...really p. at all CLASSIFICATION, 3
perish P. the Universe REVENGE, 6
they that take the sword shall p. with the sword WAR, 10
though the world p. JUSTICE, 7
weak shall p. SURVIVAL, 6
periwig with my mourning...and new p. APPEARANCE, 30
perjury P....is truth that is shamefaced TRUTH, 22
permanence love p. more than...beauty BRITISH, 3
pernicious the most p. race ENGLISH, 34
Peron If a woman like Eva P. with no ideals POLITICIANS, 75
If I had not been born P. CONTENTMENT, 5
perpetual gift of p. old age OLD AGE, 49
Literary men are...a p. priesthood WRITERS, 4
perpetuation Why should I consent to the p. of the image of this image PAINTING, 13
persecutors Wilde...p....letters page of the *Daily Telegraph* HOMOSEXUALITY, 10
perseverance the name of p. in a good cause STUBBORNNESS, 3
persistent The most p. sound...through men's history WAR, 58
person A p. may be indebted for a nose or an eye...to a great-aunt FAMILY, 15
My idea of an agreeable p. AGREEMENT, 3
the only p....I should like to know EGOTISM, 11
the only thing that can exist is an uninterested p. CURIOSITY, 5
The world regards such a p. as...an unmuzzled dog CLASSIFICATION, 1
to the cheek of a young p. EMBARRASSMENT, 1
personal obligations, both p. and public HOSTAGES, 2
They do those little p. things HABIT, 6
personalities events and p. in...history reappear HISTORY, 20
personality Simply a radio p. CHURCHILL, 8
persons God is no respecter of p. GOD, 4
I am made up of several p. CHARACTER, 17
perspective What a delightful thing this p. is ART, 29
perspire he never seemed to p. CLASS, 10
persuade Beauty...doth...p. the eyes of men BEAUTY, 35
perversion that melancholy sexual p. known as continence ABSTINENCE, 6
War is...universal p. WAR, 88
pervert Once: a philosopher; twice: a p. DEBAUCHERY, 9
p. climbs into the minds CRUELTY, 1
pessimism P. is a luxury that a Jew never can allow himself JEWS, 9
P....is just as agreeable as optimism PESSIMISM, 1
pessimist A p. is a man who PESSIMISM, 10
Scratch a p. PESSIMISM, 2
the p. fears this is true OPTIMISM, 19; PESSIMISM, 3
pessimists p. end up by desiring the things they fear PESSIMISM, 9
Peter One named P., /The other named Paul NURSERY RHYMES, 63
P. Piper picked a peck of pickled pepper NURSERY RHYMES, 39
Shock-headed P. CHILDREN, 25
thou art P. CHURCH, 1
petrified a man suffering from p. adolescence CHURCHILL, 4
petroleum Timor's p. smells better than Timorese blood OPPRESSION, 2
petticoat lay aside...modesty...and put it on again with her p. SEX, 40
pettiness I have something to expiate; /A p. REGRET, 8
petty the p. fools of rhyme TRIVIALITY, 14
petulance p. is not sarcasm PETULANCE, 2; IMPERTINENCE, 1
pews Talk about the p. and steeples RELIGION, 15
phallic the deterrent is a p. symbol NUCLEAR WEAPONS, 19
Pharisees Now is the time of P. DESTINY, 15
the scribes and P. RETRIBUTION, 6
phenomena chess-board is the world; the pieces...the p. of the universe GOD, 28
Philip Prince P....a world expert on leisure ROYALTY, 20
Philistines apostle of the P., Lord Macaulay PHILISTINISM, 2
For this class we have...the designation of P. PHILISTINISM, 1
society distributes itself into Barbarians, P., and Populace AMERICA, 1
to distinguish...the aristocratic class from the P. CLASS, 3
philosopher he who can analyze his delusion is called a p. PHILOSOPHERS, 1
I doubt if the p. lives...who could know himself...despised by a street boy PHILOSOPHERS, 5
In the p. there is nothing whatever impersonal PHILOSOPHERS, 6
never yet p. /That could endure the toothache ENDURANCE, 18
Once: a p.; twice: a pervert DEBAUCHERY, 9
Organic life...has developed...from the protozoon to the p. PROGRESS, 11
some p. has said it PHILOSOPHERS, 2
To a p. no circumstance...is too minute PHILOSOPHERS, 3
philosophers now-a-days professors of philosophy but not p. PHILOSOPHERS, 10
P. are as jealous as women PHILOSOPHERS, 9
P. never balance between profit and honesty PHILOSOPHERS, 4
the English are...the least a nation of pure p. ENGLISH, 5
till p. become kings PHILOSOPHY, 9
philosophical more p. than...curators of the museums MUSEUMS, 1; PRACTICALITY, 3
philosophy a great advantage for...p. to be...true PHILOSOPHY, 13
Art and religion first; then p. IMPORTANCE, 3
Axioms in p. are not axioms PHILOSOPHY, 8
collection of prejudices which is called political p. POLITICS, 65
dreamt of in your p. SUPERNATURAL, 13
History is p....by examples HISTORY, 10
mere touch of cold p. PHILOSOPHY, 7
necessary for a superstition to enslave a p. RELIGION, 33

new P. calls all in doubt SCIENCE, 9
Not to care for p. PHILOSOPHERS, 7
now-a-days professors of p. but not philosophers PHILOSOPHERS, 10
p. and vain deceit CHRISTIANITY, 4
P.…is a fight against…fascination PHILOSOPHY, 17
P. is not a theory PHILOSOPHY, 18
P. is the product of wonder PHILOSOPHY, 14; WONDER, 4
P. is the replacement PHILOSOPHY, 12
p. ought to…unravel people's mental blocks PHILOSOPHY, 10
Vain wisdom all, and false p. WISDOM, 19
Western p. is…a series of footnotes to Plato's p. PHILOSOPHY, 15

phobias I have three p. which…would make my life as slick as a sonnet OBSESSIONS, 1

phone Death invented the p. TECHNOLOGY, 6
how to use…a p. box ABILITY, 2

phonus is nothing but a p. bolonus APPEARANCES, 18

photograph A p. is not only an image PHOTOGRAPHY, 8
she took down the signed p. of the Kaiser WAR, 123

photography P. can never grow up if it imitates PHOTOGRAPHY, 1
p. is a…lifetime of pleasure PHOTOGRAPHY, 2
P. is truth CINEMA, 5

physic Take p., pomp HUMILITY, 10

physical a p. and metaphysical impossibility POETS, 3

physician A p. can sometimes parry the scythe of death TIME, 28
died last night of my p. DISEASE, 30
I died…of my p. DOCTORS, 8
if the p. had the same disease upon him that I have EXAMPLE, 7
p., heal thyself DOCTORS, 2
taking a place beside the p. and the priest OCCUPATIONS, 15
The p. can bury his mistakes MISTAKES, 20
the p. cutteth off a long disease DEATH, 27

physicians P. are like kings DOCTORS, 10
the help of too many p. DOCTORS, 1

physicists p. have known sin SCIENTISTS, 5
to find out anything from the theoretical p. SCIENTISTS, 3

physics Classical p.…superseded by quantum theory SCIENCE, 45
Modern P. is an instrument of Jewry SCIENCE, 42

pianist do not shoot the p. EFFORT, 7
only p. I have ever seen who did not grimace MUSICIANS, 19

piano made such a frightful din on the p. MUSICIANS, 18

Piatigorsky Gregor P. EGOTISM, 6

Picardy Roses are flowering in P. COMPLIMENTS, 9

Picasso Nothing divides them like P. ART, 18
There's no such thing as a bad P. INFERIORITY, 4

Piccadilly Crossing P. Circus LONDON, 13
Good-bye P., Farewell Leicester Square HOMESICKNESS, 8

pick Whenever you fall, p. up something OPPORTUNITY, 8

pickle weaned on a p. APPEARANCE, 22

picnic futile to attempt a p. in Eden INNOCENCE, 4

picture If you want a p. of the future OPPRESSION, 6
It's no go the p. palace INDIFFERENCE, 4

pictures book…without p. BOOKS, 12
make my p. for people CRITICS, 4
would never buy my p. PAINTING, 6

pidgin-English I include 'p.' LANGUAGE, 20

pie Amblongus P. NONSENSE, 21

piece p. of cod passes all understanding FOOD, 36
p. of divinity in us NOBILITY, 1
Prologues precede the p. PLAYS, 4
What a p. of work is a man MANKIND, 27
When a p. gets difficult MUSICIANS, 14

pieces P. of eight MONEY, 47

pie-crust Promises and p. are made to be broken PROMISES, 7

pieman Simple Simon met a p. NURSERY RHYMES, 47

pier Like Brighton p. TRAVEL, 15

Pierian Drink deep, or taste not the P. spring KNOWLEDGE, 30

pies I could eat one of Bellamy's veal p. LAST WORDS, 52; FOOD, 44

pig when they see the half p. man PROPHECY, 8

pigeons tourists…take in the Monarchy…with…the p. LONDON, 8

piggy This little p. went to market NURSERY RHYMES, 58

pigmy That shriek and sweat in p. wars TRIVIALITY, 14

pigs And whether p. have wings NONSENSE, 9
one of Epicurus' herd of p. PRESENT, 10
the virtue of p. in a litter SOCIETY, 10

pig-sty kissed her once by the p. EXPECTATION, 6

Pilate jesting P. TRUTH, 10
P.…washed his hands GUILT, 3
rather have blood on my hands…P. COMMITMENT, 4

pilgrim p. of the sky BIRDS, 11

pilgrims strangers and p. on the earth FAITH, 4

pill Protestant women may take the P. CONTRACEPTION, 8

pillar the lie has become…a p. of the State LYING, 15
triple p. of the world LOVE, 115

pills It is an age of p. DRUGS, 10

pilot Dropping the p. DISMISSAL, 9

Pimpernel That damned elusive P. ABSENCE, 9

pin If I sit on a p. /And it punctures my skin SUFFERING, 3
See a p. and pick it up SUPERSTITION, 4
you are like a p., but without…head or…*point* BORES, 3

Pinafore Captain of the *P.* CONCEIT, 9

pinch time for me to enjoy another p. of snuff EXECUTION, 1

pinching I just keep painting till I feel like p.. Then I know it's right PAINTING, 14

pine-apple p. of politeness MALAPROPISMS, 7

pinko-gray white races are…p. RACISM, 11

pint cannot put a quart in a p. cup POSSIBILITY, 2
You spend half a p. and flush two gallons WATER, 7

pious A p. man…would be an atheist SERVILITY, 4
p. bird with the scarlet breast BIRDS, 13
p. frauds of friendship FRIENDSHIP, 18

pipe Blow your p. there CONTEMPT, 2

Piper Peter P. picked a peck of pickled pepper NURSERY RHYMES, 39

pipers Wi' a hundred p. an' a', an' a' GLORY, 4

piping Helpless, naked, p. loud BIRTH, 3
P. down the valleys wild MUSIC, 12

pips squeezed – until the p. squeak RETRIBUTION, 10

piss I can p. the old boy BOASTS, 5

pissed the last four strikes we've had, it's p. down STRIKES, 5

pissing inside my tent p. out PRUDENCE, 7

pistol a p. let off at the ear PUNS, 10

pit And wretched, blind, p. ponies ANIMALS, 12

pitcher a p. of warm spit POLITICS, 29

pitchfork drive out nature with a p.…she'll be constantly running back HUMAN NATURE, 12

pith all the p. is in the postscript LETTER-WRITING, 3

pitied one has…ceased to be an object of *fear* as soon as one is p. SYMPATHY, 5

pitiless slow, sure doom falls p. and dark HUMAN CONDITION, 15

Pitt P. is to Addington POLITICIANS, 42

pity A p. beyond all telling LOVE, 152
I thought it was a p. to get up BED, 6
knock him down first, and p. him afterwards SELF-PRESERVATION, 6
My subject is War, and the p. of War POETRY, 34
P. a human face MANKIND, 6
p. for the suffering of mankind PHILOSOPHERS, 8
The Poetry is in the p. POETRY, 34
To marry a man out of p. is folly MARRIAGE, 8
To show p. is felt as a sign of contempt SYMPATHY, 5

place A p. for everything ORDER, 6
everything in its p. ORDER, 6
firm p. to stand TECHNOLOGY, 1
give p. to better men DISMISSAL, 3
Home is the p. where HOME, 4
I go to prepare a p. for you HEAVEN, 3
Never the time and the p. PERVERSITY, 2
running…to keep in the same p. NONSENSE, 8
there's no p. like home HOME, 7
the summit of Everest was hardly the p. PHOTOGRAPHY, 5
this is an awful p. PLACES, 13
Upon the p. beneath MERCY, 2

plague A p. o' both your houses CURSES, 1

plagues of all p. with which mankind are curst CHURCH, 5

plain be yourself, imperial, p. and true SINCERITY, 1
making things p. to uninstructed people was…best means of clearing…one's own mind EDUCATION, 24
Manners are…the need of the p. MANNERS, 7

plainness perfect p. of speech…perfect nobleness BIBLE, 1

plaisir *P. d'amour* LOVE, 56

plane only two emotions in a p.: boredom and terror FLYING, 3

planet I have lived some thirty years on this p. ADVICE, 16
it fell on the wrong p. WEAPONS, 2
utterly insignificant little blue green p. SCIENCE FICTION, 1

When a new p. swims into his ken DISCOVERY, 5
plans Life...happens...while you're busy making other p. LIFE, 33
The finest p. have always been spoiled SUPPORT, 2
what a man still p....shows the...injustice in his death DEATH, 36
plant Is thy love a p. /Of such weak fibre ABSENCE, 10
The infusion of a China p. DRINKS, 1
plants bottinney means a knowledge of p. EDUCATION, 14
p. left over from the Edwardian Wilderness CHANGE, 17
plashy p. fen passes the questing vole ANIMALS, 21
plate clean your p. POLITICS, 64
the silver p. on a coffin INSULTS, 32
platitude A longitude with no p. MEANING, 4
A p. is simply a truth repeated SAYINGS, 1
platitudes Literature is the orchestration of p. LITERATURE, 20
Plato P. is dear to me TRUTH, 8
Western philosophy is...a series of footnotes to P.'s philosophy PHILOSOPHY, 15
play a good p. needs no epilogue PLAYS, 10
a p. is a dynamic thing NOVELS, 16; PLAYS, 13
behold the Englishman...p. tip-and-run ENGLISH, 13
Better than a p. HOUSES OF PARLIAMENT, 6
If you p. with fire DANGER, 2
Judge not the p. PLAYS, 8; JUDGMENT, 8
p., I remember, pleas'd not the million TASTE, 7
p.'s the thing PLAYS, 11
Play up! p. up! and p. the game WAR, 76
Rehearsing a p. is making the word flesh PLAYS, 9
The little victims p. IGNORANCE, 7
this may be p. to you, 'tis death to us SERIOUSNESS, 2
unless the p. is stopped, the child cannot...go on AUDIENCES, 2
writing a good p. is difficult PLAYS, 7
play-actors p....they're a favoured race ACTORS, 3
playboy p. of the western world LOSS, 6
player poor p., /That struts and frets his hour LIFE, 45
players men and women merely p. HUMAN CONDITION, 17
to conceal the fact that the p. cannot act ACTING, 1
play-going A good many inconveniences attend p. PLAYS, 12
plays p. about rape, sodomy and drug addiction THEATRE, 7
plaything A book that furnishes no quotations is...a p. QUOTATIONS, 9
A child's a p. for an hour CHILDREN, 33
pleasant If we do not find anything p. NOVELTY, 10
lovely and p. in their lives FRIENDSHIP, 9
p. it is to have money MONEY, 18
please go anywhere I damn well p. FREEDOM, 2
he that is married careth...how he may p. his wife MARRIAGE, 26
I...do what I p. FREEDOM, 11
Music, Maestro, P. MUSIC, 30
Natural to p. CHARACTER, 7
Nothing can permanently p. PLEASURE, 10
They...say what they p. FREEDOM, 11
pleases every prospect p. MISANTHROPY, 1
one makes lovers as fast as one p. LOVE, 42
pleasing The art of p. consists in PLEASURE, 12
the surest method...of p. EXAMPLE, 3
pleasure A fool bolts p., then complains of...indigestion DEBAUCHERY, 1
a p. in the pathless woods NATURE, 3
as much p. in the reading PLEASURE, 25
Debauchee, n. One who has...pursued p. DEBAUCHERY, 3
did p. me in his top-boots SEX, 34
dissipation without p. LONDON, 7
Everyone is dragged on by their favourite p. PLEASURE, 30
gave p. to the spectators PURITANISM, 3
greatest p....to do a good action GOOD, 8
hatred is by far the longest p. LOVE AND HATE, 1
He that takes p. to hear sermons PLEASURE, 26
I make poetry and give p....because of you INSPIRATION, 4
knowledge and wonder...is an impression of p. KNOWLEDGE, 5; WONDER, 1
Love ceases to be a p. LOVE, 21
Money gives me p. MONEY, 9
No p. without pain PLEASURE, 1
no sterner moralist than P. PLEASURE, 7
P. after all is a safer guide PLEASURE, 6
P. is...intermission of pain PLEASURE, 27
P. is...seldom found where it is sought PLEASURE, 14
P. never is at home DISCONTENT, 5
p. of your company MOUNTAINS, 2
Romanticism is...literary works...affording...p. LITERATURE, 17
that p., which is undeniably the sole motive force behind the union of the sexes SEX, 14
The only sensual p. without vice MUSIC, 26
The p. of criticizing CRITICISM, 26
the p. of offering my seat to three ladies OBESITY, 3
The sight...gave me infinite p. EXECUTION, 21
The ugliest of trades have their moments of p. OCCUPATIONS, 8
understanding will...extinguish p. POETRY, 20; UNDERSTANDING, 7
what p....they have in taking their roguish tobacco SMOKING, 9
Youth is full of p. AGE, 55
pleasure-dome A stately p. decree PLEASURE, 8
sunny p. with caves of ice PLEASURE, 9
pleasures Earth fills her lap with p. NATURE, 19
interfering with the p. of others ABSTINENCE, 9
Love and all his p. SEX, 10
Mid p. and palaces though we may roam HOME, 7
No man is a hypocrite in his p. PLEASURE, 15
One half...cannot understand the p. PLEASURE, 3
One of the p. of middle age is to *find out* that one WAS right AGE, 46
P. are all alike PLEASURE, 26
p. are their only care EXPLOITATION, 2
P. newly found are sweet PLEASURE, 32
purest of human p. GARDENS, 2
The English take their p. ENGLAND, 38
the paucity of human p. HUNTING, 5
plenty but just had p. SATISFACTION, 2
that p. should attain the poor SELF-INTEREST, 2
plods plowman homeward p. his weary way DAY, 6
plot p. hath many changes PLAYS, 8
the p. thickens INTRIGUE, 1
plough To get it ready for the p. ENGLAND, 4
We p. the fields, and scatter AGRICULTURE, 1
ploughing Is my team p. AGRICULTURE, 4
plowman The p. homeward plods his weary way DAY, 6
plowshares beat their swords into p. WAR AND PEACE, 2
pluck if thy right eye offend thee, p. it out RETRIBUTION, 7
p. till time and times are done DESIRE, 18
plural in the p. and they bounce INSULTS, 28
plus *P. ça change* CONSTANCY, 3
Plymouth dreamin'...o' P. Hoe WAR, 77
pneumatic divers experiments in Mr Boyle's P. Engine SCIENTISTS, 10
poacher a p. a keeper turned inside out OCCUPATIONS, 9
pocket carried a...brick in his p. BUSINESS, 23
smile I could feel in my hip p. SEX, 15
To be played with both hands in the p. MUSIC, 42
pockets deepest p. who can risk going to law LAW, 29
the p. of the people TAXATION, 11
Podduyev life had prepared P. for living DEATH, 118
poem A long p. is a test of invention POETRY, 23
A p. lovely as a tree TREES, 8
I do not think this p. will reach its destination CRITICISM, 51
P. me no poems POETRY, 28
poems A man does not write p. POETRY, 47
My p. are hymns of praise POETRY, 46
p....for the love of Man and in praise of God POETRY, 48
that Anon, who wrote so many p. WOMEN, 91
The few bad p....created during abstinence ABSTINENCE, 8
We all write p. POETRY, 16
poet a modern p.'s fate CRITICS, 8
A true p. does not bother to be poetical POETS, 4
English love p....composed of body, soul, and mind POETS, 20
godly p. must be chaste himself POETRY, 10
lunatic, the lover, and the p. LOVE, 121; POETRY, 43
no person can be a p....without...unsoundness of mind POETRY, 27
No p., no artist of any sort, has his complete meaning alone ARTS, 3
One dislikes to see a man and p....proclaim on the streets POETS, 26
p.'s eye, in a fine frenzy POETRY, 41
p. without love POETS, 3
The most original p. now living POETS, 41
The p. and the dreamer are distinct OPPOSITES, 3

The p. gives us his essence POETRY AND PROSE, 6
The P. of Immortal Youth POETS, 58
To be a p. is a condition POETS, 6
unmourned and unknown…because they lack their sacred p. OBLIVION, 1
poetic the laws of p. truth and p. beauty POETRY, 2
poetical A true poet does not bother to be p. POETS, 4
that werges on the p. POETRY, 13
poetry Angling is somewhat like p. FISHING, 2
As civilization advances, p.…declines CIVILIZATION, 8
complexities of p. are destroyed by the media THEATRE, 5
Critics are more malicious about p. CRITICS, 9
Even when p. has a meaning POETRY, 20; UNDERSTANDING, 7
If p. comes not…as leaves to a tree POETRY, 25
I make p. and give pleasure…because of you INSPIRATION, 4
Mr Shaw…has never written any p. WRITERS, 39
no man ever talked p. POETRY, 12
no person can…enjoy p., without…unsoundness of mind POETRY, 27
One of the purposes of p. POETRY, 45
P. is a comforting piece of fiction POETRY, 29
P. is as exact a science as geometry POETRY, 15
P. is as much a part of the universe POETRY, 7
P. is baroque POETRY AND PROSE, 4
p. is…more philosophical…than history POETRY, 1
P. is not a turning loose of emotion POETRY, 14
P. is opposed to science…prose to metre POETRY AND PROSE, 1
P. is the record of the best and happiest moments POETRY, 44
P. is the spontaneous overflow of powerful feelings POETRY, 54
P. is to prose POETRY AND PROSE, 5
P. is what gets lost in translation TRANSLATION, 3
p. makes nothing happen POETRY, 5
p. reminds him of the richness POETRY, 26
P.…set to more or less lascivious music POETRY, 29
P. should be great and unobtrusive POETRY, 24
p. sinks and swoons under…prose POETRY AND PROSE, 3
P.'s unnatural POETRY, 12
p. = the best words in the best order POETRY AND PROSE, 2
p., 'The Cinderella of the Arts.' POETRY, 33
p.…to me it's the oil of life POETRY, 6
read a little p. sometimes IGNORANCE, 8
Sculpture to me is like p. ARCHITECTURE, 7
Superstition is the p. of life SUPERSTITION, 8
that is p. POETRY, 9
The difference between genuine p. POETRY, 4
the grand style arises in p. POETRY, 3
The one…p.…continually flowing is slang LANGUAGE, 8
The P. is in the pity POETRY, 34
there is p. in peaches POETRY, 18
to resuscitate the dead art /Of p. POETRY, 36
truest p. is the most feigning POETRY, 40
What is p. POETRY, 39
poets among the English P. after my death POSTERITY, 5
excellent p. that have never versified POETS, 11
if you include me among the lyric p., I'll hold my head…high PRIDE, 5
I hate the whole race…your professional p. POETS, 12
Immature p. imitate POETS, 5
nor even booksellers have put up with p. being second-rate POETS, 8
Painters and p.…licence to dare anything FREEDOM, 18
P. and painters are outside the class system POETS, 1
p. are the ones who write in words POETRY, 16
Souls of p. dead and gone PUBLIC HOUSES, 3
point you are like a pin, but without…head or…p. BORES, 3
pointless Making money is pretty p. MONEY, 21
poison food to one man is bitter p. to others TASTE, 5
strongest p. ever known POWER, 7
treatment with p. medicines DRUGS, 13
poisoned atmosphere has been p. SPORT AND GAMES, 16
poker Malice is like a game of p. NASTINESS, 9
pokers Wreathe iron p. into true-love knots POETS, 28
pole And see all sights from p. to p. SOUL, 3
Beloved from p. to p. SLEEP, 6
One step beyond the p. EXPLORATION, 3
polecat A semi-house-trained p. INSULTS, 17
Poles few virtues…the P. do not possess PLACES, 3
police Reading isn't an occupation we encourage among p. officers POLICE, 5
The p. are the only 24-hour social service POLICE, 2
The South African P. would leave no stone unturned SOUTH AFRICA, 12
policeman A p.'s lot is not a happy one POLICE, 1
park, a p. and a pretty girl HUMOUR, 5
the air of someone who is lying…to a p. POLICE, 7
The terrorist and the p. EQUALITY, 7
policemen how young the p. look AGE, 32
P. are numbered POLICE, 3
repressed sadists…become p. or butchers PUBLISHING, 6
polished p. up the handle of the big front door OFFICERS, 6
Satire should, like a p. razor keen SATIRE, 2
whole man in himself, p. and well-rounded CHARACTER, 12
polite it costs nothing to be p. DIPLOMACY, 7
p. by telling lies COURTESY, 3
time to be p. ENGLISH, 26
politeness pine-apple of p. MALAPROPISMS, 7
P. is organised indifference MANNERS, 6
Punctuality is the p. of kings PROMPTNESS, 2
political addiction of p. groups to ideas POLITICS, 27
After all, we are not p. whores POLITICS, 56
Every intellectual attitude is latently p. POLITICS, 52
Jesus was…a first-rate p. economist CHRISTIANITY, 38
most schemes of p. improvement are very laughable POLITICS, 40
one of these is the history of p. power HISTORY, 22
p. speech and writing are largely the defence of the indefensible POLITICS, 58
That points clearly to a p. career POLITICIANS, 24
the formation of the p. will of the nation POLITICS, 36
When in the course of human events, it becomes necessary for one people to dissolve…p. bonds INDEPENDENCE, 2
political correctness P. is a really inane concept POLITICAL CORRECTNESS, 4
politician a p. is an arse POLITICIANS, 3
A p. is a statesman…with an open mouth POLITICIANS, 26
A statesman is a p. who POLITICIANS, 19
A statesman is a p. who's been dead POLITICIANS, 29
at home you're just a p. POLITICIANS, 17
Coffee which makes the p. wise DRINKS, 6
like a scurvy p., seem /To see the things thou dost not. POLITICIANS, 23
p. never believes what he says POLITICIANS, 7
the p. poses as the servant POLITICIANS, 8
unfair to expect a p. to live…up to the statements he makes in public POLITICIANS, 18
politicians All p. have vanity POLITICIANS, 25
It is a pity…that more p. are not bastards POLITICIANS, 31
P.…can never forgive being ignored POLITICIANS, 30
P. neither love nor hate POLITICIANS, 6
P.…promise to build bridges POLITICIANS, 14
politics are too serious…to be left to the p. POLITICIANS, 9
There is just one rule for p. POLITICS, 28
politics An independent…wants to take the p. out of p. POLITICS, 75
A week is a long time in p. POLITICS, 92
Britain is no longer in the p. of the pendulum POLITICS, 81
History is past p. POLITICS, 66; HISTORY, 25
I am not made for p. POLITICS, 15
In p.…ask a woman POLITICIANS, 28
in p. there is no heart, only head POLITICS, 57
making p. Christian RELIGION, 49
Men who have greatness…don't go in for p. POLITICIANS, 2
P. are now nothing more than POLITICS, 41
p. are too serious…to be left to the politicians POLITICIANS, 9
P. come from man. Mercy POLITICS, 84
P. is a blood sport POLITICS, 6
P. is not an exact science POLITICS, 8
P. is not a science…but an art POLITICS, 9
P. is the art of preventing people from taking part POLITICS, 82
P. is…the only profession POLITICS, 76
P.…the systematic organisation of hatreds POLITICS, 1
p. was the second lowest profession POLITICS, 59
that men enter local p. MARRIAGE, 90
The more you read about p. POLITICS, 62
There are times in p. POLITICS, 26
they can at least pretend that p. is a game HOUSES OF PARLIAMENT, 14
War is the continuation of p. MISQUOTATIONS, 14; WAR, 30, 63

polling Now we can go to the p. booth without a bad conscience SOUTH AFRICA, 3
polloi the multitude, the *hoi p.* PUBLIC, 10
polluter intelligence is the great p. ENVIRONMENT, 5
pollution indefatigable and unsavoury engine of p. DOGS, 12
Polly P. put the kettle on NURSERY RHYMES, 40
polygamy P. was made a Sin RELIGION, 19
Pomeranian The healthy bones of a single P. grenadier DIPLOMACY, 4
pomp In lowly p. ride on to die CHRISTIANITY, 32
Pride, p., and circumstance WAR, 108
Take physic, p. HUMILITY, 10
pompous A p. woman…complaining that the head-waiter EGOTISM, 9
p. in the grave MANKIND, 9
Poms All the faces…seem to be bloody P. ENGLISH, 11
I never could cop P. INSULTS, 38
ponies And wretched, blind, pit p. ANIMALS, 12
pony I had a little p., /His name was Dapple Grey NURSERY RHYMES, 21
poodle Mr Balfour's P. HOUSES OF PARLIAMENT, 12
Pooh-Bah P. (Lord High Everything Else) TITLES, 4
poor A p. man is despised the whole world over POVERTY, 19
a p. society cannot be too p. POVERTY AND WEALTH, 8
ask of the p. that they get up and act POVERTY, 14
decent means p. RESPECTABILITY, 3
Few, save the p., feel for the p. POVERTY, 24
give to the p. MATERIALISM, 3
great men have their p. relations FAMILY, 10
Hard to train to accept being p. POVERTY, 18
I, being p., have only my dreams POVERTY, 34
I can dare to be p. POVERTY, 11
I have nothing; the rest I leave to the p. LAST WORDS, 54
inconvenient to be p. POVERTY, 5
it is p. grub, p. pay, and easy work AMERICA, 24; ENGLAND, 25
It's the p. wot gets the blame POVERTY AND WEALTH, 1
Laws grind the p. LAW, 14
only the p.…are forbidden to beg POVERTY, 10
only the p. who pay cash MONEY, 23
p. have no right to the property of the rich POVERTY AND WEALTH, 6
P. Little Rich Girl WEALTH, 10
p. relation FAMILY, 18
Resolve not to be p. POVERTY, 20
She was p. but she was honest POVERTY AND WEALTH, 1
short and simple annals of the p. POVERTY, 13
that plenty should attain the p. SELF-INTEREST, 2
the p. are our brothers and sisters POVERTY, 31
the p.…need love…have to be wanted POVERTY, 31
the p. person…thinks money would help MONEY, 29
The p.…their function…is to exercise our generosity POVERTY, 28
Though I be p., I'm honest HONESTY, 6
To be p. and independent POVERTY, 4
very p. are unthinkable POVERTY, 9
What fun it would be to be p. EXCESS, 2
poorer for richer for p. MARRIAGE, 30
poorest p. man may in his cottage bid defiance to…the Crown PRIVACY, 4
pop In England, p. art and fine art ART, 16
poplars The p. are felled TREES, 3
poppies the p. blow MEMORIALS, 8
populace society distributes itself into Barbarians, Philistines, and P. AMERICA, 1
the p. cannot exact their demands HOUSES OF PARLIAMENT, 19
this vast residuum we may…give the name of P. PUBLIC, 2
popular Nothing can render them p. CLERGY, 14
The worse I do, the more p. I get POPULARITY, 5
We're more p. than Jesus Christ POP MUSIC, 14; POPULARITY, 6
popularity I don't resent his p. POPULARITY, 8
P.?…glory's small change POPULARITY, 4
P. is a crime POPULARITY, 3
population a starving p. IRELAND, 6
P. growth…environmental damage CONSERVATION, 3
P.…increases in a geometrical ratio ECONOMICS, 16
populi *vox p., vox dei* PUBLIC, 1
populism p. that rejects anything different DEMOCRACY, 4
porcupines I shall throw two p. under you THREATS, 2
Porlock by a person on business from P. INTERRUPTIONS, 1
pornography P. is the attempt to insult sex PORNOGRAPHY, 3
p.…it is terribly, terribly boring PORNOGRAPHY, 2
p. of war WAR, 88
show that gives p. a bad name PORNOGRAPHY, 1
You don't get any p.…on the telly PORNOGRAPHY, 6
port Any p. in a storm DANGER, 1
'it would be p. if it could' ALCOHOL, 11
porter Oh, mister p., what shall I do TRAINS, 5
portion best p. of a good man's life KINDNESS, 7
portions P. and parcels of the dreadful Past TIME, 37
portrait Every man's work…is always a p. of himself ARTS, 1
Every time I paint a p. I lose a friend PAINTING, 15
not paint a p. to look like the subject ARTISTS, 13
portraits P. of famous bards and preachers PAINTING, 16
portraying What sort of God are we p. GOD, 20
posh only two p. papers on a Sunday NEWSPAPERS, 10
posies beds of roses…fragrant p. FLOWERS, 7
position only one p. for an artist WALES, 3
possessing too dear for my p. PARTING, 11
possession Marconi's most cherished p. TECHNOLOGY, 11
No human relation gives one p. in another UNITY, 10
P. is nine points LAW, 4
The p. of a book OSTENTATION, 2
the p. of it is intolerable MATERIALISM, 19
possessions Not the owner of many p. will you be right to call happy HAPPINESS, 9
p. for a moment of time LAST WORDS, 22
possibility How great a p. POETS, 25
too much of a sceptic to deny the p. of anything SCEPTICISM, 2
possible something is p., he is…right SCIENCE, 6
the art of the p. POLITICS, 13
post p. of honour is a private station VICE, 1
post-chaise I would spend my life in driving briskly in a p. PLEASURE, 16
posterity doing something for p. POSTERITY, 2
The nations which have put mankind and p. most in their debt NATIONS, 2
Think of your p. POSTERITY, 1
Thy p. shall sway ENGLAND, 13
postgraduate The British p. student is a lonely forlorn soul EDUCATION, 31
post-Natal is it p. depression SOUTH AFRICA, 7
postscript all the pith is in the p. LETTER-WRITING, 3
that which was most material in the p. LETTER-WRITING, 2
postures It requires one to assume such indecent p. CRICKET, 9
potent how p. cheap music is MUSIC, 16; POP MUSIC, 9
potter Who *is* the P. CREATION, 10
poultry A p. matter MONEY, 33; PUNS, 13
pound the p.…in your pocket ECONOMICS, 22
pounds My dear fellow…I only ask you for twenty-five p. BORROWING, 11
the p. will take care of themselves THRIFT, 4
two hundred p. a year MONEY, 15
pouvait *si vieillesse p.* AGE, 24
poverty a darn is…p. THRIFT, 10
crime so shameful as p. POVERTY, 8
Do you call p. a crime POVERTY, 30
from nothing to a state of extreme p. POVERTY, 26
generations…have struggled in p. to build these altars RELIGION, 53
If p. is the mother of crime, stupidity is its father CRIME, 5
It is easy enough to say that p. is no crime POVERTY, 19
Loneliness…is the most terrible p. LONELINESS, 7
Notwithstanding the p. of my…experience CONTENTMENT, 4
P. and oysters POVERTY, 6
p.…is a blunder POVERTY, 19
P. is a great enemy to human happiness POVERTY, 20
P. is an anomaly to rich people HUNGER, 2
P. is not a crime POVERTY, 2
P., therefore, was comparative POVERTY, 7
The misfortunes of p. POVERTY, 21
three great evils, boredom, vice, and p. WORK, 24
world p. is primarily a problem of two million villages POVERTY, 29
powder keep your p. dry PRUDENCE, 6
when your p.'s runnin' low PATRIOTISM, 21
powdered Stratford…suggests p. history ENGLAND, 19
power All that is literature seeks to communicate p. BOOKS, 16
As we make sex less secretive, we may rob it of its p. SEX, 56
corridors of p. POWER, 22
Germany will be…a world p. GERMANY, 14

greater the p. POWER, 8
He aspired to p. POWER, 25
If, drunk with sight of p., we loose BOASTS, 4
in office but not in p. GOVERNMENT, 14
its source of p.: ownership CAPITALISM, 6
Knowledge itself is p. KNOWLEDGE, 3
love of p. is the love of ourselves FREEDOM, 15
Men of p. have not time to read POWER, 11
one of these is the history of political p. HISTORY, 22
P.…and Liberty…are seldom upon good Terms POWER, 12; FREEDOM, 14
p. before his hair turned white was called a whizz-kid POWER, 13
P. corrupts POWER, 24
p. is apt to corrupt POWER, 19
P. is the ultimate aphrodisiac POWER, 14
P.?…like a dead sea fruit POWER, 15
P. tends to corrupt POWER, 3
p. without responsibility RESPONSIBILITY, 2, 9; JOURNALISM, 2
The accursed p. which stands on Privilege POLITICS, 4
The balance of p. POWER, 27
the blacks must oppress them today because they have p. POWER, 16
the kingdom of God is not in word, but in p. GOD, 12
they…take, who have the p. POWER, 28
War knows no p. WAR, 19
When p. narrows the areas of man's concern POETRY, 26
wrong sort of people are always in p. POWER, 29
You only have p. over people POWER, 23

powerful Guns will make us p. POWER POLITICS, 3
The rich and p. know GOD, 2

powerless Brief and p. HUMAN CONDITION, 15

powers a taste for *hidden* and *forbidden* p. SCIENCE, 31
Headmasters have p. EDUCATION, 12
the p. of a first-rate man and the creed of a second-rate man POLITICIANS, 1

pox You will die either on the gallows, or of the p. REPARTEE, 5

practical Compassion is…an absolutely p. belief SOCIALISM, 8
meddling with any p. part of life OBJECTIVITY, 2
P. men…are usually the slaves of some defunct economist INFLUENCE, 6

practice a thing may look evil in theory…in p. excellent THEORY, 1
P. makes perfect EXPERIENCE, 5

practiced thirty-seven years I've p. GENIUS, 8

practise P. what you preach EXAMPLE, 1
two kinds of morality…one which we preach but do not p. MORALITY, 13

praise bury Caesar, not to p. him EVIL, 16
Damn with faint p. CRITICISM, 40
envy is a kind of p. ENVY, 6
if we p. ourselves fearlessly, something will always stick PRAISE, 2
I will p. any man that will p. me FLATTERY, 7
Let us with a gladsome mind /P. the Lord GOD, 37
My poems are hymns of p. POETRY, 46
Pavilioned in splendour, and girded with p. GOD, 23
People…only want p. CRITICISM, 34
P. the Lord and pass the ammunition WAR, 37
The moment you p. a book BOOKS, 26
this blest man, let his just p. be given COMPLIMENTS, 8
To refuse p. PRAISE, 6
we but p. ourselves in other men PRAISE, 5

praises He who p. everybody INSINCERITY, 2
The idiot who p.…every country but his own DISCONTENT, 2
yet he p. those who follow different paths DISCONTENT, 4

praising advantage of…p.…oneself PRAISE, 4

pram sombre enemy of good art than the p. BABIES, 1

pray p. for you at St Paul's PRAYER, 16
P. to God and say the lines ACTING, 5
watch and p. IMPERFECTION, 4
when ye p., use not vain repetitions PRAYER, 4

praye Fare well…and p. for me FAMILY, 25

prayed I wish that God had not given me what I p. for DISAPPOINTMENT, 7

prayer More things are wrought by p. PRAYER, 17
P. makes the Christian's armour bright PRAYER, 10
storms of p. EXCESS, 14
The people's p. DREAMS, 5
The p. that…heals the sick FAITH, 10

prayers better than good men's p. PRAYER, 7

prayeth He p. well PRAYER, 8

prays man p.…for a miracle PRAYER, 18

preach two kinds of morality…one which we p. but do not practise MORALITY, 13

preachers Portraits of famous bards and p. PAINTING, 16
P. say, Do as I say, not as I do EXAMPLE, 7

preaching A woman's p. is like a dog's walking on his hinder legs WOMEN, 41

precedency the point of p. between a louse and a flea POETS, 9

precedent A p. embalms a principle EXAMPLE, 6

precious Right is more p. RIGHT, 4
so p. that it must be rationed FREEDOM, 27

precisely thinking too p. on th' event COWARDICE, 7

pre-cognitive Love means the p. flow LOVE, 81

predestination Free Will and P. DESTINY, 5

predicament Life…is a p. LIFE, 42

predictions cut back on p. DOCTORS, 6
Dreams and p. DREAMS, 1

prefabricated a better word than…p. WORDS, 6

preferable There are only opinions, some of which are p. TRUTH, 29

preferment P.'s door PROMOTION, 1

preferred he…coming after me is p. before me CHRISTIANITY, 11

pregnancy quite lawful for a Catholic woman to avoid p. by…mathematics CONTRACEPTION, 5
to imagine that p. was ever intended to be a sickness PREGNANCY, 2

pregnant a little inflation is like being a little p. ECONOMICS, 10

prejudge I do not…p. the past PREJUDICE, 6

prejudice I am free of all p. HATE, 3
skilled appeals to religious p. EVOLUTION, 10

prejudices collection of p. which is called political philosophy POLITICS, 65
Common sense is the collection of p. PREJUDICE, 3
freedom to print…proprietor's p. JOURNALISM, 30

premise fundamental p. of a revolution REVOLUTION, 8

pre-natal the greatness of Russia is only her p. struggling RUSSIA, 4

preparation life…seems to me p. for something that never happens LIFE, 55
no p. is thought necessary POLITICS, 76

prepare I go to p. a place for you HEAVEN, 3
I p. for a journey…as though for death TRAVEL, 17

prerogative p. of the eunuch RESPONSIBILITY, 14

presbyter P. is but old Priest writ large RELIGION, 45

prescribed the taking of things p. PATIENTS, 1

presence A certain person may have…a wonderful p. CHARACTER, 21

present an un-birthday p. GIFTS, 3
novelists the story of the p. NOVELS, 6
P. mirth hath present laughter PRESENT, 13
to know nothing but the p., or nothing but the past CONSERVATISM, 4

preserve p. one last male thing MASCULINITY, 2

president American…prepared to run for P. POLITICS, 83
anybody could become P. POLITICIANS, 4
I'd rather be right than p. RIGHT, 3
nobody is strongminded around a P. SERVILITY, 6
one thing about being P. POWER, 10
P. spends…time kissing people PERSUASION, 4
the P. is dead, but the Government lives ASSASSINATION, 2
We are all the P.'s men LOYALTY, 7

press a gentleman of the P. JOURNALISM, 17
Never lose your temper with the P. SELF-CONTROL, 7
would not say that our P. is obscene JOURNALISM, 20

presume Dr Livingstone, I p. GREETINGS, 3
Know then thyself, p. not God to scan SELF-KNOWLEDGE, 5

pretending p. to be wicked HYPOCRISY, 18

pretty a p. girl who naked is NAKEDNESS, 3
One girl can be p. BEAUTY, 18
There's only one p. child CHILDREN, 2

Preux Saint P. never kicked the fireirons IMPERFECTION, 5

preventing Politics is the art of p. people from taking part POLITICS, 82

prevention P. is better than cure PRUDENCE, 4

prevents Nothing p. us from being natural SPONTANEITY, 4
Time…p. everything from happening TIME, 41

prey lord of all things, yet a p. to all HUMAN CONDITION, 14

price a better p. than old mistresses PAINTING, 1
Courage is the p.…for granting peace COURAGE, 12

her p. is far above rubies WOMEN, 17
P. of Herald three cents daily NEWSPAPERS, 3; TELEGRAMS, 4
p. which is too great to pay for peace WORLD WAR I, 28
The p....for pursuing any profession DISILLUSION, 1
the p. of everything and the value of nothing CYNICISM, 5
those men have their p. CORRUPTION, 10
Who never knew the p. of happiness HAPPINESS, 33
prick If you p. us, do we not bleed EQUALITY, 22
p. the sides of my intent AMBITION, 16
pride A mother's p. EXPECTATION, 5
contempt on all my p. HUMILITY, 13
Is P., the never-failing vice of fools PRIDE, 8
it is p., but understood in a different way PRIDE, 11
P. and Truth...That long to give themselves for...youth AGE, 71
P. goeth before destruction MISQUOTATIONS, 10; PRIDE, 1
p. that licks the dust SERVILITY, 5
So sleeps the p. of former days IRELAND, 13
the kind of p. least likely to offend MODESTY, 5
There is false modesty, but there is no false p. PRIDE, 9
Pride and Prejudice I had not seen *P.* WRITERS, 36
prides His Royal Highness...p. himself upon...the excellent harvest ARROGANCE, 7
priest A p. sees people at their best OCCUPATIONS, 1
For a p. to turn a man when he lies a-dying PERSUASION, 3
Presbyter is but old P. writ large RELIGION, 45
p. is a man who is called Father CATHOLICISM, 1
rid me of this turbulent p. ASSASSINATION, 4
taking a place beside the physician and the p. OCCUPATIONS, 15
That waked the p. all shaven and shorn NURSERY RHYMES, 57
That whisky p. CLERGY, 8
priest-craft e'r P. did begin RELIGION, 19
priesthood Literary men are...a perpetual p. WRITERS, 4
priests All things, oh p., are on fire FIRE, 1
I always like to associate with a lot of p. CLERGY, 1
treen chalices and golden p. CLERGY, 9
prima They are for p. donnas or corpses FLOWERS, 11
prime having lost...your p. MARRIAGE, 71
One's p. is elusive AGE, 58
prime minister society...pays a harlot 25 times as much as it pays its P. INJUSTICE, 14
that of P. is filled by fluke POLITICIANS, 21
when a British P. sneezed BRITAIN, 12
prime ministers rogue elephant among British p. POLITICIANS, 65
primitive The classics are only p. literature CLASSICS, 6
primroses smiles, /Wan as p. FLOWERS, 5
Prince of Wales first P....not to have a mistress ADULTERY, 6
who's danced with the P. SNOBBERY, 4
princes mine were p. of the earth JEWS, 2
p. learn no art truly, but...horsemanship HORSES, 7
principal It is not my interest to pay the p. BORROWING, 10
principle A precedent embalms a p. EXAMPLE, 6
except from some strong p. MOTIVE, 4
the most useful thing about a p....sacrificed to expediency EXPEDIENCY, 4
the p. seems the same WATER, 1
you never can tell. That's a p. PRINCIPLES, 4
principles All universal moral p. are idle fancies MORALITY, 14
And wrote 'P. of Political Economy' ECONOMICS, 3
easier to fight for one's p. PRINCIPLES, 1
If one sticks too rigidly to one's p. PRINCIPLES, 2
miracle...which subverts all the p. of his understanding CHRISTIANITY, 29
The p. of a free constitution GOVERNMENT, 10
The p. of logic and metaphysics are true PHILOSOPHY, 1
Whenever two good people argue over p. PRINCIPLES, 3
whether I embrace your lordship's p. or your mistress REPARTEE, 5
print decomposing in the eternity of p. CRITICISM, 55
news that's fit to p. NEWSPAPERS, 9
pleasant, sure, to see one's name in p. BOOKS, 10
The big p. giveth and the fine p. taketh away BUSINESS, 20
The large p. giveth COMMERCIALISM, 4
printers those books by which the p. have lost BOOKS, 19
printing Gunpowder, P., and the Protestant Religion CIVILIZATION, 3
priorities The language of p. SOCIALISM, 2
prison an extraordinarily pleasant p. LEXICOGRAPHY, 1
Anyone who has been to...public school will...feel...at home in p. EDUCATION, 62
Stone walls do not a p. make IMPRISONMENT, 4
the true place for a just man is also a p. JUSTICE, 24
The world...is but a large p. EXECUTION, 23
prisoner I object to your being taken p. ROYALTY, 21
Peace took them all p. WAR AND PEACE, 9
P., God has given you good abilities THEFT, 3
prisoners If this is the way Queen Victoria treats her p. IMPRISONMENT, 11
p. cannot enter into contracts SOUTH AFRICA, 9
p. of addiction and...prisoners of envy MATERIALISM, 10
prisons not enough p....in Palestine to hold all the Jews JEWS, 10
P. are built with stones of Law HYPOCRISY, 4
privacy a right to share your p. in a public place PRIVACY, 5
That should assure us of...forty-five minutes of undisturbed p. INATTENTION, 2
private He was meddling too much in my p. life PSYCHIATRY, 12
P. Means is dead PUNS, 20
Scientific discovery is a p. event SCIENCE, 29
sex has been a very p., secretive activity SEX, 56
The grave's a fine and p. place DEATH, 82
Travel is the most p. of pleasures TRAVEL, 19
Whatsoever...the p. calamity, I hope it will not interfere with the public business of the country FIRE, 3
when religion is allowed to invade...p. life RELIGION, 43
privilege a defender of p. PESSIMISM, 2
an Englishman's heaven-born p. of doing as he likes PUBLIC, 2
The accursed power which stands on P. POLITICS, 4
prize Men p. the thing ungain'd DESIRE, 14
Not all that tempts your wand'ring eyes...is lawful p. TEMPTATION, 6
prizes just miss the p. at the flower show MEDIOCRITY, 3
The world continues to offer glittering p. RUTHLESSNESS, 6
P.R.O partly a liaison man and partly P. BUSINESS, 4
problem ineffectual liberal's p. LIBERALISM, 1
Not every p. someone has with his girlfriend CAPITALISM, 8
P. children tend to grow up into p. adults FAMILY, 11
the p. as I see it LANGUAGE, 6
problems Among the many p....the choice of the moment WRITERS, 21
There are two p. in my life POLITICIANS, 5
procession A torchlight p. ALCOHOL, 46
prodigal P. of Ease WORLD-WEARINESS, 1
producing Man...consumes without p. CAPITALISM, 10
production Capitalist p. begets...its own negation CAPITALISM, 9
profession Politics is...the only p. POLITICS, 76
The price...for pursuing any p. DISILLUSION, 1
professional will not support...p. slavery EXPLOITATION, 4
professor A p. is one who talks in someone else's sleep ACADEMICS, 1
professors American p. like their literature clear and cold LITERATURE, 11
Culture is an instrument wielded by p. CULTURE, 3
duty of government to protect all...p. GOVERNMENT, 23
now-a-days p. of philosophy but not philosophers PHILOSOPHERS, 10
profit count as p. every day that Fate allows you PRESENT, 8
No p. grows where is no pleasure EDUCATION, 49
Philosophers never balance between p. and honesty PHILOSOPHERS, 4
trouble with the p. system BUSINESS, 27
profound turbid look the most p. WRITING, 18
progeny A p. of learning MALAPROPISMS, 3
progress All p. is based PROGRESS, 2; EXTRAVAGANCE, 2
Man's 'p.' is but a gradual discovery PROGRESS, 12
Our p..../Is trouble and care LIFE, 34
P....depends on retentiveness HISTORY, 23
'p.' is simply a comparative PROGRESS, 3
the things which government does...social p. GOVERNMENT, 32
What p....In the Middle Ages PSYCHOLOGY, 1
What we call p. is PROGRESS, 5
progression Without Contraries is no p. CONFLICT, 4
prohibition Communism is like p. COMMUNISM, 6
proletarian you are polite to a p. you...bolster up the capitalist system POLITICS, 88
proletariat The dictatorship of the p. MARXISM, 5
the p. will...wage a class struggle for Socialism CLASS, 18
prologues P. precede the piece PLAYS, 4

prolonged the War is being deliberately p. WAR, 103
promise A p. made is a debt unpaid PROMISES, 5
rarely…one can see in a little boy the p. of a man CHILDREN, 20
promised Only do always in health what you have often p. to do when you are sick ILLNESS, 14
promises P. and pie-crust are made to be broken PROMISES, 7
young man of p. CHURCHILL, 3
promisin' Once you were so p. SHYNESS, 3
promptly He gives twice who gives p. PROMPTNESS, 4
pronounce foreigners…spell better than they p. PRONUNCIATION, 3; SPELLING, 2
last words which I should p. in this Academy ARTISTS, 18
p. foreign names as he chooses PRONUNCIATION, 1
spell it Vinci and p. it Vinchy PRONUNCIATION, 3; SPELLING, 2
pronouncements Science should leave off making p. SCIENCE, 24
propaganda P.…consists in nearly deceiving your friends PROPAGANDA, 1
propagated If human beings could be p.…aristocracy would be…sound ARISTOCRACY, 7
propagation Women exist…solely for the p. of the species WOMAN'S ROLE, 5
propensities the silk stockings and white bosoms… excite my amorous p. LUST, 3
proper He never does a p. thing without…an improper reason MORALITY, 17
The p. study of Mankind is Man SELF-KNOWLEDGE, 5
property poor have no right to the p. of the rich POVERTY AND WEALTH, 6
P. has its duties CAPITALISM, 2
P. is organised robbery CAPITALISM, 13
P. is theft CAPITALISM, 12
The future is the only kind of p. SLAVERY, 1
the right of governing was not p. but a trust GOVERNMENT, 9
prophecies bring about the verification of his own p. PROPHECY, 13
prophet A historian is a p. in reverse HISTORIANS, 6
a p. is not without honour HONOUR, 1
there arose not a p.…like unto Moses PROPHECY, 2
The sons of the p. were brave men and bold COURAGE, 1
proportion strangeness in the p. BEAUTY, 7
proportional representation P.…fundamentally counter-democratic POLITICS, 43
proposes Man p. GOD, 30
proposition undesirable to believe a p. SCEPTICISM, 4
propriety The p. of…having improper thoughts MORALITY, 4
prose anything except bad p. PROSE, 2
architecture like p. ARCHITECTURE, 7
difference between…p. and metrical composition POETRY AND PROSE, 7
I can only write p. today POETRY AND PROSE, 8
I have been talking p. for over forty years PROSE, 3
no one hears his own remarks as p. PROSE, 1
Poetry is opposed to science…p. to metre POETRY AND PROSE, 1
Poetry is to p. POETRY AND PROSE, 5
poetry sinks and swoons under…p. POETRY AND PROSE, 3
P.…can bear a great deal of poetry POETRY AND PROSE, 3
p. = words in their best order POETRY AND PROSE, 2
the p. for God LANGUAGE, 13
to write good p. is an affair of good manners POETRY AND PROSE, 4
prosper Treason doth never p. TREASON, 3
prosperitee A man to have ben in p. MISFORTUNE, 7
him that stood in greet p. MISFORTUNE, 6
prosperity P. doth best discover vice MISFORTUNE, 3
prostitute I don't think a p. is more moral WOMEN, 61
prostitutes the small nations like p. DIPLOMACY, 13
prostitution P.…keeps her out of trouble SEX, 23
P.…provides fresh air and wholesome exercise SEX, 23
protect p. the writer BUREAUCRACY, 1
protest lady doth p. too much EXCESS, 8
Protestant A P. with a horse NATIONALITY, 2
Gunpowder, Printing, and the P. Religion CIVILIZATION, 3
I am the P. whore RELIGION, 30
P. women may take the Pill CONTRACEPTION, 8
Too much counterpoint; what is worse, P. counterpoint CRITICISM, 3
Protestantism The chief contribution of P. to human thought PROTESTANTISM, 1
Protestants God knows how you P.…have any sense of direction CATHOLICISM, 12
P. protesting against Protestantism CATHOLICISM, 7
Proteus P. rising from the sea DISCONTENT, 10
protozoon Organic life…has developed…from the p. to the philosopher PROGRESS, 11
proud Death be not p. DEATH, 44
He who does not need to lie is p. LYING, 13
I am p. to have a son PRIDE, 10
no guarantee…you will not be p. of the feat HUMILITY, 4
p. me no prouds GRATITUDE, 4
too p. to fight WAR, 133; WORLD WAR I, 26
Yes; I am p. PRIDE, 7
proudest the moment of greatest humiliation is…when the spirit is p. PRIDE, 6
Proust Where is the P. of Papua POLITICAL CORRECTNESS, 2
prove p. anything by figures STATISTICS, 1
proved p. upon our pulses PHILOSOPHY, 8
What is now p. was…imagined PROOF, 2
proverb A p. is much matter SAYINGS, 4
no p. to you till your life has illustrated it EXPERIENCE, 17
p. is one man's wit and all men's wisdom SAYINGS, 6
proverbs p. provide them with wisdom STUPIDITY, 9
provided Add: 'p. he is really dead' ADMIRATION, 6
providence a kind of P. will…end…the acts of God DISASTER, 2
fathom the inscrutable workings of P. REPARTEE, 4
that P. dictates with the assurance of a sleepwalker TINY, 12
This is the temple of P. LUCK, 7
providential a case /of P. interference LUCK, 12
province all knowledge to be my p. KNOWLEDGE, 4
provinces The reluctant obedience of distant p. DIPLOMACY, 16
provincial worse than p. – he was parochial WRITERS, 60
provincialism rather be taken in adultery than…p. FASHION, 4
provocations To great evils we submit; we resent little p. TRIVIALITY, 9
provoke p. not your children FATHERS, 3
P. /The years OLD AGE, 53
provoked an opportunity of being p. PROVOCATION, 1
provokes No one p. me with impunity RETRIBUTION, 2
prude twenty is no age to be a p. PRUDERY, 2
prudence freedom of speech, freedom of conscience, and the p. never to practise…them FREEDOM, 51
Psyche Your mournful P. SOUL, 9
psychiatrist And a p. is the man who collects the rent PSYCHIATRY, 11
Anybody who goes to see a p. PSYCHIATRY, 4
A p. is a man who goes to the Folies-Bergère PSYCHIATRY, 9
the century of the p.'s couch PSYCHIATRY, 8
psychiatrists P. classify a person as neurotic PSYCHIATRY, 10
psychic p. development of the individual PSYCHIATRY, 3
psychological historian fits a man for p. analysis PSYCHOLOGY, 2
There is no such thing as p. CHARACTER, 20
psychology Children…have no use for p.. They detest sociology BOOKS, 39
psychopathologist the p. the unspeakable PSYCHIATRY, 7
psychotic A p. is the man who lives in it PSYCHIATRY, 11
Psychiatrists classify a person as…p. PSYCHIATRY, 10
puberty We are all American at p. NATIONALITY, 10
public a more mean, stupid…ungrateful animal than the p. PUBLIC, 13
a right to share your privacy in a p. place PRIVACY, 5
enjoy a p. school EDUCATION, 13
false to his friends…true to the p. HONESTY, 3
flinging a pot of paint in the p.'s face CRITICISM, 45
give the p. what they want to see and they'll come out for it FUNERALS, 8
If the British p. falls for this…it will be…bonkers POLITICS, 32
I hope it will not interfere with the p. business of the country FIRE, 3
Never lose your temper with…the p. SELF-CONTROL, 7
not describe holding p. office GOVERNMENT, 1
Not even a p. figure POLITICIANS, 50
obligations, both personal and p. HOSTAGES, 2
p. school, where…learning was painfully beaten into him EDUCATION, 43
strike against p. safety STRIKES, 2
The p. be damned. I am working for my stockholders CAPITALISM, 15

The p. buys its opinions as it buys its meat PUBLIC, 7
The p. doesn't give a damn MUSIC, 7
The P. is an old woman PUBLIC, 8
three things…the p. will always clamour for NOVELTY, 3
transform this society without a major extension of p. ownership SOCIALISM, 9
twenty years of marriage make her…like a p. building MARRIAGE, 132
publicity Any p. is good p. ADVERTISING, 1
public school Anyone who has been to…p. will…feel…at home in prison EDUCATION, 62
Keats's vulgarity with a P. accent CRITICISM, 28
the p. system all over EDUCATION, 61
public schools p. are the nurseries of all vice EDUCATION, 16
public transport more money spent on p. CARS, 2
publish I'll p., right or wrong PUBLISHING, 3
P. and be damned PUBLISHING, 11
p. and be sued PUBLISHING, 8
published not so much p. as carried screaming NEWSPAPERS, 16
you may destroy whatever you haven't p. PUBLISHING, 7
publisher Barabbas was a p. PUBLISHING, 4
publishers those with irrational fear of life become p. PUBLISHING, 6
publishing I would have done an easier job like p. PUBLISHING, 2
p. faster than you think PUBLISHING, 10
puffeth knowledge p. up, but charity edifieth CHARITY, 7; KNOWLEDGE, 8
pulse two people with one p. LOVE, 86
pulses proved upon our p. PHILOSOPHY, 8
pumpkin coach has turned into a p. DISILLUSION, 3
pun A man who could make so vile a p. PUNS, 3
punctuality P. is the politeness of kings PROMPTNESS, 2
P. is the virtue of the bored PROMPTNESS, 5
punished Am I not p. enough in not being born an Englishman NATIONALITY, 9
Men are rewarded and p. not for what they do MOTIVE, 6
Those who offend us are generally p. REVENGE, 14
punishing p. anyone who comes between them MARRIAGE, 110
punishment Corporal p. is…humiliating for him who gives it PUNISHMENT, 13
let the p. fit the crime PUNISHMENT, 10
P. is not for revenge PUNISHMENT, 8
Virtue is its own p. RIGHTEOUSNESS, 2
punishments In nature there are neither rewards nor p. NATURE, 11
pupils Time is a great teacher, but…kills all its p. TIME, 11
puppy Frogs and snails /And p.-dogs' tails NURSERY RHYMES, 65
purchasers a pattern to encourage p. BUSINESS, 23
pure Because my heart is p. INTEGRITY, 7
p. as the driven slush PURITY, 2
purgatory the p. of men ENGLAND, 17
puritan A p.'s a person who pours righteous indignation PURITANISM, 1
The P. hated bear-baiting PURITANISM, 3
To the P. all things are impure PURITANISM, 2
puritanism P. – The haunting fear that someone… may be happy PURITANISM, 4
purity I have laboured to refine our language to grammatical p. LANGUAGE, 14
purple-stained And p. mouth ALCOHOL, 37
purpose holding hostages achieves no useful, constructive p. HOSTAGES, 1
p. of God and the doom assigned DESTINY, 23
the creature hath a p. and its eyes are bright PURPOSE, 5
You seem to have no real p. in life AMBITION, 5
purse consumption of the p. MONEY, 42
Put money in thy p. MONEY, 43
pussy Ding dong, bell, /P.'s in the well NURSERY RHYMES, 9
P. cat, p. cat, where have you been NURSERY RHYMES, 41
put I p. away childish things CHARITY, 6
p. up with bad things TOLERANCE, 8
pygmies wars of the p. will begin WORLD WAR II, 16
pyjamas I in p. for the heat WEATHER, 16
pylons P., those pillars /Bare TECHNOLOGY, 13
pyramid bottom of the economic p. POVERTY, 27
pyramids Books are made…like p. BOOKS, 18
Pyrenees The fleas that tease in the high P. NONSENSE, 3

Q

quack uses his words as a q. uses his remedies VERBOSITY, 4
quad *I* am always about in the Q. EXISTENCE, 1
no one about in the Q. EXISTENCE, 4
quadrupeds Dogs, like horses, are q. ANIMALS, 15
Quakers I was beaten up by Q. SHYNESS, 1
qualifications actor.…q., including no money ACTORS, 6
qualities attempts to display q. which he does not possess DECEPTION, 3
q.…necessary for success upon the stage ACTING, 11
quantity *abstract reasoning concerning q. or number* PHILOSOPHY, 3
a prodigious q. of mind INDECISION, 3
quarks Three q. for Muster Mark NONSENSE, 14
quarrel a q. in a far-away country WORLD WAR II, 1
a q. in the streets is…to be hated ARGUMENTS, 11
It takes…one to make a q. ARGUMENTS, 9
Out of the q.…we make rhetoric POETRY, 55
q. at the same time MARRIAGE, 98
q.…energies displayed in it are fine ARGUMENTS, 11
The justice of my q. JUSTICE, 16
quarrelled I did not know that we had ever q. ARGUMENTS, 16
I have q. with my wife MARRIAGE, 92
quarrels q. which vivify its barrenness LOVE, 64
Q. would not last ARGUMENTS, 13
quart cannot put a q. in a pint cup POSSIBILITY, 2
Quebec written those lines than take Q. POETRY, 53
queen Fella belong Mrs Q. LANGUAGE, 20
he…happened to marry the Q. ROYALTY, 35
how very different from the home life of our own dear Q.! ROYALTY, 2
isn't a bad bit of goods, the Q. COMPLIMENTS, 1
I've been to London to look at the q. NURSERY RHYMES, 41
I would not be a q. /For all the world ROYALTY, 34
Move Q. Anne? Most certainly not MEMORIALS, 12
sorrier for my good knights' loss than for…my fair q. LOSS, 3
the British warrior q. BRITAIN, 7
The Q. of Hearts /She made some tarts NURSERY RHYMES, 51
The q. was in the parlour, /Eating bread and honey NURSERY RHYMES, 48
queenly She keeps on being Q. AFFECTATION, 3
queens for q. I might have enough LOSS, 3
queer All the world is q. SUBJECTIVITY, 5
girls are so q. WOMEN, 8
the q. old Dean SPOONERISMS, 4
There's nowt so q. DIFFERENCE, 6
thou art a little q. SUBJECTIVITY, 5
queerer the universe is…q. than we *can* suppose UNIVERSE, 7
questing plashy fen passes the q. vole ANIMALS, 21
question a good q. for you to ask DIPLOMACY, 9
A timid q. will…receive a confident answer SHYNESS, 2
man who sees both sides of a q. OBJECTIVITY, 5
Nature has never put the fatal q. PURPOSE, 4
No q. is ever settled /Until ARGUMENTS, 19
not a wise q. for me to answer DIPLOMACY, 9
q.…which I have not been able to answer WOMEN, 33
That is the Irish Q. IRELAND, 6
that is the q. SUICIDE, 12
the q. that we do not know KNOWLEDGE, 29
To be, or not to be: that is the q. LANGUAGE, 6
questioning Q. is not the mode of conversation CONVERSATION, 4
questionings Those obstinate q. DOUBT, 8
questions all q. are open OBJECTIVITY, 3
I do not answer q. like this without being paid MASCULINITY, 1
make two q. grow where only one RESEARCH, 6
queue An Englishman…forms an orderly q. of one ENGLISH, 23
quiet Anythin' for a q. life PEACE, 7
Here, where the world is q. PEACE, 15
quietness unravish'd bride of q. SILENCE, 9
quince dined on mince, and slices of q. FOOD, 34
quintessence this q. of dust MANKIND, 27
quotable It's better to be q. than…honest QUOTATIONS, 13
quotation Classical q. is the *parole* of literary men QUOTATIONS, 4
Every q. contributes something QUOTATIONS, 5
q. is a national vice QUOTATIONS, 14
the great spring of happy q. QUOTATIONS, 6

To say that anything was a q. QUOTATIONS, 11
quotations A book that furnishes no q. is...a plaything QUOTATIONS, 9
a list of q. QUOTATIONS, 8
good thing...to read books of q. QUOTATIONS, 1
It needs no dictionary of q. EYES, 1
q. very slightly wrong QUOTATIONS, 10
quote can q. Shakespeare in an economic crisis SHAKESPEARE, 15
quotes q....give us a nodding acquaintance with the originator QUOTATIONS, 15

R

rabbit The r. has a charming face RABBITS, 1
rabbits a tale of four little r. RABBITS, 2
except to shoot r. and hit his father on the jaw NASTINESS, 5
race A loftier r. KNOWLEDGE, 33
I wish I loved the Human R. MANKIND, 22
my opinion of the human r. MANKIND, 17
Slow and steady wins the r. HASTE, 7
races human species...composed of two distinct r. BORROWING, 5
the r. of Europe are melting AMERICA, 42
Rachmaninov R.'s immortalizing totality was his scowl MUSICIANS, 20
racially not r. pure are mere chaff RACISM, 13
racing happy state of getting the victor's palm without the dust of r. VICTORY, 6
racists makes the r. look like the rebels POLITICAL CORRECTNESS, 4
rack Leave not a r. behind MORTALITY, 17
radical A r. is a man IDEALISM, 6
I never dared be r. when young YOUTH, 7
The r. invents the views....the conservative adopts them CONSERVATISM, 7
radicals Few r. have good digestions POLITICS, 14
radio I had the r. on NAKEDNESS, 7
Simply a r. personality CHURCHILL, 8
Radio 4 What do we want? R. TELEVISION AND RADIO, 1
radioactive The Irish Sea is naturally r. ECOLOGY, 6
rage all Heaven in a r. IMPRISONMENT, 1
R., rage, against the dying of the light DEATH, 126
rages the weight of r. SPOONERISMS, 1
rags no scandal like r. POVERTY, 8
only men in r..../Mistake themselves for carpet bags ETIQUETTE, 5
railing R. at life, and yet afraid of death OLD AGE, 13
railway when they think they are alone in r. carriages HABIT, 6
raiment they parted his r., and cast lots FORGIVENESS, 5
rain A Hard R.'s A-Gonna Fall PESSIMISM, 5
drop of r. maketh a hole in the stone PERSISTENCE, 7
droppeth as the gentle r. MERCY, 2
falls not hail, or r., or any snow AFTERLIFE, 10
He comes in the terrible R. CHRISTIANITY, 39
R. before seven WEATHER, 2
R., rain, go away WEATHER, 3
singing in the r. WEATHER, 12
rainbow mystery of a r. SCIENCE, 28
Somewhere over the r. DESIRE, 8
the R. gave thee birth BIRDS, 3
raineth it r. on the just JUSTICE, 4
rains It never r. but it pours MISFORTUNE, 2
rainy Keep something for a r. day THRIFT, 2
when it is not r. WEATHER, 8
raise My God shall r. me up FAITH, 17
Now he will r. me to be a martyr MARTYRDOM, 1
rake every woman is at heart a r. WOMEN, 64
lene...as is a r. HORSES, 4
rallying-point The party is the r. for the...working class COMMUNISM, 9
Ralph R. wept for the end of innocence INNOCENCE, 5
Ramadan month of R. shall ye fast RELIGION, 38
Randolph the only part of R. that was not malignant INSULTS, 41
Range Rovers creche...happens between two R. POLITICS, 67
rapidly but not so r. TIME, 9
rapist r. remains a r. MARRIAGE, 77
rapists All men are r. MEN, 4
rapping r. at my chamber door SUPERNATURAL, 12
rapture a r. on the lonely shore NATURE, 3
The first fine careless r. BIRDS, 1
rare as r. things will, it vanished TRANSIENCE, 9
keep it shut up...like a r., r. fiddle NAKEDNESS, 5
rascal Get down you dirty r. NURSERY RHYMES, 23
rascals R., would you live for ever WAR, 39
rat Mr Speaker, I smell a r. MIXED METAPHORS, 4
That killed the r. NURSERY RHYMES, 57
ratchet politics of the pendulum, but of the r. POLITICS, 81
rather It's all been r. lovely LAST WORDS, 43
rationalized Happiness...should never be r. HAPPINESS, 7
rats R.! /They fought the dogs ANIMALS, 5
ravages What do the r. of time not injure AGE, 33
raven Quoth the R., 'Nevermore' EVIL, 13
ravished He...r. this fair creature SEX, 19
raw the working-class which, r. and half-developed PUBLIC, 2
razor Satire should, like a polished r. keen SATIRE, 2
razors R. pain you SUICIDE, 7
reach a man's r. should exceed his grasp AMBITION, 3
reactionaries r. are paper tigers POLITICS, 53
read A lonesome man...who does not know how to r. READING, 4
A man ought to r. just as inclination leads him READING, 8
beautiful...for someone who could not r. AMERICA, 7
books....criticized and r. by people who don't understand them BOOKS, 25
do *you* r. books *through* READING, 7
Education...has produced a vast population able to r. READING, 16
everybody wants to have r. LITERATURE, 18
he had r. of the effects of smoking SMOKING, 16
He writes as fast as they can r. WRITERS, 56
His books were r. BOOKS, 6; PUNS, 1
I have never r. it EUROPE, 7
In my early years I r. very hard KNOWLEDGE, 25
I've just r. that I am dead OBITUARIES, 2
King George will be able to r. that SIGNATURES, 2
Men of power have not time to r. POWER, 11
R., mark, learn and inwardly digest LEARNING, 3
sooner r. a time-table...than nothing NOVELS, 10
When I want to r. a novel NOVELS, 3
will bear to be r. twice...was thought twice WRITING, 32
reader A r. seldom peruses a book with pleasure WRITERS, 1
not to inform the r. BUREAUCRACY, 1
send the r. to the dictionary STYLE, 4
the r....is the respondent READING, 19
readers his r. are proud to live in it WRITERS, 7
The human race...many of my r. HUMAN CONDITION, 5
to trade a hundred contemporary r. for POSTERITY, 6
wished longer by its r. LITERATURE, 9
reading as much pleasure in the r. PLEASURE, 25
a substitute for r. it OSTENTATION, 2
a tragedy and therefore not worth r. PLAYS, 2
but I prefer r. READING, 14
half learned the art of r. READING, 2
If a book is worth r. BOOKS, 35
I have led a life of business so long that I have lost my taste for r. READING, 17
I loitered my life away, r. books DISCONTENT, 3
I shall lose no time in r. it INATTENTION, 1
Peace is poor r. WAR AND PEACE, 7
R....ingenious device for avoiding thought READING, 6
R. isn't an occupation we encourage among police officers POLICE, 5
R. is to the mind READING, 15
R. maketh a full man READING, 1
The r. of all good books LITERATURE, 3
There are two motives for r. a book READING, 13
When I am not walking, I am r. READING, 9
ready critics all are r. made CRITICS, 2
I have but ninepence in r. money CONVERSATION, 2
ready-made Why not...r. WORDS, 6
Reagan disastrous fire in President R.'s library both books were destroyed INSULTS, 20
real I could have become a r. painter LAST WORDS, 39
It's the r. thing ADVERTISING, 16
Nothing ever becomes r. till it is experienced EXPERIENCE, 17
whether Zelda and I are r. FICTION, 2
realistic he is going to make 'a r. decision' DECISION, 3
reality art...r. which is...in our minds ARTS, 6
As far as the laws of mathematics refer to r. MATHEMATICS, 3
by r. I mean shops like Selfridges REALITY, 5
Cannot bear very much r. REALITY, 3

statesmen of the world...are far more dangerous, and far more estranged from...r. NUCLEAR WEAPONS, 10
The whole of art is an appeal to a r. ARTS, 6
realize I saw it, but I did not r. it PERCEPTION, 4
realm A worse king never left a r. undone ROYALTY, 8
realms travell'd in the r. of gold TRAVEL, 14
reap sown the wind...r. the whirlwind RETRIBUTION, 5
whatsoever a man soweth, that shall he also r. RETRIBUTION, 4
reaper a R. whose name is Death DEATH, 79
reaping No, r. PUNS, 2
reappear all great events and personalities in...history r. HISTORY, 20
reason A man who does not lose his r. REASON, 4
Faith consists in believing when it is beyond the power of r. to believe FAITH, 19
happiness is not an ideal of r. HAPPINESS, 13
He never does a proper thing without...an improper r. MORALITY, 17
he who destroys a good book, kills r. BOOKS, 27
Human r. won. Mankind won VICTORY, 8
it was neither rhyme nor r. CRITICISM, 35
man...is R.'s slave PASSION, 1
nothing is law that is not r. LAW, 22
not to r. why OBEDIENCE, 4
Once the people begin to r. PUBLIC, 18
Only r. can convince us OBJECTIVITY, 3
R. is itself a matter of faith REASON, 2
r. not the need NECESSITY, 5
R., Observation, and Experience SCIENCE, 22
right deed for the wrong r. MOTIVE, 2
The madman...has lost everything except his r. MADNESS, 3
the r. of the case LAW, 22
The ruling passion conquers r. still PASSION, 6
who turns mad for a r. MADNESS, 2
woman's r. WOMEN, 71
reasonable Act of God...*something which no r. man could have expected* DISASTER, 3
figure of 'The R. Man' LAW, 16
Who kills a man kills a r. creature BOOKS, 27
reasoners most plausible r. THINKING, 4
reasoning *abstract r. concerning quantity or number* PHILOSOPHY, 3
reasons Metaphysics is the finding of bad r. METAPHYSICS, 2
never give your r. JUDGMENT, 11
r. for not printing any list of subscribers FRANKNESS, 2
The heart has its r. MOTIVE, 5
two r. for drinking THIRST, 1
rebel how to r. and conform at the same time YOUTH, 5
What is a r. REBELLION, 2
rebellion A little r. now and then REBELLION, 5
little r....is a good thing POLITICS, 37
rebels makes the racists look like the r. POLITICAL CORRECTNESS, 4
recall The Gods themselves cannot r. their gifts IRREVOCABILITY, 2
receipts How were the r. today in Madison Square Garden LAST WORDS, 6
receive whoso shall r. one such little child CHILDREN, 14
received freely ye have r., freely give GENEROSITY, 3; GIFTS, 2
receiver your wife...is a r. of stolen goods INSULTS, 21
reception men that...hinder the r. of every work CRITICS, 10
recession R. when...neighbour loses his job ECONOMICS, 19; UNEMPLOYMENT, 3
unemployment and the r. have been the price...to get inflation down UNEMPLOYMENT, 1
reckon'd beggary in the love that can be r. LOVE, 116
reckoning take you...at your own r. SELF-RESPECT, 3
recognize did not r. me by my face PUNISHMENT, 15
recoils Revenge...back on itself r. REVENGE, 13
recompense R. injury with justice KINDNESS, 1
reconcile How r. this world...with...my imagining BLINDNESS, 2
It takes a long while for a...trustful person to r. himself to...God FAITH, 15
recounting calms one's grief by r. it SORROW, 4
recreation woman accepted cooking...but man... made of it a r. FOOD, 46
red Coral is far more r. ANALOGY, 3
it's not even r. brick, but white tile CLASS, 26
leeches have r. blood LAST WORDS, 17
R. Badge of Courage COURAGE, 7
Red lips are not so r. WAR, 82
R. sky at night WEATHER, 4
The people's flag is deepest r. SOCIALISM, 3
The sand of the desert is sodden r. WAR, 76
thin r. line tipped with steel WAR, 95
redemption married past r. MARRIAGE, 53
red-hot The Last of the R. Mamas SINGERS, 3
redundancy hiring taxis...handing out r. notices to its own workers INCOMPETENCE, 2
redwood Nixon...would cut down a r. tree POLITICIANS, 73
reeling R. and Writhing EDUCATION, 9
references Always verify your r. RESEARCH, 4
refined One of those r. people CLASS, 6
reflection a r. of the British Museum Reading Room INTELLECTUALS, 8
reform All r....will prove unavailing CHANGE, 2
Any attempt to r. the university EDUCATION, 25
r. for me will be when the milk isn't sour RUSSIA, 3
reformation Every r. must have its victims SUFFERING, 12
refreshed The tree of liberty must be r. FREEDOM, 21
refuge God is the immemorial r. of the incompetent GOD, 35
Idleness...the r. of weak minds IDLENESS, 3
Patriotism is the last r. PATRIOTISM, 17
refuse To r. praise PRAISE, 6
refused She r. to begin the 'Beguine' PETULANCE, 1
refute I r. it *thus* PHILOSOPHY, 5
regardless r. of their doom IGNORANCE, 7
regime No r. has ever loved great writers WRITERS, 23
regiment led his r. from behind COWARDICE, 3
register history...the r. of the...misfortunes of mankind HISTORY, 16
I want to r. a complaint COMPLAINTS, 5
registry marriage in a r. office MARRIAGE, 7
regret I have seldom spoken with greater r. MISQUOTATIONS, 6
My r. /Becomes an April violet SORROW, 25
R. is an appalling waste of energy REGRET, 9
remember and r. REGRET, 6
wild with all r. NOSTALGIA, 20
regrets the Cup that clears /TO-DAY of past R. PRESENT, 5
The follies which a man r. REGRET, 12
rehearsing R. a play is making the word flesh PLAYS, 9
reign Better to r. in Hell POWER, 17
reigned I have r. with your loves ROYALTY, 14
reigns king r., but does not govern MONARCHY, 26
reject If you r. me on account of my religion PREJUDICE, 1
rejoice new sights of Nature made me r. NATURE, 7
related A group of closely r. persons FAMILY, 22
relation If a man's character is to be abused...there's nobody like a r. to do the business FAMILY, 33
No human r. gives one possession in another UNITY, 10
relations Fate chooses your r. FAMILY, 9; FRIENDS, 6
great men have their poor r. FAMILY, 10
relationship rapist...irrespective of his r. with his victim MARRIAGE, 77
relaxation r. from one...labour by taking up another CHANGE, 7
relief For this r. much thanks COMFORT, 2
There is a certain r. in change CHANGE, 12
thou wilt give thyself r. LIFE, 35
religion a feeling of inward tranquillity which r. is powerless to bestow CLOTHES, 5
Art and r. first; then philosophy IMPORTANCE, 3
As to r....duty of government to protect all GOVERNMENT, 23
brothels with bricks of R. HYPOCRISY, 4
Fascism is a r. FASCISM, 2
If you reject me on account of my r. PREJUDICE, 1
Love is my r. LOVE AND DEATH, 3
Many people think they have r. RELIGION, 35
Men will wrangle for r. RELIGION, 16
no reason to bring r. into it RELIGION, 48
Not a r. for gentlemen RELIGION, 12
Nothing is so fatal to r. as indifference INDIFFERENCE, 2
One r. is as true as another RELIGION, 10
One's r....yours is Success SUCCESS, 5
R. /Has made an honest woman of the supernatural RELIGION, 25; SUPERNATURAL, 8
R. is an illusion RELIGION, 24
R. is by no means a proper subject RELIGION, 13
R. is love RELIGION, 67
R....is the opium of the people RELIGION, 42
r. of feeble minds SUPERSTITION, 7
r. of Socialism SOCIALISM, 2

R.'s in the heart PRAYER, 13
Science without r. is lame RELIGION, 22; SCIENCE, 14
Sensible men are all of the same r. RELIGION, 18
talks loudly against r. RELIGION, 54
that God is interested only…in r. GOD, 48
To become a popular r. RELIGION, 33
when r. is allowed to invade…private life RELIGION, 43
when r. was strong…men mistook magic for medicine MEDICINE, 10
religions a country with thirty-two r. and only one sauce AMERICA, 34
sixty different r., and only one sauce ENGLAND, 10
The r. we call false were once true RELIGION, 23
religious frequently mistake for deep r. conviction RELIGION, 4
a r. animal RELIGION, 9
first, r. and moral principles EDUCATION, 2
not r.-good VIRTUE, 9
r. outlook on life RELIGION, 36
skilled appeals to r. prejudice EVOLUTION, 10
tabloids…have a r. affairs correspondent NEWSPAPERS, 9
To be at all is to be r. RELIGION, 11
relished the taste by which he is…r. WRITING, 37
reluctant The r. obedience of distant provinces DIPLOMACY, 16
remarkable nothing left r. /Beneath the visiting moon MOURNING, 11
remedies Extreme r.…for extreme diseases REMEDIES, 10
He that will not apply new r. INNOVATION, 1
Not even r. can master DISEASE, 35
Our r. oft in ourselves do lie SELF-RELIANCE, 8
paralyse it by encumbering it with r. REMEDIES, 13
r.…suggested for a disease REMEDIES, 7
remedy a r. for everything except death REMEDIES, 6
a sovereign r. to all diseases SMOKING, 2
Force is not a r. FORCE, 1
r. is worse than the disease DISEASE, 9; REMEDIES, 2
Tis a sharp r., but a sure one EXECUTION, 25
remember I only r. what I've learnt KNOWLEDGE, 35
I r., I r. NOSTALGIA, 9; INNOCENCE, 6
Oh! don't you r. sweet Alice, Ben Bolt MEMORY, 7
one man to r. me LAST WORDS, 59
r. and regret REGRET, 6
R. me when I am gone away MEMORY, 13
she did not r.…her jewelry PRUDENCE, 9
The world will little note, nor long r. MEMORIALS, 6
we shall be glad to r. even these hardships ENDURANCE, 22
We will r. them MEMORIALS, 3
When I meet a man whose name I can't r. MEMORY, 5
remembered By this may I r. be /When I should be forgotten MEMORIALS, 1
I r. my God GOD, 46
remembrance day of jubilation, a day of r. GERMANY, 8
r. of things past REGRET, 18
reminiscences the old have r. AGE, 50
remorse r. for what you have thought about your wife MARRIAGE, 99
remove all faith, so that I could r. mountains CHARITY, 6
Renaissance the R. was…the green end of one of civilization's hardest winters CIVILIZATION, 5
render husband r. unto the wife due benevolence MARRIAGE, 24
rendezvous a r. with Death DEATH, 103
renegades Political r. always start their career of treachery POLITICIANS, 15
renewal urban r. in New York City EDUCATION, 25
rent r. an MP just like…a London taxi POLITICIANS, 12
they r. out my room EXPEDIENCY, 1
repair the landlord does not intend to r. LAST WORDS, 2
repartee A majority is always the best r. MAJORITY, 2
repast A new r., or an untasted spring PLEASURE, 2
repay whatsoever thou spendest more…I will r. CHARITY, 8
repeal the r. of bad or obnoxious laws LAW, 15
repeat History does not r. itself HISTORY, 6
obliged to imitate himself, and to r. IMITATION, 5
repeated A platitude is simply a truth r. SAYINGS, 1
repent Do you…, my Love,/ r. PARTING, 8
r. at leisure MARRIAGE, 38
repentance A Christian…feels /R. on a Sunday HYPOCRISY, 19
There's no r. in the grave DEATH, 130
with the morning cool r. REGRET, 13
repetition constant r. will finally succeed in imprinting an idea PUBLIC, 14
History is an endless r. HISTORY, 11
replenished His intellect is not r. IGNORANCE, 13
replied And I r., 'My Lord.' RELIGION, 31
reporter A r. is a man who has renounced everything JOURNALISM, 25
I am a r. ATHEISM, 6
reporting Language is not simply a r. device for experience LANGUAGE, 28
reprehend If I r. any thing MALAPROPISMS, 8
representation Proportional R.…is fundamentally counter-democratic POLITICS, 43
Taxation without r. REPRESENTATION, 1
reproductions accurate r. of Anne Hathaway's cottage HOUSES, 3
I've seen colour r. PHILISTINISM, 5
republic An aristocracy in a r. is like a chicken ARISTOCRACY, 10
the r. of letters MANKIND, 1
republican sold Ulster to buy off the fiendish r. scum LAND, 18
The R. form of Government POLITICS, 70
Republicans Please assure me that you are all R. POLITICS, 60
republics Revolts, r., revolutions POLITICS, 78
repulsive Roundheads (Right but R.) HISTORY, 27
reputability Conspicuous consumption…is a means of r. MATERIALISM, 20
reputation ever written out of r. but by himself REPUTATION, 2
it is better for the r. ORTHODOXY, 3
O, I have lost my r. REPUTATION, 7
r. doesn't really matter to…media REPUTATION, 7
R. is a bubble REPUTATION, 3
spotless r. REPUTATION, 9
Until you've lost your r., you never realize…what freedom really is REPUTATION, 5
requests thou wilt grant their r. PRAYER, 6
requires all the Human Frame r. FOOD, 7
research R.! A mere excuse for idleness RESEARCH, 2
The aim of r. is the discovery of the equations RESEARCH, 3
The outcome of any serious r. RESEARCH, 6
resent I don't r. his popularity POPULARITY, 8
To great evils we submit; we r. little provocations TRIVIALITY, 9
resentment It is very difficult to get up r. BITTERNESS, 2
reservoir a gigantic r. of good will AMERICA, 38
residuum this vast r. we may…give the name of Populace PUBLIC, 2
resist r. everything except temptation TEMPTATION, 10
there is almost nothing to r. at all ENGLISH, 21
resisting fond of r. temptation TEMPTATION, 3
resolution In war, r. WAR AND PEACE, 3
native hue of r. CONSCIENCE, 5
resources statistics, born to consume r. STATISTICS, 3
respect A child deserves the maximum r. CHILDREN, 29
Civilization is…equal r. for all men CIVILIZATION, 1
old-fashioned r. for the young RESPECT, 5
The English have no r. for their language ENGLISH, 32
those /Who err each other must r. LOVE, 98
We must r. the other fellow's religion TOLERANCE, 5
We owe r. to the living RESPECT, 4
When people do not r. us we are sharply offended SELF-RESPECT, 4
respectable R. means rich RESPECTABILITY, 3
r., middle-class…lady AUDIENCES, 4
riff-raff apply to what is r. CLASS, 16
respecter God is no r. of persons GOD, 4
respects no man much r. himself SELF-RESPECT, 4
respondent the reader…is the r. READING, 19
responsibility In dreams begins r. RESPONSIBILITY, 17
no sense of r. at the other BABIES, 5
No sex without r. SEX, 33
power without r. RESPONSIBILITY, 2, 9; JOURNALISM, 2
responsible An idea isn't r. for the people IDEAS, 5
character is something for which people are r. CHARACTER, 11
every man is r. for his face APPEARANCE, 6
No man is r. for his father FATHERS, 7
r. and the irresponsible classes CLASS, 17
r. and wrong RESPONSIBILITY, 5; RIGHTEOUSNESS, 6
You are r. for your rose RESPONSIBILITY, 12
rest All the r. have thirty-one NURSERY RHYMES, 56
get rid of the r. of her WOMEN, 85
I have nothing; the r. I leave to the poor LAST WORDS, 54

leave the r. to the Gods DUTY, 2
Seek home for r. HOME, 9
The r. is silence DEATH, 104
To toil and not to seek for r. SELFLESSNESS, 2
restaurants Great r. are...nothing but mouth-brothels FOOD, 48
rested God...r. on the seventh day SUNDAY, 1
restless r. who will volunteer for anything SOLDIERS, 4
restore Time may r. us POETS, 17
rests our heart is not quiet until it r. in Thee HUMAN CONDITION, 2
result the long r. of Time EXPERIENCE, 19
resurrection I am the r., and the life CHRISTIANITY, 16
retain To expect a man to r. everything that he has ever read MEMORY, 15
reticulated Anything r. or decussated at equal distances WORDS, 12
retire can't put off being young until you r. MONEY, 30
retreat A mistress should be like a...r. SEX, 67
retrograde All that is human must r. PROGRESS, 6
return I shall r. DETERMINATION, 11
returning R. were as tedious as go o'er GUILT, 7
reveal words...half r. and half conceal WORDS, 21
revealeth he r. the deep and secret things GOD, 7
Revelations It ends with R. BIBLE, 11
revelry a sound of r. by night MERRYMAKING, 2
revels Our r. now are ended MORTALITY, 17
revenge A man that studieth r. REVENGE, 5
he took his r. by speaking ill ENVY, 9
if you wrong us, shall we not r. EQUALITY, 22
R., at first though sweet REVENGE, 13
R....back on itself recoils REVENGE, 13
R. is a dish REVENGE, 2
R. is a...wild justice REVENGE, 4
R. is sweet REVENGE, 3
terrible r. by the culture of the Negroes POP MUSIC, 15
revenue name a virtue that brings in as much r. SMOKING, 14
reverence a little more r....and not so much astonishment SINGING, 3
reverse popular music...made giant strides in r. POP MUSIC, 10
reviewers R....would have been poets CRITICS, 3
reviewing Prolonged...r. of books involves constantly *inventing* reactions CRITICISM, 36
revolts R., republics, revolutions POLITICS, 78
revolution Britain...is going to be forged in the white heat of this r. SOCIALISM, 15
Britain is not...easily rocked by r. BRITAIN, 8
fundamental premise of a r. REVOLUTION, 8
he'd go to church, start a r. – *something* MATERIALISM, 15
Hitler has carried out a r. on our lines FASCISM, 1
restating our socialism in terms of the scientific r. SOCIALISM, 15
R. by its very nature REVOLUTION, 9
Russia is a collapse, not a r. RUSSIA, 5
The r. eats POLITICS, 61
The word 'r.' is a word for which you kill REVOLUTION, 10
We invented the R. REVOLUTION, 11
revolutionary fierce and r. in a bathroom AMERICANS, 7
If you feed people just with r. slogans PROMISES, 4
I would be a r. myself POVERTY, 12
Patriotism...is a r. duty PATRIOTISM, 30
r. right DEMOCRACY, 11
revolutions All modern r. have ended REVOLUTION, 2
Revolts, republics, r. POLITICS, 78
R. are always verbose REVOLUTION, 7
state of mind which creates r. REVOLUTION, 1
revolver I reach for my r. PHILISTINISM, 4
reward The avoidance of taxes...still carries...r. TAXATION, 8
The r. of a thing well done SATISFACTION, 3
To labour and not ask for any r. SELFLESSNESS, 2
Vice is its own r. VICE, 6
rewarded Men are r. and punished not for what they do MOTIVE, 6
rewards In nature there are neither r. nor punishments NATURE, 11
Reynolds When...R. died /All Nature was degraded ARTISTS, 11
rhetoric Out of the quarrel...we make r. POETRY, 55
rheumatism r. is to the heart DISEASE, 23
Screw up the vise...you have r. DISEASE, 4
Rhine The Watch on the R. RIVERS, 4
rhyme it was neither r. nor reason CRITICISM, 35
outlive this powerful r. POETRY, 42
R. being no necessary adjunct or true ornament POETRY, 31
the petty fools of r. TRIVIALITY, 14
rhyming troublesome...bondage of R. POETRY, 32
rhythm r. imposes unanimity upon the divergent MUSIC, 32
rib the r....made he a woman WOMEN, 15
ribbon The blue r. of the turf HORSES, 5
rich a r. man shall hardly enter into...heaven WEALTH, 8
A r. man's joke is always funny FLATTERY, 3
as easy to marry a r. woman as a poor woman MARRIAGE, 120
as well off as if he were r. WEALTH, 4
If you can...count your money you are not...r. man WEALTH, 15
It's the r. wot gets the gravy POVERTY AND WEALTH, 1
nor a r. society too r. POVERTY AND WEALTH, 8
no sin but to be r. HYPOCRISY, 15
poor have no right to the property of the r. POVERTY AND WEALTH, 6
Poor Little R. Girl WEALTH, 10
Respectable means r. RESPECTABILITY, 3
r. are different from us WEALTH, 12
r. beyond the dreams of avarice WEALTH, 21
R. men's houses are seldom beautiful WEALTH, 3
so large, /So friendly, and so r. AMERICA, 2
The r. and powerful know GOD, 2
The r. are the scum of the earth WEALTH, 9
The r. man has his motor car ENVY, 2
the wretchedness of being r. WEALTH, 26
Victim of a r. man's game POVERTY AND WEALTH, 1
whether to be r. in things MATERIALISM, 9
you have to live with r. people WEALTH, 26
richer for r. for poorer MARRIAGE, 30
R. than all his tribe LOVE, 128
riches Infinite r. in a little room WEALTH, 19
R. are for spending EXTRAVAGANCE, 1
R. have wings WEALTH, 11
r. to be a valuable thing WEALTH, 27
the chief employment of r. consists in the parade of r. OSTENTATION, 6; WEALTH, 25
richesses *l'embarras des r.* EXCESS, 1
richest He is the r. author that ever grazed WRITERS, 61
Richmond On R. Hill there lives a lass ADMIRATION, 7
rid gladly...am I r. of it all SEX, 54
glad to get r. of it STUPIDITY, 8
riddle a r. wrapped in a mystery inside an enigma RUSSIA, 3
glory, jest, and r. of the world HUMAN CONDITION, 14
R. of destiny PURPOSE, 6
ride just a r. LIFE, 28
R. on! r. on in majesty CHRISTIANITY, 32
rides He who r. a tiger AMBITION, 1
we look for happiness in boats and carriage r. TRAVEL, 12
ridicule he who endeavours to r. other people RIDICULE, 3
R. often checks what is absurd RIDICULE, 4
R....smothers that which is noble RIDICULE, 4
ridiculous a fine sense of the r. HUMOUR, 1
a step from the sublime to the r. DECLINE, 6
no spectacle so r. MORALITY, 10
The profession of letters...in which one can make no money without being r. WRITING, 28
The sublime and the r. OPPOSITES, 7
riding Commuter...r. to and from his wife TRAINS, 6; TRAVEL, 25
riff-raff r. apply to what is respectable CLASS, 16
rifles stuttering r.' rapid rattle WORLD WAR I, 18
rift the...r. between the sexes SEXES, 22
Riga There was a young lady of R. ANIMALS, 1
right All's r. with the world PERFECTION, 2
better to be irresponsible and r. RESPONSIBILITY, 5; RIGHTEOUSNESS, 6
Every man has a r. to utter what he thinks truth FREEDOM, 22
I am not and never have been, a man of the r. POLITICIANS, 66
I disapprove of what you say, but I will defend...your r. to say it FREEDOM, 52
I'd rather be r. than president RIGHT, 3
It will all come r. in the wash OPTIMISM, 4
Keep r. on to the end of the road PERSISTENCE, 8
Liberty is the r. to do everything FREEDOM, 36
Minorities...are almost always in the r. MINORITY, 3
no r. to strike against public safety STRIKES, 2
No, this r. hand shall work it all off WRITING, 30
One of the pleasures of middle age is to *find out* that one WAS r. AGE, 46

'orthodoxy'...no longer means being r. ORTHODOXY, 2
our country, r. or wrong PATRIOTISM, 8
publish, r. or wrong PUBLISHING, 3
R. is more precious RIGHT, 4
r. mindfulness, r. contemplation RELIGION, 8
r. of all...duty of some SEPARATION, 4
r. to have a child MOTHERHOOD, 3
settled r. ARGUMENTS, 19
something is possible, he is...r. SCIENCE, 6
The customer is always r. BUSINESS, 18
The man who gets angry...in the r. way...is commended ANGER, 1
The minority is always r. MAJORITY, 3; MINORITY, 2
The r. divine of kings to govern wrong MONARCHY, 17
the r. to be consulted MONARCHY, 2
the r. to criticize Shakespeare CRITICISM, 47
Those who believe that they are exclusively in the r. SELF-CONFIDENCE, 1
Ulster will be r. IRELAND, 4
Women would rather be r. than reasonable WOMEN, 54

righteous leave r. ways behind RIGHTEOUSNESS, 3

righteousness He made r. readable EDITORS, 2
The eternal *not ourselves* that makes for r. RIGHTEOUSNESS, 1
the r. of the scribes and Pharisees RETRIBUTION, 6

righter much r. than one knew at say 17 or 23 AGE, 46

rights human beings are born free...dignity and r. HUMAN RIGHTS, 1
The Sovereign has, under a constitutional monarchy... three r. MONARCHY, 2

ring Don't carry away that arm till I have...my r. PRACTICALITY, 6
One R. to rule them all POWER, 26
R. down the curtain LAST WORDS, 55
r. is worn away by use PERSISTENCE, 11
The r. so worn...is yet of gold APPEARANCE, 10
They now *r.* the bells WAR, 121

rings R. on her fingers and bells on her toes NURSERY RHYMES, 42

riot A r. is at bottom REBELLION, 6
triumph in putting down the r. CHINA, 10

ripe Cherry r. BUSINESS, 13
we r. and r. LIFE, 46

ripeness R. is all ENDURANCE, 17

ripp'd mother's womb untimely r. BIRTH, 9

rise Early to r. and early to bed BED, 9
in the name of Jesus...r. up and walk REMEDIES, 3
nobody who does not r. early BED, 4
Thanks to words, we have been able to r. above the brutes WORDS, 11

risk a bank that would lend money to such a poor r. BORROWING, 2
deepest pockets who can r. going to law LAW, 29

risks what r. you take...to find money in a desk THEFT, 4

Ritz like the R. hotel JUSTICE, 17

river build your House of Parliament upon the r. HOUSES OF PARLIAMENT, 19
can't step into the same r. twice CHANGE, 10
Fame is like a r. FAME, 2
Ol' man r. RIVERS, 2
On either side the r. lie ARTHURIAN LEGEND, 2
On the breast of the r. of Time HUMAN CONDITION, 1
the r. of knowledge has too often turned back on itself SCIENCE, 24
The vanity of human life is like a r. LIFE, 41

road All I seek...the r. below me TRAVEL, 21
a r....that does not go through the intellect EMOTION, 1
Does the r. wind up-hill ENDURANCE, 15
free as the r. FREEDOM, 17
Keep right on to the end of the r. PERSISTENCE, 8
On the r. to Mandalay PLACES, 9
people who stay in the middle of the r. COMPROMISE, 2
tell us of the R. DEATH, 50
the Golden R. to Samarkand KNOWLEDGE, 14
There is a r. from the eye to the heart EMOTION, 1
the rolling English r. TRAVEL, 5
They shut the r. through the woods TIME, 23

roads all r. lead to France WAR, 119
How many r. must a man walk down EXPERIENCE, 13
New r.: new ruts PROGRESS, 4
Two r. diverged CHOICE, 2

roam Mid pleasures and palaces though we may r. HOME, 7

roamin' R. in the gloamin' SCOTLAND, 6

roar luck to give the r. CHURCHILL, 5

roast the learned r. an egg FOOD, 45

rob Why r. one to feed the other DEATH, 68

robb'd He that is r., not wanting what is stol'n IGNORANCE, 14

robbed We was r. INJUSTICE, 8
when you've r. a man of everything POWER, 23

Robbins President R. was so well adjusted to his environment ADAPTABILITY, 3

robes R. and furr'd gowns hide all APPEARANCES, 21

robin A r. redbreast in a cage IMPRISONMENT, 1
Our little English r. BIRDS, 13
R. Gray, he was gudeman to me MARRIAGE, 19
Who killed Cock R. NURSERY RHYMES, 68

robot the modern conception of a r. POLITICIANS, 47

rock R. and roll or Christianity POPULARITY, 6
R. Around the Clock POP MUSIC, 13
R. of ages, cleft for me RELIGION, 59
upon this r. I will build my church CHURCH, 1
With my little stick of Blackpool r. FOOD, 24

rocked R. in the cradle of the deep SEA, 11

rock'n'roll Give me that r. music POP MUSIC, 2
R. is part of a pest POP MUSIC, 1

rocks The hand that r. the cradle INFLUENCE, 10

rod he that spareth his r. hateth his son CHILDREN, 15
rule them with a r. of iron LEADERSHIP, 2
spare the r. PUNISHMENT, 6; INDULGENCE, 1

rode and r. madly off in all directions NONSENSE, 15

rodent-like music critics....small and r. with padlocked ears CRITICS, 18

Roland *Childe R. to the Dark Tower came* SUMMONS, 4

role he saw his r. as being that of Moses LEADERSHIP, 5

roll R. up that map PEACE, 13

rolled bottoms of my trousers r. OLD AGE, 17

rolling Like a r. stone TRAVEL, 7
The r. English drunkard TRAVEL, 5

Rolls She has a R. body and a Balham mind STUPIDITY, 11

Rolls Royce always using a small car to drive to the dockyard instead of my R. ROYALTY, 25

Roma *R. locuta est* AUTHORITARIANISM, 1

Roman noblest R. of them all NOBILITY, 4
the Holy R. Empire was neither holy, nor R., nor an empire NATIONS, 3
The Papacy is not other than the Ghost of the deceased R. Empire CATHOLICISM, 5
the R. people had but one neck RUTHLESSNESS, 1

romance The r. of *Tom Jones* NOVELS, 5
Twenty years of r. makes a woman look like a ruin MARRIAGE, 132

Romans Friends, R., countrymen, lend me your ears EVIL, 16
which came first, the Greeks or the R. IGNORANCE, 5

romantic The charm is purely r. IDEALISM, 7

Romanticism R. is...presenting people with the literary works...affording...the greatest...pleasure LITERATURE, 17

Rome I lov'd R. more PATRIOTISM, 28
R. has spoken; the case is concluded AUTHORITARIANISM, 1
R.'s gross yoke /Drops off INFLUENCE, 1
R. shall perish REVENGE, 9
R.'s just a city like anywhere else EUROPE, 1
R. was not built PATIENCE, 5
The farther you go from the church of R. PROTESTANTISM, 3
When in R. CONFORMITY, 2
when R. falls – the World EUROPE, 5

Romeo Romeo! wherefore art thou R. NAMES, 6

room All I want is a r. somewhere DESIRE, 10
before my little r. FLOWERS, 2
I have only slipped away into the next r. AFTERLIFE, 5
Infinite riches in a little r. WEALTH, 19
no r. for them in the inn CHRISTMAS, 7
The perpetual struggle for r. and food SURVIVAL, 3
There is always r. at the top AMBITION, 18
who sneaked into my r. at three o'clock this morning COMPLAINTS, 5

rooms being old is having lighted r. OLD AGE, 25

Roosevelt the kind of nation that President R. hoped for AMBITION, 10

roost Curses...always come home to r. CURSES, 2

root love of money is the r. of all evil MONEY, 11
the r. of all sins DRUNKENNESS, 14
Though leaves are many, the r. is one AGE, 72

rope Give a thief enough r. RETRIBUTION, 1

rose a r. /By any other name NAMES, 7
A r. without a thorn ADMIRATION, 7
At Christmas I no more desire a r. SUITABILITY, 4
killing as the canker to the r. CORRUPTION, 4
Like a r., she has lived as long as roses live TRANSIENCE, 17
mighty lak' a r. BABIES, 6
One perfect r. MATERIALISM, 16
R.…where some buried Caesar bled FLOWERS, 4
That which sets…The budding r. above the r. full blown FRENCH REVOLUTION, 4
the last r. of summer FLOWERS, 9
You are responsible for your r. RESPONSIBILITY, 12
rosebuds Gather ye r. while ye may PRESENT, 6
roses a wreath of r. FLOWERS, 1
days of wine and r. TRANSIENCE, 11
Everything's Coming Up R. PERFECTION, 8
Flung r., r. riotously MEMORY, 6
hand that gives you r. GENEROSITY, 1
I will make thee beds of r. FLOWERS, 7
I would like my r. to see you COMPLIMENTS, 5
Nor does a…gardener scent his r. POETS, 4
not a bed of r. MARRIAGE, 114
Plant thou no r. DEATH, 99
Ring-a-ring o'r. NURSERY RHYMES, 43
R. are flowering in Picardy COMPLIMENTS, 9
Send two dozen r. to Room 424 LOVE, 89
so with r. overgrown GARDENS, 10
The lilies and r. were all awake LOVE, 134
Treaties are like r. and young girls DIPLOMACY, 10
rot lie in cold obstruction, and to r. DEATH, 107
we r. and r. LIFE, 46
Rotarians The astronauts!…R. in outer space SPACE, 8
rotten r. in the state of Denmark CORRUPTION, 7
rotting Damn you, England. You're r. ENGLAND, 32
rough-hew R. them how we will DESTINY, 19
round R. and round the garden /Like a teddy bear NURSERY RHYMES, 44
r., neat, not gaudy GARDENS, 9
The trivial r., the common task SIMPLICITY, 4
roundabouts What's lost upon the r. LOSS, 2
Roundheads R. (Right but Repulsive) HISTORY, 27
roving we'll go no more a r. DEBAUCHERY, 4
row Row upon r. with strict impunity DEATH, 122
rowed All r. fast BOATS, 2
Rowley Heigh ho! says R. NURSERY RHYMES, 1
royal A R. Commission is a broody hen BUREAUCRACY, 6
Once in r. David's city CHRISTMAS, 2
trying not to be different in the sense of being r. ROYALTY, 25
rub R.-a-dub-dub, /Three men in a tub NURSERY RHYMES, 45
there's the r. SUICIDE, 12
try to r. up against money MONEY, 40
rubbish fancy poncy r. TASTE, 2
rubies her price is far above r. WOMEN, 17
the price of wisdom is above r. WISDOM, 6
Rubinstein Arthur R. EGOTISM, 6
rubs sentimentality…r. you up the wrong way SENTIMENTALITY, 4
rude Fifty lovelies in the r. OPPORTUNITY, 18
The right people are r. IMPERTINENCE, 3
rue With r. my heart is laden NOSTALGIA, 11
rug Stop…those dogs…peeing on my cheapest r. DOGS, 9
rugby R. Union which is a distillation SPORT AND GAMES, 23
ruin for the r. of our sex MEN, 11
I am inclined to notice the r. in things EUROPE, 13
Twenty years of romance makes a woman look like a r. MARRIAGE, 132
ruined Such another victory and we are r. VICTORY, 14
ruining they will end by r. our idea FASCISM, 1
ruins r. that Cromwell knocked about a bit INNUENDO, 2
rule A little r., a little sway TRANSIENCE, 12
English should give Ireland home r. IRELAND, 17
I don't believe in black majority r. RACISM, 28
Irish Home R. is conceded IRELAND, 18
One Ring to r. them all POWER, 26
R. all England under a hog INSULTS, 14
r. them with a rod of iron LEADERSHIP, 2
safer to obey than to r. OBEDIENCE, 3
The first r. in opera is the first r. in life SELF-RELIANCE, 6
ruler I am the R. of the Queen's Navee OFFICERS, 6
rulers R. of the Queen's Navee OFFICERS, 7
rules R. and models destroy genius and art RULES, 2
r. of the game are what we call the laws of Nature GOD, 28
the hand that r. the world INFLUENCE, 10
there are no golden r. RULES, 3
two golden r. for an orchestra MUSIC, 7
ruleth the cry of him that r. among fools WISDOM, 3
ruling The state is an instrument…of the r. class STATE, 5
rum r., sodomy, and the lash NAVY, 2
Yo-ho-ho, and a bottle of r. ALCOHOL, 60
rumble R. thy bellyful WEATHER, 20
rumour Where r. of oppression and deceit SOLITUDE, 3
run Gwine to r. all night HORSES, 6
He can r., but he can't hide ESCAPE, 2
You cannot r. with the hare LOYALTY, 3
runcible ate with a r. spoon FOOD, 34
He weareth a r. hat NONSENSE, 19
runners like r. hand on the torch of life MORTALITY, 15
running drive out nature with a pitchfork…she'll be constantly r. back HUMAN NATURE, 12
it takes all the r. *you* can do, to keep in the same place NONSENSE, 8
rush *R. hour:* that hour when CARS, 5; TRAVEL, 18
rushes Green grow the r. O LOVE, 32
Ruskin I doubt that art needed R. CRITICS, 17
Russia For us in R. communism is a dead dog COMMUNISM, 7
going in without the help of R. WORLD WAR II, 22
R. is a collapse, not a revolution RUSSIA, 5
the greatness of R. is only her pre-natal struggling RUSSIA, 4
Why will America not reach out…to R. DIPLOMACY, 8
Russian Scratch the R. and…find the Tartar RUSSIA, 6
the R. people have become RUSSIA, 11
Russians our decadence and the R.' DECLINE, 12
test the R., not the bombs NUCLEAR WEAPONS, 6
rustling r. in unpaid-for silk CONTENTMENT, 7
rut It's not good enough…getting into a state of r. WRITERS, 49
people getting into a state of r. CRITICISM, 14
ruts New roads: new r. PROGRESS, 4
rye Coming through the r. LOVE, 34

S

Sabbath never broke the S., but for Gain SIN, 13
the child that is born on the S. day /Is bonny and blithe, and good and gay NURSERY RHYMES, 34
sabotage All business sagacity reduces itself…to…s. BUSINESS, 25
sack Either back us or s. us SUPPORT, 3
sacred the human body is s. MANKIND, 36
sacrifice A woman will always s. herself WOMEN, 50
s.…of the devil's leavings VIRTUE, 15
this war…which did not justify the s. of a single mother's son WAR, 83
sacrificed the most useful thing about a principle…s. to expediency EXPEDIENCY, 4
sad Becoming an Anglo-Catholic must…be a s. business CATHOLICISM, 11
being kind /Is all the s. world needs RELIGION, 70; KINDNESS, 6
when thou art absent I am s. LOVE, 93
sadder A s. and a wiser man WISDOM, 13
sadists repressed s.…become policemen or butchers PUBLISHING, 6
sadness Good day s. SORROW, 7
S.…a form of fatigue SORROW, 9
safe Better be s. than sorry CAUTION, 1
make the world s. for diversity DIFFERENCE, 8
The only way to be absolutely s. CAUTION, 13
safeguard the s. of the west VENICE, 4
safer s. to obey than to rule OBEDIENCE, 3
safest Just when we are s. WORRY, 8
safety Safe though all s.'s lost WAR, 19
s. is in our speed HASTE, 6
sage without hardness will be s. FUTURE, 1
said a great deal to be s. /For being dead DEATH, 26
Nothing has yet been s. that's not been s. before ORIGINALITY, 5
they do not know what they have s. SPEECHES, 3
'Tis s. that some have died for love LOVE AND DEATH, 7
When a thing has been s. and s. well QUOTATIONS, 3
sailor No man will be a s. BOATS, 9
Tinker, /Tailor, /Soldier, /S. NURSERY RHYMES, 60
sailors opening time in the S. Arms PUBLIC HOUSES, 4
S. have a port OCCUPATIONS, 6
saint before we *know* he is a s., there will have to be miracles PROOF, 4

I consider myself superior to the s., the scientist NOVELS, 9
never a s. took pity on /My soul SOLITUDE, 2
S. Preux never kicked the fireirons IMPERFECTION, 5
St Ives As I was going to S. NURSERY RHYMES, 3
saints All are not s. HYPOCRISY, 1
many bodies of the s. which slept arose LAST WORDS, 11
sake Art for art's s. ART, 6
sakes king…men have made for their own s. MONARCHY, 18
salad My s. days YOUTH, 15
salary The s. of the chief executive BUSINESS, 11
this is the week I earn my s. MERIT, 5
sales Today's s. should be better than yesterday's BUSINESS, 2
Salkeld I am married to Beatrice S., a painter CHILDREN, 7
sally a sudden s. RIVERS, 6
There's none like pretty S. LOVE, 36
salmon cider and tinned s. FOOD, 51
serve both cod and s. PUNS, 11
the choice between smoked s. and tinned s. FOOD, 54
salt nobody likes having s. rubbed into their wounds AGGRAVATION, 2
S. water and absence LOVE, 9
speech…seasoned with s. SPEECH, 3
salvation There is no s. outside the church RELIGION, 3
The s. of mankind RESPONSIBILITY, 13
Sam Play it, S. MISQUOTATIONS, 11; NOSTALGIA, 2
Samaritan But a certain S.…had compassion on him CHARITY, 8
No one would have remembered the Good S. MONEY, 49
ready enough to do the S. CHARITY, 20
Samarkand the Golden Road to S. KNOWLEDGE, 14
same he is much the s. ILLNESS, 1
It will be all the s. WORRY, 3
it would be all the s. a hundred years hence TRIVIALITY, 3
principle seems the s. WATER, 1
we must all say *the s.* UNITY, 12
we're all made the s. SIMILARITY, 4
samite Clothed in white s. ARTHURIAN LEGEND, 3
Samuel When they circumcised Herbert S. INSULTS, 27
sanction Happiness is the only s. of life HAPPINESS, 22
sand and throws…s. in their eyes SLEEP, 10
draw a line in the s. MIDDLE EAST, 4
The s. of the desert is sodden red WAR, 76
They wept…to see /Such quantities of s. SEASIDE, 1
throw the s. against the wind FUTILITY, 5
World in a grain of s. WONDER, 2
sane Show me a s. man and I will cure him for you MADNESS, 6
sans S. teeth, sans eyes, sans taste, sans every thing OLD AGE, 38
Sappho Where burning S. loved EUROPE, 3
sarcasm petulance is not s. PETULANCE, 2; IMPERTINENCE, 1
S.…the language of the devil SARCASM, 1
sardines Life is…like a tin of s. LIFE, 10
sat The…gentleman has s. so long on the fence NONCOMMITMENT, 3
Satan And S. trembles PRAYER, 10
beheld S. as lightning fall from heaven DEVIL, 2
S. exalted sat, by merit raised DEVIL, 10
S. finds…mischief…/For idle hands IDLENESS, 10
S., Nick, or Clootie DEVIL, 6
satanic author of the S. Verses book…sentenced to death RELIGION, 37
satire hard not to write s. SATIRE, 1
S. is a sort of glass SATIRE, 3
S. should, like a polished razor keen SATIRE, 2
satirists S. should be heard and not seen CRITICISM, 48
satisfaction complacency and s.…in…a new-married couple MARRIAGE, 75
the s. of knowing that we are avenged REVENGE, 14
satisfied his soul is s. with what is assigned to him CONTENTMENT, 1
The superior man is s. SUPERIORITY, 2
Saturday betwixt /A S. and Monday SUNDAY, 3
Died on S. NURSERY RHYMES, 49
S.'s child works hard for his living NURSERY RHYMES, 34
what he did on S. HYPOCRISY, 19
satyr man is…either a stoic or a s. AGE, 45
sauce a country with thirty-two religions and only one s. AMERICA, 34
Art is not a special s. ART, 14
sixty different religions, and only one s. ENGLAND, 10
The best s. in the world HUNGER, 4
savage a time when Britain had a s. culture CIVILIZATION, 2
s. place! as holy and enchanted SUPERNATURAL, 6
soothe a s. breast MUSIC, 15
The young man who has not wept is a s. AGE, 51; WISDOM, 20
savaged s. by a dead sheep INSULTS, 18
savait *Si jeunesse s.* AGE, 24
save S. your breath SPEECH, 1
To s. a man's life against his will is…killing him KILLING, 3
saved he that endureth to the end shall be s. PERSISTENCE, 4
they only s. the world HEROISM, 2
saviour But it's 'S. of 'is country' when the guns SOLDIERS, 1
saw I came; I s.; God conquered VICTORY, 16
I came, I s., I conquered VICTORY, 1
I s. it, but I did not realize it PERCEPTION, 4
Saxon The S. is not like us Normans NATIONALITY, 6
say cannot s. what you have to s. in twenty minutes SPEECHES, 1
if we s. that we have no sin, we deceive SIN, 5
I have nothing to s., I am saying it POETRY, 9
Preachers s., Do as I s., not as I do EXAMPLE, 7
S. it with flowers FLOWERS, 10
s. what you have to s., and then sit down SPEECHES, 6
The great consolation…is to s. what one thinks FRANKNESS, 3
They are to s. what they please FREEDOM, 11
they do not know what they are going to s. SPEECHES, 3
What have we to s. to India COMMUNICATION, 4
When you have nothing to s. SILENCE, 4
saying S. is one thing ACTION, 5
when…speaking, they do not know what they are s. SPEECHES, 3
sayings Dr Johnson's s. WRITERS, 57
His s. are generally like women's letters LETTER-WRITING, 3
scab The itch of disputing…the s. of churches RELIGION, 71
scaffold no middle course between the throne and the s. MONARCHY, 7
scandal In England there is only silence or s. ENGLAND, 27
It is a public s. that gives offence MORALITY, 11
s. by a woman…proved liar POLITICS, 33
There's no s. like rags POVERTY, 8
scape who shall s. whipping MERIT, 6
scarce S., sir. Mighty scarce WOMEN, 82
scare A good s. is worth more ADVICE, 1
scarecrows Logical consequences are the s. of fools LOGIC, 3
scarlet His sins were s. BOOKS, 6; PUNS, 1
pious bird with the s. breast BIRDS, 13
though your sins be as s. FORGIVENESS, 4
scatter We plough the fields, and s. AGRICULTURE, 1
scenery Mountains…the beginning and the end of all natural s. MOUNTAINS, 3
S. is fine HUMAN NATURE, 16
scenes I'll come no more behind your s., David LUST, 3
sceptic too much of a s. to deny the possibility of anything SCEPTICISM, 2
scepticism s. kept her from being an atheist SCEPTICISM, 5
sceptred this s. isle ENGLAND, 36
Sch… S. you know who ADVERTISING, 17
Scheherazade S.…a woman saving her head SELF-PRESERVATION, 11
schemes best laid s. o' mice an' men DISAPPOINTMENT, 2
schizophrenia if God talks to you, you have s. MADNESS, 15
S. cannot be understood PSYCHIATRY, 6
schizophrenic S. behaviour…a special strategy PSYCHIATRY, 5
scholar the last humiliation of an aged s. OLD AGE, 15
scholars great men have not commonly been great s. GREATNESS, 8
S. and gentlemen HONOUR, 7
S. dispute ARGUMENTS, 7
school enjoy a public s. EDUCATION, 13
Example is the s. of mankind EXAMPLE, 2
fleshly s. of Poetry POETS, 2
If every day in the life of a s. EDUCATION, 30
never gone to s. may steal from a freight car EDUCATION, 46
nothing on earth…so horrible as a s. EDUCATION, 51
public s., where…learning was painfully beaten into him EDUCATION, 43
The Stealthy S. of Criticism CRITICISM, 43
The world is but a s. of inquiry CURIOSITY, 6
Three little maids from s. CHILDREN, 23
till he's been to a good s. EDUCATION, 47
schoolboy a s.'s barring out POLITICS, 78

every s. repeating my words POSTERITY, 8
I see a s. when I think of him POETS, 61
schoolboys 'tis the s. that educate my son EDUCATION, 15
schoolmaster Every s. after the age of 49 EDUCATION, 40
schoolmasters Let s. puzzle their brain ALCOHOL, 29
schools a hundred s. of thought contend CHINA, 8
Public s. are the nurseries of all vice EDUCATION, 16
There is now less flogging in our great s. EDUCATION, 27
We class s....into four grades EDUCATION, 59
schoolteacher The s....ludicrously overpaid as an educator EDUCATION, 41
science A s. which hesitates to forget SCIENCE, 46
Christian S. explains all cause and effect as mental RELIGION, 20
drawback that s....invented after I left school SCIENCE, 5
god of s....has given us the atomic bomb SCIENCE, 25
great tragedy of S. SCIENCE, 21
In everything that relates to s. SCIENCE, 26
Language is only the instrument of s. LANGUAGE, 16
lastly s. IMPORTANCE, 3
Learn to innure yourself to drudgery in s. EDUCATION, 42
only applications of s. SCIENCE, 32
Poetry is opposed to s....prose to metre POETRY AND PROSE, 1
Politics is not an exact s. POLITICS, 8
Politics is not a s....but an art POLITICS, 9
s....a refinement of everyday thinking SCIENCE, 13
S. fiction is no more written for scientists FICTION, 1
S. has 'explained' nothing SCIENCE, 19
s. is essentially international SCIENCE, 8
s. is...neither a potential for good nor for evil SCIENCE, 39
S. is nothing but trained and organized common sense SCIENCE, 20
S. is the great antidote SCIENCE, 40
s....is...the interplay between nature and ourselves NATURE, 10
S. must begin with myths MYTHS, 1; SCIENCE, 34
S. robs men of wisdom SCIENCE, 43
S. should leave off making pronouncements SCIENCE, 24
s. was the only career worth following WORK, 10
S. without conscience SCIENCE, 36
S. without religion is lame RELIGION, 22; SCIENCE, 14
Should we force s. down the throats SCIENCE, 35
the essence of s. SCIENCE, 1
the fairy tales of s. EXPERIENCE, 19
the greatest collective work of s. SCIENCE, 2
The highest wisdom has but one s. MANKIND, 34
the Holy Trinity of S. SCIENCE, 22
The term S. should not be given to anything SCIENCE, 44
when religion was strong and s. weak, men mistook magic for medicine MEDICINE, 10
science fiction great grey holy book of s. SCIENCE FICTION, 3
S. is the search for a definition of mankind SCIENCE FICTION, 2
sciences Books must follow s. BOOKS, 4
Do you...believe that the s. would...have...grown if the way had not been prepared by magicians SCIENCE, 31
no such things as applied s. SCIENCE, 32
scientific restating our socialism in terms of the s. revolution SOCIALISM, 15
S. discovery is a private event SCIENCE, 29
Traditional s. method has always been SCIENCE, 33
scientist I consider myself superior to the saint, the s. NOVELS, 9
When a distinguished but elderly s. states SCIENCE, 6
scientists find myself in the company of s. SCIENTISTS, 1
true men of action...the s. SCIENTISTS, 2
scissor-man The great, long, red-legged s. PUNISHMENT, 12
scope this man's art, and that man's s. DISCONTENT, 8
scorer when the One Great S. comes SPORT AND GAMES, 20; VICTORY, 15
scorn Silence is the...perfect expression of s. SILENCE, 13
scorned fury like a woman s. LOVE AND HATE, 3
Scotchman A S. must be a very sturdy moralist SCOTS, 3
Much may be made of a S. SCOTS, 5
never met with any one S. but what was a man of sense SCOTS, 8
the noblest prospect which a S. ever sees SCOTLAND, 4
what it is that makes a S. happy ALCOHOL, 34
Scotchmen trying...to like S. SCOTS, 7
Scotland I do indeed come from S. SCOTS, 4
I'll be in S. afore ye SCOTLAND, 1
Seeing S., Madam SCOTLAND, 5
Switzerland...an inferior sort of S. SWITZERLAND, 3
Scots S., wha hae wi' Wallace bled WAR, 20
Scotsman A young S. of your ability BRITISH, 1
S. on the make SCOTS, 2
the grandest moral attribute of a S. SCOTS, 1
to distinguish between a S. with a grievance SCOTS, 11
Scott C. P. S. EDITORS, 2
scoundrel given them to such a s. WEALTH, 27
Patriotism...the last refuge of the s. PATRIOTISM, 4
scratch S. my back HELP, 4
S. the Russian and...find the Tartar RUSSIA, 6
screech plastic Buddha jars out a Karate s. TECHNOLOGY, 6
screen A wide s....makes a bad film twice as bad CINEMA, 7
scribble Always s., s., s. WRITING, 9
scribbling My s. pays me zero francs per line – not including the white spaces WRITING, 29
script If it's a good s. MONEY, 12
Scripture devil can cite S. QUOTATIONS, 12
scrofulous s. French novel NOVELS, 1
sculptor not a great s. or painter can be an architect ARCHITECTURE, 9
sculpture S. to me is like poetry ARCHITECTURE, 7
scum of the s. of the earth ARMY, 5
The rich are the s. of the earth WEALTH, 9
scutcheon I bear no other s. JOURNALISM, 17
sea all the s. were ink NONSENSE, 1
Alone on a wide wide s. SOLITUDE, 2
change their clime...who rush across the s. TRAVEL, 12
Down to a sunless s. PLEASURE, 8
espouse the everlasting s. VENICE, 5
fishes live in the s. RUTHLESSNESS, 5
For all at last return to the s. SEA, 2
For those in peril on the s. SEA, 14
grow a little crazy...like all men at s. MADNESS, 5
kings of the s. DEPARTURE, 2
Learn the secret of the s. SEA, 9
like throwing water into the s. CHARITY, 11
men and s. interpenetrate ENGLAND, 11
Out of the s. came he SUN, 1
Over the s. to Skye ROYALTY, 5
Owl and the Pussy-Cat went to s. NONSENSE, 20
precious stone set in the silver s. ENGLAND, 36
s., trembling with a long line of radiance SEA, 12
Stick...to your desks and never go to s. OFFICERS, 7
The s. is calm to-night SEA, 1
The s.! the s. SEA, 15
The voice of the s. speaks to the soul SEA, 3
to the English that of the s. EUROPE, 15
We are as near to heaven by s. as by land LAST WORDS, 32; SEA, 5
when they can see nothing but s. DISCOVERY, 3
why the s. is boiling hot NONSENSE, 9
sea-change doth suffer a s. DEATH, 108
seagreen The s. Incorruptible POLITICIANS, 43
seagulls s. are following a trawler EXPECTATION, 1
sealed My lips are s. SECRECY, 2
sea-life When men come to like a s. SEA, 6
seam And sew a fine s. NURSERY RHYMES, 8
seamen There were gentlemen and...s. in the navy of Charles the Second NAVY, 3
the s. were not gentlemen NAVY, 3
search in s. of a great perhaps LAST WORDS, 56
s. for knowledge PHILOSOPHERS, 8
s. the land of living men ADMIRATION, 12
seas I must down to the s. again SEA, 10
That guard our native s. NAVY, 1
the waters called he S. CREATION, 3
seaside Beside the S. SEASIDE, 3
the drawback of all s. places SEASIDE, 2
season a perfectly ghastly s....for you Spanish dancers CHARITY, 5
Only in the mating s. ANIMALISM, 6
S. of mists and mellow fruitfulness SEASONS, 12
to every thing there is a s. TIME, 12
seasoned speech...s. with salt SPEECH, 3
seasons a man for all s. ADAPTABILITY, 4
Four s. fill the measure SEASONS, 10
seat the pleasure of offering my s. to three ladies OBESITY, 3
seated S....at the organ MUSIC, 39
sea-water Wealth is like s. GREED, 9
second The constitution...first and s. class citizens CLASS, 40
second-hand Would you buy a s. car TRUST, 5

second-rate an infallible sign of the s. INFERIORITY, 3
nor even booksellers have put up with poets' being s. POETS, 8
the creed of a s. man POLITICIANS, 1
secret a s. in the Oxford sense SECRECY, 10
a s. way...of getting at a boy EVIL, 8
bread eaten in s. is pleasant SECRECY, 5
I know that's a s. SECRECY, 8
it is no sin to sin in s. MORALITY, 11
joys of parents are s. FAMILY, 6
Learn the s. of the sea SEA, 9
not to give way to it in s. TELEVISION AND RADIO, 2
s. of reaping the greatest fruitfulness...from life DANGER, 6
Three may keep a s. SECRECY, 9
We have discovered the s. of life SCIENCE, 7
when it ceases to be a s. LOVE, 21
secreted Not in Utopia.../Or some s. island FRENCH REVOLUTION, 5
secretive As we make sex less s., we may rob it of its power SEX, 56
secrets Conversation...elicits s. from us CONVERSATION, 8
sect paradise for a s. FANATICISM, 2
sedate, sober, silent, serious, sad-coloured s. RELIGION, 32
secure only place where a man can feel...s. MEN, 6
The past, at least, is s. PAST, 9
security only freedom can make s. secure FREEDOM, 41
Sedan in a flood of tears and a S. chair HUMOUR, 37
sedge s. has wither'd from the lake ILLNESS, 10
seducers evil men and s. EVIL, 4
see change we think we s. NOVELTY, 2
Come up and s. me some time' MISQUOTATIONS, 23
complain we cannot s. COMPLAINTS, 1
I s. none coming out MISTRUST, 2
It is...at my age I now begin to s. things as they really are LAST WORDS, 25
My business is to paint...what I s. PAINTING, 17
s....into a hypocrite HYPOCRISY, 8
seem to s. things thou dost not POLITICIANS, 23
there shall no man s. me, and live GOD, 11
Why don't you come up sometime and s. me INVITATIONS, 3
seed Fair s.-time had my soul SOUL, 12
I do not want to die...until I have...cultivated the s. ACHIEVEMENT, 6
In s. time learn, in harvest teach SUITABILITY, 1
seeing S. is believing BELIEF, 2
seek I will undoubtedly have to s....gainful employment GOVERNMENT, 1
To toil and not to s. for rest SELFLESSNESS, 2
We s. him here, we s. him there ABSENCE, 9
We s./ it, ere it comes to light PERVERSITY, 3
seem Things are not always what they s. APPEARANCES, 5
seen Who has s. the wind WEATHER, 18
sees fool s. not the same tree WISDOM AND FOOLISHNESS, 5
What, when drunk, one s. in other women COMPLIMENTS, 7
Seine Today I spat in the S. WORLD WAR II, 23
seize S. the day PRESENT, 7
seldom s. attribute common sense AGREEMENT, 4
selected s....not on the basis of their grandmothers NAZISM, 3
selection Natural S. EVOLUTION, 6
self All censure of a man's s. SELF, 10
nothing...is greater...than one's s. SELF, 20
sickness enlarges the dimensions of a man's s. ILLNESS, 11
to thine own s. be true BORROWING, 8; INTEGRITY, 6
self-adjusting No man...who has wrestled with a s. card table TECHNOLOGY, 14
self-assertion Self-sufficiency at home, s. abroad NEWSPAPERS, 14
self-denial S. is not a virtue SELF-DENIAL, 1
self-employed I'm s. ROYALTY, 27
self-indulgence her favourite form of s. WOMEN, 50
write an essay on 's.' SELF, 16
self-interest S. speaks all sorts of tongues SELF-INTEREST, 6
selfish all Governments are s. GOVERNMENT, 8
a man becomes slack and s. MARRIAGE, 115
French governments more s. than most GOVERNMENT, 8
I have been a s. being all my life SELFISHNESS, 1
preserve the s. molecules known as genes SURVIVAL, 3
self-love S. is the greatest of all flatterers CONCEIT, 14
S. seems so often unrequited CONCEIT, 13
S....unrequited SELF, 12
true s. and social are the same SELF-KNOWLEDGE, 6
self-made A s. man...believes in luck SELF-MADE MEN, 3
a s. man who owed his lack of success to nobody SELF-MADE MEN, 2
self-praise S. is no recommendation PRAISE, 1
Selfridges by reality I mean shops like S. REALITY, 5
self-sufficiency S. at home, self-assertion abroad NEWSPAPERS, 14
self-sufficient know how to be s. SELF-RELIANCE, 7
selling A best-seller...because it was s. well FAME, 5
semed he s. bisier than he was APPEARANCES, 10
senators Do you pray for the s., Dr Hale POLITICIANS, 13
green-rob'd s. of mighty woods TREES, 7
senile a sign that they now consider him s. OLD AGE, 15
seniors earnest advice from my s. ADVICE, 16
sensations life of s. rather than of thoughts SENSATION, 1
sense because Americans won't listen to s. AMERICANS, 6
between a man of s. and his books BOOKS, 14
Common s. is the collection of prejudices PREJUDICE, 3
drowsy numbness pains my s. MELANCHOLY, 7
Let's talk s. to the American people ENDURANCE, 19
Money is like a sixth s. MONEY, 35
seldom attribute common s. AGREEMENT, 4
Take care of the s. MEANING, 2
The sound must seem an echo to the s. WRITING, 26
trained and organized common s. SCIENCE, 20
senses If Parson lost his s. ANIMALS, 12
sensible S. men are all of the same religion RELIGION, 18
sensitive more s. one is to great art ART, 3
sensual The only s. pleasure without vice MUSIC, 26
sent If this belief from heaven be s. MANKIND, 39
sentence S. first – verdict afterwards INJUSTICE, 4
structure of the...British s. GRAMMAR, 3
sentences The most attractive s. are not perhaps the wisest LANGUAGE, 25
sentiment Sentimentality is only s. SENTIMENTALITY, 4
sentimentality S. is a superstructure covering brutality SENTIMENTALITY, 2
S. is only sentiment SENTIMENTALITY, 4
s....rubs you up the wrong way SENTIMENTALITY, 4
sentiments high s. always win in the end NOBILITY, 3
sentinels men...who stand as s. in the avenues of fame CRITICS, 10
separation prepare for a s. SEPARATION, 4
they should declare the causes which impel them to...s. INDEPENDENCE, 2
September Clear in the cool S. morn AMERICA, 37
Thirty days hath S., /April, June, and November NURSERY RHYMES, 56
Septuagint The S. minus the Apostles NUMBERS, 4
sepulchre To famous men all the earth is a s. FAME, 20
sepulchres whited s. HYPOCRISY, 3
seraphs Mammon wins his way where S. might despair MATERIALISM, 4
serious a damned s. business WAR, 125
A joke's a very s. thing HUMOUR, 7
a noble nature...treats...a s. subject POETRY, 3
Mix a little foolishness with your s. plans FOOLISHNESS, 14
they are too *s.* FRANCE, 14
seriously Everything must be taken s., nothing tragically PERSPECTIVE, 4
sermons Ever since his s. were discontinued SERMONS, 2
He found in stones the s....hidden there POETS, 59
He that takes pleasure to hear s. PLEASURE, 26
serpent that old s. DEVIL, 4
the s. beguiled me SEXES, 2
servant for the last time in my life, Your Humble S. ARGUMENTS, 17
The cracked looking glass of a s. IRELAND, 10
the politician poses as the s. POLITICIANS, 8
thou good and faithful s. SERVICE, 1
servants Few men have been admired by their s. ADMIRATION, 8
good s., but bad masters PASSION, 4
half of them prefer hiring their s. for life SLAVERY, 2
he wouldn't have white s. RACISM, 24
part of English middle-class education is devoted to the training of s. EDUCATION, 65
S. should not be ill CLASS, 7
Socialists treat their s. with respect POLITICS, 77
We teachers can only help...as s. EDUCATION, 38
serve capacity to permit his ministers to s. him ROYALTY, 28
They also s. who only stand and wait SERVICE, 4

served I must have things daintily s. ETIQUETTE, 1
Youth will be s. SATISFACTION, 1
service I will see you in the vestry after s. CLERGY, 13
Small s. is true s. SERVICE, 5
serviettes kiddies have crumpled the s. ETIQUETTE, 1
Sesame Open S. SUPERNATURAL, 2
sessions s. of sweet silent thought REGRET, 18
set all, except their sun, is s. EUROPE, 3
best plain s. VIRTUE, 1
sets on which the sun never s. BRITISH EMPIRE, 6
setting clouds that gather round the s. sun MORTALITY, 21
settled No question is ever s. /Until ARGUMENTS, 19
Thank God, that's s. BORROWING, 9
settlement coach and six horses through the Act of S. IRELAND, 16
seven his acts being s. ages HUMAN CONDITION, 17
S. swans a-swimming NURSERY RHYMES, 55
seventh God…rested on the s. day SUNDAY, 1
seventy Being over s. is like being engaged in a war OLD AGE, 43
Being s. is not a sin OLD AGE, 29
Oh, to be s. again LUST, 4; OLD AGE, 14
sever a tie that only death can s. MARRIAGE, 83
severe if prolonged it cannot be s. SUFFERING, 13
sewage piped growing volumes of s. into the sea ENVIRONMENT, 2
sewer s. in a glass-bottomed boat CORRUPTION, 9
sex As we make s. less secretive, we may rob it of its power SEX, 56
both of them were extremely interested in s. SEX, 32
Christian view of s. SEX, 50
Continental people have s. life ENGLISH, 24
farmyard world of s. ANIMALISM, 2
How can I…dislike a s. to which Your Majesty belongs MISOGYNY, 5
If s. is such a natural phenomenon SEX, 37
if there was a third s. MEN, 13
In the s.-war thoughtlessness is the weapon of the male SEXES, 6
Is s. dirty SEX, 1
it's s. with someone you love SEX, 3
Literature is mostly about having s. LITERATURE, 12
meant us to have group s. SEX, 8
Money, it turned out, was exactly like s. MONEY, 8; SEX, 7
much more fundamental than s. MONEY, 19
no more weakness than is natural to her s. WOMEN, 78
No s. without responsibility SEX, 33
Personally I know nothing about s. SEX, 21
Pornography is the attempt to insult s. PORNOGRAPHY, 3
professed tyrant to their s. MISOGYNY, 6
s. has been a very private, secretive activity SEX, 56
S. is one of the nine reasons for reincarnation SEX, 38
S. is something I really don't understand SEX, 51
S. is the biggest nothing SEX, 61
S.'…'is the gateway to life. SEX, 6
s.…must itself be subject…to evolution SEXES, 3
the s. novel is now normal NOVELS, 14
we English have s. on the brain ENGLISH, 27; SEX, 43
sexes husbands and wives…belong to different s. SEXES, 8
more difference within the s. than between them SEXES, 5
that pleasure, which is undeniably the sole motive force behind the union of the s. SEX, 14
the…rift between the s. is…widened SEXES, 22
sexton went and told the s. PUNS, 5
sexual avowed purpose is to excite s. desire PORNOGRAPHY, 4
Industrial relations are like s. relations INDUSTRIAL RELATIONS, 2
music throatily…s. MUSIC, 25
sexuality no essential s. SEXES, 28
shabby For tamed and s. tigers ANIMALS, 12
shade a green thought in a green s. OBLIVION, 3
inviolable s. HOPE, 4
No s., no shine, no butterflies, no bees MONTHS, 10
Nothing grows well in the s. GREATNESS, 5
the s. /Of that which once was great REGRET, 23
shadow be caves…in which his s. will be shown GOD, 39
lose the substance by grasping at the s. GREED, 4
unhappy s. SORROW, 3
Who live under the s. of a war WAR, 111
Your s. at morning FEAR, 9
shadows brooding tragedy and its dark s. can be lightened HISTORY, 14
half sick of s. MARRIAGE, 119
shak'd when degree is s. ORDER, 4
Shakespeare after S. and Milton are fogotten POETS, 51
A strange, horrible business…good enough for S.'s day CRITICISM, 50
Besides S. and me, who do you think there is CONCEIT, 15
I despise S. SHAKESPEARE, 16
myriad-minded S. SHAKESPEARE, 3
reading S. by flashes of lightning CRITICISM, 9
S.…grammar school kids LITERATURE, 4
S., I come LAST WORDS, 19
S. is…really very good SHAKESPEARE, 8
S. never had six lines together without a fault SHAKESPEARE, 9
S. – the nearest thing SHAKESPEARE, 14
S., undoubtedly wanted taste SHAKESPEARE, 18
sweetest S., Fancy's child SHAKESPEARE, 13
the making up of a S. or a Milton WRITERS, 5
the right to criticize S. CRITICISM, 47
tried lately to read S. SHAKESPEARE, 4
We can say of S. SHAKESPEARE, 7
When I read S. I am struck SHAKESPEARE, 12
Wonderful women!…how much we…owe to S. SHAKESPEARE, 17
shaking After s. hands with a Greek MISTRUST, 1
all these great interests entrusted to the s. hand POLITICIANS, 77
Shakspeare who speak the tongue /That S. spake FREEDOM, 54
Shalimar Pale hands I loved beside the S. LOVE, 70
shambles Our civilization is founded on the s. DEATH, 63
shame expense of spirit in a waste of s. LUST, 7
Neither s. nor physical pain have any…effect PUNISHMENT, 13
shamefaced Perjury…is truth that is s. TRUTH, 22
shape hearts of Men…should have a virtue to s. their life MANKIND, 33
shapely important for a theory to be s. THEORY, 5
share s. in the good fortunes of the mighty INJUSTICE, 2
sharp those who have stout hearts and s. swords RUTHLESSNESS, 6
shaves man who s. and takes a train TRAINS, 6; TRAVEL, 25
Shaw Bernard S. WRITERS, 64
G. B. S. POPULARITY, 9
George Bernard S. is sadly miscast CRITICISM, 48
George Too S. To Be Good WRITERS, 87
Mr S.…has never written any poetry WRITERS, 39
S. CRITICISM, 48
S. has no enemies…disliked by…friends WRITERS, 92
S. relished every opportunity WRITERS, 42
S. replied 'I'll wait for you to grow up WRITERS, 37
Shaw's S. judgements are often scatterbrained WRITERS, 31
she s. is my country still PATRIOTISM, 6
shears marriage…resembles a pair of s. MARRIAGE, 110
shedding without s. of blood is no remission EXECUTION, 2
sheep A s. in s.'s clothing WEAKNESS, 3
Baa, baa, black s. NURSERY RHYMES, 4
good shepherd giveth his life for the s. CHRISTIANITY, 15
hungry s. look up, and are not fed CORRUPTION, 3
like lost s. SIN, 8
make a man by standing a s. PUBLIC, 4
not armies…but flocks of s. DELUSION, 3
savaged by a dead s. INSULTS, 18
s. had already made its statement ART, 10
The mountain s. are sweeter GREED, 7
The s.'s in the meadow NURSERY RHYMES, 28
the wolf in the s.'s clothing APPEARANCES, 8; DECEPTION, 2
useless for the s. to pass resolutions in favour of vegetarianism ARGUMENTS, 9
shelf The dust and silence of the upper s. NEGLECT, 3
Shelley S. and Keats were…up to date in…chemical knowledge POETS, 7
S. and Keats were…up to date in…chemical knowledge SCIENCE, 17
S. had a hyper-thyroid face APPEARANCE, 36
S.'s nature is utterly womanish POETS, 45
the right sphere for S.'s genius POETS, 14
shells With silver bells and cockle s. GARDENS, 1
shelter Our s. from the stormy blast RELIGION, 64
shepherd Go, for they call you, S., from the hill SUMMONS, 1
I am the good s. CHRISTIANITY, 15
This is the weather the s. shuns WEATHER, 14

shepherds Governments needs to have both s. and butchers GOVERNMENT, 31
s. abiding in the field CHRISTMAS, 8
s. watch'd their flocks CHRISTMAS, 18
Sherard S. Blaw, the dramatist who had discovered himself WRITERS, 80
sherry With first-rate s. flowing into second-rate whores MEDIOCRITY, 7
shift for coming down let me s. for myself EXECUTION, 18
shilling I'm sorry to hear that, sir, you don't happen to have the s. about you now, do you BEQUESTS, 2
shimmy Put thy s. on, Lady Chatterley PARTING, 7
shine shine on, s. on, harvest moon MOON, 6
shining A woman of so s. loveliness BEAUTY, 40
shins long dresses…cover a multitude of s. CLOTHES, 18
ship A whale s. was my Yale College EDUCATION, 35
being in a s. is being in a jail BOATS, 9
Don't give up the s. LAST WORDS, 42
S. me somewheres east of Suez DESIRE, 9
The s. follows Soviet custom CLASS, 34
ships Heart of oak are our s. COURAGE, 13
I spied three s. come sailing by CHRISTMAS, 3
little s. of England brought the Army home BOATS, 8; WORLD WAR II, 20
S. that pass in the night TRANSIENCE, 16
something wrong with our bloody s. BOATS, 1
stately s. go on NOSTALGIA, 21
the face that launch'd a thousand s. BEAUTY, 25
We've got the s., we've got the men, we've got the money too PATRIOTISM, 16
shipwreck husbands and wives make s. of their lives MARRIAGE, 50
shirt no s. or collar ever comes back twice NEGLECT, 2
shit People will swim through s. GREED, 10
the sun shining ten days a year and s. in the streets ENGLAND, 21
when you s.? Singing, it's the same thing SINGING, 1
shock Anybody can s. a baby SIMPLICITY, 7
deliberately set out to s. THEATRE, 12
shocked how to be amused rather than s. AGE, 16
shock-headed S. Peter CHILDREN, 25
shocking little man wears a s. bad hat CLOTHES, 20
shocks s. /That flesh is heir to SUICIDE, 12
shoemaker I take my shoes from the s. RELIGION, 28
shoes before you let the sun in, mind it wipes its s. CLEANNESS, 2
I take my s. from the shoemaker RELIGION, 28
s. and ships and sealing wax NONSENSE, 9
shoot do not s. the pianist EFFORT, 7
except to s. rabbits and hit his father on the jaw NASTINESS, 5
if a man hit you, you could s. him VIOLENCE, 2
It is not the business of generals to s. one another OFFICERS, 14
S., if you must, this old gray head PATRIOTISM, 32
they could s. me in my absence JUSTICE, 2
shooting A bit of s. takes your mind off IRELAND, 3; VIOLENCE, 1
war minus the s. SPORT AND GAMES, 18
shop All English s. assistants are Miltonists SERVICE, 3
A man must keep a little back s. SOLITUDE, 12
shop-keepers A nation of s. BRITAIN, 2; ENGLISH, 28
shopping Today you're unhappy?…Go s. MATERIALISM, 15
shore adieu! my native s. DEPARTURE, 4
waves make towards the pebbled s. TIME, 34
Shoreditch When I grow rich, /Say the bells of S. LONDON, 2
shores eternal whisperings around Desolate s. SEA, 8
short Good things, when s., are twice as good BREVITY, 1
Is not life…too s.…to bore ourselves BOREDOM, 6
it will take a long while to make it s. WRITING, 33
Life is too s. to do anything…one can pay others to do WORK, 13
make the beat keep time with s. steps FUNERALS, 1
s. and simple annals of the poor POVERTY, 13
the life of man, solitary, poor, nasty, brutish, and s. HUMAN CONDITION, 11
We have s. time to stay, as you TRANSIENCE, 14
shortage a s. of coal and fish…at the same time INCOMPETENCE, 1
shorter not had the time to make it s. VERBOSITY, 5
s. by a head ROYALTY, 15
shortest I never realized that I'd end up being the s. knight of the year PUNS, 19; TITLES, 8
the s. works are always the best BREVITY, 4
shot had them all s. LAST WORDS, 46; RUTHLESSNESS, 4
he once s. a bookseller PUBLISHING, 5
shots God is on the side…of the best s. POWER POLITICS, 8
They really are bad s. ASSASSINATION, 3
shoulder-blade I have a left s. CONCEIT, 10
shoulders it is by standing on the s. of giants PROGRESS, 9
shout S. with the largest MAJORITY, 1
show I have that within which passes s. MOURNING, 12
I often wish they would s. off a little more OSTENTATION, 4
showers Sweet April s. MONTHS, 12
shows All my s. are great BOASTS, 3; CONCEIT, 11
shreds A thing of s. and patches SINGERS, 2
Shrewsbury They hang us now in S. jail: /The whistles blow forlorn EXECUTION, 11
shriek That s. and sweat in pigmy wars TRIVIALITY, 14
shrine Melancholy has her…s. MELANCHOLY, 8
shrink all the boards did s. WATER, 2
shuffled s. off this mortal coil SUICIDE, 12
the human pack is s. and cut EDUCATION, 31
shut when I was there it seemed to be s. PLACES, 5
shy Why so s., my pretty Thomasina SHYNESS, 3
shyness S. is *common* SHYNESS, 6
S. is just egotism out of its depth SHYNESS, 4
sick A person seldom falls s. HUMAN NATURE, 10
being s. with other people singing PARTIES, 7
Dante makes me s. LAST WORDS, 13
I am s. at heart COMFORT, 2
if you don't object if I'm s. SMOKING, 1
make any man s. to hear her INSINCERITY, 3
The prayer that…heals the s. FAITH, 10
The s. man is a parasite of society PATIENTS, 2
the wary fox said…to the s. lion MISTRUST, 5
We have on our hands a s. man DECLINE, 7
sickness in s. and in health MARRIAGE, 30
Love is a s. LOVE, 45
s. enlarges the dimensions of a man's self ILLNESS, 11
S., sin and death…do not originate in God RELIGION, 21
Sidcup If only I could get down to S. PROOF, 5
side A door is what a dog is…on the wrong s. of DOGS, 10
a s. dish he hadn't ordered CONTEMPT, 3
He who knows only his own s.…knows little SUBJECTIVITY, 4
Time is on our s. PROGRESS, 7
sides Do not…write on both s. of the paper EXAMINATIONS, 2
said on both s. OBJECTIVITY, 1
We…assume that everything has two s. SUBJECTIVITY, 7
sighed They s. for the dawn and thee LOVE, 134
sighs over the Bridge of S. into eternity DEATH, 74
S. are the natural language of the heart SPEECH, 15
sight a s. to make an old man young BEAUTY, 38
Out of s. ABSENCE, 2
we walk by faith, not by s. FAITH, 5
Who ever loved, that loved not at first s. FIRST IMPRESSIONS, 6
sightless clapped the glass to his s. eye BLINDNESS, 6
sights And see all s. from pole to pole SOUL, 3
few more impressive s. in the world SCOTS, 2
sign Never s. a walentine SIGNATURES, 1
s. of an ill-spent youth SPORT AND GAMES, 22
writing a letter and forgetting to s. his name INSULTS, 5
significant s. form ART, 4
signifying S. nothing LIFE, 45
signing I am s. my death warrant PROPHECY, 3
sign language S. is the equal of speech LANGUAGE, 22
silence Come to me in the s. of the night NOSTALGIA, 18
foster-child of s. and slow time SILENCE, 9
In England there is only s. or scandal ENGLAND, 27
looking for the s. in somebody PHOTOGRAPHY, 3
Make him a bishop, and you will s. him CLERGY, 5
occasional flashes of s. INSULTS, 35
S. is as full of potential wisdom SILENCE, 8
S. is become his mother tongue SILENCE, 6
S. is the best tactic SILENCE, 10
S. is the perfectest herald of joy SILENCE, 12
S. is the…perfect expression of scorn SILENCE, 13
s. sank /Like music SILENCE, 3
Sorrow and s. are strong ENDURANCE, 9
That man's s. is wonderful to listen to SILENCE, 7
The cruellest lies are…told in s. SILENCE, 14
The dust and s. of the upper shelf NEGLECT, 3
the impression that their normal condition is s. SILENCE, 11
the more absolute s. of America ENGLAND, 24
the rest is s. DEATH, 104
With s. and tears SEPARATION, 2

silent burst /Into that s. sea EXPLORATION, 1
the great s. majority MAJORITY, 5
the man who can be s. in several languages DIPLOMACY, 11
thereon one must remain s. SILENCE, 15
silicon If s. had been a gas EXAMINATIONS, 3
silk rustling in unpaid-for s. CONTENTMENT, 7
s., too often hides eczema STYLE, 2
the s. stockings and white bosoms...excite my amorous propensities LUST, 3
silks Whenas in s. my Julia goes CLOTHES, 8
silly A s. remark can be made in Latin LANGUAGE, 5
it's lovely to be s. at the right moment FOOLISHNESS, 14
some damned s. thing in the Balkans BOSNIA AND HERCEGOVINA, 2
silver First of...Georgian s. goes POLITICS, 49
for a handful of s. BETRAYAL, 2
s. and gold have I none REMEDIES, 3
S. buckles on his knee NURSERY RHYMES, 5
S. threads among the gold OLD AGE, 35
The s. apples of the moon DESIRE, 18
When every...thing you hold /Is made of s., or of gold ECONOMICS, 9
silvery the s. adamant walls of life's exclusive city DEATH, 75
Silvia Who is S.? What is she ADMIRATION, 16
Simon Simple S. met a pieman NURSERY RHYMES, 47
simple A s. race POETS, 10
short and s. annals of the poor POVERTY, 13
Teach us delight in s. things GOOD, 7
simplicity O holy s. SIMPLICITY, 3
simplify ability to s. means SIMPLICITY, 2
S., s. SIMPLICITY, 8
simplifying s. something by destroying nearly everything CIVILIZATION, 4
sin A branch of the s. of drunkenness DRUNKENNESS, 14
All s. tends to be addictive SIN, 2
a more dreadful record of s. than...countryside SIN, 12
A private s. is not so prejudicial SIN, 10
beauty is only s. deep BEAUTY, 34
Being seventy is not a s. OLD AGE, 29
He that is without s. MISQUOTATIONS, 8; SIN, 4
if we say that we have no s., we deceive SIN, 5
it is no s. to s. in secret MORALITY, 11
nicest boy who ever committed the s. of whisky ALCOHOL, 59
no s. but to be rich HYPOCRISY, 15
no s. except stupidity STUPIDITY, 15
people who can s. with a grin SIN, 17
Sickness, s. and death...do not originate in God RELIGION, 21
S. brought death DEATH, 46; SIN, 14
than that one soul...should commit one single venial s. SIN, 18
They are written as if s. were to be taken out...by...sleep SERMONS, 1
which taketh away the s. of the world CHRISTIANITY, 12
your s. will find you out SIN, 7
sincere Some of the worst men in the world are s. SINCERITY, 3
sincerest Imitation...s. of flattery IMITATION, 2
sincerity A little s. is a dangerous thing SINCERITY, 6
style, not s., is the vital thing STYLE, 7
sinecure a widow...is a kind of s. EXPEDIENCY, 7
sinews Anger is one of the s. of the soul ANGER, 4
sing Can't act. Can't s. ACTORS, 8
Did certain persons die before they s. SINGERS, 1
I'd like to teach the world to s. ADVERTISING, 12
I will s. of the sun WOMEN, 66
S. a song of sixpence NURSERY RHYMES, 48
The Welsh...just s. WELSH, 4
singed s. the Spanish king's beard WAR, 35
singing s. in the rain WEATHER, 12
To hear the lark...s..../From his watch-tower in the skies BIRDS, 8
when you shit? S., it's the same thing SINGING, 1
single a s. man in possession of a good fortune must be in want of a wife MARRIAGE, 10
begins with a s. step BEGINNING, 1
Behold her, s. in the field SOLITUDE, 16
singular Ball...how very s. NAMES, 1
sink The s. is the great symbol of the bloodiness of family life FAMILY, 24
sinn'd More s. against than sinning INJUSTICE, 12
sinners At such an hour the s. are still in bed SIN, 19
It's your combination s....who dishonour the vices VICE, 10
sinning nothing so artificial as s. nowadays SIN, 15
sins atone for the s. of your fathers INJUSTICE, 7
from Expensive S. refrain SIN, 13
gravest s. it was possible for a gentlewoman to commit READING, 18
her s., which are many, are forgiven FORGIVENESS, 6; SIN, 6
His s. were scarlet BOOKS, 6; PUNS, 1
One of the unpardonable s...., is...to go about unlabelled CLASSIFICATION, 1
she must not reheat his s. for breakfast FORGIVENESS, 11
though your s. be as scarlet FORGIVENESS, 4
Sir I am S. Oracle EGOTISM, 8
Sirens Blest pair of S. POETRY, 30
sister I kissed her little s. UNFAITHFULNESS, 4
no friend like a s. FAMILY, 29
sisters And so do his s. FAMILY, 14
little s. to all the world WOMEN, 28
O! men with s. dear WOMEN, 40
sit I will s. down now PROPHECY, 4
men s. and hear each other groan HUMAN CONDITION, 12
nobody can tell you when to s. down POWER, 10
say what you have to say, and then s. down SPEECHES, 6
So I did s. and eat LOVE, 68
sitting Are you s. comfortably? Then I'll begin BEGINNING, 13
by s. down round you HOUSES OF PARLIAMENT, 19
I do most of my work s. down HUMOUR, 34
situation s. excellent. I shall attack WAR, 36
six Candidates should not attempt more than s. BIBLE, 2
S. geese a-laying NURSERY RHYMES, 55
s. of one and half-a-dozen of the other SIMILARITY, 5
two and two do not make s. LAST WORDS, 70
sixpence He found a crooked s. against a crooked stile NURSERY RHYMES, 52
I love s., jolly little s. NURSERY RHYMES, 22
Sing a song of s. NURSERY RHYMES, 48
The Moon and S. BOOK, SONG, AND PLAY TITLES, 17
sixpences there go two-and-forty s....to one guinea MERIT, 4
sixth Money is like a s. sense MONEY, 35
sixty at the rate of s. minutes an hour TIME, 24
close-up of a woman past s. APPEARANCE, 4
Men come of age at s. AGE, 60
S. horses wedged in a /chimney JOURNALISM, 24
sixty-five I have been drinking it for s. years and I am not dead DRINKS, 9
sixty-three Sexual intercourse began /In nineteen s. SEX, 29
size I am not this s., really OBESITY, 4
skating s. over thin ice HASTE, 6
skeleton Every family has a s. in the cupboard FAMILY, 2
ski unbecoming for a cardinal to s. badly SPORT AND GAMES, 11
skies looks commercing with the s. SOUL, 10
look up at the s. STARS, 3
skill In arguing too, the parson own'd his s. KNOWLEDGE, 17
S. without imagination is craftsmanship ART, 27
skin I've Got You Under My S. LOVE, 100
never...sell the bear's s. ANTICIPATION, 6
There is more than one way to s. a cat DIFFERENCE, 4
skinning When you are s. your customers BUSINESS, 14
skins beauty of their s. SEXES, 23
skipper s. had taken his little daughter BOATS, 11
skirt a woman...ought to lay aside...modesty with her s. SEX, 40
skittles Life isn't all beer and s. LIFE, 30
sky a Friend for little children /Above the bright blue s. GOD, 36
inverted Bowl we call The S. DESTINY, 9
Which prisoners call the s. IMPRISONMENT, 7
Skye Over the sea to S. ROYALTY, 5
slack a man becomes s. and selfish MARRIAGE, 115
slamming little girls...s. doors CHILDREN, 10
slander it is always said of s. that something always sticks PRAISE, 2
slang All s. is metaphor LANGUAGE, 9
The one...poetry...continually flowing is s. LANGUAGE, 8
slapped anyone who s. us...would get his head kicked off REVENGE, 12
slave Be not the s. of Words WORDS, 5
came to America in s. ships EQUALITY, 12
commerce between master and s. is...exercise of...boisterous passions SLAVERY, 5
man...is Reason's s. PASSION, 1
s. for livelihood ENVY, 3
slavery will not support...professional s. EXPLOITATION, 4

slaves In a consumer society there are...two kinds of s. MATERIALISM, 10
love, an...intercourse between tyrants and s. LOVE AND FRIENDSHIP, 2
Practical men...s. of some defunct economist INFLUENCE, 6
S. cannot breathe in England SLAVERY, 3
that the masters willingly concede to s. SLAVERY, 1
slaying the s. of a beautiful hypothesis by an ugly fact SCIENCE, 21
slays moves, and mates, and s. DESTINY, 7
sleave ravell'd s. of care SLEEP, 15
sleek you will come and find me fat and s. PRESENT, 10
sleep amount of s. required SLEEP, 11
A professor is one who talks in someone else's s. ACADEMICS, 1
Better s. with a sober cannibal than a drunken Christian DRUNKENNESS, 16
Every time you s. with a boy AIDS, 5; ILLNESS, 5
haven't been to s. for over a year SLEEP, 19
How do people go to s. SLEEP, 14
Let me s. the s. of the earth SOLITUDE, 14
Now I lay me down to s. SLEEP, 2
Our birth is but a s. METAPHYSICS, 5
our little life /Is rounded with a s. MORTALITY, 17
s. begins for weary /mortals SLEEP, 18
S. is good, death is better PESSIMISM, 6
s.! it is a gentle thing SLEEP, 6
S....knows not Death SLEEP, 16
S. that knits up the ravell'd sleave SLEEP, 15
The past was a s. BEGINNING, 7
They are written as if sin were to be taken out...by...s. SERMONS, 1
To s., perchance to dream SUICIDE, 12
we must s. REST, 2
youth would s. out the rest YOUTH, 16
sleepin' Capten, art tha s. there below WAR, 77
sleeping fuss about s. together...sooner go to my dentist SEX, 62
Let s. dogs lie TACT, 2
S. as quiet as death OLD AGE, 46
There will be s. enough DEATH, 12
we have only awakened a s. giant WORLD WAR II, 31
sleeps eats, s. and watches the television WOMAN'S ROLE, 2
She s. alone at last EPITAPHS, 1
sleepwalker that Providence dictates with the assurance of a s. DESTINY, 12
sleepy Come, let's to bed /Says S.-head NURSERY RHYMES, 7
sleeve let the last man...brush the Channel with his s. WAR, 105
slick I have three phobias which...would make my life as s. as a sonnet OBSESSIONS, 1
slimy thousand thousand s. things GUILT, 4
slings s. and arrows of outrageous fortune SUICIDE, 12
slip he gave us all the s. ABSENCE, 5
There's many a s. ALCOHOL, 6
slipped I have only s. away into the next room AFTERLIFE, 5
slippers Same old s. MARRIAGE, 76
slipping Time is s. underneath TIME, 18
slitty If you stay much longer you will go back with s. eyes RACISM, 25
slob just a lucky s. from Ohio ACTORS, 13
slogan democracy is just a s. DEMOCRACY, 5
slogans If you feed people just with revolutionary s. PROMISES, 4
Slough Come, friendly bombs, and fall on S. ENGLAND, 4
the s. was Despond DESPAIR, 2
slow On a s. boat to China BOATS, 10
S. and steady wins the race HASTE, 7
S. but sure PERSISTENCE, 3
Tarry a while, says S. NURSERY RHYMES, 7
too swift arrives as tardy as too s. LOVE, 114
with a s. deliberate carelessness READING, 10
slug-horn the s. to my lips I set SUMMONS, 4
slum if you've seen one city s. POVERTY, 3
slumber A s. did my spirit seal IMMORTALITY, 7
Love itself shall s. on MEMORY, 17
Oft in the stilly night, /Ere S.'s chain NOSTALGIA, 14
slumbers Golden s. kiss your eyes SLEEP, 7
slush pure as the driven s. PURITY, 2
smack much more indecent...than a good s. PUNISHMENT, 14
small Errors look so very ugly in persons of s. means POVERTY AND WEALTH, 5
From s. beginnings BEGINNING, 3
In Western Europe there are now only s. countries EUROPE, 12
Microbe is so very s. SMALLNESS, 2
Popularity?...glory's s. change POPULARITY, 4
S. is beautiful BEAUTY, 4
The best things come in s. parcels SMALLNESS, 1
virtue's still far too s. VIRTUE, 6
smaller accepts a s. as a favour INJUSTICE, 3
someone s. than oneself ABILITY, 3; PRUDENCE, 8
these have s. fleas to bite 'em PARASITES, 3
small-talking Where in this s. world MEANING, 4
smartness the s. of an attorney's clerk INSULTS, 15
smarts No creature s....as a fool FOOLISHNESS, 17
smattering A s. of everything KNOWLEDGE, 12
smell rose...would s. as sweet NAMES, 7
Sweet S. of Success SUCCESS, 12
smells the only dead thing that s. sweet PAST, 7
smile a s. I could feel in my hip pocket SEX, 15
A s. that snapped back after using APPEARANCE, 20
Cambridge people rarely s. CAMBRIDGE, 2
s. at perils past PAST, 6
S. at us, pay us, pass us ENGLISH, 12
s., s., s. OPTIMISM, 13
the vain tribute of a s. POETS, 10
smiled the soldiers he s. at WAR, 102
smiles She is Venus when she s. COMPLIMENTS, 2
s., /Wan as primroses FLOWERS, 5
The s., the tears, /Of boyhood's years NOSTALGIA, 14
smite whosoever shall s. thee on thy right cheek ENEMIES, 2
Smith Chuck it, S. RELIGION, 15
The s., a mighty man is he OCCUPATIONS, 10
smoke Don't screw around, and don't s. HEALTH AND HEALTHY LIVING, 5
no woman should marry...a man who does not s. ABSTINENCE, 10
resembling the horrible Stygian s. of the pit SMOKING, 7
S., my friend SMOKING, 15
There's no s. without fire GOSSIP, 4
smoking he had read of the effects of s. SMOKING, 16
resolve to give up s., drinking and loving ABSTINENCE, 5
s. at such a rate SMOKING, 11
s. can play a valuable role in a society SMOKING, 13
s. cigars and...drinking of alcohol before, after, and...during ALCOHOL, 21; SMOKING, 4
What a blessing this s. is SMOKING, 6
why he doesn't stop s. SMOKING, 17
smooth course of true love never did run s. LOVE, 119
many cities had rubbed him s. TRAVEL, 10
smyler The s. with the knyf HYPOCRISY, 7
snail said a whiting to a s. HASTE, 5
s.'s on the thorn PERFECTION, 2
snails Frogs and s. /And puppy-dogs' tails NURSERY RHYMES, 65
snake A s. came to my water-trough WEATHER, 16
There's a s. hidden in the grass DANGER, 7
snapper-up s. of unconsidered trifles BUSINESS, 19
snare a s. in which the feet of women have always become readily entangled WOMEN, 5
Snark For the S. *was* a Boojum NONSENSE, 6
sneezed Not to be s. at IMPORTANCE, 1
when a British Prime Minister s. BRITAIN, 12
snipe well-shot woodcock, partridge, s. HUNTING, 1
snob He who meanly admires...is a S. SNOBBERY, 7
impossible, in our condition of society, not to be sometimes a S. SNOBBERY, 8
no s. welcomes another SNOBBERY, 1
snobbish Don't be s., we seek to abolish CLASS, 21
snobs His hatred of s. SNOBBERY, 5
snore s. and you sleep alone SLEEP, 5
snorer can't hear himself s. SLEEP, 17
snotgreen The s. sea SEA, 7
snow both its national products, s. and chocolate, melt SWITZERLAND, 1
I used to be S. White PURITY, 6
The s. hath retreated SEASONS, 28
the wrong kind of s. TRAINS, 8
wish a s. in May SUITABILITY, 4
snows the s. of yesteryear NOSTALGIA, 22
snub Vile s.-nose, flat-nosed ass APPEARANCE, 31
snuff time for me to enjoy another pinch of s. EXECUTION, 1
so It is s.. It is not s. ARGUMENTS, 5

soap S. and education…are more deadly EDUCATION, 56
soar to run, though not to s. IMAGINATION, 9
sober a s. colouring from an eye MORTALITY, 21
as s. as a Judge DRUNKENNESS, 12
Better sleep with a s. cannibal than a drunken Christian DRUNKENNESS, 16
England should be compulsorily s. FREEDOM, 31
he that will go to bed s. ALCOHOL, 27
How do you look when I'm s. CLOTHES, 11
My mother, drunk or s. PATRIOTISM, 5
one sees in Garbo s. COMPLIMENTS, 7
sedate, s., silent, serious, sad-coloured sect RELIGION, 32
Tomorrow we'll be s. DRUNKENNESS, 3
sociable I am a s. worker SOCIETY, 2
Society is no comfort to one not s. SOCIETY, 8
social Man is a s. animal SOCIETY, 9
our s. spheres have been widely different SNOBBERY, 11
the things which government does…s. progress GOVERNMENT, 32
the…world was stumbling…in s. blindness BLINDNESS, 2
to enter s. life on tiptoe FOOTBALL, 7
true self-love and s. are the same SELF-KNOWLEDGE, 6
socialising I'm not very good at ordinary s. SELF-RELIANCE, 5
socialism Marxian S. must always remain a portent MARXISM, 2
Only s. would put up with it SOCIALISM, 5
religion of S. SOCIALISM, 2
restating our s. in terms of the scientific revolution SOCIALISM, 15
s.…alien to the British character SOCIALISM, 14
S. can only arrive by bicycle SOCIALISM, 4
S. with a human face COMMUNISM, 2
the proletariat will…wage a class struggle for S. CLASS, 18
the worst advertisement for S. is its adherents SOCIALISM, 11
to banish…the dark divisive clouds of Marxist s. MARXISM, 6
To the ordinary working man…S. SOCIALISM, 12
Under s. *all* will govern SOCIALISM, 10
socialists intelligent people…are s. SOCIALISM, 1
S. treat their servants with respect POLITICS, 77
We are all S. now SOCIALISM, 7
what are you s. going to do about me SOCIALISM, 6
societies range of human s. in time, the other in space MANKIND, 16
society a free s.…where it is safe to be unpopular FREEDOM, 50
a poor s. cannot be too poor POVERTY AND WEALTH, 8
A s.…of individuals…capable of original thought IDEAS, 6
Comedy, we may say, is s. HUMOUR, 24
if it be our clothes alone which fit us for s. CLOTHES, 4
impossible, in our condition of s., not to be sometimes a Snob SNOBBERY, 8
In a consumer s. there are…two kinds of slaves MATERIALISM, 10
it proved that I was in a civilized s. EXECUTION, 21
Mankind is a closed s. MANKIND, 25
Man was formed for s. SOCIETY, 3
Never speak disrespectfully of S. SNOBBERY, 12
no intellectual s. can flourish where a Jew feels…uneasy JEWS, 7
no new baby in the womb of our s. RUSSIA, 5
nothing to distinguish human s. from the farm-yard MANKIND, 29
only possible s. is oneself MISANTHROPY, 4
S., friendship, and love SOLITUDE, 4
S. goes on and on and on IDEAS, 4
S. is no comfort /To one not sociable SOCIETY, 8
S. is now one polish'd horde BORES, 2
s.…pays a harlot 25 times as much as it pays its Prime Minister INJUSTICE, 14
s., where none intrudes NATURE, 3
so famous, that it would permit me…to break wind in s. FAME, 3
The history of all…s. is the history of class struggles CLASS, 22
the ideal of a democratic and free s. RACISM, 22
There are two classes in good s. CLASS, 29
The sick man is a parasite of s. PATIENTS, 2
the transition from the…'closed s.'…to the 'open s.' SOCIETY, 6
transform this s. without a major extension of public ownership SOCIALISM, 9
sociology Children…detest s. BOOKS, 39
socks His s. compelled one's attention CLOTHES, 15
sod off I don't want you here – now s. INSULTS, 2
Sodom S. and…Gomorrah PUNISHMENT, 3
the men of S. were wicked HOMOSEXUALITY, 1
sodomy Comedy, like s., is an unnatural act HUMOUR, 12
rum, s., and the lash NAVY, 2
sofa rather lie on a s. than sweep beneath it LAZINESS, 1
soft I'm not hard – I'm frightfully s. CHARACTER, 24
our love…of the mind does not make us s. RESULTS, 4
softened subjects are s. and sentimentalised too much ARTISTS, 15
solar the whole s. and stellar systems COMFORT, 1
sold never hate a song that has s. half a million copies POP MUSIC, 3
soldier a chocolate cream s. SOLDIERS, 6
Ben Battle was a s. bold PUNS, 8
I never expect a s. to think SOLDIERS, 7
in the s. is flat blasphemy INJUSTICE, 11
s. who hated war MIDDLE EAST, 13
The summer s. and the sunshine patriot COWARDICE, 6
Tinker, /Tailor, /S., /Sailor NURSERY RHYMES, 60
soldiers English s. fight like lions OFFICERS, 8
Old s. never die OCCUPATIONS, 4
S. are citizens of death's grey land SOLDIERS, 5
soliciting supernatural s. SUPERNATURAL, 14
solitary Man is not a s. animal SOCIETY, 7
solitude In s. alone can he know true freedom SOLITUDE, 12
In s. /What happiness SOLITUDE, 10
so companionable as s. SOLITUDE, 13
s.! where are the charms SOLITUDE, 5
the bliss of s. SOLITUDE, 15
Whosoever is delighted in s. SOLITUDE, 1
Solomon S. Grundy, /Born on a Monday NURSERY RHYMES, 49
solution A difficulty for every s. BUREAUCRACY, 7
total s. of the Jewish question NAZISM, 1
some I…may be s. time LAST WORDS, 48
s. more than others SIMILARITY, 4
You can fool s. of the people all the time DECEPTION, 4
s. may be looking CONSCIENCE, 4
somebody looking for the silence in s. PHOTOGRAPHY, 3
someone I wouldn't be…talking to s. like you SNOBBERY, 3
like sleeping with s. else's wife NEWSPAPERS, 4
Somerset corroboration…in the records of S. House HUMILITY, 11
something Everybody was up to s. INTRIGUE, 2
S. must be done UNEMPLOYMENT, 4
S. nasty in the woodshed EVIL, 9
sometime Why don't you come up s. and see me INVITATIONS, 3
somewhere 'Tis always morning s. BEGINNING, 10
son An only s., sir, might expect more indulgence FATHERS, 4
I've examined your s.'s head, Mr Glum STUPIDITY, 12
the S. of man coming…with power DOOMSDAY, 2
sonatas The s. of Mozart are unique MUSIC, 43
song I have a s. to sing O SINGING, 2
the s. that is sung in our hearts MUSIC, 34
Who loves not wine, woman and s. PLEASURE, 20
songs Sing no sad s. DEATH, 99
Where are the s. of Spring SEASONS, 11
sonne soft was the s. SEASONS, 14
sonnet I have three phobias which…would make my life as slick as a s. OBSESSIONS, 1
s. is a moment's monument POETRY, 38
son-of-a-bitch The poor s. WRITERS, 74
sons I have a wife, I have s. FAMILY, 21
Now we are all s. of bitches NUCLEAR WEAPONS, 1
S. of Belial had a Glorious Time TREASON, 2
sophistry it can contain nothing but s. and illusion PHILOSOPHY, 3
Universities incline wits to s. and affectation EDUCATION, 4
sores Lazarus…laid at his gate, full of s. POVERTY AND WEALTH, 2
sorrow Down, thou climbing s. SORROW, 22
in s. thou shalt bring forth children SEXES, 2
Much in s., oft in woe ENDURANCE, 24
One for s. SUPERSTITION, 3
Parting is such sweet s. PARTING, 10
Pure and complete s. is as impossible EMOTION, 6
S. and silence are strong ENDURANCE, 9
S. is tranquillity remembered in emotion SORROW, 14
s. makes us wise SORROW, 24
Tears of eternity and s. SORROW, 10

There is no greater s. SORROW, 6
Through the night of doubt and s. ENDURANCE, 5
sorrows When s. come, they come not single spies MISFORTUNE, 17
sort that like that s. of place OXFORD, 5
Soudan to you, Fuzzy-Wuzzy, at your 'ome in the S. RACISM, 16
sought Love s. is good LOVE, 127
Pleasure is...seldom found where it is s. PLEASURE, 14
soul And never once possess our s. SOUL, 3
Anger is one of the sinews of the s. ANGER, 4
Artists are not engineers of the s. ART, 12
a...s. like season'd timber VIRTUE, 11
become a living s. DEATH, 134
company...have neither a s. to lose nor a body to kick BUSINESS, 22
education is a leading out of what is...in the pupil's s. EDUCATION, 55
Education is...the s. of a society EDUCATION, 11
Fair seed-time had my s. SOUL, 12
His s. is marching on MEMORIALS, 4
his s. is satisfied with what is assigned to him CONTENTMENT, 1
I am positive I have a s. SOUL, 11
I am the captain of my s. RESPONSIBILITY, 8
Impropriety is the s. of wit HUMOUR, 19
In mystery our s. abides SOUL, 2
I pray the Lord my s. to keep SLEEP, 2
Man has no Body distinct from his S. SOUL, 4
My s. in agony SOLITUDE, 2
my s. is white RACISM, 5
Never mind about my s....get my tie right PAINTING, 5
No coward s. is mine COURAGE, 3
passion in the human s. MUSIC, 29
Raises from Hell a human s. HELL, 1
real dark night of the s. SOUL, 6
seal the hushed casket of my s. SLEEP, 13
than that one s....should commit one single venial sin SIN, 18
The British postgraduate student is a lonely forlorn s. EDUCATION, 31
The dark night of the s. SOUL, 8
the...essence of a human s. BOOKS, 11
the eyes are the windows of the s. EYES, 1
the iron enter into his s. BITTERNESS, 3
the iron has entered his s. NONCOMMITMENT, 3
the largest and most comprehensive s. SHAKESPEARE, 5
The Life and S., the man who will never go home PARTIES, 9
The s. hath not her generous aspirings SMOKING, 10
the s. is not more than the body SELF, 20
the s. of a martyr with the intellect of an advocate POLITICIANS, 35
The s. started at the knee-cap ANIMALISM, 5
The S. that rises with us, our life's Star METAPHYSICS, 5
The voice of the sea speaks to the s. SEA, 3
Thy rapt s. sitting in thine eyes SOUL, 10
Thy s. was like a star, and dwelt apart NOBILITY, 7
souls Above the vulgar flight of common s. SUPERIORITY, 8
damp s. of the housemaids MELANCHOLY, 5
Our s. have sight of that immortal sea METAPHYSICS, 6
s. of five hundred Sir Isaac Newtons SCIENTISTS, 9; WRITERS, 5
S. of poets dead and gone PUBLIC HOUSES, 3
Stars...robbed men of their s. STARS, 1
The s. of women are so small MISOGYNY, 1
Two s. dwell, alas! in my breast CONFLICT, 6
Two s. with but a single thought LOVE, 85
sound full of s. and fury LIFE, 45
s. of a great Amen MUSIC, 39
The hills are alive with the s. of music MUSIC, 22
The most persistent s....through men's history WAR, 58
The s. must seem an echo to the sense WRITING, 26
The s. of the English county families ARISTOCRACY, 15
the trumpet shall s. DEATH, 28
whispering s. of the cool colonnade TREES, 3
sounding s. brass CHARITY, 6
sounds Music is the arithmetic of s. MUSIC, 17
the s. will take care of themselves MEANING, 2
soup concludes that it will...make better s. IDEALISM, 4
S. of the evening, beautiful S. FOOD, 13
Take the s. away FOOD, 27
sour How s. sweet music is ORDER, 5
I am sure the grapes are s. ENVY, 4
source her Majesty...must not...look upon me as a s. of income TAXATION, 7
sourest sweetest things turn s. CORRUPTION, 8
south beaker full of the warm S. ALCOHOL, 37
go s. in the winter READING, 3; TRAVEL, 8
hardly be a town in the S. of England ENGLAND, 31
South Africa S., renowned both far and wide SOUTH AFRICA, 4
S. will not allow the double standards SOUTH AFRICA, 1
you have mandated us to change S. SOUTH AFRICA, 11
South African The S. Police would leave no stone unturned SOUTH AFRICA, 12
South Africans You won't force S. SOUTH AFRICA, 2
southern mother bore me in the s. wild RACISM, 5
sovereign he will have no s. MONARCHY, 9
That s. of insufferables WRITERS, 34
The S. has, under a constitutional monarchy...three rights MONARCHY, 2
When I forget my s. LOYALTY, 10
Soviet as spiteful to me in the American press as the S. press NEWSPAPERS, 14
Communism is S. power plus the electrification COMMUNISM, 4
The ship follows S. custom CLASS, 34
sow Ireland is the old s. IRELAND, 9
like a s. that hath overwhelm'd all her litter HUMOUR, 27
soweth whatsoever a man s., that shall he also reap RETRIBUTION, 4
sown A lovelier flower /...was never s. DEATH, 133
soya workers' flats in fields of s. beans FUTURE, 2
space annihilate but s. and time LOVE, 99
In the United States there is more s. AMERICA, 32
Outer s. is no place SPACE, 2
range of human societies in time, the other in s. MANKIND, 16
S. is almost infinite SPACE, 7
S. isn't remote at all SPACE, 5
spaceship passenger on the s., Earth SPACE, 3
spade When I see a s. I call it a s. SNOBBERY, 11
Spain Farewell and adieu to you, Ladies of S. PARTING, 3
not left to S. MARTYRDOM, 4
spam he wanted steak and they offered s. DISAPPOINTMENT, 5
span Life's short s. forbids us...far-reaching hopes MORTALITY, 13
Spaniards the S. seem wiser than they are APPEARANCES, 9
time to win this game, and to thrash the S. SPORT AND GAMES, 5; WAR, 34
Spanish I speak S. to God LANGUAGE, 7
singed the S. king's beard WAR, 35
spare I can't s. this man; he fights OFFICERS, 9
S. all I have WORLD-WEARINESS, 2
S. the rod CHILDREN, 1; INDULGENCE, 1; PUNISHMENT, 6
Woodman, s. that tree TREES, 11
spareth he that s. his rod hateth his son CHILDREN, 15
sparrow a s. alight upon my shoulder...I was more distinguished by that HONOUR, 6
I, said the S., /With my bow and arrow NURSERY RHYMES, 68
It is a city where you can see a s. fall IRELAND, 14
Sparrowhawks S., Ma'am REMEDIES, 14
sparrows one of the s....flew...through the hall LIFE, 9
spasm a lonely s. of helpless agongy DEATH, 63
spat So he stood up and s. on the ceiling HUMOUR, 33
Today I s. in the Seine WORLD WAR II, 23
speak I didn't s. up NAZISM, 5
I only s. right on SPEECHES, 5
Let him now s. OPPORTUNITY, 11
more than a moral duty to s. one's mind FRANKNESS, 4
Never s. ill of the dead DEATH, 8
province of knowledge to s. KNOWLEDGE, 19; WISDOM, 18
some...s....before they think IMPETUOSITY, 2
S. softly and carry a big stick POWER POLITICS, 6
s. to God as if men were listening RIGHTEOUSNESS, 8
S. when you are spoken to SPEECH, 2; MANNERS, 2
time to think before I s. SPEECH, 8
When I think, I must s. WOMEN, 69
Whereof one cannot s. SILENCE, 15
speaking An Englishman's way of s. CLASS, 19
People talking without s. FUTILITY, 10
when...s., they do not know what they are saying SPEECHES, 3
specialist called a nerve s. because it sounds better PSYCHIATRY, 13

S. – A man who knows more and more about less and less EXPERTS, 5
specialists s.…tend to think in grooves EXPERTS, 6
species the idea of its death as a s. NUCLEAR WEAPONS, 9
the one s. I wouldn't mind seeing vanish DOGS, 3
Women exist…solely for the propagation of the s. WOMAN'S ROLE, 5
spectacle Life is not a s. LIFE, 42
spectator a S. of mankind OBJECTIVITY, 2
spectre Communism continued to haunt Europe as a s. COMMUNISM, 10
speculation If the world were good for…s. SPECULATION, 2
speech An after-dinner s. should be like a lady's dress SPEECHES, 2
freedom of s. and expression HUMAN RIGHTS, 4
freedom of s., freedom of conscience, and the prudence never to practise…them FREEDOM, 51
I dreamt that I was making a s. SPEECHES, 4
let thy s. be short SPEECH, 4
perfect plainness of s.…perfect nobleness BIBLE, 1
Sign language is the equal of s. LANGUAGE, 22
S. is silver SILENCE, 2
s. only to conceal their thoughts HUMAN NATURE, 24
s.…seasoned with salt SPEECH, 3
S. was given to man to disguise his thoughts SPEECH, 16
The most precious things in s. SPEECH, 13
The true use of s. SPEECH, 9
the whole earth was…of one s. UNITY, 6
True and False are attributes of s., not of things TRUTH, 29
speeches every government…should have its old s. burned GOVERNMENT, 28
he tries on s. like a man trying on ties POLITICIANS, 49
Many have been the wise s. of fools WISDOM AND FOOLISHNESS, 6
solved by s. and majority votes POWER POLITICS, 2
Statesmen are far too busy making s. THINKING, 7
speechless *The Times* is s. NEWSPAPERS, 5
speed safety is in our s. HASTE, 6
s. was faster than light SCIENCE, 3
spell s. it Vinci and pronounce it Vinchy PRONUNCIATION, 3; SPELLING, 2
spend s. a single day really well GOOD, 6
spendest whatsoever thou s. more…I will repay CHARITY, 8
spending Getting and s. WASTE, 3
Riches are for s. EXTRAVAGANCE, 1
spent Nought's had, all's s. CONTENTMENT, 6
When I consider how my light is s. BLINDNESS, 5
spermatozoa million million s., /All of them alive SEX, 27
spheres Fifty-five crystal s. geared to God's crankshaft UNIVERSE, 13
our social s. have been widely different SNOBBERY, 11
spice Sugar and s. /And all that's nice NURSERY RHYMES, 65
Variety's the very s. of life CHANGE, 4
spider said a s. to a fly INVITATIONS, 1
spies sorrows…come not single s. MISFORTUNE, 17
spilt the blood that she has s. REVENGE, 9
spin rare attainments…but…can she s. WOMAN'S ROLE, 3
spinning from eternity s. the thread of your being DESTINY, 2
Spinoza The Jews have produced…Christ, S., and myself CONCEIT, 16
spires City with her dreaming s. OXFORD, 2
spirit and an haughty s. before a fall PRIDE, 1
Give me the s. APPEARANCES, 20
Hail to thee, blithe S. BIRDS, 10
history of the human s. CULTURE, 1
into thy hands I commend my s. LAST WORDS, 10
Music that gentlier on the s. lies MUSIC, 51
my s. found outlet in the air FLYING, 1
s.… of a sound mind FEAR, 2
the flesh lusteth against the S. COMPROMISE, 3
the fruit of the S. is love, joy, peace CHRISTIANITY, 8
the meanest…deeds require s. and talent INSENSITIVITY, 3
The s. burning but unbent DETERMINATION, 7
the s.…is willing IMPERFECTION, 4
the S. of God moved upon…the waters CREATION, 2
the s. that always denies DENIAL, 1
Th' expense of s. in a waste of shame LUST, 7
spiritualist If the dead talk to you, you are a s. MADNESS, 15
spit a pitcher of warm s. POLITICS, 29
I am not going to s. on the deck DEPARTURE, 3
spiteful as s. to me in the American press NEWSPAPERS, 14
I like to write when I feel s. WRITING, 19
spits Who s. against the wind CONFORMITY, 1
spleen S. can subsist on any kind of food ANGER, 5
splendour Pavilioned in s., and girded with praise GOD, 23
splinters teeth like s. APPEARANCE, 7
split They s. the atom by firing particles at SCIENCE, 18
when I s. an infinitive…it stays s. GRAMMAR, 2
spoil Don't s. the ship ECONOMICS, 1
s. the child PUNISHMENT, 6; INDULGENCE, 1
spoke s. among your wheels OBSTRUCTION, 1
spoken Speak when you're s. to MANNERS, 2
spontaneity s. is fundamental in art and football FOOTBALL, 4
spontaneous set a high value on s. kindness FRIENDSHIP, 19
the Immaculate Conception was s. combustion CATHOLICISM, 9
Worrying is the most natural and s. of…functions WORRY, 12
spoof even the weather forecast seemed to be some kind of s. WEATHER, 17
spoon And the dish ran away with the s. NURSERY RHYMES, 14
S. feeding…teaches us nothing but the shape of the spoon EDUCATION, 19
spoons diners-out from whom we guard our s. MISTRUST, 8
let us count our s. MISTRUST, 6
the faster we counted our s. MISTRUST, 4
sport Blood s. is brought to its ultimate refinement JOURNALISM, 18
In love as in s., the amateur status LOVE, 63
kill us for their s. DESTINY, 20
Serious s. has nothing to do with fair play SPORT AND GAMES, 18
s. would be as tedious as to work LEISURE, 4
The national s. of England ENGLISH, 35
The only athletic s. I ever mastered SPORT AND GAMES, 10
to make s. for our neighbours RIDICULE, 1
value life less than s. WEAPONS, 8
sportsman But He was never…/A S. HUNTING, 8
spot Out, damned s. GUILT, 8
spotless s. reputation REPUTATION, 9
spots or the leopard his s. CHANGE, 1
sprang I s. to the stirrup HORSES, 3
sprat Throw out a s. CHANCE, 1
spreading Under the s. chestnut tree OCCUPATIONS, 10
spring A new repast, or an untasted s. PLEASURE, 2
as short a S.; /As quick a growth to meet decay TRANSIENCE, 14
By chilly finger'd s. FLOWERS, 5
can S. be far behind SEASONS, 21
Drink deep, or taste not the Pierian s. KNOWLEDGE, 30
flowers that bloom in the s. APPEARANCE, 16
hounds of s. are on winter's traces SEASONS, 22
In the S. a young man's fancy SEASONS, 24
In the s.…your lovely Chloë APPEARANCE, 32
lived light in the s. LIFE, 4
Now S., sweet laxative of Georgian strains SEASONS, 6
S. and summer did happen in Cambridge CAMBRIDGE, 4
S. has returned SEASONS, 17
S. is come home SEASONS, 26
s. now comes unheralded by the return of the birds ECOLOGY, 1
S.…stipple leaves with sun SEASONS, 19
there would be S. no more DECLINE, 11
They call it easing the S. WEAPONS, 7
The year's at the s. PERFECTION, 2
Thrice welcome, darling of the s. BIRDS, 14
Where are the songs of S. SEASONS, 11
spring-board poets use reality as a s. into space POETS, 56
spur A s. in the head INSPIRATION, 1
Fame is the s. FAME, 14
spurs Let the boy win his s. SELF-RELIANCE, 5
spurts They move forward in s. CHILDREN, 19
square Shed his blood…given a s. deal JUSTICE, 21
squares walk on the lines or the s. SUPERSTITION, 9
squeezed The Germans…are going to be s., as a lemon RETRIBUTION, 10
squire Bless the s. and his relations CLASS, 9
stable It's too late to shut the s. door REGRET, 2
staff I'll break my s. RENUNCIATION, 4
stage All the world's a s. HUMAN CONDITION, 17
Don't put your daughter on the s. THEATRE, 8
If this were play'd upon a s. REALITY, 6
no man dies for love, but on the s. LOVE AND DEATH, 2
qualities…necessary for success upon the s. ACTING, 11
the Attic s. LIFE, 6

this great s. of fools HUMAN CONDITION, 18
we go quite off this s. DEATH, 96
stagecoach You will hear more good things on...a s. from London to Oxford INTELLECTUALS, 6
stair As I was going up the s. NONSENSE, 22
stairs he had known many kicked down s. PROMOTION, 2
walks up the s. of his concepts MANKIND, 30
stake To the thumbscrew and the s. MARTYRDOM, 4
Stalin If Mr S. dies DIPLOMACY, 9
S. hates the guts of POLITICIANS, 70
stammer You persisted...like a s. PERSISTENCE, 9
stamp If we can't s. out literature PHILISTINISM, 7
the indelible s. of his lowly origin EVOLUTION, 4
to order a new s....with my face on it TRIVIALITY, 11
stand a firm place to s. TECHNOLOGY, 1
no time to s. and stare IDLENESS, 4
s. not upon the order of...going DISMISSAL, 8
S. your ground...if they mean to have a war, let it begin here WAR, 84
They also serve who only s. and wait SERVICE, 4
We s. today on the edge of a new frontier BEGINNING, 12
standards South Africa will not allow the double s. SOUTH AFRICA, 1
stands S. the Church clock NOSTALGIA, 3
star a s. or two beside MOON, 2
Being a s. has made it possible FAME, 7
Bright s., would I were steadfast STARS, 4
Go, and catch a falling s. NONSENSE, 11
Hitch your wagon to a s. AMBITION, 8
one s. differeth from another...in glory ASTRONOMY, 1
Remember you are a s. ACTORS, 4
Someday I'll wish upon a s. DESIRE, 7
Sunset and evening s. DUTY, 5
that same s., /That fitful, fiery Lucifer STARS, 6
The desire of the moth for the s. HUMOUR, 40
The Soul that rises with us, our life's S. METAPHYSICS, 5
Thy soul was like a s., and dwelt apart NOBILITY, 7
Twinkle, twinkle, little s. STARS, 5
we have seen his s. in the east CHRISTMAS, 9
stare no time to stand and s. IDLENESS, 4
Stark Molly S. sleeps a widow WAR, 113
Starkie There was a young woman called S. RACISM, 1
starry the s. heaven above me WONDER, 3
Under the wide and s. sky DEATH, 120
stars Clad in the beauty of a thousand s. BEAUTY, 26
Hard and high to the s. AMBITION, 2
he made the s. also CREATION, 4; STARS, 2
I'll hold my head so high it'll strike the s. PRIDE, 5
Look at the s. STARS, 3
One sees the mud, and one the s. OPTIMISM, 21
some of us are looking at the s. OPTIMISM, 28
Some s....Fell like a falling tear STARS, 7
S....robbed men of their souls STARS, 1
strives to touch the s. AMBITION, 17
Tempt not the s. DESTINY, 11
The s. grew bright in the winter sky ANIMALS, 13
the Stone that puts the S. to Flight DAY, 5
The Syrian s. look down DEATH, 19
We are merely the s.' tennis-balls DESTINY, 24
what is the s. CURIOSITY, 7
star-spangled 'Tis the s. banner AMERICA, 21
start Wrong from the s. POETRY, 36
starts make certain it never s. NUCLEAR WEAPONS, 3
starve Let not poor Nelly s. LAST WORDS, 15
starving all around you people are s. CAPITALISM, 11
state a s. in the proper sense of the word CAPITALISM, 7
attacking an ex-secretary of s. CHURCHILL, 1
I am the S. MONARCHY, 15
In a free society the s....administers justice among men STATE, 3
not good enough to have just any old s. MIDDLE EAST, 2
O Lord, to what a s....those who love Thee RELIGION, 56
Our object in the construction of the s. REPUBLIC, 1
reinforcement of the power of the S. REVOLUTION, 2
So long as the s. exists there is no freedom STATE, 2
S. socialism is totally alien SOCIALISM, 14
the lie has become...a pillar of the S. LYING, 15
The S., in choosing men...takes no notice of their opinions LOYALTY, 6
The s. is an instrument...of the ruling class STATE, 5
the s....Man is in GOD, 39
The worth of a S. STATE, 4
stately go back to thy s. homes of England PARTING, 7
lunatic asylums...the s. homes STATELY HOMES, 5
S. Homes of England ope their doors STATELY HOMES, 1
The S. Homes of England ARISTOCRACY, 6; STATELY HOMES, 2, 3, 4
statement Any general s. is like a cheque GENERALIZATIONS, 3
states S., like men, have their growth POLITICS, 44
statesman abroad you're a s. POLITICIANS, 17
A politician is a s....with an open mouth POLITICIANS, 26
A s. is a politician who POLITICIANS, 19, 29
definition of a constitutional s. POLITICIANS, 1
if you agree with him he is a s. POLITICIANS, 16
statesmen S. are far too busy making speeches THINKING, 7
s....estranged from reality NUCLEAR WEAPONS, 10
static class people as s. and dynamic SEXES, 29
novel is a s. thing NOVELS, 16; PLAYS, 13
station honour is a private s. VICE, 1
stationmaster The s.'s whiskers are of a Victorian bushiness APPEARANCE, 43
stations always know our proper s. CLASS, 9
statistics Facts speak louder than s. FACTS, 3; STATISTICS, 11
He uses s. as a drunken man uses lamp-posts STATISTICS, 4
lies, damned lies and s. STATISTICS, 2
s., born to consume resources STATISTICS, 3
S. will prove anything STATISTICS, 6
There are two kinds of s. STATISTICS, 10
unrewarded millions without whom S. would be a bankrupt science STATISTICS, 8
we must study s. STATISTICS, 7
You cannot feed the hungry on s. STATISTICS, 5
statue that *my* s. should be moved, which I should much dislike MEMORIALS, 12
there's a s. inside every block of stone OBESITY, 8
statues worth a million s. NAKEDNESS, 3
stay S., stay, /Until the hasting day /Has run TRANSIENCE, 14
stay-at-home Sweet S. CONTENTMENT, 2
steak he wanted s. and they offered spam DISAPPOINTMENT, 5
when you've got s. at home MARRIAGE, 89
steaks smell of s. in passageways FOOD, 20
steal A man who will s. *for* me will s. *from* me LOYALTY, 8
thou shalt not s. GOD, 10
stealing hanged for s. horses EXAMPLE, 5
steals what can plead that man's excuse / Who s. a common from a goose THEFT, 1
Who s. my purse s. trash REPUTATION, 8
stealth Do good by s. GOOD, 14
greatest pleasure I know, is to do a good action by s. GOOD, 8
stealthy The S. School of Criticism CRITICISM, 43
steamer tossing about in a s. from Harwich BOATS, 6
steel arm'd with more than complete s. JUSTICE, 16
the cold s. WAR, 1
When the foeman bares his s. COWARDICE, 4
steep When things are s., remember to stay level-headed SELF-CONTROL, 4
steeple clock in the s. strikes one ALCOHOL, 68
steeples Talk about the pews and s. RELIGION, 15
Till you have drench'd our s. WEATHER, 19
steer You just press the accelerator to the floor and s. left SPORT AND GAMES, 24
Stein There's a wonderful family called S. HUMOUR, 31
stellar the whole solar and s. systems COMFORT, 1
step a s. from the sublime to the ridiculous DECLINE, 6
one small s. for man SPACE, 1
One s. forward, two steps back PROGRESS, 8
only the first s....is difficult BEGINNING, 8
That's one small s. for man MISQUOTATIONS, 5
The first s. BEGINNING, 5
step-mother a kind parent...or a merciless s. NATURE, 13
Stepney When will that be? /Say the bells of S. LONDON, 2
stepp'd in blood s. in so far GUILT, 7
stick if we praise ourselves fearlessly, something will always s. PRAISE, 2
kind of burr; I shall s. PERSISTENCE, 12
Speak softly and carry a big s. POWER POLITICS, 6
sticks it is always said of slander that something always s. PRAISE, 2
S. and stones INSULTS, 1
stiff a s. upper lip COURAGE, 5
stigma Any s....to beat a dogma PUNS, 4
stile He found a crooked sixpence against a crooked s. NURSERY RHYMES, 52
I'm sitting on the s., Mary NOSTALGIA, 8

still And if she's not gone /She lives there s. NURSERY RHYMES, 53
a s. small voice GOD, 13; SUICIDE, 13
A s. tongue SILENCE, 1
Even when conversing he could not keep s. WRITERS, 76
of his own opinion s. YIELDING, 2
S. waters run deep APPEARANCES, 4
stilly Oft in the s. night, /Ere Slumber's chain NOSTALGIA, 14
sting O death, where is thy s. DEATH, 28
O death! where is thy s. DEATH, 94
stings stroke a nettle, /And it s. you for your pains DECISION, 1
stirrup I sprang to the s. HORSES, 3
stitch A s. in time ANTICIPATION, 1
stoat I...catch a glimpse of a s. PURPOSE, 5
stockholders The public be damned. I am working for my s. CAPITALISM, 15
stockings the silk s. and white bosoms...excite my amorous propensities LUST, 3
stoic man is...either a s. or a satyr AGE, 45
stole That title from a better man I s. IMITATION, 6
stolen not wanting what is s. IGNORANCE, 14
Stolen sweets are always sweeter, /S. kisses much completer THEFT, 7
S. sweets are best THEFT, 5
s. waters are sweet SECRECY, 5
stolen goods your wife...is a receiver of s. INSULTS, 21
stomach A hungry s. has no ears HUNGER, 8
An army marches on its s. FOOD, 43
my s. must just digest in its waistcoat ALCOHOL, 57
No one can worship God...on an empty s. BUSINESS, 29
The way to a man's heart is through his s. FOOD, 22
use a little wine for thy s.'s sake ALCOHOL, 13
with enforcing morality on the s. ILLNESS, 8
You can't think rationally on an empty s. THINKING, 6
stomachs Napoleon's armies used to march on their s. HISTORY, 30; HUMOUR, 55
stone and youth s. dead WAR, 101
Constant dripping hollows out a s. PERSISTENCE, 10
Dripping water hollows out a s. PERSISTENCE, 11
he that is without sin...let him first cast a s. SIN, 4
if someone throws a s. FORGIVENESS, 4
Jackson standing like a s. wall DETERMINATION, 5
Like a rolling s. TRAVEL, 7
precious s. set in the silver sea ENGLAND, 36
raised not a s. FUNERALS, 11
Virtue is like a rich s. VIRTUE, 1
Stonehenge bring S. to Nyasaland CIVILIZATION, 2
stones He found in s. the sermons...hidden there POETS, 59
s. kissed by the English dead WAR, 82
stoop A constitutional king must learn to s. MONARCHY, 14
stoops When lovely woman s. to folly GULLIBILITY, 2
stop come to the end: then s. ORDER, 2
s. everyone from doing it PERVERSITY, 4
S. the World, I Want to Get Off WORLD-WEARINESS, 5
time...must have a s. DEATH, 111
when the kissing had to s. KISSING, 1
stopped man has s. moving EVOLUTION, 2
s. short – never to go again CLOCKS, 3
stops The buck s. here RESPONSIBILITY, 16
storage A library is thought in cold s. BOOKS, 38
stories She likes s. that make her cry SENTIMENTALITY, 5
storm After a s. comes a calm OPTIMISM, 1
a mighty s....to freshen us up CHANGE, 3
lovers fled away into the s. DEPARTURE, 7
S. in a Teacup TRIVIALITY, 2
storms s. of prayer EXCESS, 14
story A cruel s. runs on wheels CRUELTY, 4
brother-in-law wrote an unusal murder s. BOOKS, 43
Not that the s. need be long WRITING, 33
novel tells a s. NOVELS, 4
Tell me the old, old s. CHRISTIANITY, 27
The s. is like the wind SENSATION, 2
stout those who have s. hearts and sharp swords RUTHLESSNESS, 6
stoutness I see no objection to s. OBESITY, 7
Stowe S., Harriet Beecher INFLUENCE, 8
straight If Michelangelo had been s. HOMOSEXUALITY, 11
I tell them s. DISEASE, 5
straight-jacket the discredited s. of the past POLITICS, 74
strain'd quality of mercy is not s. MERCY, 2
strait matters not how s. the gate RESPONSIBILITY, 8
straitened to face s. circumstances at home POVERTY, 22
Strand I walk down the S. FASHION, 3
Let's all go down the S. LONDON, 4
wandering on a foreign s. HOMESICKNESS, 6
strange A s., horrible business...good enough for Shakespeare's day CRITICISM, 50
it's a jolly s. world CONFUSION, 1
laughing and jeering at everything...s. ENGLISH, 30
pass my declining years saluting s. women OLD AGE, 31
The Law of England is a very s. one LAW, 8
truth is always s. TRUTH, 18
strangeness s. in the proportion BEAUTY, 7
stranger Look, s., at this island now DISCOVERY, 2
S. than fiction TRUTH, 18
strangers better s. SEPARATION, 6
s. and pilgrims on the earth FAITH, 4
the kindness of s. CHARITY, 23
strangle task of the Liberal party is to s. it at birth POLITICS, 68
strangled down which ideas are lured and...s. BUREAUCRACY, 4
Stratford S....suggests powdered history ENGLAND, 19
S. trades on Shakespeare EUROPE, 1
strawberries innocent as s. INNOCENCE, 9
We may say of angling as Dr Boteler said of s. FISHING, 5
strawberry My good man, I'm not a s. ACCIDENTS, 3
straws Errors, like S. TRUTH, 24
strayed s. from thy ways SIN, 8
straying s. away from the church RELIGION, 7
stream Still glides the S. CONSTANCY, 5
Time is but the s. I go a-fishing in TIME, 38
street don't do it in the s. SEX, 9
I doubt if the philosopher lives...who could know himself...despised by a s. boy PHILOSOPHERS, 5
streets a quarrel in the s. is...to be hated ARGUMENTS, 11
S. full of water VENICE, 1
The s. of London LONDON, 1
strength Credulity is...the child's s. INNOCENCE, 7
My s. is as the s. of ten INTEGRITY, 7
s. and fury PATIENCE, 11
S. through joy NAZISM, 3
We are not now that s. DETERMINATION, 15
strenuous doctrine of the s. life WORK, 20
stress s. and the violence is worse at home VIOLENCE, 8
stretched things which he s. LYING, 18
strides popular music...made giant s. in reverse POP MUSIC, 10
strife God and Nature then at s. NATURE, 15
With phantoms an unprofitable s. LIFE AND DEATH, 13
strike If you s. a child VIOLENCE, 7
no right to s. against the public safety STRIKES, 2
S. while the iron is hot OPPORTUNITY, 7
themselves must s. the blow FREEDOM, 6
the twenty-four-hour s. STRIKES, 4
where ever you meet with a passage...s. it out WRITING, 15
strikes the last four s. we've had, it's pissed down STRIKES, 5
Strindberg S. when you have a temperature LITERATURE, 13
string chewing little bits of S. FOOD, 8
strings 'There are s.', said Mr Tappertit, 'in the human heart...' EMOTION, 2
stripling yon pale s. EXPECTATION, 5
strive I s. to be brief, and I become obscure BREVITY, 2
men should s. to learn HUMAN CONDITION, 21
needst not s. /...to keep alive KILLING, 2
To s., to seek, to find, and not to yield DETERMINATION, 15
strives s. to touch the stars AMBITION, 17
stroke man fears...only the s. of death DEATH, 21
none so fast as s. BOATS, 2
strong be s. and of a good courage GOD, 8
disarm the s. and arm the weak INJUSTICE, 6
how sublime.../To suffer and be s. ENDURANCE, 10
Sorrow and silence are s. ENDURANCE, 9
S. enough to answer back to desires CHARACTER, 12
s. enough to bear the misfortunes of others MISFORTUNE, 14
the errors of those who think they are s. MISTAKES, 3
the s. shall thrive SURVIVAL, 6
the wall is s. IMPRISONMENT, 10
woe unto them that...follow s. drink ALCOHOL, 12
strongest S. minds /...the noisy world /Hears least MIND, 11
strongminded nobody is s. around a President SERVILITY, 6
strove I s. with none LIFE AND DEATH, 9
struck Certain women should be s. regularly WOMEN, 25

structure s. of the...British sentence GRAMMAR, 3
struggle each man must s., lest the moral law become...separated MORALITY, 1
manhood a s. AGE, 19
The perpetual s. for room and food SURVIVAL, 3
the s. for existence EVOLUTION, 5
struggles The history of all...society is the history of class s. CLASS, 22
struggling the greatness of Russia is only her pre-natal s. RUSSIA, 4
strumpet a s.'s fool LOVE, 115
struts player that s. and frets LIFE, 45
stubborn s. spear-men COURAGE, 18
student an over-ambitious essay by a second-year s. CRITICS, 15
a s. to the end of my days LEARNING, 5
He was...a s. of history EXPERIENCE, 18
studies S. serve for delight EDUCATION, 5
study much s. is a weariness of the flesh BOOKS, 8
s. what you most affect EDUCATION, 49
The proper s. of Mankind is Man SELF-KNOWLEDGE, 5
the result of previous s. FLATTERY, 2
studying By s. the masters EXPERTS, 1
stuff Ambition should be made of sterner s. AMBITION, 15
such s. as dreams are made on MORTALITY, 17
The future is made of the same s. FUTURE, 8
to s. a mushroom HOUSEWORK, 2
stumble they s. that run fast HASTE, 11
stumbling the...world was s....in social blindness BLINDNESS, 2
stupid anger makes us all s. ANGER, 6
clever man...came of...s. people INTELLIGENCE, 2
he ceased to be mad he became merely s. REMEDIES, 11
Living in England...must be like being married to a s....wife ENGLAND, 18
s. are cocksure...intelligent full of doubt DOUBT, 7
The s. neither forgive FORGIVENESS, 16
To be clever enough to get...money, one must be s. MATERIALISM, 6
stupidity Against s. the gods...struggle in vain STUPIDITY, 14
Human S. consists in having lots of ideas STUPIDITY, 10
If poverty is the mother of crime, s. is its father CRIME, 5
It is a s....to busy oneself with the correction of the world IMPROVEMENT, 3
no sin except s. STUPIDITY, 15
Stygian resembling the horrible S. smoke of the pit SMOKING, 7
ye S. set LUST, 5
style s. is the man himself STYLE, 1
s., not sincerity, is the vital thing STYLE, 7
s....often hides eczema STYLE, 2
the grand s. arises in poetry POETRY, 3
The s. is the man WRITING, 2
styles All s. are good except the tiresome sort STYLE, 6
subject a noble nature...treats...a serious s. POETRY, 3
Every s.'s duty is the King's MONARCHY, 19
Her Majesty is not a s. ROYALTY, 12
the individual s....'has nothing to do with the laws but to obey them.' LAW, 17
subjects Although there exist many thousand s. CONVERSATION, 1
subjunctive S. to the last, he preferred GRAMMAR, 9
sublime a step from the s. to the ridiculous DECLINE, 6
Beethoven's Fifth Symphony is the most s. noise MUSIC, 21
how s..../To suffer and be strong ENDURANCE, 10
The s. and the ridiculous OPPOSITES, 7
submerged speak for the inarticulate and the s. JOURNALISM, 4
submit To great evils we s.; we resent little provocations TRIVIALITY, 9
subscribers reasons for not printing any list of s. FRANKNESS, 2
subsequence physicians...mistake s. for consequence DOCTORS, 5
substance faith is the s. of things hoped for FAITH, 3
lose the s. by grasping at the shadow GREED, 4
substantial he that chiefly owes himself...is the s. Man SELF-RELIANCE, 3
substantives tell the s. from the adjectives POLITICS, 50
substitute a s. for reading it OSTENTATION, 2
no s. for talent TALENT, 4
substitutes and finally a single dictator s. himself COMMUNISM, 11
subtle Time, the s. thief of youth AGE, 41
suburbia I come from s. SUBURBIA, 1
subverts a continued miracle in his own person, which s. all the principles of his understanding CHRISTIANITY, 29
succeed don't s., try, try again. Then quit REALISM, 2
If at first you don't s. PERSISTENCE, 5
If they s., they fail HOMOSEXUALITY, 3
I'm...ugly enough to s. on my own INDEPENDENCE, 1
It is not enough to s. RUTHLESSNESS, 7
Never having been able to s. in the world ENVY, 9
those who ne'er s. SUCCESS, 8
to s. unconventionally ORTHODOXY, 3
succeeds Nothing s. SUCCESS, 1
Whenever a friend s. ENVY, 8
success a self-made man who owed his lack of s. to nobody SELF-MADE MEN, 2
I thought that s. spelled happiness HAPPINESS, 15
I was never affected by the question of the s. SELF-CONFIDENCE, 2
no s. like failure FAILURE, 2
not in mortals to command s. SUCCESS, 3
no very lively hope of s. PRAYER, 16
only place where s. comes before work SUCCESS, 15; WORK, 22
religion...yours is S. SUCCESS, 5
secret of my s. JEALOUSY, 4
s. and miscarriage are empty sounds DISILLUSION, 4
s....by dint of hard work EFFORT, 5; SUCCESS, 13
s. depends...upon individual initiative and exertion EFFORT, 5; SUCCESS, 13
S. is counted sweetest SUCCESS, 8
Sweet Smell of S. SUCCESS, 12
The moral flabbiness born of...S. SUCCESS, 9
The penalty of s. SUCCESS, 4
two to make a marriage a s. MARRIAGE, 102
successful It was very s. WEAPONS, 2
we do everything we can to appear s. SUCCESS, 14
sucker a s. born every minute GULLIBILITY, 1
suckle To s. fools TRIVIALITY, 12
sucks s. the nurse asleep SUICIDE, 11
suddenly No one...s. became depraved DEBAUCHERY, 6
sued publish and be s. PUBLISHING, 8
Suez Ship me somewheres east of S. DESIRE, 9
the S. Canal was flowing through my drawing room POLITICS, 23
suffer courage to love...courage to s. LOVE, 140
how sublime.../To s. and be strong ENDURANCE, 10
If s. we must, let's s. on the heights SUFFERING, 8
Rather s. than die SUFFERING, 10
s. fools gladly WISDOM AND FOOLISHNESS, 4
suffered love a place the less for having s. SUFFERING, 4
suffering A man who fears s. SUFFERING, 11
Madness and s. can set themselves no limit MADNESS, 11
pity for the s. of mankind PHILOSOPHERS, 8
sympathize with everything, except s. SYMPATHY, 6
The prime goal is to alleviate s., and not to prolong life MEDICINE, 1
we cannot be created for this sort of s. AFTERLIFE, 6
sufficient s. unto the day is the evil thereof WORRY, 7
sugar like sulphuric acid and s. VIRTUE AND VICE, 3
S. and spice /And all that's nice NURSERY RHYMES, 65
suicide committed s. 25 years after his death DIARIES, 3
If you must commit s. SUICIDE, 1
Never murder a man who is committing s. SUICIDE, 14
Not only is s. a sin SUICIDE, 3
s. in this man's town SUICIDE, 10
S. is the worst form of murder SUICIDE, 4
thought of s. is a great...comfort SUICIDE, 6
suit in a light so dim he would not have chosen a s. by it LOVE, 38
My s. is pale yellow. My nationality is French NORMALITY, 2
suitable no s. material to work on OBEDIENCE, 2
Sukey S. take it off again NURSERY RHYMES, 40
sulphur land of Calvin, oat-cakes, and s. SCOTLAND, 8
Puffed its s. to the sunset TRAINS, 1
sulphuric like s. acid and sugar VIRTUE AND VICE, 3
sultry common where the climate's s. ADULTERY, 1
sum *Cogito, ergo s.* THINKING, 3
sumer S. is icumen in SEASONS, 1
summer after many a s. dies the swan MORTALITY, 19
All on a s. day FOOD, 12
Beauty sat with me all the s. day BEAUTY, 11
Before the war...it was s. all the year round NOSTALGIA, 16

Made glorious s. OPTIMISM, 23
murmur of a s.'s day SEASONS, 3
Now the peak of s.'s past TRANSIENCE, 10
Spring and s. did happen in Cambridge CAMBRIDGE, 4
s. afternoon…two most beautiful words SEASONS, 8
S. has set in SEASONS, 7
the last rose of s. FLOWERS, 9
The s. talk stopped SEASONS, 4
summit the s. of Everest was hardly the place PHOTOGRAPHY, 5
summons when Fate s. MORTALITY, 5
summum *S. bonum* GOOD, 3
sun all, except their s. is set EUROPE, 3
aweary of the s. WORLD-WEARINESS, 8
before you let the s. in, mind it wipes its shoes CLEANNESS, 2
better is he…who hath not seen the evil work…under the s. EVIL, 3
between me and the s. REPARTEE, 2
Busy old fool, unruly S. SUN, 2
Fear no more the heat o' th' s. MORTALITY, 16
Follow thy fair s. SORROW, 3
Furnish'd and burnish'd by Aldershot s. ADMIRATION, 1
it were better for s. and moon to drop from heaven SIN, 18
I will sing of the s. WOMEN, 66
let not the s. go down upon your wrath PUNISHMENT, 1; SIN, 3
Light breaks where no s. shines EMOTION, 5
My s. sets OPTIMISM, 16
nothing like the s. ANALOGY, 3
on which the s. never sets BRITISH EMPIRE, 6
So sicken waning moons too near the s. MOON, 4
Spring…stipple leaves with s. SEASONS, 19
s. and the moon was gone out of the heavens POETS, 23
s. came dazzling thro' the leaves CHIVALRY, 11
s. had risen to hear him crow ARROGANCE, 3
S. remains fixed in the centre ASTRONOMY, 2
Thank heavens the s. has gone in LAST WORDS, 64
The kiss of s. for pardon GARDENS, 7
The people – could you patent the s. DISCOVERY, 7
there is no new thing under the s. NOVELTY, 1
There rises the s. of Austerlitz WAR, 74
The S. came up upon the left SUN, 1
The s. does not set in my dominions ROYALTY, 30
the s. shining ten days a year and shit in the streets ENGLAND, 21
this s. of York OPTIMISM, 23
To have enjoy'd the s. LIFE, 4
we cannot make our s. /Stand still LOVE, 88
with peaches and women, it's…the side next the s. that's tempting TEMPTATION, 8
sunburn S. is very becoming APPEARANCE, 9
Sunday A Christian…feels /Repentance on a S. HYPOCRISY, 19
Buried on S. NURSERY RHYMES, 49
only two posh papers on a S. NEWSPAPERS, 10
The feeling of S. is the same everywhere SUNDAY, 5
sung I have s. women in three cities WOMEN, 66
sunk thanks to words, we have often s. to the level of the demons WORDS, 11
sunless Down to a s. sea PLEASURE, 8
sunlight s. as a kind of cosmetic effulgence SUN, 4
sunset a s.-touch WORRY, 8
Puffed its sulphur to the s. TRAINS, 1
S. and evening star DUTY, 5
s. breezes shiver BOATS, 14
sunsets I have a horror of s. SUN, 3
superfluous that controversy is either s. or hopeless ARGUMENTS, 12
superior I consider myself s. to the saint, the scientist NOVELS, 9
One is not s.…because one sees the world in an odious light CYNICISM, 1
The French want no-one to be their *s.* PRIDE, 11
superiority their insolent and unfounded airs of s. FRANCE, 15
The s. of one man's opinion over another's OPINIONS, 3
superiors equality…with our s. EQUALITY, 5
In America everybody is of the opinion that he has no social s. EQUALITY, 20
superlative we have not settled the s. PROGRESS, 3
Super-Mac Introducing S. POLITICIANS, 76
superman I teach you the S. SUPERIORITY, 9
supernatural Religion /Has made an honest woman of the s. RELIGION, 25; SUPERNATURAL, 8
This s. soliciting SUPERNATURAL, 14
superstition necessary for a s. to enslave a philosophy RELIGION, 33
S. is the poetry of life SUPERSTITION, 8
S. is the religion of feeble minds SUPERSTITION, 7
S. sets the whole world in flames SUPERSTITION, 11
superstitions new truths…end as s. NOVELTY, 4
s. of the human mind PURITY, 4
superstructure Sentimentality is a s. covering brutality SENTIMENTALITY, 2
supp'd I have s. full with horrors WORLD-WEARINESS, 7
support atheist…no invisible means of s. ATHEISM, 5
s. me when I am…wrong SUPPORT, 4
suppressed must be s. CHINA, 2
supreme Our s. governors, the mob PUBLIC, 20
Supremes cutlery and furniture…swing like the S. DESIGN, 7
sups He who s. with the devil CAUTION, 4
surgeons Human beings, yes, but not s. MEDICINE, 11
surmise with a wild s. DISCOVERY, 5
surpassed Man is something that is to be s. SUPERIORITY, 9
surprised it is *I* who am s.; you are merely astonished WORDS, 22
the audience want to be s.…by things that they expect PLAYS, 3
surrender No terms except…s. WAR, 43
we shall never s. WORLD WAR II, 4
survey When I s. the wondrous Cross HUMILITY, 13
survival the S. of the Fittest EVOLUTION, 7
without victory there is no s. VICTORY, 2
survive as fitted to s.…as a tapeworm EVOLUTION, 9
obligation to s. is owed…to that cosmos SURVIVAL, 6
only the Fit s. SURVIVAL, 6
Out of their cataclysm but one poor Noah /Dare hope to s. SEX, 27
survived I s. SELF-PRESERVATION, 9
survives Education is what s. EDUCATION, 54
suspect I rather s. her of being in love LOVE AND MARRIAGE, 2
suspected New opinions are always s. NOVELTY, 5
suspense This s. is terrible EXPECTATION, 7
suspension willing s. of disbelief POETRY, 11
suspicion Caesar's wife must be above s. INTEGRITY, 2
people under s. are better moving JUDGMENT, 10
suspicions strong s. that Crippen London cellar murderer TELEGRAMS, 9
S. amongst thoughts SUSPICION, 1
swagman Once a jolly s. camped by a billy-bong PLACES, 12
swains all our s. commend her ADMIRATION, 16
swallow One s. does not make a summer PROOF, 1
swallowed death is s. up in victory DEATH, 28
swallows I hate a man who s. it FOOD, 32
one master-passion…/s. up the rest PASSION, 5
swan after many a summer dies the s. MORTALITY, 19
Sweet S. of Avon SHAKESPEARE, 11
What time is the next s. MISTAKES, 15
Swanee 'Way down upon de S. Ribber HOMESICKNESS, 3
swans S. sing before they die SINGERS, 1
sway A little rule, a little s. TRANSIENCE, 12
swear s. not by the moon UNFAITHFULNESS, 5
swear-word A foreign s. is LANGUAGE, 24
sweat blood, toil, tears and s. EFFORT, 3
it is only because miners s. their guts out SUPERIORITY, 10
That shriek and s. in pigmy wars TRIVIALITY, 14
sweats Falstaff s. to death OBESITY, 10
sweet Heard melodies are s. MUSIC, 27
How s. are looks that ladies bend WOMEN, 76
if TODAY be s. TIME, 18
Is trifle sufficient for s. FOOD, 9
Pleasures newly found are s. PLEASURE, 32
Revenge, at first though s. REVENGE, 13
so s. as Melancholy MELANCHOLY, 2
S. childish days NOSTALGIA, 24
S. day, so cool, so calm DAY, 8
S. Smell of Success SUCCESS, 12
s. will be the flower PATIENCE, 9
that bitter beer that tastes s. IMMORTALITY, 5
sweeter The mountain sheep are s. GREED, 7
sweetes' S. li'l' feller BABIES, 6
sweetest Success is counted s. SUCCESS, 8
s. things turn sourest CORRUPTION, 8
s. thing that ever grew /Beside a human door ADMIRATION, 18
sweetness Culture is the passion for s. and light CULTURE, 2
He who works for s. and light PERFECTION, 1

waste its s. on the desert air WASTE, 2
sweets Stolen s. are always sweeter, /Stolen kisses much completer THEFT, 7
Stolen s. are best THEFT, 5
swift Too s. arrives as tardy as too slow LOVE, 114
swimming s. under water WRITING, 7
swine a s. to show you where the truffles are VULGARITY, 1
Come in, you Anglo-Saxon s. INSULTS, 7
pearls before s. FOOLISHNESS, 9
swing S., swing together BOATS, 4
swings we pulls up on the s. LOSS, 2
Swiss if the S. had designed these mountains MOUNTAINS, 4; SWITZERLAND, 4
The S.…are not a people so much as a…business SWITZERLAND, 2
Swithin St. S.'s Day, if thou dost rain WEATHER, 5
Switzerland Austria is S.…with history added EUROPE, 14
In S. they had brotherly love SWITZERLAND, 5
S.…an inferior sort of Scotland SWITZERLAND, 3
swollen mere existence is s. to a horror IDEALISM, 3
sword for all they that take the s. MISQUOTATIONS, 9
Islam unashamedly came with a s. RELIGION, 51
more cruel…the pen than the s. WRITING, 4
nation shall not lift up s. against nation WAR AND PEACE, 2
pen is mightier than the s. WRITING, 3
s. sleep in my hand ENGLAND, 5
the bank was mightier than the s. LIBERALISM, 3
they that take the s. shall perish with the s. WAR, 10
swords beat their s. into plowshares WAR AND PEACE, 2
those who have stout hearts and sharp s. RUTHLESSNESS, 6
swound Like noises in a s. SEA, 4
Sydney There was the vast town of S. PLACES, 10
symbolism Loss of the Royal Family's s. MONARCHY, 8
symmetry S. is tedious BOREDOM, 4
thy fearful s. ANIMALS, 4
sympathetic To be s. without discrimination SYMPATHY, 2
sympathize s. with everything, except suffering SYMPATHY, 6
sympathy failed to inspire s. in men WOMEN, 14
machine-gun riddling her hostess with s. SYMPATHY, 3
S.…lay over the gathering like a woolly blanket SYMPATHY, 1
symptom common s. of immaturity ORIGINALITY, 7
symptoms One of the s. of approaching nervous breakdown WORK, 21
syne For auld lang s. FRIENDSHIP, 13
Syrian The S. stars look down DEATH, 19
system Christianity accepted…a metaphysical s. CHRISTIANITY, 30
I'm not interested in the bloody s. CHARITY, 14
systems Our little s. have their day TRANSIENCE, 18
the whole solar and stellar s. COMFORT, 1

T

table A man is…better pleased when he has a good dinner upon his t. WOMAN'S ROLE, 4
crumbs which fell from the rich man's t. POVERTY AND WEALTH, 2
patient etherized upon a t. DEPARTURE, 6
put them at a t. together FEAR, 5
tableau history…a t. of crimes and misfortunes HISTORY, 35
tables It is not your trade to make t. CRITICISM, 20
tabloids t.…have a religious affairs correspondent NEWSPAPERS, 9
tact Social t. is TACT, 3
T. consists in knowing TACT, 5
tactic Silence is the best t. SILENCE, 10
tae Here's t. us wha's like us INDIVIDUALITY, 1
tail A case of the t. dogging the wag HUMOUR, 53
The only man who really needs a t. coat CLOTHES, 17
tailor I go to a better t. than any of you CLOTHES, 3
Tinker, /T., /Soldier, /Sailor NURSERY RHYMES, 60
tails t. you lose VICTORY, 5
'taint That's right. 'T. yours, and 't. mine PUNS, 21
tainted the supply is not t. JOURNALISM, 27
take T. care of the sense MEANING, 2
T. things as they come WORRY, 4
They have to t. you in HOME, 4
they…t., who have the power POWER, 28
You can't t. it with you WEALTH, 2
takes It t. all sorts OPPOSITES, 1
taking not winning but t. part VICTORY, 4
tale A t. never loses GOSSIP, 1
a t. /Told by an idiot LIFE, 45
Life is as tedious as a twice-told t. LIFE, 44
t. to tell of the hardihood, endurance, and courage of my companions ENDURANCE, 16
thereby hangs a t. LIFE, 46
talent A best-seller is the gilded tomb of a mediocre t. BOOKS, 40
a country full of genius, but with absolutely no t. IRELAND, 11
any man who has no t. ENGLISH, 4
Middle age snuffs out more t. TALENT, 3
T. alone cannot make a writer WRITERS, 9
T. develops in quiet places CHARACTER, 11; TALENT, 2
T. does what it can TALENT AND GENIUS, 3
t. instantly recognizes genius MEDIOCRITY, 4; TALENT AND GENIUS, 2
the difference between t. and genius TALENT AND GENIUS, 1
the meanest…deeds require spirit and t. INSENSITIVITY, 3
the most extraordinary collection of t. TALENT, 5
There is no substitute for t. TALENT, 4
There is no such thing as a great t. without great will-power DETERMINATION, 4
the t. of flattering with delicacy FLATTERY, 2
talents If you have great t., industry will improve them WORK, 19
the difference between our t. and our expectations DISAPPOINTMENT, 1
talk If you can t. with crowds and keep your virtue IDEALISM, 2
my ministers t. – as long as they do what I say AUTHORITARIANISM, 7
never t. about anything except me TELEGRAMS, 13
Teas, /Where small t. dies CONVERSATION, 9
the need to t. is a primary impulse IMPETUOSITY, 1
think too little…t. too much VERBOSITY, 3
Two may t.…yet never really meet FRIENDSHIP, 14
We have ways of making men t. MISQUOTATIONS, 4
we never t. about anything except me CONCEIT, 23
when I hear anyone t. of Culture PHILISTINISM, 4
When two Englishmen meet, their first t. is of the weather ENGLISH, 20; WEATHER, 15
women should t. an hour SEXES, 1
you wished him to t. on for ever POETS, 38
talked He t. on for ever POETS, 38
The more you are t. about, the more you…wish to be t. about FAME, 18
There is only one thing…worse than being t. about FAME, 24
talker A good listener is a good t. with a sore throat CONVERSATION, 11
a non-stop t. to whom someone has given a typewriter WRITERS, 35
Nothing is more despicable than a professional t. VERBOSITY, 4
talkers fluent t. THINKING, 4
talking for thirty-five years he had not stopped t. SCIENTISTS, 17
Frenchman must be always t. FRANCE, 9
good newspaper…is a nation t. to itself JOURNALISM, 23
I wouldn't be…t. to someone like you SNOBBERY, 3
People t. without speaking FUTILITY, 10
T. and eloquence are not the same SPEECH, 11
T. of Michelangelo WOMEN, 31
While we're t., time will have meanly run on PRESENT, 9
tall Let our children grow t. TALENT, 7
tally-ho Maybe it's that t. lads attitude INSULTS, 38
tambourine Hey! Mr T. Man LEISURE, 3
tame the tongue can no man t. SPEECH, 6
tamper Who am I to t. with a masterpiece CONCEIT, 27
tangerine t. trees and marmalade skies IMAGINATION, 8
tank leading from the top of a t. RUSSIA, 8
tankard heart which grief hath cankered/…remedy – the T. ALCOHOL, 18
tanned getting more t. and more tired ROYALTY, 26
tapeworm as fitted to survive…as a t. EVOLUTION, 9
Tara's through T. halls IRELAND, 13
tarmac t. over the whole of England CONSERVATION, 2
tarnished neither t. nor afraid COURAGE, 6
tarry having lost…your prime, /You may for ever t. MARRIAGE, 71
Tartar Scratch the Russian and…find the T. RUSSIA, 6
tarts He's lost us the t.' vote RESPONSIBILITY, 6; JOURNALISM, 16
she made some t. FOOD, 12

The Queen of Hearts /She made some t. NURSERY RHYMES, 51
Tarzan Me? T. CINEMA, 14
task No t. is a long one but the t. on which one dare not start BEGINNING, 6
The trivial round, the common t. SIMPLICITY, 4
Tasmanians the T....are now extinct ADULTERY, 7
taste bad t. is better than no t. TASTE, 1
different t. in jokes is a...strain on the affections HUMOUR, 11
Drink deep, or t. not the Pierian spring KNOWLEDGE, 30
Every one to his t. DIFFERENCE, 2
great common sense and good t. CHARACTER, 23
I suspect his t. in higher matters FOOD, 32
no t. when you married me TASTE, 8
people who always go on about...good t. TASTE, 6
Shakespeare, undoubtedly wanted t. SHAKESPEARE, 18
T. is the feminine of genius TASTE, 3
the bouquet is better than the t. ALCOHOL, 49
the t. by which he is...relished WRITING, 37
The t. was that of the little crumb of madeleine MEMORY, 11
Things sweet to t. prove...sour REGRET, 14
willing to t. any drink once DRINKS, 3
tasted Sir, you have t. two whole worms SPOONERISMS, 5
Some books are to be t. BOOKS, 3
tastes It is like a cigar....it never t. quite the same LOVE, 145
Our t. greatly alter TASTE, 4
There is no accounting for t. DIFFERENCE, 5
taught a woman who knows all...that can be t. KNOWLEDGE, 9
I forget what I was t. KNOWLEDGE, 35
tavern A t. chair is the throne PUBLIC HOUSES, 1
he has...opened a t. for his friends PARASITES, 1
nothing...by which so much happiness is produced as by a good t. PUBLIC HOUSES, 2
There is a t. in the town PARTING, 2
tawney that t. weed tobacco SMOKING, 8
tax A hateful t. TAXATION, 6
For God's sake, madam, don't say that in England for... they will surely t. it TAXATION, 12
hardest thing...to understand is income t. TAXATION, 3
taxation T. without representation REPRESENTATION, 1
taxes collect legal t. from illegal money TAXATION, 2
Death and t. and childbirth EXPEDIENCY, 5
read my lips, no new t. TAXATION, 1
The avoidance of t....still carries...reward TAXATION, 8
taxi done almost every human activity inside a t. BOASTS, 1
taxis hiring t....handing out redundancy notices to its own workers INCOMPETENCE, 2
taxpayer The t. is someone who works for the federal government TAXATION, 10
Tay Beautiful Railway Bridge of the Silv'ry T. DISASTER, 4
tea Dinner, Lunch and T. FOOD, 7
honey still for t. NOSTALGIA, 3
it is just like having a cup of t. SEX, 46
sometimes counsel take – and sometimes T. DRINKS, 7
Take some more t. LANGUAGE, 4
T. for Two, and Two for T. DRINKS, 5
we drink too much t. DRINKS, 8
When I makes t. I makes t. HUMOUR, 41
teach Don't t. your grandmother ADVICE, 2
For every person wishing to t. EDUCATION, 48
He who shall t. the child to doubt DOUBT, 3
It is no matter what you t. them first EDUCATION, 26
You can't t. an old dog OLD AGE, 2
teacher Experience is a good t. EXPERIENCE, 6
Time is a great t., but...kills all its pupils TIME, 11
teachers We t. can only help...as servants EDUCATION, 38
teaches He who cannot, t. EDUCATION, 52
teacup Storm in a T. TRIVIALITY, 2
team Is my t. ploughing AGRICULTURE, 4
team games The British, being brought up on t. HOUSES OF PARLIAMENT, 14
tear Every t. from every eye SORROW, 1
Some stars...Fell like a falling t. STARS, 7
tears blood, toil, t. and sweat EFFORT, 3
foolish t. upon my grave HYPOCRISY, 16
He spoke, and loos'd our heart in t. POETS, 16
If you have t., prepare to shed them SORROW, 21
in a flood of t. and a Sedan chair HUMOUR, 37
mine own t. /Do scald SUFFERING, 14
No t. in the writer WRITING, 8
our t. /Thaw not the frost MOURNING, 14
shed t. when they would devour HYPOCRISY, 2
T., idle tears SORROW, 26
T. such as angels weep SORROW, 12
T. were to me SORROW, 5
The bitterest t....are for words...unsaid REGRET, 20
the land of t. SORROW, 19
The smiles, the t., /Of boyhood's years NOSTALGIA, 14
the women whose eyes have been washed...with t. WOMEN, 28
Violet Elizabeth dried her t. THREATS, 1
With silence and t. SEPARATION, 2
teas T., /Where small talk dies CONVERSATION, 9
tease The fleas that t. in the high Pyrenees NONSENSE, 3
tea-stirring t. times PRESENT, 11
teatray Like a t. in the sky NONSENSE, 5
teche gladly wolde he lerne, and gladly t. CHARACTER, 5
technological For t. man it is time TECHNOLOGY, 10
technology t....indistinguishable from magic TECHNOLOGY, 3
tedious People are either charming or t. CHARM, 4
They shorten t. nights SEX, 10
tedium t. is the very basis of mourning BOREDOM, 4
teeth I had braces on my t. and got high marks APPEARANCE, 24
I have let dentists ride roughshod over my t. TEETH, 1
I'll dispose of my t. as I see fit TEETH, 2
It is necessary to clean the t. frequently ETIQUETTE, 2
natural false t. TEETH, 3
take the bull between the t. MIXED METAPHORS, 3
taking out his false t. and hurling them at his wife MARRIAGE, 51
They will steal the very t. out of your mouth THEFT, 2
to lose one's t. is a catastrophe TEETH, 5
white sharp t. SUPERNATURAL, 16
teething they escaped t. TEETH, 4
teetotaller a beer t., not a champagne t. ALCOHOL, 54
no woman should marry a t. ABSTINENCE, 10
teetotallers T. lack the sympathy ABSTINENCE, 3
telephone I don't know his t. number NUMBERS, 2
telephone-exchange brain...more than a t. MIND, 7
television but to do it on t. TELEVISION AND RADIO, 2
eats, sleeps and watches the t. WOMAN'S ROLE, 2
stay at home and see bad t. for nothing CINEMA, 6
T. brought the brutality of war TELEVISION AND RADIO, 4; WAR, 65
T. is more interesting than people TELEVISION AND RADIO, 1
T.? No good will come TELEVISION AND RADIO, 5
T....permits you to be entertained in your living room TELEVISION AND RADIO, 3
tell do not t. them so WISDOM, 12
How could they t. POLITICIANS, 68
people who love to t. us what to do ENGLISH, 22
T. the truth TRUTH, 3
you must not kiss and t. SECRECY, 7
you never can t.. That's a principle PRINCIPLES, 4
telly People will cross the road...to say 'We saw you on the t.' TELEVISION AND RADIO, 2
You don't get any pornography...on the t. PORNOGRAPHY, 6
Téméraire She's the Fighting T. BOATS, 14
temper A tart t. never mellows with age CHARACTER, 13
if I were not king, I should lose my t. ROYALTY, 23
Never lose your t. with the Press SELF-CONTROL, 7
temperament artistic t. is a disease ARTS, 2
temperance by t. they all mean the opposite ABSTINENCE, 11
I prefer t. hotels ALCOHOL, 64
She belongs to a T. Society ABSTINENCE, 11
tempests On whom Thy t. fell all night OLD AGE, 22
That looks on t. LOVE, 123
temple in the very t. of delight MELANCHOLY, 8
The Arab who builds...a hut out of...a t....is more philosophical MUSEUMS, 1; PRACTICALITY, 3
the veil of the t. was rent in twain LAST WORDS, 11
This is the t. of Providence LUCK, 7
tempora *O t.! O mores!* CUSTOM, 1
temporary force alone is but *t.* FORCE, 2
temptation blessed is the man that endureth t. TEMPTATION, 4
I never resist t. TEMPTATION, 9
lead us not into t. PRAYER, 4
over-fond of resisting t. TEMPTATION, 3
resist everything except t. TEMPTATION, 10
The last t. MOTIVE, 2
The only way to get rid of a t. TEMPTATION, 11
'You oughtn't to yield to t..' TEMPTATION, 7
temptations in spite of all t....He remains an Englishman NATIONALITY, 5

tempting with peaches and women, it's...the side next the sun that's t. TEMPTATION, 8
ten only t. PUBLIC, 16
our dykes...are t. feet deep BOASTS, 6
T. pipers piping NURSERY RHYMES, 55
Yes, about t. minutes SERMONS, 3
tender T. Is the Night BOOK, SONG, AND PLAY TITLES, 6
tenderness Their flowers the t. of patient minds WAR, 81
ten-dollar He thinks I don't know the t. words STYLE, 5
tenement I inhabit a weak, frail, decayed t. LAST WORDS, 2
tennis playing t. with the net down POETRY, 17
tennis-balls We are merely the stars' t. DESTINY, 24
1066 1066 And All That HISTORY, 28
tent inside my t. pissing out PRUDENCE, 7
tentacles dear octopus from whose t. we never quite escape FAMILY, 31
terminological t. inexactitude LYING, 7
terms No t. except...surrender WAR, 43
terrible It is well that war is so t. WAR, 61
t. thing for a man to find out HONESTY, 13
terribles *Les enfants t.* YOUTH, 8
terror added another t. to death BIOGRAPHY, 4
Christianity has made of death a t. CHRISTIANITY, 36
terrorism t. inflicted on society by crime figures CRIME, 8
terrorist The t. and the policeman EQUALITY, 7
terrorists All t....end up with drinks at the Dorchester POLITICS, 24
test Martyrdom is the t. FREEDOM, 22
text great t. in Galatians BIBLE, 3
Thackeray W. M. T. CLERGY, 17
Thames Sweet T.! run softly RIVERS, 5
the T. is liquid history RIVERS, 1
What is there to make so much of in the T. RIVERS, 3
thank Don't bother to t. me CHARITY, 5
not going to t. anybody GRATITUDE, 3
T. me no thankings GRATITUDE, 4
thankful I am...t. for not having married MARRIAGE, 80
thanks For this relief much t. COMFORT, 2
I am glad...he t. God for anything GRATITUDE, 2
T. MEMORY, 12
thanksgiving With proud t. MOURNING, 3
that 1066 And All T. HISTORY, 28
Thatcher Blimpish patriotism in the mode of Margaret T. PATRIOTISM, 19
Margaret T.'s great strength CLASS, 38
Mrs T....looking like Queen Victoria POLITICIANS, 74
Thatcherism characteristic of T. SOCIETY, 1
thcream I'll t., an' t....till I'm thick THREATS, 1
theatre Farce is the essential t. THEATRE, 9
For the t. one needs long arms ACTING, 4
nobody goes to the t. unless he...has bronchitis AUDIENCES, 1
T. director: a person ACTING, 1
t. in the year 2000 COMMERCIALISM, 2
theatrical one may fail to find happiness in t. life DANCING, 8
theft Property is t. CAPITALISM, 12
theologian This stranger is a t. GUIDANCE, 2
theorems About binomial t. MATHEMATICS, 5
the world can be expressed in...arguments...axioms and t. THEORY, 3
theory A t. can be proved by experiment THEORY, 2
a thing may look evil in t. THEORY, 1
it's...more important for a t. to be shapely, than...true THEORY, 5
no path leads from experiment to...t. THEORY, 2
Philosophy is not a t. PHILOSOPHY, 18
t. is all grey REALITY, 4; THEORY, 4
the scream is sometimes a t. THEORY, 7
therapeutic have such immense t. value MEDICINE, 8
thick Through t. and thin FAITHFULNESS, 2
thicken other things than dissipation...t. the features APPEARANCE, 40
thickens plot t. INTRIGUE, 1
thief Time, the subtle t. of youth AGE, 41
thin Enclosing every t. man, there's a fat man APPEARANCE, 39
in every fat man a t. one OBESITY, 5
One can never be too t. WEALTH, 29
there's a t. man inside every fat man OBESITY, 8
There were times my pants were so t. POVERTY, 32
t. red line tipped with steel WAR, 95
Through thick and t. FAITHFULNESS, 2
thing call that t. under your hat a head INSULTS, 19
good t., to make it too common ENGLAND, 37
It is a far, far, better t. that I do EXECUTION, 6
something between a t. and a thought PAINTING, 8
The play's the t. PLAYS, 11
the t. which is good PUNISHMENT, 1; SIN, 3
thing-in-itself The t., the will-to-live, exists...in every being SURVIVAL, 5
things be without some of the t. you want HAPPINESS, 20
Glorious t. of thee are spoken HEAVEN, 7
no t., only processes REALITY, 1
T. are entirely what they appear to be APPEARANCES, 19
To talk of many t. NONSENSE, 9
think apparatus with which we t. MIND, 1
I cannot sit and t. READING, 9
I exist by what I t. THINKING, 9
I never t. of the future FUTURE, 6
I paint objects as I t. them ARTISTS, 17
I t. him so, because I t. him so WOMEN, 71
I t. therefore I am THINKING, 3
I t. with my hands PRACTICALITY, 4
Many people would sooner die than t. THINKING, 8
not so t. as you drunk DRUNKENNESS, 19
publishing faster than you t. PUBLISHING, 10
some...speak...before they t. IMPETUOSITY, 2
There exist some evils so terrible...that we dare not t. of them MISFORTUNE, 12
T. of your posterity POSTERITY, 1
t. only this of me WAR, 18
t. too little...talk too much VERBOSITY, 3
time to t. before I speak SPEECH, 8
To know how to say what others only...t. SPEECH, 7
We haven't the money, so we've got to t. RESEARCH, 5
When I t. of all the books I have read LIFE, 55
You can't t. rationally on an empty stomach THINKING, 6
thinkers not always the justest t. THINKING, 4
thinking In order to draw a limit to t. THINKING, 13
It ain't t. about it ACTION, 13
one prolonged effort to prevent oneself t. THINKING, 5
Plain living and high t. are no more DECLINE, 14
T. is to me the greatest fatigue in the world THINKING, 11
t. makes it so THINKING, 10
try t. of love LOVE, 58; SLEEP, 9
We are t. beings INTELLECT, 4
thinks He t. too much...dangerous MISTRUST, 9
never t. of me PARTING, 2
The great consolation...is to say what one t. FRANKNESS, 3
third if there was a t. sex MEN, 13
T. time lucky SUPERSTITION, 5
to help Britain to become a T. Programme BRITAIN, 14
third rate And t. conversation MEDIOCRITY, 7
tolerance of the t. MEDIOCRITY, 1
thirst earned his t. and the right to quench it MEN, 7
the t. to come THIRST, 2
thirsty He that goes to bed t. rises healthy ALCOHOL, 30
thirty T. days hath November MONTHS, 9
T. days hath September MONTHS, 4; NURSERY RHYMES, 56
T. millions, mostly fools ENGLISH, 9
thistle I have always plucked a t. and planted a flower REPUTATION, 4
Thomasina Why so shy, my pretty T. SHYNESS, 3
thorn A rose without a t. ADMIRATION, 7
thorough How...t. these Germans always managed to be GERMANY, 15
thoroughness with the t. of a mind that reveres details UNDERSTANDING, 9
thou Book of Verse – and T. CONTENTMENT, 3
thought a green t. in a green shade OBLIVION, 3
A library is t. in cold storage BOOKS, 38
A society...of individuals...capable of original t. IDEAS, 6
A t. is often original ORIGINALITY, 3
conversation must be an exchange of t. CONVERSATION, 7
evil is wrought by want of t. EVIL, 10
Learning without t. is labour lost KNOWLEDGE, 10
My t. is *me* THINKING, 9
Only a residual fraction is t. BUREAUCRACY, 8
pale cast of t. CONSCIENCE, 5
Reading...ingenious device for avoiding t. READING, 6
sessions of sweet silent t. REGRET, 18
silent form, dost tease us out of t. ETERNITY, 3
something between a thing and a t. PAINTING, 8
T. must be divided against itself UNDERSTANDING, 8
t. only to justify their injustices HUMAN NATURE, 24

t. without learning is perilous KNOWLEDGE, 10
Two souls with but a single t. LOVE, 85
What was once t. IDEAS, 1
will bear to be read twice...was t. twice WRITING, 32
thoughtless t. are rarely wordless SPEECH, 12
thoughtlessness In the sex-war t. is the weapon of the male SEXES, 6
thoughts Great t. come from the heart THINKING, 12
Keep off your t. from things that are past PAST, 8
man whose second t. are good THINKING, 1
our life is what our t. make it LIFE, 8
sensations rather than of t. SENSATION, 1
speech only to conceal their t. HUMAN NATURE, 24
Speech...to disguise...t. SPEECH, 16
Suspicions amongst t. SUSPICION, 1
the meanest flower...can give /T. NATURE, 21
To understand God's t. STATISTICS, 7
we ought to control our t. SELF-CONTROL, 3
thousand I can draw for a t. pounds CONVERSATION, 2
I could be a good woman if I had five t. MONEY, 48
if I were a t. years old MEMORY, 2
One t. years more. That's all *Homo sapiens* has MANKIND, 35
the face that launch'd a t. ships BEAUTY, 25
The thought of two t. people crunching celery FOOD, 49
Victory has a t. fathers SUCCESS, 10
What's a t. dollars MONEY, 33; PUNS, 13
thread from eternity spinning the t. of your being DESTINY, 2
threads well-belovèd's hair has t. of grey AGE, 70
threat one can...see in a little girl the t. of a woman CHILDREN, 20
three A committee should consist of t. men DEMOCRACY, 21
There are only t. events in a man's life LIFE AND DEATH, 8
there are only t. things to see PHILISTINISM, 5
thought t. times before taking action CAUTION, 10
T. French hens NURSERY RHYMES, 55
t. fundamental truths OBJECTIVITY, 3
T. little maids from school CHILDREN, 23
t. o'clock in the morning courage COURAGE, 24
T. o'clock is always too late or too early DAY, 13
t. of us in this marriage ADULTERY, 5
t. things...the public will always clamour for NOVELTY, 3
T. years she grew DEATH, 133
we galloped all t. HORSES, 3
who sneaked into my room at t. o'clock this morning COMPLAINTS, 5
threefold a t. cord is not quickly broken UNITY, 5
£300 let loose upon the world with £300 BRITISH, 1
three-pipe a t. problem SMOKING, 5
three-sided if triangles invented a god, they would make him t. RELIGION, 47
thrift extravagance...t. and adventure THRIFT, 5
T. has nearly killed her THRIFT, 6
thrive strong shall t. SURVIVAL, 6
throat A good listener is a good talker with a sore t. CONVERSATION, 11
throats cutting each other's t. SLAVERY, 2
throne A man may build...a t. of bayonets POWER POLITICS, 4
A tavern chair is the t. PUBLIC HOUSES, 1
barge...like a burnished t. ADMIRATION, 13
High on a t. of royal state DEVIL, 10
It helps...to remind your bride that you gave up a t. for her MARRIAGE, 134
no middle course between the t. and the scaffold MONARCHY, 7
royal t. of kings ENGLAND, 36
something behind the t. MONARCHY, 16
throve that on which it t. /Falls off LOVE, 136
throw t. an egg into an electric fan AMBITION, 9
t. away the dearest thing he ow'd DEATH, 110
thrush That's the wise t. BIRDS, 1
Thucydides the historical works of T. NEWSPAPERS, 6
thumbscrew To the t. and the stake MARTYRDOM, 4
thunder laugh as I pass in t. WEATHER, 24
Thurlow No man...so wise as T. looked APPEARANCES, 14
Thursday T.'s child has far to go NURSERY RHYMES, 34
Took ill on T. NURSERY RHYMES, 49
'Twas on a Holy T. CHILDREN, 17
thyself Be so true to t. INTEGRITY, 1
Know then t., presume not God to scan SELF-KNOWLEDGE, 5
Resolve to be t. SELF-KNOWLEDGE, 1
Tiananmen demonstrations from Chengdu to T. Square CHINA, 4
Tiber married to the only man north of the T.... untidier than I am MARRIAGE, 130
the River T. foaming with much blood PROPHECY, 11, 14; RACISM, 26
Tiberius Had T. been a cat CATS, 1
tickle a feather to t. the intellect PUNS, 10
ticky-tacky They're all made out of t. HOUSES, 4
tide a t. in the affairs of men OPPORTUNITY, 16
ever lived in the t. of times REGRET, 16
the full t. of human existence is at Charing-Cross LONDON, 9
The t. is full SEA, 1
The western t. crept up DROWNING, 1
tides the waters of the heart /Push in their t. EMOTION, 5
tidings good t. of great joy CHRISTMAS, 8
tie Never mind about my soul...get my t. right PAINTING, 5
tiger It is not the ape, nor the t. HUMAN NATURE, 23
The atom bomb is a paper t. NUCLEAR WEAPONS, 12
T.! T.! burning bright ANIMALS, 4
tigers Dictators ride to and fro upon t. AUTHORITARIANISM, 3
For tamed and shabby t. ANIMALS, 12
reactionaries are paper t. POLITICS, 53
tightrope You may reasonably expect a man to walk a t. safely NUCLEAR WEAPONS, 17
tile it's not even red brick, but white t. CLASS, 26
timber a...soul like season'd t. VIRTUE, 11
replacing some of the t. used up by my books TREES, 6
Timbuctoo On the plains of T. CLERGY, 17
time a book to kill t. CRITICISM, 32
Aging...the only...way to live a long t. LONGEVITY, 1
A Good T. Was Had by All PLEASURE, 28
And t., that takes survey of all the world, /Must have a stop DEATH, 111
annihilate but space and t. LOVE, 99
Art is long, and T. is fleeting MORTALITY, 14
As if you could kill t. TIME, 39
As t. goes by TIME, 20
As T. Goes By NOSTALGIA, 2
a t. to be born, and a t. to die TIME, 12
big man has no t. FAME, 9
But get me to the church on t. MARRIAGE, 79
chronicle of wasted t. HISTORY, 32
do not squander t. TIME, 19
Even such is T. FAITH, 17
For technological man it is t. TECHNOLOGY, 10
Had we but world enough, and t. SHYNESS, 5
He hath shook hands with t. DEATH, 51
Hurry! I never hurry. I have no t. to hurry HASTE, 12
I haven't got t. to be tired WORK, 27
I...may be some t. LAST WORDS, 48
inaudible and noiseless foot of T. TIME, 33
time irretrievable t. is flying TIME, 40
I shall lose no t. in reading it INATTENTION, 1
It is only t. that weighs TIME, 29
it's for such a long t. DEATH, 88
killing t. /Is only...another of the multifarious ways /By which T. kills us TIME, 36
make the beat keep t. with short steps FUNERALS, 1
Men talk of killing t. TIME, 13
moment of t. LAST WORDS, 22
My t. has not yet come POSTERITY, 9
Never before have we had so little t. HASTE, 9
Never the t. and the place PERVERSITY, 2
not had the t. to make it shorter VERBOSITY, 5
No t. like the present PRESENT, 1
no t. to stand and stare IDLENESS, 4
not of an age, but for all t. SHAKESPEARE, 10
O aching t. TIME, 21
On the breast of the river of T. HUMAN CONDITION, 1
peace for our t. PEACE, 6
peace in our t., O Lord PEACE, 4
pluck till t. and times are done DESIRE, 18
range of human societies in t., the other in space MANKIND, 16
Redeem thy mis-spent t. PRESENT, 12
That passed the t. TIME, 9
The art of medicine is generally a question of t. MEDICINE, 6
The Bird of T....little way /To fly TIME, 17
the long result of T. EXPERIENCE, 19
The man is killing t. TIME, 26
the original good t. that was had by all PROMISCUITY, 1
There is a t. and place TIME, 3
'The t. has come,' the Walrus said NONSENSE, 9

the t. of my departure is at hand FAITH, 6
the t. will come when you will hear me PROPHECY, 4
this bank and shoal of t. ENDING, 5
those feet in ancient t. ENGLAND, 5
t. and chance happeneth to them all CHANCE, 2
T. and the hour runs through TIME, 32
T. and tide TIME, 4
t. as a tool not as a couch TIME, 22
T. driveth onward fast TIME, 37
T. drops in decay TIME, 42
T. flies, death urges TIME, 44
T. goes by: reputation increases OLD AGE, 21
T. had robbed her of her personal charms DISEASE, 18
T. hath, my lord, a wallet at his back TIME, 35
T. is a great healer TIME, 5
T. is a great teacher, but...kills all its pupils TIME, 11
T. is but the stream I go a-fishing in TIME, 38
T. is like a river made up of the events which happen TRANSIENCE, 2
t. is money BUSINESS, 10
T. is on our side PROGRESS, 7
T. is slipping underneath our Feet TIME, 18
T....is something you're only given when...you don't need it TIME, 14
T. is the creator TIME, 7
t. is the greatest innovator INNOVATION, 1
T. is too large TIME, 30
T. may restore us POETS, 17
T. present and time past TIME, 16
T....prevents everything from happening TIME, 41
t. quietly kills them TIME, 13
T.'s up for Sir John, an' for little Lady Jane PARTING, 7
T.'s winged chariot AGE, 38
T., the subtle thief of youth AGE, 41
T. was away and somewhere else LOVE, 86
T. whereof the memory of man MEMORY, 3
T. will tell TIME, 6
T. wounds all heels TIME, 27
To choose t. is to save t. TIME, 8
to waste my t. making money MONEY, 4
We have short t. to stay, as you TRANSIENCE, 14
We take no note of t. TIME, 43
What do the ravages of t. not injure AGE, 33
While we're talking, t. will have meanly run on PRESENT, 9
Work expands so as to fill the t. WORK, 15
timeliness the t. of the gift PROMPTNESS, 1
times It was the best of t. FRENCH REVOLUTION, 1
logic of our t. DECLINE, 3
The good old t. NOSTALGIA, 5
the true old t. are dead NOSTALGIA, 19
We live in stirring t. PRESENT, 11
Times one copy of *The T.* NEWSPAPERS, 6
The T. has made many ministries NEWSPAPERS, 1
The T. is speechless NEWSPAPERS, 5
time-table I would sooner read a t. NOVELS, 10
Timor T.'s petroleum smells better than Timorese blood OPPRESSION, 2
tim'rous Wee...t. beastie ANIMALS, 7
timshel Hebrew word...*t.*...gives a choice CHOICE, 5
tinker T., /Tailor, /Soldier, /Sailor NURSERY RHYMES, 60
tinkling a t. cymbal CHARITY, 6
chime of words t. in...a few fastidious people PURPOSE, 7
tinned t. food is a deadlier weapon WEAPONS, 3
tinsel Strip the phoney t. off Hollywood APPEARANCES, 17
tip-and-run watch him play t. ENGLISH, 13
Tipperary a long, long way to T. HOMESICKNESS, 8
tipping Do they allow t. on the boat MONEY, 34
tipster A racing t. who only reached Hitler's level of accuracy HITLER, 7
tiptoe T. through the tulips FLOWERS, 3
tired getting more tanned and more t. ROYALTY, 26
Give me your t..../Your huddled masses AMERICA, 22
I haven't got time to be t. WORK, 27
I'm t. of Love MONEY, 9
Life...process of getting t. LIFE, 16
tiresome All styles are good except the t. sort STYLE, 6
Being orderly...can be excessively t. ORDER, 1
Titian Nobody cares much at heart about T. ARTISTS, 20
title Because of my t., I was the first COURAGE, 2
That t. from a better man I stole IMITATION, 6
title-page The book written against fame...has the author's name on the t. HYPOCRISY, 9
titles I've been offered t....get one into disreputable company TITLES, 11
Kinquering Congs their t. take SPOONERISMS, 3
T. distinguish the mediocre TITLES, 10
toast I had never had a piece of t....But fell...on the buttered side PERVERSITY, 5
toasted cheese – t., mostly DREAMS, 13
tobacco leave off t. SMOKING, 10
never since have I wasted any more time on t. SMOKING, 19
that tawney weed t. SMOKING, 8
T., divine, rare, superexcellent SMOKING, 2
T. drieth the brain SMOKING, 22
We shall not refuse t. the credit of being...medical SMOKING, 18
what pleasure...they have in taking their roguish t. SMOKING, 9
who lives without t. SMOKING, 12
today here t., and gone tomorrow TRANSIENCE, 3
He who can call t. his own PRESENT, 4
if T. be sweet TIME, 18
Its history dates from t. ROYALTY, 39
the Cup that clears /T. of past Regrets PRESENT, 5
they will listen t., they will listen tomorrow PROMISES, 4
wiser t. than...yesterday MISTAKES, 12
toddle I'd t. safely home WAR, 101
toe that old enemy the gout /Had taken him in t. PUNS, 6; ILLNESS, 7
the light fantastic t. DANCING, 7
together And the loved one all t. PERVERSITY, 2
two people living t. for 25 years without having a cross word MARRIAGE, 69
We must...all hang t. UNITY, 9
toil as some men t. after virtue SMOKING, 11
blood, t., tears and sweat EFFORT, 3
Horny-handed sons of t. WORK, 11
they t. not WORRY, 6
To t. and not to seek for rest SELFLESSNESS, 2
tolerance lead this people into war and they'll forget...t. WAR, 135
tolerant Eddy was a tremendously t. person WELSH, 1
tolerate the greater part of the law is learning to t. fools LAW, 19
toleration t. produced...religious concord RELIGION, 27
toll'd The sexton t. the bell PUNS, 5
tolls for whom the bell t. DEATH, 45
Tolstoy Their teacher had advised them not to read T. novels INDOCTRINATION, 1
Tom T., he was a piper's son NURSERY RHYMES, 61
T., T., the piper's son NURSERY RHYMES, 62
tomb A best-seller is the gilded t. of a mediocre talent BOOKS, 40
drink a dozen of Claret on my T. ALCOHOL, 35
Tom Jones The romance of *T.* NOVELS, 5
Tommy Little T. Tucker, /Sings for his supper NURSERY RHYMES, 31
Oh, it's T. this, an' T. that SOLDIERS, 2
tomorrow assure him that he'd live t. DESTINY, 17
Drop...what t. may bring...count as profit every day that Fate allows you PRESENT, 8
here today and gone t. TRANSIENCE, 3
jam t. PROMISES, 3
let us eat and drink; for t. we...die TRANSIENCE, 7
Never put off till t. PROCRASTINATION, 1
T., and t., and t. LIFE, 45
t. is another day HOPE, 7; OPTIMISM, 9
tom-tit little t. sang Willow BIRDS, 4
tone Take the t. of the company CONFORMITY, 3
tongue A burning forehead, and a parching t. PASSION, 3
a sharp t. is the only edged tool CHARACTER, 13
him whose strenuous t. /Can burst Joy's grape MELANCHOLY, 8
hold your t. and let me love SILENCE, 5
neither eye to see, nor t. to speak HOUSES OF PARLIAMENT, 11
One t. is sufficient for a woman EDUCATION, 36; WOMEN, 53
saying right off what comes to my t. IMPETUOSITY, 1
Silence is become his mother t. SILENCE, 6
the t. can no man tame SPEECH, 6
the t. is a little member SPEECH, 5
the use of my oracular t. MALAPROPISMS, 8
who speak the t. /That Shakspeare spake FREEDOM, 54
tongues Self-interest speaks all sorts of t. SELF-INTEREST, 6
Tony T....he immatures with age INSULTS, 45

too You can have t. much MODERATION, 2
tool a sharp tongue is the only edged t. CHARACTER, 13
time as a t., not as a couch TIME, 22
tools Give us the t. WORLD WAR II, 9
tool-using Man is a t. animal TECHNOLOGY, 2
tooth t. for t. RETRIBUTION, 3
toothache man with t.…teeth are sound ENVY, 7
philosopher that could endure the t. ENDURANCE, 18
top I shall be like that tree; I shall die from the t. DECLINE, 10
I started at the t. and worked my way down DECLINE, 13
looking at the men at the t. AMBITION, 6
People at the t. of the tree EDUCATION, 57
Room at the T. BOOK, SONG, AND PLAY TITLES, 5
There is always room at the t. AMBITION, 18
top-boots did pleasure me in his t. SEX, 34
torch like runners hand on the t. of life MORTALITY, 15
Truth, like a t. TRUTH, 28
tormentor it is I who am my t. SELF, 15
torments I cannot help it…infinity t. me INFINITY, 2
torrent When the t. sweeps a man against a boulder THEORY, 7
Tory a deep burning hatred for the T. Party POLITICS, 7
end up in the T. knackery POLITICIANS, 15
Every Briton is at heart a T. POLITICS, 5
to what is called the T.…called the Conservative, party POLITICS, 20
tossed you t. and gored several persons CONVERSATION, 3
total *t. solution* of the Jewish question NAZISM, 1
totter t. towards the tomb OLD AGE, 37
touch facility to do such things at the t. of a button TECHNOLOGY, 8
keep the Nelson t. PATRIOTISM, 22
mere t. of cold philosophy PHILOSOPHY, 7
only t. the hem of his garment REMEDIES, 4
sunset t. WORRY, 8
t. of a vanish'd hand NOSTALGIA, 21
Wound with a t. SATIRE, 2
tourist Only on the third class t. class passengers' deck CLASS, 24
the most vulgar…is the British t. BRITISH, 7
tourists t.…take in the Monarchy…with…the pigeons LONDON, 8
toves slithy t. did gyre NONSENSE, 7
towels never darken my t. again DISMISSAL, 5; HUMOUR, 45
tower Childe Roland to the Dark T. SUMMONS, 4
towering the height of his own t. style POETS, 27
towers The cloud-capp'd t. MORTALITY, 17
town man made the t. COUNTRYSIDE, 2
toy but a childish t. IGNORANCE, 11
trade Every man to his t. OCCUPATIONS, 2
God will pardon me. It is His t. LAST WORDS, 36
half a t. and half an art LITERATURE, 7
It is not your t. to make tables CRITICISM, 20
man must serve his time to every t. CRITICS, 2
no nation was ever ruined by t. BUSINESS, 9
Two of a t. can ne'er agree ARGUMENTS, 6
trades The ugliest of t. have their moments of pleasure OCCUPATIONS, 8
trading t. on the blood of my men EXPLOITATION, 3
tradition We don't want t. HISTORY, 13
traffic the t. of Jacob's ladder HEAVEN, 13
tragedie go litel myn t. BOOKS, 13
T. is to seyn a certeyn storie MISFORTUNE, 6
tragedies There are two t. in life DESIRE, 15
t. are finish'd by a death THEATRE, 6
tragedy a t. and therefore not worth reading PLAYS, 2
brooding t. and its dark shadows can be lightened HISTORY, 14
farce brutalized becomes t. THEATRE, 9
great t. of Science SCIENCE, 21
That is their t. SEXES, 30
the wine was a farce and the food a t. FOOD, 47
T. is if I cut my finger THEATRE, 5
We participate in a t. THEATRE, 10
what t. means THEATRE, 14
world is a comedy to those who think, a t. to those who feel LIFE, 53
You *may* abuse a t. CRITICISM, 20
You're a bloody t. POLITICIANS, 64
tragically Everything must be taken seriously, nothing t. PERSPECTIVE, 4
train man who shaves and takes a t. TRAINS, 6; TRAVEL, 25
The only way…of catching a t. TRAINS, 2
trained t. and organized common sense SCIENCE, 20
trains t. all night groan on the rail EXECUTION, 11
tramp He began to think the t. a fine…fellow FAMILIARITY, 6
the Lady Is a T. DECLINE, 2
the t. of the twenty-two men SPORT AND GAMES, 2
trampling t. out the vintage where the grapes of wrath GOD, 26
tranquilizer The t. of greatest value ALCOHOL, 42
tranquillity Sorrow is t. remembered in emotion SORROW, 14
tranquillizer What is dangerous about the t. DRUGS, 9
tranquillizers if t. could be bought as easily and cheaply as aspirin DRUGS, 8
transform t. this society without…extension of public ownership SOCIALISM, 9
transformation The universe is t. LIFE, 8
transit *Sic t. gloria mundi* GLORY, 3
transition I expect no very violent t. HEAVEN, 10
translation original is unfaithful to the t. TRANSLATION, 1
Poetry is what gets lost in t. TRANSLATION, 3
translations T. (like wives) are seldom faithful TRANSLATION, 2
transplanted Many ideas grow better when t. into another mind IDEAS, 3
trapeze daring young man on the flying t. SPORT AND GAMES, 15
trappings the t. and the suits of woe MOURNING, 12
trash Who steals my purse steals t. REPUTATION, 8
travel To t. hopefully is…better…than to arrive ANTICIPATION, 7
T. broadens the mind TRAVEL, 1
travel for t.'s sake TRAVEL, 22
T., in the younger sort TRAVEL, 2
T. is the most private of pleasures TRAVEL, 19
T. light THEFT, 6
wherever the wind takes me I t. as a visitor FREEDOM, 19
travelled I t. among unknown men HOMESICKNESS, 9
traveller a t. from an antique land MEMORIALS, 11
A t. would sit down SOUTH AFRICA, 6
from whose bourn no t. returns AFTERLIFE, 9
travelling The grand object of t. TRAVEL, 13
T. is…like talking with men of other centuries TRAVEL, 6
travels A man t. the world over HOME, 6
He t. fastest SELF, 4
too old to go again to my t. ROYALTY, 10
trawler seagulls are following a t. EXPECTATION, 1
treachery Political renegades always start their career of t. POLITICIANS, 15
tread fools rush in where angels fear to t. HASTE, 8
frightful fiend…behind him t. FEAR, 6
Where'er you t. ADMIRATION, 11
treason If *this* be t., make the most of it TREASON, 4
T. doth never prosper TREASON, 3
T. was no Crime TREASON, 2
treasure Preserve it as your chiefest t. BOOKS, 7
purest t. mortal times afford REPUTATION, 9
treasures lay not up…t. upon earth WEALTH, 7
Treasury the Vatican, the T. and the miners DIPLOMACY, 2
treaties T. are like roses and young girls DIPLOMACY, 10
treatment remind those responsible for the t. of tuberculosis DISEASE, 41
treaty hand that signed the t. bred a fever SIGNATURES, 3
tree A billboard lovely as a t. TREES, 12
A poem lovely as a t. TREES, 8
as the twig is bent, the t.'s inclined EDUCATION, 44
If poetry comes not…as leaves to a t. POETRY, 25
I shall be like that t.; I shall die from the top DECLINE, 10
only God can make a t. TREES, 9
Rock-a-bye baby on the t. top SLEEP, 4
same t. that a wise man sees WISDOM AND FOOLISHNESS, 5
spare the beechen t. TREES, 2
The difference between a gun and a t. TREES, 13
the fruit /Of that forbidden t. SIN, 16
The t. of liberty must be refreshed FREEDOM, 21
the t. of life GARDENS, 3
the t. of the knowledge of good and evil GARDENS, 3
t. of life is green REALITY, 4; THEORY, 4
treen In old time we had t. chalices and golden priests CLERGY, 9
trees Loveliest of t., the cherry TREES, 5
T. are poems CONSERVATION, 4
Trelawny shall T. die EXECUTION, 10

tremble Our hand will not t. RUSSIAN REVOLUTION, 1
t. like a guilty thing surprised DOUBT, 8
trembled And t. with fear at your frown MEMORY, 7
trembles And Satan t. PRAYER, 10
trenches digging t. and trying on gas-masks WORLD WAR II, 1
trial T. by jury...a delusion JUSTICE, 5
triangles if t. invented a god, they would make him three-sided RELIGION, 47
tribe Abou Ben Adhem (may his t. increase!) DREAMS, 12
Mankind is not a t. MANKIND, 12
Richer than all his t. LOVE, 128
tribute the vain t. of a smile POETS, 10
trick When in doubt, win the t. SPORT AND GAMES, 9
trifle Is t. sufficient for sweet FOOD, 9
trifles observance of t. TRIVIALITY, 5
snapper-up of unconsidered t. BUSINESS, 19
trigger Whose Finger do you want on the T. GOVERNMENT, 3
Trinian's Though loaded firearms were strictly forbidden at St T. WEAPONS, 9
Trinity I the T. illustrate DRINKS, 2
the Holy T. of Science SCIENCE, 22
Triton Old T. blow his wreathed horn DISCONTENT, 10
triumph One more devils'-t. and sorrow for angels DAMNATION, 1
t. in putting down the riot CHINA, 10
We t. without glory VICTORY, 3
triumphed So I t. ere my passion PASSION, 8
trivial mighty contests rise from t. things RESULTS, 5
pursuit of the t. MEDIOCRITY, 1
The t. round, the common task SIMPLICITY, 4
triviality you're deluded by t. DELUSION, 5
Trojan open that Pandora's Box...T. 'orses will jump out MIXED METAPHORS, 1
Trojans Do not trust the horse, T. MISTRUST, 11
troops t. of unrecording friends LIFE, 50
trot I don't t. it out and about VIRTUE, 6
trouble a lot of t. in his life WORRY, 10
A t. shared WORRY, 1
a woman is on a...hunt for t. MARRIAGE, 50
if you're on drugs then you're in t. DRUGS, 3
it saves me the t. of liking them NASTINESS, 2
man...is...full of t. HUMAN CONDITION, 3
telling one's t. does not make it better DISILLUSION, 5
Our progress.../Is t. and care LIFE, 34
Prostitution...keeps her out of t. SEX, 23
troubled let not your heart be t. PEACE, 2
troubles Don't meet t. half-way WORRY, 2
I have had t. enough MISFORTUNE, 5
pack up your t. in your old kit-bag OPTIMISM, 13
take arms against a sea of t. SUICIDE, 12
troublesome t....bondage of Rhyming POETRY, 32
trousers bottoms of my t. rolled OLD AGE, 17
I shall wear white flannel t. OLD AGE, 18
man should never put on his best t. FREEDOM, 20
She is trying to wear the t. of Winston Churchill POLITICIANS, 39
trout as when you find a t. in the milk PROOF, 6
trowel laid on with a t. EXCESS, 9
Troy from the shores /of T. came destined an exile ENDURANCE, 23
Now there are fields where T. once was DECLINE, 8
true a great advantage for...philosophy to be...t. PHILOSOPHY, 13
All one's inventions are t. POETRY, 15
A thing is not necessarily t. MARTYRDOM, 5
because a novel's invented, it isn't t. NOVELS, 12
Be so t. to thyself INTEGRITY, 1
be yourself, imperial, plain and t. SINCERITY, 1
false to his friends...t. to the public HONESTY, 3
Geometry is not t. MATHEMATICS, 8
He said t. things WORDS, 3
if they keep on saying it...it will be t. JOURNALISM, 8
it's...more important for a theory to be shapely, than...t. THEORY, 5
Journalists say a thing that they know isn't t. JOURNALISM, 8
Many a t. word TRUTH, 2
Mr. Speaker, I said the honorable member was a liar it is t. and I am sorry for it APOLOGIES, 4
No man worth having is t. to his wife UNFAITHFULNESS, 7
One religion is as t. as another RELIGION, 10
Small service is t. service SERVICE, 5
The religions we call false were once t. RELIGION, 23
to thine own self be t. BORROWING, 8; INTEGRITY, 6
T. and False are attributes of speech, not of things TRUTH, 29
T. love never grows old LOVE, 11
t. to you, darlin', in my fashion FAITHFULNESS, 5
truism is...none the less t. SAYINGS, 7
whatsoever things are t. VIRTUE, 4
truffles a swine to show you where the t. are VULGARITY, 1
truism A t. is on that account none the less true SAYINGS, 7
truly A t. great man GREATNESS, 1
trumpet the t. shall sound DEATH, 28
trunkless Two vast and t. legs of stone MEMORIALS, 11
trust I don't t. him. We're friends FRIENDSHIP, 11
Never t. a husband too far TRUST, 4
never t. a woman AGE, 67
Never t. the man who...hath injured you TRUST, 2
the one God whose worshippers...still t. in Him LUCK, 7
the right of governing was not property but a t. GOVERNMENT, 9
time for open t. GERMANY, 10
t. ye not in a friend TRUST, 1
Where large sums of money are concerned...t. nobody MONEY, 17
trustful It takes a long while for a...t. person to reconcile himself to...God FAITH, 15
trusting it never extended to t. him HITLER, 2
truth And seek for t. in the groves of Academe EDUCATION, 22
any t. but from a clear perception TRUTH, 32
A platitude is simply a t. repeated SAYINGS, 1
Appearances are not...a clue to the t. APPEARANCES, 13
a short armistice with t. TRUTH, 17
A t. that's told with bad intent TRUTH, 14
a t. universally acknowledged MARRIAGE, 10
Beauty is t., t. beauty BEAUTY, 24; TRUTH, 33
before the t. has got its boots on LYING, 6
cheated into passion, but...reasoned into t. TRUTH, 25
cinema is t. twenty-four times a second CINEMA, 5
Cynicism is an unpleasant way of saying the t. CYNICISM, 2
dearer still is t. TRUTH, 8
economical with the t. LYING, 3
Every man has a right to utter what he thinks t. FREEDOM, 22
few enthusiasts...speak the t. ENTHUSIASM, 2
hard to believe...a man is telling the t. LYING, 10
He believes...that there *is* such a thing as t. POLITICIANS, 35
I am the way, the t., and the life CHRISTIANITY, 17
if the people...can be reached with the t. DEMOCRACY, 16
If you do not tell the t. about yourself HONESTY, 14
in the end the t. will conquer TRUTH, 48
it cannot compel anyone to tell the t. LAW, 8
It takes two to speak the t. TRUTH, 44
Let us begin by committing ourselves to the t. TRUTH, 38
loving Christianity better than T. CHRISTIANITY, 22
mainly he told the t. LYING, 18
Much t. is spoken...more...concealed TRUTH, 21
My way of joking is to tell the t. TRUTH, 41
Nobody speaks the t. when LYING, 5
No poet ever interpreted nature...as a lawyer interprets t. LAW, 13
not even Marx is more precious...than the t. TRUTH, 46
Now I may wither into the t. AGE, 72
Perjury...is t. that is shamefaced TRUTH, 22
Photography is t. CINEMA, 5
polite by telling the t. COURTESY, 3
Pride and T....That long to give themselves for wage AGE, 71
put him in possession of t. TRUTH, 34
Some men love t. so much TRUTH, 16
speaking nothing but the t. HONESTY, 13
the laws of poetic t. and poetic beauty POETRY, 2
the t. is not in us SIN, 5
THE T. IS OUT THERE TRUTH, 43
T. is so seldom the sudden light TRUTH, 20
the t. of imagination IMAGINATION, 7; TRUTH, 31
the t. shall make you free TRUTH, 12
the unclouded face of t. suffer wrong JOURNALISM, 27
The worst enemy of t. and freedom MAJORITY, 4
those who live...believe...to be the t. HONESTY, 5
to the dead we owe only t. RESPECT, 4
T. be veiled OPTIMISM, 24
T. comes out in wine ALCOHOL, 47
T. fears no trial TRUTH, 4
T. has no special time of its own TRUTH, 39

t. is always strange TRUTH, 18
T. is on the march TRUTH, 49
T. is stranger TRUTH, 5
T. is...the test of experience TRUTH, 27
T., like a torch TRUTH, 28
T., Sir, is a cow SCEPTICISM, 3
T. sits upon the lips of dying men TRUTH, 9
T. telling is not compatible with the defence of the realm TRUTH, 40
t. that makes men free TRUTH, 7
T. will out TRUTH, 6
Two half-truths do not make a t. HALF MEASURES, 1
whatever remains, however improbable, must be the t. TRUTH, 23
What is t. TRUTH, 10, 13
When t. is discovered by someone else TRUTH, 42
whilst the great ocean of t. lay all undiscovered before me DISCOVERY, 6
who ever knew T. put to the worse TRUTH, 36
You can only find t. with logic LOGIC, 2; TRUTH, 19
truths All great t. begin as blasphemies NOVELTY, 9
all t. are half-t. TRUTH, 47
commonplaces are the great poetic t. TRIVIALITY, 13
He was a man of two t. LYING, 12
new t....begin as heresies NOVELTY, 4
The only t. which are universal TRUTH, 45
There are no new t. NOVELTY, 7
The...schoolboy is now familiar with t. for which Archimedes SCIENCE, 37
those three fundamental t. OBJECTIVITY, 3
t. being in and out of favour NOVELTY, 2
try t. everything once EXPERIENCE, 7
T., try again PERSISTENCE, 5
tu *Et t., Brute* LAST WORDS, 12; BETRAYAL, 7
tub Rub-a-dub-dub, /Three men in a t. NURSERY RHYMES, 45
tubby a t. little chap OBESITY, 13
tuberculosis remind those responsible for the treatment of t. DISEASE, 41
Tuesday Christened on T. NURSERY RHYMES, 49
T.'s child is full of grace NURSERY RHYMES, 34
tulips Tiptoe through the t. FLOWERS, 3
tumbler He who drinks a t. of London water WATER, 9
tune There's many a good t. AGE, 2
Whistle a Happy T. WHISTLING, 2
tunes I do not see...why the devil should have all the good t. MUSIC, 23
tunnel light at the end of the t....of an oncoming train PESSIMISM, 8
turbot would give the price of a large t. for it BOOKS, 37
turbulent rid me of this t. priest ASSASSINATION, 4
turf The blue ribbon of the t. HORSES, 5
turn I wouldn't have left a t. unstoned CRITICISM, 53
One good t. deserves another HELP, 3
turning Life is a maze in which we take the wrong t. LIFE, 19
The lady's not for t. INFLEXIBILITY, 3
turnip he had rather /Have a t. than his father NONSENSE, 13
twain never the t. shall meet OPPOSITES, 4
twang the triumphant t. of a bedspring SEX, 47
Tweedledee Tweedledum said T. /Had spoiled his nice new rattle WAR, 23
Tweedledum T. and Tweedledee /Agreed to have a battle WAR, 23
twelve I was born at the age of t. CINEMA, 3
T. lords a-leaping NURSERY RHYMES, 55
twentieth the t. century will be...the century of Fascism FASCISM, 2
T. Century Blues MELANCHOLY, 4
twenty the first t. years YOUTH, 18
The United States...are t. years in advance of this country AMERICA, 17
twenty-five My dear fellow...I only ask you for t. pounds BORROWING, 11
twenty-four There are only t. hours in the day TIME, 2
the t. hour day TIME, 10
the t.-hour strike STRIKES, 4
twenty-nine t. distinct damnations BIBLE, 3
twenty-two the tramp of the t. men SPORT AND GAMES, 2
twice can't step into the same river t. CHANGE, 10
desire to be praised t. over PRAISE, 6
Literature...something that will be read t. LITERATURE, 1; JOURNALISM, 14
no shirt or collar ever comes back t. NEGLECT, 2
will bear to be read t....was thought t. WRITING, 32
you shall drink t. while I drink once DRUNKENNESS, 20
twig as the t. is bent, the tree's inclined EDUCATION, 44
twilight T. grey DAY, 11
twinkle T. twinkle little bat NONSENSE, 5
T., twinkle, little star STARS, 5
twinkling in the t. of an eye DEATH, 28
twist last t. of the knife LIFE, 23
two Great God grant that twice t. be not four PRAYER, 18
if we knew one, we knew t. METAPHYSICS, 3
It takes t. ARGUMENTS, 1
It takes t. to speak the truth TRUTH, 44
It takes t. to tango COMPROMISE, 1
make t. questions grow where only one RESEARCH, 6
One step forward, t. steps back PROGRESS, 8
Tea for T., and T. for Tea DRINKS, 5
The formula 'T. and t. make five' PHILOSOPHY, 2
t. and t. do not make six LAST WORDS, 70
T. nations POVERTY AND WEALTH, 4
T. of a trade can ne'er agree ARGUMENTS, 6
T. turtle doves NURSERY RHYMES, 55
what can t. do against so many AUDIENCES, 6
two-faced I grant you that he's not t. NASTINESS, 8
twopenny I don't care a t. damn INDIFFERENCE, 6
typewriter a non-stop talker to whom someone has given a t. WRITERS, 35
tyrannize better that a man should t. over his bank balance TYRANNY, 4
tyranny Ecclesiastic t.'s the worst CHURCH, 5
kingship approaches t. it is near its end TYRANNY, 5
They that are discontented under *monarchy*, call it *t.* GOVERNMENT, 12
Where laws end, t. begins TYRANNY, 6
tyrant professed t. to their sex MISOGYNY, 6
tyrants all men would be t. TYRANNY, 1
love, an...intercourse between t. and slaves LOVE AND FRIENDSHIP, 2
the English seem...to act with the barbarity of t. IRELAND, 19
'Twixt kings and t. there's this difference TYRANNY, 2

U

U U and Non-U CLASS, 28
ugliest The u. of trades have their moments of pleasure OCCUPATIONS, 8
uglification Ambition, Distraction, U., and Derision EDUCATION, 9
ugliness the u. of adults, in a child's eyes CHILDREN, 36
ugly an intimate knowledge of its u. side DISILLUSION, 1
better to be first with an u. woman BEAUTY, 12
I'm...u. enough to succeed on my own INDEPENDENCE, 1
There are no u. women, only lazy ones BEAUTY, 31
There is nothing u. BEAUTY, 16
Ulster sold U. to buy off the fiendish republican scum IRELAND, 18
U. will fight; U. will be right IRELAND, 4
Ulysses on this earth to read *U.* LEISURE, 2
umblest I am the 'u. person SERVILITY, 2
umbrella The unjust steals the just's u. JUSTICE, 4
unacceptable u. face of capitalism CAPITALISM, 4
unacted than nurse u. desires DESIRE, 3
unanimity Our agenda is now exhausted....we find ourselves in such complete u. AGREEMENT, 6
unartificial Surely you don't mean by u. insemination SEX, 59
unassuming u. common-place /Of Nature FLOWERS, 13
unavailing All reform...will prove u. CHANGE, 2
unawares happened u. to look at her husband MARRIAGE, 12
unbaptized Fraser...left his children u. CHRISTIANITY, 46
unbearable in victory u. OFFICERS, 3
unbecoming nothing...so u. to a woman WOMEN, 89
u. the character of an officer OFFICERS, 1
un-birthday an u. present GIFTS, 3
unbowed My head is bloody, but u. ENDURANCE, 6
unbribed seeing what /the man will do /u. JOURNALISM, 33
uncertainty I have known u. UNCERTAINTY, 2
unchartered Me this u. freedom tires FREEDOM, 53
unchivalrous just a bit u. CHIVALRY, 2
unclouded the u. face of truth suffer wrong JOURNALISM, 27
unclubable A very u. man CHARACTER, 16
uncomely Nakedness is u. NAKEDNESS, 1
unconcern Is not a Patron, my Lord, one who looks with u. on a man struggling for life PATRONAGE, 2

unconfined let joy be u. DANCING, 1
unconquerable the u. hope HOPE, 4
unconscionable most u. time dying DEATH, 38
unconventionally to succeed u. ORTHODOXY, 3
uncreative oblivion which awaits the u. mind SCIENTISTS, 11
undecorated No part of the walls is left u. EXCESS, 5
undefeated Walter Mitty, the u. EXECUTION, 28
under U. the greenwood tree COUNTRYSIDE, 9
underdogs never find an Englishman among the u. ENGLAND, 41
underestimate they u. the cumulative effect POLITICAL CORRECTNESS, 5
underestimated effect of boredom is...u. BOREDOM, 5
underground Johnny u. IDEALISM, 5
Just the other day in the U. OBESITY, 3
underprivileged Compassion is not a sloppy, sentimental feeling for people who are u. SOCIALISM, 8
understand books...criticized and read by people who don't u. them BOOKS, 25
child of five would u. this SIMPLICITY, 5
if he could make *me* u....it would be clear to all UNDERSTANDING, 10
I u. only because I love LOVE, 138; UNDERSTANDING, 12
never u. everything UNDERSTANDING, 1
not to weep at them, nor to hate them, but to u. them UNDERSTANDING, 11
people...may not be made to u. UNDERSTANDING, 4
When men u. what each other mean ARGUMENTS, 12
Wot do they u. DISCONTENT, 6
You suddenly u. something...in a new way LEARNING, 6
understanding a candle of u. UNDERSTANDING, 2
a man of u. WISDOM, 7
God grant him peace...but never u. MONARCHY, 3
Most men...give evidence against their own u. SPEECH, 10
piece of cod passes all u. FOOD, 36
the peace of God, which passeth all u. BLESSING, 5
u. will...extinguish pleasure POETRY, 20; UNDERSTANDING, 7
We need more u. of human nature HUMAN NATURE, 14
understood Only one man ever u. me UNDERSTANDING, 6
undertakers I have nothing against u. personally OCCUPATIONS, 12
undertaking The love of life is necessary to...any u. ENTHUSIASM, 5
undiscovered whilst the great ocean of truth lay all u. before me DISCOVERY, 6
undone estate o' th' world were now u. WORLD-WEARINESS, 8
left u. those things SIN, 9
Things hitherto u. should be given...a wide berth ORIGINALITY, 1
uneasy U. lies the head that wears a crown MONARCHY, 22
uneatable the unspeakable in full pursuit of the u. HUNTING, 9
uneducated Democracy...government by the u. ARISTOCRACY, 5; DEMOCRACY, 3
unemployment u. and the recession have been the price...to get inflation down UNEMPLOYMENT, 1
unendurable A society...of individuals...capable of original thought would probably be u. IDEAS, 6
unequal Men are made by nature u. EQUALITY, 9
unexamined The u. life SELF, 14
unexpected Old age is the most u. OLD AGE, 47
unfaithful better to be u. FAITHFULNESS, 1
original is u. to the translation TRANSLATION, 1
unfortunates one of those u. to whom death is EXPLANATIONS, 1
ungain'd Men prize the thing u. more DESIRE, 14
unhappily The bad end u. THEATRE, 14
unhappy A moment of time may make us u. for ever SORROW, 8
don't believe one can ever be u. for long SELF, 17
each u. family is u. in its own way FAMILY, 34
It is better that some should be u. EQUALITY, 14
making their remaining years u. MANKIND, 15
most u. kind of misfortune HAPPINESS, 6
one is u. one becomes moral SORROW, 17
the instinct for being u. SORROW, 20
Today you're u.?...Go shopping MATERIALISM, 15
U. the land that has no heroes HEROISM, 3
unheralded spring now comes u. by the return of the birds ECOLOGY, 1
unicorn The lion and the u. NURSERY RHYMES, 50
uniform love that loves a scarlet coat /Should be more u. PUNS, 7
The u. 'e wore CLOTHES, 10
uniformity let use be preferred before u. HOUSES, 1
uninstructed making things plain to u. people was...best means of clearing...one's own mind EDUCATION, 24
uninteresting no...u. subject CURIOSITY, 5
union that pleasure, which is undeniably the sole motive force behind the u. of the sexes SEX, 14
To make a u. with Great Britain WORLD WAR II, 24
U. is strength UNITY, 2
unite Workers of the world, u. MARXISM, 3
united U. we stand UNITY, 3
United States In the U. there is more space AMERICA, 32
so near to the U. AMERICA, 11
The best immediate defence of the U. WORLD WAR II, 26
The U....are twenty years in advance of this country AMERICA, 17
The U. has to move very fast AMERICA, 20
The U. is like a gigantic boiler AMERICA, 16
The U....six hours behind AMERICA, 17
U. of Europe EUROPE, 6
universal Aunt Edna is u. AUDIENCES, 4
There is no u. law SPONTANEITY, 3
universe birth of the U. UNIVERSE, 12
chess-board is the world; the pieces...the phenomena of the u. GOD, 28
I accept the u. UNIVERSE, 4
I don't pretend to understand the U. UNIVERSE, 3
Life exists in the u. SCIENCE, 23
no hint throughout the u. /Of good or ill NECESSITY, 8
Perish the U. REVENGE, 6
take his attention away from the u. PRAYER, 11
the better ordering of the u. UNIVERSE, 1
the u. and all that surrounds it UNIVERSE, 6
the u. is expanding and contracting SELF-INTEREST, 3
The u. is not hostile UNIVERSE, 9
the u. is...queerer than we *can* suppose UNIVERSE, 7
The u. is transformation LIFE, 8
The u....more like a great thought UNIVERSE, 10
The u. ought to be presumed too vast UNIVERSE, 11
The visible u. was an illusion UNIVERSE, 2
u. go to all the bother of existing UNIVERSE, 8
universities mortifying fate of most English u. NOVELTY, 6
The King, observing...the state of both his u. CAMBRIDGE, 6; OXFORD, 6
U. are the cathedrals of the modern age EDUCATION, 32
U. incline wits to sophistry and affectation EDUCATION, 4
university Any attempt to reform the u. EDUCATION, 25
it is necessary to go to a u....to become a successful writer WRITERS, 3
u., where it was carefully taken out EDUCATION, 43
unjust The u. steals the just's umbrella JUSTICE, 4
unkind Thou art not so u. INGRATITUDE, 4
unkindness I tax not you, you elements, with u. WEATHER, 20
unknown apart from the known and the u. METAPHYSICS, 4
Give me a light that I may tread safely into the u. FAITH, 11
I travelled among u. men HOMESICKNESS, 9
the U. Prime Minister POLITICIANS, 34
To go into the u. DEATH, 127
unmourned and u. OBLIVION, 1
unlabelled unpardonable sins...to go about u. CLASSIFICATION, 1
unlike the Jews bring the u. into the heart of *every milieu* JEWS, 15
The law of dislike for the u. JEWS, 15
unluckily the good u. THEATRE, 14
unmarried to keep u. MARRIAGE, 107
unmotivated The u. action SPONTANEITY, 2
unmuzzled The world regards such a person as...an u. dog CLASSIFICATION, 1
unnatural so u. as the commonplace TRIVIALITY, 7
unobtrusive Poetry should be great and u. POETRY, 24
unpaid A promise made is a debt u. PROMISES, 5
unpardonable One of the u. sins...to go about unlabelled CLASSIFICATION, 1
unperfect He was u., unfinished, inartistic WRITERS, 60
unpleasant Cynicism is an u. way of saying the truth CYNICISM, 2
without mentioning a single book, or *in fact anything u.* BOOKS, 32
unpopular a free society...where it is safe to be u. FREEDOM, 50
unprofitable How weary, stale, flat, and u. WORLD-WEARINESS, 6

unpronouncables unspellables killing the u. BOSNIA AND HERCEGOVINA, 4
unreason a liberal education at the Colleges of U. REASON, 1
unrecording troops of u. friends LIFE, 50
unremembered u. acts /Of kindness and of love KINDNESS, 7
unremitting That u. humanity DICKENS, 1
unrequited Self-love seems so often u. CONCEIT, 13
unsaid tears...are for words...u. REGRET, 20
unsatisfied It is exquisite, and it leaves one u. SMOKING, 23
unsavoury indefatigable and u. engine of pollution DOGS, 12
unsealed my lips are not yet u. SECRECY, 2
unseemly an u. exposure of the mind NASTINESS, 3
unseen to deny the existence of an u. kingdom is bad SPECULATION, 1
unselfishness nothing...quite matches the sympathetic u. of an oyster PERFECTION, 7; SELFLESSNESS, 3
unshriven I am curious to see what happens...to one who dies u. LAST WORDS, 50
unsoundness no person can be a poet...without... u. of mind POETRY, 27
unspeakable the psychopathologist the u. PSYCHIATRY, 7
the u. in full pursuit of the uneatable HUNTING, 9
unspellables u. killing the unpronouncables BOSNIA AND HERCEGOVINA, 4
unstoned I wouldn't have left a turn u. CRITICISM, 53
untidier married to the only man north of the Tiber...u. than I am MARRIAGE, 130
untravelled Gleams that u. world EXPERIENCE, 20
untruth The camera...an accessory to u. PHOTOGRAPHY, 4
unupblown Nurse u. BREVITY, 9
unused left over from last year u. ADVICE, 8
unwashed The great U. PUBLIC, 5
unwholesome Boys...are u. companions for grown people CHILDREN, 32
up *How to be one u.* ONE-UPMANSHIP, 3
I saw it at a disadvantage – the curtain was u. CRITICISM, 54
u. with which I will not put GRAMMAR, 4
upbringing the u. a nun would envy INNOCENCE, 8
upper Like many of the u. class ARISTOCRACY, 2
the person that...has the u. hand will inevitably give place to another CHARACTER, 17
the u. classes /Have still the u. hand ARISTOCRACY, 6; STATELY HOMES, 2
upper-middle Shirley Williams...a member of the u. class CLASS, 38
upright man of life u. RIGHTEOUSNESS, 4
upstairs U. and downstairs NURSERY RHYMES, 13
Uriah U....made a ghastly writhe SERVILITY, 3
urine machine for turning...wine of Shiraz into u. MANKIND, 7
urn Can storied u..../Back to its mansion call the fleeting breath DEATH, 57
US U. is a truly monstrous force AMERICA, 28
usage if u. so choose, with whom resides the decision WORDS, 10
use force themselves into general u. TRAINS, 7
let u. be preferred before uniformity HOUSES, 1
what is the u. of a book BOOKS, 12
What is the u. of a new-born child PURPOSE, 2
useful not merely...u. and ornamental PURPOSE, 8
the most u. thing about a principle EXPEDIENCY, 4
useless All Art is quite u. ART, 33
A u. life is an early death PURPOSE, 3
most beautiful things...are the most u. BEAUTY, 33
uses all the u. of this world WORLD-WEARINESS, 6
usual Business as u. BRITISH, 5
Utopia Not in U..../Or some secreted island FRENCH REVOLUTION, 5
U-turn U. if you want to INFLEXIBILITY, 3

V

vacant In v. or in pensive mood SOLITUDE, 15
vacation a change of nuisances is as good as a v. CHANGE, 14
vacuum A v. can only exist...by the things which enclose it SCIENCE, 16
vagabond a fugitive and a v. PUNISHMENT, 2
vaguery For V. in the Field INCOMPETENCE, 3
vain generous aspirings implanted in her in v. SMOKING, 10
thou shalt not take the name of...God in v. GOD, 10
V. are the thousand creeds BELIEF, 3
V. wisdom all, and false philosophy WISDOM, 19
vale *ave atque v.* GREETINGS, 1
valet No man is a hero to his v. FAMILIARITY, 2
valiant v. never taste of death but once COWARDICE, 9
valid drunkenness would be...supremely v. DRUNKENNESS, 13
valley One sees great things from the v. PERSPECTIVE, 2
valleys Piping down the v. wild MUSIC, 12
valour The better part of v. is discretion SELF-PRESERVATION, 8
valuable riches to be a v. thing WEALTH, 27
value All knowledge is of itself of some v. KNOWLEDGE, 23
Friendship...has no survival v. FRIENDSHIP, 22
the price of everything and the v. of nothing CYNICISM, 5
values ideas are of more importance than v. INTELLECTUALS, 4
Victorian v....were the v. when our country MORALITY, 22
Van Gogh V.'s ear for music INSULTS, 44
vanished as rare things will, it v. TRANSIENCE, 9
vanity all is v. and vexation of spirit TRANSIENCE, 5
The v. of human life is like a river LIFE, 41
v. and love...universal characteristics WOMEN, 22
V. dies hard CONCEIT, 17
V. of vanities GREATNESS, 14; WISDOM, 23
V. plays lurid tricks CONCEIT, 6
vanquished redress of the grievances of the v. WAR, 27
variable light-headed, v. men MARRIAGE, 113
varies quality of moral behaviour v. MORALITY, 7
variety a sad v. of woe SORROW, 15
custom stale her infinite v. ADMIRATION, 14
V.'s the very spice of life CHANGE, 4
various man so v., that he seem'd to be HUMAN NATURE, 9
vary money appears to v. MONEY, 26
vasectomy V. means not ever having to say you're sorry CONTRACEPTION, 1
vast The universe ought to be presumed too v. UNIVERSE, 11
Vatican One of the best warehouses I ever see was the V. EUROPE, 21
the V., the Treasury and the miners DIPLOMACY, 2
V. is an oppressive regime CHURCH, 3
vaulting 'Fan v.'...belongs to the 'Last-supper-carved-on-a-peach-stone' ARCHITECTURE, 5
veal I could eat one of Bellamy's v. pies LAST WORDS, 52; FOOD, 44
vegetables you must talk to your v. GARDENS, 5
vegetarianism useless for the sheep to pass resolutions in favour of v. ARGUMENTS, 9
v. is the only road to salvation of some HEALTH AND HEALTHY LIVING, 9
vegetarians V. have wicked, shifty eyes PREJUDICE, 4
vegetate When I am in the country I wish to v. COUNTRYSIDE, 5
veil the v. of the temple was rent in twain LAST WORDS, 11
the v. which those who live call life DEATH, 114
v. of indifference COLD WAR, 4
v. which those who live /Call life LIFE, 47
veils v. of the morning PEACE, 17
Velasquez Why drag in V. CONCEIT, 22
venerability If you live long enough, the v. factor creeps in LONGEVITY, 3
vengeance No one delights more in v. than a woman REVENGE, 11; WOMEN, 42
venial than that one soul...should commit one single v. sin SIN, 18
Venice She only went to V. INSULTS, 24
V. is like eating...chocolate liqueurs VENICE, 2
V., the eldest Child of Liberty VENICE, 3
ventured Nothing v. OPPORTUNITY, 5
Venus She is V. when she smiles COMPLIMENTS, 2
verb a v. meaning 'to believe falsely' BELIEF, 8
verbose Revolutions are always v. REVOLUTION, 7
verbosity inebriated with...his own v. VERBOSITY, 2
Verdi strains of V. will come back to you tonight HUMOUR, 47
verdict Sentence first – v. afterwards INJUSTICE, 4
verification bring about the v. of his own prophecies PROPHECY, 13
verify Always v. your references RESEARCH, 4
veritas *In vino v.* ALCOHOL, 47
vermin lower than v. POLITICS, 7
vernal One impulse from a v. wood LEARNING, 10
Versailles a lady at the court of V. LANGUAGE, 26
verse Curst be the v. POETRY, 35
Having v. set to music POETRY, 50
If Galileo had said in v. that the world moved POETRY, 19
no v. can give pleasure...that is written by drinkers of water WATER, 6
Writing free v. POETRY, 17

verses v....as a literary performance POETRY, 52
versified excellent poets that have never v. POETS, 11
versifiers now swarm many v. POETS, 11
vertical The v. man POSTERITY, 3
vessel the weaker v. MARRIAGE, 28
vestry I will see you in the v. after service CLERGY, 13
vex they die to v. me CLERGY, 12
with no deep researches v. the brain CLARITY, 1
vexation all is vanity and v. of spirit TRANSIENCE, 5
viable I'm v. from ten o'clock till five BUSINESS, 4
vice extremism in the defence of liberty is no v. EXCESS, 4
Hypocrisy is the most...nerve-racking v. HYPOCRISY, 11
Is Pride, the never-failing v. of fools PRIDE, 8
no v. but beggary HYPOCRISY, 15
Prosperity doth best discover v. MISFORTUNE, 3
public schools are the nurseries of all v. EDUCATION, 16
quotation is a national v. QUOTATIONS, 14
The only sensual pleasure without v. MUSIC, 26
there is no distinction between virtue and v. MISTRUST, 6
This v. brings in one hundred million francs...every year SMOKING, 14
three great evils, boredom, v., and poverty WORK, 24
V. and virtues are products VIRTUE AND VICE, 3
V. is its own reward VICE, 6
V. is often clothed APPEARANCES, 6
V. itself lost half its evil VICE, 5
When v. prevails VICE, 1
vices It's your combination sinners...who dishonour the v. VICE, 10
one of the v. of our age ARMY, 4
small v. do appear APPEARANCES, 21
virtues and v. couple with one another VIRTUE AND VICE, 1
virtues are...v. in disguise VIRTUE AND VICE, 2
We make ourselves a ladder out of our v. VICE, 2
Vichy There's something V. about the French FRANCE, 12
vicious can't expect a boy to be v. EDUCATION, 47
He was a v. man, but very kind CHARACTER, 15
victim a v. of any kind ACTORS, 10
more easily fall v. to a big lie LYING, 8
v. must be found /I've got a little list PUNISHMENT, 9
victims Every reformation must have its v. SUFFERING, 12
Man is the only animal...on friendly terms with the v....he eats HYPOCRISY, 6
The little v. play IGNORANCE, 7
There are born v. MURDER, 8
v. who respect their executioners RESPECT, 3
victor happy state of getting the v.'s palm without the dust of racing VICTORY, 6
Victoria If this is the way Queen V. treats her prisoners IMPRISONMENT, 11
Mrs Thatcher...looking like Queen V. POLITICIANS, 74
take a ticket at V. Station FREEDOM, 2
Victorian the most antagonistic to the V. age WRITERS, 93
V. values...were the values when our country MORALITY, 22
Victorians The V. had not been anxious to go away TRAVEL, 26
victories Peace hath her v. WAR AND PEACE, 11
victorious Send him v. BRITAIN, 6
victory Before Alamein we never had a v. WORLD WAR II, 15
death is swallowed up in v. DEATH, 28
every v. turns into a defeat DISILLUSION, 2
in v. unbearable OFFICERS, 3
In...war it is not right that matters, but v. WAR, 47
let there be v. WORLD WAR I, 11
O grave! where is thy v. DEATH, 94
Such another v. and we are ruined VICTORY, 14
to gain such a v. as this VICTORY, 18
'twas a famous v. VICTORY, 17
V. at all costs VICTORY, 2
v. for all the people of South Africa SOUTH AFRICA, 10
V. has a thousand fathers SUCCESS, 10
v. under the belly of a Cossack's horse RUSSIAN REVOLUTION, 3
without v. there is no survival VICTORY, 2
vidders be very careful o' v. CAUTION, 11
vieillesse si v. pouvait AGE, 24
Vietnam To win in V. WAR, 112
V. was lost in the living rooms of America TELEVISION AND RADIO, 4; WAR, 65
view modern v. of life is always to seek what is more convenient DISEASE, 37
vigilance eternal v. FREEDOM, 9
vile only man is v. MISANTHROPY, 1
orgies are v. DEBAUCHERY, 8
vilest the v. specimens of human nature are...found among demagogues POLITICS, 46
village the world in the image of a global v. TECHNOLOGY, 9
villages world poverty is primarily a problem of two million v. POVERTY, 29
villains Children should acquire...heroes and v. from fiction HISTORY, 3
God should go before such v. GOD, 44
vine With v. leaves in his hair RETURN, 2
vino *In v. veritas* ALCOHOL, 47
vintage O, for a draught of v. ALCOHOL, 36
trampling out the v. where the grapes of wrath GOD, 26
violate men never v. the laws of God without suffering the consequences RETRIBUTION, 9
violence v. in Northern Ireland IRELAND, 12
v. in the movies can be cool VIOLENCE, 10
v. masquerading as love VIOLENCE, 6
violent I expect no very v. transition HEAVEN, 10
virtue in ambition is v. VIRTUE, 2
violet My regret /Becomes an April v. SORROW, 25
violets Good God, I forgot the v. FLOWERS, 6
violin an orangutang trying to play the v. MARRIAGE, 17
If the Almighty himself played the v. EGOTISM, 6
virgin a v. shall conceive CHRISTIANITY, 9
fashionable...to be a v. SEX, 11
v. territory for whorehouses AMERICA, 6
virginity Age...nor custom stale her infinite v. PURITY, 5
a little more v., if you don't mind ACTING, 12
that v. could be a virtue PURITY, 4
virgins everyone is back to v. again SEX, 13
virtue adversity doth best discover v. MISFORTUNE, 3
as some men toil after v. SMOKING, 11
Crime, like v., has its degrees CRIME, 6
Fine words...seldom associated with v. SERVILITY, 1
forbearance ceases to be a v. TOLERANCE, 1
greatest offence against v. VIRTUE, 10
hearts of Men...should have a v. to shape their life MANKIND, 33
Let the blessing...be...upoon all that are lovers of v. FISHING, 3
moderation in the pursuit of justice is no v. EXCESS, 4
Most men admire /V. VIRTUE, 14
much v. in If POSSIBILITY, 3
My v.'s still far too small VIRTUE, 6
name a v. that brings in as much revenue SMOKING, 14
next to impossible is the exercise of v. VIRTUE, 8
no v. like necessity NECESSITY, 6
Self-denial is not a v. SELF-DENIAL, 1
there is no distinction between v. and vice MISTRUST, 6
to practise five things...constitutes perfect v. VIRTUE, 7
V. consisted in VIRTUE, 5
v. in ambition is violent VIRTUE, 2
v. in the creator is not the same as v. in the creature CREATION, 12
V. is its own punishment RIGHTEOUSNESS, 2
V. is like a rich stone VIRTUE, 1
Woman's v. is man's greatest invention SEXES, 21
virtues ape-like v. without which EDUCATION, 13
few v....the Poles do not possess PLACES, 3
greater v. to sustain good fortune LUCK, 11
No one gossips about...secret v. GOSSIP, 8
Vice and v. are products VIRTUE AND VICE, 3
v. and vices couple with one another VIRTUE AND VICE, 1
v. are...vices in disguise VIRTUE AND VICE, 2
v. /We write in water MEMORIALS, 10
What men call social v....virtue of pigs in a litter SOCIETY, 10
virtuous the v. poor POVERTY, 33
When men grow v. in their old age VIRTUE, 15
who can find a v. woman WOMEN, 17
virus cross between a very severe v. ACTORS, 22
visage Sir Launcelot saw her v., but he wept not greatly SORROW, 11
vise Screw up the v....you have rheumatism DISEASE, 4
vision I have a v. of the future FUTURE, 2
The young men's v., and the old men's dream DREAMS, 5
turn to the wider v. of the Commonwealth POLITICS, 47
visionary Whither is fled the v. gleam METAPHYSICS, 5

visits Its v., /Like those of angels DEATH, 32
vital *v. lampada* MORTALITY, 15
vitality a symptom of deficient v. EXCESS, 13
The lower one's v. ART, 3
vitamins the right proteins and v. HEALTH AND HEALTHY LIVING, 4
they are crazy about v. or about roughage HEALTH AND HEALTHY LIVING, 9
vivify quarrels which v. its barrenness LOVE, 64
vocal His v. cords were kissed by God OPERA, 7
vogue It is charming to totter into v. AGE, 65
voice a bird of the air shall carry the v. SECRECY, 3
a still small v. GOD, 13; SUICIDE, 13
Conscience is the inner v. CONSCIENCE, 4
The higher the v. INTELLECT, 6
The melting v. through mazes running MUSIC, 33
The v. of the intellect is a soft one INTELLECT, 2
v. of the people is the v. of God PUBLIC, 1
voices Music, when soft v. die MEMORY, 17
Two v.…one is of the sea, /One of the mountains FREEDOM, 55
volcano dancing on a v. REVOLUTION, 5
explode at last in a fiery v. in one's great toe DISEASE, 17
vole plashy fen passes the questing v. ANIMALS, 21
Voltaire One does not arrest V. RESPECT, 2
volunteer restless who will v. for anything SOLDIERS, 4
volunteers V. usually fall into two groups SOLDIERS, 4
Volvo taxed and insured V. country SPORT AND GAMES, 21
vomit If…Orientals…drank a liquor which…made them v. ALCOHOL, 17
To write a diary…returning to one's own v. DIARIES, 4
vorsprung V. durch technik ADVERTISING, 19
vote He's lost us the tarts' v. RESPONSIBILITY, 6; JOURNALISM, 16
I shall not v.…I do not aspire to advise DEMOCRACY, 22
One man shall have one v. DEMOCRACY, 2
v. is the most powerful instrument DEMOCRACY, 8
voted I always v. at my party's call POLITICIANS, 10
voter there is a model Labour v.…is patronizing POLITICS, 42
votes disadvantage of merely counting v. DEMOCRACY, 7
solved by speeches and majority v. POWER POLITICS, 2
vow better…not v., than…vow and not pay PROMISES, 1
vox *V. populi, v. dei* PUBLIC, 1
vulgar Above the v. flight of common souls SUPERIORITY, 8
dislike the French from…v. antipathy FRANCE, 15
Funny without being v. CRITICISM, 15
the most v.…is the British tourist BRITISH, 7
the sign of a v. mind ARROGANCE, 1
The v. boil…an egg FOOD, 45
v. is to use a gold toothpick VULGARITY, 4
war…is looked upon as v. WAR, 130
vulgarity One can love a certain kind of v. for its own sake VULGARITY, 2
v. begins at home VULGARITY, 5
vulgarize That fellow would v. the day of judgment VULGARITY, 3
vulgarizing Death…It's the only thing we haven't succeeded in completely v. DEATH, 62

W

wabe gyre and gimble in the w. NONSENSE, 7
wag A case of the tail dogging the w. HUMOUR, 53
Every man has…an ambition to be a w. HUMOUR, 16
wage One man's w. rise is another man's price increase ECONOMICS, 23
waggle can you w. your ears BOOKS, 5
Wagner W. has lovely moments CRITICISM, 44
W. is the Puccini of music MUSICIANS, 12
wagon Hitch your w. to a star AMBITION, 8
Wagstaff a disgrace to our family name of W. FAMILY, 23
waistcoat my stomach must just digest in its w. ALCOHOL, 57
wait They also serve who only stand and w. SERVICE, 4
W. and see PATIENCE, 7
waiting people w. for you stand out far less clearly CLARITY, 2
There was I, w. at the church MARRIAGE, 78
w. for the cock to crow BETRAYAL, 4
wake hope is…the dream of those that w. HOPE, 9
waking w. from a troubled dream AFTERLIFE, 4
walentine Never sign a w. SIGNATURES, 1
Wales From W. /Whose nightingales WALES, 4
trace…the disasters of English history to…W. WALES, 5
W.…genuinely more classless WALES, 1
walk in the name of Jesus…rise up and w. REMEDIES, 3
I w. down the Strand FASHION, 3
not once in all my life have I gone out for a w. HEALTH AND HEALTHY LIVING, 3
Or w. with Kings IDEALISM, 2
w. on the lines or the squares SUPERSTITION, 9
We must learn to w. before we can run PATIENCE, 6
Where'er you w. ADMIRATION, 11
walking I'm w. backwards till Christmas NONSENSE, 23
I nauseate w. COUNTRYSIDE, 1
I were w. with destiny DESTINY, 4
simple w. from one point to another TRAVEL, 4
W. My Baby Back Home LOVE, 142
w. round him has always tired me INSULTS, 6
When I am not w., I am reading READING, 9
walks She w. in beauty BEAUTY, 14
wall Either that w. paper goes, or I do LAST WORDS, 73
Humpty Dumpty sat on a w. NURSERY RHYMES, 18
it is your business, when the w. next door catches fire NEIGHBOURS, 4
W. is the name – Max W. HUMOUR, 57
With our backs to the w.…each…must fight on to the end WAR, 44
With our backs to the w. WORLD WAR I, 12
wallet a crowd like that…brings a lump to my w. MATERIALISM, 22
Time hath…a w. at his back TIME, 35
wallop the cod's w. is always fresh made COMMUNISM, 5
walls by faith the w. of Jericho fell down FAITH, 2
No part of the w. is left undecorated EXCESS, 5
Stone w. do not a prison make IMPRISONMENT, 4
W. have ears GOSSIP, 6
walrus The W. and the Carpenter SEASIDE, 1
Walt Disney Christian presence…W. Theme Park COMMERCIALISM, 1
waltzing You'll come a-w., Matilda PLACES, 12
wandered I w. lonely as a cloud FLOWERS, 14
wanderer A w. is man from his birth HUMAN CONDITION, 1
wandering Poor w. one RETURN, 1
W. in a vast forest at night GUIDANCE, 2
w. minstrel I SINGERS, 2
wankers We're all w. underneath SEX, 18
want be without some of the things you w. HAPPINESS, 20
Economy is going without something you do w. THRIFT, 8
evil is wrought by w. of thought EVIL, 10
for w. of a nail NEGLECT, 1; PRUDENCE, 3
freedom from w. HUMAN RIGHTS, 4
give the public what they w. to see and they'll come out for it FUNERALS, 8
If you w. a thing well done SELF-RELIANCE, 1
I w. to be alone.' MISQUOTATIONS, 17
The w. of a thing is perplexing enough MATERIALISM, 19
What does a woman w. WOMEN, 33
What do we w.? Radio 4 TELEVISION AND RADIO, 1
wanted bought things because she w. 'em WOMEN, 84
Every man is w. HUMAN CONDITION, 7
I have w. only one thing to make me happy DISCONTENT, 3
wanting stop w. something you get it DESIRE, 17
wants Man w. but little MORTALITY, 24
war Against the beautiful…one can wage a pitiless w. BEAUTY, 19
All diplomacy is a continuation of w. DIPLOMACY, 14
all's fair in love and w. JUSTICE, 8
An empire founded by w. WAR, 70
As long as w. is regarded as wicked WAR, 130
Before the w.…it was summer all the year round NOSTALGIA, 16
Being over seventy is like being engaged in a w. OLD AGE, 43
could lose the w. in an afternoon OFFICERS, 4
defeat without a w. WORLD WAR II, 3
do in the Great W., Daddy WORLD WAR I, 6
done very well out of the w. HOUSES OF PARLIAMENT, 4
except the British W. Office WAR, 109
Great Britain is going to make w. on a kindred nation WORLD WAR I, 3
him who desires peace, prepare for w. WAR AND PEACE, 13
I could have lost the w. in an afternoon WAR, 52
I'd like to see the government get out of w. altogether WAR, 46
I don't care for w. WAR, 75
If we lose this w. WAR, 33
I make w. on the living REVENGE, 8

In a civil w., a general must know WAR, 89
In starting and waging a w. it is not right that matters, but victory WAR, 47
In w.... there are no winners WAR, 25
is a w. to end w. WORLD WAR I, 15
It is well that w. is so terrible WAR, 61
lead this people into w. and they'll forget... tolerance WAR, 135
Lenin was the first to discover that capitalism 'inevitably' caused w. CAPITALISM, 14
let slip the dogs of w. WAR, 107
life is more interesting in w. than in peace WAR AND PEACE, 10
makes a good w. makes a good peace WAR AND PEACE, 8
My subject is W., and the pity of W. POETRY, 34
never was a good w. WAR AND PEACE, 6
No one can guarantee success in w. WAR, 29
Now w. has a bad conscience WAR, 54
Older men declare w. WAR, 49
only twenty seconds of w. to destroy him WAR, 7
on this wall will hang my weapons and my lyre, discharged from the w. SEX, 25
Stand your ground... if they mean to have a w., let it begin here WAR, 84
Television brought the brutality of w. TELEVISION AND RADIO, 4; WAR, 65
that devil's madness – W. WAR, 106
the... barbarity of w.... forces men WAR, 55
The first casualty when w. comes WAR, 53
The quickest way of ending a w. WAR, 80
there was w. in heaven DEVIL, 4
the second rule of w. WAR, 71
The W. between Men and Women SEXES, 26
the W. is being deliberately prolonged WAR, 103
the w. of the giants is over WORLD WAR II, 16
The w. we have just been through WAR, 134
The wrong w., at the wrong place WAR, 13
they'll give a w. and nobody will come WAR, 97
this liking for w. WAR, 8
this massed multitude of silent witnesses to... w. WAR, 41
This w.... is a w. to end w. WAR, 62
this w.... which did not justify the sacrifice WAR, 83
Those who can win a w. well WAR AND PEACE, 4
w. can only be abolished through w. WAR, 64
w. ended, the explosions stopped WAR AND PEACE, 9
W. even to the knife WAR, 22
W. hath no fury like a non-combatant WAR, 69
W. is, after all, the universal perversion WAR, 88
W. is an organized bore WAR, 48
W. is capitalism WAR, 115
W. is hell WAR, 110
W. is like love WAR, 16
W. is not an adventure WAR, 96
W. is Peace OPPOSITES, 5
W. is the continuation of politics MISQUOTATIONS, 14; WAR, 30, 63
W. is too important OFFICERS, 5
W. is war WAR, 78
W. knows no power WAR, 19
W. makes rattling good history WAR AND PEACE, 7
w. minus the shooting SPORT AND GAMES, 18
W. should belong to the tragic past WAR, 85
w. which... left nothing to be desired WAR, 15
W. will never cease until babies WAR, 66
we are... in the midst of a cold w. COLD WAR, 2
We are not at w. with Egypt MIDDLE EAST, 7
We have all lost the w. WAR, 60
What they could do with round here is a good w. WAR, 14
when there was w., he went PUBLIC, 3
When the rich wage w. POVERTY AND WEALTH, 7
when they learn how we began this w. WORLD WAR II, 25
When you're at w. you think about a better life WAR AND PEACE, 14
Who live under the shadow of a w. WAR, 111
wards key deftly in the oiled w. SLEEP, 13
Ware And I should dine at W. MARRIAGE, 42
warehouses One of the best w. I ever see was the Vatican EUROPE, 21
Waring What's become of W. ABSENCE, 5
warmongers w. who... have others pull the chestnuts out of the fire POLITICS, 71
warmth No w., no cheerfulness, no healthful ease MONTHS, 10
warn the right... to w. MONARCHY, 2
warned my Friends, be w. by me FOOD, 7
warning will it come without w. /Just as I'm picking my nose LOVE, 18
warrior the British w. queen BRITAIN, 7
wars All w. are planned by old men WAR, 92
All w. are popular for the first thirty days WAR, 104
end to the beginnings of all w. WAR, 94
Just like an old liberal /Between the w. LIBERALISM, 3
military don't start w. WAR, 129
my w. /Were global WAR, 90
No kingdom has... had as many... w. as the kingdom of Christ CHRISTIANITY, 34
Still w. and lechery SEX, 53
W. are not won by evacuations WORLD WAR II, 14
W. cannot be fought with nuclear weapons NUCLEAR WEAPONS, 13
W., conflict, it's all business WAR, 26
w., horrible w. PROPHECY, 14
warts pimples, w., and everything as you see me REALISM, 1
war-war To jaw-jaw is better than to w. DIPLOMACY, 5
wary the w. fox said... to the sick lion MISTRUST, 5
wash Don't w. your dirty linen GOSSIP, 2
I do, and I also w. and iron them HOUSEWORK, 5
washed Pilate... w. his hands GUILT, 3
washing painting a face and not w. APPEARANCE, 15
wasps w. and hornets break through LAW, 28
waste biggest w. of water in the country CONSERVATION, 6
Far too good to w. on children YOUTH, 17
The years to come seemed w. of breath FLYING, 4
W. not, want not WASTE, 1
wasted most w. of all days LAUGHTER, 6
wasting she did not believe in w. her effects THREATS, 1
watch Either he's dead or my w. has stopped DEATH, 83
keeping w. over their flock by night CHRISTMAS, 8
The W. on the Rhine RIVERS, 4
w. and pray IMPERFECTION, 4
why not carry a w. CLOCKS, 1
watch-dog to hear the w.'s honest bark DOGS, 5
watched A w. pot PATIENCE, 1
watches 'Tis with our judgments as our w. OPINIONS, 4
watchmaker I should have become a w. NUCLEAR WEAPONS, 5
watchman only one man... can count on steady work – the night w. THEATRE, 2
watch-tower To hear the lark... From his w. in the skies BIRDS, 8
water better deeds /Shall be in w. writ MEMORIALS, 2
biggest waste of w. in the country WATER, 7
Dripping w. hollows out a stone PERSISTENCE, 11
half the landscape is... covered by useless w. SEASIDE, 2
He who drinks a tumbler of London w. WATER, 9
Human beings were invented by w. WATER, 8
I came like W. LIFE AND DEATH, 6
if I were under w. I would scarcely kick MELANCHOLY, 6
impressions... lasting as... an oar upon the w. INSIGNIFICANCE, 1
It is with our passions as it is with fire and w. PASSION, 4
Like a bridge over troubled w. COMFORT, 4
like throwing w. into the sea CHARITY, 11
no verse can give pleasure... that is written by drinkers of w. WATER, 6
Streets full of w. TELEGRAMS, 3; VENICE, 1
the w. that was made wine ALCOHOL, 14
virtues we write in w. MEMORIALS, 10
w. flowed like champagne ABSTINENCE, 4
W. is H_2O, hydrogen two parts, oxygen one SCIENCE, 27
w., is unsuitable in colour WATER, 5
w. still keeps falling over WATER, 1
W., water, every where WATER, 2
Water, w., every where WATER, 2
when I makes w. I makes w. HUMOUR, 41
watering a-w. the last year's crop FUTILITY, 6
Waterloo Battle of W. WAR, 79, 127
Every man meets his W. DEFEAT, 6
waters dreadful noise of w. in my ears DROWNING, 2
stolen w. are sweet SECRECY, 5
the earth shall be full... as the w. cover the sea PEACE, 1
the Spirit of God moved upon... the w. CREATION, 2
the w. of the heart /Push in their tides EMOTION, 5
water-trough A snake came to my w. WEATHER, 16
Watson Mr W., come here; I want you SUMMONS, 3
waves the w. make towards the pebbled shore TIME, 34
waxworks w. inhabited by gramophones WORDS, 15
way A man... is *so* in the w. MEN, 5

blow out your candle...to find your w. GUIDANCE, 2
catch the nearest w. KINDNESS, 4
I am the w., the truth, and the life CHRISTIANITY, 17
in every war they kill you a new w. PROGRESS, 10
plowman homeward plods his weary w. DAY, 6
The w. to a man's heart LOVE, 10
The w. to dusty death LIFE, 45
though hell should bar the w. DETERMINATION, 13
w. of all flesh DEATH, 39; HUMAN NATURE, 21
woman has her w. SEXES, 11
ways She dwelt among the untrodden w. LONELINESS, 9
We have w. of making men talk MISQUOTATIONS, 4
wayside If you see anybody fallen by the w. CHARITY, 18
we put it down a w. SPELLING, 1
weak A w., diffusive, weltering, ineffectual man POETS, 24
Beauty stands /In the admiration...of w. minds BEAUTY, 28
concessions of the w. YIELDING, 1
disarm the strong and arm the w. INJUSTICE, 6
Idleness...the refuge of w. minds IDLENESS, 3
I inhabit a w., frail, decayed tenement LAST WORDS, 2
Is thy love a plant /Of such w. fibre ABSENCE, 10
Like all w. men...an exaggerated stress DECISION, 2
surely the w. shall perish SURVIVAL, 6
The w. have one weapon MISTAKES, 3
weaker the w. vessel MARRIAGE, 28
weakest The w. goes to the wall WEAKNESS, 1
weakness no more w. than is natural to her sex WOMEN, 78
weaknesses I have got lots of human w. IMPERFECTION, 13
Never support two w. VICE, 10
touch his w. with a delicate hand IMPERFECTION, 8
weal I will govern according to the common w. MONARCHY, 13
wealth God shows his contempt for w. WEALTH, 22
His w. a well-spent age RIGHTEOUSNESS, 5
Outshone the w. of Ormus and of Ind DEVIL, 10
the insolence of w. WEALTH, 17
W. has never been a sufficient source of honour OSTENTATION, 3
W. I ask not TRAVEL, 21
W. is like sea-water GREED, 9
W. is not without its advantages WEALTH, 13
when the nation depended on agriculture for its w. ECONOMICS, 18
Where w. and freedom reign, contentment fails BUSINESS, 12
wealthy Where some people are very w. and others have nothing GOVERNMENT, 4
weaned w. on a pickle APPEARANCE, 22
weapon art is not a w. ART, 12
In the sex-war thoughtlessness is the w. of the male SEXES, 6
The weak have one w. MISTAKES, 3
tinned food is a deadlier w. WEAPONS, 3
weapons books are w. BOOKS, 34
If sunbeams were w. ENVIRONMENT, 3
on this wall will hang my w. and my lyre, discharged from the war SEX, 25
wear I...chose my wife...for...such qualities as would w. well MARRIAGE, 66
I want you to w. me LOVE, 54
you'll w. your eyes out STARING, 2
weariest The w. nights...must...end ENDURANCE, 11
weariness much study is a w. of the flesh BOOKS, 8
The w., the fever, and the fret HUMAN CONDITION, 12
weary Art thou w. SORROW, 13
let us not be w. in well doing RETRIBUTION, 4
weather even the w. forecast seemed to be some kind of spoof WEATHER, 17
Give me books, fruit, French wine and fine w. PLEASURE, 17
I like the w. WEATHER, 8
This is the w. the cuckoo likes WEATHER, 13
This is the w. the shepherd shuns WEATHER, 14
When two Englishmen meet, their first talk is of the w. ENGLISH, 20; WEATHER, 15
weather-eye Keep your w. open CAUTION, 7
weather-wise Some are w. WISDOM, 16
web The w. of our life is of a mingled yarn GOOD AND EVIL, 4
webs Laws are like spider's w. LAW, 27
weddings w. is sadder than funerals MARRIAGE, 21
Wednesday Married on W. NURSERY RHYMES, 49
W.'s child is full of woe NURSERY RHYMES, 34
wee W....tim'rous beastie ANIMALS, 7
weed that tawney w. tobacco SMOKING, 8
What is a w. GOOD, 5
weeds Lilies that fester smell far worse than w. CORRUPTION, 8
nature runs either to herbs, or to w. HUMAN NATURE, 2
Worthless as wither'd w. BELIEF, 3
week A w. is a long time in politics POLITICS, 92
Of all the days that's in the w. SUNDAY, 3
the greatest w. in the history of the world SPACE, 6
weekendmanship that basic w. should contain... Important Person Play ONE-UPMANSHIP, 2
weep By the waters of Babylon we sit down and w. AMERICA, 36
Fair daffodils, we w. to see TRANSIENCE, 14
For men must work, and women must w. SEXES, 14
not to w. at them, nor to hate them, but to understand them UNDERSTANDING, 11
She must w. or she will die MOURNING, 16
so that I do not w. LAUGHTER, 4
Tears such as angels w. SORROW, 12
w. for her sins at the other ADULTERY, 3
W. no more, my lady HOMESICKNESS, 2
weeping Do you hear the children w. SORROW, 2
Why are you w.? Did you imagine that I was immortal LAST WORDS, 44
weigh my innocence begins to w. me down INNOCENCE, 2
weighed thou art w. in the balances, and art found wanting JUDGMENT, 1
weight the w. of rages SPOONERISMS, 1
welcome Advice is seldom w. ADVICE, 6
Love bade me w. GUILT, 5
Thrice w., darling of the spring BIRDS, 14
well as w. off as if he were rich WEALTH, 4
At last I am going to be w. LAST WORDS, 62
do not speak w. of yourself MODESTY, 4
I am not w.; pray get me...brandy FIRST IMPRESSIONS, 3
lov'd not wisely, but too w. LOVE, 128
nothing...and did it very w. HOUSES OF PARLIAMENT, 10
reward of a thing w. done SATISFACTION, 3
There are two things which I am confident I can do very w. CRITICISM, 18
the world's work...is done by men who do not feel...w. ILLNESS, 4
We never do anything w. ACHIEVEMENT, 5
worth doing w. EXCELLENCE, 1
well-bred a w. sort of emotional anarchy CLASSIFICATION, 2
well-dressed The sense of being w. CLOTHES, 5
well-knownness The celebrity...known for his w. FAME, 4
well-rounded whole man in himself, polished and w. CHARACTER, 12
well-spent as rare as a w. one BIOGRAPHY, 2
well-written A w. Life BIOGRAPHY, 2
Welsh but he wouldn't put up with the W. WELSH, 1
The W....just sing WELSH, 4
Wembley W., adj. Suffering from a vague *malaise* HUMOUR, 39
wen the fate of the great w. LONDON, 5
Wenceslas Good King W. looked out CHRISTMAS, 15
wench beside the w. is dead SEX, 35
Wenlock Edge On W. the wood's in trouble...the Wrekin heaves TREES, 4
went as cooks go she w. HUMOUR, 54
wept They w. like anything to see SEASIDE, 1
young man who has not w. AGE, 51; WISDOM, 20
west closing time in the gardens of the W. CAPITALISM, 1
East is East, and W. is W. OPPOSITES, 4
Go W., young man EXPLORATION, 2
the safeguard of the w. VENICE, 4
western W. philosophy is...a series of footnotes to Plato's philosophy PHILOSOPHY, 15
westerns W. are closer to art CINEMA, 13
wet joly whistle wel y-w. ALCOHOL, 20
out of these w. clothes and into a dry Martini ALCOHOL, 67
whale A w. ship was my Yale College EDUCATION, 35
Very like a w. AGREEMENT, 5
what Aye, and w. then PROOF, 3
W. is truth TRUTH, 10
wheat An editor...separates the w. from the chaff EDITORS, 3
wheel bound upon a w. of fire SUFFERING, 14
wheels A cruel story runs on w. CRUELTY, 4
spoke among your w. OBSTRUCTION, 1
when have they fixed the where and w. EXECUTION, 10
w. a man should marry MARRIAGE, 14
where have they fixed the w. and when EXECUTION, 10
to die, and go we know not w. DEATH, 107

W. are you now LOVE, 70
W. were you fellows when the paper was blank EDITORS, 1
where'er W. you tread ADMIRATION, 11
W. you walk ADMIRATION, 11
wherefore There is occasions and causes why and w. EXPLANATIONS, 2
w. art thou Romeo NAMES, 6
whey Eating her curds and w. NURSERY RHYMES, 30
Whig Sir, I perceive you are a vile W. POLITICS, 39
Whigs caught the W. bathing POLITICS, 22
whim The strangest w. SUICIDE, 2
whimper not with a bang but a w. ENDING, 3
whipping W. and abuse are like laudanum CRUELTY, 5
who shall scape w. MERIT, 6
whirlwind sown the wind…reap the w. RETRIBUTION, 5
whisker can't speak above a w. PUNS, 12
whisky nicest boy who ever committed the sin of w. ALCOHOL, 59
That w. priest CLERGY, 8
with education and w. the price it is CHARACTER, 26
whispered it's w. every where SECRECY, 8
whispering w. sound of the cool colonnade TREES, 3
whisperings It keeps eternal w. around SEA, 8
whistle I heard the bullets w. WAR, 122
So was hir joly w. wel y-wet ALCOHOL, 20
W. a Happy Tune WHISTLING, 2
W. and she'll come to you SUMMONS, 2
whistled a young man who would…play his music and be w. at for it MUSIC, 19
whistles They hang us now in Shrewsbury jail: / The w. blow forlorn EXECUTION, 11
whistling W. aloud to bear his courage up WHISTLING, 1
white architecture…contemplate it…are those…with a w. stick and a dog ARCHITECTURE, 6
Britain…is going to be forged in the w. heat of this revolution SOCIALISM, 15
'E was w., clear w., inside APPEARANCES, 16
If the w. man *says* he does RACISM, 19
it's not even red brick, but w. tile CLASS, 26
I used to be Snow W. PURITY, 6
I want to be the w. man's brother RACISM, 14
makes a Negro unpleasant to w. folk RACISM, 23
my soul is w. RACISM, 5
One black, and one w., and two khaki RACISM, 1
so-called w. races RACISM, 11
Take up the W. Man's burden RACISM, 15
the silk stockings and w. bosoms…excite LUST, 3
The w. man knows how to make everything CHARITY, 19
When a w. man in Africa RACISM, 18
When the w. man came we had the land RACISM, 12
Whitehall W.…our attempts to be fair to everybody BRITAIN, 3
White House gathered together at the W. TALENT, 5
Log-cabin to W. ACHIEVEMENT, 8
no whitewash at the W. TRUTH, 37
standing between Nixon and the W. POLITICIANS, 57
whites because the w. oppressed us yesterday POWER, 16
the w. of their eyes WAR, 87
whitewash no w. at the White House TRUTH, 37
whither w. thou goest, I will go LOYALTY, 5
Whitman Walt W. who laid end to end POETS, 50
whizz-kid power before his hair turned white was called a w. POWER, 13
who W. is Silvia ADMIRATION, 16
w. you are, you aren't anybody FAME, 17
whole a w. is that which has a beginning, a middle, and an end PLAYS, 1
if she knew the w. of it LOVE, 141
the greatest happiness of the w. REPUBLIC, 1
whom for w. the bell tolls DEATH, 45
'W. are you?' said he GRAMMAR, 1
whore a w. in the kitchen and a cook in bed MARRIAGE, 67
I am the Protestant w. RELIGION, 30
the morals of a w., and the manners of a dancing master CRITICISM, 22
the old man does not care for the young man's w. TASTE, 4
The woman's a w. PROMISCUITY, 3
'Tis Pity She's a w. BOOK, SONG, AND PLAY TITLES, 9
You can lead a w. to culture PUNS, 16
whorehouses virgin territory for w. AMERICA, 6
whores After all, we are not political w. POLITICS, 56
With first-rate sherry flowing into second-rate w. MEDIOCRITY, 7
whoreson w. zed INSULTS, 34
whoso W. would be a man CONFORMITY, 4
why For every w. ARGUMENTS, 3
occasions and causes w. and wherefore EXPLANATIONS, 2
they knew not w. WAR, 21
W. should I go FUNERALS, 7
wicked As long as war is regarded as w. WAR, 130
no peace…unto the w. PEACE, 2; PUNISHMENT, 5
the men of Sodom were w. HOMOSEXUALITY, 1
There is a w. inclination OLD AGE, 24
to see men w. REGRET, 21
wickedness blunders usually do more to shape history than…w. MISTAKES, 17
men alone are quite capable of every w. EVIL, 7
The w. of the world VICE, 4
wide a yearning for all that is w. AMERICA, 19
Things hitherto undone should be given…a w. berth ORIGINALITY, 1
Widnes attached even to W. ENGLAND, 39
widow a w.…is a kind of sinecure EXPEDIENCY, 7
better to be the w. of a hero than the wife of a coward COURAGE, 15
Tonight the American flag floats…or Molly Stark sleeps a w. WAR, 113
you, my dear, will be my w. JEALOUSY, 3
widows When w. exclaim loudly against second marriages MARRIAGE, 58
wife A loving w. will do anything MARRIAGE, 96
A man should not insult his w. publicly MARRIAGE, 125
A man who's untrue to his w. INTELLECTUALS, 2
better to be the widow of a hero than the w. of a coward COURAGE, 15
Caesar's w. must be above suspicion INTEGRITY, 2
chose my w.…for…qualities as would wear well MARRIAGE, 66
Commuter…riding to and from his w. TRAINS, 6; TRAVEL, 25
Here lies my w. MARRIAGE, 52
He that has no w. ADVICE, 4
he that is married careth…how he may please his w. MARRIAGE, 26
He that loves not his w. and children MARRIAGE, 118
His w. could eat no lean NURSERY RHYMES, 25
his w. is beautiful and his children smart TOLERANCE, 5
If a man stays away from his w. MARRIAGE, 45
I have a w., I have sons FAMILY, 21
I have quarrelled with my w. MARRIAGE, 92
light w. doth make a heavy husband MARRIAGE, 104
man…shall cleave unto his w. WOMEN, 15
Mother to dozens, /And nobody's w. BABIES, 4
My w. hath something in her gizzard PROVOCATION, 1
My w.…is troubled with her lonely life WOMEN, 60
My w. won't let me MARRIAGE, 78
No man worth having is true to his w. UNFAITHFULNESS, 7
one w. and hardly any mistresses MARRIAGE, 101
remorse for what you have thought about your w. MARRIAGE, 99
single man…must be in want of a w. MARRIAGE, 10
stop them catching AIDS…the w. AIDS, 4
taking out his false teeth and hurling them at his w. MARRIAGE, 51
that a man lay down his w. for a friend FRIENDSHIP, 21
that monstrous animal a husband and w. MARRIAGE, 57
The first w. is matrimony MARRIAGE, 6
The husband frae the w. despises MARRIAGE, 32
the w.…the weaker vessel MARRIAGE, 28
the w. who made Britain great again…has to get her husband to sign her tax form FEMINISM, 13
When a man opens the car door for his w. MARRIAGE, 94
Whose w. shall it be ADULTERY, 9
w. had been unfaithful to me UNFAITHFULNESS, 3
with a w. to tell him what to do LAZINESS, 2
Would you allow your w.…to read this book PRUDERY, 1
your w.…is a receiver of stolen goods INSULTS, 21
wifehood w. and motherhood are but incidental relations WOMEN, 73
wig man with a w. to keep order APPEARANCE, 38
wild an old, w., and incomprehensible man POLITICIANS, 77
mother bore me in the southern w. RACISM, 5
Wilde Oscar W. did not dive very deeply WRITERS, 53
W. grew into a Pierrot WRITERS, 40

W. performed his life WRITERS, 30
W....persecutors...letters page of the *Daily Telegraph* HOMOSEXUALITY, 10
W.'s voice was of the brown velvet order WRITERS, 43
wilderness a little w. GARDENS, 10
a lodge in some vast w. SOLITUDE, 3
plants left over from the Edwardian W. CHANGE, 17
the w. of this world WORLD, 2
W. is Paradise enow CONTENTMENT, 3
wild-fowl more fearful w. than your lion FEAR, 12
will complies against his w. YIELDING, 2
Do what you w. FREEDOM, 44
formation of the political w. of the nation POLITICS, 36
His right was clear, his w. was strong RIGHT, 1
John Stuart Mill /By a mighty effort of w. ECONOMICS, 3
let my w. replace reasoned judgement AUTHORITARIANISM, 4
Man has his w. SEXES, 11
The man who leaves money to charity in his w. BEQUESTS, 3
We have to believe in free w. CHOICE, 4
Where there's a w. DETERMINATION, 2
W. ye no come back again RETURN, 3
You w., Oscar, you w. IMITATION, 7
William You are old, Father W. OLD AGE, 10, 42
Willie Wee W. Winkie runs through the town NURSERY RHYMES, 64
willow a little tom-tit /Sang...W., titwillow, titwillow BIRDS, 4
willows W. whiten, aspens quiver WEATHER, 27
will-power There is no such thing as a great talent without great w. DETERMINATION, 4
will-to-live The thing-in-itself, the w., exists...in every being SURVIVAL, 5
Wilson Mr W....is the 14th Mr W. TITLES, 1
win Heads I w. VICTORY, 5
high sentiments always w. in the end NOBILITY, 3
I am certain that we will w. the election with a good majority SELF-CONFIDENCE, 6
The conventional army loses if it does not w. WAR, 57
Those who can w. a war well WAR AND PEACE, 4
wind Blow, blow, thou winter w. INGRATITUDE, 4
gone with the w. MEMORY, 6
Gone With the W. BOOK, SONG, AND PLAY TITLES, 19
It's an ill w. OPTIMISM, 3
like W. I go LIFE AND DEATH, 6
of w. and limb FAITHFULNESS, 2
O Wild West W. WEATHER, 25
so famous, that it would permit me...to break w. in society FAME, 3
The answer...is blowin' in the w. FREEDOM, 10
The story is like the w. SENSATION, 2
throw the sand against the w. FUTILITY, 5
to agitate a bag of w. FOOTBALL, 10
what w. is to fire ABSENCE, 6
wherever the w. takes me I travel as a visitor FREEDOM, 19
Who has seen the w. WEATHER, 18
words but w. WORDS, 4
windmills not giants but w. DELUSION, 2
window Serve up...and throw...out of the w. NONSENSE, 21
wine A Flask of W. CONTENTMENT, 3
A man may surely be allowed to take a glass of w. by his own fireside FIRE, 4
And drink of my Algerian w. INSULTS, 7
days of w. and roses TRANSIENCE, 11
drinks his w. 'mid laughter free PARTING, 2
drink w. you have the gout DISEASE, 38
for its poisonous w. OBLIVION, 2
Frenchmen drink w. just like ALCOHOL, 39
full of new w. DRUNKENNESS, 8
Give me books, fruit, French w. and fine weather PLEASURE, 17
good w. needs no bush PLAYS, 10
look not thou upon the w. when it is red ALCOHOL, 16
no man...having drunk old w. straightway desireth new AGE, 12; ALCOHOL, 15
the guests must be chosen as carefully as the w. ALCOHOL, 52
the water that was made w. ALCOHOL, 14
the w. is in, the wit is out DRUNKENNESS, 7
the w. was a farce and the food a tragedy FOOD, 47
This w. upon a foreign tree AGRICULTURE, 6
Truth comes out in w. ALCOHOL, 47
use a little w. for thy stomach's sake ALCOHOL, 13
What is man...a...machine for turning...the red w. of Shiraz into urine MANKIND, 7
When the w. is in ALCOHOL, 7
white w. came up with the fish ETIQUETTE, 4
Who loves not w., woman and song PLEASURE, 20
W. comes in at the mouth AGE, 73
w. is a mocker DRUNKENNESS, 9
wingèd Doth the w. life destroy PLEASURE, 5
Time's w. chariot AGE, 38
wings Fear lent w. to his feet FEAR, 13
the w. of a dove SOLITUDE, 4
whether pigs have w. NONSENSE, 9
wink I will w. and hold out mine iron COWARDICE, 8
never came a w. too soon NOSTALGIA, 9
winners In war...there are no w. WAR, 25
winning All I think about is w. that bleedin' title SUCCESS, 6
not w. but taking part VICTORY, 4
W. isn't everything, but wanting to win is VICTORY, 9
Winston It hasn't taken W. long to get used to American ways CHURCHILL, 1
The first time you meet W. CHURCHILL, 6
W. has devoted the best years of his life CHURCHILL, 7
W.'s back TELEGRAMS, 2
W. with his hundred-horse-power mind CHURCHILL, 2
winter human beings say that they enjoy the w. SEASONS, 2
It is a w.'s tale SEASONS, 25
No one thinks of w. SEASONS, 13
the furious w.'s rages MORTALITY, 16
The stars grew bright in the w. sky ANIMALS, 13
the w. is past SEASONS, 5
W. is icummen in SEASONS, 16
w. of our discontent OPTIMISM, 23
wintry sailed the w. sea BOATS, 11
wisdom follies as the special evidences of our w. PRIDE, 12
If one is too lazy to think...never attain w. WISDOM, 14
in much w. is much grief KNOWLEDGE, 6; WISDOM, 2
Knowledge can be communicated but not w. WISDOM, 17
Love is the w. of the fool LOVE, 74
privilege of w. to listen KNOWLEDGE, 19; WISDOM, 18
proverb is one man's wit and all men's w. SAYINGS, 6
proverbs provide them with w. STUPIDITY, 9
Silence is...full of potential w. SILENCE, 8
The highest w. has but one science MANKIND, 34
The only infallible criterion of w. SUCCESS, 7
the palace of W. EXCESS, 3
the price of w. is above rubies WISDOM, 6
therefore get w. WISDOM, 8
Vain w. all, and false philosophy WISDOM, 19
want of human w. WAR, 59
W. be put in a silver rod WISDOM, 10
w....cometh by opportunity of leisure LEISURE, 1; WISDOM, 4
w. excelleth folly, as...light excelleth darkness WISDOM AND FOOLISHNESS, 2
W. has taught us to be calm and meek REVENGE, 10
W. in minds attentive KNOWLEDGE, 11; WISDOM, 15
W. is not additive DEMOCRACY, 6
w. of the crocodiles HYPOCRISY, 2
w....sweetly doth...order all things WISDOM, 9
with how little w. the world is governed GOVERNMENT, 21
with the ancient is w. OLD AGE, 6; WISDOM, 5
wise A w. man will make more opportunities OPPORTUNITY, 9
Coffee which makes the politician w. DRINKS, 6
How very weak the very w. GREATNESS, 14; WISDOM, 23
Many have been the w. speeches of fools WISDOM AND FOOLISHNESS, 6
more of the fool than of the w. HUMAN NATURE, 3
No man...so w. as Thurlow looked APPEARANCES, 14
sorrow makes us w. SORROW, 24
The only wretched are the w. IGNORANCE, 12
the w. forgive FORGIVENESS, 16
To be w. and love LOVE, 125
where ignorance is bliss, /'Tis folly to be w. IGNORANCE, 6
w. man makes his own decisions WISDOM AND FOOLISHNESS, 1
wisely deserves the name of happy who knows how to use the gods' gifts w. HAPPINESS, 9
lov'd not w., but too well LOVE, 128
wiser Be w. than other people WISDOM, 12
foreigner should...be w. than ourselves PRIDE, 12
sadder and a w. man WISDOM, 13
The French are w. than they seem APPEARANCES, 9
the old have rubbed it into the young that they are w. OLD AGE, 28

w. to-day than...yesterday MISTAKES, 12
wisest The most attractive sentences are not perhaps the w. LANGUAGE, 25
wish Conscience is...rejection of a...w. CONSCIENCE, 2
Justice is the...perpetual w. JUSTICE, 14
most...w. they were the only one alive EGOTISM, 2
Someday I'll w. upon a star DESIRE, 7
The w. to hurt CRUELTY, 1
The w. to spread those opinions that we hold ENGLISH, 7
wished consummation devoutly to be w. SUICIDE, 12
wishful There is w. thinking in Hell as well as on earth DESIRE, 11
wit An ounce of a man's own w. WISDOM, 22
Attic w. HUMOUR, 22
a w. out of two half-wits FOOLISHNESS, 16
Brevity is the soul of w. BREVITY, 7
cause that w. is in other men HUMOUR, 27
fancy w. will come STUPIDITY, 13
His foe was folly and his weapon w. HUMOUR, 15
I have neither w., nor words, nor worth SPEECHES, 5
Impropriety is the soul of w. HUMOUR, 19
love robs those who have it of their w. LOVE, 46
Music-hall songs provide the dull with w. STUPIDITY, 9
proverb is one man's w. and all men's wisdom SAYINGS, 6
To the Greeks the Muse gave native w. CLASSICS, 4
True w. is nature to advantage dress'd HUMOUR, 23
wine is in, the w. is out DRUNKENNESS, 7
W. that can creep SERVILITY, 5
witch thou shalt not suffer a w. to live SUPERNATURAL, 3
witches I have ever believed...that there are w. SUPERNATURAL, 4
wither Age cannot w. her ADMIRATION, 14
wither'd w. is the garland of the war MOURNING, 11
withered lonely of heart is w. away LONELINESS, 10
within that w. which passes show MOURNING, 12
when the fight begins w. himself CONFLICT, 5
without I can do w. LUXURY, 5
witness I am a w. TRUTH, 11
thou shalt not bear false w. GOD, 10
witnesses this massed multitude of silent w. to...war WAR, 41
wits Great W....to Madness near alli'd GENIUS, 4
homely w. HOME, 8
their poetry is conceived and composed in their w. POETRY, 4
This man I thought had been a Lord among w. CRITICISM, 21
witty a very w. prologue MARRIAGE, 39
I am not only w. in myself HUMOUR, 27
stumbling on something w. MEN, 1
wives Bricklayers kick their w. to death CLASS, 37
husbands and w....belong to different sexes SEXES, 8
husbands and w. make shipwreck of their lives MARRIAGE, 50
husbands, love your w. MARRIAGE, 23
I met a man with seven w. NURSERY RHYMES, 3
O! men with mothers and w. WOMEN, 40
The others were only my w. JEALOUSY, 3
Translations (like w.) are seldom faithful TRANSLATION, 2
W. are young men's mistresses MARRIAGE, 13
you do not make the laws but...are the w....of those who do WOMEN, 37
wiving Hanging and w. goes by destiny DESTINY, 21
Wodehouse like P. G. W. dropping Jeeves WRITERS, 90
woe a sad variety of w. SORROW, 15
Much in sorrow, oft in w. ENDURANCE, 24
suits of w. MOURNING, 12
Wednesday's child is full of w. NURSERY RHYMES, 34
w. to him that is alone when he falleth FRIENDSHIP, 8
W. to the vanquished DEFEAT, 4
w. unto them that call evil good LYING, 4
w. unto them that...follow strong drink ALCOHOL, 12
wolf The boy cried 'W., w.!' LYING, 2
the w. in the sheep's clothing APPEARANCES, 8
wolf's-bane neither twist /W. OBLIVION, 2
wolves people being thrown to the w. POLITICIANS, 59
woman A diplomat...always remembers a w.'s birthday AGE, 28
A man is only as old as the w. AGE, 39
And a w. is only a w. WOMEN, 44
Any w. who understands the problems of running a home POLITICS, 79
a w. is on a...hunt for trouble MARRIAGE, 50
a w....ought to lay aside...modesty with her skirt SEX, 40
A w.'s place is in the home WOMEN, 2
a w.'s reason WOMEN, 71
A w.'s work WOMEN, 3
A w. will always sacrifice herself WOMEN, 50
a w. yet think him an angel LOVE, 137
body of a weak and feeble w. ROYALTY, 13
Christ-like heroes and w.-worshipping Don Juans MEN, 9
close-up of a w. past sixty APPEARANCE, 4
educate a w. you educate a family EDUCATION, 33
every w. is at heart a rake WOMEN, 64
Every w. is infallibly to be gained FLATTERY, 4
Every w. should marry MARRIAGE, 48
Frailty, thy name is w. WEAKNESS, 4; WOMEN, 70
God made the w. for the man WOMEN, 75
good w. if I had five thousand MONEY, 48
he has studied anatomy and dissected at least one w. MARRIAGE, 18
hell a fury like a w. scorned LOVE AND HATE, 3
I am a...*w.* – nothing more WOMEN, 80
I am a w.? When I think, I must speak WOMEN, 69
if a w. have long hair APPEARANCE, 5
If a w. like Eva Peron with no ideals POLITICIANS, 75
I had become a w. of...character CHARACTER, 6
International W.'s Day RUSSIAN REVOLUTION, 2
It is a great glory in a w. WOMEN, 78
It's a sort of bloom on a w. CHARM, 1
I would...guess that Anon...was often a w. WOMEN, 91
Man for the field and w. for the hearth SEXES, 24
Man to command and w. to obey SEXES, 24
Man with the head and w. with the heart SEXES, 24
No one delights more in vengeance than a w. REVENGE, 11; WOMEN, 42
nor w. neither MANKIND, 27
No w. has an abortion for *fun* ABORTION, 3
No w. should ever be quite accurate about her age AGE, 66
No w. so naked as...underneath her clothes NAKEDNESS, 4
Old age is w.'s hell OLD AGE, 27
Once a w. has given you her heart WOMEN, 85
one can...see in a little girl the threat of a w. CHILDREN, 20
One is not born a w. WOMEN, 13
one of w. born BIRTH, 9
One tongue is sufficient for a w. EDUCATION, 36; WOMEN, 53
She makes love just like a w. WOMEN, 29
She really is a w. just like my mum WOMEN, 67
She was a w. of mean understanding INSULTS, 4
such beauty as a w.'s eye LEARNING, 8
Than to ever let a w. in my life MISOGYNY, 3
the help and support of the w. I love LOVE, 147
the most beautiful w. I've ever seen BEAUTY, 27
The really original w....imitates a man WOMEN, 74
There was an old w. /Lived under a hill NURSERY RHYMES, 53
There was an old w. who lived in a shoe NURSERY RHYMES, 54
the rib...made he a w. WOMEN, 15
the sort of w....one would almost feel disposed to bury for nothing WOMEN, 27
the sort of w. who lives for others CHARITY, 15
The w.'s a whore PROMISCUITY, 3
The w. that deliberates is lost WOMEN, 6
the w. who is really kind to dogs WOMEN, 14
To know the *mind* of a w. LOVE, 81
Twenty years of romance makes a w. look like a ruin MARRIAGE, 132
What does a w. want WOMEN, 33
When a w. becomes a scholar WOMEN, 56
When a w. behaves like a man WOMEN, 32
When lovely w. stoops to folly GULLIBILITY, 2
who can find a virtuous w. WOMEN, 17
Who loves not wine, w. and song PLEASURE, 20
Why can't a w. be more like a man MEN, 10
Why...was I born a w. MISOGYNY, 4
will not stand...being called a w. in my own house WOMEN, 88
w. alone, can...commit them SEXES, 25
w. as old as she looks AGE, 18
w. governs America AMERICA, 25
w. has her way SEXES, 11
W. is always fickle and changing WOMEN, 86
w. is an animal that WOMEN, 49
w. is his game SEXES, 23
W. is unrivaled as a wet nurse WOMEN, 83
w....knowing anything WOMEN, 10
w. of education WOMEN, 84
W.'s at best a contradiction WOMEN, 65

w. seldom asks advice WOMEN, 7
W.'s virtue is man's greatest invention SEXES, 21
w.'s weapon is her tongue WOMEN, 36
w.'s whole existence SEXES, 4
W. was God's *second* mistake WOMEN, 55
W. will be the last thing civilized by Man WOMEN, 52
womanhood W. is the great fact in her life WOMEN, 73
woman-kind whole race of w. is...made subject to man WOMAN'S ROLE, 1
womb mother's w. /Untimely ripp'd BIRTH, 9
no new baby in the w. of our society RUSSIA, 5
teeming w. of royal kings ENGLAND, 36
women A homely face...aided many w. heavenward APPEARANCE, 3
all w. do MARRIAGE, 9
An experience of w. EXPERIENCE, 12
a snare in which the feet of w. WOMEN, 5
Because w. can do nothing except love WOMEN, 51
Few w. care to be laughed at RIDICULE, 2
God withheld the sense of humour from w. WOMEN, 21
great city...has the greatest men and w. GREATNESS, 15
I don't think men and w. were meant to live together SEXES, 9
If men knew how w. pass their time WOMEN, 39
If w. didn't exist...money...no meaning WOMEN, 57
I have sung w. in three cities WOMEN, 66
It is a sad feature...that only w....have time to write novels WRITERS, 24
Mohamed wanted equality for w. EQUALITY, 3
Monstrous Regiment of W. WOMEN, 45
Most good w. are hidden treasures WOMEN, 59
Most w. have no characters WOMEN, 63
Most w. set out to try to change a man CHANGE, 5
Music and w. I cannot but give way to MUSIC, 37
Older w. are best SEX, 20
proper function of w. WOMEN, 30
several young w....would render the Christian life intensely difficult CHRISTIANITY, 31
souls of w. are so small MISOGYNY, 1
the only advantage w. have over men...they can cry SEXES, 20
The question of the rights of w. WOMEN, 90
There are two kinds of w. WOMEN, 62
The War between Men and W. SEXES, 26
the w. come and go WOMEN, 31
the w. whose eyes have been washed...with tears WOMEN, 28
Were't not for gold and w. SIN, 20
Whatever w. do, they must do it twice as well EQUALITY, 25
When w. go wrong SEX, 63
Why are w....so much more interesting to men SEXES, 33
Why need...w. know so much WOMEN, 18
with peaches and w., it's...the side next the sun that's tempting TEMPTATION, 8
W....are either better or worse than men WOMEN, 46
W. are much more like each other WOMEN, 22
w. become like their mothers SEXES, 30
w. can live their whole lives and not know the law LAW, 10
W....care fifty times more for a marriage WOMEN, 12
w. defend themselves so poorly WOMEN, 23
w. dislike his books WRITERS, 71
W. exist...solely for the propagation WOMAN'S ROLE, 5
W. have served...as looking-glasses WOMEN, 92
W. have smaller brains than men SEXES, 19
w....ill-using them and then confessing it WOMEN, 81
W. never have young minds WOMEN, 26
w....not so young as...painted COSMETICS, 1
W. represent...matter over mind SEXES, 31
w. require both WOMEN, 19
w. should be struck...like gongs WOMEN, 25
W....the mothers of all mischief MOTHERHOOD, 2
w. who have done something with their lives MISOGYNY, 2
W. who love the same man LOVE, 20
W. would rather be right than reasonable WOMEN, 54
Wonderful w.!...how much we...owe to Shakespeare SHAKESPEARE, 17
womman worthy w. al hir lyve MARRIAGE, 35
won Human reason w.. Mankind w. VICTORY, 8
wonder knowledge and w....is an impression of pleasure KNOWLEDGE, 5; WONDER, 1
Many a man has been a w. to the world ADMIRATION, 8
Philosophy is the product of w. PHILOSOPHY, 14; WONDER, 4
the common w. of all men INDIVIDUALITY, 4
wonderful cathedrals – grand, w. RELIGION, 53
wonders His w. to perform GOD, 18
wondrous When I survey the w. Cross HUMILITY, 13
wont seen me as he was w. to see me PUNISHMENT, 15
wood about the dreadful w. /Of conscious evil GUILT, 2
would rather hew w. than be a king MONARCHY, 6
woodcock well-shot w., partridge, snipe HUNTING, 1
woodman W., spare that tree TREES, 11
w. spare the beechen tree TREES, 2
woods fresh w., and pastures new CHANGE, 16
The w. are lovely TRAVEL, 9
the w. decay and fall MORTALITY, 19
They shut the road through the w. TIME, 23
We'll to the w. no more ENDING, 4
When the green w. laugh HAPPINESS, 5
woodshed Something nasty in the w. EVIL, 9
woodworm the w. obligingly held hands HUMOUR, 38
Woolf Who's Afraid of Virginia W. BOOK, SONG, AND PLAY TITLES, 1
word better w. than prefabricated WORDS, 6
but a w. and a blow VIOLENCE, 3
Good isn't the w. CRITICISM, 16
Greeks had a W. for It LANGUAGE, 1
in the beginning was the w. WORDS, 1
in the captain's but a choleric w. INJUSTICE, 11
longest w. in the English language BUSINESS, 7
Rehearsing a play is making the w. flesh PLAYS, 9
the kingdom of God is not in w., but in power GOD, 12
the W. had breath CHRISTIANITY, 43
The w. is half Greek and half Latin TELEVISION AND RADIO, 5
What is honour? A w. HONOUR, 4
when *I* use a w. MEANING, 3
wordless thoughtless are rarely w. SPEECH, 12
words Be not the slave of W. WORDS, 5
best w. in the best order POETRY AND PROSE, 2
big emotions come from big w. STYLE, 5
by skilful arrangement of your w. WRITING, 11
Fine w. and an insinuating appearance SERVILITY, 1
fine w. butter no parsnips WORDS, 18
For w., like Nature, half reveal WORDS, 21
I always try to get as many w. VERBOSITY, 1
I put the w. down WRITING, 35
It wasn't the w. /That frightened the birds INNUENDO, 1
learn the use of living w. WORDS, 15
Man does not live by w. alone WORDS, 19
Men of few w. are the best BREVITY, 8
my w. are my own REPARTEE, 1
neither wit, nor w., nor worth SPEECHES, 5
shrank from w. WORDS, 20
thanks to w., we have often sunk to the level of the demons WORDS, 11
the barbarous, gothic times when w. had a meaning WORDS, 9
to set a chime of w. tinkling in...a few fastidious people PURPOSE, 7
uses his w. as a quack uses his remedies VERBOSITY, 4
use the most common...w. LANGUAGE, 27
W....are great foes of reality WORDS, 7
W. are like leaves VERBOSITY, 6
W. are men's daughters WORDS, 14
w. are the daughters of earth LANGUAGE, 16
W. are...the most powerful drug WORDS, 13
w. but wind WORDS, 4
w. left unsaid and deeds left undone REGRET, 20
W. may be false and full of art SPEECH, 15
w. never seen...before outside of a dictionary POETS, 50
w. once spoke...never be recall'd SPEECH, 14
You can stroke people with w. WORDS, 8
Wordsworth Mr W., a stupid man, with a...gift POETS, 52
Mr W. is never interrupted INTERRUPTIONS, 4
W.'s healing power POETS, 17
W. was a tea-time bore POETS, 57
wore w. enough for modesty CLOTHES, 2
work All w. and no play WORK, 1
dignity in w. WORK, 5
Every man's w....is always a portrait of himself ARTS, 1
For men must w., and women must weep SEXES, 14
harder you w. WORK, 17
How can I take an interest in my w. ENTHUSIASM, 1
if any would not w., neither should he eat WORK, 4
I like w.; it fascinates me IDLENESS, 6

it is poor grub, poor pay, and easy w. AMERICA, 24; ENGLAND, 25
No, this right hand shall w. it all off WRITING, 30
no w., nor device, nor knowledge...in the grave TRANSIENCE, 6; WORK, 3
one must do some w. seriously...and not merely amuse oneself WORK, 10
only place where success comes before w. SUCCESS, 15; WORK, 22
prejudice against w. CHANGE, 3
success...by dint of hard w. EFFORT, 5; SUCCESS, 13
the w. comes out more beautiful ARTS, 4
the world's w....is done by men who do not feel...well ILLNESS, 4
they must hate to w. for a living MARRIAGE, 100
To sport would be as tedious as to w. LEISURE, 4
When w. is a pleasure WORK, 9
W. banishes those three great evils WORK, 24
W....by those employees who have not yet reached...incompetence INCOMPETENCE, 4
W. expands so as to fill the time WORK, 15
W. is much more fun than fun WORK, 7
W. is necessary for man WORK, 16
W. is the curse of the drinking classes WORK, 26
W. is the grand cure WORK, 6
you can't call yourself a great w. of nature INSULTS, 42

worker a sociable w. SOCIETY, 2

workers He is used to dealing with estate w. POLITICIANS, 52
hiring taxis...handing out redundancy notices to its own w. INCOMPETENCE, 2
W. of the world, unite MARXISM, 3

workhouse The W. – always a word of shame POVERTY, 25

working God as a w. hypothesis GOD, 14
No writer before the...19th century wrote about the w. classes CLASS, 36
The party is the rallying-point for the...w. class COMMUNISM, 9
the w.-class which, raw and half-developed PUBLIC, 2
To the ordinary w. man...Socialism SOCIALISM, 12

workman A bad w. RESPONSIBILITY, 1

works all his w. RENUNCIATION, 1
faith, if it hath not w., is dead FAITH, 7
more copies of my w. are left behind WRITERS, 32
they were judged every man according to their w. JUDGMENT, 4
W. done least rapidly PERFECTION, 3

workshop England...the w. of the world ENGLAND, 16

worktime the bustle of man's w. OPTIMISM, 17

world a citizen of the w. NATIONALITY, 8
A great writer creates a w. of his own WRITERS, 7
All's right with the w. PERFECTION, 2
all the uses of this w. WORLD-WEARINESS, 6
all the w. as my parish RELIGION, 68
All the w. is queer SUBJECTIVITY, 5
All the w. loves a lover LOVE, 2
All the w.'s a stage HUMAN CONDITION, 17
a man for whom the outside w. exists CHARACTER, 9
A man travels the w. over HOME, 6
as good be out of the w. FASHION, 2
a W. in a grain of sand WONDER, 2
brave new w. /That has such people in't MANKIND, 28
chess-board is the w.; the pieces...the phenomena of the universe GOD, 28
citizen of the w. COURTESY, 2
Dear W., I am leaving you because I am bored LAST WORDS, 60
dominate the w. INFLUENCE, 11
excellent foppery of the w. MISFORTUNE, 18
Feed the W. CHARITY, 4
Germany will be...a w. power GERMANY, 14
glory, jest, and riddle of the w. HUMAN CONDITION, 14
God so loved the w. CHRISTIANITY, 13
good deed in a naughty w. GOOD, 15
Grant me paradise in this w. HEAVEN, 14
Had we but w. enough, and time SHYNESS, 5
he could not avoid making Him set the w. in motion CREATION, 11
I am the light of the w. CHRISTIANITY, 14
I called the New W. into existence AMERICA, 5
If all the w. were paper NONSENSE, 1
If the w. were good for...speculation SPECULATION, 2
If you were the only girl in the w. LOVE, 65
I have...been all round the w. TRAVEL, 3
in mourning...for the w. MOURNING, 15
in this harsh w. MOURNING, 13
Into the dangerous w. I leapt BIRTH, 3
I...pass through this w. but once MORTALITY, 11
it's a jolly strange w. CONFUSION, 1
It's the same the whole w. over POVERTY AND WEALTH, 1
joy that a man is born into the w. BIRTH, 1
little sisters to all the w. WOMEN, 28
Looks the whole w. in the face RIGHTEOUSNESS, 7
Many a man has been a wonder to the w. ADMIRATION, 8
Never having been able to succeed in the w. ENVY, 9
One w. at a time AFTERLIFE, 11
Our country is the w. AMERICA, 14
queen for all the w. ROYALTY, 34
say to all the w. 'This was a man' CHARACTER, 22
Stop the W., I Want to Get Off WORLD-WEARINESS, 5
Superstition sets the whole w. in flames SUPERSTITION, 11
the greatest week in the history of the w. SPACE, 6
the hand that rules the w. INFLUENCE, 10
The wickedness of the w. VICE, 4
The w. is becoming like a lunatic asylum MADNESS, 9
The w....is but a large prison EXECUTION, 23
The w. is but a school of inquiry CURIOSITY, 6
The w. is disgracefully managed COMPLAINTS, 2
The w. is everything that is the case LOGIC, 4
The w. is made of people who MEDIOCRITY, 3
The w. is made up for the most part of fools FOOLISHNESS, 11
The w. is too much with us WASTE, 3
the w. may talk of hereafter WAR, 31
the w. must be made safe for...fifty years WAR, 28
the w.'s mine oyster OPPORTUNITY, 17
the w., the flesh, and the devil JOURNALISM, 25; TEMPTATION, 5
the w. would not be the same NUCLEAR WEAPONS, 14
they only saved the w. HEROISM, 2
This is the way the w. ends ENDING, 3
this little w. ENGLAND, 36
This w. is very odd we see CONFUSION, 5
This w. nis but a thurghfare LIFE AND DEATH, 4
though the w. perish JUSTICE, 7
triple pillar of the w. LOVE, 115
turn your back upon the w. PERFECTION, 4
What a fine comedy this w. would be LIFE, 21
When all the w. dissolves DOOMSDAY, 5
When all the w. is young, lad YOUTH, 12
where in this small-talking w. MEANING, 4
which taketh away the sin of the w. CHRISTIANITY, 12
wilderness of this w. WORLD, 2
with how little wisdom the w. is governed GOVERNMENT, 21
w., I count it...but an hospital WORLD, 1
w. is a beautiful place HUMAN CONDITION, 8
w. is a comedy to those who think LIFE, 53
w. is charged with the grandeur of God GOD, 25
w....made safe for democracy DEMOCRACY, 24
w. will make a...path to his door FAME, 8
w. without end ETERNITY, 2

worldly The W. Hope men set their Hearts upon TRANSIENCE, 13

worlds best of possible w. OPTIMISM, 27
So many w. ACTION, 12
we live in the best of all possible w. OPTIMISM, 19; PESSIMISM, 3

worm a w. at one end and a fool at the other FISHING, 1
Even a w. will turn ENDURANCE, 1
The cut w. FORGIVENESS, 8
To tread by chance upon a w. DEATH, 91

worms Sir, you have tasted two whole w. SPOONERISMS, 5
w. have eaten them, but not for love LOVE AND DEATH, 6

wormwood her end is bitter as w. WOMEN, 16

worrying W. is the most natural and spontaneous of...functions WORRY, 12

worse Defend the bad against the w. DECLINE, 3
Dublin, though...much w. than London PLACES, 7
for better for w. MARRIAGE, 30
If my books had been any w. CINEMA, 1
The w. I do, the more popular I get POPULARITY, 5
who ever knew Truth put to the w. TRUTH, 36

worship freedom...to w. HUMAN RIGHTS, 4
No one can w. God...on an empty stomach BUSINESS, 29
O w. the King GOD, 23

worshippers the one God whose w....still trust in Him LUCK, 7

worst His w. is better than any other person's best WRITERS, 55

it was the w. of times FRENCH REVOLUTION, 1
They...like to be told the w. BRITISH, 6
we can say 'This is the w.' OPTIMISM, 22
w. kinde of infortune MISFORTUNE, 7
You do your w. WORLD WAR II, 10
worth A man's w. something CONFLICT, 5
If a job's w. doing EFFORT, 1
Paris is w. a mass PARIS, 2
The w. of a State STATE, 4
Whatever is w. doing EXCELLENCE, 1
W. seeing? yes IRELAND, 8
worthless a more w. set than Byron POETS, 12
Our parents' age...has produced us, more w. still AGE, 33
worthy is not w. to live SMOKING, 12
would He w., wouldn't he DENIAL, 4
wound Religion...the w., not the bandage RELIGION, 50
W. with a touch SATIRE, 2
wounds To fight and not to heed the w. SELFLESSNESS, 2
wrapped w. him in swaddling clothes CHRISTMAS, 7
wrapping perceive Christmas through its w. CHRISTMAS, 20
wrath let not the sun go down upon your w. PUNISHMENT, 1; SIN, 3
trampling out the vintage where the grapes of w. GOD, 26
wreathe W. iron pokers into true-love knots POETS, 28
wreckage Literature is strewn with the w. of men WRITERS, 27
Wrekin His forest fleece the W. heaves TREES, 4
wren Four Larks and a W. APPEARANCE, 19
The w. goes to't ANIMALISM, 7
Wren Sir Christopher W. /Said ARCHITECTURE, 1
wretch a w. who supports with insolence PATRONAGE, 1
I w. lay wrestling with...my God SOUL, 7
wretched love – all the w. cant of it LOVE, 64
The only w. are the wise IGNORANCE, 12
wretches feel what w. feel HUMILITY, 10
Poor naked w. WEATHER, 21
w. hang that jury-men may dine JUSTICE, 19
wring they will soon *w.* their hands WAR, 121
writ I never w., nor no man ever lov'd LOVE, 124
write A man may w. at any time PERSISTENCE, 6
as much as a man ought to w. WRITING, 34
Better to w. for yourself WRITING, 6
Do not on any account attempt to w. on both sides EXAMINATIONS, 2
he does not w. himself down WRITERS, 56
I like to w. when I feel spiteful WRITING, 19
look in thy heart and w. INSPIRATION, 5
signing his name and forgetting to w. the letter INSULTS, 5
w. and read comes by nature LITERACY, 2
w. for children...as you do for adults WRITING, 10
writer A great w. creates a world of his own WRITERS, 7
Asking a working w....about critics CRITICS, 7
A w.'s ambition should be POSTERITY, 6
Every great and original w. WRITING, 37
it is necessary to go to a university...to become a successful w. WRITERS, 3
not a w.'s business to hold opinions WRITERS, 28
No tears in the w. WRITING, 8
protect the w. BUREAUCRACY, 1
successful w....is indistinguishable AMERICA, 23
the w....is the impregnator READING, 19
writers American w. want to be...great AMERICANS, 12
As w. become more numerous READING, 5
Clear w....do not seem so deep as they are WRITING, 18
Creative w. are...greater than the causes...they represent WRITERS, 10
Irish w. – the ones that *think.* IRISH, 3
No regime has ever loved great w. WRITERS, 23
The only way for w. to meet WRITERS, 8
W., like teeth, are divided into incisors and grinders WRITERS, 2
writes He w. as fast as they can read WRITERS, 56
Moving Finger w. DESTINY, 8
writhe Uriah...made a ghastly w. SERVILITY, 3
writhing Reeling and W. EDUCATION, 9
writing All good w. is swimming under water WRITING, 7
as I had in the w. PLEASURE, 25
I wouldn't give up w. about God WRITERS, 90
the disease of w. books WRITING, 23
the incurable disease of w. WRITING, 17
the worst..., is w. about w. CRITICISM, 4
True ease in w. comes from art WRITING, 26
When a man is in doubt about...his w. POSTERITY, 4
w. an exact man READING, 1
W....is but a different name for conversation WRITING, 31
W. is like getting married MARRIAGE, 87; WRITING, 24
writings historians left blanks in their w. HISTORIANS, 5
written Books are well w., or badly w. BOOKS, 46
books...w. by people who don't understand them BOOKS, 25
w. or thought, it can be filmed CINEMA, 8
you would have been very glad if I had w. it PLAYS, 6
wromantic Cavaliers (Wrong but W.) HISTORY, 27
wrong A door is what a dog is...on the w. side of DOGS, 10
A man should...own he has been in the w. MISTAKES, 12
anxious to do the w. thing correctly ETIQUETTE, 7
History is...the w. way of living HISTORY, 11
Of course not...I may be w. UNCERTAINTY, 3
orthodoxy...practically means being w. ORTHODOXY, 2
our country, right or w. PATRIOTISM, 8
responsible and w. RESPONSIBILITY, 5; RIGHTEOUSNESS, 6
right deed for the w. reason MOTIVE, 2
sentimentality...rubs you up the w. way SENTIMENTALITY, 4
something is impossible, he is...w. SCIENCE, 6
something w. with our bloody ships BOATS, 1
support me when I am...w. SUPPORT, 4
their authors could not endure being w. CRIME, 2
The multitude is always in the w. PUBLIC, 17
The right divine of kings to govern w. MONARCHY, 17
the unclouded face of truth suffer w. JOURNALISM, 27
The w. war, at the w. place WAR, 13
When women go w. SEX, 63
W. from the start POETRY, 36
Yes, once...I thought I had made a w. decision MISTAKES, 8
wrongdoing W. can only be avoided if those who are not wronged feel the same indignation VICE, 8
wronged Not to be w. is to forgo...goodness INJUSTICE, 13
wrongs for one class to appreciate the w. of another CLASS, 32
Two w. do not make a right MISTAKES, 1

X

Xanadu In X. did Kubla Khan PLEASURE, 8
X-ray to replace X. by hearsay GOSSIP, 9

Y

yacht sink my y. to make my guests go PARTIES, 3
Yale attended the Y. promenade dance SEX, 45
A whale ship was my Y. College EDUCATION, 35
Yankee Y. Doodle came to town AMERICA, 3; NURSERY RHYMES, 69
yard a y....3.37 inches longer FRANCE, 3
yarn web of our life is of a mingled y. GOOD AND EVIL, 4
yawn When a book is boring, they y. openly BOOKS, 39
yawns grave y. for him BORES, 7
year all the y. were playing holidays LEISURE, 4
Another y.! – another deadly blow DEFEAT, 9
each day is like a y. IMPRISONMENT, 10
I said to the man who stood at the gate of the y. FAITH, 11
Let it be kept till the ninth y. PUBLISHING, 7
Not to hope for things to last for ever, is what the y. teaches TRANSIENCE, 15
That time of y. thou mayst in me behold OLD AGE, 40
two months of every y. WEATHER, 8
y.'s at the spring PERFECTION, 2
yearning a y. for all that is wide AMERICA, 19
learning, earning and y. LIFE, 38
years After long y. SEPARATION, 2
he that cuts off twenty y. of life DEATH, 105
how many y. can some people exist FREEDOM, 10
I have been talking prose for over forty y. PROSE, 3
It will keep for y. LONGEVITY, 2
One thousand y. more MANKIND, 35
world must be made safe for...fifty y. WAR, 28
Y. hence, perhaps, may dawn an age FUTURE, 1
y. of discretion AGE, 14
Yeats William Y. is laid to rest POETS, 18
yes girls...say No when they mean Y. WOMEN, 8
The bank that likes to say y. ADVERTISING, 18
yes-men I don't want any y. GOLDWYNISMS, 22
yesterday wiser to-day than...y. MISTAKES, 12
yesterdays And all our y. LIFE, 45
yesteryear snows of y. NOSTALGIA, 22
yet A young man not y. MARRIAGE, 14
but not y. PROCRASTINATION, 4
My time has not y. come POSTERITY, 9

yeti little in civilization to appeal to a Y. CIVILIZATION, 7
yid put the id back in y. JEWS, 12
yield To strive, to seek…and not to y. DETERMINATION, 15
yoghurt culture, you'll find more on… ROYALTY, 22
yo-ho-ho Y., and a bottle of rum ALCOHOL, 60
yoke good…that he bear the y. in his youth YOUTH, 2
Rome's gross y. /Drops off INFLUENCE, 1
the inevitable y. OLD AGE, 53
Yorick Alas, poor Y. MISQUOTATIONS, 22; MOURNING, 10
York Oh! the grand old Duke of Y. ARMY, 1
you For y. but not for me DEATH, 16
young aged diplomats…bored than for y. men to die DIPLOMACY, 1
ale from the Country of the Y. KNOWLEDGE, 36
All that the y. can do for the old AGE, 56
a man of about a hundred and fifty who was rather y. OLD AGE, 51
A man that is y. in years AGE, 8
a sight to make an old man y. BEAUTY, 38
can't put off being y. until you retire MONEY, 30
country of y. men AMERICA, 13
Grieve not that I die y. DEATH, 59
how y. the policemen look AGE, 32
I am sixty years y. AGE, 61
look y. till forty AGE, 20
man's friends begin to compliment him about looking y. AGE, 34
Most women are not so y. as they are painted COSMETICS, 1
old-fashioned respect for the y. RESPECT, 5
Political history is far too criminal…to be…fit…for the y. HISTORY, 3
The atrocious crime of being a y. man YOUTH, 14
The best careers advice to give to the y. OCCUPATIONS, 18
the old have rubbed it into the y. that they are wiser OLD AGE, 28
There is…an instrument to mould the minds of the y. CENSORSHIP, 2
The y. always have the same problem YOUTH, 5
the y. are so busy teaching us YOUTH, 9
The y. Cambridge group CLASSIFICATION, 2
The y. have aspirations AGE, 50
to be y. was very heaven FRENCH REVOLUTION, 3
to make me y. again SURVIVAL, 1
When all the world is y., lad YOUTH, 12
You can be y. without money MONEY, 51
Y. men make great mistakes in life YOUTH, 11
younger I…get y. every day AGE, 61
youngest not even the y. of us IMPERFECTION, 14
yourself Better to write for y. WRITING, 6
If you do not tell the truth about y. HONESTY, 14
If you hate a person, you hate…y. HATE, 5
no friends not equal to y. FRIENDS, 5
What you do not want done to y. EXAMPLE, 4
youth age and y. cannot live together AGE, 55
A y. to whom was given /So much IMPETUOSITY, 4
everything that is great…done by y. YOUTH, 6
good…that he bear the yoke in his y. YOUTH, 2
Here rests…/A y. to fortune and to fame unknown DEATH, 58
high-water mark of my y. MEMORY, 19
Home-keeping y. HOME, 8
I summon age /To grant y.'s heritage AGE, 15
it is y. that must fight and die WAR, 49
man loves the meat in his y. AGE, 54
nothing in thy y. AGE, 11
Pride and Truth…sides at y. AGE, 71
sign of an ill-spent y. SPORT AND GAMES, 22
the Jazz Age…became less and less an affair of y. AGE, 26
Thou hast nor y. nor age AGE, 53
Time, the subtle thief of y. AGE, 41
Y. is a blunder AGE, 19
Y. is a malady YOUTH, 13
Y. is something very new YOUTH, 3
Y.'s a stuff will not endure PRESENT, 13
Y. will be served SATISFACTION, 1
Y. will come…beat on my door YOUTH, 10
y. would sleep out the rest YOUTH, 16
youthe Withouten other companye in y. MARRIAGE, 35
Yukon Law of the Y. SURVIVAL, 6
Yuletide at Y. men /are the more murderous CHRISTMAS, 13

Z

zeal Not too much z. MODERATION, 4
zed whoreson z. INSULTS, 34
zero My scribbling pays me z. francs per line WRITING, 29
zoo the city…is a human z. MANKIND, 18
Zürich the little gnomes of Z. MONEY, 52